GOLF
Annual 2002
Statistics • Results • Player Profiles
Foreword by Darren Clarke

Compiled by Dan Roebuck
Designed and edited by Joe Conboy

Published in 2001 by Outlook Press
Raceform, Compton, Newbury, Berkshire RG20 6NL
Outlook Press is an imprint of Raceform Ltd, a wholly owned
subsidiary of MGN Ltd

Copyright © Outlook Press 2001

A catalogue record for this book is available from the British
Library.

ISBN 1 901100 83 9

Printed by Omnia Books, Glasgow

Cover photograph of Darren Clarke © Associated Press

CONTENTS

THE MAJORS

WORLD GOLF CHAMPIONSHIP EVENTS

OTHER EVENTS

FOREWORD

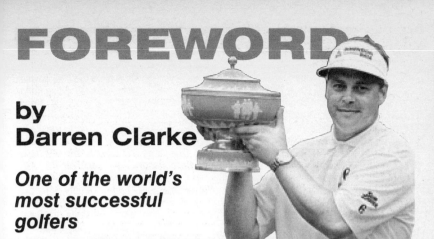

by
Darren Clarke

One of the world's most successful golfers

WHILE I'll be having my usual small wager with Lee Westwood on who finishes higher in the Order of Merit, the shrewder of you will be using this book to make a few quid at the bookies' expense.

All the facts, figures, birdies and bogeys are listed in the third edition of the *RFO Guide to Golf* for you to make your golf betting pay.

With every 2001 tournament result from both the European and US Tours listed, plus Players to Note, Course Profiles and Ten Year Form for 200 pros, this superb statistical record of last year and more is all you need.

This guide will remind you of where I shot 60 and equalled not only the European Tour record for the lowest 18 hole score but also the number of birdies and consecutive birdies in one round.

Unfortunately for me, it will also remind you of when I shot 77-78 to miss the cut by a mile and officially finish 147th. Good, bad or ugly, it's all here.

So if you enjoy watching, playing or betting on golf, you should find something of interest in the *RFO Guide to Golf*.

As for my bet with Lee, well let's just say I'm quietly confident and that 2002 will hopefully see a Major breakthrough.

EUROPEAN TOUR SCHEDULE 2002

DATE	TOURNAMENT	LOCATION
22-25 Nov	BMW Asian Open	Westin Resort Ta Shee, Taiwan
29 Nov-2 Dec	Omega Hong Kong Open	Hong Kong GC, Hong Kong
10-13 Jan	South African Open	The Country Club, Durban, South Africa
17-20 Jan	Alfred Dunhill Championship	Houghton GC Johannesburg, South Africa
24-27 Jan	Johnnie Walker Classic	Lake Karrinyup CC Perth, Australia
31 Jan-3 Feb	Heineken Classic	Royal Melbourne GC Victoria, Australia
7-10 Feb	The ANZ Championship	The Lakes Golf Club Sydney, Australia
20-24 Feb	WGC – Accenture Match Play	La Costa Resort & Spa Carlsbad, CA, USA
21-24 Feb	Caltex Singapore Masters	Laguna National G&CC, Singapore
28 Feb-3 Mar	Carlsberg Malaysian Open	Royal Selangor GC Kuala Lumpur, Malaysia
7-10 Mar	Dubai Desert Classic	Emirates GC, Dubai
14-17 Mar	Qatar Masters	Doha GC, Qatar
21-24 Mar	Madeira Island Open	Santo da Serra, Madeira
28-31 Mar	Open de Canarias	El Cortijo Club de Campo Gran Canarias
4-7 Apr	Algarve Open de Portugal	TBC, Portugal
11-14 Apr	**MASTERS TOURNAMENT**	Augusta National, Georgia, USA
19-21 Apr	The Seve Ballesteros Trophy	Druids Glen Wicklow, Ireland
25-28 Apr	Open de Espana	TBC, Spain
2-5 May	Novotel Perrier Open de France	Le Golf National Paris, France
9-12 May	B&H International Open	The De Vere Belfry, Sutton Coldfield, England
16-19 May	Deutsche Bank – SAP Open	TPC of Europe, St. Leon-Rot Heidelberg, Germany
23-26 May	Volvo PGA Championship	Wentworth Club, Surrey, England
30 May-2 Jun	Victor Chandler British Masters	Woburn, Milton Keynes, England
6-9 Jun	The Compass Group English Open	Marriott Forest of Arden, England
13-16 Jun	**US OPEN CHAMPIONSHIP**	Bethpage State Park Farmingdale, NY, USA
20-23 Jun	The Great North Open	De Vere Slaley Hall Northumberland, England
27-30 Jun	Murphy's Irish Open	Fota Island, Cork, Ireland
4-7 Jul	Smurfit European Open	The K Club, Dublin, Ireland
11-14 Jul	The Scottish Open at Loch Lomond	Loch Lomond, Glasgow, Scotland
18-21 Jul	**131st OPEN GOLF CHAMPIONSHIP**	Muirfield, East Lothian, Scotland
25-28 Jul	The TNT Open	Hilversumsche GC, Hilversum, Netherlands
1-4 Aug	Volvo Scandinavian Masters	Kungsangen Stockholm, Sweden
8-11 Aug	The Celtic Manor Resort Wales Open	The Celtic Manor Resort, Wales
15-18 Aug	North West of Ireland Open	Ballyliffin GC, Co Donegal, Ireland
15-18 Aug	**US PGA CHAMPIONSHIP**	Hazeltine National GC, Chaska, MN, USA
22-25 Aug	Gleneagles Scottish PGA Championship	The Gleneagles Hotel, Scotland
22-25 Aug	WGC – NEC Invitational	Sahalee CC, Redmond, WA, USA
29 Aug-1 Sep	BMW International Open	Golfclub Munchen Nord-Eichenried Munich, Germany
5-8 Sep	Omega European Masters	Crans-sur-Sierre, Switzerland
12-15 Sep	Linde German Masters	Gut Larchenhof, Cologne, Germany
19-22 Sep	WGC – American Express Championship	Mount Juliet, Kilkenny, Ireland
27-29 Sep	THE 34TH RYDER CUP	The De Vere Belfry, Sutton Coldfield, England
3-6 Oct	TBA	
10-13 Oct	Trophee Lancome	Saint-Nom-La-Breteche, Paris, France
17-20 Oct	Cisco World Match Play Championship*	Wentworth Club, Surrey, England
24-27 Oct	Telefonica Open de Madrid	Club de Campo Madrid, Spain
31 Oct-3 Nov	Atlanet Italian Open	Is Molas Sardinia, Italy
7-10 Nov	Volvo Masters Andalucia	TBC, Spain
12-15 Dec	WGC – EMC2 World Cup*	Vista Vallarta, Puerto Vallarta, Mexico

* Not part of the European Tour

Sponsored by Stan James

DATE	TOURNAMENT	LOCATION
3-6 Jan	Mercedes Championships	*Plantation Course, Kapalua, HI*
10-13 Jan	Sony Open in Hawaii	*Waialae CC, Honolulu, HI*
16-20 Jan	Bob Hope Chrysler Classic	*PGA West-Arnold Palmer Private Course, CA*
24-27 Jan	Phoenix Open	*TPC of Scottsdale, Scottsdale, AZ*
31 Jan-3 Feb	AT&T Pebble Beach National Pro-Am	*Pebble Beach Golf Links, CA*
7-10 Feb	Buick Invitational	*Torrey Pines GC, LaJolla, CA*
14-17 Feb	Nissan Open	*Riviera CC, Pacific Palisades, CA*
20-24 Feb	WGC – Accenture Match Play	*La Costa Resort & Spa Carlsbad, CA*
21-24 Feb	Touchstone Energy Tucson Open	*Omni Tucson NGR & Spa Tucson, AZ*
28 Feb-3 Mar	Genuity Championship	*Doral Golf Resort & Spa, Miami, FL*
7-10 Mar	Honda Classic	*TPC at Heron Bay, Coral Springs, FL*
14-17 Mar	Bay Hill Invitational	*Bay Hill Club & Lodge, Orlando, FL*
21-24 Mar	The Players Championship	*Sawgrass, Ponte Vedra Beach, FL*
28-31 Mar	Shell Houston Open	*TPC at The Woodlands, TX*
4-7 Apr	BellSouth Classic	*TPC at Sugarloaf, Duluth, GA*
11-14 Apr	**MASTERS TOURNAMENT**	*Augusta National, GA*
18-21 Apr	Worldcom Classic	*Harbour Town GL, Hilton Head Island, SC*
25-28 Apr	Greater Greensboro Chrysler Classic	*Forest Oaks CC, Greensboro, NC*
2-5 May	Compaq Classic of New Orleans	*English Turn CC, New Orleans, LA*
9-12 May	Verizon Byron Nelson Classic	*TPC at Four Seasons, Irving, TX*
16-19 May	MasterCard Colonial	*Colonial CC, Fort Worth, TX*
23-26 May	Memorial Tournament	*Muirfield Village GC, Dublin, OH*
30 May-2 Jun	Kemper Insurance Open	*TPC at Avenel, Potomac, MD*
6-9 Jun	Buick Classic	*Westchester CC, Harrison, NY*
13-16 Jun	**US OPEN CHAMPIONSHIP**	*Bethpage State Park Farmingdale, NY*
20-23 Jun	Canon Greater Hartford Open	*TPC at River Highlands, Cromwell, CT*
27-30 Jun	FedEx St. Jude Classic	*TPC at Southwind, Memphis, TN*
4-7 Jul	Advil Western Open	*Cog Hill GCC, Lemont, IL*
11-14 Jul	Greater Milwaukee Open	*Brown Deer Park GC, Milwaukee, WI*
18-21 Jul	**131st OPEN GOLF CHAMPIONSHIP**	*Muirfield, East Lothian, Scotland*
18-21 Jul	B.C. Open	*En-Joie GC, Endicott, NY*
25-28 Jul	John Deere Classic	*TPC at Deere Run, Silvas, IL*
1-4 Aug	The International	*Castle Pines GC, Castle Rock, CO*
8-11 Aug	Buick Open	*Warwick Hills GCC, Grand Blanc, MI*
15-18 Aug	**US PGA CHAMPIONSHIP**	*Hazeltine National GC, Chaska, MN,*
22-25 Aug	WGC – NEC Invitational	*Sahalee CC, Redmond, WA*
22-25 Aug	Reno-Tahoe Open	*Montreux GCC, Reno, NV*
29 Aug-1 Sep	Air Canada Championship	*Northview GCC, Surrey, BC*
5-8 Sep	Bell Canadian Open	*Angus Glen GC, Markham, Ontario*
12-15 Sep	SEI Pennsylvania Classic	*Waynesborough CC, Paoli, PA*
19-22 Sep	WGC – American Express Championship	*Mount Juliet, Kilkenny, Ireland*
19-22 Sep	Tampa Bay Classic	*Westin Innisbrook Resort, Palm Harbor, FL*
27-29 Sep	THE 34TH RYDER CUP	*The De Vere Belfry, Sutton Coldfield, England*
26-29 Sep	Texas Open at LaCantera	*LaCantera GC, San Antonio, TX*
3-6 Oct	Michelob Championship	*Kingsmill GC, Williamsburg, VA*
9-13 Oct	Invensys Classic at Las Vegas	*TPC at Summerlin, Las Vegas, NV*
17-20 Oct	National Car Rental Golf Classic	*Magnolia Palm, Lake Buena Vista, FL*
24-27 Oct	Buick Challenge	*Callaway Gardens Resort, Pine Mountain, GA*
31 Oct-3 Nov	The Tour Championship	*East Lake GC, Atlanta, GA*
31 Oct-3 Nov	Southern Farm Bureau Classic	*Annandale GC, Madison, MS*

EUROPEAN ORDER OF MERIT 2001

Pos	Name	Money (euros)
1	Retief GOOSEN	2,862,806.13
2	Padraig HARRINGTON	2,090,165.54
3	Darren CLARKE	1,988,055.29
4	Ernie ELS	1,716,287.45
5	Colin MONTGOMERIE	1,578,676.04
6	Bernhard LANGER	1,577,129.63
7	Thomas BJORN	1,474,802.31
8	Paul MCGINLEY	1,464,433.67
9	Paul LAWRIE	1,428,830.50
10	Niclas FASTH	1,224,587.60
11	Angel CABRERA	1,183,349.62
12	Michael CAMPBELL	1,065,464.79
13	Adam SCOTT	898,625.71
14	David HOWELL	886,146.38
15	Robert KARLSSON	877,179.66
16	Mathias GRONBERG	854,296.03
17	Peter O'MALLEY	847,547.18
18	Ian WOOSNAM	837,808.53
19	Thomas LEVET	801,747.31
20	Miguel Angel JIMENEZ	788,201.82
21	Phillip PRICE	763,862.75
22	Paul CASEY	760,692.09
23	Pierre FULKE	751,174.26
24	Ian POULTER	736,460.08
25	Ricardo GONZALEZ	721,853.25
26	Andrew OLDCORN	717,344.30
27	Sergio GARCIA	715,287.63
28	Raphael JACQUELIN	656,556.00
29	Warren BENNETT	653,472.36
30	Steve WEBSTER	648,067.88
31	Andrew COLTART	647,006.40
32	Greg OWEN	626,201.07
33	Justin ROSE	620,992.88
34	Jean HUGO	594,025.80
35	Jose Maria OLAZABAL	578,594.78
36	Dean ROBERTSON	572,927.33
37	Soren HANSEN	540,207.30
38	Fredrik JACOBSON	532,168.37
39	Anders HANSEN	500,544.31
40	David LYNN	488,289.32
41	Barry LANE	477,088.41
42	Nick O'HERN	473,828.53
43	Gary ORR	453,666.61
44	Henrik STENSON	442,150.83
45	Daren LEE	428,404.00
46	John BICKERTON	427,058.98
47	Mark MCNULTY	414,923.97
48	Anthony WALL	409,381.31
49	Richard GREEN	406,911.15
50	Soren KJELDSEN	400,696.05
51	Alex CEJKA	399,347.90
52	Lee WESTWOOD	390,612.92
53	Brian DAVIS	386,811.69
54	Peter LONARD	367,437.68
55	Greg TURNER	361,414.48
56	Ian GARBUTT	361,364.23
57	Brett RUMFORD	355,183.53
58	Roger WESSELS	354,955.72
59	Gary EVANS	352,718.60
60	Gregory HAVRET	343,180.01
61	Carl PETTERSSON	342,812.96
62	Mark MOULAND	338,102.31
63	Mikael LUNDBERG	325,407.75
64	Raymond RUSSELL	325,404.51
65	Stephen GALLACHER	321,417.69
66	Nick FALDO	315,858.17
67	Sven STRUVER	314,285.20
68	Olle KARLSSON	303,036.21
69	Tony JOHNSTONE	291,933.74
70	Markus BRIER	283,439.66
71	Jarrod MOSELEY	280,167.64
72	Bradley DREDGE	276,979.96
73	Eduardo ROMERO	274,678.95
74	Costantino ROCCA	259,565.84
75	Roger CHAPMAN	257,790.54
76	Jorge BERENDT	254,159.43
77	Jonathan LOMAS	252,135.62
78	Gary EMERSON	251,294.44
79	Des SMYTH	249,550.63
80	Joakim HAEGGMAN	248,508.35
81	John SENDEN	248,267.52
82	Peter BAKER	245,083.82
83	Henrik BJORNSTAD	238,136.12
84	Diego BORREGO	233,501.39
85	David CARTER	232,156.66
86	Jean-Francois REMESY	230,338.51
87	Simon DYSON	230,293.97
88	Trevor IMMELMAN	222,242.74
89	Ignacio GARRIDO	220,420.96
90	Stephen LEANEY	213,336.69
91	Christopher HANELL	210,742.63
92	Anders FORSBRAND	209,018.38
93	Patrik SJOLAND	202,291.66
94	Mark PILKINGTON	201,974.40
95	Paul EALES	201,806.16
96	Jamie DONALDSON	195,502.12
97	Stephen DODD	192,554.38
98	Marc FARRY	189,935.43
99	Johan RYSTROM	188,870.17
100	Jarmo SANDELIN	188,865.68

FULL EUROPEAN TOUR RESULTS FOR 2001 AND POINTERS FOR 2002 START ON PAGE 10

PLAYER PROFILES START ON PAGE 188

Pos	Name	Money ($)	Pos	Name	Money ($)
1	Tiger Woods	5,687,777	56	Brett Quigley	956,934
2	Phil Mickelson	4,403,883	57	Tim Herron	945,441
3	David Toms	3,791,595	58	Chris Smith	932,810
4	Vijay Singh	3,440,829	59	Lee Janzen	905,628
5	Davis Love III	3,169,463	60	Mark Brooks	899,444
6	Sergio Garcia	2,898,635	61	John Daly	828,914
7	Scott Hoch	2,875,319	62	Olin Browne	815,636
8	David Duval	2,801,760	63	Briny Baird	812,001
9	Bob Estes	2,795,477	64	Dennis Paulson	811,105
10	Scott Verplank	2,783,401	65	K.J. Choi	800,326
11	Mike Weir	2,777,936	66	Harrison Frazar	792,456
12	Chris DiMarco	2,595,201	67	Skip Kendall	753,701
13	Jim Furyk	2,540,734	68	David Gossett	748,126
14	Joe Durant	2,381,684	69	Paul Stankowski	743,603
15	Ernie Els	2,336,456	70	Matt Gogel	729,783
16	Robert Allenby	2,309,029	71	Glen Day	715,780
17	Mark Calcavecchia	1,991,576	72	Jeff Maggert	713,607
18	Brad Faxon	1,951,412	73	David Peoples	712,657
19	Frank Lickliter II	1,941,911	74	Brent Geiberger	711,194
20	Tom Lehman	1,907,660	75	Greg Chalmers	692,170
21	Jeff Sluman	1,841,952	76	David Berganio, Jr.	685,082
22	Bernhard Langer	1,810,363	77	Garrett Willis	684,038
23	Scott McCarron	1,793,506	78	Esteban Toledo	683,751
24	Kenny Perry	1,786,066	79	Jonathan Kaye	683,210
25	Justin Leonard	1,783,842	80	Neal Lancaster	657,580
26	Stewart Cink	1,743,028	81	Joey Sindelar	654,864
27	Steve Lowery	1,738,820	82	J.P. Hayes	622,964
28	Hal Sutton	1,723,946	83	Paul Gow	608,382
29	Billy Mayfair	1,716,002	84	Len Mattiace	592,781
30	Steve Stricker	1,676,229	85	Jerry Smith	592,030
31	Jesper Parnevik	1,574,208	86	Loren Roberts	584,072
32	Kevin Sutherland	1,523,573	87	Brandel Chamblee	582,086
33	Paul Azinger	1,509,130	88	Mike Sposa	576,312
34	Jose Coceres	1,502,888	89	Stephen Ames	574,451
35	Jerry Kelly	1,491,607	90	Edward Fryatt	572,820
36	Rocco Mediate	1,474,435	91	Chris Perry	568,391
37	Shigeki Maruyama	1,441,455	92	Jay Haas	565,141
38	Kirk Triplett	1,388,202	93	Grant Waite	539,227
39	Tom Pernice, Jr.	1,318,762	94	Bob May	534,936
40	Billy Andrade	1,313,047	95	Geoff Ogilvy	525,338
41	Brian Gay	1,299,361	96	Scott Simpson	512,530
42	Nick Price	1,286,756	97	Per-Ulrik Johansson	510,488
43	Fred Funk	1,237,004	98	J.L. Lewis	508,618
44	Steve Flesch	1,207,552	99	Carl Paulson	508,208
45	Chris Riley	1,198,225	100	John Huston	505,252
46	Joel Edwards	1,193,528			
47	Retief Goosen	1,126,985			
48	Bob Tway	1,121,858			
49	J.J. Henry	1,073,847			
50	Cameron Beckman	1,071,343			
51	Robert Damron	1,059,187			
52	Rory Sabbatini	1,038,590			
53	Dudley Hart	1,035,710			
54	John Cook	1,022,778			
55	Stuart Appleby	1,004,528			

FULL US TOUR RESULTS FOR 2001 AND POINTERS FOR 2002 START ON PAGE 88

US PLAYER PROFILES START ON PAGE 239

EUROPEAN TOUR

JOHNNIE WALKER CLASSIC

Alpine Club, Thailand, 16 Nov to 19 Nov 2000, purse 1,348,565 euros

Pos	Name	R1	R2	R3	R4	Total	To par	Money	DD(y)	DA%	GIR%	Putts
1	Tiger WOODS	68	65	65	65	263	-25	221,134	319.3	78.6	79.2	109
2	Geoff OGILVY	68	67	67	64	266	-22	147,411	n/a	n/a	n/a	n/a
3	M CAMPBELL	71	67	63	69	270	-18	83,060	282.0	69.6	70.8	102
4	R PAMPLING	68	66	67	71	272	-16	61,300	n/a	n/a	n/a	n/a
	Paul LAWRIE	67	69	67	69	272	-16	61,300	295.1	62.5	75.0	111
6	Jesper PARNEVIK	72	65	69	70	276	-12	43,122	277.5	60.7	73.6	114
	Wayne SMITH	65	70	68	73	276	-12	43,122	n/a	n/a	n/a	n/a
8	A PAINTER	71	68	73	65	277	-11	33,171	n/a	n/a	n/a	n/a
9	Lian-Wei ZHANG	72	67	69	71	279	-9	26,890	n/a	n/a	n/a	n/a
	Nick O'HERN	69	72	72	66	279	-9	26,890	n/a	67.9	63.9	109
	David PODLICH	69	70	69	71	279	-9	26,890	n/a	n/a	n/a	n/a

Pos	Name	R1	R2	R3	R4	Total	To par
12	Richard GREEN	71	70	71	68	280	-8
	P O'MALLEY	72	70	68	70	280	-8
14	Paul GOW	66	70	73	72	281	-7
	Kenny DRUCE	70	68	68	75	281	-7
	Soren HANSEN	70	69	73	69	281	-7
	Rolf MUNTZ	69	75	70	67	281	-7
18	Craig JONES	72	73	70	67	282	-6
19	C PLAPHOL	74	68	70	71	283	-5
	Sergio GARCIA	74	64	75	70	283	-5
	Brett OGLE	71	73	69	70	283	-5
	P MARKSAENG	71	70	72	70	283	-5
	L PARSONS	72	70	69	72	283	-5
	S A LINDSKOG	71	74	70	68	283	-5
	D MARUYAMA	69	72	69	73	283	-5
26	Tom GILLIS	72	68	72	72	284	-4
	Carlos RODILES	71	70	73	70	284	-4
	C CEVAER	72	69	70	73	284	-4
	Wei-Tze YEH	71	71	70	72	284	-4
30	C ROCCA	70	75	71	69	285	-3
	Shane TAIT	72	67	72	74	285	-3
	Steen TINNING	71	72	73	69	285	-3
	Peter BAKER	71	74	71	69	285	-3
	T JAIDEE	71	71	74	69	285	-3
35	Wayne RILEY	71	70	72	73	286	-2
	M HARWOOD	73	72	70	71	286	-2
	A HANSEN	72	70	71	73	286	-2
	D TERBLANCHE	75	70	71	70	286	-2
	Peter LONARD	70	69	78	69	286	-2
	Scott HEND	68	72	72	74	286	-2
41	Ian POULTER	73	72	71	71	287	-1
	No-Seok PARK	71	71	71	74	287	-1
	J MOSELEY	69	74	72	72	287	-1
	Alex CEJKA	71	71	72	73	287	-1
	Chie-Hsiang LIN	70	71	72	74	287	-1
46	Andre STOLZ	73	68	73	74	288	E
	W-Soon KANG	74	71	71	72	288	E

Pos	Name	R1	R2	R3	R4	Total	To par
	Thomas LEVET	71	70	74	73	288	E
	Satoshi OIDE	72	71	67	78	288	E
	T-Chang WANG	71	74	69	74	288	E
	R CUELLO	70	75	71	72	288	E
52	Nick FALDO	71	73	74	71	289	+1
	Michael LONG	70	71	75	73	289	+1
	T IMMELMAN	76	68	70	75	289	+1
	J LOMAS	74	69	73	73	289	+1
	C D GRAY	74	69	71	75	289	+1
	Erol SIMSEK	70	72	75	72	289	+1
58	Greg TURNER	71	70	75	74	290	+2
	G NORQUIST.	71	71	77	71	290	+2
60	Rodger DAVIS	70	73	75	73	291	+3
	Peter SENIOR	72	71	73	75	291	+3
	J Milkha SINGH	68	74	71	78	291	+3
	Chia-Yuh HONG	73	71	75	72	291	+3
	Neil KERRY	74	71	74	72	291	+3
	A MCLARDY	70	73	73	75	291	+3
	S GARDINER	69	75	74	73	291	+3
67	Wayne GRADY	73	70	75	74	292	+4
	S KJELDSEN	72	69	75	76	292	+4
	John SENDEN	73	70	74	75	292	+4
	Matthew ECOB	71	71	76	74	292	+4
	U GUSTAFSSON	73	72	68	79	292	+4
72	Olle NORDBERG	73	72	71	77	293	+5
73	Mardan MAMAT	70	73	73	78	294	+6
	Tim ELLIOTT	72	72	74	76	294	+6
	Scott LAYCOCK	70	71	79	74	294	+6
	H NYSTROM	70	74	73	77	294	+6
	N VAN RENSBURG	70	73	80	71	294	+6
	Tobias DIER	69	75	71	79	294	+6
79	S ROBINSON	74	71	76	74	295	+7
80	Yong-Jin SHIN	70	71	76	79	296	+8
81	S COLLINS	72	72	84	72	300	+12

Sponsored by Stan James

Tournament Report

Tiger Woods claimed the 2000 Johnnie Walker Classic – his tenth title of a marvellous year – closing with his third successive 65 for a 25-under par total 263.

Australian Geoff Ogilvy repeated his runner-up spot from the 1999 tournament with a splendid final round of 64, to finish three strokes adrift, while Kiwi Michael Campbell made a stout defence of his title, taking third place on 18-under par.

It was, however, another demonstration of Woods' mastery in the year 2000 and confirmed his status as the world's number one golfer.

Woods began the final day three shots clear and although first Campbell and then Ogilvy briefly closed the gap to two, the American never looked in any trouble in a flawless display.

Woods, who beat Ernie Els in a play-off to land the title in 1998, began the week with a 68 to trail Australian Wayne Smith by three strokes, but he moved into overdrive and reeled off three consecutive rounds of 65, seven-under par, to leave the field in his slipstream.

Campbell, with a course record 63 in the third round, made a bold attempt to stay in touch with the American.

Paul Lawrie, the 1999 Open champion, was the leading European, sharing fourth spot with Australian, Rodney Pampling – the player who led Lawrie's Open at Carnoustie after the first round but missed the halfway cut. Lawrie had four rounds in the sixties to record his highest finish since occupying the same position in the Dubai Desert Classic earlier in the year.

Jesper Parnevik, who pulled out of the American Express Championship the previous week due to illness, finished with a 70 to tie for sixth place.

MISSED THE CUT: David HOWELL 71 75, Henrik STENSON 73 73, Richard S JOHNSON 77 69, Christian PENA 73 73, Johan RYSTROM 71 75, Bradley KING 77 69, Martyn ROBERTS 75 71, Dean ROBERTSON 74 72, Danny ZARATE 74 72, David HIGGINS 75 71, Sam TORRANCE 71 76, Arjun ATWAL 73 74, Fredrik HENGE 75 72, Matthew LANE 74 73, Simon YATES 74 73, Thomas GOGELE 73 74, Stuart BOUVIER 76 71, Van PHILLIPS 76 71, Yong-Eun YANG 75 72, Kyi Hla HAN 75 73, Jose Manuel LARA 73 75, Thammanoon SRIROJ 74 74, Robert WILLIS 75 73, Justin COOPER 77 71, Danny CHIA 75 73, Mikael LUNDBERG 74 74, Mike CLAYTON 73 76, Marcus NORGREN 73 76, Steve WEBSTER 75 74, Scott WEARNE 68 81, Boonchu RUANGKIT 74 75, James KINGSTON 71 78, Gavin COLES 76 74, Firoz ALI 77 73, Thavorn WIRATCHANT 77 73, Andrew RAITT 77 73, Cameron PERCY 75 75, Brendan JONES 77 73, Gaurav GHEI 76 75, Paul EALES 75 76, Adrian PERCEY 76 75, Craig KAMPS 79 72, Chris GAUNT 73 78, Mike CUNNING 76 76, Sammy DANIELS 80 72, Marc FARRY 76 76, Chris WILLIAMS 79 73, Anthony KANG 76 76, Jun CHENG 77 80, Maarten LAFEBER 80 80, Felix CASAS 81 W/D.

Sponsored by Stan James

Course Profile

In 2000 (counting for the 2001 European Tour), the Alpine Golf and Sports Club (par 72, 6,989 yards) was used – a course where accuracy is more of a prerequisite than power.

The 2002 renewal takes place at the Lake Karrinyup C.C. (par 72, 7,269 yards) in Perth. The layout has hosted the Australian Open four times.

The greens are fast and the hilly terrain can make it tough on the shins. The fairways meander through bushland which can be a problem.

Players/Points to Note

●This event moves to Australia in 2001 for the first time since 1997 (and only the second time in it's history), so look for local players and those battled hardened from playing on the ANZ Tour to do well.

●**Tiger Woods** won his second Johnnie Walker Classic in 2000 (part of the 2001 European Tour) and when this event is held in Asia, he always wants to do well, as his mother is Thai and he has legions of fans in that part of the world. His stroke average for four starts in this event is 69.69.

●**Ernie Els** was the last winner of this event when it came to Australia and can boast five top ten finishes in seven starts. Only Woods has won more money from the sponsors of this event down the years.

●**Michael Campbell** is a multiple winner Down Under and has registered four top-ten finishes in the Johnnie Walker, including a victory in 1999.

●Major winners **Fred Couples**, **Greg Norman**, **Nick Faldo** and **Ian Woosnam** have all won this event, while the Aussie duo of **Robert Allenby** and **Peter O'Malley**, both winners on the two main tours last year, are multiple top-ten finishers. As are Europeans **Colin Montgomerie** and **Andrew Coltart** – both of whom have also won Down Under in the last few years.

Previous Results

1999: 1. Michael Campbell (-12), 2. Geoff Ogilvy (-11), 3. Ernie Els (-10).

1998: 1. Tiger Woods (-9), won play-off, 2. Ernie Els (-9), 3. Retief Goosen (-8).

1997: 1. Ernie Els (-10), 2. Michael Long (-9), Peter Lonard (-9).

1996: 1. Ian Woosnam (-16), won play-off, 2. Andrew Coltart (-16), 3. Wayne Riley (-13), Paul Curry (-13), Olle Karlsson (-13).

1995: 1. Fred Couples (-11), 2. Nick Price (-9), 3. Robert Allenby (-8).

ALFRED DUNHILL CHAMPIONSHIP

Houghton G.C., 18 Jan to 21 Jan 2001, purse 791,618 euros

Pos	Name	R1	R2	R3	R4	Total	To par	Money	DD(y)	DA%	GIR%	Putts
1	Adam SCOTT	67	66	65	69	267	-21	123,071	314.4	69.6	84.7	119
2	Justin ROSE	66	67	66	69	268	-20	89,577	317.3	73.2	83.3	118
3	Nick FALDO	68	65	68	68	269	-19	46,151	295.8	67.9	81.9	112
	Dean ROBERTSON	62	70	67	70	269	-19	46,151	300	76.8	83.3	115
5	Anthony WALL	69	64	70	67	270	-18	32,247	311.4	66.1	81.9	118
6	M MACKENZIE	68	68	67	68	271	-17	27,574	300.0	67.9	83.3	119
7	Brian DAVIS	69	70	69	64	272	-16	21,070	309.0	64.3	80.6	118
	Retief GOOSEN	73	68	67	64	272	-16	21,070	309.0	57.1	80.6	121
9	Sven STRUVER	71	70	69	63	273	-15	16,825	296.8	64.3	75.0	113
10	Ricardo GONZALEZ	69	64	70	71	274	-14	14,072	311.9	53.6	76.4	116
	Greg OWEN	66	70	69	69	274	-14	14,072	n/a	n/a	n/a	n/a
	Michael KIRK	68	66	69	71	274	-14	14,072	313.8	60.7	80.6	118

Pos	Name	R1	R2	R3	R4	Total	To par		Pos	Name	R1	R2	R3	R4	Total	To par
13	J Milkha SINGH	70	66	69	70	275	-13			B DAVISON	71	70	72	68	281	-7
	Steve WEBSTER	66	70	72	67	275	-13	49	Chris WILLIAMS	72	67	73	70	282	-6
	Bradley DREDGE	67	68	68	72	275	-13			Jamie SPENCE	69	69	73	71	282	-6
16	Brenden PAPPAS	68	67	73	68	276	-12			A DA SILVA	69	69	71	73	282	-6
	Carl SUNESON	70	67	72	67	276	-12			M LUNDBERG	71	70	72	69	282	-6
	J LOMAS	72	67	69	68	276	-12	53	T JOHNSTONE	69	68	71	75	283	-5
	P McGINLEY	67	71	68	70	276	-12		Deane PAPPAS	69	70	67	77	283	-5
	M GRONBERG	66	70	71	69	276	-12		M GORTANA	68	72	71	72	283	-5
21	Nic HENNING	68	69	69	71	277	-11		Mark HILTON	72	68	72	71	283	-5
	S LUDGATER	69	67	71	70	277	-11		Ian POULTER	67	72	72	72	283	-5
23	Mark McNULTY	67	70	72	69	278	-10		Paul EALES	65	74	73	71	283	-5
	Anders HANSEN	71	68	71	68	278	-10		Jean HUGO	71	67	76	69	283	-5
	Peter BAKER	73	66	67	72	278	-10		O EDMOND	70	68	72	73	283	-5
	David FAUGHT	72	67	71	68	278	-10		N CHEETHAM	70	67	76	70	283	-5
	Bobby LINCOLN	69	68	70	71	278	-10		Brett LIDDLE	70	70	72	71	283	-5
	D TERBLANCHE	68	65	72	73	278	-10	63	Ian PALMER	69	72	71	72	284	-4
	Andrew RAITT	71	68	70	69	278	-10		D FICHARDT	72	65	75	72	284	-4
	Markus BRIER	69	69	70	70	278	-10		H WALTERS	69	71	71	73	284	-4
	David HIGGINS	69	70	71	68	278	-10		Steen TINNING	71	68	74	71	284	-4
	A ROESTOFF	66	70	72	70	278	-10		R S JOHNSON	68	72	68	76	284	-4
33	M BERNARDINI	73	68	72	66	279	-9		J RYSTROM	71	69	70	74	284	-4
34	B VAUGHAN	70	71	70	69	280	-8		A KINGSTON	74	66	74	70	284	-4
	T IMMELMAN	75	66	71	68	280	-8		Robert COLES	75	66	76	67	284	-4
	P BROADHURST	66	70	71	73	280	-8		D McGUIGAN	70	66	74	74	284	-4
	Justin HOBDAY	70	67	73	70	280	-8	72	D GAMMON	72	69	72	72	285	-3
	Stephen DODD	69	70	70	71	280	-8	73	W BENNETT	69	68	72	78	287	-1
	Ian GARBUTT	68	71	73	68	280	-8		Titch MOORE	69	71	75	72	287	-1
	A FORSYTH	68	66	77	69	280	-8		Michele REALE	73	68	73	73	287	-1
41	David HOWELL	71	69	69	72	281	-7		Ryan DREYER	71	66	75	75	287	-1
	R JACQUELIN	71	68	70	72	281	-7		Trevor MOORE	69	71	75	72	287	-1
	Peter HANSSON	73	65	69	74	281	-7	78	D BOTES	72	69	75	72	288	E
	Greg HAVRET	71	68	74	68	281	-7		Erol SIMSEK	67	71	74	76	288	E
	Van PHILLIPS	69	72	73	67	281	-7	80	U VAN DEN BERG	69	70	77	73	289	+1
	Craig KAMPS	67	74	71	69	281	-7	81	N COLSAERTS	70	69	73	78	290	+2
	Simon DYSON	69	66	77	69	281	-7	82	S McCARTHY	69	71	74	77	291	+3

Tournament Report

Young guns Adam Scott and Justin Rose treated golf fans to a glimpse of the future as they battled down the stretch for top honours at the Alfred Dunhill Championship at Houghton Golf Club.

Split by a fortnight in age, the two 20-year-old's left a host of European Tour winners trailing in their wake, including multiple Major winner Nick Faldo.

It was Scott, however, that came out on top. Leading by a shot entering the final round, he birdied the last to win by a single stroke – holding his nerve to hole out from three feet after Rose's effort missed by millimetres.

The challenges of Faldo and Scotland's Dean Robertson fell away over the back nine and it was left to Scott and Rose to go head to head over the final few holes. Scott actually had a four shot lead after a birdie on the fifth, but a three-putt on the ninth and another dropped shot on the tenth saw the chasing pack close.

In a titanic struggle between the two former amateur stars the advantage was held by first one then the other.

But Scott's approach at the last made the difference. His pitch to three feet put the pressure on Rose, who needed to hole from a further two yards away.

He didn't, and the £79,000 and two-year European Tour exemption went to Scott.

Robertson's course record first round 62 had put him in control but a second day 70 gave the field a chance to get back into the contest.

MISSED THE CUT: A FORSBRAND 71 71, M MOULAND 70 72, W COETSEE 76 66, O KARLSSON 69 73, P PRICE 71 71, R MUNTZ 73 69, G ROJAS 70 72, R WESSELS 73 69, D LEE 70 72, G WHITE 68 74, 93 D FROST 70 73, W RILEY 71 72, H OTTO 74 69, G EMERSON 70 73, W DRUIAN 71 72, J OLVER 72 71, T GOGELE 72 71, M SANTI 72 71, J MASHEGO 70 73, N VANHOOTEGEM 71 72, A McLEAN 73 70, D LYNN 67 76, J BICKERTON 71 72, A CRUSE 72 71, S VAN VUUREN 71 72, S GALLACHER 66 77, G STORM 71 72, 110 S DANIELS 73 71, G HOUSTON 70 74, E BOULT 72 72, G RANKIN 73 71, J BELE 71 73, T VAN DER WALT 77 67, T LEVET 71 73, G MULLER 71 74, A ATWAL 72 73, S P WEBSTER 74 71, F HENGE 74 71, Keith HORNE 77 68, P O'BRIEN 75 70, I GARRIDO 72 73, S GREWAL 68 77, S THABANG 73 72, D VAN STADEN 77 69, P LAWRIE 76 70, M CAYEUX 72 74, J LOUGHNANE 71 75, W BRADLEY 71 75, C DAVISON 75 71, D W BASSON 76 70, D CRAWFORD 74 72, N VAN RENSBURG 76 70, C PETTERSSON 76 70, B VAUGHAN 73 74, J-F REMESY 74 73, T DODDS 75 72, R KAPLAN 75 72, D CARTER 71 76, T DIER 76 71, L SLATTERY 74 73, M MURLESS 74 74, HANSEN 76 72, O SANDYS 76 72, D PARK 73 76, C WHITELAW 74 75, S BARNES 75 74, D OWEN 75 74, D STANDER 79 71, M LAFEBER 77 73, M ARCHER 75 75, L NDWANDWE 74 76, K FERRIE 74 77, A RICHTER 73 78, I HUTCHINGS 78 75, R FLETCHER 76 DISQ.

Course Profile

Houghton Golf Club (par 72 7,309 yards) is situated in the suburbs of Johannesburg and is one of the longest layouts on the European Tour.

As it's way above sea level, though, the ball does travel further naturally.

The fairways are wide so accuracy off the tee is not a necessity.

Water comes into play on nine holes and the greens can be fast.

Two of the last five tournaments have been curtailed to 54 holes due to adverse conditions.

Players/Points to Note

●**Ernie Els** bypassed this event in 2000 and 2001 to play in America. But punters will be hoping the Big Easy returns in 2002. His big-hitting game is well suited to the venue as four top tens (from four starts) suggest. He won here in 1992 (Sunshine Tour), 1995 and 1999 and has a stroke average of 68.13 since 1995.

●**Retief Goosen** will hopefully come back to play in 2002, even though his US Open win in 2001 has now elevated his worldwide golfing status. The Goose has finished in the top ten on four occasions in seven starts.

South African veterans **Tony Johnstone** (three top tens including victory here in 1998 from seven starts), **Mark McNulty** and **David Frost** always do well here.

●Watch out for players who have been plying their trade on the Sunshine Tour, as they obviously cope with the conditions better. **Nico Van Rensburg**, **Ashley Roestoff**, **Nic Henning**, **Tjaart Van der Walt** and Houghton member **Roger Wessels** and **Richard Kaplan** have been worth following in the past.

●Former winners **Anthony Wall** and **Sven Struver**, along with **Patrik Sjoland** and **Gary Orr** look the best of the Europeans.

●**Adam Scott** will defend his crown in 2002 and should go close again, while runner up in 2001, **Justin Rose**, grew up playing courses in South Africa.

Previous Results

2000 1. Anthony Wall (-12) 2. Nick Price (-10), Gary Orr (-10).

1999 1. Ernie Els (-15) 2. Richard Kaplan (-11) 3. David Frost (-8), Stephen Leaney (-8), Steve Webster (-8), Jeev Milkha Singh (-8).

1998 1. Tony Johnstone (-17) 2. Ernie Els (-15) 3. Nick Price (-13), Retief Goosen (-13).

1997 1. Nick Price (-19), won play off, 2. David Frost (-19) 3. Nico Van Rensburg (-18).

1996 1. Sven Struver (-14) 2. David Feherty (-11), Ernie Els (-11).

MERCEDES-BENZ SOUTH AFRICAN OPEN

East London G.C., 25 Jan to 28 Jan 2001, purse 1,058,953 euros

Pos	Name	R1	R2	R3	R4	Total	To par	Money	DD(y)	DA%	GIR%	Putts
1	Mark McNULTY	69	71	69	71	280	-8	169,283	270.8	61.7	63.9	109
2	Justin ROSE	72	69	68	72	281	-7	122,823	289.9	68.3	66.7	114
3	Thomas BJORN	72	67	71	72	282	-6	63,120	279.9	53.3	62.5	111
	Roger WESSELS	67	69	72	74	282	-6	63,120	265.0	68.3	77.8	121
5	Hennie OTTO	65	70	71	77	283	-5	40,692	279.4	28.3	59.7	109
	Mikael LUNDBERG	71	67	73	72	283	-5	40,692	264.5	58.3	58.3	109
7	M MACKENZIE	76	68	77	63	284	-4	28,409	281.9	58.3	68.1	121
	B VAUGHAN	71	74	70	69	284	-4	28,409	279.0	63.3	61.1	109
9	Desvonde BOTES	70	71	74	70	285	-3	18,110	288.5	63.3	65.3	113
	Arjun ATWAL	72	70	72	71	285	-3	18,110	279.5	55.0	73.6	121
	Justin HOBDAY	70	70	70	75	285	-3	18,110	234.5	65.0	62.5	114
	Johan RYSTROM	71	71	75	68	285	-3	18,110	295.8	78.3	72.2	122
	S GALLACHER	70	71	71	73	285	-3	18,110	276.3	63.3	61.1	115
	Tobias DIER	71	66	76	72	285	-3	18,110	300.9	61.7	62.5	118
	Simon DYSON	69	72	69	75	285	-3	18,110	280.5	70.0	59.7	109

Pos	Name	R1	R2	R3	R4	Total	To par
16	David HOWELL	71	67	73	75	286	-2
	Brian DAVIS	73	70	74	69	286	-2
	Peter BAKER	72	73	75	66	286	-2
	I GARRIDO	66	73	73	74	286	-2
	Martin MARITZ	69	71	74	72	286	-2
21	M ARCHER	71	73	71	72	287	-1
	Paul McGINLEY	71	72	70	74	287	-1
	B DREDGE	67	70	74	76	287	-1
	Retief GOOSEN	71	68	73	75	287	-1
	Erol SIMSEK	72	70	75	70	287	-1
26	J Milkha SINGH	71	71	70	76	288	E
	B VAUGHAN	70	71	74	73	288	E
	T IMMELMAN	72	73	69	74	288	E
	J KINGSTON	68	74	73	73	288	E
	David LYNN	72	72	75	69	288	E
	Greg OWEN	67	69	74	78	288	E
	David PARK	74	68	76	70	288	E
	Markus BRIER	70	73	68	77	288	E
34	Grant MULLER	69	73	72	75	289	+1
	S P WEBSTER	72	71	75	71	289	+1
	Rolf MUNTZ	75	69	73	72	289	+1
	Trevor DODDS	70	73	75	71	289	+1
38	Paul EALES	71	72	74	73	290	+2
	Wayne BRADLEY	71	74	73	72	290	+2
	Daren LEE	75	70	76	69	290	+2
	A FORSYTH	74	70	69	77	290	+2
	B DAVISON	71	73	74	72	290	+2
	D McGUIGAN	74	69	70	77	290	+2
	C PETTERSSON	72	73	75	70	290	+2
45	Sven STRUVER	70	73	77	71	291	+3
	N KAMUNGEREMU	69	71	72	79	291	+3
	D CRAWFORD	70	73	76	72	291	+3
	Andre CRUSE	70	74	73	74	291	+3
	David HIGGINS	70	73	77	71	291	+3
	A ROESTOFF	72	73	75	71	291	+3
51	Wayne RILEY	69	71	79	73	292	+4
	B PAPPAS	68	72	73	79	292	+4
	Peter HANSON	72	72	78	70	292	+4
54	D VAN STADEN	75	70	73	75	293	+5
	Ian POULTER	72	70	79	72	293	+5
	Paolo QUIRICI	67	73	75	78	293	+5
	Michele REALE	71	74	75	73	293	+5
	J VAN DER MERWE	72	72	76	73	293	+5
59	Deane PAPPAS	72	70	79	73	294	+6
	J-F REMESY	70	74	78	72	294	+6
	Gary EMERSON	75	70	74	75	294	+6
	M GRONBERG	76	69	73	76	294	+6
	M WILCOX	70	71	81	72	294	+6
	Jaco VAN ZYL	75	67	72	80	294	+6
65	R JACQUELIN	71	71	76	77	295	+7
	Wallie COETSEE	72	73	71	79	295	+7
	Bobby LINCOLN	70	69	76	80	295	+7
	Ted HENDRIKS	72	73	75	75	295	+7
69	R KAPLAN	72	72	80	72	296	+8
	L NDWANDWE	73	71	74	78	296	+8
71	Ian KENNEDY	72	72	79	74	297	+9
72	Chris DAVISON	71	74	79	76	300	+12

Sponsored by Stan James

Tournament Report

Mark McNulty proved that there's no substitute for experience as the wily 47-year-old completed his 50th tournament victory as a pro by holding off the challenge of 20-somethings Justin Rose and Thomas Bjorn to land the South African Open.

One of the oldest swingers on the European Tour, he holed a 25-foot par putt on the last to pip Rose for the title. The Englishman had to settle for a second successive runners-up spot after failing to hole out from 15 feet – which would have forced a play-off.

McNulty won his first European Tour tournament before Rose was born but throughout the last round there was little to choose between them.

Lying three shots behind third round leader Hennie Otto, McNulty and Rose caught and then passed the South African – who shot 40 on the outward nine – and as the lead changed hands between them – and Roger Wessels – on the final day, it was McNulty's nerve that held.

The wind blew and the Zimbabwean seemed to take control when he made, and Rose missed, a putt from inside ten feet on the 11th. Wessels' challenge ended when he dropped shots on the final two holes.

Bjorn struggled to get to grips with the conditions while Malcolm Mackenzie's course record 63 was shot in the benign early conditions.

So it was left to McNulty to claim this title for the second time in his career and show the youngsters a trick or two.

MISSED THE CUT: A FORSBRAND 71 75, T JOHNSTONE 72 74, G LEVENSON 73 73, T MOORE 69 77, V GROENEWALD 74 72, J HUGO 74 72, K HORNE 72 74, D LAMBERT 73 73, O EDMOND 71 75, J LOMAS 71 75, R GONZALEZ 68 78, M GREEN 75 71, S LUDGATER 74 72, R STERNE 73 73, M KIRK 72 74, B PRYTZ 75 72, A HANSEN 72 75, M MURLESS 71 76, T VAN DER WALT 76 71, F HENGE 70 77, T LEVET 75 72, I HUTCHINGS 76 71, I GARBUTT 75 72, N VANHOOTEGEM 74 73, D GAMMON 75 72, J BICKERTON 76 71, T CASE 73 74, G HOUSTON 73 75, J OLVER 77 71, J RANDHAWA 73 75, V PHILLIPS 74 74, B LIDDLE 73 75, C WHITELAW 72 76, S VAN VUUREN 73 75, N VAN RENSBURG 73 75, C KAMPS 76 72, M BERNARDINI 74 74, S WEBSTER 72 77, J BELE 77 72, J SPENCE 74 75, P BROADHURST 74 75, S HANSEN 71 78, R S JOHNSON 72 77, D ROBERTSON 71 78, B SMITS 73 76, S DANIELS 76 74, D FICHARDT 73 77, G RANKIN 75 75, S FARRELL 77 73, M CAYEUX 71 79, N CHEETHAM 72 78, J MASHEGO 75 75, A BOSSERT 76 74, D TERBLANCHE 75 75, J CAYLESS 77 73, A DA SILVA 75 75, N HENNING 79 71, G STORM 73 77, R DREYER 74 76, J DONALDSON 72 78, I PALMER 77 74, R SAILER 74 78, M GORTANA 75 76, G VAN DE NEST 73 79, K FERRIE 75 76, M FLORIOLI 77 74, A RAITT 75 76, R STEWART 75 76, S THABANG 78 74, C RIES 74 78, D BREDENKAMP 78 74, C WILLIAMS 74 79, C SWART 76 78, N BARNETT 73 81, D CLARKE 77 78, O SANDYS 74 81, W DRUIAN 79 77, U VAN DEN BERG 75 82, C SUNESON 81 76, A McLEAN 80 77, P SANDERSON 82 76, N HOMANN 80 80, R WHITFIELD 84 80, K STONE DISQ.

Course Profile

Last year, the event was held at East London G.C. (par 72, 6,847 yards) in Johannesburg, one of the oldest venues in South Africa.

A short but tough track which relies on narrow fairways and wind for its defence. And the same can be said of the course that hosts the 2002 renewal – the Country Club in Durban (par 72, 7,200 yards approx).

This links-type venue gets battered by gusts from the Indian Ocean and you need accuracy off the tee to succeed.

Players/Points to Note

● Another tournament that has **Ernie Els** written all over it. He didn't play in 2000 or 2001 due to his American schedule, but hasn't finished outside the top three in three visits since 1997. He won in 1998 and also in 1992 and 1996 when it wasn't part of the European Tour.

● South African veterans **David Frost**, won this event in 1999 on his home course of Stellenbosch, **Mark McNulty**, who won this tournament last year, and **Tony Johnstone**, the 1994 champion, are always worth following.

● Again watch out for Sunshine Tour regulars such as **Nico Van Rensburg, Ashley Roestoff, Desvond Botes, Tjaart Van der Walt, Roger Wessels, Hennie Otto** and **Jean Hugo**.

● **Bernhard Langer** and **Thomas Bjorn** have been regular competitors in this event and can boast two top-ten finishes in three and four starts respectively.

● **Jeev Milkha Singh** was second here in 1999 and a respectable 37th in 2000. The hot conditions in South Africa are obviously to his liking.

● **Retief Goosen** and **Alex Cejka** have both featured in the top ten on two occasions over the past four years.

● The English pair of **Justin Rose** and **Simon Dyson** both secured top-ten finishes last season and have experience of playing in hot conditions.

● **Sven Struver** is a regular top-ten performer in South Africa.

Previous Results

2000: 1. Matthias Gronburg (-14), 2. Nick Price (-13), Darren Fichardt (-13), Ricardo Gonzalez (-13).

1999: 1. David Frost (-5), 2. Jeev Milkha Singh (-4), Scott Dunlap (-4).

1998: 1 Ernie Els (-15), 2. David Frost (-12), 3. Patrik Sjoland (-8).

1997: 1. Vijay Singh (-18), 2. Nick Price (-17), 3. Mark McNulty (-13), Fulton Allem (-13), Ernie Els (-13).

HEINEKEN CLASSIC
The Vines Resort, 1 Feb to 4 Feb 2001, purse 1,042,204 euros

Pos	Name	R1	R2	R3	R4	Total	To par	Money	DD(y)	DA%	GIR%	Putts
1	M CAMPBELL	69	70	67	64	270	-18	195,498	300.4	76.8	86.1	120
2	David SMAIL	71	72	66	66	275	-13	110,782	n/a	71.4	76.4	120
3	Nick O'HERN	66	69	69	72	276	-12	73,312	274.6	82.1	80.6	119
4	Paul DEVENPORT	71	68	69	69	277	-11	42,358	n/a	67.9	79.2	116
	Steen TINNING	69	66	72	70	277	-11	42,358	254.9	75.0	76.4	119
	Jarrod MOSELEY	70	70	70	67	277	-11	42,358	293.1	73.2	69.4	114
	D ROBERTSON	65	74	68	70	277	-11	42,358	276.3	80.4	63.9	109
8	R KARLSSON	72	66	72	70	280	-8	29,324	n/a	n/a	n/a	n/a
	Ian GARBUTT	78	66	68	68	280	-8	29,324	274.5	82.1	80.6	123
	Thomas BJORN	67	71	73	69	280	-8	29,324	277.8	64.3	79.2	121

Pos	Name	R1	R2	R3	R4	Total	To par
11	Greg TURNER	70	71	69	72	282	-6
	Kenny DRUCE	72	72	66	72	282	-6
	Peter LONARD	70	71	66	75	282	-6
	F JACOBSON	71	72	70	69	282	-6
	H NYSTROM	75	69	70	68	282	-6
16	Greg NORMAN	66	73	70	74	283	-5
	Craig PARRY	70	70	69	74	283	-5
	Brett RUMFORD	72	70	71	70	283	-5
19	Soren HANSEN	76	69	71	68	284	-4
	Phillip PRICE	75	70	69	70	284	-4
	David CARTER	73	70	71	70	284	-4
	Nathan GREEN	72	70	72	70	284	-4
23	David HOWELL	72	73	66	74	285	-3
	Justin ROSE	70	75	68	72	285	-3
	P BROADHURST	74	69	70	72	285	-3
	A GILLIGAN	71	73	69	72	285	-3
	Pierre FULKE	67	76	69	73	285	-3
	Markus BRIER	71	73	68	73	285	-3
	C HANELL	74	70	72	69	285	-3
	Brendan JONES	72	70	69	74	285	-3
	S GARDINER	71	72	71	71	285	-3
32	John WADE	73	70	70	73	286	-2
	Scott LAYCOCK	67	74	74	71	286	-2
34	Sven STRUVER	72	71	73	71	287	-1
	Wayne SMITH	69	73	72	73	287	-1
	Gary EVANS	72	73	71	71	287	-1
	L PARSONS	72	73	70	72	287	-1
	A TSCHUDIN	73	68	71	75	287	-1
39	Richard GREEN	69	76	74	69	288	E
	Andre STOLZ	73	71	70	74	288	E
	Shane TAIT	67	72	77	72	288	E
	Michael LONG	71	72	73	72	288	E
	J BICKERTON	74	66	73	75	288	E
44	A PAINTER	70	72	73	74	289	+1
	I GARRIDO	68	75	76	70	289	+1
	Bradley KING	69	74	70	76	289	+1
	G NORQUIST	71	74	68	76	289	+1
48	Peter SENIOR	69	72	73	76	290	+2
	Matthew ECOB	73	72	75	70	290	+2
	R S JOHNSON	77	68	71	74	290	+2
	J HAEGGMAN	73	71	75	71	290	+2
	M ROBERTS	73	72	70	75	290	+2
	S SCAHILL	74	70	75	71	290	+2
54	Jeff WAGNER	77	68	71	75	291	+3
	Marcus CAIN	71	73	72	75	291	+3
	Matthew LANE	72	73	73	73	291	+3
	David LYNN	72	73	73	73	291	+3
58	R PAMPLING	76	69	76	71	292	+4
59	M LAFEBER	70	73	75	75	293	+5
60	R CHAPMAN	73	67	74	80	294	+6
	John SENDEN	76	68	77	73	294	+6
	Rolf MUNTZ	72	72	72	78	294	+6
63	Stuart BOUVIER	73	71	78	73	295	+7
64	R WINCHESTER	72	73	74	77	296	+8
	Niclas FASTH	73	72	79	72	296	+8
66	H STENSON	69	74	76	78	297	+9
67	Justin COOPER	74	70	70	84	298	+10
	C HOWELL III	70	73	77	78	298	+10
	Robert FLOYD	75	69	75	79	298	+10
	James McLEAN	74	67	86	71	298	+10
71	R WESSELS	71	67	-	-	-	DISQ

16

Sponsored by Stan James

Tournament Report

A superb final day, 64 enabled Michael Campbell to successfully defend his Heineken Classic title at The Vines Resort in Perth.

The Kiwi's last round score was the lowest of the championship and the quality of golf demonstrated by Cambo blew away the field.

His five-shot winning margin was the biggest on the European Tour so far this season. Campbell, who trailed Nick O'Hern by two shots entering the final round, birdied the seventh, ninth, tenth, 11th, 13th, 16th and 18th.

But the turning point was surely the sixth, when O'Hern made a quadruple bogey eight, to fall from two ahead to two behind the eventual winner. The mighty Maori just failed to equal the course record when his eagle attempt drifted wide at the last.

David Smail's weekend 66-66 finish ensured a New Zealand one-two as the Kiwi followed up back to back wins at home with second place.

O'Hern's misdemeanours at the sixth seemed to knock the stuffing out of the left hander, but to his credit birdies at the 10th, 12th and 15th meant he hung onto third spot in his own.

Former champion Jarrod Moseley again proved the horses for courses rule applies at the Vines by finishing fourth but this was Cambo's day and he cited the work that he put into his short game as being crucial to his win – "I worked very hard on my putting on Saturday night. That made the difference."

MISSED THE CUT: C JONES 70 76, M HARWOOD 74 72, A HANSEN 74 72, S KJELDSEN 71 75, S WEBSTER 74 72, N KERRY 73 73, T ELLIOTT 72 74, I POULTER 73 73, P MITCHELL 73 73, S WEARNE 71 75, G COLES 73 73, J LOMAS 72 74, A PERCEY 75 71, T DIER 73 73, A FORSYTH 74 72, J BENEPE 72 74, N FALDO 74 73, R JACQUELIN 72 75, S COLLINS 75 72, R BACKWELL 72 75, D MACKENZIE 72 75, F HENGE 73 74, B OGLE 76 71, P O'MALLEY 73 74, V PHILLIPS 69 78, R COLES 78 69, T POWER 72 75, D HIGGINS 74 73, D LABELLE 73 74, R RAFFERTY 76 72, J M LARA 72 76, S LEANEY 75 73, S CONRAN 75 73, A BONHOMME 75 73, R WILLIS 73 75, P QUIRICI 75 73, C CEVAER 72 76, G OWEN 74 74, D PARK 72 76, T PRICE 73 75, C GAUNT 74 74, P FOWLER 77 72, G RANKIN 74 75, R BYRD 77 72, P MCWHINNEY 78 71, M PILKINGTON 76 73, R RUSSELL 76 73, D LEE 73 76, A CRAWFORD 75 74, A SCOTT 72 77, W GRADY 81 69, M NORGREN 77 73, S ALKER 76 74, A WALL 78 72, D PODLICH 76 74, A ATWAL 76 75, T MILLS 79 72, P BAKER 74 77, F CEA 76 75, E SIMSEK 74 77, K FELTON 84 67, C ROCCA 71 81, E BOULT 79 73, C RODILES 73 79, N VANHOOTEGEM 74 78, A RAITT 78 74, S GALLACHER 76 76, E WALTERS 77 75, S HEND 79 73, D BRANSDON 76 77, S ROBINSON 80 73, M WHEELHOUSE 78 75, P TATAURANGI 82 71, W-T YEH 80 73, B LANE 72 82, G SIMPSON 74 80, N GATEHOUSE 78 76, M FARRY 76 79, W RILEY 81 75, K FERRIE 80 78, T GOGELE 80 78, C PERCY 79 80, A CEJKA 77 DISQ, C D GRAY 80 W/D P SJOLAND 74 RTD.

Course Profile

The Vines (par 72, 7,058 yards) was used for this event for the past ten years and puts a premium on accuracy. The wind could also be a factor.

In 2002, the event moves to the Royal Melbourne G.C. in Victoria (par 72, 7,066 yards), an old fashioned course with a US Open feel to it. The track is a real scramblers course, with narrow fairways and small, fast greens. There are plenty of bunkers and sandy rough.

Players/Points to Note

●The most established Australian event on the European Tour but one which changes venue for the first time in 2002 – from The Vines Resort in Perth to the Royal Melbourne G.C. (the track used for the WGC Matchplay tournament in 2001).

●**Ernie Els** did everything but win this event when it was held at The Vines, throwing away a commanding lead in 1999 and posting four top-ten finishes in four starts all told. Having made the semi-final of the WGC Matchplay at Royal Melbourne in 2001 the South African's good run should continue in this event if he chooses to tee up in this event.

●**Michael Campbell** will be bidding for a hat-trick of wins in this tournament in 2002 and after defeating the field by five shots on each of his other two victories, Cambo should be backed.

●**Ian Woosnam** won this title in 1996 and followed up with sixth in 1997 and second the year after.

●**Thomas Bjorn** hasn't finished lower than 26th in five starts, won here in 1998, was runner-up in 2000 and eighth last year. In that time he's shot just five rounds over par and has a stroke average of 69.95.

●The Antipodean duo of **David Smail** and 1999 champion **Jarrod Moseley** boast two top-ten finishes each, as can **Jarmo Sandelin**.

Previous Results

_2000:_ 1. Michael Campbell (-20), 2. Thomas Bjorn (-14), 3. Alastair Forsyth (-13).

_1999:_ 1. Jarrod Moseley (-14), 2. Bernhard Langer (-13), Ernie Els (-13), Peter Lonard (-13).

_1998:_ 1. Thomas Bjorn (-8), 2. Ian Woosnam (-7), 3. Padraig Harrington (-6), Jose Maria Olazabal (-6), Peter Baker (-6), Ernie Els (-6).

_1997:_ 1. Miguel Angel Martin (-15), 2. Fred Couples (-14), 3. Marc Farry (-13), Frank Nobilo (-13), Jean Van de Velde (-13).

_1996:_ 1. Ian Woosnam (-11), 2. Jean Van de Velde (-10), Paul McGinley (-10).

GREG NORMAN HOLDEN INTERNATIONAL

The Lakes G.C., 8 Feb to 11 Feb 2001, purse 1,196,575 euros

Pos	Name	R1	R2	R3	R4	Total	To par	Money	DD(y)	DA%	GIR%	Putts
1	Aaron BADDELEY	67	68	68	68	271	-21	223,593	300.1	55.4	77.8	112
	Won play-off											
2	Sergio GARCIA	64	69	70	68	271	-21	126,703	287.3	76.8	84.7	115
3	Ian POULTER	70	69	65	68	272	-20	83,847	284.5	67.9	79.2	116
4	Greg NORMAN	66	68	71	68	273	-19	59,625	284.0	82.1	80.6	113
5	Nick O'HERN	70	69	72	65	276	-16	49,687	278.9	71.4	84.7	125
6	Jarrod MOSELEY	72	68	66	71	277	-15	42,234	279.9	64.3	73.6	115
	Peter LONARD	74	66	66	71	277	-15	42,234	283.3	69.6	77.8	115
8	Carlos RODILES	70	72	69	67	278	-14	30,557	281.4	76.8	79.2	119
	Craig PARRY	69	68	71	70	278	-14	30,557	n/a	78.6	77.8	118
	Robert KARLSSON	74	69	68	67	278	-14	30,557	292.0	73.2	81.9	123
	Phillip PRICE	66	69	74	69	278	-14	30,557	291.3	71.4	76.4	116
	Scott GARDINER	71	72	66	69	278	-14	30,557	287.5	67.9	70.8	119

Pos	Name	R1	R2	R3	R4	Total	To par		Pos	Name	R1	R2	R3	R4	Total	To par
13	Steve ALKER	66	72	71	70	279	-13			C HOWELL III	75	68	69	73	285	-7
	David SMAIL	71	68	71	69	279	-13			Nathan GREEN	67	69	77	72	285	-7
	R PAMPLING	70	71	69	69	279	-13			James McLEAN	69	67	75	74	285	-7
	Pierre FULKE	65	71	73	70	279	-13	46		Brett RUMFORD	72	67	74	73	286	-6
17	Marc FARRY	68	70	73	69	280	-12	47		Tim ELLIOTT	71	73	73	70	287	-5
	Peter BAKER	71	68	70	71	280	-12			Shane TAIT	70	68	74	75	287	-5
	David PARK	71	72	72	65	280	-12			Elliot BOULT	74	70	70	73	287	-5
	David CARTER	68	74	72	66	280	-12			Paolo QUIRICI	70	73	71	73	287	-5
21	S LEANEY	71	71	68	71	281	-11			Bob FRIEND	72	71	75	69	287	-5
	Kenny DRUCE	72	69	71	69	281	-11			Andrew RAITT	72	72	69	74	287	-5
	Justin ROSE	75	69	66	71	281	-11	53		Wayne RILEY	74	70	72	72	288	-4
	F JACOBSON	68	74	72	67	281	-11			Anthony WALL	70	71	77	70	288	-4
	Daren LEE	66	71	76	68	281	-11			Marcus CAIN	72	69	73	74	288	-4
26	Anders HANSEN	75	69	72	66	282	-10			Greg OWEN	69	72	74	73	288	-4
	D BRANSDON	70	73	66	73	282	-10			Terry PRICE	71	72	74	71	288	-4
	J HAEGGMAN	70	70	73	69	282	-10	58		R S JOHNSON	75	69	72	73	289	-3
	R RUSSELL	71	71	71	69	282	-10	59		Scott LAYCOCK	74	70	69	77	290	-2
	Adam SCOTT	70	67	74	71	282	-10			Gary EVANS	72	72	70	76	290	-2
31	R CHAPMAN	70	70	70	73	283	-9			L PARSONS	74	65	76	75	290	-2
	John SENDEN	69	72	72	70	283	-9	62		S COLLINS	68	73	75	75	291	-1
	Soren HANSEN	67	72	72	72	283	-9			R WESSELS	73	69	73	76	291	-1
	Matthew LANE	72	70	71	70	283	-9	64		Rodger DAVIS	71	72	73	76	292	E
	Peter O'MALLEY	68	74	71	70	283	-9			H STENSON	76	68	72	76	292	E
	Niclas FASTH	70	70	70	73	283	-9			P TATAURANGI	75	69	72	76	292	E
	D ROBERTSON	75	68	69	71	283	-9	67		Andre STOLZ	74	70	75	74	293	+1
	J BICKERTON	72	72	69	70	283	-9			A PAINTER	75	68	75	75	293	+1
39	M NORGREN	70	72	75	68	285	-7	69		M LAFEBER	70	72	75	77	294	+2
	S KJELDSEN	72	68	73	72	285	-7	70		Adrian PERCEY	70	74	71	80	295	+3
	Ian GARBUTT	71	72	74	68	285	-7	71		John WADE	71	72	78	76	297	+5
	David LYNN	70	71	70	74	285	-7			M ROBERTS	78	66	77	76	297	+5

Sponsored by Stan James

Tournament Report

Greg Norman has been instrumental in the rise of Aaron Baddeley to the forefront of Australian golf and it seemed appropriate that the apprentice should take the sorcerers money in the Great White's own tournament.

The 19-year-old won his first European Tour title by defeating Sergio Garcia in a play-off. But the young Aussie wouldn't have had the opportunity but for Sergio infringing the rules.

Garcia had dominated the first two rounds of the event but fell foul of a two-stroke penalty after breaching a local rule when taking an incorrect drop on the first hole of the third day.

It meant that instead of leading the tournament by two shots entering the final day he was tied with Baddeley.

The blunder must have affected Garcia who fell behind the local favourite before fighting back. After the pair both parred the last, Baddeley calmly stroked home a 15ft putt on the first extra hole after his rival had missed from just over twice that distance.

Garcia was gracious in defeat, and paid tribute to Baddeley's qualities. But after another talking to from the tournament director – this time regarding his attire – the Spaniard might not have particularly fond memories of the event. He probably felt that tournament officials were conspiring against him, letting fly with the verbal volley 'it's just that somebody didn't want me to win'. Last year's European Tour Rookie of the Year, Ian Poulter, holed a bunker shot on the 17th to help him to third.

MISSED THE CUT: R JACQUELIN 68 77, S STRUVER 70 75, G TURNER 69 76, R GREEN 70 75, R MUNTZ 74 71, E SIMSEK 74 71, M CAMPBELL 74 71, C HANELL 74 71, A FORSYTH 72 73, D LABELLE 75 70, C ROCCA 75 71, P FOWLER 70 76, J M SINGH 72 74, N KERRY 76 70, A BONHOMME 75 71, G COLES 76 70, A CEJKA 75 71, N VANHOOTEGEM 72 74, M BRIER 72 74, G NORQUIST 72 74, B LANE 73 74, S WEBSTER 73 74, S CONRAN 72 75, R BACKWELL 75 72, M LONG 71 76, J COOPER 72 75, P MITCHELL 72 75, G OGILVY 74 73, J LOMAS 74 73, C CEVAER 78 69, B KING 74 73, V PHILLIPS 73 74, S SCAHILL 76 71, R COLES 77 70, T POWER 71 76, C PERCY 74 73, A CRAWFORD 74 73, W GRADY 71 77, R WILLIS 74 74, P BROADHURST 74 74, W SMITH 72 76, D HIGGINS 78 70, T DIER 74 74, E WALTERS 73 75, N FALDO 76 73, M ECOB 77 72, T GOGELE 75 74, M PILKINGTON 75 74, P SJOLAND 76 73, D PODLICH 74 75, N GATEHOUSE 76 73, F HENGE 75 75, B JONES 74 76, R RAFFERTY 75 76, C JONES 78 73, J M LARA 77 74, D MCKENZIE 77 74, S TINNING 74 77, S WEARNE 75 76, H NYSTROM 74 77, K FELTON 73 78, C GAUNT 80 71, C PETTERSSON 73 78, D CLARK 73 78, P SENIOR 77 75, G RANKIN 77 75, B OGLE 75 77, S BOUVIER 77 75, F CEA 77 75, S ROBINSON 75 78, S HEND 76 77, R FLOYD 72 81, M CLAYTON 75 79, K FERRIE 77 77, T MILLS 71 83, B JONES 79 75, C D GRAY 78 76, G SIMPSON 81 73, A FRASER 75 79, G DODD 76 79, N CHEETHAM 81 74, M HARWOOD 76 83, R WINCHESTER 80 79, W-T YEH 77 W/D.

Course Profile

The Lakes Golf Club in Sydney (par 73, 6,904 yards) rewards accurate players as the fairways are narrow and, like the name suggests, there are plenty of water hazards to catch wayward tee and iron shots.

There are many bunkers on this course and they guard the greens well. Hitting the greens in regulation is a must.

The morning starters can have an advantage as the wind usually blows (very hard) in the afternoon.

Players/Points to Note

● This tournament won't exist in 2002 but the event which takes it's place on the schedule – the AN7 Tour Championship – will still be played at the Lakes Golf Club, the venue for the past two renewals of the Greg Norman Holden International.

● Since 1995 there have been four tournaments held at The Lakes and Antipodean players have won them all – they have filled the first two places on three occasions.

● The best of the Aussies are **Lucas Parsons**, who grew up near The Lakes and won in 2000 after placing 15th in the previous season and **Aaron Baddeley**, who came off the back of a tie for 22nd place to win in 2001 (and was ninth in the 1999 renewal)

● Other local players to follow are **Scott Gardiner** (successive top-ten finishes since 2000), **Jarrod Moseley** (33rd and sixth last two years), **Craig Parry** (1995 champion), **Nick O'Hern**, **Peter O'Malley** and **Peter Lonard**, plus veterans **Greg Norman** (who used to co-sponsor the event) and **Peter Senior**.

● Kiwis **Michael Long** and **Michael Campbell** (first and second in 1999) are also worth a punt.

● **Bernhard Langer** (third in 1999 after calling a penalty on himself) and **Phillip Price** (two top-ten finishes in the past two years) along with **Ian Poulter**, third last season after the best weekend scores, look best of the possible European challengers.

Previous Results

2000: 1. Lucas Parsons (-19), 2. Peter Senior (-15), 3. Per Ulrik Johansson and Andrew Coltart (-13).

Sergio Garcia player profile – pages 204 & 256

CARLSBERG MALAYSIAN OPEN

Saujana G.&C.C., 15 Feb to 18 Feb 2001, purse 986,387 euros

Pos	Name	R1	R2	R3	R4	Total	To par	Money	DD(y)	DA%	GIR%	Putts
1	Vijay SINGH	68	70	68	68	274	-14	163,655	n/a	n/a	n/a	n/a
2	P HARRINGTON	70	66	68	70	274	-14	109,107	256.5	73.8	73.6	120
3	Charlie WI	70	70	67	69	276	-12	55,285	n/a	n/a	n/a	n/a
	A Dan BATEMAN	72	69	68	67	276	-12	55,285	n/a	n/a	n/a	n/a
5	Soren HANSEN	69	70	70	69	278	-10	41,635	261.3	71.0	75.0	122
6	Ter-Chang WANG	69	71	68	71	279	-9	34,369	n/a	n/a	n/a	n/a
7	Maarten LAFEBER	67	72	69	72	280	-8	22,742	277.6	66.9	70.8	126
	Desvonde BOTES	72	67	71	70	280	-8	22,742	291.9	64.3	66.7	123
	M CAMPBELL	69	67	71	73	280	-8	22,742	267.9	59.1	68.1	122
	T JAIDEE	75	67	68	70	280	-8	22,742	n/a	n/a	n/a	n/a
	C PETTERSSON	72	69	67	72	280	-8	22,742	271.0	70.6	65.3	120

Pos	Name	R1	R2	R3	R4	Total	To par
12	Mardan MAMAT	70	70	70	71	281	-7
	Olle KARLSSON	73	65	72	71	281	-7
14	S KJELDSEN	70	69	72	71	282	-6
	T SRIROJ	71	67	72	72	282	-6
	Jean HUGO	75	69	73	65	282	-6
	John DALY	72	72	69	69	282	-6
18	J Manuel LARA	75	68	71	69	283	-5
	Justin HOBDAY	69	69	71	74	283	-5
	I GARRIDO	72	69	73	69	283	-5
	Robert COLES	68	73	71	71	283	-5
	Patrik SJOLAND	75	65	68	75	283	-5
	H NYSTROM	71	71	70	71	283	-5
	Yong-Eun YANG	72	70	67	74	283	-5
25	Clay DEVERS	75	67	67	75	284	-4
	W KANG	72	65	75	72	284	-4
	Alex CEJKA	75	69	69	71	284	-4
	R HUXTABLE	71	71	67	75	284	-4
	G ROSALES	72	69	74	69	284	-4
30	J-F REMESY	72	74	71	68	285	-3
	G HOUSTON	76	70	72	67	285	-3
	D TERBLANCHE	69	75	73	68	285	-3
	J BICKERTON	74	70	72	69	285	-3
34	Kyi Hla HAN	72	71	71	72	286	-2
	Wayne RILEY	73	71	70	72	286	-2
	A HANSEN	70	71	74	71	286	-2
	Felix CASAS	72	69	73	72	286	-2
	T VAN DER WALT	75	71	72	68	286	-2
	Gustavo ROJAS	75	70	74	67	286	-2
	S SCAHILL	75	71	71	69	286	-2
	Tobias DIER	71	74	71	70	286	-2
42	C ROCCA	69	76	69	73	287	-1
	Elliot BOULT	72	66	71	78	287	-1
	Arjun ATWAL	71	69	75	72	287	-1
	Anthony KANG	71	73	72	71	287	-1
	F ANDERSSON	74	70	72	71	287	-1
47	Thomas LEVET	72	72	74	70	288	E
	Erol SIMSEK	74	71	72	71	288	E
	M LUNDBERG	72	70	75	71	288	E
	Ted PURDY	72	69	72	75	288	E
51	Lian-Wei ZHANG	71	75	71	72	289	+1
	Marc FARRY	74	72	72	71	289	+1
	Jim RUTLEDGE	74	72	70	73	289	+1
	Simon YATES	72	72	70	75	289	+1
	J HAEGGMAN	75	69	71	74	289	+1
	Andrew RAITT	73	70	72	74	289	+1
	Danny ZARATE	71	71	74	73	289	+1
	Robert FLOYD	72	73	70	74	289	+1
59	C PLAPHOL	74	71	72	73	290	+2
60	Gary EVANS	70	72	75	74	291	+3
61	Chia-Yuh HONG	74	71	74	73	292	+4
	Rodrigo CUELLO	74	72	71	75	292	+4
	Graeme STORM	71	73	72	76	292	+4
	A JOHL	75	71	73	73	292	+4
	Holden KIM	73	73	74	72	292	+4
66	R NACHIMUTHU	74	71	75	73	293	+5
	M PILKINGTON	78	68	71	76	293	+5
68	S MURTHY	72	71	79	72	294	+6
69	Yu-Shu HSIEH	76	67	78	74	295	+7
70	Peter MITCHELL	71	74	78	73	296	+8
71	Frankie MINOZA	77	68	77	75	297	+9
72	Zaw MOE	69	72	78	79	298	+10
73	Stephen DODD	70	73	80	79	302	+14

Tournament Report

Vijay Singh needed three holes of a sudden death play-off to land the Malaysian Open at the expense of Padraig Harrington.

The Fijian won his ninth European Tour title at the Saujana Country Club in Kuala Lumpur despite double bogeying the 17th in regulation play – a lapse that saw Harrington get his nose in front.

The problem was the Irishman, having failed to look up at the scoreboard, didn't know. Singh birdied the last while the Ryder Cup star was too aggressive at the 17th and dropped a shot.

A play-off was required when Harrington missed a 15-foot birdie chance on the last – although he wasn't helped when a mobile phone went off as he was about to strike his putt.

It was Singh's third win in Malaysia (his first pro success actually came there) and although Harrington missed the chance to secure his fourth European Tour victory he professed himself happy with runners up spot as he was working on his swing all week.

Harrington led at the 36 and 54 holes stage and, along with Dutchman Maarten Lafeber, Dane Soren Hansen and Carl Petterson of Sweden, led the European challenge in this co-sanctioned event (Asian and European Tours).

Korean pro Charlie Wi and Ter Chang Wang of Taiwan led the home tour challenge. The hot humid conditions, with thunder and lightning stopping play twice, certainly seemed to favour the locals, as Europeans took only six of the top 17 places.

MISSED THE CUT: J Milkha SINGH 74 73, G EMERSON 77 70, S MUDA 73 74, E MEEKS 77 70, S RICHARDSON 76 71, R WESSELS 73 74, J KINGSTON 73 74, R RUSSELL 76 71, K-C LIN 76 71, N HENNING 75 72, W-T YEH 78 69, A RIZMAN (AM) 74 73, W-C LIANG 72 75, R RAFFERTY 74 74, S P WEBSTER 73 75, G HAVRET 73 75, B RUANGKIT 75 73, J BERENDT 76 72, F CEA 74 74, G NORQUIST 74 74, C HANELL 77 71, G RUSNAK 73 75, D GLEESON 75 73, D MARUYAMA 78 70, C-H CHUNG 75 73, T OH 72 76, W BENNETT 76 73, O NORDBERG 76 73, M RAMAYAH 74 75, P MARKSAENG 75 74, H TSUJIMURA 76 73, R ODA 78 71, A PITTS 73 77, T-C CHEN 74 76, C RODILES 78 72, R BALLESTEROS 76 74, J RANDHAWA 75 75, N CHEETHAM 76 74, T WIRATCHANT 77 73, W T LU 77 73, C-H LIN 77 73, S A LINDSKOG 74 76, C-C LEE 76 74, C-B LAM 74 76, P HANSON 77 74, D CHIA 79 72, M BERNARDINI 73 78, A DURAIRAJ 80 71, S BALLESTEROS 78 74, M CUNNING 77 75, S DANIELS 79 73, R ISMAIL 76 76, M SANTI 75 77, C KAMPS 77 75, G MORALES 80 73, J RYSTROM 78 75, P DEL OLMO 79 74, T HORI 76 77, H BUHRMANN 76 78, A SINGH 78 76, M SCARPA 74 80, Y-J SHIN 77 77, S SAEDIN(Am) 78 76, M MOULAND 85 70, S AKIBA 76 79, K FERRIE 77 79, S TAYLOR 80 76, P EALES 80 77, T HAVEMANN 84 73, S DYSON 79 78, S HUSSEIN (Am) 84 73, N COLSAERTS 81 77, G RANKIN 81 79, H BJORNSTAD 81 80, V BHANDARI 78 DISQ, F QUINN 77 W/D, P GUNASAGARAN 80 W/D.

Sponsored by Stan James

Course Profile

Saujana Golf and Country Club (par 72, 6,947 yards) was used in 2001, a venue that puts the premium on accuracy but also requires golfers to be physically fit.

The many elevation changes make the hike around the course tiring.

In 2002, Royal Selangor Golf Club (par 72, 6,802 yards) is the venue, which was used for the Davidoff Nations Cup (won by China – Zhang Lian-wei and Liang Wen-chong), and has tree lined fairways and small greens with subtle breaks.

Players/Points to Note

● **Padraig Harrington** has by far the best form figures since this event became part of the European Tour in 1999. His form figures read 2-4-4 and the Irishman, who also played for in the World Cup of golf in Malaysia in 1999 (finishing third with **Paul McGinley**), is the only player to boast three top-ten finishes.

● The three winners of this event (**Gerry Norquist**, **Wei Tze Yeh** and **Vijay Singh**), though, have all been Asian Tour regulars at one stage or another of their careers. The hot and humid conditions are so different to what most European based golfers are used to, which gives an advantage, especially in the early rounds, to the local players.

● **Wang Ter Chang** has form figures of 23-11-6 over the past three years and along with **Prayad Marksaeng**, **Kyi Hla Han**, **Frankie Minoza**, **Lian Wie Zhang**, **Thongchai Jaidee** and **Charlie Wi** are the best of the native Davidoff Tour players.

● Aside from Harrington, Europeans who tend to do well are the Danish duo of **Soren Hansen** (11th and fifth in the past two years) and **Soren Kjeldsen** (36-14 last two years), **Alex Cejka** (2-34-25) and **Patrik Sjoland** (23-18)

● Also watch out for former Davidoff Order of Merit winner **Simon Dyson** in 2002.

Previous Results

2000: 1. Wei-Tze Yeh (-10), 2. Padraig Harrington (-9), Craig Hainline (-9), Des Terblanche (-9).

1999: 1. Gerry Norquist (-8), 2. Alex Cejka (-5), Bob May (-5).

Vijay Singh player profile – page 281

CALTEX SINGAPORE MASTERS

Singapore Island C.C., 22 Feb to 25 Feb 2001, purse 932,992 euros

Pos	Name	R1	R2	R3	R4	Total	To par	Money	DD(y)	DA%	GIR%	Putts
1	Vijay SINGH	64	63	68	68	263	-21	154,616	n/a	n/a	n/a	n/a
2	Warren BENNETT	63	69	65	68	265	-19	103,077	286.5	48.1	68.1	108
3	Maarten LAFEBER	64	67	70	65	266	-18	52,232	282.5	50.0	83.3	121
	C MONTGOMERIE	66	67	65	68	266	-18	52,232	273.1	61.5	80.6	114
5	P HARRINGTON	63	67	71	66	267	-17	35,903	275.5	36.5	77.8	112
	Anders HANSEN	69	64	69	65	267	-17	35,903	n/a	n/a	n/a	n/a
7	Frankie MINOZA	64	61	71	72	268	-16	25,513	n/a	n/a	n/a	n/a
	Mikael LUNDBERG	69	64	64	71	268	-16	25,513	271.4	61.5	62.5	103
9	P MARKSAENG	67	63	69	70	269	-15	20,781	n/a	n/a	n/a	n/a
10	Clay DEVERS	70	65	70	65	270	-14	18,554	n/a	n/a	n/a	n/a

Pos	Name	R1	R2	R3	R4	Total	To par
11	Andrew PITTS	71	67	67	66	271	-13
	Chia-Yuh HONG	66	71	65	69	271	-13
	Keng-Chi LIN	67	69	64	71	271	-13
14	Tom GILLIS	69	66	70	67	272	-12
	Stephen DODD	69	66	66	71	272	-12
	Yong-Eun YANG	67	66	72	67	272	-12
17	C ROCCA	67	69	68	69	273	-11
	C PLAPHOL	67	66	70	70	273	-11
	Anthony ALL	64	71	65	73	273	-11
	Gary ORR	68	68	67	70	273	-11
	Robert COLES	68	69	69	67	273	-11
	H NYSTROM	67	66	70	70	273	-11
	G ROSALES	68	69	70	66	273	-11
24	J Milkha SINGH	68	68	67	71	274	-10
	Carlos RODILES	72	67	66	69	274	-10
	Zaw MOE	68	67	68	71	274	-10
	I GARRIDO	70	68	69	67	274	-10
	A COLTART	68	71	65	70	274	-10
29	J Manuel LARA	67	72	70	66	275	-9
	Steen TINNING	67	68	70	70	275	-9
	H BJORNSTAD	68	70	68	69	275	-9
	Anthony KANG	66	69	71	69	275	-9
	Gustavo ROJAS	70	67	69	69	275	-9
	S SCAHILL	68	70	70	67	275	-9
	Ted PURDY	67	70	70	68	275	-9
	Wei-Tze YEH	68	70	66	71	275	-9
	T JAIDEE	73	66	66	70	275	-9
38	Mark MOULAND	66	66	71	73	276	-8
	Justin HOBDAY	67	71	70	68	276	-8
	Eric MEEKS	68	70	67	71	276	-8
	G NORQUIST	69	68	71	68	276	-8
	Gary RUSNAK	67	71	67	71	276	-8
43	Richard GREEN	65	71	70	71	277	-7
	Olivier EDMOND	67	64	76	70	277	-7
	M SCARPA	66	72	70	69	277	-7
46	David HOWELL	69	69	73	67	278	-6
	Arjun ATWAL	69	69	68	72	278	-6
	Charlie WI	69	67	73	69	278	-6
	Alex CEJKA	68	69	71	70	278	-6
	A Dan BATEMAN	70	69	75	64	278	-6
51	W-Soon KANG	72	67	71	69	279	-5
	Paul EALES	68	69	72	70	279	-5
	M MURUGIAH	68	70	71	70	279	-5
	B RUANGKIT	71	67	67	74	279	-5
	Jorge BERENDT	69	68	71	71	279	-5
	D TERBLANCHE	66	72	72	69	279	-5
	M PILKINGTON	67	70	70	72	279	-5
	R RUSSELL	69	69	72	69	279	-5
	Graeme STORM	71	67	70	71	279	-5
	Unho PARK	70	68	73	68	279	-5
61	Olle NORDBERG	70	69	69	72	280	-4
	Peter MITCHELL	71	68	71	70	280	-4
	Rafael PONCE	69	70	72	69	280	-4
	Paul STREETER	71	66	72	71	280	-4
	T-Chang WANG	70	69	72	69	280	-4
	P DEL OLMO	69	64	72	75	280	-4
67	A JOHL	72	67	72	70	281	-3
	Ted OH	69	68	74	70	281	-3
69	J KINGSTON	72	67	72	71	282	-2
	D MARUYAMA	69	70	72	71	282	-2
71	Elliot BOULT	69	69	74	71	283	-1
72	Aaron MEEKS	67	71	71	75	284	E
	Yong-Jin SHIN	69	70	73	72	284	E
	Chih-Bing LAM	69	70	74	71	284	E
75	H TSUJIMURA	70	69	71	76	286	+2
76	R BALLESTEROS	71	68	72	76	287	+3

Sponsored by Stan James

Tournament Report

For the second successive week, Vijay Singh proved too good for the combined strength of the Asian and European Tours by winning the Singapore Masters at the Bukit Course at the Singapore Island Country Club.

The Fijian won the second leg of the 'Asian Swing' in convincing style. He started the final day with a one stroke lead over Frankie Minoza, who earlier in the week shot a course record 61 (and a new Asian Tour low to boot), and birdies on the first and fourth saw the US Masters champion pull further clear.

But with Colin Montgomerie, fresh from a win in Australia, and Warren Bennett hard on Singh's heels, the Fijian couldn't let up until the last. Bennett's chip in from the edge of the green on the 18th was a case of too little too late though. Still, the prolific Challenge Tour winner edged out Monty, who, after bogeying the first two holes, found the task of overhauling Singh too much.

The wet heat was again a factor and it took a day or two before the Europeans who hadn't played in Malaysia to get to grips with the conditions.

Martin Lafeber seemed to cope well with the humidity, though, as the Dutchman secured third place a week after doing likewise in Malaysia.

Padraig Harrington also deserves a mention in dispatches. The Irishman, finished a creditable fifth, despite the fact that he called a penalty on himself on the 16th after his ball moved on address.

MISSED THE CUT: M CUNNING 71 69, P HANSON 71 69, G EMERSON 71 69, J RUTLEDGE 68 72, G HAVRET 73 67, V BHANDARI 72 68, S YATES 71 69, S TAYLOR 71 69, C PETTERSSON 74 66, A FORSBRAND 73 68, P TERAVAINEN 69 72, J-F REMESY 69 72, M MAMAT 72 69, J RANDHAWA 69 72, R HUXTABLE 69 72, W T LU 70 71, R CUELLO 72 69, C HANELL 71 70, S AKIBA 67 74, R FLOYD 70 71, E-W POH 68 73, H KIM 71 70, R ODA 72 69, K H HAN 72 70, T SRIROJ 70 72, Y-S HSIEH 69 73, A SINGH 71 71, J HUGO 73 69, J ROBINSON 72 70, O KARLSSON 66 76, S RICHARDSON 70 72, B DREDGE 71 71, F CEA 71 71, C-H LIN 71 71, K DINO 69 73, D BOTES 74 69, F CASAS 72 71, S P WEBSTER 72 71, J RYSTROM 70 73, M SANTI 69 74, N CHEETHAM 73 70, T WIRATCHANT 70 73, S A LINDSKOG 69 74, J STEWART 73 70, G HOUSTON 71 73, T LEVET 70 74, G HANRAHAN 72 72, K-K LIM 73 71, T-C CHEN 74 71, S KJELDSEN 75 70, G MORALES 74 71, M BERNARDINI 73 72, S DYSON 75 70, C-H CHUNG 71 74, S DANIELS 72 74, T VAN DER WALT 76 70, C-C LEE 71 75, T HORI 74 72, D TAKI 73 73, SUSUMU ABE 74 72, L-W ZHANG 75 72, K FERRIE 74 73, E C POH 78 70, D ZARATE 75 73, R BEST 76 72, S BALLESTEROS 72 77, N COLSAERTS 77 74, F ANDERSSON 75 76,

Course Profile

Singapore Island Country Club (par 71, 6,751 yards) was used in 2001. A short inland course with small, flat greens, last used for the 1993 Johnnie Walker Classic won by Nick Faldo.

In 2002, the event moves to the Laguna Golf and Country Club, a new (1991) layout that is currently undergoing some restoration but which does feature water on 12 of the 18 holes of it's championship course.

Nico Van Rensburg won the Merlion Masters there in 1995.

Players/Points to Note

●Another co-sanctioned event between the Asian and European Tours and punters should again look to the local players. Next season this event will be before the Malaysian Open so there won't be any time for the European contingent to acclimatise to the conditions (as they did last year when the five of the top six players were from Europe).

●Also, as this event comes straight after the WGC Matchplay event in the calendar, it's hard to imagine many of the top players coming over to compete (as they did last year).

●The best of the Davidoff Tour personnel are likely to be **Charlie Wi**, **Thongchai Jaidee**, **Thaworn Wiratchant**, **Arjun Atwal**, **Vivek Bhandari** and **Frankie Minoza** (who shot a new Asian Tour low of 61 in the second round of the event last year - his 36-hole total of 125 was also a record).

●Also watch out for the American duo of **Andrew Pitts** (winner of the 2001 Taiwan Open) and **Craig Hainline**, who are experienced Asian Tour players who have performed well in Singapore before.

●European players with local knowledge are Scotland's **Simon Yates** and **Daniel Chopra** of Sweden, who won the Mercuries Masters in 2001.

●Former Davidoff Order of Merit winner **Simon Dyson** is expected to put up a good show as is European Tour pro **Patrik Sjoland** and South African **James Kingston**.

Warren Bennett player profile – page 188

DUBAI DESERT CLASSIC

Emirates G.C., 1 Mar to 4 Mar 2001, purse 1,619,414 euros

Pos	Name	R1	R2	R3	R4	Total	To par	Money	DD(y)	DA%	GIR%	Putts
1	Thomas BJORN	64	66	67	69	266	-22	265,152	284.4	64.3	66.7	104
2	Tiger WOODS	64	64	68	72	268	-20	138,184	312.6	60.7	80.6	111
	P HARRINGTON	66	69	64	69	268	-20	138,184	274.6	64.3	86.1	118
4	Ian WOOSNAM	69	68	64	69	270	-18	73,503	273.8	67.9	76.4	112
	M GRONBERG	68	68	66	68	270	-18	73,503	282.5	60.7	66.7	108
6	J Milkha SINGH	67	66	67	71	271	-17	51,706	283.1	46.4	56.9	94
	Brian DAVIS	69	65	67	70	271	-17	51,706	282.0	67.9	65.3	104
8	T IMMELMAN	66	73	68	65	272	-16	39,774	280.0	62.5	76.4	112
9	Elliot BOULT	69	69	70	65	273	-15	32,243	292.5	62.5	68.1	108
	Paul McGINLEY	70	64	67	72	273	-15	32,243	289.6	75.0	72.2	111
	Angel CABRERA	66	70	65	72	273	-15	32,243	312.9	57.1	68.1	110

Pos	Name	R1	R2	R3	R4	Total	To par
12	Eamonn DARCY	68	67	70	69	274	-14
	J-F REMESY	68	68	68	70	274	-14
	Anders HANSEN	70	66	67	71	274	-14
	Richard GREEN	67	73	67	67	274	-14
	Greg OWEN	70	68	67	69	274	-14
17	A OLDCORN	71	66	68	70	275	-13
	David LYNN	70	71	66	68	275	-13
	Lee WESTWOOD	66	70	69	70	275	-13
	Retief GOOSEN	70	68	67	70	275	-13
21	Gary EMERSON	70	67	65	74	276	-12
	C MONTGOMERIE	69	70	65	72	276	-12
	R CLAYDON	67	70	71	68	276	-12
	Phillip PRICE	66	72	69	69	276	-12
	R GONZALEZ	71	67	69	69	276	-12
	Paul LAWRIE	70	67	71	68	276	-12
	J BICKERTON	68	67	70	71	276	-12
28	Jamie SPENCE	72	66	68	71	277	-11
	Soren HANSEN	69	69	68	71	277	-11
	Rolf MUNTZ	71	69	66	71	277	-11
	D ROBERTSON	69	68	69	71	277	-11
	T JAIDEE	73	67	68	69	277	-11
33	A FORSBRAND	71	67	72	68	278	-10
	T JOHNSTONE	71	69	63	75	278	-10
	W BENNETT	70	69	69	70	278	-10
	Sven STRUVER	71	68	68	71	278	-10
	John SENDEN	68	71	67	72	278	-10
	T VAN DER WALT	68	72	70	68	278	-10
	N COLSAERTS	70	70	65	73	278	-10
	J MOSELEY	69	70	70	69	278	-10
	A COLTART	70	69	70	69	278	-10
	Wei-Tze YEH	70	70	67	71	278	-10
43	Des SMYTH	69	69	68	73	279	-9
	David HOWELL	69	69	72	69	279	-9
	Carl SUNESON	69	72	65	73	279	-9
	Tobias DIER	68	72	67	72	279	-9
47	I GARRIDO	68	73	67	72	280	-8

Pos	Name	R1	R2	R3	R4	Total	To par
	R WESSELS	70	70	70	70	280	-8
	B DREDGE	70	65	73	72	280	-8
	Robert COLES	68	70	68	74	280	-8
51	L-Wei ZHANG	70	69	70	72	281	-7
	Carlos RODILES	67	70	72	72	281	-7
	R RUSSELL	68	69	72	72	281	-7
	M BERNARDINI	70	70	70	71	281	-7
55	S WEBSTER	71	70	68	73	282	-6
	W-Soon KANG	72	69	71	70	282	-6
	F JACOBSON	70	71	66	75	282	-6
58	Mark ROE	71	69	71	72	283	-5
	Ross BAIN	71	69	71	72	283	-5
	J Manuel LARA	66	72	68	77	283	-5
	Jean HUGO	70	67	71	75	283	-5
	Michele REALE	72	69	70	72	283	-5
	Gary EVANS	70	66	72	75	283	-5
	Darren CLARKE	71	69	70	73	283	-5
	Peter LONARD	68	71	72	72	283	-5
66	Thomas LEVET	73	68	72	71	284	-4
	D BORREGO	72	69	73	70	284	-4
68	Mark McNULTY	66	74	71	74	285	-3
	J RYSTRUM	69	70	72	74	285	-3
	C HANELL	71	70	69	75	285	-3
71	C ROCCA	70	71	70	75	286	-2
	R JACQUELIN	67	72	71	76	286	-2
	Per HAUGSRUD	70	71	77	68	286	-2
	Peter MITCHELL	68	72	73	73	286	-2
	T GOGELE	69	70	73	74	286	-2
	L PARSONS	70	70	73	73	286	-2
77	M LAFEBER	70	69	74	74	287	-1
	Justin ROSE	71	71	70	75	287	-1
	Daren LEE	71	70	70	76	287	-1
80	J HAEGGMAN	71	67	77	73	288	E
	J SANDELIN	69	72	72	75	288	E
82	Ian POULTER	71	69	72	77	289	+1

Tournament Report

Tiger Woods must still be wondering how he let Thomas Bjorn come from behind to snatch the Dubai Desert Classic title from his grasp.

The World No.1 was a shot clear standing on the 17th tee in the final round. But the Dane's birdie to Woods' par meant that the duo, who had played the previous three rounds together, went to the last hole on equal terms. Bjorn, with the honour, put pressure on his playing partner by finding the fairway with his drive at the tricky 18th.

Then, the calm, composed Woods that we had witnessed winning the previous three Major titles was transformed into a Sunday morning hacker, as he went first right then left, from trees to rough, and eventually to water, as his third shot came up woefully short.

A penalty stroke and two putts made for a double bogey seven and a tie for second place with Ireland's Padraig Harrington. We should take nothing away from Bjorn, though, as the player who counts Dubai as his winter home coped well with the huge galleries that followed Woods and himself throughout the tournament.

His focus was absolute and commitment total as he never fell more than two shots behind Woods.

But this event will always be known as the one in which Tiger proved human. It was only the fourth time that he hadn't won in the 27 times he had been leading going into the final round of an event and his last hole antics gave hope to us all.

MISSED THE CUT: Roger CHAPMAN 70 72, Malcolm MACKENZIE 73 69, Peter SENIOR 69 73, Barry LANE 71 71, Anthony WALL 71 71, Felix CASAS 68 74, Mats HALLBERG 71 71, Jyoti RANDHAWA 71 71, Pierre FULKE 73 69, Des TERBLANCHE 71 71, Patrik SJOLAND 71 71, Niclas FASTH 74 68, David CARTER 71 71, Adam SCOTT 70 72, Robert FLOYD 67 75, Santiago LUNA 70 73, Marc FARRY 70 73, Tom GILLIS 73 70, Desvonde BOTES 70 73, Henrik STENSON 69 74, Steen TINNING 70 73, Jonathan LOMAS 70 73, Wayne RILEY 73 71, Roger WINCHESTER 69 75, Robert KARLSSON 71 73, Alex CEJKA 72 72, Van PHILLIPS 73 71, Andrew RAITT 69 75, David PARK 69 75, Henrik NYSTROM 73 71, Ronan RAFFERTY 72 73, Peter BAKER 76 69, Paul EALES 73 72, Paolo QUIRICI 71 74, Olivier EDMOND 69 76, Gerry NORQUIST 72 73, Mikko ILONEN 71 74, Simon DYSON 75 70, Martin MARITZ 71 74, David GILFORD 71 75, Mark O'MEARA 72 74, Richard S JOHNSON 73 73, Markus BRIER 75 71, Alastair FORSYTH 72 74, Seve BALLESTEROS 74 73, Mark DAVIS 70 77, Christian CEVAER 73 74, Mikael LUNDBERG 71 76, Gordon BRAND JNR. 74 74, JosÈ RIVERO 73 75, Graham RANKIN 73 75, Massimo SCARPA 76 72, David HIGGINS 72 76, Ross MCFARLANE 72 77, Ian GARBUTT 76 73, Francisco CEA 77 72, Erol SIMSEK 77 72, Neil WEBB 74 75, Soren KJELDSEN 78 72, Fredrik HENGE 74 76, Hamad MUBARAK (AM) 74 76, Nicolas VANHOOTEGEM 78 73.

Course Profile

The Emirates Golf Club (par 72, 7,127 yards) host venue for this event from 1989-1998 returned to stage the tournament last year and will do so again in 2002.

The fairways are wide and the greens large and flat. The grain is strong, however, and putts can be difficult to read.

It's only defence is the wind - which can blow extremely hard. The course was lengthened after the 1998 renewal. Water comes into play on ten of the holes.

Players/Points to Note

●**Colin Montgomerie** won this event in 1996 and can boast five top-ten finishes in this tournament. He is 80-under par in 11 starts and has taken away over 353,000 Euros from the sponsors' coffers down the years - the most. He's a regular visitor to Dubai as he is in the process of designing a golf course there (Emirates Hills which could be used for this tournament in 2003).

●**Paul McGinley** has five top-ten finishes in ten appearances, while **Ian Woosnam** also plays well in desert surroundings and has form figures of 5-2-7-4 for the last four renewals of this event at Emirates G.C..

●Last year's champion **Thomas Bjorn** must be considered to win again. The Dane winters in Dubai and knows most of the courses well. His 2001 success came off the back of 13th position in 2000.

●**Ernie Els** is an occasional visitor to Dubai and hasn't finished out of the top ten (he won in 1994) in four starts. The South African has a stroke average of 68.50.

●**Greg Norman** can top that with a 64.44 stroke average in 16 rounds.

●**Lee Westwood** boasts three top-ten finishes while **Angel Cabrera** has twice finished in the ten.

●**Peter Baker**, **Retief Goosen** and **David Gilford** have also performed well in this event before.

Previous Results

_2000:_ 1. Jose Coceres (-14), 2. Paul McGinley (-12), Patrik Sjoland (-12).

_1999:_ 1. David Howell (-13), 2. Lee Westwood (-9), 3. Mark James (-8), Paul McGinley (-8).

_1998:_ 1. Jose Maria Olazabal (-19), 2. Stephen Allan (-16), 3. Robert Karlsson (-15), Ernie Els (-15).

_1997:_ 1. Richard Green (-16), won play-off, 2. Greg Norman (-16), Ian Woosnam (-16).

_1996:_ 1. Colin Montgomerie (-18), 2. Miguel Angel Jimenez (-17), 3. Robert Willis (-14).

QATAR MASTERS

Doha G.C., 8 Mar to 11 Mar 2001, purse 808,986 euros

Pos	Name	R1	R2	R3	R4	Total	To par	Money	DD(y)	DA%	GIR%	Putts
1	Tony JOHNSTONE	68	70	66	70	274	-14	133,832	274.8	57.1	56.9	100
2	R KARLSSON	63	70	70	73	276	-12	89,218	300.5	46.4	72.2	112
3	Elliot BOULT	68	67	72	71	278	-10	50,267	302.3	39.3	80.6	120
4	Olivier EDMOND	65	70	71	73	279	-9	37,098	287.1	62.5	77.8	122
	D ROBERTSON	67	69	68	75	279	-9	37,098	269.3	67.9	70.8	114
6	John SENDEN	69	73	68	71	281	-7	26,097	n/a	n/a	n/a	n/a
	Angel CABRERA	66	70	67	78	281	-7	26,097	302.5	55.4	72.2	119
8	Anders HANSEN	71	69	71	71	282	-6	16,541	293.3	76.8	73.6	118
	Steve WEBSTER	71	70	73	68	282	-6	16,541	300.9	62.5	80.6	128
	R GONZALEZ	67	71	70	74	282	-6	16,541	299.1	51.8	76.4	121
	Greg OWEN	69	71	69	73	282	-6	16,541	291.0	64.3	79.2	126
	David HIGGINS	70	72	72	68	282	-6	16,541	268.1	55.4	62.5	111

Pos	Name	R1	R2	R3	R4	Total	To par
13	Ian WOOSNAM	71	70	71	71	283	-5
	M LAFEBER	69	73	68	73	283	-5
	Paul McGINLEY	71	67	71	74	283	-5
	Rolf MUNTZ	70	69	74	70	283	-5
	F JACOBSON	70	71	69	73	283	-5
	David CARTER	69	71	74	69	283	-5
	Martin MARITZ	70	69	70	74	283	-5
20	R CHAPMAN	72	71	72	69	284	-4
	J MOSELEY	67	74	75	68	284	-4
	David LYNN	67	71	70	76	284	-4
23	Thomas BJORN	69	71	70	75	285	-3
	Daren LEE	67	72	75	71	285	-3
	L PARSONS	73	70	68	74	285	-3
	M BERNARDINI	66	73	71	75	285	-3
27	Eamonn DARCY	69	68	72	77	286	-2
	Des SMYTH	71	71	68	76	286	-2
	S KJELDSEN	70	71	71	74	286	-2
	Carl SUNESON	69	71	73	73	286	-2
	M GRONBERG	68	72	70	76	286	-2
	Paul LAWRIE	68	70	69	79	286	-2
	Peter LONARD	69	74	72	71	286	-2
	Van PHILLIPS	67	72	75	72	286	-2
	C PETTERSSON	70	69	75	72	286	-2
36	David HOWELL	68	71	73	75	287	-1
	L-Wei ZHANG	70	70	70	77	287	-1
	Brian DAVIS	71	67	72	77	287	-1
	T GOGELE	71	71	70	75	287	-1
	R WESSELS	66	73	74	74	287	-1
41	Craig HAINLINE	70	73	69	76	288	E
	T IMMELMAN	70	68	73	77	288	E
	Neil CHEETHAM	69	71	73	75	288	E
	Stephen DODD	68	73	75	72	288	E
	I GARRIDO	72	68	70	78	288	E
46	Mark ROE	72	70	70	77	289	+1
	J-F REMESY	71	70	67	81	289	+1
	Fredrik HENGE	72	71	71	75	289	+1
	R S JOHNSON	69	70	73	77	289	+1
	J RYSTROM	68	71	73	77	289	+1
	Jorge BERENDT	71	71	72	75	289	+1
	M SCARPA	66	73	73	77	289	+1
	B DREDGE	72	71	69	77	289	+1
	M PILKINGTON	63	79	72	75	289	+1
	A COLTART	71	69	75	74	289	+1
	M BLACKEY	70	72	75	72	289	+1
57	R CLAYDON	69	74	72	75	290	+2
	H NYSTROM	67	71	75	77	290	+2
59	Tom GILLIS	67	76	75	73	291	+3
	G HAVRET	71	69	73	78	291	+3
	Soren HANSEN	67	73	75	76	291	+3
	J ROBINSON	71	69	73	78	291	+3
	Michele REALE	70	73	73	75	291	+3
	J LOMAS	71	72	74	74	291	+3
	Markus BRIER	66	70	73	82	291	+3
	Patrik SJOLAND	69	74	71	77	291	+3
67	Sven STRUVER	70	73	76	73	292	+4
	Kenneth FERRIE	68	74	75	75	292	+4
	H STENSON	70	70	70	82	292	+4
	Tobias DIER	71	70	72	79	292	+4
71	Marc FARRY	71	70	72	80	293	+5
72	M FLORIOLI	71	70	74	79	294	+6
73	Santiago LUNA	73	70	77	75	295	+7
	Barry LANE	68	75	77	75	295	+7
75	R JACQUELIN	69	71	75	81	296	+8
76	Hennie OTTO	71	72	71	-	-	DISQ

Tournament Report

On a windswept Doha course, Tony Johnstone produced a superb final round of 70 to win the Qatar Masters from Robert Karlsson.

The Zimbabwean pro, who had thought of giving up the game just a few weeks earlier, started the last day in fine style by chipping in at the first for an eagle three to take a share of the lead.

And with the local Shamal wind preventing anyone from shooting a score low enough to put the pressure on the 21-year tour veteran, he simply played solid golf, making just two bogeys all day.

The gusty conditions played into Johnstone's hands. Never the longest of hitters, the fact that no one else could blast their Callaways from off the tee meant Johnstone wasn't handicapped. He cited the help he received from coach Simon Holmes and eye specialist cum sports psychologist Dr Ken West as a reason he won and also that he grew up playing on windy, sandy courses in Durban when at university.

His putting was certainly better than it had been earlier this season and his all round excellent short game came to his aid on more than one occasion.

Karlsson was the third round leader, and, along with Mark Pilkington, set a new course record of 63 on Thursday. But the Swede could only manage a 73 in the last round, the eagle he needed at the 18th to force a play-off failing to materialise.

MISSED THE CUT: Peter FOWLER 75 69, Warren BENNETT 72 72, Anthony WALL 71 73, Graham RANKIN 72 72, Peter HANSON 70 74, Per HAUGSRUD 67 77, Peter MITCHELL 71 73, Paolo QUIRICI 71 73, Joakim HAEGGMAN 74 70, Ian GARBUTT 71 73, Christian CEVAER 72 72, Raymond RUSSELL 71 73, Christopher HANELL 72 72, Malcolm MACKENZIE 74 71, Ronan RAFFERTY 69 76, Costantino ROCCA 71 74, Wayne RILEY 73 72, Garry HOUSTON 69 76, Desvonde BOTES 72 73, Justin ROSE 70 75, Olle KARLSSON 74 71, Andrew RAITT 72 73, Niclas FASTH 73 72, Simon DYSON 72 73, Brett RUMFORD 72 73, Peter BAKER 70 76, Jean HUGO 73 73, Gary EVANS 68 78, Steven RICHARDSON 71 75, Jarmo SANDELIN 73 73, Fredrik ANDERSSON 71 75, Nic HENNING 72 74, Hank KUEHNE 71 75, Jose RIVERO 71 76, Tjaart VAN DER WALT 73 74, Justin HOBDAY 72 75, Nicolas COLSAERTS 72 75, Diego BORREGO 69 78, Nicolas VANHOOTEGEM 71 76, Gustavo ROJAS 67 80, Ross McFARLANE 73 75, Shaun P WEBSTER 73 75, Tomas Jesus MUOZ 71 77, Johan SKOLD 73 75, David PARK 70 78, Alastair FORSYTH 73 75, Andrew SHERBORNE 73 76, Mark DAVIS 73 76, Marcello SANTI 73 76, Des TERBLANCHE 75 74, Paul STREETER 72 77, Wei-Tze YEH 73 76, R BYRD 78 72, M TUNNICLIFF 74 76, D GILFORD 77 74, H BJORNSTAD 76 75, M JONZON 75 76, M MOULAND 72 80, R BAIN 72 81,G STORM 76 77, R WINCHESTER 77 77, G PUGH 77 77, I POULTER 77 W/D, P PRICE 78 W/D.

Course Profile

Doha Golf Club (par 72, 7,110 yards) is a long, punishing venue. The length of the layout means big hitters can prosper but the ball must be kept in play.

The fairways are relatively wide but the rough is thick. The putting surfaces are large with subtle slopes.

There are plenty of hazards on the layout for golfers to worry about but this event is invariably won and lost in the air.

Wind is a major factor and only players who can handle blustery conditions will succeed.

Players/Points to Note

●The Qatar Masters is just four-years-old and the only player to finish in the top 15 in each of its renewals is **Ian Woosnam**. The Welshman has yet to win but has form figures of 9-8-2-13 – easily the best. Woosie is 28-under in 16 rounds and has a stroke average of 70.25.

●**Rolf Muntz** won in 2000 after a top ten position in 1998 and was an encouraging 13th when defending his title. The Dutchman has a stroke average of 69.75 – the best – and is 27-under in three visits.

●The wind (Shamal) is a huge factor at Doha Golf Club and it is no surprise to see that the majority of names on the trophy have won in windy conditions before. **Paul Lawrie** went on to a win an Open, **Tony Johnstone** grew up playing wind battered desert courses in South Africa, while **Andrew Coltart** has links experience from his Dunhill Cup days. The wind usually comes in the afternoon so morning tee times can be a bonus

●**Soren Kjeldsen** can boast two top-ten finishes in four starts and came 27th last year. **Dean Robertson** (fourth last year), **Patrik Sjoland** (2-11-19-59), **Paul McGinley**, **Van Phillips**, **Angel Cabrera** and **Steve Webster** have all posted high finishes in the past and could be worth following in 2002.

Previous Results

2000: 1. Rolf Muntz (-8), 2. Ian Woosnam (-3), 3. Eduardo Romero and Stephen Leaney (+1).

1999: 1. Paul Lawrie (-20), 2. Soren Kjeldsen (-13), Phillip Price (-13).

1998: 1. Andrew Coltart (-18), 2. Andrew Sherborne (-16), Patrik Sjoland (-16).

Tony Johnstone player profile – page 213

MADEIRA ISLAND OPEN

Santo de Serra, 15 Mar to 18 Mar 2001, purse 558,115 euros

Pos	Name	R1	R2	R3	R4	Total	To par	Money	DD(y)	DA%	GIR%	Putts
1	Des SMYTH	66	70	68	66	270	-18	91,660	292.0	78.6	83.3	115
2	John BICKERTON	67	67	69	69	272	-16	61,110	n/a	n/a	n/a	n/a
3	M FLORIOLI	68	68	65	73	274	-14	26,125	296.9	71.4	76.4	117
	Stephen DODD	71	67	66	70	274	-14	26,125	278.5	53.6	79.2	117
	M SCARPA	69	68	70	67	274	-14	26,125	290.0	60.7	86.1	123
	Niclas FASTH	69	63	72	70	274	-14	26,125	n/a	n/a	n/a	n/a
7	P MAGNEBRANT	70	70	69	66	275	-13	15,125	n/a	n/a	n/a	n/a
	David LYNN	68	71	64	72	275	-13	15,125	309.5	75.0	72.2	113
9	J Manuel LARA	68	68	71	69	276	-12	11,660	301.1	73.2	75.0	114
	Craig HAINLINE	69	70	65	72	276	-12	11,660	294.3	73.2	86.1	123

Pos	Name	R1	R2	R3	R4	Total	To par
11	Gary EMERSON	69	67	72	70	278	-10
	Peter MITCHELL	72	70	70	66	278	-10
	Gary CLARK	71	68	71	68	278	-10
	J SANDELIN	69	69	73	67	278	-10
15	A OLDCORN	67	69	69	74	279	-9
	Peter FOWLER	69	68	71	71	279	-9
	Steve WEBSTER	74	68	68	69	279	-9
	Simon KHAN	68	73	69	69	279	-9
	Francis VALERA	73	65	70	71	279	-9
	Graeme STORM	71	71	68	69	279	-9
21	Santiago LUNA	70	72	67	71	280	-8
	Eric CARLBERG	69	72	70	69	280	-8
	Fredrik HENGE	70	68	69	73	280	-8
	Stuart LITTLE	72	66	70	72	280	-8
	J ROBINSON	68	72	69	71	280	-8
	Ian GARBUTT	71	67	72	70	280	-8
27	Philip GOLDING	67	72	69	73	281	-7
	Gary ORR	71	72	70	68	281	-7
29	M MACKENZIE	66	73	70	73	282	-6
	Simon HURD	73	69	67	73	282	-6
	A FORSYTH	69	75	69	69	282	-6
32	M OLANDER	75	68	70	70	283	-5
	H STENSON	70	66	73	74	283	-5
	T GOGELE	72	72	71	68	283	-5
	Andrew BEAL	73	70	70	70	283	-5
	R CLAYDON	70	72	72	69	283	-5
	B HAFTHORSSON	69	71	74	69	283	-5
	Markus BRIER	68	68	71	76	283	-5
	David CARTER	68	74	70	71	283	-5
	Nic HENNING	73	71	69	70	283	-5
41	M MOULAND	70	69	70	75	284	-4
	Philip WALTON	67	75	70	72	284	-4
	M PENDARIES	70	71	68	75	284	-4
	Greg OWEN	69	74	71	70	284	-4
	Johan SKOLD	67	71	75	71	284	-4
	Lee S JAMES	72	68	71	73	284	-4
47	S BALLESTEROS	71	68	70	76	285	-3
	S P WEBSTER	72	71	71	71	285	-3
	Hennie OTTO	68	71	74	72	285	-3
	J HAWKSWORTH	71	73	71	70	285	-3
	S D HURLEY	70	73	69	73	285	-3
	M LACKEY	68	75	71	71	285	-3
	Hank KUEHNE	67	76	71	71	285	-3
54	Richard BLAND	70	73	73	70	286	-2
	Robin BYRD	71	70	73	72	286	-2
	Dennis EDLUND	74	70	67	75	286	-2
	R SJOBERG	68	73	73	72	286	-2
	S SCAHILL	68	74	73	71	286	-2
59	Wayne RILEY	71	72	73	71	287	-1
	S KJELDSEN	70	70	71	76	287	-1
	Jose ROMERO	74	67	72	74	287	-1
62	J-F LUCQUIN	71	71	73	73	288	E
	Jorge BERENDT	68	72	75	73	288	E
	Stuart CAGE	69	70	73	76	288	E
	B TEILLERIA	72	67	76	73	288	E
66	David HOWELL	70	73	72	74	289	+1
	Gregory HAVRET	69	75	72	73	289	+1
	F ANDERSSON	72	72	72	73	289	+1
	Iain PYMAN	75	69	74	71	289	+1
	Marcus KNIGHT	70	72	73	74	289	+1
71	Sam WALKER	74	70	75	71	290	+2
72	S RICHARDSON	72	71	75	73	291	+3
	A SOBRINHO	72	71	75	73	291	+3
	D ROBERTSON	69	72	79	71	291	+3
75	Mats LANNER	73	71	75	73	292	+4
	Kenneth FERRIE	72	72	71	77	292	+4
77	R Jan DERKSEN	73	71	77	72	293	+5
	U GUSTAFSSON	70	72	75	76	293	+5
79	Paul SHERMAN	72	71	81	75	299	+11
80	Paddy GRIBBEN	70	71	73	-	-	DISQ

Sponsored by Stan James

Tournament Report

Fittingly, the day after St Patrick's Day, Irishman Des Smyth became the oldest winner on the European Tour by lifting the Madeira Island Open title at Santo da Serra Golf Club in Santa Cruz.

At 48 years and 34 days – 22 days older than Neil Coles when the Englishman won the Sanyo Open in 1982 – Smyth used all his experience and not a little style to fend off the chasing pack.

Three behind entering the final round, a mercurial escape from the trees at the seventh, which yielded a birdie, was soon followed up with under par scores at the tenth and then at the 11th, when a glorious 4-iron approach to five inches gifted him an eagle.

A bogey at the 13th gave the field some hope but a hat-trick of birdies from the 14th put distance between the former Ryder Cup star and John Bickerton – who eventually was to claim runners up place (for the third time in his European Tour career).

The Midlander's challenge faltered on the 11th. From the tee, Bickerton found the edge of the water, and, Van de Velde style, off came the socks and shoes – this time to actually play the shot. Further problems followed however, and although it was his only bogey of the round it would prove critical.

Third round leader Massimo Florioli could only manage a last day 73 to fall back into a share of third spot with fellow Italian Massimo Scarpa, last year's champion Niclas Fasth and England's David Lynn.

MISSED THE CUT: Knud STORGAARD 76 69, Martin ERLANDSSON 75 70, Paul NILBRINK 71 74, Peter HANSON 73 72, Lionel ALEXANDRE 72 73, Andrew MARSHALL 72 73, Paul AFFLECK 77 68, Michele REALE 73 72, Van PHILLIPS 74 71, Paul STREETER 72 73, Robert COLES 70 75, Sean CORTE-REAL 71 74, Charles CHALLEN 73 72, Angel MATALLANA 71 74, Thomas NORRET 73 72, Carl PETTERSSON 73 72, Alberto BINAGHI 74 72, J CARVALHOSA 75 71, Soren HANSEN 68 78, Jesus Maria ARRUTI 74 72, Marcello SANTI 73 73, Nick TAYLOR 72 74, Gordon BRAND JNR. 68 79, Gary MURPHY 71 76, Kalle BRINK 67 80, Mark FOSTER 77 70, Robert MCGUIRK 74 73, Sebastien BRANGER 72 75, Per NYMAN 73 74, Christophe POTTIER 75 72, Adam MEDNICK 72 75, Gustavo ROJAS 74 73, Andrew BUTTERFIELD 71 76, M PILKINGTON 73 74, S DELAGRANGE 73 74, R DRUMMOND 73 75, M DAVIS 72 76, M ELIASSON 76 72, P HAUGSRUD 71 77, R GILLOT 72 76, A SHERBORNE 73 76, D SILVA 73 76, J M CAZAL-RIBEIRO 74 75, S CASTRO-FERREIRA 75 74, A McLEAN 71 78, C BENIANS 73 77, J HEPWORTH 74 76, F WIDMARK 76 74, N CHEETHAM 78 73, G BARUFFALDI 76 75, F GUERMANI 73 78, D DRYSDALE 76 75, M CAPONE 75 76, D FREITAS 77 75, L CLAVERIE 74 78, P EDMOND 77 76, M JONZON 78 75, M PERSSON 74 80, J DIAS 78 76, J JOHNSON 76 79, J P SOUSA (AM) 78 78, A DANTAS DA SILVA 75 82, J UMBELINO (Am) 79 86, G RANKIN RETD.

Course Profile

Santa da Serra Golf Club (par 72, 6,661 yards) is over 2,300 feet above sea level on the top of a mountain.

The venue dips and rises, making for lies above and below players' feet.

The greens are difficult to read and the fog and mist that can engulf the layout make for treacherous play.

The wind is the layout's best defence. Gusts can throw seemingly perfect shots off line.

Selecting the right club and shot is a tricky business.

Players/Points to Note

●Should **Niclas Fasth** return in 2002, the young Swede will be a must for any staking plan. I Ie won this event in 2000, finished third in 2001 and is now a much better player. He finished second in the Open and will be playing for Europe in the Ryder Cup in 2002, so should be able to see off what is always a mediocre field to win this event.

●**John Bickerton**'s form figures at Santo da Serra read 13-14-4-5-2 and always has this event on his schedule.

●**Fredrik Jacobson** has yet to win this event but has finished in the top-ten three times in four starts. He is 14-under and has a strike average of 70.92 in this event.

●**Diego Borrego** boasts similar stats – three top tens, 17-under and a stroke average of 70.87.

●**Peter Mitchell** won here in 1997 and has finished in the top ten on two other occasions in seven appearances in the event. He was 11th in this event last year – his second highest finish of 2001.

●**Mats Lanner** is a dual winner of this event, while **Thomas Gogele** and **Carl Suneson** have both registered three top-ten finishes.

●Don't forget the Swedish influence. There have been four Swedish winners in nine Madeira Island Opens. Maybe the scenery reminds them of home.

Previous Results

2000: 1. Niclas Fasth (-9), 2. Ross Drummond (-7), Mark Davis (-7), Richard S Johnson (-7).

1999: 1. Pedro Linhart (-12), 2. Mark James (-11), 3. David Howell (-9).

1998: 1. Mats Lanner (-11), 2. Stephen Scahill (-10), 3. Andrew Beal (-9).

1997: 1. Peter Mitchell (-12), 2. Fredrik Jacobson (-11), 3. Andrew Coltart (-10).

1996: 1. Jarmo Sandelin (-9), 2. Paul Affleck (-8), 3. Five players tied.

SAO PAULO BRAZIL OPEN

Sao Paulo G.C., 22 Mar to 25 Mar 2001, purse 760,017 euros

Pos	Name	R1	R2	R3	R4	Total	To par	Money	DD(y)	DA%	GIR%	Putts
1	Darren FICHARDT	67	61	67	-	195	-18	125,000	283.0	64.1	87.0	85
2	R S JOHNSON	68	67	65	-	200	-13	55,926	278.5	59.0	81.5	84
	Jose COCERES	68	64	68	-	200	-13	55,926	271.7	56.4	87.0	90
	Brett RUMFORD	66	65	69	-	200	-13	55,926	286.5	41.0	75.9	82
5	R JACQUELIN	66	70	65	-	201	-12	29,025	286.2	74.4	85.2	89
	Nic HENNING	70	64	67	-	201	-12	29,025	278.0	69.2	77.8	83
7	Anthony WALL	71	67	64	-	202	-11	22,500	287.7	59.0	81.5	86
8	S D HURLEY	69	69	65	-	203	-10	16,087	278.7	66.7	74.1	84
	Neil CHEETHAM	69	67	67	-	203	-10	16,087	272.0	59.0	72.2	83
	M BLACKEY	67	68	68	-	203	-10	16,087	270.2	69.2	72.2	83
	C HANELL	68	65	70	-	203	-10	16,087	272.5	61.5	72.2	83

Pos	Name	R1	R2	R3	R4	Total	To par
12	Robin BYRD	68	69	67	-	204	-9
13	Gustavo ROJAS	67	68	70	-	205	-8
	Daren LEE	68	68	69	-	205	-8
15	Philip WALTON	69	66	71	-	206	-7
	Kenneth FERRIE	70	67	69	-	206	-7
	T GOGELE	70	67	69	-	206	-7
	M FLORIOLI	69	68	69	-	206	-7
	Tomas J MUOZ	71	66	69	-	206	-7
20	Peter FOWLER	70	70	67	-	207	-6
	W BENNETT	70	68	69	-	207	-6
	Carlos RODILES	69	71	67	-	207	-6
	E PESENTI	71	69	67	-	207	-6
	D BORREGO	68	67	72	-	207	-6
	B TEILLERIA	70	68	69	-	207	-6
	A ROCHA	74	69	64	-	207	-6
27	Thomas LEVET	67	71	70	-	208	-5
	Per NYMAN	65	73	70	-	208	-5
	Jorge BERENDT	75	66	67	-	208	-5
	Angel ROMERO	70	69	69	-	208	-5
31	Mark ROE	67	70	72	-	209	-4
	Jesus AMAYA	69	70	70	-	209	-4
	Andrew BEAL	68	73	68	-	209	-4
	Olle KARLSSON	70	71	68	-	209	-4
	C POTTIER	72	71	66	-	209	-4
	Johan SKOLD	70	65	74	-	209	-4
	Erol SIMSEK	67	71	71	-	209	-4
	Hank KUEHNE	67	69	73	-	209	-4
	C PETTERSSON	74	69	66	-	209	-4
40	B VAUGHAN	72	67	71	-	210	-3
	C RAVETTO	69	69	72	-	210	-3
	Henrik STENSON	75	67	68	-	210	-3
	J HAEGGMAN	70	70	70	-	210	-3
	Francisco CEA	70	69	71	-	210	-3
	Jose ADERBAL	67	71	72	-	210	-3
	A ARMAGOST	69	71	70	-	210	-3

Pos	Name	R1	R2	R3	R4	Total	To par
47	M OLANDER	68	70	73	-	211	-2
	S SCAHILL	73	68	70	-	211	-2
	Paul STREETER	71	68	72	-	211	-2
	Andrew RAITT	73	67	71	-	211	-2
	Gary CLARK	69	71	71	-	211	-2
	M MOLINA	70	69	72	-	211	-2
	S SYKORA	73	69	69	-	211	-2
54	G HAVRET	73	66	73	-	212	-1
	R GONZALEZ	70	67	75	-	212	-1
	Han LEE	71	68	73	-	212	-1
	R BARCELLOS	75	65	72	-	212	-1
58	Santiago LUNA	67	72	74	-	213	E
	M PENDARIES	69	73	71	-	213	E
	Felix LUBENAU	73	69	71	-	213	E
	S DRUMMOND	70	73	70	-	213	E
	H BJORNSTAD	71	68	74	-	213	E
	Paul EALES	72	71	70	-	213	E
	Marcello SANTI	73	70	70	-	213	E
	C CHALLEN	69	74	70	-	213	E
	R GONZALEZ	71	72	70	-	213	E
	S FERNANDEZ	72	71	70	-	213	E
68	Van PHILLIPS	75	68	71	-	214	+1
	Simon KHAN	73	70	71	-	214	+1
	M JONZON	68	69	77	-	214	+1
	M BERNARDINI	68	70	76	-	214	+1
	G ACOSTA	70	73	71	-	214	+1
73	J ROBINSON	72	71	72	-	215	+2
	Paul DWYER	70	69	76	-	215	+2
	E ANDERSSON	69	73	73	-	215	+2
76	Hennie OTTO	72	69	75	-	216	+3
77	J Priscilo DINIZ	73	70	74	-	217	+4
78	Peter HANSON	72	71	75	-	218	+5
	Sergio BRASIL	72	70	76	-	218	+5
80	Tom GILLIS	71	67	-	-	-	RETD

Tournament Report

In a tournament reduced to 54 holes because of thunderstorms throughout the whole four days, Darren Fichardt's blistering Friday 61 set up a maiden European Tour victory for the 25-year-old South African in the Sao Paulo Brazilian Open.

The Pretorian was well in control after his superb second day score – which included eight birdies and an eagle – but had to wait nearly 48 hours to start what would be his final round. The rain fell heavily every afternoon and severely disrupted play but Fichardt showed good degree of patience to win.

The recent winner of the Sunshine Tour's Player's Championship got off to a nervy final round start by bogeying the second.

And with Brett Rumford picking up a shot at the same time Fichardt's lead was suddenly down to one. However, drawing on a new mental toughness that had been instilled in him by his sports psychologist wife Natasha, Fichardt preceded to birdie four of the next five holes from the fifth to again put daylight between himself and his nearest pursuers.

Jose Coceres did mount a challenge on the back nine but the Argentinean only got as close as three shots behind, and a curling 30-foot putt on the 16th from Fichardt effectively sealed victory.

Along with Rumford and Coceres, Sweden's Richard Johnson shared second spot. First round leader Per Nyman faltered badly after an opening day 65, as the Swede followed up with rounds of 73 and 70.

MISSED THE CUT: Craig HAINLINE 75 69, Miguel FERNANDEZ 70 74, Craig COWPER 74 70, Robert COLES 73 71, Simon DYSON 72 72, John WADE 72 73, Jose Manuel LARA 70 75, Shaun P WEBSTER 74 71, Pedro Rodolfo MARTINEZ 74 71, Christian CEVAER 73 72, Carl RICHARDSON 71 74, Fabiano DOS SANTOS 73 72, Dave BISHOP 70 75, Mark MOULAND 74 72, Rafael NAVARRO 74 72, Jose Maria CAZAL-RIBEIRO 75 71, Olivier EDMOND 73 73, Jonathan LOMAS 73 73, Steven RICHARDSON 73 73, Simon HURD 72 74, David HIGGINS 68 78, Ivo LEAO (AM) 77 69, Mike CAPONE 73 73, Fredrik ANDERSSON 75 72, Raul FRETES 73 74, Mikael LUNDBERG 76 71, M LIMA 74 73, J HOBDAY 71 77, D EDLUND 75 73, M PILKINGTON 76 72, L THOMPSON 75 73, C DLUHOSCH 76 72, J ABE 78 70, A CEJKA 74 75, R FELIZARDO 76 73, R DINIZ 75 74, R McGUIRK 73 77, N COLSAERTS 76 74, A J PEDRO 72 78, D DE LIMA 74 76, S WHIFFIN 73 78, Ricardo GOES 75 76, Roberto GOMEZ (Am) 78 74, S CORTE-REAL 77 76,L MARTINS 79 74, M DIAMOND 75 79, I PYMAN 76 78, H PAIK 81 73, C VANDERLEY 78 76, I DE LIMA 76 78, A C BARCELLOS 77 78, G ANTUNES 72 85, A GONZALEZ 83 75, S BERGNER 82 78, R GILLOT 78 RETD, A FRANCO 74 RETD, J HEALEY 80 RETD, S DELAGRANGE 73 RETD, D DONAHUE 75 W/D, M R SILVA 72 RETD, L MENEZES 80 W/D.

Course Profile

The Sao Paulo Golf Club (par 71, 6,646 yards) isn't long but has narrow tree-lined fairways that reward accurate, straight hitting play.

However, last year, due to the lack of rain, the rough wasn't as long or as punishing as it was in 2000.

Unusually, it has five par threes and four par fives – but the longest hole is a monster – the third, at over 600 yards.

The greens are firm and fast.

Players/Points to Note

● The European Tour did not list the Sao Paulo Brazil Open on its schedule when released in October 2001. But that is not to say that it will not form part of the tour for 2002, as there are still some gaps in the calendar. There has been a European Tour sanctioned event at Sao Paulo Golf Club for the past two years.

● South American players will obviously have an advantage as they will be used to the conditions. Argentinean stars such as **Eduardo Romero** (who holds the course record along with **Darren Fichardt** and was third in 2000), **Jose Coceres**, **Angel Cabrera**, **Jorge Berendt** (third in 2001 and 13th in 2000) and **Ricardo Gonzalez** will always be worth following.

● Top class Brazilian golfers are a little thin on the ground but Paraguay's **Pedro Martinez** came third in 2000.

● Plenty of European Tour pros head over the Atlantic for this event and as nine of the top 12 in 2000 and seven of the top 11 in 2001 came from this continent they can be worth following.

● The European players with the best form over the past two years are **Richard Johnson** (11th and second) and **Matthew Blackey** (13th and eighth).

● And watch out for little known American **Robin Byrd** who has placed 22nd and 12th in this event.

Previous Results

2000: 1. Padraig Harrington (-14), 2. Gerry Norquist (-12), 3. Five players tied.

Jose Coceres player profile – page 247

OPEN DE ARGENTINA

Jockey Club, 29 Mar to 1 Apr 2001, purse 794,704 euros

Pos	Name	R1	R2	R3	R4	Total	To par	Money	DD(y)	DA%	GIR%	Putts
1	Angel CABRERA	67	65	69	67	268	-12	130,697	309.8	62.5	81.9	123
2	Carl PETTERSSON	65	69	67	69	270	-10	87,127	286.0	46.4	65.3	109
3	Graeme STORM	68	66	69	69	272	-8	49,092	n/a	n/a	n/a	n/a
4	Mark MOULAND	69	68	69	68	274	-6	30,859	273.9	51.8	62.5	111
	Costantino ROCCA	71	67	65	71	274	-6	30,859	274.8	53.6	68.1	116
	H BJORNSTAD	70	70	66	68	274	-6	30,859	283.0	46.4	76.4	122
	Matthew BLACKEY	66	70	71	67	274	-6	30,859	263.0	76.8	63.9	112
8	V FERNANDEZ	69	72	65	69	275	-5	16,155	n/a	n/a	n/a	n/a
	Hennie OTTO	70	67	68	70	275	-5	16,155	287.9	58.9	77.8	126
	Olle KARLSSON	65	69	72	69	275	-5	16,155	279.5	41.1	58.3	106
	Daren LEE	72	66	67	70	275	-5	16,155	259.3	55.4	69.4	117
	Nic HENNING	70	69	71	65	275	-5	16,155	269.1	62.5	69.4	117

Pos	Name	R1	R2	R3	R4	Total	To par
13	Anthony WALL	68	70	68	70	276	-4
	R GONZALEZ	70	64	69	73	276	-4
	Ruben ALVAREZ	71	72	66	67	276	-4
	Angel FRANCO	64	72	71	69	276	-4
	C HANELL	70	69	69	68	276	-4
18	E ROMERO	70	66	69	72	277	-3
	J Manuel LARA	65	71	71	70	277	-3
	Thomas LEVET	69	70	70	68	277	-3
	Paul EALES	69	69	70	69	277	-3
	T Jesus MUOZ	69	66	67	75	277	-3
	M ANSELMO (Am)	73	64	70	70	277	-3
24	S D HURLEY	73	64	70	71	278	-2
	M FLORIOLI	71	68	70	69	278	-2
26	D FICHARDT	68	72	70	69	279	-1
	M FERNANDEZ	73	69	71	66	279	-1
	D BORREGO	69	72	71	67	279	-1
	Francisco CEA	69	70	70	70	279	-1
	Johan SKOLD	73	68	66	72	279	-1
	M MOLINA	70	69	66	74	279	-1
	M LUNDBERG	66	72	72	69	279	-1
	Martin LONARDI	72	70	73	64	279	-1
	Julio ZAPATA	69	69	68	73	279	-1
35	Craig HAINLINE	71	70	70	69	280	E
	Jorge BERENDT	70	65	69	76	280	E
	Erol SIMSEK	65	71	71	73	280	E
	Dave BISHOP	67	71	69	73	280	E
39	Mark ROE	73	65	75	68	281	+1
	John WADE	73	67	70	71	281	+1
	R S JOHNSON	65	71	73	72	281	+1
	N COLSAERTS	75	67	71	68	281	+1
	H CARBONETTI	71	67	70	73	281	+1
	Gustavo ROJAS	72	70	69	70	281	+1
	Van PHILLIPS	71	71	69	70	281	+1
	S SCAHILL	69	67	73	72	281	+1
47	R JACQUELIN	72	71	65	74	282	+2
	Jesus AMAYA	71	70	70	71	282	+2
	Marcello SANTI	72	69	72	69	282	+2
	J LOMAS	70	72	72	68	282	+2
	Andrew RAITT	70	68	70	74	282	+2
	Simon HURD	72	69	70	71	282	+2
	Ariel LICERA	67	71	76	68	282	+2
	A ROCHA	74	68	69	71	282	+2
55	Dennis EDLUND	71	70	72	70	283	+3
	Gary CLARK	69	69	70	75	283	+3
	Michael JONZON	72	67	71	73	283	+3
	Hank KUEHNE	72	71	69	71	283	+3
	Ramon FRANCO	68	74	69	72	283	+3
60	Kenneth FERRIE	70	72	71	71	284	+4
	Carlos RODILES	73	67	75	69	284	+4
	Gregory HAVRET	72	70	72	70	284	+4
	Simon KHAN	70	71	71	72	284	+4
	Ariel CAETE	73	65	72	74	284	+4
	R COCERES	70	71	71	72	284	+4
66	Olivier EDMOND	70	73	69	73	285	+5
	E ARGIRO	69	70	75	71	285	+5
68	T GOGELE	75	68	67	76	286	+6
	D DONAHUE	74	69	76	67	286	+6
70	C MONASTERIO	74	66	75	72	287	+7
	Esteban ISASI	72	69	71	75	287	+7
	Damian HALE	72	71	72	72	287	+7
73	Tim HEGNA	73	70	73	72	288	+8
74	S RICHARDSON	72	71	72	74	289	+9
75	C CEVAER	69	72	76	73	290	+10
	F ANDERSSON	69	74	77	70	290	+10
77	Adan SOWA	72	71	75	73	291	+11
	Andrew BEAL	72	71	76	72	291	+11
	F CHIESA (Am)	70	73	72	76	291	+11
80	Simon DYSON	72	71	75	74	292	+12
81	Philip WALTON	72	70	79	73	294	+14

Tournament Report

After four runners-up finishes on the European Tour, Angel Cabrera finally dropped his maiden tag when proving too strong for the field in the Open de Argentina.

The popular Argentinean won this co-sanctioned event (between the European and South American Tours) in front of his own fans by getting the better of Swede, Carl Pettersson, down the stretch.

The pair were in the final group after starting the day as joint leaders. But after Pettersson had gone ahead following a birdie at the first, a two-shot swing on the next, with Cabrera shooting birdie to the Swede's bogey, saw the Argentinean take the lead.

He never let the advantage slip. Cabrera was always in control and although Pettersson, who was playing only his ninth European Tour event, applied some pressure to his playing partner by picking up shots on the 15th and 16th, the eventual winner responded with birdies of his own.

Cabrera dedicated his win to mentor and fellow pro Eduardo Romero, who helped him financially in his early days on the circuit.

Pettersson, the European Amateur champion of 2000, had to settle for second.

Another European Tour rookie, Graeme Storm, was third after a last day 69, while Mark Mouland was the only other player to shoot four sub-70 rounds. The Welshman finished fourth alongside Henrik Bjornstad, Costantino Rocca and Matthew Blackey.

MISSED THE CUT: R BYRD 73 71, J ROBINSON 72 72, R GOMEZ 73 71, G PIOVANO 75 69, A ARMAGOST 73 71, P FOWLER 74 71, H STENSON 74 71, J HAEGGMAN 72 73, R CLAYDON 74 71, A CEJKA 72 73, N CHEETHAM 68 77, R FRETES 72 73, B TEILLERIA 75 70, S LUNA 73 73, A SAAVEDRA 74 72, M GUZMAN 70 76, J ABBATE 75 71, R ECHENIQUE 71 75, D A VANCSIK 71 75, M CAPONE 70 76, F MONTOVIA 71 75, F RUBERLEI 73 73, M A RODRIGUEZ 74 72, S FERNANDEZ 72 74, C CARRANZA (Am) 70 76, C MACHADO 72 74, L CARBONETTI 77 70, J HOBDAY 72 75, D HIGGINS 72 75, E RIVAS 76 71, W A MIRANDA 72 75, A ROMERO 78 69, J MADERO (Am) 73 74, M OLANDER 78 70, M PILKINGTON 74 74, R GONZALEZ 73 75, O SOLIS 73 75, A ROMERO 74 74, N BOLLINI (Am) 74 74, F ALEMAN (Am) 76 72, R ALARCON 72 77, P STREETER 70 79, M BERNARDINI 73 76, B RUMFORD 76 73, H LEE 76 73, M RUIZ 75 74, H ORDONEZ 72 77, D NUNEZ 78 71, A FERNANDEZ 76 74, P BENZADON 74 76, P LOPEZ 77 73, E PESENTI 75 76, P R MARTINEZ 74 77, G ACOSTA 73 78, R RODRIGUEZ 77 74, M SORIA 74 77, R CHAVES 76 75, A GIANNONE 78 74, J L ALONSO 79 74, F MOLINA 79 74, R MONTENEGRO 77 76, A ORTIZ 77 76, F AMICO 79 74, M O'CURRY (Am) 79 74, P MONETTI 78 75, M ISLA 81 73, F DEL GROSSO (Am) 80 76, O REINO 75 80, J CANTERO 76 81, M CABRERA 75 82, M CHAVES 76 82, J L LOZINA 79 80, G G LLANO 74 85, S P WEBSTER 73 RETD, R COLES RETD.

Course Profile

The Jockey Club (par 70, 6,635 yards) in Buenos Aires hosted the event in 2001 and was also used for the World Cup of Golf in 2000.

The crowds can get big and boisterous and usually follow the local players.

The layout is short but as the fairways are tree lined. Accuracy over length is required.

The greens are small and fast and, if players don't hit them in regulation, can find it tough to get up and down.

Players to Note

● The European Tour did not list the Open de Argentina on its schedule when released in October 2001. But that it not to say that it will not form part of the tour for 2002, as there are still some gaps in the calendar. The European Tour sanctioned the event in Argentina for the first time last season.

● Not surprisingly, an Argentinean won this event in its inaugural running. **Angel Cabrera** had played well at the Jockey Club in 2000 (when partnering **Eduardo Romero** in the World Cup of Golf to second place behind the USA pairing **Tiger Woods** and **David Duval**) and with the help of the local support was successful in the Open de Argentina in 2001.

● Other Argentineans that will have an obvious chance of success if this event does appear on the calendar in 2002 are **Jose Coceres**, **Jorge Berendt**, **Ricardo Gonzalez**, **Gustavo Rojas** and Romero, who was beaten in a play-off in 2000 for this event and has won his national Open many times.

● And don't rule out 55-year-old **Vicente Fernandez**, who inflicted that play-off defeat on Romero and was eighth in 2001.

● Experienced European players that did well last season were **Costantino Rocca** and **Mark Mouland**. While European Tour rookies **Graeme Storm**, **Carl Pettersson** and **Henrik Bjornstad** also showed up well.

Angel Cabrera player profile – page 192

Carl Pettersson player profile – page 225

33

MOROCCAN OPEN

Royal Golf Sar Es Salam, 12 Apr to 15 Apr 2001, purse 651,336 euros

Pos	Name	R1	R2	R3	R4	Total	To par	Money	DD(y)	DA%	GIR%	Putts
1	Ian POULTER	71	67	69	70	277	-15	106,506	281.1	69.6	65.3	103
2	David LYNN	72	72	68	67	279	-13	71,004	288.6	64.3	73.6	115
3	Peter LONARD	71	75	66	68	280	-12	40,007	294.5	67.9	72.2	114
4	Thomas LEVET	73	68	70	71	282	-10	29,526	277.4	666.1	69.4	116
	S GALLACHER	72	72	70	68	282	-10	29,526	287.9	60.7	75.0	117
6	Gary EVANS	70	75	66	72	283	-9	20,770	269.4	46.4	70.8	115
	Greg OWEN	73	70	70	70	283	-9	20,770	287.0	73.2	73.6	116
8	Peter HANSON	73	71	68	72	284	-8	13,708	n/a	n/a	n/a	n/a
	Paul McGINLEY	67	75	70	72	284	-8	13,708	281.5	60.7	80.6	122
	Federico BISAZZA	72	71	69	72	284	-8	13,708	n/a	n/a	n/a	n/a
	Hank KUEHNE	71	71	71	71	284	-8	13,708	n/a	n/a	n/a	n/a

Pos	Name	R1	R2	R3	R4	Total	To par
12	R KARLSSON	70	71	70	74	285	-7
13	Gary EMERSON	73	72	68	73	286	-6
	Paolo QUIRICI	73	69	71	73	286	-6
15	Kenneth FERRIE	72	73	75	67	287	-5
	Craig HAINLINE	68	72	73	74	287	-5
	Olivier EDMOND	71	72	70	74	287	-5
	Sam WALKER	69	76	67	75	287	-5
19	A SHERBORNE	72	72	70	74	288	-4
	Peter FOWLER	74	72	68	74	288	-4
	A MARSHALL	72	74	71	71	288	-4
	Jean HUGO	71	74	70	73	288	-4
	C POTTIER	73	69	71	75	288	-4
24	Wayne RILEY	71	74	73	71	289	-3
	S KJELDSEN	71	72	71	75	289	-3
	J-F LUCQUIN	73	73	70	73	289	-3
	Carl SUNESON	74	71	72	72	289	-3
	B DREDGE	70	76	70	73	289	-3
	A COLTART	75	72	71	71	289	-3
	Simon DYSON	72	73	72	72	289	-3
31	R CHAPMAN	72	74	68	76	290	-2
	R JACQUELIN	71	75	70	74	290	-2
	B VAUGHAN	76	71	73	70	290	-2
	Hennie OTTO	74	70	72	74	290	-2
	T IMMELMAN	74	74	71	71	290	-2
	H BJORNSTAD	71	74	69	76	290	-2
	S D HURLEY	77	69	71	73	290	-2
	G HAVRET	73	70	72	75	290	-2
	R SJOBERG	74	70	72	74	290	-2
	M JONZON	68	75	72	75	290	-2
	Erol SIMSEK	71	75	72	72	290	-2
	Tobias DIER	71	75	73	71	290	-2
43	A FORSBRAND	73	71	73	74	291	-1
	G RANKIN	73	75	70	73	291	-1
	M FLORIOLI	74	69	72	76	291	-1
	Gustavo ROJAS	75	70	72	74	291	-1
	Francis VALERA	73	74	70	74	291	-1
48	Marc FARRY	71	74	70	77	292	E
	Elliot BOULT	75	72	73	72	292	E
	Justin ROSE	75	71	69	77	292	E
	M SCARPA	72	73	72	75	292	E
	Nic HENNING	76	70	72	74	292	E
	James McLEAN	74	68	74	76	292	E
54	Mark ROE	76	72	74	71	293	+1
	J-F REMESY	72	74	73	74	293	+1
	Jose ROMERO	73	72	75	73	293	+1
	D DE VOOGHT	72	71	74	76	293	+1
	Paul STREETER	72	76	71	74	293	+1
	Gary CLARK	76	72	71	74	293	+1
	David PARK	69	73	74	77	293	+1
	A EL HALI (Am)	74	74	70	75	293	+1
62	M MACKENZIE	72	70	73	79	294	+2
	R RUSSELL	71	75	76	72	294	+2
	N DOUGHERTY	76	69	73	76	294	+2
65	J RYSTROM	73	73	74	75	295	+3
	Andrew BEAL	76	71	73	75	295	+3
	Stephen DODD	75	73	70	77	295	+3
	Adam MEDNICK	73	75	73	74	295	+3
	J BICKERTON	74	70	75	76	295	+3
70	Philip WALTON	71	71	75	79	296	+4
	Peter MITCHELL	75	72	74	75	296	+4
	Markus BRIER	74	74	75	73	296	+4
	M BLACKEY	73	72	76	75	296	+4
74	Nils ROERBAEK	73	75	75	74	297	+5
	Dennis EDLUND	76	71	71	79	297	+5
76	John WADE	75	71	74	78	298	+6
	R CLAYDON	78	70	74	76	298	+6
	A FORSYTH	73	72	79	74	298	+6
79	Andrew RAITT	72	74	77	76	299	+7
	B TEILLERIA	74	73	70	82	299	+7
81	Neil CHEETHAM	68	76	74	82	300	+8
	Juan A VIZCAYA	76	72	79	73	300	+8
83	R WINCHESTER	75	73	75	78	301	+9
84	P EDMOND	72	76	73	81	302	+10
85	R DRUMMOND	72	76	75	81	304	+12

Tournament Report

A bright future is assured and a future Ryder Cup place a possibility for Ian Poulter, the Englishman who claimed the Moroccan Open at Royal Golf Sar Es Salam in Rabat.

Last season's Rookie of the Year won his second European Tour title of his career dominating the weekend play. Two shots clear after a Friday best of 67, Poulter then doubled his lead with a Saturday 69.

The chasing pack, headed by David Lynn and Peter Lonard, all made challenges to Poulter, who had as many birdie opportunities as he had in the previous three days but failed to take most them. Lynn made five birdies from holes five to 11 and could have got to within a stroke of Poulter but for a missed chance on the last, while Lonard threatened with three birdies from the turn. But neither could quite catch the 25-year-old from Hertfordshire.

Whenever his driver got him into to trouble his putter would get him out of it, holing efforts from all distances to save par on the closing holes. Lynn 's closing 67 was the joint lowest score of the day (matched by Keith Ferrie) and second was the Stoke professional's best finish on Tour.

Lonard was third with Scotland's Stephen Gallacher and Thomas Levet from France tied for fourth. First round leader Paul McGinley dropped to eighth place, while there was an encouraging debut for amateur Nick Dougherty. The Chorley teenager made the cut and looks certain to star for the Walker Cup team later in the year.

MISSED THE CUT: Santiago LUNA 71 78, Mark MOULAND 72 77, Robert Jan DERKSEN 71 78, Mark FOSTER 74 75, Jamie SPENCE 76 73, Amine O JOUDAR 74 75, Mattias NILSSON 72 77, Marcello SANTI 76 73, Christian CEVAER 72 77, Simon HURD 75 74, Fredrik ANDERSSON 76 73, Lee S JAMES 76 73, Fredrik HENGE 72 78, Per NYMAN 74 76, Ignacio GARRIDO 72 78, Francisco CEA 75 75, Paddy GRIBBEN 72 78, Mark DAVIS 75 76, Steven RICHARDSON 77 74, Stephen SCAHILL 77 74, Mark PILKINGTON 73 78, Iain PYMAN 79 72, Eric CARLBERG 77 75, Andreas LINDBERG 73 79, Renaud GUILLARD 74 78, Paul NILBRINK 71 81, Shaun P WEBSTER 77 75, Michele REALE 74 78, Gary MURPHY 75 78, Younes EL HASSANI 78 75, Knud STORGAARD 76 77, Lionel ALEXANDRE 78 75, Carlos RODILES 73 80, Alberto BINAGHI 77 76, Richard GILLOT 77 76, Kamal GARTITE 77 76, Rachid EL HALI 78 76, Sebastien BRANGER 79 75, Chris BENIANS 79 75, Nicolas COLSAERTS 77 77, Jeremy ROBINSON 77 77, Thomas GOGELE 76 78, Mustapha EL KHERRAZ 79 75, David HOWELL 77 78, Jorge BERENDT 77 78, Henrik NYSTROM 80 75, Ismael BENDIAB 81 74, Mike CAPONE 78 77, Mohamed MAKROUNE 78 78, Robin BYRD 79 77, Alex CEJKA 77 79, Marco BERNARDINI 76 80, Johan SKOLD 82 75, Gordon BRAND JNR. 81 77, Garry HOUSTON 82 76, Stuart CAGE 76 82, Karim GUESSOUS 80 79, Barry LANE 78 83, MÅrten OLANDER 80 81.

Sponsored by Stan James

Course Profile

The Dar-es-Salem course (par 73, 7,329 yards) in Rabat hosted this event in 2001 and has been used three times before (1987, 1992 and 1996) to stage this tournament. It is a long layout that favours the big hitters.

The fairways are relatively wide and the greens fast and undulating.

One feature of the course is its long par threes – three of the four are over 200 yards – the second hole measures 232 yards. The wind can be a factor.

Players/Points to Note

● The European Tour did not list the Moroccan Open on its schedule when released in October 2001. But that it not to say that it will not form part of the tour for 2002, as there are still some gaps in the calendar. The Moroccan Open has featured on the European Tour for the past 10 years.

● **Robert Karlsson** hasn't won this event but has superb form figures. From 1992 to 1998 his finishing positions are 2-4-3-3-MC-6-2. He missed the 1999 and 2000 renewals but was back in 2001 to place 12th – he could have won but for a last round 74. He has a stroke average of 70.93 and is 36-under par for 30 competitive rounds.

● **David Gilford** is the only dual winner of this event (1992 and 1993) and only Karlsson has taken more money out of the sponsors coffers than the Crewe pro.

● The two players with the best recent records are **Ian Poulter** (second and first over the past two seasons) and **Thomas Levet** (second and fourth).

● **Tony Johnstone** revels in the heat of Africa and although his best position in this event is fifth, he has had four top-tens in seven starts.

● **Andrew Coltart**, **David Lynn**, **Eduardo Romero**, **Stephen Leaney**, **Roger Chapman** and former winner **Anders Forbrand** and **Petter Hedblom** have all excellent records.

Previous Results

2000: 1. Jamie Spence (-22), 2. Ian Poulter (-18), Thomas Levet (-18), Sebastien Delagrange (-18).

1999: 1. Miguel Angel Martin (-12), won play-off, 2. David Park (-12), 3. Klas Eriksson (-9).

1998: 1. Stephen Leaney (-17), 2. Robert Karlsson (-9), 3. Mathias Gronberg (-6).

1997: 1. Clinton Whitelaw (-11), 2. Roger Chapman (-9), Wayne Riley (-9), Darren Cole (-9).

1996: 1. Peter Hedblom (-7), 2. Eduardo Romero (-6), 3. Santiago Luna (-5), Wayne Westner (-5).

PGA Golf de Catalunya, 19 Apr to 22 Apr 2001, purse 1,221,402 euros

Pos	Name	R1	R2	R3	R4	Total	To par	Money	DD(y)	DA%	GIR%	Putts
1	Robert KARLSSON	68	68	71	70	277	-11	200,000	286.4	67.9	79.2	120
2	J-F REMESY	66	72	75	66	279	-9	133,330	268.6	78.6	79.2	119
3	M Angel JIMINEZ	71	69	70	70	280	-8	67,560	263.4	78.6	66.7	114
	Soren HANSEN	68	71	70	71	280	-8	67,560	278.4	62.5	68.1	115
5	Peter MITCHELL	71	72	71	67	281	-7	42,960	273.1	78.6	80.6	124
	J HAEGGMAN	70	71	71	69	281	-7	42,960	277.6	51.8	68.1	113
	Gustavo ROJAS	72	69	74	66	281	-7	42,960	264.4	69.6	72.2	117
8	R JACQUELIN	74	71	72	65	282	-6	30,000	276.8	62.5	79.2	124
9	M MACKENZIE	72	67	74	70	283	-5	21,274	274.4	58.9	70.8	117
	Justin ROSE	70	73	72	68	283	-5	21,274	276.0	71.4	75.0	123
	Gary EMERSON	71	69	71	72	283	-5	21,274	279.3	58.9	69.4	114
	D HOSPITAL	70	74	70	69	283	-5	21,274	n/a	n/a	n/a	n/a
	Jean HUGO	70	72	69	72	283	-5	21,274	289.4	62.5	79.2	121
	Stephen SCAHILL	70	68	74	71	283	-5	21,274	284.6	62.5	80.6	123
	Jarmo SANDELIN	70	66	76	71	283	-5	21,274	264.8	60.7	66.7	113

Pos	Name	R1	R2	R3	R4	Total	To par
16	W BENNETT	69	70	75	70	284	-4
	Sergio GARCIA	69	73	71	71	284	-4
	Steve WEBSTER	69	70	73	72	284	-4
	J LOMAS	70	69	74	71	284	-4
	Peter LONARD	71	72	72	69	284	-4
	Andrew RAITT	67	68	79	70	284	-4
	C PETTERSSON	67	69	74	74	284	-4
23	G BRAND JNR.	71	72	73	69	285	-3
	M Angel MARTIN	70	71	70	74	285	-3
	S KJELDSEN	71	69	71	74	285	-3
	G HAVRET	75	70	71	69	285	-3
	T GOGELE	68	72	76	69	285	-3
	Olle KARLSSON	72	71	74	68	285	-3
	Greg OWEN	70	73	73	69	285	-3
	A COLTART	69	68	79	69	285	-3
	D ROBERTSON	71	70	71	73	285	-3
32	A OLDCORN	64	73	78	71	286	-2
	J Manuel LARA	70	73	70	73	286	-2
	David GILFORD	71	71	73	71	286	-2
	D BOTES	69	71	77	69	286	-2
	N COLSAERTS	76	69	74	67	286	-2
	J MOSELEY	70	74	72	70	286	-2
	Ian GARBUTT	68	74	73	71	286	-2
	N VANHOOTEGEM	75	70	72	69	286	-2
	Darren CLARKE	67	68	72	79	286	-2
	R RUSSELL	72	69	76	69	286	-2
42	Des SMYTH	70	72	75	70	287	-1
	J Maria ARRUTI	73	68	74	72	287	-1
	Neil CHEETHAM	73	71	74	69	287	-1
	Peter O'MALLEY	73	69	75	70	287	-1
	F JACOBSON	72	72	73	70	287	-1
	S GALLACHER	72	72	69	74	287	-1
	C HANELL	71	73	69	74	287	-1
49	A FORSBRAND	76	69	73	70	288	E
	Sven STRUVER	72	72	74	70	288	E
	Michele REALE	73	71	76	68	288	E
	Gary EVANS	71	74	74	69	288	E
	Phillip PRICE	70	74	71	73	288	E
	C CEVAER	76	69	74	69	288	E
	Van PHILLIPS	74	70	72	72	288	E
	David LYNN	69	75	73	71	288	E
	Graeme STORM	70	71	75	72	288	E
58	David HOWELL	72	72	75	70	289	+1
	Anders HANSEN	75	69	72	73	289	+1
	D BORREGO	69	72	74	74	289	+1
	I GARRIDO	71	73	75	70	289	+1
	Markus BRIER	75	70	73	71	289	+1
	Simon DYSON	72	71	75	71	289	+1
64	A SHERBORNE	73	68	73	76	290	+2
	G RANKIN	67	72	74	77	290	+2
	R BALLESTEROS	70	73	72	75	290	+2
	J BICKERTON	71	67	77	75	290	+2
	Erol SIMSEK	74	69	79	68	290	+2
	M LUNDBERG	69	76	73	72	290	+2
	A FORSYTH	72	72	78	68	290	+2
71	Santiago LUNA	73	71	76	71	291	+3
	John SENDEN	74	71	75	71	291	+3
	Patrik SJOLAND	74	71	75	71	291	+3
	Daren LEE	71	71	78	71	291	+3
75	Carlos RODILES	67	77	76	72	292	+4
	Fernando ROCA	71	73	71	77	292	+4
	F ANDERSSON	70	74	75	73	292	+4
78	M MOULAND	74	71	76	72	293	+5
79	J RYSTROM	72	72	78	72	294	+6
	Francis VALERA	69	72	77	76	294	+6
81	Juan QUIROS	72	73	78	72	295	+7
82	T WHITEHOUSE (Am)	71	74	79	74	298	+10
83	Brian DAVIS	72	73	81	76	302	+14

Sponsored by Stan James

Tournament Report

A controlled performance by Robert Karlsson, coupled with Darren Clarke's nightmare Sunday 79, gave the Swede victory in the Via Digital Spanish Open at El Saler Golf Club in Valencia.

Karlsson secured his fourth European Tour title on this links course in Valencia by two shots from Jean Francois Remesy after Clarke, who was tied with the Swede going into the final round, racked up a rather less than perfect ten on the par five 15th.

The Ulsterman was still in contention prior to his double figure score on the 564-yard dogleg hole. But having found the trees with his second shot, Clarke decided to hack out of what seemed an unplayable lie.

Three swipes later he eventually dislodged the ball and then three misjudged chips and a couple of putts saw Clarke score ten – and drop from third to 32nd.

In truth, Karlsson, who took the lead after a birdie at the first, would probably have won anyway. The Swede dropped only five shots all week and the golfing gods were certainly looking down upon him as he found the trees and two bunkers before saving par on the sixth.

After Clarke's aberrations on the 15th there was no-one left to challenge Karlsson who won his first European Tour title in Valencia six years ago.

After benign conditions over the first two days scores were sent soaring when the winds struck on Friday. Frenchman Remesy's last day 66 saw him steal second spot from Miguel Angel Jimenez of Spain and Dane Soren Hansen.

MISSED THE CUT: W RILEY 77 69, J RIVERO 71 75, I WOOSNAM 74 72, A SALTO 73 73, J M OLAZABAL 69 77, J M CARRILES 73 73, J SPENCE 71 75, S TINNING 72 74, J BERENDT 75 71, T J MUOZ 72 74, D TERBLANCHE 69 77, F CEA 73 73, R CHAPMAN 75 72, C ROCCA 75 72, M LAFEBER 74 73, H OTTO 74 73, R S JOHNSON 75 72, L CLAVERIE 72 75, R WESSELS 73 74, R COLES 72 75, D CARTER 72 75, D DARCY 75 73, G HOUSTON 75 73, S P WEBSTER 74 74, P BAKER 76 72, H BJORNSTAD 74 74, P QUIRICI 76 72, R CLAYDON 74 74, R MUNTZ 75 73, S RICHARDSON 75 73, M PILKINGTON 75 73, R RAFFERTY 75 73, R QUIROS 78 71, T IMMELMAN 75 74, I POULTER 72 77, J HOBDAY 75 74, C SUNESON 74 75, H NYSTROM 76 73, T LEVET 73 77, S DODD 77 73, D PARK 73 77, D HIGGINS 74 76, A PONS GARCIA-CON 75 75, M ROE 75 76, E DE LA RIVA 76 75, F BISAZZA 72 79, N FASTH 78 73, L PARSONS 76 75, I GINER 78 73, A GOMEZ PASTRANA 72 79, M BERNARDINI 73 78, H KUEHNE 74 77, B LANE 81 71, M FARRY 73 79, P HANSON 74 78, M FLORIOLI 75 77, J C AGUERO 75 78, F HENGE 79 75, G ORR 80 74, T DIER 78 76, M J TOMAS (Am) 77 77, S BALLESTEROS 76 79, M DAVIS 76 79, E BOULT 74 81, J A VIZCAYA 78 77, S TORRANCE 77 79, H STENSON 77 79, O SANCHEZ 79 78, N HENNING 75 82, D COMIN (Am) 87 83 170 26 R WINCHESTER 83 76, K FERRIE 83 W/D, M SANTI 79 RETD.

Course Profile

Last season's renewal took place at the El Saler (par 72, 7,095 yards) course near Valencia. The layout had been used to stage the championship in 1984 and 1989 (both won by Bernhard Langer).

It is a links course that is built into the coastline and one that can be seriously affected by the wind – as all links courses should be. It does meander inland as there are a few holes that have tree lined fairways, although many of the landing areas are generous.

Players/Points to Note

● With this tournament changing its venue from year to year, pinpointing course form seems irrelevant – especially as the host course for next year's renewal has still to be decided. One thing is for certain though – don't back a Spaniard. In the last 29 years only one Spanish player has managed to win his own national championship – **Seve Ballesteros**. Whether it's the pressure from the home crowd or media, or just the fact they are trying to hard, they don't seem to win.

● The big Spanish names do come and play here though and **Jose Maria Olazabal** can boast five top-ten finishes in this event. And **Sergio Garcia** (who always takes times out from his US schedule to play), **Miguel Angel Jimenez**, **Miguel Angel Martin**, **Santiago Luna** and **Ignacio Garrido** have all gone close to winning recently.

● Big names rarely play in this event but both **Colin Montgomerie** and **Bernhard Langer** (twice) are former champions.

● **Thomas Bjorn** has won twice in Spain (this title in 1998), as has last year's winner **Robert Karlsson**. While other former champions with impressive stroke averages in this event are **Jarmo Sandelin** and **Padraig Harrington**.

● **Eduardo Romero** has seven top-ten finishes since 1990 to his name in this event, including a win in 1991, while a fully fit **Gary Orr** could go well in 2002.

Previous Results

2000: 1. Brian Davis (-14), 2. Markus Brier (-11), 3. Eduardo Romero (-10), Peter Baker (-10).

1999: 1. Jarmo Sandelin (-21), 2. Miguel Angel Jimenez (-17), Ignacio Garrido (-17), Paul McGinley (-17).

1998: 1. Thomas Bjorn (-21), 2. Greg Chalmers (-20), Jose Maria Olazabal (-20).

1997: 1. Mark James (-11), won play-off, 2. Greg Norman (-11), 3. Eduardo Romero (-10), Jarmo Sandelin (-10).

1996: 1. Padraig Harrington (-16), 2. Gordon Brand Jnr (-12), 3. Rolf Muntz (-10).

ALGARVE OPEN DE PORTUGAL

Quinta do Lago, 26 Apr to 29 Apr 2001, purse 1,013,392 euros

Pos	Name	R1	R2	R3	R4	Total	To par	Money	DD(y)	DA%	GIR%	Putts
1	Phillip PRICE	72	67	70	64	273	-15	166,660	289.0	60.7	79.2	115
2	P HARRINGTON	64	70	71	70	275	-13	86,855	299.6	55.4	90.3	127
	Sven STRUVER	70	70	65	70	275	-13	86,855	284.5	60.7	79.2	117
4	Ignacio GARRIDO	69	68	70	70	277	-11	42,466	274.0	55.4	84.7	124
	Stephen SCAHILL	70	69	66	72	277	-11	42,466	294.4	60.7	77.3	122
	Alastair FORSYTH	68	68	72	69	277	-11	42,466	301.1	60.7	76.4	120
7	Alex CEJKA	70	73	70	65	278	-10	27,500	295.9	58.9	77.8	116
	Brett RUMFORD	74	68	67	69	278	-10	27,500	290.5	66.1	75.0	116
9	David HOWELL	67	70	69	73	279	-9	18,233	276.8	46.4	63.9	108
	Warren BENNETT	70	70	70	69	279	-9	18,233	291.0	48.2	77.8	121
	David GILFORD	66	70	69	74	279	-9	18,233	285.8	66.1	77.8	118
	Russell CLAYDON	70	72	71	66	279	-9	18,233	272.5	58.9	72.2	113
	Niclas FASTH	66	72	68	73	279	-9	18,233	294.8	51.8	73.6	116
	Simon DYSON	69	69	67	74	279	-9	18,233	286.9	51.8	75.0	117

Pos	Name	R1	R2	R3	R4	Total	To par
15	Brian DAVIS	71	71	73	65	280	-8
	Elliot BOULT	67	73	69	71	280	-8
	Roger WESSELS	73	68	66	73	280	-8
	M LUNDBERG	70	72	69	69	280	-8
19	Santiago LUNA	71	70	72	68	281	-7
	Anders HANSEN	68	71	69	73	281	-7
	M LAFEBER	72	71	71	67	281	-7
	Richard GREEN	71	72	69	69	281	-7
	T IMMELMAN	68	73	67	73	281	-7
	David PARK	70	71	69	71	281	-7
	Patrik SJOLAND	67	72	70	72	281	-7
	N DOUGHERTY	71	72	71	67	281	-7
27	R CHAPMAN	68	70	72	72	282	-6
	Greg TURNER	69	74	69	70	282	-6
	Hennie OTTO	71	73	70	68	282	-6
	Henrik STENSON	70	73	68	71	282	-6
	J ROBINSON	71	68	72	71	282	-6
	Paolo QUIRICI	73	71	71	67	282	-6
	J HAEGGMAN	68	72	68	74	282	-6
	Markus BRIER	70	72	69	71	282	-6
	A COLTART	75	68	68	71	282	-6
37	M MACKENZIE	70	72	68	73	283	-5
	S KJELDSEN	73	70	69	71	283	-5
	D BOTES	73	69	71	70	283	-5
	G HAVRET	71	72	75	65	283	-5
	Robin BYRD	72	71	67	73	283	-5
	Paul McGINLEY	71	69	70	73	283	-5
	R GONZALEZ	68	71	68	76	283	-5
44	A FORSBRAND	70	69	71	74	284	-4
	Ian WOOSNAM	74	70	69	71	284	-4
	Peter FOWLER	71	69	71	73	284	-4
	Steve WEBSTER	69	74	70	71	284	-4
	Francisco CEA	71	73	66	74	284	-4
	J SANDELIN	72	71	69	72	284	-4
	H NYSTROM	72	71	71	70	284	-4
	J BICKERTON	69	73	70	72	284	-4
	David HIGGINS	66	77	72	69	284	-4
53	M MOULAND	70	70	73	72	285	-3
	Justin ROSE	70	71	74	70	285	-3
	M SCARPA	76	66	74	69	285	-3
	Gustavo ROJAS	72	69	70	74	285	-3
	B DREDGE	72	71	71	71	285	-3
	R RUSSELL	72	71	69	73	285	-3
	M BLACKEY	68	75	71	71	285	-3
60	Mark DAVIS	70	74	72	70	286	-2
	Justin HOBDAY	70	70	76	70	286	-2
	Paul EALES	74	70	69	73	286	-2
	J RYSTROM	71	73	74	68	286	-2
	M GRONBERG	72	71	74	69	286	-2
	T Jesus MUOZ	68	75	70	73	286	-2
	David LYNN	66	75	76	69	286	-2
67	Manuel PIERO	75	68	72	72	287	-1
	D HOSPITAL	70	73	72	72	287	-1
	Jorge BERENDT	68	75	68	76	287	-1
	Paul STREETER	72	72	68	75	287	-1
	Hank KUEHNE	71	69	73	74	287	-1
72	A OLDCORN	70	74	72	72	288	E
	Ian POULTER	67	76	75	70	288	E
	R WINCHESTER	69	74	71	74	288	E
75	Kenneth FERRIE	68	74	70	77	289	+1
	N CAMPINO (Am)	72	71	74	72	289	+1
	D PRICE (Am)	70	73	72	74	289	+1
78	S P WEBSTER	70	74	71	75	290	+2
	C CEVAER	71	70	76	73	290	+2
	Andrew RAITT	70	74	73	73	290	+2
81	Craig HAINLINE	72	69	73	77	291	+3
82	Jose RIVERO	70	74	76	73	293	+5

Tournament Report

Phillip Price finally scratched a seven-year itch by winning his second European Tour title at Quinto do Lago.

In 1994, the Welshman won his first tour event, also the Portuguese Open, and after eight runners up positions between, finally got his head in front for a second time. Lying in 15th place at the start of the final day – and four shots off the pace, Price carded a superb Sunday 64. Five birdies in the first six holes set up his win.

And he repeated the trick on the homeward nine, chipping in from off the green on the 16th and holing putts from 12, 15 and 22 feet. Price needed just 26 putts in his final round and saw off some exalted company to pick up the £104,000 first place prize.

Pre-tournament favourite Colin Montgomerie missed the cut, the first time he had failed to make the weekend's play in successive tour events for three seasons (Monty had bowed out of the Masters at the halfway stage on his last outing).

First round leader Padraig Harrington failed to break 70 after his opening 64 and struggled on the greens on the final day to finish second alongside Sven Struver. The German who, along with Harrington, David Gilford, Stephen Scahill and Simon Dyson, led going into the final round went out in 38, although he picked up birdies on three of the last six holes to record his highest finish of the season.

MISSED THE CUT: Sam TORRANCE 71 74, Gary MURPHY 72 73, Jose Manuel LARA 74 71, Jean-Francois REMESY 71 74, Graham RANKIN 70 75, Peter HANSON 72 73, Colin MONTGOMERIE 73 72, Stephane CASTRO FERREIRA 73 72, Massimo FLORIOLI 72 73, Jonathan LOMAS 74 71, Ian GARBUTT 74 71, Nicolas VANHOOTEGEM 75 70, Steven RICHARDSON 68 77, Gary ORR 70 75, Greg OWEN 71 74, Fredrik ANDERSSON 73 72, Christopher HANELL 72 73, Eamonn DARCY 75 71, Barry LANE 73 73, Garry HOUSTON 71 75, Peter MITCHELL 72 74, Richard S JOHNSON 70 76, D TERBLANCHE 73 73, F JACOBSON 69 77, J SKOLD 69 77, A SOBRINHO 72 74, D CARTER 73 73, S GALLACHER 74 72, C PETTERSSON 74 72, A ROCHA 72 74, R RAFFERTY 73 74, W RILEY 70 77, F HENGE 71 76, G EMERSON 71 76, H BJORNSTAD 75 72, J HUGO 72 75, D BORREGO 72 75, V PHILLIPS 72 75, F VALERA 73 74, P WALTON 74 74, M FARRY 73 75, S TINNING 73 75, R MUNTZ 74 74, R COLES 76 72, D ROBERTSON 74 74, N HENNING 72 76, G STORM 73 75, N CHEETHAM 74 75, S DODD 71 78, S CORTE-REAL 73 76, G BRAND JNR. 75 75, D SMYTH 73 77, J JOHNSON 74 76, C RODILES 73 77, M REALE 77 73, M PILKINGTON 70 80, D LEE 74 76, P BAKER 77 74, R SOARES (Am) 74 77, M McLEAN 77 75, J CARVALHOSA 71 81, H SANTOS (Am) 75 77, P LAWRIE 75 77, B HAFTHORSSON 78 74, T CRUZ (Am) 75 78, N TAYLOR 80 75, N CAVALHEIRO 77 81, J DIAS 79 79, A DANTAS DA SILVA 80 82, D SILVA 79 84, M A MARTIN 75 RETD, J SPENCE 82 W/D, O KARLSSON RETD, M JONZON 81 W/D.

Course Profile

The Quinto do Lago course (par 72, 7,096 yards) was used for the first time since 1990 last year. The fact that Colin Montgomerie won his first European Tour title there should tell you that long straight hitters prosper.

The venue for next season's event has yet to be confirmed but there is every chance it could move back to Le Meridien Penina (par 72, 6,875 yards), which hosted the event between 1998-2000.

Another track which favours accurate strikers of the ball.

Players/Points to Note

●The Portuguese Open was **Gary Orr**'s first win on the European Tour. And as he was only just coming back from illness in 2001 you can ignore his poor showing in 2000. This event, in fact, has a habit of throwing up first time tour winners (three of the last five – and last year's champion, **Phillip Price**, was winless for nine years, so he nearly comes into that category).

●**Phillip Price** is the only dual winner of this tournament since 1990 (1994 and 2001) and has also finished as runner up. **David Gilford** won this event in 1993 has finished runner up twice.

●**Peter Mitchell**'s form figures read 18-18-25-DQ-58-17-27-53-WIN-19-18-MC from 1990 – ultra consistent stats mark him out as one to follow despite his poor season last year.

●**Ignacio Garrido** has three top-five finishes to his name in this event while fellow Spaniards **Miguel Angel Jimenez** and **Santiago Luna** also have fine records in this tournament.

●**Van Phillips** missed the cut last year but prior to that hadn't finished lower than 29th in four starts in this event and won in 1999.

●**John Bickerton** can boast three top-20 finishes over the past four years, including second place in 1999.

●Others with a decent record in the tournament are **Tony Johnstone**, **Jose Coceres**, **Anthony Wall**, **Niclas Fasth** and **Wayne Riley**.

Previous Results

2000: 1. Gary Orr (-13), 2. Phillip Price (-12), 3. Tony Johnstone (-9), Brian Davis (-9), Paul McGinley (-9).

1999: 1. Van Phillips (-12), won play-off, 2. John Bickerton (-12), 3. Robert Karlsson (-9), Alex Cejka (-9), Santiago Luna (-9).

1998: 1. Peter Mitchell (-18), 2. David Gilford (-17), Jarmo Sandelin (-17).

1997: 1. Michael Jonzon (-19), 2. Ignacio Garrido (-16), 3. Paul Broadhurst (-13).

1996: 1. Wayne Riley (-13), 2. Mark Davis (-11), Martin Gates (-11).

NOVOTEL PERRIER OPEN DE FRANCE

Lyon G.C., 3 May to 6 May 2001, purse 1,317,442 euros

Pos	Name	R1	R2	R3	R4	Total	To par	Money	DD(y)	DA%	GIR%	Putts
1	J Maria OLAZABAL	66	69	66	67	268	-12	216,660	266.6	63.5	83.3	120
2	Costantino ROCCA	68	69	64	69	270	-10	96,940	266.6	78.8	73.6	116
	Greg TURNER	69	67	67	67	270	-10	96,940	263.1	78.8	73.6	115
	Paul EALES	66	69	67	68	270	-10	96,940	n/a	n/a	n/a	n/a
5	Gregory HAVRET	67	67	69	68	271	-9	55,120	n/a	n/a	n/a	n/a
6	Marc FARRY	68	65	71	68	272	-8	45,500	n/a	n/a	n/a	n/a
7	Anders HANSEN	66	68	70	69	273	-7	33,540	n/a	n/a	n/a	n/a
	Paul McGINLEY	72	67	69	65	273	-7	33,540	270.1	76.9	73.6	119
	Ian GARBUTT	68	71	70	64	273	-7	33,540	259.0	76.9	73.6	117
10	Alex CEJKA	67	70	70	67	274	-6	21,505	277.9	71.2	70.8	116
	Neil CHEETHAM	67	69	66	72	274	-6	21,505	270.1	65.4	69.4	114
	Jorge BERENDT	66	71	69	68	274	-6	21,505	262.1	73.1	65.3	110
	Paul LAWRIE	71	67	67	69	274	-6	21,505	273.6	61.5	68.1	117
	John BICKERTON	70	67	66	71	274	-6	21,505	261.4	78.8	70.8	113
	Paddy GRIBBEN	68	68	68	70	274	-6	21,505	283.4	71.2	79.2	124
	James McLEAN	65	71	69	69	274	-6	21,505	n/a	n/a	n/a	n/a

Pos	Name	R1	R2	R3	R4	Total	To par
17	S KJELDSEN	70	68	71	66	275	-5
	S LEANEY	72	67	66	70	275	-5
	Anthony WALL	69	68	67	71	275	-5
	D BOTES	67	68	71	69	275	-5
	D HOSPITAL	69	67	66	73	275	-5
	R WINCHESTER	66	69	72	68	275	-5
	J HAEGGMAN	68	70	67	70	275	-5
	Peter O'MALLEY	72	67	70	66	275	-5
	M PILKINGTON	70	66	69	70	275	-5
	Brett RUMFORD	68	70	69	68	275	-5
27	A FORSBRAND	65	70	70	71	276	-4
	E ROMERO	67	73	68	68	276	-4
	Philip WALTON	68	71	68	69	276	-4
	Richard GREEN	68	69	70	69	276	-4
	H WALTERS	69	68	70	69	276	-4
	R CLAYDON	68	68	68	72	276	-4
	D BORREGO	69	68	69	70	276	-4
	Tobias DIER	69	71	70	66	276	-4
35	A MARSHALL	66	71	70	70	277	-3
	F ANDERSSON	68	71	69	69	277	-3
37	Peter HANSON	71	65	72	70	278	-2
	S P WEBSTER	68	71	65	74	278	-2
	J LOMAS	65	72	69	72	278	-2
	Robert COLES	67	69	71	71	278	-2
41	Mark ROE	72	67	71	69	279	-1
	Mark DAVIS	67	68	77	67	279	-1
	John SENDEN	69	68	72	70	279	-1
	Peter BAKER	69	68	71	71	279	-1
	H BJORNSTAD	72	68	63	76	279	-1
	Per NYMAN	68	72	75	64	279	-1
	R GONZALEZ	70	68	69	72	279	-1
	I GARRIDO	68	69	71	71	279	-1
	C CEVAER	69	71	67	72	279	-1
	Daren LEE	64	71	68	76	279	-1
	Nic HENNING	73	66	70	70	279	-1
52	W BENNETT	65	73	75	67	280	E
	Olivier EDMOND	70	69	71	70	280	E
	Andrew RAITT	69	71	72	68	280	E
	F DELAMONTAGNE (Am)	72	68	71	69	280	E
56	R DRUMMOND	67	72	72	70	281	+1
	Jose RIVERO	68	70	71	72	281	+1
	Gary MURPHY	70	69	73	69	281	+1
	J ROBINSON	67	69	74	71	281	+1
	Olle KARLSSON	70	69	69	73	281	+1
61	M Angel MARTIN	71	69	68	74	282	+2
	Gary EVANS	68	67	76	71	282	+2
	T Jesus MUOZ	69	70	71	72	282	+2
	David PARK	70	68	74	70	282	+2
	Erol SIMSEK	67	72	72	71	282	+2
66	J MOSELEY	63	75	74	71	283	+3
	Van PHILLIPS	68	72	72	71	283	+3
	N JOAKIMIDES	67	73	68	75	283	+3
69	G HOUSTON	66	71	76	71	284	+4
	Elliot BOULT	69	70	70	75	284	+4
	Hennie OTTO	69	70	75	70	284	+4
	Jamie SPENCE	69	70	69	76	284	+4
73	Barry LANE	71	68	74	72	285	+5
	Justin HOBDAY	67	72	73	73	285	+5
75	T GOGELE	69	70	74	73	286	+6
76	M FLORIOLI	68	72	72	75	287	+7
77	Michele REALE	69	70	78	71	288	+8
78	T IMMELMAN	71	69	77	75	292	+12
	L ALEXANDRE	69	70	80	73	292	+12
	Chris BENIANS	69	71	76	76	292	+12

Tournament Report

A 19th European Tour title came Jose Maria Olazabal's way at Lyon Golf Club, as the two-time US Masters champion won the Open de France on a soaked Sangliers course.

It was a win that lifted the Spaniard up to sixth in the Ryder Cup standings and should give Sam Torrance less of a headache when the Scot announces his team later in the year. Olazabal, who had been playing more on the US Tour over the past few months, trailed halfway leader Marc Farry by two shots after the second round.

And when Saturday's play failed to get underway on time because of bad weather it wasn't until Sunday that Ollie made his move.

A third round 66 put him on level terms with Costantino Rocca – who won the Lyon Open here in 1993. The pair duelled throughout the last day and it wasn't until the back nine that Olazabal took a grip on the championship.

When Rocca found the greenside bunker on the 15th the Italian's challenge was over, and although Greg Turner at one stage drew level with Olazabal a double bogey on the 16th put paid to the Kiwi's chances.

A superb pitch on the last set up a birdie for Olazabal, who won by two shots despite admitting that he hadn't been comfortable with his game and that he felt he should have been striking the ball better.

Paul Eales shared second place alongside Rocca and Turner, while three time French Amateur champion and tour rookie Gregory Havret claimed fifth.

MISSED THE CUT: M MOULAND 73 68, R RAFFERTY 70 71, R JACQUELIN 72 69, J VAN DE VELDE 71 70, T LEVET 72 69, D EDLUND 70 71, M SANTI 69 72, S SCAHILL 71 70, B CORNUT 71 70, J M KULA 76 65, M JONZON 71 70, M BLACKEY 72 69, B TEILLERIA 72 69, M DIEU 71 71, J M CARRILES 72 70, K FERRIE 69 73, J ROMERO 73 69, R SJOBERG 71 71, R RUSSELL 67 75, G STORM 68 74, S WALKER 68 74, R PELLICIOLI (Am) 72 70, J HUGO 72 71, A CABRERA 72 71, S HURD 69 74, F CUPILLARD 72 71, C PETTERSSON 72 71, D GILFORD 73 71, R SABARROS 69 75, M LAFEBER 73 71, G EMERSON 68 76, D HIGGINS 69 75, C HANELL 71 73, M CAPONE 71 73, J M LARA 70 75, A LINDBERG 73 72, P NILBRINK 73 72, C HAINLINE 72 73, A BINAGHI 71 74, N COLSAERTS 72 73, S DODD 71 74, F TARNAUD 78 67, M SCARPA 71 74, G ROJAS 74 71, D MOONEY 72 73, M ILONEN 71 74, R GUILLARD 72 74, R BYRD 72 74, A BEAL 71 75, P STREETER 74 72, F VALERA 72 75, B LECUONA (Am) 70 77, P FOWLER 75 73, D FICHARDT 72 76, S BRANGER 75 74, F AUMONIER 79 70, P SJOLAND 73 77, O CHABAUD (Am) 77 73, C POTTIER 74 77, R GILLOT 72 80, P LIMA (Am) 76 76, J SKOLD 75 80, N DELBOS (Am) 77 79, S BALLESTEROS 74 RETD, S LUNA 67 W/D, R MCFARLANE 75 W/D, G RANKIN 69 DISQ, S D. HURLEY 79 W/D, P MITCHELL 72 RETD, S DELAGRANGE 71 RETD.

Course Profile

In 2001 the tournament moved to Lyon Golf Club Villette d'Anthon (par 70, 7,352 yards). A venue in the south of France which is long and demanding.

In 2002, the event returns to at Le Golf National (par 72 7,098 yards) near Paris, which staged the French Open from 1991-1998 and 2000. It is a tough layout and one which can play longer than its yardage suggests – especially if the rains come (which they usually do).

Players/Points to Note

●**Retief Goosen** loves playing in France as his record from 1993 in this tournament testifies – 15-DNP-55-3-Win-16-Win-36-DNP. He is 48 under par with a stroke average of 70.00 and if he does return to play in this event in 2002 he is a must for staking plans

●**Greg Turner** finished runner-up in 1999 and 2001 and has also been placed in the top dozen on three other occasions.

●**Costantino Rocca** boasts four top-four finishes in the French Open in his last nine starts in the event, including a win in 1993. **Paul McGinley** has finished in the top ten on four occasions.

●There has been no French winner of this tournament in the modern era and while **Jean Van de Velde** has come close (two top-ten finishes), the home crowd might be looking to **Gregory Havret** to end their drought of native champions. Fifth last year, Havret in a former French Amateur champion who won the Italian Open last season.

●**Eduardo Romero** won this event in 1991 and has a stroke average of 70.55 from his last 38 rounds here.

●**Jarmo Sandelin**, **Andrew Coltart**, **Alex Cejka**, **Michael Campbell** have all performed well in this event recently while tour veterans **Santiago Luna**, **Jamie Spence**, **Paul Broadhurst** and **Sam Torrance** could be worth another throw of the dice in 2002.

Previous Results

2000: 1. Colin Montgomerie (-16), 2. Jonathan Lomas (-14), 3. Rodger Davis (-11).

1999: 1. Retief Goosen (-12), won play-off, 2. Greg Turner (-12), 3. Santiago Luna (-9), Jose Coceres (-9).

1998: 1. Sam Torrance (-12), 2. Bernhard Langer (-10), Mathew Goggin (-10), Olivier Edmond (-10), Massimo Florioli (-10).

1997: 1. Retief Goosen (-17), 2. Jamie Spence (-14), 3. Four players tied.

1996: 1. Robert Allenby (-16), won play-off, 2. Bernhard Langer (-16), 3. Retief Goosen (-14).

BENSON & HEDGES INTERNATIONAL OPEN

De Vere Belfry, 10 May to 13 May 2001, purse 1,624,384 euros

Pos	Name	R1	R2	R3	R4	Total	To par	Money	DD(y)	DA%	GIR%	Putts
1	Henrik STENSON	66	68	71	70	275	-13	267,917	286.8	65.0	70.8	109
2	Paul McGINLEY	66	72	70	70	278	-10	139,625	280.6	71.7	70.8	115
	Angel CABRERA	70	70	69	69	278	-10	139,625	307.3	46.7	65.3	111
4	Olle KARLSSON	69	71	68	73	281	-7	80,378	275.6	53.3	56.9	104
5	Desvonde BOTES	69	69	72	72	282	-6	68,160	281.4	56.7	65.3	112
6	Richard GREEN	72	70	70	71	283	-5	56,264	267.0	95.0	83.3	127
7	Eduardo ROMERO	70	74	66	74	284	-4	37,231	282.0	65.0	70.8	121
	David HOWELL	69	70	73	72	284	-4	37,231	273.8	55.0	63.0	114
	R JACQUELIN	68	74	72	70	284	-4	37,231	275.0	60.0	70.8	120
	Thomas BJORN	69	68	75	72	284	-4	37,231	275.6	46.7	55.6	107
	Retief GOOSEN	71	68	74	71	284	-4	37,231	277.8	61.7	75.0	123

Pos	Name	R1	R2	R3	R4	Total	To par
12	C MONTGOMERIE	73	69	71	72	285	-3
	Ian GARBUTT	72	70	72	71	285	-3
	Phillip PRICE	70	74	67	74	285	-3
	Jorge BERENDT	75	67	70	73	285	-3
	Patrik SJOLAND	69	73	71	72	285	-3
	N DOUGHERTY	72	72	70	71	285	-3
	Paul CASEY	72	73	71	69	285	-3
19	P HARRINGTON	68	72	76	70	286	-2
	R S JOHNSON	73	71	74	68	286	-2
	J MOSELEY	70	69	72	75	286	-2
	J RYSTROM	72	70	75	69	286	-2
	D BORREGO	68	73	74	71	286	-2
	Paul LAWRIE	70	71	74	71	286	-2
	Brett RUMFORD	72	71	71	72	286	-2
	A BADDELEY	69	72	69	76	286	-2
27	J Milkha SINGH	72	69	71	75	287	-1
	J Manuel LARA	72	73	69	73	287	-1
	J M OLAZABAL	67	75	72	73	287	-1
	Sven STRUVER	74	66	75	72	287	-1
	M Angel JIMINEZ	72	70	71	74	287	-1
	Peter MITCHELL	76	69	69	73	287	-1
	Darren CLARKE	69	76	68	74	287	-1
	Robert COLES	70	73	74	70	287	-1
35	C ROCCA	73	71	74	70	288	E
	Jose RIVERO	72	67	76	73	288	E
	Mark MCNULTY	70	74	73	71	288	E
	Elliot BOULT	68	73	77	70	288	E
	Nick O'HERN	70	75	71	72	288	E
	R CLAYDON	71	68	74	75	288	E
	Markus BRIER	73	72	71	72	288	E
42	David GILFORD	68	73	73	75	289	+1
	Steve WEBSTER	71	73	69	76	289	+1
	Anthony WALL	69	72	76	72	289	+1
	Peter BAKER	71	71	75	72	289	+1
	H BJORNSTAD	72	72	71	74	289	+1
	R KARLSSON	71	73	72	73	289	+1
	J LOMAS	72	72	70	75	289	+1
	D ROBERTSON	71	70	72	76	289	+1
	H NYSTROM	70	70	71	78	289	+1
	S GALLACHER	69	74	72	74	289	+1
52	J-F REMESY	71	70	73	76	290	+2
	S KJELDSEN	71	74	72	73	290	+2
	Paul EALES	73	72	73	72	290	+2
	Francisco CEA	70	72	72	76	290	+2
	M BERNARDINI	73	70	73	74	290	+2
57	Eamonn DARCY	75	67	75	74	291	+3
	B LANGER	72	69	73	77	291	+3
	Ian WOOSNAM	71	69	74	77	291	+3
	Marc FARRY	70	75	69	77	291	+3
	Fredrik HENGE	70	72	74	75	291	+3
	J VAN DE VELDE	72	73	74	72	291	+3
	Lee WESTWOOD	73	68	76	74	291	+3
64	Jean HUGO	69	76	73	74	292	+4
	Pierre FULKE	75	68	77	72	292	+4
	R GONZALEZ	71	70	80	71	292	+4
	Graeme STORM	76	68	73	75	292	+4
68	Peter HANSON	73	72	75	73	293	+5
	G HAVRET	72	72	71	78	293	+5
	Stephen DODD	73	72	77	71	293	+5
	N VANHOOTEGEM	68	73	76	76	293	+5
	David LYNN	72	73	74	74	293	+5
73	Santiago LUNA	72	73	73	76	294	+6
	Carl SUNESON	74	70	73	77	294	+6
	Greg OWEN	72	72	75	75	294	+6
76	Steen TINNING	75	68	79	74	296	+8
77	Gary EMERSON	69	73	83	73	298	+10
78	David CARTER	74	70	77	80	301	+13
79	Sam TORRANCE	68	70	-	-	-	W/D

Tournament Report

Last season's Challenge Tour Order of Merit winner, Henrik Stenson, showed maturity beyond his years to hold off a high class field to land the Benson and Hedges International Open at the De Vere Belfry.

The 25-year-old Swede, in his rookie season, became the sixth first time winner on the European Tour. It was a superb display of front running golf.

He led from start to finish and drew upon his experience from winning on the Challenge Tour – where each of his three victories last year also came when he was leading going into he final round – to succeed for the first time on the European Tour.

A first round 66 saw Stenson share the lead with Paul McGinley after day one but by the time Sunday came around the Swede was three clear of the Irishman as well as Olle Karlsson and Angel Cabrera.

A double bogey at the ninth gave the chasing pack some hope but when Stenson produced a Mickelson-esque flop shot to hole in for an eagle at the next and then followed up with birdie at the 11th to move five clear, the contest was all but over.

McGinley didn't make many mistakes but his lack of birdies on the final day failed to put any real pressure on Stenson and he ended up sharing second place with Cabrera.

The Argentinean also needed a fast start to the last day but his birdie blast happened too late, picking up shots on the 15th and 16th.

MISSED THE CUT: S LYLE 74 72, W BENNETT 72 74, S HANSEN 74 72, G ROJAS 73 73, M MACKENZIE 72 75, T GILLIS 74 73, J SENDEN 73 74, J ROSE 74 73, J HOBDAY 70 77, R BALLESTEROS 71 76, M REALE 74 73, M GRONBERG 74 73, M SCARPA 76 71, D TERBLANCHE 71 76, P LONARD 72 75, S SCAHILL 77 70, B DREDGE 72 75, D PARK 75 72, R RUSSELL 71 76, N FASTH 72 75, T DIER 77 70, R CHAPMAN 71 77, W RILEY 71 77, P SENIOR 71 77, B DAVIS 75 73, O EDMOND 75 73, A COLTART 76 72, N HENNING 75 73, M CAMPBELL 71 77, S LEANEY 68 81, G RANKIN 72 77, H OTTO 74 75, I POULTER 74 75, T LEVET 74 75, N COLSAERTS 73 76, R WINCHESTER 73 76, P QUIRICI 73 76, P O'MALLEY 74 75, A RAITT 72 77, J SANDELIN 74 75, J BICKERTON 76 73, G BRAND JNR. 78 72, C RODILES 75 75, Z SCOTLAND (Am) 77 73, P GRIBBEN 70 80, A FORSYTH 78 72, C PETTERSSON 75 75, C MASON 77 74, D J RUSSELL 78 73, B LANE 78 73, C STRANGE 78 73, N CHEETHAM 74 77, R WESSELS 75 76, G ORR 75 76, M MOULAND 73 79, M ROE 74 78, M LUNDBERG 80 72, S DYSON 79 73, S BALLESTEROS 75 78, C CEVAER 77 76, V PHILLIPS 75 78, D HIGGINS 81 72, R McFARLANE 80 74, D FICHARDT 76 78, G EVANS 80 74, F JACOBSON 79 75, P BROADHURST 71 84, C HALL 80 76, T GOGELE 75 82, J McLEAN 81 79, L PARSONS 77 86, M DAVIS RETD, M LAFEBER 79 W/D, T IMMELMAN 74 DISQ, P WESSELINGH 78 RETD, D LEE 79 W/D, A SCOTT 76 RETD.

Course Profile

The Brabazon course (par 72, 7,118 yards) at the Belfry has undergone many changes over the past few years but still remains a course that put the emphasis on accuracy over distance.

The greens are small but the fairways were narrower than usual in 2001 as the Ryder Cup was scheduled to play there – expect the same.

Aggressive but controlled players prosper. The venue was used for the English Open from 1979 to 1983 and from 1989 to 1992.

Players/Points to Note

● **Colin Montgomerie** has finished in the top ten of this event on seven occasions since 1990, winning in 1999. He also won three and a half points from the 1993 Ryder Cup matches at The Belfry. Montgomerie was 12th here in 2001 despite not being in the best of form. He is certainly a player to note here.

● **Jose Maria Olazabal** has won this event twice (2000 and 1990) and since 1990 has a stroke average of 71.23 (in ten starts). His win at The Belfry came 14 years after he finished 15th at the Midlands course in the Lawrence Batley International in 1986.

● **Eduardo Romero** posted another top-ten finish in 2001 to take his haul to three. Patrik Sjoland has a sub-71 stroke average (and three top tens) in five starts in this tournament, while **Angel Cabrera** has finished in the top ten three times (in five appearances) including an excellent second last year.

● **Bernhard Langer** is a dual former winner, while **Ian Woosnam** boasts a win at The Belfry in the 1986 Lawrence Batley International.

● **Darren Clarke** and **Miguel Angel Jimenez**, plus veterans **Sam Torrance** and **Russell Claydon** have also posted multiple top-ten finishes.

● Three young guns exploded onto the Benson and Hedges scene last season – the winner **Henrik Stenson**, former US College star **Paul Casey** (12th) and the amateur player **Nick Dougherty** (12th).

Previous Results

2000: 1. Jose Maria Olazabal (-13), 2. Phillip Price (-10), 3. Jose Coceres (-5), Andrew Coltart (-5).

1999: 1. Colin Montgomerie (-15), 2. Angel Cabrera (-12), Per-Ulrik Johansson (-12).

1998: 1. Darren Clarke (-15), 2. Santiago Luna (-12), 3. Massimo Florioli (-11), Thomas Bjorn (-11).

1997: 1. Bernhard Langer (-12), 2. Ian Woosnam (-10), 3. Lee Westwood (-8).

1996: 1. Stephen Ames (-5), 2. Jon Robson (-4), 3. Derrick Cooper (-3).

DEUTSCHE BANK – SAP OPEN TPC OF EUROPE

St Leon Rot Heidelburg, 17 May to 20 May 2001, purse 2,720,220 euros

Pos	Name	R1	R2	R3	R4	Total	To par	Money	DD(y)	DA%	GIR%	Putts
1	Tiger WOODS	69	68	63	66	266	-22	450,000	n/a	n/a	n/a	n/a
2	M CAMPBELL	62	65	73	70	270	-18	300,000	n/a	n/a	n/a	n/a
3	Soren KJELDSEN	70	67	69	65	271	-17	152,005	267.8	82.1	81.9	113
	Peter O'MALLEY	71	68	63	69	271	-17	152,005	266.0	83.9	80.6	113
5	P HARRINGTON	70	69	64	70	273	-15	96,660	281.4	78.6	84.3	122
	Andrew COLTART	68	69	68	68	273	-15	96,660	281.3	55.4	84.7	119
	Mikael LUNDBERG	69	69	69	66	273	-15	96,660	273.6	62.5	81.9	116
8	Nick O'HERN	69	69	66	70	274	-14	63,990	270.8	75.0	73.6	112
	Henrik STENSON	71	68	63	72	274	-14	63,990	282.4	75.0	81.9	121
10	Richard GREEN	68	69	69	69	275	-13	48,397	271.4	83.5	81.9	119
	C MONTGOMERIE	70	66	69	70	275	-13	48,397	n/a	n/a	n/a	n/a
	Paul McGINLEY	69	65	72	69	275	-13	48,397	275.6	75.0	81.9	118
	John BICKERTON	69	67	73	66	275	-13	48,397	272.5	76.8	76.4	114

Pos	Name	R1	R2	R3	R4	Total	To par
14	E ROMERO	66	67	66	77	276	-12
	Peter BAKER	71	70	68	67	276	-12
	M Angel JIMINEZ	69	69	68	70	276	-12
	Phillip PRICE	71	70	66	69	276	-12
	R GONZALEZ	73	67	68	68	276	-12
	Retief GOOSEN	72	68	64	72	276	-12
20	W BENNETT	68	70	67	73	278	-10
	Greg TURNER	71	71	69	67	278	-10
	A CABRERA	69	70	68	71	278	-10
	Peter LONARD	70	71	68	69	278	-10
24	D FICHARDT	71	69	70	69	279	-9
	Thomas LEVET	74	67	72	66	279	-9
	Darren CLARKE	76	67	69	67	279	-9
	Gustavo ROJAS	66	72	69	72	279	-9
28	M Angel MARTIN	69	70	69	72	280	-8
	Ian WOOSNAM	66	72	73	69	280	-8
	Justin ROSE	70	69	73	68	280	-8
	Paul EALES	68	71	66	75	280	-8
	Ernie ELS	66	71	72	71	280	-8
	M GRONBERG	69	68	72	71	280	-8
	Greg OWEN	68	70	72	70	280	-8
	Patrik SJOLAND	71	70	70	69	280	-8
	Daren LEE	70	68	69	73	280	-8
37	Mark McNULTY	69	73	68	71	281	-7
	Peter MITCHELL	74	67	73	67	281	-7
	R KARLSSON	71	71	69	70	281	-7
	Paul LAWRIE	72	70	69	70	281	-7
	D ROBERTSON	69	68	72	72	281	-7
	L PARSONS	66	75	68	72	281	-7
43	A HANSEN	74	69	70	69	282	-6
	Carl SUNESON	67	76	70	69	282	-6
	Niclas FASTH	74	69	71	68	282	-6
	Adam SCOTT	74	68	70	70	282	-6
47	B LANGER	72	71	70	70	283	-5
	Anthony WALL	72	71	69	71	283	-5
	Steen TINNING	70	70	68	75	283	-5
	Soren HANSEN	70	73	66	74	283	-5
	Andrew RAITT	70	69	75	69	283	-5
52	M MACKENZIE	71	69	69	75	284	-4
	John SENDEN	70	71	72	71	284	-4
	J MOSELEY	72	71	68	73	284	-4
	Ian GARBUTT	73	70	70	71	284	-4
	Lee WESTWOOD	66	71	70	77	284	-4
57	J-F REMESY	75	66	75	69	285	-3
	J M OLAZABAL	70	71	71	73	285	-3
	Olivier EDMOND	71	67	71	76	285	-3
	J SANDELIN	70	69	70	76	285	-3
	C HANELL	70	73	70	72	285	-3
	Tobias DIER	71	71	74	69	285	-3
63	Marc FARRY	70	70	73	73	286	-2
	Brian DAVIS	70	69	71	76	286	-2
	Jamie SPENCE	71	71	72	72	286	-2
	Gary ORR	71	71	71	73	286	-2
	David PARK	73	69	75	69	286	-2
68	D BORREGO	71	72	73	71	287	-1
	C CEVAER	72	69	75	71	287	-1
70	Eamonn DARCY	71	72	74	71	288	E
	Des SMYTH	74	69	71	74	288	E
	Alex CEJKA	73	68	73	74	288	E
73	E CANONICA	72	71	69	77	289	+1
	Thomas BJORN	67	75	71	76	289	+1
75	Mikko ILONEN	71	72	72	77	292	+4

Tournament Report

Despite trailing Michael Campbell by ten shots at the halfway stage, Tiger Woods once again conjured up golf unlikely to be played by anyone else on the planet to win the Deutsche Bank – SAP Open TPC of Europe at St Leon-Rot in Heidelberg.

It was the World No.1's 35th worldwide win and one that was achieved with a borrowed driver. Woods had snapped the shaft of his on Saturday night and looked to Adam Scott, whom he shares the same coach with, for a replacement.

Campbell's opening 62 saw the Kiwi blaze a trail over the opening two days but Woods repsonded on Saturday with a 63. However, the third round leader was veteran Argentinean pro Eduardo Romero.

But when Romero faded with a Sunday 77, it was the two Nike sponsored players who went head to head in the last round. Firstly Woods took the lead, making eagle at the first, but then six straight pars let in Campbell, who picked up three shots in four holes.

A double bogey at the seventh by the Kiwi meant Woods again held the upper hand, and so it went on, with the advantage see-sawing between the two players. Then, Woods produced the shot of the tournament, holing a 7-iron from 175 yards at the 13th. The crowd, as they say, went wild.

The New Zealander was stunned and could find no extra. At the end a shell shocked Campbell lost by four shots. Soren Kjeldsen and Peter O'Malley tied for third.

MISSED THE CUT: S LUNA 71 73, J RIVERO 71 73, J M SINGH 74 70, S LEANEY 74 70, G EMERSON 75 69, R WINCHESTER 73 71, J RYSTROM 71 73, V PHILLIPS 71 73, S SCAHILL 75 69, B DREDGE 72 72, E SIMSEK 74 70, G BRAND JNR. 74 71, C ROCCA 72 73, D HOWELL 70 75, D GILFORD 76 69, S WEBSTER 71 74, T GOGELE 71 74, R CLAYDON 72 73, M REALE 71 74, M SCARPA 76 69, I GARRIDO 73 72, R WESSELS 74 71, R RUSSELL 74 71, C PETTERSSON 71 74, W RILEY 76 70, P SENIOR 72 74, J M LARA 74 72, R JACQUELIN 70 76, S STRUVER 75 71, F HENGE 73 73, N COLSAERTS 71 75, J LOMAS 74 72, H NYSTROM 75 71, S GALLACHER 72 74, C MONK 71 75, W HUGET 74 72, A FORSYTH 76 70, R CHAPMAN 74 73, T JOHNSTONE 73 74, A OLDCORN 72 75, C RODILES 75 72, S WITTKOP 73 74, P QUIRICI 76 71, D CARTER 75 72, P CASEY 78 69, B LANE 75 73, T IMMELMAN 75 73, R S JOHNSON 73 75, F CEA 74 74, A FORSBRAND 73 76, R RAFFERTY 75 74, O KARLSSON 76 73, P FULKE 72 77, N VANHOOTEGEM 74 75, R MUNTZ 73 76, F JACOBSON 71 78, M LAFEBER 73 77, R GEILENBERG 79 71, J HUGO 73 77, J HAEGGMAN 78 72, D J GEALL 72 78, D LYNN 74 76, M McLEAN 77 74, P FOWLER 73 78, M DAVIS 75 76, M BERNARDINI 76 75, B RUMFORD 74 77, I POULTER 74 78, D HIGGINS 80 72, M SIEM 78 75, A ROCHA 78 75, T SCHUSTER 79 75, D TERBLANCHE 78 77, S BALLESTEROS 76 80, E BOULT 78 78, M ROE 78 79, G HAVRET 82 75, D BOTES 73 RETD, P BROADHURST 82 W/D, G EVANS 78 RETD, S P BROWN 86 RETD.

Sponsored by Stan James

Course Profile

Last season saw this event played at St Leon Rot (par 72, 7,207 yards) for only the second time – but the Heidelberg venue will be used again in 2002.

Accuracy off the tee is the key to scoring well, but length also helps.

The fairways aren't particularly tight but the rough is usually punishing and any wayward drives will be in trouble.

The greens are big and water comes into play on many of the holes.

Players/Points to Note

●**Tiger Woods** gets paid a lot of money by the sponsors just to play in this event but always gives value for money. He won in 1999, was third in 2000 and came back to win in superb style last season. He has yet to hit a round over 70 – let alone over the par of 72 – and has won nearly 900,000 euros from this event alone. In three starts his only loss came when the event was played at Gut Kaden – next year the tournament is at St Leon Rot – where Tiger is undefeated.

●**Darren Clarke** has the best record in terms of top-ten finishes since this event found a home in Germany. The Ulsterman has registered four top tens in seven starts and is 67-under par in that time.

●**Lee Westwood** has won twice (both victories coming at Gut Kaden), but he has missed two cuts in between those victories and was a lowly 52nd last year.

●**Colin Montgomerie** did win this event (the TPC of Europe) when it was held in Portugal (1989) and, since it moved to Germany, can boast four top-ten finishes in six starts.

●Others with good records are **Bernhard Langer, Miguel Angel Jimenez, Paul McGinley, Retief Goosen, Gary Orr, Jarmo Sandelin, David Howell, Brian Davis, Padraig Harrington** and **Michael Canpbell**.

Previous Results

2000: 1. Lee Westwood (-15), 2. Emanuele Canonica (-12), 3. Ian Woosnam (-11), Tiger Woods (-11), Jean Van de velde (-11).

1999: 1. Tiger Woods (-15), 2. Retief Goosen (-12), 3. Nick Price (-11).

1998: 1. Lee Westwood (-23), 2. Darren Clarke (-22), 3. Mark O'Meara (-19).

1997: 1. Ross McFarlane (-6), 2. Gordon Brand Jnr (-5), Anders Forsbrand (-5).

1996: 1. Frank Nobilo (-18), 2. Colin Montgomerie (-17), 3. Darren Clarke (-14).

VOLVO PGA CHAMPIONSHIP

Wentworth G.C., 25 May to 28 May 2001, purse 3,276,959 euros

Pos	Name	R1	R2	R3	R4	Total	To par	Money	DD(y)	DA%	GIR%	Putts
1	Andrew OLDCORN	66	66	69	71	272	-16	544,521	280.3	60.7	63.9	102
2	Angel CABRERA	63	71	72	68	274	-14	363,014	297.1	64.3	61.1	101
3	Nick FALDO	72	66	70	67	275	-13	204,524	270.3	71.4	56.9	105
4	Phillip PRICE	65	69	72	71	277	-11	138,745	278.8	55.4	55.6	101
	M GRONBERG	71	69	72	65	277	-11	138,745	281.4	60.7	47.2	99
	M CAMPBELL	70	70	67	70	277	-11	138,745	277.9	60.7	59.7	108
7	Vijay SINGH	73	65	70	70	278	-10	98,014	303.3	55.4	76.4	123
8	Peter BAKER	67	72	75	65	279	-9	73,402	278.5	66.1	73.6	115
	Darren CLARKE	72	69	68	70	279	-9	73,402	284.9	64.3	68.1	114
	Gary ORR	74	67	69	69	279	-9	73,402	272.1	69.6	70.8	117

Pos	Name	R1	R2	R3	R4	Total	To par
11	J M OLAZABAL	72	68	67	73	280	-8
	S WEBSTER	67	68	72	73	280	-8
	D ROBERTSON	68	68	75	69	280	-8
14	John SENDEN	71	67	72	71	281	-7
	Niclas FASTH	69	68	69	75	281	-7
	Simon DYSON	68	72	72	69	281	-7
17	Richard GREEN	73	68	70	71	282	-6
	Anthony WALL	70	70	72	70	282	-6
	C MONTGOMERIE	73	69	69	71	282	-6
	Paul LAWRIE	69	68	72	73	282	-6
21	Ian WOOSNAM	71	68	73	71	283	-5
	Anders HANSEN	71	70	72	70	283	-5
	Stephen LEANEY	70	64	74	75	283	-5
	Gary EMERSON	70	69	71	73	283	-5
	M LUNDBERG	67	72	70	74	283	-5
26	R JACQUELIN	69	68	74	73	284	-4
	Thomas LEVET	72	71	72	69	284	-4
	Peter O'MALLEY	69	71	71	73	284	-4
	Paul McGINLEY	66	74	73	71	284	-4
	Ian GARBUTT	71	71	70	72	284	-4
	D BORREGO	72	70	69	73	284	-4
32	S KJELDSEN	71	66	72	76	285	-3
	Justin ROSE	72	69	73	71	285	-3
	J HAEGGMAN	68	73	74	70	285	-3
	Greg OWEN	69	74	68	74	285	-3
	Markus BRIER	72	71	71	71	285	-3
	A COLTART	68	69	71	77	285	-3
	Adam SCOTT	70	69	74	72	285	-3
39	H STENSON	76	66	71	73	286	-2
	Ernie ELS	70	72	68	76	286	-2
	Rolf MUNTZ	71	67	74	74	286	-2
	Thomas BJORN	68	69	72	77	286	-2
	H NYSTROM	69	72	72	73	286	-2
	C HANELL	72	71	72	71	286	-2
45	Eamonn DARCY	72	71	71	73	287	-1
	Des SMYTH	70	68	75	74	287	-1
	P HARRINGTON	67	75	69	76	287	-1
	Carlos RODILES	69	70	78	70	287	-1
	Steen TINNING	70	73	73	71	287	-1
	J LOMAS	72	67	73	75	287	-1
	N VANHOOTEGEM	69	71	72	75	287	-1
	David LYNN	72	71	75	69	287	-1
	Patrik SJOLAND	70	73	74	70	287	-1
	J BICKERTON	69	71	76	71	287	-1
55	P BROADHURST	69	74	73	72	288	E
	David HIGGINS	72	71	74	71	288	E
	A FORSYTH	67	73	75	73	288	E
58	M Angel MARTIN	69	70	75	75	289	+1
	D McGRANE	68	72	70	79	289	+1
	Nick O'HERN	66	71	78	74	289	+1
	Soren HANSEN	71	70	73	75	289	+1
	R RUSSELL	72	69	76	72	289	+1
63	W BENNETT	71	68	76	75	290	+2
	Jean HUGO	72	70	75	73	290	+2
	E CANONICA	71	70	72	77	290	+2
	Peter LONARD	71	71	72	76	290	+2
67	R KARLSSON	72	70	73	76	291	+3
	Alex CEJKA	73	70	75	73	291	+3
	Pierre FULKE	71	70	79	71	291	+3
70	Gary EVANS	71	71	77	74	293	+5
71	J SANDELIN	71	72	73	78	294	+6
72	J Milkha SINGH	76	67	76	80	299	+11

Tournament Report

A journeyman pro he might be but Andrew Old-corn proved he has a star quality about him by holding off the late challenge of Angel Cabrera and a rejuvenated Nick Faldo to land the Volvo PGA Championship at Wentworth.

It was the biggest win of the Edinburgh based, Bolton born pro's career and one which propels him into Ryder Cup team reckoning. It was his third European Tour win and his first since capturing the Jersey Open in 1995.

Two opening 66's saw Oldcorn take the lead after the second round, a Saturday 69 meant he had a five-stroke advantage going into the final round.

Oldcorn got off to a nervy start and had to wait until the 12th for his first birdie – and this after dropping shots at the seventh and ninth. Faldo, meanwhile, was charging.

A birdie at the 12th, his fourth of the round, saw the six-time Major winner close to within a shot, and with the crowd behind him, and Fanny Suneson on his bag, memories of the time Faldo overhauled Greg Norman to win the 1996 US Masters came flooding back. But it wasn't enough as Oldcorn steadied himself, birdied two of the last six holes and held on.

Cabrera, who led after the first round following superb opening 63, nudged out Faldo for second place when he made eagle at the last, and also went to the top of the Order of Merit. Phillip Price, Mathais Gronberg and Michael Campbell finished for a tie for fourth.

MISSED THE CUT: A FORSBRAND 72 72, W RILEY 70 74, J RIVERO 75 69, M FARRY 71 73, S STRUVER 68 76, T GOGELE 75 69, P QUIRICI 72 72, D TERBLANCHE 76 68, D PARK 72 72, R GOOSEN 74 70, L PARSONS 72 72, C PETTERSSON 74 70, G BRAND JNR. 72 73, S LYLE 76 69, R RAFFERTY 72 73, S TORRANCE 71 74, D GILFORD 69 76, M LAFEBER 73 72, P MITCHELL 70 75, P EALES 71 74, P WESSELINGH 74 71, S WOOD 71 74, F JACOBSON 72 73, J BEVAN 73 72, D LEE 72 73, S GALLACHER 70 75, T JOHNSTONE 71 75, S LUNA 75 71, M McNULTY 74 72, M A JIMINEZ 75 71, R WINCHESTER 72 74, I GARRIDO 75 71, L WESTWOOD 73 73, G J BRAND 73 74, R DRUMMOND 75 72, M PIERO 74 73, B LANE 70 77, J SPENCE 78 69, R S JOHNSON 73 74, J MOSELEY 74 73, R GONZALEZ 76 71, M HAZELDEN 77 70, R WESSELS 73 74, B DREDGE 75 72, M PLUMMER 74 73, S BALLESTEROS 76 72, B LANGER 76 72, E ROMERO 74 74, G TURNER 71 77, D FICHARDT 75 73, D BOTES 74 74, C HISLOP 78 70, M ROE 72 77, I POULTER 72 77, C SUNESON 78 71, V PHILLIPS 75 74, T ANDERSEN 75 74, C ROCCA 71 79, K SPURGEON 81 69, O EDMOND 78 72, M SCARPA 75 75, P SIMPSON 76 74, G NORQUIST 75 75, M ALLEN 77 73, B MARCHBANK 77 74, J VAN DE VELDE 71 80, B CAMERON 78 73, D J RUSSELL 78 74, P WAY 76 76, D HOWELL 78 74, C GILLIES 72 80, M REALE 78 74, F CEA 76 76, D CARTER 77 75, W-T YEH 73 79, J-F REMESY 72 81, S HAMILL 82 71, M JAMES 77 79, R MCFARLANE 82 77, I ELLIS 78 85, P SENIOR 78 W/D, M DAVIS 70 RETD, B DAVIS 76 RETD, C HALL 82 RETD.

Course Profile

Wentworth (par 72, 7,047 yards) requires accuracy and length off the tee – which is why it's perfect for Monty and Els – as the fairways are narrow but the layout long, especially if it rains.

The last two holes are both par fives so the outcome of the tournament can rest on them. Subtle changes over the past few years has made the run-in tougher.

The greens have subtle contours and, when the sun shines, can be firm and fast.

Players/Points to Note

●**Colin Montgomerie** has been nearly unbeatable at Wentworth in recent seasons. He has won this event in three of the last four occasions that he has teed up in it, has only finished outside of the top ten twice since 1990 and has also won the World Matchplay tournament on this track. His stroke average is 69.40 in his last 48 rounds, he is an astonishing 125-under par in that time and has won over 1.3 million Euros.

●**Ernie Els** has a house at Wentworth and is a regular player of this tournament. He has four top-ten finishes in seven starts in this event and has also won the World Matchplay tournament which is held here three times.

●**Bernhard Langer** is also a three-time winner of this tournament (1987, 1993 and 1995).

●It was great to see **Nick Faldo** back to form here in 2001, finishing third. Outside of Monty, he is the only player with a sub-70 stroke average.

●**Angel Cabrera** equalled the course record last season on his way to second and, along with fellow Argentinean **Eduardo Romero**, can be backed with confidence in this event.

●Also watch out for **Jose Maria Olazabal, Lee Westwood, Darren Clarke, Patrick Sjoland, Retief Goosen, Michael Campbell, Gary Orr** and **Ian Woosnam**, who won the World Matchplay in 2001.

Previous Results

2000: 1. Colin Montgomerie (-17), 2. Darren Clarke (-14), Andrew Coltart (-14) and Lee Westwood (-14).

1999: 1. Colin Montgomerie (-18), 2. Mark James (-13), 3. Paul Eales (-12).

1998: 1. Colin Montgomerie (-14), 2. Patrik Sjoland (-13), Ernie Els (-13), Gary Orr (-13).

1997: 1. Ian Woosnam (-13), 2. Nick Faldo (-11), Ernie Els (-11), Darren Clarke (-11).

1996: 1. Costantino Rocca (-14), 2. Nick Faldo (-12), Paul Lawrie (-12).

VICTOR CHANDLER BRITISH MASTERS

Woburn, 31 May to 3 Jun 2001, purse 2,082,918 euros

Pos	Name	R1	R2	R3	R4	Total	To par	Money	DD(y)	DA%	GIR%	Putts
1	Thomas LEVET	69	69	67	69	274	-14	345,079	297.9	85.7	80.6	121
	Won play-off											
2	David HOWELL	68	65	68	73	274	-14	154,394	303.5	71.4	75.0	117
	R KARLSSON	66	67	69	72	274	-14	154,394	298.1	67.9	69.4	114
	M GRONBERG	69	70	67	68	274	-14	154,394	301.1	78.6	79.2	113
5	Olle KARLSSON	71	70	68	69	278	-10	87,789	288.8	51.8	62.5	109
6	R GONZALEZ	70	73	67	69	279	-9	67,291	327.5	66.1	73.6	120
	Niclas FASTH	74	69	66	70	279	-9	67,291	313.0	67.9	77.8	120
8	Anthony WALL	70	68	69	73	280	-8	49,071	303.3	78.6	63.9	111
	Lee WESTWOOD	69	70	67	74	280	-8	49,071	306.0	64.3	68.1	115
10	Roger WESSELS	70	68	72	71	281	-7	41,410	287.3	64.3	62.5	109

Pos	Name	R1	R2	R3	R4	Total	To par
11	M MACKENZIE	70	70	66	76	282	-6
	F JACOBSON	70	71	75	66	282	-6
	Erol SIMSEK	68	73	73	68	282	-6
14	M MOULAND	70	73	72	68	283	-5
	Ian WOOSNAM	69	73	72	69	283	-5
	W BENNETT	70	72	72	69	283	-5
	Sven STRUVER	68	73	71	71	283	-5
	Richard GREEN	73	71	70	69	283	-5
	Jean HUGO	72	72	70	69	283	-5
	Rolf MUNTZ	72	70	70	71	283	-5
	Adam SCOTT	67	74	71	71	283	-5
22	Mark McNULTY	70	66	76	72	284	-4
	Greg TURNER	70	72	73	69	284	-4
	S LEANEY	72	72	73	67	284	-4
	Justin ROSE	70	70	73	71	284	-4
	Peter MITCHELL	72	69	74	69	284	-4
27	John SENDEN	71	69	78	67	285	-3
	C MONTGOMERIE	68	71	74	72	285	-3
	Thomas BJORN	69	75	69	72	285	-3
	David PARK	72	71	71	71	285	-3
	J BICKERTON	69	73	72	71	285	-3
	David CARTER	76	66	72	71	285	-3
	Paul CASEY	71	69	69	76	285	-3
34	Sandy LYLE	69	72	72	73	286	-2
	Brian DAVIS	70	74	66	76	286	-2
	Nick O'HERN	69	70	72	75	286	-2
	Steen TINNING	72	72	71	71	286	-2
	Alex CEJKA	71	71	71	73	286	-2
	Peter O'MALLEY	71	71	71	73	286	-2
	Jorge BERENDT	70	71	72	73	286	-2
	Greg OWEN	68	74	73	71	286	-2
42	Mark ROE	73	70	72	72	287	-1
	David GILFORD	72	72	71	72	287	-1
	Ian GARBUTT	71	73	72	71	287	-1
	Darren CLARKE	70	72	71	74	287	-1
	M CAMPBELL	74	70	69	74	287	-1
47	S TORRANCE	72	72	66	78	288	E
	Fredrik HENGE	70	72	74	72	288	E
	Gary EVANS	74	69	73	72	288	E
	Markus BRIER	72	72	70	74	288	E
	A COLTART	70	68	75	75	288	E
	C HANELL	74	70	76	68	288	E
53	Peter FOWLER	71	69	77	72	289	+1
	Patrik SJOLAND	71	73	69	76	289	+1
	D ROBERTSON	72	70	70	77	289	+1
	Simon DYSON	73	71	71	74	289	+1
57	Des SMYTH	72	72	71	75	290	+2
	Ian POULTER	72	70	74	74	290	+2
	Carlos RODILES	72	70	76	72	290	+2
	Per HAUGSRUD	72	71	72	75	290	+2
	J MOSELEY	73	71	74	72	290	+2
	J ROBINSON	72	72	71	75	290	+2
	T GOGELE	70	72	73	75	290	+2
	R CLAYDON	73	70	69	78	290	+2
	David LYNN	69	74	73	74	290	+2
66	A OLDCORN	71	73	74	73	291	+3
	M SCARPA	72	71	76	72	291	+3
68	M BERNARDINI	68	74	79	71	292	+4
69	C ROCCA	72	70	73	78	293	+5
70	Elliot BOULT	73	71	70	81	295	+7
71	Neil CHEETHAM	73	71	73	79	296	+8
72	D FICHARDT	74	68	80	75	297	+9
73	E DARCY	68	75	77	78	298	+10
	T JOHNSTONE	72	72	76	78	298	+10

Tournament Report

In the biggest play-off on the European Tour for eight years, Thomas Levet outlasted Mathias Gronberg, Robert Karlsson and David Howell to win the British Masters at Woburn after three extra holes.

The Frenchman won for the first time outside his native country and fully deserved his success after coming back from four shots down entering the final round.

Howell and Karlsson had dominated the previous three days and were the last pairing on the final day, separated by shot, the Englishman with the advantage.

But Levet got into contention with a string of outward nine birdies. And even though he looked a bit ragged at times, he found water at the 12th but recovered to make par and dropped at shot at the 16th, Levet got up and down on the last hole of regulation play to join Gronberg on 14 under.

The Swede's chances of winning in normal play were dashed with mistakes at the 15th and 17th. Howell, whose previously hot putter went ice cold and Karlsson, who failed to find anything extra during the final day, faltered, shooting 73 and 72 respectively to join the play-off.

But, after they both bogeyed the first extra hole, just Levet, who missed a four-foot putt to win the event, and Gronberg remained. Then, from over twice that distance, Levet holed to keep the play-off alive and a birdie on the third extra hole was enough for the Frenchman to secure his second European Tour win.

MISSED THE CUT: B Lane 73 72, M Farry 73 72, R Jacquelin 71 74, S Webster 72 73, P Hanson 73 72, P Broadhurst 75 70, P Baker 72 73, C Suneson 73 72, D Borrego 74 71, A Raitt 74 71, B Dredge 75 70, R Russell 69 76, D Lee 73 72, G Brand Jnr. 73 73, J M Singh 72 74, A Hansen 71 75, C Hainline 73 73, G Hutcheon 73 73, N Colsaerts 72 74, M Florioli 72 74, J Lomas 73 73, T J Muoz 77 69, S Richardson 74 72, M Blackey 73 73, D Higgins 72 74, A Forsyth 74 72, A Forsbrand 74 73, W Riley 69 78, P Walton 73 74, S Kjeldsen 71 76, J Spence 74 73, S Hansen 76 71, P Quirici 73 74, C Cevaer 73 74, R Goosen 73 74, G Norquist 73 74, B Teilleria 72 75, L Parsons 71 76, G Murphy 74 74, G Houston 73 75, G Rojas 73 75, S Scahill 76 72, H Nystrom 69 79, N Henning 76 72, G Storm 77 71, M James 72 77, G Rankin 78 71, S P Webster 74 75, R Byrd 76 74, R Winchester 72 77, J Rystrom 75 74, N Vanhootegem 71 78, R Coles 75 74, F Valera 75 74, F Andersson 76 73, T Dier 74 75, R Rafferty 72 78, P Eales 73 77, M Jonzon 75 75, W-T Yeh 76 74, H Otto 75 76, J Haeggman 76 75, S Gallacher 74 77, B Rumford 77 74, R Chapman 74 78, M Lafeber 76 76, G Emerson 75 77, S Dodd 76 76, K Ferrie 72 81, M Santi 78 75, M Pilkington 75 78, S Walker 78 75, S Hurd 73 81, F Cea 78 76, M Piero 77 78, O Edmond 76 79, L Batchelor 77 80, V Phillips 82 75, P Streeter 77 80, S Luna 78 RETD, M A Martin 75 RETD, J Rivero 72 DISQ.

Sponsored by Stan James

Course Profile

The Marquess course at Woburn (par 72, 7,214 yards) was used for the first time for a tournament last season.

It only opened in 2000 and is similar to the Dukes course that staged this event between 1985 to 1994, then from 1999 to 2000. Fairways are generous but the tree lined nature of them mean that wayward shots can be severely punished.

Players can run their approach shots onto the greens. Club and shot selection is paramount.

Players/Points to Note

●**Colin Montgomerie** has posted seven top-ten finishes in this event since 1990. He is 107-under par in 48 competitive rounds in that time (only eight rounds have been over par) and his complete form figures from 1990 read 15-33-24-12-3-7-9-2-Win-2-3-27.

●**Mark McNulty** is a Woburn specialist. The Zimbabwean won on the track in 1987 and hasn't finished worse than 22th in six appearances at the Buckinghamshire layout over the past 11 years.

●**Ian Woosnam**, **Nick Faldo** and **Peter Baker** are all former Woburn winners.

●**Paulo Qurici** missed the cut last year but the Swiss player had shot just one round over par in his previous 16 in this event and from 1997 has form figures of 15-4-32-16, before failing to make the weekend in 2001.

●Veteran Zimbabwean **Tony Johnstone** also has a great record in this event. Five top-ten finishes since 1990 suggests the Zimbabwean should be considered if in form.

●**Bernhard Langer**, **Stephen Leaney**, **Thomas Bjorn**, **Miguel Angel Martin**, **Ray Russell** and **Gary Orr** have all played well in this event in the past.

●Last season saw a number of new names come to the fore, and after posting low scores in 2001, the likes of **Thomas Levet**, **David Howell**, **Anthony Wall**, **Jean Hugo** and **Adam Scott** could be worth following again.

Previous Results

2000: 1. Gary Orr (-21), 2. Per-Ulrik Johansson (-19), 3. Colin Montgomerie (-18).

1999: 1. Bob May (-19), 2. Colin Montgomerie (-18), 3. Christopher Hanell (-16).

1998: 1. Colin Montgomerie (-7), 2. Eduardo Romero (-6), Pierre Fulke (-6).

1997: 1. Greg Turner (-13), 2. Colin Montgomerie (-12), 3. Mark Roe (-9).

1996: 1. Robert Allenby (-4), won play-off, 2. Miguel Angel Martin (-4), 3. Costantino Rocca (-3).

COMPASS GROUP ENGLISH OPEN

Forest of Arden, 7 Jun to 10 Jun 2001, purse 1,352,287 euros

Pos	Name	R1	R2	R3	R4	Total	To par	Money	DD(y)	DA%	GIR%	Putts
1	Peter O'MALLEY	70	69	70	66	275	-13	223,373	288.6	73.2	75.0	118
2	R JACQUELIN	73	67	66	70	276	-12	148,904	297.8	71.4	68.1	111
3	Adam SCOTT	67	70	67	73	277	-11	83,901	303.0	75.0	80.6	122
4	Jean HUGO	70	68	68	73	279	-9	67,013	311.9	67.9	58.3	106
5	Steve WEBSTER	73	69	73	66	281	-7	44,363	296.5	51.8	68.1	112
	Darren CLARKE	74	72	67	68	281	-7	44,363	292.0	71.4	69.4	117
	Lee WESTWOOD	77	67	68	69	281	-7	44,363	298.5	55.4	68.1	114
	Retief GOOSEN	75	71	65	70	281	-7	44,363	296.0	48.2	68.1	113
9	Ian POULTER	72	71	69	70	282	-6	30,022	302.3	64.3	66.7	113
10	Paul McGINLEY	73	69	70	71	283	-5	26,805	283.6	67.9	62.7	114

Pos	Name	R1	R2	R3	R4	Total	To par		Pos	Name	R1	R2	R3	R4	Total	To par
11	Greg OWEN	77	70	66	71	284	-4		44	Mark McNULTY	70	76	72	74	292	+4
12	Jorge BERENDT	72	72	73	68	285	-3			Brian DAVIS	73	74	73	72	292	+4
	M SCARPA	70	69	74	72	285	-3			Nick O'HERN	73	76	72	71	292	+4
	David LYNN	74	70	70	71	285	-3			Carl SUNESON	75	73	75	69	292	+4
	Paul CASEY	73	72	72	68	285	-3			Gary EVANS	74	69	72	77	292	+4
16	R CHAPMAN	75	70	69	72	286	-2			David CARTER	74	73	73	72	292	+4
	J ROBINSON	75	67	71	73	286	-2			David HIGGINS	76	73	71	72	292	+4
	Ian GARBUTT	72	77	69	68	286	-2		51	Peter HANSON	74	71	73	75	293	+5
	Paul LAWRIE	70	77	69	70	286	-2			Peter MITCHELL	71	73	73	76	293	+5
	R RUSSELL	76	69	68	73	286	-2			J RYSTROM	71	75	74	73	293	+5
	J BICKERTON	79	70	64	73	286	-2			M PILKINGTON	76	70	73	74	293	+5
	A FORSYTH	73	72	68	73	286	-2		55	Greg TURNER	72	75	75	72	294	+6
23	C ROCCA	69	73	73	72	287	-1			R WESSELS	73	73	72	76	294	+6
	Anthony WALL	70	75	69	73	287	-1			Gary ORR	76	71	75	72	294	+6
	M BERNARDINI	68	72	69	78	287	-1		58	G BRAND JNR.	76	73	71	75	295	+7
26	A OLDCORN	67	76	73	72	288	E			Sandy LYLE	77	72	74	72	295	+7
	David GILFORD	74	71	73	70	288	E			Philip WALTON	75	72	76	72	295	+7
	Justin ROSE	72	67	70	79	288	E			Paolo QUIRICI	73	74	74	74	295	+7
	Peter BAKER	77	68	71	72	288	E		62	Wayne RILEY	78	71	74	74	297	+9
	J LOMAS	71	78	71	68	288	E			Peter FOWLER	73	71	74	79	297	+9
	Stephen DODD	72	70	73	73	288	E			Hennie OTTO	71	73	77	76	297	+9
	Francisco CEA	72	74	70	72	288	E		65	Marc FARRY	74	66	81	77	298	+10
33	Barry LANE	74	74	72	69	289	+1			S LEANEY	71	77	73	77	298	+10
	Tobias DIER	73	71	73	72	289	+1			P BROADHURST	76	73	77	72	298	+10
35	David HOWELL	69	76	72	73	290	+2			Gary EMERSON	73	74	74	77	298	+10
	A HANSEN	77	71	75	67	290	+2			B DREDGE	72	76	74	76	298	+10
	Dennis EDLUND	77	69	71	73	290	+2			Francis VALERA	77	72	72	77	298	+10
	Phillip PRICE	74	75	70	71	290	+2		71	T JOHNSTONE	77	71	75	76	299	+11
	S GALLACHER	74	71	72	73	290	+2			G RANKIN	72	73	74	80	299	+11
40	D J RUSSELL	76	70	70	75	291	+3			A MARSHALL	74	74	74	77	299	+11
	W BENNETT	73	74	75	69	291	+3			Neil CHEETHAM	76	71	75	77	299	+11
	Steen TINNING	72	73	70	76	291	+3		75	Wei-Tze YEH	73	74	75	78	300	+12
	Nic HENNING	73	71	74	73	291	+3		76	Robert COLES	75	72	77	77	301	+13

Sponsored by Stan James

Tournament Report

Peter O'Malley is no stranger to fast finishes – just remind Colin Montgomerie of the Australian's blistering end to the Scottish Open in 1992 – and the man from Down Under was again ripping it up down the stretch at the Forest of Arden to win the English Open.

O'Malley was five behind overnight leader Adam Scott at the start of the final round and still trailed his young compatriot and Frenchman Raphel Jacquelin at the turn. But birdie putts from 25 feet at the tenth and 15 feet at the 11th were sunk, before a 60-foot eagle attempt dropped to put the Aussie ahead.

Scott started badly, letting three shots go in the first four holes and, with Jean Hugo and Justin Rose also failing to keep pace with O'-Malley, it was left to Jacquelin to battle gamely on.

The Frenchman got back on level terms with O'Malley when he sank a 30-footer on the 16th and really needed a birdie or better on the par five 17th.

It wasn't to be, however, and he could only muster a par. A bogey at the last after finding sand meant that Jacquelin finished second – still his best finish on tour and the £88,880 was his biggest pay day.

For O'Malley, it was his third European Tour win of his career and the near £250,000 prize was his fattest cheque. Scott eventually finished third, again throwing away a final round lead. South African Hugo was fourth.

MISSED THE CUT: M MOULAND 79 71, K FERRIE 79 71, C HAINLINE 76 74, T IMMELMAN 77 73, H WALTERS 78 72, J SPENCE 75 75, M FLORIOLI 76 74, V PHILLIPS 72 78, M BRIER 73 77, S TORRANCE 73 78, J-F REMESY 76 75, G HOUSTON 80 71, D HOSPITAL 76 75, M NILSSON 76 75, J MOSELEY 76 75, C HALL 76 75, J HAEGGMAN 78 73, P WESSELINGH 76 75, S RICHARDSON 75 76, S SCAHILL 79 72, M JONZON 79 72, M LUNDBERG 71 80, B RUMFORD 76 75, O SANDYS 77 74, E DARCY 76 76, M MACKENZIE 77 75, M A MARTIN 77 75, E CARLBERG 76 76, H STENSON 80 72, G HAVRET 72 80, C BENIANS 77 75, R WINCHESTER 74 78, R CLAYDON 78 74, C CEVAER 76 76, F ANDERSSON 74 78, A COLTART 78 74, P GRIBBEN 76 76, S GARDINER 77 75, M ROE 77 76, M LAFEBER 80 73, S P WEBSTER 78 75, N COLSAERTS 73 80, M SANTI 79 74, P STREETER 76 77, E SIMSEK 73 80, M JAMES 80 74, F HENGE 80 74, T J MUOZ 77 77, H NYSTROM 81 73, M BLACKEY 81 73, S DYSON 76 78, A CEJKA 79 76, S CAGE 80 75, A RAITT 73 82, L PARSONS 75 80, G STORM 81 74, D SMYTH 78 78, J ROMERO 84 72, O KARLSSON 80 76, R BYRD 78 79, D LEE 76 81, M WATKINS 74 83, P EALES 80 78, P NYMAN 79 79, S D. HURLEY 82 77, M CAPONE 83 76, R S JOHNSON 76 84, G ROJAS 75 85, J HAWKSWORTH 77 84, A BEAL 78 86, A McLEAN 83 81, S WALKER 79 86, R DRUMMOND 79 DISQ, C MASON 84 RETD, E BOULT 86 W/D, C MONTGOMERIE 76 RETD, O EDMOND DISQ, M REALE W/D, D ROBERTSON 80 RETD, C HANELL DISQ.

Sponsored by Stan James

Course Profile

The Forest of Arden course (par 72, 7,182 yards) has been extensively remodelled over the past few years.

A number of the greens were made bigger, with more slopes and subtle breaks added and they tend to get trickier in the afternoon. Good putting is a key to victory.

The course is long so the bigger hitters should prosper, especially as the width of most of the fairways is generous.

Aggressive players and those who can make lots of birdies prosper.

Players/Points to Note

●**Darren Clarke** has posted six top-ten finishes in his last 11 starts. His wins have come at both the Hanbury Manor layout (used between 1997 and 1999) and the Forest of Arden venue - which has hosted the past two renewals and this event from 1993 to 1996). The British Masters was also held at the Forest of Arden track in 1997 and 1998, when Clarke was 12th and 20th respectively.

●**Colin Montgomerie** won at the Forest of Arden in 1994 and followed that success with runners up spot in 1995 and 1996. In 2000 the Scotsman was eighth, he didn't play last year. Monty won the British Masters in 1998 and was second the previous year

●**Peter O'Malley**'s win in 2001 was no fluke, the Aussie was 10th in 2000 and was also placed in the top 20 of the British Masters at the Forest of Arden in 1997 and 1998.

●**Greg Turner** has three top-20 finishes at the Forest of Arden course in this tournament and the Kiwi won the British Masters in 1997.

●**Gary Orr** can boast four top-ten finishes in nine starts in this event, while **Steve Webster**, **Stephen Leaney**, **Anthony Wall**, **Lee Westwood**, **Retief Goosen**, **Constantino Rocca** and **Russell Claydon** can usually be relied upon for a decent finish.

Previous Results

2000: 1. Darren Clarke (-13), 2. Mark James (-12), Michael Campbell (-12).

1999: 1. Darren Clarke (-20), 2. John Bickerton (-18), 3. Stephen Leaney (-14), David Carter (-14).

1998: 1. Lee Westwood (-17), 2. Greg Chalmers (-15), Olle Karlsson (-15).

1997: 1. Per-Ulrik Johansson (-19), 2. Dennis Edlund (-17), 3. Jay Townsend (-16), Steve Webster (-16).

1996: 1. Robert Allenby (-10), 2. Ross McFarlane (-9), Colin Montgomerie (-9).

GREAT NORTH OPEN

Slaley Hall, 21 Jun to 24 Jun 2001, purse 1,311,089 euros

Pos	Name	R1	R2	R3	R4	Total	To par	Money	DD(y)	DA%	GIR%	Putts
1	Andrew COLTART	68	68	69	72	277	-11	217,209	281.9	48.3	76.4	117
2	S GALLACHER	76	67	67	68	278	-10	113,190	288.8	66.7	68.1	113
	Paul CASEY	71	66	72	69	278	-10	113,190	305.0	61.7	73.6	118
4	Steve WEBSTER	73	68	71	67	279	-9	55,346	307.8	56.7	70.8	112
	Bradley DREDGE	69	67	72	71	279	-9	55,346	285.5	65.0	61.1	108
	Daren LEE	66	74	69	70	279	-9	55,346	287.9	66.7	63.9	110
7	Ian POULTER	73	68	73	66	280	-8	39,098	289.8	63.3	66.7	107
8	Peter FOWLER	71	71	70	69	281	-7	23,632	287.0	56.7	61.1	107
	Jamie SPENCE	68	70	70	73	281	-7	23,632	275.0	61.7	63.9	110
	Gregory HAVRET	73	68	70	70	281	-7	23,632	299.3	70.0	65.3	111
	Soren HANSEN	71	70	72	68	281	-7	23,632	296.0	70.0	73.6	117
	Andrew BEAL	72	69	68	72	281	-7	23,632	271.0	61.7	62.5	107
	C POTTIER	76	69	70	66	281	-7	23,632	292.8	60.0	69.4	112
	D ROBERTSON	73	70	69	69	281	-7	23,632	284.0	71.7	79.2	122
	Lucas PARSONS	71	69	69	72	281	-7	23,632	304.4	66.7	68.1	112
	Scott GARDINER	69	71	69	72	281	-7	23,632	301.5	56.7	59.7	105

Pos	Name	R1	R2	R3	R4	Total	To par
17	Justin ROSE	70	70	72	70	282	-6
	Gary EVANS	70	74	69	69	282	-6
	F JACOBSON	73	69	69	71	282	-6
20	W BENNETT	72	71	69	71	283	-5
	Richard GREEN	75	64	72	72	283	-5
	Carlos RODILES	72	70	73	68	283	-5
	Jean HUGO	75	71	68	69	283	-5
	Brett RUMFORD	74	71	66	72	283	-5
25	G BRAND JNR.	70	74	69	71	284	-4
	R CHAPMAN	69	72	72	71	284	-4
	Elliot BOULT	74	70	69	71	284	-4
	Marcello SANTI	72	72	72	68	284	-4
	Per NYMAN	72	72	70	70	284	-4
	Olle KARLSSON	74	65	72	73	284	-4
	J LOMAS	73	70	71	70	284	-4
	N VANHOOTEGEM	72	66	72	74	284	-4
33	A OLDCORN	69	72	71	73	285	-3
	Greg TURNER	69	74	73	69	285	-3
	Paul NILBRINK	75	71	70	69	285	-3
	H BJORNSTAD	73	72	68	72	285	-3
	Robin BYRD	73	71	71	70	285	-3
	Carl WATTS	73	71	73	68	285	-3
39	Mark ROE	72	70	75	69	286	-2
	David GILFORD	73	70	73	70	286	-2
	Garry HOUSTON	74	70	69	73	286	-2
	Fredrik HENGE	76	69	68	73	286	-2
	N COLSAERTS	71	73	69	73	286	-2
	M SCARPA	73	71	68	74	286	-2
	Roger WESSELS	71	75	70	70	286	-2
	N DOUGHERTY	70	73	72	71	286	-2
47	Peter BAKER	70	71	77	69	287	-1
	Greg OWEN	72	70	72	73	287	-1
49	Mats LANNER	74	68	71	75	288	E
	Barry LANE	76	69	74	69	288	E
	S DRUMMOND	75	71	74	68	288	E
	Francis VALERA	76	70	70	72	288	E
	Erol SIMSEK	74	69	74	71	288	E
54	John WADE	74	67	76	72	289	+1
	M PENDARIES	71	71	74	73	289	+1
	Hennie OTTO	74	71	71	73	289	+1
	Francisco CEA	75	70	71	73	289	+1
	David CARTER	74	68	70	77	289	+1
59	Brian DAVIS	75	71	74	70	290	+2
	S P WEBSTER	71	73	72	74	290	+2
	M ARCHER	75	71	75	69	290	+2
	Richard BLAND	72	70	72	76	290	+2
63	Mark JAMES	74	71	76	70	291	+3
	R McFARLANE	74	71	71	75	291	+3
	Craig HAINLINE	73	73	71	74	291	+3
	Simon DYSON	72	68	77	74	291	+3
67	J ROBINSON	70	73	75	74	292	+4
	David LYNN	75	70	74	73	292	+4
	M PILKINGTON	71	73	74	74	292	+4
	Iain PYMAN	74	72	74	72	292	+4
71	M NILSSON	73	70	74	76	293	+5
	M FLORIOLI	75	70	74	74	293	+5
73	Gordon J BRAND	71	74	77	73	295	+7
74	David ORR	72	71	79	76	298	+10
75	Paul EALES	74	71	80	78	303	+15

Tournament Report

Andrew Coltart finally broke free of a log jammed leaderboard to win a thrilling Great North Open at De Vere Slaley Hall in Northumberland.

The Scot, who recently celebrated his 31st birthday, claimed his second European Tour title by a shot from Stephen Gallacher and Paul Casey. Coltart had led by three strokes going into the last day, but bogeys at eight and nine saw him slip behind four players.

Gallacher and Casey, along with Bradley Dredge and Daren Lee all made determined outward nine moves and after Coltart faltered they could all smell victory. But the Scot refused to give up and, after getting up and down from a bunker to birdie the 11th, he rolled in a 20-footer to catch Lee who, at that stage, was out on his own in front at 11-under.

Casey's challenge ended when he took seven on the par five 11th, while Lee's bid for glory was to fade over the final few holes after dropping shots on the 17th and 18th.

Gallacher, who was in danger of missing the cut after a first round 76, was also unable to get to 11 under at the end of play. And with Bradley Dredge shooting a double bogey six on the last, Coltart required a par on the 18th to win.

A solid iron shot onto the final green, set up a regulation four for the Scot, and the win meant he rocketed to eighth in the Ryder Cup standings.

MISSED THE CUT: Philip ARCHER 75 72, Graham RANKIN 73 74, Paul BROADHURST 78 69, Stephen DODD 75 72, Jorge BERENDT 74 73, Christian CEVAER 73 74, Gustavo ROJAS 76 71, Stephen SCAHILL 74 73, Simon WAKEFIELD 78 69, Fredrik ANDERSSON 74 73, Joakim RASK 75 72, Matthew BLACKEY 74 73, Gary MURPHY 78 70, Eric CARLBERG 75 73, Russell WEIR 74 74, Peter HANSON 77 71, Trevor IMMELMAN 77 71, Andrew MARSHALL 76 72, Carl SUNESON 77 71, Raimo SJOBERG 78 70, Nic HENNING 78 70, Craig HISLOP 72 76, Paddy GRIBBEN 74 74, Andreas LINDBERG 77 72, Hennie WALTERS 75 74, Philip GOLDING 74 75, Chris BENIANS 78 71, Neil CHEETHAM 78 71, Eamonn DARCY 78 72, Mark MOULAND 75 75, Jose Manuel LARA 77 73, Gary EMERSON 76 74, Tomas Jesus MUOZ 76 74, Andrew RAITT 74 76, Robert COLES 78 72, Michael JONZON 77 73, Marco BERNARDINI 74 76, G STORM 74 76, M MACKENZIE 76 75, Philip WALTON 79 72, P SHERMAN 76 75, K FERRIE 79 72, S D. HURLEY 78 73, M REALE 72 79, Freddy VALENTI 79 72, C GANE 78 74, I KEENAN 78 74, S CAGE 77 75, W-T YEH 76 76, P MITCHELL 78 75, C GOODFELLOW 77 76, J MCLEAN 83 70, J HARRISON 76 78, R WALKER (Am) 80 74, P STREETER 79 75, C CHALLEN 81 73, M NESBIT 79 75, R McGUIRK 78 77, D EDLUND 79 76, L WESTWOOD 81 74, D CLARK 81 75, J ROMERO 84 74, R CLAYDON 85 73, M CAPONE 80 78, M CAIN 78 81, S RICHARDSON 81 79, A McLEAN 78 82, W RILEY 75 DISQ, D BORREGO 78 RETD.

Course Profile

Slaley Hall (par 72, 7,088 yards) has been used exclusively for this tournament since it began in 1996.

Bad weather has hit the tournament on more than one occasion and any rain can make the course play long. The greens are small and well guarded.

This layout may only have three par fives but it still favours the big hitters. The front nine are generally tougher than the back.

Accuracy is needed with the driver on holes 1-9 but not from the turn.

Players/Points to Note

● If we forgive him last year's spectacular missed cut, **Lee Westwood** is a must back if he returns to play in this event in 2002. Prior to last season's horror show, he finished in the top five of this event in his last three starts. He was third in 1997, fifth in 1999 and won in 2000.

● **Andrew Coltart** had been placed in the top 20 on three occasions (and had not missed a cut) before winning in 2001.

● This event takes place the week after the US Open so it's unlikely **Retief Goosen** will tee up in it, but if he does, back him. He didn't play in 2000 or 2001 but won the inaugural event in 1996 and was second in 1997 and 1999. His stroke average is 68.92.

● **Jamie Spence** is worth following in this event if in form. His worst finish is 11th, with his complete form figures since 1996 reading: 9-6-11-6-8. He was tied third in 1998 before the tournament was abandoned.

● **Gary Evans** finished 17th last year, fourth in 1996, 19th in 1999 and was in tied third spot in 1998 before the tournament was prematurely ended.

● **Andrew Oldcorn** and **David Carter** can boast two top six places each, while **Emanuelle Canonica**, **Ian Poulter** and **Ricardo Gonzalez** should also be noted in this event.

Previous Results

2000: 1. Lee Westwood (-12), 2. Fredrik Jacobson (-9), 3. Emmanuelle Canonica (-7), Daren Clarke (-7).

1999: 1. David Park (-14), 2. David Carter (-13), Retief Goosen (-13).

1998: N/A

1997: 1. Colin Montgomerie (-18), 2. Retief Goosen (-13), 3. Lee Westwood (-12).

1996: 1. Retief Goosen (-11), 2. Ross Drummond (-9), 3. Robert Lee (-7).

MURPHY'S IRISH OPEN

Fota Island, 28 Jun to 1 Jul 2001, purse 1,600,000 euros

Pos	Name	R1	R2	R3	R4	Total	To par	Money	DD(y)	DA%	GIR%	Putts
1	C MONTGOMERIE	63	69	68	66	266	-18	266,660	289.8	78.8	75.0	111
2	P HARRINGTON	67	72	68	64	271	-13	119,310	292.6	57.7	76.4	118
	Darren CLARKE	70	72	65	64	271	-13	119,310	303.3	75.0	70.8	114
	Niclas FASTH	68	71	69	63	271	-13	119,310	296.9	51.9	76.4	117
5	Thomas BJORN	66	69	72	66	273	-11	67,840	285.8	80.8	79.2	120
6	Gary EMERSON	68	70	67	69	274	-10	48,000	312.0	65.4	66.7	112
	R KARLSSON	71	69	67	67	274	-10	48,000	299.9	55.8	61.1	119
	Adam SCOTT	68	69	66	71	274	-10	48,000	309.9	63.5	68.1	115
9	David HOWELL	68	70	71	66	275	-9	29,173	290.5	59.6	63.9	111
	Barry LANE	68	67	72	68	275	-9	29,173	280.8	67.3	72.2	118
	Ian POULTER	69	69	71	66	275	-9	29,173	290.6	63.5	72.2	119
	Steen TINNING	69	68	72	66	275	-9	29,173	279.8	78.8	70.8	113
	Thomas LEVET	68	67	72	68	275	-9	29,173	283.3	71.2	63.9	113
	Andrew COLTART	67	71	69	68	275	-9	29,173	288.1	67.3	65.3	113

Pos	Name	R1	R2	R3	R4	Total	To par
15	G BRAND JNR.	68	69	71	68	276	-8
	Ian WOOSNAM	73	69	70	64	276	-8
	Steve WEBSTER	67	71	72	66	276	-8
	Anthony WALL	67	67	71	71	276	-8
	Justin ROSE	70	70	69	67	276	-8
20	M MOULAND	71	70	67	69	277	-7
	Marc FARRY	72	65	71	69	277	-7
	John SENDEN	67	70	71	69	277	-7
	Ian GARBUTT	70	71	69	67	277	-7
	Gary EVANS	66	70	73	68	277	-7
	M SCARPA	67	73	67	70	277	-7
26	G HAVRET	69	71	69	69	278	-6
	C POTTIER	70	69	72	67	278	-6
	Peter LONARD	73	68	71	66	278	-6
	C PETTERSSON	68	72	72	66	278	-6
30	Phillip PRICE	75	65	73	66	279	-5
	Jorge BERENDT	68	73	71	67	279	-5
	Paul LAWRIE	71	66	72	70	279	-5
	David LYNN	71	65	75	68	279	-5
	R RUSSELL	71	69	71	68	279	-5
35	S KJELDSEN	69	73	72	66	280	-4
	S LEANEY	71	70	70	69	280	-4
	Andrew BEAL	70	70	68	72	280	-4
	J LOMAS	72	70	70	68	280	-4
	I GARRIDO	68	72	68	72	280	-4
	Gary ORR	72	69	70	69	280	-4
	D ROBERTSON	67	70	73	70	280	-4
	J BICKERTON	67	72	69	72	280	-4
	Simon DYSON	70	72	69	69	280	-4
44	Sandy LYLE	68	72	70	71	281	-3
	C ROCCA	70	72	70	69	281	-3
	Peter O'MALLEY	71	70	69	71	281	-3
	Stephen DODD	69	72	71	69	281	-3
48	J-F REMESY	69	73	69	71	282	-2
	Fredrik HENGE	65	70	70	77	282	-2
	H BJORNSTAD	66	74	67	75	282	-2
	Paul McGINLEY	69	73	66	74	282	-2
	H NYSTROM	70	72	71	69	282	-2
	M LUNDBERG	69	72	73	68	282	-2
54	Peter FOWLER	73	69	70	71	283	-1
	W BENNETT	72	67	72	72	283	-1
	Sven STRUVER	67	74	68	74	283	-1
57	R JACQUELIN	68	71	73	72	284	E
	Francisco CEA	70	71	72	71	284	E
59	Daren LEE	70	70	73	72	285	+1
60	A OLDCORN	73	69	73	71	286	+2
	F JACOBSON	70	72	70	74	286	+2
	Wei-Tze YEH	72	70	75	69	286	+2
63	Eamonn DARCY	65	75	72	75	287	+3
64	Carlos RODILES	71	71	74	72	288	+4
	R BALLESTEROS	70	71	74	73	288	+4
	Erol SIMSEK	68	72	73	75	288	+4
67	T GOGELE	70	72	72	75	289	+5
	M BERNARDINI	72	70	69	78	289	+5
69	Patrik SJOLAND	73	68	70	80	291	+7
70	G RANKIN	70	70	74	81	295	+11

Sponsored by Stan James

Tournament Report

We had to wait until July but finally Colin Montgomerie won his first European Tour title of the season by claiming the Irish Open – 57 weeks after his last success on his home tour.

The seven time Order of Merit winner had looked a shadow of his former self this season, his non-winning Euro streak his worst drought for a decade, but the Scot proved that he's not finished yet by dominating an event he had won twice before.

In fact, in claiming a hat-trick of victories he joins Seve Ballesteros, Nick Faldo and Bernhard Langer in an elite club of golfers who have won the Irish Open three times. After setting a new course record of 63 in the first round, Monty never looked back.

Only once did he give the field a chance to close on him during a final round 66. On the eighth, he found water and, after taking a penalty drop, had to sign for a six.

His nearest challenger, Adam Scott, who started the day three shots adrift of the leader, couldn't take advantge, though, as the young Aussie only managed a bogey five himself. Ahead on the golf course, Thomas Bjorn was charging, going out in 31, but a double bogey at the 13th pulled in the Dane's reins.

It was left to local heroes Padraig Harrington and Darren Clarke, along with Niclas Fasth, to provide the last day excitement. The trio shot 64, 64 and 63 respectively to share second.

MISSED THE CUT: A FORSBRAND 72-71, T JOHNSTONE 73 70, D McGRANE 70 73, T IMMELMAN 71 72, P BAKER 71 72, O KARLSSON 71 72, M REALE 69 74, D BORREGO 72 71, C CEVAER 72 71, G ROJAS 73 70, F HOWLEY 72 71, M BRIER 70 73, L PARSONS 72 71, T DIER 73 70, S GARDINER 74 69, R CHAPMAN 70 74, S LUNA 74 70, D SMYTH 71 73, J M OLAZABAL 69 75, R GREEN 70 74, N O'HERN 73 71, R WINCHESTER 72 72, S GALLACHER 73 71, A FORSYTH 71 73, B RUMFORD 70 74, C MORIARTY (Am) 68 76, M A MARTIN 69 76, M ROE 71 74, P WALTON 72 73, C SUNESON 73 72, R CLAYDON 72 73, D HIGGINS 75 70, Z SCOTLAND (Am) 70 75, W RILEY 71 75, D GILFORD 73 73, S HAMILL 72 74, O EDMOND 74 72, A CEJKA 70 76, B DREDGE 72 74, K NOLAN 71 75, M MACKENZIE 75 72, R RAFFERTY 74 73, R McFARLANE 74 73, H STENSON 71 76, S QUINLIVAN 77 70, J HUGO 72 75, R S JOHNSON 76 71, N COLSAERTS 69 78, J MOSELEY 70 77, N VANHOOTEGEM 76 71, V PHILLIPS 74 73, G OWEN 72 75, D PARK 76 71, N HENNING 73 74, P CASEY 69 78, S TORRANCE 73 75, D FICHARDT 75 73, P EALES 75 75, J RYSTROM 72 76, M GRONBERG 72 76, D CARTER 72 76, C HANELL 75 73, M LAFEBER 77 72, D HOSPITAL 71 78, R MUNTZ 77 72, A RAITT 72 77, R COLES 75 74, J SANDELIN 73 76, J DWYER 69 80, S BALLESTEROS 77 73, E BOULT 77 73, H OTTO 73 77, A McCORMICK (Am) 75 75, P BROADHURST 73 78, P QUIRICI 76 75, N CHEETHAM 75 76, S SCAHILL 73 78, D WALKER 79 73, D TERBLANCHE 76 76, P GRIBBEN 74 78, R WESSELS 74 79, M ALLAN 72 81, J DIGNAM 74 81, R SYMES 80 78, P MITCHELL 73 W/D.

Sponsored by Stan James

Course Profile

Fota Island (par 71, 6,927 yards) staged this event for the first time in 2001 and will again host the Irish Open in 2002.

The layout, which was initially developed by British Open champion, Christy O'Connor Jnr, and Great Britain and Ireland Walker Cup captain, Peter McEvoy, was remodelled in 1999 and was in superb condition for the tournament.

The greens are particularly receptive and are similar to those found on Australian courses. The greens are huge and undulating (some featuring three tiers).

Players/Points to Note

●**Colin Montgomerie** captured his first European Tour tournament title of 2001 in this event and, since missing the cut in 1990, hasn't finished lower than 24th. He won at Druids Glen in 1996 and 1997 at Fota Island last year and can boast eight top-ten finishes in the 90s.

●**Lee Westwood** has form figures of 7-2-15-7 from 1996 to 1999. He has a stroke average of 70.82 in six appearances in the event.

●The last time an Irishman won this event was back in 1982 (John O'Leary) but **Darren Clarke** and **Padraig Harrington** are getting closer. The pair finished tied second last year and it won't be long before one of them, or **Paul McGinley**, alters that statistic.

●**Jose Maria Olazabal** has played in this event on seven of its last 12 renewals - never finishing outside the top ten. If it's on his schedule in 2002, he can't be discounted.

●**David Carter** has fond memories of this event, as it was the first European Tour tournament he won. In seven starts in this event he has been placed in the top 25 on four occasions.

●**Angel Cabrera**'s long game is well suited to Irish venues used for this event as two top tens in four starts suggest.

●Also watch out for multiple top-ten finishers **Peter Baker**, **Thomas Bjorn**, **Miguel Angel Martin** and **Peter Lonard** next year.

Previous Results

2000: 1. Patrik Sjoland (-14), 2. Fredrik Jacobsen (-12), 3. Paul McGinley (-10), Rolf Muntz (-10).

1999: 1. Sergio Garcia (-16), 2. Angel Cabrera (-13), 3. Jarrod Moseley (-11).

1998: 1. David Carter (-6), won play-off, 2. Colin Montgomerie (-6), 3. Peter Baker (-4), John McHenry (-4).

1997: 1. Colin Montgomerie (-15), 2. Lee Westwood (-8), 3. Nick Faldo (-6).

1996: 1. Colin Montgomerie (-5), 2. Andrew Oldcorn (-4), Wayne Riley (-4).

The K Club, 5 Jul to 8 Jul 2001, purse 3,426,434 euros

Pos	Name	R1	R2	R3	R4	Total	To par	Money	DD(y)	DA%	GIR%	Putts
1	Darren CLARKE	68	68	71	66	273	-15	553,727	288.3	69.6	72.2	106
2	Ian WOOSNAM	69	66	73	68	276	-12	247,751	275.8	58.9	70.8	109
	P HARRINGTON	70	67	69	70	276	-12	247,751	289.0	62.5	70.8	113
	Thomas BJORN	73	71	65	67	276	-12	247,751	279.0	66.1	65.3	106
5	Mark MOULAND	70	71	68	68	277	-11	140,869	291.3	75.0	70.8	115
6	H BJORNSTAD	67	68	70	73	278	-10	107,978	286.3	64.3	61.1	104
	Retief GOOSEN	69	70	73	66	278	-10	107,978	291.8	62.5	77.8	121
8	Bernhard LANGER	71	70	69	69	279	-9	71,265	286.9	75.0	77.8	121
	Phillip PRICE	70	72	70	67	279	-9	71,265	287.8	73.2	61.1	108
	R GONZALEZ	69	70	70	70	279	-9	71,265	305.4	48.2	61.1	109
	D ROBERTSON	70	72	69	68	279	-9	71,265	273.9	76.8	66.7	112

Pos	Name	R1	R2	R3	R4	Total	To par
12	M Angel MARTIN	71	71	67	71	280	-8
	C ROCCA	70	69	69	72	280	-8
	R JACQUELIN	70	70	72	68	280	-8
	Richard GREEN	70	70	70	70	280	-8
	Thomas LEVET	72	68	69	71	280	-8
	M GRONBERG	68	70	73	69	280	-8
	Paul LAWRIE	70	72	68	70	280	-8
	Daren LEE	70	70	71	69	280	-8
20	C MONTGOMERIE	68	72	69	72	281	-7
	Gary EVANS	73	67	72	69	281	-7
	Paul CASEY	69	68	71	73	281	-7
23	Sven STRUVER	75	70	69	68	282	-6
	S LEANEY	71	69	71	71	282	-6
	T IMMELMAN	74	68	70	70	282	-6
	R KARLSSON	72	70	69	71	282	-6
	R WESSELS	69	72	69	72	282	-6
	J SANDELIN	69	71	65	77	282	-6
	M CAMPBELL	67	70	71	74	282	-6
30	David HOWELL	69	71	71	72	283	-5
	Anders HANSEN	74	68	71	70	283	-5
	Olle KARLSSON	72	73	69	69	283	-5
	C HANELL	72	72	70	69	283	-5
34	A FORSBRAND	73	72	66	73	284	-4
	Marc FARRY	70	75	70	69	284	-4
	M LAFEBER	67	72	73	72	284	-4
	Angel CABRERA	71	73	66	74	284	-4
	A COLTART	72	71	69	72	284	-4
	M LUNDBERG	67	65	72	80	284	-4
40	Mark ROE	72	72	71	70	285	-3
	J LOMAS	76	69	71	69	285	-3
	Peter O'MALLEY	71	73	72	69	285	-3
	M SCARPA	67	71	73	74	285	-3
	Brett RUMFORD	68	77	73	67	285	-3
45	Eamonn DARCY	69	72	70	75	286	-2
	John SENDEN	71	74	70	71	286	-2
	Soren HANSEN	71	69	70	76	286	-2
	J HAEGGMAN	72	72	70	72	286	-2
	Rolf MUNTZ	71	71	71	73	286	-2
	Peter LONARD	73	71	71	71	286	-2
	Niclas FASTH	69	75	68	74	286	-2
52	Brian DAVIS	70	70	72	75	287	-1
	Stephen DODD	73	72	68	74	287	-1
	Markus BRIER	73	70	70	74	287	-1
	R RUSSELL	72	73	68	74	287	-1
	A FORSYTH	70	75	75	67	287	-1
	Scott GARDINER	74	70	70	73	287	-1
58	E ROMERO	72	72	70	74	288	E
	Greg TURNER	71	74	73	70	288	E
	Steen TINNING	72	73	71	72	288	E
	Greg OWEN	70	69	71	78	288	E
62	Santiago LUNA	72	73	71	73	289	+1
	W BENNETT	70	73	74	72	289	+1
	Ian GARBUTT	71	69	73	76	289	+1
	Lee WESTWOOD	71	74	73	71	289	+1
	S GALLACHER	74	69	74	72	289	+1
	Adam SCOTT	75	70	71	73	289	+1
68	G BRAND JNR.	71	73	71	75	290	+2
	J-F REMESY	71	72	75	72	290	+2
	Jamie SPENCE	71	74	70	75	290	+2
	G HAVRET	76	68	72	74	290	+2
	Olivier EDMOND	71	73	71	75	290	+2
	Alex CEJKA	72	71	73	74	290	+2
	D TERBLANCHE	70	72	74	74	290	+2
	Alan McLEAN	73	71	71	75	290	+2
76	D McGRANE	73	72	72	74	291	+3
	P BROADHURST	78	67	68	78	291	+3
	N VANHOOTEGEM	73	72	71	75	291	+3
	Simon DYSON	73	69	75	74	291	+3
80	R CHAPMAN	75	70	66	81	292	+4
	Paul EALES	71	72	74	75	292	+4
82	Steve WEBSTER	72	69	79	73	293	+5
	David CARTER	72	73	69	79	293	+5
	Wei-Tze YEH	73	70	77	73	293	+5
85	R S JOHNSON	74	71	75	74	294	+6
86	David GILFORD	75	69	74	77	295	+7
	M BERNARDINI	74	70	74	77	295	+7
88	Gary EMERSON	71	73	72	80	296	+8
89	Wayne RILEY	75	70	77	79	301	+13
90	Ian POULTER	71	74	78	79	302	+14
91	S SCAHILL	71	73	76	83	303	+15

Sponsored by Stan James

Tournament Report

19 years after John O'Leary won the Irish Open in 1982, Darren Clarke produced a superb Sunday 66 to end the hoodoo that had afflicted Irish golfers on their home fairways by claiming the European Open at the K-Club in Dublin.

The packed galleries roared on Clarke who, in winning, exorcised the demons that descended on him two years ago on the same course.

Then, he shot a third round 60 to lead by six shots, only to fall apart during the final round, losing to his great friend Lee Westwood. This time around it was Clarke who came from behind to win.

The Ulsterman trailed Mikael Lundberg by three strokes going into the last day, a triple bogey on the 17th on Saturday seemingly blowing his chances of glory.

But consecutive birdies on the fourth, fifth and sixth, where a wayward approach shot looked destined for trouble but after cannoning into a tree the ball bounced onto the putting surface, saw him move into contention.

Further outward birdies at the eighth and ninth saw Clarke take control. Lundberg was soon to fade and his last day 80 relegated the Swede to 34th place.

Harrington, lying fourth after 54 holes, was also struggling to find his rhythm and when Clarke picked up a shot at the 16th, the win was in the bag.

Finishing second alongside Harrington was Ian Woonam and Thomas Bjorn, who picked up a diamond necklace worth Ir£100,000 for shooting 14 under for the par fives in the week.

MISSED THE CUT: Jose RIVERO 72 74, Carlos RODILES 76 70, Peter BAKER 71 75, Paolo QUIRICI 72 74, Paul MCGINLEY 72 74, Ignacio GARRIDO 73 73, Gustavo ROJAS 68 78, Erol SIMSEK 71 75, Mark JAMES 77 70, Tony JOHNSTONE 75 72, Barry LANE 75 72, Soren KJELDSEN 70 77, Anthony WALL 72 75, Miguel Angel JIMENEZ 70 77, D HOSPITAL 74 73, J HUGO 74 73, N CHEETHAM 73 74, C CEVAER 71 76, G ORR 74 73, D HIGGINS 74 73, G STORM 74 73, S HAMILL 74 74, V PHILLIPS 75 73, F JACOBSON 72 76, D LYNN 74 74, J BICKERTON 74 74, L PARSONS 73 75, T DIER 74 74, S LYLE 73 76, M MACKENZIE 74 75, S TORRANCE 74 75, B VAUGHAN 76 73, D BORREGO 76 73, B DREDGE 77 72, H NYSTROM 73 76, G NORQUIST 78 71, S BALLESTEROS 78 72, D SMYTH 75 75, P WALTON 76 74, J RYSTROM 77 73, J M OLAZABAL 79 72, R WINCHESTER 78 73, M REALE 76 75, D PARK 75 76, J DWYER 78 73, A BADDELEY 75 76, J ROSE 78 74, F HENGE 75 77, T GOGELE 79 73, C SUNESON 74 78, F CEA 79 73, A MURRAY 78 75, M PIERO 76 77, A RAITT 74 79, N HENNING 78 75, C PETTERSSON 77 76, J MOSELEY 76 78, E BOULT 72 83, P SJOLAND 77 78, R RAFFERTY 83 73, J DIGNAM 77 80, D FICHARDT 76 82, A OLDCORN 77 W/D, G RANKIN DISQ, H STENSON RETD.

Course Profile

The Arnold Palmer designed K-Club (par 72, 7,227 yards) will stage the Ryder Cup in 2006 and is a long venue that favours the big hitters.

Water comes into play on all bar five of the holes so any wayward shots can put some big numbers on a golfer's scorecard. The greens are large but are well protected.

Dublin gets its fair share of rain at this time of year and this can make the course play longer.

Players/Points to Note

●**Darren Clarke** became the first Irish winner on home soil for 19 years when he won the European Open in 2001. He should have won here in 1999 but threw away a six shot lead going into the last. He also shot the course record of 60 that year. Since 1996 his form figures read 25-4-2-7-1.

●**Lee Westwood** won in 1999 and 2000 but his 2001 woes continued at the K-Club where he was placed 62nd.

●**Constantino Rocca** finished in the top five of four of the first five (1995-1999) European Opens held at the K-Club (his other finish was tenth). The Italian finished 12th in 2001 to continue his good run in this event.

●**Angel Cabrera** was a disappointing 34th last year but hadn't finished outside the top six in the previous three renewals.

●**Paul Lawrie**'s worst finishing position has been 15th over the past three years.

●**Bernhard Langer** won the inaugural event at the K-Club, while **Matthias Gronberg** is another past champion. Both players have had further top-ten finishes in the last two years.

●**Per-Ulrik Johansson** has won this event twice (1996 and 1997) and has finished in the top ten on two other occasions.

●**Thomas Bjorn** has finished in the top ten on three occasions, while others to note are **Steve Webster**, **Dean Robertson** and **Paul Casey**.

Previous Results

2000: 1. Lee Westwood (-12), 2. Angel Cabrera (-11), 3. Per-Ulrik Johansson (-10).

1999: 1. Lee Westwood (-17), 2. Peter O'Malley (-14), Darren Clarke (-14).

1998: 1. Mathias Gronberg (-13), 2. Miguel A. Jimenez (-3), Phillip Price (-3).

1997: 1. Per-Ulrik Johansson (-21), 2. Peter Baker (-15), 3. Jose Maria Olazabal (-14), Raymond Russell (-14).

1996: 1. Per-Ulrik Johansson (-11), 2. Costantino Rocca (-10), 3. Roger Chapman (-9), Andrew Coltart (-9).

SCOTTISH OPEN AT LOCH LOMOND

Loch Lomond, 12 Jul to 15 Jul 2001, purse 3,666,057 euros

Pos	Name	R1	R2	R3	R4	Total	To par	Money	DD(y)	DA%	GIR%	Putts
1	Retief GOOSEN	62	69	66	71	268	-16	610,998	286.4	80.4	86.1	121
2	Thomas BJORN	68	67	69	67	271	-13	407,332	275.0	75.0	72.2	108
3	Barry LANE	70	65	69	68	272	-12	174,137	273.9	87.5	81.9	118
	Paul McGINLEY	68	67	67	70	272	-12	174,137	280.1	85.7	80.6	117
	John DALY	68	68	66	70	272	-12	174,137	n/a	n/a	n/a	n/a
	Adam SCOTT	65	68	67	72	272	-12	174,137	286.6	87.5	77.8	120
7	Darren CLARKE	69	67	68	69	273	-11	109,981	278.9	85.7	77.8	119
8	Jesper PARNEVIK	71	69	65	70	275	-9	86,885	276.9	82.1	72.2	118
	M GRONBERG	73	70	65	67	275	-9	86,885	270.1	83.9	70.8	113
10	Jose COCERES	69	72	69	66	276	-8	73,321	274.4	91.1	75.0	119

Pos	Name	R1	R2	R3	R4	Total	To par
11	M HOEY (Am)	71	71	71	64	277	-7
	Greg OWEN	72	68	68	69	277	-7
	Brett RUMFORD	73	65	71	68	277	-7
14	Sergio GARCIA	69	69	69	71	278	-6
	Soren HANSEN	72	71	64	71	278	-6
	Geoff OGILVY	69	73	69	67	278	-6
	F JACOBSON	69	70	68	71	278	-6
	Niclas FASTH	67	71	66	74	278	-6
	Tom LEHMAN	70	66	74	68	278	-6
	Daren LEE	70	67	73	68	278	-6
21	J M OLAZABAL	70	73	65	71	279	-5
	A HANSEN	69	71	70	69	279	-5
	Ian POULTER	69	72	71	67	279	-5
	R GONZALEZ	74	69	68	68	279	-5
	Peter LONARD	69	71	71	68	279	-5
	J BICKERTON	72	69	71	67	279	-5
	Simon DYSON	69	73	68	69	279	-5
28	G CHALMERS	70	66	75	69	280	-4
	S WEBSTER	69	70	69	72	280	-4
	Anthony WALL	67	70	70	73	280	-4
	Carlos RODILES	68	73	69	70	280	-4
	C MONTGOMERIE	70	67	69	74	280	-4
	R S JOHNSON	73	70	67	70	280	-4
	J RYSTROM	73	69	68	70	280	-4
	Angel CABRERA	68	74	70	68	280	-4
	D ROBERTSON	73	69	70	68	280	-4
37	J Milkha SINGH	71	71	70	69	281	-3
	Sven STR‹VER	73	69	66	73	281	-3
	Justin ROSE	67	70	72	72	281	-3
	C PETTERSSON	69	71	68	73	281	-3
41	Nick FALDO	70	73	69	70	282	-2
	R JACQUELIN	70	67	76	69	282	-2
	M Angel JIMINEZ	70	72	68	72	282	-2
	Peter O'MALLEY	72	71	69	70	282	-2
	David LYNN	68	75	67	72	282	-2
	David CARTER	70	69	72	71	282	-2
47	W BENNETT	71	68	75	69	283	-1
	John SENDEN	69	72	73	69	283	-1
	Colin GILLIES	69	69	72	73	283	-1
50	Thomas LEVET	72	67	72	73	284	E
	J MOSELEY	65	75	68	76	284	E
	C CEVAER	70	73	73	68	284	E
53	E CANONICA	71	70	71	73	285	+1
	Ian GARBUTT	68	74	72	71	285	+1
	A COLTART	72	70	73	70	285	+1
	Erol SIMSEK	69	74	70	72	285	+1
57	Gary ORR	69	71	72	74	286	+2
	M CAMPBELL	71	68	74	73	286	+2
59	David HOWELL	70	69	72	76	287	+3
	Peter BAKER	72	69	73	73	287	+3
61	A OLDCORN	71	69	78	70	288	+4
	T GOGELE	68	70	78	72	288	+4
	D BORREGO	72	67	72	77	288	+4
64	A McLARDY	71	70	75	73	289	+5
	Jamie SPENCE	73	70	72	74	289	+5
66	S SCAHILL	73	69	75	73	290	+6
67	Greg NORMAN	68	71	74	78	291	+7
68	M MOULAND	70	67	78	77	292	+8
69	Sandy LYLE	72	70	74	78	294	+10
70	B DREDGE	73	69	76	77	295	+11
71	B LANGER	70	69	-	-	-	W/D

Sponsored by Stan James

Tournament Report

Winning is fast becoming a habit for Retief Goosen, as the South African added the Scottish Open at Loch Lomond to his victory haul just weeks after securing his first Major title.

As in the US Open, the Goose led from start to finish and, again a little like his win at Southern Hills, he stumbled over the line by dropping shots on the last two holes.

But Goosen had too much in hand and won by three strokes, going further clear at the top of the Order of Merit in the process.

A first round 62 saw the South African lead after day one and, although Adam Scott, who finished each of the first three rounds in second place, tried as he might to close the gap, the young Aussie couldn't overhaul Goosen, fading to finish third. Again it was his putting that let him down.

There was some consolation for Scott, though, as he did enough to book a place in next week's Open at Lytham.

Goosen gave notice that he wasn't for catching by posting birdies at the second and sixth holes on Sunday. A string of pars followed the turn for home and, although it wasn't exciting, it was a controlled performance by the Springbok.

Thomas Bjorn's fast finishing 67, helped by four birdies on the back nine, secured second spot for the Dane with Barry Lane, in his best finish of the season, Paul McGinley and John Daly sharing third with Scott.

MISSED THE CUT: G BRAND JNR. 70 74, B MARCHBANK 73 71, C ROCCA 68 76, E ROMERO 69 75, I WOOSNAM 70 74, D GILFERT 71 73, G TURNER 73 71, M LAFEBER 72 72, P BROADHURST 72 72, G HAVRET 76 68, P PRICE 73 71, D PARK 71 73, M BRIER 72 72, R RUSSELL 70 74, L WESTWOOD 72 72, C HANELL 74 70, A FORSBRAND 71 74, M A MARTIN 74 71, J RIVERO 73 72, R WEIR 74 71, M FARRY 74 71, R GREEN 71 74, E BOULT 65 80, T IMMELMAN 68 77, C SUNESON 73 72, J LOMAS 73 72, G EVANS 67 78, M SCARPA 74 71, I GARRIDO 71 74, N VANHOOTEGEM 74 71, S LUNA 72 74, M ROE 72 74, S LEANEY 76 70, H BJORNSTAD 71 75, H NYSTROM 73 73, S KJELDSEN 75 72, P EALES 72 75, P QUIRICI 71 76, J HAEGGMAN 77 70, P LAWRIE 70 77, A FORSYTH 77 70, S O'HARA 71 76, J McLEAN 76 71, R DRUMMOND 75 73, W RILEY 74 74, S TORRANCE 76 72, D HOSPITAL 73 75, J HUGO 72 76, R WINCHESTER 71 77, F CEA 77 71, S GALLACHER 69 79, T DIER 79 69, T JOHNSTONE 74 75, C PARRY 75 74, M REALE 74 75, P FULKE 77 72, W-T YEH 73 76, E DARCY 74 76, B DAVIS 76 74, R MUNTZ 79 71, R WESSELS 75 75, M LUNDBERG 74 76, D HIGGINS 74 77, P CASEY 76 75, J QUINNEY (Am) 75 76, D SMYTH 79 73, F HENGE 77 75, D FICHARDT 75 78, H STENSON 76 77, O EDMOND 72 81, D TERBLANCHE 76 77, M BERNARDINI 74 79, S BALLESTEROS 79 75, L PARSONS 81 73, J SANDELIN 76 79, G NORQUIST 77 84, R CHAPMAN 72 DISQ, R RAFFERTY 80 W/D, J-F REMESY 80 W/D, G EMERSON 75 RETD, S TINNING 75 W/D, A CEJKA 67 DISQ, V PHILLIPS 74 DISQ, A RAITT 74 RETD, P SJOLAND 79 RETD.

Sponsored by Stan James

Course Profile

This Tom Weiskopf designed Loch Lomond Golf Club (par 71, 7,050 yards) is well liked by the players who rate it among the best in Europe.

The greens are always in immaculate condition and were re-laid after the Solheim Cup in October 2000.

There are plenty of risk/reward and although the fairways are relatively generous, loose shots can be punished.

The course favours the big hitters and can play long after rain. The wind can also be a factor.

Players/Points to Note

●**Retief Goosen's** win in 2001 came as no surprise. He can now boast four top-ten finishes in five starts, is 38-under to par on those appearances and has a stroke average of 69.10. The South African also holds the course record of 62 – which he set in 1997 and equalled in 2001.

●**Colin Montgomerie** spoiled his record slightly last year when he could only manage a share of 28th. Prior to that he wasn't placed outside the top ten in five starts. His win in this event in 1999 was particularly sweet, as it was his first European Tour success in his native Scotland. In 28 competitive rounds he is 42-under par.

●**Thomas Bjorn** won the inagural Loch Lomond event, was runner up in 2001 and has yet to finish worse than 32nd.

●**Tom Lehman** won in 1997, was ninth the following year, third in 2000 and 14th last term.

●**Lee Westwood, Darren Clarke, Jepser Parnevik, Eduardo Romero** and **Michael Campbell** are multiple top-ten finishers.

●**Robert Allenby** played this event from 1996 to 1999 and posted form figures of 3-13-2-14.

●This tournament offers entry to the Open for players not already eligible if they finish in the top eight - a big carrot for some of the lesser lights of the European Tour.

Previous Results

2000: 1. Ernie Els (-11), 2. Tom Lehman (-10), 3. Colin Montgomerie (-9).

1999: 1. Colin Montgomerie (-16), 2. Michael Jonzon (-13), Sergio Garcia (-13), Mats Lanner (-13).

1998: 1. Lee Westwood (-8), 2. Eduardo Romero (-4), Ian Woosnam (-4), David Howell (-4), Dennis Edlund (-4), Robert Allenby (-4).

1997: 1. Tom Lehman (-19), 2. Ernie Els (-14), 3. Retief Goosen (-12).

1996: 1. Thomas Bjorn (-7), 2. Jean Van de Velde (-6), 3. Robert Allenby (-3).

TNT DUTCH OPEN

Noordwijkse G.C., 26 Jul to 29 Jul 2001, purse 1,800,000 euros

Pos	Name	R1	R2	R3	R4	Total	To par	Money	DD(y)	DA%	GIR%	Putts
1	Bernhard LANGER	69	67	67	66	269	-15	300,000	290.9	67.9	76.4	115
Won play-off												
2	Warren BENNETT	68	67	67	67	269	-15	200,000	304.6	69.6	75.0	115
3	M Angel JIMINEZ	71	65	71	66	273	-11	112,680	299.3	67.9	73.6	114
4	Barry LANE	71	67	66	70	274	-10	76,440	287.9	67.9	75.0	115
	Anders HANSEN	69	67	75	63	274	-10	76,440	294.4	55.4	66.7	104
	R RUSSELL	68	68	69	69	274	-10	76,440	295.6	78.6	76.4	118
7	Greg TURNER	68	65	71	71	275	-9	49,500	296.0	69.6	75.0	118
	R GONZALEZ	67	65	75	68	275	-9	49,500	318.6	67.9	65.3	109
9	A OLDCORN	70	65	72	69	276	-8	36,480	292.5	55.4	70.8	115
	P HARRINGTON	67	67	71	71	276	-8	36,480	324.8	64.3	77.8	118
	Stephen LEANEY	71	67	70	68	276	-8	36,480	289.5	69.6	75.0	118

Pos	Name	R1	R2	R3	R4	Total	To par		Pos	Name	R1	R2	R3	R4	Total	To par
12	Ian GARBUTT	69	71	71	66	277	-7			Paul McGINLEY	71	70	67	75	283	-1
	Ernie ELS	68	70	75	64	277	-7			C CEVAER	70	67	72	74	283	-1
14	R JACQUELIN	68	71	69	70	278	-6			David HIGGINS	70	71	67	75	283	-1
	Peter BAKER	66	68	74	70	278	-6	45	G HAVRET	72	69	72	71	284	E
	H BJORNSTAD	73	64	72	69	278	-6		J LOMAS	70	68	76	70	284	E
	R WINCHESTER	72	66	72	68	278	-6		Stephen DODD	70	71	72	71	284	E
	Peter O'MALLEY	73	68	69	68	278	-6		Gary ORR	71	68	72	73	284	E
	Gary EVANS	69	71	69	69	278	-6		David PARK	68	72	74	70	284	E
20	S WEBSTER	71	69	71	68	279	-5		F ANDERSSON	71	68	73	72	284	E
	B DREDGE	70	70	71	68	279	-5		A COLTART	66	69	79	70	284	E
	D ROBERTSON	66	68	72	73	279	-5		Daren LEE	72	68	70	74	284	E
	S GARDINER	68	73	71	67	279	-5		J BICKERTON	70	69	73	72	284	E
24	Philip WALTON	69	68	70	73	280	-4		A FORSYTH	70	71	71	72	284	E
	John SENDEN	69	70	69	72	280	-4		A BADDELEY	72	69	74	69	284	E
	D BOTES	69	70	70	71	280	-4	56	J M CARRILES	68	72	73	72	285	+1
	T Jesus MUOZ	74	67	65	74	280	-4		Paolo QUIRICI	67	72	73	73	285	+1
	D TERBLANCHE	69	71	74	66	280	-4		Darren CLARKE	68	70	73	74	285	+1
29	R CHAPMAN	70	69	72	70	281	-3		Graeme STORM	71	68	71	75	285	+1
	J HAEGGMAN	70	69	71	71	281	-3	60	Olle KARLSSON	67	70	74	75	286	+2
	M JONZON	68	68	76	69	281	-3		M LUNDBERG	67	72	69	78	286	+2
32	Peter FOWLER	69	71	72	70	282	-2	62	N BOYSEN (Am)	64	75	77	71	287	+3
	Mark McNULTY	71	67	72	72	282	-2	63	Mark ROE	69	69	73	77	288	+4
	D FICHARDT	68	66	70	78	282	-2		Carl SUNESON	69	70	76	73	288	+4
	Peter HANSON	70	69	72	71	282	-2		C POTTIER	68	72	73	75	288	+4
	Jamie SPENCE	69	70	70	73	282	-2	66	Hennie OTTO	71	70	74	74	289	+5
	Soren HANSEN	70	71	70	71	282	-2		J STEENKAMER	75	64	75	75	289	+5
	Rolf MUNTZ	71	68	71	72	282	-2		M BERNARDINI	69	71	72	77	289	+5
	Richard STERNE	67	67	73	75	282	-2	69	Eamonn DARCY	70	71	76	73	290	+6
40	J MOSELEY	67	73	74	69	283	-1		Elliot BOULT	74	63	75	78	290	+6
	Per NYMAN	73	67	69	74	283	-1	71	G BRAND JNR.	72	69	77	73	291	+7

Tournament Report

Bernhard Langer ended a four-year winless streak by capturing the TNT Open at Noordwijkse Golf Club in Holland.

The German overcame Warren Bennett in a play-off after the first extra hole to not only win the event, that was formerly known as the Dutch Open, for a third time but also put himself in the frame for a tenth Ryder Cup appearance. Langer and Bennett played in the final group and dominated the last day.

The pair were separated by just a shot at the start of the last day, with the Englishman clear, and after feeling each other out over the outward nine, the pair let loose after the turn. Bennett came home in 31, Langer in 30, as the Anglo-German two-ball blitzed the inward nine. It was Langer's birdies at the 16th and 17th, though, that set up a play-off.

The 18th was played as the first, and what turned out to be the last, extra hole. Both players found the fairway with their drives and were on the green in regulation. Bennett went for glory, charging his first putt four feet past the hole. Langer was more conservative and, after holing out for par, it was up to Bennett to sink his knee-trembler.

He missed and Langer took the prize. The pair finished four shots clear of Miguel Angel Jimenez, whose last day 66 wasn't enough. Neither was Anders Hansen's swashbuckling Sunday 63, the Dane ending up with a share of fourth spot with Ray Russell and Barry Lane.

MISSED THE CUT: M JAMES 73 69, M MOULAND 73 69, J M SINGH 70 72, S KJELDSEN 74 68, M LAFEBER 71 71, G HOUSTON 68 74, B VAUGHAN 73 69, R BYRD 69 73, D BORREGO 69 73, M VAN DEN BERG (Am) 72 70, F JACOBSON 71 71, D CARTER 73 69, W RILEY 76 67, N KRAAIJ 70 73, M FARRY 72 71, S P WEBSTER 72 71, I POULTER 71 72, F HENGE 71 72, J HAWKSWORTH 74 69, D CHAND 74 69, J ROBINSON 73 70, J RYSTROM 70 73, R CLAYDON 72 71, M REALE 71 72, M GRONBERG 73 70, J BERENDT 73 70, P STREETER 70 73, D LYNN 72 71, M ILONEN 72 71, J RIVERO 75 69, D SMYTH 73 71, D GILFORD 74 70, S STRUVER 71 73, B GEE 74 70, G OGILVY 72 72, N CHEETHAM 77 67, N VANHOOTEGEM 70 74, S RICHARDSON 70 74, S SCAHILL 72 72, R COLES 73 71, M BLACKEY 73 71, T DIER 71 73, T IMMELMAN 73 72, R S JOHNSON 76 69, F CEA 72 73, F VALERA 74 71, M PILKINGTON 72 73, N HENNING 69 76, M CAPONE 70 75, C RIES (Am) 76 69, T JOHNSTONE 74 72, R BUSCHOW (Am) 75 71, C HAINLINE 67 79, G EMERSON 76 70, C VAN DER VELDE 74 72, R WECHGELAER 74 72, C HANELL 74 72, M MACKENZIE 74 73, R RAFFERTY 77 70, R MILLER 73 74, B DAVIS 75 72, P BROADHURST 67 80, M FLORIOLI 78 69, S GALLACHER 76 71, N VAN RENSBURG 76 71, M SANTI 79 69, A BEAL 72 76, I VAN WEERELT (Am) 73 75, C ROCCA 75 74, S LOVEY 76 73, P LONARD 71 78, S CROSBY 75 74, L WESTWOOD 74 76, E SIMSEK 73 77, G VAN DER VALK (Am) 76 74, T GOGELE 75 76, O EDMOND 76 75, S LUNA 68 84, H BENSDORP 74 78, L PARSONS 79 73, P SJOLAND 78 76, N COLSAERTS 81 76, G RANKIN 80 W/D, M SCARPA 73 RETD, V PHILLIPS 70 DISQ.

Sponsored by Stan James

Course Profile

Last year Noordwijkse Golf Club staged this event (par 71, 6,751 yards). Next to the North Sea, it is a typical links venue which can be affected by the wind and rain but is fairly defenceless in benign conditions.

Hilversumche Golf Club (par 71, 6,636 yards) is another short track but despite being inland gives a good impression of a links layout. The fairways are undulating and give the golfers the opportunity to bump and run their shots onto the green.

Players/Points to Note

● **Bernhard Langer** is undoubtedly the king of this event. The German won this event last year and was successful in 1984 and 1992. He finished runner up in 1991 and 2000 and is 65-under par in eight starts since 1990. None of Langer's wins have come at Hilversumche Golf Club, though, venue for next year's renewal.

● **Lee Westwood**'s win did come at Hilversumche and despite missing the cut last year his career statistics for the TNT/Dutch Open read – 45-under in seven appearances and three top 11 finishes – including a win and third place twice.

● **Stephen Leaney**'s record in this tournament is superb. The Aussie won in 1998 and 2000 and finished 15th and ninth in his other two starts.

● **Darren Clarke** has only finished outside the top 20 once on his last six outings. He has a stroke average of 69.630 in his last six starts.

● **Angel Cabrera** has finished in the top eight of this tournament in three of the last four years he has taken part.

● **John Huston** usually plays here after contesting the British Open. Since 1990, the American has made seven appearances, never finishing lower than 33rd and registering six top-16 finishes.

● **Miguel Angel Jimenez, Mark Mouland, Mark McNulty, Sven Struver** are past Hilversumche winners, while **Anders Hanson** can boast two top-20 finishes recently.

Previous Results

2000: 1. Stephen Leaney (-19), 2. Bernhard Langer (-15), 3. Mathias Gronberg (-14), Angel Cabrera (-14), Lee Westwood (-14).

1999: 1. Lee Westwood (-15), 2. Gary Orr (-14), 3. Eduardo Romero, Jarrod Moseley (-13).

1998: 1. Stephen Leaney (-18), 2. Darren Clarke (-17), 3. Nick Price (-16), Lee Westwood (-16).

1997: 1. Sven Struver (-18), 2. Russell Claydon (-15), 3. Roger Chapman (-13), Angel Cabrera (-13).

1996: 1. Mark McNulty (-18), 2. Scott Hoch (-17), 3. Frank Nobilo (-15), Raymond Russell (-15).

VOLVO SCANDINAVIAN MASTERS

Barseback G&CC, 2 Aug to 5 Aug 2001, purse 1,837,527 euros

Pos	Name	R1	R2	R3	R4	Total	To par	Money	DD(y)	DA%	GIR%	Putts
1	C MONTGOMERIE	66	69	69	70	274	-14	300,000	285.9	70.0	73.6	110
2	Ian POULTER	70	65	68	72	275	-13	156,340	279.4	38.3	70.8	110
	Lee WESTWOOD	67	67	69	72	275	-13	156,340	287.5	46.7	65.3	108
4	Warren BENNETT	67	70	69	70	276	-12	65,664	289.8	65.0	83.3	122
	Dennis EDLUND	69	67	71	69	276	-12	65,664	266.6	43.3	68.1	108
	J HAEGGMAN	71	67	70	68	276	-12	65,664	300.1	51.7	69.4	109
	Jarmo SANDELIN	68	74	68	66	276	-12	65,664	271.4	55.0	66.7	107
	Adam SCOTT	69	72	67	68	276	-12	65,664	303.5	58.3	73.6	115
9	Peter HANSON	70	72	66	69	277	-11	35,100	283.3	65.0	72.2	113
	Soren HANSEN	66	73	68	70	277	-11	35,100	276.6	61.7	70.8	110
	Peter HEDBLOM	66	70	68	73	277	-11	35,100	n/a	n/a	n/a	n/a
	Thomas BJORN	68	72	67	70	277	-11	35,100	290.8	51.7	70.8	113

Pos	Name	R1	R2	R3	R4	Total	To par
13	F ANDERSSON	69	71	71	67	278	-10
	Niclas FASTH	67	69	72	70	278	-10
	M CAMPBELL	69	70	70	69	278	-10
16	A FORSBRAND	72	69	67	71	279	-9
	T JOHNSTONE	71	69	70	69	279	-9
	Jo RYSTROM	67	72	71	69	279	-9
	Olivier EDMOND	68	74	68	69	279	-9
	Darren CLARKE	66	70	70	73	279	-9
	Peter LONARD	71	68	69	71	279	-9
22	R CHAPMAN	69	69	72	70	280	-8
	R JACQUELIN	68	75	68	69	280	-8
	S WEBSTER	71	68	70	71	280	-8
25	Wayne RILEY	71	68	71	71	281	-7
	Thomas LEVET	67	72	67	75	281	-7
	Ian GARBUTT	71	71	69	70	281	-7
	Pierre FULKE	68	71	71	71	281	-7
29	C ROCCA	68	72	71	71	282	-6
	Brian DAVIS	71	71	69	71	282	-6
	Anthony WALL	63	76	71	72	282	-6
	J MOSELEY	70	71	66	75	282	-6
	Peter O'MALLEY	70	71	68	73	282	-6
	Paul LAWRIE	69	71	65	77	282	-6
	C PETTERSSON	74	68	70	70	282	-6
36	David HOWELL	73	70	66	74	283	-5
	J PARNEVIK	71	72	69	71	283	-5
	A HANSEN	71	72	70	70	283	-5
	S KJELDSEN	69	72	71	71	283	-5
	Fredrik HENGE	71	69	69	74	283	-5
	Peter BAKER	72	70	72	69	283	-5
	Carl SUNESON	68	74	72	69	283	-5
	Alex CEJKA	73	70	70	70	283	-5
	I GARRIDO	71	71	72	69	283	-5
	R RUSSELL	70	74	71	68	283	-5
	S GALLACHER	70	70	69	74	283	-5
47	D BOTES	71	68	72	73	284	-4
	P BROADHURST	71	73	69	71	284	-4
	P-U JOHANSSON	72	72	68	72	284	-4
	C CEVAER	71	69	73	71	284	-4
	S RICHARDSON	74	66	72	72	284	-4
	C HANELL	70	72	72	70	284	-4
53	G BRAND JNR.	72	71	72	70	285	-3
	Mark ROE	72	71	71	71	285	-3
	Mark McNULTY	70	71	70	74	285	-3
	Jamie SPENCE	69	74	70	72	285	-3
	Gary EVANS	72	71	72	70	285	-3
	B DREDGE	68	74	73	70	285	-3
59	Ian WOOSNAM	70	74	73	69	286	-2
	Marc FARRY	71	72	71	72	286	-2
	Richard GREEN	69	74	70	73	286	-2
	Steen TINNING	73	71	73	69	286	-2
	Peter MITCHELL	72	70	72	72	286	-2
	R GONZALEZ	71	73	75	67	286	-2
	F JACOBSON	71	73	71	71	286	-2
	Greg OWEN	73	71	70	72	286	-2
	David CARTER	70	70	73	73	286	-2
68	Hennie OTTO	69	74	74	70	287	-1
	H BJORNSTAD	73	70	71	73	287	-1
	N COLSAERTS	71	71	73	72	287	-1
	Olle KARLSSON	71	73	73	70	287	-1
72	Greg TURNER	72	72	74	70	288	E
	Carlos RODILES	72	71	71	74	288	E
74	M NORGREN	73	69	74	73	289	+1
	G HAVRET	67	73	75	74	289	+1
	R WINCHESTER	75	69	69	76	289	+1
	Van PHILLIPS	70	74	72	73	289	+1
	S SCAHILL	72	67	73	77	289	+1
	M JONZON	71	70	74	74	289	+1
80	H STENSON	70	74	74	72	290	+2
81	D TERBLANCHE	70	72	77	73	292	+4
82	T Jesus MUOZ	70	74	73	76	293	+5
83	N LEMKE (Am)	72	72	75	75	294	+6
84	M MACKENZIE	70	74	-	-	-	DISQ
	A OLDCORN	69	75	-	-	-	DISQ

Sponsored by Stan James

Tournament Report

It wasn't quite by the winning margin Colin Montgomerie enjoyed over the field the last time he won the Scandinavian Masters but the Scot still prevailed, this time by a single stroke, to win this event for the third time in his career.

In 1999, Monty led the best of the European Tour a merry dance at the Barseback course in Malmo to win by nine shots.

Two years on, the challenges were only the minimum distance away at stumps. It was as tight as the scoreline suggests but it shouldn't have been.

Monty started the day a shot behind defending champion, Lee Westwood, and Ian Poulter but pulled level ahead of the pack at the 11th, when a superb approach to two feet presented him with a tap in for birdie.

The Scot then picked up shots on two of the next three holes and by the time he was standing on the 17th tee, had pulled four strokes clear.

However, nervous bogeys on the final two holes gave Westwood and Poulter a chance. Westwood had the opportunity to force a play-off with birdies at either of the last two holes.

But last year's Order of Merit winner missed from 15 feet on the 17th and found only the packed galleries with his hooked 6-iron approach at the 18th and had to settle for par. Poulter, playing in the final group with Westwood, left his challenge too late, picking up his only birdie of the last day at the last hole.

MISSED THE CUT: Mark MOULAND 72 73, Sam TORRANCE 67 78, Barry LANE 72 73, Maarten LAFEBER 70 75, Paul NIL-BRINK 71 74, Justin ROSE 72 73, Per NYMAN 71 74, Michele REALE 76 69, Jonathan LOMAS 74 71, Phillip PRICE 75 70, Roger WESSELS 72 73, Paul STREETER 70 75, Robert COLES 70 75, David PARK 70 75, Lucas PARSONS 72 73, Per HAUGSRUD 73 73, Mathias GRONBERG 72 74, Diego BOR-REGO 75 71, Nicolas VANHOOTEGEM 73 73, John BICKER-TON 72 74, Mikael LUNDBERG 73 73, Alastair FORSYTH 75 71, Aaron BADDELEY 73 73, Paul CASEY 72 74, Santiago LUNA 74 73, Trevor IMMELMAN 78 69, Thomas GOGELE 72 75, Robert KARLSSON 74 73, Raimo SJOBERG 75 72, Massimo SCARPA 72 75, Mark PILKINGTON 73 74, Nic HENNING 76 71, Simon DYSON 72 75, Jose RIVERO 71 77, John SENDEN 74 74, Gary EMERSON 72 76, Olle NORDBERG 74 74, Paul EALES 75 73, Paolo QUIRICI 75 73, Jorge BERENDT 75 73, Francisco CEA 71 77, Erol SIMSEK 71 77, Niklas BRUZELIUS (Am) 75 73, Par NILSSON (Am) 71 77, Anders HULTMAN (Am) 74 75, Ge-off OGILVY 72 77, Gustavo ROJAS 73 76, Mikko ILONEN 75 74, Willhelm SCHAUMAN (Am) 74 75, Elliot BOULT 72 78, Mar-cello SANTI 77 73, Neil CHEETHAM 73 77, Tobias DIER 72 78, Graeme STORM 77 73, Peter MALMGREN 78 73, Richard S JOHNSON 76 75, Stephen DODD 75 76, Pehr MAGNEBRANT 77 74, Markus BRIER 74 77, Daren LEE 75 76, Lars JOHANSSON (Am) 76 75, Marco BERNARDINI 76 75, Sven STRUVER 75 77, Darren FICHARDT 79 73, David HIGGINS 77 75, Garry HOUS-TON 77 76, Patrik SJOLAND 74 79, Hank KUEHNE 73 82, Mats LANNER 79 77, Henrik NYSTROM 80 80, Rolf MUNTZ 78 W/D.

Sponsored by Stan James

Course Profile

Barseback Golf Club (par 72, 7,323 yards) staged this event last year (for the fifth time) and is a long but unusual course which switches styles from parkland to links (four holes around the turn next to a fjord) and back again.

Kungsangen Golf Club (par 72, 6,724 yards) is scheduled to host this tournament next year for the third time (after 1998 and 2000). It isn't a long course but puts a premium on accuracy with long irons.

Players/Points to Note

●**Colin Montgomerie** completed a hat-trick of Scandinavian Masters victories last season and his complete record in this event reads Win-40-7-12-2-12-8-16-Win-17-Win. He has finished in the top five of this event six times in the last 11 years. The Scot is 103-under par in that time and has a stroke average of 69.57. None of the Scot's wins, however, have come at next year's venue – Kungsangen Golf Club.

●**Lee Westwood** returned to form in 2001 in this tournament when taking a share of second place and he has never finished lower than 20th – winning the last renewal at Kungsangen in 2000.

●**Vijay Singh** makes the occasional visit and is always worth backing – as a win and a sub-70 stroke average suggests. **Paul Broadhurst** can boast four top-ten finishes in this event, while **Ian Poulter** and **Adam Scott** represent the younger generation who should go close after excellent performances in 2001.

●Scandinavian golfers have a superb record in this event, as you would expect (nine of the top 15 last season). **Jesper Parnevik** has won this event twice (1995 and 1998) and has also finished second and third.

●Other 'local' players to note are **Thomas Bjorn, Joakim Haeggman, Jarmo Sandelin, Robert Karlsson, Per-Ulrik Johansson, Michael Jonzon, Dennis Edlund, Niclas Fasth, Henrik Stenson, Soren Hansen** and **Soren Kjeldsen**.

Previous Results

2000: 1. Lee Westwood (-14), 2. Michael Camp-bell (-11), 3. Raymond Russell (-10).

1999: 1. Colin Montgomerie (-20), 2. Jesper Parnevik (-11), 3. Bob May (-10), Geoff Ogilvy (-10).

1998: 1. Jesper Parnevik (-11), 2. Darren Clarke (-8), 3. Stephen Field (-7).

1997: 1. Joakim Haeggman (-18), 2. Ignacio Garrido (-14), 3. Mats Hallberg (-13), Peter Baker (-13).

1996: 1. Lee Westwood (-7), won play-off, 2. Paul Broadhurst, Russell Claydon (-7).

CLETIC MANOR RESORT WALES OPEN

Celtic Manor Resort, 9 Aug to 12 Aug 2001, purse 1,228,124 euros

Pos	Name	R1	R2	R3	R4	Total	To par	Money	DD(y)	DA%	GIR%	Putts
1	Paul McGINLEY	67	71	-		138	-6	201,685	275.8	75.0	72.2	56
Won play-off												
2	Paul LAWRIE	67	71	-	-	138	-6	105,102	269.3	75.0	75.0	57
	Daren LEE	69	69	-	-	138	-6	105,102	258.5	89.3	86.1	62
4	A FORSBRAND	72	67	-	-	139	-5	51,389	263.8	85.7	77.8	60
	Mark PILKINGTON	68	71	-	-	139	-5	51,389	275.5	78.6	88.9	62
	J DONALDSON	68	71	-	-	139	-5	51,389	n/a	n/a	n/a	n/a
7	Anders HANSEN	72	68	-	-	140	-4	36,303	269.0	92.9	80.6	61
8	Steve WEBSTER	74	67	-	-	141	-3	24,020	275.0	71.4	61.1	54
	Nick O'HERN	70	71	-	-	141	-3	24,020	260.0	71.4	69.4	57
	Thomas LEVET	71	70	-	-	141	-3	24,020	258.8	75.0	66.7	58
	Roger WESSELS	68	73	-	-	141	-3	24,020	257.5	75.0	66.7	55
	Gary ORR	67	74	-	-	141	-3	24,020	258.8	89.3	66.7	55
	Nic HENNING	73	68	-	-	141	-3	24,020	258.5	67.9	63.9	56

Pos	Name	R1	R2	R3	R4	Total	To par
14	K SPURGEON	72	70	-	-	142	-2
	Sven STRUVER	72	70	-	-	142	-2
	J MOSELEY	70	72	-	-	142	-2
	Phillip PRICE	70	72	-	-	142	-2
	Simon DYSON	73	69	-	-	142	-2
	S GARDINER	69	73	-	-	142	-2
20	Santiago LUNA	72	71	-	-	143	-1
	W BENNETT	72	71	-	-	143	-1
	S KJELDSEN	70	73	-	-	143	-1
	John SENDEN	72	71	-	-	143	-1
	G RANKIN	68	75	-	-	143	-1
	Ian POULTER	71	72	-	-	143	-1
	Jean HUGO	72	71	-	-	143	-1
	J ROBINSON	73	70	-	-	143	-1
	J LOMAS	73	70	-	-	143	-1
	I GARRIDO	72	71	-	-	143	-1
	Simon HURD	69	74	-	-	143	-1
	David HIGGINS	73	70	-	-	143	-1
	A FORSYTH	72	71	-	-	143	-1
33	A OLDCORN	69	75	-	-	144	-1
	Mark ROE	70	74	-	-	144	-1
	Marc FARRY	71	73	-	-	144	-1
	Mark McNULTY	77	67	-	-	144	-1
	T IMMELMAN	72	72	-	-	144	-1
	Justin ROSE	71	73	-	-	144	-1
	Fredrik HENGE	72	72	-	-	144	-1
	R WINCHESTER	68	76	-	-	144	-1
	Per NYMAN	72	72	-	-	144	-1
	Alex CEJKA	74	70	-	-	144	-1
	D TERBLANCHE	77	67	-	-	144	-1
	David LYNN	69	75	-	-	144	-1
	M JONZON	70	74	-	-	144	-1
	J BICKERTON	71	73	-	-	144	-1
	Paul CASEY	74	70	-	-	144	-1
	C PETTERSSON	74	70	-	-	144	-1
49	Ian WOOSNAM	73	72	-	-	145	-1
	J Milkha SINGH	75	70	-	-	145	-1
	Barry LANE	71	74	-	-	145	-1
	Anthony WALL	72	73	-	-	145	-1
	Dennis EDLUND	72	73	-	-	145	-1
	T GOGELE	70	75	-	-	145	-1
	Olivier EDMOND	75	70	-	-	145	-1
	Gary EVANS	72	73	-	-	145	-1
	Jorge BERENDT	74	71	-	-	145	-1
	T Jesus MUOZ	70	75	-	-	145	-1
	Markus BRIER	72	73	-	-	145	-1
	F ANDERSSON	72	73	-	-	145	-1
	David CARTER	70	75	-	-	145	-1
	S GALLACHER	74	71	-	-	145	-1
	M BERNARDINI	73	72	-	-	145	-1
	C WILLIAMS (Am)	74	71	-	-	145	-1
65	Wayne RILEY	70	76	-	-	146	-1
	Gary MURPHY	71	75	-	-	146	-1
	M LAFEBER	72	74	-	-	146	-1
	Richard GREEN	73	73	-	-	146	-1
	Marcus HIGLEY	70	76	-	-	146	-1
	G HOUSTON	73	73	-	-	146	-1
	D BOTES	73	73	-	-	146	-1
	S D HURLEY	75	71	-	-	146	-1
	Andrew BEAL	74	72	-	-	146	-1
	M SCARPA	74	72	-	-	146	-1
	S RICHARDSON	74	72	-	-	146	-1
	Sion E BEBB	72	74	-	-	146	-1
	S SCAHILL	72	74	-	-	146	-1
	B DREDGE	73	73	-	-	146	-1
	David PARK	72	74	-	-	146	-1
	J SANDELIN	71	75	-	-	146	-1
	Erol SIMSEK	72	74	-	-	146	-1

Sponsored by Stan James

Tournament Report

Pual McGinley won a three-man, five-hole play-off to capture the Wales Open at the Celtic Manor Resort and take a step closer to Sam Torrance's Ryder Cup team.

The event was curtailed to 36 holes after heavy rain forced regulation play to be abandoned after the second round – which wasn't completed until late on Saturday.

Further rain on Sunday meant it was impossible to play a full 18 holes, so the European Tour took the decision, for the first time in their history, to settle the event by way of a play-off (other 36-hole weather shortened tournaments were awarded to the halfway leader).

McGinley, Paul Lawrie and Daren Lee, the only man to shoot two sub 70 rounds in regulation play, headed to the 12th hole, a par three 211-yard affair, which was used exclusively for the extra-time decider.

Lee had the first chance to win but missed from nine feet after a superb tee shot. Back the trio went, after pars all round. The second attempt saw Lawrie drop out after three-putting, McGinley missed from six feet minutes later, so the Irishman and Englishman went back for a third time.

Bogey fours followed for the pair after they both found the bunker. Lee holed a six-footer to stay alive on the fourth time the 12th was played but failed to repeat the trick when the duo teed up for a fifth time, handing the title to McGinley when the Irishman got up and down from the bunker.

MISSED THE CUT: Gordon BRAND JNR. 75 72, Des SMYTH 74 73, David GILFORD 77 70, Craig HAINLINE 72 75, Jamie SPENCE 75 72, Peter BAKER 75 72, Robin BYRD 74 73, Marcello SANTI 73 74, Stephen DODD 77 70, Ian GARBUTT 74 73, Diego BORREGO 73 74, Nicolas VANHOOTEGEM 72 75, Robert COLES 75 72, Graeme STORM 73 74, Sam TORRANCE 72 76, Shaun P WEBSTER 73 75, Gary EMERSON 72 76, Steen TINNING 76 72, Russell CLAYDON 73 75, Raymond RUSSELL 72 76, Mikael LUNDBERG 69 79, David HOWELL 72 77, Carl SUNESON 75 74, Rolf MUNTZ 76 73, Gustavo ROJAS 73 76, Paul STREETER 73 76, Andrew COLTART 76 73, Dean ROBERTSON 75 74, Lucas PARSONS 71 78, Tobias DIER 73 76, M MACKENZIE 77 73, N CHEETHAM 76 74, M REALE 75 75, F CEA 75 75, H NYSTROM 75 75, M BLACKEY 72 78, M PLUMMER 78 72, M GRIFFITHS (Am) 73 77, M CAIN 75 76, H OTTO 73 78, A MARSHALL 77 74, J ROMERO 73 78, P FOWLER 77 75, B VAUGHAN 74 78, P BROADHURST 79 73, N COLSAERTS 77 75, R DINSDALE 78 74, B TEILLERIA 78 74, M CAPONE 73 79, R MCFARLANE 75 78, P EALES 77 76, M FLORIOLI 78 75, C CEVAER 75 78, D DIXON 74 79,V PHILLIPS 76 78, P WALTON 78 77, J-F REMESY 75 80, S WALKER 78 77, I CAMPBELL (Am) 77 78, R DRUMMOND 78 79, R DAVIS 81 77, P SJOLAND 79 79, T JOHNSTONE 75 RETD, M MOULAND 74 W/D, P MITCHELL 75 RETD, A RAITT 76 RETD, C HANELL 75 W/D, P GRIBBEN RETD, E DARCY RETD.

Course Profile

Robert Trent Jones designed The Celtic Manor venue (par 72, 7,324 yards) which opened in 1999.

It is a long, physically demanding venue that does favours big hitters but players also have to be accurate with their drives.

The layout is built in and around a valley so, as well as steep sided fairways, there are also flat landing areas. Unorthodox lies have to be combatted.

The layout runs along the River Usk and water comes into play on eight holes.

Players/Points to Note

●The Wales Open has been on the European Tour schedule for the past two years but a big increase in prize money and a change of date in the calendar saw last season's event attract a better field. Unfortunately, poor weather forced the event to be cut to 36 holes.

●Celtic Manor Resort will stage the 2010 Ryder Cup and it would come as no surprise if this event gets a bigger following. Expect more star names to play at one of the best new courses in the country.

●The Welsh are a fiercely patriotic bunch and it is surely only a matter of time before one of their own wins this event. **Phillip Price** is the obvious player to advise. He lives just around the corner and has played the layout many times. Price was fifth in the inaugural event in 2000 and came 14th last year.

●**Ian Woosnam** should have won in 2000, after leading going into the final round, but could manage only third. After winning the World Matchplay at Wentworth in 2001, though, a more confident Woosie will surely fancy his chances in 2002.

●Other home players such as **David Park**, **Mark Mouland** and **Paul Affleck** could also be worth following if in form.

●**Nick O'Hern** has finished in the top ten twice, while **John Senden** has had two top 20s.

Previous Results

2000: 1. Steen Tinning (-15), 2. David Howell (-14), 3. Ian Woosnam (-12), Fredrik Jacobson (-12).

Paul McGinley player profile – page 220

NORTH WEST OF IRELAND OPEN

Slieve G.C., 16 Aug to 19 Aug 2001, purse 357,560 euros

Pos	Name	R1	R2	R3	R4	Total	To par	Money	DD(y)	DA%	GIR%	Putts
1	Tobias DIER	66	68	66	71	271	-17	58,330	282.1	67.9	83.3	116
2	Stephen DODD	67	68	68	69	272	-16	38,880	290.0	73.2	83.3	121
3	Mark PILKINGTON	68	69	69	68	274	-14	21,910	301.5	87.5	86.1	128
4	Mattias ELIASSON	67	70	72	68	277	-11	16,170	n/a	n/a	n/a	n/a
	J HEPWORTH	68	69	72	68	277	-11	16,170	n/a	n/a	n/a	n/a
6	Peter HANSON	75	65	67	71	278	-10	8,797	274.6	62.5	77.8	118
	D HOSPITAL	70	69	73	66	278	-10	8,797	269.9	55.4	66.7	120
	Peter HEDBLOM	71	67	70	70	278	-10	8,797	303.8	69.6	88.9	133
	David HIGGINS	69	71	69	69	278	-10	8,797	275.1	69.6	70.8	114
	A LJUNGGREN	72	71	66	69	278	-10	8,797	n/a	n/a	n/a	n/a
	Graeme STORM	69	73	70	66	278	-10	8,797	275.1	60.7	72.2	119

Pos	Name	R1	R2	R3	R4	Total	To par
12	R Jan DERKSEN	68	68	69	74	279	-9
	Kenneth FERRIE	70	68	73	68	279	-9
	J Maria ARRUTI	65	72	70	72	279	-9
	Johan SKOLD	71	69	69	70	279	-9
	Joakim RASK	71	72	68	68	279	-9
17	C CEVAER	74	69	67	70	280	-8
	J DONALDSON	69	69	72	70	280	-8
19	Niels KRAAIJ	72	71	71	67	281	-7
	D McGRANE	70	70	72	69	281	-7
	Grant DODD	68	70	75	68	281	-7
	Graham RANKIN	71	70	70	70	281	-7
	R GUILLARD	76	68	67	70	281	-7
	T IMMELMAN	71	71	70	69	281	-7
	J ROBINSON	73	71	68	69	281	-7
	J RYSTROM	71	73	67	70	281	-7
	Andrew RAITT	74	68	67	72	281	-7
	M JONZON	68	70	71	72	281	-7
29	Klas ERIKSSON	72	69	71	70	282	-6
	Gary MURPHY	72	70	73	67	282	-6
	Kalle BRINK	72	70	71	69	282	-6
	Gary EVANS	72	72	68	70	282	-6
	M BLACKEY	70	69	71	72	282	-6
34	Peter FOWLER	72	71	74	66	283	-5
	Euan LITTLE	74	70	68	71	283	-5
	S D HURLEY	71	71	70	71	283	-5
	R SJOBERG	72	71	73	67	283	-5
38	G HUTCHEON	68	72	74	70	284	-4
	Alberto BINAGHI	71	70	71	72	284	-4
	Philip GOLDING	74	69	70	71	284	-4
	M NILSSON	72	68	73	71	284	-4
	D DE VOOGHT	74	70	67	73	284	-4
43	Des SMYTH	72	72	72	69	285	-3
	Robin BYRD	73	68	72	72	285	-3
	M TUNNICLIFF	72	71	71	71	285	-3
	G BARUFFALDI	72	68	74	71	285	-3
	Robert COLES	74	70	71	70	285	-3
	B HAFTHORSSON	72	72	72	69	285	-3
49	Paul NILBRINK	72	71	69	74	286	-2
	Craig HAINLINE	72	70	71	73	286	-2
	Chris GANE	75	67	69	75	286	-2
	Dennis EDLUND	69	69	75	73	286	-2
	Simon KHAN	73	66	76	71	286	-2
	Alan McLEAN	71	73	72	70	286	-2
55	K STORGAARD	70	72	73	72	287	-1
	Michele REALE	70	70	71	76	287	-1
	F BISAZZA	75	69	69	74	287	-1
	G PIETROBONO	71	71	77	68	287	-1
	Carlos LARRAIN	74	68	73	72	287	-1
	S DELAGRANGE	70	74	72	71	287	-1
	Nic HENNING	71	73	68	75	287	-1
62	Eric CARLBERG	70	74	70	74	288	E
	P GOTTFRIDSON	71	73	72	72	288	E
	Marcello SANTI	73	69	72	74	288	E
	Jose ROMERO	71	71	74	72	288	E
	F HOWLEY	75	68	75	70	288	E
	S WAKEFIELD	69	71	73	75	288	E
68	P PURHONEN	74	67	74	74	289	+1
	Ian HUTCHINGS	75	68	72	74	289	+1
70	A MARSHALL	67	74	74	75	290	+2
	M VIBE-HASTRUP	71	70	78	71	290	+2
	W HUGET	70	72	73	75	290	+2
	T NORRET	73	70	76	71	290	+2
74	Jorge BERENDT	72	72	72	75	291	+3
	D NOUAILHAC	70	71	74	76	291	+3
	John MELLOR	75	67	74	75	291	+3
	Kariem BARAKA	73	70	77	71	291	+3
78	M OLANDER	73	71	79	69	292	+4
	G HOUSTON	74	70	76	72	292	+4
	Stuart LITTLE	70	74	75	73	292	+4
81	John DIGNAM	69	75	74	75	293	+5
	David DIXON	71	71	77	74	293	+5
83	M BERNARDINI	72	69	72	82	295	+7
84	R WINCHESTER	73	70	78	75	296	+8
85	A BUTTERFIELD	75	68	80	74	297	+9
86	Philip WALTON	71	71	-	-	-	RETD

Sponsored by Stan James

Tournament Report

Germany's Tobias Dier became the eighth first-time winner on the 2001 European Tour when he captured the North West of Ireland Open by finishing a stroke ahead of playing partner Stephen Dodd of Wales.

Dier, who last year shot a course record 65 on his way to finishing fourth in this event, continued his love affair with the Slieve Russell Hotel, Golf and Country Club, shooting a closing 71 for a 17-under par total of 271 to finish one clear of Dodd with Mark Pilkington, also of Wales, a further two shots adrift.

Dodd briefly closed the gap to just one shot with a birdie on the par three fourth hole as Dier bogeyed but the German pulled clear again with back to back birdies on the next two holes and then moved four clear with a third birdie of the round on the ninth.

After bogeying the 15th Dier remained three ahead and seemed destined for his first title until the 17th where he bogeyed as Dodd birdied to close the gap to a solitary shot playing the par five last.

Dier played his approach first, hitting a two iron to 30 feet but Dodd followed with the same club to 15 feet to set up a dramatic finale. The German putted first, leaving his putt dead for a birdie four but Dodd still had the chance to take the tournament into a play-off but his putt didn't turn as much as he thought and narrowly slipped by the cup.

MISSED THE CUT: Alvaro SALTO 72 73, Sean QUINLIVAN 75 70, Adam MEDNICK 76 69, Paul STREETER 74 71, Mikael PILTZ 74 71, Fredrik ANDERSSON 73 72, Lee S JAMES 75 70, Benoit TEILLERIA 75 70, Knut EKJORD 74 71, Fredrik WIDMARK 73 72, Ashley ROESTOFF 74 71, Andrew SHERBORNE 73 73, John WADE 74 72, Scott DRUMMOND 73 73, Robert McGUIRK 74 72, Massimo FLORIOLI 74 72, Christophe POTTIER 71 75, Massimo SCARPA 72 74, Steven RICHARDSON 73 73, Gustavo ROJAS 74 72, Grant HAMERTON 73 73, Pascal EDMOND 75 71, Kalle VAINOLA 73 74, Jean-Francois LUCQUIN 74 73, Andrew BEAL 75 72, Carl WATTS 76 71, Stephen SCAHILL 74 73, Gary CLARK 73 74, Iain PYMAN 74 73, Michael ALLAN 76 71, David ORR 73 74, Mike CAPONE 76 71, Wayne RILEY 72 76, Paul SHERMAN 73 75, Marcus CAIN 77 71, Martin ERLANDSSON 77 71, Peter LAWRIE 75 73, Nils ROERBAEK 76 72, Pehr MAGNEBRANT 76 72, Francesco GUERMANI 77 71, Andre BOSSERT 71 77, Paul DWYER 72 76, Tony EDLUND 75 73, Simon HURD 74 74, Ola ELIASSON 76 72, Bjorn PETTERSSON 72 76, Hank KUEHNE 76 72, Magnus PERSSON 74 75, Mark FOSTER 74 75, Shaun P WEBSTER 78 72, Hennie WALTERS 76 74, Richard BLAND 78 72, Benn BARHAM 77 73, Franck AUMONIER 75 75, Sam WALKER 77 74, Paul BROADHURST 78 74, Chris BENIANS 74 78, Neil CHEETHAM 76 76, Charles CHALLEN 76 76, Per LARSSON 77 76, Richard GILLOT 76 77, Sebastien BRANGER 80 73, David WALKER 77 76, Andre CRUSE 77 76, Thomas HAVEMANN 79 74, John DWYER 78 78, Liam MCCOOL 79 79, Michael ARCHER 74 W/D, Luis CLAVERIE RETD, Paddy GRIBBEN 73 RETD.

Sponsored by Stan James

Course Profile

In 2000, the Slieve Russell Hotel Golf Club (par 72, 7,053 yards) was the venue for this tournament.

The course has generous fairways so distance rather than accuracy off the tee is more important.

The greens have some devilish slopes on them but are relatively slow. In 2002, the event will move to Ballyliffin Golf Club (par 72, 7,102 yards) in county Donegal.

A links venue that meanders among sand dunes with most holes having well-guarded greens.

Players/Points to Note

● This is a co-sanctioned event between the full European Tour and the Challenge Tour. The two tours provide half the field each. The top end of the Challenge Tour is probably as good as the lower end of the full tour, so always consider those players that are in the top ten of the Challenge Tour Order of Merit. Especially those who have won recently as the confidence of success might just push them to glory in this event.

● **Tobias Dier** won in 2001, 12 months after placing fourth, so it shouldn't have been that much of a surprise.

● **Gary Emerson** has finished 11th and seventh in 1999 and 2000 renewals respectively. Only once has he shot an over par score leaving him with a stroke average of 70.13.

● **Stephen Dodd** has played all three North West of Ireland Open's to date and is getting progressively better – as form figures of 40-32-2 suggest

● **Gary Murphy** shared the lead after the second round in 2000 with the Kilkenny golfer eventually finishing seventh. That followed up 35th position in 1999. Last year he was 29th.

● **Trevor Immelman** has placed 15th and 19th on his last two starts in this event while **Fredrik Henge**, **Mark Pilkington**, **Graeme Storm**, **Grant Dood** and **Jesus Maria Arruti** can boast two top-30 finishes.

Previous Results

2000: 1. Massimo Scarpa (-13), 2. Mikael Lundberg (-12), 3. Andrew Beal (-11).

1999: 1. Costantino Rocca (-12), 2. Padraig Harrington (-10), 3. Paul Broadhurst (-9), Gary Evans (-9), Des Smyth (-9).

Stephen Dodd player profile – page 196

SCOTTISH PGA

Gleneagles, 23 Aug to 26 Aug 2001, purse 1,599,464 euros

Pos	Name	R1	R2	R3	R4	Total	To par	Money	DD(y)	DA%	GIR%	Putts
1	Paul CASEY	69	69	67	69	274	-14	263,034	283.3	63.5	76.4	114
2	Alex CEJKA	71	67	66	71	275	-13	175,361	280.8	61.5	80.6	118
3	David HOWELL	70	71	66	70	277	-11	98,799	267.6	61.5	75.0	116
4	Gary EVANS	66	67	77	68	278	-10	67,023	280.0	69.2	81.9	124
	Christian CEVAER	72	71	69	66	278	-10	67,023	262.5	63.5	69.4	110
	C PETTERSSON	75	66	70	67	278	-10	67,023	284.1	65.4	66.7	113
7	Peter HANSON	74	64	69	72	279	-9	38,430	273.1	61.5	68.1	114
	Jonathan LOMAS	66	74	70	69	279	-9	38,430	274.3	78.8	76.4	119
	D TERBLANCHE	73	70	70	66	279	-9	38,430	269.0	67.3	70.8	114
	S GALLAGHER	67	71	69	72	279	-9	38,430	284.1	65.4	70.8	114

Pos	Name	R1	R2	R3	R4	Total	To par
11	M MOULAND	65	70	73	72	280	-8
	A OLDCORN	70	67	73	70	280	-8
	Des SMYTH	71	71	68	70	280	-8
	Justin ROSE	67	71	68	74	280	-8
	P O'MALLEY	68	72	70	70	280	-8
	S SCAHILL	69	74	69	68	280	-8
	David HIGGINS	67	71	70	72	280	-8
18	R CHAPMAN	72	70	70	69	281	-7
	Gary MURPHY	68	69	70	74	281	-7
	R WESSELS	69	72	68	72	281	-7
	Paul LAWRIE	75	69	69	68	281	-7
22	M MACKENZIE	75	66	70	71	282	-6
	Mark ROE	73	71	69	69	282	-6
	Greg TURNER	69	67	75	71	282	-6
	P BROADHURST	68	69	73	72	282	-6
	J RYSTRUM	72	69	67	74	282	-6
	David LYNN	69	70	72	71	282	-6
	Simon DYSON	69	70	69	74	282	-6
29	R KARLSSON	70	69	70	74	283	-5
	Stephen DODD	73	70	70	70	283	-5
	Ian GARBUTT	70	72	70	71	283	-5
	N VANHOOTEGEM	73	65	69	76	283	-5
	J SANDELIN	72	66	72	73	283	-5
	J DONALDSON	69	71	71	72	283	-5
35	Peter FOWLER	66	68	78	72	284	-4
	Carlos RODILES	69	67	75	73	284	-4
37	Mark JAMES	72	71	70	72	285	-3
	S TORRANCE	68	74	70	73	285	-3
	Brian DAVIS	72	72	69	72	285	-3
	Anthony WALL	69	74	70	72	285	-3
	Jamie SPENCE	71	68	72	74	285	-3
	R CLAYDON	70	72	74	69	285	-3
	Rolf MUNTZ	69	72	74	70	285	-3
	Andrew RAITT	73	67	72	73	285	-3
	D ROBERTSON	72	69	73	71	285	-3
	N DOUGHERTY	70	74	70	71	285	-3
47	R DRUMMOND	71	72	71	72	286	-2
	S KJELDSEN	71	68	71	76	286	-2
	T IMMELMAN	71	73	70	72	286	-2
	Colin GILLIES	74	66	70	76	286	-2
51	Wayne RILEY	69	72	72	74	287	-1
	W BENNETT	67	75	72	73	287	-1
	David PARK	73	70	70	74	287	-1
	M PILKINGTON	72	69	74	72	287	-1
	R RUSSELL	71	70	68	78	287	-1
56	Eamonn DARCY	73	69	73	73	288	E
	A FORSBRAND	68	70	80	70	288	E
	S P WEBSTER	70	72	74	72	288	E
	Olivier EDMOND	68	74	73	73	288	E
	Robert ARNOTT	74	66	71	77	288	E
61	B MARCHBANK	75	69	71	74	289	+1
	D BOTES	71	70	74	74	289	+1
	Daren LEE	72	71	74	72	289	+1
64	Santiago LUNA	71	72	74	73	290	+2
	G HOUSTON	74	70	71	75	290	+2
	John SENDEN	72	70	70	78	290	+2
	Olle KARLSSON	72	72	73	73	290	+2
68	David GILFORD	74	70	74	73	291	+3
	G RANKIN	74	70	73	74	291	+3
	M GRONBERG	73	71	75	72	291	+3
71	Sandy LYLE	72	71	75	74	292	+4
	Jean HUGO	73	71	72	76	292	+4
73	Neil CHEETHAM	74	70	72	77	293	+5
74	G HAVRET	69	73	75	77	294	+6
	Paul EALES	70	74	78	72	294	+6
76	R WINCHESTER	73	70	79	73	295	+7
77	Craig HAINLINE	72	72	75	77	296	+8
	Soren HANSEN	74	69	77	76	296	+8
	Van PHILLIPS	75	69	77	75	296	+8

Sponsored by Stan James

Tournament Report

On only his 11th European Tour start as a professional, Paul Casey won the Scottish PGA Championship at Gleneagles. The 24-year-old former US College amateur star produced a last round 69 to over haul overnight leader Alex Cejka by a shot with David Howell two shots further adrift.

At the halfway stage, victory looked unlikely for Casey as he trailed Gary Evans by five shots. But Casey's third round 67 put him in contention, Evans slipped away carding a score ten shots worse. There was still work to do, though, as Cejka, after a Saturday 66, led. The first shake up on the leaderbaord came at the third, when Casey birdied and Cejka bogeyed, the two shot swing in saw the Surrey based pro take the lead.

But the German wouldn't give up and got back on level terms. And when Howell holed his second shot from just over 100 yards at the 13th, there was suddenly a three-way tie for first place.

Howell's challenge faded down the stretch, however, and when Casey went two ahead following a birdie at the 16th, time was running out for Cejka. The gap did close to one when the German picked up a shot on the 17th but Casey showed few nerves when rolling in an eight-footer on the last to win by a single stroke.

Evans held on to fourth spot along with Swede Carl Pettersson and Frenchman Christian Cevaer, whose weekend scores of 69-66 weren't bettered.

MISSED THE CUT: M GRAY 75 70, E BOULT 74 71, H BJORN-STAD 75 70, P STREETER 71 74, F JACOBSON 77 68, F CEA 76 69, A COLTART 71 74, M BLACKEY 74 71, B TEILLERIA 75 70, M BERNARDINI 74 71, A FORSYTH 69 76, T JOHN-STONE 73 73, H STENSON 74 72, T LEVET 74 72, P MITCHELL 73 73, N COLSAERTS 71 75, J ROBINSON 76 70, M SANTI 73 73, C SUNESON 74 72, F ANDERSSON 72 74, D CARTER 74 72, M LUNDBERG 71 75, B HUME 73 73, R GREEN 70 77, G LAW 76 71, F HENGE 70 77, P BAKER 74 73, M FLO-RIOLI 74 73, R COLES 75 72, G OWEN 78 69, J STEVEN-SON 77 70, S O'HARA 72 75, M LAFEBER 77 71, R S JOHNSON 75 73, M REALE 71 77, T J MUOZ 78 70, S HENDERSON 72 76, E SIMSEK 73 75, N HENNING 75 73, S LEANEY 75 74, J MOSELEY 74 75, J BERENDT 77 72, S RICHARDSON 78 71, L PARSONS 72 77, K PHILLIPS 75 74, B RUMFORD 76 73, K HARRISON 76 73, C LEE 77 72, H NYSTROM 76 74, C RONALD 74 76, C HANELL 74 76, G STORM 74 76, S STRU-VER 76 75, J CHILLAS 77 74, D BORREGO 74 77, B DREDGE 72 79, A CRERAR 75 76, S SMITH 72 79, G ROJAS 76 76, P SJOLAND 77 75, G BRAND JNR. 79 74, R WEIR 78 75, B VAUGHAN 78 75, G EMERSON 79 74, J GREAVES 77 77, M URQUHART 77 77, G MCINNES 78 76, M WARREN (Am) 78 76, M LOFTUS 79 77, D J RUSSELL 80 77, N SCOTT-SMITH 76 83, S McALLISTER 85 77, S ORR 83 80, R RAFFERTY DISQ, S WEBSTER 71 DISQ, T GOGELE RETD, M SCARPA 81 W/D.

Sponsored by Stan James

Course Profile

The PGA Centenary Course (which used to be known as the Monarch's course, par 72, 7,060 yards) was designed by Jack Nicklaus and is one of Scotland's longest inland layouts.

When the weather is bad, the course can play tough and long.

The fairways are undulating but aren't particularly narrow. The rough, though, isn't maintained and is punishing.

The weather can be a factor and the wind has got up in recent renewals. Hitting fairways seems the key to victory.

Players/Points to Note

●This tournament started life as a weak event which took its field from both the European Tour and some 70 or so Scottish professionals. But it is getting a better reputation. **Colin Montgomerie** nearly played here last year and although it is once again opposite a WGC event in America in 2002 (as it has been for the past two renewals), the decent prize money on offer and the superb course which stages the event should see a good field.

●The young guns of the European Tour took this event by storm last year, with **Paul Casey** winning and high finishes for **Carl Pettersson** and **Justin Rose**.

●**Grant Hammerton** has had two top-11 finishes in this event. **Andrew Oldcorn** has placed 11th in 2000 and 2001. **Jonathon Lomas** can also boast two top-20 finishes over the past two years.

●**Rolf Muntz** was second at Gleneagles in 1999 and 20th in 2000, although he only placed 37th last year.

●**Roger Chapman** has finished in the top 25 on three occasions.

●The Monarch course at Gleneagles is used for this event but one of the other courses and the Scottish golf complex was used to host the Scottish Open from 1987 to 1994. The winners there include **Ian Woosnam** (twice), **Barry Lane** and **Peter O'Malley**.

Previous Results

2000: 1. Pierre Fulke (-17), 2. Henrik Nystrom (-15), Raphael Jaquelin (-11).

1999: 1. Warren Bennett (-6), won play-off, 2. Rolf Muntz (-6), 3. Klas Eriksson (-5), Roger Winchester (-5).

Paul Casey player profile – page 193

BMW INTERNATIONAL OPEN

Golfclub Munchen, 30 Aug to 2 Sep 2001, purse 1,824,192 euros

Pos	Name	R1	R2	R3	R4	Total	To par	Money	DD(y)	DA%	GIR%	Putts
1	John DALY	63	64	68	66	261	-27	300,000	315.1	69.6	81.9	112
2	P HARRINGTON	69	63	62	68	262	-26	200,000	280.4	71.4	83.3	110
3	Thomas LEVET	70	66	64	68	268	-20	112,680	281.8	67.9	84.7	119
4	R RUSSELL	68	66	66	69	269	-19	76,440	264.1	69.6	81.9	113
	D ROBERTSON	64	69	69	67	269	-19	76,440	272.8	82.1	77.8	112
	C HANELL	71	65	66	67	269	-19	76,440	274.0	62.5	76.4	110
7	Sergio GARCIA	67	67	69	67	270	-18	46,440	293.1	62.5	69.4	108
	Justin ROSE	67	69	68	66	270	-18	46,440	285.1	66.1	75.0	110
	Paul CASEY	69	67	69	65	270	-18	46,440	282.5	58.9	76.4	113
10	Soren KJELDSEN	65	70	71	65	271	-17	33,360	271.4	66.1	73.6	113
	Paul MCGINLEY	70	66	68	67	271	-17	33,360	276.1	67.9	77.8	113
	David CARTER	69	66	68	68	271	-17	33,360	280.0	82.1	87.5	124

Pos	Name	R1	R2	R3	R4	Total	To par
13	J M OLAZABAL	70	62	70	70	272	-16
	R JACQUELIN	68	67	70	67	272	-16
	C MONTGOMERIE	69	69	68	66	272	-16
16	B LANGER	67	69	69	68	273	-15
	W BENNETT	69	68	69	67	273	-15
	P O'MALLEY	71	67	66	69	273	-15
	Thomas BJORN	65	67	65	76	273	-15
	C PETTERSSON	66	69	70	68	273	-15
21	Alex CEJKA	69	66	69	70	274	-14
	R GONZALEZ	67	68	69	70	274	-14
23	Sandy LYLE	69	71	71	65	276	-12
	Stephen DODD	69	70	69	68	276	-12
	F JACOBSON	68	66	68	74	276	-12
	F ANDERSSON	69	68	69	70	276	-12
	Retief GOOSEN	68	69	68	71	276	-12
	M LUNDBERG	72	68	70	66	276	-12
	Adam SCOTT	67	64	77	68	276	-12
30	Greg TURNER	69	70	71	67	277	-11
	A HANSEN	69	69	70	69	277	-11
	Steen TINNING	74	66	69	68	277	-11
	J RYSTROM	67	70	70	70	277	-11
	R CLAYDON	70	70	72	65	277	-11
	Paul LAWRIE	70	70	69	68	277	-11
	S GALLACHER	67	70	68	72	277	-11
37	Mark MOULAND	68	68	70	72	278	-10
	Ian WOOSNAM	69	67	71	71	278	-10
	Barry LANE	69	69	70	70	278	-10
	John SENDEN	68	67	70	73	278	-10
	G HAVRET	68	70	70	70	278	-10
	Jorge BERENDT	69	67	71	71	278	-10
	Robert COLES	72	66	68	72	278	-10
	Markus BRIER	72	68	70	68	278	-10
	Brett RUMFORD	68	68	69	73	278	-10
46	D BOTES	70	70	69	70	279	-9
	Carl SUNESON	72	68	70	69	279	-9
	R WESSELS	66	70	72	71	279	-9
	Gary ORR	68	69	71	71	279	-9
	Mikko ILONEN	71	68	68	72	279	-9
	A FORSYTH	68	66	74	71	279	-9
	N DOUGHERTY	71	68	68	72	279	-9
53	M LAFEBER	72	68	71	69	280	-8
	Richard GREEN	63	69	75	73	280	-8
	J HAEGGMAN	67	71	71	71	280	-8
	R KARLSSON	70	68	71	71	280	-8
	I GARRIDO	68	72	71	69	280	-8
	S SCAHILL	71	66	71	72	280	-8
	Graeme STORM	71	69	68	72	280	-8
60	A OLDCORN	67	69	70	75	281	-7
	E ROMERO	71	67	71	72	281	-7
	P MITCHELL	68	70	72	71	281	-7
	Greg OWEN	69	67	74	71	281	-7
	David PARK	68	71	74	68	281	-7
	Niclas FASTH	67	71	71	72	281	-7
	J BICKERTON	67	68	72	74	281	-7
67	T JOHNSTONE	66	71	72	73	282	-6
	Marc FARRY	67	67	75	73	282	-6
	Brian DAVIS	68	68	74	72	282	-6
	T IMMELMAN	70	69	69	74	282	-6
	Pierre FULKE	69	71	72	70	282	-6
	David LYNN	70	69	70	73	282	-6
73	J LOMAS	66	71	74	72	283	-5
74	Soren HANSEN	68	70	78	68	284	-4
75	Mark JAMES	72	67	74	72	285	-3
76	J SANDELIN	69	71	70	76	286	-2
77	A COLTART	69	71	74	73	287	-1
78	Sven STRUVER	71	69	76	73	289	+1
79	Patrik SJOLAND	74	66	78	76	294	+6

Sponsored by Stan James

Tournament Report

The focus was meant to be on the scramble for Ryder Cup places but instead John Daly took centre stage to win for the first time in six years.

The 1995 Open champion captured the BMW International with a European Tour record low score of 27-under and saw off the challenge of Padraig Harrington – the sixth time this term that the Irishman has found one player too good.

The top ten in the Ryder Cup points table didn't change despite the fact Phillip Price, currently in tenth place, missed the cut at the Nord Eichenried.

So the drama was confined to 'Big' John, who certainly seems to be winning his battle with the booze – he's been teetotal for 13 months, and Harrington, who between them produced some fantastic golf at the Munich venue. Daly led from day one, after an opening 63, followed up with a 64 on day two.

Amazingly, though, it was Harrington who led going into the final round after a flawless Saturday 62. And after trading birdies through the final round the pair were deadlocked at 26-under standing on the par five last. Then disaster struck the Irishman as he found water with his second shot and had to take a penalty.

Daly comfortably birdied the last to take the spoils. Frenchman, Thomas Levet, was a distant third, while Dean Robertson's tie for fourth, along with Ray Russell and Christopher Hanell, just wasn't enough to hoist him into the Ryder Cup reckoning.

MISSED THE CUT: M ROE 71 70, P HANSON 69 72, C RODILES 72 69, M A JIMENEZ 67 74, P QUIRICI 71 70, P PRICE 71 70, D BORREGO 69 72, T J MUOZ 69 72, D TERBLANCHE 70 71, N HENNING 70 71, S DYSON 71 70, S BALLESTEROS 70 72, S LUNA 70 72, W RILEY 69 73, P PLATZ 77 65, S LEANEY 71 71, A WALL 72 70, H BJORNSTAD 74 68, P EALES 71 71, T DIER 71 71, A FORSBRAND 71 72, D SMYTH 72 71, P FOWLER 69 74, D GILFORD 74 69, E BOULT 69 74, F HENGE 70 73, R S JOHNSON 73 70, N COLSAERTS 73 70, M SIEM 75 68, J MOSELEY 69 74, M SCARPA 72 71, V PHILLIPS 74 69, B DREDGE 70 73, F CEA 69 74, D LEE 71 72, I POULTER 73 71, G EMERSON 72 72, J HUGO 71 73, O KARLSSON 76 68, M REALE 71 73, M GRONBERG 74 70, H NYSTROM 69 75, K BARAKA 70 74, S WITTKOP 73 72, M FLORIOLI 70 75, G ROJAS 70 75, A RAITT 69 76, W HUGET 69 76, G BRAND JNR. 72 74, S TORRANCE 75 71, J SPENCE 73 73, T GOGELE 77 69, O EDMOND 71 75, E CANONICA 74 72, C CEVAER 72 74, M PILKINGTON 73 73, D HIGGINS 73 73, N CHEETHAM 74 73, C REIMBOLD (Am) 78 69, M MACKENZIE 70 78, P BAKER 75 73, N VANHOOTEGEM 73 75, M BERNARDINI 73 75, M ZOLLER (Am) 73 75, D HOWELL 72 77, S WEBSTER 75 74, D FICHARDT 75 76, F LUBENAU 74 77, L FRACASSI 79 73, R WINCHESTER 76 76, C GRENIER 76 76, J A VIZCAYA 77 76, J-F REMESY 76 79, D J GEALL 81 74, C GUNTHER 75 85, J BOECKX 79 82, P BROADHURST 77 W/D.

Course Profile

The Nord Eichenried layout (par 72, 6,914 yards) has staged this event between 1989 and 1993 and from 1997 onwards.

The emphasis is on a golfer's short game. And consequently those players who have hot putters can go low. The greens are flat and run true, which makes for easy scoring.

The fairways are wide with the rough of average height. There have been one or two changes over the past few years (the odd tree planted here and there) but nothing major.

Players/Points to Note

●This is the only event based in Germany that **Bernhard Langer** hasn't won. But boy has he gone close. His complete form figures from 1991 read 15-2-3-14-2-16-12-4-15-2-16. A run that includes only two rounds over par. He is 154-under par for those 11 starts and has a stroke average of 68.33.

●**Thomas Bjorn** won in 2000, after he'd finished fifth, sixth and 34th on his previous three visits. He was in contention when defending his title last year before a final round 74 blew his chances.

●**Padraig Harrington** has yet to finish lower than 20th at Nord Eichenried and has posted four top-ten finishes in five starts in this event. The Irishman, who was second last year, has great memories of this tournament and course, as he clinched his first Ryder Cup place here.

●**Colin Montgomerie** has won this event on it's current track. He's also posted four other top-six finishes in this tournament.

●**John Daly** will surely be back to defend his title next year and, after his record breaking total in 2001, he'll be a player to follow.

●**Robert Karlsson**, **Gary Orr**, **Ignacio Garrido**, **Peter Baker**, **Miguel Angel Jimenez** and **Joakim Haeggman** have enjoyed multiple top-ten finishes.

●Younger players to go well in 2002 could be **Paul Casey**, **Carl Petterson**, **Justin Rose** and **Adam Scott**.

Previous Results

2000: 1. Thomas Bjorn (-20), 2. Bernhard Langer (-17), 3. Carl Suneson (-16).

1999: 1. Colin Montgomerie (-20), 2. Padraig Harrington (-17), 3. Jarrod Moseley (-16).

1998: 1. Russell Claydon (-18), 2. Jamie Spence (-17), 3. Thomas Gogele (-16).

1997: 1. Robert Karlsson (-24), 2. Carl Watts (-24), 3. Colin Montgomerie (-23).

1996: 1. Marc Farry (-12), 2. Richard Green (-11), 3. Padraig Harrington (-10), Russell Claydon (-10), David Higgins (-10).

OMEGA EUROPEAN MASTERS

Crans-sur-Sierre, 6 Sep to 9 Sep 2001, purse 1,520,142 euros

Pos	Name	R1	R2	R3	R4	Total	To par	Money	DD(y)	DA%	GIR%	Putts
1	R GONZALEZ	65	67	68	68	268	-16	250,000	315.5	59.6	73.6	114
2	Soren HANSEN	70	65	68	68	271	-13	166,660	298.6	61.5	77.8	117
3	Craig STADLER	69	69	67	68	273	-11	84,450	N/A	N/A	N/A	N/A
	Gary ORR	67	66	71	69	273	-11	84,450	282.9	71.2	68.1	111
5	F JACOBSON	68	71	65	70	274	-10	63,600	293.9	59.6	72.2	117
6	Stephen SCAHILL	67	67	68	74	276	-8	48,750	281.9	71.2	68.1	113
	Greg OWEN	68	67	68	73	276	-8	48,750	305.6	67.3	73.6	123
8	G BRAND JNR.	66	71	71	69	277	-7	35,550	282.8	61.5	70.8	118
	Peter FOWLER	69	71	69	68	277	-7	35,550	281.9	63.5	70.8	117
10	E ROMERO	72	67	71	68	278	-6	27,800	301.5	67.3	73.6	120
	David GILFORD	67	66	72	73	278	-6	27,800	289.4	65.4	68.1	111
	R JACQUELIN	68	70	72	68	278	-6	27,800	289.3	71.2	70.8	122

Pos	Name	R1	R2	R3	R4	Total	To par
13	Francis VALERA	69	72	67	71	279	-5
	Markus BRIER	69	67	70	73	279	-5
	J DONALDSON	71	72	66	70	279	-5
16	Greg TURNER	67	71	71	71	280	-4
	S LEANEY	67	71	72	70	280	-4
	J ROBINSON	70	72	70	68	280	-4
	P O'MALLEY	68	71	67	74	280	-4
	Ernie ELS	71	72	68	69	280	-4
	L WESTWOOD	70	69	69	72	280	-4
	S O'HARA	74	64	71	71	280	-4
23	M MOULAND	69	72	72	68	281	-3
	Barry LANE	72	69	69	71	281	-3
	Brian DAVIS	68	71	71	71	281	-3
	J M CARRILES	73	68	70	70	281	-3
	Paul EALES	68	69	70	74	281	-3
	J HAEGGMAN	71	68	73	69	281	-3
	David PARK	69	71	70	71	281	-3
	F ANDERSSON	68	70	70	73	281	-3
	D ROBERTSON	66	70	74	71	281	-3
	David CARTER	73	67	69	72	281	-3
	Adam SCOTT	69	69	72	71	281	-3
34	Justin ROSE	69	69	72	72	282	-2
	M GRONBERG	70	72	68	72	282	-2
	C HANELL	69	71	70	72	282	-2
37	S TORRANCE	72	71	71	69	283	-1
	Gary MURPHY	69	69	72	73	283	-1
	Elliot BOULT	70	72	71	70	283	-1
	T GOGELE	66	75	71	71	283	-1
	J RYSTROM	69	74	69	71	283	-1
	Alex CEJKA	70	72	69	72	283	-1
	David LYNN	68	70	73	72	283	-1
	David HIGGINS	71	70	71	71	283	-1
	Paul CASEY	76	67	65	75	283	-1
46	Nick FALDO	70	72	70	72	284	E
	Marc FARRY	70	70	71	73	284	E
	T IMMELMAN	70	69	72	73	284	E
	M A JIMINEZ	73	68	73	70	284	E
	Olle KARLSSON	71	69	70	74	284	E
	E CANONICA	70	72	70	72	284	E
	Van PHILLIPS	69	69	74	72	284	E
53	Mark JAMES	71	70	71	73	285	+1
	Santiago LUNA	71	70	69	75	285	+1
	W BENNETT	68	69	74	74	285	+1
	S P WEBSTER	69	71	69	76	285	+1
	S GALLACHER	71	69	74	71	285	+1
58	Sandy LYLE	72	70	71	73	286	+2
	Jean HUGO	72	68	74	72	286	+2
	R CLAYDON	72	71	72	71	286	+2
	C CEVAER	71	71	72	72	286	+2
	H NYSTROM	66	73	75	72	286	+2
	G STORM	71	72	68	75	286	+2
64	R CHAPMAN	72	70	71	74	287	+3
	David HOWELL	71	72	73	71	287	+3
	A HANSEN	73	69	70	75	287	+3
	R WINCHESTER	71	76	69	71	287	+3
	Ian GARBUTT	72	69	73	73	287	+3
69	Carlos RODILES	71	72	70	75	288	+4
70	Wayne RILEY	74	67	73	75	289	+5
	Gary EMERSON	71	72	71	75	289	+5
72	I GARRIDO	67	72	75	76	290	+6
73	M LAFEBER	72	71	77	71	291	+7
	P MITCHELL	71	71	71	78	291	+7
	Nic HENNING	72	66	74	79	291	+7
76	S BALLESTEROS	72	71	76	74	293	+9
77	Philip WALTON	68	73	74	80	295	+11
	M SCARPA	70	73	78	77	298	+14
79	Kim FELTON	70	73	77	79	299	+15
80	Thomas BJORN	66	71	-	-	-	W/D

Sponsored by Stan James

Tournament Report

Ricardo Gonzalez kept the European Masters title in Argentinean hands by following up compatriot Eduardo Romero's win of 12 months ago.

It was his first victory on the European Tour and was achieved in emphatic style. The big-hitting 31-year-old led from day one and completed a three-shot win over Denmark's Soren Hansen with ease. Starting the final day two strokes clear Stephen Scahill and the field never got any closer.

Gonzalez dominated the event, which attracted some big names like Lee Westwood and Ernie Els, his powerful driving and fine putting touch always keeping him ahead of his rivals.

He put the result beyond doubt when picking up biridies at three of the first nine holes, dropping just one shot in the process – his only error of the day coming at the sixth. And with Scahill having a nightmare on the 14th – when he signed for a triple-bogey seven, no serious back-nine challenger emerged.

The Kiwi, though, did pass the £100,000 seasonal earning barrier, to make sure of his playing rights for next year. Craig Stadler, on his first visit to the Swiss course for 16 years, shared third place with Gary Orr. And for a moment it looked like the 'Walrus' might be able to run Gonzalez close after two early birdies. But the American's challenge faded. Orr's third place was his best of the season.

MISSED THE CUT: L-W ZHANG 72 72, A WALL 76 68, G HOUSTON 73 71, P QUIRICI 74 70 C SUNESON 75 69, J BERENDT 74 70, A RAITT 69 75, F CEA 72 72, M BLACKEY 72 72, M BERNARDINI 73 71, K H HAN 73 72, M MACKENZIE 72 73, R RAFFERTY 76 69, D FICHARDT 76 69, C HAINLINE 72 73, S REALE 72 73, O EDMOND 74 71, M SANTI 70 75, M REALE 74 71, N VANHOOTEGEM 70 75, S RICHARDSON 71 74, M PILKINGTON 73 72, T DIER 73 72, R STERNE 69 76, E DARCY 72 74, M ROE 75 71, J-F REMESY 74 72, J SPENCE 75 71, J MOSELEY 74 72, J LOMAS 74 72, T J MUOZ 72 74, P STREETER 73 73, B DREDGE 76 70, R COLES 73 73, J BICKERTON 74 72, E SIMSEK 73 73, C MOODY 71 76, S STRUVER 72 75, K FERRIE 74 73, G HAVRET 77 70, R S JOHNSON 74 73, M KNIGHT 71 76, M LUNDBERG 71 76, A FORSBRAND 73 75, N COLSAERTS 74 74, M FLORIOLI 73 76, N CHEETHAM 77 71, S DODD 74 74, J SANDELIN 72 76, P SJOLAND 75 73, M PIERO 74 75, B RUMFORD 72 77, R ZIMMERMANN (Am) 76 73, M LOFTUS 74 75, J HAWKES 75 75, R BYRD 76 74, R BALLESTEROS 75 75, R MUNTZ 77 73, R GOJAS 77 73, N DOUGHERTY 73 77, P BROADHURST 78 73, T WEISS (Am) 74 77, R de SOUSA (Am) 75 77, C PETTERSSON 76 76, A FORSYTH 74 79, J CLEMENT (Am) 81 73, H-N WONG 80 74, S REY 84 73, A CHOPARD 80 78, S MAIO (Am) 79 80, J BLATTI 81 80, M CHATELAIN 84 81, P HANSON 73 W/D, I POULTER 80 W/D, D TERBLANCHE 79 W/D, D ZURSCHMITTEN (Am)DISQ.

Course Profile

Extensive changes were made to the Crans-sur-Sierre course (par 71, 6,857 yards) in Switzerland before and after the 1998 renewal.

Some fairways were re-shaped putting more of an emphasis on accuracy but the main differences are on the greens.

Seve Ballesteros has made the putting surfaces tough.

They resemble the up turned saucer variety used on US Open layouts.

At over 5,000 feet above sea level even the short hitters can knock it out there.

Players/Points to Note

●**Ricardo Gonzelez**'s win in 2001 maintained the Argentinean's grip on this tournament. 12 months earlier, **Eduardo Romero** was successful and who's to say **Angel Cabrera** won't win in 2002?

●Romero has the best record of that trio in this event, having won twice (2000 and 1994) and also posted three other top-ten finishes in the 90s.

●**Darren Clarke** has yet to win this tournament but in nine starts in the event he has finished in the top ten on six occasions. His form figures from 1993 read 6-70-6-7-6-3-28-3.

●**Thomas Bjorn** has found just one player too good for him in the 1999 and 2000 renewals of this event and also finished seventh in 1996.

●**Patrik Sjoland** has a similar record to Bjorn with three top-ten finishes in five starts.

●**Colin Montgomerie** holds the course and 72-hole tournament records of 61 and 260.

●**Costantino Rocca**, **Sven Struver** and **Mathias Gronberg** are former champions with two other top-ten finishes since 1990.

●**Miguel Angel Jimenez** has finished in the top ten four times since 1990. Gary Orr has had three top-ten finishes and is yet to miss a cut in eight visits.

●**Ernie Els** should tee-up here in 2002 at the behest of his sponsors and has the game to go better than the 16th position he gained last term.

Previous Results

2000: 1. Eduardo Romero (-23), 2. Thomas Bjorn (-13), 3. Darren Clarke (-12).

1999: 1. Lee Westwood (-14), 2. Thomas Bjorn (-12), 3. Alex Cejka (-8).

1998: 1. Sven Struver (-21), won play-off, 2. Patrik Sjoland (-21), 3. Darren Clarke (-19).

1997: 1. Costantino Rocca (-18), 2. Robert Karlsson (-17), Scott Henderson (-17).

1996: 1. Colin Montgomerie (-24), 2. Sam Torrance (-20), 3. Paul Curry (-17).

TROPHEE LANCOME

Saint-Nom-la-Breteche, 20 Sep to 23 Sep 2001, purse 1,455,874 euros

Pos	Name	R1	R2	R3	R4	Total	To par	Money	DD(y)	DA%	GIR%	Putts
1	Sergio GARCIA	68	65	68	65	266	-18	239,782	283.4	67.9	80.6	115
2	Retief GOOSEN	64	71	65	67	267	-17	159,855	286.4	53.6	76.4	112
3	Jean HUGO	66	68	69	66	269	-15	90,062	294.6	62.5	73.6	111
4	Gary EMERSON	66	70	66	69	271	-13	71,934	267.1	69.6	70.8	108
5	Niclas FASTH	68	66	66	71	272	-12	61,000	279.3	60.7	77.8	116
6	R JACQUELIN	68	71	68	66	273	-11	46,757	282.6	78.6	80.6	123
	Anthony WALL	68	65	70	70	273	-11	46,757	281.6	71.4	73.6	116
8	Ian WOOSNAM	68	71	69	66	274	-10	32,322	277.1	67.9	77.8	119
	T IMMELMAN	70	72	67	65	274	-10	32,322	278.3	60.7	76.4	118
	Henrik NYSTROM	70	66	69	69	274	-10	32,322	274.1	73.2	77.8	119

Pos	Name	R1	R2	R3	R4	Total	To par
11	S WEBSTER	66	68	71	70	275	-9
	Phillip PRICE	70	67	66	72	275	-9
	Adam SCOTT	69	70	65	71	275	-9
14	M MOULAND	75	67	69	65	276	-8
	Sven STRUVER	69	68	70	69	276	-8
	S P WEBSTER	67	68	69	72	276	-8
	David LYNN	70	71	64	71	276	-8
	A COLTART	66	71	66	73	276	-8
	Graeme STORM	71	65	69	71	276	-8
20	R S JOHNSON	70	72	67	68	277	-7
	Greg OWEN	68	70	73	66	277	-7
	J BICKERTON	68	71	71	67	277	-7
23	M MACKENZIE	69	70	70	69	278	-6
	Paul EALES	69	70	69	70	278	-6
	R CLAYDON	68	73	69	68	278	-6
	J LOMAS	69	71	70	68	278	-6
	Markus BRIER	73	66	67	72	278	-6
	D ROBERTSON	69	71	66	72	278	-6
	David CARTER	72	67	68	71	278	-6
30	Mark ROE	66	66	75	72	279	-5
	Mark McNULTY	71	68	68	72	279	-5
	J MOSELEY	71	71	70	67	279	-5
	Per NYMAN	74	67	73	65	279	-5
	Jorge BERENDT	69	68	68	74	279	-5
	C CEVAER	73	67	67	72	279	-5
	Angel CABRERA	72	68	67	72	279	-5
	Gary ORR	66	73	71	69	279	-5
38	Santiago LUNA	71	68	68	73	280	-4
	Thomas LEVET	68	72	71	69	280	-4
	E CANONICA	72	67	71	70	280	-4
	D BORREGO	70	71	69	70	280	-4
	F ANDERSSON	71	68	70	71	280	-4
43	Jose RIVERO	71	71	67	72	281	-3
	G RANKIN	69	72	68	72	281	-3
	J HAEGGMAN	69	71	70	71	281	-3
	Van PHILLIPS	70	68	72	71	281	-3
	Brett RUMFORD	70	72	69	70	281	-3
	S GARDINER	66	73	70	72	281	-3
49	Peter HANSON	71	68	69	74	282	-2
	Peter BAKER	67	72	71	72	282	-2
	J ROBINSON	71	69	75	67	282	-2
	M SCARPA	69	72	67	74	282	-2
	Robert COLES	67	70	69	76	282	-2
54	E ROMERO	67	72	69	75	283	-1
	J VAN DE VELDE	70	69	71	73	283	-1
	Carl SUNESON	69	72	72	70	283	-1
	R KARLSSON	67	72	72	72	283	-1
	B DREDGE	71	71	70	71	283	-1
	F JACOBSON	71	67	68	77	283	-1
	Erol SIMSEK	69	72	70	72	283	-1
	M LUNDBERG	66	73	73	71	283	-1
	Simon DYSON	69	68	70	76	283	-1
63	G BRAND JNR.	71	69	71	73	284	E
	A OLDCORN	71	67	72	74	284	E
65	Barry LANE	72	69	71	73	285	+1
	M LAFEBER	71	71	72	71	285	+1
	S LEANEY	70	72	69	74	285	+1
	G HOUSTON	69	68	76	72	285	+1
	P MITCHELL	71	71	70	73	285	+1
	Ian GARBUTT	73	69	73	70	285	+1
71	R RUSSELL	75	67	69	75	286	+2
	C PETTERSSON	70	71	68	77	286	+2
73	Olivier DAVID	71	71	69	76	287	+3
74	David GILFORD	68	73	72	75	288	+4
	N COLSAERTS	68	73	73	76	290	+6
76	David HOWELL	71	71	74	76	292	+8
	Olivier EDMOND	73	69	75	75	292	+8
78	M PENDARIES	73	69	76	77	295	+11

Tournament Report

Sergio Garcia's electric finish at Saint Nom La Breteche was enough to overhaul a stuttering Retief Goosen to win the Lancome Trohpy in Paris.

It was the young Spaniard's third European Tour title and his first since 1999. And make no mistake, although the South African did make mistakes on the last two holes, this was an event Garcia won, not lost by Goosen. El Nino was four down with four to play but conjured up an unbelievable run of three birdies from the 15th. Garcia holed from 15 foot each time.

Goosen couldn't respond and after three-putting the 17th for a bogey five the pair were level. Then, after pulling his tee shot on the last into a bunker, Goosen failed to make par, his attempt at the last curling in then out of the cup, leaving Garica two putts for victory.

The Spaniard needed them both as he snatched an unlikely win from underneath Goosen's nose. The Springbok started the day a shot clear of Garcia and Sweden's Niclas Fasth and, at one stage, birdied five holes in a row to secure a seemingly impossible position to lose from.

But, although he stumbled over the line when winning at Southern Hills and at Loch Lomond this term, this time Goosen wouldn't get away with a slack finish. Another South African, Jean Hugo managed to a last day 66 to claim third place, while Gary Emerson produced a Sunday 69 to place fourth - his best career finish.

MISSED THE CUT: Henrik STENSON 71 72, Fredrik HENGE 70 73, Colin MONTGOMERIE 75 68, Henrik BJORNSTAD 72 71, Soren HANSEN 72 71, Massimo FLORIOLI 73 70, Olle KARLSSON 71 72, Didier DE VOOGHT 71 72, Paul LAWRIE 72 71, David PARK 72 71, David HIGGINS 74 69, Christopher HANELL 68 75, Roger CHAPMAN 69 75, Costantino ROCCA 74 70, Marc FARRY 73 71, Soren KJELDSEN 73 71, Roger WINCHESTER 72 72, Johan RYSTROM 73 71, Neil CHEETHAM 71 73, Michele REALE 70 74, Stephen DODD 73 71, Gustavo ROJAS 73 71, Mark PILKINGTON 70 74, Daren LEE 74 70, Lucas PARSONS 76 68, Stephen GALLACHER 72 72, Alastair FORSYTH 73 71, Tony JOHNSTONE 68 77, Paul BROADHURST 72 73, Gregory HAVRET 71 74, Steven RICHARDSON 71 74, Paul STREETER 71 74, Sebastien DELAGRANGE 78 67, Matthew BLACKEY 73 72, Benoit TEILLERIA 71 74, Tobias DIER 74 71, Philippe LIMA (Am) 72 73, Des SMYTH 75 71, Paolo QUIRICI 69 77, Christophe POTTIER 72 74, Patrik SJOLAND 71 75, Jeev Milkha SINGH 76 71, Gary MURPHY 74 73, Marcello SANTI 76 71, Nicolas VANHOOTEGEM 73 74, Rolf MUNTZ 71 76, Francisco CEA 74 73, Marco BERNARDINI 72 75, Peter FOWLER 75 73, Jean-Francois REMESY 77 71, Elliot BOULT 72 76, Andrew RAITT 73 75, Stephen SCAHILL 71 78, Jamie DONALDSON 73 76, Eamonn DARCY 79 W/D, Wayne RILEY 80 W/D, Jamie SPENCE 77 RETD, Carlos RODILES 80 W/D, Gary EVANS 72 DISQ, Ignacio GARRIDO 72 RETD.

Sponsored by Stan James

Course Profile

Saint Nom la Breteche Golf Club (par 71 6,903 yards) near Paris has been used to host this tournament since it's inclusion on the European Tour in 1970.

It's rated as one of the best parkland courses on the continent and one that puts a premium on accurate iron play.

The fairways are generous but extremely wayward tee shots will find the trees that line the layout and some punishing rough. Interestingly, the last hole is a par three.

Players/Points to Note

●**Colin Montgomerie** has registered six top-ten finishes in this event from 1990. In that time he is 90-under to par and has a stroke average of 68.78. His win came in 1995 and he has also finished runner-up on three occasions.

●**Retief Goosen** won in 2000 and should have successfully defended his title in 2001 but for a late charge from **Sergio Garcia**.

●**Miguel Angel Jimenez** has had four top-ten positions and won here in 1999. Since 1990 his stroke average is 69.98.

●**Ian Woosnam** is a dual winner of this tournament (1987 and 1993) while **Jarmo Sandelin** has one of the best recent records with form figures of 2-2-6-MC-DNP since 1997.

●**Alex Cejka** has a stroke average of 69.38 in four starts while **Anthony Wall**, **Jose Maria Olazabal**, **Eduardo Romero** and **David Gilford** also have sub-70 stroke averages in this event. **Lee Westwood** has three top-ten finishes in six starts.

●Because of the terrorists attacks in America, all of US Tour stars stayed away from this event – including **Tiger Woods**. The sponsors, though do dig deep to bring over a few big names from the States and they should be back next year. Garcia, **Vijay Singh**, **Jesper Parnevik**, **Frank Nobilo** and **Mark O'Meara** are current US Tour pros who have won this event.

Previous Results

_2000:_ 1. Retief Goosen (-13), 2. Michael Campbell (-12), Darren Clarke (-12).

_1999:_ 1. Pierre Fulke (-14), 2. Ignacio Garrido (-13), 3. Santiago Luna (-12), Greg Owen (-12), Colin Montgomerie (-12).

_1998:_ 1. Miguel Angel Jimenez (-11), 2. Mark O'Meara (-9), David Duval (-9), Greg Turner (-9), Jarmo Sandelin (-9).

_1997:_ 1. Mark O'Meara (-13), 2. Jarmo Sandelin (-12), 3. Greg Norman (-11), Peter O'Malley (-11).

_1996:_ 1. Jesper Parnevik (-12), 2. Colin Montgomerie (-7), 3. Ross Drummond (-6).

GERMAN MASTERS

Gut Larchenhof, 4 Oct to 7 Oct 2001, purse 2,700,000 euros

Pos	Name	R1	R2	R3	R4	Total	To par	Money	DD(y)	DA%	GIR%	Putts
1	Bernhard LANGER	67	64	68	67	266	-22	450,000	279.0	76.8	81.9	112
2	Fredrik JACOBSON	67	66	67	67	267	-21	234,510	279.8	46.4	75.0	105
	John DALY	71	67	64	65	267	-21	234,510	316.6	60.7	81.9	114
4	Roger CHAPMAN	67	69	67	66	269	-19	124,740	294.3	69.6	81.9	115
	Greg OWEN	65	68	67	69	269	-19	124,740	295.1	62.5	76.4	113
6	Gary ORR	70	67	66	67	270	-18	87,750	277.3	82.1	83.3	116
	David LYNN	68	66	68	68	270	-18	87,750	285.4	62.5	79.2	114
8	Ian WOOSNAM	69	68	66	68	271	-17	63,990	281.3	57.1	69.4	106
	Paul McGINLEY	70	67	68	66	271	-17	63,990	282.5	58.9	81.9	117
10	Robert KARLSSON	67	69	69	68	273	-15	46,980	296.6	53.6	63.9	101
	Gary EVANS	71	65	66	71	273	-15	46,980	287.5	67.9	81.9	121
	Roger WESSELS	67	70	65	71	273	-15	46,980	273.1	73.2	69.4	109
	R RUSSELL	71	67	67	68	273	-15	46,980	267.3	78.6	81.9	116
	Retief GOOSEN	68	68	67	70	273	-15	46,980	297.4	73.2	76.4	117

Pos	Name	R1	R2	R3	R4	Total	To par
15	Marc FARRY	72	65	66	71	274	-14
	S WEBSTER	70	68	65	71	274	-14
	Ian POULTER	67	69	67	71	274	-14
	C MONTGOMERIE	70	70	68	66	274	-14
19	A FORSBRAND	73	69	64	69	275	-13
	P HARRINGTON	70	67	67	71	275	-13
	Barry LANE	68	70	68	69	275	-13
	Peter O'MALLEY	69	70	66	70	275	-13
	Markus BRIER	70	70	65	70	275	-13
	M CAMPBELL	72	68	68	67	275	-13
25	T IMMELMAN	68	72	69	67	276	-12
	M Angel JIMINEZ	68	69	68	71	276	-12
	Jean HUGO	70	72	68	66	276	-12
	R WINCHESTER	68	70	72	66	276	-12
	Van PHILLIPS	68	69	72	67	276	-12
	Niclas FASTH	72	69	68	67	276	-12
	Paul CASEY	72	69	67	68	276	-12
32	W BENNETT	68	66	71	72	277	-11
	A HANSEN	70	68	70	69	277	-11
	S KJELDSEN	70	67	72	68	277	-11
	S LEANEY	67	66	67	77	277	-11
	Pierre FULKE	67	70	69	71	277	-11
	Darren CLARKE	68	67	71	71	277	-11
	Rolf MUNTZ	70	71	70	66	277	-11
	J SANDELIN	67	69	70	71	277	-11
	Mikko ILONEN	69	67	72	69	277	-11
41	Mark McNULTY	68	72	70	68	278	-10
	John SENDEN	66	72	68	72	278	-10
	Carl SUNESON	70	69	68	71	278	-10
	R GONZALEZ	66	70	73	69	278	-10
	David CARTER	73	68	67	70	278	-10
46	David HOWELL	70	70	69	70	279	-9
	M LAFEBER	72	68	72	67	279	-9
	Anthony WALL	71	69	70	69	279	-9
	Justin ROSE	72	66	68	73	279	-9
	H STENSON	67	69	73	70	279	-9
	J VAN DE VELDE	73	68	67	71	279	-9
	J LOMAS	69	68	71	71	279	-9
	Ian GARBUTT	74	65	70	70	279	-9
	M GRONBERG	67	74	69	69	279	-9
	Paul LAWRIE	71	70	67	71	279	-9
	W HUGET	70	68	70	71	279	-9
	N DOUGHERTY	69	72	66	72	279	-9
58	J-F REMESY	68	70	72	70	280	-8
	Thomas LEVET	71	71	69	69	280	-8
	Lucas PARSONS	69	70	69	72	280	-8
61	Santiago LUNA	71	69	70	71	281	-7
	Des SMYTH	71	71	72	67	281	-7
	Brian DAVIS	67	74	69	71	281	-7
	Alex CEJKA	74	67	67	73	281	-7
	I GARRIDO	72	70	70	69	281	-7
	H NYSTROM	65	73	70	73	281	-7
	S GALLACHER	72	70	72	67	281	-7
68	T JOHNSTONE	71	71	71	69	282	-6
	J M OLAZABAL	69	71	68	74	282	-6
70	J LUPPRIAN	70	70	70	73	283	-5
	Marcel SIEM	72	70	71	70	283	-5
	M SCARPA	72	68	74	69	283	-5
	A COLTART	72	69	72	70	283	-5
	Nick CASSINI	73	68	70	72	283	-5
75	L WESTWOOD	72	70	69	73	284	-4
	Adam SCOTT	70	71	73	70	284	-4
77	E CANONICA	70	71	71	73	285	-3
78	D FICHARDT	68	74	75	69	286	-2
	Gary EMERSON	71	71	70	74	286	-2
80	G BRAND JNR.	70	69	73	75	287	-1
81	Mark JAMES	72	70	72	80	294	+6

Tournament Report

For the 11th time in his career Bernhard Langer was successful on home soil as the veteran Ryder Cup star won the Linde German Masters at Gut Larchenof in Cologne.

It was the fourth time that the German had won his 'own' event – he co-promotes the tournament – and was his 39th European Tour success in his 390th start.

Langer's other wins in Germany include five German Opens, one Honda Open and one Deutsche Bank-SAP Open TPC of Europe.

A record crowd saw the local hero hold off determined challenges from both John Daly and Sweden's Fredrik Jacobson.

Langer took the lead after a 64 on Friday and was never headed over the weekend.

He started the last day holding a one shot advantage over Jacobson, Stephen Leaney and Greg Owen.

The biggest threat to the eventual winner, though, came from Daly. The American played the last 45 holes in 20-under par. But even his last day 65 wasn't enough.

Daly – winner of the BMW International Open on his last visit to Europe – had gathered a head of steam, eagling the 13th and birdieing the 15th and 16th to reach 21-under par. However, he was unable to make another birdie over the closing two holes to force a play-off.

There were only a few anxious moments for Langer. At the 17th the German's wayward second shot seemed to have entered a water hazard. But, luckily for him, his ball stopped just short.

And despite finding a bunker at the last, which resulted in Langer dropping his only shot of the day, he managed to fend off Daly.

Jacobson's challenge looked a real one when he holed from 105 yards for an eagle at the third but, having missed birdie opportunities on the par five 13th and 15th holes, he had to settle for second.

Owen dropped to a share of fourth with Roger Chapman, who won three gold coins for shooting the most birdies in the week.

MISSED THE CUT: Seve BALLESTEROS 72 71, Nick O'HERN 74 69, Ralf GEILENBERG 69 74, Jarrod MOSELEY 74 69, Steven RICHARDSON 70 73, Patrik SJOLAND 75 68, Christopher HANELL 73 70, Marco BERNARDINI 73 70, Raphael JACQUELIN 76 68, Sven STRUVER 73 71, Jamie SPENCE 75 69, Paolo QUIRICI 74 70, Dean ROBERTSON 70 74, Erol SIMSEK 69 75, Kalle VAINOLA 72 73, Peter MITCHELL 72 74, Thomas GOGELE 72 74, Tobias DIER 78 68, Patrick PLATZ 76 71, Soren HANSEN 74 73, David PARK 73 74, John BICKERTON 72 75, Peter BAKER 77 71, Alastair FORSYTH 73 75, Kariem BARAKA 73 76, Christoph GUNTHER 74 80, Andrew OLDCORN W/D

Course Profile

The Jack Nicklaus designed Gut Larchenhof course (par 72 7,209 yards) in Cologne has been used for this tournament for the last four years.

It is an expansive layout (it was lengthened after the 1998 event) which can play even longer as a number of the par fours (5,6, 17 and 18) usually play into the wind.

The greens can be quick and are large with tough pin positions. Water comes into play on a number of holes.

Players/Points to Note

● **Bernhard Langer's** management company co-sponsors this event and recently he's been the major benefactor of the prize money he helped to put up. The German won this event last year and can also boast victories in 1989, 1991 and 1997. Langer has posted six other top-ten finishes since 1990, is 170-under to par and has a stroke average of 68.38. In 47 competitive rounds he has shot over par just once.

● **Colin Montgomerie** has not finished lower than 15th in the last five renewals of this event. Since 1996 the Scot's form figures read 4-2-Win-9-3-15. In that time he hasn't shot one round over par.

● **Padraig Harrington** has yet to finish lower than 19th at Gut Larchenhof and has four top-ten finishes in six starts in this event, including a play-off defeat in 1999. He has yet to shoot an over par round in this tournament.

● **Jose Maria Olazabal** won this event in 1988 and can boast top-ten finishes on five occasions.

● **Sergio Garcia** won in 1999 and followed up with a share of 17th spot in 2000.

● **Thomas Bjorn**, **Paul McGinley**, **Robert Karlsson** and **Ian Woosnam** have all finished in the top ten on three occasions in the last decade.

● **Retief Goosen** and **Michael Campbell** (2000 champion) are consistently good performers in this event.

Previous Results

2000: 1. Michael Campbell (-19), 2. Jose Coceres (-18), 3. Padraig Harrington (-15), Colin Montgomerie (-15).

1999: 1. Sergio Garcia (-11) won play-off, 2. Padraig Harrington, (-11) Ian Woosnam (-11).

1998: 1. Colin Montgomerie (-22), 2. Vijay Singh (-21), Robert Karlsson (-21).

1997: 1. Bernhard Langer (-21), 2. Colin Montgomerie (-15), 3. Thomas Bjorn (-14).

1996: 1. Darren Clarke (-24), 2. Mark Davis (-23), 3. Paul Broadhurst (-22).

CANNES OPEN

Cannes Mougin G.C., 11 Oct to 14 Oct 2001, purse 550,000 euros

Pos	Name	R1	R2	R3	R4	Total	To par	Money	DD(y)	DA%	GIR%	Putts
1	Jorge BERENDT	67	66	67	68	268	-20	92,500	287.9	75.0	76.4	111
2	J VAN DE VELDE	70	66	68	65	269	-19	61,660	291.5	67.9	75.0	112
3	Santiago LUNA	70	66	68	68	272	-16	28,675	n/a	n/a	n/a	n/a
	Thomas LEVET	69	66	69	68	272	-16	28,675	314.0	55.4	87.5	123
	A MARSHALL	65	68	69	70	272	-16	28,675	282.4	71.4	79.2	116
6	Warren BENNETT	66	66	70	71	273	-15	16,650	301.4	64.3	80.6	120
	Johan RYSTROM	67	71	69	66	273	-15	16,650	308.0	69.6	77.8	117
	Ignacio GARRIDO	69	67	67	70	273	-15	16,650	308.0	76.8	84.7	122
9	H BJORNSTAD	65	68	70	71	274	-14	12,432	301.0	69.6	80.6	121
10	Shaun WEBSTER	68	72	67	68	275	-13	9,948	283.1	75.0	77.8	117
	Paul EALES	67	70	68	70	275	-13	9,948	284.1	87.5	86.1	122
	F ANDERSSON	70	68	67	70	275	-13	9,948	291.9	75.0	72.2	110
	M BLACKEY	69	70	66	70	275	-13	9,948	272.1	82.1	81.9	118

Pos	Name	R1	R2	R3	R4	Total	To par
14	R JACQUELIN	69	65	71	71	276	-12
	Carl SUNESON	68	67	71	70	276	-12
	Bradley DREDGE	68	67	71	70	276	-12
	David PARK	64	75	71	66	276	-12
18	Van PHILLIPS	67	69	69	72	277	-11
	Lucas PARSONS	62	73	72	70	277	-11
	Richard STERNE	71	71	68	67	277	-11
	Steven O'HARA	67	69	71	70	277	-11
	Martin MARITZ	71	69	68	69	277	-11
23	J ROBINSON	66	76	71	65	278	-10
	R WINCHESTER	69	69	68	72	278	-10
	Jose ROMERO	70	68	71	69	278	-10
	Roger WESSELS	66	70	73	69	278	-10
	Paddy GRIBBEN	71	69	67	71	278	-10
28	Wayne RILEY	66	69	75	69	279	-9
	Garry HOUSTON	71	68	68	72	279	-9
	Tomas MUNOZ	71	71	67	70	279	-9
	D TERBLANCHE	72	68	72	67	279	-9
	Robert COLES	68	70	73	68	279	-9
	David HIGGINS	70	72	69	68	279	-9
	Simon DYSON	71	67	71	70	279	-9
	David DIXON	69	69	70	71	279	-9
36	L ALEXANDRE	68	69	70	73	280	-8
	Fredrik HENGE	67	68	74	71	280	-8
	G HAVRET	72	70	70	68	280	-8
39	A FORSBRAND	68	74	71	68	281	-7
	Mark MOULAND	71	67	69	74	281	-7
	Marc FARRY	71	70	71	69	281	-7
	J-F REMESY	69	70	71	71	281	-7
	T GOGELE	73	67	71	70	281	-7
	Stephen DODD	67	71	71	72	281	-7
	M PILKINGTON	68	69	75	69	281	-7
	F CUPILLARD	70	67	72	72	281	-7
	Daren LEE	69	69	73	70	281	-7
	C HANELL	71	69	72	69	281	-7
	Scott GARDINER	68	70	68	75	281	-7
50	Peter FOWLER	72	69	71	70	282	-6
	N VANHOOTEGEM	71	69	70	72	282	-6
	H NYSTROM	72	69	71	70	282	-6
53	E CANONICA	71	68	71	73	283	-5
	N KALOUGUINE	71	71	71	70	283	-5
	Erol SIMSEK	70	67	72	74	283	-5
	Graeme STORM	70	69	70	74	283	-5
57	J M CARRILES	69	73	71	71	284	-4
	Peter HANSON	69	71	75	69	284	-4
	P BROADHURST	70	68	70	76	284	-4
	R CLAYDON	71	70	73	70	284	-4
61	D HOSPITAL	71	71	74	71	287	-1
	Marcello SANTI	70	71	71	75	287	-1
	Michele REALE	71	69	76	71	287	-1
64	Gary EVANS	70	67	70	81	288	E
	A FORSYTH	69	72	74	73	288	E
66	Gustavo ROJAS	72	69	70	78	289	+1
67	Robin BYRD	72	67	75	76	290	+2
68	Olivier EDMOND	70	72	72	77	291	+3
69	Patrik SJOLAND	72	69	81	71	293	+5
70	B CORNUT	71	70	76	78	295	+7
71	R KARLSSON	70	71	-	-	-	W/D

Sponsored by Stan James

Tournament Report

Jorge Berendt won the first European Tour event of his career as the Argentinean held off Jean Van de Velde to capture the Cannes Open in the south of France.

The tournament, a late replacement on the schedule for the Estoril Open, saw a dramatic final day as local favourite Van de Velde put in a last day charge only to fall a shot shy of what eventually was required.

In winning, Berendt became the third Argentinean winner of a European Tour event this season.

The 37-year-old opened with scores of 67 and 66 and then was helped on the way to a third round 67 by a superb eagle two on the 9th, when he managed to hole from 137 yards. He led by two shots from Andy Marshall and Warren Bennett after Saturday's play.

But with Van de Velde flying through the field – he made six birdies and an eagle in his equal (with Jeremy Robinson) best of the day 65 – Berendt had plenty to do over the back nine, and was in fact left to make a par at the last to win.

A nervous second shot failed to find the putting green, but a wonderful chip to two feet and a tap in for a four meant the Argentinean had done enough.

Berendt, who followed in the footsteps of fellow Argentineans Angel Cabrera and Ricardo Gonzalez as winners on the European Tour this season, pocketed the 92,500 euro (£57,319) first prize to move from 111th to 77th on the Volvo Order of Merit and secured a two-year exemption.

Van De Velde's second place prize money ensured his tour card for next season.

Marshall birdied the last three holes to claim third place but a double bogey on the 18th, when an errant drive came close to the clubhouse, saw Bennett slip to share sixth place with Johan Rystrom and Ignacio Garrido.

MISSED THE CUT: Gordon BRAND JNR. 70 73, Soren KJELDSEN 69 74, Richard S JOHNSON 73 70, Neil CHEETHAM 69 74, Massimo SCARPA 73 70, Steven RICHARDSON 72 71, David CARTER 72 71, Nic HENNING 72 71, Mark ROE 72 72, Nick O'HERN 70 74, Jean Pierre CIXOUS 71 73, Graham RANKIN 74 71, Ricardo GONZALEZ 72 73, Stuart CAGE 73 72, Paul STREETER 75 70, Eamonn DARCY 76 70, Dennis EDLUND 68 78, Massimo FLORIOLI 75 71, Per NYMAN 72 74, Diego BORREGO 71 75, Andrew COLTART 75 71, Mikael LUNDBERG 75 71, Nick DOUGHERTY 73 73, Chris BENIANS 74 73, Francisco CEA 72 75, Maarten LAFEBER 74 74, Andrew BEAL 75 74, Alexandre BALICKI 78 72, Carlos RODILES 73 78, Richard McEVOY 75 77, Gary BIRCH JNR 76 79, Sebastien DELAGRANGE 79 71, Peter MITCHELL 76 W/D, Nicolas COLSAERTS 71 RETD, Olle KARLSSON 69 RETD, Andrew RAITT 75 RETD, Marco BERNARDINI 75 RETD

Course Profile

In a marvellous effort by the staff at Cannes Mougin Golf Club (par 72, 6,830 yards) the course was pulled into shape just nine days after getting the go ahead for the event to take place.

The wind and rain usually come to the South of France in October and as this layout is only short with generous fairways, the weather is its biggest defence.

The greens are undulating but the rough was grown relatively high in 2001.

Players/Points to Note

●The Cannes Open was a late replacement for the Estoril Open on the European Tour Schedule and was played on the Cannes Mougin layout which was used for this event between 1984 and 1994. Hats off to Andrew Chandler and his International Sports Management group for getting this tournament on – with the help of Nigel Robertson who pumped around £500,00 into the event. As yet the European Tour hasn't found a slot for this event on the 2002 schedule.

●Both **Jean Van de Velde** and **Santiago Luna** placed in the top five of this event the last time it was held at Cannes Mougins in 1994 and were second and third respectively in 2001.

●**Thomas Levet** won the last Cannes Open, although at Royal Mougins and was third in the 2001 renewal.

●Veteran Zimbabwean **Mark McNulty** has a superb record at this track. Twice a winner (1988 and 1990) he has also finished second and third. Another Southern African pro, **Tony Johnstone** holds the course record (62). **Lucas Parsons** also shot 62 in 2001.

●**Ian Woosnam**, **Costantino Rocca**, **David Carter**, **Paul Eales** and **Ignacio Garrido** have performed well in this event over the years.

●If this tournament does make it onto the 2002 schedule and is still supported by the ISM team, expect the likes of **Lee Westwood** and **Darren Clarke** to play.

Previous Results

2000: N/A
1999: 1. Jean-Francois Remesy (-2), 2. Massimo Floroili (Ev), Andrew Coltart (Ev), David Carter (Ev).

Thomas Levet player profile – page 217

DUNHILL LINKS CHAMPIONSHIP

St Andrews, 18 Oct to 22 Oct 2001, purse 5,457,660 euros

Pos	Name	R1	R2	R3	R4	Total	To par	Money	DD(y)	DA%	GIR%	Putts
1	Paul LAWRIE	71	68	63	68	270	-18	881,250	299.1	67.0	90.0	122
2	Ernie ELS	65	70	68	68	271	-17	587,496	311.4	62.0	89.0	122
3	David HOWELL	67	68	69	68	272	-16	330,997	300.1	66.0	79.0	116
4	Jean HUGO	68	70	69	66	273	-15	264,375	299.1	72.0	74.0	110
5	P HARRINGTON	67	67	72	69	275	-13	175,016	286.9	72.0	78.0	116
	C MONTGOMERIE	71	68	69	67	275	-13	175,016	300.5	84.0	88.0	126
	Peter O'MALLEY	71	67	68	69	275	-13	175,016	287.4	82.0	88.0	124
	Paul CASEY	69	70	66	70	275	-13	175,016	318.5	66.0	78.0	121
9	Paul McGINLEY	67	64	71	74	276	-12	103,106	301.5	80.0	86.0	126
	M GRONBERG	68	70	71	67	276	-12	103,106	n/a	n/a	n/a	n/a
	Retief GOOSEN	69	69	69	69	276	-12	103,106	n/a	n/a	n/a	n/a
	J DONALDSON	68	66	74	68	276	-12	103,106	n/a	84.0	88.0	128

Pos	Name	R1	R2	R3	R4	Total	To par
13	Brian DAVIS	65	68	72	72	277	-11
	Thomas BJORN	70	67	71	69	277	-11
	M PILKINGTON	69	69	71	68	277	-11
	Brett RUMFORD	72	67	68	70	277	-11
17	Justin ROSE	69	68	74	67	278	-10
	Wayne SMITH	71	74	67	66	278	-10
	E CANONICA	66	74	69	69	278	-10
	David LYNN	71	69	69	69	278	-10
	Greg OWEN	70	67	72	69	278	-10
	Patrik SJOLAND	71	66	72	69	278	-10
	Lucas PARSONS	72	68	69	69	278	-10
24	Darren CLARKE	72	67	70	70	279	-9
	J BICKERTON	69	70	69	71	279	-9
	David DIXON	69	70	72	68	279	-9
27	Jarrod MOSELEY	67	70	71	72	280	-8
	R GONZALEZ	67	70	72	71	280	-8
29	E ROMERO	70	71	72	68	281	-7
	R JACQUELIN	72	68	74	67	281	-7
	M A JIMINEZ	70	70	69	72	281	-7
	J KINGSTON	74	67	70	70	281	-7
	Daren LEE	68	70	71	72	281	-7
	David CARTER	71	73	69	68	281	-7
35	A FORSBRAND	71	64	76	71	282	-6
	Barry LANE	68	72	74	68	282	-6
	R KARLSSON	70	70	73	69	282	-6
	Ian GARBUTT	72	69	68	73	282	-6
	I GARRIDO	67	72	74	69	282	-6
	H NYSTROM	70	66	74	72	282	-6
	N DOUGHERTY	68	68	73	73	282	-6
	Adam SCOTT	72	68	75	67	282	-6
43	S KJELDSEN	68	72	71	73	284	-4
	J LOMAS	67	73	72	72	284	-4
	Graeme STORM	71	74	70	69	284	-4
	Brett QUIGLEY	68	69	73	74	284	-4
	Scott GARDINER	72	67	75	70	284	-4
48	T JOHNSTONE	67	66	80	72	285	-3
	Gary ORR	75	67	71	72	285	-3
	Van PHILLIPS	75	68	69	73	285	-3
	F JACOBSON	73	66	75	71	285	-3
52	M LAFEBER	71	74	70	71	286	-2
	Roger WESSELS	72	69	73	72	286	-2
	M LUNDBERG	74	68	72	72	286	-2
	Simon DYSON	70	72	71	73	286	-2
56	Jorge BERENDT	70	72	73	72	287	-1
	Peter LONARD	71	68	76	72	287	-1
	Markus BRIER	70	72	69	76	287	-1
59	J F REMESY	72	74	69	73	288	E
	Omar SANDYS	65	71	74	78	288	E
61	Steve WEBSTER	70	70	75	75	290	2
	David SMAIL	70	70	75	75	290	2
	Jamie SPENCE	69	74	72	75	290	2
64	Sam TORRANCE	69	70	76	76	291	3

The following players failed to play the fourth round

Pos	Name	R1	R2	R3	R4	Total
65	Ian WOOSNAM	71	74	69	RTD	214
66	Arjun ATWAL	68	72	73	WD	213
67	Santiago LUNA	72	72	72	-	216
	Mark McNULTY	75	72	69	-	216
	Sven STR‹VER	71	71	74	-	216
	Anthony WALL	75	71	70	-	216
	B VAUGHAN	76	68	72	-	216
	Henrik STENSON	72	71	73	-	216
	Thomas LEVET	74	67	75	-	216
	J HAEGGMAN	71	72	73	-	216
	R CLAYDON	71	74	71	-	216
	Phillip PRICE	71	69	76	-	216
	Pierre FULKE	71	66	79	-	216
	D TERBLANCHE	74	71	71	-	216
	A FORSYTH	74	70	72	-	216
	Richard STERNE	74	67	75	-	216

Sponsored by Stan James

Tournament Report

Paul Lawrie returned to the scene of his greatest triumph to win the inaugural Dunhill Links Challenge in Scotland.

St Andrews, Kingsbarns and Carnoustie were the host courses used for this pro-am event and it was, of course, the latter that saw Lawrie win the Open Championship in 1999. Bad weather meant a fifth day was needed to finish the tournament.

But that didn't matter to the Scot, who hadn't won an event since that Major victory two years, as he rolled in a 40-foot putt through the 'Valley of Sin' on the 18th at St Andrews to deny Ernie Els.

Lawrie started the day at 14-under alongside Paul McGinley and looked to be coasting to victory after he took a two shot lead at the turn over Els and David Howell.

But seven pars and a bogey at the infamous Road Hole looked to have given Els the edge. Needing a birdie to win and a par to force a play-off, Lawrie's precision 40-footer raced down, through and up the valley before found the middle of the cup.

It was just reward for Lawrie who had played well all week but found his putter cold more often than not. Howell claimed third place while South African Jean Hugo secured another top high finish by placing fourth.

The exciting end to the event certainly more than made up for the disappointment of the previous four days, which were besotted by delays because of rain and fog.

MISSED THE CUT: M ROE 67 73, R GREEN 71 71, N O'HERN 76 68, J VAN DE VELDE 71 73, J HOBDAY 73 72, P EALES 73 72, S HANSEN 69 72, C SUNESON 71 69, N VANHOOTEGEM 71 70, F CEA 72 74, D PARK 75 70, M MARITZ 70 71, S LEANEY 77 66, G EVANS 71 67, D BORREGO 71 74, R MUNTZ 68 70, M ILONEN 75 72, S O'HARA 74 68, S LYLE 74 72, J M SINGH 72 72, D GILFORD 70 74, T MOORE 77 72, R WINCHESTER 74 66, C CEVAER 75 71, A COLTART 69 70, S GALLACHER 75 70, D McGUIGAN 68 72, G TURNER 70 72, D FICHARDT 75 71, P MITCHELL 75 71, R S JOHNSON 72 71, J RANDHAWA 72 71, O EDMOND 71 72, A CABRERA 78 73, B DREDGE 75 74, C KAMPS 69 72, P FOWLER 69 74, J M OLAZABAL 73 71, I POULTER 76 71, T GOGELE 72 74, L WESTWOOD 73 76, M CAMPBELL 74 72, R CHAPMAN 75 68, D SMYTH 74 75, P BAKER 76 74, M SCARPA 78 69, D HIGGINS 72 72, T DIER 71 75, M CUNNING 73 73, S ELKINGTON 71 73, D BOTES 78 73, G EMERSON 74 74, A HANSEN 74 72, R RUSSELL 76 75, N GREEN 70 75, T IMMELMAN 73 73, W-T YEH 71 74, P BROADHURST 69 76, F HENGE 74 74, D LAMBERT 74 72, A ROESTOFF 75 78, R RAFFERTY 76 78, G MULLER 80 75, M FARRY 78 70, M JAMES 81 70, K DRUCE 82 73, K FELTON 75 79, H BUHRMANN 80 77, G BRAND JNR. 79 73, E DARCY 77 RETD, W RILEY 76 70, C RODILES 76 74, J SANDELIN 76 78, E SIMSEK 73 77, C HANELL 73 68, N VAN RENSBURG 78 76.

Course Profile

The Old Course (par 72, 7,2215 yards), Carnoustie (par 72, 7,361 yards) and Kingsbarns (par 72, 7,126 yards) are all classic links courses.

The Old Course has huge double greens and wide fairways littered with pot bunkers.

Carnoustie was savage in 1999 for the British Open but the rough won't be as punishing as it was then – the weather will be, though.

Kingsbarns is the most exposed venue of the three with the North Sea visible from nearly every hole.

Players/Points to Note

● The Alfred Dunhill Links was a new tournament in 2001, replacing the old Dunhill Cup. And after being criticised (rather unfairly) in some quarters the European Tour have yet to make a decision as to whether it will be on in 2002. There is space in the calendar, so hopefully it will. In 2001 the purse was massive and prize money did count towards the Order Of Merit.

● The event was played over three links courses - the Old Course at St Andrews, Carnoustie and Kingsbarns – each of the three layouts was played once with the last round played at St Andrews. The event was run as a Pro-Am, similar to the Pebble Beach event in America.

● The format suits some players and not others, they will have to play with an amateur for a few days and that can take a lot of patience. The weather was dreadful last year and the event took in a fifth day – those that can handle the elements should prosper.

● Last year, we highlighted the following players – **Paul Lawrie, Darren Clarke, Michael Campbell, Retief Goosen, Padraig Harrington, Greg Turner** and **Angel Cabrera** from the European Tour, and **Craig Parry, Paul Azinger, Jesper Parnevik** and **Ernie Els** from the US Tour. The same players are worth noting for 2002 if the tournament makes it on to the schedule.

Paul Lawrie player profile – page 216

Ernie Els player profile – pages 199 & 252

TELIFONICA OPEN DE MADRID

Club de Campo, 25 Oct to 28 Oct 2001, purse 1,400,000 euros

Pos	Name	R1	R2	R3	R4	Total	To par	Money	DD(y)	DA%	GIR%	Putts
1	Retief GOOSEN	66	64	66	68	264	-20	233,330	289.1	66.1	84.7	114
	Won play-off											
2	Steve WEBSTER	68	62	68	66	264	-20	155,550	297.3	80.4	81.9	115
3	Brian DAVIS	66	64	73	62	265	-19	78,820	289.1	67.9	63.9	100
	Diego BORREGO	69	65	64	67	265	-19	78,820	285.0	76.8	83.3	117
5	Markus BRIER	67	68	66	66	267	-17	59,360	284.3	69.6	69.4	105
6	Jeev M SINGH	72	67	65	64	268	-16	39,340	278.4	69.6	72.2	110
	Anders HANSEN	68	69	65	66	268	-16	39,340	285.0	75.0	69.4	109
	Darren CLARKE	67	69	65	67	268	-16	39,340	294.9	76.0	73.6	113
	Robert COLES	66	69	69	64	268	-16	39,340	284.1	66.1	68.1	107
10	Thomas BJORN	68	71	66	64	269	-15	26,880	273.0	67.9	70.8	110
	Angel CABRERA	68	69	65	67	269	-15	26,880	309.4	67.9	77.8	115

Pos	Name	R1	R2	R3	R4	Total	To par
12	Richard GREEN	69	67	65	69	270	-14
	Van PHILLIPS	68	67	69	66	270	-14
	David LYNN	68	66	68	68	270	-14
	J BICKERTON	69	67	68	66	270	-14
16	J M OLAZABAL	69	67	68	67	271	-13
	Carlos RODILES	65	70	67	69	271	-13
	Gary EMERSON	70	68	68	65	271	-13
	Phillip PRICE	66	69	67	69	271	-13
	Greg OWEN	67	70	66	68	271	-13
21	Barry LANE	66	72	66	68	272	-12
	R JOHNSON	73	65	67	67	272	-12
	I GARRIDO	70	67	71	64	272	-12
	Bradley DREDGE	70	68	65	69	272	-12
25	P HARRINGTON	63	72	69	69	273	-11
	J M CARRILES	72	68	69	64	273	-11
	F ANDERSSON	69	65	71	68	273	-11
	H NYSTROM	67	67	72	67	273	-11
	S GALLACHER	64	70	70	69	273	-11
	David HIGGINS	67	62	69	75	273	-11
31	Des SMYTH	65	73	67	69	274	-10
	M A JIMENEZ	65	67	70	72	274	-10
	Ian GARBUTT	69	71	70	64	274	-10
	A FORSYTH	69	67	71	67	274	-10
35	E ROMERO	70	67	72	66	275	-9
	M LAFEBER	71	69	68	67	275	-9
	R WINCHESTER	71	65	72	67	275	-9
	C PETTERSSON	70	70	67	68	275	-9
39	Santiago LUNA	72	68	67	69	276	-8
	David HOWELL	70	69	65	72	276	-8
	Mark McNULTY	70	69	69	68	276	-8
	Peter MITCHELL	70	69	68	69	276	-8
	J RYSTROM	67	67	71	71	276	-8
	E CANONICA	70	70	67	69	276	-8
	Brett RUMFORD	71	69	66	70	276	-8
46	H BJORNSTAD	70	69	72	66	277	-7
	T GOGELE	68	68	73	68	277	-7
	Stephen DODD	71	65	72	69	277	-7
49	Wayne RILEY	71	67	66	74	278	-6
	Mark ROE	67	70	70	71	278	-6
	D FICHARDT	72	68	66	72	278	-6
	P BROADHURST	72	68	69	69	278	-6
	Gary ORR	70	68	68	72	278	-6
	M BLACKEY	72	67	72	67	278	-6
	N DOUGHERTY	71	67	71	69	278	-6
56	A MARSHALL	66	68	77	68	279	-5
57	Juan QUIROS	70	70	70	70	280	-4
	Alvaro SALTO	69	68	73	70	280	-4
	Marc FARRY	67	71	71	71	280	-4
	H STENSON	71	68	70	71	280	-4
	Olle KARLSSON	71	69	70	70	280	-4
	Rolf MUNTZ	71	69	72	68	280	-4
	David PARK	68	69	74	69	280	-4
	Paul CASEY	69	70	72	69	280	-4
65	J F REMESY	70	68	73	70	281	-3
	Soren HANSEN	69	69	72	71	281	-3
	Michele REALE	68	70	72	71	281	-3
	Fernando ROCA	67	68	76	70	281	-3
	Graeme STORM	66	72	73	70	281	-3
70	Lucas PARSONS	69	70	70	73	282	-2
71	M PILKINGTON	70	69	74	72	285	+1
72	Mark JAMES	69	71	72	80	292	+8

Sponsored by Stan James

Tournament Report

Retief Goosen became the first South African winner of the Volvo Order of Merit since Dale Hayes in 1975 by beating Steve Webster at the third hole of a sudden-death play-off to capture the Telefonica Open de Madrid.

The 32-year-old US and Scottish Open Champion was winning for the third time this season and victory meant that his nearest persurer for the Harry Vardon Trophy, Darren Clarke, couldn't catch him with one tournament left.

The Irishman made a bold challenge to close the gap on Goosen but had to be content with a share of sixth place in Madrid as the South African closed out the second play-off victory of the most productive season of his career.

Goosen and Webster were tied on a 20-under par total of 264, with the former making a birdie two at the third extra hole to secure the title.

Goosen, leader by two after 54 holes, seemed to have secured the title when he birdied the 17th to ease ahead of Webster, who had six birdies and one bogey on his card.

But he bogeyed the last to open the door once more and it was Webster who had the first stab at glory at the 18th, the first extra hole. He punched his approach within five feet of the hole but failed to hit his putt with enough conviction to hole it.

Both players returned to the 18th and made solid par fours before returning to the 17th, which Goosen had birdied minutes earlier. This time, he hit a nine-iron to eight feet and, after Webster had used his three-wood to putt close from the fringe, the man who won the US Open title after a play-off rolled in his putt for another high class victory.

MISSED THE CUT: Sandy LYLE 71 70, Sam TORRANCE 70 71, Anthony WALL 70 71, John SENDEN 74 67, Jean VAN DE VELDE 73 68, Nicolas VANHOOTEGEM 70 71, Marco BERNARDINI 72 69, Malcolm MACKENZIE 68 74, Jose RIVERO 70 72, Greg TURNER 68 74, Soren KJELDSEN 70 72, Trevor IMMELMAN 73 69, Gregory HAVRET 72 70, Gary EVANS 70 72, Christian CEVAER 70 72, Des TERBLANCHE 69 73, Peter LONARD 72 70, Francisco CEA 74 68, Mikael LUNDBERG 70 72, Pablo MARTIN BENAVIDES 68 74, Mark MOULAND 71 72, Shaun P WEBSTER 71 72, Jesus Maria ARRUTI 72 71, Carl SUNESON 72 71, Massimo SCARPA 71 72, Jarmo SANDELIN 76 67, David CARTER 71 72, Erol SIMSEK 70 73, Tony JOHNSTONE 72 72, Fredrik HENGE 71 73, Domingo HOSPITAL 74 70, Simon DYSON 68 76, Raul BALLESTEROS 72 73, Jorge BERENDT 71 74, Juan A VIZCAYA 75 70, Gonzalo FERNANDEZ CASTAN 73 72, Neil CHEETHAM 72 74, Seve BALLESTEROS 72 75, Peter HANSON 74 73, Carlos BALMASEDA 75 72, Peter BAKER 76 72, Olivier EDMOND 74 74, Gustavo ROJAS 76 75, Manuel PIERO 77 76, Juan Carlos PIERO 74 79, Roger CHAPMAN 76 RETD, Desvonde BOTES 75 W/D, Raymond RUSSELL 77 RETD

Course Profile

Club de Campo in Madrid (par 71 6,957 yards) has staged this tournament for the past two years and will do so again in 2002.

It also staged the Spanish Open in 1996 won by Padraig Harrington.

The course is a parkland style layout that has tree-lined fairways and rewards accuracy off the tee.

Its undulating greens and sloping fairways make it test with the putter and long irons.

Most of the greens are well protected by bunkers.

Players/Points to Note

● This tournament has come under the Turespana Masters banner recently. The Turespana Masters has been played at numerous venues over the years but under its new guise as the 'Madrid Open' has found a home at Club de Campo since 2000.

● With so many changes of venue the only constant in this event is the fact that Spanish players have a superb record in it. Four of the last six champions have been home players.

● Club de Campo was used to stage the 1996 Spanish Open, which was won by **Padraig Harrington**, and the Irishman made it two wins from two visits by capturing this title in 2000. In 2001 he opened up with a sparkling 63 only to fade to 25th.

● **Miguel Angel Jimenez** won in 1998 and 1999 (in Malaga and Mallorca). When going for the hat-trick he could only manage seventh, though, and was 31st in 2001. He has six top-20 performances in this event in all of its guises.

● **Jose Maria Olazabal** won this event in 1997 and finished runner-up in 1994. In six starts Ollie has finished in the top-20 on five occasions.

● **Diego Borrego** (winner in 1996 and three top-5 finishes since) was third in this event in 2001. Other Spaniards to note are **Ignacio Garrido**, **Carlos Rodiles** and **Francisco Cea**.

Previous Results

2000: 1. Padraig Harrington (-17), 2. Gary Orr (-15), 3. Per-Ulrik Johansson (-14).

1999: 1. Miguel Angel Jimenez (-24), 2. Steve Webster (-20), 3. Raphael Jacquelin (-19).

1998: 1. Miguel Angel Jimenez (-9), 2. Miguel Angel Martin (-7), 3. Katsuyoshi Tomori (-6), Paul McGinley (-6).

1997: 1. Jose Maria Olazabal (-20), 2. Lee Westwood (-18), 3. Eduardo Romero (-16), Paul Broadhurst (-16).

1996: 1. Diego Borrego (-17), 2. Tony Johnstone (-17), 3. Peter Baker (-13).

ATLANET ITALIAN OPEN

Is Molas, 1 Nov to 4 Nov 2001, purse 1,000,000 euros

Pos	Name	R1	R2	R3	R4	Total	To par	Money	DD(y)	DA%	GIR%	Putts
1	Gregory HAVRET	65	66	68	69	268	-20	166,660	288.3	73.2	86.1	115
2	Bradley DREDGE	69	66	65	69	269	-19	111,110	290.9	71.4	69.4	103
3	Mark ROE	63	69	73	66	271	-17	47,500	278.8	71.4	76.4	107
	S P WEBSTER	70	67	66	68	271	-17	47,500	276.6	75.0	75.0	110
	Ian POULTER	67	69	68	67	271	-17	47,500	291.6	66.1	81.9	116
	Diego BORREGO	70	66	65	70	271	-17	47,500	286.4	87.5	86.1	117
7	Steve WEBSTER	68	67	68	69	272	-16	27,500	301.1	80.4	86.1	123
	Henrik STENSON	67	70	68	67	272	-16	27,500	278.4	75.0	72.2	110
9	David HOWELL	71	66	68	68	273	-15	18,820	293.5	83.9	84.7	120
	T IMMELMAN	70	67	65	71	273	-15	18,820	296.3	71.4	77.8	113
	Michele REALE	63	73	68	69	273	-15	18,820	301.0	87.5	76.4	117
	Markus BRIER	70	66	70	67	273	-15	18,820	276.6	78.6	76.4	113
	F ANDERSSON	65	72	67	69	273	-15	18,820	280.5	75.0	75.0	113

Pos	Name	R1	R2	R3	R4	Total	To par
14	Sven STRUVER	66	68	64	76	274	-14
	Stephen DODD	70	68	68	68	274	-14
	Mikko ILONEN	68	71	66	69	274	-14
17	W BENNETT	70	71	68	66	275	-13
	S GRAPPASONNI	70	65	69	71	275	-13
	Richard GREEN	72	69	66	68	275	-13
	Anthony WALL	66	71	72	66	275	-13
	J VAN de VELDE	67	65	74	69	275	-13
	J LOMAS	68	72	70	65	275	-13
23	Santiago LUNA	69	70	68	69	276	-12
	J ROBINSON	70	68	70	68	276	-12
	Carl SUNESON	73	68	69	66	276	-12
	N VAN HOOTEGEM	70	69	68	69	276	-12
	Robert COLES	72	68	69	67	276	-12
	R RUSSELL	66	70	70	70	276	-12
29	J RYSTROM	66	70	71	70	277	-11
	Gary EVANS	70	70	66	71	277	-11
	Patrik SJOLAND	69	71	66	71	277	-11
32	R RAFFERTY	68	69	69	72	278	-10
	E ROMERO	66	70	75	67	278	-10
	R SJOHNSON	70	70	70	68	278	-10
	Marcello SANTI	68	74	69	67	278	-10
	M SCARPA	70	69	64	75	278	-10
	S GALLACHER	67	71	69	71	278	-10
38	R CHAPMAN	67	69	72	71	279	-9
	Peter HANSON	71	66	70	72	279	-9
	Robin BYRD	68	72	68	71	279	-9
	Olle KARLSSON	72	70	66	71	279	-9
	C CEVAER	69	66	71	73	279	-9
	Lucas PARSONS	68	71	68	72	279	-9
44	S SOFFIETTI	68	73	68	71	280	-8
	H BJORNSTAD	71	68	70	71	280	-8
	S RICHARDSON	67	73	72	68	280	-8
	Tony EDLUND	69	73	70	68	280	-8
	Peter LONARD	69	70	69	72	280	-8
49	A FORSYTH	70	70	71	70	281	-7
50	M MACKENZIE	70	70	73	69	282	-6
	Mark MOULAND	70	71	70	71	282	-6
	Elliot BOULT	71	70	74	67	282	-6
	R WINCHESTER	73	68	70	71	282	-6
	Angel CABRERA	72	68	67	75	282	-6
	M PILKINGTON	69	69	72	72	282	-6
56	A TADINI	71	69	69	74	283	-5
	P BROADHURST	70	72	71	70	283	-5
	E CANONICA	71	70	71	71	283	-5
	David PARK	72	67	73	71	283	-5
	G PIETROBONO	67	70	74	72	283	-5
	Daren LEE	72	69	72	70	283	-5
62	Dennis EDLUND	70	71	74	69	284	-4
	Simon HURD	73	69	72	70	284	-4
	L BERNARDINI	70	72	70	72	284	-4
65	Neil CHEETHAM	70	70	72	73	285	-3
	E DELARIVA	72	68	75	70	285	-3
67	Paolo TERRENI	73	69	71	73	286	-2
	Stefano REALE	71	70	73	72	286	-2
	T GOGELE	70	71	74	71	286	-2
	Nic HENNING	74	68	70	74	286	-2
71	A ROMANO (Am)	69	71	79	70	289	E
72	Paul EALES	73	69	74	75	291	+2
	M RIGONE (Am)	75	67	76	73	291	+2

Sponsored by Stan James

Tournament Report

On a day of high drama, Gregory Havret held his nerve to shoot a final round of 69, three-under par, for a winning total of 268, 20-under par.

Havret's win meant he became the second Frenchman to win on the 2001 European Tour. It was his maiden title in his rookie season.

Havret finished one clear of Bradley Dredge, who carded a final round of 69 with the defending champion Ian Poulter, Diego Borrego, Shaun Webster and Mark Roe sharing third place on 17-under par.

Havret started the final round a shot off the lead but immediately moved to the top of the leaderboard with birdie on the first hole. He three-putted the sixth for his only bogey of the round but it was not until the 11th that he started to pull ahead when he pitched to ten feet.

A third birdie of the day followed on the par three 14th, his eight iron shot finishing ten feet from the hole and then he moved to 20-under par with his final birdie of the day on the par five 16th, chipping to three feet.

Dredge came flying out of the blocks with an eagle on the first followed by a birdie on the third but his charge faltered when he drove out of bounds on the fifth on his way to running up a double bogey six.

He bounced back with two birdies in the last four holes but was unable to catch Havret as he closed with a 69. It was still his best finish on the European Tour.

For Roe it meant he climbed from 131st in the Volvo Order of Merit to 111th to retain his playing privileges for an 18th season on the European Tour. Christian Cevaer held on to the all important 115th place after holding off the challenges of those behind him by finishing in joint 38th place.

MISSED THE CUT: Greg TURNER 72 71, Justin ROSE 72 71, Massimo FLORIOLI 69 74, Russell CLAYDON 75 68, David HIGGINS 72 71, Marco BERNARDINI 72 71, Emmanuele LATTANZI 73 71, Christophe RAVETTO 73 71, Andrea MAESTRONI 71 73, Peter MITCHELL 74 70, Paolo QUIRICI 70 74, Francesco GUERMANI 70 74, Sean WHIFFIN 70 74, Van PHILLIPS 74 70, David CARTER 70 74, Alessandro NAPOLEONI 73 72, Gary MURPHY 72 73, Olivier EDMOND 71 74, Rolf MUNTZ 72 73, Charles CHALLEN 70 75, Edoardo MOLINARI (Am) 74 71, Guido VAN DER VALK 74 71, Wayne RILEY 74 72, Giuseppe CALI 74 72, Roby PAOLILLO 76 70, Fredrik HENGE 72 74, Gianluca BARUFFALDI 74 72, Jorge BERENDT 73 73, Gustavo ROJAS 77 69, Alan McLEAN 72 74, Francesco MOLINARI 76 71, Marco SOFFIETTI 74 74, Peter BAKER 77 71, Carl PETTERSSON 72 76, Maarten LAFEBER 75 74, Roberto ZAPPA 70 79, Graeme STORM 73 76, Sandy LYLE 76 74, Peter FOWLER 71 79, Matthew BLACKEY 75 75, Ralph MILLER 75 77, Renaud GUILLARD 74 78, Andrea BASCIU 78 75, Richard GILLOT 74 80, Raphael VANBEGIN 72 85, Erol SIMSEK 70 RETD, Mikael LUNDBERG 77 W/D.

Course Profile

The Is Molas (par 72, 7,013 yards) layout in Sardinia will be used for this tournament for the next six years. The wind is the venue's only real defence as there is no rough to speak of.

The fairways are wide so big, but wayward hitters aren't punished. As this event comes late in the calendar the greens can look a little bit pale, but they still run true.

The fairways are usually hard due to the lack of rain and watering system.

Players/Points to Note

●**Ian Poulter** has a superb record at Is Molas – he won the Italian Open held there in 2000 (a year after placing seventh in the Is Molas Challenge) and was third in 2001.

●**Bradley Dredge** won the Is Molas Challenge in 1999 and was second in the 2001 Italian Open.

●**Costantino Rocca** has finished in the top ten on four occasions but never won his national Open and it's worth pointing out that it's over 20 years since an Italian was successful in the Italian Open.

●**Patrik Sjoland** won a rain shortened Italian Open in 1998 and can also boast finishing positions of second, 12th, 20th and 29th (his worst finish) in five starts.

●**Jose Maria Olazabal** has five top-ten finishes in eight starts since 1990.

●**Vijay Singh** and **Mark James** are previous course winners, while **Thomas Levet** and **Massimo Scarpa** has had two top-20 finishes in the Is Molas Challenge.

●In 2002, like 2001, this event will be the last regular tournament of the season – so watch out for players who are around the 115 mark on the Order of Merit. A good performance in the Italian Open can secure their playing rights for the next season – as it did for **Mark Roe** in 2001. **Eduardo Romero**, **Padraig Harrington**, **Greg Turner** and **Dean Robertson** are others to note.

Previous Results

2000: 1. Ian Poulter (-21), 2. Gordon Brand Jnr (-20), 3. Richard Green (-18), Francisco Cea (-18).

1999: 1. Dean Robertson (-17), 2. Padraig Harrington (-16), 3. Phillip Price (-15), Russell Claydon (-15), Gary Evans (-15).

1998: 1. Patrik Sjoland (-21), 2. Jose Maria Olazabal (-18), Joakim Haeggman (-18).

1997: 1. Bernhard Langer (-15), 2. Jose Maria Olazabal (-14), 3. Darren Clarke (-11).

1996: 1. Jim Payne (-9), 2. Patrik Sjoland (-8), 3. Miguel Angel Jimenez (-7), Jonathan Lomas (-7), Lee Westwood (-7).

VOLVO MASTERS

Montecastillo G.C., 8 Nov to 11 Nov 2001, purse 3,234,479 euros

Pos	Name	R1	R2	R3	R4	Total	To par	Money	DD(y)	DA%	GIR%	Putts
1	P HARRINGTON	67	71	-	66	204	-12	539,074	281.7	61.9	75.0	86
2	Paul MCGINLEY	66	69	-	70	205	-11	359,383	276.3	81.0	83.3	94
3	Adam SCOTT	67	74	-	65	206	-10	202,478	294.2	66.7	74.1	85
4	R KARLSSON	71	68	-	68	207	-9	137,357	296.3	54.8	55.6	78
	M GRONBERG	70	67	-	70	207	-9	137,357	284.8	64.3	66.7	85
	D CLARKE	70	68	-	69	207	-9	137,357	292.8	71.4	79.6	94
7	Tony JOHNSTONE	69	72	-	67	208	-8	83,449	276.3	69.0	83.3	96
	Bernhard LANGER	69	70	-	69	208	-8	83,449	270.8	54.8	83.3	96
	C MONTGOMERIE	71	69	-	68	208	-8	83,449	276.2	81.0	79.6	90
10	David HOWELL	69	73	-	67	209	-7	61,455	294.0	57.1	68.5	85
	Retief GOOSEN	68	75	-	66	209	-7	61,455	287.3	78.6	79.6	91

Pos	Name	R1	R2	R3	R4	Total	To par
12	Greg TURNER	72	70	-	68	210	-6
	Gary EVANS	69	71	-	70	210	-6
	Roger WESSELS	70	70	-	70	210	-6
	D ROBERTSON	69	72	-	69	210	-6
16	J M OLAZABAL	69	70	-	72	211	-5
	Phillip PRICE	70	73	-	68	211	-5
	Angel CABRERA	69	73	-	69	211	-5
	Peter LONARD	65	78	-	68	211	-5
20	Steve WEBSTER	70	71	-	71	212	-4
21	Soren HANSEN	72	73	-	68	213	-3
	Charlie WI	70	72	-	71	213	-3
	Niclas FASTH	72	67	-	74	213	-3
24	R GONZALEZ	71	76	-	67	214	-2
	Paul LAWRIE	74	73	-	67	214	-2
	David LYNN	71	71	-	72	214	-2
27	Nick O'HERN	69	72	-	74	215	-1
	J BICKERTON	73	75	-	67	215	-1
	C PETTERSSON	70	74	-	71	215	-1
30	Brian DAVIS	68	75	-	73	216	E
	M A JIMNEZ	70	74	-	72	216	E
	M CAMPBELL	73	72	-	71	216	E
33	Anthony WALL	72	71	-	74	217	+1
	S GALLACHER	70	76	-	71	217	+1
35	Mark MOULAND	70	74	-	74	218	+2
	Barry LANE	71	75	-	72	218	+2
	Mark McNULTY	69	74	-	75	218	+2
	R JACQUELIN	72	74	-	72	218	+2
	S KJELDSEN	70	75	-	73	218	+2
	Richard GREEN	72	71	-	75	218	+2
	Thomas LEVET	69	76	-	73	218	+2
	Jean HUGO	72	72	-	74	218	+2
	Greg OWEN	73	76	-	69	218	+2
44	Pierre FULKE	73	72	-	74	219	+3
	Thomas BJORN	73	69	-	77	219	+3
	F JACOBSON	73	77	-	69	219	+3
	A COLTART	70	76	-	73	219	+3
	M LUNDBERG	73	74	-	72	219	+3
49	Ian POULTER	64	81	-	76	221	+5
	Ian GARBUTT	71	76	-	74	221	+5
	Paul CASEY	76	74	-	71	221	+5
52	Sven STRUVER	72	79	-	71	222	+6
	Anders HANSEN	69	74	-	79	222	+6
	Lee WESTWOOD	69	76	-	77	222	+6
55	R RUSSELL	70	77	-	76	223	+7
56	Justin ROSE	69	83	-	72	224	+8
	Henrik STENSON	81	73	-	70	224	+8
58	P O'MALLEY	77	74	-	74	225	+9
	Brett RUMFORD	70	81	-	74	225	+9
60	Gregory HAVRET	79	79	-	77	226	+10
61	Olle KARLSSON	72	79	-	76	227	+11
62	Daren LEE	75	78	-	75	228	+12
63	S BALLESTEROS	79	80	-	71	230	+14
64	Ian WOOSNAM	74	77	-	-		DISQ
65	W BENNETT	72	78	-	-		W/D
66	Gary ORR	77	80	-	-		W/D

Sponsored by Stan James

Tournament Report

After finishing runner up on seven occasions this season, Padraig Harrington finally got his nose out in front and stayed there, by winning the Volvo Masters in Jerez, Spain.

The last event of the season not only brought the Irishman his maiden 2001 success, but also, second place (where else) in the Order of Merit. The most consistent performer of the year was rewarded with his win in a tournament that was shortened to 54 holes, due to bad weather over the first three days.

And Harrington achieved it by defeating good friend Paul McGinley down the stretch. In a final day full of drama four players had the chance of victory.

Adam Scott set the clubhouse target after a superb last day 65, which brought him to ten under, despite three putting the 16th green.

That hole also saw the demise of Darren Clarke, whom Harrington overtook in the Order of Merit, as the Ulsterman found water with his second shot and had to sign for a bogey six. So it was left to the two Dubliners to vie for supremacy over the closing holes.

McGinley had led by two going into the final day but mistakes early on in his round saw him drop back into the pack.

Playing the last, Harrington made a 20-foot putt to take the lead. Minutes later, McGinley had a slightly longer putt to take the tournament to extra time, but his effort missed, handing the glory to his World Cup team-mate.

WINNER . . . Irish ace, Padraig Harrington

Sponsored by Stan James

Course Profile

Montecastillo Golf Club (par 72 7,069 yards) in Spain has been used for this event for the past five years.

It is a Jack Nicklaus-designed course that has forgiving fairways making low scores the norm. The large greens yield plenty of birdie opportunities.

The wind can be a factor but overall it is the players' form with their irons that is most important. The site for the 2002 renewal was tbc at time of writing.

Players/Points to Note

●The top 55 from the Order of Merit plus the last five champions and six invitees make up the field – there is no halfway out.

●**Darren Clarke** has a superb record in this event since it moved to Montecastillo. In five starts, he has finished in the top 15 every time. His form figures from 1997 15-5-Win-2-4. In that time he has shot just two rounds over par. He also shares the course record (with **Per-Ulrik Johansson** and **Michael Campbell**) of 63.

●**Jose Maria Olazabal** isn't punished for his erratic driving so much at this venue and it shows. In the three times he has completed the event at it's current home he has finished third, seventh and fifth and 16th.

●Last year's winner, **Padraig Harrington**, had posted four successive top-20 finishes at Montecastillo (including two runners-up places), as had **Colin Montgomerie** and **Bernhard Langer**, who shared seventh place in 2001.

●**Peter O'Malley** (three top tens), **Andrew Coltart** (two top tens) and **Ian Woosnam** also have decent records at the track.

●In what must be no more than a coincidence, no player has ever won this title twice since its inception in 1988. The roll of champions is impressive and all of them have been excellent players but surely someone will win this tournament again.

Previous Results

2000: 1. Pierre Fulke (-16), 2. Darren Clarke (-15), 3. Lee Westwood (-13), Michael Campbell (-13).

1999: 1. Miguel Angel Jimenez (-19), 2. Bernhard Langer (-17), Padraig Harrington (-17), Retief Goosen (-17).

1998: 1. Darren Clarke (-17), 2. Andrew Coltart (-15), 3. Colin Montgomerie (-14).

1997: 1. Lee Westwood (-16), 2. Padraig Harrington (-13), 3. Jose Maria Olazabal (-12).

1996: 1. Mark McNulty (-8), 2. Sam Torrance (-1), Wayne Westner (-1), Jose Coceres (-1), Lee Westwood (-1).

MERCEDES CHAMPIONSHIP

Plantation, Kapalua, 11 Jan to 14 Jan 2001, purse $3,500,000

Pos	Name	R1	R2	R3	R4	Total	To par	Money	DD(y)	DA%	GIR%	Putts
1	Jim FURYK	69	69	69	67	274	-18	$630,000	244.4	75	82	114
2	Rory SABBATINI	69	69	65	72	275	-17	$380,000	270.9	75	83	124
3	Ernie ELS	68	66	73	69	276	-16	$203,000	257.3	77	89	128
	Vijay SINGH	71	67	67	71	276	-16	$203,000	264.0	70	88	126
5	John HUSTON	74	67	69	67	277	-15	$140,000	261.4	92	92	124
6	Rocco MEDIATE	70	69	70	69	278	-14	$126,000	255.5	63	81	117
7	David DUVAL	73	71	65	70	279	-13	$118,000	272.3	75	83	127
8	Michael CLARK II	69	70	72	69	280	-12	$99,000	256.9	73	85	126
	Justin LEONARD	67	73	69	71	280	-12	$99,000	244.9	75	90	127
	David TOMS	70	71	67	72	280	-12	$99,000	247.8	85	90	125
	Tiger WOODS	70	73	68	69	280	-12	$99,000	274.3	73	86	129

Pos	Name	R1	R2	R3	R4	Total	To par		Pos	Name	R1	R2	R3	R4	Total	To par
12	Billy ANDRADE	69	70	69	73	281	-11		23	Brad FAXON	71	70	71	73	285	-7
	Stewart CINK	69	71	69	72	281	-11			J PARNEVIK	76	66	72	71	285	-7
	D PAULSON	70	72	67	72	281	-11		25	Hal SUTTON	70	74	73	69	286	-6
	Mike WEIR	70	70	68	73	281	-11		26	Tom LEHMAN	74	73	71	71	289	-3
16	Kirk TRIPLETT	71	73	68	70	282	-10			T SCHERRER	74	71	72	72	289	-3
17	Paul AZINGER	70	70	68	75	283	-9		28	Robert ALLENBY	72	74	73	71	290	-2
	Chris DIMARCO	71	73	69	70	283	-9			Phil MICKELSON	72	73	72	73	290	-2
19	Carlos FRANCO	70	76	68	70	284	-8		30	S VERPLANK	74	73	71	73	291	-1
	Dudley HART	70	77	69	68	284	-8		31	Jim CARTER	80	72	72	72	296	+4
	Loren ROBERTS	74	69	71	70	284	-8		32	Notah BEGAY III	75	76	71	75	297	+5
	Duffy WALDORF	70	70	71	73	284	-8		33	Steve LOWERY	80	73	71	75	299	+7

Tournament Report

Jim Furyk showed no signs of ring rustiness to win the Mercedes Championship at the Plantation Course in Kapalua, Hawaii.

The 30-year-old hadn't swung a club in anger for two months because of injury, but sunk an eight-foot putt on the last to post an 18-under clubhouse target.

Furyk, who qualified for this 'winners from the previous year only' tournament by claiming the Doral Ryder Open in gusty conditions, again had to get the better of the elements.

And after completing 72 holes fully expected to have to take part in a play-off. That was because South African Rory Sabbatini had what looked like a gimme to force extra time.

However, from three feet, Sabbatini somehow contrived to miss and Furyk looked as surprised as anyone to win. Furyk, though, was the only player to shoot four sub-70 rounds and battled back from four strokes down at the start of the final day's play.

His charge started at the fifth, when he rolled in a 60-footer for eagle and when he did make errors he managed to get up and down in regulation. It was the third time Furyk had won in Hawaii.

Els missed relatively short putts on five occasions on the back nine and after a poor approach shot on the last the Big Easy's chance had gone. Sabbatini played solid golf all day but the birdies wouldn't come.

Then his miss on the last coupled with Furyk's birdie meant the event slipped from his grasp.

Course Profile

The Plantation course at Kapalua (par 73, 7,263 yards) is long and as it's built into the side of a mountain the terrain can be punishing on a golfers limbs. You have to be physically fit to win around here.

The greens are some of the biggest on Tour (at around 9,500 square feet on average), which means you have to putt well.

The biggest factor, though, is the wind, which can blow as hard as it did at Carnoustie in 1999.

Players/Points to Note

●This tournament is only open to the winners of last year's US Tour events. The field, therefore, will be small and for those of you who like an each way punt, this tournament usually offers plenty of value.

●**Tiger Woods** loves to beat the best and, as every tournament winner from the previous year on Tour takes part in this event, you can be sure the World No.1 will be up for this one. The length of the course suits Tiger down to a tee, so to speak. In three visits to Kapalua Woods hasn't finished outside the top eight.

●**David Duval** is another big hitter whose game should prosper here, his form figures read 1-3-7 at this event since it moved to Kapalua. He also shares the course record (63) at the layout.

●**Vijay Singh**'s low-ball striking is perfect for this windy track (form figures at Kapalua of 4-8-3). Also with the huge greens, his skill in judging long putts is vital.

●Last year's champion **Jim Furyk** also won on this course in 1996, when it hosted the Kapalua International. Furyk also won the Hawaiian Open in 1997, so obviously likes playing in these Pacific islands.

●**Davis Love** will be back in this event in 2002 and is a fine Hawaii performer. Love was eighth in this event in 1999.

Previous Results

2000: 1. Tiger Woods (-16), won play-off, 2. Ernie Els (-16), 3. David Duval (-12).

1999: 1. David Duval (-26), 2. Billy Mayfair (-17), Mark O'Meara (-17).

1998: 1. Phil Mickelson (-17), 2. Mark O'Meara (-16), Tiger Woods (-16).

1997 1. *Tiger Woods (-14), won play-off, 2. Tom Lehman (-14), 3. Guy Boros (-9). Played over 54 holes.

1996 Mark O'Meara (-17) Nick Faldo (-14), Scott Hoch (-14).

TOUCHSTONE ENERGY TUCSON OPEN

Omni Tuscon Resort, 11 Jan to 14 Jan 2001, purse $3,000,000

Pos	Name	R1	R2	R3	R4	Total	To par	Money	DD(y)	DA%	GIR%	Putts
1	Garrett WILLIS	71	69	64	69	273	-15	$540,000	285.3	64	68	106
2	K SUTHERLAND	67	72	67	68	274	-14	$324,000	278.9	68	76	113
3	Bob TWAY	73	69	67	66	275	-13	$174,000	270.4	59	72	112
	Geoff OGILVY	67	72	68	68	275	-13	$174,000	284.1	73	78	114
5	Cliff KRESGE	72	67	71	66	276	-12	$105,375	275.9	73	72	110
	K.J. CHOI	70	70	70	66	276	-12	$105,375	286.5	61	75	115
	Greg KRAFT	74	65	69	68	276	-12	$105,375	267.0	73	72	110
	Mark WIEBE	69	67	66	74	276	-12	$105,375	278.4	66	78	117
9	Rich BEEM	70	69	71	67	277	-11	$72,000	287.1	57	72	115
	Jeff MAGGERT	70	68	70	69	277	-11	$72,000	272.9	64	71	109
	Bernhard LANGER	68	69	70	70	277	-11	$72,000	274.1	70	76	116
	Steve FLESCH	72	69	66	70	277	-11	$72,000	289.8	73	68	113
	Harrison FRAZAR	68	73	66	70	277	-11	$72,000	282.3	68	71	113
	Mark HENSBY	69	68	69	71	277	-11	$72,000	277.9	70	76	117

Pos	Name	R1	R2	R3	R4	Total	To par
15	Jerry KELLY	70	69	70	69	278	-10
	M CALCAVECCHIA	71	71	67	69	278	-10
	Hunter HAAS	71	68	68	71	278	-10
	Brandt JOBE	72	69	66	71	278	-10
	Glen HNATIUK	71	69	66	72	278	-10
20	Craig KANADA	70	70	72	67	279	-9
	Bob BURNS	70	70	70	69	279	-9
	Fred FUNK	70	73	67	69	279	-9
	Mike SPOSA	71	70	69	69	279	-9
	Russ COCHRAN	71	69	68	71	279	-9
	Chris RILEY	69	70	68	72	279	-9
26	Tim CLARK	67	73	71	69	280	-8
	Robert GAMEZ	69	70	72	69	280	-8
	Jay Don BLAKE	70	72	68	70	280	-8
	Paul GOYDOS	70	71	69	70	280	-8
	Len MATTIACE	70	71	68	71	280	-8
	Fred COUPLES	71	69	68	72	280	-8
32	Jonathan KAYE	72	68	71	70	281	-7
	S McCARRON	71	69	71	70	281	-7
	Willie WOOD	67	75	69	70	281	-7
	Olin BROWNE	68	74	69	70	281	-7
	Ben FERGUSON	74	70	66	71	281	-7
	Kaname YOKOO	68	70	72	71	281	-7
	David PEOPLES	71	70	72	68	281	-7
	Tim HERRON	67	76	66	72	281	-7
	Mike REID	73	67	68	73	281	-7
41	Jim McGOVERN	74	67	70	71	282	-6
	Tommy TOLLES	71	70	71	70	282	-6
	Chris PERRY	70	74	68	70	282	-6
	N LANCASTER	68	76	68	70	282	-6
45	Grant WAITE	71	71	71	70	283	-5
	Larry MIZE	73	70	70	70	283	-5
	Andrew MAGEE	70	66	70	77	283	-5
48	Lee PORTER	69	65	76	74	284	-4
	Carl PAULSON	70	68	74	72	284	-4

Pos	Name	R1	R2	R3	R4	Total	To par
	Chris TIDLAND	71	70	72	71	284	-4
	John DALY	70	72	71	71	284	-4
	Stephen AMES	69	71	73	71	284	-4
	Mark WURTZ	74	70	69	71	284	-4
	J GALLAGHER	70	73	72	69	284	-4
	Glen DAY	67	76	73	68	284	-4
56	Jeff HART	70	73	69	73	285	-3
	Craig BARLOW	71	70	72	72	285	-3
	B SCHWARZROCK	72	71	66	76	285	-3
	Jason GORE	71	72	72	70	285	-3
	J GALLAGHER	72	72	73	68	285	-3
61	Sean MURPHY	70	71	70	75	286	-2
	Ronnie BLACK	70	69	75	72	286	-2
	Steve JONES	70	66	72	78	286	-2
	Kenny PERRY	73	71	70	72	286	-2
	Stephen ALLAN	76	67	73	70	286	-2
	T PERNICE JR	74	70	73	69	286	-2
67	Donnie HAMMOND	70	73	71	73	287	-1
	John COOK	71	71	74	71	287	-1
	Tom PURTZER	73	70	74	70	287	-1
70	Ted TRYBA	72	71	71	74	288	E
71	Jeff BREHAUT	71	70	73	75	289	+1
	Mike SPRINGER	71	72	72	74	289	+1
	Matt GOGEL	72	72	73	72	289	+1
	John RIEGGER	73	71	73	72	289	+1
75	S ELKINGTON	70	74	70	76	290	+2
	Brad ELDER	72	71	76	71	290	+2
77	D STOCKTON	73	71	76	71	291	+3
78	Y MIZUMAKI	70	74	73	75	292	+4
79	Robert DAMRON	71	73	74	75	293	+5
80	Rick FEHR	70	74	76	74	294	+6
81	B CHEESMAN	73	71	79	72	295	+7
82	E CANONICA	69	72	77	78	296	+8
83	C BECKMAN	72	70	73	-		WD

Sponsored by Stan James

Tournament Report

Garrett Willis, just a month out of Q-School and playing in his first US Tour event, was the shock winner of the Touchstone Energy Tucson Open at the Omni Tucson National in Arizona.

The 27-year-old rookie looked as surprised as everyone else as he managed to fend off the attentions of Kevin Sutherland to secure a maiden victory and a two year tour exemption that goes with it.

Willis didn't manage to finish any of his last nine tournaments on the Buy.com Tour in the 2000 for one reason or another (he missed five cuts, withdrew from three events and was disqualified in another).

But after claiming 11th spot in the Q-School was determined to give the full tour a go. Willis had to come from behind to win, as Mark Wiebe held a two shot advantage on him going into the final round. But as Wiebe fell away the challenge was to come from Sutherland, who birdied the 14th and the 16th to set the clubhouse target of 14 under.

Willis appeared to be fading down the stretch, the last of his five birdies came at the 12th hole, and nerves were definitely a factor when he missed a four foot putt on the 17th. And when he left his approach to the last some 60 feet of the flag, Sutherland could have been forgiven for thinking he might get a second chance.

But Willis wasn't to be denied, confidently two putting for the win.

MISSED THE CUT: Curtis STRANGE 68 77, Bob MAY 73 72, Pete JORDAN 72 73, Joey SINDELAR 75 70, Tommy ARMOUR III 75 70, Robin FREEMAN 75 70, Esteban TOLEDO 74 71, Brent GEIBERGER 74 71, Per Ulrik JOHANSSON 74 71, Michael MUEHR 71 74, Keith CLEARWATER 72 73, Don POOLEY 74 71, Jay WILLIAMSON 74 71, Craig PERKS 74 71, Tripp ISENHOUR 74 71, Dan FORSMAN 72 74, Edward FRYATT 72 74, Sam RANDOLPH 73 73, Craig PARRY 73 73, J.P. HAYES 77 69, Paul STANKOWSKI 74 72, Chris SMITH 76 70, Brett UPPER 74 72, Marco DAWSON 73 73, Joe DURANT 73 73, Spike MCROY 73 73, Billy MAYFAIR 76 70, Brian WILSON 75 71, Rocky WALCHER 74 72, Jerry SMITH 73 74, Lee JANZEN 75 72, Ian LEGGATT 77 70, Danny ELLIS 73 74, Steve PATE 76 71, Shaun MICHEEL 78 69, Mathew GOGGIN 74 73, Ben BATES 73 74, J.J. HENRY 72 75, Kent JONES 70 77, Briny BAIRD 75 72, J.L. LEWIS 72 76, Woody AUSTIN 76 72, Dicky PRIDE 70 78, Richie COUGHLAN 78 70, Jeff SLUMAN 76 73, Kiernan MATTSON 75 74, Craig A. SPENCE 73 76, Fred WADSWORTH 73 76, Jay SYNKELMA 75 74, Joe OGILVIE 72 78, Gary NICKLAUS 73 77, Joe OZAKI 74 76, Toru TANIGUCHI 74 76, Jeremy ANDERSON 72 78, Casey MARTIN 74 76, Jeff KERN 77 73, Kevin JOHNSON 80 70, Andrew McLARDY 77 73, Kelly GRUNEWALD 74 76, Bradley HUGHES 79 72, Craig STADLER 76 75, Tom BYRUM 80 72, Fuzzy ZOELLER 79 73, Jeff JULIAN 75 77, Brian GAY 79 75, Paul Gow 78 77, David MORLAND IV 75 80, Brian KONTAK 82 74, Kevin WENTWORTH 79 77, Charley HOFFMAN 82 76, David SUTHERLAND 72 WD, David BERGANIO 77 WD,

Sponsored by Stan James

Course Profile

Although in the middle of the desert, the Tucson National (par 72, 7,109 yards) isn't a typical desert course. There are some big mature trees throughout the layout that almost resembles a European Tour parkland course.

It's long, and can favour the big hitters but the 663 yard par five 15th hole, is inaccessible to all in two. Still, those players who can play the par fives well will be in with a strong chance of success.

Players/Points to Note

● In 2002, like last year, the Touchstone Energy Tucson Open will play opposite the Mercedes Championship. Meaning that all the best players will not be competing

● Like last year, the field will be weak but this has always been a championship that is a breeding ground for the future. For veterans **Craig Stadler** and **Bruce Lietzke**, this tournament provided them with their first win US Tour in the 70s and 80s respectively, while **Phil Mickeslon** won this event as an amateur in 1991. **Garret Willis** was the 20-something pro that won last year, watch for them **Charles Howell**, **Bryce Molder**, **Ty Tryon**, **Matt Kuchar**, **Ed Fryatt**, **Matt Gogel** and **Rory Sabbatini** and in 2002.

● Of the rest, **Bob Tway** has six top-ten finishes in 15 starts here (including third last year). **Mike Reid** is another veteran who can boast multiple top-dozen finishes.

● **Jim Carter** had won a college event as an amateur on this course before winning in 2000.

● **Corey Pavin** has finished in the top ten four times in seven starts, while veteran **Tom Watson** can also boast a top-ten strike rate of over 50%.

● Interesting competitors last year who haven't normally teed up in this event were **Bernhard Langer** (ninth) and **Fred Couples** (26th). **Steve Flesch** and **Paul Stankowski** also have good records in this tournament.

Previous Results

2000: 1. Jim Carter (-19), 2. Chris DiMarco (-17), Jean Van De Velde (-17), Tom Scherrer (-17).

1999: 1. Gabriel Hjertstedt (-12), won play-off, 2. Tommy Armour III (-12), 3. Mike Reid (-11), Kirk Triplett (-11).

1998: 1. David Duval (-19), 2. Justin Leonard (-15), David Toms (-15).

1997: 1. Jeff Sluman (-13), 2. Steve Jones (-12), 3. Brad Bryant (-11), Paul Stankowski (-11).

1996: 1. Phil Mickelson (-14), 2. Bob Tway (-12), 3. Four players tied.

SONY OPEN

Waialae Country Club, 18 Jan to 21Jan 2001, purse $4,000,000

Pos	Name	R1	R2	R3	R4	Total	To par	Money	DD(y)	DA%	GIR%	Putts
1	Brad FAXON	64	64	67	65	260	-20	$720,000	283.9	52	67	103
2	Tom LEHMAN	66	67	65	66	264	-16	$432,000	295.0	52	78	114
3	Ernie ELS	68	65	65	69	267	-13	$272,000	283.9	41	75	113
4	Billy ANDRADE	69	69	66	65	269	-11	$192,000	284.0	57	68	113
5	Briny BAIRD	68	70	68	65	271	-9	$135,600	282.3	57	81	120
	Greg CHALMERS	69	69	66	67	271	-9	$135,600	292.8	59	83	123
	Fred FUNK	66	69	69	67	271	-9	$135,600	285.9	70	60	110
	N Joe OZAKI	66	70	68	67	271	-9	$135,600	287.6	66	69	113
	Loren ROBERTS	67	67	69	68	271	-9	$135,600	266.0	52	60	108
10	Tom BYRUM	68	70	67	67	272	-8	$96,000	278.5	77	68	112
	Brian GAY	71	65	70	66	272	-8	$96,000	282.6	66	57	107
	Davis LOVE III	70	68	65	69	272	-8	$96,000	306.8	57	68	112
	Jeff SLUMAN	66	73	66	67	272	-8	$96,000	290.5	59	64	108

Pos	Name	R1	R2	R3	R4	Total	To par
14	Stephen AMES	68	68	68	69	273	-7
	Jim FURYK	66	67	69	71	273	-7
	John HUSTON	68	66	69	70	273	-7
	Spike McROY	66	69	71	67	273	-7
	S MICHEEL	67	68	69	69	273	-7
19	Michael CLARK II	72	66	69	67	274	-6
	Carlos FRANCO	66	67	69	72	274	-6
	Duffy WALDORF	73	66	70	65	274	-6
22	B HUGHES	67	66	71	71	275	-5
	Vijay SINGH	68	70	67	70	275	-5
	Chris DiMARCO	67	69	67	72	275	-5
	Scott DUNLAP	68	68	68	71	275	-5
	Steve LOWERY	68	70	69	68	275	-5
	S MARUYAMA	69	66	70	70	275	-5
	Craig PARRY	69	69	66	71	275	-5
29	Robert ALLENBY	70	67	68	71	276	-4
	Jim CARTER	70	69	68	69	276	-4
	K.J. CHOI	68	70	69	69	276	-4
	Joe DURANT	68	69	68	71	276	-4
	Jerry KELLY	69	65	73	69	276	-4
	F LANGHAM	66	69	69	72	276	-4
	Jerry SMITH	71	66	67	72	276	-4
	Kaname YOKOO	70	66	72	68	276	-4
37	Stuart APPLEBY	72	67	69	69	277	-3
	D BERGANIO Jr.	71	66	67	73	277	-3
	Bill GLASSON	67	68	68	74	277	-3
	J.L. LEWIS	66	69	70	72	277	-3
	Jeff MAGGERT	69	70	69	69	277	-3
	David PEOPLES	67	70	73	67	277	-3
43	Olin BROWNE	67	68	71	72	278	-2
	Cliff KRESGE	68	68	70	72	278	-2
	R SABBATINI	71	68	66	73	278	-2
	Esteban TOLEDO	71	66	73	68	278	-2
47	Steve ALLAN	70	69	69	71	279	-1
	Dudley HART	69	70	70	70	279	-1
	Larry MIZE	64	71	71	73	279	-1
	Ted TRYBA	68	70	75	66	279	-1
51	Bob BURNS	68	70	69	73	280	E
	R COUGHLAN	65	71	70	74	280	E
	Craig BARLOW	69	67	75	69	280	E
	Pete JORDAN	68	71	72	69	280	E
	Corey PAVIN	73	66	71	70	280	E
	Chris PERRY	67	72	68	73	280	E
57	John COOK	71	68	70	72	281	+1
	John RIEGGER	68	70	75	68	281	+1
59	Paul GOYDOS	68	71	71	72	282	+2
	K GRUNEWALD	71	68	74	69	282	+2
	Chris SMITH	70	69	68	75	282	+2
	Garrett WILLIS	68	70	68	76	282	+2
63	John DALY	64	72	76	71	283	+3
	F LICKLITER II	71	66	74	72	283	+3
	Sean MURPHY	66	71	70	76	283	+3
66	J.J. HENRY	67	71	72	74	284	+4
	P JACOBSEN	69	64	75	76	284	+4
68	J ANDERSON	72	67	75	71	285	+5
	Michael MUEHR	68	70	75	72	285	+5
	Gary NICKLAUS	66	71	70	78	285	+5

Sponsored by Stan James

Tournament Report

Brad Faxon led the field a merry dance at the Waialae Country Club in Hawaii to land the Sony Open by four shots. It was Faxon's eighth US Tour win and one that came from the front.

The 39-year-old led from start to finish, with Tom Lehman his nearest challenger in the end and Ernie Els a further three shots adrift. It was Lehman that asked the most questions of Faxon. Three down at the start of the day Lehman got to within one stroke of the eventual winner after six holes but couldn't catch Faxon and faded over the back nine.

Faxon started as he meant to go on, chipping in from 30 yards at the second. And two monster birdies plus an eagle secured the victory. Els, like last week in the Mercedes Championship, flattered to deceive. A third round 65 meant he was tied for second with Lehman after Saturday's play but a final day 69 was a lacklustre effort from the South African.

Faxon opened up with successive 64s to post a commanding halfway lead and the $720,000 winners cheque was the biggest of his career. Lehman must be sick of the sight of Faxon, as the pair met in the WGC Matchplay Championship in Melbourne just a few weeks ago, Faxon again coming out on top.

Billy Andrade's fast-finishing 65 ensured the 36-year-old placed fourth on his own. Duffy Waldorf, along with Andrade and Faxon, was the only other player to shoot 65 on the Sunday.

MISSED THE CUT: Tommy ARMOUR III 69 71, Cameron BECKMAN 68 72, Notah BEGAY III 70 70, Stewart CINK 70 70, Joel EDWARDS 71 69, Paul GOW 70 70, Neal LANCASTER 66 74, Andrew MAGEE 68 72, Andrew McLARDY 68 72, Tom PERNICE Jr. 72 68, Lee PORTER 70 70, Chris RILEY 69 71, Rich BEEM 71 70, Jay Don BLAKE 69 72, Emanuele CANONICA 66 75, Brandel CHAMBLEE 69 72, Robin FREEMAN 72 69, Brian HENNINGER 69 72, Ryuji IMADA 74 67, Tripp ISENHOUR 73 68, Per Ulrik JOHANSSON 68 73, Kevin JOHNSON 69 72, Matt KUCHAR 71 70, Len MATTIACE 72 69, Dennis PAULSON 73 68, Tom SCHERRER 70 71, Tommy TOLLES 69 72, Paul AZINGER 72 70, Harrison FRAZAR 71 71, Edward FRYATT 70 72, Mark HENSBY 71 71, Bob MAY 69 73, Chris TIDLAND 73 69, Doug BARRON 74 69, Steve JONES 70 73, Bobby KALINOWSKI 69 74, Jesper PARNEVIK 69 74, Hidemichi TANAKA 67 76, Jeff GALLAGHER 76 68, Jimmy GREEN 77 67, Glen Hnatiuk 72 72, Kent Jones 75 69, Greg KRAFT 70 74, Rocky WALCHER 70 74, Danny ELLIS 70 75, Keiichiro FUKABORI 72 73, Jason GORE 71 74, David MORLAND IV 78 67, Geoff OGILVY 71 74, Carl PAULSON 73 72, Nobuhito Sato 71 74, Jay WILLIAMSON 74 71, David ISHII 73 73, Jim M. JOHNSON 72 74, Jeff JULIAN 74 72, Ben FERGUSON 77 70, Mathew GOGGIN 73 74, Craig PERKS 74 73, Brian SASADA 70 78, Brian WILSON 71 77, Woody AUSTIN 75 74, Mike HULBERT 76 73, Ian LEGGATT 78 71, Joe OGILVIE 75 74, Scott SIMPSON 80 70, Craig STADLER 75 75, Douglas BOHN 78 73, Hunter HAAS 76 75, Matthew HALL 74 77, Brandan KOP 77 76, Fred WADSWORTH 74 79, Tommy KIM 80 79, Skip KENDALL 72 W/D, Russ COCHRAN 81 W/D.

Course Profile

After John Huston's record breaking success the Waialae Country Club (par 70, 7,060 yards) course was toughened up by changing the par from 70 to 72.

However, the prerequisite for winning hasn't altered. If you hit the greens in regulation more often than not, you'll be in with a chance of winning.

The greens are bigger than average and run true. The course isn't long so the big hitters have less of an advantage. The wind can be a factor.

Players/Points to Note

● This used to be a tournament where scoring was low and birdies were easy. But after **John Huston**'s runaway success in 1998, officials decided to toughen up the course.

● Prior to 1999, anyone could come here and shoot low but, since then, only experienced pros (**Jeff Sluman**, **Paul Azinger** and **Brad Faxon**) have won.

● Azinger won in 2000 and can boast nine top-ten finishes in this tournament.

● Faxon should have won here in 1996 before capturing the title in 2001.

● John Huston will have positive associations with this event after his win in record breaking win in 1998. He also favours the Bermuda grass greens.

● **Tom Lehman** has finished in the top six here on six occasions and has been in with a shout of victory on each occasion.

● **Davis Love** still holds the course record, courtesy of a second round 60 in 1994 and has four top-ten finishes in six visits, plus a victory on these Pacific Islands before.

● **Jim Furyk** has won three times in Hawaii while **Ernie Els**, **Jesper Parnevik** and **Stuart Appleby** have good records here. **Corey Pavin** is the only dual winner (1986 and 1987) of this event still on Tour.

● Watch out for Hawaiian resident **Scott Simpson** who missed his first Hawaiian Open for 22 years last season through injury.

Previous Results

2000: 1. Paul Azinger (-19), 2. Stuart Appleby (-12), 3. John Huston (-10), Jesper Parnevik (-10).
1999: 1. Jeff Sluman (-9), 2. Five players tied.
1998: 1. John Huston (-28), 2. Tom Watson (-21), 3. Trevor Dodds (-20).
1997: 1. Paul Stankowski (-17), won play-off, 2. Jim Furyk (-17), Mike Reid (-17).
1996: 1. Jim Furyk (-11), won play-off, 2. Brad Faxon (-11), 3. Steve Stricker (-10).

93

PHOENIX OPEN

TPC of Scottsdale, 25 Jan to 28 Jan 2001, purse $4,000,000

Pos	Name	R1	R2	R3	R4	Total	To par	Money	DD(y)	DA%	GIR%	Putts
1	M CALCAVECCHIA	65	60	64	67	256	-28	$720,000	287.0	79	78	105
2	Rocco MEDIATE	68	63	64	69	264	-20	$432,000	284.9	71	72	107
3	Steve LOWERY	69	67	64	68	268	-16	$272,000	284.0	73	76	116
4	Scott VERPLANK	64	66	70	70	270	-14	$192,000	281.8	75	78	117
5	Chris DiMARCO	68	67	65	71	271	-13	$152,000	288.0	61	64	106
	Tiger WOODS	65	73	68	65	271	-13	$152,000	307.8	64	75	118
7	Tom LEHMAN	64	70	69	69	272	-12	$129,000	282.5	66	76	116
	Steve STRICKER	71	62	72	67	272	-12	$129,000	278.6	71	76	115
9	Stewart CINK	65	66	71	71	273	-11	$104,000	276.4	70	75	115
	John DALY	67	70	70	66	273	-11	$104,000	301.8	61	75	116
	Fred FUNK	68	69	70	66	273	-11	$104,000	269.1	77	74	117
	David TOMS	69	69	68	67	273	-11	$104,000	274.6	80	72	115

Pos	Name	R1	R2	R3	R4	Total	To par
13	Edward FRYATT	66	69	72	67	274	-10
	Sergio GARCIA	67	71	70	66	274	-10
	Billy MAYFAIR	68	71	70	65	274	-10
	Chris PERRY	65	70	72	67	274	-10
	Nick PRICE	70	70	69	65	274	-10
18	F LICKLITER II	70	66	70	69	275	-9
19	H FRAZAR	67	71	72	66	276	-8
	Paul GOYDOS	70	68	72	66	276	-8
	S MARUYAMA	69	65	72	70	276	-8
22	Stephen AMES	69	68	71	69	277	-7
23	Bob BURNS	69	65	72	72	278	-6
	Fred COUPLES	67	70	72	69	278	-6
	Steve FLESCH	67	71	71	69	278	-6
	M GOGGIN	67	68	74	69	278	-6
	Mark HENSBY	70	69	70	69	278	-6
	Tim HERRON	69	70	71	68	278	-6
	Jonathan KAYE	71	69	71	67	278	-6
	Frank NOBILO	65	69	72	72	278	-6
	Steve PATE	65	71	76	66	278	-6
	Mike WEIR	66	74	69	69	278	-6
33	Steve JONES	70	70	71	68	279	-5
	Davis LOVE III	68	66	77	68	279	-5
	S McCARRON	67	65	73	74	279	-5
36	T ARMOUR III	68	67	72	73	280	-4
	Brad ELDER	64	75	71	70	280	-4
	Brian GAY	67	68	74	71	280	-4
	Matt GOGEL	69	71	71	69	280	-4
	Brandt JOBE	72	67	71	70	280	-4
	Bob MAY	66	71	72	71	280	-4
	Vijay SINGH	71	69	69	71	280	-4
	Hal SUTTON	72	66	75	67	280	-4
44	Jay Don BLAKE	70	67	76	68	281	-3
	Joe DURANT	70	68	73	70	281	-3
	Glen HNATIUK	71	67	69	74	281	-3
	Andrew MAGEE	66	71	72	72	281	-3
	Len MATTIACE	71	69	73	68	281	-3
49	Stuart APPLEBY	72	66	72	72	282	-2
	Nolan HENKE	69	70	72	71	282	-2
	Joel EDWARDS	70	70	71	71	282	-2
	Dan FORSMAN	70	65	71	76	282	-2
	Skip KENDALL	71	68	71	72	282	-2
	David PEOPLES	67	68	76	71	282	-2
55	Steve ALLAN	72	66	71	74	283	-1
	Paul AZINGER	72	68	70	73	283	-1
	B HENNINGER	67	73	73	70	283	-1
	B HUGHES	69	69	71	74	283	-1
	P STANKOWSKI	69	67	72	75	283	-1
60	G CHALMERS	68	71	75	70	284	E
	M CLARK II	68	71	73	72	284	E
	M A JIMENEZ	68	70	73	73	284	E
	J M OLAZABAL	68	72	73	71	284	E
	Kenny PERRY	68	68	75	73	284	E
65	Scott DUNLAP	69	70	72	74	285	+1
	B McCALLISTER	66	72	76	71	285	+1
	Jim CARTER	67	72	70	77	286	+2
	F LANGHAM	69	69	74	76	288	+4
	Olin BROWNE	68	69	79	73	289	+5
70	B GEIBERGER	68	72	77	73	290	+6
	J.P. HAYES	70	69	74	77	290	+6

Sponsored by Stan James

Tournament Report

A 46-year-old US Tour record fell when Mark Calcavecchia won the Phoenix Open at TPC of Scottsdale in Arizona.

Calc notched an amazing 28-under par score of 256 to break the 72 hole low for a US Tour event. The previous best was 257, set in 1955 by Mike Souchak at the Texas Open.

Not surprisingly, Calcavecchia destroyed the field, Rocco Mediate was a distant second some eight shots back.

The first round headlines, though, were stolen by Andrew Magee, whose tee shot on the 332-yard par four 17th saw the ball find it's way into the hole, via the putter of Tom Byrum.

Byrum was walking off the green when Magee's effort caught the heel and ricocheted into the cup. The second round was all about the 1989 Open champion.

Calc, who trailed by a shot after day one, fired a Friday 60, his lowest ever score and one that would see daylight open up between him and the field. At the same time Tiger Woods, who started the day level with Calcavecchia, shot a one-over par 73.

Calc got to 17-under at the halfway stage but didn't let up. His iron play was superb and his putter red hot as he went for more birdies. A third round 64 followed and with no challengers in sight he cruised to a record win by carding a Sunday 67.

It was the third time Calcavecchia had won at Scottsdale following success at the Arizona track in 1989 and 1992.

MISSED THE CUT: Rich BEEM 74 67, Ronnie BLACK 75 66, Tim CLARK 70 71, Doug DUNAKEY 75 66, Ernie ELS 69 72, Chris ENDRES 69 72, Robin FREEMAN 68 73, Lee JANZEN 72 69, Neal LANCASTER 71 70, Justin LEONARD 71 70, Jesper PARNEVIK 67 74, Tom PURTZER 68 73, Chris RILEY 72 69, Glen DAY 71 71, Gabriel HJERTSTEDT 76 66, Pete JORDAN 72 70, Spike McROY 71 71, Ted TRYBA 72 70, Grant WAITE 70 72, Duffy WALDORF 71 71, Briny BAIRD 69 74, Tom BYRUM 71 72, David DUVAL 70 73, Carlos FRANCO 73 70, Bill GLASSON 70 73, Matt McDOUGALL 69 74, Shaun MICHEEL 75 68, Phil MICKELSON 71 72, Bob TWAY 72 71, Mark WIEBE 70 73, Ben CRENSHAW 76 68, Robert DAMRON 72 72, Bob ESTES 75 69, Joe OGILVIE 70 74, Rory SABBATINI 72 72, Tom SCHERRER 73 71, Billy ANDRADE 71 74, Doug BARRON 69 76, Peter JACOBSEN 71 74, Tom PERNICE, Jr. 76 69, Jerry SMITH 75 70, Craig A. SPENCE 70 75, Kevin SUTHERLAND 75 70, Kirk TRIPLETT 73 72, Jay WILLIAMSON 74 71, Don YRENE 71 74, Robert ALLENBY 74 72, Woody AUSTIN 70 76, Brandel CHAMBLEE 74 72, Mark O'MEARA 72 74, Jeff QUINNEY 72 74, Esteban TOLEDO 72 74, Brian WILSON 75 71, Gary NICKLAUS 70 77, Jean VAN DE VELDE 75 73, Jimmy GREEN 73 76, Brett UPPER 71 78, Notah BEGAY III 72 78, Jeff GOVE 74 W/D, Dennis PAULSON 74 W/D, Garrett WILLIS 75 W/D.

Sponsored by Stan James

Course Profile

TPC at Scottsdale (par 71, 7,089 yards) is a links type of course in the middle of the desert.

However, as well as the shotmaking skills that are necessary on a links course, players have to be accurate off the tee, as there are innumerable bunkers and wasteland areas throughout the layout to catch stray shots.

Large and boisterous galleries (that usually get behind the local golfers) are the norm, so players have to be able to handle the crowd.

Players/Points to Note

● Before **Mark Calcavecchia** won here in 2001 he had the best stroke average in this tournament. After his success last term that figure is now 68.44. Calc posted a record 72-hole low when winning – 256, one stroke better than Mike Souchak shot in the 1955 Texas Open – and won this event for the third time (following wins in 1989 and 1992). He has finished in the top ten on eight occasions. Calc's 60 in the second round equalled the course record (set by New Zealander Grant Waite).

● **Rocco Mediate**'s won in 1999 and was runner-up last year. He's missed the cut here just once in the the dozen years and has seven top-ten finishes in 14 starts.

● **Justin Leonard** ranks this event as one of his personal favourites. The Texan was runner-up in 1996 and 1999. Scottsdale resident **Tom Lehman**'s local knowledge served him well last year and in previous seasons, as six top-ten finishes suggests.

● Former winners **Jesper Parnevik, Hal Sutton, Phil Mickelson** and **Lee Janzen** have all figured in the top ten of this event on more than one occasion.

● And also watch out for **David Toms, Scott Verplank, Mike Weir** and **John Daly** in 2002.

● Since the tournament moved to Scottsdale in 1987 eight of the 14 champions have been Major winners.

Previous Results

2000: 1. Tom Lehman (-14), 2. Robert Allenby (-13), Rocco Mediate (-13).

1999: 1. Rocco Mediate (-11), 2. Justin Leonard (-9), 3. Tiger Woods (-8).

1998: 1. Jesper Parnevik (-15), 2. Tommy Armour III (-12), Steve Pate (-12), Brent Geiberger (-12), Tom Watson (-12).

1997: 1. Steve Jones (-26), 2. Jesper Parnevik (-15), 3. Nick Price (-14).

1996: 1. Phil Mickelson (-15), won play-off, 2. Justin Leonard (-15), 3. Tom Scherrer (-14).

AT & T PEBBLE BEACH NATIONAL PRO-AM

Pebble Beach Golf Links, 1 Feb to 4 Feb 2001, purse $4,000,000

Pos	Name	R1	R2	R3	R4	Total	To par	Money	DD(y)	DA%	GIR%	Putts
1	Davis LOVE III	71	69	69	63	272	-16	$720,000	277.0	64	78	114
2	Vijay SINGH	66	68	70	69	273	-15	$432,000	267.9	82	75	110
3	Olin BROWNE	68	69	65	73	275	-13	$232,000	254.9	84	78	116
	Phil MICKELSON	70	66	66	73	275	-13	$232,000	269.4	84	76	116
5	Ronnie BLACK	67	68	70	71	276	-12	$160,000	259.9	73	72	114
6	Craig BARLOW	67	71	67	72	277	-11	$139,000	265.5	68	69	111
	Glen DAY	68	75	69	65	277	-11	$139,000	249.3	84	74	111
8	Jerry KELLY	69	68	68	73	278	-10	$112,000	266.0	63	72	118
	F LANGHAM	70	70	70	68	278	-10	$112,000	244.5	77	74	114
	Frank NOBILO	70	70	67	71	278	-10	$112,000	264.8	77	74	116
	Mike WEIR	70	70	65	73	278	-10	$112,000	263.6	73	71	117

Pos	Name	R1	R2	R3	R4	Total	To par
12	S McCARRON	68	73	65	73	279	-9
13	Brad FAXON	71	67	69	73	280	-8
	Tim HERRON	67	70	74	69	280	-8
	Mike SPRINGER	72	70	71	67	280	-8
	Kirk TRIPLETT	71	69	70	70	280	-8
	Grant WAITE	70	73	71	66	280	-8
	Tiger WOODS	66	73	69	72	280	-8
	Kenny PERRY	70	70	69	71	280	-8
20	D BERGANIO JR.	64	73	71	73	281	-7
	K SUTHERLAND	72	69	70	70	281	-7
	Willie WOOD	67	69	73	72	281	-7
23	Steve FLESCH	71	72	66	73	282	-6
	Jonathan KAYE	69	73	68	72	282	-6
	J M OLAZABAL	71	76	67	68	282	-6
	Garrett WILLIS	71	74	69	68	282	-6
27	K.J. CHOI	68	72	72	71	283	-5
	Edward FRYATT	66	72	74	71	283	-5
	Matt GOGEL	69	62	81	71	283	-5
	Joe OGILVIE	72	73	68	70	283	-5
	John RIEGGER	73	68	70	72	283	-5
	Esteban TOLEDO	72	70	72	69	283	-5
	Jerry SMITH	71	70	69	73	283	-5
	Jeff HART	73	69	71	70	283	-5
	David TOMS	70	69	70	74	283	-5
36	Jay Don BLAKE	70	67	72	75	284	-4
	Scott DUNLAP	71	71	69	73	284	-4
	Brad ELDER	66	69	75	74	284	-4
	Kevin JOHNSON	67	72	72	73	284	-4
	T PERNICE, JR.	70	69	72	73	284	-4
	Hal SUTTON	70	71	73	70	284	-4
	R JOHNSON	67	71	72	74	284	-4
43	Mark JOHNSON	65	74	73	73	285	-3
	Corey PAVIN	71	69	71	74	285	-3
	K WENTWORTH	72	71	71	71	285	-3
	Fuzzy ZOELLER	73	68	73	71	285	-3
47	Paul AZINGER	72	70	71	73	286	-2
	P JACOBSEN	71	74	68	73	286	-2
	Dan FORSMAN	71	70	73	72	286	-2
	Mike HEINEN	70	73	71	72	286	-2
	Joey SINDELAR	73	68	71	74	286	-2
	Chris SMITH	71	71	71	73	286	-2
53	R COUGHLAN	74	71	68	74	287	-1
	G HALLBERG	71	73	70	73	287	-1
55	Woody AUSTIN	74	70	70	74	288	E
	T SCHERRER	68	67	73	80	288	E
	Craig STADLER	68	71	73	76	288	E
	T ISENHOUR	71	70	73	74	288	E
59	M CLARK II	73	71	70	75	289	+1
	Sergio GARCIA	68	70	75	76	289	+1
	F LICKLITER II	69	66	78	76	289	+1
	Mark O'MEARA	73	70	70	76	289	+1
63	Chris DiMARCO	70	73	70	77	290	+2
	Scott GUMP	71	68	75	76	290	+2
	D HAMMOND	70	69	75	76	290	+2
	Pete JORDAN	69	72	71	78	290	+2
	J McGOVERN	70	69	71	80	290	+2
	P STANKOWSKI	70	72	71	77	290	+2
	C BECKMAN	72	72	67	80	291	+3
	Jeff MAGGERT	72	71	70	78	291	+3
	S ELKINGTON	70	71	73	77	291	+3
72	J PARNEVIK	72	70	71	80	293	+5

Tournament Report

Davis Love refused to accept defeat as he came from seven shots behind to win the title.

Love hadn't won for nearly three years but remembered how Tiger Woods had come from a similar position to claim victory in this event in 2000. Using that as inspiration, he set off an a last-day birdie barrage that would see him card a score of 63 to overhaul Vijay Singh, Phil Mickelson and Olin Browne.

The fightback started from the off. Love played the first seven holes in eight-under par, making birdie at every hole bar the second, where he lobbed in from just over 100 yards for an eagle. His iron play was superb to the turn and only twice did he need to putt from more than 10 feet for birdie on the outward nine.

He set the clubhouse target at 16-under and then watched as his nearest pursuers failed to take their chances. Singh was just one stoke off the lead when he stood on the 17th tee. But the Fijian's tee shot at the par three hole drifted on the wind, over the green onto the rocks below. His chance has gone.

Mickelson picked up shots at the 16th and 17th but a double bogey at the last meant the left-hander's challenge was over. Browne was the joint leader along with Mickelson after 54 holes but, like Lefty, he shot a Sunday 73.

MISSED THE CUT: B BATES 72 68 75, B CHEESMAN 68 71 76, B GAY 72 74 69, K GIBSON 73 66 76, P GOYDOS 73 74 68, F WADSWORTH 73 71 71, M WIEBE 71 71 73, K YOKOO 72 75 68, M BROOKS 73 68 75, E CANONICA 73 72 71, J HAAS 70 70 76, J.J. HENRY 73 72 71, S KENDALL 69 72 75, C RILEY 74 70 72, J WILLIAMSON 71 73 72, J BREHAUT 75 70 72, M CALCAVECCHIA 76 73 68, J DALY 69 69 79, H FRAZAR 74 74 69, C KRESGE 71 72 74, T LEHMAN 68 78 70, J LEONARD 76 72 69, C MARTIN 72 69 76, M MUEHR 69 73 75, A OBERHOLSER 75 72 70, L PORTER 70 72 75, B QUIGLEY 73 69 75, B FABEL 76 73 69, D FROST 71 73 74, M HULBERT 70 74 74, C KANADA 73 74 71, G KRAFT 72 69 77, A MAGEE 71 74 73, R MEDIATE 73 70 75, S MICHEEL 72 71 75, G OGILVY 67 74 77, N J OZAKI 70 72 76, B SCHWARZROCK 69 75 74, J VAN DE VELDE 71 73 74, F ALLEM 72 78 69, T ARMOUR III 65 80 74, R FREEMAN 70 76 76, A MA JIMENEZ 73 75 71, P-U JOHANSSON 73 73 73, M KUCHAR 72 75 72, S RANDOLPH 70 76 73, C A SPENCE 71 74 74, B CLAAR 76 73 71, J EDWARDS 75 70 75, D ELLIS 72 77 71, R GAMEZ 73 69 78, K GRUNEWALD 76 74 70, H HAAS 73 75 72, N LANCASTER 73 74 73, E LIPPERT 70 75 75, M LOWE 71 76 73, A McLARDY 69 78 73, T PURTZER 73 72 75, M REID 73 73 74, L RINKER 74 72 74, D STOCKTON, Jr. 72 76 72, J ANDERSON 75 75 71, B ANDRADE 71 71 79, B BAIRD 71 76 74, P GOW 72 74 75, B WILSON 71 76 74, R ZOKOL 76 73 72, K CLEARWATER 72 77 73, J GREEN 76 70 76, S KELLY 71 74 77, G NICKLAUS 76 75 71, C TIDLAND 73 76 73, R WALCHER 76 75 71, P CASEY 76 76 71, S LYLE 77 73 73, M STANDLY 75 70 78, K JONES 71 78 75, A MILLER 74 74 76, D PRIDE 74 78 72, S SCOTT 74 75 75, S SEAR 73 78 73, J SUMMERHAYS 74 76 74, J GALLAGHER 69 80 76, R MALTBIE 75 74 76, S MURPHY 75 71 79, T TOLLES 75 76 74, B FERGUSON 75 72 79, J GALLAGHER, Jr. 77 74 75, D GOSSETT 71 83 72, L HINKLE 77 79 70, J DELSING 74 78 75, G HJERTSTEDT 76 77 74, I LEGGATT 74 76 78, B HULL 78 75 76, R BIN 78 75 81 234, B R BROWN 77 76 83 236, J GORE W/D 72 74 146, M SPOSA D 71 78 149, D DUNAKEY 71 73 71, S McROY 71 72 72, D DUVAL 75 70 71, G HNATIUK 72 71 73, C PERKS 72 71 73, J JULIAN 72 75 71, D MORLAND IV 75 74 70, B LANGER 74 77 72, S SIMPSON 74 75 74, T CLARK 79 W/D.

Course Profile

Pebble Beach (par 72, 6,816 yards) is used twice (the cut is made after three rounds) and is a spectacular layout with forgiving fairways but tiny greens.

Spyglass Hill (par 72, 6,858 yards) is the toughest track of the trio used, with accuracy off the tee and fairway a prerequisite.

Poppy Hills (par 72, 6,833 yards) is also another tight course with sloping fairways making for difficult second shots to large but undulating greens. Bad weather nearly always affects the event.

Players/Points to Note

● **Tiger Woods** is the only player to have a sub-70 stroke average in this tournament and won at Pebble Beach twice in 2000 (this event and the US Open).

● **Mark O'Meara** is dubbed 'The Prince of the Pebble' due to his superb record in the tournament. He's won it five times, recorded eight top-ten finishes in total, and is 58-under par for 20 visits.

● **David Duval** holds the course record at Pebble Beach (62).

● **Paul Azinger**'s five top-ten finishes are worth mentioning, while **Jesper Parnevik** named his daughter Pebble after the course so must like playing at the Monterrey track.

● **Davis Love** has played consistently well in this event and prior to his win in 2001 he posted seven top-30 finishes in nine starts.

● **Jim Furyk**, **Vijay Singh**, **Phil Mickelson**, **Tom Lehman**, **David Duval** and **Brad Faxon** all have good records here. **Steve Stricker** and **Dan Forsman** hold the course record at Spyglass Hill (64), **Clark Dennis** boasts likewise at Poppy Hills (63).

● The pro-am format can put a lot of golfers off their game and, unlike the other pro-ams, the top-25 amateurs get to play with the pros on the final round.

● It's interesting that since 1985, except for **Brett Ogle** and **Phil Mickelson**, all the winners (including 2001) had previously won a pro-am event.

Previous Results

2000: 1. Tiger Woods (-15), 2. Matt Gogel (-13), Vijay Singh (-13).

1999: 1. Payne Stewart (-10), 2. Frank Lickliter (-9), 3. Craig Stadler (-7).

1998: 1. *Phil Mickelson (-14), 2. Tom Pernice Jr (-13), 3. Jim Furyk (-12), Paul Azinger (-12), J.P. Hayes (-12). Played over 54 holes.

1997: 1. Mark O'Meara (-20), 2. Tiger Woods (-19), David Duval (-19).

1996: 1. *Jeff Maggert (-8), 2. Loren Roberts (-7), Steve Jones (-7), Davis Love III (-7). Played over 36 holes.

BUICK INVITATIONAL

Torrey Pines, 8 Feb to 11 Feb 2001, purse $3,500,000

Pos	Name	R1	R2	R3	R4	Total	To par	Money	DD(y)	DA%	GIR%	Putts
1	Phil MICKELSON	68	64	71	66	269	-19	$630,000	286.8	66	74	114
2	Frank LICKLITER II	68	67	68	66	269	-19	$308,000	295.6	70	75	111
	Davis LOVE III	65	67	70	67	269	-19	$308,000	303.0	59	74	115
4	Tiger WOODS	70	67	67	67	271	-17	$168,000	304.3	59	74	112
5	Brent GEIBERGER	64	69	70	69	272	-16	$133,000	271.5	57	74	110
	Mike WEIR	68	67	68	69	272	-16	$133,000	286.5	61	72	112
7	Jay WILLIAMSON	68	69	71	65	273	-15	$109,083	264.8	45	69	108
	Jay Don BLAKE	68	68	68	69	273	-15	$109,083	264.5	68	76	113
	Greg KRAFT	69	68	66	70	273	-15	$109,083	265.9	48	78	115
10	C BECKMAN	70	68	68	68	274	-14	$87,500	283.0	59	72	113
	Harrison FRAZAR	68	68	70	68	274	-14	$87,500	287.6	55	81	119
	Chris SMITH	66	70	71	67	274	-14	$87,500	296.4	52	75	117

Pos	Name	R1	R2	R3	R4	Total	To par
13	Brandt JOBE	69	70	67	69	275	-13
	Tom LEHMAN	68	68	69	70	275	-13
	S MARUYAMA	69	69	69	68	275	-13
	J M OLAZABAL	68	68	70	69	275	-13
	Mike SPOSA	70	68	69	68	275	-13
	K SUTHERLAND	70	68	69	68	275	-13
	J VAN DE VELDE	70	67	69	69	275	-13
20	J.L. LEWIS	71	66	69	70	276	-12
	D PAULSON	69	66	69	72	276	-12
	Chris RILEY	67	71	70	68	276	-12
	B SCHWARZROCK	67	71	70	68	276	-12
	Bob TWAY	68	69	70	69	276	-12
25	B LANGER	71	69	67	70	277	-11
	Frank NOBILO	67	70	69	71	277	-11
27	Ronnie BLACK	71	68	69	70	278	-10
	Steve JONES	68	71	71	68	278	-10
	Corey PAVIN	68	72	68	70	278	-10
	Fred FUNK	68	69	69	72	278	-10
	J.J. HENRY	73	66	69	70	278	-10
	Bob MAY	71	68	67	72	278	-10
	Billy MAYFAIR	73	66	68	71	278	-10
	D MORLAND IV	67	69	68	74	278	-10
	Chris TIDLAND	67	68	71	72	278	-10
36	Joe DURANT	69	70	71	69	279	-9
	R FREEMAN	69	70	73	67	279	-9
	Jason GORE	72	69	70	68	279	-9
	T PERNICE, Jr.	73	65	71	70	279	-9
	Jeff SLUMAN	71	70	69	69	279	-9
41	Rich BEEM	70	71	72	67	280	-8
	Bob ESTES	70	71	68	71	280	-8
	Michael MUEHR	67	73	70	70	280	-8
	N Joe OZAKI	68	70	72	70	280	-8
	Chris PERRY	67	72	70	71	280	-8
	Lee PORTER	72	68	68	72	280	-8
	Hal SUTTON	72	67	72	69	280	-8
48	K.J. CHOI	69	65	74	73	281	-7

Pos	Name	R1	R2	R3	R4	Total	To par
	John DALY	71	69	70	71	281	-7
	B McCALLISTER	71	68	71	71	281	-7
	Toru TANIGUCHI	72	65	72	72	281	-7
	Doug BARRON	70	66	69	76	281	-7
	Fred COUPLES	70	71	72	68	281	-7
54	Bob BURNS	70	69	72	71	282	-6
	Hunter HAAS	70	69	72	71	282	-6
	Glen HNATIUK	69	71	73	69	282	-6
	Steve LOWERY	73	67	73	69	282	-6
58	Stephen AMES	70	69	73	71	283	-5
	D BERGANIO, Jr.	70	69	73	71	283	-5
	Jeff BREHAUT	72	69	74	68	283	-5
	Brad FAXON	67	69	72	75	283	-5
	Edward FRYATT	70	71	69	73	283	-5
	Paul GOYDOS	72	69	71	71	283	-5
	Tripp ISENHOUR	71	68	73	71	283	-5
	Craig KANADA	68	73	72	70	283	-5
	Skip KENDALL	68	71	72	72	283	-5
	Spike McROY	68	70	73	72	283	-5
	Ted TRYBA	69	72	70	72	283	-5
69	Jeff GALLAGHER	71	70	72	71	284	-4
	Mark O'MEARA	68	73	73	70	284	-4
	P STANKOWSKI	68	67	71	78	284	-4
72	Craig BARLOW	69	70	75	71	285	-3
	Mark HENSBY	71	70	74	70	285	-3
	Esteban TOLEDO	69	70	68	78	285	-3
75	Jerry KELLY	71	70	68	77	286	-2
	Tommy TOLLES	67	73	73	73	286	-2
	Kirk TRIPLETT	71	65	76	74	286	-2
78	J ANDERSON	70	70	70	77	287	-1
	Kent JONES	73	68	74	72	287	-1
	R WALCHER	70	70	74	73	287	-1
81	R DAMRON	70	71	75	72	288	E
82	M GOGGIN	71	70	76	73	290	+2
	Fuzzy ZOELLER	71	69	75	75	290	+2
84	Sean MURPHY	72	68	78	73	291	+3
	D STEPHENS	69	72	76	80	297	+8

Sponsored by Stan James

Tournament Report

It's not that often that a double bogey is enough to win a play-off but that was the case for Phil Mickelson, who claimed the Buick Invitational after mistake ridden 'extra time' at Torrey Pines, San Diego.

Defending champion Mickelson, along with Frank Lickliter and Davis Love needed a play-off to separate them after scores of 66, 66 and 67 respectively. Love, the overnight leader by one, had an opportunity to win on the last hole of regulation play and the first of the play-off but missed them both.

And it was no surprise to see Love bow out at the second extra hole, after he found the bunker on the 16th. So Mickelson and Lickliter, who also both had chances to win the event in regulation play, moved to the 425-yard 17th – and that's where the fun began.

Both players hit their tee shots into a ravine on the left and then hit provisionals, presuming their original balls would not be found. But both were, so the duo had to go back to the tee to play again. Lickliter found the fairway with his drive but Mickelson's effort was drifting left again.

However, after cannoning off a tree the ball settled in the rough. Both men found the green with their approaches, with Lickliter 12 feet away and Mickelson twice that distance. Lefty two-putted for a six, but Lickliter, unbelievably missed his putt for victory and the one back from just four feet, handing the title to Mickelson.

MISSED THE CUT: Fulton ALLEM 70 72, Tommy ARMOUR III 73 69, Tom BYRUM 67 75, Greg CHALMERS 76 66, Jeffrey CRANFORD 73 69, Ben CRENSHAW 72 70, Joel EDWARDS 74 68, Brad ELDER 74 68, Bill GLASSON 72 70, Jay HAAS 72 70, Bradley HUGHES 74 68, Per Ulrik JOHANSSON 70 72, Ian LEGGATT 74 68, Andrew McLARDY 69 73, John RIEGGER 72 70, Craig STADLER 71 71, Grant WAITE 72 70, Steve ALLAN 72 71, Doug DUNAKEY 76 67, Steve FLESCH 71 72, Brian GAY 69 74, Kelly GRUNEWALD 72 71, Jeff HART 73 70, Lee JANZEN 70 73, Miguel A. JIMENEZ 72 71, Jeff JULIAN 73 70, Craig PERKS 75 68, Scott SIMPSON 71 72, Dane STATON 71 72, David TOMS 72 71, Duffy WALDORF 70 73, Richie COUGHLAN 70 74, Danny ELLIS 72 72, Gabriel HJERTSTEDT 72 72, Charley HOFFMAN 67 77, Toshi IZAWA 71 73, David PEOPLES 72 72, Loren ROBERTS 73 71, Ben FERGUSON 70 75, Paul HOLTBY 72 73, Kevin JOHNSON 70 75, Kevin NA 75 70, Mark BROOKS 72 74, Brandel CHAMBLEE 72 74, Jim FURYK 73 73, J.P. HAYES 73 73, Brian HENNINGER 74 72, Jonathan KAYE 71 75, Steve STRICKER 74 72, Fred WADSWORTH 74 72, Brian WILSON 74 72, Stuart APPLEBY 70 77, Emanuele CANONICA 73 74, Tim HERRON 74 73, Keith CLEARWATER 77 71, Paul GOW 69 79, Rory SABBATINI 75 73, Neal LANCASTER 74 74, Steve PATE 76 73, Woody AUSTIN 77 74, Billy Ray BROWN 76 75, Scott MAHLBERG 76 75, Magnus CARLSSON 76 76, Cliff KRESGE 75 77, Dicky PRIDE 76 76, Stan WATKINS 75 77, Michael FERGIN 78 75, John LIEBER 81 74, Kaname YOKOO 74 W/D, John COOK W/D, Carl PAULSON W/D.

Course Profile

Both the North Course (par 72, 6,874 yards) and the South Course (par 72, 7,055 yards) are played alternatively in the first two rounds then the latter is played twice over the weekend.

The South Course is a shot or so harder than the North Course. The two tracks are similar, both having small greens and both requiring players to have a good iron game.

The hot, windy conditions can cause the greens to run extremely fast on both courses.

Players/Points to Note

● **Phil Mickelson** first visited Torrey Pines as a little boy, when he came with his parents to watch the San Diego Open. The venue was also the scene of his high school golf days and as a 17-year-old he qualified to play in the 1988 Buick Invitational. The left-hander also won his first tournament as a pro here just eight months after leaving the amateur ranks. In 12 starts in this event he's won the most money, won three times, has two other top-ten finishes and has a stroke average of 69.41.

● **Tiger Woods'** form figures now read 3-1-2-4 in four starts (stroke average of 67.73), and, as usual, the 'Phenom' can never be discounted. He won the World Junior Championships at Torrey Pines (as did Mickeslon and **Craig Stadler**) and also holds the course record (62) on the South Course.

● **Davis Love** has enjoyed four top-ten finishes in 11 visits is a former winner and has a sub-70 stroke average.

● **Brent Geiberger** has yet to finish lower than 25th in four starts and was fifth last season. And **Kevin Sutherland** and **Skip Kendall** have good records in relatively few starts.

● **Jay Don Blake**, **Steve Pate**, **Scott Simpson** and Stadler are former winners and serial top-ten finishes. **Mark Brooks** holds the North Course record of 61.

Previous Results

2000: 1. Phil Mickelson (-18), 2. Shigeki Maruyama (-14), Tiger Woods (-14).

1999: 1. Tiger Woods (-22), 2. Billy Ray Brown (-20), 3. Bill Glasson (-18).

1998: 1. *Scott Simpson (-12), won play-off, 2. Skip Kendall (-12), 3. Tiger Woods (-11), Davis Love III (-11), Kevin Sutherland (-11). Played over 54 holes.

1997: 1. Mark O'Meara (-13), 2. Seven players tied.

1996: 1. Davis Love III (-19), 2. Phil Mickelson (-17), 3. Five players tied.

BOB HOPE CHRYSLER CLASSIC

La Quinta, 15 Feb to 18 Feb 2001, purse $3,500,000

Pos	Name	R1	R2	R3	R4	R5	Total	To par	Money	DD(y)	DA%	GIR%	Putts
1	Joe DURANT	65	61	67	66	65	324	-36	$630,000	281.3	81	87	135
2	Paul STANKOWSKI	67	64	65	69	63	328	-32	$378,000	288.9	64	72	129
3	M CALCAVECCHIA	64	66	69	65	66	330	-30	$238,000	295.0	66	77	137
4	Brad FAXON	66	67	70	65	65	333	-27	$144,666	280.6	70	77	138
	Scott VERPLANK	66	68	70	62	67	333	-27	$144,666	277.1	74	83	145
	Bob TWAY	68	62	68	68	67	333	-27	$144,666	277.7	74	82	140
7	F LICKLITER II	70	66	64	68	66	334	-26	$112,875	282.4	71	73	133
	Tom PERNICE, Jr.	64	68	66	70	66	334	-26	$112,875	283.4	64	79	138
9	Billy MAYFAIR	71	62	67	69	66	335	-25	$98,000	270.82	69	74	134
	K SUTHERLAND	64	67	66	67	71	335	-25	$98,000	279.0	69	82	137

Pos	Name	R1	R2	R3	R4	R5	Total	To par
11	Brad ELDER	67	68	67	66	69	337	-23
	Robert GAMEZ	73	72	64	67	61	337	-23
	M A JIMENEZ	68	62	68	68	71	337	-23
	Kevin JOHNSON	66	73	67	65	66	337	-23
	J.L. LEWIS	69	67	71	63	67	337	-23
	Jeff MAGGERT	64	70	71	65	67	337	-23
	Jeff SLUMAN	67	69	66	66	69	337	-23
18	B GEIBERGER	65	70	68	68	67	338	-22
	S McCARRON	70	68	63	69	68	338	-22
	Chris PERRY	68	68	72	64	66	338	-22
	David TOMS	67	68	66	69	68	338	-22
22	H FRAZAR	63	71	69	67	69	339	-21
	Jim FURYK	68	68	67	69	67	339	-21
	Jason GORE	65	73	70	66	65	339	-21
	B McCALLISTER	69	66	67	66	71	339	-21
26	Steve ALLAN	66	70	67	67	70	340	-20
	John COOK	72	67	69	69	63	340	-20
	Jerry KELLY	67	67	68	71	67	340	-20
	Spike McROY	68	68	72	62	70	340	-20
30	Stuart APPLEBY	67	68	69	68	69	341	-19
	Jay Don BLAKE	66	75	66	68	66	341	-19
	Robert DAMRON	68	70	67	66	70	341	-19
	Glen DAY	64	67	72	71	67	341	-19
	Fred FUNK	69	68	71	68	65	341	-19
	Mathew GOGGIN	68	67	71	68	67	341	-19
	Jay HAAS	69	70	65	72	65	341	-19
	Joey SINDELAR	70	73	64	68	66	341	-19
38	Chris SMITH	65	64	69	69	75	342	-18
	Steve STRICKER	70	67	66	69	70	342	-18
40	Robin FREEMAN	71	67	72	66	67	343	-17
	Lee JANZEN	70	68	70	68	67	343	-17
	Justin LEONARD	69	69	67	69	69	343	-17
	Loren ROBERTS	72	70	70	65	66	343	-17
	Hal SUTTON	70	74	66	65	68	343	-17
	Mark WIEBE	71	68	69	68	67	343	-17
46	G CHALMERS	69	66	71	65	73	344	-16
	David GOSSETT	66	69	68	69	72	344	-16
	D HAMMOND	71	65	67	70	71	344	-16
	Skip KENDALL	66	71	73	67	67	344	-16
	Garrett WILLIS	65	72	67	71	69	344	-16
51	Stephen AMES	64	71	69	73	68	345	-15
	David DUVAL	65	68	70	68	74	345	-15
	N LANCASTER	67	69	70	68	71	345	-15
	D MORLAND IV	69	73	66	68	69	345	-15
	Brian WILSON	70	68	68	70	69	345	-15
56	Fred COUPLES	72	66	72	67	69	346	-14
	Bob ESTES	66	69	68	70	73	346	-14
	Brandt JOBE	71	69	65	72	69	346	-14
	J M OLAZABAL	71	69	70	67	69	346	-14
	Kirk TRIPLETT	72	64	65	73	72	346	-14
	Ted TRYBA	66	72	73	66	69	346	-14
62	Robert ALLENBY	65	69	72	68	73	347	-13
	Billy ANDRADE	69	73	66	67	72	347	-13
	Paul AZINGER	72	70	67	67	71	347	-13
	C BECKMAN	64	76	67	70	70	347	-13
	A McLARDY	66	69	71	70	71	347	-13
67	Russ COCHRAN	71	66	71	66	74	348	-12
	Joe OGILVIE	69	71	67	70	71	348	-12
	Fuzzy ZOELLER	68	69	67	70	74	348	-12
70	Mark BROOKS	69	71	70	67	72	349	-11
	Olin BROWNE	69	67	71	70	72	349	-11
	Shaun MICHEEL	74	65	71	67	72	349	-11
73	Rich BEEM	72	72	65	67	74	350	-10
74	Rory SABBATINI	71	68	66	71	76	352	-8
75	Jonathan KAYE	73	69	66	68	80	356	-4

Tournament Report

Another US Tour event, another US Tour record is broken. This time Joe Durant made a mockery of the concept of par by breaking the 90-hole tournament record by returning a score of 324 – an astonishing 36-under total – to win the Bob Hope Chrysler Classic in California.

In perfect conditions on perfect courses, Durant took control after a second day 61. And a bogey free, seven-birdie 65 saw him complete the job, winning by four shots from Paul Stankowski with Mark Calcavecchia two shots further adrift in third. Durant is arguably the most improved player on tour this season.

At one stage he was struggling to make pro golf pay and took up a regular job, selling insurance, to keep the wolf from the door. But after working hard on his short game and adding extra length off the tee, one of the best ball strikers on tour is back in business.

Stankowski's Sunday 63 was only enough to pull two shots back on Durant and on a day of low scoring, only 14 of the 75 golfers who made the cut failed to break par, there was no surprise that someone had a chance to break 60.

That man was Robert Gamez. The 32-year-old needed to birdie each of the last two holes for a 59. But he left an eight-footer short on the 17th and his chance was gone, eventually signing for a 61 after seeing another birdie chance slip by on the last.

MISSED THE CUT: Tommy ARMOUR III 69 71 69 69, Doug BARRON 72 68 69 69, Tom BYRUM 72 67 73 66, Stewart CINK 71 67 72 68, Michael CLARK II 70 72 66 70, Steve FLESCH 73 70 71 64, Bradley HUGHES 70 68 71 69, Peter JACOBSEN 72 69 71 66, Steve JONES 75 68 67 68, Sandy LYLE 70 67 74 67, Len MATTIACE 70 69 68 71, Rocco MEDIATE 74 67 69 68, Frank NOBILO 68 71 69 70, Steve PATE 70 70 68 70, Brian GAY 67 69 70 73, Paul GOYDOS 70 69 71 69, Brian HENNINGER 71 67 74 67, Andrew MAGEE 71 69 69 70, Dennis PAULSON 71 72 68 68, Kenny PERRY 71 64 69 75, Woody AUSTIN 72 70 69 69, Bob Burns 67 73 69 71, Matt GOGEL 70 68 73 69, J.P. HAYES 69 71 74 66, Scott HOCH 69 70 72 69, Kent JONES 71 71 68 70, Esteban TOLEDO 70 68 72 70, Pete JORDAN 68 75 67 71, Scott SIMPSON 71 67 71 72, Briny BAIRD 69 72 70 71, David FROST 68 67 71 76, Ian LEGGATT 71 71 67 73, Tommy TOLLES 69 72 72 69, Gary NICKLAUS 72 70 74 67, Curtis STRANGE 71 70 70 72, Keith FERGUS 71 72 69 72, Jimmy GREEN 73 71 71 69, John HUSTON 69 69 74 72, Jerry SMITH 74 72 69 69, Brandel CHAMBLEE 68 70 75 72, Greg KRAFT 70 73 72 71, Bruce LIETZKE 73 75 70 69, Mark HENSBY 71 72 76 71, Larry MIZE 71 69 74 76, Gabriel HJERTSTEDT 69 78 72 75, Dave STOCKTON, Jr. 72 69 81 75, Jeffrey CRANFORD 74 77 77 70, Arnold PALMER 81 79 75 71, Doug SANDERS 81 82 77 73, Bob MAY 67 71 66 W/D, Dudley HART 68 69 75 D, Jay WILLIAMSON 77 71 72 W/D, Fulton ALLEM 75 79 W/D, Jesper PARNEVIK W/D.

Sponsored by Stan James

Course Profile

Four courses are used with the host course played twice (and crucially on the final day).

In 2001, the PGA West course was the host layout. The PGA West (par 72, 6,950 yards) is generally the second easiest of the four and five par fives.

Bermuda Dunes (par 71, 6,829 yards) is the second toughest with Indian Wells (par 72, 6,478 yards) the easiest.

In 2002, Tamarisk (par 72, 6,881 yards) is back on the roster for the first time since 1999.

Players/Points to Note

● With four courses used over five rounds, punters betting in running should be aware of just which layouts their selections have played. Also, be wary of scores posted in the earlier rounds on the host course, as the pin positions are usually a lot tougher on the last day as previously the cups were cut to aid the amateurs.

● Look for players who can go low. **Joe Durant** broke all kinds of records on his way to victory here last year.

● **David Duval** shot 59 (on the PGA West layout) to win in 1999. Duval, in fact, has the best scoring average at this tournament (68.03).

● **Jesper Parnevik** can obviously handle the pro-celebrity nature of this event – his father Bo is one of Sweden's best known comics, so is at home amongst the gags of Joe Pesci and co. – as his victory in 2000 proved.

● **Fred Couples** has finished in the top ten of this event on seven occasions and is 247-under par in 17 visits.

● **Scott Hoch**, winner here in 1994, can boast similar figures – seven top 10s and -238 in 18 starts. Dual winners **John Cook** and **Corey Pavin** are outsiders to follow while **John Huston**, **Mark O'Meara** and **Tom Kite** can also boast multiple top-ten finishes.

Previous Results

2000: 1. Jesper Parnevik (-27), 2. Rory Sabbatini (-26), 3. J L Lewis (-25), David Toms (-25).

1999: 1. David Duval (-26), 2. Steve Pate (-25), 3. John Huston (-24).

1998: 1. Fred Couples (-28), won play-off, 2. Bruce Lietzke (-28), 3. Andrew Magee (-27).

1997: 1. John Cook (-33), 2. Mark Calcavecchia (-32), 3. Jesper Parnevik (-28).

1996: 1. Mark Brooks (-23), 2. John Huston (-22), 3. Scott Hoch (-21).

NISSAN OPEN

Riviera Country Club, 22 Feb to 25 Feb 2001, purse $3,400,000

Pos	Name	R1	R2	R3	R4	Total	To par	Money	DD(y)	DA%	GIR%	Putts
1	Robert ALLENBY	73	64	69	70	276	-8	$612,000	263.1	71	72	115

Won play-off

Pos	Name	R1	R2	R3	R4	Total	To par	Money	DD(y)	DA%	GIR%	Putts
2	B CHAMBLEE	68	68	73	67	276	-8	$204,000	252.4	75	58	105
	Toshi IZAWA	73	68	69	66	276	-8	$204,000	278.1	86	69	114
	Dennis PAULSON	70	68	68	70	276	-8	$204,000	256.8	63	63	109
	Jeff SLUMAN	68	69	70	69	276	-8	$204,000	268.3	77	74	118
	Bob TWAY	67	71	70	68	276	-8	$204,000	257.1	70	67	111
7	E CANONICA	68	70	71	68	277	-7	$113,900	281.6	64	65	114
8	D BERGANIO, Jr.	71	67	70	70	278	-6	$91,800	255.4	73	65	112
	Jerry KELLY	72	69	70	67	278	-6	$91,800	256.1	75	69	114
	Neal LANCASTER	69	68	71	70	278	-6	$91,800	246.9	73	67	117
	Davis LOVE III	68	67	68	75	278	-6	$91,800	272.8	71	57	107
	Chris PERRY	68	68	72	70	278	-6	$91,800	261.3	80	65	111

Pos	Name	R1	R2	R3	R4	Total	To par
13	G CHALMERS	67	70	71	71	279	-5
	Jeff MAGGERT	71	70	68	70	279	-5
	J PARNEVIK	70	68	71	70	279	-5
	Craig BARLOW	68	68	70	73	279	-5
	Scott DUNLAP	71	69	68	71	279	-5
	Michael MUEHR	74	63	70	72	279	-5
	Tiger WOODS	71	68	69	71	279	-5
20	Rich BEEM	70	72	68	70	280	-4
	Stewart CINK	69	69	70	72	280	-4
	Edward FRYATT	67	73	72	68	280	-4
	Corey PAVIN	71	68	67	74	280	-4
	Nick PRICE	68	70	69	73	280	-4
25	Jeff BREHAUT	72	70	70	69	281	-3
	Robin FREEMAN	72	69	70	70	281	-3
	Sergio GARCIA	66	72	71	72	281	-3
	Paul GOW	69	70	71	71	281	-3
	M A JIMENEZ	69	66	73	73	281	-3
	Rocco MEDIATE	67	70	74	70	281	-3
	Frank NOBILO	72	69	70	70	281	-3
	B SCHWARZROCK	66	75	69	71	281	-3
33	T ARMOUR III	70	71	70	71	282	-2
	C BECKMAN	72	68	71	71	282	-2
	K.J. CHOI	69	71	72	70	282	-2
	B HUGHES	67	71	73	71	282	-2
	Kevin JOHNSON	69	69	75	69	282	-2
	J.L. LEWIS	73	69	67	73	282	-2
	Billy MAYFAIR	68	69	72	73	282	-2
	Tom SCHERRER	66	71	72	73	282	-2
	Esteban TOLEDO	70	72	69	71	282	-2
	Scott VERPLANK	72	70	71	69	282	-2
43	Mark BROOKS	70	71	72	70	283	-1
	Andrew MAGEE	70	70	71	72	283	-1
	Len MATTIACE	70	68	74	71	283	-1
	S McCARRON	68	68	76	71	283	-1
	Chris RILEY	68	70	76	69	283	-1
	P STANKOWSKI	70	71	72	70	283	-1
	Ted TRYBA	72	70	71	70	283	-1
	Brian WILSON	71	71	71	70	283	-1
51	S ELKINGTON	69	71	71	73	284	E
	Jason GORE	69	71	73	71	284	E
	B GEIBERGER	69	71	68	76	284	E
	J.P. HAYES	69	72	72	71	284	E
	Scott SIMPSON	75	66	72	71	284	E
	K SUTHERLAND	71	71	71	71	284	E
57	Jay Don BLAKE	71	68	74	72	285	+1
	Olin BROWNE	73	68	71	73	285	+1
	John DALY	69	73	70	73	285	+1
	Ben FERGUSON	71	69	73	72	285	+1
	S MARUYAMA	67	69	75	74	285	+1
	Duffy WALDORF	71	70	73	71	285	+1
63	Jay HAAS	70	71	72	73	286	+2
	Peter JACOBSEN	71	71	71	73	286	+2
	Steve LOWERY	71	69	73	73	286	+2
66	Dan FORSMAN	72	70	70	75	287	+3
	Rory SABBATINI	72	69	75	71	287	+3
68	Doug BARRON	71	67	75	75	288	+4
	John COOK	71	70	71	76	288	+4
	Hunter HAAS	70	72	68	78	288	+4
	Tripp ISENHOUR	72	70	73	73	288	+4
	Justin LEONARD	71	70	72	75	288	+4
	T PERNICE, Jr.	69	70	77	72	288	+4
74	Steve PATE	71	69	74	75	289	+5
	Dicky PRIDE	71	70	72	76	289	+5
76	N Joe OZAKI	67	74	75	74	290	+6
77	Sean MURPHY	72	68	74	79	293	+9
	Gary BIRCH, Jr.	70	72	75	76	293	+9
79	Doug DUNAKEY	71	70	73	80	294	+10
	Russ COCHRAN	70	70	79	W/D		

Tournament Report

Robert Allenby likes play-offs. He must do, as he won his seventh tournament of his career by way of extra holes when claiming the Nissan Open at the Riviera Country Club in Los Angeles.

Six players tied for first place after regulation play ended, meaning this event would host the equal biggest play-off in US Tour history – matching the sextet of pros that took part in the play-off for the 1994 GTE Byron Nelson Classic. Allenby, Toshi Izawa, Brandel Chamblee, Bob Tway, Jeff Sluman and Dennis Paulson were the half dozen players that would contest sudden death, but there could have been more.

Overnight leader, David Love, dropped four shots in the last four holes, Chris Perry bogeyed three of the last four and Michael Muehr also held the lead on the back nine. Amazingly the play-off lasted just one hole.

The six players teed up at the tough 18th, where only one birdie had been made all day, with the rain continuing to fall, as it had been all day. Izawa was the only man to find the fairway from the tee but just Allenby and Tway managed to make the putting surface in two.

The Aussie's 3-wood from over 220 yards was perfect and came to rest five feet from the hole. And when the other quartet failed to conjure up anything special from off the green, and Tway had left his 35-footer short, Allenby stroked his effort home keep his unbeaten play-off record intact.

MISSED THE CUT: Joel EDWARDS 71 72, Brad ELDER 70 73, David FROST 70 73, Fred FUNK 73 70, Matt GOGEL 71 72, Kent JONES 71 72, Craig KANADA 72 71, Frank LICKLITER II 69 74, Spike McROY 70 73, Larry MIZE 70 73, Tom PURTZER 71 72, Jerry SMITH 71 72, Mike WEIR 69 74, Garrett WILLIS 69 74, Woody AUSTIN 70 74, Jim CARTER 70 74, Michael CLARK II 72 72, J.J. HENRY 73 71, Mark HENSBY 72 72, Scott HOCH 70 74, Jose Maria OLAZABAL 70 74, Mark WIEBE 71 73, Jay WILLIAMSON 75 69, Keith CLEARWATER 73 72, Fred COUPLES 73 72, Ben CRENSHAW 70 75, Bob ESTES 73 72, Dudley HART 72 73, Andrew McLARDY 77 68, Craig PERKS 73 72, Lee PORTER 71 74, John RIEGGER 72 73, Brad BENKEY 76 70, Danny ELLIS 72 74, Mathew GOGGIN 74 72, Paul GOYDOS 72 74, Jimmy GREEN 73 73, Jeff HART 72 74, Shaun MICHEEL 72 74, Hidemichi TANAKA 73 73, Jeremy ANDERSON 74 73, David GOSSETT 74 73, Kelly GRUNEWALD 74 73, Jim McGOVERN 73 74, Phil MICKELSON 73 74, Joe OGILVIE 73 74, Chris TIDLAND 76 71, Kirk TRIPLETT 66 81, Toru TANIGUCHI 73 75, Fred WADSWORTH 74 74, Per Ulrik JOHANSSON 72 77, Cliff KRESGE 74 75, Ted SCHULZ 74 75, Chris SMITH 71 78, Craig STADLER 71 78, Kaname YOKOO 75 74, Bobby KALINOWSKI 77 73, Ron KRAMER 77 73, Steve ALLAN 74 78, Rocky WALCHER 75 78, Brian HENNINGER 78 76, Jeffrey CRANFORD 81 77, Tam BRONKEY 80 81, Pete JORDAN 76 W/D.

Sponsored by Stan James

Course Profile

The Riviera Club (par 71, 7,078 yards) has hosted this event in all but one of the last 16 years (in 1998 Valhalla G.C took over).

Its US Open-type set up means putting the ball on the fairway is a prerequisite. The rough can be punishing.

The type of grass used on the fairways, Kikuyu, means bump and run shots are impossible. However, the ball sits up on the fairway allowing for perfect lies every time.

Players/Points to Note

●**Davis Love** doesn't tee up in this event every year but has the perfect game for the venue and should have won last year (fading to eighth). He can boast two seconds and a third in this event and, should he play in 2002, must be backed.

●This is one of **Fred Couples'** favourite tournaments, barring injury he will be playing in it for the 21st time in 2002. He has won this tournament twice (1990 and 1992), come runner up three times, is 89-under par in 20 visits, is one of the few players to boast a scoring average under 70 in this event and has finished in the top ten on nine occasions.

●**Ernie Els'** relaxed approach aided him in winning in 1999. The South African is well suited to this US Open type venue where keeping the ball in play is vital.

●The more experienced professionals have good records here such as **Craig Stadler**, **Tom Kite**, **Mark Calcavecchia**, **Corey Pavin** (all previous winners) and **Mike Reid** (four top tens).

●**Ted Tryba**, the course record holder courtesy of a 61 in the third round in 1999, and **Bob Estes**, top tens in '98 and '99 also go well.

●**David Duval** has the powerful game for the venue, while **Jeff Sluman** is a grinder who performs well on tough courses.

Previous Results

2000: 1. Kirk Triplett (-12), 2. Jesper Parnevik (-11), 3. Robin Freeman (-10).

1999: 1. Ernie Els (-14), 2. Ted Tryba (-12), Tiger Woods (-12), Davis Love III (-12).

1998: 1. Billy Mayfair (-12), won play-off, 2. Tiger Woods (-12), 3. Stephen Ames (-9).

1997: 1. Nick Faldo (-12), 2. Craig Stadler (-9), 3. Scott Hoch (-8).

1996: 1. Craig Stadler (-6), 2. Mark Brooks (-5), Fred Couples (-5), Scott Simpson (-5), Mark Wiebe (-5).

GENUITY CHAMPIONSHIP

Doral Blue Course, 1 Mar to 4 Mar 2001, purse $4,500,000

Pos	Name	R1	R2	R3	R4	Total	To par	Money	DD(y)	DA%	GIR%	Putts
1	Joe DURANT	68	70	67	65	270	-18	$810,000	293.1	84	84	119
2	Mike WEIR	62	70	69	71	272	-16	$486,000	287.4	70	64	103
3	Vijay SINGH	70	71	66	67	274	-14	$234,000	286.3	68	71	110
	Jeff SLUMAN	69	66	69	70	274	-14	$234,000	279.5	68	71	109
	Hal SUTTON	66	66	70	72	274	-14	$234,000	281.6	79	78	114
6	Davis LOVE III	65	70	69	71	275	-13	$162,000	310.5	68	74	116
7	Nick PRICE	71	68	71	67	277	-11	$150,750	290.8	71	68	114
8	Billy ANDRADE	67	67	74	70	278	-10	$126,000	288.8	68	61	108
	Bob ESTES	68	69	71	70	278	-10	$126,000	281.9	64	67	111
	Lee PORTER	69	69	69	71	278	-10	$126,000	280.1	73	65	109
	Chris SMITH	69	66	76	67	278	-10	$126,000	295.5	73	79	121

Pos	Name	R1	R2	R3	R4	Total	To par
12	Craig BARLOW	67	70	70	72	279	-9
	G CHALMERS	67	66	75	71	279	-9
	Stewart CINK	64	66	75	74	279	-9
	Esteban TOLEDO	70	69	68	72	279	-9
	Scott VERPLANK	67	71	69	72	279	-9
17	Ben BATES	67	69	72	72	280	-8
	Jim FURYK	69	72	66	73	280	-8
	Billy MAYFAIR	68	69	71	72	280	-8
	J PARNEVIK	68	70	71	71	280	-8
21	Glen DAY	64	71	74	72	281	-7
	Lee JANZEN	67	67	77	70	281	-7
	Geoff OGILVY	72	67	69	73	281	-7
	David TOMS	73	68	71	69	281	-7
25	B CHAMBLEE	73	65	72	72	282	-6
	K.J. CHOI	65	72	73	72	282	-6
	Robert DAMRON	69	72	71	70	282	-6
	Ernie ELS	66	71	72	73	282	-6
	Jerry KELLY	69	69	71	73	282	-6
	Skip KENDALL	68	73	69	72	282	-6
	J.L. LEWIS	69	69	71	73	282	-6
	Chris PERRY	71	68	70	73	282	-6
	Grant WAITE	70	65	73	74	282	-6
34	Stuart APPLEBY	67	72	74	70	283	-5
	C BECKMAN	69	71	71	72	283	-5
	Brad ELDER	69	72	73	69	283	-5
	Brian GAY	71	70	69	73	283	-5
	Greg KRAFT	67	72	69	75	283	-5
	Steve STRICKER	69	72	70	72	283	-5
40	Steve ALLAN	69	72	72	71	284	-4
	S ELKINGTON	68	70	73	73	284	-4
	Matt GOGEL	71	70	71	72	284	-4
	Paul GOW	67	73	71	73	284	-4
	Glen HNATIUK	72	69	68	75	284	-4
	Pete JORDAN	69	71	70	74	284	-4
	Craig KANADA	67	71	70	76	284	-4
	B LANGER	68	70	73	73	284	-4
	Steve LOWERY	68	73	69	74	284	-4
	H TANAKA	71	69	72	72	284	-4
50	Robert ALLENBY	66	67	75	77	285	-3
	Ronnie BLACK	70	70	74	71	285	-3
	Joel EDWARDS	68	69	75	73	285	-3
	Fred FUNK	72	68	68	77	285	-3
	John HUSTON	69	72	70	74	285	-3
	N LANCASTER	73	64	75	73	285	-3
	Frank NOBILO	72	68	78	67	285	-3
	Joe OGILVIE	67	72	76	70	285	-3
58	Steve FLESCH	65	72	78	71	286	-2
	H FRAZAR	65	71	81	69	286	-2
	Justin LEONARD	71	70	73	72	286	-2
	Mike SPOSA	68	73	72	73	286	-2
	Bob TWAY	69	70	71	76	286	-2
	Briny BAIRD	71	70	75	71	287	-1
63	Jim CARTER	68	68	75	76	287	-1
	David DUVAL	69	69	77	72	287	-1
	Edward FRYATT	70	68	79	70	287	-1
	Mathew GOGGIN	68	71	74	74	287	-1
	S MARUYAMA	70	66	74	77	287	-1
	D MORLAND IV	69	71	75	72	287	-1
	Kenny PERRY	68	72	74	73	287	-1
	Larry RINKER	68	70	75	74	287	-1
72	Russ COCHRAN	69	71	72	76	288	E
	Doug DUNAKEY	74	67	78	69	288	E
	Nick FALDO	72	69	75	72	288	E
	Shaun MICHEEL	68	69	75	76	288	E
	John RIEGGER	69	71	71	77	288	E
77	Chris RILEY	70	69	75	75	289	+1
	Kaname YOKOO	66	75	76	72	289	+1
79	Andy BEAN	66	74	77	77	294	+6
	Stephen AMES	67	72	68		W/D	

Tournament Report

Joe Durant battled with the elements and Doral Country Club's infamous Blue Monster course to win the Genuity Championship from Canada's Mike Weir by two strokes.

In 20mph winds on the final day, Durant claimed his second US Tour win of the season by shooting a superb 65. The drama unfolded at the turn.

Weir, who led by two going into the final round, found sand at the par three ninth and, after discovering his ball was plugged, did well to sign for a bogey.

Then, on the next hole, he dropped another shot. This time he found a fairway bunker with his tee shot and failed to make par. Ahead of him on the golf course Durant made birdie on the 603 yard 12th to take the outright lead for the first time in the tournament. Weir was unable to make a single birdie on the back nine and Durant came home unchallenged.

Vijay Singh carded a Sunday 67 for a share of third place with Jeff Sluman and Hal Sutton. Davis Love, who played in the final pairing with Weir, struggled to a 71 and slipped to sixth. It was the third successive time that Love had played in the last group this term and failed to win.

Durant not only picked up a cheque for $810,000, the biggest pay day of his career, but also went top of the Money List – a position that meant he had also qualified to play in this year's US Masters.

MISSED THE CUT: Michael CLARK II 71 71, John COOK 72 70, Scott DUNLAP 71 71, Tripp ISENHOUR 72 70, Franklin LANGHAM 73 69, Gary NICKLAUS 71 71, Scott SIMPSON 73 69, Rich BEEM 73 70, Olin BROWNE 72 71, Chris DiMARCO 74 69, David FROST 69 74, Jason GORE 69 74, Mark HENSBY 73 70, Scott HOCH 70 73, Bradley HUGHES 73 70, Jack NICKLAUS 70 73, Tom SCHERRER 73 70, Brent SCHWARZROCK 73 70, Curtis STRANGE 70 73, Tommy TOLLES 73 70, Jay WILLIAMSON 71 72, Tommy ARMOUR III 71 73, David BERGANIO, Jr. 74 70, Jay Don BLAKE 77 67, Michael BRADLEY 73 71, Carlos FRANCO 72 72, Jeff HART 71 73, J.J. HENRY 70 74, Mike HULBERT 71 73, Jimmy GREEN 73 72, Hunter HAAS 71 74, Kevin JOHNSON 73 72, Blaine McCALLISTER 75 70, David PEOPLES 73 72, Woody AUSTIN 71 75, Richie COUGHLAN 72 74, Bill GLASSON 74 72, Tim HERRON 74 72, Jonathan KAYE 73 73, Mark McCUMBER 70 76, Michael MUEHR 73 73, Naomichi Joe OZAKI 72 74, Fulton ALLEM 70 77, Gene FIEGER 74 73, Robert FORD 77 70, James DRISCOLL 75 73, Brandt Jobe 73 75, Per Ulrik JOHANSSON 76 72, Cliff KRESGE 74 74, Len MATTIACE 74 74, Adam SPRING 76 72, Ben FERGUSON 70 79, Dudley HART 74 75, Chris TIDLAND 74 75, Ted TRYBA 72 77, Jeff BREHAUT 70 80, Emanuele CANONICA 74 77, Garrett WILLIS 73 78, Gabriel HJERTSTEDT 74 78, James VARGAS 75 77, Justin HICKS 78 75, Sean MURPHY 74 79, Billy Ray BROWN 77 80, Daniel GRANNAN Jr. 75 82.

Course Profile

The Blue Monster (par 72, 7,125 yards), as Doral's Blue course is dubbed, isn't a place for the inexperienced – as the list of winners testifies.

It's long, requires accuracy and with water coming into play on half of the holes, golfers need plenty of bottle. The greens are slightly bigger than average.

During the round you must both fade and draw the ball, run the ball up, and hit high parachute shots, onto the greens. The wind can be a factor.

Players/Points to Note

●This is the first event on the Florida Swing of the US Tour and Florida residents go well. Only two of the last 13 winners (**Steve Elkington** in 1997 and 1999) weren't based in Florida. The Bermuda Grass greens seem to be the key. They are used on most courses in Florida. Incidentally, Elkington grew up in Australia where Bermuda Grass greens are the norm.

●And as we're mentioning Australians, **Robert Allenby**'s win in 2000 was the sixth time a player from Down Under was successful. Elkington has won twice and **Greg Norman** three times. Norman doesn't play many US Tour events these days but should always be noted in this event. He holds the course record (62), can boast six top-ten finishes in 12 starts, is 107-under par and has taken over $1.1million out of the sponsors coffers in prize money.

●**Jim Furyk** equalled the low 72-hole score when successful in 2000, while John Huston is another former winner who goes well.

●Serial top-ten finishers are **Fred Couples** (6), **Scott Hoch** (5), **Davis Love** (4) and **Mark Calcavecchia** (4).

●**Vijay Singh**, **Ernie Els** and, inevitably, **Tiger Woods** all have the game for the venue and will surely win here sooner rather than later.

●Also, keep an eye out for Australia's **Greg Chalmers**, **Nick Price**, **Mike Weir** and **Chris Smith**.

Previous Results

2000: 1. Jim Furyk (-23), 2. Franklin Langham (-21), 3. Nick Price (-18).
1999: 1. Steve Elkington (-13), 2. Greg Kraft (-12), 3. Five players tied.
1998: 1. Michael Bradley (-10), John Huston (-9), Billy Mayfair (-9).
1997: 1. Steve Elkington (-13), 2. Larry Nelson (-11), Nick Price (-11).
1996: 1. Greg Norman (-19), 2. Michael Bradley (-17), Vijay Singh (-17).

HONDA CLASSIC

TPC at Herron Bay, 8 Mar to 11 Mar 2001, purse $3,200,000

Pos	Name	R1	R2	R3	R4	Total	To par	Money	DD(y)	DA%	GIR%	Putts
1	Jesper PARNEVIK	65	67	66	72	270	-18	$576,000	296.1	52	63	99
2	Craig PERKS	67	70	68	66	271	-17	$238,933	279.6	45	65	102
	M CALCAVECCHIA	67	68	66	70	271	-17	$238,933	287.5	70	86	116
	Geoff OGILVY	65	72	65	69	271	-17	$238,933	297.3	61	72	107
5	Joe DURANT	67	71	66	69	273	-15	$121,600	284.4	86	76	113
	Joel EDWARDS	69	67	68	69	273	-15	$121,600	281.5	64	81	116
7	Stuart APPLEBY	68	70	67	69	274	-14	$96,400	300.3	77	75	111
	Steve FLESCH	69	70	67	68	274	-14	$96,400	291.1	63	74	111
	Jim FURYK	70	72	67	65	274	-14	$96,400	272.6	73	72	107
	Kaname YOKOO	71	69	69	65	274	-14	$96,400	280.6	77	72	108

Pos	Name	R1	R2	R3	R4	Total	To par
11	Fulton ALLEM	66	71	68	70	275	-13
	Skip KENDALL	68	70	67	70	275	-13
	S McCARRON	69	71	68	67	275	-13
	Adam SCOTT	70	68	67	70	275	-13
	Tommy TOLLES	71	69	67	68	275	-13
	John DALY	71	65	67	72	275	-13
	Chris SMITH	67	68	69	71	275	-13
18	Chris DiMARCO	69	73	68	66	276	-12
	Glen HNATIUK	70	70	67	69	276	-12
	John HUSTON	68	67	71	70	276	-12
	Joey SINDELAR	70	71	69	66	276	-12
	Mike SPOSA	70	71	69	66	276	-12
	Garrett WILLIS	70	69	69	68	276	-12
	Briny BAIRD	69	68	67	72	276	-12
	Brad FAXON	69	67	69	71	276	-12
	Hal SUTTON	69	68	67	72	276	-12
27	Ben FERGUSON	65	75	70	67	277	-11
	Gene FIEGER	68	73	69	67	277	-11
	Tom LEHMAN	68	72	70	67	277	-11
	Esteban TOLEDO	69	73	68	67	277	-11
	Brian GAY	70	67	68	72	277	-11
	Pete JORDAN	69	70	67	71	277	-11
	B LANGER	66	73	68	70	277	-11
	Spike McROY	67	69	69	72	277	-11
	Phil MICKELSON	69	70	67	71	277	-11
	Joe OGILVIE	67	72	69	69	277	-11
	Kenny PERRY	69	71	69	68	277	-11
	P STANKOWSKI	68	69	71	69	277	-11
39	Dan FORSMAN	67	70	65	76	278	-10
	Carlos FRANCO	69	68	68	73	278	-10
	Jeff HART	68	72	68	70	278	-10
	Lee JANZEN	70	69	64	75	278	-10
	N LANCASTER	69	68	70	71	278	-10
	Shaun MICHEEL	70	68	66	74	278	-10
	Mark O'MEARA	72	69	69	68	278	-10
	Ty TRYON	67	73	70	68	278	-10
47	Mark BROOKS	67	75	70	67	279	-9
	Jim CARTER	70	71	65	73	279	-9
	John COOK	69	70	69	71	279	-9
	Marco DAWSON	72	68	70	69	279	-9
	Doug DUNAKEY	70	71	65	73	279	-9
	H FRAZAR	72	70	69	68	279	-9
	J GALLAGHER Jr.	66	72	70	71	279	-9
	Dudley HART	70	71	69	69	279	-9
	J.P. HAYES	66	71	72	70	279	-9
	Mark WIEBE	73	69	70	67	279	-9
57	Craig BARLOW	69	69	68	74	280	-8
	P U JOHANSSON	71	71	69	69	280	-8
	Jonathan KAYE	69	71	68	72	280	-8
	Craig PARRY	73	69	71	67	280	-8
61	C BECKMAN	72	69	68	72	281	-7
	Bill GLASSON	69	71	69	72	281	-7
	Paul GOW	70	71	72	68	281	-7
	G HJERTSTEDT	67	72	73	69	281	-7
	Kevin JOHNSON	67	70	71	73	281	-7
	D MORLAND IV	70	70	67	74	281	-7
67	Stephen AMES	70	70	73	69	282	-6
	Tim HERRON	69	71	72	70	282	-6
	Tripp ISENHOUR	67	74	70	71	282	-6
	J WILLIAMSON	71	71	69	71	282	-6
71	Mathew GOGGIN	73	68	67	75	283	-5
	Cliff KRESGE	71	70	72	70	283	-5
73	D BERGANIO Jr.	72	69	71	72	284	-4
	Jeff BREHAUT	71	71	70	72	284	-4
	Robin FREEMAN	72	68	71	73	284	-4
76	R COUGHLAN	71	71	72	71	285	-3
	Jimmy GREEN	69	73	72	71	285	-3
	Hunter HAAS	66	71	71	77	285	-3
	Scott SIMPSON	66	76	71	72	285	-3

Tournament Report
Despite a bogey at the last, Jesper Parnevik won his fifth US Tour title by winning the Honda Classic at Heron Bay in Florida.

The Swede led by three going into the final round and a level par 72 was enough to hold off Craig Perks, Geoff Ogilvy and Mark Calcavecchia.

Parnevik had undergone hip surgery in the close season and his wife had also given birth to their fourth child but he showed few signs of ring rustiness when blazing a trail over the first three days courtesy of scores of 65, 67 and 66.

Sunday's round proved to be different, though, as the field came right back at Parnevik, and by the turn he trailed Ogilvy by a shot. But the Swede fought back to the top of the leaderboard by picking up a shot on the 11th.

With Ogilvy bogeying the 15th and 18th and Perks, whose 66 was the best Sunday score of the top four, also dropping a shot on the last, only Calcavecchia had a chance of victory as the final group came to the 72nd hole.

Calc, who was only just back from surgery on a damaged knee and had earlier made double bogey on the sixth, had to sink a 15-footer to force a play-off. But he saw his putt lip out and had to settle for second.

The relief on Parnevik's face was for all to see and the European Ryder Cup star hung on to claim his first win of the season.

MISSED THE CUT: Rich BEEM 70 73, Bradley HUGHES 69 74, Kent JONES 75 68, Craig KANADA 71 72, Greg KRAFT 68 75, Rob LABRITZ 72 71, Ian LEGGATT 71 72, Andrew MAGEE 70 73, Michael MUEHR 69 74, David PEOPLES 69 74, Tom PERNICE Jr. 70 73, Brian WATTS 73 70, Fuzzy ZOELLER 71 72, K.J. CHOI 73 71, Robert GAMEZ 74 70, Brian HENNINGER 71 73, Mark HENSBY 69 75, Steve JONES 72 72, Andrew McLARDY 72 72, Gary NICKLAUS 69 75, Jerry SMITH 71 73, Fred WADSWORTH 70 74, Kevin WENTWORTH 72 72, Aaron BADDELEY 76 69, Robert DAMRON 70 75, Bob ESTES 72 73, Matt GOGEL 75 70, Greg TOWNE 71 74, Rocky WALCHER 71 74, Jeremy ANDERSON 76 70, Paul CASEY 73 73, Brad ELDER 74 72, J.J. HENRY 71 75, Mike HULBERT 77 69, Carl PAULSON 69 77, Notah BEGAY III 75 72, Keith CLEARWATER 76 71, Glen DAY 74 73, Jeff MAGGERT 69 78, Blaine McCALLISTER 73 74, Sean MURPHY 74 73, Dicky PRIDE 70 77, Brian WILSON 74 73, Jorge BENEDETTI 71 77, Mike DONALD 73 75, Peter JACOBSEN 74 74, Dave STOCKTON Jr. 75 73, Ted TRYBA 73 75, Steve ALLAN 73 76, Tom BYRUM 72 77, Barry CHEESMAN 72 77, Danny ELLIS 73 76, Kelly GRUNEWALD 77 73, Mark McCUMBER 75 75, Justin PETERS 72 78, Lee PORTER 73 77, Paul GOYDOS 74 77, Craig A. SPENCE 72 79, Jeff JULIAN 77 75, Billy Ray BROWN 81 73, Emanuele CANONICA 76 80, Ray BOONE 81 76, Steve PATE 71 W/D, John RIEGGER 72 W/D, Chris TIDLAND W/D.

Course Profile
TPC at Heron Bay (par 72, 7,268 yards) has staged this event since 1997. This is a long course so big hitters go well.

There are over 100 bunkers on the layout, although few are deep, so players with a good touch from the sand prosper.

The course is usually set up fairly easily as when the wind blows it can play tough.

It is a young venue, with few mature trees, so a number of the holes are exposed.

Players/Points to Note
● **Vijay Singh** has recorded one win and one runner-up spot since this tournament moved to Heron Bay in 1997. The wind can affect this tournament so the Fijian's low ball striking is perfect.

● **Stuart Appleby** has a great record in this event, posting three top tens in five starts, including a win here 1997. **Mark Calcavecchia** has won this tournament twice, including at its present venue and was fourth in 2001. Both Appleby (also seventh in 2001) and Calcavecchia have good records on TPC courses – they have eight wins between them.

● **Davis Love** rarely plays this event but has yet to miss a cut and can boast three top-ten finishes. He has finished fourth and 19th in his two starts in the last ten years. Love also shares the course record (64) along with **Craig Parry**, **Tommy Armour** and **Hal Sutton**.

● Sutton is another player that performs well on TPC courses as is **Nick Price**, **David Duval** and **Phil Mickelson**.

● **Colin Montgomerie** probably won't play in 2002 but if he does he is worth considering given his two top-five finishes in the late '90s.

● The rejuvenated **John Daly** could go well in 2002 as could **Joe Durant**, **Harrison Frazar** and **Geoff Ogilvy**. All have showed up well in recent Honda Classics.

Previous Results
2000: 1. Dudley Hart (-19), 2. J P Hayes (-18), Kevin Wentworth (-18).

1999: 1. Vijay Singh (-11), 2. Payne Stewart (-11), 3. Eric Booker (-8), Doug Dunakey (-8), Carlos Franco (-8), Mark O'Meara (-8).

1998: 1. Mark Calcavecchia (-18), 2. Vijay Singh (-15), 3. Colin Montgomerie (-13).

1997: 1. Stuart Appleby (-14), 2. Michael Bradley (-13), Payne Stewart (-13).

1996: 1. Tim Herron (-17), 2. Mark McCumber (-13), 3. Nick Price (-12), Payne Stewart (-12), Lee Rinker (-12).

BAY HILL INVITATIONAL

Bay Hill Club, 15 Mar to 18 Mar 2001, purse $3,500,000

Pos	Name	R1	R2	R3	R4	Total	To par	Money	DD(y)	DA%	GIR%	Putts
1	Tiger WOODS	71	67	66	69	273	-15	$630,000	279.1	71	71	113
2	Phil MICKELSON	66	72	70	66	274	-14	$378,000	278.8	75	61	102
3	Grant WAITE	66	71	72	69	278	-10	$238,000	288.1	64	61	106
4	Sergio GARCIA	71	66	68	74	279	-9	$137,812	293.8	88	74	115
	Steve LOWERY	68	70	70	71	279	-9	$137,812	274.5	77	75	118
	Greg NORMAN	69	71	68	71	279	-9	$137,812	268.0	75	67	110
	Vijay SINGH	71	70	66	72	279	-9	$137,812	281.9	73	63	107
8	Paul GOYDOS	68	68	73	71	280	-8	$91,000	266.1	82	54	102
	Scott HOCH	68	72	69	71	280	-8	$91,000	267.6	82	71	114
	Lee JANZEN	67	72	69	72	280	-8	$91,000	266.1	77	69	114
	Dennis PAULSON	66	75	69	70	280	-8	$91,000	281.1	68	64	109
	Chris PERRY	71	66	69	74	280	-8	$91,000	266.8	79	68	110
	Jeff SLUMAN	67	74	68	71	280	-8	$91,000	275.3	68	63	107

Pos	Name	R1	R2	R3	R4	Total	To par
14	H FRAZAR	70	70	68	73	281	-7
15	Paul AZINGER	71	70	71	70	282	-6
	Fred FUNK	70	72	71	69	282	-6
17	Robert DAMRON	72	66	73	72	283	-5
	Bob ESTES	69	74	69	71	283	-5
	Gary NICKLAUS	71	70	71	71	283	-5
	Lee WESTWOOD	71	72	68	72	283	-5
	Brandt JOBE	70	73	66	74	283	-5
	S McCARRON	67	70	71	75	283	-5
23	Fulton ALLEM	70	67	73	74	284	-4
	Olin BROWNE	70	75	68	71	284	-4
	Dan FORSMAN	72	71	69	72	284	-4
	Skip KENDALL	70	75	67	72	284	-4
	F LICKLITER II	70	71	70	73	284	-4
	Rocco MEDIATE	77	67	67	73	284	-4
	Frank NOBILO	72	69	70	73	284	-4
	Steve PATE	66	73	71	74	284	-4
31	D BERGANIO, Jr.	70	71	70	74	285	-3
	M CALCAVECCHIA	66	72	75	72	285	-3
	K SUTHERLAND	73	69	69	74	285	-3
34	Robert ALLENBY	72	72	74	68	286	-2
	G CHALMERS	71	70	73	72	286	-2
	Nick FALDO	72	72	68	74	286	-2
	Retief GOOSEN	72	72	71	71	286	-2
	Tripp ISENHOUR	69	72	75	70	286	-2
	B LANGER	72	70	70	74	286	-2
40	Tim HERRON	68	72	73	74	287	-1
	N Joe OZAKI	74	71	69	73	287	-1
	Carl PAULSON	72	70	70	75	287	-1
43	Jay Don BLAKE	72	72	73	71	288	E
	B CHAMBLEE	73	70	69	76	288	E
	Tom LEHMAN	71	71	68	78	288	E
	Kenny PERRY	73	72	69	74	288	E
47	Brad FAXON	75	70	75	69	289	+1
	Peter JACOBSEN	73	72	71	73	289	+1
	Loren ROBERTS	72	71	71	75	289	+1
	J VAN DE VELDE	69	76	72	72	289	+1
51	K.J. Choi	71	72	70	77	290	+2
	Brad ELDER	69	73	77	71	290	+2
	David FROST	68	70	75	77	290	+2
	C MONTGOMERIE	75	69	75	71	290	+2
	Geoff OGILVY	69	72	70	79	290	+2
56	Notah BEGAY III	73	72	71	75	291	+3
	Joe DURANT	70	75	73	73	291	+3
	Brian GAY	72	72	70	77	291	+3
	J.L. LEWIS	74	70	76	71	291	+3
	Corey PAVIN	71	73	70	77	291	+3
	David TOMS	71	74	73	73	291	+3
62	Ernie ELS	73	70	74	75	292	+4
	Len MATTIACE	70	75	71	76	292	+4
64	Stephen AMES	74	70	72	77	293	+5
	Kirk TRIPLETT	69	74	75	75	293	+5
66	Craig BARLOW	68	76	75	75	294	+6
	Steve STRICKER	74	70	77	73	294	+6
68	Fred COUPLES	73	70	73	79	295	+7
	Craig PARRY	71	73	72	79	295	+7
	Adam SCOTT	71	74	75	75	295	+7
71	Jay HAAS	72	72	76	76	296	+8
	Gary KOCH	73	71	72	80	296	+8
	T PERNICE Jr.	70	74	77	75	296	+8
	P STANKOWSKI	72	72	77	75	296	+8

Sponsored by Stan James

Tournament Report

Tiger Woods ended his so called slump by scrambling to victory in the Bay Hill Invitational at the Bay Hill Country Club in Florida.

The World No.1 hadn't won for seven tournaments this season – a run that had the media claiming Woods' dominance of golf might be over.

But Tiger's success reminded us all that the winner of the last three Majors still has plenty to offer. It was a hard fought victory and one that required a little luck.

Woods started the day in the lead after a Saturday 66 and his challenger throughout Sunday was Phil Mickelson, who teed off for his final round four strokes behind Woods.

The left hander, though, caught the third round leader just after the turn, with birdies at the 11th and 12th.

And with Tiger struggling with his driver – he hit only one fairway with his biggest club all day – Mickelson went ahead when he rolled in a ten-footer on the 15th for birdie.

A thrilling duel then took place with Woods hauling back Mickelson on two occasions down the stretch.

Woods was spraying the ball all over the place it was only his miraculous short game that kept him in it. Then came the luck all golfers need to win tournaments.

Woods' drive on the 18th went left but hit a spectator, and after landing near a cart path he received a free drop.

From it, Woods launched a superb 5-iron from 195 yards to 15 feet, and duly sank the putt for victory.

MISSED THE CUT: Billy ANDRADE 74 72, J.J. HENRY 74 72, Miguel A. JIMENEZ 76 70, Franklin LANGHAM 73 73, Joey SINDELAR 74 72, Curtis STRANGE 75 71, Esteban TOLEDO 71 75, Jay WILLIAMSON 73 73, Robert GAMEZ 72 75, Brent GEIBERGER 72 75, Justin LEONARD 73 74, Andrew MAGEE 74 73, Billy MAYFAIR 74 73, Mark O'MEARA 75 72, Phillip PRICE 76 71, Tom SCHERRER 76 71, Ronnie BLACK 75 73, Steve JONES 79 69, Greg KRAFT 77 71, Blaine McCALLISTER 73 75, Duffy WALDORF 70 78, Jeremy ANDERSON 72 77, Charles Howell III 74 75, Larry MIZE 81 68, Jose Maria OLAZABAL 75 74, Tom PURTZER 77 72, John DALY 77 73, Glen DAY 77 73, Chris DiMARCO 76 74, Carlos FRANCO 75 75, Stuart APPLEBY 70 81, Andy BEAN 76 75, Michael CAMPBELL 73 78, Jim CARTER 80 71, Scott DUNLAP 77 74, Craig STADLER 79 72, Mark BROOKS 76 76, J.P. HAYES 72 80, Fuzzy ZOELLER 81 72, Steve FLESCH 76 78, D.A. WEIBRING 81 73, Jonathan KAYE 79 76, Garrett WILLIS 79 77, Mike HULBERT 78 79, Darren CLARKE 80 78, Will FRANTZ 79 80, Mikko ILONEN 78 82, Arnold PALMER 85 78.

Course Profile

The Arnold Palmer-designed Bay Hill Club and Lodge (par 72, 7,239 yards) in Orlando is long and as well as length off the tee, you have to be fairly straight to win here.

But don't discount the short hitters as the roll-call of champions suggests that you need more than booming tee shots to succeed.

The finishing five holes are arguably the toughest on the US Tour. The greens are larger than average and can host tricky pin positions.

Players/Points to Note

● **Tiger Woods** first played in the Bay Hill event in 1994 and the event is usually on the World No.1's schedule. In 2002 he will be going for a hat-trick of victories – a feat that hasn't been achieved before.

● **Davis Love** hasn't won this event but has finished runner-up on three occasions. In 15 starts he has registered seven top-ten finishes and is a record 69-under par.

● **Loren Roberts** won here in 1994 and 1995 and can boast five top-ten finishes. He obviously enjoys the fact that the greens are bigger than usual at Bay Hill, so can demonstrate his considerable skill with the flat stick.

● **Robert Damron** consistently performs well at Bay Hill and can boast four top-30 finishes in his last five starts. A Bay Hill resident his parents live by the course and he can also count designer and owner of the layout, Arnold Palmer, as a personal friend.

● **Scott Hoch** is a member at Bay Hill, while former winners and multiple top-ten finishers **Paul Goydos** and **Andrew Magee** will go well at a big prices.

● **Bernhard Langer** has the best record of the Europeans (with six top-ten finishes), who often come in preparation for the following week's Players Championship.

● **Tim Herron**, **Steve Lowery** and **Sergio Garcia** are also worth noting in this event.

Previous Results

2000: 1. Tiger Woods (-18), 2. Davis Love III (-14), 3. Skip Kendall (-13).

1999: 1. Tim Herron (-14) won play-off, 2. Tom Lehman (-14), 3. Davis Love III (-13).

1998: 1. Ernie Els (-14), 2. Jeff Maggert (-10), Bob Estes (-10).

1997: 1. Phil Mickelson (-16), 2. Stuart Appleby (-13), 3. Payne Stewart (-12), Mark O'Meara (-12), Omar Uresti (-12).

1996: 1. Paul Goydos (-13), 2. Jeff Maggert (-12), 3. Tom Purtzer (-11).

THE PLAYERS CHAMPIONSHIP

TPC at Sawgrass, 22 Mar to 25 Mar 2001, purse $6,000,000

Pos	Name	R1	R2	R3	R4	Total	To par	Money	DD(y)	DA%	GIR%	Putts
1	Tiger WOODS	72	69	66	67	274	-14	$1,080,000	288.3	63	69	109
2	Vijay SINGH	67	70	70	68	275	-13	$648,000	279.4	73	74	111
3	Bernhard LANGER	73	68	68	67	276	-12	$408,000	262.5	61	74	111
4	Jerry KELLY	69	66	70	73	278	-10	$288,000	268.9	79	79	120
5	Billy MAYFAIR	68	72	70	71	281	-7	$228,000	264.3	77	65	112
	Hal SUTTON	72	71	68	70	281	-7	$228,000	264.4	75	68	116
7	Paul AZINGER	66	70	74	72	282	-6	$187,000	269.8	68	72	114
	Scott HOCH	67	70	71	74	282	-6	$187,000	268.4	64	65	115
	Frank LICKLITER II	72	72	70	68	282	-6	$187,000	281.0	75	63	108
10	Joe DURANT	73	73	67	70	283	-5	$156,000	266.4	77	71	114
	Nick PRICE	70	74	71	68	283	-5	$156,000	258.1	75	72	118

Pos	Name	R1	R2	R3	R4	Total	To par
12	Tom LEHMAN	71	71	72	70	284	-4
	J M OLAZABAL	71	76	68	69	284	-4
	David TOMS	70	77	66	71	284	-4
15	M CAMPBELL	72	71	69	73	285	-3
	Scott DUNLAP	70	73	73	69	285	-3
	F LANGHAM	73	71	71	70	285	-3
18	Lee JANZEN	77	67	69	73	286	-2
	Jonathan KAYE	67	72	76	71	286	-2
	Kenny PERRY	71	66	74	75	286	-2
21	Robert ALLENBY	68	75	71	73	287	-1
	Jim FURYK	72	75	72	68	287	-1
	J.P. HAYES	72	69	76	70	287	-1
	Tim HERRON	73	74	71	69	287	-1
	Corey PAVIN	73	72	69	73	287	-1
26	Angel CABRERA	72	70	74	72	288	E
	Darren CLARKE	75	70	72	71	288	E
	Brad FAXON	72	74	73	69	288	E
	Skip KENDALL	68	78	69	73	288	E
	N Joe OZAKI	77	68	72	71	288	E
31	D PAULSON	74	70	73	72	289	+1
	Kirk TRIPLETT	72	71	76	70	289	+1
33	Stuart APPLEBY	74	73	75	68	290	+2
	Fred FUNK	70	71	77	72	290	+2
	P HARRINGTON	70	75	73	72	290	+2
	Phil MICKELSON	73	68	72	77	290	+2
	Craig PARRY	71	73	76	70	290	+2
	Jeff SLUMAN	72	71	75	72	290	+2
	Mark WIEBE	73	73	69	75	290	+2
40	Steve FLESCH	70	73	76	72	291	+3
	Brian GAY	73	74	72	72	291	+3
	C MONTGOMERIE	71	71	75	74	291	+3
	Bob TWAY	72	73	74	72	291	+3
44	Billy ANDRADE	72	73	74	73	292	+4
	Tom KITE	70	73	75	74	292	+4
	S McCARRON	71	75	77	69	292	+4
	P STANKOWSKI	72	74	73	73	292	+4
	Scott VERPLANK	69	75	72	76	292	+4
	Mike WEIR	77	69	72	74	292	+4
50	Jay Don BLAKE	74	73	73	73	293	+5
	Jim CARTER	69	73	75	76	293	+5
	Nick FALDO	73	73	75	72	293	+5
	Sergio GARCIA	73	74	74	72	293	+5
	Steve JONES	72	71	72	78	293	+5
55	Tom BYRUM	73	71	75	75	294	+6
	John COOK	71	72	75	76	294	+6
	Chris DiMARCO	74	73	74	73	294	+6
58	G CHALMERS	71	73	72	79	295	+7
	Fred COUPLES	71	75	70	79	295	+7
	Glen HNATIUK	74	70	71	80	295	+7
	Steve PATE	72	72	76	75	295	+7
	Chris RILEY	71	75	73	76	295	+7
	K SUTHERLAND	71	74	73	77	295	+7
	J WILLIAMSON	78	69	77	71	295	+7
65	Mark BROOKS	71	74	76	76	297	+9
	Greg KRAFT	73	71	72	81	297	+9
	Rocco MEDIATE	73	73	75	76	297	+9
68	Paul GOYDOS	73	74	76	75	298	+10
	Carl PAULSON	74	73	76	75	298	+10
70	B GEIBERGER	72	75	82	70	299	+11
	Mathew GOGGIN	72	75	72	80	299	+11
	Ian WOOSNAM	73	73	81	72	299	+11
73	Brad ELDER	69	72	81	78	300	+12
	Robin FREEMAN	73	72	79	76	300	+12
	J.L. LEWIS	73	72	78	77	300	+12

LANGER

Tournament Report

The tournament the pros call the 'Fifth Major' went to the player that had won the previous three, as Tiger Woods held off Vijay Singh's late surge to land the Players Championship at TPC at Sawgrass.

All talk of a slump was firmly over as Woods, who lost out in a head to head battle with Hal Sutton in this event in 2000, caught overnight, two-shot leader Jerry Kelly after just two holes, after chipping in from 70 feet on the second.

He then went clear of his playing partner after four holes and was never headed. When play had to be halted on Sunday night (the start to the final round was delayed), Woods was a shot clear of both Kelly and Singh having played through nine holes. When play resumed on Monday the challenge was to come from Singh.

The Fijian caught Woods by the 13th but disaster was to strike at the par four 14th, when Singh took a triple bogey – an errant drive finding water. But he was to bounce back by shooting eagle and then birdie on the 16th and 17th respectively.

A missed birdie opportunity at the last by Singh, moments after Woods nearly ended in the water on the infamous island green 17th hole, meant that Tiger could bogey the last and still win. He needed that two-shot cushion as his drive on the 18th found the rough and a five was all he could muster.

Bernhard Langer's Sunday 67 meant that the German edged out Kelly for third.

MISSED THE CUT: Michael CLARK II 73 75, Robert DAMRON 76 72, Dudley HART 70 78, Bradley HUGHES 74 74, Neal LANCASTER 76 72, Davis LOVE III 72 76, Steve STRICKER 74 74, Jean VAN DE VELDE 75 73, Duffy WALDORF 77 71, Lee WESTWOOD 73 75, Carlos FRANCO 73 76, Matt GOGEL 74 75, Brian HENNINGER 71 78, Greg NORMAN 75 74, Jesper PARNEVIK 70 79, David PEOPLES 71 78, Brandel CHAMBLEE 75 75, Bob ESTES 72 78, Miguel A. JIMENEZ 75 75, Justin LEONARD 74 76, Jeff MAGGERT 70 80, Tom PURTZER 71 79, Tom SCHERRER 76 74, Fulton ALLEM 74 77, Notah BEGAY III 79 72, Mark CALCAVECCHIA 74 77, John DALY 73 78, Doug DUNAKEY 75 76, Ernie ELS 76 75, Edward FRYATT 74 77, Steve LOWERY 73 78, Blaine McCALLISTER 77 74, Esteban TOLEDO 74 77, Doug BARRON 77 75, Len MATTIACE 80 72, Shaun MICHEEL 73 79, Mark O'MEARA 78 74, Joe OGILVIE 72 80, Garrett WILLIS 74 78, Stephen AMES 78 75, Harrison FRAZAR 79 74, Brandt JOBE 76 77, Paul LAWRIE 75 78, Loren ROBERTS 76 77, Craig STADLER 78 75, Grant WAITE 75 78, Russ COCHRAN 74 80, Glen DAY 78 76, Jimmy GREEN 76 78, John HUSTON 75 79, Andrew MAGEE 74 80, Thomas BJORN 76 79, Olin BROWNE 76 79, Jerry SMITH 77 78, Ben CRENSHAW 78 78, Retief GOOSEN 79 77, Gary NICKLAUS 79 77, Woody AUSTIN 78 79, Stewart CINK 78 79, Pete JORDAN 76 81, Larry MIZE 76 81, Eduardo ROMERO 78 79, Rory SABBATINI 74 84, Bob BURNS 76 83, Bill GLASSON 77 86, Joel EDWARDS 72 D, Tommy ARMOUR III W/D.

Course Profile

TPC at Sawgrass (par 72, 7,093 yards) in Florida is one of the toughest courses used on Tour.

Water comes into play on the final three holes and players need nerves of steel to finish with two pars on the par three 17th, which features an island green, and the punishing par four 18th.

The greens are smaller than average and the key to winning is hitting the fairways and the putting surfaces in regulation.

Players/Points to Note

●After form figures of 31-35-10-2, **Tiger Woods** finally won the only major title that had eluded him. He won the 1994 Amateur Championship at Sawgrass and dominated the final round in 2001. He could do likewise in 2002.

●**David Duval** has the perfect power game for the layout and is rarely intimidated by the shots required to win at Sawgrass. He was the champion in 1999 but missed out through injury in 2001.

●**Tom Lehman** is yet to win at Sawgrass but has the lowest stroke average of 70.88. In nine starts he has finished in the top ten, four times (and the top 15 another four times), and to par, is 40-under – the lowest of anyone who's played in the event.

●**Ernie Els** can boast top-20 finishes in five of the last six renewals, while dual winners **Fred Couples**, **Steve Elkington** and **Hal Sutton** are also worth considering if in form.

●**Nick Price** is another former winner who always goes well, as eight top-ten finishes suggest.

●**Bernhard Langer** and **Colin Montgomerie** can boast five and four top-ten finishes respectively and look the best chance of a European win in 2002.

●Experienced golfers win this event. Since 1993 all the champions has already won at least three times on the US Tour and all bar one had won a Major.

Previous Results

_2000:_ 1. Hal Sutton (-10), 2. Tiger Woods (-9), 3. Five players tied.

_1999:_ 1. David Duval (-3), 2. Scott Gump (-1), 3. Nick Price (Ev).

_1998:_ 1. Justin Leonard (-10), 2. Tom Lehman (-8), Glen Day (-8).

_1997:_ 1. Steve Elkington (-16), 2. Scott Hoch (-9), 3. Loren Roberts (-8).

_1996:_ 1. Fred Couples (-18), 2. Colin Montgomerie (-14), Tommy Tolles (-14).

BELL SOUTH CLASSIC

TPC at Sugarloaf, 29 Mar to 1 Apr 2001, purse $3,300,000

Pos	Name	R1	R2	R3	R4	Total	To par	Money	DD(y)	DA%	GIR%	Putts
1	Scott McCARRON	68	67	72	73	280	-8	$594,000	287.5	80	78	121
2	Mike WEIR	76	67	73	67	283	-5	$356,400	282.6	84	69	116
3	Phil MICKELSON	70	66	73	75	284	-4	$171,600	284.0	66	64	111
	Dennis PAULSON	72	65	72	75	284	-4	$171,600	282.8	61	69	116
	Chris SMITH	73	70	72	69	284	-4	$171,600	291.4	66	72	123
6	Stewart CINK	70	71	71	73	285	-3	$103,290	277.0	79	76	124
	Chris DiMARCO	68	67	73	77	285	-3	$103,290	281.3	66	71	119
	Mathew GOGGIN	69	73	69	74	285	-3	$103,290	299.4	79	71	119
	C HOWELL III	70	68	74	73	285	-3	$103,290	297.3	79	67	115
	Joey SINDELAR	73	70	72	70	285	-3	$103,290	290.3	68	74	121

Pos	Name	R1	R2	R3	R4	Total	To par
11	Scott DUNLAP	74	65	75	72	286	-2
	Brandt JOBE	68	74	73	71	286	-2
	Jerry KELLY	69	69	72	76	286	-2
	Skip KENDALL	74	67	73	72	286	-2
	Davis LOVE III	70	71	71	74	286	-2
	Shaun MICHEEL	72	71	70	73	286	-2
17	H FRAZAR	73	68	73	73	287	-1
	David TOMS	69	69	74	75	287	-1
19	K.J. CHOI	72	70	69	77	288	E
	Steve FLESCH	68	75	71	74	288	E
21	Jeff BREHAUT	70	68	78	73	289	+1
	Bob BURNS	73	70	73	73	289	+1
	Billy MAYFAIR	70	70	74	75	289	+1
	J PARNEVIK	72	71	75	71	289	+1
25	Gary NICKLAUS	73	69	76	72	290	+2
	Mike SPOSA	69	70	77	74	290	+2
27	Doug BARRON	74	67	73	77	291	+3
	John DALY	69	71	76	75	291	+3
	S MARUYAMA	69	73	75	74	291	+3
	Greg NORMAN	73	67	76	75	291	+3
	J M OLAZABAL	73	70	71	77	291	+3
	Craig PARRY	71	70	74	76	291	+3
	Scott SIMPSON	73	69	73	76	291	+3
34	Marco DAWSON	67	72	79	74	292	+4
	K GRUNEWALD	71	71	75	75	292	+4
	Mark HENSBY	69	72	73	78	292	+4
	A McLARDY	71	70	78	73	292	+4
	T PERNICE, Jr.	73	70	75	74	292	+4
	Kaname YOKOO	68	69	77	78	292	+4
40	Bradley HUGHES	73	70	75	75	293	+5
	F LICKLITER II	70	68	72	83	293	+5
	Bob TWAY	72	70	74	77	293	+5
43	B McCALLISTER	70	71	78	75	294	+6
44	Ernie ELS	74	67	81	73	295	+7
45	Robin FREEMAN	72	70	74	80	296	+8
46	M CLARK II	71	72	80	74	297	+9
	Pierre FULKE	72	70	78	77	297	+9
	Ted TRYBA	70	69	79	79	297	+9
49	Robert DAMRON	71	69	79	79	298	+10
	Andrew MAGEE	73	69	76	80	298	+10
51	Kevin JOHNSON	73	70	75	81	299	+11
52	T ARMOUR III	72	67	84	78	301	+13

Made the cut but did not play final 36 holes

Pos	Name	R1	R2	R3	R4	Total
53	Billy ANDRADE	71	73	-	-	144
	C BECKMAN	72	72	-	-	144
	D BERGANIO Jr.	70	74	-	-	144
	Kevin BLANTON	74	70	-	-	144
	Bill GLASSON	74	70	-	-	144
	J.J. HENRY	72	72	-	-	144
	John HUSTON	73	71	-	-	144
	Steve JONES	72	72	-	-	144
	Jeff JULIAN	72	72	-	-	144
	Cliff KRESGE	69	75	-	-	144
	Jeff MAGGERT	74	70	-	-	144
	Len MATTIACE	70	74	-	-	144
	D MORLAND IV	71	73	-	-	144
	Craig PERKS	73	71	-	-	144
	Duffy WALDORF	72	72	-	-	144
68	Briny BAIRD	74	71	-	-	145
	Rich BEEM	76	69	-	-	145
	S ELKINGTON	74	71	-	-	145
	Edward FRYATT	72	73	-	-	145
	Jeff HART	72	73	-	-	145
	Nolan HENKE	70	75	-	-	145
	G HJERTSTEDT	72	73	-	-	145
	Glen HNATIUK	75	70	-	-	145
	P U JOHANSSON	71	74	-	-	145
	J.L. LEWIS	73	72	-	-	145
	Dick MAST	74	71	-	-	145
	Michael MUEHR	75	70	-	-	145
	David PEOPLES	71	74	-	-	145
	Tom SCHERRER	75	70	-	-	145
	Jerry SMITH	76	69	-	-	145
	Chris TIDLAND	71	74	-	-	145
	Grant WAITE	72	73	-	-	145
	J WILLIAMSON	72	73	-	-	145
69	Retief GOOSEN	69	74	-	-	W/D

Sponsored by Stan James

Tournament Report

Scott McCarron had to win the BellSouth Classic the hard way. After Thursday's play was washed out, 36 holes were to be completed at TPC at Sugarloaf – a long course that winds it's way through hilly terrain – on Sunday.

But McCarron was up to the task and won his third US Tour event by three shots from Canadian Mike Weir.

The scoring reflected the gruelling conditions, which were made worse by wind and rain, as McCarron's one-over par total for the last two rounds was enough for victory.

McCarron led at the halfway stage courtesy of opening scores of 68 and 67 and was prepared more than most to take on the elements – and the 20-mile hike around 36 holes.

Ernie Els signed for a last round 81, Frank Lickliter an 83, while Retief Goosen withdrew after just two holes on Sunday.

McCarron did have his problems and dropped three shots in four holes on the back nine of his final round – and also had to play left handed to scrape a bogey when his ball settled behind a tree. Only Weir threatened.

The Canadian conjured up a magical last round 67 – the best of the day and one of only four sub-70 Sunday scores – and got to within three strokes of the eventual winner.

But a 40-foot birdie putt dropped at the 16th for McCarron and victory was practically his. Phil Mickelson, Dennis Paulson and Chris Smith, after shooting a last round 69, shared third spot.

MISSED THE CUT: Jose COCERES 76 70, Russ COCHRAN 74 72, Paul GOW 73 73, Kent JONES 72 74, Matt KUCHAR 74 72, Spike McROY 70 76, Frank NOBILO 74 72, Paul STANKOWSKI 74 72, Kevin SUTHERLAND 75 71, Tommy TOLLES 73 73, Garrett WILLIS 73 73, Doug DUNAKEY 77 70, Dudley HART 77 70, Brian HENNINGER 72 75, Tim HERRON 73 74, Pete JORDAN 77 70, Franklin LANGHAM 74 73, Chris PERRY 72 75, Chris RILEY 75 72, Brent SCHWARZROCK 74 73, Rocky WALCHER 74 73, Tom BYRUM 76 72, Hunter HAAS 72 76, J.P. HAYES 75 73, Craig KANADA 77 71, Joe OGILVIE 76 72, John RIEGGER 74 74, Tim WEINHART 75 73, Jeremy ANDERSON 74 75, Andy BEAN 77 72, Matt GOGEL 72 77, Jason GORE 81 68, Miguel A. JIMENEZ 77 72, James MASON 76 73, Carl PAULSON 79 70, Lee PORTER 74 75, Dicky PRIDE 73 76, Jay Don BLAKE 72 78, Larry MIZE 74 76, Sean MURPHY 77 73, Corey PAVIN 77 73, Clark SPRATLIN 78 72, Brian WILSON 78 72, Jace BUGG 74 77, Ben FERGUSON 73 78, Jimmy GREEN 77 74, Tripp ISENHOUR 77 74, Joel EDWARDS 78 74, David FROST 75 77, Steve ALLAN 81 72, Woody AUSTIN 77 76, Chris RIEVE 81 73, Jean VAN DE VELDE 83 72, Ian WOOSNAM D 74 74, Neal LANCASTER W/D 76 76, Brent GEIBERGER W/D 77 77.

Course Profile

TPC at Sugarloaf (par 72, 7,259 yards) is a favourite of a lot of pros.

The terrain is similar to that at Augusta, with big mature trees and streams running throughout the layout (water comes into play on eight holes). The emphasis is definitely on hitting the ball a long way.

There are plenty of subtle slopes on the fairways that can run errant drives into trouble.

If betting in running, watch out for the super risk/reward par five finishing hole.

Players/Points to Note

●**David Duval** has the best record at this tournament and course. He won the event in 1999, in a record low 72-hole score of 270. Prior to that he recorded four consecutive top-15 finishes, including a second and a third place. In 1995, he should have won this event as an amateur. He led going into the final round by two shots but fell away with a Sunday 79.

●**Stewart Cink**'s form figures over the past three years read 5-2-10-6. He enjoyed playing at Sugarloaf so much that he built a home on the grounds and now lives there.

●**Scott McCarron**'s win last year was no fluke. His game is perfectly suited to Sugarloaf and he now has two wins at the venue.

●Prior to last year (when he didn't play the last two rounds due to bad weather), **John Huston** had never been out of the top five in three visits to Sugarloaf.

●**David Toms** has also shot only three rounds over par - this time in five starts at the course. He has finished in the top 20 on four occasions.

Outsiders to consider would be **Chris DiMarco**, **Brian Henninger**, **Steve Flesch** (10-36-3), **Jay Don Blake** and **Joey Sindelaar**.

●**Tiger Woods**, winner in 1998, holds the course record of 63 along with **Duffy Waldorf**.

Previous Results

2000: 1. Phil Mickelson (-11), won play-off, 2. Gary Nicklaus (-11), 3. Kenny Perry (-9), Harrison Frazar (-9).

1999: 1. David Duval (-18), 2. Stewart Cink (-16), 3. John Huston (-15), Rory Sabbatini (-15).

1998: 1. Tiger Woods (-17), 2. Jay Don Blake (-16), 3. Esteban Toledo (-14), Steve Flesch (-14).

1997: 1. Scott McCarron (-14), 2. Lee Janzen (-11), Brian Henninger (-11), David Duval (-11).

1996: 1. Paul Stankowski (-8), won play-off, 2. Brandel Chamblee (-8), 3. Nick Price (-6), David Duval (-6).

WORLDCOM CLASSIC

Hilton Head Island G.C., 12 Apr to 15 Apr 2001, purse $3,500,000

Pos	Name	R1	R2	R3	R4	Total	To par	Money	DD(y)	DA%	GIR%	Putts
1	Jose COCERES	68	70	64	71	273	-11	$630,000	264.1	93	79	109
Won play-off												
2	Billy MAYFAIR	65	68	69	71	273	-11	$378,000	263.9	88	60	103
3	Bernhard LANGER	69	69	67	69	274	-10	$168,000	269.6	82	68	110
	Carl PAULSON	71	63	71	69	274	-10	$168,000	283.5	91	63	107
	Vijay SINGH	65	68	67	74	274	-10	$168,000	280.4	75	63	104
	Scott VERPLANK	68	67	69	70	274	-10	$168,000	264.8	82	65	108
7	Steve FLESCH	71	69	72	63	275	-9	$109,083	282.0	80	58	102
	Mark BROOKS	66	69	71	69	275	-9	$109,083	247.5	84	51	101
	Davis LOVE III	68	67	71	69	275	-9	$109,083	294.9	80	67	112
10	Billy ANDRADE	66	67	73	70	276	-8	$91,000	268.4	84	61	105
	Stewart CINK	69	71	70	66	276	-8	$91,000	275.0	75	63	109

Pos	Name	R1	R2	R3	R4	Total	To par
12	Paul AZINGER	69	71	68	69	277	-7
	Thomas BJORN	69	70	71	67	277	-7
	M CAMPBELL	72	65	69	71	277	-7
	Brad ELDER	66	69	72	70	277	-7
	David FROST	69	69	72	67	277	-7
	Rocco MEDIATE	66	71	74	66	277	-7
	Dudley HART	66	71	69	71	277	-7
	Len MATTIACE	68	68	68	73	277	-7
	D PAULSON	71	68	67	71	277	-7
21	Fulton ALLEM	73	67	71	67	278	-6
	Stephen AMES	71	69	69	69	278	-6
	Joe DURANT	69	68	72	69	278	-6
	Lee JANZEN	69	71	67	71	278	-6
	Bob MAY	69	71	70	68	278	-6
	Corey PAVIN	69	70	69	70	278	-6
	Mike SPOSA	67	67	70	74	278	-6
28	John COOK	69	66	73	71	279	-5
	Glen DAY	70	68	67	74	279	-5
	Joel EDWARDS	74	65	72	68	279	-5
	Glen HNATIUK	67	72	75	65	279	-5
	Scott HOCH	67	69	71	72	279	-5
	Tom LEHMAN	66	66	72	75	279	-5
	J PARNEVIK	68	69	72	70	279	-5
	Chris SMITH	71	66	72	70	279	-5
	Ted TRYBA	69	70	70	70	279	-5
	D.A. WEIBRING	69	73	68	69	279	-5
38	M CALCAVECCHIA	66	71	71	72	280	-4
	Fred FUNK	68	72	72	68	280	-4
	Greg NORMAN	69	71	71	69	280	-4
	Mark WIEBE	71	71	70	68	280	-4
42	G CHALMERS	66	71	69	75	281	-3
	Doug DUNAKEY	65	71	76	69	281	-3
	Bob ESTES	70	69	67	75	281	-3
	Brian GAY	67	71	72	71	281	-3
	Skip KENDALL	72	66	71	72	281	-3
	Steve LOWERY	71	68	73	69	281	-3
	Bob TWAY	69	68	73	71	281	-3
49	John DALY	73	66	67	76	282	-2
	Nick PRICE	70	72	69	71	282	-2
51	Nick FALDO	70	71	70	72	283	-1
	Carlos FRANCO	67	72	76	68	283	-1
	Chris RILEY	68	68	75	72	283	-1
	Tom SCHERRER	69	70	70	74	283	-1
55	T ARMOUR III	66	74	73	71	284	E
	C BECKMAN	70	69	74	71	284	E
	N LANCASTER	67	75	70	72	284	E
	Garrett WILLIS	70	68	72	74	284	E
59	T BARRANGER	68	73	69	75	285	+1
	P HARRINGTON	70	71	72	72	285	+1
	Shaun MICHEEL	72	69	72	72	285	+1
62	Craig BARLOW	73	69	73	71	286	+2
	B CHAMBLEE	70	71	72	73	286	+2
	Jay HAAS	71	71	72	72	286	+2
	Loren ROBERTS	67	73	72	74	286	+2
66	Bob BURNS	68	74	75	70	287	+3
	M CLARK II	73	68	72	74	287	+3
	Brad FAXON	69	72	77	69	287	+3
	F LANGHAM	69	70	76	72	287	+3
	Jeff SLUMAN	67	71	73	76	287	+3
71	Jay Don BLAKE	74	68	73	73	288	+4
	Chris PERRY	72	70	73	73	288	+4
73	Robert DAMRON	71	71	72	75	289	+5
74	Jimmy GREEN	71	71	72	76	290	+6
75	Robert ALLENBY	71	69	74	78	292	+8

Sponsored by Stan James

Tournament Report

Jose Coceres became the first Argentinean to win on the US Tour since 1968 when he defeated Billy Mayfair in a play-off for the World-Com Classic at Harbour Town Links, Hilton Head, South Carolina.

The 11-year veteran of the European Tour needed five extra holes to end the determined challenge of Mayfair.

The pair had started the day tied for second place behind Vijay Singh. But when the Fijian fell away after a final round 74 (eventually sharing third place alongside Bernhard Langer, Carl Paulson and Scott Verplank), both had chances to win in regulation play.

Mayfair at one stage had a two-stroke advantage but, after an errant drive, on the 11th had to sign for a double bogey to slip back into a tie for the lead.

Coceres birdied the 16th to put pressure on Mayfair who only just made par at the last by holing a 15-footer. In the end, both shot final round 71s to send the tournament into extra time.

Two holes of the play-off were possible on Sunday before darkness descended and play was suspended. The duo came back on Monday morning with Mayfair having the first chance to win.

But the 34-year-old, who once defeated Tiger Woods in a sudden death affair, missed a six-foot putt to win on the second extra hole of the day and the fourth of the play-off.

Coceres' chance would come minutes later, as the Argentinean made no mistake from five feet after a glorious approach to claim victory.

MISSED THE CUT: Aaron BADDELEY 70 73, David BERGANIO Jr. 73 70, K.J. CHOI 71 72, Sergio GARCIA 72 71, John HUSTON 73 70, Kevin JOHNSON 70 73, Jerry KELLY 72 71, Frank NOBILO 72 71, Geoff OGILVY 73 70, Steve PATE 69 74, David PEOPLES 72 71, Craig PERKS 73 70, Tom PERNICE Jr. 69 74, Gabriel HJERTSTEDT 74 70, Tom PURTZER 72 72, Jerry SMITH 70 74, Jim CARTER 74 71, Steve ELKINGTON 71 74, Edward FRYATT 73 72, Mathew GOGGIN 75 70, Tim HERRON 75 70, Blaine McCALLISTER 70 75, Gary NICKLAUS 74 71, Joey SINDELAR 72 73, Doug BARRON 75 71, Bob BOYD 75 71, Russ COCHRAN 74 72, Tim DUNLAVEY 74 72, Per Ulrik JOHANSSON 73 73, Pete JORDAN 73 73, Joe OGILVIE 74 72, Adam SCOTT 71 75, Tom WATSON 71 75, Briny BAIRD 76 71, Robin FREEMAN 76 71, Brian HENNINGER 72 75, Cliff KRESGE 75 72, Justin LEONARD 76 71, Frank LICKLITER II 68 79, Esteban TOLEDO 72 75, Rory SABBATINI 71 77, Kaname YOKOO 74 75, Scott DUNLAP 75 74, Larry MIZE 74 75, Lee PORTER 70 79, Rich BEEM 76 74, Spike McROY 72 78, Rod PAMPLING 79 71, Woody AUSTIN 79 72, Jay WILLIAMSON 75 76, Tony BRANHAM 75 78, Matt GOGEL 81 75, Fuzzy ZOELLER 81 76, Ben CRENSHAW 76 82, David EDWARDS 82 77, Bradley HUGHES 72 D, Peter JACOBSEN W/D, Craig STADLER W/D.

Sponsored by Stan James

Course Profile

Extensive work on the Hilton Head Island Golf Club (par 72, 6,973 yards) continued right up until the 2001 renewal.

Pete Dye, original designer and overseer of the restorations, didn't change the characteristics of the layout too much and most of the changes met with the players' approval.

The track is still narrow and has small greens, although perhaps they are flatter now.

Players have to have a good short game to win here and be able to hit the greens in regulation.

Players/Points to Note

● **Davis Love** is the undisputed king of Harbour Town. He has won this event on four occasions ('87, '91, '92 and '98), has four other top-ten finishes, is 67-under par in 16 visits and has a stroke average of 69.78.

● **Loren Roberts** holds the low 72-hole score of 265. A score he shot when winning in 1996. The small, tricky greens are perfect for Roberts, who has also finished in the top ten on two other occasions.

● **Tom Lehman** can boast the lowest scoring average of 69.63 and three top tens in ten starts.

● **Nick Price**, the 1997 champion, has five top tens in 15 starts. **David Frost** is a multiple top-ten finisher (five) and holds the course record of 61. **Greg Norman** can match Frost's top-ten count.

● Prior to missing the cut in 2001, **John Huston**'s form figures read 10-5-9.

● **Glen Day** followed up his runner-up position in 1998 with a win 12 months later. **Ernie Els** has three top tens in four visits.

● **Stewart Cink** won on his first outing at Hilton Head and followed up last season with a share of tenth.

● This is the event directly after the US Masters and anyone who was in contention there usually doesn't perform well in this event (if they tee-up at all).

Previous Results

2000: 1. Stewart Cink (-14), 2. Tom Lehman (-12), 3. Six players tied.

1999: 1. Glen Day (-10) won play-off, 2. Jeff Sluman (-10), Payne Stewart (-10).

1998: 1. Davis Love III (-18), 2. Glen Day (-11), 3. Payne Stewart (-8), Phil Mickelson (-8).

1997: 1. Nick Price (-15), 2. Jesper Parnevik (-9), Brad Faxon (-9).

1996: 1. Loren Roberts (-19), 2. Mark O'Meara (-16), 3. Scott Hoch (-14).

SHELL HOUSTON OPEN

The Woodlands, 19 Apr to 22 Apr 2001, purse $3,400,000

Pos	Name	R1	R2	R3	R4	Total	To par	Money	DD(y)	DA%	GIR%	Putts
1	Hal SUTTON	70	68	71	69	278	-10	$612,000	270.9	82	68	111
2	Joe DURANT	67	69	71	74	281	-7	$299,200	277.3	91	71	114
	Lee JANZEN	67	68	73	73	281	-7	$299,200	275.5	80	63	110
4	John COOK	69	72	72	69	282	-6	$149,600	266.5	73	65	113
	Justin LEONARD	71	70	72	69	282	-6	$149,600	275.1	73	57	105
6	Len MATTIACE	72	69	73	69	283	-5	$113,900	278.4	73	61	109
	Billy MAYFAIR	70	72	71	70	283	-5	$113,900	267.1	86	64	112
	Vijay SINGH	73	70	69	71	283	-5	$113,900	285.1	75	63	110
9	Chris DiMARCO	69	70	71	74	284	-4	$88,400	272.8	59	56	105
	Ben FERGUSON	72	71	68	73	284	-4	$88,400	271.6	64	54	104
	K SUTHERLAND	69	69	72	74	284	-4	$88,400	273.0	73	61	112
	David TOMS	73	68	73	70	284	-4	$88,400	278.3	73	67	114

Pos	Name	R1	R2	R3	R4	Total	To par
13	Stewart CINK	73	70	71	71	285	-3
	Joel EDWARDS	70	69	73	73	285	-3
	Brian GAY	74	70	68	73	285	-3
16	Phil BLACKMAR	70	72	71	73	286	-2
	Marco DAWSON	71	69	73	73	286	-2
	David FROST	72	72	71	71	286	-2
	Paul GOW	73	72	68	73	286	-2
	Scott HOCH	72	72	67	75	286	-2
	Chris RILEY	71	71	72	72	286	-2
22	Fred COUPLES	68	76	72	71	287	-1
	Nick FALDO	75	70	70	72	287	-1
	Carlos FRANCO	72	71	68	76	287	-1
	S MARUYAMA	73	72	72	70	287	-1
26	J ANDERSON	72	72	72	72	288	E
	Jim CARTER	72	69	77	70	288	E
	John DALY	71	69	73	75	288	E
	David DUVAL	72	70	72	74	288	E
	B HENNINGER	74	69	74	71	288	E
	Brandt JOBE	69	73	74	72	288	E
	F LICKLITER II	75	68	71	74	288	E
	Chris SMITH	71	72	70	75	288	E
	T PERNICE, Jr.	70	67	74	77	288	E
35	Briny BAIRD	74	71	72	72	289	+1
	D MORLAND IV	72	69	72	76	289	+1
	Carl PAULSON	68	73	76	72	289	+1
	Scott SIMPSON	72	71	74	72	289	+1
	Mike SPOSA	75	70	68	76	289	+1
	Esteban TOLEDO	71	73	69	76	289	+1
41	G CHALMERS	71	72	74	73	290	+2
	Brad ELDER	75	68	71	76	290	+2
	Robert GAMEZ	71	70	75	74	290	+2
	Bradley HUGHES	71	72	74	73	290	+2
	Tim THELEN	75	70	70	75	290	+2
46	Stephen AMES	72	71	75	73	291	+3
	Tom BYRUM	74	71	69	77	291	+3
	Fred FUNK	72	70	76	73	291	+3
	J.J. HENRY	71	74	71	75	291	+3
	Joe OGILVIE	72	69	76	74	291	+3
	Jerry SMITH	71	72	73	75	291	+3
	Brian WILSON	73	72	71	75	291	+3
	Kaname YOKOO	69	76	75	71	291	+3
54	Jeff BREHAUT	73	72	74	73	292	+4
	Jimmy GREEN	70	71	76	75	292	+4
	Craig KANADA	69	76	74	73	292	+4
	Andrew MAGEE	70	71	73	78	292	+4
	Shaun MICHEEL	72	71	68	81	292	+4
	Garrett WILLIS	74	70	76	72	292	+4
60	Doug BARRON	75	67	75	76	293	+5
	Matt GOGEL	70	69	79	75	293	+5
62	Robert ALLENBY	69	74	70	81	294	+6
	K.J. CHOI	73	71	74	76	294	+6
	Greg KRAFT	73	72	69	80	294	+6
	Lee PORTER	73	72	72	77	294	+6
	Adam SCOTT	68	73	77	76	294	+6
67	T ARMOUR III	73	72	76	74	295	+7
	P STANKOWSKI	73	69	80	73	295	+7
	R THOMPSON	75	70	75	75	295	+7
70	Cliff KRESGE	70	72	79	75	296	+8
	Steve PATE	72	73	81	70	296	+8
72	J.P. HAYES	72	70	74	81	297	+9
73	J GALLAGHER	71	71	74	83	299	+11

Tournament Report

Hal Sutton had always wanted to win the Houston Open and after two near misses – he was runner-up in 1994 and 1999 – the 19-year US Tour veteran would not be denied in 2001.

Sutton overhauled Joe Durant, the overnight leader by two, by shooting a Sunday 69, one of only four sub-70 scores on the final day, to win his 14th US Tour title. On a tough last day at TPC at Woodlands the turning point for Sutton wasn't a birdie or an eagle but a bogey.

After finding water at the seventh with his approach, Sutton needed to hole from 25 feet to escape with no more than a single dropped shot. And sink it he did to stay in contention. Two birdies followed in the next three holes, thanks to accurate iron play and dead-eye putting.

And with Durant and Lee Janzen faltering, Sutton led by two strokes after 10 holes. Although Durant would get to within a shot of Sutton, a bogey at the 16th would effectively seal the win for the Shreveport pro.

Janzen started the day just one stroke off the lead but he let four shots go on the outward nine, due to two bogeys and a double bogey, to trail by four at the turn.

Durant, a two-time US Tour winner this season, and Janzen posted final rounds of 74 and 73 respectively and eventually missed out by three shots. John Cook and Justin Leonard carded Sunday 69s to share fourth spot.

MISSED THE CUT: Stuart APPLEBY 76 70, Woody AUSTIN 73 73, Craig BARLOW 73 73, Cameron BECKMAN 72 74, Emanuele CANONICA 71 75, Brandel CHAMBLEE 74 72, Steve ELKINGTON 76 70, Edward Fryatt 75 71, Bill GLASSON 73 73, Charles HOWELL III 73 73, Kent JONES 71 75, Jerry KELLY 72 74, Ian LEGGATT 71 75, Jim McGOVERN 75 71, Gary NICKLAUS 71 75, Curtis STRANGE 74 72, Kevin WENTWORTH 74 72, Jay WILLIAMSON 75 71, Mark BROOKS 76 71, Doug DUNAKEY 74 73, Kelly GRUNEWALD 74 73, Jeff HART 75 72, Mike HEINEN 73 74, Per Ulrik JOHANSSON 75 72, Pete JORDAN 76 71, Skip KENDALL 74 73, Blaine McCALLISTER 75 72, Kenny PERRY 76 71, John RIEGGER 73 74, Jeff SLUMAN 75 72, D STOCKTON Jr. 78 69, T TRYBA 75 72, M WIEBE 76 71, H FRAZAR 75 73, M HENSBY 72 76, J JULIAN 74 74, A McLARDY 73 75, B SCHWARZROCK 72 76, T TOLLES 71 77, K CLEARWATER 78 71, D FORSMAN 75 74, M GOGGIN 73 76, M GORTANA 73 76, J HAAS 74 75, G HJERTSTEDT 74 75, J.L. LEWIS 78 71, M MUEHR 76 73, C STADLER 73 76, R FEHR 74 76, B GEIBERGER 75 75, G HNATIUK 78 72, C A. SPENCE 74 76, S ALLAN 76 75, R BEEM 77 74, O BROWNE 75 76, E FIORI 73 78, R FREEMAN 77 74, J KAYE 77 74, B MAY 75 76, G MCDOWELL 78 73, D PEOPLES 76 75, C CRAIG 76 76, H HAAS 76 76, B NUTT 75 77, C PERKS 78 74, C TIDLAND 74 78, D ELLIS 80 74, S JONES 73 81, J MAGGERT 78 76, J SINDELAR 76 78, R WALCHER 75 79, J BURNS 79 76, K JOHNSON 80 75, D PRIDE 74 81, M KULLBERG 76 80, S MURPHY 78 78, J GORE 77 80, T ISENHOUR 74 83, S JURGENSEN 84 74, B R BROWN 88 82, N LANCASTER 77 W/D, L ROBERTS 81 W/D.

Sponsored by Stan James

Course Profile

TPC at Woodlands (par 72, 7,018 yards) is a Texas-style golf course that requires skill with the Texas wedge. The greens are big and undulating.

If the sun shines, long hitters have an advantage but if the rains comes (and it often does) then a premium is put on accuracy.

The wind can also blow hard, so low-ball strikers should be considered. Water comes into play on eight of the holes.

The crowd will always support the home state players.

Players/Points to Note

●**Hal Sutton**'s form figures since 1992 read 2-41-48-4-6-2-29-1, and after winning last year he proclaimed that this was the title he wanted to win 'more than any other'. Sutton has a great record on other TPC courses.

●**Jeff Maggert** is a regular visitor to The Woodlands and has finished as runner-up on three occasions.

●**David Duval** won in 1998 and has the powerful, straight hitting game to prosper again.

●**Scott Hoch** has finished in the top-ten five times in 11 starts.

●**Fred Funk** won here in 1992, holds the course record of 62 and has the straight hitting game to go well again. He has a house at the Woodlands so obviously likes the surroundings.

●Antipodeans have a good record here. **Allenby** and **Appleby** have won the past two renewals and prior to that three other Aussies and one Kiwi have succeeded. **Vijay Singh** has finished in the top ten on four occasions.

●**Jerry Kelly** missed the cut in 2001 but, prior to that, could boast four top-30 finishes from five starts including two top-six places.

●Native Texans also go well, such as **Maggert** and **Mark Brooks** (who won here in 1996 and has three top-ten finishes to his name).

●And don't discount **Fred Couples**, who has never missed a cut here. **J.P Hayes** and **Jonathan Kaye** are also worth noting.

Previous Results

_2000:_ 1. Robert Allenby (-13), won play-off, 2. Craig Stadler (-13), 3. Joel Edwards (-12), Loren Roberts (-12).

_1999:_ 1. Stuart Appleby (-9), 2. John Cook (-8), Hal Sutton (-8).

_1998:_ 1. David Duval (-12), 2. Jeff Maggert (-11), 3. Fred Couples (-10).

_1997:_ 1. Phil Blackmar (-12), won play-off, 2. Kevin Sutherland (-12), 3. Steve Elkington (-10).

_1996:_ 1. Mark Brooks (-14), won play-off, 2. Jeff Maggert (-14), 3. David Duval (-13).

GREATER GREENSBORO CHRYSLER CLASSIC
Forest Oaks C.C., 26 Apr to 29 Apr 2001, purse $3,500,000

Pos	Name	R1	R2	R3	R4	Total	To par	Money	DD(y)	DA%	GIR%	Putts
1	Scott HOCH	68	68	67	69	272	-16	$630,000	285.6	75	74	109
	Brett QUIGLEY	68	71	67	67	273	-15	$308,000	293.6	63	61	102
	Scott SIMPSON	66	69	70	68	273	-15	$308,000	269.5	54	61	104
4	D BERGANIO Jr.	70	66	68	71	275	-13	$131,950	298.5	80	56	103
	K.J. CHOI	72	66	70	67	275	-13	$131,950	300.4	59	67	106
	G HJERTSTEDT	70	69	67	69	275	-13	$131,950	294.6	66	65	105
	Jerry KELLY	67	70	67	71	275	-13	$131,950	290.9	77	69	107
	Jeff MAGGERT	69	67	70	69	275	-13	$131,950	292.3	79	65	104
9	Olin BROWNE	71	67	69	69	276	-12	$94,500	278.8	79	60	101
	Jim FURYK	69	72	66	69	276	-12	$94,500	260.1	80	69	108
	Kaname YOKOO	71	69	65	71	276	-12	$94,500	287.5	64	72	113

Pos	Name	R1	R2	R3	R4	Total	To par
12	Rich BEEM	71	65	70	71	277	-11
	Mike SPOSA	68	66	70	73	277	-11
	K SUTHERLAND	69	72	65	71	277	-11
	P TATAURANGI	69	72	66	70	277	-11
	Brian WATTS	70	68	69	70	277	-11
17	Matt KUCHAR	72	68	70	68	278	-10
	Esteban TOLEDO	70	69	69	70	278	-10
19	Briny BAIRD	75	67	66	71	279	-9
	D HAMMOND	71	68	69	71	279	-9
	S McCARRON	69	68	72	70	279	-9
	David PEOPLES	70	72	70	67	279	-9
	Joey SINDELAR	68	70	70	71	279	-9
24	Stephen AMES	68	70	72	70	280	-8
	Dudley HART	67	70	70	73	280	-8
	Kenny PERRY	69	69	70	72	280	-8
	Hal SUTTON	70	71	68	71	280	-8
	Omar URESTI	71	65	73	71	280	-8
29	Stuart APPLEBY	71	70	68	72	281	-7
	Jim CARTER	71	68	73	69	281	-7
	Marco DAWSON	71	70	72	68	281	-7
	Edward FRYATT	74	68	66	73	281	-7
	J LANKFORD	67	73	69	72	281	-7
	Frank NOBILO	69	71	69	72	281	-7
	Steve STRICKER	70	70	72	69	281	-7
36	M CALCAVECCHIA	73	69	69	71	282	-6
	Trevor DODDS	70	69	69	74	282	-6
	Scott DUNLAP	68	73	69	72	282	-6
	S GANGLUFF	71	70	72	69	282	-6
	Jonathan KAYE	68	69	73	72	282	-6
	N LANCASTER	69	72	71	70	282	-6
	Ian LEGGATT	68	74	68	72	282	-6
	Lee PORTER	71	69	70	72	282	-6
	B SCHWARZROCK	71	68	70	73	282	-6
	S VERPLANK	73	67	71	71	282	-6
	Cliff KRESGE	71	69	68	74	282	-6
47	Russ COCHRAN	69	71	72	71	283	-5
	Robert DAMRON	67	71	70	75	283	-5
	Glen DAY	70	71	68	74	283	-5
	K GRUNEWALD	69	73	70	71	283	-5
	Tripp ISENHOUR	74	65	68	76	283	-5
	Craig KANADA	71	67	72	73	283	-5
	Jim McGOVERN	73	69	72	69	283	-5
54	Joel EDWARDS	70	69	73	72	284	-4
	S ELKINGTON	71	69	73	71	284	-4
	Fred FUNK	70	70	70	74	284	-4
	Jimmy GREEN	72	69	70	73	284	-4
	Pete JORDAN	72	70	70	72	284	-4
	Greg KRAFT	68	72	72	72	284	-4
	Andrew MAGEE	71	70	69	74	284	-4
61	A BADDELEY	67	74	66	78	285	-3
	Jeff BREHAUT	69	71	74	71	285	-3
	Robin FREEMAN	69	69	73	74	285	-3
	Mathew GOGGIN	70	72	68	75	285	-3
	Shaun MICHEEL	67	74	74	70	285	-3
66	Hunter HAAS	72	70	73	71	286	-2
	Kevin JOHNSON	71	71	73	71	286	-2
	John RIEGGER	73	67	74	72	286	-2
	Willie WOOD	70	70	73	73	286	-2
70	Spike McROY	67	71	74	75	287	-1
	D MORLAND IV	70	70	70	77	287	-1
	Michael MUEHR	70	68	78	71	287	-1
73	Mike HEINEN	70	70	77	71	288	E
	Mike SPRINGER	73	69	72	74	288	E
	J WILLIAMSON	73	69	74	72	288	E
76	Mike HULBERT	75	67	71	76	289	+1
77	Steve ALLAN	72	68	72	78	290	+2
	Ted TRYBA	71	70	73	76	290	+2
79	Garrett WILLIS	70	68	71	82	291	+3

Tournament Report

Scott Hoch won for the first time in nearly four years by shooting four sub-70 rounds to claim the Greater Greensboro Chrysler Classic at Forest Oaks Country Club in North Carolina.

The 22-year US Tour veteran won his ninth career US Tour title despite bogeying the last hole. By then, though, Hoch had the win in the bag and his last day 69 matched his best Sunday score of the season.

Hoch had started the week complaining that the rough was too short. The long but wayward drivers of the ball would have the advantage over someone like him who relies on accuracy. But he wasn't moaning after 72 holes.

He started the last day one shot clear of David Berganio and after six straight pars secured his first birdie of the round at the seventh. The pack were getting closer, and after the outward nine there were as many as ten players in contention.

But Hoch managed to make birdies on three of the five holes after the turn, holing from four, eight and 12 feet. Brett Quigley's Sunday's 67 was the best of the day, along with KJ Choi (who eventually finished fourth), and it was enough to hoist him into second place alongside first round leader Scott Simpson.

It was Simpson's best finish not only of the season but for well over two years, as he missed all of last term with injury.

Halfway leader Mike Sposa faded with weekend scores of 70 and 73.

MISSED THE CUT: Woody AUSTIN 72 71, Ronnie BLACK 71 72, Bill GLASSON 70 73, Jason GORE 73 70, Gary HALLBERG 71 72, Nolan HENKE 71 72, Bradley HUGHES 72 71, Brandt Jobe 71 72, Sandy LYLE 74 69, Andrew McLARDY 74 69, Mark O'MEARA 69 74, Craig PERKS 69 74, Jerry SMITH 70 73, Andy BEAN 71 73, Emanuele CANONICA 71 73, Paul GOW 71 73, Glen HNATIUK 71 73, Per Ulrik JOHANSSON 69 75, John MAGINNES 70 74, Blaine McCALLISTER 74 70, Dave STOCKTON, Jr. 71 73, Ken TANIGAWA 72 72, Grant WAITE 71 73, Fuzzy ZOELLER 72 72, Bob BURNS 73 70, Stewart CINK 71 74, Tim DUNLAVEY 70 75, Ben FERGUSON 73 72, Jeff HART 74 71, Skip KENDALL 72 73, Naomichi Joe OZAKI 75 70, Dicky PRIDE 71 74, Chris TIDLAND 70 75, Brian WILSON 76 69, Ben BATES 70 76, Keith CLEARWATER 71 75, Doug DUNAKEY 69 77, Matt GOGEL 75 71, K JONES 74 72, C PERRY 77 69, C RILEY 74 72, T SCHERRER 74 72, T TOLLES 73 73, K WENTWORTH 75 71, M CLARK II 72 75, B ELDER 76 71, D ELLIS 76 71, R GAMEZ 74 73, J.L. LEWIS 73 74, J OGILVIE 74 73, G OGILVY 73 74, C PAULSON 72 75, M REID 77 70, B HENNINGER 74 74, S MARUYAMA 75 73, C A. SPENCE 75 73, J ANDERSON 73 76, B FRITSCH 74 75, S GUMP 74 75, R WALCHER 76 73, B ANDRADE 76 74, J.J. HENRY 71 77, C STUTTS 76 74, D FORSMAN 79 72, J GALLAGHER Jr. 73 79, J JULIAN 76 76, R MORTON 72 81, L RINKER 76 77, J GALLAGHER 78 76, B R BROWN 83 87, D BARRON W/D 72 72, R COUGHLAN W/D 74 74, T PURTZER D 75 75, S MURPHY W/D 76 76, R FEHR W/D, M HENSBY W/D, P STANKOWSKI W/D.

Sponsored by Stan James

Course Profile

Forest Oaks Country Club (par 72, 7,062 yards) offers differing elevations from tee to tee, so selecting the right club is paramount.

If the weather is poor before the tournament the rough can grow quite high, so straight hitters can prosper – although in 2001 Scott Hoch complained the rough wasn't long enough (but still won).

The par fives are there to score low on. The greens are bigger than average, while water comes into play on four of the holes.

Players/Points to Note

● **Dudley Hart**'s best position here is only third but he is 58-under (the best to par score of anyone still on the US Tour) in ten visits to Forest Oaks. He now has four top-ten finishes.

● **Jeff Sluman** has never won this event but always plays well. He has registered seven top-ten finishes in 15 starts.

● **Jim Furyk**'s form figures here read 7-14-11-2-42-9 over the past six years and he has a stroke average of 70.41.

● **Jesper Parnevik** won here in 1999 and was eighth when defending his crown in 2000. He enjoys the venue and can deal with the, shall we say, exuberance, that goes with the big crowds that always come to Forest Oaks.

● **Davis Love** rarely plays this event these days, but if he includes it on his schedule then must be considered. He shares the course record at Forest Oaks (62 – along with **Mark O'Meara** and **Jeff Maggert**) and won here in 1992 when he needed to (to earn a US Masters berth).

● The unruly nature of some of the paying public, which comes courtesy of what they're drinking, can upset some players but spur on others. Someone like **Tim Herron** (who has a laid back nature) can prosper. Also look out for former champion **Hal Sutton**, **Steve Stricker**, **Scott Verplank** and **Neal Lancaster**.

Previous Results

2000: 1. Hal Sutton (-14), 2. Andrew Magee (-11), 3. Mark Calcavecchia (-10), Dudley Hart (-10).

1999: 1. Jesper Parnevik (-23), 2. Jim Furyk (-21), 3. Jeff Maggert (-15).

1998: 1. Trevor Dodds (-12), won play-off, 2. Scott Verplank (-12), 3. Bob Estes (-11).

1997: 1. Frank Nobilo (-14), won play-off, 2. Brad Faxon (-14), 3. Kirk Triplett (-13).

1996: 1. Mark O'Meara (-14), 2. Duffy Waldorf (-12), 3. Steve Stricker (-10).

BTM)   C. CAMBELL

COMPAQ CLASSIC OF NEW ORLEANS

English Turn G.&C.C., 3 May to 6 May 2001, purse $4,000,000

Pos	Name	R1	R2	R3	R4	Total	To par	Money	DD(y)	DA%	GIR%	Putts
1	David TOMS	66	73	63	64	266	-22	$720,000	281.5	73	76	103
2	Phil MICKELSON	66	66	64	72	268	-20	$432,000	293.0	75	69	102
3	Ernie ELS	67	69	65	68	269	-19	$272,000	290.9	70	71	108
4	Harrison FRAZAR	68	65	66	71	270	-18	$192,000	285.3	61	74	107
5	Brian GAY	66	66	70	69	271	-17	$152,000	266.6	72	64	101
	Chris SMITH	73	66	66	66	271	-17	$152,000	285.3	73	78	112
7	C HOWELL III	69	71	63	69	272	-16	$134,000	285.8	63	81	118
8	Stephen AMES	69	70	65	69	273	-15	$116,000	287.5	64	68	106
	Frank LICKLITER II	67	71	67	68	273	-15	$116,000	279.1	89	78	113
	Steve LOWERY	71	67	66	69	273	-15	$116,000	284.3	77	71	107

Pos	Name	R1	R2	R3	R4	Total	To par
11	David PEOPLES	68	69	71	66	274	-14
	G CHALMERS	70	71	66	67	274	-14
	Joe DURANT	67	71	68	68	274	-14
	Dudley HART	71	70	65	68	274	-14
	Scott HOCH	69	72	63	70	274	-14
	Bob MAY	67	73	66	68	274	-14
	Jeff SLUMAN	69	72	66	67	274	-14
18	David DUVAL	69	68	69	69	275	-13
	Joel EDWARDS	69	69	70	67	275	-13
	Brad FABEL	67	70	67	71	275	-13
	Jerry KELLY	68	67	71	69	275	-13
	T PERNICE, Jr.	66	74	68	67	275	-13
23	S MARUYAMA	67	71	70	68	276	-12
	Nick PRICE	69	69	69	69	276	-12
	Bob TWAY	69	71	68	68	276	-12
26	Danny ELLIS	73	66	70	68	277	-11
	Jeff HART	70	69	69	69	277	-11
	N LANCASTER	70	71	65	71	277	-11
	J.L. LEWIS	69	69	74	65	277	-11
	Steve STRICKER	69	72	65	71	277	-11
	Chris TIDLAND	66	69	71	71	277	-11
32	Scott DUNLAP	69	72	67	70	278	-10
	Brian WATTS	64	72	71	71	278	-10
34	John COOK	70	71	67	71	279	-9
	Bill GLASSON	68	73	70	68	279	-9
	Kirk TRIPLETT	68	71	69	71	279	-9
	Woody AUSTIN	68	72	65	74	279	-9
	K CLEARWATER	65	70	72	72	279	-9
	Russ COCHRAN	68	74	66	71	279	-9
	Carlos FRANCO	69	68	70	72	279	-9
	Paul GOW	70	70	66	73	279	-9
	G HJERTSTEDT	70	70	66	73	279	-9
43	B HENNINGER	68	70	67	75	280	-8
	B McCALLISTER	69	69	68	74	280	-8
	Kenny PERRY	64	77	69	70	280	-8
	Scott SIMPSON	68	71	67	74	280	-8
	Hal SUTTON	67	73	68	72	280	-8
	S VERPLANK	67	73	69	71	280	-8
	Brian WILSON	65	70	74	71	280	-8
50	C BECKMAN	72	70	70	69	281	-7
	Jim CARTER	65	71	75	70	281	-7
	Robin FREEMAN	71	68	71	71	281	-7
53	Pete JORDAN	71	70	70	71	282	-6
	P STANKOWSKI	61	77	72	72	282	-6
	Jonathan KAYE	69	73	64	76	282	-6
56	Fulton ALLEM	69	72	70	72	283	-5
	B GEIBERGER	68	73	70	72	283	-5
	Craig KANADA	71	70	72	70	283	-5
	Greg NORMAN	70	72	71	70	283	-5
	Dicky PRIDE	71	69	69	74	283	-5
61	M CLARK II	70	71	68	75	284	-4
	Marco DAWSON	71	71	68	74	284	-4
	Tommy TOLLES	67	75	69	73	284	-4
	Ted TRYBA	67	72	71	74	284	-4
	Mike WEIR	68	74	74	68	284	-4
66	John RIEGGER	69	73	71	72	285	-3
	Grant WAITE	71	69	70	75	285	-3
	Kaname YOKOO	70	72	67	76	285	-3
69	Bradley HUGHES	70	70	69	77	286	-2
70	Andrew MAGEE	68	73	73	73	287	-1
	A McLARDY	70	71	72	74	287	-1
72	Mathew GOGGIN	69	73	75	74	291	+3

Tournament Report

The crowd came to cheer one of their own and weren't disappointed when local favourite David Toms produced a superb Sunday 64 to overhaul Phil Mickelson to win the Compaq Classic at English Turn in New Orleans.

For Toms it was his fifth US Tour victory, for Mickelson it was the second time he has finished as runner-up this season. The left hander dominated the second and third rounds and led going into the last day. And after a three-week break since finishing third in the US Masters, looked set for victory.

But he hadn't banked on Toms' last day surge. After getting to the turn in two-under, Toms ripped up the back nine. He birdied ten, eagled 11 and then picked up shots on 16 and 18 to set the clubhouse target of 266.

His putt on the last from 30 feet sent the crowd wild after it went up a ridge and rattled into the cup. Mickelson had already dropped a shot by the time he racked up a triple bogey at the fifth. A hooked tee shot found the trees and then his attempt to chip out failed.

Mickelson fought back with birdies on the next two holes. But further birdies weren't forthcoming and when he found water at the 15th his challenge was over. Ernie Els was the only player to shoot four sub-70 rounds and finished third. First round plaudits went to Paul Stankowski who broke the course record with a 61.

MISSED THE CUT: Briny BAIRD 71 72, Rodney BUTCHER 71 72, Mark CALCAVECCHIA 71 72, Emanuele CANONICA 72 71, K.J. CHOI 69 74, Richie COUGHLAN 71 72, Chris DiMARCO 73 70, Kevin JOHNSON 71 72, Len MATTIACE 70 73, Scott McCARRON 70 73, Michael MUEHR 69 74, Brett QUIGLEY 69 74, Kevin SUTHERLAND 74 69, Tim THELEN 72 71, Garrett WILLIS 71 72, Jeff BREHAUT 70 74, Glen DAY 70 74, Kelly GRUNEWALD 66 78, Hunter HAAS 70 74, Craig STADLER 71 73, Mike STANDLY 69 75, Fuzzy ZOELLER 67 77, Craig BARLOW 68 77, Rich BEEM 73 72, Aaron BENGOECHEA 71 74, Jay Don BLAKE 72 73, David FROST 70 75, Edward FRYATT 70 75, Matt GOGEL 73 72, Cliff KRESGE 73 72, Ian LEGGATT 71 74, Shaun MICHEEL 71 74, Jack NICKLAUS 73 72, Frank NOBILO 68 77, Craig PARRY 73 72, Brent SCHWARZROCK 70 75, Rocky WALCHER 72 73, Chip BECK 71 75, Steve FLESCH 70 76, Jason GORE 71 75, Mark HENSBY 68 78, Tim HERRON 70 76, Franklin LANGHAM 69 77, Sean MURPHY 72 74, Esteban TOLEDO 70 76, Jay WILLIAMSON 71 75, Jeremy ANDERSON 70 77, Tommy ARMOUR III 71 76, Aaron BADDELEY 73 74, Jose COCERES 71 76, Steve ELKINGTON 73 74, Jimmy GREEN 74 73, Joey GULLION 74 73, J.P. HAYES 73 74, Kent JONES 75 72, Joe OGILVIE 73 74, Jerry SMITH 73 74, Tom Byrum 74 74, Jeff JULIAN 72 76, Steve PATE 75 73, Lee PORTER 70 78, Doug DUNAKEY 73 76, Ben FERGUSON 75 74, Mike HULBERT 76 73, Robert DAMRON 73 77, Brad FAXON 71 79, Jeff GALLAGHER 78 72, Kelly GIBSON 73 77, J.J. HENRY 76 74, D MORLAND IV 73 77, Naomichi Joe OZAKI 76 74, Geoff OGILVY 71 80, Steve JONES 75 77, Gary NICKLAUS 74 78, David S. LEE 73 80, Carl PAULSON 77 76, Craig PERKS 75 79, Steve ALLAN 76 79, John DACKSON 80 77, Leigh BRANNAN 80 80, Doug BARRON 70 W/D, Mark WIEBE 72 W/D, Cliff BAILEY W/D, Tripp ISENHOUR W/D.

Sponsored by Stan James

Course Profile

English Turn Golf Club (par 72, 7,116 yards) in New Orleans is a deceptively long and tough course.

The front nine seems short enough but on the way back the players have to cover 3,650 yards. Long hitters who can hit the ball high will prosper.

But you have to be able to master the greens, which are difficult to read as their are many subtle undulations. Water comes into play on nearly all the holes.

Players/Points to Note

● **Carlos Franco** missed out on the a third win in a row in 2001, finishing 34th but having played at English Turn three times and won twice is still impressive. In 12 rounds at the course he has shot over 69 just twice. This was the Paraguayan's first US Tour win 1999 and the course is perfect for his strengths.

● **Steve Flesch** spoiled his superb record here last year by missing the cut, but, prior to that, had finished second twice and sixth in three starts.

● **Harrison Frazar** enjoys playing at this time of the year and his length of the tee is handy on this course. His form figures in four starts read 42-2-3-4.

● **Steve Lowery** has registered four top-eight finishes in the last six years. **Greg Norman** has five top-ten finishes to his name in eight starts, while **Scott McCarron** won in 1996 and has finished in the top 20 on three other occasions.

● **Scott Hoch** hasn't finished lower than 21st in eight starts since 1991.

● The big names have bypassed this event in recent years but **Phil Mickelson** and **Ernie Els** showed up last season to claim second and third respectively and both have the game to win here. As do **Vijay Singh** and **Hal Sutton**.

● **David Toms** had vociferous support from the crowd last season and Louisiana golfers always go well.

Previous Results

2000: 1. Carlos Franco (-18), won play-off, 2. Blaine McCallister (-18), 3. Harrison Frazar (-17).

1999: 1. Carlos Franco (-19), 2. Steve Flesch (-17), Harrison Frazar (-17).

1998: 1. Lee Westwood (-15), 2. Steve Flesch (-12), 3. Four players tied.

1997: 1. Brad Faxon (-16), 2. Bill Glasson (-13), Jesper Parnevik (-13).

1996: 1. Scott McCarron (-13), 2. Tom Watson (-8), 3. Tommy Tolles (-7).

VERIZON BYRON NELSON CLASSIC

TPC at Four Seasons, 10 May to 13 May 2001, purse $4,500,000

Pos	Name	R1	R2	R3	R4	Total	To par	Money	DD(y)	DA%	GIR%	Putts
1	Robert DAMRON	66	64	67	66	263	-17	$810,000	271.9	70	85	116
Won play-off												
2	Scott VERPLANK	62	67	68	66	263	-17	$486,000	268.0	79	75	110
3	David DUVAL	64	65	70	67	266	-14	$234,000	306.3	72	69	108
	Nick PRICE	69	65	65	67	266	-14	$234,000	272.5	82	74	110
	Tiger WOODS	66	68	69	63	266	-14	$234,000	310.9	61	72	112
6	Justin LEONARD	68	69	61	69	267	-13	$156,375	281.8	68	67	107
	Brian WATTS	68	68	63	68	267	-13	$156,375	279.5	77	82	118
8	Sergio GARCIA	71	68	64	65	268	-12	$130,500	302.3	72	75	113
	David PEOPLES	66	69	67	66	268	-12	$130,500	285.3	63	69	109
	Kenny PERRY	68	65	67	68	268	-12	$130,500	297.6	63	78	119

Pos	Name	R1	R2	R3	R4	Total	To par
11	Rich BEEM	69	66	68	66	269	-11
	Glen DAY	66	68	69	66	269	-11
	Brad FAXON	70	65	67	67	269	-11
	David FROST	72	66	65	66	269	-11
	Dudley HART	67	66	69	67	269	-11
	Tim HERRON	64	70	67	68	269	-11
	Fred COUPLES	71	63	66	69	269	-11
	Vijay SINGH	67	64	67	71	269	-11
	Esteban TOLEDO	66	71	63	69	269	-11
	David TOMS	68	71	62	68	269	-11
	Mike WEIR	66	68	65	70	269	-11
22	T ARMOUR III	66	67	70	67	270	-10
	Olin BROWNE	69	67	64	70	270	-10
	Ted TRYBA	68	67	73	62	270	-10
25	Len MATTIACE	69	70	64	68	271	-9
	Chris RILEY	64	69	71	67	271	-9
	P STANKOWSKI	71	67	68	65	271	-9
28	Russ COCHRAN	65	70	70	67	272	-8
	Scott DUNLAP	66	73	67	66	272	-8
	B GEIBERGER	68	68	68	68	272	-8
	J.L. LEWIS	68	67	70	67	272	-8
	F LICKLITER II	68	66	66	72	272	-8
	Phil MICKELSON	72	66	68	66	272	-8
	Loren ROBERTS	70	65	69	68	272	-8
	Hal SUTTON	68	70	66	68	272	-8
	Kirk TRIPLETT	70	67	67	68	272	-8
37	Mark BROOKS	69	67	67	70	273	-7
	Chris DiMARCO	71	67	67	68	273	-7
	Jim FURYK	72	66	66	69	273	-7
	Scott McCARRON	68	69	66	70	273	-7
	Scott SIMPSON	69	70	67	67	273	-7
	Grant WAITE	69	66	67	71	273	-7
43	Robert ALLENBY	70	68	66	70	274	-6
	Stuart APPLEBY	67	68	70	69	274	-6
	Jim CARTER	68	67	67	72	274	-6
	John COOK	69	70	67	68	274	-6
	Steve FLESCH	69	68	70	67	274	-6
	Brian GAY	68	68	69	69	274	-6
	Andrew MAGEE	69	68	68	69	274	-6
	S MARUYAMA	69	70	66	69	274	-6
51	Tom BYRUM	68	71	69	67	275	-5
	Jose COCERES	71	68	70	66	275	-5
	H FRAZAR	68	67	72	68	275	-5
	Perry ARTHUR	70	68	65	72	275	-5
	Craig BARLOW	66	71	69	69	275	-5
	Dan FORSMAN	69	70	67	69	275	-5
	G HJERTSTEDT	66	69	69	71	275	-5
	Bob MAY	65	69	68	73	275	-5
	Rocco MEDIATE	67	69	67	72	275	-5
	Steve PATE	70	68	66	71	275	-5
	D.A. WEIBRING	70	68	69	68	275	-5
62	Steve LOWERY	67	70	68	71	276	-4
	J PARNEVIK	70	64	68	74	276	-4
	Chris SMITH	71	68	65	72	276	-4
65	Kevin JOHNSON	69	70	69	69	277	-3
	Michael MUEHR	67	67	72	71	277	-3
	Rory SABBATINI	70	67	71	69	277	-3
68	G CHALMERS	67	70	70	71	278	-2
	Fred FUNK	68	71	70	69	278	-2
	Bradley HUGHES	75	64	66	73	278	-2
	Joe OGILVIE	69	66	72	71	278	-2
	B SCHWARZROCK	67	70	72	69	278	-2
73	Briny BAIRD	71	68	70	70	279	-1
	C BECKMAN	70	65	68	76	279	-1
	B CHAMBLEE	66	71	72	70	279	-1
	B MAYFAIR	65	70	74	70	279	-1
77	Edward FRYATT	67	65	73	75	280	E
	Jerry SMITH	69	70	66	75	280	E
79	Jason GORE	65	69	72	76	282	+2
	Glen HNATIUK	70	64	72	76	282	+2
	Larry MIZE	67	70	75	70	282	+2
82	J WILLIAMSON	69	70	75	69	283	+2
83	E CANONICA	71	65	72	76	284	+4

Tournament Report

Robert Damron emerged as the winner of a four-hole play-off against Scott Verplank to land the Byron Nelson Classic at Las Colinas in Irving, Texas.

It was the 28-year-old's first win on the US Tour and one that saw the recently married Damron collect $810,000. Verplank led from day one after an opening 62 and was joined at the top of the leaderboard after the second round by Damron. The eventual winner had his fair share of luck during regulation play. On the 14th he found the trees with his drive but the ball stopped just short of a hazard.

Then, despite the pleas of his caddie to play safe, Damron rifled an eight-iron towards the green – It found the bunker but he still managed to save par with a shot from the sand to 12 inches. Verplank birdied three of the last four holes to make the play-off.

But when extra time came, Verplank's putting touch deserted him. He had chances to win from 15 and 20 feet twice but didn't take them. And when Damron rolled in a 15-footer of his own, after a superb 7-iron approach on the fourth extra hole, Verplank couldn't match his effort.

Damron certainly won on merit and fended off some of the biggest names in golf. Tiger Woods, David Duval and Nick Price, who went out in 31 before fading on the inward nine, all challenged on the last day but could only tie for third.

MISSED THE CUT: Jeff BREHAUT 73 67, Michael CONNELL 69 71, Bob ESTES 69 71, Jimmy GREEN 73 67, Steve JONES 69 71, Jonathan KAYE 68 72, Greg KRAFT 72 68, Shaun MICHEEL 73 67, Craig PERKS 71 69, Tom PURTZER 72 68, Kevin SUTHERLAND 70 70, Tommy TOLLES 73 67, Jimmy WALKER 72 68, Fulton ALLEM 70 71, Bob BURNS 71 70, Joel EDWARDS 69 72, Robin FREEMAN 70 71, Paul GOYDOS 70 71, Charles HOWELL III 73 68, Lee JANZEN 72 69, Pete JORDAN 72 69, Neal LANCASTER 73 68, Blaine McCALLISTER 72 69, Spike McROY 73 68, Dennis PAULSON 71 70, Bob TWAY 71 70, Billy ANDRADE 72 70, Michael CLARK II 72 70, Ben CRENSHAW 71 71, John DALY 71 71, Carlos FRANCO 74 68, Bill GLASSON 72 70, Hunter HAAS 73 69, Mark HENSBY 66 76, Brandt JOBE 72 70, Cliff KRESGE 72 70, Franklin LANGHAM 74 68, Tom LEHMAN 73 69, Gary NICKLAUS 70 72, Corey PAVIN 74 68, Troy REISER 73 69, Mike SPOSA 70 72, Tim THELEN 73 69, Brad ELDER 72 71, Per Ulrik JOHANSSON 72 71, Skip KENDALL 71 72, Billy TUTEN 74 69, Kaname YOKOO 75 68, Steve ALLAN 66 78, Brian HENNINGER 77 67, Tim HOBBY 72 72, Jeff MAGGERT 72 72, Craig PARRY 72 72, Craig STADLER 74 70, Doug DUNAKEY 73 72, Ernie ELS 75 70, Mark McCUMBER 74 71, Lee PORTER 72 73, Mark WIEBE 72 73, Garrett WILLIS 70 75, David BERGANIO Jr. 76 70, Tom PERNICE Jr. 74 72, Woody AUSTIN 73 74, Paul EARNEST 69 78, J.P. HAYES 73 74, K.J. CHOI 74 74, Edward LOAR 73 76, Tom SCHERRER 73 77, Ed FIORI 76 75, Mathew GOGGIN 78 73, Carl WORLEY Jr. 79 79, Jay Don BLAKE W/D, Geoff OGILVY D.

Course Profile

TPC at Four Seasons, Las Colinas (par 70, 7,017 yards) is used for one of the first rounds and the weekend.

Players don't have to be long but accuracy is important here, the greens are bigger than average for the US Tour. The layout has been toughened up over the past 18 months.

Cottonwood Valley (par 70, 6,846 yards) is used for just one of the first two rounds and is easier than Las Colinas by around a shot.

Players/Points to Note

● **Tiger Woods** won this event in 1997 and it is usually on the World No.1's schedule. Since winning, Tiger's form figures 12-7-3-4. He normally comes into this event fresh after a break and is the man to beat – as usual.

● **Phil Mickelson** has an excellent record in this event. His play-off defeat in 2000 came after three top-12 finishes in his four previous starts – including a win in 1996. And the left-hander was 28th last year.

● **Sergio Garcia**'s three top-15 places in three visits, mark the young Spaniard one to consider, especially as no-one bettered his weekend scores in 2001.

● **Loren Roberts** (winner in 1999 and joint holder of the 72 hole record – 262) obviously has the game for the venue.

● **Hal Sutton** has come second twice and third once.

● **Nick Price** notched his fifth top-ten finish in this event last year (and his tenth top-20 spot) and won this event back in 1991. A fit **Scott Simpson** (1993 champion) could go well here in 2002.

● **Bob Estes** has a good record here, while **Paul Stankowski**, **Blaine McAllister** and **Chris Perry** have finished in the top 20 more often than not in recent years.

● Don't be surprised if there is another play-off in 2002 – extra holes have been needed 14 times since 1970.

Previous Results

2000: 1. Jesper Parnevik (-11), won play-off, 2. Davis Love III (-11), Phil Mickelson (-11).

1999: 1. Loren Roberts (-18), won play-off, 2. Steve Pate (-18), 3. Four players tied.

1998: 1. John Cook (-15), 2. Hal Sutton (-12), Fred Couples (-12), Harrison Frazar (-12).

1997: 1. Tiger Woods (-17), 2. Lee Rinker (-15), 3. Tom Watson (-13), Dan Forsman (-13).

1996: 1. Phil Mickelson (-15), 2. Craig Parry (-13), 3. David Duval (-12).

MASTERCARD COLONIAL

Colonial Country Club, 17 May to 20 May 2001, purse $4,000,000

Pos	Name	R1	R2	R3	R4	Total	To par	Money	DD(y)	DA%	GIR%	Putts
1	Sergio GARCIA	69	69	66	63	267	-13	$720,000	257.3	73	76	114
2	Brian GAY	66	69	69	65	269	-11	$352,000	287.6	63	67	109
	Phil MICKELSON	65	68	66	70	269	-11	$352,000	308.1	61	74	116
4	Glen DAY	68	72	64	66	270	-10	$192,000	303.4	68	60	104
5	Justin LEONARD	69	67	70	66	272	-8	$146,000	292.3	52	67	111
	S MARUYAMA	72	65	65	70	272	-8	$146,000	302.1	52	61	108
	Brett QUIGLEY	69	64	66	73	272	-8	$146,000	320.9	61	65	111
8	Rocco MEDIATE	72	62	69	70	273	-7	$116,000	287.9	57	72	116
	Corey PAVIN	68	64	73	68	273	-7	$116,000	294.1	70	58	107
	David TOMS	67	70	66	70	273	-7	$116,000	288.5	57	75	119

Pos	Name	R1	R2	R3	R4	Total	To par
11	P-U JOHANSSON	69	68	68	69	274	-6
	J PARNEVIK	70	69	67	68	274	-6
	Vijay SINGH	69	68	69	68	274	-6
	Mike SPOSA	71	66	67	70	274	-6
15	Robert ALLENBY	72	68	65	70	275	-5
	G CHALMERS	71	69	67	68	275	-5
	Tom LEHMAN	67	68	68	72	275	-5
	Jeff SLUMAN	71	64	69	71	275	-5
	Kirk TRIPLETT	68	67	70	70	275	-5
20	Fred FUNK	70	68	67	71	276	-4
	Billy MAYFAIR	71	68	69	68	276	-4
22	Jim CARTER	73	67	68	69	277	-3
	Jim FURYK	65	71	69	72	277	-3
	B McCALLISTER	71	64	71	71	277	-3
	S McCARRON	68	67	72	70	277	-3
26	Fulton ALLEM	68	73	67	70	278	-2
	Stephen AMES	68	71	66	73	278	-2
	Rich BEEM	70	68	71	69	278	-2
	Stewart CINK	71	70	67	70	278	-2
	Brad ELDER	70	71	67	70	278	-2
	Bob ESTES	68	73	64	73	278	-2
	B GEIBERGER	68	69	72	69	278	-2
	Kenny PERRY	72	67	70	69	278	-2
34	Jose COCERES	70	67	70	72	279	-1
	John COOK	71	71	70	67	279	-1
	Jonathan KAYE	71	65	70	73	279	-1
	Tom KITE	68	71	69	71	279	-1
	Joe OGILVIE	75	66	68	70	279	-1
	Geoff OGILVY	70	70	68	71	279	-1
40	B CHAMBLEE	71	66	73	70	280	E
	Chris DiMARCO	71	71	66	72	280	E
	J.L. LEWIS	71	67	69	73	280	E
	Frank NOBILO	70	68	72	70	280	E
	Joey SINDELAR	74	67	72	67	280	E
	Hal SUTTON	73	69	66	72	280	E
46	David DUVAL	69	68	73	71	281	+1
	Steve FLESCH	69	69	69	74	281	+1
	Brandt JOBE	71	70	68	72	281	+1
	Skip KENDALL	69	68	73	71	281	+1
	Greg KRAFT	69	69	71	72	281	+1
	Bob TWAY	75	67	66	73	281	+1
52	David FROST	73	69	70	70	282	+2
	Bob MAY	70	72	69	71	282	+2
54	Craig BARLOW	72	70	69	72	283	+3
	Scott DUNLAP	69	71	68	75	283	+3
	H FRAZAR	73	65	69	76	283	+3
	Len MATTIACE	74	68	70	71	283	+3
58	Robert DAMRON	70	71	73	70	284	+4
	J.P. HAYES	73	67	68	76	284	+4
	Bruce LIETZKE	71	71	69	73	284	+4
	Mike WEIR	70	71	68	75	284	+4
62	Briny BAIRD	72	68	71	74	285	+5
	Mark BROOKS	67	72	72	74	285	+5
	Steve PATE	70	70	69	76	285	+5
	Brian WILSON	70	70	74	71	285	+5
66	K CLEARWATER	72	70	68	76	286	+6
67	D.A. WEIBRING	69	71	72	75	287	+7
68	Ronnie BLACK	69	70	74	75	288	+8
69	Tim HERRON	70	71	75	74	290	+10
70	Tom PURTZER	70	69	73	79	291	+11
71	D STOCKTON, Jr.	70	71	77	76	294	+14

Tournament Report

Sergio Garcia registered his first US Tour win by coming from behind to capture the Mastercard Colonial title at Colonial Country Club in Fort Worth, Texas.

The Spaniard shot a last day 63 to race from five behind at the start of the round to win by two after 72 holes, defeating overnight leader Phil Mickelson, who carded a Sunday 70, and Brian Gay, who finished with an impressive 65.

Garcia played the outward nine in a swashbuckling 29 – six-under par. And his birdie on the ninth, coupled with Mickelson's eight meant he closed to the gap to two.

Then, Mickelson missed from first two and then three feet, the lead then changed hands for the first time since Friday as Garcia picked up a shot at the 13th – his only back nine birdie. Mickelson managed to hang onto Garcia's coat tails until the 17th, when another three-footer lipped out.

It was the third time that the left hander had found one player too good this season. And worryingly for Mickelson, he revealed that he had "a mental block on Sundays on the backside."

Not a particularly good frame of mind to be in with the US Open approaching.

For Garcia, a Major will surely come sooner rather than later. It almost seemed inevitable that the Spaniard would win after such a superb run to the turn.

The locals were certainly behind him, the cheers could be heard by Mickelson, playing two holes behind, throughout Garcia's opening birdie barrage.

Glen Day claimed fourth spot after weekend scores of 64 and 66 – his 130 total bettered only by Garcia.

MISSED THE CUT: Olin BROWNE 70 73, Fred COUPLES 72 71, Edward FRYATT 73 70, Franklin LANGHAM 72 71, Nick PRICE 71 72, Esteban TOLEDO 71 72, Billy ANDRADE 72 72, Brad FAXON 75 69, Kazuhiko HOSOKAWA 73 71, Lee JANZEN 73 71, Steve JONES 73 71, Chris PERRY 74 70, Chris SMITH 73 71, Brian WATTS 74 70, Stuart APPLEBY 76 69, Joe DURANT 75 70, Joel EDWARDS 72 73, Matt GOGEL 72 73, Fuzzy ZOELLER 73 72, Michael CLARK II 74 72, Andrew MAGEE 73 73, Jeff MAGGERT 69 77, Spike McROY 72 74, Duffy WALDORF 74 72, Ben CRENSHAW 76 71, Kaname YOKOO 72 75, Mike HULBERT 74 74, Tom PERNICE Jr. 72 76, Dave STOCKTON 79 70, Jerry KELLY 75 75, Ian Baker FINCH 74 77, Greg NORMAN 76 75, Dennis PAULSON 71 80, Dan POHL 76 75, Rod CURL 80 72, Chris RILEY 79 73, Mark CALCAVECCHIA 81 72, Carl PAULSON 72 81, Hunter HAAS 80 74, Dudley HART 71 W/D, Scott VERPLANK 74 W/D, Carlos FRANCO 76 W/D, David BERGANIO Jr. 77 W/D, Rory SABBATINI 79 W/D.

Course Profile

The Colonial Country Club (par 70, 7,080 yards) at Fort Worth, Texas usually rewards accurate golfers. A player who is even a little wild with the driver will struggle to succeed.

Players have to move the ball both ways and have some imagination with their second shots to find the small well guarded greens.

The putting surfaces are a little firmer than they used to be so are faster. Players who rank high in the GIR stats will prosper.

Players/Points to Note

●**Phil Mickelson**'s success broke the mould of experienced pros winning this event. Throughout the '90s, no player under the age of 35 took the title. And the left-hander should have won last year. He led going into the final round but choked to let in Sergio Garcia, who incidentally has the perfect game for the venue – as he proved by taking advantage of Mickelson's lapse.

●**Jeff Sluman** hasn't won this event but has taken sizeable purses down the years. In 13 starts, he has had two seconds, one third and five top-ten finishes – he hasn't been out of the top 15 on his last six visits.

●**Nick Price** came back from seven shots down to win this event in 1994 (the Zimbabwean has finished in the top ten on four other visits).

●**Stewart Cink**'s five visits to Fort Worth has gained him a stroke average of 68.90.

●**Kirk Triplett** has finished in the top 25 here on seven occasions from 11 starts

●**Jim Furyk** can boast three top-ten finishes in the last five years. **Davis Love**, **Mark Calcavecchia**, **Craig Parry**, **Fred Funk** and **John Cook** can are all multiple top-ten finishers who have yet to win.

●**Corey Pavin** is the veteran with the best record – six top tens in 17 starts (including two victories).

Previous Results

2000: 1. Phil Mickelson (-12), 2. Stewart Cink (-10), Davis Love III (-10).

1999: 1. Olin Browne (-8), 2. Five players tied.

1998: 1. Tom Watson (-15), 2. Jim Furyk (-13), 3. Jeff Sluman (-11).

1997: 1. David Frost (-15), 2. Brad Faxon (-13), David Ogrin (-13).

1996: 1. Corey Pavin (-8), 2. Jeff Sluman (-6), 3. Rocco Mediate (-5).

KEMPER INSURANCE OPEN

TPC at Avenel, 24 May to 27 May 2001, purse $3,500,000

Pos	Name	R1	R2	R3	R4	Total	To par	Money	DD(y)	DA%	GIR%	Putts
1	F LICKLITER II	69	65	66	68	268	-16	$630,000	276.9	82	79	114
2	J.J. HENRY	65	71	67	66	269	-15	$378,000	283.9	89	78	116
3	Bradley HUGHES	70	63	72	67	272	-12	$182,000	274.4	84	79	121
	Spike McROY	71	66	67	68	272	-12	$182,000	261.8	82	82	119
	Phil MICKELSON	68	67	72	65	272	-12	$182,000	297.1	75	78	119
6	Tim HERRON	69	68	68	69	274	-10	$117,250	272.4	70	76	118
	Scott HOCH	68	70	66	70	274	-10	$117,250	257.3	88	75	117
	P U JOHANSSON	68	69	66	71	274	-10	$117,250	272.5	84	72	116
9	Chris DiMARCO	65	70	68	72	275	-9	$94,500	275.5	86	68	111
	Dan FORSMAN	68	67	67	73	275	-9	$94,500	256.3	82	72	112
	B SCHWARZROCK	68	67	71	69	275	-9	$94,500	281.5	79	71	115

Pos	Name	R1	R2	R3	R4	Total	To par
12	Robert ALLENBY	69	67	67	73	276	-8
	Chris RILEY	67	69	69	71	276	-8
14	C BECKMAN	69	69	69	70	277	-7
	C HOWELL III	71	65	71	70	277	-7
	Brian WATTS	72	67	69	69	277	-7
17	Fred FUNK	71	69	71	67	278	-6
	Jay HAAS	69	67	71	71	278	-6
	Frank NOBILO	66	72	71	69	278	-6
	Craig PARRY	70	70	71	67	278	-6
	P TATAURANGI	68	68	71	71	278	-6
22	Bill GLASSON	73	68	72	66	279	-5
	Lee JANZEN	71	68	69	71	279	-5
	Greg KRAFT	71	70	69	69	279	-5
	Esteban TOLEDO	70	71	73	65	279	-5
	Bob ESTES	66	69	73	71	279	-5
	Matt GOGEL	71	70	69	69	279	-5
	Mike HEINEN	72	69	67	71	279	-5
	K HOSOKAWA	70	65	73	71	279	-5
	Lee PORTER	66	68	71	74	279	-5
31	Stuart APPLEBY	65	71	70	74	280	-4
	B CHAMBLEE	72	69	70	69	280	-4
	Kevin JOHNSON	68	68	71	73	280	-4
	Skip KENDALL	69	68	71	72	280	-4
	Ian LEGGATT	71	69	71	69	280	-4
	Steve LOWERY	68	68	71	73	280	-4
37	Briny BAIRD	69	68	72	72	281	-3
	Jeff BREHAUT	73	68	68	72	281	-3
	D HAMMOND	71	66	73	71	281	-3
	Jeff JULIAN	69	66	76	70	281	-3
	Mark O'MEARA	67	73	72	69	281	-3
	Brett QUIGLEY	69	68	77	67	281	-3
	Willie WOOD	67	70	74	70	281	-3
44	Mark BROOKS	69	72	70	71	282	-2
	Gary NICKLAUS	69	70	72	71	282	-2
	T PERNICE, Jr.	70	68	70	74	282	-2
47	Mark HENSBY	71	68	73	71	283	-1
	Larry MIZE	72	69	73	69	283	-1
	Carl PAULSON	71	68	73	71	283	-1
	Loren ROBERTS	70	70	70	73	283	-1
	M BRADLEY	70	71	71	71	283	-1
	Pete JORDAN	71	70	69	73	283	-1
53	Woody AUSTIN	68	73	70	73	284	E
	Bob BURNS	69	72	69	74	284	E
	Jim CARTER	71	68	72	73	284	E
	Justin LEONARD	68	68	78	70	284	E
57	Chris TIDLAND	68	73	70	74	285	+1
	Tommy TOLLES	68	69	69	79	285	+1
59	Ben CRENSHAW	70	70	74	72	286	+2
60	Brad ELDER	71	66	72	78	287	+3
	Steve FLESCH	68	73	72	74	287	+3
62	Ben BATES	69	71	74	75	289	+5
63	Steve ALLAN	70	71	77	75	293	+9

Made the cut but did not play final 36 holes

Pos	Name	R1	R2	R3	R4	Total
64	Doug BARRON	73	69	-	-	142
	Jay Don BLAKE	69	73	-	-	142
	Jason GORE	72	70	-	-	142
	Glen HNATIUK	72	70	-	-	142
	Cliff KRESGE	71	71	-	-	142
	Jim McGOVERN	69	73	-	-	142
	Shaun MICHEEL	73	69	-	-	142
	Michael MUEHR	69	73	-	-	142
	Joey SINDELAR	69	73	-	-	142
	Mike SPOSA	70	72	-	-	142
	Duffy WALDORF	68	74	-	-	142
71	T ARMOUR III	69	67	-	-	D

Sponsored by Stan James

Tournament Report

Try as he might to throw the tournament away, Frank Lickliter somehow ended up winning the Kemper Insurance Open at TPC at Avenel in Maryland.

It was the third time in succession that the event went to a first-time winner and the tenth occasion since 1980. But boy did he do it the hard way. With thunderstorms forcing the event into a fifth day, Lickliter found himself three shots clear with three to play, after making birdies at the 12th and 14th when play resumed on Monday.

But bogeys at the 16th and 17th and a wayward approach on 18 seemed to be the making of one of golf's most spectacular collapses. But a chip and a putt from off the green saved Lickliter's blushes and saw him win by a stroke from J.J Henry. Lickliter made his move on Friday, when a second round 65 took him to within one shot of halfway leader Bradley Hughes.

A third round 66 saw Lickliter top the leaderboard. Henry was pushing Lickliter all the way on Sunday and got level with the eventual winner before play was halted on Sunday. He lost his momentum, however, and when play resumed the next day was unable to take advantage of Lickliter's aberrations over the closing holes.

Hughes along with Spike McRoy, who had to return on Monday to play one shot – a 25 foot birdie chance which he duly sank – and Phil Mickelson, who shot a best of the round 65, shared third.

MISSED THE CUT: C BECK 71 72, B CHEESMAN 75 68, J DURANT 73 70, G HJERTSTEDT 76 67, B JOBE 69 74, K JONES 74 69, C PAVIN 70 73, A BADDELEY 70 74, D ELLIS 71 73, C KANADA 71 73, B MAYFAIR 73 71, A McLARDY 78 66, N J OZAKI 74 70, S SIMPSON 76 68, R COUGHLAN 72 73, J GULLION 74 71, J HART 71 74, T ISENHOUR 74 71, J KAYE 73 72, S MURPHY 72 73, J OGILVIE 73 72, D PAULSON 73 72, D PEOPLES 71 74, S STRICKER 72 73, K TRIPLETT 69 76, T TRYBA 74 71, G WAITE 73 72, M WIEBE 73 72, C BARLOW 75 71, C BOWDEN 71 75, O BROWNE 72 74, J DALY 72 74, M DAWSON 76 70, R FREEMAN 73 73, P GOYDOS 73 73, K GRUNEWALD 69 77, P STANKOWSKI 71 75, C STRANGE 70 76, R WALCHER 77 69, J ANDERSON 73 74, R BEEM 72 75, H HAAS 71 76, B HENNINGER 72 75, M SPRINGER 74 73, K WENTWORTH 71 76, R FEHR 76 72, J MAGGERT 70 78, A PAINTER 73 75, D SCHULTZ 75 73, J GALLAGHER Jr. 75 74, J GREEN 74 75, M REID 75 74, T SCHERRER 72 77, C SULLIVAN 74 75, B FERGUSON 79 71, E FRYATT 78 72, D MORLAND IV 77 73, C BLUM 80 71, N HENKE 76 75, D STOCKTON Jr. 79 73, P GOW 78 75, R GAMEZ 76 78, J STONE 79 75, F LANGHAM 80 75, E EGLOFF 81 75, D PONCHOCK 75 82, T BYRUM 70 W/D, S DUNLAP 70 D, G CHALMERS 71 D, P DICKINSON 72 W/D, C PERRY 72 W/D, D PRIDE 72 W/D, D DUNAKEY 73 W/D, Jay WILLIAMSON 73 W/D, B WILSON 73 W/D, J RIEGGER 74 W/D, M McCUMBER 75 W/D, G HALLBERG 76 W/D, N LANCASTER 77 W/D, M HULBERT 78 W/D, S AMES 79 D.

Course Profile

You need a good short game to be successful at TPC at Avenel (par 71, 7,005 yards), mainly because if shots to the small greens are just a touch off line they are punished.

So leads can come and go and accurate players with a good touch on and around the greens do well. Luck can certainly play its part.

Accuracy over length is the key on this course specialists' track.

Players/Points to Note

●**Stuart Appleby** regularly plays this tournament. He hasn't missed an event since he started playing here in 1996, and has never finished worse than 31st and won in 1998. The Aussie holds the course record of 63 and has a stroke average of 69.25. He has only shot five rounds over par in 24 played.

●**Justin Leonard** had not finished worse than 25th in this tournament prior to missing the cut in 2001 – and he has played this event every year since turning pro in 1994. He won in 1997 and was second in 2000.

●**Steve Stricker** won here in 1996 and has posted two top-ten finishes since. He is a proven scrambler, who does better than most when things go wrong. And given the unlucky kicks and bounces that Avenel usually dishes out, that is a big advantage.

●**Scott Hoch** is a multiple top-ten finisher (nine in 20 starts) as are former winners **Lee Janzen** and **Bill Glasson**.

●Big names usually swerve the event but **Phil Mickelson** did show up in 2002 to place third (his third top-20 finish in four starts).

●**Tim Herron** has played well at Avenel before and can boast three top-seven finishes in four starts, while **Per-Ulrik Johansson** played well on his debut last year and could spring a surprise in 2002.

Previous Results

_2000:_ 1. Tom Scherrer (-13), 2. Greg Chalmers (-11), Kazuhiko Hosokawa (-11), Franklin Langham (-11), Justin Leonard (-11), Steve Lowery (-11).

_1999:_ 1. Rich Beem (-10), 2. Bill Glasson (-9), Bradley Hughes (-9).

_1998:_ 1. Stuart Appleby (-10), 2. Scott Hoch (-9), 3. Five players tied.

_1997:_ 1. Justin Leonard (-10), 2. Mark Wiebe (-9), 3. Four players tied.

_1996:_ 1. Steve Sricker (-14), 2. Grant Waite (-11), Brad Faxon (-11), Mark O'Meara (-11), Scott Hoch (-11).

MEMORIAL TOURNAMENT

Muirfield Village, 31 May to 3 Jun 2001, purse $4,100,000

Pos	Name	R1	R2	R3	R4	Total	To par	Money	DD(y)	DA%	GIR%	Putts
1	Tiger WOODS	68	69	68	66	271	-17	$738,000	276.6	82	76	116
2	Paul AZINGER	68	67	69	74	278	-10	$360,800	245.5	73	68	111
	Sergio GARCIA	68	69	70	71	278	-10	$360,800	273.0	86	74	118
4	Stewart CINK	72	69	67	71	279	-9	$196,800	260.4	66	75	116
5	Vijay SINGH	70	66	73	71	280	-8	$155,800	271.9	79	72	118
	Toru TANIGUCHI	68	74	69	69	280	-8	$155,800	250.9	82	72	116
7	Kenny PERRY	72	69	71	69	281	-7	$127,783	264.9	86	76	118
	Robert ALLENBY	69	69	70	73	281	-7	$127,783	256.1	82	74	118
	Stuart APPLEBY	67	71	69	74	281	-7	$127,783	264.6	77	61	104
10	Scott HOCH	70	69	69	74	282	-6	$110,700	253.1	86	68	109

Pos	Name	R1	R2	R3	R4	Total	To par
11	Steve FLESCH	72	67	71	73	283	-5
	Fred FUNK	71	68	71	73	283	-5
	Lee JANZEN	74	71	71	67	283	-5
	K SUTHERLAND	69	72	71	71	283	-5
15	Fred COUPLES	72	75	72	65	284	-4
	C HOWELL III	73	68	70	73	284	-4
	Peter LONARD	75	69	71	69	284	-4
	Gary NICKLAUS	72	72	70	70	284	-4
	Jeff SLUMAN	67	73	73	71	284	-4
20	G CHALMERS	72	68	71	74	285	-3
	John COOK	72	68	72	73	285	-3
	John DALY	73	68	75	69	285	-3
	Jay HAAS	68	76	72	69	285	-3
24	Mark BROOKS	72	72	72	70	286	-2
	Jim FURYK	69	69	74	74	286	-2
	Skip KENDALL	73	70	72	71	286	-2
	Len MATTIACE	72	67	73	74	286	-2
	N Joe OZAKI	69	69	74	74	286	-2
	S VERPLANK	66	72	72	76	286	-2
30	Brad FAXON	70	71	75	71	287	-1
	Jonathan KAYE	71	71	74	71	287	-1
	J PARNEVIK	68	75	73	71	287	-1
	Chris DiMARCO	74	70	74	69	287	-1
	Justin LEONARD	71	73	74	69	287	-1
	Grant WAITE	68	71	72	76	287	-1
	Mike WEIR	72	69	71	75	287	-1
37	S MARUYAMA	70	75	70	73	288	E
	Steve STRICKER	74	70	72	72	288	E
	Bob TWAY	72	72	68	76	288	E
40	M CALCAVECCHIA	69	73	74	73	289	+1
	D PAULSON	68	74	70	77	289	+1
	Mike SPOSA	68	78	72	71	289	+1
43	David FROST	71	72	75	72	290	+2
	Billy MAYFAIR	68	74	76	72	290	+2
	Garrett WILLIS	72	70	73	75	290	+2
46	A BADDELEY	71	73	73	74	291	+3
	Rich BEEM	71	70	76	74	291	+3
	David PEOPLES	74	72	74	71	291	+3
49	J.P. HAYES	71	76	74	71	292	+4
	F LANGHAM	74	73	73	72	292	+4
	Andrew MAGEE	74	70	74	74	292	+4
	P STANKOWSKI	72	71	74	75	292	+4
53	Hal SUTTON	71	71	75	76	293	+5
	Bob MAY	75	71	76	71	293	+5
	Carl PAULSON	71	73	76	73	293	+5
56	Robert DAMRON	74	71	70	79	294	+6
	S KATAYAMA	71	76	76	71	294	+6
	Frank NOBILO	73	72	77	72	294	+6
	Chris SMITH	66	71	81	76	294	+6
60	Brian GAY	71	74	78	72	295	+7
	Cliff KRESGE	71	75	74	75	295	+7
	Rory SABBATINI	73	69	77	76	295	+7
63	Billy ANDRADE	72	71	74	79	296	+8
	Ernie ELS	69	75	75	77	296	+8
	Duffy WALDORF	68	75	80	73	296	+8
66	Steve LOWERY	72	70	78	77	297	+9
67	Carlos FRANCO	69	74	77	78	298	+10
68	H FRAZAR	76	71	75	78	300	+12
69	Curtis STRANGE	71	75	77	78	301	+13
70	Esteban TOLEDO	76	70	82	74	302	+14

Sponsored by Stan James

Tournament Report

A three-shot swing on the fifth hole of the last round enabled Tiger Woods to win the Memorial Tournament from Paul Azinger and Sergio Garcia at Muirfield Village Golf Club, Dublin, Ohio.

It was the third time in succession that Woods had won the Memorial and his 37th victory as a professional.

After starting the final round a stroke behind Azinger, who had led after both the second and third rounds, Woods set about overhauling his playing partner at the par five fifth in amazing style.

Azinger's second shot had already found water when Woods launched a 2-iron from 250 yards, carrying the pond at the front of the green, that landed six feet from the pin.

Woods made eagle to Azinger's bogey and the World No.1 took the lead for the first time. Azinger just couldn't compete and faded to a final round two over par score of 74.

Garcia, who started the day two behind Woods and three behind Azinger, also failed to match anything Woods could produce and posted a last day 71 for a share of second.

The key to Woods' win was the way he played the par fives. His big hitting game set up plenty of birdie and eagle chances on the long holes which he duly took.

Tiger played them in 14-under par. Apart from Woods only Toru Taniguchi carded a final round in the 60s, the Japanese pro claiming fifth place alongside Vijay Singh, a shot adrift of Stewart Cink in fourth.

First round leader Scott Verplank fell away after an opening 66 to drop to 24th after 72 holes.

Woods became the first player in the history of the Memorial tournament to win the title for a third time (in 2000 event he was the first plater to successfully defend it).

His margin of victory in 2001, was bigger than his previous two victories and, in fact, was the biggest in the tournament's 25-year history.

Sponsored by Stan James

Course Profile

The back nine at Muirfield Village Golf Club (par 72, 7,221 yards) in Dublin, Ohio is where this tournament will be won and lost.

The two par fives are there to make eagles on but any errant shots can see some big numbers appear on your scorecard. Accuracy and length are the two prerequisites.

Long, narrow fairways with punishing rough and small greens dominate the layout.

If the weather is dry the greens get quicker.

Players/Points to Note

● This tournament is regarded as Jack Nicklaus' tournament. But it may as well belong to **Tiger Woods**, as the World No.1 has won the last three renewals. In 2002, look no further than Tiger to make it four in a row. Woods' victories certainly give credence to the suggestion that players who have won Majors tend to win at Muirfield Village. The field is always top class, the course tough and the stats are that eight of the last nine champions have won Majors.

● **David Duval** has yet to finish outside the top 30 in this event – a run that stretches back to 1994. He has come second and third twice. He will surely win this event sooner or later.

● **Ernie Els** is dual US Open winner, so his game is well suited to Muirfield Village as five top-15 finishes suggest **Vijay Singh** has been placed in the top five twice since winning in 1997.

● **Paul Azinger** was second in 2001 and has posted five top-ten finishes in this event in his career.

● **Justin Leonard** (who won the 1992 US Amateur championship here), **Tom Lehman**, **Mark Calcavecchia** and **Davis Love** have decent records in this event.

● Outsiders to follow would be **Steve Lowery** and **Steve Flesch** – who both have the game for the venue.

Previous Results

_2000:_ 1. Tiger Woods (-19), 2. Ernie Els (-14), Justin Leonard (-14).

_1999:_ 1. Tiger Woods (-15), 2. Vijay Singh (-13), 3. Olin Browne (-9), David Duval (-9), Carlos Franco (-9).

_1998:_ 1. Fred Couples (-17), 2. Andrew Magee (-13), 3. David Duval (-12).

_1997:_ 1. *Vijay Singh (-14), 2. Greg Norman (-12), Jim Furyk (-12). Played over 54 holes.

_1996:_ 1. Tom Watson (-14), 2. David Duval (-12), 3. David Frost (-10), Mark O'Meara (-10).

FEDEX ST JUDE CLASSIC

TPC at Southwind, 7 Jun to 10 Jun 2001, purse $3,500,000

Pos	Name	R1	R2	R3	R4	Total	To par	Money	DD(y)	DA%	GIR%	Putts
1	Bob ESTES	61	66	69	71	267	-17	$630,000	280.6	64	69	104
2	Bernhard LANGER	69	65	68	66	268	-16	$378,000	269.6	82	75	110
3	Tom LEHMAN	69	68	66	66	269	-15	$203,000	282.6	73	74	112
	Scott McCARRON	66	65	66	72	269	-15	$203,000	287.4	72	65	107
5	John DALY	69	65	63	73	270	-14	$127,750	311.3	84	74	117
	Paul GOYDOS	66	67	69	68	270	-14	$127,750	272.5	73	64	101
	Curtis STRANGE	65	67	69	69	270	-14	$127,750	266.3	77	71	109
8	Jesper PARNEVIK	67	64	71	69	271	-13	$105,000	283.0	80	71	110
	Nick PRICE	68	67	69	67	271	-13	$105,000	277.8	80	75	111
10	Nick FALDO	66	70	67	69	272	-12	$91,000	268.3	91	79	118
	Scott HOCH	68	68	67	69	272	-12	$91,000	278.8	80	69	110

Pos	Name	R1	R2	R3	R4	Total	To par
12	Ben BATES	70	69	70	64	273	-11
	Bob BURNS	71	67	67	68	273	-11
	Chris DiMARCO	66	69	69	69	273	-11
	Jay HAAS	69	68	70	66	273	-11
	Len MATTIACE	69	69	67	68	273	-11
	Billy MAYFAIR	69	67	68	69	273	-11
	Craig PARRY	67	66	72	68	273	-11
19	K.J. CHOI	67	66	72	69	274	-10
	Jose COCERES	68	69	67	70	274	-10
	Mathew GOGGIN	69	69	65	71	274	-10
22	Brandt JOBE	68	68	72	67	275	-9
	Pete JORDAN	71	66	70	68	275	-9
	B SCHWARZROCK	64	67	75	69	275	-9
	Ted TRYBA	67	69	69	70	275	-9
	Joel EDWARDS	67	67	71	70	275	-9
	Glen HNATIUK	69	70	64	72	275	-9
28	David GOSSETT	67	70	70	69	276	-8
	Bob MAY	69	68	69	70	276	-8
30	Russ COCHRAN	69	66	71	71	277	-7
	Bill GLASSON	68	71	68	70	277	-7
	P U JOHANSSON	70	65	73	69	277	-7
	Steve JONES	71	67	72	67	277	-7
	J.L. LEWIS	68	70	70	69	277	-7
	Scott SIMPSON	71	66	72	68	277	-7
	Mike SPOSA	70	68	70	69	277	-7
37	Stewart CINK	70	69	71	68	278	-6
	Jimmy GREEN	71	66	71	70	278	-6
	Shaun MICHEEL	68	66	72	72	278	-6
	John RIEGGER	65	70	73	70	278	-6
	Chris TIDLAND	71	68	68	71	278	-6
42	B CHAMBLEE	68	70	74	67	279	-5
	R COUGHLAN	64	72	71	72	279	-5
	Robert DAMRON	68	67	73	71	279	-5
	K GRUNEWALD	67	69	77	66	279	-5
	Cliff KRESGE	66	72	73	68	279	-5
	Frank NOBILO	70	67	69	73	279	-5
	Jeff SLUMAN	68	69	69	73	279	-5
49	Notah BEGAY III	68	70	71	71	280	-4
	Tom BYRUM	64	70	72	74	280	-4
	Angel CABRERA	71	67	73	69	280	-4
	J.P. HAYES	66	70	71	73	280	-4
53	B CHEESMAN	67	70	72	72	281	-3
	A McLARDY	68	71	74	68	281	-3
	Jerry SMITH	69	69	72	71	281	-3
	David TOMS	70	68	73	70	281	-3
	J VAN DE VELDE	69	70	69	73	281	-3
58	Brad ELDER	66	69	75	72	282	-2
	Hunter HAAS	68	71	68	75	282	-2
	Kent JONES	71	66	75	70	282	-2
	Sean MURPHY	66	69	74	73	282	-2
	Tommy TOLLES	65	74	68	75	282	-2
63	B COCHRAN	67	69	74	73	283	-1
	Jason GORE	69	69	76	69	283	-1
65	Bart BRYANT	70	68	68	78	284	E
	D MORLAND IV	71	66	74	73	284	E
67	Joe OGILVIE	69	70	71	75	285	+1
68	Jeff HART	70	68	75	73	286	+2
	Spike McROY	71	66	73	76	286	+2
70	Rob BRADLEY	70	69	73	75	287	+3

Tournament Report

It was a tournament full of comebacks and Bob Estes, who hadn't won for 162 starts, managed the biggest return to form of the lot to win Fedex St Jude Classic at TPC at Southwind in Memphis.

It was Estes' second win of his career and his first since 1994 and was achieved by leading from start to finish, denying Bernhard Langer, who was notching his best US Tour finish for six years by placing second and Tom Lehman and Scott McCarron who tied for third.

There were also top-five positions for John Daly and Curtis Strange – their highest US Tour finishes for three and four years respectively. Estes, using a new driver, opened up with a course record equalling 61 and was always in control. Only once did he give the chasing pack any hope on the final day.

Four clear with five to play Estes bogeyed the 14th and 15th, and with Langer ahead of him on the course picking up a shot at the 16th, the eventual winner's lead was down to one. But Estes was to hang on.

At the par five 16th he managed to find the bunker with his second shot as he went for the green in two, and when he blasted out through the green a par looked in doubt. But a chip and a putt saw him make five and two controlled pars later, Estes was getting his hands on the trophy and the winner's cheque of $630,000.

MISSED THE CUT: Doug BARRON 72 68, David BERGANIO Jr. 71 69, Danny ELLIS 72 68, Edward FRYATT 70 70, Brian HENNINGER 68 72, Mike HULBERT 72 68, Tripp ISENHOUR 71 69, Neal LANCASTER 73 67, Jose Maria OLAZABAL 72 68, Craig PERKS 70 70, Tom PERNICE Jr. 72 68, Loren ROBERTS 71 69, Kirk TRIPLETT 71 69, Steve ALLAN 67 74, Ryan DILLON 70 71, Steve ELKINGTON 72 69, Dan FORSMAN 71 70, Brian GAY 70 71, Kelly GIBSON 69 72, J.J. HENRY 70 71, Miguel A. JIMENEZ 72 69, Greg KRAFT 70 71, Ian LEGGATT 71 70, Phil MICKELSON 70 71, Larry MIZE 73 68, D PRIDE 72 69, K SUTHERLAND 69 72, B BAIRD 69 73, C BECKMAN 72 70, M CLARK II 72 70, G DAY 72 70, J GALLAGHER Jr. 69 73, P GOW 72 70, M HENSBY 71 71, J McGOVERN 73 69, M MUEHR 71 71, S PATE 68 74, L PORTER 71 71, D STOCKTON Jr. 72 70, G WILLIS 67 75, F ALLEM 72 71, J ANDERSON 73 70, J COOK 71 72, R FREEMAN 69 74, G HJERTSTEDT 71 72, L JANZEN 77 66, K JOHNSON 73 70, S KATAYAMA 70 73, J KAYE 69 74, M McCUMBER 73 70, E TOLEDO 72 71, J WILLIAMSON 69 74, W AUSTIN 72 72, J D BLAKE 73 71, J BREHAUT 69 75, B HUGHES 71 73, D PEOPLES 73 71, B FERGUSON 70 75, C KANADA 72 73, J KELLY 78 67, N J OZAKI 73 72, K WENTWORTH 73 72, B WILSON 75 70, W WOOD 73 72, S POPE 71 75, R FEHR 73 74, A MAGEE 73 74, J RESTINO 75 72, A BEAN 74 74, R WALCHER 78 70, R GAMEZ 73 76, B R BROWN 75 75, C FRANCO 70 80, J JULIAN 72 78, J PATE 75 75, T ARMOUR III 76 75, E FIORI 76 75, D DUNAKEY 77 75, J MAGGERT 77 75, B OLSEN 77 75, Z PATTEN 74 78, E CANONICA 79 74, C A SPENCE 76 77, J PASCHAL 78 77, R BEEM 72 W/D, J SINDELAR 72 W/D.

Course Profile

Low scoring is always probable at TPC at Southwind (par 72, 7,030 yards) as there are few bunkers or hazards to capture tee shots.

The course is long and does favour the big hitters but you have to rank high in the greens in regulations stats to succeed.

The rough can be punishing as can the conditions – fitness and patience will help.

It can get extremely hot in Memphis in June, so players who can handle the heat prosper.

Players/Points to Note

●**Nick Price** has won this event twice (1993 and 1998) and has a stroke average of 68.95. He is a massive 125-under par for his 15 starts in the event. Those stats were helped by a solid eighth place last year

●**Robert Damron**'s record at Southwind is superb. Although he has yet to win, in five attempts at the title he has posted three top-ten finishes. Only poor weekend scores prevented another high placing in 2001.

●**Chris DiMarco** has been placed in the top 15 of this event from three starts as has Tim Herron.

●**Kirk Triplett** has had six top-20 finishes in 10 visits to Southwind. **Craig Parry**'s six visits have yielded two top-ten finishes and the Aussie was 12th in 2001. **Glen Day** can boast three top-ten finishes.

●Others with good records in this event include 2001 champion **Bob Estes**, **David Toms**, **Scott Hoch** and **Tom Lehman**. Veteran, **Jay Haas**, was 12th in 2001 – his eighth top-15 finish.

●Most players who do well here can handle the hot, sticky conditions that affect the area at this time of year. The 2000 champion, **Notah Begay**, always plays his best golf in the summer months, while second-placed **Bob May** who was second in 2000 and 28th in 2001 hails from Las Vegas.

Previous Results

_2000:_ 1. Notah Begay III (-13), 2. Chris DiMarco (-12), Bob May (-12).

_1999:_ 1. Ted Tryba (-19), 2. Tim Herron (-17), Tom Lehman (-17).

_1998:_ 1. Nick Price (-16), won play-off, 2. Jeff Sluman (-16), 3. Glen Day (-14).

_1997:_ 1. Greg Norman (-16), 2. Dudley Hart (-15), 3. Craig Parry (-14), Robert Damron (-14).

_1996:_ 1. John Cook (-26), 2. John Adams (-19), 3. Kenny Perry (-18).

BUICK CLASSIC

Westchester C.C., 21 Jun to 24 Jun 2001, purse $3,500,000

Pos	Name	R1	R2	R3	R4	Total	To par	Money	DD(y)	DA%	GIR%	Putts
1	Sergio GARCIA	68	67	66	67	268	-16	$630,000	n/a	n/a	n/a	n/a
2	Scott HOCH	67	68	68	68	271	-13	$378,000	n/a	n/a	n/a	n/a
3	Billy ANDRADE	70	69	68	66	273	-11	$182,000	n/a	n/a	n/a	n/a
	Stewart CINK	65	72	69	67	273	-11	$182,000	n/a	n/a	n/a	n/a
	J.P. HAYES	68	69	67	69	273	-11	$182,000	n/a	n/a	n/a	n/a
6	Brad FAXON	69	72	66	67	274	-10	$121,625	n/a	n/a	n/a	n/a
	Vijay SINGH	67	70	70	67	274	-10	$121,625	n/a	n/a	n/a	n/a
8	Robert ALLENBY	69	68	74	64	275	-9	$105,000	n/a	n/a	n/a	n/a
	Russ COCHRAN	71	68	67	69	275	-9	$105,000	n/a	n/a	n/a	n/a
10	Jay WILLIAMSON	70	72	65	69	276	-8	$94,500	n/a	n/a	n/a	n/a

Pos	Name	R1	R2	R3	R4	Total	To par
11	Olin BROWNE	71	71	69	67	278	-6
	K SUTHERLAND	70	70	69	69	278	-6
13	S ELKINGTON	70	68	72	69	279	-5
	Craig PARRY	71	69	67	72	279	-5
	G HJERTSTEDT	68	70	68	73	279	-5
16	Paul AZINGER	71	70	68	71	280	-4
	Chris SMITH	72	70	69	69	280	-4
	Tiger WOODS	75	66	68	71	280	-4
19	Steve ALLAN	69	71	72	69	281	-3
	Jim FURYK	71	72	67	71	281	-3
	P-U JOHANSSON	69	69	72	71	281	-3
	Skip KENDALL	72	70	69	70	281	-3
	J.L. LEWIS	72	71	69	69	281	-3
	Chris PERRY	70	73	69	69	281	-3
	Mark WIEBE	68	68	73	72	281	-3
26	Stuart APPLEBY	73	68	70	71	282	-2
	David DUVAL	71	73	68	70	282	-2
	H FRAZAR	71	67	72	72	282	-2
	Paul GOW	71	68	72	71	282	-2
	Jay HAAS	68	73	72	69	282	-2
	Frank NOBILO	73	69	69	71	282	-2
32	C BECKMAN	72	69	72	70	283	-1
	John COOK	69	73	69	72	283	-1
	Fred COUPLES	72	68	70	73	283	-1
	David FROST	70	71	72	70	283	-1
	Ian LEGGATT	70	69	71	73	283	-1
37	T ARMOUR III	74	69	71	70	284	E
	Tom BYRUM	69	69	75	71	284	E
	Danny ELLIS	72	72	68	72	284	E
	Nick FALDO	73	68	70	73	284	E
	Brian GAY	71	71	71	71	284	E
	B GEIBERGER	70	69	73	72	284	E
	Matt GOGEL	70	71	71	72	284	E
	Glen HNATIUK	71	68	71	74	284	E
	Kevin JOHNSON	69	70	74	71	284	E
	Jonathan KAYE	70	74	71	69	284	E
47	Rich BEEM	74	67	71	73	285	+1
	Edward FRYATT	70	71	74	70	285	+1
	Loren ROBERTS	72	72	71	70	285	+1
50	Jim McGOVERN	70	72	74	70	286	+2
	Tom PERNICE Jr.	71	69	71	75	286	+2
52	B CHAMBLEE	73	69	74	71	287	+3
	D PAULSON	71	73	74	69	287	+3
	Corey PAVIN	69	72	71	75	287	+3
	Dicky PRIDE	71	72	71	73	287	+3
56	Jim CARTER	73	67	72	76	288	+4
	Steve FLESCH	71	73	70	74	288	+4
	Jason GORE	73	69	68	78	288	+4
	Jeff HART	69	71	73	75	288	+4
	Jerry KELLY	72	72	73	71	288	+4
	Justin LEONARD	69	75	72	72	288	+4
	Jerry SMITH	77	66	74	71	288	+4
63	Bob ESTES	72	69	73	75	289	+5
	Brian WATTS	69	73	70	77	289	+5
65	D BERGANIO Jr.	69	73	71	77	290	+6
	Brad ELDER	73	67	78	72	290	+6
	Kent JONES	76	67	74	73	290	+6
	D MORLAND IV	71	73	70	76	290	+6
69	M CAMPBELL	72	72	75	72	291	+7
	Tripp ISENHOUR	72	66	79	74	291	+7
	Gary NICKLAUS	73	71	74	73	291	+7
	Brett QUIGLEY	70	73	72	76	291	+7
	Chris RILEY	73	71	74	73	291	+7
	R WALCHER	74	70	74	73	291	+7
75	Larry MIZE	72	72	72	76	292	+8
76	Mike REID	76	68	74	75	293	+9
77	Jeff JULIAN	73	71	75	76	295	+11
	B SCHWARZROCK	71	73	78	73	295	+11
79	K CLEARWATER	73	70	78	75	296	+12
	Tom LEHMAN	72	68	72	-	-	D

Sponsored by Stan James

Tournament Report

Sergio Garcia's win in the Buick Classic saw the Spaniard not only claim his second US Tour title of his career but also climb to number five in the world standings – a position that makes him the highest ranked European.

Garcia's previous Stateside success saw him come from behind to win but at Westchester Country Club 'El Nino' won from the front. Garcia led by two shots going into the final round and saw off the challengers one by one to win by three stokes from Scott Hoch.

This was in stark contrast to last year when the Spaniard faltered down the stretch – having held a three shot advantage with seven holes to play he failed to win. One year on, Garcia showed maturity beyond his 21 years by coping with rain and the inevitable delays that go with bad weather.

He is still an aggressive golfer – as 21 birdies, seven bogeys and an eagle in his 72 holes suggest – but when he controls his game he is good enough to win any tournament.

It was the perfect reply to those that suggested Garcia would never be a serious contender on a regular basis if he continued to be taught by his father and to use a swing that many felt was flawed. The re-grips and waggles that were so in evidence during the final round of the US Open were still on display in New York but they didn't stop him winning.

MISSED THE CUT: Ben BATES 74 71, Craig BOWDEN 75 70, Jeff BREHAUT 73 72, Scott DUNLAP 72 73, Ben FERGUSON 75 70, Fred FUNK 70 75, Ken GREEN 73 72, Lee JANZEN 73 72, Pete JORDAN 71 74, Steve LOWERY 73 72, Joe OGILVIE 74 71, Craig PERKS 72 73, Rory SABBATINI 71 74, Tommy TOLLES 75 70, Duffy WALDORF 72 73, Garrett WILLIS 73 72, Jeremy ANDERSON 69 77, Jay Don BLAKE 73 73, Len MATTIACE 74 72, Blaine McCALLISTER 75 71, Andrew McLARDY 73 73, Phil TATAURANGI 72 74, Bob BURNS 73 74, Jose COCERES 72 75, Mathew GOGGIN 74 73, J.J. HENRY 76 71, Mark HENSBY 73 74, John HUSTON 74 73, Craig KANADA 76 71, Spike McROY 72 75, Michael MUEHR 75 72, Geoff OGILVY 73 74, Ted TRYBA 72 75, Bob TWAY 81 66, Jean VAN DE VELDE 75 72, Grant WAITE 73 74, Emanuele CANONICA 76 72, Barry CHEESMAN 72 76, Richie COUGHLAN 74 74, Robert GAMEZ 74 74, Rick HARTMANN 74 74, Bradley HUGHES 73 75, Willie WOOD 79 69, Woody AUSTIN 79 70, Joel EDWARDS 74 75, Rick FEHR 76 73, Pierre FULKE 77 72, Jimmy GREEN 74 75, Dave STOCKTON Jr. 77 72, Chris TIDLAND 71 78, Brian WILSON 71 78, Kaname YOKOO 75 74, Doug BARRON 77 73, Doug DUNAKEY 78 72, Joe DURANT 76 74, Craig A. SPENCE 73 77, Dan FORSMAN 75 76, Kelly GRUNEWALD 77 74, Miguel A. JIMENEZ 74 75, Greg KRAFT 76 75, Shaun MICHEEL 77 74, Sean MURPHY 73 78, Mike MEEHAN 74 78, Charles BOLLING 80 73, Bart BRYANT 71 82, Neal LANCASTER 77 76, Robin FREEMAN 78 76, Rob LABRITZ 75 81, Colin AMARAL 77 80, Ben CRENSHAW 75 82, Mike LAUDIEN 80 77, Hunter HAAS 75 83, Joey SINDELAR W/D 74 74, S MARUYAMA W/D 75 75, Rocco MEDIATE W/D 75 75, Fulton ALLEM W/D.

Course Profile

Westchester Country Club (par 71, 6,722 yards) in New York isn't long but is a tough test of golf and requires accuracy both off the tee and fairway.

Heavy rough awaits errant tee shots while some of the smallest, and fastest, greens on the US Tour make hitting the putting surfaces in regulation a must.

The style of the set up is similar to US Open venues – so watch out for players who perform well in the season's second Major.

Players/Points to Note

●**Ernie Els** made his debut in this tournament at this venue 1994, finishing second. Since then, he has won twice and finished fourth and fifth. He withdrew in 1998 and 2001 and posted his worst finish in 1999 when 22nd. His game is ideal for the track as his stroke average of 68.79 (he is 53-under for his seven starts) suggests.

●**Vijay Singh** is another dual winner (1993 - his first win on the US Tour – and 1995) and has yet to finish outside of the top 25 in nine attempts on the title.

●**Dennis Paulson** was defending the title he won in 2000 last year and was perhaps not focusing 100% on his golf last year when finishing 52nd (the responsibilities of being a champion involves a lot of flesh pressing and duties away from the course). But he was second in 1999 and a hassle free good show is expected in 2002.

●**Sergio Garcia** should have won in 2000, when throwing a lead away down the stretch but was back to win in 2001.

●**Duffy Waldorf**, **Lee Janzen** and **Billy Andrade** are previous winners who have recorded multiple top-ten finishes, while **Jim Carter**, **Stewart Cink**, **Bob Estes**, **David Duval** and **Jeff Maggert** are yet to lift the trophy but have gone close on several occasions.

Previous Results

2000: 1. Dennis Paulson (-8), won play-off, 2. David Duval (-8), 3. Sergio Garcia (-7).

1999: 1. Duffy Waldorf (-8), won play-off, 2. Dennis Paulson (-8), 3. Chris Perry (-7), Scott Hoch (-6).

1998: 1. *J.P. Hayes (-12), won play-off, 2. Jim Furyk (-12) 3. Tom Lehman (-9). Won after 54 holes.

1997: 1. Ernie Els (-16), 2. Jeff Maggert (-14), 3. Jim Furyk (-10), Robert Damron (-10).

1996: 1. Ernie Els (-13), 2. Tom Lehman (-5), Jeff Maggert (-5), Steve Elkington (-5), Craig Parry (-5).

CANON GREATER HARTFORD OPEN

TPC at River Highlands, 28 Jun to 1 Jul 2001, purse $2,800,000

Pos	Name	R1	R2	R3	R4	Total	To par	Money	DD(y)	DA%	GIR%	Putts
1	Phil MICKELSON	67	68	61	68	264	-16	$558,000	325.0	80	75	111
2	Billy ANDRADE	68	65	66	66	265	-15	$344,800	296.5	66	79	113
3	D BERGANIO Jr	67	66	64	69	266	-14	$161,200	290.1	77	81	116
	Chris DiMARCO	65	67	66	68	266	-14	$161,200	287.8	73	67	106
	Dudley HART	70	63	70	63	266	-14	$161,200	289.4	72	64	105
6	Tom PERNICE Jr	68	68	66	65	267	-13	$111,600	293.9	68	65	107
7	Olin BROWNE	68	71	67	63	269	-11	$83,921	286.7	80	79	117
	Tripp ISENHOUR	69	70	67	63	269	-11	$83,921	279.5	75	72	112
	Frank LICKLITER II	65	69	68	67	269	-11	$83,921	282.8	82	71	113
	S MARUYAMA	63	69	73	64	269	-11	$83,921	286.9	73	69	109
	Kenny PERRY	68	68	70	63	269	-11	$83,921	306.5	86	74	114
	Kirk TRIPLETT	68	71	65	65	269	-11	$83,921	274.5	82	81	120
	Jerry KELLY	67	65	69	68	269	-11	$83,921	281.0	70	78	114

Pos	Name	R1	R2	R3	R4	Total	To par
14	Paul AZINGER	70	64	69	67	270	-10
	Tim HERRON	66	68	67	69	270	-10
	Hal SUTTON	67	67	69	67	270	-10
17	Mark BROOKS	66	69	68	68	271	-9
	Joe OGILVIE	68	64	70	69	271	-9
	Scott SIMPSON	65	67	70	69	271	-9
	K SUTHERLAND	68	67	68	68	271	-9
	Scott VERPLANK	72	67	71	61	271	-9
22	Jay DON BLAKE	64	68	72	68	272	8
	John DALY	67	70	70	65	272	-8
	Edward FRYATT	65	72	68	67	272	-8
	Billy MAYFAIR	70	70	68	64	272	-8
	David DUVAL	67	66	70	69	272	-8
	Frank NOBILO	67	66	70	69	272	-8
	Geoff OGILVY	67	68	69	68	272	-8
29	Briny BAIRD	67	69	70	67	273	-7
	M CALCAVECCHIA	68	68	71	66	273	-7
	David FROST	69	68	69	67	273	-7
	C HOWELL III	66	72	70	65	273	-7
	Jonathan KAYE	62	71	72	68	273	-7
	J WILLIAMSON	66	72	70	64	273	-7
	Paul GOW	67	69	68	69	273	-7
36	J ANDERSON	70	67	71	66	274	-6
	Jim CARTER	68	68	71	67	274	-6
	Brian GAY	68	72	68	66	274	-6
	Steve PATE	68	67	71	68	274	-6
	Doug DUNAKEY	67	65	71	71	274	-6
	Jay HAAS	71	68	68	67	274	-6
	Jeff SLUMAN	67	69	69	69	274	-6
	Duffy WALDORF	71	69	65	69	274	-6
44	Len MATTIACE	67	69	72	67	275	-5
45	C BECKMAN	70	70	69	67	276	-4
	Joel EDWARDS	73	67	66	70	276	-4
	Jimmy GREEN	66	73	70	67	276	-4
	A McLARDY	66	71	72	67	276	-4
	Chris SMITH	70	66	72	68	276	-4

Pos	Name	R1	R2	R3	R4	Total	To par
50	Kevin JOHNSON	68	71	67	71	277	-3
	J.L. LEWIS	70	70	69	68	277	-3
	Larry MIZE	65	72	71	69	277	-3
	Carl PAULSON	68	69	71	69	277	-3
	Esteban TOLEDO	66	74	71	66	277	-3
55	M CLARK II	69	69	69	71	278	-2
	Nick FALDO	66	73	72	67	278	-2
	Andrew MAGEE	67	71	71	69	278	-2
	Corey PAVIN	69	71	71	67	278	-2
	David PEOPLES	71	68	69	70	278	-2
	Chris TIDLAND	70	70	69	69	278	-2
61	K CLEARWATER	71	67	73	68	279	-1
	Jim FURYK	72	67	71	69	279	-1
	Jeff HART	74	66	69	70	279	-1
	Glen HNATIUK	73	67	71	68	279	-1
	Bradley HUGHES	69	71	69	70	279	-1
	Sean MURPHY	67	73	74	65	279	-1
67	Woody AUSTIN	69	71	70	70	280	E
	Bart BRYANT	70	69	74	67	280	E
	S ELKINGTON	68	72	69	71	280	E
	Pete JORDAN	69	66	73	72	280	E
	Ian LEGGATT	67	73	71	69	280	E
	P STANKOWSKI	67	72	70	71	280	E
73	Greg KRAFT	68	72	74	67	281	+1
	Chris RILEY	65	70	78	68	281	+1
75	E CANONICA	71	68	71	72	282	+2
	Robin FREEMAN	73	67	74	68	282	+2
77	K GRUNEWALD	69	70	75	69	283	+3
	Dicky PRIDE	68	71	74	70	283	+3
79	Spike McROY	68	71	76	69	284	+4
80	John HUSTON	71	68	71	75	285	+5
	N LANCASTER	69	69	74	73	285	+5
82	B GEIBERGER	70	69	78	69	286	+6
	F LANGHAM	70	67	78	71	286	+6
84	Kent JONES	71	65	77	74	287	+7
85	Mathew GOGGIN	67	72	72	77	288	+8

Tournament Report

After blowing chances to win in four events this season with back nine disasters, Phil Mickelson finally remembered how to close out a tournament by holding off the challenge of Billy Andrade to capture the Canon Greater Hartford Open title at TPC at River Highlands in Cromwell.

Perhaps significantly, this was the first time that Mickelson teed it up at the Connecticut venue for seven seasons, and after spending the last few weeks practising visualising techniques to help him mentally, he managed to produce some must see golf to win by a stroke.

It was his Saturday 61, the lowest score Mickelson had carded in tournament golf, that helped set up the win – his second of the season and 19th of his career. And although the winning distance was the minimum margin, the victory was easier than that suggested. Mickelson made just one bogey all weekend and knew that par on the final three holes would be enough.

Andrade was too far behind approaching the last few holes and his birdie-birdie finish only ensured him of second place. Dudley Hart, David Berganio and Chris DiMarco tied for third. On a day of low scoring only two of the top-49 players didn't manage to break 70 and there were four 63s and a 61 (carded by Scott Verplank).

Mickelson's win moved him closer to Tiger Woods at the top of the Money List, his seasonal total boosted to over $3.5million – courtesy of two wins, three seconds and four third places.

MISSED THE CUT: Marco DAWSON 67 74, D MORLAND IV 71 70, John RIEGGER 69 72, Joey SINDELAR 67 74, David SMAIL 70 71, Jean VAN DE VELDE 69 72, Fulton ALLEM 65 77, Craig BOWDEN 69 73, Ed FIORI 69 73, Bill GLASSON 73 69, Paul GOYDOS 70 72, Gabriel HJERTSTEDT 71 71, Craig KANADA 74 68, Skip KENDALL 71 71, Michael MUEHR 69 73, Mike SPOSA 68 74, Kaname YOKOO 69 73, Ben FERGUSON 71 72, Dan FORSMAN 72 71, Jason GORE 74 69, J.P. HAYES 72 71, J.J. HENRY 70 73, Mark HENSBY 68 75, Per Ulrik JOHANSSON 70 73, Wayne LEVI 72 71, Mark McCUMBER 70 73, Steve AL-LAN 72 72, Craig BARLOW 70 74, Stewart CINK 68 76, Brad ELDER 70 74, Brad FAXON 72 72, Ken GREEN 74 70, Hunter HAAS 73 71, Gary NICKLAUS 70 74, Jim SALINETTI 74 70, Rocky WALCHER 71 73, D.A. WEIBRING 72 72, Garrett WILLIS 74 70, Greg CHALMERS 72 73, K.J. CHOI 69 76, Richie COUGH-LAN 72 73, Tony KELLEY 73 72, Blaine McCALLISTER 70 75, John RESTINO 75 70, Grant WAITE 72 73, Brian WILSON 71 74, Tommy ARMOUR III 75 71, Jeff BREHAUT 69 77, Steve FLESCH 68 78, Steve JONES 71 75, Jeff JULIAN 74 72, Craig PERKS 69 77, Tommy TOLLES 72 74, Fuzzy ZOELLER 72 74, Danny ELLIS 72 75, Peter JACOBSEN 74 73, Cliff KRESGE 74 73, Davis LOVE III 77 70, Jerry SMITH 72 75, Billy DOWNES 70 78, William LINK IV 74 74, Lee PORTER 73 75, Ted TRY-BA 73 75, Kevin GIANCOLA 75 74, Matt ROSENFELD 74 76, Phil BLACKMAR 78 73, Bob BURNS 76 75, Fran MARRELLO 83 72, Doug BARRON 71 W/D, Tom SCHERRER 75 W/D, Tom BYRUM 77 W/D.

Course Profile

TPC at River Highlands (par 70, 6,820 yards) isn't really at typical TPC venue. A lot of the greens are smaller than usual, and they are raised, making them into a scramblers delight.

Many shots that look good will run off the putting surfaces – getting up and down in essential – but players who figure highly in the GIR stats will do well.

With galleries over 100,000 over the four days, successful players have to be able to handle the boisterous crowd.

Players/Points to Note

● **Mark Calcavecchia** has done everything but win this event. He is 100-under par in 20 visits, can boast seven top-five finishes and has a stroke average of 68.94. He has a real affection for this tournament and this course. He could have arguably won in 1982, 1990, 1996, 1997, 1999 and 2000. His sister lives close by to the course. Next season may be the year he finally succeeds.

● **Stewart Cink**'s form figures in this event from 1997 read Win-2-8-14-MC. He has only shot two over-par rounds in 22 and has an incredible stroke average of 67.73.

● **Kirk Triplett** has registered five top-11 finishes in his last seven starts, while veterans **Kenny Perry** and **Paul Azinger** both have multiple top-ten finishes to their name.

● **Chris DiMarco**'s form figures from 1998 read 25-20-5-3.

● **Davis Love** usually plays well in this event if he includes it in his schedule as does **Justin Leonard**.

● Some big names have won this event (**Greg Norman**, **Nick Price**, **Curtis Strange** and **Lee Trevino**) but these days the field is invariably sub-standard and it has become known as a first-time winners tournament (three of the last five). Last year, though, saw Phil Mickelson tee up for the first time here in seven years – and he duly won.

Previous Results

2000: 1. Notah Begay III (-20), 2. Mark Calcavecchia (-19), 3. Kirk Triplett (-16).

1999: 1. Brent Geiberger (-18), 2. Skip Kendall (-15), 3. Mark Calcavecchia (-14), Justin Leonard (-14), Ted Tryba (-14).

1998: 1. Olin Browne (-14), won play-off, 2. Stewart Cink (-14), Larry Mize (-14).

1997: 1. Stewart Cink (-13), 2. Brandel Chamblee (-12), Jeff Maggert (-12), Tom Byrum (-12).

1996: 1. D.A. Weibring (-14), 2. Tom Kite (-10), 3. Dicky Pride (-9), Fuzzy Zoeller (-9), Mark Calcavecchia (-9).

ADVIL WESTERN OPEN

Cog Hill G.&C.C., 5 Jul to 8 Jul 2001, purse $3,600,000

Pos	Name	R1	R2	R3	R4	Total	To par	Money	DD(y)	DA%	GIR%	Putts
1	Scott HOCH	69	68	66	64	267	-21	$648,000	295.6	86	74	107
2	Davis LOVE III	66	67	69	66	268	-20	$388,800	315.5	59	81	113
3	B CHAMBLEE	69	67	70	69	275	-13	$208,800	287.4	72	76	113
	Mike WEIR	71	70	67	67	275	-13	$208,800	304.6	64	71	113
5	Jerry KELLY	67	73	69	67	276	-12	$136,800	284.6	68	76	117
	Rory SABBATINI	71	68	70	67	276	-12	$136,800	312.1	64	69	116
7	Steve FLESCH	71	70	67	69	277	-11	$112,200	292.6	61	71	112
	Dudley HART	70	70	69	68	277	-11	$112,200	300.4	66	71	114
	K SUTHERLAND	70	70	69	68	277	-11	$112,200	289.5	66	79	120
10	Matt GOGEL	69	74	66	69	278	-10	$82,800	297.4	66	74	115
	Frank LICKLITER II	70	71	70	67	278	-10	$82,800	295.5	64	65	111
	Vijay SINGH	69	70	70	69	278	-10	$82,800	308.3	64	69	114
	Steve STRICKER	72	70	68	68	278	-10	$82,800	292.8	56	68	111
	Mark WIEBE	65	74	67	72	278	-10	$82,800	287.4	63	79	119

Pos	Name	R1	R2	R3	R4	Total	To par
15	Bob ESTES	70	68	71	70	279	-9
	Brian GAY	74	68	67	70	279	-9
	Billy MAYFAIR	72	70	67	70	279	-9
	Carl PAULSON	68	71	72	68	279	-9
	S VERPLANK	69	69	70	71	279	-9
20	Stephen AMES	72	69	68	71	280	-8
	Brad FAXON	68	70	72	70	280	-8
	David FROST	72	71	70	67	280	-8
	Justin LEONARD	69	72	70	69	280	-8
	Frank NOBILO	68	69	72	71	280	-8
	Joe OGILVIE	71	67	73	69	280	-8
	Kenny PERRY	68	74	70	68	280	-8
	Chris SMITH	71	68	71	70	280	-8
	Tiger WOODS	73	68	68	71	280	-8
	C BECKMAN	71	72	66	71	280	-8
	Bob TWAY	68	74	67	71	280	-8
31	John COOK	69	72	72	68	281	-7
	Jonathan KAYE	69	71	75	66	281	-7
	Tom LEHMAN	74	68	70	69	281	-7
	Bob MAY	72	70	74	65	281	-7
	S McCARRON	69	73	72	67	281	-7
	Hal SUTTON	70	71	70	70	281	-7
37	Briny BAIRD	70	71	70	71	282	-6
	Robert DAMRON	70	72	68	72	282	-6
	Joey GULLION	72	69	71	70	282	-6
	C HOWELL III	72	69	73	68	282	-6
	Joey SINDELAR	72	69	70	71	282	-6
42	Bob BURNS	71	68	72	72	283	-5
	G CHALMERS	69	74	72	68	283	-5
	Brandt JOBE	70	70	72	71	283	-5
	Ian LEGGATT	69	73	70	71	283	-5
	Shaun MICHEEL	70	72	67	74	283	-5
	Phil MICKELSON	66	74	67	76	283	-5
	Larry MIZE	70	73	69	71	283	-5
	David TOMS	67	73	73	70	283	-5
50	Glen HNATIUK	71	69	73	71	284	-4
	Nick PRICE	72	71	68	73	284	-4
52	J.J. HENRY	74	69	71	71	285	-3
	Tim HERRON	70	73	72	70	285	-3
	Skip KENDALL	71	72	72	70	285	-3
	Loren ROBERTS	70	69	73	73	285	-3
	Mark WILSON	71	67	73	74	285	-3
57	Russ COCHRAN	72	69	73	72	286	-2
	B GEIBERGER	69	73	70	74	286	-2
	J.L. LEWIS	69	71	74	72	286	-2
60	Rich BEEM	70	73	75	69	287	-1
	K.J. CHOI	71	71	76	69	287	-1
	Robin FREEMAN	74	69	69	75	287	-1
63	Jim CARTER	71	72	74	71	288	E
	Kevin JOHNSON	70	73	76	69	288	E
	Jeff MAGGERT	70	71	70	77	288	E
	Chris PERRY	74	68	74	72	288	E
67	Ted TRYBA	71	72	74	72	289	+1
68	Craig KANADA	74	69	73	74	290	+2
	Gary NICKLAUS	71	72	74	73	290	+2
70	S MARUYAMA	72	71	76	75	294	+6
	J VAN DE VELDE	73	70	76	75	294	+6

Tournament Report

Scott Hoch pushed himself into the Ryder Cup picture by capturing the Advil Western Open title at Cog Hill in Illinois.

It was the second win of the season for the 45-year-old, who had been complaining of tendinitis in his left wrist before the off. He got the better of another ailing golfer, Davis Love – who had just been suffering with a neck injury since mid-April, by a shot. Neither player had practised that much before the event but it didn't seem to matter as they dominated the weekend play.

Love was ahead at the halfway stage and led by a stoke going into the final round from Hoch. The two, playing in the last group, went head to head on Sunday. Love seemed to be in control but Hoch kept close.

On the 15th Hoch made a crucial birdie to stay within one shot of Love by rolling in an 18-foot putt. He then drew level when Love could only bogey the 17th, after a poor 7-iron approach. And then on the 18th and final hole, Love hooked his drive nearly out of bounds, and when he eventually found the green missed a 12-footer for par.

Hoch needed to hole from 18 inches for the win and didn't disappoint. Hoch birdied 12 of the last 22 holes and became the first player aged 45 or over to win on the US Tour for over 10 years. Mike Weir and Brandel Chamblee tied for third – eight shots behind the winner.

MISSED THE CUT: Tommy ARMOUR III 72 72, Craig BARLOW 71 73, Chip BECK 74 70, Jay Don BLAKE 72 72, Jeff BREHAUT 73 71, Mark BROOKS 71 73, Olin BROWNE 71 73, Marco DAWSON 71 73, Carlos FRANCO 74 70, Hunter HAAS 73 71, Per-Ulrik JOHANSSON 74 70, Steve LOWERY 73 71, Spike McROY 74 70, G OGILVY 69 75, S SIMPSON 74 70, T TOLLES 70 74, D WALDORF 72 72, S ALLAN 73 72, B ANDRADE 73 72, S APPLEBY 71 74, W AUSTIN 72 73, D BARRON 76 69, G DAY 71 74, J EDWARDS 73 72, J GORE 69 76, G HJERTSTEDT 73 70, C KRESGE 74 71, A MAGEE 76 69, M McCUMBER 73 72, K TRIPLETT 73 72, M CLARK II 72 74, J DURANT 72 74, M HENSBY 75 71, G KRAFT 71 75, L MATTIACE 74 72, C PARRY 71 75, C PERKS 74 72, J SLUMAN 75 71, J SMITH 71 75, G WILLIS 71 75, R ALLENBY 74 73, J ANDERSON 75 72, E FRYATT 70 77, J GREEN 71 76, J.P. HAYES 75 72, P JACOBSEN 72 75, S PATE 72 75, T PERNICE Jr. 77 70, M SPOSA 71 76, S UTLEY 75 72, T BYRUM 71 77, S DUNLAP 74 74, B GLASSON 74 74, M GOGGIN 72 76, L JANZEN 77 71, D MORLAND IV 74 74, M MUEHR 72 76, L PORTER 74 74, T PURTZER 73 75, B ELDER 74 75, N LANCASTER 74 75, B SCHWARZROCK 75 74, P STANKOWSKI 73 76, G WAITE 76 73, D.A. WEIBRING 73 76, H FRAZAR 73 77, B HENNINGER 76 74, F LANGHAM 74 76, D PEOPLES 74 76, E TOLEDO 71 79, B FERGUSON 75 76, R FLOYD 75 76, M SMALL 78 73, B HUGHES 76 76, P JORDAN 77 75, M KIRK 74 78, C TIDLAND 74 78, K YOKOO 73 79, P GOYDOS 76 77, M HARRIGAN 75 79, D LUCCHESI 76 78, D DUNAKEY 76 80, P GOW 77 82, K VANKO 82 84, E CANONICA W/D 74 74.

Sponsored by Stan James

LONARD - JOBE. (2003)

Course Profile

Most pros enjoy playing the Dubsdread Course at Cog Hill Golf Club (par 72, 7,073 yards), the venue for this event since 1991, which offers plenty of scoring opportunities on it's four par fives and large greens.

The putting surfaces have subtle undulations and players need to be accurate with their second shots to create birdie chances.

Hitting the greens in regulation is the key. Big, mature oaks line the fairways and there are plenty of bunkers to catch wayward shots.

Players/Points to Note

● **Nick Price** has won this event twice (1993 and 1994 – the only player in the last 34 years to gain back-to-back successes) and has been beaten in a play-off twice (1986 and 2000).

● **Tiger Woods** has also had two tournament wins (1997 and 1999). The World No.1 always enjoys playing in tournaments with a history and as this one is the oldest on the PGA Tour (the US and British Open's may have been around for longer but are run by different associations), it's an event that Woods holds in high regard.

● **Jim Furyk** has finished in the top seven on three occasions in the last four years.

● **Stuart Appleby** missed the cut in 2001 but finished in the top 20 on five successive occasions from 1996.

● **Steve Stricker** ran away with victory in 1996 – he won by eight shots the most since 1952 – so will always have fond memories of the event. Another top-ten finish (his third) came Stricker's way in 2001.

● **Justin Leonard** has yet to finish lower than 26th in eight starts and has been placed in the top ten, four times.

● **Vijay Singh** has finished in the top ten in three of the last four renewals.

Mike Weir has twice finished in the top three twice in three starts.

Previous Results

2000: 1. Robert Allenby (-14), won play-off, 2. Nick Price (-14), 3. Jim Furyk (-12), Greg Kraft (-12), Shigeki Maruyama (-12).

1999: 1. Tiger Woods (-15), 2. Mike Weir (-12), 3. Brent Geiberger (-11).

1998: 1. Joe Durant (-17), 2. Vijay Singh (-15), 3. Dudley Hart (-11), Lee Janzen (-11).

1997: 1. Tiger Woods (-13), 2. Frank Nobilo (-10), 3. Jeff Sluman (-9), Justin Leonard (-9), Steve Lowery (-9).

1996: 1. Steve Stricker (-18), 2. Billy Andrade (-10), Jay Don Blake (-10).

GREATER MILWAUKEE OPEN

Brown Deer Park, 12 Jul to 15 Jul 2001, purse $3,100,000

Pos	Name	R1	R2	R3	R4	Total	To par	Money	DD(y)	DA%	GIR%	Putts
1	S MARUYAMA	68	65	67	66	266	-18	$558,000	289.1	58	74	108
Won play-off												
2	C HOWELL III	66	69	67	64	266	-18	$334,800	311.0	75	71	107
3	J.P. HAYES	69	66	71	63	269	-15	$179,800	302.3	67	74	114
	Tim HERRON	69	69	64	67	269	-15	$179,800	310.0	69	78	116
5	K.J. CHOI	70	68	66	66	270	-14	$105,090	292.8	63	72	113
	Harrison FRAZAR	70	68	62	70	270	-14	$105,090	303.8	67	65	109
	Brent GEIBERGER	65	68	70	67	270	-14	$105,090	298.1	81	72	114
	B McCALLISTER	69	65	70	66	270	-14	$105,090	279.9	63	68	108
	Kenny PERRY	66	63	71	70	270	-14	$105,090	308.3	87	79	118
10	Jay HAAS	64	71	69	67	271	-13	$71,300	300.4	62	63	106
	Scott HOCH	67	68	68	68	271	-13	$71,300	298.5	69	71	115
	Steve LOWERY	72	69	66	64	271	-13	$71,300	304.6	77	67	110
	Jeff SLUMAN	67	68	64	72	271	-13	$71,300	289.4	44	63	108
	Bob TWAY	69	72	66	64	271	-13	$71,300	292.0	67	71	114

Pos	Name	R1	R2	R3	R4	Total	To par
15	Skip KENDALL	73	67	65	67	272	-12
	David PEOPLES	71	68	66	67	272	-12
	Steve STRICKER	68	66	69	69	272	-12
18	T ARMOUR III	73	66	67	67	273	-11
	Brian CLAAR	68	68	71	66	273	-11
	Glen DAY	72	69	66	66	273	-11
	Jonathan KAYE	70	71	65	67	273	-11
	Michael MUEHR	69	70	67	67	273	-11
	Brett QUIGLEY	72	67	67	67	273	-11
	Tom BYRUM	70	67	66	70	273	-11
25	R COUGHLAN	69	70	67	68	274	-10
	Carlos FRANCO	71	66	68	69	274	-10
	C A. SPENCE	68	65	70	71	274	-10
28	Briny BAIRD	67	67	73	68	275	-9
	Brad ELDER	68	67	70	70	275	-9
	Paul GOYDOS	72	68	68	67	275	-9
	F LICKLITER II	73	66	70	66	275	-9
	Jay Don BLAKE	67	69	67	72	275	-9
	Marco DAWSON	65	69	68	73	275	-9
	Bradley HUGHES	68	70	67	70	275	-9
	D.A. WEIBRING	65	75	70	65	275	-9
36	John RIEGGER	71	66	69	70	276	-8
	Woody AUSTIN	71	70	70	65	276	-8
	Craig BARLOW	72	69	69	66	276	-8
	Jimmy GREEN	67	73	69	67	276	-8
	Cliff KRESGE	72	65	67	72	276	-8
	N LANCASTER	71	70	68	67	276	-8
	Jim McGOVERN	70	70	68	68	276	-8
	Corey PAVIN	70	68	70	68	276	-8
	Loren ROBERTS	74	67	67	68	276	-8
	Scott SIMPSON	71	70	64	71	276	-8
	Chris SMITH	66	66	72	72	276	-8
47	Jerry KELLY	68	71	67	71	277	-7
	Larry MIZE	68	72	68	69	277	-7
	Joe OGILVIE	75	65	67	70	277	-7
	Lee PORTER	70	69	67	71	277	-7
	C BECKMAN	72	68	71	66	277	-7
	Robert DAMRON	72	69	67	69	277	-7
	Dan FORSMAN	71	70	68	68	277	-7
	Tom PURTZER	71	70	67	69	277	-7
	Jerry SMITH	69	70	65	73	277	-7
56	Bob BURNS	68	69	69	72	278	-6
	Doug DUNAKEY	75	66	70	67	278	-6
	Scott GUMP	70	69	69	70	278	-6
	Pete JORDAN	70	71	70	67	278	-6
	Steve PATE	66	71	68	73	278	-6
61	Joel EDWARDS	70	69	71	69	279	-5
	Brad FABEL	69	69	67	74	279	-5
	D HAMMOND	69	70	68	72	279	-5
	J.J. HENRY	72	69	70	68	279	-5
	Peter JACOBSEN	69	72	66	72	279	-5
	Chris PERRY	68	70	66	75	279	-5
	Craig STADLER	69	66	73	71	279	-5
	Fuzzy ZOELLER	69	71	68	71	279	-5
69	Rich BEEM	70	68	72	70	280	-4
	Craig BOWDEN	68	70	69	73	280	-4
	M BRADLEY	69	72	70	69	280	-4
	Sean MURPHY	70	71	71	68	280	-4
	Esteban TOLEDO	68	66	71	75	280	-4
	Brian WATTS	66	70	73	71	280	-4
75	Brandt JOBE	67	70	69	75	281	-3
	F LANGHAM	69	71	71	70	281	-3
	Craig PERKS	70	69	69	73	281	-3
	Mike REID	69	71	74	67	281	-3
	Mike STANDLY	70	70	73	68	281	-3
80	Spike McROY	68	73	69	72	282	-2
	D STOCKTON Jr.	68	72	68	74	282	-2
82	Gary NICKLAUS	70	71	72	70	283	-1
	Ted TRYBA	72	69	72	70	283	-1
84	Mark WILSON	71	67	70	76	284	E
85	Dicky PRIDE	71	70	73	71	285	+1
86	Tripp ISENHOUR	69	70	73	74	286	+2
	Kevin JOHNSON	73	68	76	69	286	+2
88	Jeff HART	69	71	75	72	287	+3

Sponsored by Stan James

Tournament Report

Nine-time Japanese Tour winner Shegeki Maruyama managed to secure his first US Tour success by defeating Charlies Howell in a play-off for the Greater Milwaukee Open at Brown Deer Park Golf Club.

It was the first victory by a Japanese professional on the United States mainland and it was achieved despite misjudging his approach to the last in regulation play when he hit his ball into the stands. He missed an 18-footer that would have given him the win on the 72nd hole, instead extra time beckoned after Howell had birdied six of the last seven holes of his final round.

The 2000 NCAA champion couldn't take that sort of form into the play-off, however, as he needed four shots just to get the ball on the green at the first extra hole. And after Howell had missed a seven-foot par putt, Maruyama had two strokes to win from inside that distance and made no mistake with his first strike. Maruyama had led going into the final round and looked set to destroy the field by picking up five shots in the first ten holes but he played the next eight in level par to give the chasing pack a chance.

Howell actually started the day in fifth place and, although he just failed to win for the first time as a professional, the second place prize money of $334,800 was enough to earn him his playing rights for next season. JP Hayes and Tim Herron tied for third.

MISSED THE CUT: Ben BATES 70 72, Michael CLARK II 71 71, Hunter HAAS 72 70, Andrew MAGEE 69 73, Mark McCUMBER 72 70, Frank NOBILO 72 70, Tom PERNICE Jr. 70 72, Joey SINDELAR 72 70, Omar URESTI 72 70, Jay WILLIAMSON 69 73, Danny ELLIS 70 73, Ben FERGUSON 72 71, Robin FREEMAN 71 72, Paul GOW 73 70, Kent JONES 73 70, Dick MAST 75 68, Shaun MICHEEL 69 74, Phil TATAURANGI 75 68, Jeff BREHAUT 72 72, Robert GAMEZ 72 72, Ian LEGGATT 72 72, Charles RAULERSON 74 70, Chris RILEY 71 73, Jeff SCHMID 72 72, Jim SCHUMAN 73 71, Garrett WILLIS 73 71, Gary HALLBERG 69 75, Mike HEINEN 73 72, Craig KANADA 70 75, Mike SPRINGER 73 72, Doug BARRON 75 71, Keith CLEARWATER 77 69, Mathew GOGGIN 74 72, Nolan HENKE 70 76, Glen HNATIUK 72 74, Mike HULBERT 70 76, D MORLAND IV 69 77, Dave SPENGLER 72 74, Ronnie BLACK 74 73, Barry CHEESMAN 76 71, Jay DELSING 73 74, Jim GALLAGHER Jr. 74 73, Brian HENNINGER 76 71, Mark HENSBY 76 71, Jeff JULIAN 74 73, John RESTINO 74 73, Brent SCHWARZROCK 73 74, Willie WOOD 72 75, Nick GILLIAM 70 78, Kelly GRUNEWALD 76 72, Brian WILSON 74 74, Larry RINKER 76 73, Greg KRAFT 77 73, Jake REEVES 76 74, Tom SCHERRER 75 75, Tommy TOLLES 72 78, Jedd McLUEN 78 73, Jason GORE 74 78, Rocky WALCHER 76 76, Steve ALLAN 72 82, Jeremy ANDERSON 76 78, Andy BEAN 79 76, CJ BROCK 79 76, Brad PECK 78 80, Roy LIVINGSTON 83 77, Mark WIEBE 72 W/D, Grant WAITE 76 W/D, Russ COCHRAN W/D.

Course Profile

Brown Deer Park Golf Club in Milwaukee (par 71, 6,739 yards) is an old style venue that you and I could score fairly well on and the pros can rip up like a pitch and putt layout.

It is short, so the longer hitters have no real advantage, and has five par threes.

The rough has been grown higher recently putting an emphasis on getting the ball on the putting surface in regulation.

Good putters prosper.

Players/Points to Note

●**Loren Roberts** has won this event twice and his 72-hole total of 260 in 2000 broke the four round record at Brown Deer Park. He always played this event (19 starts and five top-ten finishes) and is considered one of their own by the Milwaukee crowd.

●**Scott Hoch** and **Jeff Sluman** also come under that category – both have won and have numerous top-ten finishes (including 2001) in 14 starts apiece. And as far as Hoch is concerned with this tournament usually the week before the British Open – and with many of the US stars skipping this event in preparation for it – he's doubly keen to do well. He rarely plays in the UK and tries to make a point of winning in the US when the big tournaments are on in Europe.

●**Mark Calcavecchia** has skipped this event for the last two years but played in the previous 20 – posting nine top-ten finishes.

●**Jerry Kelly** is the local hero and is desperate to win his home tournament.

●**Steve Lowery** holds the course record at Brown Deer Park (61 in 1999) and can boast four top-ten finishes in his last six visits.

●**Andrew Magee**, **Steve Stricker**, **Nolan Henke**, **Frank Lickliter** and **Chris Perry** have also played consistently well over the past five years, posting multiple top-ten finishes.

Previous Results

2000: 1. Loren Roberts (-24), 2. Franklin Langham (-16), 3. Mathew Goggin (-15), J P Hayes (-15), Steve Pate (-15), Kenny Perry (-15).

1999: 1. Carlos Franco (-20), 2. Tom Lehman (-18), 3. Jerry Kelly (-16).

1998: 1. Jeff Sluman (-19), 2. Steve Stricker (-18), 3. Mark Calcavecchia (-16), Nolan Henke (-16), Chris Perry (-16).

1997: 1. Scott Hoch (-16), 2. Loren Roberts (-15), David Sutherland (-15).

1996: 1. Loren Roberts (-19), won play-off, 2. Jerry Kelly (-19), 3. Four players tied.

B C OPEN

En-Joie Golf Club, 19 Jul to 22 Jul 2001, purse $2,000,000

Pos	Name	R1	R2	R3	R4	Total	To par	Money	DD(y)	DA%	GIR%	Putts
1	Jeff SLUMAN	67	68	65	66	266	-22	$360,000	297.0	61	78	103
2	Paul GOW	69	65	66	66	266	-22	$216,000	297.5	72	78	110
3	Jonathan KAYE	67	65	70	67	269	-19	$136,000	303.0	68	79	111
4	Jay HAAS	68	68	66	68	270	-18	$96,000	296.5	66	74	109
5	Steve PATE	69	69	67	66	271	-17	$80,000	286.9	57	78	112
6	Stephen AMES	70	70	69	63	272	-16	$69,500	296.8	75	83	119
	Jim McGOVERN	67	66	68	71	272	-16	$69,500	309.3	68	74	110
8	Brett QUIGLEY	67	62	72	72	273	-15	$60,000	314.1	59	71	113
	Brian WATTS	66	72	67	68	273	-15	$60,000	303.9	70	61	102
10	Trevor DODDS	74	67	69	64	274	-14	$52,000	293.6	66	68	108
	Brad FABEL	66	71	69	68	274	-14	$52,000	289.4	57	69	108

Pos	Name	R1	R2	R3	R4	Total	To par
12	Ronnie BLACK	67	69	69	70	275	-13
	Edward FRYATT	65	68	73	69	275	-13
	C HOWELL III	70	71	68	66	275	-13
	Tim THELEN	73	66	68	68	275	-13
	Ted TRYBA	68	68	69	70	275	-13
17	M BRADLEY	71	68	68	69	276	-12
	Brad ELDER	72	65	69	70	276	-12
	Jerry SMITH	69	66	71	70	276	-12
	D.A. WEIBRING	67	69	72	68	276	-12
	Dan FORSMAN	70	68	68	70	276	-12
	John RIEGGER	71	64	69	72	276	-12
23	Ben BATES	70	69	68	70	277	-11
	Cliff KRESGE	70	69	70	68	277	-11
	Esteban TOLEDO	69	69	70	69	277	-11
	Omar URESTI	70	69	69	69	277	-11
27	Brad BRYANT	68	71	69	70	278	-10
	B CHEESMAN	70	70	69	69	278	-10
	K CLEARWATER	69	71	67	71	278	-10
	Joel EDWARDS	73	66	68	71	278	-10
	Ed FIORI	69	67	74	68	278	-10
	Mark HENSBY	66	66	70	76	278	-10
	Bradley HUGHES	70	69	68	71	278	-10
	Ian LEGGATT	73	66	69	70	278	-10
	Craig PARRY	69	68	69	72	278	-10
	Chris RILEY	70	71	69	68	278	-10
37	J ANDERSON	71	69	69	70	279	-9
	Jonathan BYRD	69	70	70	70	279	-9
	M CARNEVALE	67	73	65	74	279	-9
	Doug DUNAKEY	67	70	70	72	279	-9
	Michael MUEHR	68	70	72	69	279	-9
	Gene SAUERS	68	73	67	71	279	-9
	D STOCKTON Jr.	71	65	71	72	279	-9
	Brian WILSON	72	68	70	69	279	-9
	Ty TRYON	65	72	72	70	279	-9
46	Ben CURTIS	68	73	68	71	280	-8
	J.J. HENRY	71	66	73	70	280	-8
	Sam RANDOLPH	68	72	70	70	280	-8
	Willie WOOD	71	69	71	69	280	-8
50	Jay DELSING	70	69	71	71	281	-7
	Pete JORDAN	71	70	71	69	281	-7
	B McCALLISTER	71	68	72	70	281	-7
	Bobby WADKINS	71	70	71	69	281	-7
	Mike SPOSA	67	67	72	75	281	-7
	Chris TIDLAND	67	73	70	71	281	-7
56	Scott GUMP	71	68	74	69	282	-6
	Nolan HENKE	71	69	70	72	282	-6
	Glen HNATIUK	73	66	71	72	282	-6
	Mike HULBERT	67	73	71	71	282	-6
	Dicky PRIDE	73	68	68	73	282	-6
61	Steve ALLAN	74	67	71	71	283	-5
	Andy BEAN	68	69	73	73	283	-5
	Danny ELLIS	71	70	69	73	283	-5
	D HAMMOND	69	70	68	76	283	-5
	Kent JONES	72	66	73	72	283	-5
	Bob LOHR	69	69	73	72	283	-5
67	Woody AUSTIN	69	70	70	75	284	-4
	Jeff HART	66	73	72	73	284	-4
	Sean MURPHY	68	68	72	76	284	-4
70	Bart BRYANT	69	69	74	73	285	-3
	M HATALSKY	75	64	72	74	285	-3
	Dick MAST	70	71	68	76	285	-3
73	Doug BARRON	69	68	73	76	286	-2
	Wayne LEVI	69	69	73	75	286	-2
	John MORSE	72	69	72	73	286	-2
76	Dave BARR	69	71	72	75	287	-1
	Robin FREEMAN	67	72	72	76	287	-1
	Mike HEINEN	68	68	72	79	287	-1
79	Tim CONLEY	68	70	74	76	288	E
80	Jason GORE	69	72	74	74	289	+1
81	Marco DAWSON	70	71	75	74	290	+2
	Jeff JULIAN	71	69	72	78	290	+2
	Greg TWIGGS	71	66	76	77	290	+2
	Stan UTLEY	73	68	74	75	290	+2
85	Ernie GONZALEZ	68	73	76	83	300	+3
86	Garrett WILLIS	66	72	-	-	D	

Tournament Report

After six play-off defeats Jeff Sluman finally managed to win a tournament by way of extra holes when he got the better of Paul Gow to claim the BC Open at the En-Joie Golf Club in New York.

With all the big names away playing the British Open, this was an opportunity for some of the lesser lights to shine. And Sluman and Gow took centre stage by dominating the weekend play.

The pair posted Saturday scores of 65 and 66 respectively to tie for the lead after the third round. And for much of the last round there was little between them.

Sluman, though, looked like he had the title in the bag after Gow could only manage a bogey at the 17th hole to hand his rival a two shot lead heading to the last.

But Sluman, though, fired his approach to the 18th over the green and failed to get up and down and signed for a five. Gow meanwhile, had rolled in a birdie putt to send the contest into extra time.

Sluman was also in trouble on the first extra hole but salvaged par to keep his hopes alive.

Then, on the second hole, Sluman stroked in an eight-foot birdie putt, to which Gow had no answer, to win his fifth US Tour career win. For Gow, second place was the Australian's highest ever finish on the US Tour. Jonathan Kaye was third – two shots behind the play-off competitors, while veteran pro Jay Haas was fourth.

MISSED THE CUT: Brian CLAAR 68 74, Jimmy GREEN 72 70, Tripp ISENHOUR 68 74, Craig KANADA 71 71, James A. McLEAN 72 70, David OGRIN 69 73, Dan POHL 69 73, Tom SCHERRER 71 71, Mike SPRINGER 72 70, Craig STADLER 70 72, Mike STANDLY 68 74, Mike SULLIVAN 71 71, Curt BYRUM 73 70, Kelly GRUNEWALD 73 70, Terry HATCH 70 73, Mark PFEIL 74 69, Craig A. SPENCE 69 74, Rocky WALCHER 77 66, Jim BENEPE 72 72, Hunter HAAS 72 72, Len MATTIACE 71 73, Don POOLEY 72 72, Jack RENNER 74 70, Larry RINKER 74 70, Alex ROCHA 72 72, Don BELL 68 77, Dennis COLLIGAN 70 75, Mike DONALD 71 74, Keith FERGUS 77 68, Bill GLASSON 73 72, Brent SCHWARZROCK 71 74, Richie COUGHLAN 72 74, Fred FUNK 78 68, Jim GALLAGHER Jr. 72 74, Gary NICKLAUS 73 73, Tommy TOLLES 75 71, Matt ABBOTT 72 75, Jay WILLIAMSON 72 75, Ben FERGUSON 71 77, Dave RUMMELLS 76 72, Gary HALLBERG 76 73, Greg POWERS 74 76, Adam RUSHIN 72 78, Phil TATAURANGI 79 71, Guy BOROS 81 71, Dan HALLDORSON 79 73, Robert GAMEZ 76 77, Chris GONZALES 76 77, Bobby COLE 77 78, Jay TURCSIK 79 76, Paul ZUREK 80 75, Richie KARL 78 78, Neal LANCASTER D 70 70, Shaun MICHEEL 76 W/D, Joey SINDELAR 76 W/D, Ken GREEN W/D, Gabriel HJERTSTEDT W/D, Barry JAECKEL D.

Course Profile

The En Joie Golf Club (par 72, 6,947 yards) in New York has been redesigned in recent years, with some of the greens increased in size by 25%.

Off the tee, accurate golfers prosper, as the fairways are tree lined and can punish errant drives. Water hazards come into play on ten holes.

The final holes require a lot of bottle and it is perhaps easier to defend a lead than come from behind to win.

Players/Points to Note

● **Jeff Sluman**'s win last year came as no surprise as he had already placed in the top ten of this event on seven occasions in 16 starts. He had finished as runner-up twice and had missed the cut just once in his career.

● **Brad Faxon** has won this twice (in 1999 and 2000) but didn't go for a three-peat as he was playing in the British Open.

● **Fred Funk** should have won in 2000, carded the course record of 61 in the 1999 and did win in 1996. His accurate style is well suited to this tight track.

● **Chris Perry**, **Bill Glasson**, **Nolan Henke** and **Blaine McCallister** are all past winners with multiple top-ten finishes. Perry and Henke have also finished second. **Skip Kendall** and **Jonathan Kaye** have also got decent records in this event.

● This tournament is opposite the British Open in 2002, so a weak field will contest the event again. Of the last 12 champions, four were winning their first regular US Tour tournament.

● The last two champions, though, have been stalwarts of the US Tour for a long time and with the British Open getting all the headlines, it may be their way of reminding the public that they are still around.

● Younger players to note in 2002 are **Charles Howell** and **Ed Fryatt**.

Previous Results

2000: 1. Brad Faxon (-18), 2. Esteban Toledo (-17), 3. Bill Glasson (-14), Glen Hnatiuk (-14).

1999: 1. Brad Faxon (-15), won play-off, 2. Fred Funk (-15), 3. Rory Sabbatini (-14).

1998: 1. Chris Perry (-15), 2. Peter Jacobsen (-12), 3. Nolan Henke (-11).

1997: 1. Gabriel Hjerstedt (-13), 2. Lee Rinker (-12), Chris Perry (-12), Andrew Magee (-12).

1996: 1. Fred Funk (-16), won play-off, 2. Pete Jordan (-16), 3. Patrick Burke (-13), Tiger Woods (-13). Played over 54 holes.

JOHN DEERE CLASSIC

TPC at Deere Run, 26 Jul to 29 Jul 2001, purse $2,800,000

Pos	Name	R1	R2	R3	R4	Total	To par	Money	DD(y)	DA%	GIR%	Putts
1	David GOSSETT	67	64	68	66	265	-19	$504,000	288.4	75	81	114
2	Briny BAIRD	69	65	66	66	266	-18	$302,400	287.1	93	83	117
3	Pete JORDAN	69	68	65	65	267	-17	$190,400	273.3	84	76	111
4	Jeff SLUMAN	70	65	68	65	268	-16	$134,400	301.9	73	82	117
5	Matt GOGEL	68	66	67	68	269	-15	$106,400	309.3	84	71	109
	Ian LEGGATT	67	68	68	66	269	-15	$106,400	289.5	72	76	116
7	P STANKOWSKI	67	67	66	70	270	-14	$93,800	300.5	70	71	107
8	Woody AUSTIN	69	66	69	67	271	-13	$84,000	285.1	72	72	112
	Brian CLAAR	66	69	66	70	271	-13	$84,000	286.6	77	74	112
10	Barry CHEESMAN	71	67	66	68	272	-12	$67,200	277.3	75	76	117
	Paul GOW	65	69	69	69	272	-12	$67,200	297.8	79	74	116
	Bradley HUGHES	69	65	66	72	272	-12	$67,200	291.9	77	72	112
	Jerry SMITH	65	69	67	71	272	-12	$67,200	274.1	73	64	109

Pos	Name	R1	R2	R3	R4	Total	To par
14	John RIEGGER	67	69	72	65	273	-11
15	Olin BROWNE	68	71	65	70	274	-10
	Edward FRYATT	66	67	69	72	274	-10
	Bill GLASSON	72	69	67	66	274	-10
	Kent JONES	68	64	73	69	274	-10
	Steve JONES	70	67	66	71	274	-10
	N LANCASTER	69	71	67	67	274	-10
	Steve LOWFRY	66	70	67	71	274	-10
	S McCARRON	70	69	67	68	274	-10
	A McLARDY	64	71	70	69	274	-10
	Kirk TRIPLETT	73	68	66	67	274	-10
25	Bart BRYANT	68	70	69	68	275	-9
	Brad ELDER	68	69	69	69	275	-9
	D HAMMOND	68	70	69	68	275	-9
	C HOWELL III	70	69	66	70	275	-9
29	Matt KUCHAR	69	66	73	68	276	-8
	Tommy TOLLES	67	72	69	68	276	-8
	Steve ALLAN	65	76	68	67	276	-8
	D BERGANIO Jr.	70	67	67	72	276	-8
	Fred FUNK	70	70	69	67	276	-8
	Bob MAY	67	67	70	72	276	-8
35	Spike McROY	70	69	69	69	277	-7
	Craig PERKS	69	70	69	69	277	-7
	Doug BARRON	69	70	68	70	277	-7
	C BECKMAN	70	70	71	66	277	-7
	Glen DAY	67	68	70	72	277	-7
	Brad FABEL	69	71	70	67	277	-7
	Scott GUMP	69	72	70	66	277	-7
	Len MATTIACE	70	71	68	68	277	-7
	D MORLAND IV	66	68	73	70	277	-7
	Craig PARRY	68	69	71	69	277	-7
	Lee PORTER	70	68	69	70	277	-7
46	M CHRISTENSEN	67	70	70	71	278	-6
	Kevin JOHNSON	71	71	66	70	278	-6
	Dicky PRIDE	70	70	69	69	278	-6
	Brett QUIGLEY	67	72	70	69	278	-6
	J WILLIAMSON	71	66	70	71	278	-6
	Willie WOOD	69	69	72	68	278	-6
52	Dan FORSMAN	70	71	66	72	279	-5
	Jimmy GREEN	69	69	71	70	279	-5
	Jim McGOVERN	69	70	68	72	279	-5
	Michael MUEHR	74	67	69	69	279	-5
	B SCHWARZROCK	70	71	69	69	279	-5
	D.A. WEIBRING	69	71	70	69	279	-5
58	J ANDERSON	69	72	68	71	280	-4
	Shaun MICHEEL	70	69	67	74	280	-4
	Esteban TOLEDO	69	70	72	69	280	-4
61	Ronnie BLACK	72	69	70	70	281	-3
	Jim CARTER	70	70	73	68	281	-3
	Gary HALLBERG	67	71	73	70	281	-3
	B HENNINGER	71	67	71	72	281	-3
	John HUSTON	72	68	68	73	281	-3
	J.L. LEWIS	64	72	69	76	281	-3
	Gary NICKLAUS	73	66	69	73	281	-3
68	M BRADLEY	70	68	71	73	282	-2
	Jason GORE	68	70	75	69	282	-2
	Jeff HART	69	71	71	71	282	-2
	Joey SINDELAR	70	71	70	71	282	-2
	Chris ZAMBRI	73	67	68	74	282	-2
73	H FRAZAR	73	68	71	71	283	-1
74	M CARNEVALE	69	72	70	73	284	E
	Tim HERRON	69	72	70	73	284	E
	Craig KANADA	71	69	67	77	284	E
	Brian WATTS	69	67	73	75	284	E
78	Joe OGILVIE	71	70	75	69	285	+1
	Fuzzy ZOELLER	70	71	73	71	285	+1
80	D STOCKTON Jr.	67	74	74	71	286	+2
81	Guy BOROS	68	73	75	71	287	+3
	Nolan HENKE	71	70	73	73	287	+3
83	Ben BATES	70	71	71	76	288	+4
84	Jeff JULIAN	71	70	75	76	292	+8

Sponsored by Stan James

Tournament Report

David Gossett became the seventh first time winner on the US Tour this season – and the first since Tiger Woods in 1996 to post victory playing under a sponsor's exemption – by claiming the John Deere Classic title at Deere Run in Illinois.

Gossett shot a 59 in Q-School but failed to get his card and has had to rely on sponsors invites for his previous five US Tour starts this season. But after sharpening up his skills on the Buy.Com Tour this term he dominated the action at the Silvis track, leading after Friday's play and never being headed.

The chasing pack did challenge on the last day, though, as Briny Baird, who started the day a shot adrift of Gossett at the start of the final round (along with Paul Stankowski and Bradley Hughes) and Pete Jordan hauled themselves level with the eventual winner at one stage or another.

Firstly, Jordan would get on equal terms when he birdied the seventh and then Baird would also share parity with Gossett after picking up a shot at the 14th. But when Gossett birdied the 15th he stayed out in front for good.

Another birdie at the par three 16th, which took him to 19 under par, effectively sealed the win. Five of the top six shot 66 or better on a day where low scoring was the norm. Baird was second, despite taking a bogey at the 16th, while Jordan, whose weekend total of 130 wasn't bettered, took third.

MISSED THE CUT: Bob BURNS 71 71, Jay DELSING 71 71, Rick FEHR 74 68, David FROST 69 73, Tom PERNICE Jr. 70 72, Chris SMITH 70 72, Mike STANDLY 71 71, Chris TIDLAND 73 69, Ted TRYBA 71 71, Bob TWAY 70 72, Chip BECK 69 74, Rich BEEM 71 72, Michael CLARK II 74 69, Doug DUNAKEY 70 73, Danny ELLIS 69 74, Robert GAMEZ 72 71, Mike HEINEN 72 71, Mike HULBERT 69 74, Brandt JOBE 72 71, Andrew MAGEE 70 73, Larry MIZE 72 71, Dan POHL 70 73, Brian WILSON 75 68, Robert DAMRON 71 73, Robin FREEMAN 73 71, Ken GREEN 72 72, Greg KRAFT 71 73, Sam RANDOLPH 71 73, John RESTINO 73 71, Chris RILEY 72 72, Grant WAITE 73 71, Keith CLEARWATER 74 71, Ben FERGUSON 70 75, Mathew GOGGIN 72 73, Cliff KRESGE 75 70, Sean MURPHY 73 72, Phil TATAURANGI 73 72, Rocky WALCHER 73 72, Ed FIORI 75 71, Tripp ISENHOUR 73 73, Carl PAULSON 74 72, Larry RINKER 76 70, Gene SAUERS 71 75, Tom SCHERRER 74 72, Craig A. SPENCE 73 73, Mike SPOSA 70 76, Mike DONALD 74 73, John SHAWVER 72 75, Stan UTLEY 74 73, Stephen AMES 72 76, John BERMEL 77 71, Jim GALLAGHER Jr. 75 73, Paul GOYDOS 74 74, Mike SPRINGER 76 72, Mike SULLIVAN 74 74, Blaine McCALLISTER 74 75, Mike REID 72 77, Richie COUGHLAN 76 74, Brian CONSER 77 74, Tom MILLER 76 75, Chris O'CONNELL 74 77, Emanuele CANONICA 74 78, Dave RUMMELLS 75 77, Andy BEAN 76 77, Dan HALLDORSON 78 75, Kevin KEMP 76 80, Kelly GRUNEWALD 71 W/D, Charlie RYMER 73 W/D, Mark HENSBY 75 W/D, David PEOPLES 76 W/D, Craig BARLOW W/D, Dave BARR W/D.

Course Profile

TPC at Deere Run (par 71, 7,183 yards) in Silvis, Illinois This layout runs along the top of a ridge and can be seriously affected by stiff winds.

Power isn't the key to success but with only moderate rough, players can get away with some loose tee shots.

Accuracy, though, will still be needed to a degree with the driver.

The greens are large and some prowess with the putter is required.

Players/Points to Note

●2000 was the first time the John Deere Classic was held at TPC Deere Run. In 2000 and 2001, this event was won by players who had yet to win on the US Tour. The best players over the past two years are:

●**Kirk Triplett** was 15th last year and second in 2000. **Charles Howell**'s form figures since 2000 are 3-25, **Neal Lancaster**'s 8-15, **Steve Lowery**'s 5-15, **Bill Glasson**'s 12-15 and **Steve Jones**' 12-15. **Tim Herron** was seventh in 2000 and had played the layout non-competitively.

●Triplett and Jones both had form in this event prior to it moving to Deere Run. Triplett had two top-ten finishes before his was beaten in a play-off in 2000. Jones was fifth in 1999, 12 months after winning.

●Of the players that have done well in this event over the past decade or so, the best records belong to:

DA Weibring – who has won this event on three occasions, is 124-under par in 21 starts and has finished in the top ten eight times. DA should know the venue well as he designed it. **David Frost** – a former dual winner (1992 and 1993 – the only time a defending champion has been successful) and multiple top-ten finisher (5). **Scott Hoch** – 1980 and 1984 champion and eight top tens in 14 starts.

Previous Results

2000: 1. Michael Clark II (-19), won play-off, 2. Kirk Triplett (-19), 3. Charles Howell III (-18).

1999: 1. J. L. Lewis (-19), won play-off, 2. Mike Brisky (-19), 3. Kirk Triplett (-16), Brian Henninger (-16).

1998: 1. Steve Jones (-17), 2. Scott Gump (-16), 3. Kenny Perry (-15).

1997: 1. David Toms (-15), 2. Jimmy Johnston (-12), Brandel Chamblee (-12), Robert Gamez (-12).

1996: 1. Ed Fiori (-12), 2. Andrew Magee (-10), 3. Chris Perry (-9), Steve Jones (-9).

143

THE INTERNATIONAL PRESENTED BY QWEST

Castle Pines Golf Club, 2 Aug to 5 Aug 2001, purse $4,000,000

Pos	Name	R1	R2	R3	R4	To par	Money
1	Tom PERNICE Jr.	+12	+12	+9	+1	+34	$720,000
2	Chris RILEY	+16	+5	+8	+4	+33	$432,000
3	Ernie ELS	+9	+7	+10	+6	+32	$208,000
	Chris DiMARCO	+7	+13	+8	+4	+32	$208,000
	Vijay SINGH	+9	+9	+12	+2	+32	$208,000
6	Brett QUIGLEY	+9	+6	+2	+13	+30	$139,000
	Brad FAXON	+8	+10	+4	+8	+30	$139,000
8	Woody AUSTIN	+11	+8	+8	+1	+28	$124,000
9	Mark O'MEARA	+12	+3	+4	+8	+27	$112,000
	Edward FRYATT	+9	+11	+2	+5	+27	$112,000

Pos	Name	R1	R2	R3	R4	To par
11	C HOWELL	+11	+8	+8	-1	+26
	Sergio GARCIA	+7	+12	+7	0	+26
	Kenny PERRY	0	+10	+11	+5	+26
14	Tim HERRON	+9	+11	+2	+3	+25
15	J M OLAZABAL	+12	+5	0	+7	+24
	Bob MAY	+3	+8	+6	+7	+24
	Kirk TRIPLETT	+10	+7	+3	+4	+24
18	Jay Don BLAKE	+7	+1	+10	+5	+23
	Steve FLESCH	+6	+8	+6	+3	+23
20	S McCARRON	+13	+3	0	+6	+22
	Steve JONES	+6	+2	+10	+4	+22
	Duffy WALDORF	+13	0	+5	+4	+22
	Justin LEONARD	+7	+12	+3	0	+22
24	H FRAZAR	+11	+2	+3	+5	+21
	David DUVAL	+11	+5	+2	+3	+21
26	Stewart CINK	+8	+14	-4	+2	+20
	Rory SABBATINI	+14	0	+5	+1	+20
28	C BECKMAN	+5	+2	+9	+3	+19
	J VAN DE VELDE	+8	+2	+10	-1	+19
	Stuart APPLEBY	+2	+12	+9	-4	+19
31	Ted TRYBA	+3	+12	+4	-1	+18
32	B GEIBERGER	+12	+8	-3	0	+17
33	Stephen AMES	+3	+7	+7	-1	+16
34	Spike McROY	+4	+5	+7	-1	+15
	Bill GLASSON	+6	+7	+3	-1	+15
	Lee JANZEN	+17	-1	+4	-5	+15
37	Paul GOW	+7	+8	+1	-5	+11

FAILED TO QUALIFY FOR SUNDAY

Pos	Name	R1	R2	R3	R4	To par
38	Billy ANDRADE	+5	+8	+2	-	+15
	John HUSTON	+7	+7	+1	-	+15
	Bob TWAY	+7	+3	+5	-	+15
	Briny BAIRD	+1	+7	+7	-	+15

Pos	Name	R1	R2	R3	R4	To par
42	John COOK	+9	+4	+1	-	+14
	Chris TIDLAND	+1	+10	+3	-	+14
	Jeff BREHAUT	0	+9	+5	-	+14
45	P STANKOWSKI	+3	+9	+1	-	+13
	D BERGANIO	+9	+3	+1	-	+13
	Mike SPOSA	+5	+3	+5	-	+13
	K. J. CHOI	+10	+7	4	-	+13
	Jay HAAS	+1	+7	+5	-	+13
	Jerry KELLY	+4	+3	+6	-	+13
51	Russ COCHRAN	+7	+4	+1	-	+12
	Jim McGOVERN	+2	+8	+2	-	+12
	Joey SINDELAR	+9	+4	-2	-	+11
	Greg NORMAN	+5	+5	+1	-	+11
	Craig STADLER	+6	+3	+2	-	+11
	David PEOPLES	+8	0	+3	-	+11
57	Angel CABRERA	+5	+6	-1	-	+10
	Glen DAY	+1	+6	+3	-	+10
59	Lee PORTER	+3	+8	-2	-	+9
	Tommy TOLLES	+11	0	-2	-	+9
	Jonathan KAYE	+5	+5	-1	-	+9
62	Tripp ISENHOUR	+8	+4	-4	-	+8
	Mathew GOGGIN	+11	+4	-7	-	+8
	Craig PARRY	+1	+6	+1	-	+8
65	Shaun MICHEEL	+11	-1	-3	-	+7
	Glen HNATIUK	-1	+11	-3	-	+7
67	Olin BROWNE	+7	+4	-5	-	+6
	Bob BURNS	+8	+1	-3	-	+6
	Dan FORSMAN	+6	+2	-2	-	+6
	Chris SMITH	+8	-1	-1	-	+6
71	Phil MICKELSON	+11	+5	-11	-	+5
72	Andrew MAGEE	+5	+6	-9	-	+2
	S ELKINGTON	+1	+6	-5	-	+2

Tournament Report

Of the 37 players that played the final round of The International, Tom Pernice outscored just three of them.

But that didn't stop the 41-year-old journeyman pro from completing victory in this modified Stableform scoring system event at Castle Pines Golf Club in Colorado.

Pernice had netted 33 points in the first three rounds, where players receive eight points for an albatross, five for eagle, two for birdie, zero for par, minus one for bogey and minus three for double bogey or worse.

And it meant that the single point he managed on the final day was just enough to hang on for victory. Not surprisingly, it was Pernice's ability to scramble pars and bogeys on the last day that secured his win.

He was particularly grateful for a miracle recovery on the 16th, when he escaped with just one dropped point instead of what looked like a certain minus three score.

After finding the bunker on the par three hole, his first effort to blast out failed, but with the ball in an even worse lie he managed to hoist it from the sand to within inches of the hole. He tapped in for bogey.

None of the stars names could manage a double figure score on the final day and when they did have the chances to close on Pernice they failed – notably when Vijay Singh drove into the water on the 17th when just one behind the eventual winner.

Castle Pines regular Phil Mickelson put in one of his worst performances in the event in 2001. Having been a very consistent player in this tournament over the years, the left hander inexplicably fell away after bagging 16 points over the first two days.

MISSED THE CUT: Steve ALLAN, Tommy ARMOUR III, Craig BARLOW, Rich BEEM, Mark CALCAVECCHIA, Emanuele CANONICA, Jim CARTER, Greg CHALMERS, Michael CLARK II, Jose COCERES, John DALY, Doug DUNAKEY, Brad ELDER, Bob ESTES, Rick FEHR, Ben FERGUSON, Robin FREEMAN, Jim GALLAGHER, Jr., Brian GAY, Matt GOGEL, Jason GORE, David GOSSETT, Paul GOYDOS, Jimmy GREEN, Ken GREEN D, Hunter HAAS, Gary HALLBERG, Dudley HART, Jeff HART, Brian HENNINGER, J.J. HENRY, Bradley HUGHES, Mike HULBERT, Brandt JOBE, Kevin JOHNSON, Pete JORDAN, Craig KANADA, Skip KENDALL, Greg KRAFT, Cliff KRESGE, Neal LANCASTER, Franklin LANGHAM, J.L. LEWIS, Steve LOWERY, Len MATTIACE, Billy MAYFAIR, Larry MIZE, D MORLAND IV, David MUEHR, Gary NICKLAUS, Frank NOBILO, Joe OGILVIE, Steve PATE, Corey PAVIN, Craig PERKS, Mike REID, John RIEGGER, Eduardo ROMERO, Clarence ROSE, Tom SCHERRER, Jeev Milkha SINGH, David SMAIL, Steve STRICKER, Kevin SUTHERLAND, Esteban TOLEDO, David TOMS, Grant WAITE, Mark WIEBE, Jay WILLIAMSON, Garrett WILLIS, Brian WILSON.

Course Profile

The Castle Pines course (par 72, 7,559 yards) is long but as it's over 6,000 feet above sea level the ball travels further.

Players with little experience at the track can find it hard to judge just how far their shots might go.

Jack Nicklaus designed the layout and golfers have to be physically fit, as there are plenty of elevation changes between holes.

The greens are large and fast, and the fairways relatively narrow.

Players/Points to Note

●The modified stableford scoring system rewards aggressive, attacking play. So before making your selection, check out the eagle and birdie leaders statistics.

●**Phil Mickelson** could only manage 71st in 2001 – his second worst finish ever in this event. But his overall record his superb from 1992 his form figures read 15-Win-10-MC-16-Win-2-16-2-71. Mickelson also has the most amount of points gained in this event (48, along with **Ernie Els**) and the biggest winning margin (eight in 1993).

●Els has five top-five finishes in this event and won here in 2000. The layout is perfect for the South African. As it is for **Vijay Singh**, who was third last year and won here in 1998.

●**Brad Faxon** isn't massive off the tee but his prowess with the putter means he can make plenty of birdies. He won in 1993 and has five top-ten finishes.

●**Sergio Garcia** will win this event one day and his form figures suggest he is getting closer – 13-14-11. **Jose Maria Olazabal** won here in 1991 and always plays well in this event (he was 15th last year).

●**Stuart Appleby**, **David Duval** and **Tiger Woods** all have the game for the venue.

●Decent outside bets in 2002 would be **Ed Fryatt** and **Chris Riley**, both of whom have placed in the top 15 in the last two renewals.

Previous Results

2000: 1. Ernie Els (48), 2. Phil Mickelson (44), 3. Stuart Appleby (41).

1999: 1. David Toms (47), 2. David Duval (44), 3. Stephem Ames (43).

1998: 1. Vijay Singh (47), 2. Willie Wood (41), Phil Mickelson (41).

1997: 1. Phil Mickelson (48), 2. Stuart Appleby (41), 3. Skip Kendall (38).

1996: 1. Clarence Rose (31), won play-off, 2. Brad Faxon (31), 3. Bob Tway (30), Michael Bradley (30).

BUICK OPEN
Warwick Hills G.&C.C., 9 Aug to 12 Aug 2001, purse $3,100,000

Pos	Name	R1	R2	R3	R4	Total	To par	Money	DD(y)	DA%	GIR%	Putts
1	Kenny PERRY	66	64	64	69	263	-25	$558,000	308.0	68	81	112
2	Chris DiMARCO	68	67	65	65	265	-24	$272,800	295.3	77	85	114
	Jim FURYK	64	69	66	66	265	-24	$272,800	291.5	73	78	107
4	Dudley HART	68	70	65	64	267	-21	$136,400	310.3	61	78	109
	Tom PERNICE Jr.	68	67	66	66	267	-21	$136,400	305.1	59	78	111
6	Brian GAY	70	67	66	65	268	-20	$107,725	281.6	75	81	109
	P HARRINGTON	67	67	65	69	268	-20	$107,725	310.3	72	83	116
8	Ian LEGGATT	66	68	69	66	269	-19	$93,000	302.0	64	76	116
	Jeff MAGGERT	69	66	68	66	269	-19	$93,000	300.6	75	86	118
10	Justin LEONARD	69	68	63	70	270	-18	$74,400	293.9	73	75	110
	Frank LICKLITER II	68	70	69	63	270	-18	$74,400	302.8	70	78	111
	Phil MICKELSON	65	70	71	64	270	-18	$74,400	301.1	64	76	115
	Bob TWAY	68	65	67	70	270	-18	$74,400	295.8	70	79	111

Pos	Name	R1	R2	R3	R4	Total	To par
14	Stephen AMES	69	66	68	68	271	-17
	Tom BYRUM	73	63	67	68	271	-17
	Skip KENDALL	69	70	66	66	271	-17
	Billy MAYFAIR	69	70	71	61	271	-17
	Craig PERKS	66	68	68	69	271	-17
	S VERPLANK	68	67	68	68	271	-17
20	Brian WILSON	67	70	64	71	272	-16
21	Woody AUSTIN	67	68	68	70	273	-15
	Russ COCHRAN	68	71	68	66	273	-15
	Fred FUNK	73	63	72	65	273	-15
	B HENNINGER	64	71	70	68	273	-15
	Loren ROBERTS	69	69	67	68	273	-15
	Jeff SLUMAN	68	69	68	68	273	-15
27	John COOK	66	68	70	70	274	-14
	J WILLIAMSON	70	65	69	70	274	-14
29	Craig BARLOW	70	69	71	65	275	-13
	Brandt JOBE	72	68	69	66	275	-13
	Ben BATES	69	66	69	71	275	-13
	Stewart CINK	73	67	67	68	275	-13
	D HAMMOND	67	69	70	69	275	-13
	J VAN DE VELDE	66	71	70	68	275	-13
35	Jim CARTER	68	70	68	70	276	-12
	Katsumune IMAI	69	70	71	66	276	-12
	Jonathan KAYE	67	67	71	71	276	-12
	David TOMS	68	69	70	69	276	-12
	Stuart APPLEBY	68	71	64	73	276	-12
	Jay Don BLAKE	67	68	70	71	276	-12
	Steve FLESCH	66	70	67	73	276	-12
	Larry MIZE	67	71	67	71	276	-12
43	Olin BROWNE	69	71	70	67	277	-11
	Bob BURNS	71	69	69	68	277	-11
	B CHEESMAN	72	65	75	65	277	-11
	Rocco MEDIATE	70	68	71	68	277	-11
	G CHALMERS	67	72	68	70	277	-11
	N LANCASTER	68	72	68	69	277	-11
49	Paul AZINGER	70	70	70	68	278	-10
	M CLARK II	71	69	69	69	278	-10
	Joel EDWARDS	67	69	69	73	278	-10
	David FROST	68	70	71	69	278	-10
	Jay HAAS	70	69	69	70	278	-10
	David PEOPLES	66	69	69	74	278	-10
	Brett QUIGLEY	68	65	72	73	278	-10
	Heath SLOCUM	73	66	70	69	278	-10
57	Briny BAIRD	66	72	69	72	279	-9
	Glen DAY	69	70	70	70	279	-9
	Brad ELDER	69	70	74	66	279	-9
	Paul GOW	68	71	71	69	279	-9
	Spike McROY	69	71	71	68	279	-9
62	J.P. HAYES	70	70	68	72	280	-8
	Tripp ISENHOUR	70	69	73	68	280	-8
	Mark O'MEARA	67	72	72	69	280	-8
	Dicky PRIDE	69	66	74	71	280	-8
66	Jerry SMITH	70	69	69	73	281	-7
67	D BERGANIO Jr.	68	71	73	70	282	-6
	Jeff BREHAUT	68	71	71	72	282	-6
69	Joe OGILVIE	72	67	72	72	283	-6
	Craig A. SPENCE	71	69	78	65	283	-6
71	Carlos FRANCO	73	67	71	73	284	-4
	J ANDERSON	71	66	W/D			

Tournament Report

Kenny Perry ended the third day of the Buick Open with a five-stroke lead on the field but admitted he got precious little sleep on the night before the final round.

He showed no signs of anxiety on Sunday, though, as he went on to land his fourth US Tour victory of his career at Warwick Hills.

By the time Perry had arrived on the course the fireworks on it had already started. Billy Mayfair ripped up the back nine on the Michigan track, coming home in 27 shots – nine under, a US Tour record for nine holes.

Mayfair's 18-hole score of 61 was also a tournament record and his birdie/eagle streak of eight holes also a US Tour best. It lifted him up from 56th to 14th place.

But it wasn't to affect Perry, who built his overnight lead courtesy of scores of 64 twice on Friday and Saturday, in the process setting a new first on the US Tour himself – that of scoring 29 for nine holes twice in the same tournament. And with such a lead he just needed to keep his golf neat and tidy to land his first win for six years.

That he did with a controlled 69 to win by two strokes from Jim Furyk and Chris DiMarco, both of whom jumped into the top dozen of the Ryder Cup standings. On a day of low scoring only seven of the 71 players who made the cut failed to break par.

MISSED THE CUT: Bart BRYANT 71 70, Mark CALCAVECCHIA 70 71, Joe DURANT 70 71, Danny ELLIS 73 68, Robin FREEMAN 72 69, Retief GOOSEN 70 71, Greg KRAFT 70 71, Cliff KRESGE 72 69, Jose Maria OLAZABAL 73 68, Naomichi Joe OZAKI 70 71, Brent SCHWARZROCK 70 71, Esteban TOLEDO 69 72, Duffy WALDORF 72 69, Garrett WILLIS 72 69, Willie WOOD 70 71, Glen HNATIUK 75 67, J.L. LEWIS 73 69, Andrew MAGEE 69 73, Frank NOBILO 72 70, Craig PARRY 74 68, C PERRY 72 70, L PORTER 71 71, J RESTINO 75 67, H SUTTON 72 70, T ARMOUR III 72 71, B CRENSHAW 73 70, R GAMEZ 74 69, K GRUNEWALD 72 71, G HJERTSTEDT 71 72, J McGOVERN 71 72, D MORLAND IV 69 74, M SPOSA 73 70, C TIDLAND 71 72, J COCERES 68 76, J GORE 74 70, P GOYDOS 72 72, J GREEN 72 72, H HAAS 73 71, J HART 73 71, P-U JOHANSSON 75 69, C KANADA 72 72, M MUEHR 73 71, C PAULSON 70 74, T RAKOTZ 70 74, M STANDLY 72 72, P TATAURANGI 71 73, B WATTS 73 71, K WENTWORTH 72 72, D BRIGGS 75 70, P JACOBSEN 73 72, A McLARDY 73 72, S MURPHY 70 75, S PATE 73 72, T TANIGUCHI 70 75, T TRYBA 74 71, S ALLAN 72 74, B FERGUSON 74 72, B GEIBERGER 73 73, K JOHNSON 71 75, K JONES 69 77, J SINDELAR 75 71, B CAIRNS 73 74, M DAWSON 74 73, M GOGEL 73 74, P JORDAN 73 74, F LANGHAM 73 74, J McPHERSON 75 72, R WALCHER 75 72, R ALLENBY 72 76, T LEHMAN 71 77, G NICKLAUS 73 75, R COUGHLAN 76 73, B FAXON 73 76, D STOCKTON, Jr. 76 74, R DAMRON 76 75, D DUNAKEY 74 77, T TOLLES 75 76, J GNIEWEK 75 77, M GOGGIN 77 76, S SALL 79 74, E CANONICA 80 76, D PING 81 86, M McCUMBER 77 W/D, D BARRON 79 W/D.

Course Profile

Length is an obvious advantage at Warwick Hills Golf Club in Michigan (par 72, 7,127 yards) but by no means a necessity. Players with a good putting touch can also prosper.

The course is long, though, and the fairways generous with what little rough there is not particularly high.

Hitting the bigger than average greens in regulation helps.

Most players will feel comfortable on the course and scores will be low.

Players/Points to Note

●Big hitters are usually the sort of players that do well at the Buick Opon.

●**Tom Pernice**, who has won at the monster Castle Pines course in Colorado, has won here, as has **Vijay Singh** (1997 champion) and **Fred Couples** (1994). The pair boast six top-ten finishes between them.

●**Ernie Els** has a stroke average of 68.81 in four visits, **Hal Sutton** has the length and accurate iron play to prosper.

●**Phil Mickelson** was tenth last year after a fast-finishing 64 – posting his second successive top-ten position. **Tiger Woods'** record here is 8-4-DNP-11-DNP.

●**Kenny Perry** was 16th in 2000 before winning in 2001. **Justin Leonard** won here in 1996 and tenth here in 2001.

●**Rocco Mediate's** form figures now read 8-29-9-Win-43 over the past five years.

●**Brad Faxon**, **Fred Funk** (joint course record holder – 62 – with **Jim Furyk**) and **Scott Hoch** have 15 top-tens between them, suggesting it's not just the power players that can succeed.

●**Furyk**, in fact, hasn't finished lower than 38th in seven visits and can count five top-16 finishes. **Woody Austin** won in 1995 and has finished in the top 15 three times since.

●Look for players who can shoot really low scores as there are always plenty of birdies on offer at the Warwick Hills venue. Grinders don't tend to win here.

Previous Results

2000: 1. Rocco Mediate (-20), 2. Chris Perry (-19), 3. Hal Sutton (-17).

1999: 1. Tom Pernice Jr (-18), 2. Tom Lehman (-17), Ted Tryba (-17), Bob Tway (-17).

1998: 1. Billy Mayfair (-17), 2. Scott Verplank (-15), 3. Andrew Magee (-14).

1997: 1. Vijay Singh (-15), 2. Six players tied.

1996: 1. Justin Leonard (-22), 2. Chip Beck (-17), 3. Four players tied.

Montreux G.&C.C., 23 Aug to 26 Aug 2001, purse $3,000,000

Pos	Name	R1	R2	R3	R4	Total	To par	Money	DD(y)	DA%	GIR%	Putts
1	John COOK	69	64	74	64	271	-17	$540,000	290.6	80.4	75.0	109
2	Jerry KELLY	66	68	67	71	272	-16	$324,000	293.9	87.5	72.2	110
3	Bryce MOLDER	70	65	67	71	273	-15	$204,000	293.3	78.6	72.2	109
4	C HOWELL III	68	66	69	71	274	-14	$144,000	305.8	87.5	80.6	119
	Justin LEONARD	71	69	69	66	275	-13	$114,000	279.1	94.6	72.2	110
	Duffy WALDORF	71	67	69	68	275	-13	$114,000	302.9	89.3	72.2	110
7	Dan FORSMAN	71	68	68	69	276	-12	$93,500	285.6	80.4	75.0	112
	J.P. HAYES	68	68	71	69	276	-12	$93,500	287.6	85.7	77.8	118
	Tim HERRON	66	70	71	69	276	-12	$93,500	313.1	83.9	81.9	120
10	Steve FLESCH	67	74	67	69	277	-11	$78,000	298.5	83.9	75.0	117
	Brian GAY	69	69	69	70	277	-11	$78,000	266.9	85.7	73.6	113

Pos	Name	R1	R2	R3	R4	Total	To par
12	Edward FRYATT	65	73	71	69	278	-10
	Bob TWAY	68	69	72	69	278	-10
14	Mark BROOKS	73	67	73	66	279	-9
	Corey PAVIN	69	72	71	67	279	-9
	Chris RILEY	70	71	68	70	279	-9
17	John DALY	71	71	69	69	280	-8
	John RIEGGER	69	70	69	72	280	-8
19	D BERGANIO, Jr.	66	68	74	73	281	-7
	Joel EDWARDS	67	70	75	69	281	-7
	N LANCASTER	71	68	72	70	281	-7
	Mark O'MEARA	66	72	73	70	281	-7
	Brian WATTS	64	71	71	75	281	-7
24	C BECKMAN	71	67	71	73	282	-6
	Brad ELDER	72	69	72	69	282	-6
	B GEIBERGER	71	67	70	74	282	-6
	G HJERTSTEDT	71	67	72	72	282	-6
	S McCARRON	70	70	73	69	282	-6
	J VAN DE VELDE	71	70	72	69	282	-6
30	Bart BRYANT	71	67	73	72	283	-5
	Hunter HAAS	76	66	68	73	283	-5
	Tripp ISENHOUR	70	72	72	69	283	-5
	Kent JONES	72	70	71	70	283	-5
	Ian LEGGATT	72	70	75	66	283	-5
	Craig PERKS	71	70	74	68	283	-5
36	Jim CARTER	68	67	72	77	284	-4
	Robin FREEMAN	67	72	75	70	284	-4
	Jeff HART	71	71	72	70	284	-4
	Jonathan KAYE	71	66	71	76	284	-4
	Greg KRAFT	71	71	73	69	284	-4
	Michael MUEHR	72	70	75	67	284	-4
	Craig STADLER	71	68	71	74	284	-4
	Chris TIDLAND	70	68	73	73	284	-4
44	Ben BATES	68	69	73	75	285	-3
	G CHALMERS	72	70	72	71	285	-3
	Lee JANZEN	70	65	75	75	285	-3
	Billy MAYFAIR	70	69	74	72	285	-3
	A McI ARDY	72	70	71	72	285	-3
	Jeff SLUMAN	68	73	69	75	285	-3
50	Ronnie BLACK	68	73	74	71	286	-2
	Lee PORTER	73	65	75	73	286	-2
	Brett QUIGLEY	72	65	74	75	286	-2
	Mike SPOSA	69	71	73	73	286	-2
	Esteban TOLEDO	73	68	76	69	286	-2
55	D HAMMOND	72	69	75	71	287	-1
	J.L. LEWIS	71	70	72	74	287	-1
	Carl PAULSON	70	72	68	77	287	-1
58	Danny ELLIS	69	71	75	73	288	E
	B HENNINGER	68	74	78	68	288	E
	Glen HNATIUK	70	72	75	71	288	E
61	Steve ALLAN	67	69	79	74	289	+1
	Woody AUSTIN	71	66	75	77	289	+1
63	Craig KANADA	70	71	76	73	290	+2
	Brian WILSON	69	72	73	76	290	+2
65	Rich BEEM	74	68	77	72	291	+3
	Joe OGILVIE	73	69	71	78	291	+3
	Dicky PRIDE	71	70	73	73	291	+3
68	Ben FERGUSON	70	72	79	71	292	+4
69	B SCHWARZROCK	69	72	77	75	293	+5
70	T ARMOUR III	72	68	79	80	299	+11

Tournament Report

John Cook was as surprised as anyone when he produced a final round 64 to steal the Reno Tahoe Open title from underneath Jerry Kelly's nose at Montreux Golf Club in Reno.

Surprised firstly because he played so poorly on the Saturday, when a third round 74 saw him fall from first place at halfway to fifth – six strokes behind Kelly at the start of Sunday's play. And surprised secondly because Kelly was still leading by one with just three holes to play. Disaster struck on the 16th hole for Kelly.

Having failed to find the putting surface on the par three 163 yard hole, he proceeded to fluff two chips from the rough and then missed a three-foot putt, eventually signing for a triple bogey. Kelly fell two behind clubhouse leader Cook and then missed a birdie opportunity on the 17th hole and narrowly failed to hole from 95 yards for eagle at the last.

He had to settle for runner-up position and has yet to win on the full tour. The two veteran pros have more than 26 years on the US Tour between them and managed to fend off the attentions of the next generation of golfers to place first and second.

Two 22-year-olds, Bryce Molder and Charles Howell, finished third and fourth respectively, impressively putting down markers for the future. Cook's win was his 11th on the US Tour and the $540,000 winner's cheque took his career earnings to over $9 million.

MISSED THE CUT: Jeff BREHAUT 72 71, K.J. CHOI 76 67, Michael CLARK II 72 71, Russ COCHRAN 70 73, Fred COUPLES 74 69, Jay HAAS 71 72, Peter LONARD 73 70, David PEOPLES 72 71, Paul STANKOWSKI 74 69, Kevin SUTHERLAND 72 71, Ted TRYBA 70 73, Billy ANDRADE 73 71, Emlyn AUBREY 71 73, Craig BARLOW 69 75, Jay Don BLAKE 70 74, Bob BURNS 68 76, Jay DELSING 73 71, Luke DONALD 75 69, Bill GLASSON 72 72, Mathew GOGGIN 69 75, Kelly GRUNEWALD 69 75, J.J. HENRY 74 70, Skip KENDALL 73 71, Blaine McCALLISTER 72 72, Jim McGOVERN 72 72, Spike McROY 71 73, Nick O'HERN 73 71, Chris SMITH 74 70, Brad FABEL 74 71, Per Ulrik JOHANSSON 74 71, Bob MAY 72 73, Chris PERRY 74 71, Joey SINDELAR 72 73, Garrett WILLIS 72 73, Tom BYRUM 74 72, Richie COUGHLAN 71 75, Peter JACOBSEN 73 73, Dave STOCKTON Jr. 74 72, Kevin WENTWORTH 72 74, Jay WILLIAMSON 71 75, Kaname YOKOO 67 79, David FROST 72 75, Robert GAMEZ 71 76, Paul GOW 74 73, Jeff MAGGERT 72 75, David MORLAND IV 67 80, Mike REID 75 72, Mark WURTZ 76 71, Richard BARCELO 74 74, Jason GORE 74 74, Bradley HUGHES 78 70, Brandt JOBE 73 75, Shawn KELLY 76 72, Andrew MAGEE 74 74, Geoff OGILVY 70 78, Tom SCHERRER 68 80, Jerry SMITH 76 72, Phil TATAURANGI 74 74, Craig A. SPENCE 73 76, Mark HENSBY 75 75, Pete JORDAN 74 76, Cliff KRESGE 73 77, Rocky WALCHER 75 75, Mark WIEBE 74 76, Chris ZAMBRI 76 74, Brandel CHAMBLEE 75 76, Keith CLEARWATER 77 74, Paul GOYDOS 74 77, Tommy TOLLES 73 78, Barry CHEESMAN 74 78, Sean MURPHY 78 74, Heath SLOCUM 77 75, Doug DUNAKEY 79 74, Jimmy GREEN 76 77, Mike HULBERT 75 78, Shaun MICHEEL 76 78, Paul WIGHTMAN 81 75, Bryson YOUNG 80 77, Rick LEIBOVICH 79 79, Emanuele CANONICA 79 85, Jeremy ANDERSON 69 W/D, Tim THELEN 71 D, Nick FALDO 75 W/D, Marco DAWSON 77 W/D, Fred FUNK 78 W/D, Rocco MEDIATE W/D.

Sponsored by Stan James

Course Profile

Montreux Golf Club (par 72, 7,552 yards) in Nevada is way above sea level and the ball flies through the air with the greatest of ease.

The yardages look big but play shorter. Still, you have to be confident enough with your driver to be able to go for it.

The 'Bear Trap', the stretch of holes between six and eight, over 1,100 yards, needs to be covered in 11 shots to make par.

The fairways are relatively narrow.

Players/Points to Note

●This is a new tour event that has only been contested three times – 1999, 2000 and 2001. And like the previous two years this event will be played opposite the WGC Invitational. So many of the top players will not be competing.

●Only four players can boast two top-ten finishes in this event. **David Toms** was seventh in 2000 and second in 1999 – although he surely won't be playing in 2002 given his rise up to superstar status in the game (after his USPGA Championship win). **John Cook** won here in 2001 after placing fourth in 1999.

●**Duffy Waldorf**'s form figures read 24-4-5. **Steve Flesch** has finished seventh and tenth in the last two renewals.

●**Fred Funk** has two top-25 spots in this tournament and, although the course is long, you still need accuracy off the tee – which Funk excels in.

●**Chris Perry**, **Scott Verplank**, **Jerry Kelly**, **Brian Henninger**, **Notah Begay**, **Franklin Langham** and **Jean Van de Velde** (beaten in a play-off in 2000) have all performed well in this event in it's young life.

●Only the Sprint International can be compared with this event in terms of altitude. That tournament is played just a few weeks before this one, so look for anyone with a good record at Castle Pines to go well at Montreux.

Previous Results

2000: 1. Scott Verplank (-13), won play-off, 2. Jean Van de Velde (-13), 3. Bob May (-12).
1999: 1. Notah Begay III (-14), 2. Chris Perry (-11), David Toms (-11).

John Cook player profile – page 248

AIR CANADA CHAMPIONSHIP

Northview G.&C.C., 30 Aug to 2 Sep 2001, purse $3,400,000

Pos	Name	R1	R2	R3	R4	Total	To par	Money	DD(y)	DA%	GIR%	Putts
1	Joel EDWARDS	65	67	68	65	265	-19	$612,000	261.6	87.5	75.0	108
2	Steve LOWERY	73	65	68	66	272	-12	$367,200	273.3	66.1	72.2	110
3	Fred FUNK	70	67	67	69	273	-11	$197,200	259.8	78.6	70.8	113
	Matt KUCHAR	68	66	72	67	273	-11	$197,200	269.3	58.9	58.3	102
5	Brent GEIBERGER	66	70	70	68	274	-10	$124,100	263.1	76.8	66.7	110
	David GOSSETT	67	68	69	70	274	-10	$124,100	269.3	73.2	62.5	106
	K SUTHERLAND	70	69	68	67	274	-10	$124,100	273.1	69.6	72.2	115
8	Bob ESTES	69	69	69	68	275	-9	$82,025	263.6	57.1	65.3	106
	Edward FRYATT	72	67	66	70	275	-9	$82,025	272.0	75.0	58.3	104
	J.J. HENRY	67	72	66	70	275	-9	$82,025	271.6	78.6	81.9	120
	Brett QUIGLEY	68	70	67	70	275	-9	$82,025	279.1	66.1	69.4	114
	Chris RILEY	66	71	71	67	275	-9	$82,025	264.5	78.6	69.4	111
	B SCHWARZROCK	68	68	69	70	275	-9	$82,025	268.0	80.4	68.1	114
	Jerry SMITH	71	70	67	67	275	-9	$82,025	269.6	62.5	65.3	108
	Grant WAITE	70	68	65	72	275	-9	$82,025	271.8	62.5	75.0	119

Pos	Name	R1	R2	R3	R4	Total	To par
16	D PAULSON	70	69	70	67	276	-8
	John RIEGGER	70	71	68	67	276	-8
	Joey SINDELAR	71	67	69	69	276	-8
19	Ben FERGUSON	67	71	67	72	277	-7
	J PARNEVIK	67	71	72	67	277	-7
21	Craig BARLOW	67	71	69	71	278	-6
	Danny ELLIS	69	69	70	70	278	-6
	Tripp ISENHOUR	71	69	67	71	278	-6
	S MARUYAMA	68	68	73	69	278	-6
	S McCARRON	67	72	70	69	278	-6
	David PEOPLES	70	70	68	70	278	-6
	Esteban TOLEDO	69	70	70	69	278	-6
	Brian WILSON	72	68	70	68	278	-6
29	T ARMOUR III	67	69	71	72	279	-5
	Tony CAROLAN	72	68	69	70	279	-5
	David FROST	69	72	70	68	279	-5
	J.P. HAYES	69	71	71	68	279	-5
	Tim HERRON	71	68	74	66	279	-5
	Bob MAY	70	70	69	70	279	-5
	Rory SABBATINI	67	70	71	71	279	-5
	Chris TIDLAND	67	70	71	71	279	-5
37	Jim CARTER	72	68	69	71	280	-4
	Peter JACOBSEN	69	71	72	68	280	-4
	N LANCASTER	68	72	70	70	280	-4
	D MORLAND IV	68	71	70	71	280	-4
	Tom PERNICE Jr.	68	69	72	71	280	-4
	J VAN DE VELDE	72	69	72	67	280	-4
43	Woody AUSTIN	71	68	70	72	281	-3
	Jay Don BLAKE	70	71	68	72	281	-3
	Guy BOROS	70	68	72	71	281	-3
	B HENNINGER	70	69	73	69	281	-3
	C HOWELL III	68	73	68	72	281	-3
	Gary NICKLAUS	71	70	68	72	281	-3
	Lee PORTER	69	68	73	71	281	-3
	Brian WATTS	72	67	71	71	281	-3
	Kaname YOKOO	69	69	70	73	281	-3
52	K.J. CHOI	73	68	72	69	282	-2
	Paul GOYDOS	70	70	70	72	282	-2
	Pete JORDAN	68	71	72	71	282	-2
	Craig STADLER	69	70	71	72	282	-2
56	Dan FORSMAN	69	71	75	68	283	-1
	Brandt JOBE	67	70	70	76	283	-1
	Heath SLOCUM	67	71	75	70	283	-1
59	Jeff BREHAUT	70	71	77	66	284	E
	Greg KRAFT	65	71	74	74	284	E
	Steve PATE	70	68	73	73	284	E
62	Michael COMBS	68	69	77	71	285	+1
	J DRISCOLL	70	68	75	72	285	+1
	Todd F. FANNING	68	70	73	74	285	+1
	P-U JOHANSSON		68	66	76	75	285	+1
	John RESTINO	69	72	70	74	285	+1
67	Bart BRYANT	70	70	75	71	286	+2
	Mark HENSBY	68	73	74	71	286	+2
	Steve JONES	68	72	74	72	286	+2
	Ted TRYBA	70	71	72	73	286	+2
71	B CHAMBLEE	68	71	73	76	288	+4
	D STOCKTON Jr.	70	71	77	70	288	+4
73	Carlos FRANCO	68	73	73	75	289	+5

Tournament Report

Joel Edwards is the epitome of a journeyman pro. But 12 years making his living from the sport on such tours as the Lone Star Tour in Dallas hasn't dampened his appetite for the game.

And when finally his chance came to win on the full tour he grabbed it with both hands. His win in the Air Canada Championship was for "the guys that are playing the Buy.com Tour and the Golden Bear Tour" and should prove as inspiration for all those golfers plying their trade on the lesser tours – just as he has done for over a decade.

Edwards led from start to finish, kicking off with an opening 65 and then following up with rounds of 67, 68 and 65. He eventual won by seven shots from Steve Lowery, with Matt Kuchar and Fred Funk one stroke further back in a tie for third.

It was, in fact, the second biggest winning margin on the US Tour so far this season. Edwards started the day three shots clear of New Zealander Grant Waite and knew that it would take something special from someone else to deny him. But the doubts did creep in when he bogeyed the fifth hole of the final round – his first dropped shot in 47 holes.

Funk was now just two behind but Edwards responded with birdies on the seventh and eighth holes. Edwards' 72-hole total of 265 equalled the tournament record at Northview Golf Club in British Columbia.

MISSED THE CUT: Ben BATES 72 70, Cameron BECKMAN 74 68, Keith CLEARWATER 70 72, Luke DONALD 71 71, Doug DUNAKEY 71 71, Bill GLASSON 72 70, Gary HALLBERG 68 74, Glen HNATIUK 73 69, Jerry KELLY 71 71, Ian LEGGATT 71 71, J.L. LEWIS 71 71, Peter LONARD 71 71, Andrew MAGEE 70 72, Carl PAULSON 70 72, Mike REID 69 73, Rocky WALCHER 74 68, Steve ALLAN 70 73, Dave BARR 71 72, Barry CHEESMAN 71 72, Erik COMPTON 68 75, Richie COUGHLAN 73 70, Scott DUNLAP 70 73, Jason GORE 72 71, Jeff MAGGERT 70 73, Craig MATTHEW 71 72, Bryce MOLDER 72 71, Michael MUEHR 72 71, Bryn PARRY 70 73, Craig PERKS 73 70, Jeff QUINNEY 73 70, Ray STEWART 73 70, Briny BAIRD 73 71, Mathew GOGGIN 70 74, Craig KANADA 71 73, Blaine McCALLISTER 67 77, Jim McGOVERN 72 72, Shaun MICHEEL 73 71, Geoff OGILVY 69 75, Phil TATAURANGI 72 72, Mike WEIR 73 71, Robert GAMEZ 74 71, Gabriel HJERTSTEDT 76 69, Jeff JULIAN 72 73, Andrew McLARDY 73 72, Sean MURPHY 73 72, Nick O'HERN 70 75, Dicky PRIDE 68 77, Mike SPOSA 71 74, Kevin WENTWORTH 76 69, Jeremy ANDERSON 70 76, Aaron BADDELEY 74 72, Doug BARRON 73 73, Paul DEVENPORT 69 77, Kevin JOHNSON 72 74, Kent JONES 74 72, Tommy TOLLES 75 71, Rich BEEM 69 78, Greg CHALMERS 70 77, Brad ELDER 71 76, Paul GOW 70 77, Jeff HART 75 73, Bradley HUGHES 73 75, Mark SLAWTER 76 72, Paul STANKOWSKI 71 77, Stephen AMES 73 76, Robin FREEMAN 78 71, Jim GALLAGHER Jr. 78 71, Kelly GRUNEWALD 74 75, Hunter HAAS 74 75, Lee JANZEN 72 77, Jon MILLS 73 76, Tom SCHERRER 71 78, Bob BURNS 71 79, Craig A. SPENCE 73 77, Spike McROY 71 80, Mark WIEBE 76 75, Aaron BARBER 76 76, Bart TURCHIN 77 76, Notah BEGAY III 77 80, Ted BACH 82 77, Billy Ray BROWN 81 84, Jay WILLIAMSON 71 W/D, Russ COCHRAN 73 W/D.

Course Profile

Northview's Ridge Course (par 71, 7,072 yards) was designed by Arnold Palmer.

It isn't long but big hitters tend to do well there, as there are some juicy risk reward par fives than can yield eagles.

Players who can control their long irons also do well and because of the narrow-ish fairways you can't be too wayward off the tee.

This venue in Canada has been used for all the Air Canada Championship renewals.

Players/Points to Note

●**Mike Weir**, a native Canadian always plays well here – as form figures since 1996 of 5-MC-6 Win-38-MC suggest. He has a stroke average of 68.95 and is 41-under par in six visits.

●**Bob Estes** can always be relied upon for a good score. In five visits to Northview he has finished in the top ten on four occasions. He has a stroke average of 68.56.

●**Russ Cochran** has finished in the top ten three times, **Andrew Magee** has two top tens as does 1997 champion **Mark Calcavecchia**, who also holds the 72-hole record (265) at Northview (along with Brandel Chamblee).

●**Scott McCarron** holds the course record of 61. **Brent Geiberger** has four top-12 finishes in five starts.

●There have been only six Air Canada Championships (in one guise or another) and five of them have been won by players' claiming their first US Tour title.

●Course form is not necessary as both **Mark Calcavecchia** and **Rory Sabbatini** (winners in 1997 and 1998) hadn't been placed in the top ten prior to their wins.

●In 2002, this championship signals the start of the 'Fall Finish' – a separate money list running from this event to the end of the season. Around $250,00 is up for grabs to the golfer who can top the Fall Finish rankings.

Previous Results

2000: 1. Rory Sabbatini (-16), 2. Grant Waite (-15), 3. Mark Calcavecchia (-14).

1999: 1. Mike Weir (-18), 2. Fred Funk (-16), 3. Carlos Franco (-14).

1998: 1. Brandel Chamblee (-19), 2. Payne Stewart (-16), 3. Lee Porter (-13).

1997: 1. Mark Calcavecchia (-19), 2. Andrew Magee (-18), 3. Bob Estes (-17).

1996: 1. Guy Boros (-12), 2. Emlyn Aubrey (-11), Lee Janzen (-11), Taylor Smith (-11).

BELL CANADIAN OPEN

Royal Montreal G.C., 6 Sep to 9 Sep 2001, purse $3,800,000

Pos	Name	R1	R2	R3	R4	Total	To par	Money	DD(y)	DA%	GIR%	Putts
1	Scott VERPLANK	70	63	66	67	266	-14	$684,000	279.8	71.4	72.2	113
2	Bob ESTES	69	65	67	68	269	-11	$334,400	280.4	51.8	68.1	109
	Joey SINDELAR	66	69	69	65	269	-11	$334,400	307.5	57.1	79.2	118
4	John DALY	66	74	64	66	270	-10	$182,400	329.0	55.4	75.0	118
	Sergio GARCIA	69	68	65	69	271	-9	$138,700	305.0	69.6	68.1	113
	Paul GOW	67	67	66	71	271	-9	$138,700	298.5	58.9	70.8	114
	D MORLAND IV	69	63	73	66	271	-9	$138,700	296.5	50.0	63.9	106
8	Robert ALLENBY	70	68	69	65	272	-8	$98,800	294.8	64.3	69.4	116
	D BERGANIO Jr.	69	68	69	66	272	-8	$98,800	298.8	67.9	72.2	116
	K.J. CHOI	67	68	69	68	272	-8	$98,800	298.3	67.9	72.2	116
	Matt GOGEL	65	67	71	69	272	-8	$98,800	286.6	58.9	68.1	111
	Dudley HART	69	68	71	64	272	-8	$98,800	299.3	42.9	66.7	109
	Michael MUEHR	65	70	68	69	272	-8	$98,800	286.6	41.1	66.7	108

Pos	Name	R1	R2	R3	R4	Total	To par
14	Fulton ALLEM	70	71	67	66	274	-6
	Brad FAXON	70	67	69	68	274	-6
	J.J. HENRY	72	68	66	68	274	-6
	Dicky PRIDE	67	64	69	74	274	-6
15	Luke DONALD	71	69	68	67	275	-5
	Brian GAY	70	71	65	69	275	-5
	Ian LEGGATT	70	71	65	69	275	-5
	Mike SPOSA	70	69	71	65	275	-5
	Steve STRICKER	67	68	69	71	275	-5
20	Nick PRICE	69	69	70	68	276	-4
	Stuart APPLEBY	72	67	66	71	276	-4
	Fred FUNK	69	68	70	69	276	-4
	Jay HAAS	73	68	67	68	276	-4
	P-U JOHANSSON	68	72	67	69	276	-4
	Bob TWAY	69	72	66	69	276	-4
	Tiger WOODS	65	73	69	69	276	-4
27	Olin BROWNE	70	68	71	68	277	-3
	Robin FREEMAN	71	66	73	67	277	-3
	Mark O'MEARA	66	68	72	71	277	-3
	Jeff SLUMAN	73	68	64	72	277	-3
31	S ELKINGTON	68	69	72	69	278	-2
	Robert GAMEZ	70	70	70	68	278	-2
	Jimmy GREEN	68	70	76	64	278	-2
	Jeff JULIAN	68	68	73	69	278	-2
	Steve PATE	69	69	70	70	278	-2
	Mike WEIR	68	69	69	72	278	-2
	Glen HNATIUK	69	70	67	72	278	-2
	Len MATTIACE	68	71	67	72	278	-2
	Shaun MICHEEL	70	67	66	75	278	-2
40	Ronnie BLACK	68	70	71	70	279	-1
	M CARNEVALE	68	71	70	70	279	-1
	Jose COCERES	73	64	69	73	279	-1
	David GOSSETT	71	68	68	72	279	-1
	D HAMMOND	69	71	73	66	279	-1
	Jim McGOVERN	65	73	68	73	279	-1
	Spike McROY	69	69	67	74	279	-1
	J PARNEVIK	71	67	74	67	279	-1
	Willie WOOD	71	67	72	69	279	-1
49	Joel EDWARDS	74	66	70	70	280	E
	Sam RANDOLPH	69	68	65	78	280	E
	Kaname YOKOO	68	70	69	73	280	E
52	Steven ALKER	68	73	71	69	281	+1
	Jeff BREHAUT	70	70	73	68	281	+1
	N LANCASTER	72	69	71	69	281	+1
	Justin LEONARD	71	70	70	70	281	+1
	A McLARDY	69	71	67	74	281	+1
	Jerry SMITH	70	71	67	73	281	+1
58	Jim CARTER	70	71	72	69	282	+2
	Cliff KRESGE	73	67	71	71	282	+2
	Chris TIDLAND	70	70	68	74	282	+2
61	Mike HULBERT	73	67	70	73	283	+3
	Craig PERKS	72	65	71	75	283	+3
	G PADDISON (Am)	70	67	72	74	283	+3
64	Ben BATES	72	68	70	74	284	+4
	Steve JONES	68	67	72	77	284	+4
	Scott SIMPSON	71	70	71	72	284	+4
67	Heath SLOCUM	70	67	76	72	285	+5
68	J.L. LEWIS	69	72	72	73	286	+6
	Brian WATTS	72	68	75	71	286	+6
70	R COUGHLAN	72	68	70	78	288	+8
71	Geoff OGILVY	72	67	72	78	289	+9
72	Derek GILLESPIE	67	74	70	79	290	+10
73	K WENTWORTH	69	71	76	77	293	+13
	F LICKLITER II	70	68	70	-	-	WD

Tournament Report

There were one or two eyebrows raised when Curtis Strange announced that Scott Verplank would be one of his wild card picks for the US Ryder Cup team.

But the only thing raised at the end of the Bell Canadian Open at Royal Montreal Golf Club were Verplank's arms in victory celebration, as the Ryder Cup rookie proved that Strange has got his selection policy spot on.

Verplank won for the fourth time in his career and was probably motivated by the criticism that had been aired by some sections of the press regarding his inclusion in the Ryder Cup team.

Verplank took over at the top of the leaderboard after a Saturday 66 and, although he was caught on the final day, he was never passed and managed to win by three shots from Joey Sindelaar and Bob Estes.

Verplank was hauled back twice during Sunday's play, firstly by Australian Paul Gow and then by John Daly, who was blazing a trail ahead of the third round leader by shooting a superb 30 to the turn. But a ten-foot birdie on the ninth gave Verplank the outright lead again and he wasn't to give it up.

There was still work to do though and after he went three clear with three to play he foolishly dropped two shots by double bogeying the 15th hole. But a two shot swing in his favour was to follow as Estes bogeyed the last while Verplank birdied the 17th.

MISSED THE CUT: Tommy ARMOUR III 74 68, Angel CABRERA 68 74, Danny ELLIS 74 68, Edward FRYATT 71 71, Pete JORDAN 69 73, Peter LONARD 70 72, Larry RINKER 68 74, Craig A. SPENCE 73 69, Stephen AMES 72 71, Scott DUNLAP 71 72, Todd F. FANNING 75 68, Mike HEINEN 73 70, Rob McMILLAN 71 72, Sean MURPHY 73 70, Carl PAULSON 70 73, Tom PERNICE Jr. 72 71, Lee PORTER 70 73, Vijay SINGH 72 71, Aaron BARBER 72 72, Paul DEVENPORT 71 73, Dan FORSMAN 68 76, David FROST 75 69, Mark HENSBY 74 70, Gabriel HJERTSTEDT 75 69, Kevin JOHNSON 73 71, Richard MASSEY 74 70, Bryce MOLDER 73 71, Gary NICKLAUS 70 74, John RESTINO 71 73, Mark SLAWTER 71 73, Mark WIEBE 73 71, Brian WILSON 75 69, Jace BUGG 71 74, Barry CHEESMAN 72 73, Brian CLAAR 73 72, Doug DUNAKEY 73 72, Brad ELDER 73 72, Brad FABEL 75 70, Ben FERGUSON 71 74, Jim GALLAGHER Jr. 73 72, Nolan HENKE 74 71, Matt KUCHAR 73 72, Craig MATTHEW 74 71, John ROBERTSON 75 70, Michael BRADLEY 73 73, Mathew GOGGIN 73 73, Kelly GRUNEWALD 72 74, Tripp ISENHOUR 73 73, Brandt JOBE 76 70, Frank NOBILO 72 74, Brett QUIGLEY 74 72, Dave STOCKTON Jr. 75 71, Phil TATAURANGI 73 73, Woody AUSTIN 75 72, Dave BARR 72 75, Doug BARRON 74 73, Tom BYRUM 77 70, Keith CLEARWATER 75 72, Lee CURRY 71 76, Hunter HAAS 79 68, Kent JONES 74 73, Greg KRAFT 76 71, Hal SUTTON 74 73, Tommy TOLLES 72 75, Jason GORE 74 74, Scott GUMP 74 74, Dennis PAULSON 72 76, Graham COOKE 77 72, Bradley HUGHES 76 73, Jon MILLS 77 72, Bob BURNS 74 76, Dave CHRISTENSEN 71 79, Rocky WALCHER 76 74, Mike SPRINGER 76 75, Steve ALLAN 80 73, John DREWERY 77 78, Chris DICKSON 74 84 158 Don HACHEY 77 83, Grant WAITE D.

Course Profile

The Blue course at the Montreal Golf Club (par 70, 6,859 yards), which was used last year, isn't long but can play longer than its yardage because a number of it's holes are played directly into the wind.

In 2002, the Angus Glen Golf Club (par 72, 7,300 yards approx) in Markham, Ontario is being used. It's a championship course built in 1995 that has rolling terrain, wide fairways, deep bunkers and many hollows surrounding the greens. A solid short game is required.

Players/Points to Note

●The Canadian Open is usually played at Glen Abbey Golf Club (all bar three tournaments since 177) but wasn't last year and won't be in 2002. So obviously, course form is skinny. In fact, as this event moves to a venue that has never been used before it is non-existent.

●**Nick Price** has finished in the top ten on eight occasions and won this event in both 1991 and 1994.

●**Hal Sutton** has enjoyed six top-ten finishes and won here in 1999.

●**Sergio Garcia** has performed well at the two different venues used over the last two seasons. The young Spaniard was third on his debut in this event in 2000 and followed up with fifth in 2001.

●**Tiger Woods**' last missed cut came in this event but he exorcised that particular demon by winning this event in 2000.

●**Scott Verplank** has an excellent record in this event and his win in 2001 came as no surprise. Verplank has posted three top-15 finishes in his previous five starts in this tournament.

●**Brad Faxon, Jesper Parnevik** and **Justin Leonard** have all finished in the top ten on more than one occasion over the last decade.

●**Dudley Hart** and **Scott Dunlap** can boast four top-15 finishes each.

●Young players who impressed in 2001 were **JJ Henry, Matt Gogel** and **Luke Donald**.

Previous Results

_2000:_ 1. Tiger Woods (-22), 2. Grant Waite (-21), 3. Sergio Garcia (-15).

_1999:_ 1. Hal Sutton (-13), 2. Dennis Paulson (-10), 3. Four players tied.

_1998:_ 1. Billy Andrade (-13), won play-off, 2. Bob Friend (-13), 3. Mike Hulbert (-12).

_1997:_ 1. Steve Jones (-5), 2. Greg Norman (-4), 3. Phil Tataurangi (-3).

_1996:_ 1. *Dudley Hart (-14), 2. David Duval (-13), 3. Tom Byrum (-11), Taylor Smith (-11), Scott Dunlap (-11). Played over 54 holes.

Laurel Valley G.C., 20 Sep to 23 Sep 2001, purse $3,300,000

Pos	Name	R1	R2	R3	R4	Total	To par	Money	DD(y)	DA%	GIR%	Putts
1	Robert ALLENBY	70	65	66	68	269	-19	594,000	291.5	77	82	116
2	Rocco MEDIATE	69	68	67	68	272	-16	290,400	286.1	80	79	118
	Larry MIZE	73	67	67	65	272	-16	290,400	261.4	77	75	109
4	K SUTHERLAND	76	65	64	68	273	-15	158,400	274.6	64	75	110
5	Nick PRICE	66	71	68	69	274	-14	132,000	281.0	77	79	114
6	Steve ELKINGTON	70	68	69	70	277	-11	110,550	273.8	70	76	114
	Matt GOGEL	70	73	66	68	277	-11	110,550	258.9	79	71	111
	Jay WILLIAMSON	74	68	67	68	277	-11	110,550	275.3	77	74	115
9	Glen HNATIUK	70	73	66	69	278	-10	95,700	265.9	80	85	123
10	C BECKMAN	70	71	65	73	279	-9	89,100	269.4	59	71	111
11	Jim FURYK	72	72	68	68	280	-8					
	Chris DiMARCO	69	70	69	72	280	-8					
	Robert GAMEZ	70	73	73	64	280	-8					
	Jay HAAS	74	66	66	74	280	-8					
	Jeff HART	70	71	68	71	280	-8					
	C HOWELL III	68	74	66	72	280	-8					
	P STANKOWSKI	70	72	70	68	280	-8					
18	Olin BROWNE	69	71	72	69	281	-7					
	Fred FUNK	69	68	70	74	281	-7					
	Joe OGILVIE	75	69	72	65	281	-7					
	Jerry SMITH	71	69	72	69	281	-7					
22	Stuart APPLEBY	76	64	73	69	282	-6					
	M DAWSON	69	74	67	72	282	-6					
	Steve FLESCH	69	67	74	72	282	-6					
	Brian GAY	71	70	72	69	282	-6					
	John HUSTON	71	71	71	69	282	-6					
	John RIEGGER	72	72	70	68	282	-6					
28	Jeff BREHAUT	72	72	69	70	283	-5					
	Tim HERRON	72	68	70	73	283	-5					
	Greg KRAFT	72	68	72	71	283	-5					
	Jeff SLUMAN	72	67	71	73	283	-5					
	Willie WOOD	70	70	71	72	283	-5					
33	Billy ANDRADE	70	73	70	71	284	-4					
	Tom BYRUM	69	73	70	72	284	-4					
	John COOK	72	70	71	71	284	-4					
	P-U JOHANSSON	67	73	71	73	284	-4					
	S MARUYAMA	72	69	72	71	284	-4					
38	Jonathan KAYE	70	72	71	72	285	-3					
	A McLARDY	74	68	70	73	285	-3					
	Duffy WALDORF	75	69	69	72	285	-3					
41	M CLARK II	69	73	71	73	286	-2					
	Chris SMITH	72	69	71	74	286	-2					
	Ted TRYBA	74	70	66	76	286	-2					
	Bob TWAY	70	73	71	72	286	-2					
	Brian WATTS	70	72	71	73	286	-2					
46	Briny BAIRD	69	71	73	74	287	-1					
	J.L. LEWIS	71	70	75	71	287	-1					
	Steve LOWERY	71	68	76	72	287	-1					
	Len MATTIACE	71	71	72	73	287	-1					
	Corey PAVIN	72	72	73	70	287	-1					
	Tommy TOLLES	74	70	73	70	287	-1					
52	Brian CLAAR	73	69	76	70	288	E					
	Edward FRYATT	71	71	73	73	288	E					
	Lee JANZEN	72	72	72	72	288	E					
55	K GRUNEWALD	73	69	73	74	289	+1					
	Kevin JOHNSON	71	72	72	74	289	+1					
	Lee PORTER	71	70	75	73	289	+1					
58	Paul AZINGER	70	74	72	74	290	+2					
	Jerry KELLY	71	68	73	78	290	+2					
	David PEOPLES	75	69	73	73	290	+2					
61	Andrew MAGEE	72	72	71	76	291	+3					
	Carl PAULSON	70	74	75	72	291	+3					
	Mike REID	70	72	76	73	291	+3					
	Scott VERPLANK	74	70	72	75	291	+3					
65	M CALCAVECCHIA	69	73	78	72	292	+4					
	David FROST	70	69	70	83	292	+4					
	Heath SLOCUM	71	71	72	78	292	+4					
68	John DALY	70	71	82	70	293	+5					
69	Dan FORSMAN	71	71	73	79	294	+6					
70	John RESTINO	72	71	78	75	296	+6					
71	Ryan DILLON	71	72	81	77	301	+13					

Sponsored by Stan James

Tournament Report

Robert Allenby joined an elite club when winning the Marconi Pennsylvania Classic at Laurel Valley Golf Club in Lignier.

With his success the Australian became only the third golfer to boast two US Tour wins in each of the last two seasons, along with Tiger Woods and Phil Mickelson. Allenby, who has needed a play-off to win in each of his previous three US Tour victories, dominated the event after the second round, when a Friday 65 took him clear of the field. He eventually won by three shots from Larry Mize and Rocco Mediate.

Allenby's iron play was superb. His second round 65 included no birdie putts from more than ten feet. He kept putting the ball close throughout the last round, keeping local favourite Mediate at arms length.

Mediate, who started Sunday's play three shots down, tried hard to close the gap, but when a 35-foot eagle attempt on the third hole lipped out, you sensed it wasn't to be his day. Three consecutive birdies around the turn saw Allenby effectively seal victory.

Mediate, who is a member of the Laurel Valley club, was second alongside Mize, who shot a best of the day 65. Keith Sutherland, who shot the best final three round score, claimed fourth spot, while first round leader Nick Price finished fifth. The event took place in a sombre atmosphere, as it was the first US Tour tournament after the terrorist attacks in New York.

MISSED THE CUT: S ALLAN 75 70, K.J. CHOI 72 73, G DAY 71 74, D HART 73 72, B JOBE 77 68, J JULIAN 71 74, C KANADA 74 71, C KRESGE 73 72, F LICKLITER II 72 73, P LONARD 73 72, C PARRY 72 73, L ROBERTS 75 70, R SABBATINI 74 71, V SINGH 73 72, C TIDLAND 71 74, F ALLEM 71 75, C BARLOW 74 72, R COUGHLAN 74 72, L DONALD 71 75, S DUNLAP 76 70, D ELLIS 74 72, G HJERTSTEDT 72 74, S HOCH 73 73, S KENDALL 76 70, J McGOVERN 70 76, M MUEHR 72 74, C PERKS 73 73, J ABER 73 74, B BATES 73 74, M HENSBY 75 72, I LEGGATT 75 72, B McCALLISTER 78 69, S McROY 72 75, G WILLIS 74 73, S WOODARD 75 72, R BEEM 76 72, M BROOKS 73 75, B CHEESMAN 76 72, S CINK 74 74, R DAMRON 76 72, B GLASSON 72 76, S MICHEEL 75 73, C STRANGE 76 72, W AUSTIN 73 76, B BURNS 74 75, M GOGGIN 72 77, J GORE 72 77, P GOYDOS 76 73, J GREEN 73 76, B HUGHES 76 73, M SPRINGER 74 75, D STOCKTON Jr 75 74, B WILSON 75 74, K YOKOO 74 75, T ARMOUR III 76 74, J D BLAKE 76 74, B ELDER 77 73, B FABEL 79 71, R FREEMAN 78 72, S MURPHY 77 73, G NICKLAUS 78 72, B HENNINGER 74 77, K JONES 78 73, D PRIDE 73 78, C A SPENCE 77 74, J ANDERSON 74 78, T ISENHOUR 77 75, J MAZZA 73 79, J SINDELAR 73 79, K WENTWORTH 73 79, S WHEATCROFT 75 77, M WIEBE 79 73, N LANCASTER 74 79, B MAYFAIR 78 75, F NOBILO 76 77, T SCHERRER 79 74, E TOLEDO 73 81, B WESTFALL 80 74, B CARMEN 80 75, K CLEARWATER 79 76, B FERGUSON 74 82, T PERNICE Jr 78 78, R WALCHER 79 77, P JORDAN W/D 76, R BLACK W/D 77, D MORLAND IV W/D 79, A PALMER W/D.

Sponsored by Stan James

Course Profile

Laurel Valley Golf Club (par 72, 7,261 yards) is an old style country club layout.

Arnold Palmer redesigned the layout in 1989 and it still favours long hitters, as a course should do that's nearly 7,300 yards.

It has around 90 bunkers, many of them defending severely undulating greens.

Waynesborough Golf Club (par 71, 6,939 yards) has wide fairways and fast undualting greens.

The wind can be a major factor – especially in the afternoon.

Players/Points to Note

● The Marconi Pennsylvania Classic has only been played twice – and at different venues – so course form is slim. And, obviously, there is no historical form to go on either. This year, Laurel Valley Golf Course was used, next year the event goes back to Waynesborough Country Club – host for the inaugural running of this event in 2000.

● Most golfers enjoy going back to the state that they grew up in. They have the support of the crowd and can feel more at home. Five players who can count on local support are **Jim Furyk**, **Ted Tryba**, **Rocco Mediate**, **Scott Dunlap** and **Emlyn Aubrey**.

● The players with the best scores over the last two seasons are listed below.

● **Chris DiMarco** won at Waynesborough in 2000 and made a decent fist of defending his title in 2001 when finishing 11th.

● **Kevin Sutherland** finished 28th in 2000 and fourth in 2001.

● The top ten players in 2000 were Chris DiMarco, **Mark Calcavecchia**, **Brad Elder**, **Scott Hoch**, **Jonathan Kaye**, **Chris Perry**, **Sandy Lyle**, **Jeff Maggert**, **Loren Roberts** and **Scott Verplank**.

● A note for 2003 is that the Laurel Valley course has been compared to Bay Hill Club & Lodge in Orlando, Fla., host to the Bay Hill Invitational. Both courses were built by Dick Wilson in the '50s and redesigned by Arnold Palmer and Ed Seay.

Previous Results

2000: 1. Chris DiMarco (-14), 2. Mark Calcavecchia (-8), Brad Elder (-8), Scott Hoch (-8), Jonathan Kaye (-8), Chris Perry (-8).

Robert Allenby player profile – page 240

TEXAS OPEN

LaCantera G.C., 27 Sep to 30 Sep 2001, purse $3,000,000

Pos	Name	R1	R2	R3	R4	Total	To par	Money	DD(y)	DA%	GIR%	Putts
1	Justin LEONARD	65	64	68	69	266	-18	$540,000	301.4	76.8	75.0	108
2	J.J. HENRY	70	64	68	66	268	-16	$264,000	322.6	64.3	80.6	116
	Matt KUCHAR	67	68	64	69	268	-16	$264,000	304.9	69.7	82.0	117
4	Bob ESTES	67	68	69	67	271	-13	$132,000	285.3	67.9	77.8	113
	Tommy TOLLES	68	69	66	68	271	-13	$132,000	307.4	73.2	68.1	108
6	Steve ELKINGTON	67	70	68	67	272	-12	$104,250	311.3	76.8	75.0	117
	Kaname YOKOO	67	69	68	68	272	-12	$104,250	293.5	69.6	72.2	111
8	Bob BURNS	66	72	67	68	273	-11	$87,000	298.6	76.8	76.4	119
	David FROST	70	65	70	68	273	-11	$87,000	291.5	67.9	72.2	111
	J.L. LEWIS	71	68	69	65	273	-11	$87,000	295.9	67.9	75.0	117

Pos	Name	R1	R2	R3	R4	Total	To par		Pos	Name	R1	R2	R3	R4	Total	To par
11	J BRIGMAN	67	71	67	69	274	-10		45	Paul CASEY	71	69	68	71	279	-5
	B GEIBERGER	67	69	68	70	274	-10			Doug DUNAKEY	69	69	68	73	279	-5
	J PARNEVIK	67	66	71	70	274	-10			Paul GOYDOS	70	66	70	73	279	-5
	Carl PAULSON	66	66	68	74	274	-10			Jeff MAGGERT	71	69	72	67	279	-5
	Jerry SMITH	68	69	69	68	274	-10			S McCARRON	66	70	71	72	279	-5
	J WILLIAMSON	65	68	71	70	274	-10			Lee PORTER	69	70	70	70	279	-5
17	Jay HAAS	68	67	71	69	275	-9			Jay Don BLAKE	69	69	71	71	280	-4
	Larry MIZE	67	71	71	66	275	-9		51	Marco DAWSON	64	68	70	78	280	-4
	Joel EDWARDS	67	71	68	69	275	-9			P-U JOHANSSON						
	Carlos FRANCO	68	70	65	72	275	-9				70	68	70	72	280	-4
	Tripp ISENHOUR	68	65	72	70	275	-9			Jim McGOVERN	68	68	72	72	280	-4
	Bob MAY	68	66	71	70	275	-9			Gary NICKLAUS	71	69	70	70	280	-4
	Tom SCHERRER	69	66	67	73	275	-9			Joe OGILVIE	73	65	70	72	280	-4
24	Tom BYRUM	68	71	68	69	276	-8			D STOCKTON Jr.	70	68	72	70	280	-4
	Brian GAY	68	71	70	67	276	-8		58	Steve ALLAN	71	68	71	71	281	-3
	David GOSSETT	67	72	69	68	276	-8			John RIEGGER	69	71	70	71	281	-3
	Glen HNATIUK	68	70	69	69	276	-8			Heath SLOCUM	69	68	68	76	281	-3
	Scott SIMPSON	71	68	71	66	276	-8			D.A. WEIBRING	71	68	68	74	281	-3
	P STANKOWSKI	69	70	66	71	276	-8		62	Tim HERRON	69	68	69	76	282	-2
30	B CHAMBLEE	66	70	73	68	277	-7			Len MATTIACE	67	70	67	78	282	-2
	Danny ELLIS	70	66	71	70	277	-7		64	B CHEESMAN	69	70	72	72	283	-1
	Pete JORDAN	70	69	70	68	277	-7			Greg KRAFT	72	66	72	73	283	-1
	Andrew MAGEE	69	69	69	70	277	-7		66	Rich BEEM	70	67	73	74	284	E
	Frank NOBILO	67	73	66	71	277	-7			Robert GAMEZ	69	71	70	74	284	E
	Craig PERKS	67	69	70	71	277	-7			Lucas GLOVER	70	70	74	70	284	E
	Hal SUTTON	69	69	69	70	277	-7		69	David OGRIN	69	67	73	77	286	+2
	K.J. CHOI	68	69	68	72	277	-7			Duffy WALDORF	70	69	74	73	286	+2
	C HOWELL III	70	68	67	72	277	-7			Mark BROOKS	69	71	73	74	287	+3
	Jonathan KAYE	69	71	70	67	277	-7			Luke DONALD	67	70	76	74	287	+3
	Esteban TOLEDO	69	71	69	68	277	-7		71	Robin FREEMAN	67	73	73	74	287	+3
41	Brandt JOBE	69	70	71	68	278	-6			D PAULSON	69	70	76	72	287	+3
	Michael MUEHR	71	67	71	69	278	-6			P TATAURANGI	70	70	70	77	287	+3
	Jeff QUINNEY	69	68	72	69	278	-6		76	T ARMOUR III	68	72	74	75	289	+5
	Chris RILEY	71	67	69	71	278	-6			R COUGHLAN	72	68	75	74	289	+5

Tournament Report

Justin Leonard won the Texas Open for the second successive season by holding off JJ Henry and Matt Kuchar at LaCantera in San Antonio.

Leonard, who has practically overhauled his swing since winning here 12 months ago, went to the top of the leaderboard after a superb Friday 64 – which included 10 birdies – and never let the advantage go. It was the Texan's sixth US Tour win and took his career earnings to over $10million.

Leonard played conservatively over the final round and did just enough to keep his nearest pursuers at bay. The biggest challenge was to come from Henry. The US Tour rookie started the day five shots behind Leonard but got to within two strokes of the eventual winner when he rolled in a curling 15-footer on the par three 13th.

After trading birdies on the next hole, Leonard went three ahead when Henry misjudged a 50-foot birdie chance on the 15th and was unable to hole the putt back. Leonard, in the group behind Henry, made par when he played the same hole minutes later, after a delightful chip to three feet after a wayward approach.

A dropped shot on the 16th by Leonard gave Henry his last chance to put any pressure on the defending champion but the youngster missed an easy chance on the last and the Texan came home with something to spare. Kuchar's challenge never really got going after dropping shots on two of the first four holes.

MISSED THE CUT: Briny BAIRD 72 69, Olin BROWNE 70 71, Scott DUNLAP 68 73, Rick FEHR 72 69, Edward FRYATT 70 71, Jimmy GREEN 68 73, Jeff HART 70 71, Gabriel HJERTSTEDT 73 68, Neal LANCASTER 72 69, Shaun MICHEEL 71 70, Bryce Molder 71 70, Craig PARRY 70 71, Brett QUIGLEY 69 72, Loren ROBERTS 71 70, Willie WOOD 69 72, Cameron BECKMAN 74 68, Greg GREGORY 68 74, Jerry KELLY 71 71, Shigeki MARUYAMA 68 74, G OGILVY 76 66, M REID 72 70, R THOMPSON 70 72, T TRYBA 70 72, B WATTS 72 70, J ANDERSON 70 73, Woody AUSTIN 76 67, Brad FABEL 72 71, Ben FERGUSON 71 72, F FUNK 73 70, B HENNINGER 70 73, M HULBERT 72 71, C PAVIN 73 70, T PURTZER 73 70, B TUTEN 72 71, R WALCHER 71 72, B ELDER 71 73, J GALLAGHER, Jr. 72 72, B GLASSON 71 73, H HAAS 74 70, K JOHNSON 73 71, C KRESGE 73 71, I LEGGATT 74 70, K COX 72 73, J DALEY 73 72, D HAMMOND 74 71, M HENSBY 73 72, B McCALLISTER 69 76, S MURPHY 69 76, B CLAAR 70 76, K JONES 73 73, F LICKLITER II 72 74, D MORLAND IV 70 70, R SABBATINI 71 75, C TIDLAND 74 72, B WILSON 72 74, D FORSMAN 75 72, A McLARDY 70 77, D TOMS 74 73, B BRYANT 72 76, K CLEARWATER 72 76, J WALKER 72 76, R BLACK 75 74, S BOWMAN 72 77, J BREHAUT 71 78, M WIEBE 73 76, M SPRINGER 76 74, G WILLIS 73 77, B BATES 76 75, C KANADA 75 77, C A. SPENCE 79 73, K WENTWORTH 78 74, M GOGGIN 75 78, J JULIAN 75 81, M KULLBERG 78 80, K GRUNEWALD 69W/D, J RESTINO 73 W/D, D PEOPLES 74 W/D, D PRIDE 76 W/D, J GORE W/D.

Sponsored by Stan James

Course Profile

LaCantera Golf Club (par 72, 7,001 yards) in San Antonio, Texas has been used for the last seven renewals of this event and it features large, undulating greens. Good putting is essential.

Tom Weiskopf designed this course and as he liked to keep the ball on the fairway as a player his layout dictates that you must do much the same.

Over 75 bunkers and several fast-running streams criss-cross the course that are there to catch wayward shots.

Players/Points to Note

●**Justin Leonard** is the undisputed king of this tournament. He won in 2001, when he was defending the title he won 12 months earlier. Prior to his win in 2000 he had come second twice and posted two other top-15 finishes in four starts. He has a stroke average of 67.75 from 24 competitive rounds. As a native Texan, Leonard considers this event nearly as important as a Major championship.

●**Duffy Waldorf** has won this event twice, 1999 and 1995 and also finished fourth in 1997. Jay Haas has had three top-five finishes in the past six years (plus 17th in 2001), while **Corey Pavin**'s form figures over the same period read 11-MC-10-21-9-MC.

●**Tim Herron** won here in 1997 and has broken par in 18 of his last 24 rounds at LaCantera.

●**Nick Price** has a stroke average of 68.10 in seven starts in this tournament, while **Loren Roberts** has finished in the top ten on five occasions.

●**Charles Howell** was 15th in 2000 and was nine-under through the last 54 holes. In 2001, he was a respectable 30th. **David Toms** and **Bob Estes** both have solid records in this event.

●The third-round leader has won 12 of the last 14 events – so back whoever leads on Saturday night if betting in running.

Previous Results
2000: 1. Justin Leonard (-19), Mark Wiebe (-14), 3. Jim Gallagher Jnr (-11), Blaine McCallister (-11).

1999: 1. Duffy Waldorf (-18), won play-off, 2. Ted Tryba (-18), 3. Brent Geiberger (-17).

1998: 1. Hal Sutton (-18), 2. Justin Leonard (-17), Jay Haas (-17).

1997: 1. Tim Herron (-17), 2. Brent Geiberger (-15), Rick Fehr (-15).

1996: 1. David Ogrin (-13), 2. Jay Haas (-12), 3. Tiger Woods (-11).

MICHELOB CHAMPIONSHIP

Kingsmill Golf Club, 4 Oct to 7Oct 2001, purse $3,500,000

Pos	Name	R1	R2	R3	R4	Total	To par	Money	DD(y)	DA%	GIR%	Putts
1	David TOMS	64	70	67	68	269	-15	$630,000	271.1	71.4	68.1	109
2	Kirk TRIPLETT	67	68	69	66	270	-14	$378,000	269.4	85.7	68.1	105
3	C HOWELL III	70	65	71	67	273	-11	$203,000	278.3	62.5	70.8	111
	Esteban TOLEDO	68	67	68	70	273	-11	$203,000	256.4	71.4	62.5	105
5	Len MATTIACE	67	66	74	67	274	-10	$140,000	271.5	64.3	61.1	107
6	J.J. HENRY	65	71	72	67	275	-9	$126,000	280.6	66.1	70.8	115
7	Rich BEEM	66	70	72	68	276	-8	$101,850	279.8	66.1	76.4	122
	Jimmy GREEN	65	70	73	68	276	-8	$101,850	269.8	62.5	66.7	111
	Neal LANCASTER	65	69	70	72	276	-8	$101,850	271.0	51.8	65.3	110
	Jim McGOVERN	71	68	68	69	276	-8	$101,850	270.6	76.8	69.4	112
	Michael MUEHR	65	70	70	71	276	-8	$101,850	263.6	64.3	66.7	114

Pos	Name	R1	R2	R3	R4	Total	To par
12	Jose COCERES	71	66	67	73	277	-7
	Chris RILEY	66	67	71	73	277	-7
	Mike WEIR	69	68	72	68	277	-7
15	Jonathan KAYE	66	67	72	73	278	-6
16	Tom BYRUM	72	69	71	67	279	-5
	G CHALMERS	69	66	72	72	279	-5
	R FREEMAN	70	69	71	69	279	-5
	Skip KENDALL	68	70	73	69	280	-4
19	Greg KRAFT	68	72	68	72	280	-4
	Brett QUIGLEY	68	69	72	71	280	-4
	D STOCKTON, Jr.	70	69	67	74	280	-4
23	Robert ALLENBY	68	70	67	76	281	-3
	J ANDERSON	67	70	70	74	281	-3
	Jay Don BLAKE	69	69	74	69	281	-3
26	Luke DONALD	68	69	73	72	282	-2
	Glen HNATIUK	69	70	73	70	282	-2
	Carl PAULSON	68	66	73	75	282	-2
	Nick PRICE	70	70	71	71	282	-2
	Mike SPOSA	67	72	74	69	282	-2
	Tommy TOLLES	71	70	73	68	282	-2
32	Larry MIZE	71	69	74	69	283	-1
	Brad FABEL	69	70	73	71	283	-1
	Lee JANZEN	67	72	71	73	283	-1
	Joe OGILVIE	70	70	72	71	283	-1
	D PAULSON	70	70	73	70	283	-1
	Lee PORTER	67	70	73	73	283	-1
	K SUTHERLAND	69	69	71	74	283	-1
	P TATAURANGI	67	72	73	71	283	-1
	Ted TRYBA	71	69	72	71	283	-1
41	Briny BAIRD	68	72	70	74	284	E
	David DUVAL	73	68	72	71	284	E
	Mark O'MEARA	70	71	70	73	284	E
	Mike REID	71	69	73	71	284	E
	Curtis STRANGE	68	71	73	72	284	E
	Chris TIDLAND	69	68	75	72	284	E
47	Paul AZINGER	69	69	75	72	285	+1
	Bart BRYANT	70	70	72	73	285	+1
	Robert DAMRON	72	69	70	74	285	+1
	Steve FLESCH	70	69	73	73	285	+1
	Fred FUNK	69	68	72	76	285	+1
	Paul GOYDOS	70	70	74	71	285	+1
	Mike HULBERT	70	68	75	72	285	+1
	Bob TWAY	70	71	72	72	285	+1
55	K CLEARWATER	72	66	75	73	286	+2
	Russ COCHRAN	70	69	75	72	286	+2
	Danny ELLIS	69	69	72	76	286	+2
	Brandt JOBE	69	70	75	72	286	+2
	P-U JOHANSSON	69	70	73	74	286	+2
	Jerry KELLY	67	73	74	72	286	+2
	S MARUYAMA	65	74	76	71	286	+2
62	Ian LEGGATT	73	68	71	75	287	+3
	Spike McROY	68	69	75	75	287	+3
	Frank NOBILO	73	68	72	74	287	+3
	Willie WOOD	68	72	71	76	287	+3
66	Hunter HAAS	70	71	76	71	288	+4
	Brian WILSON	71	68	78	71	288	+4
68	Bryce MOLDER	66	71	76	76	289	+5
	John RIEGGER	67	71	72	79	289	+5
70	Jeff HART	71	69	75	77	292	+8
	Tom SCHERRER	70	71	77	74	292	+8
72	Gary NICKLAUS	71	68	78	77	294	+10

Tournament Report

David Toms won for the third time in 2001 and the sixth time since 1999 by seeing off a determined Kirk Triplett to capture the Michelob Championship at Kingsmill in Virginia.

Only Tiger Woods has won more tournaments on the US Tour than Toms in the last three seasons. And the former Buy.Com Tour player can now be talked about in the same breath as Woods, Phil Mickelson and David Duval, for he surely is, as his world ranking suggests, one of the best golfers on the planet.

Toms started the tournament in great style by taking the first round lead after a flawless 64. But a Friday 70 gave the field some hope, Toms fell to fourth behind halfway leader Len Mattiace, before he took over at the top of the leaderboard once more by carding a Saturday 67. A superb display of controlled golf followed as Toms birdied four of the first seven holes to put distance between himself and the chasing pack.

At one stage he led by four strokes but a bogey on the 17th saw his advantage cut to one, as a charging Triplett had picked up three shots in the last five holes.

But Toms made no mistake at the 18th. His drive found the perfect position on the fairway and, after making the green in regulation, calmly two-putted for a single stroke win. Esteban Toledo shared third place with Charles Howell, whose bogey-free 67 secured his third top-five finish of the season.

MISSED THE CUT: Billy ANDRADE 68 74, Tommy ARMOUR III 72 70, Olin BROWNE 70 72, Bob BURNS 71 71, Marco DAWSON 71 71, Wayne DEFRANCESCO 68 74, Dan FORSMAN 71 71, Carlos FRANCO 70 72, Jim FURYK 69 73, Lucas GLOVER 72 70, David GOSSETT 73 69, Jay HAAS 70 72, Tripp ISENHOUR 72 70, Peter JACOBSEN 69 73, SHAUN MICHEEL 71 71, Jeff SLUMAN 71 71, Jerry SMITH 72 70, Garrett WILLIS 67 75, Michael CLARK II 68 75, Jim GALLAGHER, Jr. 73 70, Robert GAMEZ 74 69, Kelly GRUNEWALD 69 74, Gabriel HJERTSTEDT 72 71, Scott HOCH 71 72, Bradley HUGHES 70 73, Zach JOHNSON 73 70, Sean MURPHY 69 74, Corey PAVIN 71 72, Chris SMITH 72 71, Craig A. SPENCE 71 72, Richie COUGHLAN 73 71, Scott DUNLAP 71 73, David FROST 72 72, Donnie HAMMOND 74 70, Matt KUCHAR 72 72, Billy MAYFAIR 70 74, Stephen AMES 73 72, Woody AUSTIN 72 73, Doug DUNAKEY 72 73, John ENGLER 69 76, Tim HERRON 71 74, Pete JORDAN 72 73, Justin LEONARD 72 73, Frank LICKLITER II 71 74, Blaine McCALLISTER 72 73, Craig PARRY 73 72, Dicky PRIDE 73 72, Grant WAITE 74 71, Jeff BREHAUT 74 72, Brian CLAAR 75 71, Steve MADSEN 68 78, Jeff MAGGERT 73 73, Andrew McLARDY 68 78, John RESTINO 73 73, Joey SINDELAR 72 74, Jay WILLIAMSON 76 70, Ronnie BLACK 70 77, Jeff JULIAN 75 72, Cliff KRESGE 72 75, Craig PERKS 73 74, Mark BROOKS 75 73, Brad ELDER 71 77, David MORLAND IV 78 70, Steve PATE 74 74, Ty TRYON 76 72, Kevin WENTWORTH 69 79, Kent JONES 73 76, Kaname YOKOO 74 75, Fulton ALLEM 74 76, Ben BATES 73 77, Mathew GOGGIN 73 77, Rocky WALCHER 76 75, Barry CHEESMAN 76 76, Craig KANADA 74 78, Jerry BURTON 79 74, Ben FERGUSON 77 76, Chris GREENWOOD 77 76, Brett BONER 77 77, Matt CANNON 80 83, Mark HENSBY 73 W/D, Kevin JOHNSON 73 W/D, David BERGANIO, Jr. W/D Dudley HART W/D.

Sponsored by Stan James

Course Profile

Kingsmill Golf Club (par 71, 6,853 yards) was designed by Pete Dye and, like many of his courses, the emphasis is put on driving the ball well. Accuracy above distance should see a player score well.

However, the last two champions can hardly be considered straight hitters, so don't discount a player who is slightly wayward off the tee.

The greens are big, so players need to get close with their irons or be in good form with their putter to succeed.

Players/Points to Note

●**David Toms** had missed the cut in four of his six starts at Kinsmill before he won in 2000. But after winning again in 2001, who's to say he wont make it the hat-trick in 2002?

●**Scott Hoch** has finished in the top ten seven times, has a stroke average of 69.55, holds the 72-hole course record of 265 and is an astonishing 112-under par in 20 starts in this tournament.

●**David Duval** has won this event twice. His stroke average is 69.58.

●**Mike Weir** missed out on a play-off in 1999 by bogeying the last, lost in extra time in 2000 and was 12th in 2001, while **Frank Lickliter** has gained a stroke average of 69.75 in six starts.

●**Robert Allenby** can boast three top-25 finishes in four starts. Loren Roberts hasn't finished lower than 35th in his last six starts at Kingsmill.

●**Fred Funk** hasn't missed a cut in this event since 1988 – and he's played all bar one in that time. He has finished in the top ten four times.

●**Bradley Hughes**, **Jeff Sluman** and **Scott Verplank** all boast multiple top-ten finishes.

●Young players that did well in 2001 were **JJ Henry** and **Charles Howell**. Also watch out for veterans such as **Curtis Strange** and **Bruce Lietzke** if they tee-up.

Previous Results

2000: 1. David Toms (-13), won play-off, 2. Mike Weir (-13), 3. Frank Lickliter (-11).

1999: 1. Notah Begay III (-10), won play-off, 2. Tom Byrum (-10), 3. Mike Weir (-9).

1998: 1. David Duval (-16), 2. Phil Tataurangi (-13), 3. Barry Cheesman (-12).

1997: 1. David Duval (-13), won play-off, 2. Duffy Waldorf (-13), Grant Waite (-13).

1996: 1. Scott Hoch (-19), 2. Tom Purtzer (-15), 3. Michael Bradley (-12), Ted Tryba (-12), Fred Funk (-12).

INVENSYS CLASSIC AT LAS VEGAS

TPC at Summerlin, 11 Oct to 14 Oct 2001, purse $3,500,000

Pos	Name	R1	R2	R3	R4	R5	Total	To par	Money	DD(y)	DA%	GIR%	Putts
1	Bob ESTES	65	66	67	68	63	329	-30	810,000	288.1	72.9	85.6	140
2	Tom LEHMAN	63	62	72	67	66	330	-29	396,000	294.7	82.9	84.4	143
	Rory SABBATINI	64	67	72	63	64	330	-29	396,000	311.1	71.4	77.8	133
4	Davis LOVE III	69	65	68	69	61	332	-27	198,000	305.4	67.1	75.6	135
	Scott McCARRON	68	65	65	63	71	332	-27	198,000	303.1	71.4	82.2	141
6	C BECKMAN	67	67	69	66	64	333	-26	162,000	294.8	61.4	80.0	140
7	John DALY	67	62	72	69	67	337	-22	135,562	321.6	64.3	83.3	150
	Craig PARRY	64	66	66	70	71	337	-22	135,562	292.3	82.9	75.6	139
	Scott VERPLANK	67	67	71	65	67	337	-22	135,562	294.0	88.6	81.1	140
	Chris RILEY	69	65	68	68	67	337	-22	135,562	306.4	54.3	61.1	n/a

Pos	Name	R1	R2	R3	R4	R5	Total	To par
11	Matt GOGEL	69	67	68	65	69	338	-21
	Kenny PERRY	71	69	67	65	66	338	-21
13	Robert ALLENBY	66	65	71	71	67	340	-19
	Chris DiMARCO	68	61	72	69	70	340	-19
	Steve FLESCH	65	67	67	74	67	340	-19
	David FROST	69	67	69	66	69	340	-19
	Brian GAY	67	69	70	66	68	340	-19
18	Jason GORE	66	68	70	69	68	341	-18
	Billy MAYFAIR	70	66	68	71	66	341	-18
20	Stewart CINK	71	71	67	66	67	342	-17
	C HOWELL III	66	68	72	69	67	342	-17
	Skip KENDALL	66	70	69	67	70	342	-17
	Bob MAY	69	66	65	72	70	342	-17
	Kaname YOKOO	71	67	70	68	66	342	-17
25	Woody AUSTIN	71	67	68	69	68	343	-16
	Andrew MAGEE	67	67	66	72	71	343	-16
	S MARUYAMA	67	68	72	70	66	343	-16
	Kirk TRIPLETT	69	66	70	70	68	343	-16
29	Stuart APPLEBY	70	69	68	72	65	344	-15
	Russ COCHRAN	67	66	76	64	71	344	-15
	John COOK	68	68	71	70	67	344	-15
	Robin FREEMAN	67	70	68	70	69	344	-15
	Lee JANZEN	67	67	68	67	75	344	-15
	Pete JORDAN	67	66	71	69	71	344	-15
	Craig KANADA	69	70	70	69	66	344	-15
	Greg KRAFT	69	65	71	71	68	344	-15
	Grant WAITE	70	68	69	67	70	344	-15
38	Glen DAY	67	68	71	68	71	345	-14
	Jeff MAGGERT	73	67	68	68	69	345	-14
	Joe OGILVIE	64	70	70	76	65	345	-14
	Carl PAULSON	68	69	71	66	71	345	-14
	K SUTHERLAND	69	67	72	73	64	345	-14
	Bob TWAY	69	68	69	70	69	345	-14
	Brian WILSON	69	69	69	68	70	345	-14
45	Joel EDWARDS	71	63	71	71	70	346	-13
46	Fulton ALLEM	68	69	66	69	75	347	-12
	Olin BROWNE	70	65	67	74	71	347	-12
	Fred COUPLES	63	64	72	72	76	347	-12
	Fred FUNK	67	69	72	67	72	347	-12
	P STANKOWSKI	69	66	71	69	72	347	-12
	Ted TRYBA	68	67	73	73	66	347	-12
52	G CHALMERS	67	69	71	67	74	348	-11
53	Jim CARTER	65	69	73	71	71	349	-10
	Jonathan KAYE	68	69	72	73	67	349	-10
	A McLARDY	68	68	72	71	70	349	-10
	David PEOPLES	69	70	68	71	71	349	-10
	Scott SIMPSON	68	69	72	70	70	349	-10
58	Tom BYRUM	70	65	72	67	76	350	-9
	Robert DAMRON	67	68	71	73	71	350	-9
	Tripp ISENHOUR	68	68	69	72	73	350	-9
	Justin LEONARD	71	68	70	70	71	350	-9
	D MORLAND IV	69	65	71	73	72	350	-9
	J PARNEVIK	69	69	70	71	71	350	-9
64	Jose COCERES	69	70	68	70	74	351	-8
	Paul GOYDOS	72	69	67	72	71	351	-8
	J.J. HENRY	70	71	67	71	72	351	-8
67	Jeff HART	71	66	71	72	72	352	-7
	Ian LEGGATT	68	67	74	73	71	353	-6
	Bob BURNS	68	68	70	74	74	354	-5
70	Jay Don BLAKE	70	68	71	71	75	355	-4
	Michael MUEHR	68	66	75	73	73	355	-4
	T PERNICE, Jr.	64	69	75	72	75	355	-4
73	B HENNINGER	72	64	73	76	74	359	E
74	Stephen AMES	68	70	69	79	74	360	+1

Tournament Report

162 US Tour starts separated Bob Estes' second win from his first but he didn't have to wait as long again for his third victory.

Just four months after he was successful in the Fedex St Jude Classic, Estes managed to capture the Invensys Classic title in Las Vegas. He started the last day of this five round tournament five shots adrift of 72-hole leader Scott McCarron, but nine birdies and nine pars in a Sunday 63 saw Estes edge out Tom Lehman and Rory Sabbatini by one stroke.

It was Estes' 17th consecutive round in the 60s and he didn't drop a shot in four of the five rounds over the four different courses this tournament is held over.

Estes picked up three shots over the first five holes but then his bid for glory looked over as his drive on the sixth landed in a bush. With the ball waist high he could either declare the lie unplayable, and take three off the tee, or take a swipe at it.

Out came the driver and after making contact with the ball it fell into the rough. A 9-iron to 45 feet gave him a slim opportunity to make par. But he managed to hole the putt to keep his challenge on course.

With McCarron dropping out of contention early with a triple bogey at the fourth, Estes outbattled Lehman, who missed birdie putts on the 17th and 18th, down the stretch to win.

MISSED THE CUT: Jeremy ANDERSON 69 73 68, Billy ANDRADE 70 68 72, Michael CLARK II 70 68 72, Tim HERRON 68 67 75, Kevin JOHNSON 71 69 70, Cliff KRESGE 69 73 68, Neal LANCASTER 70 69 71, Steve LOWERY 70 65 75, Jeff SLUMAN 68 71 71, Nick CASSINI 72 71 68, Joe DURANT 67 66 78, Ben FERGUSON 74 67 70, Steve PATE 70 69 72, Dennis PAULSON 70 70 71, Mike SPOSA 71 69 71, Rich BEEM 66 75 71, Brandel CHAMBLEE 69 68 75, Edward FRYATT 72 68 72, Steve JONES 71 71 70, John RIEGGER 71 71 70, Chris TIDLAND 69 69 74, Mark BROOKS 70 71 72, Robert GAMEZ 68 69 76, Brent GEIBERGER 69 71 73, Bill GLASSON 73 71 69, Jimmy GREEN 73 71 69, Gabriel HJERTSTEDT 71 69 73, Brandt JOBE 72 67 74, Kent JONES 67 74 72, J.L. LEWIS 69 71 73, Spike McROY 72 70 71, Mark O'MEARA 73 67 73, Craig PERKS 74 68 71, Mark CALCAVECCHIA 71 71 72, Peter JACOBSEN 73 70 71, Jeff QUINNEY 72 72 70, Duffy WALDORF 71 72 71, Steve ALLAN 72 72 71, David GOSSETT 73 69 73, Kelly GRUNEWALD 72 71 72, Per Ulrik JOHANSSON 72 71 72, Jim McGOVERN 69 68 78, Rocco MEDIATE 70 69 76, Shaun MICHEEL 72 68 75, Chris PERRY 71 68 76, Doug DUNAKEY 70 71 75, Jim FURYK 76 70 70, Hunter HAAS 78 65 74, Jerry SMITH 75 70 72, David BERGANIO, Jr. 69 73 76, Keith CLEARWATER 73 73 72, Danny ELLIS 76 66 76, Paul GOW 72 69 77, Gary NICKLAUS 71 73 74, Geoff OGILVY 75 68 75, Lee PORTER 70 73 75, Dicky PRIDE 73 71 74, Blaine McCALLISTER 75 67 77, Chris SMITH 72 75 72, Tommy ARMOUR III 71 72 78, Bradley HUGHES 74 73 76, Tom SCHERRER 75 73 75, Richie COUGHLAN 77 71 76, Scott LANDER 74 77 76, James DRISCOLL 79 72 77, Tommy TOLLES 76 69 83, Marco DAWSON D 72 69, Mark WIEBE 73 73 W/D, Mathew GOGGIN 75 76 W/D, Craig STADLER 73 73 W/D.

Sponsored by Stan James

Course Profile

Three courses are used over five days. One round each is played at TPC at Summerlin (par 72, 7,243 yards), (par 71, 7,382 yards) and Southern Highlands (par 72, 7,193 yards), then the cut is made with the last two rounds played at Summerlin.

All of the courses are long and have wide fairways – so the bigger the better off the tee. Players can really let rip.

Water comes into play on some of the holes at Southern Hills.

Players/Points to Note

●**Jim Furyk** has the best record in this event. He might have missed the cut in 2001 but he is a three-time winner (1999, 1998 and 1995), can boast a stroke average 67.84 and is 155-under par in 30 rounds. He loves the format, the courses and the weather – just about everything at this event.

●**Davis Love** was fourth in 2001 and finished in the top seven five times from 1992 to 1998 (including a win in 1993). Love shot a course record 61 at the host layout TPC Summerlin last year and, at 246-under par in 15 appearances, he is always a player to consider.

●**Jonathan Kaye** is a relative newcomer to this event but three top-ten finishes in six starts make him out as an outsider to follow in 2002.

●**Fred Couples**' form figures from 1996 read 8-9-22-10-17-46. **John Cook** is another lover of these type of events, as four top tens at Las Vegas testifies.

●**Bill Glasson**, **Paul Azinger** and **Scott Hoch** are former winners with three or more top-ten finishes in this event.

●**Phil Mickelson** and **Mark Calcavecchia**, **Romert Gamez** (born and bred Las Vegan) and **Kirk Triplett** haven't won but can also boast three top-ten finishes.

●Big hitters, like **John Daly**, have done well in the past.

Previous Results

2000: 1. Billy Andrade (-28), 2. Phil Mickelson (-27), 3. Jonathan Kaye (-26), Stewart Cink (-26).

1999: 1. Jim Furyk (-29), 2. Jonathan Kaye (-28), 3. Dudley Hart (-22).

1998: 1. Jim Furyk (-25), 2. Mark Calcavecchia (-24) 3. Scott Verplank (-22).

1997: 1. Bill Glasson (-20), 2. David Edwards (-19), Billy Mayfair (-19).

1996: 1. Tiger Woods (-27), won play-off, 2. Davis Love III (-27), 3. Kelly Gibson (-26), Mark Calcavecchia (-26).

NATIONAL CAR RENTAL GOLF CLASSIC DISNEY

Walt Disney World Resort, 18 Oct to 21 Oct 2001, purse $3,400,000

Pos	Name	R1	R2	R3	R4	Total	To par	Money	DD(y)	DA%	GIR%	Putts
1	Jose COCERES	68	65	64	68	265	-23	612,000	277.4	77	83	111
2	Davis LOVE III	67	66	67	66	266	-22	367,200	288.3	66	83	115
3	David PEOPLES	69	65	68	66	268	-20	197,200	280.3	80	86	119
	Jerry SMITH	66	66	73	63	268	-20	197,200	289.8	70	74	106
5	Steve FLESCH	73	65	66	65	269	-19	136,000	286.4	82	85	117
6	Craig PERKS	70	69	67	64	270	-18	99,328	280.0	68	72	108
	Danny ELLIS	67	68	70	65	270	-18	99,328	292.0	68	83	116
	Skip KENDALL	68	70	64	68	270	-18	99,328	271.1	77	79	114
	Scott McCARRON	65	71	65	69	270	-18	99,328	289.1	70	83	115
	Jesper PARNEVIK	71	65	67	67	270	-18	99,328	283.6	66	78	113
	Vijay SINGH	66	68	67	69	270	-18	99,328	296.1	70	81	112
	David TOMS	66	68	69	67	270	-18	99,328	282.8	77	81	115

Pos	Name	R1	R2	R3	R4	Total	To par
13	Nick PRICE	70	69	67	65	271	-17
	Stuart APPLEBY	69	67	65	70	271	-17
	Tom LEHMAN	72	66	66	67	271	-17
16	Woody AUSTIN	70	65	69	68	272	-16
	Paul AZINGER	70	69	67	66	272	-16
	John HUSTON	70	66	69	67	272	-16
	Billy MAYFAIR	68	68	68	68	272	-16
	Tiger WOODS	69	67	67	69	272	-16
21	Stewart CINK	65	70	71	67	273	-15
	B McCALLISTER	67	69	70	67	273	-15
	Tom PERNICE Jr.	68	68	70	67	273	-15
	T ARMOUR III	70	67	67	69	273	-15
	R DAMRON	71	66	70	66	273	-15
	Lee JANZEN	70	67	65	71	273	-15
	Rocco MEDIATE	73	64	68	68	273	-15
	Bob TWAY	67	69	69	68	273	-15
	Kaname YOKOO	66	65	71	71	273	-15
30	Stephen AMES	69	70	67	68	274	-14
	Lee PORTER	67	70	68	69	274	-14
32	Briny BAIRD	68	69	69	69	275	-13
	Fred COUPLES	70	68	70	67	275	-13
	Chris DiMARCO	68	70	66	71	275	-13
	R WALCHER	71	68	68	68	275	-13
36	R ALLENBY	67	71	69	69	276	-12
	Olin BROWNE	71	68	68	69	276	-12
	Bob BURNS	73	65	67	71	276	-12
	Jim CARTER	72	66	71	67	276	-12
	Greg KRAFT	70	67	69	70	276	-12
	B LANGER	67	72	67	70	276	-12
	Len MATTIACE	65	70	71	70	276	-12
	Michael MUEHR	71	67	71	67	276	-12
	Carl PAULSON	66	72	69	69	276	-12
	Mike WEIR	66	71	70	69	276	-12
46	Glen DAY	69	69	69	70	277	-11
	John RIEGGER	69	68	72	68	277	-11
	S VERPLANK	68	70	70	69	277	-11
	J WILLIAMSON	69	67	72	69	277	-11
50	Jay Don BLAKE	69	70	68	71	278	-10
	John COOK	69	69	68	72	278	-10
	Mark BROOKS	68	69	72	69	278	-10
	R SABBATINI	69	70	69	70	278	-10
	Mike SPOSA	72	67	69	70	278	-10
	Brian WILSON	66	68	73	71	278	-10
56	Jeff HART	68	71	70	70	279	-9
	B HENNINGER	70	68	71	70	279	-9
	Glen HNATIUK	70	67	74	68	279	-9
59	M CLARK II	72	64	73	71	280	-8
	M DAWSON	72	65	68	75	280	-8
	M GOGGIN	71	67	71	71	280	-8
	C HOWELL III	72	67	70	71	280	-8
	Steve LOWERY	65	71	70	74	280	-8
	M McCUMBER	69	66	70	75	280	-8
	S MICHEEL	65	70	70	75	280	-8
	Dicky PRIDE	70	69	71	70	280	-8
	Ted TRYBA	70	68	69	73	280	-8
68	Matt KUCHAR	72	67	71	72	282	-6
69	J.L. LEWIS	69	70	72	72	283	-3
70	D MORLAND IV	71	68	74	73	286	-2
	Garrett WILLIS	72	66	75	73	286	-2

Tournament Report

Neither the rain nor the presence of most of the best golfers in the world prevented Jose Coceres from winning the National Car Rental Golf Classic at Walt Disney World Resort in Florida.

After a delay of 49 minutes, the Argentinean, who was looking for his second US Tour win after claiming the Worldcom Classic in April, returned to the middle of the 18th fairway, where his ball was after driving from the last tee before a brief but heavy downpour. His approach to 30 feet seemed to set up what looked like an easy par.

But on a rain sodden green he left his first putt six feet short, as playing partner David Love, who knew a play-off was on if Coceres missed, looked on. The Argentinean rattled in his second effort to win by a shot. Coceres had led going into the final round by three strokes after a Saturday 64, but was caught by the eighth after Love put a wedge to a couple of feet and tapped in for birdie.

But Love found the trees on the next hole and dropped behind again. Love had further chances to catch Coceres but missed birdie putts on the 10th, 14th and 16th holes and failed to take advantage of a monster 328-yard drive on the 18th.

Only on the last did Coceres look like faltering but he held his nerve to win. The Argentinean is now exempt on the US Tour through 2004 and looks odds-on to take the Rookie of the Year title.

MISSED THE CUT: Jeremy ANDERSON 68 72, Brad BRYANT 70 70, Chad CAMPBELL 72 68, Russ COCHRAN 73 67, Scott DUNLAP 69 71, Brian GAY 73 67, Kelly GRUNEWALD 71 69, Scott HOCH 72 68, Brandt JOBE 70 70, Cliff KRESGE 69 71, Neal LANCASTER 68 72, Bob MAY 72 68, Larry MIZE 69 71, Frank NOBILO 71 69, Chris SMITH 69 71, Fulton ALLEM 72 69, Greg CHALMERS 70 71, Craig KANADA 71 70, Jerry KELLY 70 71, Andrew MAGEE 75 66, Spike McROY 74 67, Sean MURPHY 72 69, Loren ROBERTS 72 69, Grant WAITE 69 72, Steve ALLAN 74 68, Cameron BECKMAN 71 71, Keith CLEARWATER 71 71, Richie COUGHLAN 71 71, Joel EDWARDS 71 71, Brent GEIBERGER 72 70, Bill GLASSON 71 71, Tripp ISENHOUR 70 72, Ian LEGGATT 72 70, Andrew McLARDY 73 69, Joe OGILVIE 73 69, Kenny PERRY 72 70, Tom SCHERRER 73 69, Jeff SLUMAN 71 71, Duffy WALDORF 73 69, Doug BARRON 78 65, Doug DUNAKEY 72 71, Jason GORE 74 69, David GOSSETT 73 70, Paul GOYDOS 76 67, Mark O'MEARA 70 73, Steve PATE 72 71, Chris PERRY 69 74, Tom PURTZER 69 74, Heath SLOCUM 72 71, Ben FERGUSON 76 68, Edward FRYATT 71 73, Paul GOW 74 70, Gabriel HJERTSTEDT 71 73, Bradley HUGHES 73 71, Per Ulrik JOHANSSON 75 69, Kevin JOHNSON 76 68, Kevin SUTHERLAND 69 75, Hunter HAAS 74 71, Brandel CHAMBLEE 72 74, Mark HENSBY 77 69, Pete JORDAN 75 71, Gary NICKLAUS 73 73, Geoff OGILVY 72 74, Brad ELDER 74 73, Fred FUNK 75 72, Frank LICKLITER II 76 71, Craig PARRY 79 69, Tommy TOLLES 74 74, Jimmy GREEN 75 74, Kent JONES 79 70, Chris TIDLAND 74 75, Esteban TOLEDO 77 74, Will FRANTZ 81 74.

Course Profile

This event takes place at Walt Disney World Resort in Florida and two courses at the complex, Magnolia (par 72, 7,190 yards) and Palm (par 72, 6,957 yards) are used for each of the first two rounds, with the first-named layout played on over the final two days.

Magnolia is the more difficult of the two courses but both are relatively easy.

Length over accuracy is rewarded on both tracks with making birdies the name of the game.

Players/Points to Note

● **Tiger Woods** only finished 16th in 2001 but this is undoubtedly one of the tournaments he should be backed to win. He won this event in 1996 and 1999 and was 26th and seventh in between those successes and third in 2000. He has a six-year stroke average of 67.92.

● **John Huston** always enjoys playing on Bermuda grass and his record in this event hammers home that point. Two wins, the 72-hole record of 262 and a stroke average of 69.50 confirm his liking for this event.

● **Paul Azinger** is 194-under par in 16 outings in this event.

● **Davis Love**, **Jeff Maggert** and **Scott Hoch** have all posted multiple top-ten finishes.

● **Tom Lehman** has finished in the top 15 on three of his last four starts in this event.

● **Vijay Singh** has played in the last four NCR Classics and has never finished lower than 18th.

● **Glen Day** has finished in the top 15 on six of his last eight starts here.

● **Steve Flesch** put in one of his best performances here in 2001 (fifth), following up from second in 2000.

● Check out the birdie leaders statistics as players who can pick up lots of shots will do well. Of the last nine champions, seven had topped the birdie makers charts in the week.

Previous Results

2000: 1. Duffy Waldorf (-26), 2. Steve Flesch (-25), 3. Tiger Woods (-23).

1999: 1. Tiger Woods (-17), 2. Ernie Els (-16), 3. Franklin Langham (-14), Bob Tway (-14).

1998: 1. John Huston (-16), 2. Davis Love III (-15), 3. Brent Geiberger (-13).

1997: 1. David Duval (-18), won play-off, 2. Dan Forsman (-18), 3. Ted Tryba (-16), Len Mattiace (-16).

1996: 1. Tiger Woods (-21), 2. Payne Stewart (-20), 3. Robert Gamez (-19).

BUICK CHALLENGE

Callaway Gardens, 25 Oct to 28 Oct 2001, purse $3,400,000

Pos	Name	R1	R2	R3	R4	Total	To par	Money	DD(y)	DA%	GIR%	Putts
1	Chris DiMARCO	67	64	71	65	267	-21	612,000	270.4	73.2	73.6	102
2	David DUVAL	67	69	68	63	267	-21	367,200	301.3	60.7	68.1	105
3	Bob ESTES	71	63	69	66	269	-19	197,200	290.6	83.9	77.8	111
	Neal LANCASTER	65	67	68	69	269	-19	197,200	280.0	67.9	69.4	105
5	Davis LOVE III	68	62	69	71	270	-18	136,000	303.6	60.7	75.0	112
6	Jeff MAGGERT	67	66	72	66	271	-17	122,400	275.3	80.4	73.6	109
7	P-U-JOHANSSON	65	70	68	69	272	-16	109,650	281.5	69.6	69.4	106
	Joel EDWARDS	65	68	65	74	272	-16	109,650	277.0	82.1	70.8	108
9	Nick PRICE	70	68	69	67	274	-14	98,600	273.1	67.9	73.6	111
10	Vijay SINGH	64	67	75	69	275	-13	88,400	298.9	67.9	75.0	112
	Chris RILEY	68	69	69	69	275	-13	88,400	280.4	78.6	75.0	115

Pos	Name	R1	R2	R3	R4	Total	To par
12	C HOWELL	68	70	68	70	276	-12
	Mark O'MEARA	66	70	68	72	276	-12
14	Carlos FRANCO	67	70	72	68	277	-11
	Jeff SLUMAN	70	71	68	68	277	-11
	Shaun MICHEEL	67	70	70	70	277	-11
17	Lee JANZEN	72	68	70	68	278	-10
	Paul AZINGER	68	72	70	68	278	-10
	Glen DAY	69	71	69	69	278	-10
	Loren ROBERTS	68	72	69	69	278	-10
	B GEIBERGER	69	70	70	69	278	-10
	B HENNINGER	70	69	69	70	278	-10
23	David GOSSETT	71	70	68	70	279	-9
	Fred FUNK	70	71	71	67	279	-9
	Steve LOWERY	72	70	66	71	279	-9
	Greg KRAFT	70	70	69	70	279	-9
	S MARUYAMA	71	71	70	67	279	-9
	Kenny PERRY	71	70	72	66	279	-9
	B McCALLISTER	70	69	74	66	279	-9
	Skip KENDALL	71	70	72	66	279	-9
	Danny ELLIS	65	72	69	73	279	-9
32	T ARMOUR III	68	71	71	70	280	-8
	Bill GLASSON	70	70	70	70	280	-8
	Mike SPOSA	65	71	73	71	280	-8
	J PARNEVIK	73	69	67	71	280	-8
	Jay Don BLAKE	70	72	69	69	280	-8
	David PEOPLES	70	71	72	67	280	-8
	Bob TWAY	70	72	73	65	280	-8
39	Spike McROY	70	71	69	71	281	-7
	John RIEGGER	67	73	70	71	281	-7
	Steve FLESCH	68	69	74	70	281	-7
	D BERGANIO	69	72	71	69	281	-7
	Brad ELDER	68	74	70	69	281	-7
	E TOLEDO	68	69	76	68	281	-7
	F LICKLITER	71	70	72	68	281	-7
	S ELKINGTON	70	71	73	67	281	-7
47	K SUTHERLAND	70	69	69	74	282	-6
	Jonathan KAYE	68	68	70	76	282	-6
	Tom BYRUM	68	72	67	75	282	-6
	Briny BAIRD	68	72	74	68	282	-6
51	B HUGHES	71	68	71	73	283	-5
	Frank NOBILO	69	72	70	72	283	-5
	Stewart CINK	69	70	74	70	283	-5
	Russ COCHRAN	72	68	76	67	283	-5
55	D SUTHERLAND	70	71	69	74	284	-4
	C BECKMAN	69	71	72	72	284	-4
	M GOGGIN	68	73	71	72	284	-4
	Grant WAITE	70	71	73	70	284	-4
59	Jim CARTER	68	71	71	75	285	-3
	P JACOBSEN	73	66	72	74	285	-3
	Brad FAXON	71	71	69	74	285	-3
62	H FRAZAR	67	70	74	75	286	-2
	Larry MIZE	71	69	72	74	286	-2
	J LEONARD	68	74	71	73	286	-2
65	R SABBATINI	71	71	72	73	287	-1
	Stuart APPLEBY	70	71	74	72	287	-1
67	J.J. HENRY	68	74	73	73	288	E
68	Andrew MAGEE	74	66	71	78	289	+1
	David FROST	69	72	73	75	289	+1
70	Jose COCERES	66	75	74	77	292	+4
	Jimmy GREEN	69	72	77	74	292	+4
72	J.L. LEWIS	67	75	75	82	299	+11

Tournament Report

Chris DiMarco's putting technique may never make it into a coaching manual, but his 'Psycho Grip' was good enough to need just 26 putts during a final round 65 that set up a play-off with David Duval whom he defeated at the first extra hole to win the Buick Challenge.

The pair tied on 267 in regulation play, Duval having fired a Sunday 63 to set the clubhouse target, after both had come from behind on the final day.

Overnight leader Davis Love faded with a Sunday 70, finishing fifth behind DiMarco, Duval, Bob Estes and Neal Lancaster. DiMarco drained a 12-footer on the last in regulation play to join Duval in the play-off.

Duval meanwhile played some sublime golf on the final day and made a decent fist of defending the championship he won 12 months ago, despite not having played that much over the past six weeks.

The Open champion's first mistake of the day, though, was when it mattered – on the first hole of the play-off.

His approach to the 18th dived over the green and came to rest in a bunker. Duval blasted out to eight feet but couldn't hole his putt and as DiMarco had safely holed out for a par four, the title was the New Yorker's.

As this was the last counting event towards entry to the Tour Championship there were many subplots to the drama, with Kenny Perry managing to hang onto 30th place on the Money List with a last day 66.

MISSED THE CUT: Jerry SMITH 70 73, Geoff OGILVY 64 79, Olin BROWNE 74 69, Hal SUTTON 71 72, Jim FURYK 70 73, Tom PERNICE JR. 73 70, John COOK 68 75, Gary NICKLAUS 71 72, Sergio GARCIA 70 74, Glen HNATIUK 73 71, Steve PATE 73 71, Jerry KELLY 71 73, Garrett WILLIS 71 73, Chris SMITH 72 72, Fulton ALLEM 71 73, Scott DUNLAP 70 74, Michael MUEHR 71 73, Ted TRYBA 70 74, Ernie ELS 73 71, John DALY 71 74, Michael BRADLEY 75 70, Steve JONES 73 72, Doug DUNAKEY 72 73, Billy MAYFAIR 72 73, Kirk TRIPLETT 73 72, Michael CLARK II 70 75, Luke DONALD 71 74, Joe DURANT 75 71, Joe OGILVIE 71 75, Corey PAVIN 72 74, Paul GOYDOS 73 73, Robin FREEMAN 68 78, Edward FRYATT 76 70, Bob BURNS 70 76, Jay WILLIAMSON 72 74, Kaname YOKOO 71 75, Ian LEGGATT 74 72, K.J. CHOI 71 75, Craig PERKS 77 70, Brian GAY 70 77, Scott SIMPSON 72 75, Brandt JOBE 69 78, Gabriel HJERTSTEDT 72 76, Jerry PATE 74 74, Tom SCHERRER 75 73, Doug BARRON 73 76, Carl PAULSON 73 76, Gary HALLBERG 77 73, Billy ANDRADE 74 77, Matt GOGEL 78 74, Len MATTIACE 77 76, Paul STANKOWSKI 79 74, Billy Ray BROWN 73 81, Pete JORDAN 76 78.

Course Profile

Callaway Gardens (par 72, 7,057 yards) is a venue tailor made for the big hitters.

The four par fives are all reachable in two for the likes of Woods and Duval and can make or break a players score.

The last five champions have all played the par fives in 13-under or better.

The fairways aren't particularly narrow so not every errant tee shot is punished.

Players have to shape shots from left to right and vice versa.

Players/Points to Note

●**David Duval**'s play-off defeat in 2001 means he can boast four top-ten finishes in six starts in this event (including a win in 2000) and a stroke average of 68.70 - the lowest. He always enjoys playing in his home state of Georgia. Duval, along with **Chris DiMarco**, tied the 72-hole record in 2001.

●**Stewart Cink** was a disappointing 51st in 2001 but he has posted three top-ten finishes in the previous five years of this event. Now living in Georgia, Cink's big-hitting game is well suited to this track.

●**Scott Hoch** boasts the most top-ten finishes in this tournament – six – although he has yet to win.

●**Davis Love** jointly holds the 72-hole course record (267 with **Steve Elkington** – a dual winner, Duval and DiMarco) and hasn't been outside the top 18 in his last six visits, while **Steve Lowery** holds the course record of 60.

●**Fred Funk**, 69-under par in 11 visits, was successful here in 1995 and has finished runner-up twice since then, while **Jeff Maggert**, **Hal Sutton**, **Paul Azinger**, **David Frost** and **Jeff Sluman** have all played well here over the years.

●Outsiders to follow in 2002, if they are in good enough form, would be **Jim Carter**, **Steve Flesch**, **Skip Kendall** and **John Maginnes**.

Previous Results

2000: 1. David Duval (-19), 2. Jeff Maggert (-17), Nick Price (-17).

1999: 1. David Toms (-17), 2. Stuart Appleby (-14), 3. Jay Delsing (-12), Craig Barlow (-12), Davis Love III (-12).

1998: 1. Steve Elkington (-21), won play-off, 2. Fred Funk (-21), 3. Bill Glasson (-20).

1997: 1. Davis Love III (-21), 2. Stewart Cink (-17), 3. Steve Lowery (-16), Hal Sutton (-16).

1996: 1. Michael Bradley (-10), won play-off, 2. John Maginnes (-10), Fred Funk (-10), Davis Love III (-10), Len Mattiace (-10). Played over 36 holes.

TOUR CHAMPIONSHIP

Champions G.C., 1 Nov to 4 Nov 2001, purse $5,000,000

Pos	Name	R1	R2	R3	R4	Total	To par	Money	DD(y)	DA%	GIR%	Putts
1	Mike WEIR	68	66	68	68	270	-14	900,000	293.9	55.4	76.4	118
2	Ernie ELS	69	68	65	68	270	-14	385,000	308.8	50.0	76.4	119
	Sergio GARCIA	69	67	66	68	270	-14	385,000	299.6	53.6	72.2	113
	David TOMS	73	66	64	67	270	-14	385,000	299.8	64.3	86.1	123
5	Kenny PERRY	70	67	65	69	271	-13	202,500	306.3	57.1	86.1	125
	Scott VERPLANK	67	65	68	71	271	-13	202,500	281.1	73.2	75.0	113
7	Bob ESTES	71	66	65	70	272	-12	166,666	300.0	58.9	76.4	116
	Jim FURYK	70	71	62	69	272	-12	166,666	293.3	76.8	81.9	121
	David DUVAL	69	69	63	71	272	-12	166,666	317.4	51.8	83.3	124
10	Chris DIMARCO	69	68	69	69	275	-9	136,666	297.4	66.1	76.4	119
	Joe DURANT	73	65	67	70	275	-9	136,666	295.0	85.7	73.6	119
	B LANGER	65	68	69	73	275	-9	136,666	277.6	71.4	73.6	118

Pos	Name	R1	R2	R3	R4	Total	To par
13	Stewart CINK	70	70	67	69	276	-8
	Tiger WOODS	70	67	69	70	276	-8
15	Tom LEHMAN	69	68	72	68	277	-7
	Davis LOVE III	70	72	66	69	277	-7
17	Vijay SINGH	70	73	68	67	278	-6
18	S McCARRON	70	70	70	69	279	-5
19	M CALCAVECCHIA	71	64	69	76	280	-4
20	F LICKLITER II	65	73	69	74	281	-3
	Jeff SLUMAN	73	70	66	72	281	-3
22	R ALLENBY	76	67	67	73	283	-1
	J LEONARD	69	66	71	77	283	-1
24	S STRICKER	74	70	72	68	284	E
25	S LOWERY	67	70	73	75	285	+1
26	Brad FAXON	68	70	70	78	286	+2
	Billy MAYFAIR	72	74	72	68	286	+2
	Hal SUTTON	70	73	70	73	286	+2
29	Scott HOCH	74	71	70	72	287	+3

Tournament Report

Mike Weir must like leaving his tour victories until the final event of the year.

In 2000 he claimed the season-ending WGX AmEx Championship, 12 months on the Canadian left-hander was at it again, this time capturing the Tour Championship title – the last tournament of 2001.

Weir won a thrilling four man play-off to land his third US Tour win, defeating USPGA Champion David Toms, dual US Open winner Ernie Els and two-time 2001 US Tour champion Sergio Garcia at the first extra hole.

Weir looked to have thrown his chance of victory away when he bogeyed the 72 hole but with Toms dropping a shot on the 17th he was given a reprieve.

Els and Garcia picked up a birdie on the 18th and 17th respectively to make the play-off. Scott Verplank started the day with a one shot lead but with some of the world's best players snapping at his heels the Ryder Cup rookie was unable to keep the chasing pack at bay – eventually missing out on the extra holes by a shot, along with Kenny Perry.

The play-off quartet went back to the 18th tee but after they had played their tee shots only Weir and Toms had found the fairway - Els and Garcia were in the trees.

And when the Canadian hit his approach to six feet, the contest was all but over. None of the other could fashion a birdie, but Weir could, and he took the title, with it becoming the first non-American to win the event.

ERNIE ELS . . . just lost out in play-off

Course Profile

Champions G.C. (par 71, 7,220 yards) in Houston was used in 2001. Straight hitters prosper on this track as the fairways are narrow. The greens are huge.

In 2002, East Lake Golf Club (par 70, 6,890 yards) in Atlanta will stage the event. It also staged the Tour Championship in 1998 and 2000.

The fairways are narrow and the rough around them deep – so players who are accurate off the tee prosper. The greens and fairways can get firm and fast.

Players/Points to Note

●This event is only open to the top 30 on the Money List   there is no halfway cut. The event alternates between Champions Golf Club in Houston and the East Lake Golf Club in Atlanta. Next season in will be at the latter.

●**Vijay Singh**, who has yet to win the Tour Championship, has done everything but. The Fijian has played in this event on seven occasions and finished in the top ten on six of them. His form figures from 1995 read 6-9-10-2-9-3-17. He was 16th in 1993 and those seven appearances give him a stroke average of 69.75.

●**Phil Mickelson** won the last time this event was held at East Lake, **Tiger Woods** was second and in six starts in this event he has a stroke average of 69.67.

●**David Duval** has won at Champions G.C. and has posted five top-ten finishes in a total of seven starts.

●**Davis Love** failed to finish outside the top ten for the first time in five starts in 2001.

●**Jim Furyk** has gained a stroke average of 69.35 and three top-ten finishes in five starts.

●**Ernie Els**, **David Toms** and **Sergio Garcia** contested the thrilling play-off in 2001, won by **Mike Weir**, and all three must surely win at some stage of their careers.

Previous Results

2000: 1. Phil Mickelson (-13), 2. Tiger Woods (-11), 3. Ernie Els (-7), Nick Price (-7), Vijay Singh (-7).

1999: 1. Tiger Woods (-15), 2. Davis Love III (-11), 3. Brent Geiberger (-10).

1998: 1. Hal Sutton (-6), won play-off, 2. Vijay Singh (-6), 3. Jim Furyk (-5), Jesper Parnevik (-5).

1997: 1. David Duval (-11), 2. Jim Furyk (-10), 3. Davis Love III (-9).

1996: 1. Tom Lehman (-12), 2. Brad Faxon (-6), 3. Steve Stricker (-5).

SOUTHERN FARM BUREAU CLASSIC

Annandale G.C., 1 Nov to 4 Nov 2001, purse $2,400,000

Pos	Name	R1	R2	R3	R4	Total	To par	Money	DD(y)	DA%	GIR%	Putts
1	C BECKMAN	66	69	67	67	269	-19	432,000	283.4	83.9	80.3	112
2	Chad CAMPBELL	70	64	65	71	270	-18	259,200	283.0	73.2	75.0	108
3	Fred FUNK	65	69	69	68	271	-17	163,200	264.8	85.7	77.8	111
4	Dan FORSMAN	68	70	65	69	272	-16	115,200	267.9	91.1	70.8	110
5	Brett QUIGLEY	68	69	69	67	273	-15	96,000	296.0	75.0	77.8	114
6	K.J. CHOI	67	69	68	70	274	-14	72,600	276.8	71.4	68.1	109
	J.J. HENRY	69	67	68	70	274	-14	72,600	289.3	83.9	77.8	113
	Carl PAULSON	67	66	70	71	274	-14	72,600	280.4	82.1	72.2	109
	Dicky PRIDE	66	68	67	73	274	-14	72,600	267.4	83.9	69.4	105
	Loren ROBERTS	70	71	67	66	274	-14	72,600	265.0	91.1	77.8	112
	Chris SMITH	70	68	69	67	274	-14	72,600	291.5	75.0	86.1	119

Pos	Name	R1	R2	R3	R4	Total	To par
12	Willie WOOD	71	65	68	71	275	-13
13	N LANCASTER	69	68	70	69	276	-12
	David PEOPLES	74	67	66	69	276	-12
	Lee PORTER	72	63	72	69	276	-12
16	Russ COCHRAN	70	69	66	72	277	-11
17	Briny BAIRD	71	67	71	69	278	-10
	J GALLAGHER Jr.	72	66	72	68	278	-10
	John HUSTON	70	71	66	71	278	-10
	T ISENHOUR	71	70	70	67	278	-10
	Matt KUCHAR	70	69	68	71	278	-10
	Mike SPOSA	68	70	70	70	278	-10
23	Carlos FRANCO	72	66	72	69	279	-9
	David GOSSETT	71	70	67	71	279	-9
	Chris TIDLAND	71	67	72	69	279	-9
	Kirk TRIPLETT	67	69	70	73	279	-9
	Richard ZOKOL	69	70	68	72	279	-9
28	Tom BYRUM	71	71	68	70	280	-8
	Joel EDWARDS	69	71	69	71	280	-8
	Jimmy GREEN	68	70	74	68	280	-8
	C HOWELL III	71	68	68	73	280	-8
	Brandt JOBE	67	66	69	78	280	-8
	Pete JORDAN	70	69	69	72	280	-8
	Jeff MAGGERT	68	75	67	70	280	-8
	B McCALLISTER	69	71	67	73	280	-8
	E TOLEDO	71	68	69	72	280	-8
37	Doug BARRON	70	69	70	72	281	-7
	Bob BURNS	68	69	72	72	281	-7
	M CLARK II	72	69	69	71	281	-7
	John COOK	68	70	72	71	281	-7
	Glen DAY	72	71	68	70	281	-7
	Jason GORE	71	71	68	71	281	-7
	Lee JANZEN	72	68	69	72	281	-7
	Jerry KELLY	71	69	69	72	281	-7
	Chris RILEY	68	70	72	71	281	-7
	Heath SLOCUM	69	65	76	71	281	-7
	Garrett WILLIS	72	68	69	72	281	-7
48	Brad ELDER	71	70	70	71	282	-6
	Brian GAY	70	70	67	75	282	-6
	Glen HNATIUK	71	69	72	70	282	-6
	Andrew MAGEE	68	66	72	76	282	-6
	Steve PATE	67	74	72	69	282	-6
	Tommy TOLLES	73	65	76	68	282	-6
54	R COUGHLAN	68	71	74	70	283	-5
	Doug DUNAKEY	69	72	71	71	283	-5
	Ted TRYBA	71	69	70	73	283	-5
57	K CLEARWATER	70	72	70	72	284	-4
	Craig KANADA	69	68	74	73	284	-4
	Skip KENDALL	69	71	72	72	284	-4
	Grant WAITE	69	69	70	76	284	-4
61	Jeff BREHAUT	70	73	66	76	285	-3
	Scott DUNLAP	72	67	66	80	285	-3
	Danny ELLIS	71	71	71	72	285	-3
	S MICHEEL	71	72	69	73	285	-3
	D MORLAND IV	68	73	73	71	285	-3
	Bob TWAY	68	68	71	78	285	-3
67	Ben FERGUSON	70	71	73	72	286	-2
	B HUGHES	72	70	70	74	286	-2
	T PERNICE Jr.	70	71	74	71	286	-2
70	M GOGGIN	74	69	71	73	287	-1
71	Mark BROOKS	66	73	72	77	288	E
	Joe OGILVIE	72	71	72	73	288	E
73	Woody AUSTIN	71	70	72	76	289	+1
	Len MATTIACE	69	73	73	74	289	+1
75	Greg KRAFT	71	72	75	74	292	+4
76	R FREEMAN	70	71	71	81	293	+5

Tournament Report

Cameron Beckman won his first US Tour event by making birdie at three of the last five holes to power past Chad Campbell to claim the Southern Farm Bureau Classic title at Annandale Golf Club in Madison.

The Texan, whose earnings in the week pushed his seasonal haul to over £1million (and 50th place in the Money List), was trailing Campbell by three strokes with five holes to play but his birdie blast saw he overtake his faltering rival.

Campbell, who was playing in just his second US Tour event, had led going into the final round by two strokes after he dominated the first three days.

He had already won three times on the Buy.com Tour this season and looked comfortable with his lead until Beckman launched his late charge.

After an uninspiring outward nine, two par saving putts at 11 and 12 seemed to rejuvenate Beckman.

Birdies followed at the 14th and the 15th, with the shot he picked up at the latter, perhaps the turning point, as Campbell was in the process of bogeying.

The pair were then level at 18 under. But Beckman went ahead at the 17th when he made another birdie to Campbell's par.

The par five 18th, beckoned but with water guarding the green neither player was brave enough to go for it in two.

The pair laid up, but after finding the green in three, Campbell's long effort fell short, leaving Beckman with the simple task of two putting for the championship, which he duly did.

MISSED THE CUT: Billy ANDRADE 73 71, Paul GOYDOS 76 68, Brian HENNINGER 72 72, J.L. LEWIS 74 70, Andrew McLARDY 72 72, Michael MUEHR 71 73, Gary NICKLAUS 71 73, Harrison FRAZAR 74 71, Hunter HAAS 75 70, Sean MURPHY 75 70, Brian WILSON 74 71, Tommy ARMOUR III 72 74, Kevin JOHNSON 74 72, Cliff KRESGE 74 72, Tom PURTZER 72 74, Dave STOCKTON Jr. 71 75, Fulton ALLEM 77 70, Rich BEEM 78 69, Marco DAWSON 75 72, Kent JONES 73 74, Jeff JULIAN 78 69, Ian LEGGATT 75 72, Mark McCUMBER 75 72, Tim THELEN 73 74, Rocky WALCHER 74 73, Bill GLASSON 74 74, Craig PERKS 79 69, Brett WETTERICH 77 71, Jeff HART 75 74, Tom KITE 78 71, Bryce MOLDER 72 77, Kelly GRUNEWALD 75 75, Gabriel HJERTSTEDT 75 75, Spike McROY 74 76, Mark HENSBY 72 80, Steve ALLAN 81 73, John RESTINO 72 82, John RIEGGER 75 75, David FROST 76 76, Craig A. SPENCE D 76, Jay WILLIAMSON D 77, Frank NOBILO W/D 80, Scott SIMPSON W/D 80, Jeremy ANDERSON W/D.

Course Profile

Annandale Golf Club (par 72, 7,199 yards) in Madison is a Jack Nicklaus designed venue which has held this event for the past eight years and one on which the tour pros can shoot low scores. Three of the four par fives are reachable to almost everyone – especially the last, although there is a certain amount of bottle required as the approach shot is over water. The layout has many water hazards, in fact. The fairways are tree lined but not particularly narrow.

Players/Points to Note

●This is the last tournament of the year for the rank and file of the US Tour. The top 125 in the Money List retain their card for next season, watch out for any player hovering around that mark to play above themselves. Dan Forsman and Pete Jordan have done just that in the last two years. All the best players will be participating in the Tour Championship.

●**Fred Funk** is the classic straight hitting journeyman pro who relishes this type of event. In nine starts he has finished in the top 11 on six occasions. He has a stroke average of 68.32 in 31 competitive rounds.

●**Brian Henninger** has won this event twice – both at Annandale – and can boast three other top-20 finishes.

●**Steve Lowery**'s win in 2000 was predictable. He hadn't shot a round over par at the course in three previous visits and was fourth here in 1997.

●**Chad Campbell** was making the step up to the full tour after winning three times on the Buy.com Tour – and nearly won. Any player who has built up confidence by winning on the feeder tour will have a chance in this weak event.

●**Kirk Triplett**, **Chris DiMarco**, **Grant Waite**, **Pete Jordan** and **Blaine McAllister** can all boast multiple top-ten finishes.

Previous Results

2000: 1. Steve Lowery (-22), won play-off, 2. Skip Kendall (-22), 3. Kenny Perry (-21).

1999: 1. Brian Henninger (-14), 2. Chris DiMarco (-11), 3. Glen Day (-10), Paul Stankowski (-10), Perry Moss (-10).

1998: 1. Fred Funk (-18), 2. Tim Loustalot (-16), Franklin Langham (-16), Paul Goydos (-16).

1997: 1. Billy Ray Brown (-17), 2. Mike Standly (-16), 3. Mike Brisky (-15).

1996: 1. Willie Wood (-20), 2. Kirk Triplett (-19), 3. Scott Hoch (-17), Greg Kraft (-17).

THE MASTERS

Augusta, 5 Apr to 8 Apr 2001, purse $5,514,920

Pos	Name	R1	R2	R3	R4	Total	To par	Money	DD(y)	DA%	GIR%	Putts
1	Tiger WOODS	70	66	68	68	272	-16	$1,008,000	305.5	74.1	81.9	121
2	David DUVAL	71	66	70	67	274	-14	$604,800	290.9	69.6	72.2	114
3	P MICKELSON	67	69	69	70	275	-13	$380,800	277.6	64.3	70.8	112
4	T IZAWA	71	66	74	67	278	-10	$246,400	286.4	78.6	70.8	116
	M CALCAVECCHIA	72	66	68	72	278	-10	$246,400	284.8	69.6	72.2	114
6	B LANGER	73	69	68	69	279	-9	$181,300	273.2	69.6	70.8	113
	Jim FURYK	69	71	70	69	279	-9	$181,300	270.4	73.2	66.7	111
	Ernie ELS	71	68	68	72	279	-9	$181,300	281.5	73.2	63.8	113
	Kirk TRIPLETT	68	70	70	71	279	-9	$181,300	266.5	71.4	72.2	115
10	Brad FAXON	73	68	68	71	280	-8	$128,800	273.8	75.0	76.4	116
	S STRICKER	66	71	72	71	280	-8	$128,800	285.5	62.5	65.3	119
	M Angel JIMINEZ	68	72	71	69	280	-8	$128,800	270.1	76.8	66.7	112
	A CABRERA	66	71	70	73	280	-8	$128,800	301.1	60.7	77.8	118
	C DIMARCO	65	69	72	74	280	-8	$128,800	278.2	62.5	65.3	108

15	J M OLAZABAL	70	68	71	72	281	-7
	Paul AZINGER	70	71	71	69	281	-7
	Rocco MEDIATE	72	70	66	73	281	-7
18	Vijay SINGH	69	71	73	69	282	-6
	Tom LEHMAN	75	68	71	68	282	-6
20	Mark O'MEARA	69	74	72	68	283	-5
	J PARNEVIK	71	71	72	69	283	-5
	John HUSTON	67	75	72	69	283	-5
	Jeff MAGGERT	72	70	70	71	283	-5
24	Darren CLARKE	72	67	72	73	284	-4
25	Tom SCHERRER	71	71	70	73	285	-3
26	Fred COUPLES	74	71	73	68	286	-2
27	P HARRINGTON	75	69	72	71	287	-1
	Justin LEONARD	73	71	72	71	287	-1
	Mike WEIR	74	69	72	72	287	-1
	Steve JONES	74	70	72	71	287	-1
31	Stuart APPLEBY	72	70	70	76	288	E

	Mark BROOKS	70	71	77	70	288	E
	D WALDORF	72	70	71	75	288	E
	Lee JANZEN	67	70	72	79	288	E
	David TOMS	72	72	71	73	288	E
36	Hal SUTTON	74	69	71	75	289	+1
37	Loren ROBERTS	71	74	73	72	290	+2
	Chris PERRY	68	74	74	74	290	+2
	Scott HOCH	74	70	72	74	290	+2
40	Steve LOWERY	72	72	78	70	292	+4
	S KATAYAMA	75	70	73	74	292	+4
	F LANGHAM	72	73	75	72	292	+4
43	Dudley HART	74	70	78	71	293	+5
	Bob MAY	71	74	73	75	293	+5
	Jonathan KAYE	74	71	74	74	293	+5
46	Carlos FRANCO	71	71	77	75	294	+6
47	Robert ALLENBY	71	74	75	75	295	+7

A 'CABRERA.

MISSED THE CUT: Sergio GARCIA 70 76, Davis LOVE III 71 75, Jose COCERES 77 69, Thomas BJORN 70 76, Dennis PAULSON 73 73, Notah BEGAY III 73 73, James DRISCOLL (Am) 68 78, Sandy LYLE 74 73, Shigeki MARUYAMA 77 70, Scott VERPLANK 69 78, Joe DURANT 73 74, Jack NICKLAUS 73 75, Eduardo ROMERO 75 73, Tom WATSON 78 70, Ian WOOSNAM 71 77, Greg CHALMERS 76 72, Nick PRICE 73 75, Larry MIZE 74 74, Rory SABBATINI 73 75, Gary PLAYER 73 76, Fuzzy ZOELLER 77 72, Stewart CINK 75 74, Colin MONTGOMERIE 73 76, Paul LAWRIE 73 76, Retief GOOSEN 75 74, Steve FLESCH 74 76, Grant WAITE 79 71, Aaron BADDELEY 75 75, Nick FALDO 75 76, Raymond FLOYD 75 76, Mikko ILONEN (Am) 72 79, Seve BALLESTEROS 76 76, Craig STADLER 79 73, Charles COODY 80 72, Pierre FULKE 73 79, Greg NORMAN 71 82, Michael CAMPBELL 78 75, D J TRAHAN (Am) 78 75, Jeff QUINNEY (Am) 80 76, Greg PUGA (Am) 76 80, Arnold PALMER 82 76, Ben CRENSHAW 81 78, Tommy AARON 81 82, Billy CASPER 87 80, Gay BREWER 84 RETD, Doug FORD W/D.

A. SOTT.   J. KQLY.   I. MGINNLEY.

Sponsored by Stan James

Tournament Report

It was perhaps the greatest sporting achievement of all. Tiger Woods, having been victorious in the previous three Majors, claimed the 65th US Masters at Augusta to lay claim to the Grand Slam.

Many will argue that a slam is only a slam if all four events are won in the same year, but whether you subscribe to that opinion or not seems irrelevant.

He proved that he is without doubt the best golfer the world has ever seen.

Woods took over at the top of the leaderboard after the third round – Chris DiMarco had led since day one after opening scores of 65 and 69. But the challenges came from David Duval and Phil Mickelson on Sunday.

Duval, who started the day three behind Woods, took the lead momentarily after birdieing the eighth.

But by the time Woods had completed that hole the World No.1 was back in front.

A bogey at the 12th by Woods gave hope to Duval and Mickelson, but they both missed their chance, with the latter prone to an alarming number of blunders (he actually made the most birdies in the history of any Masters but also carded a number double bogeys).

And when Mickelson failed to make par at 16 he fell two behind Woods. Duval had also bogeyed the 16th and with Woods giving nothing away down the stretch, he faced the last knowing a par would be enough for victory.

After finding the green in two, Woods rolled in an 18-footer for a quite unique success.

GRAND SLAM . . . Tiger Woods lands his fourth Major in a row.

Course Profile

Changes are afoot to Augusta National (par 72, 6,985 yards) with 300 yards looking like it's going to be added to its length for the 2002 renewal.

But the fact remains that this is a unique golf course as it has little or no rough. Accuracy off the tee is not important but length obviously helps.

The greens can be lightning quick and good putting is a must. Patience is essential. Experienced golfers and those with nerves of steel win.

Players/Points to Note

●**Tiger Woods** created history with his Masters win in 2001 and has played the event seven times now. His full record from 1995 reads – 41-MC-Win-8-18-5-1. His win in 1997 was by a record 12 shots and he produced the lowest 72 hole score of 270. His game is tailor made for Augusta.

●**David Duval** plans his whole early season around the Masters in 2000 and in his last four starts his lowest finish has been sixth.

●**Davis Love** is yet to win a Masters title but has finished in the top ten on five occasions in 11 starts (including runner-up twice).

●**Phil Mickelson** is also a non-winner with a superb August record. The left has posted five top-ten finishes in nine starts. His magical short game will see him contest again.

●**Jose Maria Olazabal**'s short game has led him to two wins and five top-ten finishes in 14 starts.

●**Fred Couples** has never missed a cut at Augusta in 16 appearances.

●The European challenge hasn't been a strong one recently. **Colin Montgomerie** (nine appearances), **Lee Westwood** (four) and **Darren Clarke** (three) have managed just one top-ten finish each. **Jesper Parnevik** and **Sergio Garcia** are yet to trouble the leaderboard. South African, **Ernie Els** (three top tens), and Fijian, **Vijay Singh** (2000 champions), have done a lot better.

US OPEN

Southern Hills C.C., 14 Jun to 17 Jun 2001, purse $3,500,000

Pos	Name	R1	R2	R3	R4	Total	To par	Money	DD(y)	DA%	GIR%	Putts
1	Retief GOOSEN	66	70	69	71	276	-4	$900,000	298.3	67.9	66.7	115
	Won play-off											
2	Mark BROOKS	72	64	70	70	276	-4	$530,000	275.4	75.0	73.6	119
3	Stewart CINK	69	69	67	72	277	-3	$325,310	305.0	48.2	61.1	111
4	Rocco MEDIATE	71	68	67	72	278	-2	$226,777	291.9	57.1	61.1	113
5	Tom KITE	73	72	72	64	281	+1	$172,912	281.5	66.1	61.1	114
	Paul AZINGER	74	67	69	71	281	+1	$172,912	300.0	62.5	63.9	117
7	Davis LOVE III	72	69	71	70	282	+2	$125,172	309.8	51.8	55.6	113
	Vijay SINGH	74	70	74	64	282	+2	$125,172	293.1	60.7	61.1	113
	Angel CABRERA	70	71	72	69	282	+2	$125,172	307.0	60.7	54.2	106
	Phil MICKELSON	70	69	68	75	282	+2	$125,172	322.0	66.1	61.1	117
	Kirk TRIPLETT	72	69	71	70	282	+2	$125,172	282.6	75.0	61.1	116

Pos	Name	R1	R2	R3	R4	Total	To par
12	Tiger WOODS	74	71	69	69	283	+3
	Sergio GARCIA	70	68	68	77	283	+3
	Michael ALLEN	77	68	67	71	283	+3
	Matt GOGEL	70	69	74	70	283	+3
16	David DUVAL	70	69	71	74	284	+4
	Scott HOCH	73	73	69	69	284	+4
	Chris DIMARCO	69	73	70	72	284	+4
19	Corey PAVIN	70	75	68	72	285	+5
	Chris PERRY	72	71	73	69	285	+5
	Mike WEIR	67	76	68	74	285	+5
22	S VERPLANK	71	71	73	71	286	+6
	Thomas BJORN	72	69	73	72	286	+6
24	Steve LOWERY	71	73	72	71	287	+7
	Joe DURANT	71	74	70	72	287	+7
	M CALCAVECCHIA	70	74	73	70	287	+7
	Hal SUTTON	70	75	71	71	287	+7
	Tom LEHMAN	76	68	69	74	287	+7
	Olin BROWNE	71	74	71	71	287	+7
30	P HARRINGTON	73	70	71	74	288	+8
	J PARNEVIK	73	73	74	68	288	+8
	Dean WILSON	71	74	72	71	288	+8
	Bob ESTES	70	72	75	71	288	+8
	Steve JONES	73	73	72	70	288	+8
	G HJERTSTEDT	72	74	70	72	288	+8
	Darren CLARKE	74	71	71	72	288	+8
	Bob MAY	72	72	69	75	288	+8
	B MOLDER (Am)	75	71	68	74	288	+8
	J.L. LEWIS	68	68	77	75	288	+8
40	B LANGER	71	73	71	74	289	+9
	Tim HERRON	71	74	73	71	289	+9
	Briny BAIRD	71	72	70	76	289	+9
	S MICHEEL	73	70	75	71	289	+9
44	Fred FUNK	78	68	71	73	290	+10
	T IZAWA	69	74	74	73	290	+10
	B CHAMBLEE	72	71	71	76	290	+10
	Jeff MAGGERT	69	73	72	76	290	+10
	D WALDORF	75	68	69	78	290	+10
	K SUTHERLAND	73	72	73	72	290	+10
	Tom BYRUM	74	72	72	72	290	+10
51	E ROMERO	74	72	72	73	291	+11
52	Loren ROBERTS	69	76	69	78	292	+12
	C MONTGOMERIE	71	70	77	74	292	+12
	Mark WIEBE	73	72	74	73	292	+12
	Bob TWAY	75	71	72	74	292	+12
	Hale IRWIN	67	75	74	76	292	+12
	Jose COCERES	70	73	75	74	292	+12
	Scott DUNLAP	74	70	73	75	292	+12
	Brandt JOBE	77	68	71	76	292	+12
	F LICKLITER	75	71	70	76	292	+12
	J WALKER (Am)	79	66	74	73	292	+12
62	Jim FURYK	70	70	71	82	293	+13
	Dudley HART	71	73	74	75	293	+13
	Richard ZOKOL	72	71	74	76	293	+13
	Tim PETROVIC	74	71	75	73	293	+13
66	Ernie ELS	71	74	77	72	294	+14
	Peter LONARD	76	69	70	79	294	+14
	Dan FORSMAN	75	71	77	71	294	+14
	David TOMS	71	71	77	75	294	+14
	H FRAZAR	73	73	76	72	294	+14
	David PEOPLES	73	73	72	76	294	+14
72	Nick FALDO	76	70	74	75	295	+15
	F LANGHAM	75	71	75	74	295	+15
74	Anthony KANG	74	72	77	73	296	+16
	M GRONBERG	74	69	74	79	296	+16
	Gary ORR	74	72	74	76	296	+16
	T JAIDEE	73	73	72	78	296	+16
78	J MCGOVERN	71	73	77	76	297	+17
79	S GANGLUFF	74	72	78	77	301	+21

Tournament Report

You could neither watch nor turn away as Retief Goosen contrived to miss from two feet on the final hole of regulation play before returning the following day to defeat Mark Brooks in a 18-hole play-off to win the US Open.

The drama came on the last hole of the 72. Goosen, who had led all tournament after an opening 66, needed a par to win but amazingly three putted from a dozen feet, the last from no more than 24 inches.

Brooks and Stewart Cink also needed three putts on the last, the former from 40 feet, the latter from less. In fact Cink's penultimate stroke of the championship missed from 18 inches ñ a hurried effort that he thought would be meaningless given Goosen's position. It wasn't and Cink missed out on the play.

Brooks also probably wished he had, as Goosen dominated the extra round, managing to one putt seven holes on the outward nine. Goosen's birdie on the 9th put the South African in control, as Brooks hooked his drive, found the rough and eventually took bogey.

There was another two shot swing at the tenth, again in Goosen's favour, and suddenly the Springbok led by five. Game over. Justice was done, and Goosen's horror miss on the last in regulation play didn't matter.

It was a deserved first Major win for the South African whose putting was superb throughout. There were fleeting challenges from Phil Mickelson and Sergio Garcia but nervy final rounds put paid to both their chances.

MISSED THE CUT: Brad FAXON 73 74, Gary KOCH 75 72, Robert DAMRON 73 74, Mike HULBERT 75 72, Lee JANZEN 77 70, Tom PERNICE 74 73, Chad CAMPBELL 76 71, Rich BEEM 74 73, Brett QUIGLEY 71 76, Pete JORDAN 77 70, Mark O'MEARA 74 74, Nick PRICE 74 74, Steve STRICKER 73 75, Kyoung-Ju CHOI 78 70, Skip KENDALL 74 74, Robert GAMEZ 74 74, Dennis PAULSON 75 73, Jose Maria OLAZABAL 77 72, Billy ANDRADE 75 74, Toru TANIGUCHI 78 71, Robert ALLENBY 74 75, Charles HOWELL III 75 74, Carl PAULSON 73 76, Steve FLESCH 81 69, Fred COUPLES 76 74, Miguel Angel JIMENEZ 77 73, Paul LAWRIE 73 77, Kyle BLACKMAN 74 76, Joey MAXON 74 76, Ronnie BLACK 76 74, Tripp ISENHOUR 73 77, Chris GONZALEZ 75 75, Justin LEONARD 78 73, Paul GOYDOS 76 75, Donnie HAMMOND 76 75, John HUSTON 75 76, Esteban TOLEDO 74 77, Jay Don BLAKE 75 76, M SPOSA 78 73, L WESTWOOD 75 76, T FISCHER 76 75, J KRIBEL 74 77, G NICKLAUS 78 74, C RAULERSON 77 75, J FREEMAN 77 75, S KATAYAMA 77 75, J DALEY 80 72, C SMITH 74 78, J DUFNER 74 78, B KLAPPROTT 75 77, J DOUMA 77 75, J HARRIS (Am) 76 77, K JOHNSON 77 76, G DAY 77 76, B HENNINGER 75 78, M CAMPBELL 77 77, J HART 80 75, S APPLEBY (Am) 80 75, C D FRANCO 76 79, D PRIDE 77 78, J QUINNEY (Am) 82 73, S JOHNSON 82 73, B BATES 75 80, J MAGINNES 79 76, N BEGAY III 78 78, W WOOD 75 81, D CLARK 79 77, W HEFFERNAN 77 79, C ANDERSON 77 79, M SCHIENNE 78 79, J BARLOW 78 81, C WALL 81 79, G FRAKE II 84 77, P PRICE RETD, P FULKE 76 RETD, J SANDELIN 72 WD, J WILLIAMSON DISQ.

Course Profile

In 2001, Southern Hills Country Club (par 70, 6,973 yards) in Tulsa was used.

The layout is likened to the Colonial Country Club (used for the MasterCard Colonial event) and puts a premium on accurate driving and iron play.

In 2002, Bethpage State Park (The Black Course – par 71, 7,295 yards) in Farmingdale, New York.

It will probably be set up like all US Open courses – tight fairways, high rough and fast greens.

Additionally, there are plenty of strategically placed bunkers.

Players to Note

●**Tiger Woods** will always be the man to beat in the US Open as form figures of 19-18-3-1-12 suggest. His controlled long and straight hitting game is now ideal – and this after many said he'd never win a US Open.

●**Ernie Els** has won the US Open twice and can boast three other top-seven finishes. **Vijay Singh** hasn't missed a cut in the last seven US Opens and has enjoyed five top-ten finishes in that time.

●**Tom Lehman** has managed five top-ten finishes in his last ten US Opens, while Jim can boast four top-20 finishes in the last six years, including fifth place twice.

●**Colin Montgomerie** has been the best of the European challenges for the last decade (three top-three finishes). No European has won the US Open since 1970 incidentally.

●**Scott Hoch** has a superb US Open record (five top tens) and has the grinding game for the event.

Phil Mickelson hasn't finished lower than 16th in the last four years and is a brilliant scrambler – essential at the US Open.

●**Lee Janzen** has won two US Opens (with Els, the only current tour player to have won it twice), while **David Duval**'s form figures over the last three years are 7-7-8-16.

●For **Stewart Cink**, this event represents his best chance of a Major.

Retief Goosen player profile
– pages 205 & 258

OPEN GOLF CHAMPIONSHIP

Royal Lytham, 19 Jul to 22 Jul 2001, purse $5,300,859

Pos	Name	R1	R2	R3	R4	Total	To par	Money	DD(y)	DA%	GIR%	Putts
1	David DUVAL	69	73	65	67	274	-10	984,756	312.3	60.7	68.1	116
2	Niclas FASTH	69	69	72	67	277	-7	590,853	270.8	71.4	66.7	113
3	B LANGER	71	69	67	71	278	-6	232,511	291.1	66.1	63.9	116
	Ian WOOSNAM	72	68	67	71	278	-6	232,511	268.8	69.6	58.3	109
	M Angel JIMINEZ	69	72	67	70	278	-6	232,511	299.9	71.4	66.7	116
	Billy MAYFAIR	69	72	67	70	278	-6	232,511	300.3	69.6	66.7	116
	Ernie ELS	71	71	67	69	278	-6	232,511	299.5	71.4	69.4	118
	Darren CLARKE	70	69	69	70	278	-6	232,511	302.6	73.2	68.1	117
9	Sergio GARCIA	70	72	67	70	279	-5	104,630	298.6	69.6	61.1	112
	Jesper PARNEVIK	69	68	71	71	279	-5	104,630	301.6	80.4	69.4	118
	Mikko ILONEN	68	75	70	66	279	-5	104,630	292.5	60.7	58.3	107
	K SUTHERLAND	75	69	68	67	279	-5	104,630	294.5	71.4	79.2	112

Pos	Name	R1	R2	R3	R4	Total	To par
13	Des SMYTH	74	65	70	71	280	-4
	Loren ROBERTS	70	70	70	70	280	-4
	R JACQUELIN	71	68	69	72	280	-4
	C MONTGOMERIE	65	70	73	72	280	-4
	Billy ANDRADE	69	70	70	71	280	-4
	Vijay SINGH	70	70	71	69	280	-4
	Alex CEJKA	69	69	69	73	280	-4
	Retief GOOSEN	74	68	67	71	280	-4
21	Nick PRICE	73	67	68	73	281	-3
	Davis LOVE III	73	67	74	67	281	-3
23	Greg OWEN	69	68	72	73	282	-2
	M CAMPBELL	71	72	71	68	282	-2
25	E ROMERO	70	68	72	73	283	-1
	Tiger WOODS	71	68	73	71	283	-1
	Bob ESTES	74	70	73	66	283	-1
	Joe OGILVIE	69	68	71	75	283	-1
29	Barry LANE	70	72	72	70	284	E
30	Stewart CINK	71	72	72	70	285	+1
	Justin ROSE	69	72	74	70	285	+1
	S VERPLANK	71	72	70	72	285	+1
	Phillip PRICE	74	69	71	71	285	+1
	N VANHOOTEGEM	72	68	70	75	285	+1
	P MICKELSON	70	72	72	71	285	+1
	David DIXON	70	71	70	74	285	+1
37	P HARRINGTON	75	66	74	71	286	+2
	Dudley HART	74	69	69	74	286	+2
	T TANIGUCHI	72	69	72	73	286	+2
	A COLTART	75	68	70	73	286	+2
	Frank LICKLITER	71	71	73	71	286	+2
42	Mark O'MEARA	70	69	72	76	287	+3
	S STRICKER	71	69	72	75	287	+3
	Richard GREEN	71	70	72	74	287	+3
	JP HAYES	69	71	74	73	287	+3
	Paul LAWRIE	72	70	69	76	287	+3
47	Brad FAXON	68	71	74	75	288	+4
	Peter LONARD	72	70	74	72	288	+4
	Robert ALLENBY	73	71	71	73	288	+4
	Lee WESTWOOD	73	70	71	74	288	+4
	Chris DIMARCO	68	74	72	74	288	+4
	Adam SCOTT	73	71	70	74	288	+4
	Matt GOGEL	73	70	71	74	288	+4
54	J M OLAZABAL	69	74	73	73	289	+5
	Paul CURRY	72	71	71	75	289	+5
	M CALCAVECCHIA	72	70	72	75	289	+5
	Carlos FRANCO	71	71	73	74	289	+5
	Paul MCGINLEY	69	72	72	76	289	+5
	D WALDORF	70	73	69	77	289	+5
	R SABBATINI	70	69	76	74	289	+5
61	Stuart APPLEBY	69	75	72	74	290	+6
62	G BRAND JNR.	70	72	75	74	291	+7
	B CHAMBLEE	72	69	74	76	291	+7
	Pierre FULKE	69	67	72	83	291	+7
65	Neil CHEETHAM	72	72	73	78	295	+11
66	A BALICKI	69	75	75	77	296	+12
	Thomas LEVET	72	72	77	75	296	+12
68	David SMAIL	71	72	76	79	298	+14
69	Sandy LYLE	72	71	77	81	301	+17
	S HENDERSON	75	69	81	76	301	+17

Tournament Report

David Duval had gone close to winning Majors before but he finally broke his duck at Royal Lytham & St Annes by claiming the 130th Open Championship.

The former World No.1 continued the dominance of the Americans in this event and, for at least at little while, stepped out of Tiger Woods' shadow. As many as 20 players probably had designs on winning entering the final round.

There was a four-way tie at the top of the leaderboard, with Duval heading the list along with Bernhard Langer, Alex Cejka and Ian Woosnam. And with the likes of Darren Clarke, Jesper Parnevik, Colin Montgomerie, Sergio García and Ernie Els just off the pace, whoever was going to win the title would certainly earn their victory.

Duval, though, was the first to make a move, picking up a birdie at the third and then on the outwards nine's generous par fives. There was no looking back for Duval who managed to keep the field at bay.

Clarke was the only player to threaten, as when the American failed to get up and down from a bunker at the 12th, the Ulsterman rolled in a long birdie putt to close to within a stroke. Clarke's hopes were dashed at the next, however, as he made double bogey.

Niclas Fasth's 67 ensured the Swede second spot, but share a thought for Ian Woosnam, who was handed a two-shot penalty for having too many clubs in his bag but still finished third alongside five other players.

MISSED THE CUT: S FLESCH 74 71, S KJELDSEN 73 72, J LEONARD 74 71, S LEANEY 76 69, G BIRCH 75 70, J HUGO 73 72, J DURANT 75 70, P O'MALLEY 71 74, M GRONBERG 75 70, F JACOBSON 74 71, M BRIER 74 71, J BICKERTON 74 71, N FALDO 75 71, C PAVIN 71 75, B VAUGHAN 72 74, S MARUYAMA 75 71, T TESHIMA 74 72, S HANSEN 71 75, D CHAND 75 71, R KARLSSON 75 71, R COLES 73 73, M BROOKS 73 73, M CORT 77 69, D HOWELL 74 73, M WIEBE 73 74, O KARLSSON 72 75, S HOCH 75 72, M PILKINGTON 77 70, T LEHMAN 75 72, D TOMS 74 73, A BADDELEY 75 72, S WILSON (Am) 77 70, D FROST 74 74, N SATO 76 72, J COCERES 71 77, G ORR 73 75, J MAGGERT 72 76, J DALY 72 76, D LEE 76 72, D PAULSON 78 70, J B GAY 72 76, S BALLESTEROS 78 71, B CHARLES 75 74, T JACKLIN 75 74, A OLDCORN 73 76, S ELKINGTON 77 72, M MCNULTY 70 79, F COUPLES 71 78, M HOEY (Am) 73 76, B MAY 77 72, J QUINNEY (Am) 76 73, C PAULSON 72 77, N OZAKI 77 73, M WEIR 78 72, D WILSON 72 78, S DYSON 77 73, S KATAYAMA 75 75, M GRIFFITHS 73 77, N GREEN 75 75, M ROE 73 78, J KELLY 74 77, G OGILVY 76 75, S JONES 74 77, J HUSTON 76 75, T BJORN 76 75, B RUMFORD 73 78, R CHAPMAN 76 76, T WATSON 74 78, G TURNER 79 73, J FURYK 77 75, H STENSON 75 77, J VAN DE VELDE 77 75, M SANDERS 79 73,4 G RANKIN 79 75, J C AGUERO 77 77, H TANAKA 76 78, J KEMP (Am) 76 78, W RILEY 78 77, A CABRERA 80 75, M MCGUIRE 71 85, T ODATE 76 80, G PLAYER 77 82, S VALE 85 74, S CALLAN 78 82, C PERRY 78 W/D, R MEDIATE 74 W/D

Course Profile

In 2001, Royal Lytham (par 71, 6,905 yards) on the Lancashire cost hosted the tournament. It was used for the 1996 Open when Tom Lehman was successful. The wind, as with most links venues, its biggest defence.

Muirfield in East Lothian, Scotland will be the venue in 2002 – which was last used in 1992 when Nick Faldo got the better of John Cook down the stretch. And also in 1987 when Faldo was again the winner (Paul Azinger second).

Players/Points to Note

●**Tiger Woods** has the long game to overpower many of the links courses used to host the British Open. The wide fairways mean he can let loose with his driver. Even of the wind blows Woods has the imagination and all the shots to combat the elements. His form figures over the past four years read 3-7-1-25.

●**Ernie Els** hasn't finished lower than 28th in this tournament, and although he is yet to win, he has recorded six top-ten finishes.

●**Jesper Parnevik** maybe should have won in 1994 and if the Swede is to win a Major Championship then this will be it. He is a superb wind player, who can strike the ball low with his irons. In nine starts in this tournament, he has finished second twice and in the top 25 seven times.

●**David Duval** revealed just how much he enjoys coming to Britain to play in his victory speech last year and could go in again in 2002.

●**Darren Clarke** is the best bet of the British players. Seventh last year and third the season before, the Ulsterman loves links golf and was runner-up in 1997.

●**Padraig Harrington** and **Thomas Bjorn** could both stake claims in 2002 after fine performances recently.

●**Michael Campbell**, **Stuart Appleby**, **Robert Allenby** and **Craig Parry** look the best of the Australians.

> ### David Duval player profile – page 251
>
> ### Niclas Fasth player profile – page 201

US PGA CHAMPIONSHIP

Atlanta Athletic Club, 16 Aug to 19 Aug 2001, purse $5,200,000

Pos	Name	R1	R2	R3	R4	Total	To par	Money	DD(y)	DA%	GIR%	Putts
1	David TOMS	66	65	65	69	265	-15	$936,000	298.0	67.9	66.7	106
2	Phil MICKELSON	66	66	66	68	266	-14	$562,000	314.4	69.6	73.6	111
3	Steve LOWERY	67	67	66	68	268	-12	$354,000	304.5	64.3	65.3	106
4	M CALCAVECCHIA	71	68	66	65	270	-10	$222,500	287.8	53.6	81.9	122
	S KATAYAMA	67	64	69	70	270	-10	$222,500	294.3	66.1	66.7	109
6	Billy ANDRADE	68	70	68	66	272	-8	$175,000	313.0	66.1	63.9	115
7	Jim FURYK	70	64	71	69	274	-6	$152,333	286.5	60.7	70.8	119
	Scott VERPLANK	69	68	70	67	274	-6	$152,333	275.6	69.6	68.1	116
	Scott HOCH	68	70	69	67	274	-6	$152,333	274.9	62.5	69.4	117
10	David DUVAL	66	68	67	74	275	-5	$122,000	321.5	55.4	76.4	124
	Justin LEONARD	70	69	67	69	275	-5	$122,000	278.1	69.6	72.2	118
	Kirk TRIPLETT	68	70	71	66	275	-5	$122,000	275.0	73.2	80.6	123

Pos	Name	R1	R2	R3	R4	Total	To par		Pos	Name	R1	R2	R3	R4	Total	To par
13	Steve FLESCH	73	67	70	66	276	-4			G CHALMERS	68	70	69	74	281	+1
	J PARNEVIK	70	68	70	68	276	-4			Jerry KELLY	69	67	72	73	281	+1
	Ernie ELS	67	67	70	72	276	-4			Hal SUTTON	67	71	73	70	281	+1
16	Stuart APPLEBY	66	70	68	73	277	-3			Kenny PERRY	68	70	71	72	281	+1
	Mike WEIR	69	72	66	70	277	-3			L WESTWOOD	71	68	68	74	281	+1
	Dudley HART	66	68	73	70	277	-3			R SCHULLER	68	70	72	71	281	+1
	Jose COCERES	69	68	73	67	277	-3	51	Nick FALDO	67	74	71	70	282	+2
	R ALLENBY	69	67	73	68	277	-3			Ian WOOSNAM	71	70	73	68	282	+2
	Chris DIMARCO	68	67	71	71	277	-3			Joe DURANT	68	71	72	71	282	+2
22	Mark O'MEARA	72	63	70	73	278	-2			Vijay SINGH	73	68	70	71	282	+2
	S MARUYAMA	68	72	71	67	278	-2			Scott DUNLAP	69	72	70	71	282	+2
	Paul AZINGER	68	67	69	74	278	-2			Tom PERNICE	69	69	74	70	282	+2
	Paul MCGINLEY	68	72	71	67	278	-2			Chris RILEY	68	71	73	70	282	+2
	Briny BAIRD	70	69	72	67	278	-2			F LICKLITER	71	69	71	71	282	+2
	Brian GAY	70	68	69	71	278	-2	59	Brad FAXON	66	70	74	73	283	+3
	C HOWELL III	71	67	69	71	278	-2			Stewart CINK	68	72	71	72	283	+3
29	Greg NORMAN	70	68	71	70	279	-1			Phillip PRICE	68	69	76	70	283	+3
	Tiger WOODS	73	67	69	70	279	-1			Grant WAITE	64	74	73	72	283	+3
	Nick PRICE	71	67	71	70	279	-1	63	Skip KENDALL	72	67	73	72	284	+4
	K-Ju CHOI	66	68	72	73	279	-1			Thomas BJORN	67	71	73	73	284	+4
	Bob TWAY	69	69	71	70	279	-1			Jonathan KAYE	67	68	78	71	284	+4
	Carlos FRANCO	67	72	71	69	279	-1	66	Tom WATSON	69	70	76	70	285	+5
	Niclas FASTH	66	69	72	72	279	-1			S STRICKER	75	65	75	70	285	+5
	C SMITH	69	71	68	71	279	-1			R DAMRON	68	73	71	73	285	+5
37	J M OLAZABAL	71	70	68	71	280	E			R MEDIATE	71	65	73	76	285	+5
	Fred COUPLES	70	69	70	71	280	E	70	Fred FUNK	66	74	71	75	286	+6
	Davis LOVE III	71	67	65	77	280	E			S MCCARRON	69	67	73	77	286	+6
	Bob ESTES	67	65	75	73	280	E	72	John HUSTON	67	68	75	77	287	+7
	A CABRERA	69	69	70	72	280	E	73	Bob MAY	71	70	76	74	291	+11
	A COLTART	67	72	71	70	280	E	74	P STANKOWSKI	67	71	76	79	293	+13
	Retief GOOSEN	69	70	66	75	280	E	75	Steve PATE	71	69	71	83	294	+14
44	A OLDCORN	73	67	74	67	281	+1		C MONTGOMERIE	71	69	74	-	-	DISQ

Sponsored by Stan James

Tournament Report

The 83rd USPGA Championship was won by David Toms, whose safety first tactics might not have pleased the crowd, but certainly proved effective in seeing off the challenge of perennial Major runner up Phil Mickelson.

The 34-year-old also secured his Ryder Cup place and moved his career earning over he $8million mark in capturing his 6th US Tour title. After taking the lead on Saturday in spectacular fashion – he aced the par three 15th – Toms never looked back.

On three occasions, Mickelson managed to draw level during the final round as the pair duelled from the off. But Lefty could never quite get his nose out in front, Toms controlled performance epitomised by the way he played the last hole.

Mickelson, trailing by a stroke, was on the green in two, but Toms tee shot had found the first cut of rough. And with water guarding the putting surface at the front of the 18th at Atlanta Athletic Club, he had to decide whether to lay up, knowing Mickelson would have a putt to tie, or go for the green, aware that finding the wet stuff might end his chances of glory. He took the sensible option, much to the derision of the galleries.

But when his wedge onto the green settled 15 feet from the hole the pressure was back on Mickelson. And, like so often before, the World No.3 just couldn't quite finish the job. His birdie attempt slid by, leaving Toms a putt for victory – which he duly holed.

MISSED THE CUT: Stephen KEPPLER 72 70, Bernhard LANGER 69 73, Larry NELSON 68 74, Garrett WILLIS 70 72, Darren CLARKE 73 69, Mark BROOKS 71 71, Jeff MAGGERT 70 72, Olin BROWNE 70 72, Tom KITE 72 71, Loren ROBERTS 74 69, Sergio GARCIA 68 75, Jerry PATE 73 70, Gary ORR 73 70, Paul LAWRIE 69 74, Glen DAY 74 69, Kevin SUTHERLAND 73 70, Brett QUIGLEY 71 72, Adam SCOTT 71 72, David GOSSETT 72 71, Tom LEHMAN 72 72, Lee JANZEN 70 74, Eduardo ROMERO 73 72, Bruce ZABRISKI 69 76, Nick O'HERN 73 72, Billy MAYFAIR 73 72, Len MATTIACE 74 71, Tim THELEN 74 71, Carl PAULSON 72 73, Don BERRY 73 72, Tim HERRON 72 74, Ian POULTER 73 73, Dennis PAULSON 73 73, Notah BEGAY III 78 68, Steve SCHNEITER 72 74, Harrison FRAZAR 73 73, Franklin LANGHAM 70 76, Robert KARLSSON 74 73, Duffy WALDORF 75 72, John MAZZA 70 77, John ABER 74 73, Tim FLEMING 75 72, Jeff SLUMAN 72 76, Chris PERRY 74 74, Miguel Angel JIMENEZ 74 74, Mark BROWN 75 73, Michael CLARK II 70 78, Padraig HARRINGTON 75 74, Mathias GR÷NBERG 75 74, Pierre FULKE 71 78, John DALY 72 77, Craig STEVENS 73 76, Darrell KESTNER 73 77, Toru TANIGUCHI 72 78, Wayne DEFRANCESCO 76 74, Jim WOODWARD 77 73, Bob SOWARDS 78 72, Curtis STRANGE 74 77, Mark MCNULTY 71 80, Naomichi "Joe" OZAKI 78 73, Michael CAMPBELL 72 79, Ken SCHALL 74 77, Jeffrey LANKFORD 77 74, Larry W EMERY 74 78, Hidemichi TANAKA 80 73, Steve BRADY 77 76, Rory SABBATINI 78 76, James BLAIR III 80 74, Mark MIELKE 80 77, Mike NORTHERN 78 79, Dean PROWSE 78 79, Bill LOEFFLER 78 81, Robert WILKIN 86 75, Lanny WADKINS 86 85, Steve ELKINGTON 77 W/D

Course Profile

In 2001 the event was staged at Atlanta Athletic Club in Georgia (par 70, 7,213 yards). This course has narrow, tree lined fairways but is long.

Accuracy is needed with the driver and the long irons. The greens can be quick.

In 2002, Hazeltine National Golf Club (par 72, 7,149 yards) in Chaska, Minnesota will host the event.

The late Payne Stewart won the last Major to be held at the venue, defeating Scott Simpson in a play-off.

Players/Points to Note

●**Tiger Woods** won in 1999 and 2000 and despite a poor showing in 2001 he can still boast a stroke average in this event of 69.55.

●**Phil Mickelson**'s second place in 2001 was his fifth top-ten finish in nine starts.

●For **Vijay Singh** and **Davis Love** the USPGA gave them their maiden Major success, and with three top tens apiece will go close again.

●**Nick Price** has missed the cut in in this tournament just twice in 18 starts. Those appearances have yielded two USPGA wins and seven top-ten finishes in total.

●**Justin Leonard** has had four top-ten finishes in seven appearances. The Texan might have missed two of the last four cuts in this event but did go 8-5-2 from 1995 to 1997 and was tenth last year.

●**David Toms** win in 2001 fitted perfectly the make up of past USPGA winners.

Eleven of the past 14 champions have been proven winners on the regular tour, in their 30s but hadn't yet taken their chances in a Major, just like Toms. This statistic points to a **Jesper Parnevik** or a **Colin Montgomerie**, though no European has ever won this event.

●Canadian **Mike Weir** could be a live outsider in 2002 after three successive top-30 finishes.

●**Bob Estes** and **Chris DiMarco** could also spring a surprise next season.

David Toms player profile – page 286

MAJOR WINNERS SINCE 1984

THE MASTERS

All at Augusta

Year	Winner	Score	Runner(s) Up
2001	Tiger WOODS	272	David DUVAL
2000	Vijay SINGH	278	Ernie ELS
1999	Jose Maria OLAZABAL	280	Davis LOVE III
1998	Mark O'MEARA	279	David DUVAL, Fred COUPLES
1997	Tiger WOODS	270	Tom KITE
1996	Nick FALDO	276	Greg NORMAN
1995	Ben CRENSHAW	274	Davis LOVE III
1994	Jose Maria OLAZABAL	279	Tom LEHMAN
1993	Bernhard LANGER	277	Chip BECK
1992	Fred COUPLES	275	Ray FLOYD
1991	Ian WOOSNAM	277	Jose Maria OLAZABAL
1990	*Nick FALDO	278	Raymond FLOYD
1989	*Nick FALDO	283	Scott HOCH
1988	Sandy LYLE	281	Mark CALCAVECCHIA
1987	*Larry MIZE	285	Seve BALLESTEROS, Greg NORMAN
1986	Jack NICKLAUS	279	Greg NORMAN, Tom KITE
1985	Bernhard LANGER	282	Curtis STRANGE, Seve BALLESTEROS, Raymond FLOYD
1984	Ben CRENSHAW	277	Tom WATSON

US OPEN

Year	Winner	Score	Runner(s) Up	Venue
2001	*Retief GOOSEN	276	Mark BROOKS	Southern Hills
2000	Tiger WOODS	272	Ernie ELS, Miguel Angel JIMINEZ	Pebble Beach
1999	Payne STEWART	279	Phil MICKELSON	Pinehurst
1998	Lee JANZEN	280	Payne STEWART	Olympic Club
1997	Ernie ELS	276	Colin MONTGOMERIE	Congressional
1996	Steve JONES	278	Tom LEHMAN, Davis LOVE III	Oakland Hills
1995	Corey PAVIN	280	Greg NORMAN	Shinnecock
1994	*Ernie ELS	279	Loren ROBERTS, Colin MONTGOMERIE	Oakmont
1993	Lee JANZEN	272	Payne STEWART	Baltusrol
1992	Tom KITE	285	Jeff SLUMAN	Pebble Beach
1991	*Payne STEWART	282	Scott SIMPSON	Hazeltine
1990	*Hale IRWIN	280	Mike DONALD	Medinah
1989	Curtis STRANGE	278	Chip BECK, Mark McCUMBER	Oak Hill
1988	*Curtis STRANGE	278	Nick FALDO	Brookline
1987	Scott SIMPSON	277	Tom WATSON	Olympic Club
1986	Raymond FLOYD	279	Lanny WADKINS, Chip BECK	Shinnecock
1985	Andy NORTH	279	Dave BARR, T.C. CHEN	Oakland Hills
1984	*Fuzzy ZOELLER	276	Greg NORMAN	Winged Foot

* = won after play-off

Sponsored by Stan James

MAJOR WINNERS SINCE 1984

OPEN GOLF CHAMPIONSHIP

Year	Winner	Score	Runner(s) Up	Venue
2001	David DUVAL	274	Niclas FASTH	Royal Lytham
2000	Tiger WOODS	269	Thomas BJORN, Ernie ELS	St Andrews
1999	*Paul LAWRIE	290	Justin LEONARD, Jean VAN DE VELDE	Carnoustie
1998	*Mark O'MEARA	280	Brian WATTS	Royal Birkdale
1997	Justin LEONARD	272	Darren CLARKE, Jesper PARNEVIK	Royal Troon
1996	Tom LEHMAN	271	Ernie ELS	Lytham St Annes
1995	*John DALY	282	Costantino ROCCA	St Andrews
1994	Nick PRICE	268	Jesper PARNEVIK	Turnberry
1993	Greg NORMAN	267	Nick FALDO	St George's
1992	Nick FALDO	272	John COOK	Muirfield
1991	Ian BAKER-FINCH	272	Mike HARWOOD	Royal Birkdale
1990	Nick FALDO	270	Payne STEWART, Mark McNULTY	St Andrews
1989	*Mark CALCAVECCHIA	275	Wayne GRADY, Greg NORMAN	Royal Troon
1988	Seve BALLESTEROS	273	Nick PRICE	Lytham St Annes
1987	Nick FALDO	279	Paul AZINGER, Rodger DAVIS	Muirfield
1986	Greg NORMAN	280	Gordon BRAND	Turnberry
1985	Sandy LYLE	282	Payne STEWART	St George's
1984	Seve BALLESTEROS	276	Tom WATSON, Bernhard LANGER	St Andrews

US PGA CHAMPIONSHIP

Year	Winner	Score	Runner(s) Up	Venue
2001	David TOMS	265	Phil MICKELSON	Atlanta Athletic Club
2000	*Tiger WOODS	270	Bob MAY	Valhalla
1999	Tiger WOODS	277	Sergio GARCIA	Medinah
1998	Vijay SINGH	271	Steve STRICKER	Sahalee
1997	Davis LOVE III	269	Justin LEONARD	Winged Foot
1996	*Mark BROOKS	277	Kenny PERRY	Valhalla
1995	*Steve ELKINGTON	267	Colin MONTGOMERIE	Riviera
1994	Nick PRICE	269	Corey PAVIN	Southern Hills
1993	*Paul AZINGER	272	Greg NORMAN	Inverness
1992	Nick PRICE	278	John COOK, Jim GALLAGHER, Gene SAUERS, Nick FALDO	Bellerive
1991	John DALY	276	Bruce LIETZKE	Crooked Stick
1990	Wayne GRADY	282	Fred COUPLES	Shoal Creek
1989	Payne STEWART	276	Mike REID	Kemper Lakes
1988	Jeff SLUMAN	272	Paul AZINGER	Oak Tree
1987	*Larry NELSON	287	Lanny WADKINS	PGA National
1986	Bob TWAY	276	Greg NORMAN	Inverness
1985	Hubert GREEN	278	Lee TREVINO	Cherry Hills
1984	Lee TREVINO	273	Gary PLAYER, Lanny WADKINS	Shoal Creek

* = won after play-off

WGC EVENTS

ACCENTURE MATCHPLAY CHAMPIONSHIP
Metropolitan G.C., 3 Jan to 7 Jan 2001, purse $5,000,000

FINAL (36 holes)
STRICKER bt FULKE – 2 and 1
(Stricker wins $1,000,000)

THIRD PLACE PLAY–OFF (18 holes)
TANIGUCHI bt ELS – 4 and 3

SEMI–FINAL (18 holes)
FULKE bt ELS – 2 and 1
STRICKER bt TANIGUCHI – 2 and 1

QUARTER–FINAL (18 holes)
STRICKER bt O'HERN – on the 20th hole
FULKE bt FAXON – on the 19th hole
TANIGUCHI bt MARUYAMA – 2 and 1
ELS bt STADLER – 1–up

THIRD ROUND (18 holes)
FULKE bt CAMPBELL – 1 up
TANIGUCHI bt APPLEBY – 2 and 1
MARUYAMA bt MCNULTY – 4 and 3
FAXON bt LEHMAN – 1 up
O'HERN bt HART – 5 and 4
STRICKER bt LEONARD – 6 and 5
ELS bt VAN DE VELDE – on 19th hole
STADLER bt COLTART – on 19th hole

SECOND ROUND (18 holes)
ELS bt TANAKA – 1 hole
VAN DE VELDE bt GOOSEN – 4 and 3
STADLER bt PARRY – 7 and 6
COLTART bt TOMS – 3 and 2
LEHMAN bt SLUMAN – 3 and 2
FAXON bt PERRY – 1 hole
CAMPBELL bt IZAWA – 5 and 4
FULKE bt DAY – at 20th
O'HERN bt HERRON – 5 and 3
HART bt ALLENBY – 5 and 4
LEONARD bt ORR – at 20th
STRICKER bt VERPLANK – 3 and 2
TANIGUCHI bt SINGH – 1 hole
APPLEBY bt JOHANSSON – 4 and 3
MCNULTY bt LAWRIE – 5 and 4
MARUYAMA bt MAY – at 22nd

FIRST ROUND (18 holes)
David TOMS (9) bt Hirofumi MIYASE (56) – 1 up

Andrew COLTART (41) bt Phillip PRICE (24) – 3 and 2
Steve STRICKER (55) bt Padraig HARRINGTON (10) – 2 and 1
Scott VERPLANK (23) bt Brent GEIBERGER (42) – at 19th
Glen DAY (53) bt Kirk TRIPLETT (12) – 3 and 1
Pierre FULKE (21) bt Fred FUNK (44) – 5 and 4
Bob MAY (11) bt Tom SCHERRER (54) – 2 and 1
Shegeki MARUYAMA (22) bt Scott DUNLAP (43) – 2 and 1
John HUSTON (8) bt Craig STADLER (57) – 4 and 2
Craig PARRY (40) bt Dennis PAULSON (25) – at 21st
Justin LEONARD (7) bt Patrik SJOLAND (58) – 6 and 5
Gary ORR (26) bt Paul MCGINLEY (39) – 2 and 1
Michael CAMPBELL (5) bt Matthias GRONBERG (60) – 4 and 3
Toshi IZAWA (28) bt Steve PATE (37) – at 19th
Mark MCNULTY (59) bt Stewart CINK (6) – 1 up
Paul LAWRIE (27) bt Chris DIMARCO (38) – 5 and 4
Jean VAN De VELDE (49) bt Duffy WALDORF (16) – at 19th
Retief GOOSEN (17) bt Steve LOWERY (48) – 2 and 1
Robert ALLENBY (15) bt Nobuhito SATO (50) – 2 and 1
Dudley HART (18) bt Skip KENDALL (47) – 6 and 5
Chris PERRY (13) bt Jonathan KAYE (52) 2 up
Brad FAXON (45) bt Jose COCERES (20) – 3 and 2
Stuart APPLEBY (14) bt Kenny PERRY (51) – 1 up
Per Ulrik JOHANSSON (46) bt Steve FLESCH (19) – 5 and 4
Tom LEHMAN (4) bt Greg CHALMERS (61) – 2 and 1
Jeff SLUMAN (36) bt Joe OZAKI (29) – 3 and 2
Nick O'HERN (63) bt Hal SUTTON (2) – 21st hole
Tim HERRON (34) bt Franklin LANGHAM (31) – 2 and 1
Ernie ELS (1) bt Greg KRAFT (64) – 3 and 2
Hidemichi TANAKA (32) bt Bernhard LANGER (33) – 19th hole
Vijay SINGH (3) bt Kevin SUTHERLAND (62) – 4 and 2
Toru TAANIGUCHI (30) bt Bob ESTES (35) – 3 and 2

Tournament Report

Steve Stricker secured his first win since 1996 – and a cool million dollars to boot – when he defeated Pierre Fulke 2&1 in the final of the WGC Matchplay.

The Wisconsin pro came into the event as the 26th reserve but made light of his lowly ranking by getting the better of Padraig Harrington, Scott Verplank, Justin Leonard, Nick O'Hern and Toru Taniguchi before dominating the final against the Swede. Stricker took charge from the first hole and was never headed by Fulke.

The stars may have stayed away – and the fans unfortunately did too – but Stricker's ability to sink the putts that mattered and get up and down on a tricky Metropolitan GC layout was enough.

Fulke at least kept the sparse crowd interested, as he battled back from three down to just one behind with eight to play in the 36 hole final. But it wasn't enough as the two-time US Tour winner took advantage of Fulke's sloppy 2-iron approach at the 17th to win with a hole to spare.

It was an event that saw 40 players pull out for one reason or another, and left Ernie Els as the only member of the world's top seven.

The South African, though, went out at the semi final stage to Fulke. Taniguchi was the other player who made the last four.

The Japanese star put down a marker for the future and was perhaps a touch unlucky to go down to Stricker in the semi final.

STEVE STRICKER . . . took charge early

Course Profile

In 2001, the Metropolitan Golf Club (par 72, 7,066 yards) in Melbourne, Australia hosted this event for the first time. An old, traditional golf course that has small greens and is a scramblers' delight.

The La Costa resort (par 72, 7,022yards) takes over in 2002 (venue for the first two renewals and the Mercedes Championship between 1969 and 1998).

The fairways are generous so wayward tee shots aren't particularly punished.

Phil Mickelson (twice), Tiger Woods and Davis Love all won the Mercedes there.

Players/Points to Note

●Eighteen-hole matchplay can be something of a lottery and you could argue that backing the outsiders blind in all matches is the way to make a profit. Ryder and Presidents Cup records should be checked before making any selection.

●This tournament returns to La Costa in 2002 after being held in Australia last year – when nearly all the top players stayed away. All the best players will be back and the form from last year can be all but ignored – mainly because over half the golfers who teed-up in Melbourne won't be eligible 12 months on.

●The field consists of the top-ranked 64 players in the world and the draw is made so the Number One player meets No. 64 and so on.

●The best players to follow are **Tiger Woods** (superb amateur record in matchplay events and runner up at La Costa in 2000).

●**Phil Mickelson** (poor WGC Matchplay record but 6-3-2 in Ryder Cup matches and former US Amateur Champion).

●**Hal Sutton** (6-4-4 Ryder and 3-1-0 Presidents Cup records).

●**Padraig Harrington** (superb Ryder Cup debut and some fine performances in the Wentworth World Matchplay event).

●**Ernie Els** (semi-finalist last year and brilliant Wentworth Matchplay record – three wins).

●**Jeff Maggert** (tough Ryder Cup performer and winner of the inaugural WGC Matchplay event in 1999).

Previous Results

2000: 1. Darren Clarke, 2. Tiger Woods, 3. David Duval.
1999: 1. Jeff Maggert, 2. Andrew Magee, 3. John Huston.

Firestone CC, 23 Aug to 26 Aug 2001, purse $5,000,000

Pos	Name	R1	R2	R3	R4	Total	To par	Money	DD(y)	DA%	GIR%	Putts
1	Tiger WOODS	66	67	66	69	268	-12	$1,000,000	311.0	66.1	72.2	111
2	Jim FURYK	65	66	66	71	268	-12	$500,000	283.4	78.6	63.9	105
3	Darren CLARKE	66	68	68	69	271	-9	$375,000	289.3	71.4	59.7	107
4	C MONTGOMERIE	66	71	66	70	273	-7	$300,000	273.6	69.6	59.7	105
5	Stuart APPLEBY	70	64	70	70	274	-6	$201,667	283.6	57.1	56.9	105
	Davis LOVE III	68	68	70	68	274	-6	$201,667	290.3	62.5	62.5	110
	Paul AZINGER	67	70	65	72	274	-6	$201,667	279.5	60.7	58.3	109
8	Ernie ELS	67	70	66	72	275	-5	$147,500	295.3	62.5	58.3	105
	Phil MICKELSON	67	66	70	72	275	-5	$147,500	297.1	73.2	63.9	113
10	Retief GOOSEN	72	69	64	71	276	-4	$131,000	292.6	57.2	61.1	109

Pos	Name	R1	R2	R3	R4	Total	To par
11	B LANGER	69	67	68	73	277	-3
	Hal SUTTON	69	71	67	70	277	-3
13	Stewart CINK	69	67	70	72	278	-2
	Ian POULTER	67	72	69	70	278	-2
	Vijay SINGH	68	68	69	73	278	-2
	David TOMS	68	70	70	70	278	-2
17	P HARRINGTON	68	66	73	72	279	-1
	S VERPLANK	69	71	70	69	279	-1
	Pierre FULKE	73	71	65	70	279	-1
20	Carlos FRANCO	68	71	68	73	280	E
21	Scott HOCH	71	70	69	71	281	+1
	Niclas FASTH	74	67	68	72	281	+1
23	S ELKINGTON	73	68	73	68	282	+2
	R ALLENBY	68	67	75	72	282	+2
25	Mike WEIR	69	70	71	73	283	+3
26	Paul MCGINLEY	68	73	71	72	284	+4
27	David DUVAL	69	69	72	75	285	+5
28	Phillip PRICE	70	71	74	71	286	+6
29	Loren ROBERTS	72	70	67	79	288	+8
	Nick PRICE	71	70	71	76	288	+8
31	S MARUYAMA	68	75	73	73	289	+9
	Thomas BJORN	66	79	73	71	289	+9
	M CAMPBELL	71	71	75	72	289	+9
	Notah BEGAY III	77	71	72	69	289	+9
35	Greg NORMAN	65	71	74	80	290	+10
36	M A JIMINEZ	70	72	74	76	292	+12
	M CALCAVECCHIA		72	69	72	79	292	+12
38	Kirk TRIPLETT	70	70	69	-	-	DISQ
39	L WESTWOOD	70	78	-	-	-	WD

Sponsored by Stan James

Tournament Report

Tiger Woods defeated Jim Furyk after a marathon seven hole play-off to land his third consecutive WGC NEC Invitational title in Akron, Ohio.

The World No.1 also took his career earning past the $25million but was made to work extremely hard by Furyk at the Firestone Country Club for victory.

Furyk held the advantage after each of the first three rounds, and led by two shots going into the last day, but with Woods never more than two shots adrift it was no surprise that extra holes were needed when the regulation 72 were completed.

The play-off started in spectacular fashion. Furyk looked dead and buried when failing to shift his ball from the bunker at the first extra hole but amazingly holed from the sand at the second time of asking to stay alive.

Then it was Woods' turn to pull something out of the bag. Firstly he holed from 20 foot to force a second extra hole, and then chipped to inches to take the tournament to a third. Three pars a piece over the next three holes saw the pair tee off for a seventh time.

But when Furyk found the trees at the 18th, and succeeded in moving his ball just a few yards with his second shot, Woods took advantage, producing a superb birdie to win. It was Woods 29th US Tour win.

Darren Clarke, who briefly threatened with early two birdies, finished third with Colin Montgomerie fourth in a fine showing by European golfers.

PLAY-OFF . . . Jim Furyk loses out to Woods.

Course Profile

Firestone Golf Club in Ohio (par 70, 7,139 yards) is a tough course with some long par fours (seven over 450 yards) and a 625 yard par five. Not surprisingly the big hitters prosper.

Sahalee Golf Course in Washington State was used for the 1998 USPGA Championship (the par then was 70 and the yardage 6,906).

It is a tight track with tree-lined fairways. Accuracy over length succeeded. The greens are large and undulating.

Players/Points to Note

● After three years based at Firestome Country Club in Akron, Ohio, the WGC-NEC Invitational moves to Sahalee Country Club in Washington – home of the 1998 USPGA Championship won by **Vijay Singh**.

● Only players who are in the 2002 Ryder Cup sides and the 2002 Presidents Cup teams will be eligible for this event in 2002.

● **Tiger Woods** is the only winner of this event so far. In 12 rounds he is 43-under par and has a stroke average of 66.42. Woods was 10th in the 1998 USPGA Championship.

● **Phil Mickelson** (2-4-8) and **Jim Furyk** (10-4-2) are the only other two players who can boast top-ten finishes in the last three years.

● **Ernie Els**, **Paul Azinger** and **Colin Montgomerie** can boast two top-ten finishes. Azinger (13th) and Els (21st) also played well in the 1998 USPGA.

● Players who went well at Sahalee in 1998 and could make the field in 2002 include Singh (winner in 1998), **Steve Stricker** (second), **Steve Elkington** (third), **Nick Price** (fourth), **Davis Love** (seventh), **Robert Allenby** (13th) and **Brad Faxon** (13th).

● The rest are longshots to make the field but will have local knowledge of Sahalee – **Fred Couples** and **Kirk Triplett** both grew up in the area.

● The best Europeans outside Monty, are **Darren Clarke**, **Phillip Price** and **Bernhard Langer**.

Previous Results

2000: 1. Tiger Woods (-21), 2. Justin Leonard (-10), 3. Phillip Price (-10).

1999: 1. Tiger Woods (-10), 2. Phil Mickelson (-9), 3. Craig Parry (-5), Nick Price (-5).

The 34th Ryder Cup was scheduled to take place at the Belfry in September 2001 but was cancelled in the wake of the terrorists attacks in America.

It has been re-scheduled to be played September 27-29, 2002, with this biennial contest between Europe and the USA continuing in every even year.

In terms of good grace and etiquette, the competition reached it's nadir at Brookline two years ago and hopefully it will be the golf and not the antics of the players and galleries that make the headlines in 2002. I'm sure it will be.

For punters, the best piece of advice seems not to back either team outright but to have a bet on a small winning margin for both.

The 1985 contest was the last one that saw the teams separated by more than two points. It was possible in the last Ryder Cup to back 15-13 and 14 1/2-13 1/2 for both teams and the 14-14 tie at combined odds of around 13-8.

The Americans are likely to start favourites in 2002 despite the Europeans being at home. The USA did win the last time this event was held at the Belfry (1993 15-13) but were hammered 16 1/2-11 1/2 in 1985 at the Sutton Coldfield venue.

And two years later the Europeans won at Muirfield Village – the last time one side won two cups in succession.

Sam Torrance is setting up the layout to favour his team. New bunkers and trees have been added to combat the big hitters from America.

Landing areas will be narrower and players will have to think their way around the course rather than just blasting a driver off the tee and a short iron to the green. All the changes should give the Europeans a better chance.

As we already know the two teams (records below), it's interesting to note that Europe have four rookies to the USA's three. But one of America's first timers is David Toms – now a Major winner, and another, Scott Verplank, has been around a long time and has won four times on the US Tour.

The American team does look strong and the chances of the likes of Paul McGinley, Phillip Price and Niclas Fasth being in the same form as they were last summer is doubtful. Having said that, Pierre Fulke surely won't be in any worse form.

If you do fancy the Americans, wait until after the first day as they are invariably trailing and are therefore a bigger price. Players who have played in all four matches coming to the Sunday can be drained and are worth opposing in the singles.

The outright winner? It's sure to be close and I will sit on the fence and have a few quid on the aforementioned winning margin bet but, if pressed, I would go for the USA to nick it.

Ryder Cup Records of the two teams

Europe

	P	W	1/2	L
Bernhard LANGER	38	18	5	15
Lee WESTWOOD	10	4	0	6
Darren CLARKE	7	3	0	4
Jesper PARNEVIK	9	4	3	2
Padraig HARRINGTON	3	1	1	1
Colin MONTGOMERIE	23	12	4	7
Sergio GARCIA	5	3	1	1
Thomas BJORN	2	1	1	0
Paul McGINLEY	debut			
Pierre FULKE	debut			
Niclas FASTH	debut			
Phillip PRICE	debut			

USA

	P	W	1/2	L
Hal SUTTON	14	6	4	4
Phil MICKELSON	11	6	2	3
Davis LOVE	15	6	1	8
Tiger WOODS	10	3	1	6
David DUVAL	4	1	1	2
Jim FURYK	6	2	0	4
Mark CALCAVECCHIA	11	5	1	5
Paul AZINGER	13	5	2	6
Scott HOCH	3	2	1	0
David TOMS	debut			
Scott VERPLANK	debut			
Stewart CINK	debut			

Sponsored by Stan James

TAMPA BAY CLASSIC

The Tampa Bay Classic didn't take place in 2001 due to the terrorist attacks on America but the event will take place in 2002 from September 16-20.

Players/Points to Note

●The 2000 tournament was the inaugural Tampa Bay Classic and was won by **John Huston**, who used his course knowledge to good effect to win the event by three shots from **Carl Paulson**. Huston, who lives in the area and had played the Copperhead course over 100 times, admitted to feeling at home with the layout and the galleries when carding a last-round 65 to overhaul Paulson, who started the day with a two-shot lead over the field. **Frank Lickliter** and **Len Mattiace** tied for third place with **Joe Durant** fifth.

●As this event is played opposite the WGC AmEx event all the best players won't be teeing up, so this event represents a chance for some of the lesser lights to shine.

●The Copperhead course at Westin Innisbrook was used from 1990 for the JCPenney Classic, a pairs event which featured players from both the PGA and LPGA, so many of the players will know it well even though it wasn't used for a US Tour event prior to 2000.

●Previous winners in of that event include **John Daly**, **Steve Pate**, **Davis Love**, **Dan Forsman** and **Billy Andrade**.

●Florida-based players should go well as they will be comfortable with the Bermuda Grass greens and the climate at this time of year.

Course Profile

The Copperhead course at Westin Innisbrook (par 71, 7,295 yards), Tampa Bay, Florida, isn't too taxing and features wide fairways and little rough. Accuracy, therefore, is not at a premium.

The layout is long, though, so big hitters are sure to prosper. The greens are fairly flat and of average size.

The Bermuda Grass greens will certainly favour golfers who have played well on Florida courses before.

The eventual winner might just be the player who turns up with the hottest putter.

WGC AMERICAN EXPRESS CHAMPIONSHIP

The WGC American Express Championship didn't take place in 2001 due to the terrorist attacks on America but the event will go ahead in 2002 from September 16-20.

Players/Points to Note

●Eligibility – The top-ranked 50 players in the world along with any top-30 ranked player on the US Money List, top-20 player on the European Order of Merit, top-three player from the Australasian Tour OoM, top-three player from the Southern Africa Tour OoM, top-three player from the Japan Tour OoM and the money list leader from the Asian Tour. With some players qualifying under two or more categories the field is usually around 60. However, many of the top American players did not take part in the event in 2000.

●**Tiger Woods**, **Lee Westwood**, **Nick Price** and **Sergio Garcia** are the only four players to have finished in the top ten of both WGC AmEx Championships.

●**Bob May**, **Jose Maria Olazabal**, **Chris Perry** and **Scott Hoch** have all finished in the top 20 in both renewals so far.

●The 2001 tournament was scheduled to be staged at the Bellerive Country Club but the 2002 renewal will take place at Mount Juliet Estate, Thomastown, Co. Kilkenny, Ireland.

●The layout was used to host the Irish Open between 1993 and 1995. **Nick Faldo**, **Bernhard Langer** and **Sam Torrance** were the respective champions.

●Others who performed well then and might make the field in 2002 are **Robert Allenby** (two top-four positions), **Colin Montgomerie**, **Ian Woosnam**, **Michael Campbell**, **Retief Goosen** and Olazabal.

Course Profile

The Jack Nicklaus-designed course (par 72, 7,116 yards) at Mount Juliet in Ireland was used three times for the Irish Open in the early '90s and is a parkland venue that meanders it's way over rolling hills and river scenery.

The rollcall of past champions suggests you have to be an accurate driver of the ball and a good iron player to succeed.

There is no doubt this is a tough course and some of the greens have wicked slopes and undulations.

First Round (Losers £50,000)
Thomas BJORN bt Adam SCOTT 4&3
Ian WOOSNAM by Retief GOOSEN 4&3
Padraig HARRINGTON bt Nick FALDO 9&8
Sam TORRANCE bt Seve BALLESTEROS 3&2

Second Round (Losers £65,000)
Lee WESTWOOD bt Thomas BJORN 1 hole
Ian WOOSNAM bt Colin MONTGOMERIE 4&3
Padraig HARRINGTON bt Darren CLARKE 5&4
Sam TORRANCE bt Vijay SINGH 1 hole

Semi Finals (Losers £85,000)
Ian WOOSNAM bt Lee WESTWOOD 10&9
Padraig HARRINGTON bt Sam TORRANCE 4&3

Final
Ian WOOSNAM bt Padraig HARRINGTON 2&1

Prize Money
Winner £250,000,
Runner Up £120,000

Tournament Report

A vintage display by Ian Woosnam saw the Welshman win the Cisco World Matchplay Championship final, defeating Padraig Harrington 2&1. It was as if the clock had rolled back ten years as Woosie produced some superb golf, reminiscent of his 1991 US Masters win.

And after being so unlucky when penalised for having an extra club in his bag at the start of the final round of the Open when in a position to win, this success was some consolation.

Woosnam first defeated Retief Goosen 4&3 before knocking out Colin Montgomerie by the same score. A quite remarkable 10&9 victory over Lee Westwood in the semi final set up a meeting with Harrington, who had despatched Sam Torrance, Darren Clarke and Nick Faldo.

The Irishman took control of the final after shooting an estimated 61 in the morning 18 holes. But Woosie was never far away, shooting seven consecutive birdies from the second to keep in touch with Harrington. Between them they notched 21 birdies in the morning round.

At halfway, Harrington led by two but with seven to play in was all square as Woosnam battled back, helped by some wayward tee shots from the Irishman on the 25th and 27th holes.

The Welshman, who was driving the ball superbly, won the next two holes and then on the 35th hole wrapped up victory by rolling in a nine foot birdie. Harrington could hardly disguise his disappointment and finished second for the seventh time this year.

Course Profile

Wentworth (par 72, 7,047 yards) requires accuracy and length off the tee – which is why it's perfect for Monty and Els – as the fairways are narrow but the layout long – especially if it rains. The last six holes were altered slightly in 2000.

The last two holes are both par fives so the outcome of the tournament can rest on those holes. The greens have subtle contours and, when the sun shines, they can be firm and fast.

Players/Points to Note

●Twelve golfers contest the event with four seeded players and eight non-seeds. Only the eight non-seeds play in the first round, the winners going on to meet a seeded player. All matches are over 36 holes in a matchplay format. The draw can be a major factor.

●Playing 36 holes a day is tough and if you are required to play 36 holes for four consecutive days it's obviously even tougher. So this event is set up for the seeded players. In the last 17 years, 13 seeds have won.

●**Colin Montgomerie** won in 1999 and has been the losing finalist on two other occasions. He was an astonishing 37-under par for his three games in 2000 – a record for the event. He has won three of the last four Volvo PGA Championships, which are also held at Wentworth and he lives 15 minutes drive away from the course.

●**Ernie Els** won a hat-trick of World Matchplay titles between 1994 and 1996 and was a beaten finalist in 1997. His UK home is Wentworth and he also has a superb record in the Volvo PGA Championship.

●**Ian Woosnam**'s superb win in 2001 as a non-seed should ensure he gets an invite in 2002. And who's to say Woosie won't win again?

Past Results

2000: 1. Lee Westwood, 2. Colin Montgomerie, 3. Ernie Els, Vijay Singh.
1999: 1. Colin Montgomerie, 2. Mark O'Meara, 3. Padraig Harrington, Nick Price.

Sponsored by Stan James

EUROPEAN TOUR PLAYER PROFILES

Ten-Year Form Tournament Course History

Johnnie Walker Cl'   92 – Bangkok; 93 – Singapore Island; 94 – Blue Canyon; 95 – Orchard; 96 – Tanah Merah; 97 – Hope Island; 98 – Blue Canyon; 99 NA; 00 –Westin Resort; 01 – Alpine

WGC Matchplay   92-98 NA; 99-00 – LaCosta; 01 – Metropolitan

Alfred Dunhill Ch'   92-94 NA; 95 – Wanderers; 96-01 – Houghton

South African Open   92-96 NA; 97 – Glendower; 98 – Durban; 99 – Stellenbosch; 00 – Randpark; 01 – East London

Heineken Classic   92-95 NA; 96-01 – The Vines Resort

Greg Norman Int'   92-99 NA; 00-01 – The Lakes

Malaysian Open   92-98 NA; 99 – Saujana; 00 – Templer Park; 01 – Saujana

Singapore Masters   92-00 NA; 01 – Singapore Island

Dubai Desert Classic   92-98 –Emirates; 99-01 –Dubai Creek

Qatar Masters   92-97 NA; 98-01 – Doha

Madeira Island Open   92 NA; 93-96 – Campo de Golf; 97-01 – Santo da Serra

Sao Paulo Brazil' Op'   92-99 NA; 00-01 – Sao Paulo

Open de Argentina   92-00 NA; 01 – The Jockey Club

US Masters   92-01 – Augusta National

Moroccan Open   92 – Dar-es-Salem; 93-95 – Golf Royal; 96 – Dar-es-Salem; 97-99 – Golf Royal; 00 – Golf D`Amelkis; 01 – Dar-es-Salem

Open de Espana   92-93 – R.A.C.E.; 94-96 – Club de Campo; 97 – La Moraleja II; 98-99 – El Prat; 00-01 – Catalunya

Open de Portugal   92-93 – Vila Sol; 94-95 – Penha Longa; 96-97 – Aroeira; 98-00 – Le Meridien Penina; 01 – Quinta do Lago

Open de France   92-98 – Golf National; 99 – Medoc; 00 – Golf National; 01 – Lyon

B & H International   92-95 – St. Mellion; 96-99 – The Oxfordshire; 00-01 – The De Vere Belfry

Deutsche Bank   92-94 NA; 95-98 – Gut Kaden; 99 – St. Leon Rot; 00 – Gut Kaden; 01 – St. Leon Rot

Volvo PGA Champ'   92-01 – Wentworth

British Masters   92-94 – Woburn; 95-96 – Collingtree Park; 97-98 – Forest of Arden; 99-01 – Woburn

English Open   92 – The Belfry; 93-96 – Forest of Arden; 97-99 – Hanbury Manor; 00-01 – Forest of Arden

US Open   92 – Pebble Beach; 93 – Baltusrol; 94 – Oakmont; 95 – Shinnecock Hills; 96 – Oakland Hills; 97 – Congressional; 98 – The Olympic Club; 99 – Pinehurst; 00 – Pebble Beach; 01 – Southern Hills

The Great North Open   92-95 NA; 96-01 – Slaley Hall

Irish Open   92 – Killarney; 93-95 – Mount Juliet; 96-99 – Druids Glen; 00 – Ballybunion; 01 – Fota Island

European Open   92 – Sunningdale; 93-94 – East Sussex National; 95-01 – The K Club

Scot Open at Loch L   92-95 NA; 96-01 – Loch Lomond

British Open Champ'   92 – Muirfield; 93 – Royal St. George's; 94 – Turnberry; 95 – St. Andrews; 96 – Royal Lytham & St. Annes; 97 – Royal Troon; 98 – Royal Birkdale; 99 – Carnoustie; 00 – St. Andrews; 01 – Royal Lytham & St. Annes

TNT/Dutch Open   92-93 – Noordwijkse; 94-99 – Hilversumsche; 00-01 – Noordwijkse

Scandinavian Masters   92 – Barseback; 93 – Forsgardens; 94 – Drottningholm; 95 – Barseback; 96 – Forsgardens; 97 – Barseback; 98 – Kungsangen; 99 – Barseback; 00 – Kungsangen; 01 – Barseback

The Wales Open   92-99 NA; 00-01 – Celtic Manor

USPGA Champ'   92 – Bellerive; 93 – Inverness; 94 – Southern Hills; 95 – Riviera; 96 – Valhalla; 97 – Winged Foot; 98 – Sahalee; 99 – Medinah; 00 – Valhalla; 01 – Atlanta Athletic Club

NW Ireland Open   92-98 NA; 99 – Galway Bay; 00-01 – Slieve Russell Hotel

WGC NEC Inv'   92-98 NA; 99-01 – Firestone

Scottish PGA Ch'   92-98 NA; 99-01 – Gleneagles

BMW Int' Open   92-93 – Golfplatz; 94-96 – St. Eurach Land; 97-01 – Nord Eichenried

European Masters   92-01 – Crans-sur -Sierre

WGC AmEx Champ'   92-98 NA; 99-00 – Valderrama; 01 NA

Trophee Lancome   92-01 – St Nom-la-Breteche

German Masters   92-93 – Stuttgart; 94-97 – Berliner; 98-01 – Gut Larchenhof

Cannes Open   92-94 – Mougins; 95-98 - Royal Mougins; 99-00 NA; 01 – Mougins

Dunhill Links Ch'   92-00 NA; 01 – St. Andrews, Carnoustie & Kingsbarns

Masters de Madrid   92 – Malaga; 93 – Novo Sancti Petri; 94 – Montecastillo; 95 – Islantilla; 96 – El Saler; 97 – Campo de Golf; 98 –Santa Ponsa I; 99 – Malaga; 00-01 – Club de Campo

Italian Open Ch'   92 – Monticello; 93 – Modena; 94 – Marco Simone; 95 – Le Rovedine; 96 – Bergamo; 97 – Gardagolf; 98 – Castelconturbia; 99 – CircoloGolf; 00-01 – Is Molas

Volvo Masters   92-96 – Valderrama; 97-01 – Montecastillo

Peter Baker
7/10/67 – Shifnal, England

An ardent Wolves FC supporter who slipped to his worst position for a decade on the Order of Merit in 2001.

The last of his three European Tour wins came in 1993, when he actually won twice – the British Masters and the Scandinavian Masters (finishing a career best seventh on the Order of Merit and making the European Ryder Cup team).

An outstanding amateur player – he played Walker Cup golf in 1985 – Baker turned pro in 1986 and has earned over £2million in prize money.

His game is based on solid iron play and finding the greens in regulation.

Sc Av – 71.72 (116th) DD - 274.1 (156th) DA - 66.7 (57th) GIR – 70.6 (36th) PpGIR – 1.790 (96th) SS – 43.9 (169th)

	'92	'93	'94	'95	'96	'97	'98	'99	'00	'01
Johnnie Walker	-	25	19	-	MC	61	14	-	-	30
WGC Matchplay	-	-	-	-	-	-	-	-	-	-
Alfred Dunhill	-	-	-	-	-	-	-	9	14	23
S African Open	-	-	-	-	-	40	-	14	MC	16
Heineken Cl'	-	-	-	MC	MC	3	MC	58	MC	-
Greg Norman	-	-	-	-	-	-	-	-	70	17
Malaysian Open	-	-	-	-	-	-	-	-	-	-
S'pore Masters	-	-	-	-	-	-	-	-	-	-
Dubai Desert	11	9	34	39	5	53	20	35	54	MC
Qatar Masters	-	-	-	-	-	-	MC	MC	19	MC
Madeira Open	-	32	-	58	-	49	-	13	-	-
Brazil Open	-	-	-	-	-	-	-	-	-	-
Open de Arg	-	-	-	-	-	-	-	-	-	-
US Masters	-	-	MC	-	-	-	-	-	-	-
Moroccan Open	-	-	MC	-	35	MC	-	-	-	-
Open de Espana	-	8	45	4	16	57	69	25	3	MC
Open de Portugal	27	62	-	-	69	MC	7	32	34	MC
Open de France	5	MC	-	11	MC	MC	-	-	59	41
B&H I'national	MC	74	MC	MC	26	MC	24	MC	MC	42
Deutsche Bank	-	-	-	12	29	MC	MC	4	17	14
Volvo PGA	MC	34	19	25	MC	MC	41	MC	62	8
British Masters	MC	1	49	7	MC	35	55	55	77	MC
English Open	MC	21	MC	16	MC	26	20	MC	41	26
US Open	-	-	39	-	-	-	MC	-	-	-
G North Open	-	-	-	-	-	MC	-	68	36	47
Irish Open	45	34	6	4	25	MC	3	48	MC	MC
European Open	49	30	62	MC	42	2	16	35	MC	MC
Scot Open	46	-	-	-	29	57	24	MC	MC	59
British Open	-	21	55	66	-	MC	14	37	-	-
Dutch Open	50	33	31	MC	37	MC	6	-	-	14
Scandinavian	2	1	MC	MC	25	3	MC	MC	MC	36
Wales Open	-	-	-	-	-	-	-	-	29	MC
USPGA	-	MC	-	-	-	-	-	-	-	-
NW Ireland Open	-	-	-	-	-	-	-	MC	-	-
WGC NEC Inv'	-	-	-	-	-	-	-	-	-	-
Scottish PGA	-	-	-	-	-	-	-	-	-	MC
BMW Int' Open	MC	51	-	7	31	63	55	9	55	MC
European Mas'	MC	-	-	-	-	-	-	-	-	-
WGC AmEx	-	-	-	-	-	-	-	-	-	-
Troph' Lancome	62	10	30	51	21	MC	MC	-	MC	49
German Masters	68	-	20	45	5	11	69	4	66	MC
Cannes Open	-	MC	17	MC	44	MC	-	-	-	-
Dunhill Links	-	-	-	-	-	-	-	-	-	MC
Masters Madrid	-	-	-	27	3	43	-	MC	15	MC
Italian Open	60	-	-	8	-	53	5	23	5	MC
Volvo Masters	40	35	-	12	34	32	4	61	38	-

Warren Bennett
20/8/71 – Ashford, England

After an injury plagued 2000 he bounced back in 2001 by finishing in his best position in the Order of Merit since joining the European Tour in 1995.

He was perhaps unlucky not to win the Dutch Open last season, losing in a play-off to an inspired Bernhard Langer.

The European Tour title that did come his way was won in a play-off – the 1999 Scottish PGA Championship.

He won the Challenge Tour Order of Merit winner in 1998 – when he won five times. Bennett had to pull out of the 2001 World Cup because of an ankle problem. Long off the tee and a good iron player.

Sc Av – 70.37 (17th) DD - 285.1 (46th) DA - 63.9 (87th) GIR – 71.3 (25th) PpGIR – 1.773 (52nd) SS – 56.8 (65th)

	'92	'93	'94	'95	'96	'97	'98	'99	'00	'01
Johnnie Walker	-	-	-	-	-	-	-	-	-	-
WGC Matchplay	-	-	-	-	-	-	-	-	-	-
Alfred Dunhill	-	-	-	-	-	-	-	-	-	73
S African Open	-	-	-	-	-	-	-	-	-	-
Heineken Cl'	-	-	-	-	-	-	-	-	-	-
Greg Norman	-	-	-	-	-	-	-	-	-	-
Malaysian Open	-	-	-	-	-	-	-	-	-	MC
S'pore Masters	-	-	-	-	-	-	-	-	-	2
Dubai Desert	-	-	-	-	-	-	-	15	-	33
Qatar Masters	-	-	-	-	-	-	-	48	-	MC
Madeira Open	-	-	-	-	-	-	-	MC	-	-
Brazil Open	-	-	-	-	-	-	-	-	-	20
Open de Arg	-	-	-	-	-	-	-	-	-	-
US Masters	-	-	-	-	-	-	-	-	-	-
Moroccan Open	-	-	MC	-	MC	-	-	-	-	-
Open de Espana	-	-	-	-	-	-	-	58	-	16
Open de Portugal	-	-	-	-	-	MC	-	44	-	9
Open de France	-	-	-	-	-	-	-	MC	-	52
B&H I'national	-	-	-	-	-	-	-	MC	MC	MC
Deutsche Bank	-	-	-	-	-	WD	-	55	MC	20
Volvo PGA	-	-	-	-	-	-	-	13	MC	63
British Masters	-	-	-	MC	-	-	MC	-	-	14
English Open	-	-	-	-	-	-	-	MC	MC	40
US Open	-	-	-	-	-	-	-	-	-	-
G North Open	-	-	-	-	-	WD	-	8	WD	20
Irish Open	-	-	-	-	-	-	-	MC	-	54
European Open	-	-	-	-	-	-	-	WD	-	62
Scot Open	-	-	-	-	-	-	-	MC	-	47
British Open	-	72	39	-	-	-	-	MC	-	-
Dutch Open	-	-	-	-	-	MC	-	-	-	2
Scandinavian	-	-	-	-	-	-	-	-	-	4
Wales Open	-	-	-	-	-	-	-	-	MC	20
USPGA	-	-	-	-	-	-	-	-	-	-
NW Ireland Open	-	-	-	-	-	-	-	-	-	-
WGC NEC Inv'	-	-	-	-	-	-	-	-	-	-
Scottish PGA	-	-	-	-	-	-	-	1	-	51
BMW Int' Open	-	-	-	-	-	-	-	62	-	16
European Mas'	-	-	-	-	-	-	-	61	-	53
WGC AmEx	-	-	-	-	-	-	-	-	-	-
Troph' Lancome	-	-	-	-	-	-	-	-	-	-
German Masters	-	-	-	-	-	-	-	-	-	32
Cannes Open	-	-	-	-	61	-	-	-	-	6
Dunhill Links	-	-	-	-	-	-	-	-	-	-
Masters Madrid	-	-	-	-	66	-	66	-	-	-
Italian Open	-	-	-	-	-	MC	-	MC	-	17
Volvo Masters	-	-	-	-	-	-	-	-	-	WD

Jorge Berendt

19/7/64 – Formosa, Argentina

Veteran Argentinean pro who won his first European Tour event last season – the Cannes Open. Prolific winner in his home country before trying his luck in Europe in 1990.

Over the next five years he only managed to break into the top 100 of the Order of Merit once before dropping down to the Challenge Tour.

Won the Challenge Tour Grand Final to re-take his place on the full tour in 1999.

Former caddie who was inspired by the like of Eduardo Romero to take up the game. A short but straight hitter who now enjoys a two-year tour exemption courtesy of his Cannes win.

Sc Av – 71.28 (72nd) DD - 277.2 (122nd) DA - 67.6 (42nd) GIR – 69.5 (54th) PpGIR – 1.794 (104th) SS – 45.1 (164th)

	'92	'93	'94	'95	'96	'97	'98	'99	'00	'01
Johnnie Walker	21	59	-	-	-	-	-	-	-	-
WGC Matchplay	-	-	-	-	-	-	-	-	-	-
Alfred Dunhill	-	-	-	-	-	-	MC	-	-	-
S African Open	-	-	-	-	-	-	-	-	-	-
Heineken Cl'	-	-	-	-	-	-	-	-	-	-
Greg Norman	-	-	-	-	-	-	-	-	-	-
Malaysian Open	-	-	-	-	-	-	-	-	-	MC
S'pore Masters	-	-	-	-	-	-	-	-	-	51
Dubai Desert	10	MC	-	-	-	-	-	13	-	-
Qatar Masters	-	-	-	-	-	-	-	MC	46	-
Madeira Open	-	-	-	-	-	-	-	66	29	62
Brazil Open	-	-	-	-	-	-	-	-	13	27
Open de Arg	-	-	-	-	-	-	-	-	-	35
US Masters	-	-	-	-	-	-	-	-	-	-
Moroccan Open	-	MC	-	-	-	-	-	4	-	MC
Open de Espana	MC	33	-	-	-	-	-	MC	MC	MC
Open de Portugal	18	2	-	-	-	-	-	73	-	67
Open de France	MC	-	MC	-	-	-	-	5	MC	-
B&H I'national	MC	MC	-	-	-	-	-	MC	63	12
Deutsche Bank	-	-	-	-	-	-	-	63	60	-
Volvo PGA	-	45	MC	-	-	-	-	MC	-	-
British Masters	-	53	-	-	-	-	-	MC	62	34
English Open	34	59	-	-	-	-	-	-	MC	12
US Open	-	-	-	-	-	-	-	-	-	-
G North Open	-	-	-	-	-	-	74	-	-	MC
Irish Open	-	55	MC	-	-	-	-	-	MC	30
European Open	MC	13	-	-	-	-	-	45	MC	-
Scot Open	-	-	-	-	-	-	55	-	-	-
British Open	-	-	-	-	-	-	-	-	-	-
Dutch Open	-	9	-	-	-	-	-	-	41	MC
Scandinavian	MC	72	-	-	-	-	-	65	MC	MC
Wales Open	-	-	-	-	-	-	-	-	-	49
USPGA	-	-	-	-	-	-	-	-	-	-
NW Ireland Open	-	-	-	-	-	-	-	-	-	74
WGC NEC Inv'	-	-	-	-	-	-	-	-	-	-
Scottish PGA	-	-	-	-	-	-	-	-	-	MC
BMW Int' Open	MC	-	-	-	-	-	-	-	38	37
European Mas'	MC	MC	-	-	-	-	-	MC	MC	MC
WGC AmEx	-	-	-	-	-	-	-	-	-	-
Troph' Lancome	-	44	-	-	-	-	-	-	MC	30
German Masters	-	-	-	-	-	-	-	-	-	-
Cannes Open	-	-	-	-	-	-	-	-	-	1
Dunhill Links	-	-	-	-	-	-	-	-	-	56
Masters Madrid	MC	30	-	-	-	-	-	29	MC	MC
Italian Open	MC	32	-	-	-	-	-	38	64	MC
Volvo Masters	-	-	-	-	-	-	-	-	-	-

John Bickerton

23/12/69 – Redditch, England

Former Challenge Tour graduate and Q-School regular whose consistent play over the past few years has meant a trip to neither has been necessary.

The Droitwich pro is still to win on the European Tour and claimed his third runner-up place of his career in the Madeira Island Open.

Did manage to win the Gore Tex Challenge on the Challenge Tour in 1994.

His best season came in 1999 when he managed 20th position in the Order Of Merit, courtesy of six top-ten finishes.

A member of the UK team which contested the inaugural Seve Ballesteros Trophy in 2000.

Sc Av – 70.89 (38th) DD - 274.9 (147th) DA - 77.1 (3rd) GIR – 73.4 (13th) PpGIR – 1.794 (104th) SS – 53.4 (94th)

	'92	'93	'94	'95	'96	'97	'98	'99	'00	'01
Johnnie Walker	-	-	-	-	-	-	-	-	-	-
WGC Matchplay	-	-	-	-	-	-	-	-	-	-
Alfred Dunhill	-	-	-	-	-	MC	-	46	-	MC
S African Open	-	-	-	-	-	-	-	9	-	MC
Heineken Cl'	-	-	-	-	-	-	-	45	18	39
Greg Norman	-	-	-	-	-	-	-	-	MC	31
Malaysian Open	-	-	-	-	-	-	-	27	34	30
S'pore Masters	-	-	-	-	-	-	-	-	-	-
Dubai Desert	-	-	-	MC	MC	-	-	15	20	21
Qatar Masters	-	-	-	-	-	-	-	4	35	-
Madeira Open	-	MC	-	MC	MC	13	14	4	5	2
Brazil Open	-	-	-	-	-	-	-	-	-	-
Open de Arg	-	-	-	-	-	-	-	-	-	-
US Masters	-	-	-	-	-	-	-	-	-	-
Moroccan Open	-	-	MC	MC	41	24	-	49	-	65
Open de Espana	-	-	-	69	MC	-	-	MC	33	64
Open de Portugal	-	-	-	37	60	60	16	2	18	44
Open de France	-	-	-	MC	63	MC	66	-	-	10
B&H I'national	-	-	-	MC	18	MC	-	MC	66	10
Deutsche Bank	-	-	-	27	MC	MC	-	MC	35	10
Volvo PGA	-	-	-	-	MC	-	-	43	30	45
British Masters	-	-	-	35	MC	MC	8	10	55	27
English Open	-	-	-	MC	MC	-	71	2	23	16
US Open	-	-	-	-	-	-	-	-	-	-
G North Open	-	-	-	-	9	MC	-	MC	61	-
Irish Open	-	-	-	67	39	WD	-	MC	MC	35
European Open	-	-	-	24	67	-	MC	MC	MC	MC
Scot Open	-	-	-	-	-	-	-	MC	MC	21
British Open	-	-	-	MC	-	-	-	-	MC	MC
Dutch Open	-	-	-	WD	MC	MC	65	30	17	45
Scandinavian	-	-	-	MC	18	-	-	-	45	MC
Wales Open	-	-	-	-	-	-	-	-	MC	33
USPGA	-	-	-	-	-	-	-	-	-	-
NW Ireland Open	-	-	-	-	-	-	-	MC	-	-
WGC NEC Inv'	-	-	-	-	-	-	-	-	-	-
Scottish PGA	-	-	-	-	-	-	-	-	-	-
BMW Int' Open	-	-	-	28	24	-	48	4	64	60
European Mas'	-	-	-	75	WD	44	MC	20	MC	MC
WGC AmEx	-	-	-	-	-	-	-	-	-	-
Troph' Lancome	-	-	-	-	-	-	MC	MC	53	20
German Masters	-	-	-	-	-	-	-	MC	22	MC
Cannes Open	-	-	-	21	MC	MC	-	-	-	-
Dunhill Links	-	-	-	-	-	-	-	-	-	24
Masters Madrid	-	-	-	20	MC	MC	19	10	MC	12
Italian Open	-	-	-	MC	MC	32	-	MC	7	-
Volvo Masters	-	-	-	-	-	-	-	47	-	27

Thomas Bjorn
18/2/71 – Silkeborg, Denmark

Dane who in 2001 out-duelled Tiger Woods down the stretch in Dubai to claim his sixth European Tour win.

In doing so, he joined a select club of only four golf players who have come from behind to snatch victory when Woods led going into the final day of a pro tour event.

Suffered from both shoulder and neck injuries in 2001 but still finished in the top ten of the Order of Merit for a second successive season.

A big hitter and aggressive putter who will line up for the Europeans in the Ryder Cup in 2002 – his second appearance.

Sc Av – 70.19 (13th) DD - 282.3 (74th) DA - 60.8 (129th) GIR – 66.9 (98th) PpGIR – 1.731 (2nd) SS – 53.6 (92nd)

	'92	'93	'94	'95	'96	'97	'98	'99	'00	'01
Johnnie Walker	-	-	-	-	-	MC	MC	-	-	-
WGC Matchplay	-	-	-	-	-	-	-	17	9	-
Alfred Dunhill	-	-	-	-	-	-	-	-	-	-
S African Open	-	-	-	-	17	-	6	MC	-	3
Heineken Cl'	-	-	-	-	25	1	26	2	8	-
Greg Norman	-	-	-	-	-	-	-	-	-	-
Malaysian Open	-	-	-	-	-	-	-	-	-	-
S'pore Masters	-	-	-	-	-	-	-	-	-	-
Dubai Desert	-	-	-	-	7	WD	MC	53	13	1
Qatar Masters	-	-	-	-	-	-	MC	MC	-	23
Madeira Open	-	-	-	-	MC	-	-	-	-	-
Brazil Open	-	-	-	-	-	-	-	-	-	-
Open de Arg	-	-	-	-	-	-	-	-	-	-
US Masters	-	-	-	-	-	-	-	MC	28	48
Moroccan Open	-	-	-	-	64	-	35	-	-	-
Open de Espana	-	-	-	-	55	11	1	-	43	-
Open de Portugal	-	-	-	-	MC	-	-	-	-	-
Open de France	-	-	-	-	28	18	-	-	-	-
B&H I'national	-	-	-	-	WD	12	3	MC	MC	7
Deutsche Bank	-	-	-	-	18	9	13	MC	35	73
Volvo PGA	-	-	-	-	MC	19	5	-	62	39
British Masters	-	-	-	-	46	4	-	32	50	27
English Open	-	-	-	-	12	MC	41	-	17	-
US Open	-	-	-	-	68	25	MC	46	-	22
G North Open	-	-	-	-	-	-	-	-	-	-
Irish Open	-	-	-	-	MC	6	-	4	45	5
European Open	-	-	-	-	-	MC	23	MC	8	2
Scot Open	-	-	-	-	1	13	32	20	19	2
British Open	-	-	-	-	MC	MC	8	30	2	MC
Dutch Open	-	-	-	-	25	-	-	-	-	-
Scandinavian	-	-	-	-	7	-	55	52	23	9
Wales Open	-	-	-	-	-	-	-	-	-	-
USPGA	-	-	-	-	45	MC	70	-	3	63
NW Ireland Open	-	-	-	-	-	-	-	-	-	-
WGC NEC Inv'	-	-	-	-	-	-	-	-	10	31
Scottish PGA	-	-	-	-	-	-	-	-	-	-
BMW Int' Open	-	-	-	-	-	5	6	34	1	16
European Mas'	-	-	-	-	7	MC	30	2	2	WD
WGC AmEx	-	-	-	-	-	-	-	-	59	40
Troph' Lancome	-	-	-	-	MC	-	18	24	16	-
German Masters	-	-	-	-	8	3	MC	16	5	-
Cannes Open	-	-	-	-	MC	29	-	-	-	-
Dunhill Links	-	-	-	-	-	-	-	-	-	13
Masters Madrid	-	-	-	-	-	-	-	-	-	10
Italian Open	-	-	-	-	42	4	-	-	MC	-
Volvo Masters	-	-	-	-	20	15	41	7	28	44

Henrik Bjornstad
7/5/79 – Oslo, Norway

Norwegian pro who enjoyed his best season on the European Tour in 2001, finishing in the top ten on three occasions and comfortably keeping his card for 2002.

He turned pro in 1997 and made it through Q-School in 1998 to take his place on the European Tour for the first the following season.

He missed 14 out of 20 cuts, however, in his rookie season and finished a lowly 149th on the Order of Merit.

After playing just one event in 2000, Bjornstad earned his playing privileges again by way of the Q-School.

Sc Av – 71.04 (48th) DD - 285.6 (42nd) DA - 62.6 (105th) GIR – 63.9 (150th) PpGIR – 1.763 (34th) SS – 58.0 (53rd)

	'92	'93	'94	'95	'96	'97	'98	'99	'00	'01
Johnnie Walker	-	-	-	-	-	-	-	-	-	-
WGC Matchplay	-	-	-	-	-	-	-	-	-	-
Alfred Dunhill	-	-	-	-	-	-	-	-	-	-
S African Open	-	-	-	-	-	-	-	MC	-	-
Heineken Cl'	-	-	-	-	-	-	-	13	-	-
Greg Norman	-	-	-	-	-	-	-	-	-	-
Malaysian Open	-	-	-	-	-	-	-	-	-	MC
S'pore Masters	-	-	-	-	-	-	-	-	29	-
Dubai Desert	-	-	-	-	-	-	-	-	-	-
Qatar Masters	-	-	-	-	-	-	-	MC	-	MC
Madeira Open	-	-	-	-	-	-	MC	MC	-	-
Brazil Open	-	-	-	-	-	-	-	-	-	58
Open de Arg	-	-	-	-	-	-	-	-	-	4
US Masters	-	-	-	-	-	-	-	-	-	-
Moroccan Open	-	-	-	-	-	-	MC	MC	MC	31
Open de Espana	-	-	-	-	-	-	-	-	-	MC
Open de Portugal	-	-	-	-	-	-	-	-	-	MC
Open de France	-	-	-	-	-	-	-	MC	-	41
B&H I'national	-	-	-	-	-	-	-	-	-	42
Deutsche Bank	-	-	-	-	-	-	-	-	-	-
Volvo PGA	-	-	-	-	-	-	-	-	-	-
British Masters	-	-	-	-	-	-	-	MC	-	-
English Open	-	-	-	-	-	-	-	MC	-	-
US Open	-	-	-	-	-	-	-	-	-	-
G North Open	-	-	-	-	-	-	-	61	-	33
Irish Open	-	-	-	-	-	-	-	MC	-	48
European Open	-	-	-	-	-	-	-	MC	-	6
Scot Open	-	-	-	-	-	-	-	-	-	MC
British Open	-	-	-	-	-	-	-	-	-	-
Dutch Open	-	-	-	-	-	-	-	42	-	14
Scandinavian	-	-	-	-	-	-	-	MC	-	68
Wales Open	-	-	-	-	-	-	-	-	-	-
USPGA	-	-	-	-	-	-	-	-	-	-
NW Ireland Open	-	-	-	-	-	-	-	MC	-	-
WGC NEC Inv'	-	-	-	-	-	-	-	-	-	-
Scottish PGA	-	-	-	-	-	-	-	15	-	MC
BMW Int' Open	-	-	-	-	-	-	-	34	-	MC
European Mas'	-	-	-	-	-	-	-	MC	-	-
WGC AmEx	-	-	-	-	-	-	-	-	-	-
Troph' Lancome	-	-	-	-	-	-	-	-	-	MC
German Masters	-	-	-	-	41	-	-	-	-	-
Cannes Open	-	-	-	-	-	-	-	-	-	9
Dunhill Links	-	-	-	-	-	-	-	-	-	-
Masters Madrid	-	-	-	-	-	-	-	-	-	46
Italian Open	-	-	-	-	-	-	-	-	-	44
Volvo Masters	-	-	-	-	-	-	-	-	-	-

Diego Borrego

29/1/72 – Malaga, Spain

Big-hitting Spaniard whose late rush of high finishes last season secured his playing rights for 2002.

He was languishing outside the top 115 in October but third places in the last two counting events (the Madrid Open and the Italian Open) won him enough cash to continue full time on the tour.

His sole success came in 1996, when he won the Turespana Masters in a play-off, eventually finishing 30th on the Order of Merit – still his best position.

Turned pro in 1991 and had successful spells on the Challenge Tour (winning in the Leman Pro-Am in 1993 and the Perrier European Pro-Am in 1995). Sc Av – 71.18 (62nd) DD - 279.6 (102nd) DA - 66.7 (57th) GIR – 70.2 (42nd) PpGIR – 1.781 (71st) SS – 58.3 (50th)

	'92	'93	'94	'95	'96	'97	'98	'99	'00	'01
Johnnie Walker	-	-	-	-	-	-	-	-	-	-
WGC Matchplay	-	-	-	-	-	-	-	-	-	-
Alfred Dunhill	-	-	-	-	-	-	-	-	-	-
S African Open	-	-	-	-	-	-	-	-	-	-
Heineken Cl'	-	-	-	-	-	-	-	-	-	-
Greg Norman	-	-	-	-	-	-	-	-	-	-
Malaysian Open	-	-	-	-	-	-	-	-	-	-
S'pore Masters	-	-	-	-	-	-	-	-	-	-
Dubai Desert	-	-	-	MC	MC	-	-	MC	66	-
Qatar Masters	-	-	-	-	-	MC	-	MC	MC	-
Madeira Open	-	8	-	8	-	-	4	24	-	-
Brazil Open	-	-	-	-	-	-	-	48	20	-
Open de Arg	-	-	-	-	-	-	-	-	-	26
US Masters	-	-	-	-	-	-	-	-	-	-
Moroccan Open	-	MC	-	37	10	19	MC	-	-	-
Open de Espana	-	MC	MC	21	MC	MC	11	43	-	58
Open de Portugal	-	MC	-	21	26	MC	55	MC	MC	-
Open de France	-	39	-	MC	32	52	12	MC	27	-
B&H I'national	-	-	-	-	MC	MC	MC	4	MC	19
Deutsche Bank	-	-	-	-	MC	47	MC	23	MC	68
Volvo PGA	-	-	-	-	MC	37	63	WD	MC	26
British Masters	-	-	-	-	MC	-	39	MC	23	MC
English Open	-	-	-	-	-	MC	MC	MC	65	-
US Open	-	-	-	-	-	-	-	-	-	-
G North Open	-	-	-	-	-	MC	-	31	32	WD
Irish Open	-	20	-	MC	31	MC	-	MC	MC	-
European Open	-	-	-	-	63	MC	MC	55	52	MC
Scot Open	-	-	47	MC	MC	-	MC	61	-	-
British Open	-	-	-	MC	-	-	-	-	-	-
Dutch Open	-	MC	-	30	-	MC	49	MC	MC	-
Scandinavian	-	42	-	-	-	MC	MC	4	MC	-
Wales Open	-	-	-	-	-	-	-	MC	MC	-
USPGA	-	-	-	-	-	-	-	-	-	-
NW Ireland Open	-	-	-	-	-	-	-	MC	-	-
WGC NEC Inv'	-	-	-	-	-	-	-	-	-	-
Scottish PGA	-	-	-	-	-	-	-	-	-	MC
BMW Int' Open	-	-	-	-	57	55	WD	MC	MC	-
European Mas'	-	-	-	-	MC	MC	15	66	-	-
WGC AmEx	-	-	-	-	-	-	-	-	-	-
Troph' Lancome	-	-	-	-	MC	47	MC	-	46	38
German Masters	-	-	-	61	-	MC	-	66	-	-
Cannes Open	-	-	-	MC	-	MC	-	-	MC	-
Dunhill Links	-	-	-	-	-	-	-	-	-	MC
Masters Madrid	-	59	MC	55	1	7	15	40	MC	3
Italian Open	-	65	-	-	-	MC	MC	72	59	3
Volvo Masters	-	-	-	20	-	-	-	-	-	-

Markus Brier

5/7/68 – Vienna, Austria

Austrian pro who made it onto the full tour in 2000 after a string of fine performances on the Challenge Tour in the previous season.

Enjoyed a sparkling amateur career, winning the German and Swiss Amateur titles before turning pro in 1995.

Tried and failed to get on to the main tour by way of the Q-School on four occasions. But two runner-up places on the Challenge Tour in 1999 helped him to third place in the Challenge Tour Order of Merit and promotion to the European Tour.

Finished second in the Spanish Open in 2000 – his best tour finish.

Sc Av – 71.16 (58th) DD - 278.6 (111th) DA - 63.7 (88th) GIR – 66.7 (103rd) PpGIR – 1.783 (76th) SS – 43.1 (174th)

	'92	'93	'94	'95	'96	'97	'98	'99	'00	'01
Johnnie Walker	-	-	-	-	-	-	-	-	-	-
WGC Matchplay	-	-	-	-	-	-	-	-	-	-
Alfred Dunhill	-	-	-	-	-	-	-	-	MC	23
S African Open	-	-	-	-	-	-	-	-	26	26
Heineken Cl'	-	-	-	-	-	-	-	-	13	23
Greg Norman	-	-	-	-	-	-	-	-	DQ	-
Malaysian Open	-	-	-	-	-	-	-	-	-	-
S'pore Masters	-	-	-	-	-	-	-	-	-	-
Dubai Desert	-	-	-	-	-	-	-	-	MC	MC
Qatar Masters	-	-	-	-	-	-	-	-	14	59
Madeira Open	-	-	-	-	-	-	MC	-	7	32
Brazil Open	-	-	-	-	-	-	-	-	-	-
Open de Arg	-	-	-	-	-	-	-	-	-	-
US Masters	-	-	-	-	-	-	-	-	-	-
Moroccan Open	-	-	-	-	-	-	MC	-	MC	70
Open de Espana	-	-	-	-	-	-	-	-	2	58
Open de Portugal	-	-	-	-	-	-	MC	-	MC	27
Open de France	-	-	-	-	-	-	-	-	MC	-
B&H I'national	-	-	-	-	-	-	-	-	MC	35
Deutsche Bank	-	-	-	-	-	MC	-	-	45	-
Volvo PGA	-	-	-	-	-	-	-	-	MC	32
British Masters	-	-	-	-	-	-	-	-	MC	47
English Open	-	-	-	-	-	-	-	-	-	MC
US Open	-	-	-	-	-	-	-	-	-	-
G North Open	-	-	-	-	-	-	-	-	-	-
Irish Open	-	-	-	-	-	-	-	-	MC	MC
European Open	-	-	-	-	-	-	-	-	MC	52
Scot Open	-	-	-	-	-	-	-	-	MC	MC
British Open	-	-	-	-	-	-	-	-	-	MC
Dutch Open	-	-	-	-	-	-	-	-	-	-
Scandinavian	-	-	-	-	-	-	-	-	70	MC
Wales Open	-	-	-	-	-	-	-	-	MC	49
USPGA	-	-	-	-	-	-	-	-	-	-
NW Ireland Open	-	-	-	-	-	-	-	MC	-	-
WGC NEC Inv'	-	-	-	-	-	-	-	-	-	-
Scottish PGA	-	-	-	-	-	-	-	-	-	-
BMW Int' Open	-	-	-	-	-	-	-	-	MC	37
European Mas'	-	-	-	-	-	-	-	-	13	13
WGC AmEx	-	-	-	-	-	-	-	-	-	-
Troph' Lancome	-	-	-	-	-	-	-	-	68	23
German Masters	-	-	-	-	-	-	-	-	-	19
Cannes Open	-	-	-	-	-	-	-	-	-	-
Dunhill Links	-	-	-	-	-	-	-	-	-	56
Masters Madrid	-	-	-	-	-	-	-	-	25	5
Italian Open	-	-	-	-	-	-	-	-	64	9
Volvo Masters	-	-	-	-	-	-	-	-	-	-

Angel Cabrera
12/9/69 – Cordoba, Argentina

Burly Argentinean pro who finally won on the European Tour after umpteen near misses by capturing the co-sanctioned Open de Argentina title in 2001.

After finishing second in the B&H International in May he moved into the top 25 in the world rankings.

Another Argentinean who started life as a caddie before taking up the game, he was given financial assistance by Eduardo Romero in the early part of his career and dedicated his victory to his mentor.

Came to Europe in 1996 and his big hitting game has rewarded him with over £2million of prize money.

Sc Av – 69.95 (8th) DD - 303.5 (1st) DA - 59.7 (146th) GIR – 70.2 (42nd) PpGIR – 1.761 (31st) SS – 57.4 (60th)

	'92	'93	'94	'95	'96	'97	'98	'99	'00	'01
Johnnie Walker	-	-	-	-	-	-	-	-	9	-
WGC Matchplay	-	-	-	-	-	-	-	33	-	-
Alfred Dunhill	-	-	-	-	-	-	-	-	-	-
S African Open	-	-	-	-	-	-	-	-	-	-
Heineken Cl'	-	-	-	-	-	-	-	-	-	-
Greg Norman	-	-	-	-	-	-	-	-	-	-
Malaysian Open	-	-	-	-	-	-	43	-	-	-
S'pore Masters	-	-	-	-	-	-	-	-	-	-
Dubai Desert	-	-	-	-	-	10	40	25	MC	9
Qatar Masters	-	-	-	-	-	-	17	40	14	6
Madeira Open	-	-	-	-	-	-	-	-	-	-
Brazil Open	-	-	-	-	-	-	-	28	-	-
Open de Arg	-	-	-	-	-	-	-	-	-	1
US Masters	-	-	-	-	-	-	-	-	MC	10
Moroccan Open	-	-	-	-	23	MC	27	-	-	-
Open de Espana	-	-	-	-	62	MC	11	46	21	-
Open de Portugal	-	-	-	-	52	46	22	16	-	-
Open de France	-	-	-	-	45	MC	MC	26	MC	MC
B&H I'national	-	-	-	-	-	MC	MC	2	9	2
Deutsche Bank	-	-	-	-	-	24	MC	67	23	20
Volvo PGA	-	-	-	-	-	6	MC	67	51	2
British Masters	-	-	-	-	MC	8	48	38	-	-
English Open	-	-	-	-	53	MC	-	-	-	-
US Open	-	-	-	-	-	-	-	-	37	7
G North Open	-	-	-	-	17	-	-	-	-	-
Irish Open	-	-	-	-	-	MC	69	2	10	-
European Open	-	-	-	-	14	MC	5	6	2	34
Scot Open	-	-	-	-	-	16	60	15	29	28
British Open	-	-	-	-	-	51	-	4	MC	MC
Dutch Open	-	-	-	-	MC	3	MC	8	3	-
Scandinavian	-	-	-	-	-	-	-	-	-	-
Wales Open	-	-	-	-	-	-	-	-	-	-
USPGA	-	-	-	-	-	-	-	-	19	37
NW Ireland Open	-	-	-	-	-	-	-	-	-	-
WGC NEC Inv'	-	-	-	-	-	-	-	-	-	-
Scottish PGA	-	-	-	-	-	-	-	-	-	-
BMW Int' Open	-	-	-	44	31	4	-	-	-	-
European Mas'	-	-	-	23	MC	37	28	10	-	-
WGC AmEx	-	-	-	-	-	-	-	25	17	-
Troph' Lancome	-	-	-	-	MC	51	10	16	30	-
German Masters	-	-	-	-	-	-	-	11	-	-
Cannes Open	-	-	52	-	-	-	-	-	-	-
Dunhill Links	-	-	-	-	-	-	-	-	-	MC
Masters Madrid	-	-	-	-	MC	8	29	12	10	-
Italian Open	-	-	-	-	32	MC	60	MC	-	50
Volvo Masters	-	-	-	-	-	29	26	42	5	16

Michael Campbell
23/2/69 – Hawere, New Zealand

Another winning season for the Brighton-based Kiwi who successfully defended his Heineken Classic title in January. Shot a career best score of 62 in the Deutsche Bank.

But was beaten down the stretch by Tiger Woods. After bursting onto the scene in 1995 – his rookie season – when he led the Open after the third round (but faded to finish third) his form dipped over the following two years.

Back to his best over the past two seasons, winning three times in Europe and bagging a couple of ANZ Tour titles as well. Brilliant putter who sees his future in America.

Sc Av – 70.84 (36th) DD - 280.9 (91st) DA - 66.8 (54th) GIR – 69.9 (52nd) PpGIR – 1.731 (2nd) SS – 50.0 (122nd)

	'92	'93	'94	'95	'96	'97	'98	'99	'00	'01
Johnnie Walker	-	-	-	4	-	7	MC	-	1	3
WGC Matchplay	-	-	-	-	-	-	-	-	-	9
Alfred Dunhill	-	-	-	-	-	MC	-	-	-	-
S African Open	-	-	-	-	-	51	-	-	-	-
Heineken Cl'	-	-	-	-	-	45	-	MC	1	1
Greg Norman	-	-	-	-	-	-	-	-	MC	MC
Malaysian Open	-	-	-	-	-	-	-	-	-	7
S'pore Masters	-	-	-	-	-	-	-	-	-	-
Dubai Desert	-	-	-	-	3	-	MC	-	11	-
Qatar Masters	-	-	-	-	-	-	MC	-	-	-
Madeira Open	-	-	-	-	-	MC	19	-	-	-
Brazil Open	-	-	-	-	-	-	-	-	-	-
Open de Arg	-	-	-	-	-	-	-	-	-	-
US Masters	-	-	-	-	-	MC	-	-	-	MC
Moroccan Open	-	-	-	-	-	MC	-	-	-	-
Open de Espana	-	-	-	MC	55	MC	MC	25	-	-
Open de Portugal	-	-	-	-	-	MC	-	-	-	-
Open de France	-	-	-	MC	MC	MC	11	-	7	-
B&H I'national	-	-	-	15	MC	MC	52	MC	52	MC
Deutsche Bank	-	-	-	7	35	58	-	MC	26	2
Volvo PGA	-	-	-	2	MC	-	-	19	11	4
British Masters	-	MC	-	2	MC	-	19	10	-	42
English Open	-	-	-	24	31	MC	14	39	2	-
US Open	-	-	-	-	32	-	-	-	12	MC
G North Open	-	-	-	-	-	MC	-	39	-	-
Irish Open	-	-	-	12	43	MC	-	29	-	-
European Open	-	-	-	42	MC	34	-	18	34	23
Scot Open	-	-	-	-	65	-	MC	7	9	57
British Open	-	-	MC	3	DQ	-	64	MC	MC	23
Dutch Open	-	MC	-	-	-	-	MC	27	-	-
Scandinavian	-	MC	-	10	-	-	63	14	2	13
Wales Open	-	-	-	-	-	-	-	-	-	-
USPGA	-	-	-	17	MC	-	-	-	MC	MC
NW Ireland Open	-	-	-	-	-	-	-	-	-	-
WGC NEC Inv'	-	-	-	-	-	-	-	-	15	31
Scottish PGA	-	-	-	-	-	-	-	-	-	-
BMW Int' Open	-	-	-	-	-	MC	64	-	-	-
European Mas'	-	-	MC	11	50	44	-	15	10	-
WGC AmEx	-	-	-	-	-	-	-	-	9	-
Troph' Lancome	-	-	-	14	58	-	40	18	2	-
German Masters	-	-	-	57	13	-	-	30	1	19
Cannes Open	-	-	MC	35	-	MC	-	-	-	-
Dunhill Links	-	-	-	-	-	-	-	-	-	MC
Masters Madrid	-	-	-	-	-	36	19	-	-	-
Italian Open	-	-	MC	-	-	-	23	23	-	-
Volvo Masters	-	-	-	28	-	-	-	7	3	30

David Carter

16/6/72 – Johannesburg, South Africa (represents England)

South African born Englishman who slumped to his lowest position on the Order of Merit in 2001 since his debut year on the European Tour six years ago.

He managed only one top-ten finish in 2001 – in the BMW International – and never looked like the golfer that finished in the top 30 of the Order of Merit in both 1998 and 1999.

He joined the main tour in 1995 but suffered from a brain haemorrhage in 1997, when not just his career but his life was threatened.

He battled back to fitness and form and won his first title at the 1998 Irish Open.

Sc Av – 71.54 (98th) DD - 283.2 (65th) DA - 71.4 (12th) GIR – 71.9 (20th) PpGIR – 1.831 (169th) SS – 52.1 (103rd)

	'92	'93	'94	'95	'96	'97	'98	'99	'00	'01
Johnnie Walker	-	-	-	MC	MC	20	MC	-	-	-
WGC Matchplay	-	-	-	-	-	-	-	-	-	-
Alfred Dunhill	-	-	-	24	MC	44	-	51	-	MC
S African Open	-	-	-	-	-	40	-	57	-	-
Heineken Cl'	-	-	-	-	37	18	46	-	MC	19
Greg Norman	-	-	-	-	-	-	-	-	60	17
Malaysian Open	-	-	-	-	-	-	-	-	-	-
S'pore Masters	-	-	-	-	-	-	-	-	-	-
Dubai Desert	-	-	-	53	17	-	13	MC	56	MC
Qatar Masters	-	-	-	-	-	-	5	MC	14	13
Madeira Open	-	-	-	MC	3	-	-	29	-	32
Brazil Open	-	-	-	-	-	-	-	-	-	-
Open de Arg	-	-	-	-	-	-	-	-	-	-
US Masters	-	-	-	-	-	-	-	-	-	-
Moroccan Open	-	-	-	14	MC	-	-	-	-	-
Open de Espana	-	-	-	33	21	23	26	25	33	MC
Open de Portugal	-	-	-	28	27	-	10	MC	-	MC
Open de France	-	-	-	34	MC	MC	MC	-	WD	-
B&H I'national	-	-	-	-	23	MC	24	MC	28	78
Deutsche Bank	-	-	-	43	MC	9	54	31	35	MC
Volvo PGA	-	-	-	MC	46	14	-	7	38	MC
British Masters	-	-	-	54	46	MC	MC	32	62	27
English Open	-	-	-	MC	24	26	MC	3	26	44
US Open	-	-	-	-	-	-	-	-	-	54
G North Open	-	-	-	-	-	6	-	2	22	MC
Irish Open	-	-	-	33	48	15	1	21	10	82
European Open	-	-	-	50	55	5	57	70	34	41
Scot Open	-	-	-	54	61	47	23	29	-	-
British Open	-	-	-	-	-	-	42	MC	-	-
Dutch Open	-	-	-	MC	37	18	MC	-	-	MC
Scandinavian	-	-	-	35	MC	20	63	14	62	59
Wales Open	-	-	-	-	-	-	-	-	29	49
USPGA	-	-	-	-	-	-	-	-	-	-
NW Ireland Open	-	-	-	-	-	-	-	-	-	-
WGC NEC Inv'	-	-	-	-	-	-	-	-	-	-
Scottish PGA	-	-	-	-	-	-	-	-	-	MC
BMW Int' Open	-	MC	-	19	44	MC	-	34	MC	10
European Mas'	-	-	-	MC	-	MC	-	50	59	23
WGC AmEx	-	-	-	-	-	-	-	-	-	-
Troph' Lancome	-	-	-	23	MC	54	MC	MC	WD	23
German Masters	-	-	-	-	35	34	48	MC	30	41
Cannes Open	-	-	-	MC	2	2	MC	-	-	MC
Dunhill Links	-	-	-	-	-	-	-	-	-	29
Masters Madrid	-	-	-	35	49	-	-	MC	MC	MC
Italian Open	-	-	-	MC	-	-	51	13	-	MC
Volvo Masters	-	-	-	-	7	15	64	36	-	-

Paul Casey

Weybridge, England

Named Rookie of the Year for 2001 and one of England's most promising golfers who had a superb college career in the States before turning pro in late 2000.

In just his 11th start as a professional, the 24-year-old won the Scottish PGA Championship. The win guaranteed his playing privileges for two years and took his earnings as a pro to over £300,00 in just four months.

He admits that he future will probably lie in America where he had such a fine career on the college circuit.

Blessed with plenty of length off the tee.

Sc Av – 70.67 (29th) DD - 291.1 (18th) DA - 63.2 (96th) GIR – 69.0 (60th) PpGIR – 1.790 (96th) SS – 47.6 (144th)

	'92	'93	'94	'95	'96	'97	'98	'99	'00	'01
Johnnie Walker	-	-	-	-	-	-	-	-	-	-
WGC Matchplay	-	-	-	-	-	-	-	-	-	-
Alfred Dunhill	-	-	-	-	-	-	-	-	-	-
S African Open	-	-	-	-	-	-	-	-	-	-
Heineken Cl'	-	-	-	-	-	-	-	-	-	-
Greg Norman	-	-	-	-	-	-	-	-	-	-
Malaysian Open	-	-	-	-	-	-	-	-	-	-
S'pore Masters	-	-	-	-	-	-	-	-	-	-
Dubai Desert	-	-	-	-	-	-	-	-	-	-
Qatar Masters	-	-	-	-	-	-	-	-	-	-
Madeira Open	-	-	-	-	-	-	-	-	-	-
Brazil Open	-	-	-	-	-	-	-	-	-	-
Open de Arg	-	-	-	-	-	-	-	-	-	-
US Masters	-	-	-	-	-	-	-	-	-	-
Moroccan Open	-	-	-	-	-	-	-	-	-	-
Open de Espana	-	-	-	-	-	-	-	-	-	-
Open de Portugal	-	-	-	-	-	-	-	-	-	-
Open de France	-	-	-	-	-	-	-	-	-	-
B&H I'national	-	-	-	-	-	-	-	-	-	12
Deutsche Bank	-	-	-	-	-	-	-	-	-	MC
Volvo PGA	-	-	-	-	-	-	-	-	-	-
British Masters	-	-	-	-	-	-	-	-	-	27
English Open	-	-	-	-	-	-	-	-	-	12
US Open	-	-	-	-	-	-	-	-	-	-
G North Open	-	-	-	-	-	-	-	-	-	2
Irish Open	-	-	-	-	-	-	-	-	-	MC
European Open	-	-	-	-	-	-	-	-	-	20
Scot Open	-	-	-	-	-	-	-	-	-	MC
British Open	-	-	-	-	-	-	-	-	-	-
Dutch Open	-	-	-	-	-	-	-	-	-	-
Scandinavian	-	-	-	-	-	-	-	-	-	MC
Wales Open	-	-	-	-	-	-	-	-	-	33
USPGA	-	-	-	-	-	-	-	-	-	-
NW Ireland Open	-	-	-	-	-	-	-	-	-	-
WGC NEC Inv'	-	-	-	-	-	-	-	-	-	-
Scottish PGA	-	-	-	-	-	-	-	-	-	1
BMW Int' Open	-	-	-	-	-	-	-	-	-	7
European Mas'	-	-	-	-	-	-	-	-	-	37
WGC AmEx	-	-	-	-	-	-	-	-	-	-
Troph' Lancome	-	-	-	-	-	-	-	-	-	-
German Masters	-	-	-	-	-	-	-	-	-	25
Cannes Open	-	-	-	-	-	-	-	-	-	-
Dunhill Links	-	-	-	-	-	-	-	-	-	5
Masters Madrid	-	-	-	-	-	-	-	-	-	57
Italian Open	-	-	-	-	-	-	-	-	-	-
Volvo Masters	-	-	-	-	-	-	-	-	-	49

Alex Cejka

2/12/70 – Marianbad, Czech Republic (represents Germany)

Czech born German who won three times in 1995 (including the prestigious Volvo Masters) on his way to seventh place in the Order of Merit.

Has struggled in the greens in recent seasons but is superb iron player.

Had a brief spell in America and has also played on the Challenge Tour (winning four times).

Became a father for the second time in 2001, when his best finish on the main tour was second in the Scottish PGA Championship to Paul Casey.

Two-time winner of the Czech Open and based in Prague with his news reader wife.

Sc Av – 70.94 (41st) DD - 280.5 (94th) DA - 62.8 (101st) GIR – 70.1 (47th) PpGIR – 1.812 (139th) SS – 45.6 (159th)

	'92	'93	'94	'95	'96	'97	'98	'99	'00	'01
Johnnie Walker	-	-	MC	33	-	17	4	-	-	41
WGC Matchplay	-	-	-	-	-	-	-	-	-	-
Alfred Dunhill	-	-	16	MC	-	-	48	-	-	-
S African Open	-	-	-	-	-	-	9	10	-	-
Heineken Cl'	-	-	-	-	MC	25	13	18	DQ	
Greg Norman	-	-	-	-	-	-	-	47	MC	
Malaysian Open	-	-	-	-	-	-	2	34	25	
S'pore Masters	-	-	-	-	-	-	-	-	46	
Dubai Desert	-	-	16	40	MC	9	11	32	MC	
Qatar Masters	-	-	-	-	-	21	11	40	-	
Madeira Open	-	12	-	MC	-	53	-	-		
Brazil Open	-	-	-	-	-	-	-	MC		
Open de Arg	-	-	-	-	-	-	-	MC		
US Masters	-	-	-	44	-	-	-	-		
Moroccan Open	28	-	12	4	23	22	19	14	-	MC
Open de Espana	MC	-	-	-	71	MC	9	MC	-	
Open de Portugal	MC	-	MC	-	34	15	12	3	-	7
Open de France	-	-	43	MC	-	32	11	-	22	10
B&H I'national	-	10	56	-	-	-	-	-		
Deutsche Bank	-	-	MC	44	33	27	42	52	70	
Volvo PGA	-	-	64	21	65	MC	MC	34	67	
British Masters	-	-	-	-	-	MC	-	-	34	
English Open	-	71	48	-	-	-	-	-	MC	
US Open	-	-	-	51	-	-	-	-		
G North Open	-	-	-	-	-	24	-	-		
Irish Open	-	-	-	-	60	15	MC	MC		
European Open	-	-	-	MC	49	MC	68			
Scot Open	-	-	-	-	20	63	55	DQ		
British Open	-	-	11	MC	-	MC	13			
Dutch Open	-	-	60	14	-	37	-	-		
Scandinavian	-	-	-	45	-	59	-	36		
Wales Open	-	-	-	-	-	-	33			
USPGA	-	-	52	-	65	-	-			
NW Ireland Open	-									
WGC NEC Inv'	-									
Scottish PGA	-	-	-	-	-	2				
BMW Int' Open	24	19	MC	67	16	MC	MC	MC	25	21
European Mas'	-	44	17	MC	12	5	3	MC	37	
WGC AmEx	-	-	-	-	-	55	-			
Troph' Lancome	-	-	34	-	-	11	10	4	-	
German Masters	52	31	DQ	MC	-	51	WD	6	22	61
Cannes Open	-	MC	MC	-	MC	11	-	-		
Dunhill Links										
Masters Madrid	-	65	1	-	20	-	5	MC		
Italian Open	-	MC	36	-	-	MC	38	-	-	
Volvo Masters	-	-	1	60	60	12	36	38	-	

Roger Chapman

1/5/59 – Nakuru, Kenya (represents England)

Became only sixth golfer to have played 500 or more European Tour events in May at the Portuguese Open.

He has only managed to win once though, in 19 years on the main tour – the 2000 Sao Paulo Brazil Open.

Born in Kenya, he has won twice in Africa (1988 Zimbawe Open and 2000 Hassan II Trophy), although his best finish last season was only fourth – in the German Masters.

Moved his career earnings ever nearer the £2 million mark in 2001 and comfortably retained his card.

According to the stats, he has put 20 yards on his drives over the past year.

Sc Av – 71.66 (107th) DD - 291.3 (17th) DA - 66.4 (61st) GIR – 70.3 (41st) PpGIR – 1.785 (82nd) SS – 51.5 (106th)

	'92	'93	'94	'95	'96	'97	'98	'99	'00	'01
Johnnie Walker	50	71	MC	28	MC	MC	45	-	-	-
WGC Matchplay	-	-	-	-	-	-	-	-	-	-
Alfred Dunhill	-	-	-	MC	-	-	-	-		
S African Open	-	-	-	-	-	-	-	-		
Heineken Cl'	-	-	-	25	18	MC	-	50	60	
Greg Norman	-	-	-	-	-	-	-	MC	31	
Malaysian Open	-	-	-	-	-	-	-	MC	-	
S'pore Masters	-	-	-	-	-	-	-	-		
Dubai Desert	21	26	45	MC	-	12	MC	MC	32	MC
Qatar Masters	-	-	-	-	-	-	63	35	20	
Madeira Open	-	13	27	-	-	-	17	-	-	
Brazil Open	-	-	-	-	-	-	-	39	-	
Open de Arg	-	-	-	-	-	-	-	-		
US Masters	-	-	-	-	-	-	-	-		
Moroccan Open	42	13	-	10	MC	2	9	-	22	31
Open de Espana	-	8	MC	52	11	8	11	MC	27	MC
Open de Portugal	27	24	-	WD	-	65	68	39	27	
Open de France	MC	-	52	28	27	DQ	34	-	-	
B&H I'national	27	7	67	MC	23	MC	MC	65	MC	MC
Deutsche Bank	-	-	-	MC	36	67	33	35	MC	
Volvo PGA	60	24	MC	MC	41	37	MC	MC	13	-
British Masters	MC	4	16	18	24	53	43	WD	23	-
English Open	30	MC	62	3	WD	5	71	MC	47	16
US Open	-	-	-	-	-	-	-	-		
G North Open	-	-	-	25	MC	-	MC	-	25	
Irish Open	-	MC	-	72	25	26	53	DQ	32	MC
European Open	65	MC	MC	42	3	MC	61	45	39	80
Scot Open	-	-	-	20	MC	53	WD	DQ	DQ	
British Open	64	MC	-	71	-	-	MC	MC		
Dutch Open	WD	MC	48	25	3	MC	25	-	29	
Scandinavian	-	MC	MC	25	50	8	MC	MC	62	22
Wales Open	-	-	-	-	-	-	27	-		
USPGA	-	-	-	-	-	-	-	-		
NW Ireland Open	-									
WGC NEC Inv'	-									
Scottish PGA	-	-	-	-	-	9	24	22		
BMW Int' Open	27	-	24	-	-	39	26	-	MC	-
European Mas'	36	27	33	31	23	44	26	38	23	64
WGC AmEx	-									
Troph' Lancome	-	26	-	MC	MC	-	MC	DQ	MC	MC
German Masters	-	-	43	-	MC	MC	65	-	14	4
Cannes Open	-	57	MC	13	61	MC	-	-	-	
Dunhill Links	-	-	-	-	-	-	-	MC		
Masters Madrid	-	66	15	47	11	36	-	15	35	WD
Italian Open	27	-	-	-	-	-	23	-	38	
Volvo Masters	-	42	-	42	20	53	-	17	-	

Darren Clarke
14/6/68 – Dungannon, N.Ireland

Arguably the most consistent golfer in Europe over the past two seasons, having finished runner-up in the Order of Merit in 2000 and third last year.

He became the first Irishman to win a European Tour event in Ireland for 19 years when he won the European Open at the K-Club in Dublin (his seventh European Tour title).

Proved he could beat the best when defeating Tiger Woods in the WGC Matchplay final (and David Duval in the semis) in 2000 and his tough competitive nature will surely bring a Major sooner rather than later.

Long and accurate off the tee.

Sc Av – 70.02 (11th) DD - 291.8 (15th) DA - 70.1 (18th) GIR – 71.0 (30th) PpGIR – 1.742 (7th) SS – 45.0 (165th)

	'92	'93	'94	'95	'96	'97	'98	'99	'00	'01
Johnnie Walker	MC	53	28	9	14	45	-	-	-	-
WGC Matchplay	-	-	-	-	-	-	33	1	-	-
Alfred Dunhill	-	-	61	MC	-	-	-	-	-	-
S African Open	-	-	-	-	-	-	-	-	-	MC
Heineken Cl'	-	-	-	17	25	-	-	-	-	-
Greg Norman	-	-	-	-	-	3	-	-	-	-
Malaysian Open	-	-	-	-	-	-	-	MC	-	-
S'pore Masters	-	-	-	-	-	-	-	-	-	-
Dubai Desert	47	MC	26	34	MC	28	13	62	17	58
Qatar Masters	-	-	-	-	-	-	9	-	-	-
Madeira Open	-	-	-	-	-	-	-	-	-	-
Brazil Open	-	-	-	-	-	-	-	-	-	-
Open de Arg	-	-	-	-	-	-	-	-	-	-
US Masters	-	-	-	-	-	-	8	MC	40	21
Moroccan Open	4	13	-	32	-	-	-	-	-	-
Open de Espana	-	26	-	MC	71	MC	-	-	-	32
Open de Portugal	37	-	-	2	-	4	9	-	-	-
Open de France	62	-	-	-	3	-	-	-	-	-
B&H I'national	MC	24	18	34	MC	7	1	20	22	27
Deutsche Bank	-	-	-	17	3	4	2	7	15	24
Volvo PGA	54	MC	MC	49	MC	2	29	13	2	8
British Masters	-	34	WD	18	MC	12	19	10	-	42
English Open	MC	4	62	4	4	12	49	1	1	5
US Open	-	-	-	-	MC	43	43	10	53	30
G North Open	-	-	-	-	-	-	11	3	-	-
Irish Open	MC	34	67	50	43	15	MC	-	32	2
European Open	MC	8	5	MC	25	-	4	2	7	1
Scot Open	-	-	-	6	25	-	23	-	-	7
British Open	MC	39	38	31	11	2	MC	30	7	3
Dutch Open	-	MC	40	7	18	-	2	5	17	56
Scandinavian	62	17	-	MC	-	20	2	-	23	16
Wales Open	-	-	-	-	-	-	-	-	-	-
USPGA	-	-	-	-	-	MC	-	MC	9	MC
NW Ireland Open	-	-	-	-	-	-	-	-	-	-
WGC NEC Inv'	-	-	-	-	-	-	-	36	17	3
Scottish PGA	-	-	-	-	-	-	-	-	-	-
BMW Int' Open	9	-	4	56	52	-	13	-	-	-
European Mas'	MC	6	70	6	7	6	3	28	3	-
WGC AmEx	-	-	-	-	-	-	-	-	17	-
Troph' Lancome	-	16	23	14	45	MC	-	2	-	-
German Masters	-	MC	-	-	1	7	21	-	-	32
Cannes Open	WD	25	6	MC	32	-	-	-	-	-
Dunhill Links	-	-	-	-	-	-	-	-	-	24
Masters Madrid	-	12	WD	-	-	MC	-	MC	-	6
Italian Open	-	-	-	-	-	3	51	-	-	-
Volvo Masters	27	2	18	33	25	15	1	5	2	4

Andrew Coltart
12/5/70 – Dumfries, Scotland

A first European Tour win for three years came the Scottish pro's way when he claimed the Great North Open title at Slaley Hall.

However, he missed out on a second successive Ryder Cup place.

Turned pro in 1991 and won his first full tour event in 1998 – the Qatar Masters.

Also topped the Order of Merit on the ANZ Tour in 1998 and can boast two victories Down Under.

Paid £7,000 to have a practice green laid in his garden last season and his putting stats improved slightly on the previous year.

His game, though, is still based on strong, accurate iron play.

Sc Av – 71.07 (51st) DD - 279.2 (106th) DA - 60.0 (140th) GIR – 71.5 (22nd) PpGIR – 1.808 (130th) SS – 61.9 (31st)

	'92	'93	'94	'95	'96	'97	'98	'99	'00	'01
Johnnie Walker	-	65	4	2	MC	4	-	-	-	9
WGC Matchplay	-	-	-	-	-	-	-	-	-	-
Alfred Dunhill	-	-	38	8	37	-	-	-	-	-
S African Open	-	-	-	-	-	-	MC	-	-	-
Heineken Cl'	-	-	-	MC	22	15	13	25	-	-
Greg Norman	-	-	-	-	-	-	-	3	-	-
Malaysian Open	-	-	-	-	-	-	-	4	63	-
S'pore Masters	-	-	-	-	-	-	-	-	-	24
Dubai Desert	-	MC	MC	57	46	20	41	MC	33	-
Qatar Masters	-	-	-	-	-	-	1	28	MC	46
Madeira Open	-	MC	37	35	-	3	-	4	-	-
Brazil Open	-	-	-	-	-	-	-	-	-	-
Open de Arg	-	-	-	-	-	-	-	-	-	-
US Masters	-	-	-	-	-	-	-	-	-	-
Moroccan Open	-	MC	9	9	-	10	-	49	24	-
Open de Espana	-	MC	-	-	29	26	11	MC	17	23
Open de Portugal	-	MC	36	WD	39	-	-	49	-	27
Open de France	-	MC	5	-	37	MC	MC	-	7	-
B&H I'national	-	MC	MC	52	4	46	44	39	3	MC
Deutsche Bank	-	-	-	-	MC	60	MC	MC	5	-
Volvo PGA	-	-	MC	13	MC	5	47	2	32	-
British Masters	-	-	32	58	64	43	-	5	47	-
English Open	-	44	50	-	33	14	5	MC	MC	-
US Open	-	-	-	-	75	-	-	-	-	-
G North Open	-	-	-	-	17	35	-	16	18	1
Irish Open	68	MC	24	25	MC	MC	MC	-	9	-
European Open	-	MC	34	3	27	-	10	MC	34	-
Scot Open	-	-	26	31	57	29	32	53	-	-
British Open	MC	-	24	20	MC	MC	42	18	55	37
Dutch Open	-	-	13	51	17	20	MC	45	-	-
Scandinavian	-	9	MC	WD	MC	11	45	23	-	-
Wales Open	-	-	-	-	-	-	-	-	14	MC
USPGA	-	-	-	-	-	-	-	65	51	37
NW Ireland Open	-	-	-	-	-	-	-	-	-	-
WGC NEC Inv'	-	-	-	-	-	-	-	33	17	-
Scottish PGA	-	-	-	-	-	-	-	-	-	MC
BMW Int' Open	25	19	-	63	-	5	-	77	-	-
European Mas'	-	-	-	-	MC	-	-	-	-	-
WGC AmEx	-	-	-	-	-	-	-	-	17	-
Troph' Lancome	-	17	45	19	MC	57	MC	38	14	-
German Masters	-	-	33	18	7	-	26	30	70	-
Cannes Open	MC	34	4	MC	8	MC	-	-	MC	-
Dunhill Links	-	-	-	-	-	-	-	-	-	MC
Masters Madrid	61	MC	MC	42	20	-	30	-	-	-
Italian Open	-	MC	22	6	-	23	47	-	-	-
Volvo Masters	-	44	19	34	24	2	26	10	44	-

Brian Davis

2/8/74 – London, England

Made his breakthrough in 2000 by winning the Spanish Open but failed to build on that success last season.

Davis managed three top-ten finishes in 2001, with his best effort coming in his last outing – third in Madrid.

Turned pro in 1994 and made it on to the European Tour in 1997 after battling through Q-School.

A powerful driver of the ball he has lost some accuracy over the past season but retains a deft touch on the greens.

Had a fine amateur career, representing England and boys, youth and seniors level. He also played for England in the Dunhill Cup.

Sc Av – 71.09 (53rd) DD - 283.2 (65th) DA – 69.5 (150th) GIR – 65.4 (125th) PpGIR – 1.746 (10th) SS – 48.8 (137th)

	'92	'93	'94	'95	'96	'97	'98	'99	'00	'01
Johnnie Walker	-	-	-	-	-	MC	-	-	-	-
WGC Matchplay	-	-	-	-	-	-	-	-	-	-
Alfred Dunhill	-	-	-	-	-	32	MC	MC	10	7
S African Open	-	-	-	-	-	-	MC	MC	16	16
Heineken Cl'	-	-	-	-	-	-	62	-	-	-
Greg Norman	-	-	-	-	-	-	-	-	-	-
Malaysian Open	-	-	-	-	-	-	-	-	-	-
S'pore Masters	-	-	-	-	-	-	-	-	-	-
Dubai Desert	-	-	-	-	-	-	MC	MC	46	6
Qatar Masters	-	-	-	-	-	-	-	53	5	36
Madeira Open	-	-	-	-	57	67	-	-	-	-
Brazil Open	-	-	-	-	-	-	-	22	-	-
Open de Arg	-	-	-	-	-	-	-	-	-	-
US Masters	-	-	-	-	-	-	-	-	-	-
Moroccan Open	-	-	-	-	-	6	-	-	-	-
Open de Espana	-	-	-	-	-	-	69	46	1	83
Open de Portugal	-	-	-	-	-	MC	-	MC	3	15
Open de France	-	-	MC	-	-	61	MC	64	59	-
B&H I'national	-	-	-	-	-	MC	11	MC	28	MC
Deutsche Bank	-	-	-	-	-	MC	34	5	13	63
Volvo PGA	-	-	-	-	-	-	50	MC	MC	WD
British Masters	-	-	-	-	-	30	MC	MC	MC	34
English Open	-	-	-	-	-	46	MC	MC	6	44
US Open	-	-	-	-	-	-	-	-	-	-
G North Open	-	-	-	-	-	74	-	39	32	59
Irish Open	-	-	-	-	-	MC	16	52	-	-
European Open	-	-	-	-	-	5	MC	18	60	52
Scot Open	-	-	-	-	-	-	62	68	WD	MC
British Open	-	-	-	-	-	-	MC	68	MC	-
Dutch Open	-	-	-	-	-	39	11	MC	75	MC
Scandinavian	-	-	-	-	-	55	11	9	-	29
Wales Open	-	-	-	-	-	-	-	-	MC	-
USPGA	-	-	-	-	-	-	-	-	-	-
NW Ireland Open	-	-	-	-	-	-	-	-	-	-
WGC NEC Inv'	-	-	-	-	-	-	-	-	-	-
Scottish PGA	-	-	-	-	-	-	-	-	-	37
BMW Int' Open	-	-	-	-	-	MC	36	WD	25	67
European Mas'	-	-	-	-	-	MC	MC	MC	42	23
WGC AmEx	-	-	-	-	-	-	-	-	-	-
Troph' Lancome	-	-	-	-	-	-	57	31	46	-
German Masters	-	-	-	-	-	-	MC	MC	41	61
Cannes Open	-	-	-	-	-	MC	MC	-	-	-
Dunhill Links	-	-	-	-	-	-	-	-	-	13
Masters Madrid	-	-	-	-	-	36	-	MC	-	3
Italian Open	-	-	-	-	-	6	MC	MC	-	-
Volvo Masters	-	-	-	-	-	24	-	-	57	30

Stephen Dodd

15/7/66 – Cardiff, Wales

Former British Amateur Champion who has struggled since joining the paid ranks at the start of the last decade.

Last season was only his third on the European Tour and the Welshman has still to win.

He did, though, claim his highest finish in a full tour event when he came second in the North West of Ireland Open.

Last term was the best of his pro career to date, and including his runner-up position at Co. Cavan he managed to finish in the top 15 on four occasions.

Spent the early 90s on the Challenge Tour, winning twice, before debuting on the full tour in 1995.

Sc Av – 71.40 (87th) DD - 288.5 (32nd) DA – 61.9 (115th) GIR – 67.0 (94th) PpGIR – 1.779 (67th) SS – 54.4 (84th)

	'92	'93	'94	'95	'96	'97	'98	'99	'00	'01
Johnnie Walker	-	-	-	-	-	-	-	-	-	-
WGC Matchplay	-	-	-	-	-	-	-	-	-	-
Alfred Dunhill	-	-	-	-	-	-	-	MC	-	34
S African Open	-	-	-	-	-	-	-	-	-	-
Heineken Cl'	-	-	-	-	-	-	-	MC	-	-
Greg Norman	-	-	-	-	-	-	-	-	-	-
Malaysian Open	-	-	-	-	-	-	-	MC	-	73
S'pore Masters	-	-	-	-	-	-	-	-	-	14
Dubai Desert	-	-	-	-	-	-	-	-	-	-
Qatar Masters	-	-	-	-	-	-	-	MC	-	41
Madeira Open	-	-	-	MC	MC	-	56	MC	55	3
Brazil Open	-	-	-	-	-	-	-	-	-	-
Open de Arg	-	-	-	-	-	-	-	-	-	-
US Masters	-	-	-	-	-	-	-	-	-	-
Moroccan Open	-	-	-	MC	-	-	-	MC	22	65
Open de Espana	-	-	-	-	-	-	-	-	-	MC
Open de Portugal	-	-	-	-	-	-	-	MC	-	MC
Open de France	-	-	-	-	39	-	-	64	-	MC
B&H I'national	-	-	-	-	-	-	-	-	-	68
Deutsche Bank	-	-	-	-	27	-	-	-	-	-
Volvo PGA	-	-	-	-	-	-	-	-	-	-
British Masters	-	-	-	-	-	-	-	MC	-	MC
English Open	-	-	-	-	-	-	-	64	-	26
US Open	-	-	-	-	-	-	-	-	-	-
G North Open	-	-	-	20	-	-	-	71	-	MC
Irish Open	-	-	-	-	-	-	-	-	-	44
European Open	-	-	-	MC	-	-	-	-	-	52
Scot Open	-	-	-	-	-	-	-	-	-	-
British Open	-	-	-	-	-	-	-	-	-	-
Dutch Open	-	-	MC	-	-	-	-	67	-	44
Scandinavian	-	-	MC	-	-	-	-	-	-	MC
Wales Open	-	-	-	-	-	-	-	-	MC	MC
USPGA	-	-	-	-	-	-	-	-	-	-
NW Ireland Open	-	-	-	-	-	-	-	42	30	2
WGC NEC Inv'	-	-	-	-	-	-	-	-	-	-
Scottish PGA	-	-	-	-	-	-	-	15	-	29
BMW Int' Open	-	-	-	45	-	-	-	77	-	23
European Mas'	-	-	MC	-	MC	-	-	-	-	MC
WGC AmEx	-	-	-	-	-	-	-	-	-	-
Troph' Lancome	-	-	-	-	-	-	-	-	-	MC
German Masters	-	-	-	-	-	-	-	-	-	-
Cannes Open	-	-	-	-	-	-	-	-	-	39
Dunhill Links	-	-	-	-	-	-	-	-	-	-
Masters Madrid	-	-	-	47	-	-	-	MC	-	46
Italian Open	-	-	-	19	-	-	-	59	-	14
Volvo Masters	-	-	-	-	-	-	-	-	-	-

Jamie Donaldson
19/10/75 – Wales

Signed up by the International Management Group at the start of the season and enjoyed a brilliant year on the Challenge Tour, winning twice before making his mark on the full tour late in the year.

It all started to go right for the Macclesfield-based Welshman in August when he won the BMW Russian Open, then, after finishing fourth in the Wales Open on the European Tour, he won again on the Challenge Tour, this time in the Telia Grand Prix in Sweden.

Already assured a full tour card for 2002 he finished ninth in the Dunhill Links to win 100,000 euros.

Sc Av – N/A (N/A) DD – N/A (N/A) DA – N/A (N/A) GIR – N/A (N/A) PpGIR – N/A (N/A) SS – N/A (N/A)

	'92	'93	'94	'95	'96	'97	'98	'99	'00	'01
Johnnie Walker	-	-	-	-	-	-	-	-	-	-
WGC Matchplay	-	-	-	-	-	-	-	-	-	-
Alfred Dunhill	-	-	-	-	-	-	-	-	-	-
S African Open	-	-	-	-	-	-	-	-	-	MC
Heineken Cl'	-	-	-	-	-	-	-	-	-	-
Greg Norman	-	-	-	-	-	-	-	-	-	-
Malaysian Open	-	-	-	-	-	-	-	-	-	-
S'pore Masters	-	-	-	-	-	-	-	-	-	-
Dubai Desert	-	-	-	-	-	-	-	-	-	-
Qatar Masters	-	-	-	-	-	-	-	-	-	-
Madeira Open	-	-	-	-	-	-	-	-	-	-
Brazil Open	-	-	-	-	-	-	-	-	-	-
Open de Arg	-	-	-	-	-	-	-	-	-	-
US Masters	-	-	-	-	-	-	-	-	-	-
Open de Espana	-	-	-	-	-	-	-	-	-	-
Open de Portugal	-	-	-	-	-	-	-	-	-	-
Open de France	-	-	-	-	-	-	-	-	-	-
B&H I'national	-	-	-	-	-	-	-	-	-	-
Deutsche Bank	-	-	-	-	-	-	-	-	-	-
Volvo PGA	-	-	-	-	-	-	-	-	-	-
British Masters	-	-	-	-	-	-	-	-	-	-
English Open	-	-	-	-	-	-	-	-	-	-
US Open	-	-	-	-	-	-	-	-	-	-
G North Open	-	-	-	-	-	-	-	-	-	-
Irish Open	-	-	-	-	-	-	-	-	-	-
European Open	-	-	-	-	-	-	-	-	-	-
Scot Open	-	-	-	-	-	-	-	-	-	-
British Open	-	-	-	-	-	-	-	-	-	-
Dutch Open	-	-	-	-	-	-	-	-	-	-
Scandinavian	-	-	-	-	-	-	-	-	-	-
Wales Open	-	-	-	-	-	-	-	-	-	4
USPGA	-	-	-	-	-	-	-	-	-	-
NW Ireland Open	-	-	-	-	-	-	-	-	-	17
WGC NEC Inv'	-	-	-	-	-	-	-	-	-	-
Scottish PGA	-	-	-	-	-	-	-	-	-	19
BMW Int' Open	-	-	-	-	-	-	-	-	-	-
European Mas'	-	-	-	-	-	-	-	-	-	13
WGC AmEx	-	-	-	-	-	-	-	-	-	-
Troph' Lancome	-	-	-	-	-	-	-	-	-	-
German Masters	-	-	-	-	-	-	-	-	-	-
Cannes Open	-	-	-	-	-	-	-	-	-	-
Dunhill Links	-	-	-	-	-	-	-	-	-	9
Masters Madrid	-	-	-	-	-	-	-	-	-	-
Italian Open	-	-	-	-	-	-	-	-	-	-
Volvo Masters	-	-	-	-	-	-	-	-	-	-

Bradley Dredge
6/7/73 – Newport, Wales

Two-time Challenge Tour winner who went close to gaining his maiden win on the European Tour in the final regular event of last season – the Italian Open.

Second place at Is Molas in Sardinia (a venue he'd previously won at on the Challenge Tour) secured his playing rights for another season and meant a further trip to the Q-School or a drop down to the feeder tour was unnecessary.

Newport based and managed by Barry Hearn's Macthroom Golf Management team, Dredge made the 1993 Walker Cup team before turning pro in 1996.

Sc Av – 71.38 (85th) DD - 278.2 (114th) DA - 59.7 (146th) GIR – 63.2 (160th) PpGIR – 1.768 (43rd) SS – 64.3 (22nd)

	'92	'93	'94	'95	'96	'97	'98	'99	'00	'01
Johnnie Walker	-	-	-	-	-	-	-	-	-	-
WGC Matchplay	-	-	-	-	-	-	-	-	-	-
Alfred Dunhill	-	-	-	-	-	-	16	-	65	13
S African Open	-	-	-	-	-	-	MC	-	MC	21
Heineken Cl'	-	-	-	-	-	-	-	-	-	-
Greg Norman	-	-	-	-	-	-	-	-	-	-
Malaysian Open	-	-	-	-	-	-	-	-	-	-
S'pore Masters	-	-	-	-	-	-	-	-	-	MC
Dubai Desert	-	-	-	-	-	-	-	-	32	47
Qatar Masters	-	-	-	-	-	-	MC	-	75	46
Madeira Open	-	-	-	-	-	-	-	-	7	-
Brazil Open	-	-	-	-	-	-	-	-	-	-
Open de Arg	-	-	-	-	-	-	-	-	-	-
US Masters	-	-	-	-	-	-	-	-	-	-
Moroccan Open	-	-	-	-	-	-	MC	-	8	24
Open de Espana	-	-	-	-	-	-	62	-	MC	-
Open de Portugal	-	-	-	-	-	-	-	-	24	53
Open de France	-	-	-	-	-	-	MC	MC	50	-
B&H I'national	-	MC	-	-	-	-	38	-	54	MC
Deutsche Bank	-	-	-	-	-	-	MC	-	MC	MC
Volvo PGA	-	-	-	-	-	-	-	-	MC	MC
British Masters	-	-	-	-	-	-	MC	-	MC	MC
English Open	-	-	-	-	-	-	MC	-	MC	65
US Open	-	-	-	-	-	-	-	-	-	-
G North Open	-	-	-	-	-	-	-	-	45	4
Irish Open	-	-	-	-	-	-	MC	-	6	MC
European Open	-	-	-	-	-	-	MC	-	MC	MC
Scot Open	-	-	-	-	-	MC	-	MC	70	-
British Open	-	-	-	-	-	-	MC	-	-	-
Dutch Open	-	-	-	-	-	-	MC	-	-	20
Scandinavian	-	-	-	-	-	-	63	-	WD	53
Wales Open	-	-	-	-	-	-	-	-	MC	65
USPGA	-	-	-	-	-	-	-	-	-	-
NW Ireland Open	-	-	-	-	-	-	-	18	-	-
WGC NEC Inv'	-	-	-	-	-	-	-	-	-	-
Scottish PGA	-	-	-	-	-	-	-	-	36	MC
BMW Int' Open	-	-	-	-	-	-	MC	-	49	MC
European Mas'	-	-	-	-	-	-	59	-	MC	MC
WGC AmEx	-	-	-	-	-	-	-	-	-	-
Troph' Lancome	-	-	-	-	-	-	-	-	30	54
German Masters	-	-	-	-	-	-	-	-	-	-
Cannes Open	-	-	-	-	-	-	MC	-	-	15
Dunhill Links	-	-	-	-	-	-	-	-	-	MC
Masters Madrid	-	-	-	-	-	-	-	-	MC	21
Italian Open	-	-	-	-	-	-	MC	-	44	2
Volvo Masters	-	-	-	-	-	-	-	-	-	-

Simon Dyson

21/12/77 – York, England

Made his name on the Davidoff Tour, winning the Order of Merit in 2000 and claiming a whole host of player awards.

His first full season on the European Tour in 2001 wasn't so successful but the Malton based pro still managed a couple of top-ten finishes.

Had a brilliant amateur career, playing in the 1999 Walker Cup before turning pro.

Having failed to get through Q-School in 1999 he went to the Far East where he won three tournaments.

A very good footballer as a youngster and was once on the books of York City.

Sc Av – 71.84 (122nd) DD - 281.4 (84th) DA - 59.8 (143rd) GIR – 67.8 (78th) PpGIR – 1.789 (94th) SS – 42.0 (179th)

	'92	'93	'94	'95	'96	'97	'98	'99	'00	'01
Johnnie Walker	-	-	-	-	-	-	-	-	-	-
WGC Matchplay	-	-	-	-	-	-	-	-	-	-
Alfred Dunhill	-	-	-	-	-	-	-	-	-	41
S African Open	-	-	-	-	-	-	-	-	-	9
Heineken Cl'	-	-	-	-	-	-	-	-	-	-
Greg Norman	-	-	-	-	-	-	-	-	-	-
Malaysian Open	-	-	-	-	-	-	-	-	54	MC
S'pore Masters	-	-	-	-	-	-	-	-	-	MC
Dubai Desert	-	-	-	-	-	-	-	-	-	MC
Qatar Masters	-	-	-	-	-	-	-	-	-	MC
Madeira Open	-	-	-	-	-	-	-	-	-	-
Brazil Open	-	-	-	-	-	-	-	-	-	MC
Open de Arg	-	-	-	-	-	-	-	-	-	80
US Masters	-	-	-	-	-	-	-	-	-	-
Moroccan Open	-	-	-	-	-	-	-	-	-	24
Open de Espana	-	-	-	-	-	-	-	-	-	58
Open de Portugal	-	-	-	-	-	-	-	-	-	9
Open de France	-	-	-	-	-	-	-	-	-	-
B&H I'national	-	-	-	-	-	-	-	-	-	MC
Deutsche Bank	-	-	-	-	-	-	-	-	-	-
Volvo PGA	-	-	-	-	-	-	-	-	-	14
British Masters	-	-	-	-	-	-	-	-	-	53
English Open	-	-	-	-	-	-	-	-	MC	MC
US Open	-	-	-	-	-	-	-	-	-	-
G North Open	-	-	-	-	-	-	-	-	MC	63
Irish Open	-	-	-	-	-	-	-	-	32	35
European Open	-	-	-	-	-	-	-	-	-	76
Scot Open	-	-	-	-	-	-	-	-	-	21
British Open	-	-	-	-	-	-	-	-	MC	MC
Dutch Open	-	-	-	-	-	-	-	-	33	-
Scandinavian	-	-	-	-	-	-	-	-	45	MC
Wales Open	-	-	-	-	-	-	-	-	55	14
USPGA	-	-	-	-	-	-	-	-	-	-
NW Ireland Open	-	-	-	-	-	-	-	-	-	-
WGC NEC Inv'	-	-	-	-	-	-	-	-	-	-
Scottish PGA	-	-	-	-	-	-	-	-	-	22
BMW Int' Open	-	-	-	-	-	-	-	-	-	MC
European Mas'	-	-	-	-	-	-	-	-	-	-
WGC AmEx	-	-	-	-	-	-	-	-	-	-
Troph' Lancome	-	-	-	-	-	-	-	-	-	54
German Masters	-	-	-	-	-	-	-	-	-	-
Cannes Open	-	-	-	-	-	-	-	-	-	28
Dunhill Links	-	-	-	-	-	-	-	-	-	52
Masters Madrid	-	-	-	-	-	-	-	-	-	MC
Italian Open	-	-	-	-	-	-	-	-	-	-
Volvo Masters	-	-	-	-	-	-	-	-	-	-

Paul Eales

2/8/63 – Epping, England

'Slippery' made sure he didn't have to endure any last tournament anxiety this year by securing his playing rights for 2002 way before the Italian Open.

That was unlike the previous season, when 12th position in the last counting event just about preserved his 2001 playing privileges.

Despite commitments off the course, which include a burgeoning broadcast career, Eales remains competitive and his second place in the French Open last season was his best finish for six seasons.

His sole win in eight years on the European Tour came in the 1994 Extremedura Open.

Sc Av – 72.08 (143rd) DD - 265.4 (187th) DA - 72.7 (9th) GIR – 68.1 (73rd) PpGIR – 1.839 (177th) SS – 46.7 (152nd)

	'92	'93	'94	'95	'96	'97	'98	'99	'00	'01
Johnnie Walker	-	-	MC	43	12	34	MC	-	-	MC
WGC Matchplay	-	-	-	-	-	-	-	-	-	-
Alfred Dunhill	-	-	-	-	73	-	MC	MC	43	53
S African Open	-	-	-	-	-	WD	MC	-	13	38
Heineken Cl'	-	-	-	-	60	11	46	-	-	-
Greg Norman	-	-	-	-	-	-	-	-	-	-
Malaysian Open	-	-	-	-	-	-	-	-	-	MC
S'pore Masters	-	-	-	-	-	-	-	-	-	51
Dubai Desert	-	MC	MC	23	MC	-	64	-	MC	MC
Qatar Masters	-	-	-	-	-	-	27	63	MC	-
Madeira Open	-	MC	8	-	MC	MC	-	34	-	-
Brazil Open	-	-	-	-	-	-	-	-	MC	58
Open de Arg	-	-	-	-	-	-	-	-	-	18
US Masters	-	-	-	-	-	-	-	-	-	-
Moroccan Open	-	56	60	43	-	51	-	-	-	-
Open de Espana	-	MC	-	56	67	36	34	17	-	-
Open de Portugal	-	14	2	MC	MC	MC	40	68	29	60
Open de France	-	MC	11	39	-	47	-	-	MC	2
B&H I'national	-	MC	45	MC	36	46	MC	MC	MC	52
Deutsche Bank	-	-	-	-	-	53	63	MC	52	28
Volvo PGA	-	-	MC	17	21	MC	MC	3	MC	MC
British Masters	-	-	44	MC	35	MC	MC	MC	50	MC
English Open	-	MC	51	-	-	MC	14	59	MC	MC
US Open	-	-	-	-	MC	-	-	-	-	-
G North Open	-	-	-	-	-	MC	-	65	36	75
Irish Open	-	49	-	-	-	-	MC	41	MC	MC
European Open	-	21	42	MC	42	MC	49	24	64	80
Scot Open	-	-	-	-	MC	31	53	-	51	MC
British Open	-	MC	MC	-	-	-	-	MC	MC	-
Dutch Open	-	8	MC	11	18	MC	MC	30	-	-
Scandinavian	-	MC	58	46	29	55	43	52	68	MC
Wales Open	-	-	-	-	-	-	-	-	55	MC
USPGA	-	-	-	-	-	-	-	-	-	-
NW Ireland Open	-	-	-	-	-	-	-	-	-	-
WGC NEC Inv'	-	-	-	-	-	-	-	-	-	-
Scottish PGA	-	-	-	-	-	-	-	-	-	74
BMW Int' Open	-	MC	24	-	52	MC	13	-	64	MC
European Mas'	-	27	MC	MC	-	-	26	-	MC	23
WGC AmEx	-	-	-	-	-	-	-	-	-	-
Troph' Lancome	-	-	34	59	7	77	MC	MC	30	23
German Masters	-	-	DQ	6	8	68	48	57	30	-
Cannes Open	-	-	MC	MC	20	4	MC	-	-	10
Dunhill Links	-	-	-	-	-	-	-	-	-	MC
Masters Madrid	-	MC	18	-	-	-	-	MC	MC	-
Italian Open	-	MC	4	-	7	-	-	23	12	72
Volvo Masters	-	-	22	10	34	-	-	-	42	-

198

Ernie Els

17/10/69 – Johannesburg, South Africa

Two-time US Open champion whose honorary lifetime membership of the European Tour sees him play more than just the Majors and the WGC events on this side of the Atlantic.

However, Els couldn't capture a European title in 2001, so ending his run of four successive years with a victory on the European Tour.

The last of his six European wins came in the 2000 Loch Lomond Invitational.

Suffered with a back injury in the summer and turned to top sports psychologist Jos Vanstiphout after witnessing the effect the Belgian had on fellow South African Retief Goosen.

Sc Av – 69.90 (7th) DD - N/A (N/A) DA - N/A (N/A) GIR - N/A (N/A) PpGIR - N/A (N/A) SS - N/A (N/A)

	'92	'93	'94	'95	'96	'97	'98	'99	'00	'01
Johnnie Walker	-	9	16	43	6	1	2	-	3	-
WGC Matchplay	-	-	-	-	-	-	-	33	17	4
Alfred Dunhill	-	-	-	1	2	-	2	1	-	-
S African Open	-	-	-	-	-	3	1	6	-	-
Heineken Cl'	-	-	-	-	-	8	3	2	4	-
Greg Norman	-	-	-	-	-	-	-	-	-	-
Malaysian Open	-	-	-	-	-	-	-	-	-	-
S'pore Masters	-	-	-	-	-	-	-	-	-	-
Dubai Desert	-	8	1	-	-	-	3	-	-	-
Qatar Masters	-	-	-	-	-	-	-	-	-	-
Madeira Open	-	-	-	-	-	-	-	-	-	-
Brazil Open	-	-	-	-	-	-	-	-	-	-
Open de Arg	-	-	-	-	-	-	-	-	-	-
US Masters	-	-	8	MC	12	17	16	27	2	6
Moroccan Open	-	-	-	-	-	-	-	-	-	-
Open de Espana	-	2	6	-	-	-	-	-	-	-
Open de Portugal	-	-	-	-	-	-	-	-	-	-
Open de France	MC	15	-	-	-	-	-	-	-	-
B&H I'national	44	MC	MC	-	-	-	-	-	-	-
Deutsche Bank	-	-	-	-	-	-	-	5	-	28
Volvo PGA	MC	30	2	-	-	2	2	4	-	39
British Masters	11	21	5	-	-	-	-	-	-	-
English Open	-	-	-	-	-	-	-	-	-	-
US Open	-	7	1	MC	5	1	49	MC	2	66
G North Open	-	-	-	-	-	-	-	-	-	-
Irish Open	65	-	8	-	12	-	33	-	-	-
European Open	58	MC	14	-	-	-	-	-	-	-
Scot Open	MC	-	-	-	-	2	-	-	1	-
British Open	5	6	24	11	2	10	28	24	2	3
Dutch Open	32	MC	7	-	-	-	-	-	-	12
Scandinavian	-	-	-	-	-	-	-	-	-	-
Wales Open	-	-	-	-	-	-	-	-	-	-
USPGA	MC	MC	25	3	61	53	21	MC	34	13
NW Ireland Open	-	-	-	-	-	-	-	-	-	-
WGC NEC Inv'	-	-	-	-	-	-	-	5	12	8
Scottish PGA	-	-	-	-	-	-	-	-	-	-
BMW Int' Open	-	-	-	-	-	26	-	-	5	-
European Mas'	MC	-	-	-	-	-	-	-	-	16
WGC AmEx	-	-	-	-	-	-	-	40	WD	-
Troph' Lancome	-	47	-	-	-	-	-	69	-	-
German Masters	MC	10	2	-	5	-	-	-	MC	-
Cannes Open	-	-	-	-	-	-	-	-	-	-
Dunhill Links	-	-	-	-	-	-	-	-	-	2
Masters Madrid	-	-	-	-	-	-	-	-	-	-
Italian Open	-	-	-	-	-	-	-	-	-	-
Volvo Masters	-	10	-	-	-	-	8	-	-	-

Gary Emerson

26/9/63 – Bournemouth, England

Enjoyed his best season on the European Tour in 2001, registering his highest career finish – fourth in the Lancome Trophy – in the process.

Previous seasons had seen an annual battle against securing his tour card for the Salisbury based pro who tried and failed to win his playing privileges at Q-School on seven occasions.

Joined the paid ranks in 1982 after representing his country at boys and senior level as an amateur and left a job as a club pro to try his luck on the European Tour, eventually making it through Q-School in 1994.

Won the Norwegian Open on the Challenge Tour in 1998.

Sc Av – 71.94 (133rd) DD - 293.1 (11th) DA - 60.0 (140th) GIR - 62.5 (170th) PpGIR - 1.760 (27th) SS - 54.1 (87th)

	'92	'93	'94	'95	'96	'97	'98	'99	'00	'01
Johnnie Walker	-	-	-	-	-	-	-	-	-	-
WGC Matchplay	-	-	-	-	-	-	-	-	-	-
Alfred Dunhill	-	-	-	-	-	44	-	-	-	MC
S African Open	-	-	-	-	-	-	-	-	-	59
Heineken Cl'	-	-	-	-	-	-	-	57	64	-
Greg Norman	-	-	-	-	-	-	-	77	-	-
Malaysian Open	-	-	-	-	-	-	-	-	23	MC
S'pore Masters	-	-	-	-	-	-	-	-	-	MC
Dubai Desert	-	-	-	-	25	MC	-	-	MC	21
Qatar Masters	-	-	-	-	-	-	-	MC	MC	-
Madeira Open	-	-	-	62	MC	MC	45	17	29	11
Brazil Open	-	-	-	-	-	-	-	-	-	-
Open de Arg	-	-	-	-	-	-	-	-	-	-
US Masters	-	-	-	-	-	-	-	-	-	-
Moroccan Open	-	-	-	-	-	-	-	MC	MC	13
Open de Espana	-	-	-	MC	MC	16	-	54	MC	9
Open de Portugal	-	-	-	-	21	MC	-	-	70	MC
Open de France	-	-	-	MC	MC	MC	MC	MC	MC	MC
B&H I'national	MC	MC	MC	40	MC	66	-	MC	MC	77
Deutsche Bank	-	-	-	69	44	53	-	-	MC	MC
Volvo PGA	-	MC	MC	MC	46	32	-	-	17	21
British Masters	-	-	-	-	MC	MC	-	MC	73	MC
English Open	-	-	-	34	53	10	MC	33	WD	65
US Open	-	-	-	-	-	-	-	-	-	-
G North Open	-	-	-	-	MC	MC	-	31	12	MC
Irish Open	-	-	-	-	MC	-	-	MC	40	6
European Open	-	-	-	-	MC	MC	-	6	69	88
Scot Open	-	-	-	-	-	MC	-	-	MC	WD
British Open	MC	-	MC	-	MC	-	-	MC	-	-
Dutch Open	-	-	-	35	58	MC	-	MC	44	MC
Scandinavian	-	-	-	25	57	MC	-	21	MC	MC
Wales Open	-	-	-	-	-	-	-	-	MC	MC
USPGA	-	-	-	-	-	-	-	-	-	-
NW Ireland Open	-	-	-	-	-	-	-	11	7	-
WGC NEC Inv'	-	-	-	-	-	-	-	-	-	-
Scottish PGA	-	-	-	-	-	-	-	-	50	MC
BMW Int' Open	-	-	-	MC	-	MC	-	MC	WD	MC
European Mas'	-	-	-	-	61	55	-	MC	34	70
WGC AmEx	-	-	-	-	-	-	-	-	-	-
Troph' Lancome	-	-	-	-	MC	MC	-	-	30	4
German Masters	-	-	-	-	-	-	-	-	-	78
Cannes Open	-	-	-	MC	MC	-	-	-	-	-
Dunhill Links	-	-	-	-	-	-	-	-	-	MC
Masters Madrid	-	-	-	MC	60	-	MC	-	25	16
Italian Open	-	-	-	65	-	MC	-	-	-	-
Volvo Masters	-	-	-	-	-	-	-	-	-	-

Gary Evans

22/2/69 – Rushington, England

One of the brightest prospects of English golf in the early '90s after a sparkling amateur career, when he won two Lytham Trophys and the English Amateur Stroke Play Championship.

His pro career hasn't been so successful and he is still to win a European Tour event, his best finish is second in the 1992 Turespana Masters.

Three top-ten finishes last season helped towards him securing his playing rights for 2002 with fourth place in the Scottish PGA Championship his best effort. Not the longest of drivers but an accurate iron player.

Sc Av – 71.31 (74th) DD - 278.5 (112th) DA - 65.5 (68th) GIR – 71.8 (21st) PpGIR – 1.780 (69th) SS – 51.2 (109th)

	'92	'93	'94	'95	'96	'97	'98	'99	'00	'01
Johnnie Walker	50	MC	58	-	-	59	66	-	MC	-
WGC Matchplay	-	-	-	-	-	-	-	-	-	-
Alfred Dunhill	-	-	-	MC	-	MC	-	-	-	-
S African Open	-	-	-	-	-	12	65	-	-	-
Heineken Cl'	-	-	-	-	32	MC	40	63	25	34
Greg Norman	-	-	-	-	-	-	-	-	16	59
Malaysian Open	-	-	-	-	-	-	-	21	MC	60
S'pore Masters	-	-	-	-	-	-	-	-	-	-
Dubai Desert	MC	55	7	-	25	65	29	15	63	58
Qatar Masters	-	-	-	-	-	-	MC	28	59	MC
Madeira Open	-	MC	-	-	-	-	71	-	-	-
Brazil Open	-	-	-	-	-	-	-	-	MC	-
Open de Arg	-	-	-	-	-	-	-	-	-	-
US Masters	-	-	-	-	-	-	-	-	-	-
Moroccan Open	-	-	-	-	-	-	-	-	-	6
Open de Espana	46	-	MC	-	49	MC	MC	11	7	49
Open de Portugal	MC	57	17	-	WD	37	47	32	-	-
Open de France	20	55	WD	-	-	55	57	-	MC	61
B&H I'national	16	20	51	12	49	MC	11	20	DQ	MC
Deutsche Bank	-	-	-	MC	40	MC	76	42	MC	WD
Volvo PGA	4	24	61	MC	-	45	MC	MC	MC	70
British Masters	13	MC	-	MC	MC	35	55	MC	MC	47
English Open	74	26	10	16	24	MC	14	51	17	44
US Open	-	-	-	-	-	-	-	-	-	-
G North Open	-	-	-	-	4	19	-	MC	52	17
Irish Open	61	MC	33	MC	63	MC	MC	MC	MC	20
European Open	-	MC	-	-	MC	MC	MC	MC	8	20
Scot Open	52	-	-	-	MC	MC	67	MC	MC	MC
British Open	MC	MC	35	-	-	-	70	-	-	-
Dutch Open	3	33	57	WD	MC	MC	56	-	44	14
Scandinavian	MC	45	MC	-	37	20	-	21	MC	53
Wales Open	-	-	-	-	-	-	-	-	29	49
USPGA	-	-	-	-	-	-	-	-	-	-
NW Ireland Open	-	-	-	-	-	-	-	3	-	29
WGC NEC Inv'	-	-	-	-	-	-	-	-	-	-
Scottish PGA	-	-	-	-	-	-	-	11	MC	4
BMW Int' Open	MC	-	-	28	MC	MC	MC	MC	WD	-
European Mas'	-	MC	WD	-	MC	63	61	-	-	-
WGC AmEx	-	-	-	-	-	-	-	-	-	-
Troph' Lancome	-	47	-	-	MC	43	40	6	53	DQ
German Masters	MC	24	-	-	41	55	30	63	10	
Cannes Open	-	76	18	-	MC	MC	MC	-	-	64
Dunhill Links	-	-	-	-	-	-	-	-	-	MC
Masters Madrid	MC	MC	MC	-	MC	MC	-	49	19	MC
Italian Open	53	-	-	-	28	MC	47	3	21	29
Volvo Masters	40	-	-	-	-	-	47	-	12	

Nick Faldo

18/7/57 – Welwyn Garden City, England

Six-time Major winner failed to make the Ryder Cup line up for a 12th time despite some high finishes, and flashes of brilliance in 2001.

Was reunited with Fanny Suneson in May, his caddie for all of his glory years but missed only his second cut in 25 years of playing the Open two months later at Lytham.

The last of his 27 European Tour wins came in the 1993 Alfred Dunhill Open.

His best finish in 2001 came in the Volvo PGA at Wentworth when third.

He remains a superb iron player but usually fails to take his birdie chances.

Sc Av – 71.36 (83rd) DD - 271.8 (171st) DA - 71.4 (12th) GIR – 64.1 (146th) PpGIR – 1.751 (18th) SS – 50.0 (122nd)

	'92	'93	'94	'95	'96	'97	'98	'99	'00	'01
Johnnie Walker	21	1	69	-	-	4	8	-	12	52
WGC Matchplay	-	-	-	-	-	-	-	33	-	-
Alfred Dunhill	-	-	-	-	-	-	-	MC	-	3
S African Open	-	-	-	-	-	-	43	-	-	-
Heineken Cl'	-	-	-	-	-	-	-	-	-	MC
Greg Norman	-	-	-	-	-	-	-	-	-	MC
Malaysian Open	-	-	-	-	-	-	-	-	-	-
S'pore Masters	-	-	-	-	-	-	-	-	-	-
Dubai Desert	5	26	-	-	-	-	-	MC	-	-
Qatar Masters	-	-	-	-	-	-	-	-	-	-
Madeira Open	-	-	-	-	-	-	-	-	-	-
Brazil Open	-	-	-	-	-	-	-	-	-	-
Open de Arg	-	-	-	-	-	-	-	-	-	-
US Masters	13	39	32	24	1	MC	MC	MC	28	MC
Moroccan Open	-	-	-	-	-	-	-	-	-	-
Open de Espana	2	2	-	-	-	-	-	MC	-	-
Open de Portugal	-	-	-	-	-	-	-	-	-	-
Open de France	3	-	-	-	-	-	-	-	-	-
B&H I'national	3	6	2	-	2	-	-	7	-	-
Deutsche Bank	-	-	-	-	-	-	-	73	-	-
Volvo PGA	8	MC	21	12	2	2	-	59	-	3
British Masters	4	33	13	-	-	-	-	-	-	-
English Open	-	-	-	-	-	-	-	51	-	-
US Open	4	72	MC	45	16	48	MC	MC	7	72
G North Open	-	-	-	-	-	-	-	-	-	-
Irish Open	1	1	8	-	-	3	27	-	-	-
European Open	1	40	-	-	-	-	-	31	-	-
Scot Open	3	-	-	-	37	21	-	29	9	41
British Open	1	2	8	39	4	51	42	MC	41	MC
Dutch Open	-	-	-	-	-	-	-	-	-	-
Scandinavian	1	3	-	-	-	-	-	-	-	-
Wales Open	-	-	-	-	-	-	-	-	-	-
USPGA	2	3	4	31	65	MC	54	41	51	51
NW Ireland Open	-	-	-	-	-	-	-	-	-	-
WGC NEC Inv'	-	-	-	-	-	-	-	-	-	-
Scottish PGA	-	-	-	-	-	-	-	-	-	-
BMW Int' Open	-	-	-	-	-	-	-	21	-	-
European Mas'	-	8	6	-	-	6	MC	38	6	46
WGC AmEx	-	-	-	-	-	-	-	-	-	-
Troph' Lancome	17	6	7	-	25	-	6	-	12	-
German Masters	-	4	-	-	-	41	-	30	-	-
Cannes Open	-	-	-	-	-	-	-	-	-	-
Dunhill Links	-	-	-	-	-	-	-	-	-	-
Masters Madrid	-	-	-	-	-	-	-	-	-	-
Italian Open	-	-	-	-	-	-	-	-	-	-
Volvo Masters	23	25	13	-	-	-	-	36	28	-

Sponsored by Stan James

Marc Farry
3/7/59 – Paris, France

Veteran French pro whose sole success in 13 full seasons on the European Tour came in the 1996 BMW International Open.

Had his best season on the main tour in 1999 courtesy of four top-ten finishes (finishing 49th on the Order of Merit), but last term wasn't so successful as he only just scraped into the top 100.

Made a bold bid to become the first Frenchman to win the French Open in over three decades when sixth in this year's renewal in Lyon.

Can still hit the ball a long way off the tee but has struggled on the greens in recent seasons.

Sc Av – 71.83 (121st) DD - 284.6 (50th) DA - 63.5 (92nd) GIR – 64.1 (146th) PpGIR – 1.821 (154th) SS – 56.8 (65th)

	'92	'93	'94	'95	'96	'97	'98	'99	'00	'01
Johnnie Walker	-	MC	DQ	MC	MC	7	MC	-	MC	MC
WGC Matchplay	-	-	-	-	-	-	-	-	-	-
Alfred Dunhill	-	-	-	20	MC	-	-	51	-	-
S African Open	-	-	-	-	-	61	-	MC	-	-
Heineken Cl'	-	-	-	-	MC	3	MC	MC	MC	MC
Greg Norman	-	-	-	-	-	-	-	-	MC	17
Malaysian Open	-	-	-	-	-	-	-	MC	-	51
S'pore Masters	-	-	-	-	-	-	-	-	-	-
Dubai Desert	47	63	MC	-	WD	41	-	MC	MC	MC
Qatar Masters	-	-	-	-	-	-	-	40	59	71
Madeira Open	-	MC	MC	-	-	-	-	-	-	-
Brazil Open	-	-	-	-	-	-	-	-	MC	-
Open de Arg	-	-	-	-	-	-	-	-	-	-
US Masters	-	-	-	-	-	-	-	-	-	-
Moroccan Open	MC	57	55	MC	70	MC	67	-	-	48
Open de Espana	46	16	MC	-	37	MC	44	MC	MC	MC
Open de Portugal	24	MC	-	-	-	64	MC	25	-	MC
Open de France	53	MC	20	30	MC	53	6	8	MC	6
B&H I'national	MC	13	MC	25	36	MC	MC	33	MC	57
Deutsche Bank	-	-	-	-	MC	-	27	20	67	63
Volvo PGA	MC	MC	MC	-	60	37	MC	WD	MC	MC
British Masters	55	MC	44	41	MC	MC	12	26	23	MC
English Open	MC	MC	MC	-	78	-	MC	54	12	65
US Open	-	-	-	-	-	-	-	-	-	-
G North Open	-	-	-	-	MC	-	-	-	-	-
Irish Open	MC	44	MC	57	MC	MC	MC	58	32	20
European Open	18	WD	42	-	-	MC	MC	MC	28	34
Scot Open	-	-	-	37	MC	MC	43	58	MC	-
British Open	-	-	-	MC	-	-	MC	MC	-	-
Dutch Open	MC	14	MC	-	MC	59	65	-	WD	MC
Scandinavian	66	MC	53	-	-	45	WD	MC	MC	59
Wales Open	-	-	-	-	-	-	-	-	29	33
USPGA	-	-	-	-	-	-	-	-	-	-
NW Ireland Open	-	-	-	-	-	-	-	-	-	-
WGC NEC Inv'	-	-	-	-	-	-	-	-	-	-
Scottish PGA	-	-	-	-	-	-	-	-	-	-
BMW Int' Open	MC	19	60	7	1	12	MC	74	MC	67
European Mas'	22	MC	59	MC	23	71	37	4	-	46
WGC AmEx	-	-	-	-	-	-	-	-	-	-
Troph' Lancome	27	61	-	45	38	71	57	8	16	MC
German Masters	-	66	48	-	23	MC	11	17	30	15
Cannes Open	MC	72	WD	MC	26	WD	56	-	-	39
Dunhill Links	-	-	-	-	-	-	-	-	-	MC
Masters Madrid	7	38	MC	13	MC	-	-	4	60	57
Italian Open	53	55	MC	58	-	MC	31	38	-	-
Volvo Masters	-	-	-	-	48	-	61	-	-	-

Niclas Fasth
29/4/72 – Gotherburg, Sweden

Produced some superb golf to finish second in the Open Championship at Lytham and in doing so book his place in the Ryder Cup team.

It was the first time that the young Swede had played in a Major championship, but four top ten finishes earlier in the season had certainly served notice of his talent.

Won the Madeira Island Open in 2000 after six years on the European Tour. Tried to play the US and European Tours in 1998 but lost his card on both.

Found his form on the Challenge Tour when winning the 1999 Warsaw Open and gaining promotion to the full tour.

Sc Av – 70.27 (14th) DD - 289.1 (29th) DA - 60.7 (130th) GIR – 71.4 (24th) PpGIR – 1.745 (9th) SS – 59.3 (43rd)

	'92	'93	'94	'95	'96	'97	'98	'99	'00	'01
Johnnie Walker	-	-	MC	MC	MC	-	-	-	-	-
WGC Matchplay	-	-	-	-	-	-	-	-	-	-
Alfred Dunhill	-	-	-	-	-	8	-	43	-	-
S African Open	-	-	-	-	-	-	-	-	-	-
Heineken Cl'	-	-	-	-	51	MC	-	-	-	64
Greg Norman	-	-	-	-	-	-	-	-	-	31
Malaysian Open	-	-	-	-	-	-	-	-	MC	-
S'pore Masters	-	-	-	-	-	-	-	-	-	-
Dubai Desert	MC	-	60	MC	25	-	-	-	MC	MC
Qatar Masters	-	-	-	-	-	-	-	-	46	MC
Madeira Open	-	MC	-	-	MC	-	-	13	1	3
Brazil Open	-	-	-	-	-	-	-	-	-	-
Open de Arg	-	-	-	-	-	-	-	-	-	-
US Masters	-	-	-	-	-	-	-	-	-	-
Moroccan Open	-	-	MC	23	17	-	-	-	-	-
Open de Espana	-	-	-	-	-	36	-	-	7	MC
Open de Portugal	-	-	MC	MC	MC	-	-	-	14	9
Open de France	-	20	MC	-	MC	MC	-	-	-	-
B&H I'national	-	MC	MC	MC	17	-	-	-	22	MC
Deutsche Bank	-	-	63	69	36	MC	-	MC	-	43
Volvo PGA	-	-	-	30	60	MC	-	MC	-	14
British Masters	-	-	-	-	MC	WD	-	-	20	6
English Open	-	-	35	41	19	12	-	-	-	-
US Open	-	-	-	-	-	-	-	-	-	-
G North Open	-	-	-	-	-	-	-	-	-	-
Irish Open	-	-	MC	MC	MC	31	46	-	59	2
European Open	-	21	MC	14	22	WD	-	-	39	45
Scot Open	-	-	-	-	-	-	MC	-	29	14
British Open	-	-	-	-	-	-	-	-	-	2
Dutch Open	-	-	-	30	MC	-	-	-	-	-
Scandinavian	35	21	MC	46	MC	MC	MC	82	MC	13
Wales Open	-	-	-	-	-	-	-	-	-	-
USPGA	-	-	-	-	-	-	-	-	-	29
NW Ireland Open	-	-	-	-	-	-	-	-	-	-
WGC NEC Inv'	-	-	-	-	-	-	-	-	-	21
Scottish PGA	-	-	-	-	-	-	-	-	-	-
BMW Int' Open	-	7	MC	-	12	MC	-	-	25	60
European Mas'	-	57	MC	MC	12	MC	-	-	4	-
WGC AmEx	-	-	-	-	-	-	-	-	-	-
Troph' Lancome	-	-	51	-	-	-	-	-	MC	5
German Masters	-	-	-	27	-	-	-	-	63	25
Cannes Open	-	-	MC	19	MC	31	-	-	-	-
Dunhill Links	-	-	-	-	-	-	-	-	-	-
Masters Madrid	-	-	MC	-	MC	-	-	-	43	-
Italian Open	-	-	MC	MC	-	49	-	-	-	-
Volvo Masters	-	-	-	-	-	-	-	-	54	21

Anders Forsbrand

1/4/61 – Filipstad, Sweden

The first Swede to make his mark in European golf and back playing full time on the European Tour.

Fourth place in the Wales Open helped him to his highest position on the Order of Merit for four years in 2001, though even last term's performance was in stark contrast to when Forsbrand became the first Swede to play all four Majors in the same season back in 1993.

That was the year after he had finished fourth on the Order of Merit, winning three times.

The last of his six European Tour titles came in 1995 (German Masters).

Sc Av – 71.11 (54th) DD - 283.6 (59th) DA - 60.6 (131st) GIR – 71.1 (27th) PpGIR – 1.789 (94th) SS – 48.6 (139th)

	'92	'93	'94	'95	'96	'97	'98	'99	'00	'01
Johnnie Walker	10	31	MC	-	MC	27	-	-	MC	-
WGC Matchplay	-	-	-	-	-	-	-	-	-	-
Alfred Dunhill	-	-	-	-	-	8	-	-	-	MC
S African Open	-	-	-	-	29	69	-	-	-	MC
Heineken Cl'	-	-	-	MC	-	-	-	-	-	-
Greg Norman	-	-	-	-	-	-	-	-	-	-
Malaysian Open	-	-	-	-	-	-	-	-	-	-
S'pore Masters	-	-	-	-	-	-	-	-	-	MC
Dubai Desert	11	5	14	-	-	70	33	-	MC	33
Qatar Masters	-	-	-	-	-	-	13	-	-	-
Madeira Open	-	37	-	-	13	-	-	-	-	-
Brazil Open	-	-	-	-	-	-	-	-	-	-
Open de Arg	-	-	-	-	-	-	-	-	-	-
US Masters	-	11	MC	-	-	-	-	-	-	-
Moroccan Open	6	34	1	20	-	30	24	-	-	43
Open de Espana	-	26	MC	-	-	MC	MC	-	MC	49
Open de Portugal	2	-	36	-	-	MC	MC	-	29	44
Open de France	6	4	DQ	-	-	27	-	17	MC	27
B&H I'national	5	46	-	MC	DQ	MC	69	20	MC	-
Deutsche Bank	-	-	-	4	18	2	MC	MC	MC	MC
Volvo PGA	MC	MC	29	MC	MC	60	MC	MC	MC	MC
British Masters	MC	-	-	-	-	-	-	-	62	MC
English Open	MC	MC	-	24	-	46	MC	64	-	-
US Open	32	MC	-	-	33	-	-	-	-	-
G North Open	-	-	-	-	-	-	53	-	-	-
Irish Open	4	34	-	42	MC	40	MC	MC	40	MC
European Open	MC	-	12	9	-	10	MC	MC	MC	34
Scot Open	-	-	-	-	MC	MC	MC	MC	MC	-
British Open	34	MC	4	47	MC	-	-	-	-	-
Dutch Open	20	19	MC	-	-	-	-	51	-	-
Scandinavian	18	2	MC	25	65	MC	-	77	MC	60
Wales Open	-	-	-	-	-	-	-	-	-	4
USPGA	9	MC	MC	-	-	-	-	-	-	-
NW Ireland Open	-	-	-	-	-	-	-	-	-	-
WGC NEC Inv'	-	-	-	-	-	-	-	-	-	-
Scottish PGA	-	-	-	-	-	-	-	-	-	56
BMW Int' Open	2	3	14	MC	-	-	MC	MC	32	MC
European Mas'	2	11	25	50	-	-	MC	MC	17	MC
WGC AmEx	-	-	-	-	-	-	-	-	-	-
Troph' Lancome	47	-	57	-	-	-	-	-	MC	-
German Masters	-	MC	34	1	MC	MC	-	-	MC	19
Cannes Open	1	5	54	-	-	-	-	-	-	39
Dunhill Links	-	-	-	-	-	-	-	-	-	35
Masters Madrid	3	12	-	5	-	-	-	MC	-	-
Italian Open	27	MC	4	15	52	MC	WD	-	-	-
Volvo Masters	18	15	31	5	-	32	-	-	-	-

Pierre Fulke

21/2/71 – Nykoping, Sweden

Started the season by finishing second to Steve Stricker in the WGC World Matchplay tournament in Melbourne.

The $500,000 was enough to seal the Swede's place in the Ryder Cup team. His fine start to the year came after he ended 2000 on a high note – by winning the prestigious Volvo Masters (his third European Tour win).

Joined the full tour in 1993 but had to wait a further six years for his maiden victory – the 1999 Lancome Trophy. An injured wrist hampered his progress but he bounced back in 2000, first claiming the Scottish PGA Championship before going on to glory in Spain.

Sc Av – 71.87 (124th) DD - 266.0 (185th) DA - 70.3 (17th) GIR – 62.2 (176th) PpGIR – 1.739 (6th) SS – 57.4 (60th)

	'92	'93	'94	'95	'96	'97	'98	'99	'00	'01
Johnnie Walker	-	-	MC	-	-	-	-	-	-	-
WGC Matchplay	-	-	-	-	-	-	-	-	-	2
Alfred Dunhill	-	-	-	MC	-	-	-	-	-	-
S African Open	-	-	-	-	-	-	50	-	-	-
Heineken Cl'	-	-	-	-	-	MC	-	7	-	23
Greg Norman	-	-	-	-	-	-	-	-	-	13
Malaysian Open	-	-	-	-	-	-	-	33	-	-
S'pore Masters	-	-	-	-	-	-	-	-	-	-
Dubai Desert	MC	34	11	MC	MC	46	22	-	MC	-
Qatar Masters	-	-	-	-	-	-	MC	MC	-	-
Madeira Open	MC	MC	-	-	-	-	-	-	-	-
Brazil Open	-	-	-	-	-	-	-	-	-	-
Open de Arg	-	-	-	-	-	-	-	-	-	-
US Masters	-	-	-	-	-	-	-	-	-	MC
Moroccan Open	44	10	MC	MC	-	WD	-	-	-	-
Open de Espana	WD	-	-	-	36	MC	17	-	-	-
Open de Portugal	24	MC	-	-	-	-	72	-	-	-
Open de France	-	-	3	39	MC	-	MC	-	-	-
B&H I'national	MC	64	67	9	-	24	-	-	-	64
Deutsche Bank	-	-	20	MC	WD	34	WD	-	MC	-
Volvo PGA	-	-	56	MC	69	MC	MC	47	-	67
British Masters	-	MC	MC	MC	MC	2	38	11	-	-
English Open	33	10	MC	33	MC	32	MC	-	-	-
US Open	-	-	-	-	-	-	-	-	-	WD
G North Open	-	-	-	-	-	-	-	-	-	-
Irish Open	WD	MC	-	-	MC	MC	MC	MC	-	-
European Open	WD	-	MC	WD	-	28	MC	46	-	-
Scot Open	-	-	-	29	4	24	MC	MC	MC	-
British Open	-	-	MC	-	-	MC	-	30	7	62
Dutch Open	-	MC	-	50	MC	22	30	64	-	-
Scandinavian	77	MC	25	MC	12	MC	16	MC	17	25
Wales Open	-	-	-	-	-	-	-	-	29	-
USPGA	-	-	-	-	-	-	-	-	-	MC
NW Ireland Open	-	-	-	-	-	-	-	-	-	-
WGC NEC Inv'	-	-	-	-	-	-	-	-	-	17
Scottish PGA	-	-	-	-	-	-	-	-	1	-
BMW Int' Open	39	63	-	-	MC	11	-	-	MC	67
European Mas'	33	2	WD	34	MC	20	50	-	-	-
WGC AmEx	-	-	-	-	-	-	-	-	42	-
Troph' Lancome	-	MC	-	-	77	MC	1	79	-	-
German Masters	-	10	MC	MC	-	-	-	30	14	32
Cannes Open	3	5	55	MC	21	16	-	-	-	-
Dunhill Links	-	-	-	-	-	-	-	-	-	67
Masters Madrid	47	30	MC	MC	-	-	-	54	19	-
Italian Open	30	-	-	MC	-	31	54	7	-	-
Volvo Masters	-	34	-	-	-	-	60	54	1	44

Sponsored by Stan James

Stephen Gallacher
1/11/74 – Dechmont, Scotland

Nephew of former Ryder Cup captain Bernard who starred in Great Britain and Ireland's stunning Walker Cup success in 1995.

Gallacher registered his best season in 2001 since turning pro six years earlier, posting four top-ten finishes and coming close to winning his maiden European Tour title when second in the Great North Open.

After coming through Q-School in 1995 a wrist injury the following year meant his pro career was put on hold, but a successful season on the Challenge Tour in 1998 (when he won the KB Golf Challenge in the Czech Republic) saw him regain his full tour card.

Sc Av – 71.46 (91st) DD - 287.8 (34th) DA - 63.4 (94th) GIR – 70.0 (50th) PpGIR – 1.824 (159th) SS – 61.0 (41st)

	'92	'93	'94	'95	'96	'97	'98	'99	'00	'01
Johnnie Walker	-	-	-	-	-	-	-	-	-	-
WGC Matchplay	-	-	-	-	-	-	-	-	-	-
Alfred Dunhill	-	-	-	-	-	63	-	-	36	MC
S African Open	-	-	-	-	-	-	-	-	27	9
Heineken Cl'	-	-	-	-	-	-	-	-	18	MC
Greg Norman	-	-	-	-	-	-	-	-	-	-
Malaysian Open	-	-	-	-	-	-	-	-	-	-
S'pore Masters	-	-	-	-	-	-	-	-	-	-
Dubai Desert	-	-	-	-	-	-	-	4	-	-
Qatar Masters	-	-	-	-	-	-	-	15	MC	-
Madeira Open	-	-	-	63	MC	-	47	-	-	-
Brazil Open	-	-	-	-	-	-	-	-	-	-
Open de Arg	-	-	-	-	-	-	-	-	-	-
US Masters	-	-	-	-	-	-	-	-	-	-
Moroccan Open	-	-	-	64	MC	-	-	-	-	4
Open de Espana	-	-	-	37	-	-	MC	-	67	42
Open de Portugal	-	-	-	69	64	-	44	34	MC	-
Open de France	-	-	-	-	WD	-	-	37	50	-
B&H I'national	-	-	-	MC	MC	-	-	MC	5	42
Deutsche Bank	-	-	-	-	44	-	-	MC	MC	MC
Volvo PGA	-	-	-	-	-	-	-	MC	MC	MC
British Masters	-	-	-	-	-	-	-	55	MC	MC
English Open	-	-	-	-	MC	-	-	28	65	35
US Open	-	-	-	-	-	-	-	-	-	-
G North Open	-	-	-	-	WD	61	-	21	-	2
Irish Open	-	-	-	-	-	-	-	58	23	MC
European Open	-	-	-	-	-	-	-	35	39	MC
Scot Open	-	MC	-	MC	-	-	-	-	63	MC
British Open	-	-	-	MC	-	-	-	MC	-	-
Dutch Open	-	-	-	-	MC	-	-	49	-	MC
Scandinavian	-	-	-	-	MC	-	-	72	29	36
Wales Open	-	-	-	-	-	-	-	-	MC	49
USPGA	-	-	-	-	-	-	-	-	-	-
NW Ireland Open	-	-	-	-	-	-	-	35	-	-
WGC NEC Inv'	-	-	-	-	-	-	-	-	-	-
Scottish PGA	-	-	-	-	-	-	-	-	-	-
BMW Int' Open	-	-	-	-	-	-	MC	55	30	
European Mas'	-	-	-	-	-	-	MC	49	53	
WGC AmEx	-	-	-	-	-	-	-	-	-	-
Troph' Lancome	-	56	-	-	-	-	-	77	22	MC
German Masters	-	-	-	-	-	-	-	-	-	61
Cannes Open	-	-	-	-	26	MC	-	-	-	-
Dunhill Links	-	-	-	-	-	-	-	-	-	MC
Masters Madrid	-	-	-	-	MC	MC	-	MC	19	25
Italian Open	-	-	-	-	MC	61	-	66	44	32
Volvo Masters	-	-	-	-	-	-	-	-	54	33

Ian Garbutt
3/4/72 – Doncaster, England

After seven full seasons on the European Tour the Doncaster pro is yet to post a top five finish.

He did, though, equal his best finish on the full tour in 2001 when claiming seventh position in the French Open.

An accurate iron player and driver, he has always struggled on the greens. Turned pro in 1992 and spent two years on the full tour before losing his playing privileges.

After a successful season on the Challenge Tour in 1996 (when he won the UAP Grand Final) this former English Amateur champion was back amongst the big boys in 1997 and has stayed there ever since.

Sc Av – 70.91 (39th) DD - 274.6 (152nd) DA - 72.1 (11th) GIR – 72.6 (17th) PpGIR – 1.790 (96th) SS – 45.8 (157th)

	'92	'93	'94	'95	'96	'97	'98	'99	'00	'01
Johnnie Walker	-	-	-	-	-	25	-	-	-	-
WGC Matchplay	-	-	-	-	-	-	-	-	-	-
Alfred Dunhill	-	-	-	-	50	-	38	53	34	-
S African Open	-	-	-	-	-	-	-	34	MC	MC
Heineken Cl'	-	-	-	-	-	MC	32	36	MC	8
Greg Norman	-	-	-	-	-	-	-	-	8	39
Malaysian Open	-	-	-	-	-	-	-	-	-	-
S'pore Masters	-	-	-	-	-	-	-	-	-	-
Dubai Desert	-	63	-	-	34	72	55	24	MC	-
Qatar Masters	-	-	-	-	-	21	37	MC	MC	-
Madeira Open	-	52	37	-	-	MC	-	17	-	21
Brazil Open	-	-	-	-	-	-	-	-	39	-
Open de Arg	-	-	-	-	-	-	-	-	-	-
US Masters	-	-	-	-	-	-	-	-	-	-
Moroccan Open	-	53	25	-	-	-	-	-	-	-
Open de Espana	26	54	-	-	16	51	15	MC	32	-
Open de Portugal	MC	-	-	-	MC	16	16	WD	MC	-
Open de France	MC	-	-	-	MC	16	-	MC	-	7
B&H I'national	-	MC	-	-	-	52	MC	MC	34	12
Deutsche Bank	-	-	-	-	-	MC	22	23	MC	52
Volvo PGA	-	-	-	-	-	45	MC	13	MC	26
British Masters	-	-	-	-	-	35	-	MC	16	42
English Open	-	65	-	-	-	12	25	25	10	16
US Open	-	-	-	-	-	-	-	-	-	-
G North Open	-	-	-	-	-	MC	-	24	MC	-
Irish Open	-	MC	-	-	-	MC	9	36	53	20
European Open	-	-	-	-	-	WD	7	MC	MC	62
Scot Open	-	-	-	-	-	49	24	15	MC	53
British Open	-	50	-	-	-	-	-	-	52	-
Dutch Open	-	-	-	-	-	22	7	8	41	12
Scandinavian	-	MC	-	-	-	MC	MC	37	-	25
Wales Open	-	-	-	-	-	-	-	-	8	MC
USPGA	-	-	-	-	-	-	-	-	-	-
WGC NEC Inv'	-	-	-	-	-	-	-	-	-	-
Scottish PGA	-	-	-	-	-	-	-	-	-	29
BMW Int' Open	MC	MC	-	-	-	-	26	-	13	-
European Mas'	-	MC	-	-	-	32	MC	25	17	64
WGC AmEx	-	-	-	-	-	-	-	-	-	-
Troph' Lancome	-	-	-	-	-	43	MC	MC	24	65
German Masters	-	-	-	-	-	-	37	MC	30	46
Cannes Open	-	48	-	-	MC	16	-	-	-	-
Dunhill Links	-	-	-	-	-	-	-	-	-	35
Masters Madrid	-	MC	-	-	-	11	-	10	35	31
Italian Open	-	70	56	-	-	32	MC	MC	39	-
Volvo Masters	-	-	-	-	-	-	41	16	43	49

Sergio Garcia

9/1/80 – Castellon, Spain

The highest ranked European golfer at the end of the 2001 season after winning twice on the US Tour and once in Europe (the Lancome Trophy).

El Nino is now based mainly in the States but was named as a Wild Card for the European Ryder Cup team.

Turned pro in 1999 after a record breaking amateur career (claiming 19 victories) and won twice in his rookie season in Europe.

He helped Spain win the Dunhill Cup in 2000 and although his temper can sometimes get the better of him, he is surely destined to win a cabinet of Majors.

Sc Av – 69.53 (3rd) DD - 291.4 (16th) DA - 72.6 (10th) GIR – 77.1 (1st) PpGIR – 1.847 (186th) SS – 47.1 (149th)

	'92	'93	'94	'95	'96	'97	'98	'99	'00	'01
Johnnie Walker	-	-	-	-	-	-	-	-	-	19
WGC Matchplay	-	-	-	-	-	-	-	9	-	-
Alfred Dunhill	-	-	-	-	-	-	-	-	-	-
S African Open	-	-	-	-	-	-	-	-	-	-
Heineken Cl'	-	-	-	-	-	-	-	-	-	-
Greg Norman	-	-	-	-	-	-	-	-	-	2
Malaysian Open	-	-	-	-	-	-	-	-	-	-
S'pore Masters	-	-	-	-	-	-	-	-	-	-
Dubai Desert	-	-	-	-	-	-	-	31	-	-
Qatar Masters	-	-	-	-	-	-	-	MC	-	-
Madeira Open	-	-	-	-	-	-	-	-	-	-
Brazil Open	-	-	-	-	-	-	-	-	-	-
Open de Arg	-	-	-	-	-	-	-	-	-	-
US Masters	-	-	-	-	-	-	-	38	40	MC
Moroccan Open	-	-	-	-	-	-	-	-	-	-
Open de Espana	-	-	-	45	47	34	25	12	16	-
Open de Portugal	-	-	-	-	-	-	-	-	-	-
Open de France	-	-	-	-	-	-	-	-	-	-
B&H I'national	-	-	-	-	-	-	-	-	-	-
Deutsche Bank	-	-	-	-	-	-	-	20	31	-
Volvo PGA	-	-	-	-	-	-	-	19	5	-
British Masters	-	-	-	-	71	12	-	-	-	-
English Open	-	-	-	-	-	-	-	-	-	-
US Open	-	-	-	-	-	-	-	-	46	12
G North Open	-	-	-	-	-	-	-	-	-	-
Irish Open	-	-	-	-	-	-	60	1	10	-
European Open	-	-	-	-	-	-	-	49	-	-
Scot Open	-	-	-	-	-	-	57	2	-	14
British Open	-	-	-	-	MC	-	28	MC	36	9
Dutch Open	-	-	-	-	-	-	-	-	-	-
Scandinavian	-	-	-	-	-	-	-	-	-	-
Wales Open	-	-	-	-	-	-	-	-	-	-
USPGA	-	-	-	-	-	-	-	2	34	MC
NW Ireland Open	-	-	-	-	-	-	-	-	-	-
WGC NEC Inv'	-	-	-	-	-	-	-	7	-	-
Scottish PGA	-	-	-	-	-	-	-	-	-	-
BMW Int' Open	-	-	-	-	-	-	-	-	-	7
European Mas'	-	-	-	-	-	-	-	7	5	-
WGC AmEx	-	-	-	-	-	-	-	-	-	-
Troph' Lancome	-	-	-	-	65	18	-	-	-	1
German Masters	-	-	-	-	-	-	1	17	-	-
Cannes Open	-	-	-	-	-	-	-	-	-	-
Dunhill Links	-	-	-	-	-	-	-	-	-	-
Masters Madrid	-	-	-	-	-	-	-	MC	25	-
Italian Open	-	-	-	-	-	-	-	-	-	-
Volvo Masters	-	-	-	-	-	-	-	5	13	-

Ignacio Garrido

27/3/72 – Madrid, Spain

Spanish former Ryder Cup player whose sole European Tour success came in the 1997 German Open.

Last season wasn't the best for Garrido, as just two top-ten finishes saw him slip to 89th in the Order of Merit – his lowest position since joining the full tour in 1994.

He can boast four Challenge Tour victories and also won the Hassan Trophy in North Africa 1996. Used to caddie for his father, Antonio – a member of the first European Ryder Cup side who last year returned the compliment in Cannes Open.

Short off the tee but still hits plenty of greens in regulation.

Sc Av – 70.82 (34th) DD - 279.3 (105th) DA - 66.9 (52nd) GIR – 70.6 (36th) PpGIR – 1.785 (82nd) SS – 64.0 (24th)

	'92	'93	'94	'95	'96	'97	'98	'99	'00	'01
Johnnie Walker	-	-	19	-	-	-	-	-	-	-
WGC Matchplay	-	-	-	-	-	-	-	-	-	-
Alfred Dunhill	-	-	-	43	15	WD	26	22	MC	-
S African Open	-	-	-	-	20	7	34	DQ	16	-
Heineken Cl'	-	-	-	-	-	-	-	-	-	44
Greg Norman	-	-	-	-	-	-	-	-	-	-
Malaysian Open	-	-	-	-	-	-	-	-	-	18
S'pore Masters	-	-	-	-	-	-	-	-	-	24
Dubai Desert	-	-	39	20	MC	6	MC	MC	47	-
Qatar Masters	-	-	-	-	-	-	40	MC	MC	41
Madeira Open	-	-	MC	12	37	-	-	-	-	-
Brazil Open	-	-	-	-	-	-	-	75	-	-
Open de Arg	-	-	-	-	-	-	-	-	-	-
US Masters	-	-	-	-	-	-	-	MC	-	-
Moroccan Open	-	-	-	-	-	-	28	8	MC	-
Open de Espana	-	-	33	2	62	26	39	2	MC	58
Open de Portugal	-	5	33	MC	2	MC	MC	70	4	-
Open de France	-	-	8	48	52	67	WD	MC	36	41
B&H I'national	-	MC	48	45	29	-	51	-	-	-
Deutsche Bank	-	-	27	-	53	MC	MC	65	MC	-
Volvo PGA	-	-	56	MC	50	MC	56	62	MC	-
British Masters	-	-	MC	MC	43	4	-	78	-	-
English Open	-	-	35	16	MC	MC	49	39	-	-
US Open	-	-	-	-	-	-	MC	-	-	-
G North Open	-	-	-	-	-	-	-	65	-	-
Irish Open	-	46	MC	5	MC	46	33	MC	35	-
European Open	-	MC	70	55	-	37	63	5	MC	-
Scot Open	-	-	43	-	62	59	51	MC	-	-
British Open	-	-	-	MC	55	-	-	-	-	-
Dutch Open	-	40	54	MC	MC	-	37	-	-	-
Scandinavian	-	MC	35	18	2	43	37	MC	36	-
Wales Open	-	-	-	-	-	-	-	-	-	20
USPGA	-	-	-	-	41	MC	-	-	-	-
NW Ireland Open	-	-	-	-	-	-	-	-	-	-
WGC NEC Inv'	-	-	-	-	-	-	-	-	-	-
Scottish PGA	-	-	-	-	-	-	-	-	-	-
BMW Int' Open	-	-	-	6	MC	-	50	4	53	-
European Mas'	-	59	-	MC	25	MC	6	MC	72	-
WGC AmEx	-	-	-	-	-	-	-	-	-	-
Troph' Lancome	-	-	57	28	-	MC	2	30	WD	-
German Masters	-	-	MC	8	WD	MC	28	39	6	61
Cannes Open	-	-	23	13	3	46	-	-	-	6
Dunhill Links	-	-	-	-	-	-	-	-	-	35
Masters Madrid	-	-	25	35	6	8	MC	15	50	21
Italian Open	-	-	-	-	-	-	31	-	-	-
Volvo Masters	-	-	33	60	21	63	30	57	-	-

Sponsored by Stan James

Ricardo Gonzalez
24/10/69 – Corrientes, Argentina

A first European Tour win came this big hitting Argentinean pros way in 2001 at Cran-sur-Sierre, where captured the European Masters title.

It was just reward for a player who had battled back to the top level of golf after an abortive first season on the European Tour back in 1992.

He returned to Europe in 1998 to re-launch his career on the Challenge Tour, winning the Tusker Kenyan Open on his way to regaining his European Tour playing privileges.

A multiple winner in his native South America his win in Switzerland helped him to his highest Order of Merit position.

Sc Av – 70.00 (9th) DD - 303.3 (2nd) DA - 54.2 (183rd) GIR – 68.4 (71st) PpGIR – 1.760 (27th) SS – 54.3 (85th)

	'92	'93	'94	'95	'96	'97	'98	'99	'00	'01
Johnnie Walker	MC	-	-	-	-	-	-	-	-	-
WGC Matchplay	-	-	-	-	-	-	-	-	-	-
Alfred Dunhill	-	-	-	-	-	-	-	MC	18	10
S African Open	-	-	-	-	-	-	-	34	2	MC
Heineken Cl'	-	-	-	-	-	-	-	-	-	-
Greg Norman	-	-	-	-	-	-	-	-	-	-
Malaysian Open	-	-	-	-	-	-	-	-	-	-
S'pore Masters	-	-	-	-	-	-	-	-	-	-
Dubai Desert	MC	-	-	-	-	-	-	35	56	21
Qatar Masters	-	-	-	-	-	-	-	48	59	8
Madeira Open	-	-	-	-	-	-	-	-	-	-
Brazil Open	-	-	-	-	-	-	-	-	59	54
Open de Arg	-	-	-	-	-	-	-	-	-	13
US Masters	-	-	-	-	-	-	-	-	-	-
Moroccan Open	-	-	-	-	-	-	MC	-	-	-
Open de Espana	40	-	-	-	-	-	MC	MC	-	-
Open de Portugal	MC	-	-	-	-	-	9	-	37	
Open de France	MC	-	-	-	-	-	MC	22	41	
B&H I'national	-	-	-	-	-	-	MC	44	64	
Deutsche Bank	-	-	-	-	-	-	58	70	14	
Volvo PGA	-	-	-	-	-	-	-	26	MC	
British Masters	-	-	-	-	-	-	MC	-	6	
English Open	MC	-	-	-	-	-	-	4	-	
US Open	-	-	-	-	-	-	-	-	-	
G North Open	-	-	-	-	-	-	6	-	-	
Irish Open	MC	-	-	-	-	-	15	28	-	
European Open	-	-	-	-	-	-	35	46	8	
Scot Open	-	-	-	-	-	-	59	72	21	
British Open	-	-	-	-	-	-	-	-	-	
Dutch Open	-	-	-	-	-	-	20	33	7	
Scandinavian	-	-	-	-	-	-	-	11	59	
Wales Open	-	-	-	-	-	-	-	-	-	
USPGA	-	-	-	-	-	-	-	-	-	
NW Ireland Open	-	-	-	-	-	-	-	-	-	
WGC NEC Inv'	-	-	-	-	-	-	-	-	-	
Scottish PGA	-	-	-	-	-	-	-	-	-	
BMW Int' Open	MC	-	-	-	-	-	-	MC	21	
European Mas'	-	-	-	-	-	-	25	42	1	
WGC AmEx	-	-	-	-	-	-	-	-	-	
Troph' Lancome	-	-	-	-	-	-	18	MC	-	
German Masters	-	-	-	-	-	-	25	MC	41	
Cannes Open	-	-	-	-	-	-	-	-	MC	
Dunhill Links	-	-	-	-	-	-	-	-	27	
Masters Madrid	-	-	-	-	-	-	15	MC	-	
Italian Open	27	-	-	-	-	-	6	12	-	
Volvo Masters	-	-	-	-	-	-	64	7	24	

Retief Goosen
3/2/69 – Pietersburg, South African

The big hitting South African finally realised his potential in 2001 by not only winning his first Major – the US Open – but also the European Order of Merit.

A superb amateur player 'The Goose' always seemed two steps behind his great rival Ernie Els. However, last season, he finally found some consistancy with his putter and, although he stumbled over the line at Southern Hills, eventually won the Major his talent derserves.

Goosen's fine run of summer form continued into July when he kept a top class field at bay to land the Scottish Open at Loch Lomond. Those two victories helped him become the first non-European Order of Merit winner since Greg Norman in 1980.

Sc Av – 69.32 (2nd) DD - 291.0 (19th) DA - 62.7 (104th) GIR – 76.5 (4th) PpGIR – 1.738 (4th) SS – 50.0 (122nd)

	'92	'93	'94	'95	'96	'97	'98	'99	'00	'01
Johnnie Walker	-	31	MC	-	-	-	3	-	-	-
WGC Matchplay	-	-	-	-	-	-	-	-	17	17
Alfred Dunhill	-	-	46	MC	4	-	3	WD	4	7
S African Open	-	-	-	-	-	-	6	MC	5	21
Heineken Cl'	-	-	-	-	-	-	MC	-	MC	-
Greg Norman	-	-	-	-	-	-	-	-	16	-
Malaysian Open	-	-	-	-	-	-	-	-	-	-
S'pore Masters	-	-	-	-	-	-	-	-	-	-
Dubai Desert	-	2	21	8	MC	MC	46	-	-	17
Qatar Masters	-	-	-	-	-	-	5	20	-	-
Madeira Open	-	-	-	-	MC	-	4	-	-	-
Brazil Open	-	-	-	-	-	-	-	-	-	-
Open de Arg	-	-	-	-	-	-	-	-	-	-
US Masters	-	-	-	-	-	-	MC	-	40	MC
Moroccan Open	-	-	-	MC	14	-	-	-	-	-
Open de Espana	-	-	MC	65	11	MC	-	46	-	-
Open de Portugal	-	40	2	MC	46	-	-	66	-	-
Open de France	-	15	-	55	3	1	16	1	36	-
B&H I'national	-	13	26	MC	18	17	5	MC	MC	7
Deutsche Bank	-	-	MC	4	18	22	2	13	14	
Volvo PGA	-	45	37	37	21	32	MC	4	7	MC
British Masters	MC	MC	74	22	24	15	MC	10	MC	MC
English Open	-	10	3	MC	12	MC	MC	28	41	5
US Open	-	-	-	-	-	-	MC	MC	12	1
G North Open	-	-	-	1	2	-	2	-	-	
Irish Open	WD	6	36	42	-	MC	-	-	21	-
European Open	-	13	37	MC	MC	-	MC	24	28	6
Scot Open	-	-	-	-	29	3	-	10	4	1
British Open	-	MC	-	-	75	10	MC	10	41	13
Dutch Open	-	47	69	MC	18	-	WD	-	-	
Scandinavian	50	69	MC	41	-	-	43	59	-	
Wales Open	-	-	-	-	-	-	-	-	-	
USPGA Champ'	-	-	-	-	61	MC	MC	MC	37	
NW Ireland Open	-	-	-	-	-	-	-	-	-	
WGC NEC Inv'	-	-	-	-	-	-	-	24	10	
Scottish PGA	-	-	-	-	-	-	-	-	-	
BMW Int' Open	-	35	42	MC	-	-	55	-	23	
European Mas'	MC	10	-	40	25	20	-	-	-	
WGC AmEx	-	-	-	-	-	-	25	35	-	
Troph' Lancome	-	26	WD	-	38	13	57	15	1	2
German Masters	-	-	24	65	21	11	7	66	10	
Cannes Open	-	MC	42	MC	56	-	-	-	-	
Dunhill Links	-	-	-	-	-	-	-	-	9	
Masters Madrid	-	61	-	MC	8	-	MC	-	1	
Italian Open	-	MC	79	-	17	13	6	-	-	
Volvo Masters	10	52	-	51	42	49	2	22	10	

Richard Green

19/2/71 – Melbourne Australia

Left-handed Australian pro whose sole European Tour success came at the 1997 Dubai Desert Classic. Eleven top 25 finishes in 2001 helped him to his highest Order of Merit position since 1997.

The Bath based pro won four times in the mid '90s in Australasia and first came to Europe in 1996, registering four top ten finishes.

A member of the Australian World Cup team in 1998 he has struggled with his putter in recent seasons but still retains plenty of accuracy off the tee and with his irons.

Based in Bath in the UK and lists Wentworth as his favourite course.

Sc Av – 70.50 (22nd) DD - 270.5 (125th) DA - 81.9 (2nd) GIR – 75.4 (8th) PpGIR – 1.808 (131st) SS – 61.6 (33rd)

	'92	'93	'94	'95	'96	'97	'98	'99	'00	'01
Johnnie Walker	-	-	-	-	29	34	MC	-	-	12
WGC Matchplay	-	-	-	-	-	-	-	-	-	-
Alfred Dunhill	-	-	-	-	-	-	-	MC	-	-
S African Open	-	-	-	-	-	-	-	19	-	-
Heineken Cl'	-	-	-	-	5	MC	32	MC	MC	39
Greg Norman	-	-	-	-	-	-	-	MC	MC	-
Malaysian Open	-	-	-	-	-	-	-	-	-	-
S'pore Masters	-	-	-	-	-	-	-	-	-	43
Dubai Desert	-	-	-	-	-	1	MC	46	MC	12
Qatar Masters	-	-	-	-	-	-	-	53	MC	MC
Madeira Open	-	-	-	-	MC	-	-	-	-	-
Brazil Open	-	-	-	-	-	-	-	-	-	-
Open de Arg	-	-	-	-	-	-	-	-	-	-
US Masters	-	-	-	-	-	-	-	-	-	-
Moroccan Open	-	-	-	MC	-	-	-	-	-	-
Open de Espana	-	-	-	-	-	MC	-	-	60	-
Open de Portugal	-	-	-	-	-	-	-	-	-	19
Open de France	-	-	-	-	39	64	MC	34	31	27
B&H I'national	-	-	-	-	-	35	MC	7	18	6
Deutsche Bank	-	-	-	-	-	-	MC	MC	MC	10
Volvo PGA	-	-	-	-	-	MC	MC	MC	5	17
British Masters	-	-	-	-	-	59	MC	47	MC	14
English Open	-	-	-	-	-	MC	MC	MC	MC	-
US Open	-	-	-	-	-	-	-	-	-	-
G North Open	-	-	-	-	-	MC	-	61	18	20
Irish Open	-	-	-	-	-	37	46	MC	MC	MC
European Open	-	-	-	-	24	MC	MC	10	MC	12
Scot Open	-	-	-	-	6	MC	MC	MC	22	MC
British Open	-	-	-	-	-	MC	-	MC	-	42
Dutch Open	-	-	-	-	-	-	WD	MC	MC	-
Scandinavian	-	-	-	-	-	-	-	52	MC	59
Wales Open	-	-	-	-	-	-	-	-	17	65
USPGA	-	-	-	-	-	-	-	-	-	-
NW Ireland Open	-	-	-	-	-	-	-	-	-	-
WGC NEC Inv'	-	-	-	-	-	-	-	-	-	-
Scottish PGA	-	-	-	-	-	-	-	-	-	MC
BMW Int' Open	-	-	-	-	2	MC	MC	MC	-	53
European Mas'	-	-	-	-	-	-	-	MC	-	-
WGC AmEx	-	-	-	-	-	-	-	-	-	-
Troph' Lancome	-	-	-	-	45	47	-	MC	MC	-
German Masters	-	-	-	-	-	-	-	41	17	-
Cannes Open	-	-	-	-	-	MC	MC	-	-	-
Dunhill Links	-	-	-	-	-	-	-	-	-	MC
Masters Madrid	-	-	-	-	-	-	-	-	35	12
Italian Open	-	-	-	-	-	66	-	MC	3	17
Volvo Masters	-	-	-	-	-	9	46	-	40	35

Mathias Gronberg

12/3/70 – Stockholm, Sweden

Talented Swedish golfer who has scored three European Tour successes since joining the European Tour full time in 1994.

He didn't manage to add to his victory haul in 2001, but in a very consistent season, in which he only just missed out on a place in the Ryder Cup team, Gronberg claimed six top-ten finishes.

His last victory came in 2000 in the South African Open, his first, five years earlier in the European Masters.

Has tried and failed to get his US Tour card and with an American wife could see his future on the other side of the Atlantic.

Sc Av – 70.79 (33rd) DD - 282.8 (70th) DA - 62.2 (110th) GIR – 65.3 (127th) PpGIR – 1.758 (25th) SS – 64.6 (20th)

	'92	'93	'94	'95	'96	'97	'98	'99	'00	'01
Johnnie Walker	-	-	-	68	MC	MC	MC	-	-	-
WGC Matchplay	-	-	-	-	-	-	-	-	-	33
Alfred Dunhill	-	-	-	MC	43	-	9	22	14	16
S African Open	-	-	-	-	-	-	MC	MC	1	59
Heineken Cl'	-	-	-	-	MC	MC	MC	-	MC	-
Greg Norman	-	-	-	-	-	-	-	-	MC	-
Malaysian Open	-	-	-	-	-	-	-	-	11	-
S'pore Masters	-	-	-	-	-	-	-	-	-	-
Dubai Desert	-	-	-	MC	MC	MC	MC	MC	MC	4
Qatar Masters	-	-	-	-	-	-	MC	11	27	27
Madeira Open	-	-	3	9	MC	-	-	-	-	-
Brazil Open	-	-	-	-	-	-	-	-	11	-
Open de Arg	-	-	-	-	-	-	-	-	-	-
US Masters	-	-	-	-	-	-	-	-	-	-
Moroccan Open	-	-	-	55	-	8	WD	3	-	-
Open de Espana	-	-	MC	MC	4	MC	7	58	-	-
Open de Portugal	-	-	MC	42	60	-	-	-	-	60
Open de France	-	-	MC	MC	MC	-	-	47	-	-
B&H I'national	-	-	58	MC	-	-	38	20	MC	MC
Deutsche Bank	-	-	-	MC	MC	58	MC	MC	35	28
Volvo PGA	-	-	-	MC	13	70	MC	7	MC	4
British Masters	-	-	-	71	MC	WD	35	18	18	2
English Open	-	-	MC	24	40	MC	41	54	12	-
US Open	-	-	-	-	-	-	-	MC	-	74
G North Open	-	-	-	-	-	49	-	-	-	-
Irish Open	-	-	24	-	-	37	MC	66	MC	12
European Open	-	-	MC	55	42	MC	1	MC	4	12
Scot Open	-	-	-	-	MC	25	62	MC	69	8
British Open	-	-	MC	-	-	-	MC	-	-	MC
Dutch Open	-	-	DQ	-	MC	-	54	-	3	MC
Scandinavian	MC	-	48	25	57	MC	7	18	31	MC
Wales Open	-	-	-	-	-	-	-	-	-	-
USPGA	-	-	-	-	-	-	-	-	MC	MC
NW Ireland Open	-	-	-	-	-	-	-	-	-	-
WGC NEC Inv'	-	-	-	-	-	-	-	-	-	-
Scottish PGA	-	-	-	-	-	-	-	-	-	68
BMW Int' Open	-	-	47	-	9	26	MC	9	49	MC
European Mas'	-	-	MC	1	59	12	7	50	5	34
WGC AmEx	-	-	-	-	-	-	-	-	42	-
Troph' Lancome	-	-	-	14	MC	27	57	64	77	-
German Masters	-	-	-	MC	MC	41	48	MC	66	46
Cannes Open	-	-	-	MC	6	MC	21	32	-	-
Dunhill Links	-	-	-	-	-	-	-	-	-	-
Masters Madrid	-	-	30	27	30	-	-	-	50	-
Italian Open	-	-	50	-	10	53	43	23	-	-
Volvo Masters	-	-	-	42	-	-	16	-	52	4

Joakim Haeggman

28/8/69 – Kalmar, Sweden

One of the most consistent performers on the European Tour in the mid '90s and the first Swede to play on the Ryder Cup team.

The last few seasons have been a struggle for Haeggman, however, with the last of his two European Tour wins coming in 1997 at the Scandinavian Masters.

Turned pro in 1989 and after a successful career on the Challenge Tour (winning twice) he had his best year on the tour in 1993, winning the Sapanish Open and making the Ryder Cup side.

Brilliant putter, but wayward driver, his best finish in 2001 was fourth in the Scandinavian Masters.

Sc Av – 71.23 (68th) DD - 284.5 (52nd) DA - 55.3 (179th) GIR – 61.7 (180th) PpGIR – 1.748 (13th) SS – 50.0 (122nd)

	'92	'93	'94	'95	'96	'97	'98	'99	'00	'01
Johnnie Walker	MC	53	MC	37	-	15	-	-	-	-
WGC Matchplay	-	-	-	-	-	-	-	-	-	-
Alfred Dunhill	-	-	-	-	-	MC	-	-	-	-
S African Open	-	-	-	-	-	MC	-	-	-	-
Heineken Cl'	-	-	-	-	MC	-	MC	-	-	48
Greg Norman	-	-	-	-	-	-	-	-	-	26
Malaysian Open	-	-	-	-	-	-	-	-	16	51
S'pore Masters	-	-	-	-	-	-	-	-	-	-
Dubai Desert	18	9	45	23	11	12	MC	55	MC	80
Qatar Masters	-	-	-	-	-	-	40	MC	WD	MC
Madeira Open	-	-	-	-	-	-	-	MC	-	-
Brazil Open	-	-	-	-	-	-	-	-	59	40
Open de Arg	-	-	-	-	-	-	-	-	-	MC
US Masters	-	-	-	-	-	-	-	-	-	-
Moroccan Open	-	-	35	-	MC	22	-	22	-	-
Open de Espana	25	1	MC	MC	-	MC	44	40	MC	5
Open de Portugal	-	-	-	4	MC	-	-	-	11	27
Open de France	20	-	-	65	39	MC	-	-	31	17
B&H I'national	52	4	MC	MC	17	59	MC	MC	MC	-
Deutsche Bank	-	-	-	-	MC	-	13	MC	26	MC
Volvo PGA	MC	16	4	25	MC	45	MC	29	-	32
British Masters	34	6	13	27	7	-	MC	MC	-	-
English Open	24	10	MC	24	10	55	MC	64	47	MC
US Open	-	-	MC	-	-	-	-	-	-	-
G North Open	-	-	-	-	MC	-	-	-	-	-
Irish Open	-	8	MC	-	12	-	-	52	76	-
European Open	33	MC	-	8	MC	34	MC	MC	MC	45
Scot Open	20	-	-	-	54	12	47	MC	-	MC
British Open	-	MC	76	-	MC	-	36	-	-	-
Dutch Open	MC	-	-	MC	-	43	48	64	17	29
Scandinavian	26	MC	30	MC	MC	1	MC	MC	52	4
Wales Open	-	-	-	-	-	-	-	-	55	-
USPGA	-	-	MC	-	-	-	-	-	-	-
NW Ireland Open	-	-	-	-	-	-	-	-	-	-
WGC NEC Inv'	-	-	-	-	-	-	-	-	-	-
Scottish PGA	-	-	-	-	-	-	-	MC	-	-
BMW Int' Open	-	7	-	-	-	MC	-	MC	46	53
European Mas'	64	-	DQ	4	40	21	MC	MC	MC	23
WGC AmEx	-	-	-	-	-	-	-	-	-	-
Troph' Lancome	36	-	14	MC	-	36	MC	MC	-	43
German Masters	43	-	MC	6	27	-	MC	12	-	-
Cannes Open	-	-	MC	35	MC	38	11	-	-	-
Dunhill Links	-	-	-	-	-	-	-	-	-	67
Masters Madrid	49	8	-	MC	23	30	-	MC	-	-
Italian Open	-	-	-	MC	MC	-	2	23	-	-
Volvo Masters	23	35	11	37	63	32	-	-	-	-

Chris Hanell

30/5/73 – Vastervik, Sweden

After failing to gain his US Tour card, following a successful spell in college golf in the USA, this talented Swede joined the Challenge Tour in 1998.

He didn't manage to win, but did enough to place in the top 15 of the feeder tour to gain his playing privileges to the full tour in 1999.

A solid rookie season followed and his second year mirrored his first.

His third term, however, saw him slip to 91st in the Order of Merit – his lowest position in his career so far.

His best European Tour finish came in the 2000 British Masters when third.

Sc Av – 71.17 (60th) DD - 275.8 (135th) DA - 64.7 (75th) GIR – 66.7 (103rd) PpGIR – 1.800 (117th) SS – 64.0 (24th)

	'92	'93	'94	'95	'96	'97	'98	'99	'00	'01
Johnnie Walker	-	-	-	-	-	-	-	-	-	-
WGC Matchplay	-	-	-	-	-	-	-	-	-	-
Alfred Dunhill	-	-	-	-	-	-	-	33	MC	-
S African Open	-	-	-	-	-	-	-	-	13	-
Heineken Cl'	-	-	-	-	-	-	-	13	26	23
Greg Norman	-	-	-	-	-	-	-	-	12	MC
Malaysian Open	-	-	-	-	-	-	-	11	-	MC
S'pore Masters	-	-	-	-	-	-	-	-	-	MC
Dubai Desert	-	-	-	-	-	-	-	-	71	68
Qatar Masters	-	-	-	-	-	-	-	5	46	MC
Madeira Open	-	-	-	-	-	-	-	53	14	-
Brazil Open	-	-	-	-	-	-	-	-	-	8
Open de Arg	-	-	-	-	-	-	-	-	-	13
US Masters	-	-	-	-	-	-	-	-	-	-
Moroccan Open	-	-	-	-	-	-	-	-	40	-
Open de Espana	-	-	-	-	-	-	-	25	-	42
Open de Portugal	-	-	-	-	-	-	-	MC	-	MC
Open de France	-	-	-	-	-	-	-	MC	MC	MC
B&H I'national	-	-	-	-	-	-	-	51	MC	-
Deutsche Bank	-	-	-	-	-	-	-	55	MC	57
Volvo PGA	-	-	-	-	-	-	-	-	56	39
British Masters	-	-	-	-	-	-	-	3	43	47
English Open	-	-	-	-	-	-	-	64	26	DQ
US Open	-	-	-	-	-	-	-	-	-	-
G North Open	-	-	-	-	-	-	-	-	MC	-
Irish Open	-	-	-	-	-	-	-	MC	40	MC
European Open	-	-	-	-	-	-	-	MC	13	30
Scot Open	-	-	-	-	-	-	-	MC	41	MC
British Open	-	-	-	-	-	-	-	MC	-	-
Dutch Open	-	-	-	-	-	-	-	37	MC	MC
Scandinavian	-	65	MC	MC	35	-	63	65	11	47
Wales Open	-	-	-	-	-	-	-	-	-	WD
USPGA	-	-	-	-	-	-	-	-	-	-
NW Ireland Open	-	-	-	-	-	-	-	-	-	-
WGC NEC Inv'	-	-	-	-	-	-	-	-	-	-
Scottish PGA	-	-	-	-	-	-	-	-	-	MC
BMW Int' Open	-	-	-	-	-	-	-	MC	16	4
European Mas'	-	-	-	-	-	-	-	42	23	34
WGC AmEx	-	-	-	-	-	-	-	-	-	-
Troph' Lancome	-	-	-	-	-	-	-	57	MC	MC
German Masters	-	-	-	-	-	-	-	-	41	MC
Cannes Open	-	-	-	-	-	-	-	-	-	39
Dunhill Links	-	-	-	-	-	-	-	-	-	MC
Masters Madrid	-	-	-	-	-	-	-	15	35	-
Italian Open	-	-	-	-	-	-	-	MC	-	-
Volvo Masters	-	-	-	-	-	-	-	64	-	-

Anders Hansen

16/9/70 – Sonderborg, Denmark

London based Dane who enjoyed a fine college career in America before turning pro in 1995.

He also captured two Danish Amateur titles before joining the paid ranks.

Last season was his fourth full term on the European Tour and also his best.

He registered six top-ten finishes, including fourth in the TNT Dutch Open – his best European Tour finish.

An accurate golfer whose putting was first class throughout last season. Played on the Challenge Tour intermittently in the late '90s. Comes from a golfing family, with mum, dad and brother, Nicolai, all competent players.

Sc Av – 70.47 (21st) DD - 280.4 (95th) DA - 73.7 (7th) GIR – 69.4 (55th) PpGIR - 1.757 (23rd) SS – 53.3 (95th)

	'92	'93	'94	'95	'96	'97	'98	'99	'00	'01
Johnnie Walker	-	-	-	-	-	-	-	-	MC	35
WGC Matchplay	-	-	-	-	-	-	-	-	-	-
Alfred Dunhill	-	-	-	-	-	MC	-	30	10	23
S African Open	-	-	-	-	-	55	-	-	MC	MC
Heineken Cl'	-	-	-	-	-	-	-	36	25	MC
Greg Norman	-	-	-	-	-	-	-	-	6	26
Malaysian Open	-	-	-	-	-	-	-	21	-	34
S'pore Masters	-	-	-	-	-	-	-	-	-	5
Dubai Desert	-	-	-	-	-	-	-	-	MC	12
Qatar Masters	-	-	-	-	-	-	-	16	-	8
Madeira Open	-	-	-	-	MC	MC	-	17	-	-
Brazil Open	-	-	-	-	-	-	-	8	-	-
Open de Arg	-	-	-	-	-	-	-	-	-	-
US Masters	-	-	-	-	-	-	-	-	-	-
Moroccan Open	-	-	-	-	23	MC	-	28	-	-
Open de Espana	-	-	-	-	-	64	-	MC	21	58
Open de Portugal	-	-	-	-	-	MC	-	38	34	19
Open de France	-	-	-	-	-	-	-	17	15	7
B&H I'national	-	-	-	-	-	-	-	MC	14	-
Deutsche Bank	-	-	-	-	-	-	MC	-	77	43
Volvo PGA	-	-	-	-	-	-	-	-	20	21
British Masters	-	-	-	-	MC	WD	-	60	29	MC
English Open	-	-	-	-	-	-	-	39	-	35
US Open	-	-	-	-	-	-	-	-	-	-
G North Open	-	-	-	-	44	35	-	65	36	-
Irish Open	-	-	-	-	-	MC	-	48	-	-
European Open	-	-	-	-	-	-	-	MC	MC	30
Scot Open	-	-	-	-	-	-	-	-	48	21
British Open	-	-	-	-	-	-	-	MC	-	-
Dutch Open	-	-	-	-	-	67	-	20	56	4
Scandinavian	-	-	-	-	-	MC	-	-	45	36
Wales Open	-	-	-	-	-	-	-	-	29	7
USPGA	-	-	-	-	-	-	-	-	-	-
NW Ireland Open	-	-	-	-	-	-	-	6	-	-
WGC NEC Inv'	-	-	-	-	-	-	-	-	-	-
Scottish PGA	-	-	-	-	-	-	-	-	-	-
BMW Int' Open	-	-	-	-	MC	-	-	MC	-	30
European Mas'	-	-	-	-	-	44	-	MC	MC	64
WGC AmEx	-	-	-	-	-	-	-	-	-	-
Troph' Lancome	-	-	-	-	-	-	-	12	-	-
German Masters	-	-	-	-	-	-	-	-	-	32
Cannes Open	-	-	-	-	-	-	MC	MC	-	-
Dunhill Links	-	-	-	-	-	-	-	-	-	MC
Masters Madrid	-	-	-	-	-	MC	23	49	67	6
Italian Open	-	-	-	-	MC	MC	-	66	31	-
Volvo Masters	-	-	-	-	-	-	-	-	40	52

Soren Hansen

21/3/74 – Copenhagen, Denmark

No relation to another Hansen on the European Tour, Anders, this Danish pro is four years younger and can boast a win on the Challenge Tour, unlike his namesake.

Last season saw Hansen enjoy his best year on the European Tour since joining in 1999.

Five top-ten finishes came his way including second in the European Masters – hi best finish on the full tour.

He graduated to the main tour after a successful first season on the Challenge Tour – winning the Navision Open in Denmark after a three-man play-off. Straight and long off the tee.

Sc Av – 71.11 (54th) DD - 283.2 (65th) DA - 63.2 (96th) GIR – 69.1 (59th) PpGIR - 1.769 (45th) SS – 58.2 (51st)

	'92	'93	'94	'95	'96	'97	'98	'99	'00	'01
Johnnie Walker	-	-	-	-	-	-	-	-	32	14
WGC Matchplay	-	-	-	-	-	-	-	-	-	-
Alfred Dunhill	-	-	-	-	-	-	-	MC	22	MC
S African Open	-	-	-	-	-	-	-	WD	MC	MC
Heineken Cl'	-	-	-	-	-	-	-	38	-	19
Greg Norman	-	-	-	-	-	-	-	21	-	31
Malaysian Open	-	-	-	-	-	-	-	MC	11	5
S'pore Masters	-	-	-	-	-	-	-	-	-	-
Dubai Desert	-	-	-	-	-	-	-	MC	37	28
Qatar Masters	-	-	-	-	-	-	-	53	14	59
Madeira Open	-	-	-	-	-	-	-	MC	-	MC
Brazil Open	-	-	-	-	-	-	-	-	-	-
Open de Arg	-	-	-	-	-	-	-	-	-	-
US Masters	-	-	-	-	-	-	-	-	-	-
Moroccan Open	-	-	-	-	-	-	-	-	-	-
Open de Espana	-	-	-	-	-	-	-	25	43	3
Open de Portugal	-	-	-	-	-	-	-	49	-	-
Open de France	-	-	-	-	-	-	-	MC	7	-
B&H I'national	-	-	-	-	-	-	-	29	28	MC
Deutsche Bank	-	-	-	-	-	-	-	33	MC	47
Volvo PGA	-	-	-	-	-	-	-	-	MC	58
British Masters	-	-	-	-	-	-	-	60	MC	MC
English Open	-	-	-	-	-	-	-	MC	26	-
US Open	-	-	-	-	-	-	-	-	-	-
G North Open	-	-	-	-	-	-	-	MC	-	8
Irish Open	-	-	-	-	-	-	-	25	68	-
European Open	-	-	-	-	-	-	-	49	MC	45
Scot Open	-	-	-	-	-	-	-	MC	MC	14
British Open	-	-	-	-	-	-	-	-	-	MC
Dutch Open	-	-	-	-	-	-	-	MC	33	32
Scandinavian	-	-	-	-	-	-	-	MC	MC	9
Wales Open	-	-	-	-	-	-	-	-	72	-
USPGA	-	-	-	-	-	-	-	-	-	-
NW Ireland Open	-	-	-	-	-	-	-	12	-	-
WGC NEC Inv'	-	-	-	-	-	-	-	-	-	-
Scottish PGA	-	-	-	-	-	-	-	-	-	77
BMW Int' Open	-	-	-	-	-	-	-	64	25	74
European Mas'	-	-	-	-	-	-	-	MC	23	2
WGC AmEx	-	-	-	-	-	-	-	-	-	-
Troph' Lancome	-	-	-	-	-	-	-	MC	-	MC
German Masters	-	-	-	-	-	-	-	-	MC	MC
Cannes Open	-	-	-	-	-	-	-	-	-	-
Dunhill Links	-	-	-	-	-	-	-	-	-	MC
Masters Madrid	-	-	-	-	-	-	-	24	30	65
Italian Open	-	-	-	-	-	-	-	47	57	-
Volvo Masters	-	-	-	-	-	-	-	-	-	21

Padraig Harrington
31/8/71 – Dublin, Ireland

After seven second places on the European Tour in 2001, he finally broke his seasonal duck in the last event of the year, the Volvo Masters.

His win in Jerez hoisted him up to second place in the Order of Merit – his highest position.

Four European Tour wins have now come his way (the first the 1996 Spanish Open) and he can now safely regarded as one of Europe's best players.

His deadly iron play and assured putting should have arguably brought him more tournament victories.

He'll make his second Ryder Cup appearance in 2002. Former Walker Cup player.

Sc Av – 69.23 (1st) DD - 285.5 (44th) DA - 62.2 (110th) GIR – 77.1 (1st) PpGIR – 1.723 (1st) SS – 71.1 (10th)

	'92	'93	'94	'95	'96	'97	'98	'99	'00	'01
Johnnie Walker	-	-	-	-	-	27	8	-	-	-
WGC Matchplay	-	-	-	-	-	-	-	-	33	33
Alfred Dunhill	-	-	-	-	-	54	-	-	-	-
S African Open	-	-	-	-	-	27	-	-	-	-
Heineken Cl'	-	-	-	-	-	11	3	51	MC	-
Greg Norman	-	-	-	-	-	-	-	MC	-	-
Malaysian Open	-	-	-	-	-	-	-	4	2	2
S'pore Masters	-	-	-	-	-	-	-	-	-	5
Dubai Desert	-	-	-	-	-	28	64	MC	-	2
Qatar Masters	-	-	-	-	-	-	17	24	-	-
Madeira Open	-	-	-	-	48	9	-	4	-	-
Brazil Open	-	-	-	-	-	-	-	1	-	-
Open de Arg	-	-	-	-	-	-	-	-	-	-
US Masters	-	-	-	-	-	-	-	19	27	
Moroccan Open	-	-	-	-	23	38	-	-	-	-
Open de Espana	-	-	-	-	1	36	MC	54	-	-
Open de Portugal	-	-	-	-	45	MC	-	74	-	2
Open de France	-	-	-	-	-	-	-	-	-	-
B&H l'national	-	-	-	-	MC	4	59	16	DQ	19
Deutsche Bank	-	-	-	-	-	-	60	38	17	5
Volvo PGA	-	-	-	-	13	60	11	56	17	45
British Masters	-	-	-	-	MC	-	MC	-	-	-
English Open	-	-	-	-	-	MC	25	-	-	-
US Open	-	-	-	-	-	MC	32	-	5	30
G North Open	-	-	-	-	9	26	-	11	-	-
Irish Open	-	-	-	MC	7	MC	MC	28	-	2
European Open	-	-	MC	-	10	50	23	18	39	2
Scot Open	-	-	-	-	39	57	40	MC	-	-
British Open	-	-	-	-	18	5	MC	29	20	37
Dutch Open	-	-	-	-	MC	-	51	-	28	9
Scandinavian	-	-	-	-	18	6	63	21	-	-
Wales Open	-	-	-	-	-	-	-	-	-	-
USPGA	-	-	-	-	-	MC	-	-	58	MC
NW Ireland Open	-	-	-	-	-	-	-	2	-	-
WGC NEC Inv'	-	-	-	-	-	-	-	12	27	17
Scottish PGA	-	-	-	-	-	-	-	-	-	-
BMW Int' Open	-	-	-	-	3	9	-	2	20	2
European Mas'	-	-	-	-	18	63	23	-	MC	-
WGC AmEx	-	-	-	-	-	-	-	30	5	-
Troph' Lancome	-	-	-	-	7	-	MC	-	-	-
German Masters	-	-	-	-	8	27	8	2	3	19
Cannes Open	-	-	-	-	8	-	MC	-	-	-
Dunhill Links	-	-	-	-	-	-	-	-	-	5
Masters Madrid	-	-	-	-	7	-	-	-	1	25
Italian Open	-	-	-	-	10	32	43	2	-	-
Volvo Masters	-	-	-	-	29	2	16	2	14	1

Gregory Havret
25/11/76 – Paris, France

An impressive rookie season for the three time French Amateur champion who was signed up by The International Management Group at the start of the year.

Havret won the season-ending Italian Open to earn a two-year exemption on the European Tour.

He also went close to victory in the French Open when finishing fifth and posted three top-ten places last term.

Possesses massive length off the tee and is also fairly straight with the driver.

Turned pro in 1999 after a sparkling amateur career that saw him win five prestige titles.

Sc Av – 71.51 (96th) DD - 289.5 (27th) DA - 65.6 (66th) GIR – 68.2 (72nd) PpGIR – 1.795 (106th) SS – 49.5 (130th)

	'92	'93	'94	'95	'96	'97	'98	'99	'00	'01
Johnnie Walker	-	-	-	-	-	-	-	-	-	-
WGC Matchplay	-	-	-	-	-	-	-	-	-	-
Alfred Dunhill	-	-	-	-	-	-	-	-	-	41
S African Open	-	-	-	-	-	-	-	-	-	-
Heineken Cl'	-	-	-	-	-	-	-	-	-	-
Greg Norman	-	-	-	-	-	-	-	-	-	-
Malaysian Open	-	-	-	-	-	-	-	-	-	MC
S'pore Masters	-	-	-	-	-	-	-	-	-	MC
Dubai Desert	-	-	-	-	-	-	-	-	-	-
Qatar Masters	-	-	-	-	-	-	-	-	-	59
Madeira Open	-	-	-	-	-	-	-	-	-	66
Brazil Open	-	-	-	-	-	-	-	-	-	54
Open de Arg	-	-	-	-	-	-	-	-	-	60
US Masters	-	-	-	-	-	-	-	-	-	-
Moroccan Open	-	-	-	-	-	-	-	-	MC	31
Open de Espana	-	-	-	-	-	-	-	-	-	23
Open de Portugal	-	-	-	-	-	-	-	-	-	37
Open de France	-	-	-	-	-	-	MC	37	-	5
B&H l'national	-	-	-	-	-	-	-	-	-	68
Deutsche Bank	-	-	-	-	-	-	-	-	-	MC
Volvo PGA	-	-	-	-	-	-	-	-	-	-
British Masters	-	-	-	-	-	-	-	-	-	-
English Open	-	-	-	-	-	-	-	-	-	MC
US Open	-	-	-	-	-	-	-	-	-	-
G North Open	-	-	-	-	-	-	-	-	-	8
Irish Open	-	-	-	-	-	-	-	-	-	26
European Open	-	-	-	-	-	-	-	-	-	68
Scot Open	-	-	-	-	-	-	-	72	-	-
British Open	-	-	-	-	-	-	-	-	-	-
Dutch Open	-	-	-	-	-	-	-	-	-	45
Scandinavian	-	-	-	-	-	-	-	-	-	74
Wales Open	-	-	-	-	-	-	-	-	-	-
USPGA	-	-	-	-	-	-	-	-	-	-
NW Ireland Open	-	-	-	-	-	-	-	-	MC	-
WGC NEC Inv'	-	-	-	-	-	-	-	-	-	74
Scottish PGA	-	-	-	-	-	-	-	-	-	-
BMW Int' Open	-	-	-	-	-	-	-	-	-	37
European Mas'	-	-	-	-	-	-	-	MC	-	MC
WGC AmEx	-	-	-	-	-	-	-	-	-	-
Troph' Lancome	-	-	-	-	-	MC	MC	-	38	MC
German Masters	-	-	-	-	-	-	-	-	-	-
Cannes Open	-	-	-	-	-	-	-	-	-	36
Dunhill Links	-	-	-	-	-	-	-	-	-	-
Masters Madrid	-	-	-	-	-	-	-	-	-	80
Italian Open	-	-	-	-	-	-	-	-	-	1
Volvo Masters	-	-	-	-	-	-	-	-	-	60

David Howell

23/6/75 – Swindon, England

Former Walker Cup player who has only once finished outside the top 50 on the Order of Merit since turning pro in 1995.

Only just missed out on a Ryder Cup place in 2001 and enjoyed his best position on the Order of Merit when eight top ten finishes helped him claim 14th place.

He didn't add to his sole European Tour success (the 1999 Dubai Desert Classic), though. Spent some time in Australia in 1998 and won the Australian PGA Championship.

Has the same management team (ISM) as Darren Clarke and Lee Westwood. Played in the inaugural Seve Ballesteros Trophy in 2000.

Sc Av – 70.98 (44th) DD – 282.1 (77th) DA – 59.8 (143rd) GIR – 66.2 (112th) PpGIR – 1.702 (101st) SS – 47.3 (147th)

	'92	'93	'94	'95	'96	'97	'98	'99	'00	'01
Johnnie Walker	-	-	-	-	7	56	-	-		MC
WGC Matchplay	-	-	-	-	-	MC	-	-	-	-
Alfred Dunhill	-	-	8	-	-	-	-	-	43	41
S African Open	-	-	-	-	-	MC	9	-	69	16
Heineken Cl'	-	-	-	-	-	MC	8	-	MC	23
Greg Norman	-	-	-	-	-	-	-	MC	-	
Malaysian Open	-	-	-	-	-	-	27	-	-	46
S'pore Masters	-	-	-	-	-	-	-	-	-	46
Dubai Desert	-	-	-	MC	53	MC	1	64	43
Qatar Masters	-	-	-	-	-	21	28	40	36
Madeira Open	-	-	12	20	-	3	-	66
Brazil Open	-	-	-	-	-	-	-	-	-	-
Open de Arg	-	-	-	-	-	-	-	-	-	-
US Masters	-	-	-	-	-	-	-	-	-	-
Moroccan Open	-	-	-	-	-	-	24	-	MC
Open de Espana	-	-	-	5	11	46	48	58
Open de Portugal	-	-	MC	MC	16	19	MC	9
Open de France	-	-	21	23	8	-	WD	-
B&H I'national	-	58	-	59	52	MC	MC	7
Deutsche Bank	-	-	MC	MC	7	42	9	MC
Volvo PGA	-	-	MC	21	13	62	MC
British Masters	-	-	29	MC	61	MC	MC	2
English Open	-	-	MC	5	41	-	23	35
US Open	-	-	-	-	-	-	-	-	-	-
G North Open	-	-	4	MC	-	31	MC	-
Irish Open	-	-	16	40	MC	15	MC	9
European Open	-	-	MC	MC	MC	MC	MC	30
Scot Open	-	-	20	43	2	23	41	59
British Open	-	-	MC	42	45	-	MC
Dutch Open	-	11	-	30	WD	58	-
Scandinavian	-	MC	MC	34	MC	MC	36
Wales Open	-	-	-	-	-	-	MC
USPGA	-	-	-	-	-	-	-	-	-	-
NW Ireland Open	-	-	-	-	-	-	-	-	-	-
WGC NEC Inv'	-	-	-	-	-	-	-	-	-	-
Scottish PGA	-	-	-	-	-	-	-	-	-	-
BMW Int' Open	-	16	MC	37	5	20	MC
European Mas'	-	40	WD	MC	66	42	64
WGC AmEx	-	-	-	-	-	-	-	-	-	-
Troph' Lancome	-	4	36	MC	MC	70	76
German Masters	-	-	13	MC	42	22	46
Cannes Open	-	-	52	21	16	-	-
Dunhill Links	-	-	-	-	-	-	3
Masters Madrid	-	42	MC	15	MC	15	39
Italian Open	-	10	39	-	MC	21	9
Volvo Masters	-	34	21	49	36	34	10

Jean Hugo

3/12/75 – Stellenbosch, South Africa

An excellent rookie season on the European Tour for this big hitting South African.

Hugo managed four top-ten finishes on his first full term on the main tour, including third place in the Lancome Trophy.

Having turned pro in 1999 his first competitive tournament was in the Open at Carnoustie – he missed the cut by a shot.

A year on the Challenge Tour came next, and after winning the Volvo Finnish Open he was on his to earning his full tour playing privileges.

He was a superb amateur player and won the South African Amateur Championship in 1998.

Sc Av – 71.36 (83rd) DD - 297.6 (4th) DA - 61.7 (117th) GIR – 65.0 (130th) PpGIR – 1.773 (52nd) SS – 53.0 (96th)

	'92	'93	'94	'95	'96	'97	'98	'99	'00	'01
Johnnie Walker	-	-	-	-	-	-	-	-	-	-
WGC Matchplay	-	-	-	-	-	-	-	-	-	-
Alfred Dunhill	-	-	-	-	-	-	-	-	MC	53
S African Open	-	-	-	-	-	-	MC	9	34	MC
Heineken Cl'	-	-	-	-	-	-	-	-	-	-
Greg Norman	-	-	-	-	-	-	-	-	-	-
Malaysian Open	-	-	-	-	-	-	-	-	-	14
S'pore Masters	-	-	-	-	-	-	-	-	-	MC
Dubai Desert	-	-	-	-	-	-	-	-	-	58
Qatar Masters	-	-	-	-	-	-	-	-	-	MC
Madeira Open	-	-	-	-	-	-	-	-	-	-
Brazil Open	-	-	-	-	-	-	-	-	-	-
Open de Arg	-	-	-	-	-	-	-	-	-	-
US Masters	-	-	-	-	-	-	-	-	-	-
Moroccan Open	-	-	-	-	-	-	-	-	-	19
Open de Espana	-	-	-	-	-	-	-	-	-	9
Open de Portugal	-	-	-	-	-	-	-	-	-	MC
Open de France	-	-	-	-	-	-	-	-	-	-
B&H I'national	-	-	-	-	-	-	-	-	-	64
Deutsche Bank	-	-	-	-	-	-	-	-	-	MC
Volvo PGA	-	-	-	-	-	-	-	-	-	63
British Masters	-	-	-	-	-	-	-	MC	-	14
English Open	-	-	-	-	-	-	-	-	-	4
US Open	-	-	-	-	-	-	-	-	-	-
G North Open	-	-	-	-	-	-	-	-	-	20
Irish Open	-	-	-	-	-	-	-	-	-	MC
European Open	-	-	-	-	-	-	-	-	-	MC
Scot Open	-	-	-	-	-	-	-	-	-	MC
British Open	-	-	-	-	-	-	-	-	MC	MC
Dutch Open	-	-	-	-	-	-	-	-	-	-
Scandinavian	-	-	-	-	-	-	-	-	-	-
Wales Open	-	-	-	-	-	-	-	-	-	20
USPGA	-	-	-	-	-	-	-	-	-	-
NW Ireland Open	-	-	-	-	-	-	-	-	MC	-
WGC NEC Inv'	-	-	-	-	-	-	-	-	-	-
Scottish PGA	-	-	-	-	-	-	-	-	-	71
BMW Int' Open	-	-	-	-	-	-	-	-	-	MC
European Mas'	-	-	-	-	-	-	-	MC	-	58
WGC AmEx	-	-	-	-	-	-	-	-	-	-
Troph' Lancome	-	-	-	-	-	-	-	-	-	3
German Masters	-	-	-	-	-	-	-	-	-	25
Cannes Open	-	-	-	-	-	-	-	-	-	-
Dunhill Links	-	-	-	-	-	-	-	-	-	4
Masters Madrid	-	-	-	-	-	-	-	-	-	-
Italian Open	-	-	-	-	-	-	-	-	-	-
Volvo Masters	-	-	-	-	-	-	-	-	-	35

Sponsored by Stan James

Trevor Immelman

16/12/79 – Cape Town, South Africa

Immensely talented South African who enjoyed an excellent amateur career before turning pro in 1999.

Immelman won the prestigious US Public Links title before joining the paid ranks and although he missed out at Q-School in 1999 when trying to gain his full tour card, his season on the Challenge Tour turned out to be good preparation.

He won the Tusker Kenyan Open on his way to graduating to the European Tour and also won the Vodacom Players Championship on the Sunshine Tour in 2000.

Lack of accuracy of the tee was a problem in last season.

Sc Av – 71.34 (81st) DD – 282.1 (77th) DA – 58.6 (159th) GIR – 68.0 (74th) PpGIR – 1.774 (59th) SS – 62.0 (30th)

	'92	'93	'94	'95	'96	'97	'98	'99	'00	'01
Johnnie Walker	-	-	-	-	-	-	-	-	-	52
WGC Matchplay	-	-	-	-	-	-	-	-	-	-
Alfred Dunhill	-	-	-	-	-	-	-	-	MC	34
S African Open	-	-	-	51	38	MC	63	26	-	-
Heineken Cl'	-	-	-	-	-	-	-	-	-	-
Greg Norman	-	-	-	-	-	-	-	-	-	-
Malaysian Open	-	-	-	-	-	-	-	-	-	-
S'pore Masters	-	-	-	-	-	-	-	-	-	-
Dubai Desert	-	-	-	-	-	-	-	41	-	8
Qatar Masters	-	-	-	-	-	-	-	63	-	41
Madeira Open	-	-	-	-	-	-	-	-	-	-
Brazil Open	-	-	-	-	-	-	-	-	-	-
Open de Arg	-	-	-	-	-	-	-	-	-	-
US Masters	-	-	-	-	-	-	-	-	-	-
Moroccan Open	-	-	-	-	-	-	-	-	-	31
Open de Espana	-	-	-	-	-	-	-	-	-	MC
Open de Portugal	-	-	-	-	-	-	-	-	-	19
Open de France	-	-	-	-	-	-	-	-	-	78
B&H I'national	-	-	-	-	-	-	-	MC	-	DQ
Deutsche Bank	-	-	-	-	-	-	-	-	-	MC
Volvo PGA	-	-	-	-	-	-	-	-	-	-
British Masters	-	-	-	-	39	MC	-	-	-	-
English Open	-	-	-	-	-	-	-	-	-	MC
US Open	-	-	-	-	-	-	-	-	-	-
G North Open	-	-	-	-	-	-	-	MC	-	MC
Irish Open	-	-	-	-	-	-	-	-	-	MC
European Open	-	-	-	-	-	-	-	-	-	23
Scot Open	-	-	-	-	-	-	-	-	-	MC
British Open	-	-	-	-	-	-	-	-	-	-
Dutch Open	-	-	-	-	-	-	-	MC	-	MC
Scandinavian	-	-	-	-	-	-	-	-	-	MC
Wales Open	-	-	-	-	-	-	-	-	-	33
USPGA	-	-	-	-	-	-	-	-	-	-
NW Ireland Open	-	-	-	-	-	-	-	-	15	19
WGC NEC Inv'	-	-	-	-	-	-	-	-	-	-
Scottish PGA	-	-	-	-	-	-	-	MC	-	47
BMW Int' Open	-	-	-	-	-	-	-	55	-	67
European Mas'	-	-	-	-	-	-	-	MC	-	46
WGC AmEx	-	-	-	-	-	-	-	-	-	-
Troph' Lancome	-	-	-	-	-	-	-	-	-	8
German Masters	-	-	-	-	-	-	-	-	-	25
Cannes Open	-	-	-	-	-	-	-	-	-	-
Dunhill Links	-	-	-	-	-	-	-	-	-	MC
Masters Madrid	-	-	-	-	-	-	-	-	-	MC
Italian Open	-	-	-	-	-	-	-	-	-	9
Volvo Masters	-	-	-	-	-	-	-	-	-	-

Fredrik Jacobson

26/9/74 – Molndal, Sweden

Monaco based Swedish pro who won and lost his playing privileges three times before establishing himself on the European Tour in 2000.

Last season though, he was unable to show the same sort of form that brought him five top ten finishes and 25th place on the Order of Merit but he was still one of the most consistent performers on the main tour.

Jacobson is yet to win a full tour event but has come second on five occasions (including in last season's German Masters).

A prolific amateur winner, his time on the full tour will surely come soon.

Sc Av – 70.97 (43rd) DD – 282.1 (77th) DA – 55.6 (176th) GIR – 66.1 (116th) PpGIR – 1.751 (18th) SS – 69.0 (11th)

	'92	'93	'94	'95	'96	'97	'98	'99	'00	'01
Johnnie Walker	-	-	MC	-	-	-	MC	-	-	-
WGC Matchplay	-	-	-	-	-	-	-	-	-	-
Alfred Dunhill	-	-	MC	-	-	-	MC	MC	-	-
S African Open	-	-	-	-	-	-	62	MC	-	-
Heineken Cl'	-	-	-	-	-	-	MC	68	-	11
Greg Norman	-	-	-	-	-	-	-	-	-	21
Malaysian Open	-	-	-	-	-	-	-	MC	-	-
S'pore Masters	-	-	-	-	-	-	-	-	-	-
Dubai Desert	-	-	MC	-	MC	20	MC	-	-	55
Qatar Masters	-	-	-	-	-	MC	48	-	-	13
Madeira Open	-	-	-	-	2	10	10	MC	-	-
Brazil Open	-	-	-	-	-	-	-	48	-	-
Open de Arg	-	-	-	-	-	-	-	-	-	-
US Masters	-	-	-	-	-	-	-	-	-	-
Moroccan Open	-	-	MC	-	MC	-	-	31	-	-
Open de Espana	-	-	-	-	8	-	MC	MC	-	42
Open de Portugal	-	-	-	-	-	51	9	-	-	MC
Open de France	-	-	MC	-	MC	-	-	4	-	-
B&H I'national	-	-	-	-	MC	-	MC	MC	-	MC
Deutsche Bank	-	-	MC	-	MC	MC	MC	MC	MC	MC
Volvo PGA	-	-	-	-	-	-	MC	MC	-	MC
British Masters	-	-	-	-	MC	-	MC	MC	73	11
English Open	-	-	-	-	-	46	MC	MC	41	-
US Open	-	-	-	-	-	-	-	-	-	-
G North Open	-	-	-	-	26	-	MC	2	-	17
Irish Open	-	-	-	-	-	62	MC	2	-	60
European Open	-	-	-	-	-	61	MC	MC	MC	MC
Scot Open	-	-	-	-	-	-	MC	MC	-	14
British Open	-	-	-	-	-	-	-	-	MC	MC
Dutch Open	-	-	-	-	-	MC	MC	60	17	MC
Scandinavian	-	-	62	MC	MC	MC	37	MC	-	59
Wales Open	-	-	-	-	-	-	-	3	-	-
USPGA	-	-	-	-	-	-	-	-	-	-
NW Ireland Open	-	-	-	-	-	-	-	-	-	-
WGC NEC Inv'	-	-	-	-	-	-	-	-	-	-
Scottish PGA	-	-	-	-	-	-	-	9	-	MC
BMW Int' Open	-	-	38	-	57	37	MC	MC	-	23
European Mas'	-	-	-	-	32	MC	MC	17	-	5
WGC AmEx	-	-	-	-	-	-	-	-	-	-
Troph' Lancome	-	-	-	-	-	-	18	43	30	54
German Masters	-	-	-	-	-	70	42	-	-	2
Cannes Open	-	-	-	55	-	MC	-	-	-	-
Dunhill Links	-	-	-	-	-	-	-	-	-	48
Masters Madrid	-	-	-	-	MC	-	-	29	MC	MC
Italian Open	-	-	-	58	-	-	-	MC	-	-
Volvo Masters	-	-	-	-	-	-	-	-	10	44

Raphael Jacquelin
8/5/74 – Lyon, France

Having struggled on the European Tour since graduating from the Challenge Tour at the end of 1997, this French pro finally found his feet at the highest level last season.

Six top-ten finishes, including second place in the English Open – his highest full tour finish, saw him finish in 28th place on the Order of Merit – over 50 positions higher than his previous best.

He also scored a hole in one and won a BMW Z8 worth £45,000 at the BMW International.

Burst on to the European Tour scene in 1998 after three wins on the Challenge Tour.

Sc Av – 70.66 (28th) DD – 285.6 (42nd) DA – 65.0 (71st) GIR – 72.7 (16th) PpGIR – 1.804 (121st) SS – 43.9 (169th)

	'92	'93	'94	'95	'96	'97	'98	'99	'00	'01
Johnnie Walker	-	-	-	-	-	-	MC	-	-	-
WGC Matchplay	-	-	-	-	-	-	-	-	-	-
Alfred Dunhill	-	-	-	-	68	23	MC	22	41	-
S African Open	-	-	-	-	-	-	MC	MC	74	65
Heineken Cl'	-	-	-	-	-	40	-	25	MC	-
Greg Norman	-	-	-	-	-	-	-	MC	MC	-
Malaysian Open	-	-	-	-	-	-	MC	MC	-	-
S'pore Masters	-	-	-	-	-	-	-	-	-	-
Dubai Desert	-	-	-	-	-	-	MC	MC	MC	71
Qatar Masters	-	-	-	-	-	-	MC	-	MC	75
Madeira Open	-	-	-	59	49	-	39	-	-	-
Brazil Open	-	-	-	-	-	-	-	MC	5	-
Open de Arg	-	-	-	-	-	-	-	-	-	47
US Masters	-	-	-	-	-	-	-	-	-	-
Moroccan Open	-	-	-	-	MC	19	-	49	31	-
Open de Espana	-	-	MC	-	MC	MC	MC	MC	MC	8
Open de Portugal	-	-	-	-	-	12	25	-	-	-
Open de France	-	-	-	27	29	MC	59	MC	-	-
B&H I'national	-	-	-	-	-	MC	MC	MC	38	7
Deutsche Bank	-	-	-	-	-	MC	38	26	MC	-
Volvo PGA	-	-	-	-	-	MC	MC	13	26	-
British Masters	-	-	-	-	-	-	52	MC	MC	-
English Open	-	-	-	-	-	41	64	MC	2	-
US Open	-	-	-	-	-	-	-	-	-	-
G North Open	-	-	-	-	MC	-	-	-	-	-
Irish Open	-	-	-	-	-	MC	MC	MC	57	-
European Open	-	-	-	-	-	57	MC	MC	12	-
Scot Open	-	-	-	-	-	MC	MC	MC	41	-
British Open	-	-	-	-	MC	-	-	-	13	-
Dutch Open	-	-	-	-	-	11	MC	MC	MC	-
Scandinavian	-	-	-	-	-	39	45	MC	22	-
Wales Open	-	-	-	-	-	-	-	MC	-	-
USPGA	-	-	-	-	-	-	-	-	-	-
NW Ireland Open	-	-	-	-	-	-	-	-	-	-
WGC NEC Inv'	-	-	-	-	-	-	-	-	-	-
Scottish PGA	-	-	-	-	-	MC	3	-	-	-
BMW Int' Open	-	-	-	-	-	26	MC	MC	-	13
European Mas'	-	-	-	-	-	15	MC	28	-	10
WGC AmEx	-	-	-	-	-	-	-	-	-	-
Troph' Lancome	-	-	-	MC	-	DQ	72	24	-	6
German Masters	-	-	-	-	-	-	48	-	-	MC
Cannes Open	-	-	-	32	54	27	-	-	-	14
Dunhill Links	-	-	-	-	-	-	-	-	-	29
Masters Madrid	-	-	-	-	66	27	3	12	-	-
Italian Open	-	-	-	-	61	66	23	26	-	-
Volvo Masters	-	-	-	-	-	-	-	-	-	35

Miguel Angel Jimenez
5/1/64 – Malaga, Spain

Decided to try his luck in America last term and spent much of the season playing on the US Tour.

His success, though, was limited, and he failed to make the Ryder Cup team as a result of playing Stateside.

Jimenez was a stalwart of the European Tour from 1989 to 2000 winning six times (the 1999 Volvo Masters being his last victory) and claiming fourth place in the Order of Merit twice.

His was a member of the victorious 1999 and 2000 Spanish Dunhill Cup teams.

Known 'The Mechanic', his straight hitting game has brought him around £4million in prize money.

Sc Av – 70.67 (29th) DD – 276.4 (129th) DA – 70.9 (15th) GIR – 70.1 (47th) PpGIR – 1.785 (82nd) SS – 78.7 (4th)

	'92	'93	'94	'95	'96	'97	'98	'99	'00	'01
Johnnie Walker	50	9	22	MC	-	-	-	-	-	-
WGC Matchplay	-	-	-	-	-	-	-	33	5	-
Alfred Dunhill	-	-	35	-	-	-	-	-	-	-
S African Open	-	-	-	-	-	-	-	-	-	-
Heineken Cl'	-	-	-	-	-	-	-	-	-	-
Greg Norman	-	-	-	-	-	-	-	-	-	-
Malaysian Open	-	-	-	-	-	-	-	-	-	-
S'pore Masters	-	-	-	-	-	-	-	-	-	-
Dubai Desert	27	44	65	MC	2	37	MC	8	46	-
Qatar Masters	-	-	-	-	-	-	13	MC	-	-
Madeira Open	-	-	-	-	-	-	-	-	-	-
Brazil Open	-	-	-	-	-	-	-	-	-	-
Open de Arg	-	-	-	-	-	-	-	-	-	-
US Masters	-	-	MC	-	-	-	MC	49	10	-
Open de Espana	7	19	57	MC	45	16	26	2	MC	3
Open de Portugal	18	10	7	7	17	69	55	32	-	-
Open de France	60	MC	-	-	-	-	MC	23	-	-
B&H I'national	33	24	58	27	6	23	80	4	9	27
Deutsche Bank	-	-	-	29	MC	7	7	6	14
Volvo PGA	50	MC	4	12	21	54	MC	43	20	MC
British Masters	MC	MC	13	3	4	MC	19	-	-	-
English Open	-	MC	66	-	-	26	41	-	-	-
US Open	-	-	28	-	-	-	23	2	-
G North Open	-	-	-	-	-	-	-	-	-	-
Irish Open	-	-	16	MC	MC	16	21	WD	-	-
European Open	MC	13	MC	30	-	49	27	2	70	MC
Scot Open	MC	-	-	-	16	31	24	MC	MC	41
British Open	-	50	MC	85	MC	MC	MC	-	26	3
Dutch Open	15	29	1	30	WD	17	21	-	-	3
Scandinavian	MC	66	35	6	-	11	WD	-	-	-
Wales Open	-	-	-	-	-	-	-	-	-	-
USPGA	-	-	13	24	-	-	10	64	MC
NW Ireland Open	-	-	-	-	-	-	-	-	-	-
WGC NEC Inv'	-	-	-	-	-	-	27	36	36
Scottish PGA	-	-	-	-	-	-	-	-	-	-
BMW Int' Open	16	12	-	-	9	6	-	-	-	MC
European Mas'	64	2	MC	MC	7	55	7	6	21	46
WGC AmEx	-	-	-	-	-	-	-	2	25	-
Troph' Lancome	42	19	2	51	10	27	1	10	24	-
German Masters	9	24	61	24	27	MC	48	12	6	25
Cannes Open	-	MC	-	MC	-	-	27	-	-	-
Dunhill Links	-	-	-	-	-	-	-	-	-	29
Masters Madrid	7	55	5	47	42	20	1	1	7	31
Italian Open	62	-	-	-	3	MC	-	6	-	-
Volvo Masters	10	10	4	16	34	24	16	1	42	30

Tony Johnstone
2/5/56 – Bulawayo, Zimbabwe

Proved that you can teach an old dog new tricks when a radical over haul of his game bore fruit with victory in the 2001 Qatar Masters – his first European Tour win in three years (and sixth of his career).

This veteran Zimbabwean pro was on the brink of giving up tournament golf but changes to his swing, helped by eye specialist Dr Ken West, brought a change of thought and luck.

Johnstone has been on the European Tour since 1980 and can boast 22 world wide wins, his first in Europe the 1984 Portuguese Open. One of the best bunker players on tour.

Sc Av – 71.10 (112th) DD – 279.7 (99th) DA – 64.8 (74th) GIR – 63.6 (155th) PpGIR – 1.799 (115th) SS – 81.6 (2nd)

	'92	'93	'94	'95	'96	'97	'98	'99	'00	'01
Johnnie Walker	-	14	28	-	-	-	-	-	-	-
WGC Matchplay	-	-	-	-	-	-	-	-	-	-
Alfred Dunhill	-	-	-	3	8	15	1	MC	MC	53
S African Open	-	-	-	-	-	MC	38	MC	37	MC
Heineken Cl'	-	-	-	-	-	-	-	-	-	-
Greg Norman	-	-	-	-	-	-	-	-	-	-
Malaysian Open	-	-	-	-	-	-	-	-	-	-
S'pore Masters	-	-	-	-	-	-	-	-	-	-
Dubai Desert	-	MC	34	-	11	-	MC	-	20	33
Qatar Masters	-	-	-	-	-	-	48	-	69	1
Madeira Open	-	-	-	-	-	-	-	-	-	-
Brazil Open	-	-	-	-	-	-	-	-	-	-
Open de Arg	-	-	-	-	-	-	-	-	-	-
US Masters	-	MC	-	-	-	-	-	-	-	-
Moroccan Open	21	8	-	50	5	10	6	61	-	-
Open de Espana	MC	-	-	WD	MC	-	-	33	-	-
Open de Portugal	-	50	4	34	47	10	38	3	-	-
Open de France	-	6	MC	55	-	32	-	-	-	-
B&H I'national	2	42	WD	MC	MC	MC	MC	61	MC	-
Deutsche Bank	-	-	WD	MC	24	MC	MC	75	MC	-
Volvo PGA	1	6	MC	MC	13	MC	37	MC	43	MC
British Masters	2	3	MC	52	29	59	55	10	MC	73
English Open	-	-	20	MC	44	33	MC	MC	17	71
US Open	-	77	-	-	-	-	-	-	-	-
G North Open	-	-	-	-	67	-	-	-	-	-
Irish Open	22	18	20	MC	54	40	27	MC	53	MC
European Open	49	51	37	MC	MC	-	MC	-	-	MC
Scot Open	-	-	-	66	-	MC	MC	-	MC	-
British Open	34	MC	MC	MC	MC	-	79	-	MC	-
Dutch Open	32	13	MC	54	13	42	MC	MC	DQ	MC
Scandinavian	16	64	-	-	-	-	-	30	50	16
Wales Open	-	-	-	-	-	-	-	-	MC	WD
USPGA	MC	MC	MC	-	-	-	-	-	-	-
NW Ireland Open	-	-	-	-	-	-	-	-	-	-
WGC NEC Inv'	-	-	-	-	-	-	-	-	-	-
Scottish PGA	-	-	-	-	-	-	-	-	-	MC
BMW Int' Open	-	41	-	-	-	-	-	21	55	67
European Mas'	-	MC	-	35	-	-	-	-	-	-
WGC AmEx	-	-	-	-	-	-	-	-	-	-
Troph' Lancome	8	26	46	MC	51	27	MC	64	12	MC
German Masters	-	-	MC	-	48	61	MC	37	MC	68
Cannes Open	5	15	6	29	MC	-	-	-	-	-
Dunhill Links	-	-	-	-	-	-	-	-	-	48
Masters Madrid	-	-	-	-	2	-	-	-	30	MC
Italian Open	24	-	-	8	-	-	WD	-	-	-
Volvo Masters	4	51	27	16	29	53	61	49	23	7

Olle Karlsson
9/4/69 – Falkenberg, Sweden

No relation to Robert, and not as nearly prolific, this Swede is still to win on the European Tour after nine years of trying.

His career, though, has been blighted by injury, with everything from a car accident to a thumb problem keeping him out of the game over the past eight years.

But last season was the first season since 1998 that a trip to the Q-School wasn't necessary.

An excellent amateur golfer he won on the Challenge Tour before joining the full tour and was also successful in the now defunct Novotel Pairs event in 1998 (with Jarmo Sandelin).

Sc Av – 71.23 (68th) DD – 278.2 (114th) DA – 54.7 (180th) GIR – 62.8 (167th) PpGIR – 1.767 (41st) SS – 56.4 (68th)

	'92	'93	'94	'95	'96	'97	'98	'99	'00	'01
Johnnie Walker	-	MC	-	3	-	-	-	-	-	-
WGC Matchplay	-	-	-	-	-	-	-	-	-	-
Alfred Dunhill	-	-	-	35	-	-	-	-	-	MC
S African Open	-	-	-	-	MC	-	WD	-	-	-
Heineken Cl'	-	-	-	-	MC	-	-	-	-	-
Greg Norman	-	-	-	-	-	-	-	-	-	-
Malaysian Open	-	-	-	-	-	-	-	-	-	12
S'pore Masters	-	-	-	-	-	-	-	-	-	MC
Dubai Desert	-	57	MC	25	-	82	-	-	-	-
Qatar Masters	-	-	-	-	-	-	-	MC	-	MC
Madeira Open	-	24	-	4	-	-	-	-	-	-
Brazil Open	-	-	-	-	-	-	-	-	-	31
Open de Arg	-	-	-	-	-	-	-	-	-	8
US Masters	-	-	-	-	-	-	-	-	-	-
Moroccan Open	-	MC	MC	20	37	-	6	-	-	-
Open de Espana	-	MC	-	45	MC	-	11	MC	-23	-
Open de Portugal	-	33	-	-	17	-	MC	-	-	WD
Open de France	-	MC	MC	14	21	-	MC	71	-	56
B&H I'national	-	56	MC	MC	49	46	MC	57	MC	4
Deutsche Bank	-	-	34	18	-	MC	-	77	MC	MC
Volvo PGA	-	MC	-	66	WD	-	MC	43	-	-
British Masters	-	-	-	41	-	19	68	-	5	-
English Open	-	59	WD	MC	57	MC	2	7	-	MC
US Open	-	-	-	-	-	-	-	-	-	-
G North Open	-	-	-	-	-	-	-	-	14	25
Irish Open	-	6	MC	33	MC	-	MC	MC	-	MC
European Open	-	4	-	42	-	-	MC	MC	-	30
Scot Open	-	-	-	-	-	MC	40	MC	-	-
British Open	-	62	-	66	-	-	-	-	-	MC
Dutch Open	-	9	-	WD	-	-	-	71	48	60
Scandinavian	-	DQ	MC	MC	MC	-	39	WD	31	68
Wales Open	-	-	-	-	-	-	-	-	MC	-
USPGA	-	-	-	-	-	-	-	-	-	-
NW Ireland Open	-	-	-	-	-	-	-	11	-	-
WGC NEC Inv'	-	-	-	-	-	-	-	-	-	-
Scottish PGA	-	-	-	-	-	-	-	MC	5	64
BMW Int' Open	-	MC	-	-	-	-	26	-	MC	-
European Mas'	-	WD	-	15	-	MC	-	61	73	46
WGC AmEx	-	-	-	-	-	-	-	-	-	-
Troph' Lancome	-	47	-	41	-	-	33	MC	-	-
German Masters	-	44	64	-	MC	-	MC	-	-	-
Cannes Open	-	MC	MC	MC	-	-	MC	-	-	WD
Dunhill Links	-	-	-	-	-	-	-	-	-	-
Masters Madrid	-	19	-	5	55	-	-	-	-	57
Italian Open	-	-	21	-	-	-	MC	20	-	38
Volvo Masters	-	-	-	46	-	-	59	-	-	61

Robert Karlsson
3/9/69 – St Malmo, Sweden

Tall, blonde Swedish pro who kept up his record of winning in every odd numbered year since 1995 by capturing the Spanish Open title in 2001.

His victory in Valencia was his fourth European Tour win but once again Karlsson just missed out on a Ryder Cup place.

Has been on the full tour for ten years and is yet to drop out of the top 115 of the Order of Merit, and therefore have to go to Q-School.

Has tried some strange diets in the past, but confesses to eating sensibly these days.

Karlsson has a deft touch on the greens and is also a long driver.

Sc Av – 70.39 (18th) DD – 295.3 (7th) DA – 59.5 (150th) GIR – 67.2 (90th) PpGIR – 1.754 (20th) SS – 55.7 (73rd)

	'92	'93	'94	'95	'96	'97	'98	'99	'00	'01
Johnnie Walker	57	MC	22	12	-	MC	MC	-	-	-
WGC Matchplay	-									
Alfred Dunhill	-	-	-	-	MC					
S African Open	-	-	-	40						
Heineken Cl'	-	-	-	MC	20	MC	-	8		
Greg Norman	-	-	-	-	-	-	-	8		
Malaysian Open	-	-	-	-	27	-				
S'pore Masters	-									
Dubai Desert	40	44	MC	MC	62	MC	3	MC	-	MC
Qatar Masters	-	-	-	-	-	40	-	2		
Madeira Open	-	-	18							
Brazil Open	-	-	-	-	-	13	-			
Open de Arg	-									
US Masters	-									
Moroccan Open	2	4	3	3	MC	6	2	-	-	12
Open de Espana	67	-	70	MC	-	MC	26	40	-	1
Open de Portugal	-	33	17	42	MC	-	-	3	-	-
Open de France	MC	-	49	-	MC	11	-	31	-	
B&H I'national	MC	20	5	MC	MC	5	MC	51	28	42
Deutsche Bank	-	-	-	MC	-	-	11	MC	37	
Volvo PGA	MC	MC	MC	49	MC	65	21	13	13	67
British Masters	-	62	MC	35	-	-	-	MC	2	
English Open	-	MC	MC	MC	MC	22	-	13	-	
US Open	-	-	-	-	-	MC	-	-		
G North Open	-									
Irish Open	-	MC	59	MC	MC	-	MC	23	6	
European Open	2	51	53	MC	-	MC	-	4	64	23
Scot Open	20	-	-	MC	43	MC	MC	MC	-	
British Open	5	MC	-	MC	-	MC	MC	MC	MC	MC
Dutch Open	32	MC	-	MC	17	-	-			
Scandinavian	58	7	7	MC	46	38	MC	5	MC	MC
Wales Open	-	-	-	-	-	-	MC	-		
USPGA	-	-	-	-	-	65	41	-	MC	
NW Ireland Open	-									
WGC NEC Inv'	-									
Scottish PGA	-	-	-	-	-	-	-	29		
BMW Int' Open	-	-	-	-	1	43	9	38	53	
European Mas'	-	11	-	45	-	2	7	-	MC	-
WGC AmEx	-	-	-	-	-	-	53	-		
Troph' Lancome	24	-	40	MC	MC	MC	-	38	54	
German Masters	17	2	MC	15	-	30	2	-	-	10
Cannes Open	-	53	13	35	MC	-	-	-	-	WD
Dunhill Links	-	-	-	-	-	-	-	-	35	
Masters Madrid	-	MC	MC	14	-	-	43	MC	-	
Italian Open	-	38	-	MC	-	32	18	66	MC	-
Volvo Masters	23	46	-	49	-	4	26	22	-	4

Soren Kjeldsen
17/5/75 – Arhus, Denmark

Another solid season for this Danish pro who climbed to his highest position in the Order of Merit in 2001.

Third place in the Deutsche Bank tournament ensured his playing rights for a 2002 and he went on to finish 50th in the Order of Merit – his other top ten finish of last term, incidentally, was also in Germany (in the BMW International).

Turned pro n 1995 and graduated to the full tour courtesy of a superb 1997 season on the Challenge Tour (when he won once – the Finnish Open).

His game possesses accuracy off the tee and a good putting touch .

Sc Av – 71.21 (66th) DD – 272.4 (169th) DA – 66.7 (55th) GIR – 66.0 (119th) PpGIR – 1.766 (36th) SS – 45.5 (161st)

	'92	'93	'94	'95	'96	'97	'98	'99	'00	'01
Johnnie Walker	-	-	-	-	-	-	-	-	58	67
WGC Matchplay	-									
Alfred Dunhill	-	-	-	-	-	-	73	MC	MC	-
S African Open	-	-	-	-	-	-	58	43	MC	-
Heineken Cl'	-	-	-	-	-	-	-	MC	33	MC
Greg Norman	-	-	-	-	-	-	-	55	39	
Malaysian Open	-	-	-	-	-	-	-	MC	36	14
S'pore Masters	-	-	-	-	-	-	-	-	-	MC
Dubai Desert	-	-	-	-	-	-	65	MC	MC	
Qatar Masters	-	-	-	-	-	-	60	2	7	27
Madeira Open	-	-	-	-	-	-	41	73	-	59
Brazil Open	-	-	-	-	-	-	-	75	-	
Open de Arg	-									
US Masters	-									
Moroccan Open	-	-	-	-	-	-	MC	-	22	MC
Open de Espana	-	-	-	-	-	-	MC	46	MC	23
Open de Portugal	-	-	-	-	-	-	MC	MC	43	37
Open de France	-	-	-	-	-	-	11	-	31	17
B&H I'national	-	-	-	-	-	-	24	51	63	52
Deutsche Bank	-	-	-	-	-	-	MC	MC	9	3
Volvo PGA	-	-	-	-	-	-	-	MC	38	32
British Masters	-	-	-	-	-	-	12	38	69	MC
English Open	-	-	-	-	-	-	MC	39	-	
US Open	-									
G North Open	-	-	-	-	-	-	-	MC	-	
Irish Open	-	-	-	-	-	-	MC	33	MC	35
European Open	-	-	-	-	-	-	66	49	25	MC
Scot Open	-	-	-	-	-	-	-	MC	MC	MC
British Open	-	-	-	-	-	-	-	-	-	MC
Dutch Open	-	-	-	-	-	-	56	MC	17	MC
Scandinavian	-	-	-	-	-	-	39	30	MC	36
Wales Open	-	-	-	-	-	-	-	-	21	20
USPGA	-									
NW Ireland Open	-									
WGC NEC Inv'	-									
Scottish PGA	-	-	-	-	-	-	-	-	-	47
BMW Int' Open	-	-	-	-	-	-	18	21	32	10
European Mas'	-	-	-	-	-	-	MC	MC	MC	-
WGC AmEx	-									
Troph' Lancome	-	-	-	-	-	-	-	31	30	MC
German Masters	-	-	-	-	-	-	-	MC	32	
Cannes Open	-	-	-	-	-	-	MC	-	-	MC
Dunhill Links	-	-	-	-	-	-	-	-	-	43
Masters Madrid	-	-	-	-	-	-	65	MC	54	MC
Italian Open	-	-	-	-	-	-	MC	31	59	-
Volvo Masters	-	-	-	-	-	-	-	32	-	35

Sponsored by Stan James

Barry Lane

21/6/60 – Hayes, England

After winning the Anderson Consulting Matchplay title in 1995 – and a cool $1million to boot – this former Ryder Cup star went about reconstructing his swing.

Five winless seasons later, Lane finally showed some form in 2001, finishing third in the Scottish Open at Loch Lomond – his first top three position since 1995.

It is not inconceivable that he could win again, as he was one of the best iron players on the European Tour before his dip in form.

He has had four full tour victories, the last of which was the Turespana Open in 1994.

Sc Av – 71.56 (100th) DD – 276.6 (126th) DA – 65.5 (68th) GIR – 68.0 (74th) PpGIR – 1.799 (115th) SS – 41.4 (181st)

	'92	'93	'94	'95	'96	'97	'98	'99	'00	'01
Johnnie Walker	MC	25	26	-	-	45	-	-	-	-
WGC Matchplay	-	-	-	-	-	-	-	-	-	-
Alfred Dunhill	-	-	-	-	-	-	-	-	-	-
S African Open	-	-	-	-	-	MC	-	-	-	-
Heineken Cl'	-	-	-	-	-	MC	-	-	MC	MC
Greg Norman	-	-	-	-	-	-	-	-	MC	MC
Malaysian Open	-	-	-	-	-	-	-	-	-	-
S'pore Masters	-	-	-	-	-	-	-	-	-	-
Dubai Desert	6	3	18	51	34	65	MC	52	MC	MC
Qatar Masters	-	-	-	-	-	-	MC	71	19	73
Madeira Open	-	-	-	-	-	-	-	-	-	-
Brazil Open	-	-	-	-	-	-	-	-	-	-
Open de Arg	-	-	-	-	-	-	-	-	-	-
US Masters	-	-	MC	-	-	-	-	-	-	-
Moroccan Open	-	MC	-	50	-	-	-	-	-	MC
Open de Espana	-	-	-	24	-	47	MC	MC	72	MC
Open de Portugal	7	21	-	28	4	MC	MC	32	23	MC
Open de France	28	22	29	WD	MC	MC	MC	MC	MC	73
B&H I'national	MC	33	18	19	42	MC	18	33	73	MC
Deutsche Bank	-	-	-	-	36	MC	7	MC	MC	
Volvo PGA	15	NC	21	25	MC	10	MC	47	38	MC
British Masters	MC	26	20	61	46	MC	68	MC	29	MC
English Open	4	40	2	7	57	MC	MC	MC	MC	33
US Open	-	16	47	44	-	-	-	-	-	-
G North Open	-	-	-	-	-	19	-	53	-	49
Irish Open	40	-	-	33	66	23	16	52	70	9
European Open	4	MC	9	2	14	MC	10	45	55	MC
Scot Open	52	-	-	-	11	MC	MC	70	32	3
British Open	51	13	MC	20	MC	-	MC	-	-	29
Dutch Open	27	47	72	-	-	-	-	-	-	4
Scandinavian	MC	MC	54	14	50	MC	MC	59	11	MC
Wales Open	-	-	-	-	-	-	-	-	29	49
USPGA	-	71	25	63	-	-	-	-	-	-
NW Ireland Open	-	-	-	-	-	-	-	-	-	
WGC NEC Inv'	-	-	-	-	-	-	-	-	-	
Scottish PGA	-	-	-	-	-	-	-	-	-	
BMW Int' Open	-	-	WD	-	-	MC	34	11	37	
European Mas'	28	1	3	2	32	40	66	28	42	23
WGC AmEx	-	-	-	-	-	-	-	-	-	
Troph' Lancome	8	3	5	64	28	60	18	43	MC	65
German Masters	1	38	-	-	-	WD	-	WD	-	19
Cannes Open	-	8	18	WD	26	16	MC	-	-	
Dunhill Links	-	-	-	-	-	-	-	-	35	
Masters Madrid	24	-	-	8	-	-	-	20	MC	21
Italian Open	9	3	42	-	15	-	MC	54	-	-
Volvo Masters	43	15	39	28	-	-	-	-	-	35

Bernhard Langer

27/8/57 – Anhausen, Germany

Veteran German golfer who rolled back the years to win twice on the European Tour in 2001.

The 38th and 39th wins of his career in Europe came in the Dutch Open and the German Masters – his first victories for four seasons.

Langer regained his place on the Ryder Cup team that he lost in 1999 and also played superbly well in America and in the Majors. The German is well and truly back to his best.

He turned pro in 1972 and can boast two Majors wins (1985 and 1993 US Masters). A brilliant iron player and tough competitor.

Sc Av – 69.82 (5th) DD – 274.8 (150th) DA – 66.0 (63rd) GIR – 74.6 (10th) PpGIR – 1.774 (59th) SS – 78.9 (3rd)

	'92	'93	'94	'95	'96	'97	'98	'99	'00	'01
Johnnie Walker	2	-	3	23	38	7	-	-	-	-
WGC Matchplay	-	-	-	-	-	-	-	9	33	33
Alfred Dunhill	-	-	-	-	-	-	-	14	-	-
S African Open	-	-	-	-	-	4	26	10	-	
Heineken Cl'	-	-	-	-	-	11	2	-	-	
Greg Norman	-	-	-	-	-	-	-	27	-	
Malaysian Open	-	-	-	-	-	-	-	16	-	
S'pore Masters	-	-	-	-	-	-	-	-	-	
Dubai Desert	-	-	26	16	-	4	-	-	-	
Qatar Masters	-	-	-	-	-	-	-	-	-	
Madeira Open	-	-	-	-	-	-	-	-	-	
Brazil Open	-	-	-	-	-	-	-	-	-	
Open de Arg	-	-	-	-	-	-	-	-	-	
US Masters	31	1	24	31	36	7	39	11	28	6
Moroccan Open	32	-	-	-	-	-	-	-	-	
Open de Espana	-	-	5	8	-	36	MC	MC	-	
Open de Portugal	-	-	-	-	-	-	-	-	-	
Open de France	-	-	-	2	-	2	-	-	-	
B&H I'national	10	-	14	19	12	1	-	7	18	57
Deutsche Bank	-	-	1	15	MC	4	11	MC	47	
Volvo PGA	15	1	3	MC	32	29	7	17	MC	
British Masters	5	15	3	-	-	-	69	MC	-	
English Open	-	-	-	-	-	-	-	-	-	
US Open	23	MC	23	36	MC	MC	MC	-	MC	40
G North Open	-	-	-	-	-	-	-	-	-	
Irish Open	6	14	1	20	12	MC	-	33	10	-
European Open	-	-	1	38	MC	7	MC	55	8	
Scot Open	5	-	-	-	MC	-	MC	-	WD	
British Open	59	3	60	24	MC	38	MC	18	11	3
Dutch Open	1	41	-	35	-	-	27	15	2	1
Scandinavian	-	20	-	46	-	-	-	-		
Wales Open	-	-	-	-	-	-	-	-		
USPGA	40	MC	25	-	76	23	-	61	46	MC
NW Ireland Open	-	-	-	-	-	-	-	-		
WGC NEC Inv'	-	-	-	-	-	-	-	-	11	
Scottish PGA	-	-	-	-	-	-	-	-		
BMW Int' Open	2	3	14	2	16	12	4	15	2	16
European Mas'	19	WD	8	-	MC	-	-	-	-	-
WGC AmEx	-	-	-	-	-	-	48	35	-	
Troph' Lancome	8	-	24	5	15	13	MC	MC	-	
German Masters	1	4	34	2	23	1	15	9	6	1
Cannes Open	-	-	-	-	-	-	-	-		
Dunhill Links	-	-	-	-	-	-	-	-		
Masters Madrid	24	12	-	-	-	34	-	54	-	
Italian Open	-	-	-	-	-	1	-	38	-	7
Volvo Masters	8	23	1	5	16	15	6	2	14	7

Paul Lawrie

1/1/69 – Aberdeen, Scotland

After winning the Open at Carnoustie in 1999, Lawrie tried his luck in America for a while.

But a loss of form and one or two niggling injuries resulted in a poor couple of seasons.

But the Scot was back to his best late last term when he won the Dunhill Links Championship.

The conditions were windy, as they were in his three previous European Tour victories, but he seems to relish battling with the elements.

Turned pro in 1986 and joined the European Tour in 1992 after making it through Q-School, he made a superb debut in the Ryder Cup in 1999.

Sc Av – 70.54 (24th) DD – 281.2 (85th) DA – 60.3 (138th) GIR – 69.0 (60th) PpGIR – 1.760 (27th) SS – 57.1 (62nd)

	'92	'93	'94	'95	'96	'97	'98	'99	'00	'01
Johnnie Walker	MC	MC	-	-	-	MC	63	-	-	4
WGC Matchplay	-	-	-	-	-	-	-	-	5	17
Alfred Dunhill	-	-	-	-	37	-	-	-	-	-
S African Open	-	-	-	-	-	-	-	-	-	-
Heineken Cl'	-	-	-	MC	MC	-	58	-	-	-
Greg Norman	-	-	-	-	-	-	-	-	-	-
Malaysian Open	-	-	-	-	-	-	-	-	-	-
S'pore Masters	-	-	-	-	-	-	-	-	-	-
Dubai Desert	61	52	MC	MC	20	MC	MC	MC	4	21
Qatar Masters	-	-	-	-	-	-	48	1	-	27
Madeira Open	-	MC	56	12	34	20	-	25	-	-
Brazil Open	-	-	-	-	-	-	-	-	-	-
Open de Arg	-	-	-	-	-	-	-	-	-	-
US Masters	-	-	-	-	-	-	-	-	MC	MC
Moroccan Open	-	-	-	-	-	-	-	-	-	-
Open de Espana	15	MC	-	MC	-	57	28	7	-	-
Open de Portugal	50	43	36	10	17	37	40	9	-	MC
Open de France	60	14	MC	MC	34	MC	-	-	-	-
B&H I'national	MC	13	MC	MC	6	29	11	MC	MC	19
Deutsche Bank	-	-	-	58	MC	MC	10	MC	15	37
Volvo PGA	28	MC	14	MC	2	MC	MC	47	WD	17
British Masters	-	33	MC	34	46	43	MC	MC	5	-
English Open	MC	48	77	MC	MC	22	MC	17	-	16
US Open	-	-	-	-	-	-	-	-	-	MC
G North Open	-	-	-	-	-	17	-	MC	32	-
Irish Open	6	-	28	MC	54	7	MC	21	-	30
European Open	-	6	MC	9	MC	14	10	15	8	12
Scot Open	MC	-	-	-	MC	MC	MC	59	19	MC
British Open	22	6	24	56	MC	-	MC	1	MC	42
Dutch Open	MC	WD	-	MC	18	MC	21	-	-	-
Scandinavian	MC	MC	65	-	-	MC	-	-	-	29
Wales Open	-	-	-	-	-	-	-	-	-	2
USPGA	-	-	-	-	-	-	-	34	72	MC
NW Ireland Open	-	-	-	-	-	-	21	-	-	-
WGC NEC Inv'	-	-	-	-	-	-	-	21	-	-
Scottish PGA	-	-	-	-	-	-	-	16	18	-
BMW Int' Open	-	19	-	-	12	26	27	-	30	-
European Mas'	-	62	MC	17	40	MC	-	-	34	-
WGC AmEx	-	-	-	-	-	-	37	-	-	-
Troph' Lancome	-	53	-	-	8	57	18	12	-	MC
German Masters	-	MC	WD	MC	18	30	MC	-	17	46
Cannes Open	-	MC	-	MC	MC	11	-	-	-	-
Dunhill Links	-	-	-	-	-	-	-	-	-	1
Masters Madrid	70	MC	56	MC	30	-	-	MC	MC	-
Italian Open	12	-	-	-	-	MC	-	-	-	-
Volvo Masters	-	-	-	-	25	21	-	10	17	24

Daren Lee

10/1/65 – London, England

Burst onto the golfing scene in 1992 after winning the Silver Medal (awarded to the top amateur) in the 1992 Open Championship at Muirfield.

His pro career hasn't been so successful but after struggling on the European Tour for the past four years (he had three trips to the Q-School in that time), Lee comfortably retained his playing privileges for 2002 with his best season to date last year.

Three top ten finishes, including second in the Wales Open – his highest placing in a European Tour event, came his way in 2001.

Not a long hitter, but one that finds plenty of fairways.

Sc Av – 71.46 (91st) DD – 273.3 (163rd) DA – 67.7 (40th) GIR – 67.8 (78th) PpGIR – 1.808 (131st) SS – 40.7 (182nd)

	'92	'93	'94	'95	'96	'97	'98	'99	'00	'01
Johnnie Walker	-	-	-	-	-	-	-	-	-	-
WGC Matchplay	-	-	-	-	-	-	-	-	-	-
Alfred Dunhill	-	-	-	MC	MC	-	-	-	43	MC
S African Open	-	-	-	-	-	-	-	-	-	38
Heineken Cl'	-	-	-	-	-	-	-	MC	-	MC
Greg Norman	-	-	-	-	-	-	-	-	-	21
Malaysian Open	-	-	-	-	-	-	-	MC	MC	-
S'pore Masters	-	-	-	-	-	-	-	-	-	-
Dubai Desert	-	-	-	-	-	-	-	-	60	77
Qatar Masters	-	-	-	-	-	-	-	MC	-	23
Madeira Open	-	-	-	70	-	MC	51	39	18	-
Brazil Open	-	-	-	-	-	-	-	-	MC	3
Open de Arg	-	-	-	-	-	-	-	-	-	8
US Masters	-	-	-	-	-	-	-	-	-	-
Moroccan Open	-	-	MC	-	65	65	7	MC	-	-
Open de Espana	-	-	-	-	-	-	-	MC	MC	71
Open de Portugal	-	-	-	-	MC	-	7	MC	MC	41
Open de France	-	-	-	-	MC	MC	26	MC	41	-
B&H I'national	-	-	-	-	67	-	MC	-	-	WD
Deutsche Bank	-	-	-	-	63	-	-	-	-	28
Volvo PGA	-	-	-	-	-	-	-	-	-	MC
British Masters	-	-	-	-	-	MC	-	18	MC	MC
English Open	-	-	-	-	-	MC	-	MC	63	MC
US Open	-	-	-	-	-	-	-	-	-	-
G North Open	-	-	-	MC	67	-	-	39	22	4
Irish Open	-	-	-	31	-	MC	-	-	-	59
European Open	-	-	-	41	-	MC	-	-	-	12
Scot Open	-	-	-	-	-	-	-	-	-	14
British Open	68	-	-	-	-	MC	-	-	-	MC
Dutch Open	-	-	-	-	-	14	-	66	28	45
Scandinavian	-	-	-	-	-	MC	-	MC	29	MC
Wales Open	-	-	-	-	-	-	-	-	46	2
USPGA	-	-	-	-	-	-	-	-	-	-
NW Ireland Open	-	-	-	-	-	-	-	MC	51	-
WGC NEC Inv'	-	-	-	-	-	-	-	-	-	-
Scottish PGA	-	-	-	-	-	-	-	15	79	61
BMW Int' Open	-	-	-	-	-	63	-	MC	5	MC
European Mas'	-	-	-	-	-	55	-	46	49	-
WGC AmEx	-	-	-	-	-	-	-	-	-	-
Troph' Lancome	-	-	-	-	-	-	-	-	-	MC
German Masters	-	-	-	-	-	-	-	-	-	-
Cannes Open	-	-	-	-	-	WD	-	-	-	39
Dunhill Links	-	-	-	-	-	-	-	-	-	29
Masters Madrid	-	-	-	-	-	60	27	MC	MC	-
Italian Open	-	-	65	-	6	-	-	59	59	56
Volvo Masters	-	-	-	-	-	-	-	-	-	62

Sponsored by Stan James

Thomas Levet
5.9.68 – Paris, France

Unheralded Frenchman who claimed his second European Tour win by capturing the Victor Chandler British Masters after a four-man play-off.

Five other top-ten finishes resulted in 2001 becoming Levet's best season on the European Tour. He finished 19th on the Order of Merit and signed to IMG in August.

His only other European Tour win came at the 1998 Cannes Open, although he has won many non-tour professional events in France, including the Championnat de France on the Challenge Tour in 1992.

Putting has been a problem for Levet, although his approach play is first class.

Sc Av – 70.71 (31st) DD – 281.6 (82nd) DA – 61.4 (122nd) GIR – 74.3 (12th) PpGIR – 1.805 (123rd) SS – 44.4 (166th)

	'92	'93	'94	'95	'96	'97	'98	'99	'00	'01
Johnnie Walker	MC	MC	-	MC	MC	-	-	-	MC	46
WGC Matchplay	-	-	-	-	-	-	-	-	-	-
Alfred Dunhill	-	-	-	MC	MC	-	-	MC	MC	MC
S African Open	-	-	-	-	-	-	-	MC	16	MC
Heineken Cl'	-	-	-	MC	-	-	-	51	MC	-
Greg Norman	-	-	-	-	-	-	-	MC	-	-
Malaysian Open	-	-	-	-	-	-	-	21	36	47
S'pore Masters	-	-	-	-	-	-	-	-	-	MC
Dubai Desert	MC	MC	-	MC	MC	-	-	31	37	66
Qatar Masters	-	-	-	-	-	-	-	MC	54	-
Madeira Open	-	MC	-	MC	MC	-	-	34	-	-
Brazil Open	-	-	-	-	-	-	-	-	27	-
Open de Arg	-	-	-	-	-	-	-	-	-	18
US Masters	-	-	-	-	-	-	-	-	-	-
Moroccan Open	-	MC	-	MC	MC	-	-	-	2	4
Open de Espana	40	MC	MC	MC	MC	-	44	33	54	MC
Open de Portugal	10	MC	45	MC	MC	-	-	38	-	-
Open de France	MC	41	58	MC	MC	MC	MC	MC	50	MC
B&H I'national	MC	46	-	MC	49	-	MC	-	-	MC
Deutsche Bank	-	-	-	-	MC	-	MC	67	MC	24
Volvo PGA	-	61	54	4	MC	-	MC	29	MC	26
British Masters	-	MC	-	MC	MC	-	-	48	43	1
English Open	43	48	17	MC	MC	-	MC	39	MC	-
US Open	-	-	-	-	-	-	-	-	-	-
G North Open	-	-	-	-	-	-	-	31	-	-
Irish Open	MC	-	36	MC	MC	-	MC	61	20	9
European Open	-	MC	-	MC	MC	-	44	52	12	-
Scot Open	-	-	-	-	-	-	40	23	41	50
British Open	-	-	-	-	-	MC	49	-	-	66
Dutch Open	MC	47	MC	16	MC	-	MC	MC	-	-
Scandinavian	MC	MC	MC	25	MC	-	16	MC	31	25
Wales Open	-	-	-	-	-	-	MC	-	29	8
USPGA	-	-	-	-	-	-	-	-	-	-
NW Ireland Open	-	-	-	-	-	-	-	-	-	-
WGC NEC Inv'	-	-	-	-	-	-	-	-	-	-
Scottish PGA	-	-	-	-	-	-	-	-	-	MC
BMW Int' Open	50	MC	60	MC	MC	-	-	MC	46	3
European Mas'	49	MC	20	77	MC	-	MC	-	MC	-
WGC AmEx	-	-	-	-	-	-	-	-	-	-
Troph' Lancome	47	58	53	45	-	MC	18	74	63	38
German Masters	-	MC	-	MC	-	-	MC	26	MC	58
Cannes Open	MC	MC	-	MC	MC	56	1	-	-	3
Dunhill Links	-	-	-	-	-	-	-	-	-	MC
Masters Madrid	25	MC	-	MC	-	-	-	MC	MC	-
Italian Open	35	-	-	MC	46	-	23	47	MC	-
Volvo Masters	-	-	-	-	-	-	-	-	-	35

Stephen Leaney
10.3.69 – Busselton, Australia

Australian pro who may look to the US Tour in the future to continue his career. Came to Europe in 1998 after seven victories in Australia, including one as an amateur.

His early career was interrupted by injury – he had 18 months out of the game between 1993 and 1994 due to a blood clot – but since joining the European Tour full time in 1998 he has won three times.

Last season was his poorest as he managed just one top-ten finish and placed a lowly 90th in the Order of Merit.

An excellent ball striker and good putter.

Sc Av – 71.18 (62nd) DD – 275.9 (133rd) DA – 65.4 (170th) GIR – 66.4 (108th) PpGIR – 1.767 (41st) SS – 51.4 (107th)

	'92	'93	'94	'95	'96	'97	'98	'99	'00	'01
Johnnie Walker	-	-	-	-	MC	7	8	-	-	-
WGC Matchplay	-	-	-	-	-	-	-	33	-	-
Alfred Dunhill	-	-	-	-	-	-	-	3	-	-
S African Open	-	-	-	-	-	-	-	MC	-	-
Heineken Cl'	-	-	-	-	44	22	MC	MC	5	MC
Greg Norman	-	-	-	-	-	-	-	-	MC	21
Malaysian Open	-	-	-	-	-	-	-	-	-	-
S'pore Masters	-	-	-	-	-	-	-	-	-	-
Dubai Desert	-	-	-	-	-	-	-	-	MC	-
Qatar Masters	-	-	-	-	-	-	-	-	3	-
Madeira Open	-	-	-	-	-	-	-	-	-	-
Brazil Open	-	-	-	-	-	-	-	-	-	-
Open de Arg	-	-	-	-	-	-	-	-	-	-
US Masters	-	-	-	-	-	-	-	-	-	-
Moroccan Open	-	-	-	-	-	-	1	-	-	-
Open de Espana	-	-	-	-	-	-	44	-	-	-
Open de Portugal	-	-	-	-	-	-	29	-	-	-
Open de France	-	-	-	-	-	-	-	MC	22	17
B&H I'national	-	-	-	-	-	-	44	29	MC	MC
Deutsche Bank	-	-	-	-	-	-	MC	23	35	MC
Volvo PGA	-	-	-	-	-	-	16	4	43	21
British Masters	-	-	-	-	-	-	55	9	73	22
English Open	-	-	-	-	-	-	10	3	47	65
US Open	-	-	-	-	-	-	-	MC	-	-
G North Open	-	-	-	-	-	-	-	8	-	-
Irish Open	-	-	-	-	-	-	MC	15	32	35
European Open	-	-	-	-	-	-	32	55	46	23
Scot Open	-	-	-	-	-	-	62	37	22	MC
British Open	-	-	-	MC	-	-	MC	MC	MC	MC
Dutch Open	-	-	-	-	-	-	1	15	1	9
Scandinavian	-	-	-	-	-	-	25	-	-	-
Wales Open	-	-	-	-	-	-	-	-	46	-
USPGA	-	-	-	-	-	-	68	MC	-	-
NW Ireland Open	-	-	-	-	-	-	-	-	-	-
WGC NEC Inv'	-	-	-	-	-	-	-	-	-	-
Scottish PGA	-	-	-	-	-	-	-	-	-	MC
BMW Int' Open	-	-	-	-	-	-	-	-	-	MC
European Mas'	-	-	-	-	-	-	52	-	23	16
WGC AmEx	-	-	-	-	-	-	-	-	-	-
Troph' Lancome	-	-	-	-	-	-	MC	31	38	65
German Masters	-	-	-	-	-	-	-	67	56	32
Cannes Open	-	-	-	-	-	-	-	-	-	-
Dunhill Links	-	-	-	-	-	-	-	-	-	MC
Masters Madrid	-	-	-	-	-	-	-	-	-	-
Italian Open	-	-	-	-	-	-	31	-	-	-
Volvo Masters	-	-	-	-	-	-	12	32	23	-

Jonathan Lomas
7/5/68 – Chesterfield, England

Rookie of the Year in 1994, Lomas finished 77th in the Order of Merit in 2001, comfortably retaining his playing privileges for 2002.

His run of the European Tour has been unbroken since stepping up fron the Challenge Tour in 1994.

A three-time winner on the feeder tour, he claimed his maiden European Tour win in the 1996 Chemapol Trophy. Can come up with some spectacular shots.

He made the first hole in one of the 2000 season and in the Alfred Dunhill Championship and made the 4th albatross of the European Tour last term.

Sc Av – 71.19 (65th) DD – 276.6 (126th) DA – 68.3 (34th) GIR – 71.1 (27th) PpGIR – 1.805 (123rd) SS – 52.6 (99th)

	'92	'93	'94	'95	'96	'97	'98	'99	'00	'01
Johnnie Walker	-	-	50	WD	MC	50	45	-	MC	52
WGC Matchplay	-	-	-	-	-	-	-	-	-	-
Alfred Dunhill	-	-	-	-	MC	-	MC	MC	22	16
S African Open	-	-	-	-	-	MC	34	10	43	MC
Heineken Cl'	-	-	-	-	55	MC	MC	-	38	MC
Greg Norman	-	-	-	-	-	-	-	-	-	MC
Malaysian Open	-	-	-	-	-	-	-	58	-	-
S'pore Masters	-	-	-	-	-	-	-	-	-	-
Dubai Desert	-	-	4	MC	48	MC	33	35	56	MC
Qatar Masters	-	-	-	-	-	-	MC	MC	MC	59
Madeira Open	-	-	MC	-	-	-	MC	-	-	-
Brazil Open	-	-	-	-	-	-	-	-	59	MC
Open de Arg	-	-	-	-	-	-	-	-	-	47
US Masters	-	-	-	-	-	-	-	-	-	-
Moroccan Open	-	-	17	66	MC	-	-	-	-	-
Open de Espana	-	-	6	-	WD	MC	64	MC	54	16
Open de Portugal	-	-	MC	MC	MC	MC	4	MC	65	MC
Open de France	-	-	58	22	MC	MC	MC	64	2	37
B&H I'national	-	-	3	MC	MC	52	38	16	9	42
Deutsche Bank	-	-	-	63	MC	-	WD	MC	MC	MC
Volvo PGA	-	-	14	17	MC	78	41	MC	MC	45
British Masters	-	-	42	22	MC	49	39	32	MC	MC
English Open	-	-	MC	MC	MC	MC	MC	MC	MC	26
US Open	-	-	-	-	-	-	-	-	-	-
G North Open	-	-	-	-	-	19	-	39	45	25
Irish Open	-	-	MC	33	MC	55	68	52	MC	35
European Open	-	-	-	60	-	2	MC	MC	MC	40
Scot Open	-	-	-	-	4	MC	MC	MC	38	MC
British Open	-	-	11	66	-	33	-	-	-	-
Dutch Open	-	-	31	50	MC	-	11	8	WD	45
Scandinavian	-	-	-	25	MC	MC	30	-	-	MC
Wales Open	-	-	-	-	-	-	-	-	-	20
USPGA	-	-	-	-	-	-	-	-	-	-
NW Ireland Open	-	-	-	-	-	-	-	-	-	-
WGC NEC Inv'	-	-	-	-	-	-	-	-	-	-
Scottish PGA	-	-	-	-	-	-	DQ	16	7	
BMW Int' Open	-	-	MC	34	MC	74	MC	50	73	73
European Mas'	-	-	MC	MC	-	-	52	-	MC	MC
WGC AmEx	-	-	-	-	-	-	-	-	-	-
Troph' Lancome	-	-	49	-	21	22	MC	MC	58	23
German Masters	-	-	DQ	MC	48	MC	MC	WD	-	46
Cannes Open	-	-	27	42	52	MC	43	-	-	-
Dunhill Links	-	-	-	-	-	-	-	-	-	43
Masters Madrid	-	-	56	27	30	30	-	-	MC	-
Italian Open	-	-	-	58	3	17	MC	MC	31	17
Volvo Masters	-	-	40	-	20	-	-	65	-	-

Peter Lonard
17/7/67 – Sydney, Australia

Australian born Sunninghill-based pro who comfortably retained his playing privileges for 2002 despite playing in just 20 events last season.

Lonard is yet to win on the European Tour but can boast two victories on the AZ Tour, including the 1997 Eriksson Masters, when he went on to top the Australasian Order of Merit, and the Ford Open Championship in 2000.

Missed most of the 1993 and 1994 seasons after contracting Ross River Fever.

A powerful and accurate driver of the ball whose bunker stats leave plenty to be desired.

Sc Av – 70.99 (45th) DD – 286.0 (40th) DA – 68.3 (34th) GIR – 70.5 (39th) PpGIR – 1.781 (71st) SS – 49.3 (132nd)

	'92	'93	'94	'95	'96	'97	'98	'99	'00	'01
Johnnie Walker	63	-	-	-	MC	2	12	-	17	35
WGC Matchplay	-	-	-	-	-	-	-	-	-	-
Alfred Dunhill	-	-	-	-	-	-	-	10	22	-
S African Open	-	-	-	-	-	-	-	MC	26	-
Heineken Cl'	-	-	-	-	MC	41	25	2	MC	11
Greg Norman	-	-	-	-	-	-	-	-	55	6
Malaysian Open	-	-	-	-	-	-	-	-	-	-
S'pore Masters	-	-	-	-	-	-	-	-	-	-
Dubai Desert	-	-	-	-	-	-	-	-	46	58
Qatar Masters	-	-	-	-	-	-	-	-	54	27
Madeira Open	-	-	-	-	-	-	-	-	-	-
Brazil Open	-	-	-	-	-	-	-	-	28	-
Open de Arg	-	-	-	-	-	-	-	-	-	-
US Masters	-	-	-	-	-	-	-	-	-	-
Moroccan Open	-	-	-	-	-	-	-	-	-	3
Open de Espana	21	-	-	-	-	-	MC	-	-	16
Open de Portugal	10	-	-	-	-	-	-	-	-	-
Open de France	20	-	-	-	-	11	MC	-	56	-
B&H I'national	MC	-	-	-	-	MC	MC	MC	52	MC
Deutsche Bank	-	-	-	-	-	-	WD	MC	MC	20
Volvo PGA	-	-	-	-	-	MC	5	29	MC	63
British Masters	-	-	-	-	-	49	MC	-	-	-
English Open	34	-	-	-	-	33	-	25	MC	-
US Open	-	-	-	-	-	-	-	-	-	66
G North Open	-	-	-	-	-	-	-	MC	MC	-
Irish Open	MC	-	-	-	-	-	8	57	5	26
European Open	-	-	-	-	-	-	MC	10	MC	45
Scot Open	-	-	-	-	-	MC	MC	MC	72	21
British Open	-	-	-	-	-	24	-	49	-	47
Dutch Open	MC	-	-	-	-	-	17	30	MC	MC
Scandinavian	66	-	-	-	-	-	59	MC	MC	16
Wales Open	-	-	-	-	-	-	-	-	-	-
USPGA	-	-	-	-	-	-	-	-	-	-
NW Ireland Open	-	-	-	-	-	-	-	-	-	-
WGC NEC Inv'	-	-	-	-	-	-	-	-	-	-
Scottish PGA	-	-	-	-	-	-	-	-	-	-
BMW Int' Open	MC	-	-	-	-	-	-	-	-	-
European Mas'	MC	-	-	-	-	4	15	-	-	-
WGC AmEx	-	-	-	-	-	-	-	-	-	-
Troph' Lancome	-	-	-	-	-	65	15	-	-	-
German Masters	-	-	-	-	-	-	MC	-	-	-
Cannes Open	-	-	-	-	-	-	8	-	-	-
Dunhill Links	-	-	-	-	-	-	-	-	-	56
Masters Madrid	56	-	-	-	-	-	-	-	43	MC
Italian Open	-	-	-	-	-	-	MC	-	26	44
Volvo Masters	-	-	-	-	-	57	12	-	-	16

Sponsored by Stan James

Mikael Lundberg
13/8/73 – Helsingborg, Sweden

Turned pro in 1995 but only made it onto the European Tour for the first time last season.

He graduated from the Challenge Tour, after an ultra consistent 2000 season when he missed just three cuts and finished second twice.

His rookie year on the full tour started brightly, with two top ten finishes coming in his opening five starts, and his Order of Merit position of 63rd meant he comfortably retained his card.

He managed to win the 1997 Himmerland Open on the Challenge Tour and was a star amateur player. Possesses a deft touch on the greens.

Sc Av – 71.47 (94th) DD – 275.0 (144th) DA – 60.6 (131st) GIR – 63.4 (158th) PpGIR – 1.748 (13th) SS – 56.5 (67th)

	'92	'93	'94	'95	'96	'97	'98	'99	'00	'01
Johnnie Walker	-	-	-	-	-	-	-	-	-	MC
WGC Matchplay	-	-	-	-	-	-	-	-	-	-
Alfred Dunhill	-	-	-	-	-	-	-	-	-	49
S African Open	-	-	-	-	-	-	-	-	-	5
Heineken Cl'	-	-	-	-	-	-	-	-	-	-
Greg Norman	-	-	-	-	-	-	-	-	-	-
Malaysian Open	-	-	-	-	-	-	-	-	-	47
S'pore Masters	-	-	-	-	-	-	-	-	-	7
Dubai Desert	-	-	-	-	-	-	-	-	-	MC
Qatar Masters	-	-	-	-	-	-	-	-	-	-
Madeira Open	-	-	-	-	-	-	-	-	24	-
Brazil Open	-	-	-	-	-	-	-	-	-	MC
Open de Arg	-	-	-	-	-	-	-	-	-	26
US Masters	-	-	-	-	-	-	-	-	-	-
Moroccan Open	-	-	-	-	-	-	-	24	14	-
Open de Espana	-	-	-	-	-	-	-	-	-	64
Open de Portugal	-	-	-	-	-	-	-	-	-	15
Open de France	-	-	-	-	-	-	-	-	-	-
B&H I'national	-	-	-	-	-	-	-	-	-	MC
Deutsche Bank	-	-	-	-	-	-	-	-	-	5
Volvo PGA	-	-	-	-	-	-	-	-	-	21
British Masters	-	-	-	-	-	-	-	-	-	-
English Open	-	-	-	-	-	-	-	-	-	MC
US Open	-	-	-	-	-	-	-	-	-	-
G North Open	-	-	-	-	-	-	-	-	-	-
Irish Open	-	-	-	-	-	-	-	-	-	48
European Open	-	-	-	-	-	-	-	-	-	34
Scot Open	-	-	-	-	-	-	-	-	-	MC
British Open	-	-	-	-	-	-	-	-	-	-
Dutch Open	-	-	-	-	-	-	-	-	-	60
Scandinavian	-	66	54	-	-	-	-	77	-	MC
Wales Open	-	-	-	-	-	-	-	-	-	MC
USPGA	-	-	-	-	-	-	-	-	-	-
NW Ireland Open	-	-	-	-	-	MC	2	-	-	-
WGC NEC Inv'	-	-	-	-	-	-	-	-	-	-
Scottish PGA	-	-	-	-	-	-	-	-	-	MC
BMW Int' Open	-	-	-	-	-	-	-	-	-	23
European Mas'	-	-	-	-	-	-	-	-	-	MC
WGC AmEx	-	-	-	-	-	-	-	-	-	-
Troph' Lancome	-	-	-	-	-	-	-	-	-	54
German Masters	-	-	-	-	-	-	-	-	-	-
Cannes Open	-	-	-	-	-	-	-	-	-	MC
Dunhill Links	-	-	-	-	-	-	-	-	-	52
Masters Madrid	-	-	-	-	-	-	-	-	-	MC
Italian Open	-	-	-	-	-	-	-	-	-	WD
Volvo Masters	-	-	-	-	-	-	-	-	-	44

David Lynn
20/10/73 – Billinge, England

Enjoyed his best season on the European Tour in 2001, finishing 40th on the Order of Merit.

This former English amateur international managed three top-ten finishes last season, including second place in the Morrocan Open – a position that equalled his best of the European Tour.

His career on the full tour has been something of a stop start affair and his has spent some time on the Challenge Tour, winning the Danish Open in 1997.

Managed by Barry Hearn's Matchroom Sport team whose booming drives are a feature of his play.

Sc Av – 70.88 (37th) DD – 289.8 (24th) DA – 62.8 (101st) GIR – 67.8 (78th) PpGIR – 1.783 (76th) SS – 46.5 (154th)

	'92	'93	'94	'95	'96	'97	'98	'99	'00	'01
Johnnie Walker	-	-	-	-	-	-	-	-	-	-
WGC Matchplay	-	-	-	-	-	-	-	-	-	-
Alfred Dunhill	-	-	-	-	-	-	MC	-	5	MC
S African Open	-	-	-	-	-	-	48	-	-	26
Heineken Cl'	-	-	-	-	-	-	-	-	-	54
Greg Norman	-	-	-	-	-	-	-	-	-	39
Malaysian Open	-	-	-	-	-	-	-	-	48	-
S'pore Masters	-	-	-	-	-	-	-	-	-	-
Dubai Desert	-	-	-	-	-	-	MC	-	37	17
Qatar Masters	-	-	-	-	-	-	MC	-	27	20
Madeira Open	-	-	-	-	MC	MC	63	-	7	7
Brazil Open	-	-	-	-	-	-	-	-	39	-
Open de Arg	-	-	-	-	-	-	-	-	-	-
US Masters	-	-	-	-	-	-	-	-	-	-
Moroccan Open	-	-	-	-	-	-	MC	13	-	2
Open de Espana	-	-	-	-	-	-	MC	-	60	49
Open de Portugal	-	-	-	-	-	-	74	-	57	60
Open de France	-	-	-	-	-	-	MC	-	59	-
B&H I'national	-	-	-	-	-	-	48	-	38	68
Deutsche Bank	-	-	-	-	-	-	WD	-	35	MC
Volvo PGA	-	-	-	-	-	-	-	-	-	45
British Masters	-	-	-	-	-	-	MC	-	MC	57
English Open	-	-	-	-	-	-	MC	-	9	12
US Open	-	-	-	-	-	-	-	-	-	-
G North Open	-	-	-	-	44	-	-	51	36	67
Irish Open	-	-	-	-	-	-	27	-	59	30
European Open	-	-	-	-	-	-	61	-	12	MC
Scot Open	-	-	-	-	-	-	MC	-	MC	41
British Open	-	-	-	-	-	-	-	-	-	-
Dutch Open	-	-	-	-	-	-	58	-	MC	MC
Scandinavian	-	-	-	-	-	-	34	-	38	-
Wales Open	-	-	-	-	-	-	-	-	12	33
USPGA	-	-	-	-	-	-	-	-	-	-
NW Ireland Open	-	-	-	-	-	-	-	56	-	-
WGC NEC Inv'	-	-	-	-	-	-	-	-	-	-
Scottish PGA	-	-	-	-	-	-	-	MC	-	22
BMW Int' Open	-	-	-	-	-	-	51	-	32	67
European Mas'	-	-	-	-	-	-	MC	-	MC	37
WGC AmEx	-	-	-	-	-	-	-	-	-	-
Troph' Lancome	-	-	-	-	-	-	-	-	-	14
German Masters	-	-	-	-	-	-	-	-	-	6
Cannes Open	-	-	-	-	-	-	37	-	-	-
Dunhill Links	-	-	-	-	-	-	-	-	-	17
Masters Madrid	-	-	-	-	-	-	MC	-	-	12
Italian Open	-	-	-	-	-	-	10	-	78	-
Volvo Masters	-	-	-	-	-	-	-	-	-	24

Paul McGinley

16/12/66 – Dublin, Ireland

Irishman who made the Ryder Cup team for the first time after a string of impressive results in 2001, including a third European Tour win – in the Wales Open.

Notched 12 top-ten finishes last season, missing the cut just once and placing eighth in the Order of Merit – his highest finish.

Turned pro in 1991 after playing in the 1991 Walker Cup and won his first tournament on the full tour in 1996 – the Hohe Brucke Open.

Perhaps has underachieved in his career but has the talent to win many events. His game doesn't have an obvious weakness.

Sc Av – 69.82 (5th) DD – 283.3 (63rd) DA – 68.1 (38th) GIR – 75.6 (6th) PpGIR – 1.766 (36th) SS – 53.9 (89th)

	'92	'93	'94	'95	'96	'97	'98	'99	'00	'01
Johnnie Walker	37	MC	22	MC	14	MC	21	-	MC	-
WGC Matchplay	-	-	-	-	-	-	-	-	-	33
Alfred Dunhill	-	-	-	35	20	-	-	-	5	16
S African Open	-	-	-	-	-	-	-	20	-	21
Heineken Cl'	-	-	-	2	29	20	-	18	-	-
Greg Norman	-	-	-	-	-	-	-	27	-	-
Malaysian Open	-	-	-	-	-	-	21	-	-	-
S'pore Masters	-	-	-	-	-	-	-	-	-	-
Dubai Desert	53	5	51	22	48	6	33	3	2	9
Qatar Masters	-	-	-	-	-	21	16	7	13	
Madeira Open	-	27	-	-	-	-	-	46	-	
Brazil Open	-	-	-	-	-	-	-	-	-	
Open de Arg	-	-	-	-	-	-	-	-	-	
US Masters	-	-	-	-	-	-	-	-	-	
Moroccan Open	-	44	MC	24	-	-	-	-	-	
Open de Espana	MC	19	33	MC	-	53	MC	2	-	
Open de Portugal	55	MC	-	4	55	37	-	-	3	37
Open de France	12	2	5	MC	4	MC	16	-	68	7
B&H I'national	-	13	18	MC	MC	23	24	20	18	2
Deutsche Bank	-	-	-	17	7	5	22	63	9	10
Volvo PGA	31	56	MC	44	37	MC	10	MC	20	26
British Masters	MC	MC	37	54	MC	WD	10	MC	-	
English Open	78	-	MC	16	44	MC	-	-	-	10
US Open	-	-	-	-	-	MC	-	-	-	
G North Open	-	-	-	-	12	11	-	39	-	
Irish Open	26	12	MC	28	32	40	MC	MC	3	48
European Open	-	21	28	MC	14	14	20	MC	13	MC
Scot Open	-	-	-	-	29	43	32	MC	-	3
British Open	MC	MC	MC	-	14	65	MC	-	20	54
Dutch Open	-	14	15	MC	-	33	30	15	MC	40
Scandinavian	-	71	MC	14	-	34	16	-	-	
Wales Open	-	-	-	-	-	-	-	-	69	1
USPGA	-	-	-	-	-	-	MC	22		
NW Ireland Open	-	-	-	-	-	-	-	-	-	
WGC NEC Inv'	-	-	-	-	-	-	-	-	23	26
Scottish PGA	-	-	-	-	-	-	-	-	-	
BMW Int' Open	MC	MC	-	-	-	57	MC	69	-	10
European Mas'	64	33	MC	-	-	-	-	-	-	
WGC AmEx	-	-	-	-	-	-	-	-	35	
Troph' Lancome	-	-	34	14	MC	-	26	24	16	
German Masters	-	-	-	MC	5	27	6	17	14	8
Cannes Open	-	74	MC	35	20	6	MC	-	-	
Dunhill Links	-	-	-	-	-	-	-	-	9	
Masters Madrid	MC	MC	40	3	MC	-	3	-	5	
Italian Open	MC	-	-	MC	-	13	MC	-	-	
Volvo Masters	-	42	42	-	45	46	19	32	34	2

Mark McNulty

25/10/53 – Zimbabwe

Veteran Zimbabwean pro who rolled back the years to win the South African Open in 2001 – his 16th European Tour win and first for five years.

Turned pro in 1977 and has been a regular on the European Tour since 1978, finishing second on the Order of Merit in both 1987 and 1990.

He won three times in 1996, including the prestigious Volvo Masters and has won over £3million in official prize money in his career.

Has won 49 titles worldwide and his straight hitting driving game can still set up plenty of birdie opportunities.

Sc Av – 71.6 (58th) DD – 273.9 (158th) DA – 67.4 (46th) GIR – 68.7 (65th) PpGIR – 1.779 (67th) SS – 52.8 (97th)

	'92	'93	'94	'95	'96	'97	'98	'99	'00	'01
Johnnie Walker	-	-	-	-	-	-	-	61	-	
WGC Matchplay	-	-	-	-	-	-	-	-	-	9
Alfred Dunhill	-	-	-	3	MC	20	10	7	36	23
S African Open	-	-	-	-	3	7	34	24	1	
Heineken Cl'	-	-	-	-	-	-	-	-	-	
Greg Norman	-	-	-	-	-	-	-	-	-	
Malaysian Open	-	-	-	-	-	-	-	-	-	
S'pore Masters	-	-	-	-	-	-	-	-	-	
Dubai Desert	-	-	-	-	-	-	-	-	68	
Qatar Masters	-	-	-	-	-	-	-	-	-	
Madeira Open	-	-	-	-	-	-	-	-	-	
Brazil Open	-	-	-	-	-	-	-	-	-	
Open de Arg	-	-	-	-	-	-	-	-	-	
US Masters	-	-	-	MC	-	MC	-	-	-	
Moroccan Open	-	-	-	-	-	-	-	-	-	
Open de Espana	-	-	2	-	-	67	-	46	-	
Open de Portugal	-	-	-	-	-	-	-	-	-	
Open de France	-	20	-	45	-	-	-	-	-	
B&H I'national	-	MC	MC	-	MC	MC	-	MC	MC	35
Deutsche Bank	-	-	-	40	MC	MC	-	52	37	
Volvo PGA	48	5	MC	-	4	MC	37	38	34	MC
British Masters	13	19	-	-	-	-	-	18	4	22
English Open	-	-	-	-	41	10	33	17	44	
US Open	33	-	MC	-	28	-	-	-	-	
G North Open	-	-	-	-	-	-	-	-	-	
Irish Open	MC	WD	MC	-	-	-	39	MC	MC	
European Open	-	-	-	-	-	-	-	18	MC	
Scot Open	3	-	-	8	MC	MC	MC	MC	-	
British Open	28	14	11	39	14	32	MC	37	11	MC
Dutch Open	-	-	-	1	WD	MC	25	MC	32	
Scandinavian	37	1	-	-	-	-	-	-	53	
Wales Open	-	-	-	-	-	-	-	5	33	
USPGA	-	MC	15	-	MC	-	-	-	MC	
NW Ireland Open	-	-	-	-	-	-	-	-	-	
WGC NEC Inv'	-	-	-	-	-	-	-	-	-	
Scottish PGA	-	-	-	-	-	-	-	-	-	
BMW Int' Open	8	1	14	31	-	-	-	46	MC	
European Mas'	-	MC	-	-	-	-	-	34	-	
WGC AmEx	-	-	-	-	-	-	-	-	-	
Troph' Lancome	-	34	-	-	-	-	10	38	30	
German Masters	57	31	-	43	-	-	30	17	41	
Cannes Open	-	2	47	-	-	-	-	-	-	
Dunhill Links	-	-	-	-	-	-	-	-	MC	
Masters Madrid	2	-	-	-	-	-	-	-	39	
Italian Open	-	-	-	-	-	13	-	-		
Volvo Masters	32	6	6	-	1	5	36	22	34	35

Colin Montgomerie

23/6/63 – Glasgow, Scotland

Put personal problems behind him in 2001 to record three worldwide wins – two on the European Tour and one in Australia.

His success Down Under in the Australian Masters was followed up by wins in the Irish Open and the Scandinavian Masters (taking his European Tour title haul to 26).

Monty remains a world class player and still believes he can win a Major Championship. Won the Order of Merit a record seven times (1993-1999).

A naturally talented player whose strong driving game sets up plenty of birdie opportunities. Gained a little weight in the summer and reckoned it helped his timing.

Sc Av – 69.75 (4th) DD – 278.9 (108th) DA – 69.7 (24th) GIR – 75.1 (9th) PpGIR – 1.738 (4th) SS – 48.8 (137th)

	'92	'93	'94	'95	'96	'97	'98	'99	'00	'01
Johnnie Walker	21	2	6	7	-	15	-	-	-	-
WGC Matchplay	-	-	-	-	-	-	-	33	17	-
Alfred Dunhill	-	-	-	-	-	-	-	-	-	-
S African Open	-	-	-	-	-	-	-	-	-	-
Heineken Cl'	-	-	-	-	22	-	-	-	-	-
Greg Norman	-	-	-	-	-	-	-	-	-	-
Malaysian Open	-	-	-	-	-	-	-	-	-	-
S'pore Masters	-	-	-	-	-	-	-	-	-	3
Dubai Desert	40	17	15	2	1	6	10	5	46	21
Qatar Masters	-	-	-	-	-	-	-	-	-	-
Madeira Open	-	-	-	-	-	-	-	-	-	-
Brazil Open	-	-	-	-	-	-	-	-	-	-
Open de Arg	-	-	-	-	-	-	-	-	-	-
US Masters	37	52	MC	17	39	30	8	11	19	MC
Moroccan Open	-	20	-	-	-	-	-	-	-	-
Open de Espana	15	MC	1	15	MC	-	-	-	5	-
Open de Portugal	-	-	-	-	-	-	-	-	-	MC
Open de France	28	-	-	-	MC	11	23	-	1	-
B&H I'national	12	7	14	4	9	59	5	1	5	12
Deutsche Bank	-	-	-	20	2	-	10	20	6	10
Volvo PGA	10	2	37	9	7	5	1	1	1	17
British Masters	24	10	3	7	9	2	1	2	3	27
English Open	15	-	1	2	2	12	4	5	8	MC
US Open	3	33	2	28	10	2	18	15	46	52
G North Open	-	-	-	-	-	1	-	-	-	-
Irish Open	4	23	24	4	1	1	2	7	-	1
European Open	27	21	4	3	24	22	MC	15	8	20
Scot Open	-	-	-	4	10	7	1	3	28	-
British Open	MC	MC	8	MC	MC	24	MC	15	26	13
Dutch Open	15	1	4	7	-	-	-	-	-	-
Scandinavian	39	7	12	2	12	8	16	1	17	1
Wales Open	-	-	-	-	-	-	-	-	-	-
USPGA	?	33	36	2	MC	13	44	6	39	DQ
NW Ireland Open	-	-	-	-	-	-	-	-	-	-
WGC NEC Inv'	-	-	-	-	-	-	-	30	8	4
Scottish PGA	-	-	-	-	-	-	-	-	-	-
BMW Int' Open	6	-	-	-	-	3	MC	1	MC	13
European Mas'	3	8	MC	11	1	10	12	-	-	-
WGC AmEx	-	-	-	-	-	-	-	20	25	-
Troph' Lancome	21	14	4	1	2	22	11	3	46	MC
German Masters	17	MC	MC	MC	4	2	1	9	3	15
Cannes Open	3	36	2	13	-	-	-	-	-	-
Dunhill Links	-	-	-	-	-	-	-	-	-	5
Masters Madrid	3	12	-	-	-	-	-	-	-	-
Italian Open	2	-	-	-	-	-	-	-	-	-
Volvo Masters	2	1	4	2	29	8	3	16	9	7

Jarrod Moseley

6/2/72 – Perth, Australia

Australian pro who won the Heineken Classic just 18 months after joining the paid ranks.

His victory in the co-sanctioned event (by the ANZ and European Tour) earned him a two-year exemption to the European Tour.

Showed his best form in 2001 in the early stages of season, claiming top six finishes in two of his first three starts.

Was a brilliant amateur player, winning eight prestigious events in Australian, South Africa and south east Asia.

Another player who has linked up with Belgian sports psychologist Jos Vanstiphout. Put in plenty of practice on his short game over the season.

Sc Av – 71.31 (74th) DD – 283.4 (60th) DA – 62.4 (108th) GIR – 66.1 (116th) PpGIR – 1.768 (43rd) SS – 48.9 (136th)

	'92	'93	'94	'95	'96	'97	'98	'99	'00	'01
Johnnie Walker	-	-	-	-	-	-	-	-	-	41
WGC Matchplay	-	-	-	-	-	-	-	-	-	-
Alfred Dunhill	-	-	-	-	-	-	-	-	-	-
S African Open	-	-	-	-	-	-	-	-	-	-
Heineken Cl'	-	-	-	-	-	-	-	1	67	4
Greg Norman	-	-	-	-	-	-	-	-	31	6
Malaysian Open	-	-	-	-	-	-	-	-	-	-
S'pore Masters	-	-	-	-	-	-	-	-	-	-
Dubai Desert	-	-	-	-	-	-	-	-	-	33
Qatar Masters	-	-	-	-	-	-	-	-	-	20
Madeira Open	-	-	-	-	-	-	-	-	-	-
Brazil Open	-	-	-	-	-	-	-	-	-	-
Open de Arg	-	-	-	-	-	-	-	-	-	-
US Masters	-	-	-	-	-	-	-	-	-	-
Moroccan Open	-	-	-	-	-	-	-	-	-	-
Open de Espana	-	-	-	-	-	-	-	MC	48	32
Open de Portugal	-	-	-	-	-	-	-	-	-	-
Open de France	-	-	-	-	-	-	-	-	MC	66
B&H I'national	-	-	-	-	-	-	-	MC	MC	19
Deutsche Bank	-	-	-	-	-	-	-	MC	MC	52
Volvo PGA	-	-	-	-	-	-	-	MC	MC	MC
British Masters	-	-	-	-	-	-	-	MC	11	57
English Open	-	-	-	-	-	-	-	-	MC	MC
US Open	-	-	-	-	-	-	-	-	-	-
G North Open	-	-	-	-	-	-	-	53	MC	-
Irish Open	-	-	-	-	-	-	-	3	45	MC
European Open	-	-	-	-	-	-	-	18	64	MC
Scot Open	-	-	-	-	-	-	-	MC	22	50
British Open	-	-	-	-	-	-	-	MC	41	-
Dutch Open	-	-	-	-	-	-	-	3	14	40
Scandinavian	-	-	-	-	-	-	-	9	45	29
Wales Open	-	-	-	-	-	-	-	-	39	14
USPGA	-	-	-	-	-	-	-	-	-	-
NW Ireland Open	-	-	-	-	-	-	-	-	-	-
WGC NEC Inv'	-	-	-	-	-	-	-	-	-	-
Scottish PGA	-	-	-	-	-	-	-	-	-	MC
BMW Int' Open	-	-	-	-	-	-	-	3	61	MC
European Mas'	-	-	-	-	-	-	-	38	8	MC
WGC AmEx	-	-	-	-	-	-	-	25	-	-
Troph' Lancome	-	-	-	-	-	-	-	74	WD	30
German Masters	-	-	-	-	-	-	-	63	22	MC
Cannes Open	-	-	-	-	-	-	-	-	-	-
Dunhill Links	-	-	-	-	-	-	-	-	-	27
Masters Madrid	-	-	-	-	-	-	-	-	50	-
Italian Open	-	-	-	-	-	-	-	47	82	-
Volvo Masters	-	-	-	-	-	-	-	42	-	-

Mark Mouland

23/4/61 – St Athan, Wales

Having struggled on the European Tour for the past two seasons this 20-year tour veteran bounced back to form in 2001 with seven top-25 finishes to place 62nd on the Order of Merit – his equal best for over a decade.

Turned pro in 1981 and won the first of his two European Tour victories five years later in the Car Care Plan International. His second success came in 1988 at the Dutch Open.

Has represented Wales at all levels as an amateur and on seven occasions in the Dunhill Cup. Accurate iron play and good putting were features of his 2001 season.

Sc Av – 71.34 (81st) DD – 275.0 (144th) DA – 65.7 (65th) GIR – 63.7 (153rd) PpGIR – 1.773 (52nd) SS – 56.3 (69th)

	'92	'93	'94	'95	'96	'97	'98	'99	'00	'01
Johnnie Walker	-	MC	MC	MC	29	MC				
WGC Matchplay	-									
Alfred Dunhill	-	-	-	26	MC	43	33	-	MC	
S African Open	-	-	-	-	-	22	57	-		
Heineken Cl'	-	-	-	-	MC	-	MC	-		
Greg Norman	-									
Malaysian Open	-	-	-	-	-	-	-	29	MC	
S'pore Masters	-	-	-	-	-	-	-	-		38
Dubai Desert	-	MC	34	30	11	46	46	46	-	-
Qatar Masters	-	-	-	-	-	-	72	40	-	MC
Madeira Open	-	MC	66	-	-	20	-	39	MC	41
Brazil Open	-	-	-	-	-	-	-	39	-	
Open de Arg	-	-	-	-	-	-	-	-		4
US Masters	-									
Moroccan Open	45	11	MC	MC	23	-	-	WD	MC	
Open de Espana	67	37	MC	15	21	MC	51	MC	-	78
Open de Portugal	-	47	36	MC	27	9	MC	MC	43	53
Open de France	39	55	49	39	15	MC	-	MC	-	MC
B&H I'national	38	61	MC	40	59	19	7	MC	MC	-
Deutsche Bank	-	-	-	47	40	33	46	63	-	-
Volvo PGA	28	20	MC	9	MC	MC	MC	MC	-	-
British Masters	MC	21	MC	MC	35	MC	43	65	36	14
English Open	MC	WD	76	34	72	MC	36	MC	MC	MC
US Open	-									
G North Open	-	-	-	-	75	-	MC	36	MC	
Irish Open	-	-	52	WD	-	WD	MC	MC	-	20
European Open	33	60	WD	MC	MC	DQ	MC	MC	-	5
Scot Open	MC	-	-	MC	MC	MC	MC	-	68	
British Open	MC	-	MC	-						
Dutch Open	7	28	26	16	44	17	21	MC	11	MC
Scandinavian	MC	55	MC	WD	18	5	MC	MC	-	MC
Wales Open	-	-	-	-	-	-	-	-	39	WD
USPGA	-									
NW Ireland Open	-	-	-	-	-	-	-	15	-	
WGC NEC Inv'	-									
Scottish PGA	-						WD	58	11	
BMW Int' Open	MC	-	WD	34	16	12	26	27	-	37
European Mas'	36	MC	MC	61	MC	WD	61	28	17	23
WGC AmEx	-									
Troph' Lancome	-	-	-	59	55	54	55	MC	-	14
German Masters	70	62	40	-	23	41	MC	23	-	-
Cannes Open	-	MC	61	55	WD	38	16	-	39	
Dunhill Links	-									
Masters Madrid	59	MC	48	8	60	60	76	WD	-	MC
Italian Open	35	MC	-	MC	10	42	MC	MC	-	50
Volvo Masters	-	-	-	-	-	-	-	-	-	35

Nick O'Hern

18/10/71 – Perth, Australia

Left-handed Australian pro who surely would have had a better 2001 season if it wasn't for a broken wrist – which kept him out of the Open Championship and other tournaments thereafter (he'd actually played for the previous five weeks with the problem).

As it was, he still managed six top-ten finishes and 43rd place on the Order of Merit.

Yet to win on the European Tour in three seasons since moving from Australia, although he has won twice in his native country.

Possesses a solid all round game and will win sooner rather than later in Europe.

Sc Av – 71.02 (46th) DD – 273.1 (165th) DA – 70.9 (15th) GIR – 69.0 (60th) PpGIR – 1.773 (52nd) SS – 56.0 (70th)

	'92	'93	'94	'95	'96	'97	'98	'99	'00	'01
Johnnie Walker	-								24	9
WGC Matchplay	-									5
Alfred Dunhill	-									
S African Open	-									
Heineken Cl'	-					MC	40	36	MC	3
Greg Norman	-								27	5
Malaysian Open	-							11		
S'pore Masters	-									
Dubai Desert	-									
Qatar Masters	-									
Madeira Open	-							17		
Brazil Open	-									
Open de Arg	-									
US Masters	-									
Moroccan Open	-							6		
Open de Espana	-								33	
Open de Portugal	-									
Open de France	-							37	15	
B&H I'national	-							MC	28	35
Deutsche Bank	-								60	8
Volvo PGA	-								11	58
British Masters	-							52	36	34
English Open	-							MC	12	44
US Open	-									
G North Open	-							73	30	
Irish Open	-							MC	6	MC
European Open	-							24	55	
Scot Open	-								32	
British Open	-								41	
Dutch Open	-							MC		
Scandinavian	-							MC	MC	
Wales Open	-								5	8
USPGA	-									MC
NW Ireland Open	-							42		
WGC NEC Inv'	-									
Scottish PGA	-									
BMW Int' Open	-							55	MC	
European Mas'	-							9	49	
WGC AmEx	-									
Troph' Lancome	-							7		
German Masters	-									MC
Cannes Open	-									MC
Dunhill Links	-									MC
Masters Madrid	-									
Italian Open	-									
Volvo Masters	-								44	27

Sponsored by Stan James

Jose Maria Olazabal

5/2/66 – Fuenterrabia, Spain

Moved back into world's top 50 after victory in the French Open (his 19th European Tour win) but that success in Lyon turned out to be his only top-ten finish on the European Tour in 2001.

He did spend more time in America last season and also changed caddie, beginning a new relationship with caddie Phil 'Wobbly' Morbey (Ian Woosnam's former bagman) in Benson & Hedges at The Belfry in May.

This dual US Masters champion missed out on a seventh Ryder Cup place but still has one of the best short games in the world.

Sc Av – 70.62 (26th) DD – 269.6 (177th) DA – 58.0 (164th) GIR – 69.2 (58th) PpGIR – 1.744 (8th) SS – 72.2 (9th)

	'92	'93	'94	'95	'96	'97	'98	'99	'00	'01
Johnnie Walker	-	-	-	-	-	-	16	-	-	-
WGC Matchplay	-	-	-	-	-	-	5	17	-	-
Alfred Dunhill	-	-	-	-	-	-	-	-	-	-
S African Open	-	-	-	-	-	-	-	-	-	-
Heineken Cl'	-	-	-	-	-	3	-	MC	-	-
Greg Norman	-	-	-	-	-	-	-	8	-	-
Malaysian Open	-	-	-	-	-	-	-	-	-	-
S'pore Masters	-	-	-	-	-	-	-	-	-	-
Dubai Desert	-	-	-	-	-	12	1	25	24	-
Qatar Masters	-	-	-	-	-	-	17	-	-	-
Madeira Open	-	-	-	-	-	-	-	-	-	-
Brazil Open	-	-	-	-	-	-	-	-	-	-
Open de Arg	-	-	-	-	-	-	-	-	-	-
US Masters	42	7	1	14	-	12	12	1	MC	15
Moroccan Open	-	-	-	-	-	-	-	-	-	-
Open de Espana	10	4	8	15	-	11	2	MC	33	MC
Open de Portugal	-	-	-	-	-	4	-	-	-	-
Open de France	-	15	3	11	-	-	-	MC	-	1
B&H I'national	27	2	34	10	-	-	11	16	1	27
Deutsche Bank	-	-	-	-	-	-	27	-	35	57
Volvo PGA	2	10	1	-	25	19	16	10	56	11
British Masters	-	45	16	-	-	30	MC	-	-	-
English Open	-	-	-	-	-	22	-	-	-	-
US Open	MC	MC	MC	29	-	16	18	MC	12	MC
G North Open	-	-	-	-	-	-	-	-	-	-
Irish Open	-	2	4	-	-	6	9	-	10	MC
European Open	4	MC	2	-	-	3	37	-	52	MC
Scot Open	-	-	-	-	-	MC	32	-	9	21
British Open	3	MC	38	30	-	20	14	MC	31	54
Dutch Open	MC	33	26	-	-	-	-	MC	-	-
Scandinavian	2	17	-	-	-	38	MC	-	-	-
Wales Open	-	-	-	-	-	-	-	-	-	-
USPGA	MC	56	7	31	-	MC	MC	MC	4	37
NW Ireland Open	-	-	-	-	-	-	-	-	-	-
WGC NEC Inv'	-	-	-	-	-	-	-	40	10	-
Scottish PGA	-	-	-	-	-	-	-	-	-	-
BMW Int' Open	-	-	-	-	31	18	-	-	-	13
European Mas'	-	-	-	-	-	52	-	-	-	-
WGC AmEx	-	-	-	-	-	-	11	17	-	-
Troph' Lancome	6	37	5	26	-	-	-	43	38	-
German Masters	MC	6	2	-	-	4	21	26	-	68
Cannes Open	-	-	-	-	-	-	-	-	-	-
Dunhill Links	-	-	-	-	-	-	-	-	-	MC
Masters Madrid	-	8	2	20	-	1	-	MC	-	16
Italian Open	17	9	21	-	-	2	2	13	-	-
Volvo Masters	6	23	8	-	-	3	7	WD	5	16

Andrew Oldcorn

31/3/60 – Bolton, England (represents Scotland)

Bolton-born Scot who truned the form book on its head when winning the Volvo PGA Championship at Wentworth.

It was Oldcorn's third win of his European Tour career and first since 1995 (Jersey Open).

Has had a solid, if unspectacular, career since turning pro in 1983 (after winning the English Amateur crown a year earlier) claiming his first win in 1993 in the Turespana Masters.

Last year was by far and away his best and he nearly made the Ryder Cup team before finishing 26th in the Order of Merit.

Short off the tee but an accurate driver of the ball.

Sc Av – 71.03 (47th) DD – 274.8 (150th) DA – 68.1 (38th) GIR – 66.8 (102nd) PpGIR – 1.766 (36th) SS – 51.9 (104th)

	'92	'93	'94	'95	'96	'97	'98	'99	'00	'01
Johnnie Walker	-	-	-	-	-	-	-	-	-	-
WGC Matchplay	-	-	-	-	-	-	-	-	-	-
Alfred Dunhill	-	-	-	-	-	-	-	-	-	-
S African Open	-	-	-	-	-	-	-	-	-	-
Heineken Cl'	-	-	-	-	-	-	-	MC	-	-
Greg Norman	-	-	-	-	-	-	-	MC	-	-
Malaysian Open	-	-	-	-	-	-	-	-	-	-
S'pore Masters	-	-	-	-	-	-	-	-	-	-
Dubai Desert	-	57	59	40	18	10	41	MC	17	-
Qatar Masters	-	-	-	-	-	-	MC	59	WD	-
Madeira Open	-	MC	-	-	12	45	-	-	-	15
Brazil Open	-	-	-	-	-	-	-	-	-	-
Open de Arg	-	-	-	-	-	-	-	-	-	-
US Masters	-	-	-	-	-	-	-	-	-	-
Moroccan Open	-	-	-	-	-	-	-	-	-	-
Open de Espana	-	-	-	-	-	53	WD	46	-	32
Open de Portugal	-	33	MC	48	-	MC	61	25	11	72
Open de France	-	-	-	WD	MC	-	MC	-	-	-
B&H I'national	-	29	45	4	MC	19	MC	51	-	-
Deutsche Bank	-	-	MC	MC	MC	72	58	-	-	MC
Volvo PGA	50	16	57	25	69	32	MC	43	MC	1
British Masters	39	33	26	5	MC	MC	71	-	66	-
English Open	-	MC	58	MC	7	MC	MC	MC	59	26
US Open	-	-	-	-	-	-	-	-	-	-
G North Open	-	-	-	-	4	35	-	MC	5	33
Irish Open	-	34	MC	65	2	WD	70	MC	45	60
European Open	-	MC	MC	MC	MC	19	MC	28	WD	-
Scot Open	-	-	-	-	47	MC	68	68	MC	61
British Open	-	MC	WD	MC	-	77	-	-	MC	MC
Dutch Open	-	61	-	-	MC	21	8	58	9	-
Scandinavian	-	-	-	-	-	55	-	-	WD	DQ
Wales Open	-	-	-	-	-	-	-	-	17	33
USPGA	-	-	-	-	-	-	-	-	-	44
NW Ireland Open	-	-	-	-	-	-	18	-	-	-
WGC NEC Inv'	-	-	-	-	-	-	-	63	11	11
Scottish PGA	-	-	-	-	-	-	-	-	-	-
BMW Int' Open	-	19	-	-	MC	48	-	-	-	60
European Mas'	-	-	35	10	-	MC	MC	WD	-	-
WGC AmEx	-	-	-	-	-	-	-	-	-	-
Troph' Lancome	-	37	-	MC	28	22	MC	57	MC	63
German Masters	-	17	-	-	-	51	MC	MC	-	WD
Cannes Open	-	48	-	MC	MC	MC	16	-	-	-
Dunhill Links	-	-	-	-	-	-	-	-	-	-
Masters Madrid	1	MC	MC	MC	20	-	MC	MC	-	-
Italian Open	-	-	42	-	-	MC	38	7	-	-
Volvo Masters	-	39	-	28	6	-	-	-	-	-

Peter O'Malley
23/6/65 – Bathurst, Australia

Will probably be always known as the player who finished eagle, birdie, birdie, birdie, eagle (seven-under par for the last five holes) to beat Colin Montgomerie by two strokes in the 1992 Scottish Open.

However, this Aussie pro, who has been plying his trade in Europe for 12 years, got back in the winner enclosure for the first time in six years in 2001 when he captured the English Open title – his third European Tour success.

Known by his initials, 'PoM', he has been a regular winner Down Under over the years and relies on his accurate game to stay competitive.

Sc Av – 70.35 (15th) DD – 277.2 (122nd) DA – 83.7 (1st) GIR – 76.5 (4th) PpGIR – 1.803 (120th) SS – 55.8 (72nd)

	'92	'93	'94	'95	'96	'97	'98	'99	'00	'01
Johnnie Walker	10	66	26	28	59	7	4	-	12	12
WGC Matchplay	-	-	-	-	-	-	-	-	-	-
Alfred Dunhill	-	-	-	-	-	-	-	-	-	-
S African Open	-	-	-	-	-	-	-	-	-	-
Heineken Cl'	-	-	-	-	MC	16	32	19	18	MC
Greg Norman	-	-	-	-	-	-	-	-	16	31
Malaysian Open	-	-	-	-	-	-	-	-	-	-
S'pore Masters	-	-	-	-	-	-	-	-	-	-
Dubai Desert	-	-	-	-	MC	-	-	-	-	-
Qatar Masters	-	-	-	-	-	-	-	-	-	-
Madeira Open	-	-	-	-	-	-	-	-	-	-
Brazil Open	-	-	-	-	-	-	-	-	-	-
Open de Arg	-	-	-	-	-	-	-	-	-	-
US Masters	-	-	-	-	-	-	-	-	-	-
Moroccan Open	-	-	-	-	35	-	-	-	-	-
Open de Espana	-	-	27	16	MC	-	9	MC	42	
Open de Portugal	-	-	-	-	9	-	-	-	-	
Open de France	MC	15	MC	7	-	MC	-	-	7	17
B&H I'national	38	MC	MC	1	MC	MC	38	29	9	MC
Deutsche Bank	-	-	-	34	-	MC	39	23	31	3
Volvo PGA	MC	34	MC	4	57	27	MC	MC	7	26
British Masters	55	-	61	68	15	12	19	MC	20	34
English Open	19	MC	MC	MC	-	-	MC	MC	10	1
US Open	-	-	-	-	68	-	-	-	-	-
G North Open	-	-	-	-	-	-	-	4	-	-
Irish Open	11	23	52	-	25	31	16	21	73	44
European Open	70	60	MC	MC	29	MC	-	2	21	40
Scot Open	1	-	-	8	10	MC	46	MC	41	
British Open	68	-	53	MC	7	23	24	-	MC	
Dutch Open	20	19	10	25	13	-	45	-	14	14
Scandinavian	2	37	15	25	35	MC	MC	21	-	29
Wales Open	-	-	-	-	-	-	-	-	67	-
USPGA	-	-	-	-	-	-	MC	MC	-	-
NW Ireland Open	-	-	-	-	-	-	-	-	-	-
WGC NEC Inv'	-	-	-	-	-	-	-	-	-	-
Scottish PGA	-	-	-	-	-	-	-	-	-	11
BMW Int' Open	MC	51	19	57	-	45	-	34	64	16
European Mas'	MC	MC	13	25	MC	55	-	15	-	16
WGC AmEx	-	-	-	-	-	-	-	-	-	-
Troph' Lancome	-	44	-	23	-	3	7	40	58	-
German Masters	43	48	28	45	35	-	15	MC	MC	19
Cannes Open	-	36	23	29	MC	-	-	-	-	-
Dunhill Links	-	-	-	-	MC	-	-	-	-	5
Masters Madrid	-	-	-	-	30	-	-	-	-	-
Italian Open	48	23	26	-	-	MC	-	MC	-	-
Volvo Masters	50	-	-	24	-	5	4	10	34	58

Gary Orr
11/5/67 – Helensburgh, Scotland

One of the most consistent golfers on the European Tour over the last decade but one that didn't manage to win on the European Tour until the 2000 season.

Two victories in the year before last (in the Portuguese Open and the British Masters) hoisted the Scot up to 10th in the Order of Merit but last season so the Weybridge based pro slipped to 43rd.

He did, though, suffer from illness (kidney stones) last term and missed a few events in March.

Short but straight off the tee, he is a very good iron player but his putting can let him down.

Sc Av – 71.17 (60th) DD – 273.7 (161st) DA – 76.0 (4th) GIR – 73.2 (14th) PpGIR – 1.798 (113th) SS – 42.0 (179th)

	'92	'93	'94	'95	'96	'97	'98	'99	'00	'01
Johnnie Walker	-	-	41	MC	38	20	56	-	-	-
WGC Matchplay	-	-	-	-	-	-	-	-	-	17
Alfred Dunhill	-	-	-	17	-	-	26	2	-	-
S African Open	-	-	-	-	40	20	WD	16	-	-
Heineken Cl'	-	-	-	MC	MC	55	-	19	MC	-
Greg Norman	-	-	-	-	-	-	-	8	-	-
Malaysian Open	-	-	-	-	-	-	-	-	-	-
S'pore Masters	-	-	-	-	-	-	-	-	-	17
Dubai Desert	-	15	MC	MC	37	20	35	29	-	-
Qatar Masters	-	-	MC	-	-	55	MC	46	-	-
Madeira Open	44	MC	-	MC	-	-	59	-	27	-
Brazil Open	-	-	-	-	-	-	-	-	-	-
Open de Arg	-	-	-	-	-	-	-	-	-	-
US Masters	-	-	-	-	-	-	-	-	-	-
Moroccan Open	-	50	39	46	-	17	-	-	-	-
Open de Espana	37	-	MC	49	36	68	40	6	MC	
Open de Portugal	MC	17	MC	39	47	MC	38	1	MC	
Open de France	11	MC	MC	13	58	38	-	-	-	
B&H I'national	-	61	3	MC	23	40	52	33	-	MC
Deutsche Bank	-	-	-	10	15	MC	17	16	9	63
Volvo PGA	-	MC	MC	12	7	50	2	29	26	8
British Masters	-	-	37	54	MC	23	48	38	1	-
English Open	-	26	10	34	MC	10	32	7	6	55
US Open	-	-	-	-	-	-	-	-	-	74
G North Open	-	-	-	-	-	-	-	53	-	-
Irish Open	-	MC	59	20	MC	MC	6	11	-	35
European Open	-	MC	49	MC	-	MC	MC	35	34	MC
Scot Open	28	-	-	-	MC	7	46	13	57	
British Open	-	MC	MC	-	-	MC	MC	-	41	-
Dutch Open	-	33	61	MC	-	MC	-	2	WD	45
Scandinavian	-	21	MC	20	-	MC	MC	14	38	-
Wales Open	-	-	-	-	-	-	-	-	29	8
USPGA	-	-	-	-	-	-	-	-	MC	MC
NW Ireland Open	-	-	-	-	-	-	-	-	-	-
WGC NEC Inv'	-	-	-	-	-	-	-	27	-	-
Scottish PGA	-	-	-	-	-	-	-	-	-	-
BMW Int' Open	3	35	66	MC	22	MC	5	-	46	
European Mas'	6	13	61	4	25	MC	46	-	3	
WGC AmEx	-	-	-	-	-	-	-	25	30	
Troph' Lancome	19	30	41	45	MC	40	-	46	6	
German Masters	-	21	-	53	MC	7	MC	42	49	6
Cannes Open	-	MC	27	42	20	-	MC	-	-	48
Dunhill Links	-	-	-	-	-	-	-	-	-	48
Masters Madrid	19	DQ	MC	-	MC	-	8	2	49	
Italian Open	-	31	15	15	MC	MC	10	-	-	
Volvo Masters	25	36	-	13	-	49	54	59	-	

Greg Owen
19/2/72 – Mansfield, England

Started to become something of a media darling in 2001 after he was signed by the Daily Star to give its golf coverage a boost and then, following a fine Open Championship at Lytham, booked to appear on the next series of Question of Sport and Blue Peter.

Back problems have plagued his career on the course but having found out that one leg was shorter than the other he had special insoles made for his shoes.

He has yet to win on the European Tour in four years but can boast a Challenge Tour win (1996 Gosen Challenge).

Sc Av – 70.69 (31st) DD – 292.4 (13th) DA – 69.9 (22nd) GIR – 77.1 (1st) PpGIR – 1.826 (161st) SS – 60.8 (35th)

	'92	'93	'94	'95	'96	'97	'98	'99	'00	'01
Johnnie Walker	-	-	-	-	-	-	-	-	-	-
WGC Matchplay	-	-	-	-	-	-	-	-	-	-
Alfred Dunhill	-	-	-	-	-	-	23	MC	MC	10
S African Open	-	-	-	-	-	-	-	26	10	26
Heineken Cl'	-	-	-	-	-	-	MC	MC	MC	MC
Greg Norman	-	-	-	-	-	-	-	-	MC	53
Malaysian Open	-	-	-	-	-	-	-	43	-	-
S'pore Masters	-	-	-	-	-	-	-	-	-	-
Dubai Desert	-	-	-	-	-	-	-	MC	13	12
Qatar Masters	-	-	-	-	-	-	MC	63	27	8
Madeira Open	-	-	-	MC	MC	34	-	-	-	41
Brazil Open	-	-	-	-	-	-	-	3	-	-
Open de Arg	-	-	-	-	-	-	-	-	-	-
US Masters	-	-	-	-	-	-	-	-	-	-
Moroccan Open	-	-	MC	-	45	-	-	-	-	6
Open de Espana	-	-	-	MC	-	MC	MC	17	-	23
Open de Portugal	-	-	-	MC	-	51	MC	6	-	MC
Open de France	-	-	-	-	-	DQ	-	41	-	-
B&H I'national	-	-	-	-	-	33	62	44	73	
Deutsche Bank	-	-	-	-	-	MC	MC	MC	28	
Volvo PGA	-	-	-	-	-	-	MC	MC	32	
British Masters	-	-	-	-	-	7	4	20	34	
English Open	-	-	-	-	-	49	MC	MC	11	
US Open	-	-	-	-	-	-	-	-	-	-
G North Open	-	-	MC	-	-	MC	MC	47		
Irish Open	-	-	-	-	-	MC	45	MC		
European Open	-	-	-	-	28	MC	21	58		
Scot Open	-	-	-	-	-	29	MC	11		
British Open	-	-	-	-	-	MC	55	23		
Dutch Open	-	-	-	-	MC	68	7	-		
Scandinavian	-	-	-	-	MC	52	-	59		
Wales Open	-	-	-	-	-	-	-	-		
USPGA	-	-	-	-	-	-	-	-		
NW Ireland Open	-	-	-	-	-	-	-	-		
WGC NEC Inv'	-	-	-	-	-	-	-	-		
Scottish PGA	-	-	-	-	-	40	-	MC		
BMW Int' Open	-	-	-	-	55	27	5	60		
European Mas'	-	-	-	-	47	MC	49	6		
WGC AmEx	-	-	-	-	-	-	-	-		
Troph' Lancome	-	-	-	-	31	3	MC	20		
German Masters	-	-	-	-	-	51	49	4		
Cannes Open	-	-	47	-	MC	-	-	-		
Dunhill Links	-	-	-	-	-	-	-	17		
Masters Madrid	-	-	-	-	34	20	15	16		
Italian Open	-	-	MC	-	MC	MC	-	-		
Volvo Masters	-	-	-	-	-	-	17	35		

Carl Pettersson
29/8/77 – Sweden

A brilliant rookie season for this young Swede who carved out an impressive amateur career on the college circuit in America before turning pro in 2000. He managed to win his European Tour card at the first time of asking at Q-School and immediately impressed this term.

He finished seventh in the Malaysian Open and then runner-up in the Open de Argentina.

A third top-ten finish came in the Scottish PGA Championship.

Fairly long off the tee, although a little wild, he possesses a good putting touch but his bunker stats' were poor.

Sc Av – 71.18 (62nd) DD – 281.9 (81st) DA – 58.8 (158th) GIR – 64.7 (138th) PpGIR – 1.774 (59th) SS – 43.1 (174th)

	'92	'93	'94	'95	'96	'97	'98	'99	'00	'01
Johnnie Walker	-	-	-	-	-	-	-	-	-	-
WGC Matchplay	-	-	-	-	-	-	-	-	-	-
Alfred Dunhill	-	-	-	-	-	-	-	-	-	MC
S African Open	-	-	-	-	-	-	-	-	-	38
Heineken Cl'	-	-	-	-	-	-	-	-	-	-
Greg Norman	-	-	-	-	-	-	-	-	-	MC
Malaysian Open	-	-	-	-	-	-	-	-	-	7
S'pore Masters	-	-	-	-	-	-	-	-	-	MC
Dubai Desert	-	-	-	-	-	-	-	-	-	-
Qatar Masters	-	-	-	-	-	-	-	-	-	27
Madeira Open	-	-	-	-	-	-	-	-	-	MC
Brazil Open	-	-	-	-	-	-	-	-	-	31
Open de Arg	-	-	-	-	-	-	-	-	-	2
US Masters	-	-	-	-	-	-	-	-	-	-
Moroccan Open	-	-	-	-	-	-	-	-	-	-
Open de Espana	-	-	-	-	-	-	-	-	-	16
Open de Portugal	-	-	-	-	-	-	-	-	-	MC
Open de France	-	-	-	-	-	-	-	-	-	MC
B&H I'national	-	-	-	-	-	-	-	-	-	MC
Deutsche Bank	-	-	-	-	-	-	-	-	-	MC
Volvo PGA	-	-	-	-	-	-	-	-	-	MC
British Masters	-	-	-	-	-	-	-	-	-	-
English Open	-	-	-	-	-	-	-	-	-	-
US Open	-	-	-	-	-	-	-	-	-	-
G North Open	-	-	-	-	-	-	-	-	-	-
Irish Open	-	-	-	-	-	-	-	-	-	26
European Open	-	-	-	-	-	-	-	-	-	MC
Scot Open	-	-	-	-	-	-	-	-	-	37
British Open	-	-	-	-	-	-	-	-	-	-
Dutch Open	-	-	-	-	-	-	-	-	-	-
Scandinavian	-	-	-	-	-	-	-	-	-	29
Wales Open	-	-	-	-	-	-	-	-	-	33
USPGA	-	-	-	-	-	-	-	-	-	-
NW Ireland Open	-	-	-	-	-	-	-	-	-	-
WGC NEC Inv'	-	-	-	-	-	-	-	-	-	-
Scottish PGA	-	-	-	-	-	-	-	-	-	4
BMW Int' Open	-	-	-	-	-	-	-	-	-	16
European Mas'	-	-	-	-	-	-	-	-	-	MC
WGC AmEx	-	-	-	-	-	-	-	-	-	-
Troph' Lancome	-	-	-	-	-	-	-	-	-	71
German Masters	-	-	-	-	-	-	-	-	-	-
Cannes Open	-	-	-	-	-	-	-	-	-	-
Dunhill Links	-	-	-	-	-	-	-	-	-	-
Masters Madrid	-	-	-	-	-	-	-	-	-	35
Italian Open	-	-	-	-	-	-	-	-	-	MC
Volvo Masters	-	-	-	-	-	-	-	-	-	27

Mark Pilkington

17/3/78 – Bangor, Wales

Prolific amateur player whose sterling performances in the second half of last season were enough to secure the Welshman his playing privileges for 2002.

Won the Spanish and Welsh Amateur titles before turning pro in 1998.

His first taste of life on the European Tour was a bitter one as he lost his card in 1999.

But a solid year on the Challenge Tour followed and he regained his full tour card via the Q-School in 2000.

A high finish (13th) in the cash rich Dunhill Links Championship earned this long and accurate driver his card for 2002.

Sc Av – 72.04 (140th) DD – 295.7 (6th) DA – 75.1 (5th) GIR – 70.7 (34th) PpGIR – 1.843 (182nd) SS – 64.5 (21st)

	'92	'93	'94	'95	'96	'97	'98	'99	'00	'01
Johnnie Walker	-	-	-	-	-	-	-	-	-	-
WGC Matchplay	-	-	-	-	-	-	-	-	-	-
Alfred Dunhill	-	-	-	-	-	-	-	MC	-	-
S African Open	-	-	-	-	-	-	-	-	-	-
Heineken Cl'	-	-	-	-	-	-	-	MC	-	MC
Greg Norman	-	-	-	-	-	-	-	-	-	MC
Malaysian Open	-	-	-	-	-	-	-	MC	-	66
S'pore Masters	-	-	-	-	-	-	-	-	-	51
Dubai Desert	-	-	-	-	-	-	-	65	-	-
Qatar Masters	-	-	-	-	-	-	-	MC	-	46
Madeira Open	-	-	-	-	-	-	-	MC	61	MC
Brazil Open	-	-	-	-	-	-	-	-	MC	MC
Open de Arg	-	-	-	-	-	-	-	-	-	MC
US Masters	-	-	-	-	-	-	-	-	-	-
Moroccan Open	-	-	-	-	-	-	-	-	40	MC
Open de Espana	-	-	-	-	-	-	-	-	-	MC
Open de Portugal	-	-	-	-	-	-	-	MC	-	MC
Open de France	-	-	-	-	-	-	-	MC	-	17
B&H I'national	-	-	-	-	-	-	-	-	-	-
Deutsche Bank	-	-	-	-	-	-	-	-	-	-
Volvo PGA	-	-	-	-	-	-	-	-	-	-
British Masters	-	-	-	-	-	-	-	-	-	MC
English Open	-	-	-	-	-	-	-	MC	-	51
US Open	-	-	-	-	-	-	-	-	-	-
G North Open	-	-	-	-	-	-	-	MC	-	67
Irish Open	-	-	-	-	-	-	-	-	-	-
European Open	-	-	-	-	-	-	-	-	-	-
Scot Open	-	-	-	-	-	-	-	-	-	-
British Open	-	-	-	-	-	-	-	-	-	MC
Dutch Open	-	-	-	-	-	-	-	MC	-	MC
Scandinavian	-	-	-	-	-	-	-	-	-	MC
Wales Open	-	-	-	-	-	-	-	-	-	4
USPGA	-	-	-	-	-	-	-	-	-	-
NW Ireland Open	-	-	-	-	-	-	-	MC	19	3
WGC NEC Inv'	-	-	-	-	-	-	-	-	-	-
Scottish PGA	-	-	-	-	-	-	-	MC	-	51
BMW Int' Open	-	-	-	-	-	-	-	-	-	MC
European Mas'	-	-	-	-	-	-	-	-	-	MC
WGC AmEx	-	-	-	-	-	-	-	-	-	-
Troph' Lancome	-	-	-	-	-	-	-	-	-	MC
German Masters	-	-	-	-	-	-	-	-	-	-
Cannes Open	-	-	-	-	-	-	-	-	-	39
Dunhill Links	-	-	-	-	-	-	-	-	-	13
Masters Madrid	-	-	-	-	-	61	-	-	-	71
Italian Open	-	-	-	-	-	-	-	-	-	50
Volvo Masters	-	-	-	-	-	-	-	-	-	-

Ian Poulter

10/1/76 – Hitchin, England

Rookie of the Year in 2000 he didn't disappoint in his second season.

The English pro missed out on a place on the Ryder Cup team by the narrowest of margins after some superb performances last year.

He won the Morocco Open (his second European Tour success) and posted six other top-ten finishes.

His Order of Merit position jumped seven places from 31st to 24th last year.

After graduating from the Challenge Tour in 1999 (winning once) he won the Italian Open at the end of his first year on the full tour. A sound putter but wayward off the tee.

Sc Av – 71.44 (89th) DD – 285.7 (41st) DA – 60.6 (131st) GIR – 66.0 (119th) PpGIR – 1.769 (45th) SS – 58.1 (52nd)

	'92	'93	'94	'95	'96	'97	'98	'99	'00	'01
Johnnie Walker	-	-	-	-	-	-	-	-	-	41
WGC Matchplay	-	-	-	-	-	-	-	-	-	-
Alfred Dunhill	-	-	-	-	-	-	-	-	22	53
S African Open	-	-	-	-	-	-	-	-	-	54
Heineken Cl'	-	-	-	-	-	-	-	-	-	MC
Greg Norman	-	-	-	-	-	-	-	-	-	3
Malaysian Open	-	-	-	-	-	-	-	-	23	4
S'pore Masters	-	-	-	-	-	-	-	-	-	4
Dubai Desert	-	-	-	-	-	-	-	-	-	82
Qatar Masters	-	-	-	-	-	-	-	-	11	WD
Madeira Open	-	-	-	-	-	-	-	-	55	-
Brazil Open	-	-	-	-	-	-	-	-	3	-
Open de Arg	-	-	-	-	-	-	-	-	-	-
US Masters	-	-	-	-	-	-	-	-	-	-
Moroccan Open	-	-	-	-	-	-	-	-	2	1
Open de Espana	-	-	-	-	-	-	-	-	MC	MC
Open de Portugal	-	-	-	-	-	-	-	-	18	72
Open de France	-	-	-	-	-	-	-	-	73	-
B&H I'national	-	-	-	-	-	-	-	-	22	MC
Deutsche Bank	-	-	-	-	-	-	-	-	17	MC
Volvo PGA	-	-	-	-	-	-	-	-	MC	MC
British Masters	-	-	-	-	-	-	-	-	-	57
English Open	-	-	-	-	-	-	-	-	WD	9
US Open	-	-	-	-	-	-	-	-	-	-
G North Open	-	-	-	-	-	-	-	-	14	7
Irish Open	-	-	-	-	-	-	-	-	MC	7
European Open	-	-	-	-	-	-	-	-	MC	90
Scot Open	-	-	-	-	-	-	-	-	MC	21
British Open	-	-	-	-	-	-	-	-	64	-
Dutch Open	-	-	-	-	-	-	-	-	28	MC
Scandinavian	-	-	-	-	-	-	-	-	52	2
Wales Open	-	-	-	-	-	-	-	-	-	20
USPGA	-	-	-	-	-	-	-	-	-	MC
NW Ireland Open	-	-	-	-	-	-	-	MC	-	-
WGC NEC Inv'	-	-	-	-	-	-	-	-	-	13
Scottish PGA	-	-	-	-	-	-	-	MC	-	-
BMW Int' Open	-	-	-	-	-	-	-	-	38	MC
European Mas'	-	-	-	-	-	-	-	-	42	WD
WGC AmEx	-	-	-	-	-	-	-	-	-	-
Troph' Lancome	-	-	-	-	-	-	-	-	MC	-
German Masters	-	-	-	-	-	-	-	-	-	15
Cannes Open	-	-	-	-	-	-	-	-	-	-
Dunhill Links	-	-	-	-	-	-	-	-	-	MC
Masters Madrid	-	-	-	-	-	-	-	-	-	-
Italian Open	-	-	-	-	-	-	-	-	1	3
Volvo Masters	-	-	-	-	-	-	-	-	23	49

Phillip Price
21/10/66 – Pontypridd, Wales

Seven years after his first European Tour win this Welsh pro went on to claim his second tour success with victory in the 2001 Portuguese Open – the same tournament which had given him his first win.

The victory also helped him to make the Ryder Cup team for the first time.

Price has been one of the most consistent performers on the European Tour for a decade and gave Tiger Woods a fright in the 2000 WGC NEC Invitational before finishing second.

A brilliant putter and accurate driver of the ball, he turned pro in 1989.

Sc Av – 70.42 (19th) DD – 279.6 (102nd) DA – 67.0 (51st) GIR – 67.2 (90th) PpGIR – 1.746 (10th) SS – 58.8 (46th)

	'92	'93	'94	'95	'96	'97	'98	'99	'00	'01
Johnnie Walker	29	MC	WD	-	MC	17	16	-	7	-
WGC Matchplay	-	-	-	-	-	-	-	-	-	33
Alfred Dunhill	-	-	-	-	MC	22	6	MC	2	MC
S African Open	-	-	-	-	MC	46	20	58	-	-
Heineken Cl'	-	-	-	51	-	61	-	MC	19	-
Greg Norman	-	-	-	-	-	-	-	8	8	-
Malaysian Open	-	-	-	-	-	-	-	-	-	-
S'pore Masters	-	-	-	-	-	-	-	-	-	-
Dubai Desert	47	41	MC	MC	40	12	20	11	37	21
Qatar Masters	-	-	-	-	-	-	55	2	40	MC
Madeira Open	-	32	34	-	-	45	-	-	-	-
Brazil Open	-	-	-	-	-	-	-	-	-	-
Open de Arg	-	-	-	-	-	-	-	-	-	-
US Masters	-	-	-	-	-	-	-	-	-	-
Moroccan Open	10	-	48	5	56	22	-	-	-	-
Open de Espana	MC	-	8	33	45	MC	10	33	17	49
Open de Portugal	-	51	1	MC	MC	-	-	-	2	1
Open de France	53	61	WD	-	WD	-	-	-	-	-
B&H I'national	70	MC	5	MC	MC	MC	15	20	2	12
Deutsche Bank	-	-	-	-	-	47	34	MC	45	14
Volvo PGA	MC	MC	MC	17	37	MC	11	40	20	4
British Masters	MC	55	20	54	15	6	MC	MC	-	-
English Open	19	51	44	63	12	12	6	MC	-	35
US Open	-	-	-	-	-	-	-	53	-	WD
G North Open	-	-	-	-	MC	MC	-	WD	-	-
Irish Open	72	MC	MC	-	7	37	65	11	MC	30
European Open	MC	2	64	50	MC	MC	2	MC	13	8
Scot Open	MC	-	-	MC	MC	MC	15	19	MC	-
British Open	MC	-	-	-	-	-	MC	58	MC	30
Dutch Open	50	MC	WD	MC	7	MC	42	-	-	-
Scandinavian	MC	MC	-	56	MC	38	-	65	64	MC
Wales Open	-	-	-	-	-	-	-	-	-	14
USPGA	-	-	-	-	-	-	-	MC	59	-
NW Ireland Open	-	-	-	-	-	-	-	-	-	-
WGC NEC Inv'	-	-	-	-	-	-	-	-	2	28
Scottish PGA	-	-	-	-	-	-	-	-	-	-
BMW Int' Open	MC	MC	31	57	MC	6	MC	15	-	MC
European Mas'	11	MC	-	MC	MC	32	47	42	6	-
WGC AmEx	-	-	-	-	-	-	-	-	17	-
Troph' Lancome	-	WD	WD	-	25	13	-	81	6	11
German Masters	66	17	-	MC	43	13	65	42	22	-
Cannes Open	-	MC	-	MC	-	2	-	-	-	-
Dunhill Links	-	-	-	-	-	-	-	-	-	MC
Masters Madrid	33	25	48	13	-	MC	-	-	43	16
Italian Open	-	62	-	MC	36	MC	13	3	-	-
Volvo Masters	-	-	34	-	-	24	41	49	23	16

Jean-Francois Remesy
5/6/64 – Nimes, France

French pro whose sole success came in the 1999 Estoril Open.

His victory granted him a two-year exemption on the European Tour and meant he didn't have to go back to Q-School for what would have been the 13th successive year.

Last season saw the end of his exemption but he made enough cash in the early part of the year, including over 133,000euros for second place in the French Open, to retain his card for 2002.

Remesy is a former French Amateur champion who is fairly shoer off the tee but finds more fairways than most.

Sc Av – 72.16 (155th) DD – 274.4 (155th) DA – 67.3 (48th) GIR – 68.5 (68th) PpGIR – 1.810 (136th) SS – 57.1 (60th)

	'92	'93	'94	'95	'96	'97	'98	'99	'00	'01
Johnnie Walker	-	-	-	-	-	-	-	-	39	-
WGC Matchplay	-	-	-	-	-	-	-	-	-	-
Alfred Dunhill	-	-	-	-	-	-	48	-	MC	MC
S African Open	-	-	-	-	-	22	-	-	5	59
Heineken Cl'	-	-	-	-	MC	-	-	-	-	-
Greg Norman	-	-	-	-	-	-	-	-	-	-
Malaysian Open	-	-	-	-	-	-	-	-	-	30
S'pore Masters	-	-	-	-	-	-	-	-	-	MC
Dubai Desert	-	-	-	-	-	-	-	-	24	12
Qatar Masters	-	-	-	-	-	-	-	-	MC	46
Madeira Open	-	-	-	-	-	-	45	71	-	-
Brazil Open	-	-	-	-	-	-	-	8	-	-
Open de Arg	-	-	-	-	-	-	-	-	-	-
US Masters	-	-	-	-	-	-	-	-	-	-
Moroccan Open	-	-	-	-	MC	MC	-	-	-	54
Open de Espana	-	-	-	-	-	51	MC	MC	-	2
Open de Portugal	-	-	-	-	-	MC	-	-	MC	MC
Open de France	MC	-	MC	69	18	MC	17	47	-	-
B&H I'national	-	-	-	-	-	-	-	MC	9	52
Deutsche Bank	-	-	-	-	-	MC	WD	MC	WD	57
Volvo PGA	-	-	-	-	-	-	-	MC	34	MC
British Masters	-	-	-	-	-	MC	MC	MC	62	-
English Open	-	-	-	-	-	-	41	-	MC	MC
US Open	-	-	-	-	-	-	-	-	-	-
G North Open	-	-	-	-	-	MC	-	45	-	-
Irish Open	-	-	-	-	-	-	-	41	-	48
European Open	-	-	-	-	-	MC	MC	-	46	68
Scot Open	-	-	-	-	-	-	37	MC	-	WD
British Open	-	-	-	-	-	MC	MC	-	MC	-
Dutch Open	-	-	-	-	-	MC	30	30	58	-
Scandinavian	-	-	-	-	-	29	32	-	-	-
Wales Open	-	-	-	-	-	-	-	-	-	MC
USPGA	-	-	-	-	-	-	-	-	-	-
NW Ireland Open	-	-	-	-	-	-	-	-	-	-
WGC NEC Inv'	-	-	-	-	-	-	-	-	-	-
Scottish PGA	-	-	-	-	-	-	-	-	-	-
BMW Int' Open	-	-	-	-	-	-	MC	9	MC	MC
European Mas'	-	-	-	-	-	MC	MC	46	MC	MC
WGC AmEx	-	-	-	-	-	-	-	-	-	-
Troph' Lancome	-	-	-	-	-	67	MC	51	MC	MC
German Masters	-	-	-	-	-	-	42	-	58	-
Cannes Open	-	-	-	-	-	MC	11	-	39	-
Dunhill Links	-	-	-	-	-	-	-	-	-	59
Masters Madrid	-	-	-	-	-	MC	MC	-	-	65
Italian Open	-	-	-	-	-	MC	MC	-	-	-
Volvo Masters	-	-	-	-	-	-	-	49	-	-

Dean Robertson

11/7/70 – Sarnia, Canada (represents Scotland)

Scottish pro who recovered from an illness plagued 2000 to register six top-ten finishes last season and narrowly miss out on a place in the Ryder Cup team.

Robertson's seventh season on the European Tour didn't see him add to his sole success (in the 1999 Italian Open) but did re-establish him as one of the top golfers on this continent.

Played Walker Cup golf in 1993 before turning pro and is managed by Stephen Doyle – who looks after snooker star Stephen Hendry.

Has straightened up off the tee over the past year and remains an excellent putter.

Sc Av – 70.62 (26th) DD – 276.6 (126th) DA – 70.1 (18th) GIR – 67.3 (87th) PpGIR – 1.776 (64th) SS – 66.9 (15th)

	'92	'93	'94	'95	'96	'97	'98	'99	'00	'01
Johnnie Walker	-	-	-	67	-	MC	-	-	-	MC
WGC Matchplay	-	-	-	-	-	-	-	-	-	-
Alfred Dunhill	-	-	61	57	-	-	MC	-	-	3
S African Open	-	-	-	-	-	MC	MC	-	-	MC
Heineken Cl'	-	-	-	8	-	MC	MC	-	-	4
Greg Norman	-	-	-	-	-	-	-	-	-	31
Malaysian Open	-	-	-	-	-	-	MC	-	-	-
S'pore Masters	-	-	-	-	-	-	-	-	-	-
Dubai Desert	-	-	-	40	46	53	15	-	-	28
Qatar Masters	-	-	-	-	-	27	MC	-	-	4
Madeira Open	-	-	4	52	9	-	-	13	-	72
Brazil Open	-	-	-	-	-	-	-	-	-	-
Open de Arg	-	-	-	-	-	-	-	-	-	-
US Masters	-	-	-	-	-	-	-	-	-	-
Moroccan Open	-	-	-	MC	-	MC	MC	-	-	-
Open de Espana	-	-	-	-	-	MC	MC	33	12	23
Open de Portugal	-	-	-	72	MC	65	MC	-	-	-
Open de France	-	-	-	MC	15	46	WD	MC	-	-
B&H I'national	-	-	-	MC	MC	MC	44	20	44	42
Deutsche Bank	-	-	-	WD	44	51	67	63	72	37
Volvo PGA	-	-	-	MC	37	5	19	30	11	-
British Masters	-	-	-	66	WD	WD	MC	MC	WD	53
English Open	-	-	-	10	33	WD	36	7	MC	WD
US Open	-	-	-	-	-	-	-	-	-	-
G North Open	-	-	-	-	35	-	-	6	22	8
Irish Open	-	-	-	33	MC	MC	53	MC	45	35
European Open	-	-	-	9	10	50	64	67	13	8
Scot Open	-	-	-	-	39	13	MC	32	28	-
British Open	-	-	-	76	-	MC	-	49	26	-
Dutch Open	-	-	-	50	-	MC	58	50	-	20
Scandinavian	-	-	-	MC	37	45	MC	-	MC	-
Wales Open	-	-	-	-	-	-	-	-	-	MC
USPGA	-	-	-	-	-	-	-	-	-	-
NW Ireland Open	-	-	-	-	-	-	-	-	-	-
WGC NEC Inv'	-	-	-	-	-	-	-	-	-	-
Scottish PGA	-	-	-	-	-	-	-	-	MC	37
BMW Int' Open	-	-	-	52	MC	MC	MC	14	70	4
European Mas'	-	-	-	25	-	MC	-	15	10	23
WGC AmEx	-	-	-	-	-	-	-	-	-	-
Troph' Lancome	-	-	-	MC	-	MC	MC	-	7	23
German Masters	-	-	-	-	MC	-	72	MC	41	MC
Cannes Open	-	-	-	-	10	47	MC	53	-	-
Dunhill Links	-	-	-	-	-	-	-	-	-	-
Masters Madrid	-	-	-	MC	MC	MC	-	MC	MC	-
Italian Open	-	-	-	MC	46	6	51	1	53	-
Volvo Masters	-	-	-	-	-	-	-	42	28	12

Costantino Rocca

4/12/56 – Bergamo, Italy

Former Ryder Cup player with five European Tour victories to his name.

He has struggled with his game recently, however, and was ranked a lowly 152nd on the Order of Merit in 2000.

Last season saw him return to a semblance of form when he recorded two top-four finishes including second place in the French Open.

Will probably be always known for the 60-foot putt he sank on the 72nd hole of the 1995 British Open when he forced a play-off with John Daly – only to lose.

Turned pro in 1981 and joined the European Tour full time in 1990.

Sc Av – 71.33 (79th) DD – 275.5 (138th) DA – 61.3 (123rd) GIR – 66.4 (108th) PpGIR – 1.808 (131st) SS – 44.0 (168th)

	'92	'93	'94	'95	'96	'97	'98	'99	'00	'01
Johnnie Walker	38	MC	23	-	-	-	-	-	-	30
WGC Matchplay	-	-	-	-	-	-	-	-	-	-
Alfred Dunhill	-	-	-	-	8	MC	36	-	-	-
S African Open	-	-	-	-	-	MC	65	-	-	-
Heineken Cl'	-	-	-	-	-	-	-	-	-	MC
Greg Norman	-	-	-	-	-	-	-	-	-	MC
Malaysian Open	-	-	-	-	-	-	-	-	-	42
S'pore Masters	-	-	-	-	-	-	-	-	-	17
Dubai Desert	9	MC	11	52	10	-	MC	46	MC	71
Qatar Masters	-	-	-	-	-	-	60	40	MC	MC
Madeira Open	-	-	-	-	-	-	-	39	-	-
Brazil Open	-	-	-	-	-	-	-	-	MC	-
Open de Arg	-	-	-	-	-	-	-	-	-	4
US Masters	-	41	-	MC	5	MC	-	-	-	-
Open de Espana	12	12	25	15	-	15	MC	40	-	MC
Open de Portugal	-	5	10	-	-	-	-	-	MC	MC
Open de France	1	MC	4	21	18	-	26	MC	-	2
B&H I'national	12	13	MC	2	MC	-	MC	MC	28	35
Deutsche Bank	-	-	5	18	MC	17	MC	70	-	MC
Volvo PGA	24	MC	14	37	1	65	15	29	62	MC
British Masters	17	26	31	-	3	53	19	MC	MC	69
English Open	24	2	6	24	-	MC	MC	17	54	23
US Open	-	-	21	-	67	-	MC	-	-	-
G North Open	-	-	-	-	-	MC	-	-	-	-
Irish Open	-	5	-	-	-	51	-	41	MC	44
European Open	MC	2	5	2	5	10	4	-	MC	12
Scot Open	7	-	-	-	29	25	47	MC	MC	MC
British Open	55	MC	MC	2	63	MC	8	18	-	-
Dutch Open	-	MC	31	13	MC	30	5	MC	MC	MC
Scandinavian	9	-	-	-	-	38	34	59	MC	29
Wales Open	-	-	-	-	-	-	-	-	MC	-
USPGA	-	-	MC	17	52	71	MC	-	-	-
NW Ireland Open	-	-	-	-	-	-	-	1	70	-
WGC NEC Inv'	-	-	-	-	-	-	-	-	-	-
Scottish PGA	-	-	-	-	-	-	-	-	-	-
BMW Int' Open	9	MC	-	-	-	26	18	MC	-	-
European Mas'	43	-	59	2	MC	1	4	MC	MC	-
WGC AmEx	-	-	-	-	-	-	-	-	-	-
Troph' Lancome	24	26	17	9	4	-	MC	18	MC	MC
German Masters	5	14	28	-	-	4	28	51	56	-
Cannes Open	-	MC	34	21	5	-	-	-	-	-
Dunhill Links	-	-	-	-	-	-	-	-	-	-
Masters Madrid	49	6	-	2	11	-	-	37	-	-
Italian Open	MC	44	50	3	20	6	31	10	59	-
Volvo Masters	21	8	7	12	43	9	36	-	44	-

Eduardo Romero

17/7/54 – Cordoba, Argentina

Vetreran Argentinean golfer who missed the start of the 2001 season as he was bitten by a stray dog and laid low by the injury – which was somehow ironic as he's nicknamed 'El Gato' – the cat.

A seven-time European Tour winner (the last success coming in the 2000 European Masters), Romero struggled last term to continue in the same form that had seen him place in the top 30 of the Order of Merit in the previous five years.

He posted just two top-ten finishes in 2001. A multiple winner in his native South America his strength is from tee to green.

Sc Av – 70.60 (25th) DD – 284.3 (54th) DA – 64.6 (76th) GIR – 73.0 (15th) PpGIR – 1.788 (92nd) SS – 46.5 (154th)

	'92	'93	'94	'95	'96	'97	'98	'99	'00	'01
Johnnie Walker	-	-	-	-	-	-	-	-	39	-
WGC Matchplay	-	-	-	-	-	-	5	-	-	-
Alfred Dunhill	-	-	-	-	-	-	-	-	-	-
S African Open	-	-	-	-	-	-	-	-	-	-
Heineken Cl'	-	-	-	-	-	-	-	-	-	-
Greg Norman	-	-	-	-	-	-	-	-	-	-
Malaysian Open	-	-	-	-	-	-	-	-	-	-
S'pore Masters	-	-	-	-	-	-	-	-	-	-
Dubai Desert	-	-	-	20	-	29	35	32	-	-
Qatar Masters	-	-	-	-	-	55	40	3	-	-
Madeira Open	-	-	-	-	-	-	-	-	-	-
Brazil Open	-	-	-	-	-	-	-	3	-	-
Open de Arg	-	-	-	-	-	-	-	-	-	18
US Masters	-	-	-	-	-	-	-	-	-	MC
Moroccan Open	-	34	-	-	2	10	35	-	-	-
Open de Espana	4	49	MC	6	4	3	4	MC	3	-
Open de Portugal	27	11	WD	-	WD	37	4	-	-	-
Open de France	MC	DQ	MC	-	61	8	23	12	41	27
B&H I'national	12	MC	18	-	18	7	-	7	34	7
Deutsche Bank	-	-	-	-	40	-	-	52	MC	14
Volvo PGA	10	7	14	MC	10	11	54	19	56	MC
British Masters	10	21	20	MC	58	MC	2	18	-	-
English Open	MC	33	MC	-	-	26	-	-	-	-
US Open	MC	-	-	51	-	-	25	-	-	51
G North Open	-	-	-	-	-	-	-	-	-	-
Irish Open	-	44	31	-	MC	15	27	WD	6	-
European Open	MC	44	MC	-	9	10	16	35	25	58
Scot Open	MC	-	-	-	29	MC	2	7	32	MC
British Open	MC	MC	MC	85	32	7	55	-	35	25
Dutch Open	-	28	10	-	-	-	-	3	11	-
Scandinavian	-	-	-	-	-	-	-	-	-	-
Wales Open	-	-	-	-	-	-	-	-	-	-
USPGA	MC	21	-	-	41	MC	MC	MC	MC	-
NW Ireland Open	-	-	-	-	-	-	-	-	-	-
WGC NEC Inv'	-	-	-	-	-	-	-	-	-	-
Scottish PGA	-	-	-	-	-	-	-	-	-	-
BMW Int' Open	-	-	-	-	-	9	43	-	-	60
European Mas'	28	17	1	4	34	53	20	9	1	10
WGC AmEx	-	-	-	-	-	-	-	-	25	-
Troph' Lancome	3	30	17	41	33	5	MC	MC	22	54
German Masters	MC	-	-	-	43	-	-	-	56	-
Cannes Open	-	-	MC	-	-	-	-	-	-	-
Dunhill Links	-	-	-	-	-	-	-	-	-	29
Masters Madrid	3	2	18	-	MC	3	-	-	7	35
Italian Open	6	17	1	-	7	12	51	31	-	32
Volvo Masters	4	25	42	-	34	9	29	49	28	-

Justin Rose

30/7/80 – Johannesburg, South Africa (represents England)

At last beginning to fulfil the potential the world saw in 1998, when as an amateur he finished fourth in the Open Championship at Birkdale.

He had a torrid time shortly after that when he missed cut after cut and suffered from an obvious case of too much too soon.

Only after his third visit to the Q-School did Rose hit top form again, when last season he finished second in his first two starts.

It was enough to earn his card for 2002 and a further visit to San Roque wasn't necessary. Has the all-round game to win many tournaments.

Sc Av – 70.83 (35th) DD – 286.6 (37th) DA – 64.2 (81st) GIR – 70.7 (34th) PpGIR – 1.782 (74th) SS – 57.6 (58th)

	'92	'93	'94	'95	'96	'97	'98	'99	'00	'01
Johnnie Walker	-	-	-	-	-	-	-	-	-	-
WGC Matchplay	-	-	-	-	-	-	-	-	-	-
Alfred Dunhill	-	-	-	-	-	-	-	MC	59	2
S African Open	-	-	-	-	-	MC	-	-	37	2
Heineken Cl'	-	-	-	-	-	-	-	-	MC	23
Greg Norman	-	-	-	-	-	-	-	-	40	21
Malaysian Open	-	-	-	-	-	-	-	-	MC	-
S'pore Masters	-	-	-	-	-	-	-	-	-	-
Dubai Desert	-	-	-	-	-	-	-	MC	MC	77
Qatar Masters	-	-	-	-	-	-	-	MC	MC	MC
Madeira Open	-	-	-	-	-	-	-	MC	29	-
Brazil Open	-	-	-	-	-	-	-	MC	-	-
Open de Arg	-	-	-	-	-	-	-	-	-	-
US Masters	-	-	-	-	-	-	-	-	-	-
Moroccan Open	-	-	-	-	-	-	-	MC	MC	48
Open de Espana	-	-	-	-	-	-	-	-	MC	9
Open de Portugal	-	-	-	-	-	-	-	MC	70	53
Open de France	-	-	-	-	-	-	-	MC	MC	-
B&H I'national	-	-	-	-	-	-	44	MC	-	MC
Deutsche Bank	-	-	-	-	-	-	-	MC	-	28
Volvo PGA	-	-	-	-	-	-	-	-	-	32
British Masters	-	-	-	-	-	-	MC	-	MC	22
English Open	-	-	-	-	-	-	-	-	MC	26
US Open	-	-	-	-	-	-	-	-	-	-
G North Open	-	-	-	-	-	-	-	74	MC	17
Irish Open	-	-	-	-	-	-	-	-	MC	15
European Open	-	-	-	-	-	-	MC	-	46	MC
Scot Open	-	-	-	-	-	-	MC	-	-	37
British Open	-	-	-	-	-	-	4	MC	-	30
Dutch Open	-	-	-	-	-	-	MC	-	28	-
Scandinavian	-	-	-	-	-	-	MC	-	38	MC
Wales Open	-	-	-	-	-	-	-	MC	MC	33
USPGA	-	-	-	-	-	-	-	-	-	-
NW Ireland Open	-	-	-	-	-	-	-	42	19	-
WGC NEC Inv'	-	-	-	-	-	-	-	-	-	-
Scottish PGA	-	-	-	-	-	-	-	15	44	11
BMW Int' Open	-	-	-	-	-	-	MC	-	11	7
European Mas'	-	-	-	-	-	MC	MC	-	MC	34
WGC AmEx	-	-	-	-	-	-	-	-	-	-
Troph' Lancome	-	-	-	-	-	-	-	MC	-	-
German Masters	-	-	-	-	-	-	MC	-	-	46
Cannes Open	-	-	-	-	-	-	-	-	-	-
Dunhill Links	-	-	-	-	-	-	-	-	-	17
Masters Madrid	-	-	-	-	-	-	-	-	-	-
Italian Open	-	-	-	-	-	-	-	-	21	MC
Volvo Masters	-	-	-	-	-	-	-	-	-	56

Brett Rumford

27/7/77 – Australia

Along with Adam Scott and Aaron Baddeley another of Australia's talented young golfers who are taking the tours by storm.

In his first full season on the European Tour, Rumford went close to winning his first full tour title when second in the Sao Paulo Open and followed up with seventh place in the Portuguese Open.

He comfortably retained his card for 2002, finishing 57th on the Order of Merit.

He turned pro in 2000, a year after winning the Australasian Tour TPC (a pro event on the ANZ Tour). Massive off the tee and a fine iron player.

Sc Av – 71.25 (70th) DD – 289.7 (25th) DA – 69.3 (27th) GIR – 71.1 (27th) PpGIR – 1.792 (101st) SS – 78.3 (5th)

	'92	'93	'94	'95	'96	'97	'98	'99	'00	'01
Johnnie Walker	-	-	-	-	-	-	-	-	-	-
WGC Matchplay	-	-	-	-	-	-	-	-	-	-
Alfred Dunhill	-	-	-	-	-	-	-	-	-	-
S African Open	-	-	-	-	-	-	-	-	-	-
Heineken Cl'	-	-	-	-	-	-	-	-	38	16
Greg Norman	-	-	-	-	-	-	-	-	40	46
Malaysian Open	-	-	-	-	-	-	-	-	-	-
S'pore Masters	-	-	-	-	-	-	-	-	-	-
Dubai Desert	-	-	-	-	-	-	-	-	-	-
Qatar Masters	-	-	-	-	-	-	-	-	-	MC
Madeira Open	-	-	-	-	-	-	-	-	-	-
Brazil Open	-	-	-	-	-	-	-	-	-	2
Open de Arg	-	-	-	-	-	-	-	-	-	MC
US Masters	-	-	-	-	-	-	-	-	-	-
Moroccan Open	-	-	-	-	-	-	-	-	-	-
Open de Espana	-	-	-	-	-	-	-	-	-	-
Open de Portugal	-	-	-	-	-	-	-	-	-	7
Open de France	-	-	-	-	-	-	-	-	-	17
B&H I'national	-	-	-	-	-	-	-	-	-	19
Deutsche Bank	-	-	-	-	-	-	-	-	-	MC
Volvo PGA	-	-	-	-	-	-	-	-	-	-
British Masters	-	-	-	-	-	-	-	-	-	MC
English Open	-	-	-	-	-	-	-	-	54	MC
US Open	-	-	-	-	-	-	-	-	-	-
G North Open	-	-	-	-	-	-	-	-	MC	20
Irish Open	-	-	-	-	-	-	-	-	-	MC
European Open	-	-	-	-	-	-	-	-	MC	40
Scot Open	-	-	-	-	-	-	-	-	MC	11
British Open	-	-	-	-	-	-	-	-	-	MC
Dutch Open	-	-	-	-	-	-	-	-	-	-
Scandinavian	-	-	-	-	-	-	-	-	-	-
Wales Open	-	-	-	-	-	-	-	-	54	-
USPGA	-	-	-	-	-	-	-	-	-	-
NW Ireland Open	-	-	-	-	-	-	-	-	-	-
WGC NEC Inv'	-	-	-	-	-	-	-	-	-	-
Scottish PGA	-	-	-	-	-	-	-	-	-	MC
BMW Int' Open	-	-	-	-	-	-	-	-	-	37
European Mas'	-	-	-	-	-	-	-	-	34	MC
WGC AmEx	-	-	-	-	-	-	-	-	-	-
Troph' Lancome	-	-	-	-	-	-	-	-	7	43
German Masters	-	-	-	-	-	-	-	-	-	-
Cannes Open	-	-	-	-	-	-	-	-	-	-
Dunhill Links	-	-	-	-	-	-	-	-	-	13
Masters Madrid	-	-	-	-	-	-	-	-	-	39
Italian Open	-	-	-	-	-	-	-	-	-	-
Volvo Masters	-	-	-	-	-	-	-	-	-	58

Ray Russell

26/7/72 – Edinburgh, Scotland

Came strong in the second half of the season to maintain his playing privileges on the European Tour for the sixth successive year.

Fourth place in the Dutch Open and the BMW International were two of four top-ten finishes for the Scot who was involved in a bizarre incident in the English Open.

After marking his golf ball he threw it to his caddie for cleaning. His caddie missed, however, and it went in the lake and couldn't be found, costing Russell a two-shot penalty.

His sole success on the European Tour came at the 1996 Cannes Open.

Sc Av – 71.30 (73rd) DD – 270.7 (174th) DA – 64.3 (78th) GIR – 66.9 (98th) PpGIR – 1.771 (49th) SS – 58.9 (46th)

	'92	'93	'94	'95	'96	'97	'98	'99	'00	'01
Johnnie Walker	-	-	-	-	-	20	MC	-	-	-
WGC Matchplay	-	-	-	-	-	-	-	-	-	-
Alfred Dunhill	-	-	-	MC	-	-	-	-	-	-
S African Open	-	-	-	-	-	-	-	-	-	-
Heineken Cl'	-	-	-	-	-	63	MC	19	MC	MC
Greg Norman	-	-	-	-	-	-	-	-	60	26
Malaysian Open	-	-	-	-	-	-	-	-	-	MC
S'pore Masters	-	-	-	-	-	-	-	-	-	51
Dubai Desert	-	-	-	-	-	40	MC	-	41	51
Qatar Masters	-	-	-	-	-	-	-	5	69	MC
Madeira Open	-	-	-	-	-	19	-	39	-	-
Brazil Open	-	-	-	-	-	-	-	-	75	-
Open de Arg	-	-	-	-	-	-	-	-	-	-
US Masters	-	-	-	-	-	-	-	-	-	-
Moroccan Open	-	-	-	-	-	9	MC	48	-	62
Open de Espana	-	-	-	-	-	MC	MC	MC	MC	32
Open de Portugal	-	-	-	-	21	9	MC	MC	-	53
Open de France	-	-	-	-	-	MC	3	-	-	MC
B&H I'national	-	-	-	-	MC	MC	MC	MC	MC	MC
Deutsche Bank	-	-	-	-	MC	5	67	MC	MC	MC
Volvo PGA	-	-	-	-	MC	MC	MC	43	WD	58
British Masters	-	-	-	-	35	4	MC	10	10	MC
English Open	-	-	-	-	40	MC	MC	MC	59	16
US Open	-	-	-	-	-	MC	-	-	-	-
G North Open	-	-	-	-	-	-	-	MC	52	-
Irish Open	-	-	-	-	5	MC	MC	MC	40	30
European Open	-	-	-	-	24	3	MC	63	MC	52
Scot Open	-	-	-	-	47	31	MC	57	13	MC
British Open	-	-	-	-	-	38	4	MC	MC	-
Dutch Open	-	-	-	-	3	7	MC	MC	76	4
Scandinavian	-	-	-	-	37	34	MC	MC	3	36
Wales Open	-	-	-	-	-	-	-	-	72	MC
USPGA	-	-	-	-	-	-	-	-	-	-
NW Ireland Open	-	-	-	-	-	-	-	-	-	-
WGC NEC Inv'	-	-	-	-	-	-	-	-	-	-
Scottish PGA	-	-	-	-	-	-	-	11	58	51
BMW Int' Open	-	-	-	-	6	57	MC	-	32	4
European Mas'	-	-	-	-	-	-	MC	MC	-	-
WGC AmEx	-	-	-	-	-	-	-	-	-	-
Troph' Lancome	-	-	-	-	MC	32	67	MC	MC	71
German Masters	-	-	-	-	MC	57	11	51	-	10
Cannes Open	-	-	-	-	1	54	MC	-	-	-
Dunhill Links	-	-	-	-	-	-	-	-	-	MC
Masters Madrid	-	-	-	-	30	64	-	MC	15	WD
Italian Open	-	-	-	-	MC	6	MC	MC	53	23
Volvo Masters	-	-	-	-	20	61	-	-	-	55

Sponsored by Stan James

Johan Rystrom
13/1/64 – Koping, Sweden

Stalwart of the European Tour in the late 80s, the following decade wasn't so kind to the Swede as he played just 24 events between 1995 and 1999, mainly due to his failure to regain his full tour card.

Visits to Q-School weren't successful and he spent most of his playing time on the Challenge Tour.

Six top-ten finishes on the 2000 Challenge Tour, including victory in the Costa Blanca Challenge, saw him graduate to the full tour again.

Has finished second on the European Tour three times including twice in 1992 when he finished 52nd on the Order of Merit.

Sc Av – 71.39 (86th) DD – 282.1 (77th) DA – 64.9 (73rd) GIR – 69.6 (53rd) PpGIR – 1.783 (76th) SS – 57.6 (58th)

	'92	'93	'94	'95	'96	'97	'98	'99	'00	'01
Johnnie Walker	-	MC	-	-	-	-	-	-	-	MC
WGC Matchplay	-	-	-	-	-	-	-	-	-	-
Alfred Dunhill	-	-	-	-	-	-	-	-	-	63
S African Open	-	-	-	-	-	-	-	-	-	9
Heineken Cl'	-	-	-	-	-	-	-	-	-	-
Greg Norman	-	-	-	-	-	-	-	-	-	-
Malaysian Open	-	-	-	-	-	-	-	-	-	MC
S'pore Masters	-	-	-	-	-	-	-	-	-	MC
Dubai Desert	-	-	69	-	-	-	-	-	-	68
Qatar Masters	-	-	-	-	-	-	-	-	-	46
Madeira Open	-	-	-	-	-	-	63	34	69	-
Brazil Open	-	-	-	-	-	-	-	MC	-	-
Open de Arg	-	-	-	-	-	-	-	-	-	-
US Masters	-	-	-	-	-	-	-	-	-	-
Moroccan Open	-	MC	-	-	-	MC	MC	MC	-	65
Open de Espana	29	MC	MC	-	-	-	-	-	-	79
Open de Portugal	18	14	MC	-	-	-	51	-	-	60
Open de France	28	6	MC	-	-	66	37	-	-	-
B&H I'national	59	MC	-	-	-	-	-	-	-	19
Deutsche Bank	-	-	-	-	-	-	-	-	-	MC
Volvo PGA	9	MC	64	-	-	-	-	-	-	-
British Masters	MC	MC	MC	-	-	-	-	MC	-	MC
English Open	62	MC	70	-	-	-	-	MC	-	51
US Open	-	-	-	-	-	-	-	-	-	-
G North Open	-	-	-	-	-	-	16	-	-	-
Irish Open	-	-	-	-	-	-	-	-	-	MC
European Open	-	MC	37	-	-	-	-	MC	-	MC
Scot Open	-	-	-	-	-	-	-	28	-	-
British Open	MC	-	-	-	-	-	62	-	-	-
Dutch Open	46	71	MC	-	-	-	-	MC	-	MC
Scandinavian	MC	37	MC	-	-	WD	37	MC	16	-
Wales Open	-	-	-	-	-	-	-	-	-	-
USPGA	-	-	-	-	-	-	-	-	-	-
NW Ireland Open	-	-	-	-	-	-	-	-	57	19
WGC NEC Inv'	-	-	-	-	-	-	-	-	-	-
Scottish PGA	-	-	-	-	-	-	-	43	-	22
BMW Int' Open	-	-	-	-	-	-	-	MC	-	30
European Mas'	MC	67	MC	-	-	-	-	MC	-	37
WGC AmEx	-	-	-	-	-	-	-	-	-	-
Troph' Lancome	36	44	-	-	-	-	-	-	-	MC
German Masters	MC	48	MC	-	-	-	-	-	-	-
Cannes Open	MC	MC	-	-	-	MC	-	-	-	6
Dunhill Links	-	-	-	-	-	-	-	-	-	-
Masters Madrid	MC	MC	-	-	-	-	MC	-	-	39
Italian Open	MC	-	-	-	-	-	-	-	-	29
Volvo Masters	50	-	-	-	-	-	-	-	-	-

Jarmo Sandelin
10/5/67 – Imatra, Finland (represents Sweden)

Big-hitting Finnish born Swede who found himself spending more time with his young family than on the practice range during 2001.

Prior to experiencing the joy of parenthood, Monaco-based Sandelin had been performing impressively on the European Tour.

His best season so far came in 1999 with 9th place in the Order of Merit and automatic Ryder Cup qualification following victories in both the Spanish Open and German Open.

Crept into the 2001 Order of Merit top 100 thanks mainly to fourth place at the Scandinavian Masters in August. Ranked highly in last season's putting stats.

Sc Av – 71.77 (118th) DD – 276.9 (124th) DA – 63.2 (96th) GIR – 64.6 (139th) PpGIR – 1.766 (33rd) SS – 64.7 (19th)

	'92	'93	'94	'95	'96	'97	'98	'99	'00	'01
Johnnie Walker	-	-	MC	-	-	MC	-	-	-	-
WGC Matchplay	-	-	-	-	-	-	-	-	-	-
Alfred Dunhill	-	-	-	-	-	48	MC	MC	-	-
S African Open	-	-	-	-	-	MC	26	43	-	-
Heineken Cl'	-	-	-	-	-	8	7	55	-	-
Greg Norman	-	-	-	-	-	-	-	-	37	-
Malaysian Open	-	-	-	-	-	-	-	21	-	-
S'pore Masters	-	-	-	-	-	-	-	-	-	-
Dubai Desert	-	-	23	-	MC	33	15	-	24	MC
Qatar Masters	-	-	-	-	-	-	69	-	27	MC
Madeira Open	-	-	55	1	MC	-	-	-	-	11
Brazil Open	-	-	-	-	-	-	-	-	68	-
Open de Arg	-	-	-	-	-	-	-	-	-	-
US Masters	-	-	-	-	-	-	-	-	-	-
Moroccan Open	71	-	-	-	-	-	-	-	-	-
Open de Espana	-	-	42	55	3	64	1	-	67	9
Open de Portugal	-	-	MC	34	MC	2	-	-	-	44
Open de France	-	-	MC	-	-	14	11	22	MC	-
B&H I'national	-	-	65	-	-	-	MC	-	-	MC
Deutsche Bank	-	-	10	64	63	27	7	-	65	57
Volvo PGA	-	-	MC	4	54	MC	10	-	69	71
British Masters	-	-	MC	-	53	69	38	8	-	-
English Open	-	-	63	-	59	MC	MC	-	-	-
US Open	-	-	-	-	-	-	-	-	MC	WD
G North Open	-	-	-	-	MC	-	-	-	-	-
Irish Open	-	-	33	32	MC	39	MC	10	-	MC
European Open	-	-	MC	-	27	23	-	5	-	23
Scot Open	-	-	-	-	49	20	43	7	MC	-
British Open	-	-	-	76	-	-	65	31	-	-
Dutch Open	-	-	MC	-	30	-	-	-	-	-
Scandinavian	-	-	50	MC	MC	25	30	-	-	4
Wales Open	-	-	-	-	-	-	-	-	-	65
USPGA	-	-	-	-	-	-	MC	24	-	-
NW Ireland Open	-	-	-	-	-	-	-	-	-	-
WGC NEC Inv'	-	-	-	-	-	-	-	30	-	-
Scottish PGA	-	-	-	-	-	-	-	-	29	-
BMW Int' Open	-	-	2	-	12	MC	-	-	13	76
European Mas'	-	-	MC	18	40	30	-	-	MC	MC
WGC AmEx	-	-	-	-	-	-	-	20	-	-
Troph' Lancome	-	-	68	MC	2	2	6	MC	-	-
German Masters	-	-	13	37	MC	8	69	MC	-	32
Cannes Open	-	-	55	52	58	MC	-	-	-	-
Dunhill Links	-	-	-	-	-	-	-	-	-	WD
Masters Madrid	-	-	MC	23	MC	-	-	-	MC	MC
Italian Open	-	-	28	MC	12	13	31	MC	-	-
Volvo Masters	-	-	46	64	29	23	10	44	-	-

Adam Scott

16/7/80 – Adelaide, Australia

Widely tipped to be the next Tiger Woods after a stunning junior and amateur career that saw him win a multitude of titles.

Uses the same coach as Woods, Butch Harmon, and his swing is very similar.

Sees his future on the US Tour but looks destined to be a force on the European Tour after a superb first full season.

He won the Alfred Dunhill Championship and posted five other top ten finishes, although he might have won more often but for the odd last round collapse.

Massive off the tee, and accurate too, his putting was his only weakness last season.

Sc Av – 70.12 (12th) DD – 297.4 (5th) DA – 69.4 (26th) GIR – 74.6 (10th) PpGIR – 1.786 (88th) SS – 52.7 (98th)

Event	'92	'93	'94	'95	'96	'97	'98	'99	'00	'01
Johnnie Walker	-	-	-	-	-	-	-	-	-	-
WGC Matchplay	-	-	-	-	-	-	-	-	-	-
Alfred Dunhill	-	-	-	-	-	-	-	-	-	1
S African Open	-	-	-	-	-	-	-	-	-	-
Heineken Cl'	-	-	-	-	-	-	-	-	-	MC
Greg Norman	-	-	-	-	-	-	-	-	37	26
Malaysian Open	-	-	-	-	-	-	-	-	-	-
S'pore Masters	-	-	-	-	-	-	-	-	-	-
Dubai Desert	-	-	-	-	-	-	-	-	-	MC
Qatar Masters	-	-	-	-	-	-	-	-	-	-
Madeira Open	-	-	-	-	-	-	-	-	-	-
Brazil Open	-	-	-	-	-	-	-	-	-	-
Open de Arg	-	-	-	-	-	-	-	-	-	-
US Masters	-	-	-	-	-	-	-	-	-	-
Moroccan Open	-	-	-	-	-	-	-	6	-	-
Open de Espana	-	-	-	-	-	-	-	-	-	-
Open de Portugal	-	-	-	-	-	-	-	-	-	-
Open de France	-	-	-	-	-	-	-	-	-	-
B&H I'national	-	-	-	-	-	-	-	5	WD	-
Deutsche Bank	-	-	-	-	-	-	-	-	-	43
Volvo PGA	-	-	-	-	-	-	-	-	-	32
British Masters	-	-	-	-	-	-	-	-	MC	14
English Open	-	-	-	-	-	-	-	-	-	3
US Open	-	-	-	-	-	-	-	-	-	-
G North Open	-	-	-	-	-	-	-	61	-	-
Irish Open	-	-	-	-	-	-	-	-	10	6
European Open	-	-	-	-	-	-	-	-	MC	62
Scot Open	-	-	-	-	-	-	-	-	12	3
British Open	-	-	-	-	-	-	-	-	MC	47
Dutch Open	-	-	-	-	-	-	-	-	-	-
Scandinavian	-	-	-	-	-	-	-	-	-	4
Wales Open	-	-	-	-	-	-	-	-	-	-
USPGA	-	-	-	-	-	-	-	-	MC	-
NW Ireland Open	-	-	-	-	-	-	-	-	-	-
WGC NEC Inv'	-	-	-	-	-	-	-	-	-	-
Scottish PGA	-	-	-	-	-	-	-	-	-	-
BMW Int' Open	-	-	-	-	-	-	-	-	-	23
European Mas'	-	-	-	-	-	-	-	-	-	23
WGC AmEx	-	-	-	-	-	-	-	-	-	-
Troph' Lancome	-	-	-	-	-	-	-	-	-	11
German Masters	-	-	-	-	-	-	-	-	6	75
Cannes Open	-	-	-	-	-	-	-	-	-	-
Dunhill Links	-	-	-	-	-	-	-	-	-	35
Masters Madrid	-	-	-	-	-	-	-	-	-	-
Italian Open	-	-	-	-	-	-	-	-	-	-
Volvo Masters	-	-	-	-	-	-	-	-	-	3

John Senden

20/4/71 – Brisbane, Australia

Tall Australian whose first full season on Tour was 1999, having won twice on the 1998 Challenge Tour.

Prior to that, he had played on the Australasian and Asian Tours, capturing the 1996 Indonesian PGA Championship.

His best European Tour result to date is fourth in the 2000 French Open.

He was a consistent performer last season, only missing three cuts, with his best finish sixth at the Qatar Masters in March.

Took a month off towards the end of the year and now appears to see his future in the USA. Strong off the tee – both long and accurate.

Sc Av – 71.04 (48th) DD – 286.5 (39th) DA – 69.5 (25th) GIR – 67.3 (87th) PpGIR – 1.800 (117th) SS – 76.0 (7th)

Event	'92	'93	'94	'95	'96	'97	'98	'99	'00	'01
Johnnie Walker	-	-	-	-	MC	69	-	-	MC	67
WGC Matchplay	-	-	-	-	-	-	-	-	-	-
Alfred Dunhill	-	-	-	-	-	-	-	MC	22	-
S African Open	-	-	-	-	-	-	-	-	63	-
Heineken Cl'	-	-	-	-	MC	MC	MC	10	25	60
Greg Norman	-	-	-	-	-	-	-	-	MC	31
Malaysian Open	-	-	-	-	-	-	-	-	-	-
S'pore Masters	-	-	-	-	-	-	-	-	-	-
Dubai Desert	-	-	-	-	-	-	-	-	33	-
Qatar Masters	-	-	-	-	-	-	-	-	-	6
Madeira Open	-	-	-	-	-	-	MC	47	-	-
Brazil Open	-	-	-	-	-	-	-	-	-	-
Open de Arg	-	-	-	-	-	-	-	-	-	-
US Masters	-	-	-	-	-	-	-	-	-	-
Moroccan Open	-	-	-	-	-	-	-	-	-	-
Open de Espana	-	-	-	-	-	-	-	MC	33	71
Open de Portugal	-	-	-	-	-	-	-	-	-	-
Open de France	-	-	-	-	-	-	-	MC	4	41
B&H I'national	-	-	-	-	-	-	-	39	14	MC
Deutsche Bank	-	-	-	-	-	-	-	17	MC	52
Volvo PGA	-	-	-	-	-	-	-	-	77	14
British Masters	-	-	-	-	-	-	-	MC	MC	27
English Open	-	-	-	-	-	-	-	15	-	-
US Open	-	-	-	-	-	-	-	-	-	-
G North Open	-	-	-	-	-	-	-	53	MC	-
Irish Open	-	-	-	-	-	-	-	MC	MC	20
European Open	-	-	-	-	-	-	-	6	MC	45
Scot Open	-	-	-	-	-	-	-	37	60	47
British Open	-	-	-	-	-	-	-	-	-	-
Dutch Open	-	-	-	-	-	-	-	MC	MC	24
Scandinavian	-	-	-	-	-	-	-	DQ	10	MC
Wales Open	-	-	-	-	-	-	-	-	14	20
USPGA	-	-	-	-	-	-	-	-	-	-
NW Ireland Open	-	-	-	-	-	-	-	-	-	-
WGC NEC Inv'	-	-	-	-	-	-	-	-	-	-
Scottish PGA	-	-	-	-	-	-	-	-	11	64
BMW Int' Open	-	-	-	-	-	-	-	MC	64	37
European Mas'	-	-	-	-	-	-	-	MC	MC	-
WGC AmEx	-	-	-	-	-	-	-	-	-	-
Troph' Lancome	-	-	-	-	-	-	-	72	24	-
German Masters	-	-	-	-	-	-	-	-	30	41
Cannes Open	-	-	-	-	-	-	-	-	-	-
Dunhill Links	-	-	-	-	-	-	-	-	-	-
Masters Madrid	-	-	-	-	-	-	-	43	-	MC
Italian Open	-	-	-	-	-	-	-	10	-	-
Volvo Masters	-	-	-	-	-	-	-	-	-	-

Patrick Sjoland
13/5/71 – Boras, Sweden

A disappointing season in 2001 for the Marbella-based Swede who failed to hit top form.

Having turned pro in 1990, Sjoland earned his full tour card for 1996 after four visits to the Q-School.

Made solid progress over the next two years and then came his finest season to date in 1998. He won the Italian Open, took part in all four Majors and finished fifth in the Order of Merit.

Slipped back down the rankings in 1999 but captured the Hong Kong Open and then went on to achieve his second European Tour victory in the 2000 Irish Open.

Sc Av – 72.67 (182nd) DD – 267.2 (184th) DA – 55.5 (177th) GIR – 63.6 (155th) PpGIR – 1.773 (52nd) SS – 56.0 (70th)

	'92	'93	'94	'95	'96	'97	'98	'99	'00	'01
Johnnie Walker	-	-	-	-	-	-	37	-	MC	-
WGC Matchplay	-	-	-	-	-	-	-	9	-	33
Alfred Dunhill	-	-	-	-	-	-	MC	10	-	-
S African Open	-	-	-	-	-	64	3	26	MC	-
Heineken Cl'	-	-	-	-	-	-	MC	-	13	WD
Greg Norman	-	-	-	-	-	-	-	-	MC	WD
Malaysian Open	-	-	-	-	-	-	-	-	23	18
S'pore Masters	-	-	-	-	-	-	-	-	-	-
Dubai Desert	-	-	-	-	-	MC	MC	74	2	MC
Qatar Masters	-	-	-	-	-	-	2	11	19	59
Madeira Open	-	-	-	-	12	MC	-	-	-	-
Brazil Open	-	-	-	-	-	-	-	-	-	-
Open de Arg	-	-	-	-	-	-	-	-	-	-
US Masters	-	-	-	-	-	-	MC	-	-	-
Moroccan Open	-	-	-	MC	MC	-	-	14	-	-
Open de Espana	-	-	-	MC	47	26	MC	52	71	
Open de Portugal	-	-	-	55	-	34	-	-	-	19
Open de France	-	-	-	-	WD	-	-	-	-	MC
B&H I'national	-	-	-	MC	7	7	7	-	12	
Deutsche Bank	-	-	-	-	-	MC	42	-	28	
Volvo PGA	-	-	-	7	MC	2	62	MC	45	
British Masters	-	-	-	-	8	-	26	8	53	
English Open	-	-	-	MC	MC	5	-	MC	-	
US Open	-	-	-	-	-	-	MC	-	-	-
G North Open	-	-	-	29	49	-	-	-	-	
Irish Open	-	-	-	66	-	-	61	1	69	
European Open	-	-	-	55	27	-	MC	MC	MC	
Scot Open	-	-	MC	25	20	10	69	WD		
British Open	-	-	-	-	36	18	MC	-		
Dutch Open	-	-	MC	22	9	MC	-	MC		
Scandinavian	-	-	MC	MC	73	MC	31	MC		
Wales Open	-	-	-	-	-	-	-	MC		
USPGA	-	-	-	-	MC	MC	-	-		
NW Ireland Open	-	-	-	-	-	-	-	-		
WGC NEC Inv'	-	-	-	-	-	-	-	-		
Scottish PGA	-	-	-	-	-	-	-	MC		
BMW Int' Open	-	-	24	31	MC	-	MC	79		
European Mas'	-	-	32	4	2	9	59	MC		
WGC AmEx	-	-	-	-	-	-	-	-		
Troph' Lancome	-	-	33	5	33	MC	MC	MC		
German Masters	-	-	-	4	61	MC	17	MC		
Cannes Open	-	-	MC	61	49	-	-	69		
Dunhill Links	-	-	-	-	-	-	-	17		
Masters Madrid	-	-	MC	54	-	-	50	-		
Italian Open	-	-	2	12	1	20	-	29		
Volvo Masters	-	-	48	5	49	26	17	-		

Des Smyth
12/2/53 – Drogheda, Ireland

Few players have been on the Tour as long as the vastly experienced Smyth, who has won titles over three decades and became the oldest ever winner when he won the 2001 Madera Island Open at 48 years and 34 days.

Prior to that, his last win was back in 1993 at the Madrid Open.

He turned pro in 1974 having learnt his game on the links of Baltry, Co. Louth and has always been a strong player in adverse conditions.

Accurate off the tee and a good iron player, he made the Ryder Cup team as long ago as 1979 (and 1981).

Sc Av – 71.61 (101st) DD – 272.5 (168th) DA – 69.3 (27th) GIR – 71.5 (22nd) PpGIR – 1.823 (157th) SS – 60.6 (36th)

	'92	'93	'94	'95	'96	'97	'98	'99	'00	'01
Johnnie Walker	MC	-	34							
WGC Matchplay	-									
Alfred Dunhill	-	-	17	-	-					
S African Open	-	-	-	-	MC					
Heineken Cl'	-									
Greg Norman	-									
Malaysian Open	-									
S'pore Masters	-									
Dubai Desert	21	MC	MC	-	40	25	33	WD	68	43
Qatar Masters	-	-	-	-	-	-	64	MC	MC	27
Madeira Open	-	32	34	55	3	20	-	53	MC	1
Brazil Open	-									
Open de Arg	-									
US Masters	-									
Moroccan Open	-	12	48	MC	MC	-	14	-	40	-
Open de Espana	-	MC	-	MC	MC	MC	67	17	MC	42
Open de Portugal	-	21	MC	MC	14	DQ	40	25	MC	MC
Open de France	MC	MC	MC	34	MC	15	68	17	22	-
B&H I'national	23	MC	72	WD	MC	MC	52	MC	DQ	-
Deutsche Bank	-	-	-	MC	MC	MC	67	MC	70	
Volvo PGA	MC	40	29	MC	MC	65	MC	29	26	45
British Masters	31	MC	49	11	MC	MC	-	32	29	57
English Open	MC	MC	4	MC	MC	MC	MC	MC	MC	MC
US Open	-									
G North Open	-	-	-	-	-	MC	-	MC	-	
Irish Open	69	23	MC	24	MC	MC	MC	25	6	MC
European Open	27	11	MC	MC	MC	MC	61	45	60	MC
Scot Open	-	-	-	20	MC	MC	37	MC	MC	
British Open	MC	27	MC	-	DQ	-	14	MC	-	13
Dutch Open	15	41	40	MC	25	MC	MC	MC	MC	MC
Scandinavian	MC	21	MC	MC	38	25	MC	52	-	
Wales Open	-	-	-	-	-	-	-	-	MC	MC
USPGA	-									
NW Ireland Open	-	-	-	-	-	-	-	3	42	43
WGC NEC Inv'	-									
Scottish PGA	-	-	-	-	-	-	-	-	-	11
BMW Int' Open	-	-	-	-	-	-	MC	-	-	MC
European Mas'	MC	14	44	MC	MC	MC	MC	MC	MC	-
WGC AmEx	-									
Troph' Lancome	-	57	30	50	MC	65	MC	57	38	MC
German Masters	MC	MC	28	MC	-	21	-	-	-	61
Cannes Open	-	25	34	MC	-	29	MC	-	-	-
Dunhill Links	-	-	-	-	-	-	-	-	-	MC
Masters Madrid	13	8	-	8	14	36	-	61	25	31
Italian Open	-	-	-	-	-	-	WD	-	MC	-
Volvo Masters	-	46								

Henrik Stenson
5/4/76 – Gothenburg, Sweden

Dominated the 2000 Challenge Tour, recording three victories – including the Challenge Grand Final – and winning the Order of Merit, before joining the full tour last season.

Big things were expected of this Swede and he didn't disappoint, winning the prestigious B&H International and posting two other top-ten finishes to claim 44th place in the Order of Merit.

A prolific winner at amateur level, he turned pro in 1998 and finished 21st on the Challenge Tour in his first season (1999) from just seven events.

A strong iron player but weak putter last season.
Sc Av – 71.88 (127th) DD – 282.3 (74th) DA – 61.5 (121st) GIR – 70.2 (42nd) PpGIR – 1.823 (157th) SS – 54.5 (83rd)

	'92	'93	'94	'95	'96	'97	'98	'99	'00	'01
Johnnie Walker	-	-	-	-	-	-	-	-	-	MC
WGC Matchplay	-	-	-	-	-	-	-	-	-	-
Alfred Dunhill	-	-	-	-	-	-	-	-	-	-
S African Open	-	-	-	-	-	-	-	-	-	-
Heineken Cl'	-	-	-	-	-	-	-	-	-	66
Greg Norman	-	-	-	-	-	-	-	-	-	64
Malaysian Open	-	-	-	-	-	-	-	-	-	-
S'pore Masters	-	-	-	-	-	-	-	-	-	-
Dubai Desert	-	-	-	-	-	-	-	-	-	MC
Qatar Masters	-	-	-	-	-	-	-	-	-	67
Madeira Open	-	-	-	-	-	-	-	-	18	32
Brazil Open	-	-	-	-	-	-	-	-	-	40
Open de Arg	-	-	-	-	-	-	-	-	-	MC
US Masters	-	-	-	-	-	-	-	-	-	-
Moroccan Open	-	-	-	-	-	-	-	-	-	-
Open de Espana	-	-	-	-	-	MC	-	-	-	MC
Open de Portugal	-	-	-	-	-	-	-	-	-	27
Open de France	-	-	-	-	-	-	-	-	-	-
B&H I'national	-	-	-	-	-	-	-	-	-	1
Deutsche Bank	-	-	-	-	-	-	-	-	-	8
Volvo PGA	-	-	-	-	-	-	-	-	-	39
British Masters	-	-	-	-	-	-	-	-	-	-
English Open	-	-	-	-	-	-	-	-	-	MC
US Open	-	-	-	-	-	-	-	-	-	-
G North Open	-	-	-	-	-	-	-	-	-	-
Irish Open	-	-	-	-	-	-	-	-	-	MC
European Open	-	-	-	-	-	-	-	-	-	WD
Scot Open	-	-	-	-	-	-	-	-	-	MC
British Open	-	-	-	-	-	-	-	-	-	MC
Dutch Open	-	-	-	-	-	-	-	-	-	-
Scandinavian	-	-	-	-	-	-	MC	30	11	80
Wales Open	-	-	-	-	-	-	-	-	-	-
USPGA	-	-	-	-	-	-	-	-	-	-
NW Ireland Open	-	-	-	-	-	-	-	11	-	-
WGC NEC Inv'	-	-	-	-	-	-	-	-	-	-
Scottish PGA	-	-	-	-	-	-	-	-	11	MC
BMW Int' Open	-	-	-	-	-	-	-	-	-	-
European Mas'	-	-	-	-	-	-	-	-	-	-
WGC AmEx	-	-	-	-	-	-	-	-	-	-
Troph' Lancome	-	-	-	-	-	-	-	-	-	MC
German Masters	-	-	-	-	-	-	-	-	-	46
Cannes Open	-	-	-	-	-	-	-	-	-	-
Dunhill Links	-	-	-	-	-	-	-	-	-	MC
Masters Madrid	-	-	-	-	-	-	-	-	-	57
Italian Open	-	-	-	-	-	-	-	-	-	7
Volvo Masters	-	-	-	-	-	-	-	-	-	56

Sven Struver
9/8/67 – Bremen, Germany

Three-time European Tour winner who has not shown his best form since peaking at 13th in the 1998 Order of Merit.

The most productive period of his career so far, in terms of tournament results was 1996-1998, his last victory coming in a play-off for the 1998 European Masters.

After visits to the Q-School in 1990 and 1991, he developed into a consistent performer on the full tour and the highlight of his 2001 season was second place at the Open de Portugal.

Struver has often been compared to compatriot Bernhard Langer, and one of his main strengths is accuracy off the tee.
Sc Av – 71.33 (79th) DD – 274.1 (156th) DA – 67.4 (46th) GIR – 67.8 (78th) PpGIR – 1.796 (109th) SS – 38.0 (188th)

	'92	'93	'94	'95	'96	'97	'98	'99	'00	'01
Johnnie Walker	-	-	10	12	18	MC	25	-	-	-
WGC Matchplay	-	-	-	-	-	-	-	-	-	-
Alfred Dunhill	-	-	-	1	12	23	22	MC	-	9
S African Open	-	-	-	-	9	46	4	19	45	-
Heineken Cl'	-	-	-	MC	MC	55	36	25	34	-
Greg Norman	-	-	-	-	-	-	-	-	76	MC
Malaysian Open	-	-	-	-	-	-	-	-	-	-
S'pore Masters	-	-	-	-	-	-	-	-	-	-
Dubai Desert	9	51	23	MC	MC	-	46	46	MC	33
Qatar Masters	-	-	-	-	-	-	13	MC	40	67
Madeira Open	-	19	-	MC	-	-	-	-	-	-
Brazil Open	-	-	-	-	-	-	-	-	-	-
Open de Arg	-	-	-	-	-	-	-	-	-	-
US Masters	-	-	-	-	-	-	-	-	-	-
Moroccan Open	MC	20	45	-	-	-	52	-	-	-
Open de Espana	-	WD	33	MC	MC	-	MC	-	21	49
Open de Portugal	-	24	MC	MC	-	-	MC	-	-	2
Open de France	MC	20	22	15	WD	50	-	50	-	-
B&H I'national	33	18	19	MC	29	44	MC	28	27	-
Deutsche Bank	-	-	55	MC	MC	MC	MC	MC	45	MC
Volvo PGA	MC	MC	17	MC	MC	54	10	MC	MC	MC
British Masters	-	61	22	WD	15	61	26	43	14	-
English Open	-	MC	-	-	-	-	-	-	-	-
US Open	-	-	-	-	-	-	-	32	-	-
G North Open	-	-	-	-	-	-	-	11	MC	-
Irish Open	-	MC	28	-	MC	MC	46	7	32	54
European Open	-	MC	-	30	29	41	51	MC	28	23
Scot Open	-	-	-	-	59	MC	MC	MC	37	-
British Open	-	-	-	-	-	33	66	-	-	-
Dutch Open	47	-	-	WD	1	42	MC	26	MC	-
Scandinavian	14	7	46	57	MC	43	59	36	MC	-
Wales Open	-	-	-	-	-	-	-	-	-	14
USPGA	-	-	-	-	-	-	-	75	-	-
NW Ireland Open	-	-	-	-	-	-	-	-	-	-
WGC NEC Inv'	-	-	-	-	-	-	-	-	-	-
Scottish PGA	-	-	-	-	-	-	-	-	-	MC
BMW Int' Open	MC	47	7	63	52	MC	24	27	MC	78
European Mas'	5	53	52	17	59	MC	1	6	MC	MC
WGC AmEx	-	-	-	-	-	-	-	-	-	-
Troph' Lancome	-	-	-	-	21	5	MC	57	MC	14
German Masters	49	48	4	8	63	21	37	MC	41	MC
Cannes Open	-	65	MC	29	MC	38	2	-	-	-
Dunhill Links	-	-	-	-	-	-	-	-	-	MC
Masters Madrid	-	MC	MC	MC	-	36	-	MC	MC	-
Italian Open	-	32	56	-	15	MC	6	-	-	14
Volvo Masters	-	-	13	28	-	32	54	-	-	52

Greg Turner

21/2/63 – Dunedin, New Zealand

Since joining the European Tour in 1986, this experienced Kiwi has won on five occasions – his last success coming in the 1997 British Masters.

More recently he captured the 1999 Australian PGA Championship and, in 2001, he was a runner-up at the French Open.

Turner comes from a talented sporting family – he has represented New Zealand a total of 21 times in World and Dunhill Cups, while one brother, Glenn, is a former test cricketer and another, Brian, was a hockey international.

He is accurate off the tee, a good scrambler, and copes better than most with adverse weather conditions.

Sc Av – 71.07 (51st) DD – 283.1 (68th) DA – 68.6 (31st) GIR – 70.0 (50th) PpGIR – 1.761 (31st) SS – 47.9 (143rd)

	'92	'93	'94	'95	'96	'97	'98	'99	'00	'01
Johnnie Walker	-	63	-	-	MC	MC	25	-	-	58
WGC Matchplay	-	-	-	-	-	-	-	-	-	-
Alfred Dunhill	-	-	51	17	-	-	-	-	-	-
S African Open	-	-	-	-	-	-	-	-	-	-
Heineken Cl'	-	-	-	-	MC	11	35	-	6	11
Greg Norman	-	-	-	-	-	-	-	-	MC	MC
Malaysian Open	-	-	-	-	-	-	-	-	-	-
S'pore Masters	-	-	-	-	-	-	-	-	-	-
Dubai Desert	-	-	-	-	-	-	-	-	-	-
Qatar Masters	-	-	-	-	-	-	-	-	-	-
Madeira Open	-	-	-	-	-	-	-	-	-	-
Brazil Open	-	-	-	-	-	-	-	-	-	-
Open de' Arg	-	-	-	-	-	-	-	-	-	-
US Masters	-	-	-	-	-	-	-	-	-	-
Moroccan Open	-	-	-	-	-	-	-	-	-	-
Open de Espana	MC	-	-	27	-	26	MC	MC	-	-
Open de Portugal	-	MC	36	-	-	-	-	-	-	27
Open de France	12	41	54	4	7	MC	52	2	WD	2
B&H I'national	MC	50	-	34	49	13	7	57	MC	-
Deutsche Bank	-	-	-	-	35	-	MC	38	35	20
Volvo PGA	MC	7	MC	49	46	74	33	40	MC	MC
British Masters	55	50	26	11	WD	1	MC	47	MC	22
English Open	MC	48	17	-	12	MC	MC	-	12	55
US Open	-	-	-	-	-	-	-	-	-	33
G North Open	-	-	-	-	-	40	-	31	9	-
Irish Open	11	-	4	MC	MC	-	-	41	80	-
European Open	MC	40	21	MC	MC	41	-	31	MC	58
Scot Open	MC	-	-	-	11	MC	47	66	MC	-
British Open	MC	38	20	-	7	51	14	MC	-	MC
Dutch Open	10	62	MC	25	-	-	30	-	51	7
Scandinavian	11	55	MC	62	MC	20	16	9	11	72
Wales Open	-	-	-	-	-	-	-	-	-	-
USPGA	-	-	-	-	-	MC	16	MC	-	-
NW Ireland Open	-	-	-	-	-	-	-	-	-	-
WGC NEC Inv'	-	-	-	-	-	-	-	21	-	-
Scottish PGA	-	-	-	-	-	-	-	-	-	22
BMW Int' Open	MC	-	-	-	-	12	-	-	20	30
European Mas'	MC	-	-	-	MC	-	-	-	-	16
WGC AmEx	-	-	-	-	-	-	-	-	-	-
Troph' Lancome	-	37	17	14	33	32	2	MC	MC	-
German Masters	MC	MC	10	15	17	-	21	17	17	-
Cannes Open	-	-	13	42	13	MC	2	-	-	-
Dunhill Links	-	-	-	-	-	-	-	-	-	MC
Masters Madrid	-	38	30	-	7	-	-	-	-	MC
Italian Open	MC	1	2	15	7	42	13	38	-	MC
Volvo Masters	-	39	36	24	16	42	26	26	-	12

Anthony Wall

29/5/75 – London, England

Sunningdale based pro who kicked off the 2001 season making a spirited defence of his Alfred Dunhill Championship title by finishing fifth.

His victory in the previous year's event was his first full tour win.

He is the son of a London cabbie and first earned a main tour card via the Q-School in 1996 but his debut season was disrupted by glandular fever.

He recovered to make a successful return to the Q-School in 1997 and went on to achieve three top-ten finishes in 1998.

Wall is equipped with a solid all-round game, performing especially well with the putter.

Sc Av – 70.35 (15th) DD – 284.6 (50th) DA – 66.5 (59th) GIR – 70.2 (42nd) PpGIR – 1.749 (16th) SS – 51.1 (110th)

	'92	'93	'94	'95	'96	'97	'98	'99	'00	'01
Johnnie Walker	-	-	-	-	-	-	-	-	-	-
WGC Matchplay	-	-	-	-	-	-	-	-	-	-
Alfred Dunhill	-	-	-	-	MC	7	61	1	5	
S African Open	-	-	-	-	-	17	71	34	-	
Heineken Cl'	-	-	-	-	-	-	57	68	MC	
Greg Norman	-	-	-	-	-	-	-	MC	53	
Malaysian Open	-	-	-	-	-	-	-	-	-	
S'pore Masters	-	-	-	-	-	-	-	-	17	
Dubai Desert	-	-	-	-	-	-	64	8	WD	MC
Qatar Masters	-	-	-	-	-	-	MC	MC	-	MC
Madeira Open	-	-	-	-	-	MC	68	-	-	
Brazil Open	-	-	-	-	-	-	-	-	7	
Open de Arg	-	-	-	-	-	-	-	-	13	
US Masters	-	-	-	-	-	-	-	-	-	
Moroccan Open	-	-	-	-	-	MC	MC	-	-	
Open de Espana	-	-	-	-	-	-	7	WD		
Open de Portugal	-	-	-	-	-	-	6	14	-	
Open de France	-	-	-	-	-	MC	-	41	17	
B&H I'national	-	-	-	-	-	MC	MC	5	42	
Deutsche Bank	-	-	-	-	-	80	33	MC	47	
Volvo PGA	-	-	-	-	-	-	MC	MC	17	
British Masters	-	-	-	-	-	MC	38	-	8	
English Open	-	-	-	-	-	36	59	17	23	
US Open	-	-	-	-	-	-	-	-	-	
G North Open	-	-	-	-	MC	-	WD	-	-	
Irish Open	-	-	-	-	-	-	65	MC	15	
European Open	-	-	-	-	-	MC	49	MC	MC	
Scot Open	-	-	-	-	-	-	46	65	28	
British Open	-	-	-	-	-	-	-	-	-	
Dutch Open	-	-	-	-	-	-	MC	MC	WD	
Scandinavian	-	-	-	-	-	70	MC	-	29	
Wales Open	-	-	-	-	-	-	-	55	49	
USPGA	-	-	-	-	-	-	-	-	-	
NW Ireland Open	-	-	-	-	-	-	-	-	-	
WGC NEC Inv'	-	-	-	-	-	-	-	-	-	
Scottish PGA	-	-	-	-	-	-	-	-	37	
BMW Int' Open	-	-	-	-	-	MC	MC	16	MC	
European Mas'	-	-	-	-	-	68	50	-	MC	
WGC AmEx	-	-	-	-	-	-	-	-	-	
Troph' Lancome	-	-	-	-	-	7	43	63	6	
German Masters	-	-	-	-	-	28	34	51	46	
Cannes Open	-	-	-	-	-	-	-	-	-	
Dunhill Links	-	-	-	-	-	-	-	-	MC	
Masters Madrid	-	-	-	-	-	23	20	19	MC	
Italian Open	-	-	-	-	MC	-	54	-	17	
Volvo Masters	-	-	-	-	-	-	-	16	23	33

Steve Webster

17/11/75 – Nuneaton, England

Turned pro in 1995, following his rise to prominence as an amateur, culminating in 24th place and the Amateur Medal in the Open at St Andrews.

Won the Q-School at his first attempt but made a disappointing start to his full tour career, missing his first nine cuts.

He returned to the Q-School in 1996 where fourth place saw him regain his card and has made steady progress ever since, finishing as runner-up in the 1998 German Open and again at the 1999 Turespana Masters.

Last season was his best so far in terms of top-ten finishes with four.

Sc Av – 70.52 (23rd) DD – 292.4 (13th) DA – 64.3 (78th) GIR – 75.5 (7th) PpGIR – 1.795 (106th) SS – 43.6 (101st)

	'92	'93	'94	'95	'96	'97	'98	'99	'00	'01
Johnnie Walker	-	-	-	MC	-	-	-	-	-	MC
WGC Matchplay	-	-	-	-	-	-	-	-	-	-
Alfred Dunhill	-	-	-	-	MC	-	32	3	22	13
S African Open	-	-	-	-	-	-	20	14	26	MC
Heineken Cl'	-	-	-	-	MC	-	-	-	WD	MC
Greg Norman	-	-	-	-	-	-	-	-	MC	MC
Malaysian Open	-	-	-	-	-	-	-	-	-	-
S'pore Masters	-	-	-	-	-	-	-	-	-	-
Dubai Desert	-	-	-	-	MC	MC	MC	22	32	55
Qatar Masters	-	-	-	-	-	-	60	28	11	8
Madeira Open	-	-	-	-	MC	MC	-	-	-	15
Brazil Open	-	-	-	-	-	-	-	3	-	-
Open de Arg	-	-	-	-	-	-	-	-	-	-
US Masters	-	-	-	-	-	-	-	-	-	-
Moroccan Open	-	-	-	-	-	-	-	-	-	-
Open de Espana	-	-	-	MC	-	MC	66	54	-	16
Open de Portugal	-	-	-	-	MC	64	MC	49	-	44
Open de France	-	-	-	-	MC	7	52	-	-	-
B&H I'national	-	-	-	-	-	35	MC	MC	MC	42
Deutsche Bank	-	-	-	-	MC	MC	54	31	23	MC
Volvo PGA	-	-	-	-	21	-	MC	MC	75	11
British Masters	-	-	-	-	MC	MC	MC	6	23	MC
English Open	-	-	-	-	19	3	25	69	23	5
US Open	-	-	-	-	-	-	-	-	-	-
G North Open	-	-	-	-	MC	46	-	MC	-	4
Irish Open	-	-	-	-	-	MC	9	36	53	15
European Open	-	-	-	-	MC	MC	MC	MC	13	82
Scot Open	-	-	-	-	-	-	WD	46	MC	28
British Open	-	-	-	24	-	-	-	MC	-	-
Dutch Open	-	-	-	-	MC	48	MC	WD	-	20
Scandinavian	-	-	-	-	MC	14	WD	MC	17	22
Wales Open	-	-	-	-	-	-	-	-	-	8
USPGA	-	-	-	-	-	-	-	-	-	-
NW Ireland Open	-	-	-	-	-	-	-	-	-	-
WGC NEC Inv'	-	-	-	-	-	-	-	-	-	-
Scottish PGA	-	-	-	-	-	-	-	-	-	DQ
BMW Int' Open	-	-	-	-	MC	39	18	MC	MC	MC
European Mas'	-	-	-	MC	-	-	-	-	-	-
WGC AmEx	-	-	-	-	-	-	-	-	-	-
Troph' Lancome	-	-	-	-	MC	MC	MC	8	-	11
German Masters	-	-	-	-	48	-	4	51	73	15
Cannes Open	-	-	-	-	MC	MC	5	-	-	-
Dunhill Links	-	-	-	-	-	-	-	-	-	61
Masters Madrid	-	-	-	-	30	MC	-	2	54	2
Italian Open	-	-	-	-	MC	4	31	72	44	7
Volvo Masters	-	-	-	-	-	-	29	53	-	20

Roger Wessels

4/3/61 – Port Elizabeth, South Africa

Last season was another solid, if unspectacular, year for the experienced South African pro who has been playing the European Tour since 1995.

He comfortably retained his card with four top-ten finishes including third at the South African Open and tenth at both the British and German Masters.

Turned pro at the relatively late age of 26 and played the South African mini-Tour before joining the Canadian Tour for a time and winning the 1994 Canadian Masters.

The 2000 season was his most successful to date with six top-ten finishes and 37th place in the Order of Merit.

Sc Av – 71.31 (74th) DD – 275.6 (136th) DA – 64.3 (78th) GIR – 69.3 (59th) PpGIR – 1.783 (76th) SS – 43.0 (176th)

	'92	'93	'94	'95	'96	'97	'98	'99	'00	'01
Johnnie Walker	-	-	-	MC	-	-	-	-	15	-
WGC Matchplay	-	-	-	-	-	-	-	-	-	-
Alfred Dunhill	-	-	30	2	MC	MC	23	26	MC	MC
S African Open	-	-	-	-	-	-	22	MC	MC	3
Heineken Cl'	-	-	-	25	-	-	-	-	50	DQ
Greg Norman	-	-	-	-	-	-	-	-	12	62
Malaysian Open	-	-	-	-	-	-	-	-	MC	MC
S'pore Masters	-	-	-	-	-	-	-	-	-	-
Dubai Desert	-	-	-	-	65	MC	17	MC	MC	47
Qatar Masters	-	-	-	-	-	-	9	MC	MC	36
Madeira Open	-	-	-	-	-	-	-	-	-	-
Brazil Open	-	-	-	-	-	-	-	-	-	-
Open de Arg	-	-	-	-	-	-	-	-	-	-
US Masters	-	-	-	-	-	-	-	-	-	-
Moroccan Open	-	-	-	-	MC	55	MC	MC	-	-
Open de Espana	-	-	-	-	MC	MC	6	MC	MC	MC
Open de Portugal	-	-	-	-	-	MC	-	23	-	15
Open de France	-	-	-	65	-	-	34	4	-	-
B&H I'national	-	-	15	33	MC	MC	57	MC	MC	MC
Deutsche Bank	-	-	-	7	MC	5	MC	38	MC	MC
Volvo PGA	-	-	-	-	46	MC	33	29	MC	MC
British Masters	-	MC	-	-	MC	-	48	MC	MC	10
English Open	-	-	-	MC	44	MC	8	54	MC	55
US Open	-	-	-	-	-	-	-	-	-	-
G North Open	-	-	-	-	MC	6	-	53	MC	39
Irish Open	-	-	-	12	48	MC	MC	25	10	MC
European Open	-	-	-	MC	71	MC	20	63	13	23
Scot Open	-	-	-	-	MC	MC	MC	MC	51	MC
British Open	-	-	-	-	-	-	-	-	-	-
Dutch Open	-	-	-	-	52	17	58	MC	6	-
Scandinavian	-	-	-	7	45	MC	MC	MC	MC	MC
Wales Open	-	-	-	-	-	-	-	-	21	8
USPGA	-	-	-	-	-	-	-	-	-	-
NW Ireland Open	-	-	-	-	-	-	-	-	-	-
WGC NEC Inv'	-	-	-	-	-	-	-	-	-	-
Scottish PGA	-	-	-	-	-	-	-	-	-	18
BMW Int' Open	-	-	-	45	MC	-	MC	46	55	46
European Mas'	-	-	-	MC	MC	-	59	19	MC	-
WGC AmEx	-	-	-	-	-	-	-	-	-	-
Troph' Lancome	-	-	-	26	MC	-	15	24	MC	-
German Masters	-	-	-	-	MC	-	MC	MC	51	10
Cannes Open	-	-	-	-	-	-	-	-	-	23
Dunhill Links	-	-	-	-	-	-	-	-	-	52
Masters Madrid	-	-	-	-	MC	23	MC	9	-	-
Italian Open	-	-	-	MC	12	MC	23	7	-	-
Volvo Masters	-	-	-	-	-	-	29	-	7	12

Lee Westwood
24/4/73 – Worksop, England

Last season turned out to be a huge disappointment for the former world No. 5.

Having topped the Order of Merit in 2000, winning six times in the process and rounding off the season with second place at the WGC–AmEx, he experienced an alarming slump in form during 2001.

The birth of baby son Samuel disrupted his early season schedule and, having failed to add to his career tally of 14 European Tour victories in 2001, he looked set to part company with long-time coach Peter Cowan.

He will look to find his touch on the greens as he attempts to recapture his best form in 2002.

Sc Av – 71.69 (109th) DD – 284.8 (49th) DA – 59.2 (153rd) GIR – 65.1 (128th) PpGIR – 1.760 (27th) SS – 47.1 (149th)

	'92	'93	'94	'95	'96	'97	'98	'99	'00	'01
Johnnie Walker	-	-	50	51	59	66	4	-	-	-
WGC Matchplay	-	-	-	-	-	-	-	33	17	-
Alfred Dunhill	-	-	-	MC	-	-	-	-	-	-
S African Open	-	-	-	-	-	-	-	-	10	-
Heineken Cl'	-	-	-	-	MC	45	-	-	-	-
Greg Norman	-	-	-	-	-	-	-	-	-	-
Malaysian Open	-	-	-	-	-	-	MC	-	-	-
S'pore Masters	-	-	-	-	-	-	-	-	-	-
Dubai Desert	-	-	57	MC	MC	MC	6	2	4	17
Qatar Masters	-	-	-	-	-	-	21	-	-	-
Madeira Open	-	-	19	27	WD	-	-	-	-	-
Brazil Open	-	-	-	-	-	-	-	-	-	-
Open de Arg	-	-	-	-	-	-	-	-	-	-
US Masters	-	-	-	-	-	24	44	6	MC	-
Moroccan Open	-	-	-	MC	-	-	-	-	-	-
Open de Espana	-	MC	MC	8	16	-	-	-	-	-
Open de Portugal	-	-	-	60	-	-	-	-	-	-
Open de France	-	4	55	6	-	-	-	-	-	-
B&H I'national	-	-	39	MC	63	3	65	-	54	57
Deutsche Bank	-	-	-	27	55	MC	1	MC	1	52
Volvo PGA	-	-	21	25	11	9	16	56	2	MC
British Masters	-	-	-	MC	MC	MC	12	4	-	8
English Open	-	-	44	MC	MC	22	1	MC	4	5
US Open	-	-	-	-	-	19	7	MC	5	MC
G North Open	-	-	-	-	25	3	-	5	1	MC
Irish Open	-	-	43	MC	7	2	15	7	-	-
European Open	-	-	MC	24	24	-	WD	1	1	62
Scot Open	-	-	-	-	16	22	1	5	-	MC
British Open	-	-	-	93	MC	10	62	18	64	47
Dutch Open	-	-	MC	35	11	-	3	1	3	MC
Scandinavian	-	-	20	19	1	14	-	-	1	2
Wales Open	-	-	-	-	-	-	-	-	-	-
USPGA	-	-	-	-	29	MC	16	15	44	-
NW Ireland Open	-	-	-	-	-	-	-	-	-	-
WGC NEC Inv'	-	-	-	-	-	-	-	33	20	WD
Scottish PGA	-	-	-	-	-	-	-	-	-	-
BMW Int' Open	-	-	-	MC	12	-	-	-	-	-
European Mas'	-	-	WD	MC	10	-	12	1	21	16
WGC AmEx	-	-	-	-	-	-	-	4	2	-
Troph' Lancome	-	-	10	71	MC	8	71	-	7	-
German Masters	-	-	67	37	WD	6	-	11	75	-
Cannes Open	-	-	41	MC	58	-	-	-	-	-
Dunhill Links	-	-	-	-	-	-	-	-	-	MC
Masters Madrid	-	-	67	69	2	-	-	-	-	-
Italian Open	-	-	50	MC	3	6	6	-	12	-
Volvo Masters	-	-	53	-	2	1	12	30	3	52

Ian Woosnam
2/3/58 – Oswestry, Wales

The 1991 US Masters champion was involved in one of the biggest stories of last season when an oversight by caddie Miles Byrne may well have cost him the Open title.

On the final day, with Woosnam mounting a strong challenge, after a birdie at the first hole, he incurred a two-shot penalty when it emerged he was carrying 15 clubs in his bag instead of the permitted 14.

Woosnam finished third but he went on to put the disappointment behind him in stunning style by winning his third Cisco World Matchplay crown in October – his first victory since 1997.

Sc Av – 70.45 (20th) DD – 275.6 (136th) DA – 61.6 (119th) GIR – 72.3 (18th) PpGIR – 1.771 (49th) SS – 61.2 (34th)

	'92	'93	'94	'95	'96	'97	'98	'99	'00	'01
Johnnie Walker	57	14	4	-	1	14	MC	-	-	-
WGC Matchplay	-	-	-	-	-	-	33	-	-	-
Alfred Dunhill	-	-	-	-	-	-	-	-	MC	-
S African Open	-	-	-	-	7	-	50	24	-	-
Heineken Cl'	-	-	-	1	6	2	MC	-	-	-
Greg Norman	-	-	-	-	-	-	-	-	-	-
Malaysian Open	-	-	-	-	-	-	-	-	-	-
S'pore Masters	-	-	-	-	-	-	-	-	-	-
Dubai Desert	6	-	-	7	2	5	MC	MC	-	4
Qatar Masters	-	-	-	-	-	-	9	8	2	13
Madeira Open	-	-	-	-	-	-	-	-	-	-
Brazil Open	-	-	-	-	-	-	-	-	-	-
Open de Arg	-	-	-	-	-	-	-	5	-	-
US Masters	19	17	46	17	29	39	16	14	40	59
Moroccan Open	-	-	-	-	-	5	-	-	-	-
Open de Espana	MC	4	-	MC	-	-	34	-	33	MC
Open de Portugal	-	-	-	-	-	-	-	-	9	44
Open de France	-	-	-	21	-	5	-	-	-	-
B&H I'national	-	-	-	-	12	2	18	16	44	57
Deutsche Bank	-	-	-	34	29	-	17	42	3	28
Volvo PGA	31	24	MC	MC	11	1	54	26	7	21
British Masters	55	-	1	MC	5	59	12	18	11	14
English Open	-	1	10	MC	MC	-	-	-	-	-
US Open	6	52	MC	21	79	MC	MC	-	-	-
G North Open	-	-	-	-	-	-	-	-	-	-
Irish Open	33	11	-	12	17	4	9	MC	63	15
European Open	-	6	21	19	33	27	37	35	MC	2
Scot Open	-	-	-	20	39	2	MC	38	MC	-
British Open	5	50	MC	47	MC	24	55	24	68	3
Dutch Open	-	4	23	16	-	-	-	-	-	-
Scandinavian	-	-	54	10	20	MC	-	MC	17	59
Wales Open	-	-	-	-	-	-	-	3	49	-
USPGA	MC	22	9	MC	36	MC	29	MC	MC	51
NW Ireland Open	-	-	-	-	-	-	-	-	-	-
WGC NEC Inv'	-	-	-	-	-	-	-	33	-	-
Scottish PGA	-	-	-	-	-	-	-	-	-	-
BMW Int' Open	-	2	-	-	-	-	MC	15	-	37
European Mas'	49	-	-	-	-	-	-	-	-	-
WGC AmEx	-	-	-	-	-	-	-	-	-	-
Troph' Lancome	10	1	10	34	7	36	MC	43	24	8
German Masters	2	-	34	MC	MC	-	-	2	MC	8
Cannes Open	5	-	1	21	-	-	-	-	-	-
Dunhill Links	-	-	-	-	-	-	-	-	-	WD
Masters Madrid	-	-	-	-	-	-	-	-	WD	-
Italian Open	-	-	-	-	-	23	-	57	-	-
Volvo Masters	13	5	8	5	25	9	41	10	61	DQ

US TOUR PLAYER PROFILES

Ten-Year Form Tournament Course History

WGC MatchPlay   92-98 NA; 99-00 – LaCosta; 01 – Metropolitan

Mercedes Champ   92-98 – La Costa; 99-01 – Plantation Course

Tucson Open   92-96 – StarPass & Tucson National; 97-01 – Tucson National

Sony Open   92-01 – Walalae

Phoenix Open   92-01 – Scottsdale

AT&T P Beach   92-01 – Pebble Beach, Spyglass Hill & Poppy Hills

Buick Invitatn'l   92-01 – Torrey Pines

Bob Hope Cl'   92, 94, 98, 00 & 01 – PGA West (Palmer Course), Bermuda Dunes, Indian Wells & La Quinta; 93 & 99 - PGA West (Palmer Course), Bermuda Dunes, Indian Wells & Tamarisk; 95 & 97 - Indian Ridge, Bermuda Dunes, Indian Wells & La Quinta; 96 - Indian Ridge, Bermuda Dunes, Indian Wells & Tamarisk. Host courses (those used twice in the tournament) – 92, 95, 98 & 00 Bermuda Dunes; 94 & 97 Indian Wells; 93, 99 & 01 PGA West (Palmer Course); 96 Indian Ridge

Nissan Open   92-97 – Riviera; 98 – Valencia; 99-01 – Riviera

Genuity Champ   92-01 – Doral

Honda Classic   92-95 – Weston Hills; 96 – Eagle Trace; 97-01 – Heron Bay

Bay Hill Invit'l   92-01 – Bay Hill

Players Champ   92-01 – Sawgrass

BellSouth Cl'   92-96 – Atlanta; 97-01 – Sugarloaf

US Masters   92-01 – Augusta National

Worldcom Cl'   92-01 – Harbour Town

Houston Open   92-01 – The Woodlands

GG Chrysler Cl'   92-01 – Forest Oaks

Compaq Classic   92-01 – English Turn

Byron Nelson C'   92-01 – Las Colinas & Cottonwood Valley

MasterCard Cln'l   92-01 – Colonial

Kemper Ins Open   92-01 – Avenel

Memorial T'ment   92-01 – Muirfield

St. Jude Classic   92-01 – Southwind

U.S. Open   92 – Pebble Beach; 93 – Baltusrol; 94 – Oakmont; 95 – Shinnecock Hills; 96 – Oakland Hills; 97 – Congressional; 98 – The Olympic Club; 99 – Pinehurst; 00 – Pebble Beach; 01 – Southern Hills

Buick Classic   92-01 – Westchester

Canon GH Open   92-01 – River Highlands

Western Open   92-01 – Cog Hill

Gr. Milwaukee   92-93 – Tuckaway; 94-01 – Brown Deer

British Open   92 – Muirfield; 93 – Royal St. George's; 94 – Turnberry; 95 – St. Andrews; 96 – Royal Lytham & St. Annes; 97 – Royal Troon; 98 – Royal Birkdale; 99 – Carnoustie; 00 – St. Andrews; 01 – Royal Lytham & St. Annes

B.C. Open   92-01 – En-Joie

John Deere Cl'   92-99 – Oakwood; 00-01 – Deere Run

The International   92-01 – Castle Pines

Buick Open   92-01 – Warwick Hills

USPGA Champ   92 – Bellerive; 93 – Inverness; 94 – Southern Hills; 95 – Riviera; 96 – Valhalla; 97 – Winged Foot; 98 – Sahalee; 99 – Medinah; 00 – Valhalla; 01 – Atlanta Athletic Club

WGCNEC Inv'   92-01 – Firestone

Reno-Tahoe Op'   92-98 NA; 99-01 – Montreux

Air Canada Chp'   92-95 NA; 96-01 – Northview

Bell Canadian O'   92-96 – Glen Abbey; 97 – Royal Montreal; 98-00 – Glen Abbey; 01 – Royal Montreal

WGC AmEx   92-98 NA; 99-00 – Valderrama; 01 NA

Tampa Bay Cl'   92-99 NA; 00-01 – Westin Innisbrook

Marconi Penn C'   92-99 NA; 00 – Waynesborough; 01 – Laurel Valley

Texas Open   92-94 – Oak Hills; 95-01 – LaCantera

Michelob Chmp'   92-01 – Kingsmill

Invensys Classic   92-93 & 98-99 – Las Vegas, Desert Inn & Summerlin; 94-95 - Las Vegas, Las Vegas Hilton & Summerlin; 96-97 Las Vegas Hilton, Desert Inn & Summerlin; 00 – Southern Highlands, Desert Inn & Summerlin; 01 - Southern Highlands, The Canyons & Summerlin

NCR Golf Cl'   92-93 & 95-97 – Palm, Magnolia & Lake Buena Vista; 94 - Palm, Magnolia & Eagle Pines; 98-01 – Palm & Magnolia

Buick Challenge   92-01 – Callaway Gardens

SFB Classic   92-93 – Hattiesburg; 94-01 – Annandale

Tour Champ'ship   92 – Pinehurst; 93-94 – Olympic Club; 95-96 – Southern Hills; 97 – Champions; 98 – East Lake; 99 – Champions; 00 – East Lake; 01 – Champions

Robert Allenby

12/7/71 – Melbourne, Australia

Australian former European Tour pro who enjoyed his best season on the US Tour in 2001 – his third term Stateside. The two victories he gained (in the Nissan Open and the Pennsylvania Classic) meant that the Aussie was only the third person to win twice on the US Tour in 2000 and 2001. One of the best drivers of the ball in America, he is a three-time Presidents Cup team member and can boast victories on the European and ANZ Tours. Allenby has a remarkable 7-0 play-off record (three of his four US wins have come by way of extra holes).

ScAv - 70.53 (42nd) – DD - 284.7 (38th) DA - 70.0 (67th) GIR - 69.3 (33rd) – PpGIR - 1.785 (125th) SS - 43.6 (175th)

	'92	'93	'94	'95	'96	'97	'98	'99	'00	'01
WGC MatchPlay	-	-	-	-	-	-	-	-	-	17
Mercedes Ch	-	-	-	-	-	-	-	-	-	28
Tucson Open	-	-	-	-	-	-	32	64	-	-
Sony Open	-	-	-	-	-	-	-	MC	39	39
Phoenix Open	-	-	-	-	-	-	-	-	2	MC
AT&T P Beach	-	-	-	-	-	-	-	39	-	-
Buick Invitatn'l	-	-	-	-	-	-	-	30	-	-
Bob Hope Cl'	-	-	-	-	-	-	-	11	12	62
Nissan Open	-	-	-	-	-	-	-	MC	43	1
Genuity Champ	-	-	-	MC	-	-	-	-	12	50
Honda Classic	-	-	-	MC	-	-	-	46	-	-
Bay Hill Invit'l	-	-	-	31	MC	-	-	13	29	34
Players Champ	-	-	73	MC	MC	-	-	-	53	21
BellSouth Cl'	-	-	-	-	-	-	-	MC	MC	-
US Masters	-	-	-	-	-	-	-	-	-	47
Worldcom Cl'	-	-	-	WD	-	MC	-	-	MC	75
Houston Open	-	-	-	-	-	-	-	33	1	62
GG Chrysler Cl'	-	-	-	-	-	MC	-	-	-	-
Compaq Classic	-	MC	-	MC	MC	-	-	28	-	-
Byron Nelson C'	-	-	-	-	-	-	-	24	MC	43
MasterCard Cln'l	-	-	-	-	-	-	-	MC	62	15
Kemper Ins Open	-	-	MC	-	-	-	-	-	47	12
Memorial T'ment	-	MC	-	21	-	-	-	52	MC	7
St. Jude Classic	-	-	-	-	-	-	-	55	-	-
U.S. Open	-	33	-	-	-	MC	-	46	-	MC
Buick Classic	-	MC	-	-	-	-	-	-	-	8
Canon GH Open	-	MC	-	-	-	-	-	62	14	-
Western Open	-	-	-	-	-	-	-	MC	1	MC
Gr. Milwaukee	-	-	-	-	-	-	-	-	-	-
British Open	-	MC	60	15	55	10	19	-	36	47
B.C. Open	-	-	-	-	-	-	4	-	-	-
John Deere Cl'	-	-	-	-	-	-	-	-	-	-
The International	-	-	-	MC	-	37	43	31	-	-
Buick Open	-	-	-	-	-	MC	45	-	-	MC
USPGA Champ	-	MC	-	MC	MC	49	13	MC	19	16
WGCNEC Inv'	-	-	-	-	-	-	-	-	12	23
Reno-Tahoe Op'	-	-	-	-	-	-	-	-	-	-
Air Canada Chp'	-	-	-	-	-	-	28	-	27	-
Bell Canadian O'	-	-	-	-	-	-	MC	-	-	8
WGC AmEx	-	-	-	-	-	-	-	25	-	-
Tampa Bay Cl'	-	-	-	-	-	-	-	-	-	-
Marconi Penn C'	-	-	-	-	-	-	-	-	-	1
Texas Open	-	-	-	-	-	37	-	-	-	-
Michelob Chmp'	-	-	-	-	-	-	17	13	62	23
Invensys Classic	-	-	-	-	-	-	-	MC	52	13
NCR Golf Cl'	-	-	-	-	-	-	-	MC	-	36
Buick Challenge	-	-	-	-	-	-	MC	-	-	-
SFB Classic	-	-	-	-	-	-	-	51	-	-
Tour Champ'ship	-	-	-	-	-	-	-	-	16	22

Stephen Ames

28/4/64 – San Fernando, Trinidad

Trinidadian-born former European Tour pro who is based in Canada. Ames has had problems obtaining a Visa to play in the United States in the past and 2001 was only his second full season on the US Tour. He has yet to win an event Stateside but has two victories on the European Tour to his name. His win in the Beson and Hedges International in England in dreadful conditions marked him out as one to follow when the wind blows. Ames has won on the Buy.com Tour (Pensacola Open in 1991). A fine ball striker his short game can let him down.

ScAv - 71.18 (98th) – DD - 282.3 (65th) DA - 70.2 (64th) GIR - 69.1 (35th) – PpGIR - 1.772 (96th) SS - 53.4 (83rd)

	'92	'93	'94	'95	'96	'97	'98	'99	'00	'01
WGC MatchPlay	-	-	-	-	-	-	-	-	-	-
Mercedes Ch	-	-	-	-	-	-	-	-	-	-
Tucson Open	-	-	-	-	-	-	-	-	17	48
Sony Open	-	-	-	-	-	-	-	-	64	14
Phoenix Open	-	-	-	-	-	-	-	-	MC	22
AT&T P Beach	-	-	-	-	-	-	-	-	-	-
Buick Invitatn'l	-	-	-	-	-	-	-	-	41	58
Bob Hope Cl'	-	-	-	-	-	-	-	-	WD	51
Nissan Open	-	-	-	-	-	-	3	-	61	-
Genuity Champ	-	-	-	-	-	-	MC	-	8	WD
Honda Classic	-	-	-	-	-	-	57	-	19	67
Bay Hill Invit'l	-	-	-	-	-	-	10	-	38	64
Players Champ	-	-	-	-	-	-	MC	-	42	MC
BellSouth Cl'	-	-	-	-	-	-	19	-	-	-
US Masters	-	-	-	-	-	-	-	-	-	-
Worldcom Cl'	-	-	-	-	-	-	-	-	MC	21
Houston Open	-	-	-	-	-	-	10	-	17	46
GG Chrysler Cl'	-	-	-	-	-	-	30	-	MC	24
Compaq Classic	-	-	-	-	-	-	-	-	4	8
Byron Nelson C'	-	-	-	-	-	-	-	-	62	-
MasterCard Cln'l	-	-	-	-	-	-	-	-	MC	26
Kemper Ins Open	-	-	-	-	-	-	-	44	MC	DQ
Memorial T'ment	-	-	-	-	-	-	-	-	-	WD
St. Jude Classic	-	-	-	-	-	-	MC	55	-	-
U.S. Open	-	-	-	-	-	68	-	-	-	-
Buick Classic	-	-	-	-	-	-	-	66	MC	-
Canon GH Open	-	-	-	-	-	-	-	MC	MC	-
Western Open	-	-	-	-	-	-	-	MC	15	20
Gr. Milwaukee	-	-	-	-	-	-	MC	MC	-	-
British Open	-	51	-	-	55	5	24	-	-	-
B.C. Open	-	-	-	-	-	-	58	4	-	6
John Deere Cl'	-	-	-	-	-	-	-	30	23	MC
The International	-	-	-	-	-	-	-	3	8	33
Buick Open	-	-	-	-	-	-	-	63	MC	14
USPGA Champ	-	-	-	-	-	-	-	-	30	-
WGCNEC Inv'	-	-	-	-	-	-	-	-	-	-
Reno-Tahoe Op'	-	-	-	-	-	-	-	MC	-	-
Air Canada Chp'	-	-	-	-	-	-	MC	MC	MC	MC
Bell Canadian O'	-	-	-	-	-	-	13	MC	32	MC
WGC AmEx	-	-	-	-	-	-	-	-	-	-
Tampa Bay Cl'	-	-	-	-	-	-	-	-	51	-
Marconi Penn C'	-	-	-	-	-	-	-	-	WD	-
Texas Open	-	-	-	-	-	-	-	8	-	-
Michelob Chmp'	-	-	-	-	-	-	MC	13	5	MC
Invensys Classic	-	-	-	-	-	-	-	9	MC	74
NCR Golf Cl'	-	-	-	-	-	-	-	MC	MC	30
Buick Challenge	-	-	-	-	-	-	24	31	-	-
SFB Classic	-	-	-	-	-	-	-	-	-	-
Tour Champ'ship	-	-	-	-	-	-	-	-	-	-

Billy Andrade
25/1/64 – Bristol, RI

A four-time US Tour winner who became the first player to win back-to-back titles for 12 years when victorious in the 1991 Kemper and Buick Opens. Andrade has only added two wins since, the last of which came in the 2000 Invensys Classic.

A big hitter, Andrade lacks accuracy off the tee and with his irons, relying upon his occasional hot putter to get him out of trouble. A stalwart of the US Tour who turned pro in 1987 who has only twice finished outside the top 80 on the Money List in the last 14 years.

ScAv - 70.81 (65th) – DD - 280.1 (88th) DA - 66.7 (128th) GIR - 64.7 (144th) – PpGIR - 1.763 (68th) SS - 55.1 (60th)

	'92	'93	'94	'95	'96	'97	'98	'99	'00	'01
WGC MatchPlay	-	-	-	-	-	-	-	-	-	-
Mercedes Ch	-	-	-	-	-	-	-	-	-	16
Tucson Open	-	7	59	MC	-	27	59	MC	-	-
Sony Open	MC	42	-	-	MC	-	33	MC	-	4
Phoenix Open	-	27	18	MC	70	62	6	-	50	MC
AT&T P Beach	MC	9	MC	43	-	7	MC	66	MC	MC
Buick Invitatn'l	MC	-	-	50	-	11	MC	11	MC	-
Bob Hope Cl'	-	-	-	-	56	-	-	-	MC	62
Nissan Open	22	MC	57	MC	MC	-	-	23	MC	-
Genuity Champ	44	66	2	75	MC	28	MC	19	36	8
Honda Classic	41	20	27	53	MC	64	MC	-	-	-
Bay Hill Invit'l	MC	10	42	20	69	30	MC	MC	22	MC
Players Champ	MC	20	MC	8	MC	5	35	62	MC	44
BellSouth Cl'	25	7	30	7	50	67	65	23	MC	54
US Masters	54	61	-	-	-	MC	38	-	-	-
Worldcom Cl'	29	20	MC	78	MC	-	45	56	MC	10
Houston Open	-	-	-	-	-	27	-	-	-	-
GG Chrysler Cl'	MC	9	44	29	5	4	38	MC	62	MC
Compaq Classic	-	-	-	-	-	-	-	MC	-	-
Byron Nelson C'	62	-	-	10	30	15	24	MC	28	
MasterCard Cln'l	MC	-	15	64	20	73	26	24	MC	
Kemper Ins Open	41	55	MC	16	43	-	MC	MC	47	-
Memorial T'ment	14	40	26	MC	MC	10	MC	43	MC	63
St. Jude Classic	-	-	35	-	-	-	50	-	-	
U.S. Open	6	33	-	21	23	13	MC	-	-	MC
Buick Classic	20	MC	5	MC	31	12	41	35	MC	3
Canon GH Open	MC	55	8	MC	13	14	62	MC	2	
Western Open	MC	-	MC	MC	2	17	-	MC	MC	MC
Gr. Milwaukee	MC	-	-	-	12	20	9	-	70	-
British Open	25	MC	-	MC	-	70	-	MC	-	13
B.C. Open	MC	MC	70	73	-	12	16	44	-	-
John Deere Cl'	-	-	-	-	-	-	-	-	-	-
The International	24	MC	MC	MC	9	MC	MC	24	57	38
Buick Open	-	MC	MC	-	22	-	-	-	-	-
USPGA Champ	12	MC	47	MC	MC	MC	44	MC	-	6
WGCNEC Inv'	-	-	-	-	-	-	-	-	-	-
Reno-Tahoe Op'	-	-	-	-	-	-	24	MC	MC	
Air Canada Chp'	-	-	-	-	-	MC	-	-	-	-
Bell Canadian O'	-	MC	19	MC	12	-	1	MC	MC	-
WGC AmEx	-	-	-	-	-	-	-	-	-	-
Tampa Bay Cl'	-	-	-	-	-	-	-	MC	-	-
Marconi Penn C'	-	-	-	-	-	-	-	-	-	33
Texas Open	47	3	MC	59	MC	-	-	-	-	-
Michelob Chmp'	-	-	-	-	23	15	33	MC	MC	MC
Invensys Classic	40	MC	3	MC	44	19	71	MC	1	MC
NCR Golf Cl'	-	44	-	MC	-	MC	27	MC	-	-
Buick Challenge	MC	2	52	MC	30	MC	14	MC	10	MC
SFB Classic	-	-	-	4	2	13	7	7	-	MC
Tour Champ'ship	-	-	-	-	-	-	-	-	-	-

Stuart Appleby
1/4/71 – Cohuna, Australia

Australian regular on the US Tour who has based himself Stateside for the past six seasons. Appleby is long off the tee and a powerful player who has the all round game to win a Major. Won in consecutive years on the US Tour between 1997 and 1999 but hasn't managed a fourth tour win yet. His last victory was gained at the 1999 Shell Houston Open. Appleby has also won on the ANZ Tour and on the Buy.com Tour. He represented the International side in the Presidents Cup in 1998 and 2000 and is expected to make the team in 2003.

ScAv - 70.68 (52nd) – DD - 288.6 (19th) DA - 67.7 (113th) GIR - 64.8 (142nd) – PpGIR - 1.736 (15th) SS - 52.3 (93rd)

	'92	'93	'94	'95	'96	'97	'98	'99	'00	'01
WGC MatchPlay	-	-	-	-	-	-	-	33	33	9
Mercedes Ch	-	-	-	-	-	30	16	15	-	
Tucson Open	-	-	-	-	MC	48	-	-	-	-
Sony Open	-	-	-	-	31	9	-	16	2	37
Phoenix Open	-	-	-	-	MC	-	69	18	-	49
AT&T P Beach	-	-	-	-	-	-	-	53	-	-
Buick Invitatn'l	-	-	-	-	MC	-	-	-	-	MC
Bob Hope Cl'	-	-	-	-	33	-	29	43	-	30
Nissan Open	-	-	-	-	-	MC	-	-	18	-
Genuity Champ	-	-	-	-	69	MC	30	-	-	34
Honda Classic	-	-	-	-	65	1	4	9	12	7
Bay Hill Invit'l	-	-	-	-	MC	2	MC	MC	64	MC
Players Champ	-	-	-	-	-	14	MC	MC	22	33
BellSouth Cl'	-	-	-	-	MC	34	MC	10	-	-
US Masters	-	-	-	-	-	21	MC	MC	MC	31
Worldcom Cl'	-	-	-	-	-	54	MC	-	-	-
Houston Open	-	-	-	-	MC	-	-	1	MC	MC
GG Chrysler Cl'	-	-	-	-	67	19	23	-	-	29
Compaq Classic	-	-	-	-	10	-	-	WD	11	-
Byron Nelson C'	-	-	-	-	MC	-	MC	-	-	43
MasterCard Cln'l	-	-	-	-	-	MC	10	11	35	MC
Kemper Ins Open	-	-	-	-	18	14	1	6	7	31
Memorial T'ment	-	-	-	-	-	MC	MC	31	17	7
St. Jude Classic	-	-	-	-	16	-	-	63	-	-
U.S. Open	-	-	-	-	-	36	10	MC	MC	MC
Buick Classic	-	-	-	-	MC	17	-	-	-	26
Canon GH Open	-	-	-	-	30	-	-	-	32	-
Western Open	-	-	-	-	43	7	9	13	20	MC
Gr. Milwaukee	-	-	-	-	12	-	-	-	-	-
British Open	-	-	-	-	-	20	MC	MC	11	61
B.C. Open	-	-	-	-	MC	-	-	-	-	-
John Deere Cl'	-	-	-	-	-	-	-	-	-	-
The International	-	-	-	-	MC	2	29	66	3	28
Buick Open	-	-	-	-	22	-	-	25	-	35
USPGA Champ	-	-	-	-	61	MC	MC	4	16	
WGCNEC Inv'	-	-	-	-	-	-	-	23	50	5
Reno-Tahoe Op'	-	-	-	-	-	-	-	-	-	-
Air Canada Chp'	-	-	-	-	MC	-	57	-	-	-
Bell Canadian O'	-	-	-	-	34	-	-	-	-	23
WGC AmEx	-	-	-	-	-	-	30	25	-	
Tampa Bay Cl'	-	-	-	-	-	-	-	-	-	22
Marconi Penn C'	-	-	-	-	-	-	-	-	-	-
Texas Open	-	-	-	-	73	-	-	-	-	-
Michelob Chmp'	-	-	-	-	MC	-	WD	-	-	-
Invensys Classic	-	-	-	-	33	-	-	-	MC	29
NCR Golf Cl'	-	-	-	-	36	MC	-	41	13	
Buick Challenge	-	-	-	-	MC	-	2	-	65	
SFB Classic	-	-	-	-	50	-	-	-	-	65
Tour Champ'ship	-	-	-	-	-	22	-	26	7	-

Paul Azinger
6/1/60 – Holyoke, MA

The Zinger might not have won in 2001 but his comeback was complete as he was picked for the American Ryder Cup Cup team by Curtis Strange as a wild card. After battling back from cancer – which kept him out of the game in the mid '90s – Azinger was winless for five seasons. Victory in the 2000 Sony Open gave him his 12th US Tour success and restored the belief that he could compete at the highest level again. A former Major winner (1993 USPGA Championship), Azinger has a deft putting touch and will make his fourth Ryder Cup appearance in 2002.

ScAv - 70.14 (21st) – DD - 279.5 (96th) DA - 68.7 (94th) GIR - 69.2 (34th) – PpGIR - 1.768 (85th) SS - 56.7 (33rd)

	'92	'93	'94	'95	'96	'97	'98	'99	'00	'01
WGC MatchPlay	-	-	-	-	-	-	-	17	33	-
Mercedes Ch	6	3	-	-	-	-	-	-	-	17
Tucson Open	-	-	-	-	-	-	-	-	-	-
Sony Open	2	3	-	4	11	9	MC	MC	1	MC
Phoenix Open	12	39	-	22	21	26	MC	14	MC	55
AT&T P Beach	3	MC	-	57	-	7	3	10	61	47
Buick Invitatn'l	-	-	-	-	20	MC	57	-	-	-
Bob Hope Cl'	-	-	-	-	-	24	MC	-	-	62
Nissan Open	-	6	-	MC	-	-	-	MC	-	-
Genuity Champ	MC	2	-	58	MC	MC	15	-	-	-
Honda Classic	WD	-	-	MC	-	-	-	MC	-	-
Bay Hill Invit'l	51	MC	-	31	27	47	MC	33	-	15
Players Champ	29	6	-	MC	MC	14	MC	MC	17	7
BellSouth Cl'	-	MC	-	-	MC	-	-	MC	49	-
US Masters	31	MC	-	17	18	28	5	MC	28	50
Worldcom Cl'	-	3	-	68	32	MC	WD	-	25	12
Houston Open	-	-	-	-	77	-	-	-	-	-
GG Chrysler Cl'	9	1	-	MC	WD	9	38	17	26	-
Compaq Classic	-	-	-	-	-	19	-	-	-	-
Byron Nelson C'	-	-	-	-	-	-	-	-	-	-
MasterCard Cln'l	-	-	-	-	-	-	-	-	-	-
Kemper Ins Open	-	-	-	-	33	-	MC	-	-	-
Memorial T'ment	14	1	-	MC	49	46	-	19	5	2
St. Jude Classic	10	MC	-	-	-	7	6	10	-	-
U.S. Open	33	3	-	MC	67	28	14	12	12	5
Buick Classic	3	MC	-	40	MC	DQ	24	35	-	16
Canon GH Open	MC	MC	-	15	49	MC	47	20	-	14
Western Open	-	-	-	29	55	MC	-	-	-	-
Gr. Milwaukee	-	-	-	-	60	-	-	-	-	-
British Open	59	59	-	MC	MC	MC	MC	-	7	-
B.C. Open	-	-	-	-	-	-	MC	-	-	-
John Deere Cl'	10	-	-	-	-	-	-	-	-	-
The International	-	-	-	-	-	-	-	-	-	-
Buick Open	-	-	MC	-	-	-	MC	21	49	-
USPGA Champ	33	1	MC	31	31	29	13	41	24	22
WGCNEC Inv'	-	-	-	-	-	-	-	8	5	-
Reno-Tahoe Op'	-	-	-	-	-	-	WD	-	-	-
Air Canada Chp'	-	-	-	-	-	-	-	-	-	-
Bell Canadian O'	15	MC	-	MC	-	44	51	9	10	-
WGC AmEx	-	-	-	-	-	-	-	-	-	-
Tampa Bay Cl'	-	-	-	-	-	-	-	-	-	-
Marconi Penn C'	-	-	-	-	-	-	-	-	-	58
Texas Open	-	-	15	-	-	-	-	-	-	-
Michelob Chmp'	-	-	-	-	-	MC	-	-	58	47
Invensys Classic	8	3	-	74	8	-	20	56	-	-
NCR Golf Cl'	38	60	33	28	18	-	17	10	16	-
Buick Challenge	-	-	19	MC	20	MC	-	6	8	-
SFB Classic	-	-	-	-	-	-	-	-	-	17
Tour Champ'ship	1	21	-	-	-	-	-	-	11	-

Briny Baird
11/5/72 – Miami Beach, FL

Miami-based golfer who turned professional in 1995 and played in just his second full season on the US Tour in 2001. Baird played on the Buy.com Tour in 2000 after losing his card at the end of the 1999 season – after managing just one top-30 finish. And on the feeder tour he won the Monterey Classic before going on to finish third on the Money List. A long and accurate iron player, he showed good form in mid-summer when rewarded with second place in the John Deere Classic – a finish that practically ensured his playing rights for 2002.

ScAv - 70.76 (62nd) – DD - 281.8 (67th) DA - 70.5 (59th) GIR - 69.8 (27th) – PpGIR - 1.780 (117th) SS - 50.9 (113th)

	'92	'93	'94	'95	'96	'97	'98	'99	'00	'01
WGC MatchPlay	-	-	-	-	-	-	-	-	-	-
Mercedes Ch	-	-	-	-	-	-	-	-	-	-
Tucson Open	-	-	-	-	-	-	-	28	-	MC
Sony Open	-	-	-	-	-	-	-	MC	-	5
Phoenix Open	-	-	-	-	-	-	-	-	-	MC
AT&T P Beach	-	-	-	-	-	-	-	MC	-	MC
Buick Invitatn'l	-	-	-	-	-	-	-	MC	-	-
Bob Hope Cl'	-	-	-	-	-	-	-	-	-	MC
Nissan Open	-	-	-	-	-	-	-	-	-	-
Genuity Champ	-	-	-	-	-	-	-	34	-	63
Honda Classic	-	-	-	-	-	-	-	46	-	18
Bay Hill Invit'l	-	-	-	-	-	-	-	-	-	-
Players Champ	-	-	-	-	-	-	-	-	-	-
BellSouth Cl'	-	-	-	-	-	-	-	MC	-	68
US Masters	-	-	-	-	-	-	-	-	-	-
Worldcom Cl'	-	-	-	-	-	-	-	-	-	MC
Houston Open	-	-	-	-	-	-	-	MC	-	35
GG Chrysler Cl'	-	-	-	-	-	-	-	63	-	19
Compaq Classic	-	-	-	-	-	-	-	35	-	MC
Byron Nelson C'	-	-	-	-	-	-	-	-	-	73
MasterCard Cln'l	-	-	-	-	-	-	-	-	-	62
Kemper Ins Open	-	-	-	-	-	-	-	MC	-	37
Memorial T'ment	-	-	-	-	-	-	-	-	-	-
St. Jude Classic	-	-	-	-	-	-	-	MC	-	MC
U.S. Open	-	-	-	-	-	-	-	-	-	40
Buick Classic	-	-	-	-	-	-	-	MC	-	-
Canon GH Open	-	-	-	-	-	-	-	WD	-	29
Western Open	-	-	-	-	-	-	-	42	-	37
Gr. Milwaukee	-	-	-	-	-	-	-	MC	-	28
British Open	-	-	-	-	-	-	-	-	-	-
B.C. Open	-	-	-	-	-	-	-	-	-	-
John Deere Cl'	-	-	-	-	-	-	-	30	-	2
The International	-	-	-	-	-	-	-	MC	-	38
Buick Open	-	-	-	-	-	-	-	33	-	57
USPGA Champ	-	-	-	-	-	-	-	-	-	22
WGCNEC Inv'	-	-	-	-	-	-	-	-	-	-
Reno-Tahoe Op'	-	-	-	-	-	-	-	MC	-	-
Air Canada Chp'	-	-	-	-	-	-	-	MC	-	MC
Bell Canadian O'	-	-	-	-	-	-	-	64	-	-
WGC AmEx	-	-	-	-	-	-	-	-	-	-
Tampa Bay Cl'	-	-	-	-	-	-	-	-	-	-
Marconi Penn C'	-	-	-	-	-	-	-	-	-	46
Texas Open	-	-	-	-	-	-	-	71	-	MC
Michelob Chmp'	-	-	-	-	-	-	-	59	-	41
Invensys Classic	-	-	-	-	-	-	-	MC	-	-
NCR Golf Cl'	-	-	-	-	-	-	-	MC	-	32
Buick Challenge	-	-	-	-	-	-	-	MC	-	46
SFB Classic	-	-	-	-	-	-	-	31	-	17
Tour Champ'ship	-	-	-	-	-	-	-	-	-	-

Sponsored by Stan James

Cameron Beckman
15/2/70 – Minneapolis, MN

For the first time since 1998 Beckman won't have to go back to Q-School. After gaining his 1999, 2000 and 2001 playing rights by way of the qualifying tournament, Beckman could boast the longest active streak in golf for Q-School graduates, but after his best year on tour in 2001 he won't need to go back to the six round nerve jangler. Beckman is a powerful driver of the ball with a surprisingly good putting touch. He won for the first time on the US Tour by capturing the season ending Southern Farm Bureau Classic title.

ScAv - 70.65 (48th) – DD - 285.4 (32nd) DA - 66.9 (125th) GIR - 68.0 (42nd) – PpGIR - 1.746 (27th) SS - 53.2 (85th)

	'92	'93	'94	'95	'96	'97	'98	'99	'00	'01
WGC MatchPlay	-	-	-	-	-	-	-	-	-	-
Mercedes Ch	-	-	-	-	-	-	-	-	-	-
Tucson Open	-	-	-	-	-	-	-	MC	-	WD
Sony Open	-	-	-	-	-	-	-	24	MC	MC
Phoenix Open	-	-	-	-	-	-	-	-	-	-
AT&T P Beach	-	-	-	-	-	-	-	MC	-	69
Buick Invitatn'l	-	-	-	-	-	-	-	MC	MC	10
Bob Hope Cl'	-	-	-	-	-	-	-	-	-	62
Nissan Open	-	-	-	-	-	-	-	MC	-	33
Genuity Champ	-	-	-	-	-	-	-	-	-	34
Honda Classic	-	-	-	-	-	-	-	74	MC	61
Bay Hill Invit'l	-	-	-	-	-	-	-	-	-	-
Players Champ	-	-	-	-	-	-	-	-	-	-
BellSouth Cl'	-	-	-	-	-	-	-	MC	-	54
US Masters	-	-	-	-	-	-	-	-	-	-
Worldcom Cl'	-	-	-	-	-	-	-	-	-	55
Houston Open	-	-	-	-	-	-	-	45	MC	MC
GG Chrysler Cl'	-	-	-	-	-	-	-	63	MC	-
Compaq Classic	-	-	-	-	-	-	-	MC	MC	50
Byron Nelson C'	-	-	-	-	-	-	-	MC	-	73
MasterCard Cln'l	-	-	-	-	-	-	-	-	-	-
Kemper Ins Open	-	-	-	-	-	-	-	61	MC	14
Memorial T'ment	-	-	-	-	-	-	-	-	-	-
St. Jude Classic	-	-	-	-	-	-	-	MC	84	MC
U.S. Open	-	-	-	-	-	-	-	-	MC	-
Buick Classic	-	-	-	-	-	-	-	MC	57	32
Canon GH Open	-	-	-	-	-	-	-	62	73	45
Western Open	-	-	-	-	-	-	-	MC	69	20
Gr. Milwaukee	-	-	-	-	-	-	-	MC	22	47
British Open	-	-	-	-	-	-	-	-	-	-
B.C. Open	-	-	-	-	-	-	-	-	-	-
John Deere Cl'	-	-	-	-	-	-	-	52	66	35
The International	-	-	-	-	-	-	-	-	-	28
Buick Open	-	-	-	-	-	-	-	54	28	-
USPGA Champ	-	-	-	-	-	-	-	-	-	-
WGCNEC Inv'	-	-	-	-	-	-	-	-	-	-
Reno-Tahoe Op'	-	-	-	-	-	-	-	17	MC	24
Air Canada Chp'	-	-	-	-	-	-	-	MC	MC	MC
Bell Canadian O'	-	-	-	-	-	-	-	MC	20	-
WGC AmEx	-	-	-	-	-	-	-	-	-	-
Tampa Bay Cl'	-	-	-	-	-	-	-	-	19	-
Marconi Penn C'	-	-	-	-	-	-	-	-	28	10
Texas Open	-	MC	-	-	38	MC	38	14	MC	-
Michelob Chmp'	-	-	-	-	-	-	-	MC	15	-
Invensys Classic	-	-	-	-	-	-	-	MC	MC	6
NCR Golf Cl'	-	-	-	-	-	-	-	MC	MC	-
Buick Challenge	-	-	-	-	-	-	-	13	14	54
SFB Classic	-	-	-	-	-	-	-	31	60	1
Tour Champ'ship	-	-	-	-	-	-	-	-	-	-

David Berganio, Jr.
14/1/69 – Los Angeles, CA

After a poor debut on the US Tour in 1997 Berganio spent a couple of seasons on the Buy.com Tour honing his skills. Four top ten finishes and a win (in the Omaha Classic) in the 2000 season gave the LA golfer his full tour playing privileges for 2001. And four years after his first, but ultimately abortive, assault on the main tour, he made his mark with a string of fine performances. Berganio is another player who relies on length off the tee but does manage to find the fairways more often than not. If anything, it's his bunker play that lets him down.

ScAv - 70.93 (67th) – DD - 285.5 (31st) DA - 70.9 (52nd) GIR - 67.1 (73rd) – PpGIR - 1.769 (87th) SS - 51.7 (100th)

	'92	'93	'94	'95	'96	'97	'98	'99	'00	'01
WGC MatchPlay	-	-	-	-	-	-	-	-	-	-
Mercedes Ch	-	-	-	-	-	-	-	-	-	-
Tucson Open	MC	68	-	-	MC	MC	-	MC	-	WD
Sony Open	-	-	-	-	-	WD	-	-	-	37
Phoenix Open	-	-	-	-	-	MC	-	-	-	-
AT&T P Beach	-	-	-	-	-	-	-	-	-	20
Buick Invitatn'l	-	-	-	-	-	MC	MC	35	48	58
Bob Hope Cl'	-	-	-	-	-	45	-	-	-	-
Nissan Open	-	-	-	-	MC	MC	-	-	-	8
Genuity Champ	-	-	-	-	-	50	-	-	-	MC
Honda Classic	-	-	-	-	-	MC	-	-	-	73
Bay Hill Invit'l	-	-	-	-	-	WD	-	-	-	31
Players Champ	-	-	-	-	-	-	-	-	-	-
BellSouth Cl'	-	-	-	-	-	-	-	-	-	54
US Masters	MC	-	-	-	-	MC	-	-	-	-
Worldcom Cl'	-	-	-	-	-	-	-	-	-	MC
Houston Open	-	-	-	-	-	MC	-	-	-	-
GG Chrysler Cl'	-	-	-	-	-	37	-	-	-	4
Compaq Classic	-	-	-	-	-	-	-	-	-	-
Byron Nelson C'	-	-	-	-	-	19	-	-	-	MC
MasterCard Cln'l	-	-	-	-	-	-	-	-	-	WD
Kemper Ins Open	-	-	-	-	-	MC	-	-	-	MC
Memorial T'ment	-	-	-	-	-	-	-	-	-	MC
St. Jude Classic	-	-	-	-	-	53	-	-	-	MC
U.S. Open	-	MC	47	-	16	-	-	28	MC	-
Buick Classic	-	-	-	-	-	33	WD	62	29	65
Canon GH Open	-	-	-	-	-	-	-	-	-	3
Western Open	-	-	-	-	-	MC	-	-	-	-
Gr. Milwaukee	-	-	-	-	-	34	-	-	-	-
British Open	-	-	-	-	-	-	-	-	-	-
B.C. Open	-	MC	MC	-	-	MC	-	-	-	-
John Deere Cl'	-	48	WD	-	-	MC	-	-	-	29
The International	-	-	-	-	-	50	-	-	-	45
Buick Open	-	-	-	-	-	MC	39	74	47	67
USPGA Champ	-	-	-	-	-	-	-	-	-	-
WGCNEC Inv'	-	-	-	-	-	-	-	-	-	-
Reno-Tahoe Op'	-	-	-	-	-	-	-	-	-	19
Air Canada Chp'	-	-	-	-	-	24	-	-	-	-
Bell Canadian O'	-	-	-	-	-	-	-	-	-	8
WGC AmEx	-	-	-	-	-	-	-	-	-	-
Tampa Bay Cl'	-	-	-	-	-	-	-	-	-	-
Marconi Penn C'	-	-	-	-	-	-	-	-	-	-
Texas Open	-	-	-	-	46	MC	-	-	-	-
Michelob Chmp'	-	-	-	-	-	29	-	-	-	WD
Invensys Classic	-	-	-	-	-	50	-	-	-	MC
NCR Golf Cl'	-	-	-	-	-	WD	-	-	-	-
Buick Challenge	-	-	-	-	-	9	-	-	-	38
SFB Classic	-	MC	-	-	-	46	-	-	-	-
Tour Champ'ship	-	-	-	-	-	-	-	-	-	-

Mark Brooks

Date & Birthplace
25/3/61 – Ft. Worth, TX

Veteran Texas pro who hasn't won since landing the USPGA Championship in 1996. He burst back onto the scene in 2001, however, with his performance at the US Open, when he finished as runner-up to Retief Goosen and perhaps should have won. Short but accurate with his driver, Brooks has won seven times on the US Tour. His putting kept him in contention at Southern Hills and his second place there was one of only two top-ten finishes in 2001. Represented the USA in the 1996 Presidents Cup and is a former Texas Amateur champion.

ScAv - 71.24 (105th) – DD - 265.5 (191st) DA - 74.3 (15th) GIR - 63.8 (163rd) - PpGIR - 1.798 (167th) SS - 54.2 (73rd)

	'92	'93	'94	'95	'96	'97	'98	'99	'00	'01
WGC MatchPlay	-	-	-	-	-	-				
Mercedes Ch	MC	-	15	-	17					
Tucson Open	MC	18	22	58	MC	-	48	MC	MC	-
Sony Open	8	30	32	7	21	MC	-	-	-	-
Phoenix Open	-	MC	-	26	26	47	MC	53	-	
AT&T P Beach	25	21	MC	21	-	MC	22	MC	7	MC
Buick Invitatn'l	-	45	-	-	-	-	-	-	MC	
Bob Hope Cl'	28	-	44	7	1	34	MC	43	36	70
Nissan Open	39	MC	MC	MC	2	63	-	9	52	43
Genuity Champ	11	MC	49	MC	50	50	-	MC	36	-
Honda Classic	3	77	39	-	-	MC	12	36	47	
Bay Hill Invit'l	3	WD	21	20	MC	-	MC	64	-	MC
Players Champ	9	MC	MC	MC	MC	7	MC	10	57	65
BellSouth Cl'	-	-	35	66	-	-	-	-	-	-
US Masters	MC	MC	-	MC	MC	MC	38	40	31	
Worldcom Cl'	MC	39	-	MC	77	-	45	43	-	7
Houston Open	5	MC	75	32	1	67	MC	MC	5	MC
GG Chrysler Cl'	10	12	29	-	23	-	-	-	-	-
Compaq Classic	-	10	44	MC	47	27	19	62	17	-
Byron Nelson C'	62	50	8	11	6	64	MC	MC	7	37
MasterCard Cln'l	4	20	42	MC	46	22	53	65	MC	62
Kemper Ins Open	6	-	1	MC	-	53	-	-	-	45
Memorial T'ment	5	-	7	38	26	MC	48	59	33	24
St. Jude Classic	-	10	MC	11	72	MC	MC	MC	MC	-
U.S. Open	44	46	MC	-	16	MC	57	MC	MC	2
Buick Classic	65	34	8	-	-	33	32	72	-	-
Canon GH Open	53	MC	MC	MC	MC	40	12	46	48	17
Western Open	29	13	MC	20	8	MC	MC	27	76	MC
Gr. Milwaukee	3	MC	18	MC	-	WD	-	-	-	-
British Open	55	-	20	3	5	MC	66	62	MC	MC
B.C. Open	-	MC	-	-	-	-	-	-	-	-
John Deere Cl'	MC	31	59	-	-	-	-	-	-	-
The International	-	46	-	21	55	37	56	54	-	-
Buick Open	-	27	MC	-	MC	74	15	-	-	-
USPGA Champ	15	MC	MC	31	1	MC	56	16	MC	MC
WGCNEC Inv'										
Reno-Tahoe Op'	-	-	-	-	-	-	9	MC	14	
Air Canada Chp'	-	-	-	-	-	-	52	-	-	
Bell Canadian O'	22	-	14	26	MC	MC	29	-		
WGC AmEx										
Tampa Bay Cl'	-	-	-	-	-	-	WD	-		
Marconi Penn C'	-	-	-	-	-	MC	MC			
Texas Open	7	MC	71	MC	36	MC	MC	38	MC	71
Michelob Chmp'	-	25	-	-	MC	17	50	WD	MC	
Invensys Classic	MC	MC	14	30	67	47	51	65	MC	MC
NCR Golf Cl'	-	-	37	-	MC	19	44	-	50	
Buick Challenge	-	2	41	MC	MC	MC	58	13	MC	WD
SFB Classic	-	-	-	-	-	-	MC	-	71	
Tour Champ'ship	27	-	29	-	27	-	-	-	-	-

Olin Browne

22/5/59 – Washington, DC

Failed to add to his haul of two US Tour wins in 2001 – his last success came in 1999 when he won the MasterCard Colonial. A typical fairways and greens journeyman pro who has made over $3million in prize money since turning pro in 1984. Browne won consistently on the Buy.com Tour throughout the 90s (four wins) before securing his first full tour title in 1998 (Canon Greater Hartford Open). A fluent Spanish speaker, Browne is far from you average pro and lists politics as one of his interests. Best performance in 2001 came at the AT&T when third.

ScAv - 70.60 (45th) – DD - 275.0 (145th) DA - 75.8 (6th) GIR - 68.3 (49th) - PpGIR - 1.755 (50th) SS - 47.1 (143rd)

	'92	'93	'94	'95	'96	'97	'98	'99	'00	'01
WGC MatchPlay	-	-	-	-	-	-	-	-	33	-
Mercedes Ch	-	-	-	-	-	-	-	-	21	-
Tucson Open	4	-	6	-	56	27	MC	65	-	32
Sony Open	52	-	32	-	MC	MC	7	-	34	43
Phoenix Open	67	-	MC	-	48	MC	22	-	MC	69
AT&T P Beach	MC	58	MC	-	-	MC	MC	-	MC	3
Buick Invitatn'l	MC	-	-	61	70	WD-	-	-	-	
Bob Hope Cl'	44	-	MC	-	MC	79	MC	-	16	70
Nissan Open	MC	-	MC	-	44	67	-	-	MC	57
Genuity Champ	37	-	-	-	WD	23	44	51	MC	
Honda Classic	MC	-	MC	-	21	45	39	MC	MC	-
Bay Hill Invit'l	MC	-	-	-	71	29	74	29	23	
Players Champ	-	-	-	-	MC	MC	MC	77	MC	
BellSouth Cl'	-	-	13	-	MC	WD	MC	-	-	
US Masters	-	-	-	-	-	MC	52	-	-	
Worldcom Cl'	-	-	-	30	-	MC	MC	-		
Houston Open	-	MC	-	-	MC	17	51	-	MC	
GG Chrysler Cl'	MC	-	-	MC	MC	-	MC	56	9	
Compaq Classic	MC	-	-	27	57	-	-	-	-	
Byron Nelson C'	-	MC	-	57	19	MC	24	MC	22	
MasterCard Cln'l	-	-	-	-	MC	1	MC	MC	-	
Kemper Ins Open	65	MC	73	-	43	58	72	MC	34	MC
Memorial T'ment	-	-	-	-	-	-	3	13	MC	
St. Jude Classic	MC	-	-	-	-	-	-	-	-	
U.S. Open	-	-	47	-	101	5	43	MC	-	24
Buick Classic	MC	-	MC	-	53	MC	54	MC	MC	11
Canon GH Open	79	-	61	-	25	MC	1	26	32	7
Western Open	29	-	45	-	47	MC	MC	68	23	-
Gr. Milwaukee	MC	-	62	-	7	52	-	9	-	-
British Open	-	-	-	-	-	-	-	-	-	-
B.C. Open	MC	-	59	-	-	-	-	-	-	-
John Deere Cl'	57	-	MC	-	-	18	70	-	44	50
The International	WD	-	MC	-	MC	28	32	8	43	67
Buick Open	35	-	56	-	7	MC	-	MC	-	43
USPGA Champ	-	-	-	-	-	53	62	49	-	MC
WGCNEC Inv'										
Reno-Tahoe Op'	-	-	-	-	-	-	-	63	MC	
Air Canada Chp'	-	-	-	MC	-	-	-	46	-	
Bell Canadian O'	MC	-	68	-	57	MC	-	-	20	30
WGC AmEx										
Tampa Bay Cl'	-	-	-	-	-	-	-	MC	-	
Marconi Penn C'	-	-	-	-	-	-	-	28	18	
Texas Open	MC	-	MC	-	28	-	-	MC	-	MC
Michelob Chmp'	73	-	-	-	9	63	-	-	53	MC
Invensys Classic	68	-	MC	-	22	67	-	32	22	46
NCR Golf Cl'	MC	-	33	-	42	6	-	57	66	36
Buick Challenge	MC	-	52	-	14	MC	-	MC-	-	-
SFB Classic	-	-	50	-	-	-	-	51	-	-
Tour Champ'ship	-	-	-	-	-	-	-	-	-	-

244

Mark Calcavecchia

12/6/60 – Laurel, NE

Calc proved that he is still among the best golfers in the world in 2001 by regaining a Ryder Cup place (next year will be his first appearance for over a decade) and breaking all manor of records when winning the Phoenix Open – his 10th US Tour victory. The 1989 Open champion is long off the tee and a good putter. The Florida based pro has won over $13million in his career and still has the appetite for the game. His fourth place in the Masters was his best finish in a Major since winning at Troon in 1989.

ScAv – 70.40 (32nd) – DD – 282.2 (28th) DA – 66.5 (132nd) GIR – 67.6 (62nd) – PpGIR – 1.747 (30th) SS – 55.6 (50th)

	'92	'93	'94	'95	'96	'97	'98	'99	'00	'01
WGC MatchPlay	-	-	-	-	-	-	-	33	9	-
Mercedes Ch	-	10	-	24	-	6	20	-	-	-
Tucson Open	WD	MC	MC	32	MC	-	31	-	-	15
Sony Open	69	MC	-	14	-	45	-	-	-	-
Phoenix Open	1	MC	18	7	4	4	MC	26	7	1
AT&T P Beach	MC	MC	-	13	-	20	-	21	20	MC
Buick Invitatn'l	-	-	9	2	8	MC	57	-	-	-
Bob Hope Cl'	MC	-	-	33	2	19	MC	59	3	-
Nissan Open	50	MC	-	41	-	-	76	MC	-	-
Genuity Champ	69	24	16	33	74	MC	30	78	73	-
Honda Classic	17	38	MC	47	33	37	1	74	7	2
Bay Hill Invit'l	21	MC	42	53	4	14	4	MC	46	31
Players Champ	73	MC	23	18	29	24	4	10	MC	MC
BellSouth Cl'	-	2	MC	1	45	51	59	MC	MC	-
US Masters	31	17	MC	41	15	17	16	MC	-	4
Worldcom Cl'	-	MC	-	-	-	-	-	-	-	38
Houston Open	MC	-	-	59	18	-	-	-	-	-
GG Chrysler Cl'	-	12	33	5	MC	-	-	-	3	36
Compaq Classic	-	MC	-	-	-	-	35	MC	MC	-
Byron Nelson C'	55	8	20	16	51	MC	MC	51	MC	-
MasterCard Cln'	10	11	12	8	MC	72	41	26	8	MC
Kemper Ins Open	6	59	-	-	-	-	-	-	-	-
Memorial T'ment	71	WD	54	2	14	14	7	24	41	40
St. Jude Classic	75	55	-	-	-	-	-	-	-	-
U.S. Open	33	25	MC	MC	MC	MC	MC	MC	-	24
Buick Classic	-	-	-	-	-	27	17	72	-	-
Canon GH Open	26	30	MC	MC	3	5	16	3	2	29
Western Open	48	59	3	25	77	17	MC	-	-	-
Gr. Milwaukee	39	2	3	MC	40	20	3	8	MC	-
British Open	28	14	11	24	40	10	35	MC	26	54
B.C. Open	-	MC	-	-	-	-	-	-	-	-
John Deere Cl'	57	-	10	-	-	-	-	-	-	-
The International	MC	2	8	26	MC	25	MC	39	14	MC
Buick Open	-	-	-	-	-	-	-	-	-	MC
USPGA Champ	48	31	MC	MC	36	23	44	61	34	4
WGCNEC Inv'	-	-	-	-	-	-	-	12	-	36
Reno-Tahoe Op'	-	-	-	-	-	-	-	21	-	-
Air Canada Chp'	-	-	-	-	1	-	21	3	-	-
Bell Canadian O'	34	45	2	45	7	-	13	25	48	-
WGC AmEx	-	-	-	-	-	-	-	-	10	-
Tampa Bay Cl'	-	-	-	-	-	-	-	-	-	-
Marconi Penn C'	-	-	-	-	-	-	-	-	2	65
Texas Open	-	33	-	DQ	62	-	-	-	-	-
Michelob Chmp'	-	-	-	-	-	-	-	45	25	-
Invensys Classic	MC	-	39	3	4	2	MC	MC	MC	-
NCR Golf Cl'	-	47	-	-	-	-	-	-	-	-
Buick Challenge	-	13	MC	-	55	-	66	-	-	-
SFB Classic	-	-	-	-	-	-	-	9	-	-
Tour Champ'ship	-	7	24	27	15	4	29	-	11	19

Greg Chalmers

11/10/73 – Sydney, Australia

Australian former European Tour pro who is getting closer to a breakthrough in the United States every year. Last season was his third full term on the US Tour with his best finish fifth at the Sony Open. Honed his skills on the ANZ Tour (two wins, including the Australian Open) before trying his luck in Europe (one Challenge Tour win and two European Tour runners-up positions) and then America. Left-handed with a fine temperament and a excellent short game. Former Australian Amateur champion who was nicknamed 'Snake' when playing on the ANZ Tour.

ScAv – 70.74 (60th) – DD – 278.6 (106th) DA – 69.1 (82nd) GIR – 65.8 (103rd) – PpGIR – 1.754 (46th) SS – 56.8 (31st)

	'92	'93	'94	'95	'96	'97	'98	'99	'00	'01
WGC MatchPlay	-	-	-	-	-	-	-	-	-	33
Mercedes Ch	-	-	-	-	-	-	-	-	-	-
Tucson Open	-	-	-	-	-	-	-	MC	25	-
Sony Open	-	-	-	-	-	-	-	MC	MC	5
Phoenix Open	-	-	-	-	-	-	-	-	MC	60
AT&T P Beach	-	-	-	-	-	-	-	MC	-	-
Buick Invitatn'l	-	-	-	-	-	-	-	MC	MC	MC
Bob Hope Cl'	-	-	-	-	-	-	-	32	28	46
Nissan Open	-	-	-	-	-	-	-	30	18	13
Genuity Champ	-	-	-	-	-	-	-	10	45	12
Honda Classic	-	-	-	-	-	-	-	46	57	-
Bay Hill Invit'l	-	-	-	-	-	-	-	MC	-	34
Players Champ	-	-	-	-	-	-	-	-	9	58
BellSouth Cl'	-	-	-	-	-	-	-	MC	-	-
US Masters	-	-	-	-	-	-	-	-	25	42
Worldcom Cl'	-	-	-	-	-	-	-	-	-	MC
Houston Open	-	-	-	-	-	-	-	MC	MC	41
GG Chrysler Cl'	-	-	-	-	-	-	-	MC	MC	-
Compaq Classic	-	-	-	-	-	-	-	73	-	11
Byron Nelson C'	-	-	-	-	-	-	-	51	33	68
MasterCard Cln'l	-	-	-	-	-	-	-	-	35	15
Kemper Ins Open	-	-	-	-	-	-	-	65	2	DQ
Memorial T'ment	-	-	-	-	-	-	-	35	45	20
St. Jude Classic	-	-	-	-	-	-	-	MC	-	-
U.S. Open	-	-	-	-	-	-	-	-	-	-
Buick Classic	-	-	-	-	-	-	-	22	MC	-
Canon GH Open	-	-	-	-	-	-	-	MC	58	MC
Western Open	-	-	-	-	-	-	-	17	MC	42
Gr. Milwaukee	-	-	-	-	-	-	-	28	-	-
British Open	-	-	-	-	-	57	-	-	-	-
B.C. Open	-	-	-	-	-	-	-	39	-	-
John Deere Cl'	-	-	-	-	-	-	-	41	MC	-
The International	-	-	-	-	-	-	-	51	11	MC
Buick Open	-	-	-	-	-	-	-	MC	16	43
USPGA Champ	-	-	-	-	-	-	MC	-	4	44
WGCNEC Inv'	-	-	-	-	-	-	-	-	-	-
Reno-Tahoe Op'	-	-	-	-	-	-	-	37	-	44
Air Canada Chp'	-	-	-	-	-	-	-	21	31	MC
Bell Canadian O'	-	-	-	-	-	-	-	15	4	-
WGC AmEx	-	-	-	-	-	-	-	-	-	-
Tampa Bay Cl'	-	-	-	-	-	-	-	-	-	-
Marconi Penn C'	-	-	-	-	-	-	-	-	-	-
Texas Open	-	-	-	-	-	-	-	MC	-	-
Michelob Chmp'	-	-	-	-	-	-	-	24	MC	16
Invensys Classic	-	-	-	-	-	-	-	44	60	52
NCR Golf Cl'	-	-	-	-	-	-	-	MC	-	MC
Buick Challenge	-	-	-	-	-	-	-	MC	8	-
SFB Classic	-	-	-	-	-	-	-	21	-	-
Tour Champ'ship	-	-	-	-	-	-	-	-	-	-

Brandel Chamblee
2/7/62 – St. Louis, MO

Turned pro in 1985 and was an original member of the Buy.com Tour (then Hogan Tour) in 1990, claiming his first win as a pro – the New England Classic. Since 1993 has always made the top 125 on the Money List and thus has retained his card. Chamblee's only success in 177 US Tour starts was in the 1998 Greater Vancouver Open (now Air Canada Championship), although he did lose a play-off for the 1996 BellSouth Classic. His bunker play improved out of all recognition last season but the best part of his game has been his accuracy off the tee.
ScAv - 71.24 (105th) – DD - 273.9 (153rd) DA - 70.1 (65th) GIR - 63.9 (159th) – PpGIR - 1.790 (144th) SS - 60.1 (16th)

	'92	'93	'94	'95	'96	'97	'98	'99	'00	'01
WGC MatchPlay	-	-	-	-	-	-	-	-		
Mercedes Ch	-	-	-	-	-	-	-	16	-	-
Tucson Open	23	MC	52	12	MC	67	WD	45	36	-
Sony Open	69	MC	-	-	31	27	11	48	-	MC
Phoenix Open	-	-	39	66	35	22	58	MC	18	MC
AT&T P Beach	MC	9	-	-	-	-	MC	-	-	-
Buick Invitatn'l	25	29	24	8	MC	38	MC	-	52	MC
Bob Hope Cl'	-	-	16	MC	-	-	-	66	MC
Nissan Open	MC	MC	72	25	26	-	20	15	10	2
Genuity Champ	-	-	75	-	72	MC	-	-	-	25
Honda Classic	16	MC	3	59	MC	60	-	-	-	-
Bay Hill Invit'l	-	-	42	-	-	MC	5	10	43
Players Champ	-	69	MC	MC	MC	42	MC	66	MC
BellSouth Cl'	-	13	70	7	2	25	65	-	MC
US Masters	-	-	-	-	-	-	18	-	-
Worldcom Cl'	-	-	MC	71	30	MC	MC	-	62
Houston Open	14	MC	MC	46	-	MC	36	-	MC	MC
GG Chrysler Cl'	WD	MC	44	MC	-	MC	-	-	MC	-
Compaq Classic	57	MC	-	-	-	-	-	MC	-
Byron Nelson C'	MC	33	42	16	10	43	MC	24	7	73
MasterCard Cln'l	-	-	MC	MC	MC	-	53	33	-	40
Kemper Ins Open	36	MC	-	-	-	58	-	-	47	31
Memorial T'ment	-	-	-	MC	MC	-	5	MC	-	-
St. Jude Classic	78	31	MC	5	MC	MC	26	-	-	42
U.S. Open	MC	-	-	-	-	-	MC	46	61	44
Buick Classic	65	34	MC	-	-	27	-	-	-	52
Canon GH Open	MC	MC	26	WD	12	2	MC	-	-	-
Western Open	38	MC	WD	MC	MC	MC	35	68	-	3
Gr. Milwaukee	31	62	29	MC	-	-	-	22	35	-
British Open	-	-	MC	-	-	-	-	-	-	62
B.C. Open	58	MC	-	-	-	-	30	-	-
John Deere Cl'	MC	14	31	-	61	2	MC	-	-
The International	MC	MC	71	MC	-	68	12	-	MC	-
Buick Open	MC	-	-	-	-	-	8	-	-	-
USPGA Champ	-	-	MC	MC	MC	-	MC	-	-
WGCNEC Inv'	-	-	-	-	-	-	-	-	-
Reno-Tahoe Op'	-	-	-	-	-	-	MC	-	MC
Air Canada Chp'	-	-	-	-	MC	1	MC	-	71
Bell Canadian O'	MC	10	59	29	-	-	-	-	-
WGC AmEx	-	-	-	-	-	-	-	-	-
Tampa Bay Cl'	-	-	-	-	-	-	-	-	-
Marconi Penn C'	-	-	-	-	-	-	-	MC	-
Texas Open	54	27	46	22	MC	MC	37	MC	68	30
Michelob Chrmp'	23	46	58	-	MC	-	-	-	-
Invensys Classic	MC	MC	73	MC	74	-	10	6	22	MC
NCR Golf Cl'	MC	-	-	MC	MC	19	MC	13	MC
Buick Challenge	23	64	41	-	MC	6	24	MC	MC
SFB Classic	-	32	11	-	46	-	-	-	-
Tour Champ'ship	-	-	-	-	-	-	-	-	-

K.J. Choi
5/9/70 – Seoul, Korea

Became the first Korean to earn a US Tour card after getting through Q-School in 1999. His rookie season saw him post one top-ten finish – in the Air Canada Championship and another trip to the qualifying tournament had to be endured. Last season, though, saw Choi post five top-ten finishes and comfortably retain his playing privileges. Always long off the tee, the biggest improvement in his game in 2001 has been on the greens. His putting figures in 2000 ranked him outside the top 160, now he ranks a respectable 74th. A first win on the tour could come next season.
ScAv - 70.62 (46th) – DD - 283.1 (59th) DA - 63.8 (173rd) GIR - 65.9 (100th) – PpGIR - 1.765 (74th) SS - 50.7 (116th)

	'92	'93	'94	'95	'96	'97	'98	'99	'00	'01
WGC MatchPlay	-	-	-	-	-	-	-	-		
Mercedes Ch	-	-	-	-	-	-	-	-	-	-
Tucson Open	-	-	-	-	-	-	-	-	69	5
Sony Open	-	-	-	-	-	-	-	-	MC	29
Phoenix Open	-	-	-	-	-	-	-	-	-	-
AT&T P Beach	-	-	-	-	-	-	-	-	MC	27
Buick Invitatn'l	-	-	-	-	-	-	-	-	MC	48
Bob Hope Cl'	-	-	-	-	-	-	-	-	-	-
Nissan Open	-	-	-	-	-	-	-	-	-	-
Genuity Champ	-	-	-	-	-	-	-	-	21	25
Honda Classic	-	-	-	-	-	-	-	-	MC	MC
Bay Hill Invit'l	-	-	-	-	-	-	-	-	-	51
Players Champ	-	-	-	-	-	-	-	-	-	-
BellSouth Cl'	-	-	-	-	-	-	-	-	69	19
US Masters	-	-	-	-	-	-	-	-	-	-
Worldcom Cl'	-	-	-	-	-	-	-	-	-	MC
Houston Open	-	-	-	-	-	-	-	-	MC	62
GG Chrysler Cl'	-	-	-	-	-	-	-	-	MC	4
Compaq Classic	-	-	-	-	-	-	-	-	74	MC
Byron Nelson C'	-	-	-	-	-	-	-	-	41	MC
MasterCard Cln'l	-	-	-	-	-	-	-	-	-	-
Kemper Ins Open	-	-	-	-	-	-	-	-	MC	-
Memorial T'ment	-	-	-	-	-	-	24	-	MC
St. Jude Classic	-	-	-	-	-	-	-	-	MC	19
U.S. Open	-	-	-	-	-	-	-	-	-	MC
Buick Classic	-	-	-	-	-	-	-	-	64	-
Canon GH Open	-	-	-	-	-	-	-	-	76	MC
Western Open	-	-	-	-	-	-	-	-	63	60
Gr. Milwaukee	-	-	-	-	-	-	-	-	47	5
British Open	-	-	-	-	-	MC	49	-	-
B.C. Open	-	-	-	-	-	-	-	-	MC	-
John Deere Cl'	-	-	-	-	-	-	-	-	-	-
The International	-	-	-	-	-	-	-	-	48	45
Buick Open	-	-	-	-	-	-	-	-	47	-
USPGA Champ	-	-	-	-	-	-	-	-	-	29
WGCNEC Inv'	-	-	-	-	-	-	-	-	-	-
Reno-Tahoe Op'	-	-	-	-	-	-	-	-	12	MC
Air Canada Chp'	-	-	-	-	-	-	-	-	8	52
Bell Canadian O'	-	-	-	-	-	-	-	-	60	8
WGC AmEx	-	-	-	-	-	-	-	-	-	-
Tampa Bay Cl'	-	-	-	-	-	-	-	-	MC	-
Marconi Penn C'	-	-	-	-	-	-	-	-	18	MC
Texas Open	-	-	-	-	-	-	-	-	-	30
Michelob Chrmp'	-	-	-	-	-	-	-	-	MC	-
Invensys Classic	-	-	-	-	-	-	-	-	MC	-
NCR Golf Cl'	-	-	-	-	-	-	-	-	MC	-
Buick Challenge	-	-	-	-	-	-	-	-	MC	MC
SFB Classic	-	-	-	-	-	-	-	-	29	6
Tour Champ'ship	-	-	-	-	-	-	-	-	-	-

246

Stewart Cink

21/5/73 – Huntsville, AL

A big guy at 6'4" and over 200lbs, Cink didn't win in 2001 but went agonisingly close in the US Open. He missed a tiddler on the last hole that would have seen him make the play-off.

His fine run of summer form earned him a place in the USA Ryder Cup team. His two wins on the full tour came in the 2000 MCI (now WorldCom) Classic and the 1997 Canon Greater Hartford Open. Long off the tee, the best part about his game is his accurate iron play that sets up plenty of birdie opportunities.

ScAv - 70.27 (25th) – DD - 281.7 (69th) DA - 64.0 (171st) GIR - 69.8 (27th) – PpGIR - 1.768 (85th) SS - 54.5 (66th)

	'92	'93	'94	'95	'96	'97	'98	'99	'00	'01
WGC MatchPlay	-	-	-	-	-	-	-	9	33	33
Mercedes Ch	-	-	-	-	-	-	6	-	-	12
Tucson Open	-	-	-	-	-	27	-	-	-	-
Sony Open	-	-	-	-	-	-	-	MC	-	MC
Phoenix Open	-	-	-	-	-	MC	MC	10	10	9
AT&T P Beach	-	-	-	-	-	MC	25	-	61	-
Buick Invitatn'l	-	-	-	-	-	-	13	26	28	-
Bob Hope Cl'	-	-	-	-	-	9	6	24	MC	MC
Nissan Open	-	-	-	-	-	27	-	62	5	20
Genuity Champ	-	-	-	-	-	20	4	57	-	12
Honda Classic	-	-	-	-	-	MC	12	-	-	-
Bay Hill Invit'l	-	-	-	-	-	38	36	-	6	-
Players Champ	-	-	-	-	-	-	42	MC	33	MC
BellSouth Cl'	-	-	-	68	-	MC	5	2	10	6
US Masters	-	-	-	-	MC	23	27	28	MC	-
Worldcom Cl'	-	-	-	-	-	-	-	-	1	10
Houston Open	-	-	-	-	-	-	-	-	-	13
GG Chrysler Cl'	-	-	-	-	-	MC	-	40	-	MC
Compaq Classic	-	-	-	-	-	MC	-	-	-	-
Byron Nelson C'	-	-	-	-	-	48	MC	-	MC	-
MasterCard Cln'l	-	-	-	-	-	15	41	21	2	26
Kemper Ins Open	-	-	-	-	-	-	-	22	20	-
Memorial T'ment	-	-	-	-	43	MC	38	24	45	4
St. Jude Classic	-	-	-	-	-	16	-	-	33	37
U.S. Open	-	-	-	-	16	13	10	32	8	3
Buick Classic	-	-	-	-	-	6	47	MC	-	3
Canon GH Open	-	-	-	18	-	1	2	8	14	MC
Western Open	-	-	-	-	-	MC	-	-	-	-
Gr. Milwaukee	-	-	-	-	-	12	-	-	-	-
British Open	-	-	-	-	-	66	MC	41	30	-
B.C. Open	-	-	-	5	-	12	MC	-	-	-
John Deere Cl'	-	-	-	MC	-	-	-	-	-	-
The International	-	-	-	-	-	33	21	MC	MC	26
Buick Open	-	-	-	-	-	-	15	MC	MC	29
USPGA Champ	-	-	-	-	-	MC	MC	3	15	59
WGCNEC Inv'	-	-	-	-	-	-	-	-	7	13
Reno-Tahoe Op'	-	-	-	-	-	-	-	9	-	-
Air Canada Chp'	-	-	-	-	-	-	56	-	-	-
Bell Canadian O'	-	-	-	-	-	13	-	-	-	-
WGC AmEx	-	-	-	-	-	-	-	4	-	-
Tampa Bay Cl'	-	-	-	-	-	-	-	-	-	-
Marconi Penn C'	-	-	-	-	-	-	-	-	-	MC
Texas Open	-	-	-	-	-	-	11	54	19	-
Michelob Chmp'	-	-	-	45	-	46	25	-	-	-
Invensys Classic	-	-	-	12	MC	16	22	3	20	-
NCR Golf Cl'	-	-	-	-	-	51	11	-	21	-
Buick Challenge	-	-	58	9	2	MC	6	18	50	-
SFB Classic	-	-	-	21	MC	-	-	-	-	-
Tour Champ'ship	-	-	-	-	23	-	18	13		

Jose Coceres

14/8/63 – Chaco, Argentina

Argentine former European Tour pro who earned over $1.5million in his rookie season on the US Tour. Amazingly, he won twice, in the WorldCom and NCR Classics, but didn't post any other top ten finishes. Like many Argentinean golfers, he started life as a caddie and taught himself the game. Came to Europe in 1991 and won twice in a decade of consistent play, netting over £1.6million before trying his luck in America. An extremely accurate driver of the ball and an excellent bunker player his shortness off the tee can be a disadvantage.

ScAv - 70.41 (36th) – DD - 274.0 (151st) DA - 75.6 (8th) GIR - 67.7 (58th) PpGIR - 1.778 (108th) SS - 63.7 (5th)

	'92	'93	'94	'95	'96	'97	'98	'99	'00	'01
WGC MatchPlay	-	-	-	-	-	-	-	-	-	33
Mercedes Ch	-	-	-	-	-	-	-	-	-	-
Tucson Open	-	-	-	-	-	-	-	-	-	-
Sony Open	-	-	-	-	-	-	-	-	-	-
Phoenix Open	-	-	-	-	-	-	-	-	-	-
AT&T P Beach	-	-	-	-	-	-	-	-	-	-
Buick Invitatn'l	-	-	-	-	-	-	-	-	-	-
Bob Hope Cl'	-	-	-	-	-	-	-	-	-	-
Nissan Open	-	-	-	-	-	-	-	-	-	-
Genuity Champ	-	-	-	-	-	-	-	-	-	-
Honda Classic	-	-	-	-	-	-	-	-	-	-
Bay Hill Invit'l	-	-	-	-	-	-	-	-	-	-
Players Champ	-	-	-	-	-	-	-	-	-	-
BellSouth Cl'	-	-	-	-	-	-	-	-	-	MC
US Masters	-	-	-	-	-	-	-	-	-	MC
Worldcom Cl'	-	-	-	-	-	-	-	-	-	1
Houston Open	-	-	-	-	-	-	-	-	-	-
GG Chrysler Cl'	-	-	-	-	-	-	-	-	-	-
Compaq Classic	-	-	-	-	-	-	-	-	-	MC
Byron Nelson C'	-	-	-	-	-	-	-	-	-	51
MasterCard Cln'l	-	-	-	-	-	-	-	-	-	34
Kemper Ins Open	-	-	-	-	-	-	-	-	-	-
Memorial T'ment	-	-	-	-	-	-	-	-	-	-
St. Jude Classic	-	-	-	-	-	-	-	-	-	19
U.S. Open	-	-	-	-	-	-	-	-	-	52
Buick Classic	-	-	-	-	-	-	-	-	-	MC
Canon GH Open	-	-	-	-	-	-	-	-	-	-
Western Open	-	-	-	-	-	-	-	-	-	-
Gr. Milwaukee	-	-	-	-	-	-	-	-	-	-
British Open	45	-	-	96	MC	44	-	-	36	MC
B.C. Open	-	-	-	-	-	-	-	-	-	-
John Deere Cl'	-	-	-	-	-	-	-	-	-	-
The International	-	-	-	-	-	-	-	-	-	MC
Buick Open	-	-	-	-	-	-	-	-	-	MC
USPGA Champ	-	-	-	-	-	-	-	-	MC	16
WGCNEC Inv'	-	-	-	-	-	-	-	-	-	-
Reno-Tahoe Op'	-	-	-	-	-	-	-	-	-	-
Air Canada Chp'	-	-	-	-	-	-	-	-	-	-
Bell Canadian O'	-	-	-	-	-	-	-	-	-	43
WGC AmEx	-	-	-	-	-	-	-	14	-	-
Tampa Bay Cl'	-	-	-	-	-	-	-	-	-	-
Marconi Penn C'	-	-	-	-	-	-	-	-	-	-
Texas Open	-	-	-	-	-	-	-	-	-	-
Michelob Chmp'	-	-	-	-	-	-	-	-	-	12
Invensys Classic	-	-	-	-	-	-	-	-	-	64
NCR Golf Cl'	-	-	-	-	-	-	-	-	-	1
Buick Challenge	-	-	-	-	-	-	-	-	-	70
SFB Classic	-	-	-	-	-	-	-	-	-	-
Tour Champ'ship	-	-	-	-	-	-	-	-	-	-

John Cook
2/10/57 – Toledo, OH

Surprised even himself by winning the Reno Tahoe Open in 2001 – his first US Tour win since 1998 but the 11th of his 22-year career as a pro. His first victory came in 1981 – the Bing Crosby National Pro-Am (now AT&T) – defeating Bobby Clampett in a play-off. Still competitive, Cook remains one of the most accurate drivers of the ball on the US Tour. Never the biggest of hitters, he relies upon his ability to hit fairways and greens in regulation to give him a chance of birdies. He has won twice internationally and is a former Ryder Cup player (1993).

ScAv - 70.72 (57th) – DD - 270.7 (174th) DA - 76.6 (4th) GIR - 72.9 (3rd) – PpGIR - 1.755 (50th) SS - 47.4 (142nd)

	'92	'93	'94	'95	'96	'97	'98	'99	'00	'01
WGC MatchPlay	-	-	-	-	-	-	-	33	-	-
Mercedes Ch	-	5	-	-	-	8	4	22	-	-
Tucson Open	-	-	17	40	MC	73	-	MC	67	
Sony Open	1	MC	MC	MC	MC	MC	-	38	22	57
Phoenix Open	-	-	MC	-	-	-	-	-	-	-
AT&T P Beach	12	52	MC	50	-	MC	56	-	-	-
Buick Invitatn'l	25	63	31	58	MC	29	-	MC	MC	WD
Bob Hope Cl'	1	12	21	MC	MC	1	MC	MC	MC	26
Nissan Open	32	-	MC	MC	MC	-	36	50	MC	68
Genuity Champ	-	-	-	28	36	9	MC	MC	MC	
Honda Classic	-	39	-	MC	MC	MC	-	15	41	47
Bay Hill Invit'l	MC	17	42	53	-	-	-	-	-	-
Players Champ	MC	MC	23	WD	MC	22	13	58	MC	55
BellSouth Cl'	-	-	MC	-	-	-	-	-	-	-
US Masters	54	39	46	MC	-	MC	43	MC	-	-
Worldcom Cl'	29	8	18	-	56	7	62	43	MC	28
Houston Open	-	-	11	9	27	MC	2	MC	4	
GG Chrysler Cl'	2	20	22	MC	74	MC	-	-	-	-
Compaq Classic	-	-	-	-	-	MC	-	54	34	
Byron Nelson C'	-	11	MC	32	36	12	1	MC	MC	43
MasterCard Cln'l	6	-	9	MC	-	-	5	11	8	34
Kemper Ins Open	-	-	-	-	58	-	52	-	-	
Memorial T'ment	48	12	3	MC	56	46	31	35	68	20
St. Jude Classic	-	55	10	5	1	39	MC	-	33	MC
U.S. Open	13	25	5	62	16	36	MC	60	MC	-
Buick Classic	-	-	-	-	11	-	41	5	32	
Canon GH Open	-	7	9	45	-	-	-	-	44	-
Western Open	-	-	43	35	21	MC	MC	-	31	
Gr. Milwaukee	-	-	-	-	-	18	-	-	-	
British Open	2	MC	55	40	-	MC	-	-	-	-
B.C. Open	-	-	-	-	-	-	-	-	-	-
John Deere Cl'	-	-	WD	59	-	-	-	12	-	-
The International	-	-	MC	53	9	-	MC	MC	42	
Buick Open	19	40	-	MC	33	29	23	-	32	27
USPGA Champ	2	6	4	MC	47	23	9	MC	-	-
WGCNEC Inv'	-	-	-	-	-	-	-	-	-	-
Reno-Tahoe Op'	-	-	-	-	-	-	4	MC	1	
Air Canada Chp'	-	-	-	-	-	-	-	-	-	-
Bell Canadian O'	-	WD	-	MC	-	MC	-	-	-	
WGC AmEx	-	-	-	-	-	-	-	-	-	-
Tampa Bay Cl'	-	-	-	-	-	-	33	-	-	
Marconi Penn C'	-	-	-	-	-	-	-	-	3	
Texas Open	-	MC	21	75	-	-	-	-	-	
Michelob Chrmp'	MC	-	-	-	7	MC	65	19	-	
Invensys Classic	1	23	MC	14	19	40	36	MC	5	29
NCR Golf Cl'	46	7	70	15	18	10	19	77	62	50
Buick Challenge	-	-	-	-	-	-	-	38	MC	
SFB Classic	-	-	-	-	-	-	-	-	37	
Tour Champ'ship	13	-	-	11	20	21	-	-	-	

John Daly
28/4/66 – Carmichael, CA

Off the booze and back on track, Daly had his best season for six years in 2001. The two-time Major winner didn't manage to add to his four US Tour victories but he did win on the European Tour, in the BMW International in Germany – his first success anywhere since his 1995 Open win at St Andrews. Daly still has his demons but is learning to control them and has such a fine all-round game that another Major win wouldn't come as a surprise. Massive off the tee, although still wild, he has a sublime touch on and around the greens.

ScAv - 70.74 (60th) – DD - 306.7 (1st) DA - 60.7 (188th) GIR - 67.3 (70th) – PpGIR - 1.752 (42nd) SS - 46.9 (144th)

	'92	'93	'94	'95	'96	'97	'98	'99	'00	'01
WGC MatchPlay	-	-	-	-	-	-	-	-	-	-
Mercedes Ch	21	-	-	20	30	-	-	-	-	-
Tucson Open	-	-	MC	-	55	18	20	WD	48	
Sony Open	-	-	78	-	27	-	53	-	63	
Phoenix Open	63	MC	-	MC	-	-	12	14	72	9
AT&T P Beach	-	MC	-	-	-	-	MC	-	-	MC
Buick Invitatn'l	-	-	-	-	MC	16	MC	-	48	
Bob Hope Cl'	MC	-	-	-	7	-	MC	21	MC	-
Nissan Open	8	26	-	41	17	-	4	-	MC	57
Genuity Champ	50	29	-	58	MC	MC	-	MC	MC	
Honda Classic	59	20	4	80	57	-	4	27	16	11
Bay Hill Invit'l	51	35	21	72	MC	35	53	-	78	MC
Players Champ	72	MC	MC	-	19	WD	MC	WD	48	MC
BellSouth Cl'	-	-	1	12	MC	-	MC	-	-	27
US Masters	19	3	48	45	29	-	33	52	MC	-
Worldcom Cl'	-	-	MC	-	13	-	-	MC	-	49
Houston Open	-	17	7	MC	-	-	-	51	MC	26
GG Chrysler Cl'	-	74	MC	-	-	76	-	66	-	-
Compaq Classic	-	51	MC	-	-	-	-	-	-	
Byron Nelson C'	29	-	-	41	MC	-	77	67	MC	MC
MasterCard Cln'l	MC	-	-	MC	-	-	-	WD	-	-
Kemper Ins Open	2	DQ	31	-	10	70	MC	MC	34	MC
Memorial T'ment	MC	70	71	-	73	74	-	WD	MC	20
St. Jude Classic	MC	16	MC	-	58	-	DQ	MC	MC	5
U.S. Open	MC	33	MC	45	27	WD	53	68	WD	-
Buick Classic	-	MC	-	-	-	-	-	-	-	
Canon GH Open	-	DQ	MC	37	21	76	-	MC	22	
Western Open	MC	MC	-	47	-	-	-	-	-	
Gr. Milwaukee	-	-	67	-	MC	-	-	-	-	
British Open	75	14	81	1	66	-	MC	-	MC	MC
B.C. Open	1	58	-	MC	-	-	-	-	-	
John Deere Cl'	MC	-	-	-	-	-	MC	-	MC	-
The International	5	62	MC	-	-	WD	-	-	-	MC
Buick Open	-	-	-	MC	-	-	-	-	-	
USPGA Champ	82	51	MC	MC	MC	29	MC	-	-	-
WGCNEC Inv'	-	-	-	-	-	-	-	-	-	-
Reno-Tahoe Op'	-	-	-	-	-	-	-	MC	MC	17
Air Canada Chp'	-	-	-	-	-	-	MC	-	-	
Bell Canadian O'	12	-	-	-	MC	-	-	MC	-	4
WGC AmEx	-	-	-	-	-	-	-	-	-	-
Tampa Bay Cl'	-	-	-	-	-	-	-	-	-	-
Marconi Penn C'	-	-	-	-	-	-	-	MC	68	
Texas Open	-	-	WD	66	MC	-	76	-	-	
Michelob Chrmp'	-	-	-	-	-	-	-	-	-	-
Invensys Classic	MC	-	-	-	-	53	37	-	7	
NCR Golf Cl'	-	-	MC	-	42	-	WD	-	51	-
Buick Challenge	8	WD	-	67	MC	MC	-	MC	63	MC
SFB Classic	-	-	-	-	-	-	-	36	50	-
Tour Champ'ship	-	-	-	-	-	-	-	-	-	-

Robert Damron

27/10/72 – Pikeville, KY

A first US Tour win came Damron's way in 2001 - his sixth season on the main tour. His breakthrough came in the Verizon Byron Nelson Classic. He gained early advice from Arnold Palmer (Damron is a member at the Bay Hill Club the seven-time Major winner owns) and has comfortably retained his card over the past five years. Prior to his win Damron hadn't posted a top-ten finish in 2001 and he failed to do so after his success. He isn't the longest of hitters but is extremely accurate. He slipped nearly 100 places in the putting rankings last year.

ScAv - 71.56 (127th) – DD - 276.3 (126th) DA - 72.9 (27th) GIR - 65.1 (132nd) - PpGIR - 1.788 (138th) SS - 56.2 (38th)

	'92	'93	'94	'95	'96	'97	'98	'99	'00	'01
WGC MatchPlay	-	-	-	-	-	-	-	-	-	-
Mercedes Ch	-	-	-	-	-	-	-	-	-	-
Tucson Open	-	-	-	-	-	MC	14	-	MC	79
Sony Open	-	-	-	-	-	MC	-	71	-	-
Phoenix Open	-	-	-	-	-	27	49	MC	MC	-
AT&T P Beach	-	-	-	-	-	33	WD	-	MC	MC
Buick Invitatn'l	-	-	-	-	-	MC	16	MC	-	81
Bob Hope Cl'	-	-	-	-	-	20	35	MC	28	30
Nissan Open	-	-	-	-	-	MC	-	56	MC	-
Genuity Champ	-	-	-	-	-	5	DQ	44	12	25
Honda Classic	-	-	-	-	-	41	MC	27	7	MC
Bay Hill Invit'l	-	-	-	-	-	11	29	4	MC	17
Players Champ	-	-	-	-	-	53	MC	52	3	MC
BellSouth Cl'	-	-	-	-	-	-	-	MC	-	49
US Masters	-	-	-	-	-	-	-	-	-	-
Worldcom Cl'	-	-	-	-	-	70	50	70	34	73
Houston Open	-	-	-	-	-	MC	-	-	-	-
GG Chrysler Cl'	-	-	-	-	-	4	72	48	MC	47
Compaq Classic	-	-	-	-	-	48	12	51	17	MC
Byron Nelson C'	-	-	-	-	-	MC	35	60	33	1
MasterCard Cln'l	-	-	-	-	-	54	69	39	50	58
Kemper Ins Open	-	-	-	-	-	MC	-	-	-	-
Memorial T'ment	-	-	-	-	-	21	11	-	25	56
St. Jude Classic	-	-	-	-	-	3	7	MC	7	42
U.S. Open	-	-	-	-	-	-	-	-	63	MC
Buick Classic	-	-	-	-	-	3	41	80	-	-
Canon GH Open	-	-	-	-	-	77	MC	-	-	-
Western Open	-	-	MC	-	-	-	20	49	41	37
Gr. Milwaukee	-	-	-	-	-	-	MC	73	35	47
British Open	-	-	-	-	-	MC	-	-	-	-
B.C. Open	-	-	-	-	-	56	-	-	-	-
John Deere Cl'	-	-	-	-	-	-	-	10	33	MC
The International	-	-	-	-	-	MC	56	MC	MC	-
Buick Open	-	-	-	-	-	-	MC	MC	-	MC
USPGA Champ	-	-	-	-	-	MC	MC	-	74	66
WGCNEC Inv'	-	-	-	-	-	-	-	-	-	-
Reno-Tahoe Op'	-	-	-	-	-	-	-	32	-	-
Air Canada Chp'	-	-	-	-	-	21	-	74	-	-
Bell Canadian O'	-	-	-	-	-	44	25	64	-	-
WGC AmEx	-	-	-	-	-	-	-	-	-	-
Tampa Bay Cl'	-	-	-	-	-	-	-	-	MC	-
Marconi Penn C'	-	-	-	-	-	-	-	-	MC	MC
Texas Open	-	-	-	-	-	-	-	54	-	-
Michelob Chmp'	-	-	-	-	-	MC	WD	17	30	47
Invensys Classic	-	-	-	-	-	MC	12	6	MC	58
NCR Golf Cl'	-	-	-	-	-	MC	27	57	MC	21
Buick Challenge	-	-	-	-	-	MC	MC	44	32	WD
SFB Classic	-	-	-	-	-	-	-	-	-	-
Tour Champ'ship	-	-	-	-	-	-	-	-	-	-

Glen Day

16/11/65 – Mobile, AL

Eight full years on the full tour have brought just one win for Glen Day, who was once dubbed 'All Day' as he used to be one of the slowest players on the US Tour. Spent the early part of his professional career in the Far East and won the Malaysian Open in 1990. Competed in the 1993 Open Championship before he had played a US Tour event. His sole win came in 1999 in the MCI (now WorldCom) Classic. Short but straight off the tee, Day is one of the best putters around. His best performance in 2001 was fourth in the Mastercard Colonial.

ScAv - 71.03 (81st) – DD - 273.3 (159th) DA - 72.6 (29th) GIR - 65.1 (132nd) – PpGIR - 1.735 (13th) SS - 54.3 (68th)

	'92	'93	'94	'95	'96	'97	'98	'99	'00	'01
WGC MatchPlay	-	-	-	-	-	-	-	33	33	17
Mercedes Ch	-	-	-	-	-	-	-	-	8	-
Tucson Open	-	-	46	MC	MC	43	-	-	-	48
Sony Open	-	-	MC	MC	-	-	-	-	MC	-
Phoenix Open	-	-	-	MC	WD	-	6	44	-	MC
AT&T P Beach	-	-	69	-	-	9	22	53	20	6
Buick Invitatn'l	-	-	19	MC	MC	MC	49	-	-	-
Bob Hope Cl'	-	-	11	MC	MC	61	24	37	16	30
Nissan Open	-	-	-	71	44	-	74	-	-	-
Genuity Champ	-	-	-	MC	14	45	MC	10	MC	21
Honda Classic	-	-	35	24	-	MC	-	-	MC	MC
Bay Hill Invit'l	-	-	10	WD	9	MC	MC	MC	52	MC
Players Champ	-	-	MC	MC	MC	61	2	MC	MC	MC
BellSouth Cl'	-	MC	MC	-	19	30	7	-	-	-
US Masters	-	-	-	-	-	-	-	MC	19	-
Worldcom Cl'	-	-	MC	MC	29	42	2	1	61	28
Houston Open	-	-	-	-	-	-	-	-	-	-
GG Chrysler Cl'	-	-	44	41	MC	19	-	-	-	47
Compaq Classic	-	-	12	49	27	43	3	7	13	MC
Byron Nelson C'	-	-	MC	11	18	71	25	67	13	11
MasterCard Cln'l	-	-	30	33	56	10	41	51	55	4
Kemper Ins Open	-	-	-	WD	MC	MC	-	-	-	-
Memorial T'ment	-	-	MC	MC	-	10	11	43	41	MC
St. Jude Classic	-	-	MC	21	13	WD	3	25	25	MC
U.S. Open	-	-	MC	MC	-	-	23	MC	MC	MC
Buick Classic	-	-	MC	-	24	-	-	-	-	-
Canon GH Open	-	-	9	MC	49	MC	-	MC	-	-
Western Open	-	-	45	52	4	71	MC	9	71	MC
Gr. Milwaukee	-	-	41	MC	22	MC	-	-	-	18
British Open	-	MC	-	-	-	MC	MC	MC	-	-
B.C. Open	-	-	22	MC	-	MC	-	-	-	-
John Deere Cl'	-	-	-	-	-	-	-	-	23	35
The International	-	-	MC	17	MC	MC	-	MC	-	57
Buick Open	-	-	-	-	-	-	39	19	32	57
USPGA Champ	-	-	15	MC	41	MC	29	MC	51	MC
WGCNEC Inv'	-	-	-	-	-	-	-	-	-	-
Reno-Tahoe Op'	-	-	-	-	-	-	-	-	-	-
Air Canada Chp'	-	-	-	-	-	MC	28	-	-	-
Bell Canadian O'	-	-	19	45	52	WD	4	29	60	-
WGC AmEx	-	-	-	-	-	-	-	DQ	-	-
Tampa Bay Cl'	-	-	-	-	-	-	-	-	MC	-
Marconi Penn C'	-	-	-	-	-	-	-	-	MC	MC
Texas Open	-	-	MC	-	-	-	-	-	-	-
Michelob Chmp'	-	-	2	11	56	MC	-	79	MC	-
Invensys Classic	-	-	MC	7	44	MC	WD	15	MC	38
NCR Golf Cl'	-	-	7	37	13	10	11	7	6	46
Buick Challenge	-	-	41	12	68	MC	30	44	-	17
SFB Classic	-	-	DQ	18	12	-	-	3	36	37
Tour Champ'ship	-	-	-	-	-	-	-	18	-	-

Chris DiMarco

23/8/68 – Huntington, NY

New Yorker who has come good in the late part of the last two seasons to record victories. In 2000 he managed to win for the first time on the US Tour when landing the Pennsylvania Classic. Then, just over 12 months, later he won the Buick Challenge, defeating David Duval in a play-off. A former Buy.com Tour player (he won the 1997 Ozarks Open), DiMarco enjoyed his best year in 2001, winning and posting nine other top-ten finishes. Neither long off the tee nor accurate with his driver, DiMarco relies on superb iron play and a deadly putting touch.

ScAv - 69.87 (10th) – DD - 278.8 (104th) DA - 65.9 (137th) GIR - 70.6 (15th) – PpGIR - 1.734 (12th) SS - 59.6 (17th)

	'92	'93	'94	'95	'96	'97	'98	'99	'00	'01
WGC MatchPlay	-	-	-	-	-	-	-	-	-	33
Mercedes Ch	-	-	-	-	-	-	-	-	-	17
Tucson Open	-	-	59	MC	-	-	MC	77	2	-
Sony Open	-	-	66	MC	-	-	MC	MC	22	22
Phoenix Open	-	-	-	MC	-	-	47	54	61	5
AT&T P Beach	-	-	MC	MC	-	-	-	-	18	63
Buick Invitatn'l	-	-	MC	54	-	-	-	-	-	-
Bob Hope Cl'	-	-	MC	28	-	-	69	69	MC	-
Nissan Open	-	-	-	MC	-	-	43	MC	31	-
Genuity Champ	-	-	43	MC	-	46	70	69	MC	
Honda Classic	-	-	59	66	69	-	22	12	41	18
Bay Hill Invit'l	-	-	57	MC	-	MC	-	MC	MC	-
Players Champ	-	-	-	MC	-	-	46	MC	55	
BellSouth Cl'	-	-	MC	MC	-	MC	10	63	6	
US Masters	-	-	-	-	-	-	-	-	10	
Worldcom Cl'	-	-	-	37	-	-	MC	-	-	
Houston Open	-	-	MC	-	-	MC	21	45	9	
GG Chrysler Cl'	-	-	56	19	-	MC	57	53	-	
Compaq Classic	-	-	7	60	-	MC	47	43	MC	
Byron Nelson C'	-	-	42	67	-	35	3	49	37	
MasterCard Cln'l	-	-	-	-	-	-	-	MC	40	
Kemper Ins Open	-	-	75	51	-	14	MC	28	9	
Memorial T'ment	-	-	-	-	-	-	19	MC	30	
St. Jude Classic	-	-	15	MC	-	26	MC	2	12	
U.S. Open	-	-	-	-	-	32	-	16		
Buick Classic	-	-	MC	MC	-	MC	MC	-	-	
Canon GH Open	-	-	MC	MC	-	25	20	5	3	
Western Open	-	-	MC	MC	-	MC	MC	-	-	
Gr. Milwaukee	-	-	-	MC	-	31	MC	-	-	
British Open	-	-	-	-	-	-	MC	47		
B.C. Open	-	-	32	MC	26	-	9	30	-	
John Deere Cl'	-	-	MC	24	-	-	-	-	-	
The International	-	-	6	42	-	MC	61	35	3	
Buick Open	-	-	51	24	-	39	MC	MC	2	
USPGA Champ	-	-	-	-	-	41	15	16		
WGCNEC Inv'	-	-	-	-	-	-	-	-	-	
Reno-Tahoe Op'	-	-	-	-	-	-	21	-		
Air Canada Chp'	-	-	-	MC	-	28	48	-		
Bell Canadian O'MC	-	MC	MC	30	-	9	44	MC	-	
WGC AmEx	-	-	-	-	-	-	25	-		
Tampa Bay Cl'	-	-	-	-	-	-	33	-		
Marconi Penn C'	-	-	-	-	-	-	1	11		
Texas Open	-	-	46	WD	-	-	-	-	-	
Michelob Chmp'	-	-	MC	MC	-	MC	MC	-	-	
Invensys Classic	-	-	MC	MC	-	MC	MC	5	13	
NCR Golf Cl'	-	-	63	49	-	MC	17	18	32	
Buick Challenge	-	-	MC	-	-	MC	-	23	1	
SFB Classic	-	-	3	MC	-	35	2	-		
Tour Champ'ship	-	-	-	-	-	-	-	18	10	

Joe Durant

7/4/64 – Pensacola, FL

From journeyman pro to back-to-back US Tour winner in the space of a few months, Durant's game was nothing out of the ordinary until the early part of 2001. Then victories in the Bob Hope Classic and the Genuity Championship catapulted this one time Buy.com Tour never-has-been to the top of the Money List. An invite to the Masters followed and Durant only just missed out on a place in the USA Ryder Cup team. Always known as one of the best ball strikers on the tour, he added some distance off the tee and required the mental strength to win.

ScAv - 70.45 (39th) – DD - 280.4 (84th) DA - 81.1 (1st) GIR - 72.1 (5th) – PpGIR - 1.774 (101st) SS - 45.4 (160th)

	'92	'93	'94	'95	'96	'97	'98	'99	'00	'01
WGC MatchPlay	-									
Mercedes Ch	-						-	18	-	-
Tucson Open	-	MC	-	-	24	-	-	-	MC	MC
Sony Open	-	MC	-	-	-	9	MC	38	MC	29
Phoenix Open	-	-	-	-	MC	MC	-	MC	44	
AT&T P Beach	-	-	-	-	MC	-	MC	-	-	
Buick Invitatn'l	-	47	-	-	MC	49	-	-	MC	36
Bob Hope Cl'	-	MC	-	-	-	MC	-	MC	1	
Nissan Open	-	MC	-	-	-	-	-	-	-	
Genuity Champ	-	-	-	-	MC	-	-	-	1	
Honda Classic	-	-	-	-	5	52	-	61	5	
Bay Hill Invit'l	-	-	-	-	47	-	-	-	56	
Players Champ	-	-	-	-	MC	76	-	10		
BellSouth Cl'	-	MC	-	-	MC	MC	MC	53	-	
US Masters	-	-	-	-	-	MC	-	4		
Worldcom Cl'	-	-	-	-	MC	-	57	21		
Houston Open	-	-	-	-	12	MC	60	2		
GG Chrysler Cl'	-	-	-	MC	48	-	MC	-		
Compaq Classic	-	-	-	-	62	9	11			
Byron Nelson C'	-	-	-	64	-	MC	MC	-		
MasterCard Cln'l	-	-	-	MC	30	-	MC			
Kemper Ins Open	-	MC	-	-	MC	21	MC	47	MC	
Memorial T'ment	-	-	-	-	-	35	-	MC		
St. Jude Classic	-	-	-	46	12	-	11	-		
U.S. Open	-	-	-	-	32	MC	-	24		
Buick Classic	-	-	MC	63	MC	42	MC			
Canon GH Open	-	MC	-	17	16	34	18	-		
Western Open	-	-	42	1	MC	51	MC			
Gr. Milwaukee	-	-	34	65	55	7	-			
British Open	-	-	-	MC	-	-	MC			
B.C. Open	-	MC	-	MC	-	-	MC	-		
John Deere Cl'	-	MC	-	-	-	12	55	-		
The International	-	-	71	-	-	-	-			
Buick Open	-	-	59	-	-	-	MC			
USPGA Champ	-	-	-	40	-	-	51			
WGCNEC Inv'	-									
Reno-Tahoe Op'	-	-	-	-	50	77	-			
Air Canada Chp'	-	24	-	48	13	-				
Bell Canadian O'	-	52	-	MC	-	-	-			
WGC AmEx	-	-	-	-	-	5	-			
Tampa Bay Cl'	-	-	-	-	-	5	-			
Marconi Penn C'	-	-	-	-	-	-	-			
Texas Open	-	MC	-	62	-	MC	48	-		
Michelob Chmp'	-	MC	-	19	-	-	-			
Invensys Classic	-	MC	-	40	MC	9	MC			
NCR Golf Cl'	-	-	7	70	MC	MC	-			
Buick Challenge	-	72	-	28	MC	44	38	MC		
SFB Classic	-	MC	-	70	-	51	-	-		
Tour Champ'ship	-									10

David Duval
9/11/71 – Jacksonville, FL

After a number of near misses, Duval finally made his Major breakthrough in 2001 by winning the Open Championship at Royal Lytham. After 18 months in the shadow of Tiger Woods the former World No.1 looks set to win many more Major titles in the next decade. He has won 13 US Tour titles in total, managing to win at least once in every season since 1997. Duval is massive off the tee but wasn't particularly accurate with his driver in 2001 as he has been in previous years. His all-round game, though, is top class.

ScAv - 69.73 (7th) – DD - 296.7 (5th) DA - 65.3 (148th) GIR - 69.1 (35th) – PpGIR - 1.773 (98th) SS - 54.5 (66th)

	'92	'93	'94	'95	'96	'97	'98	'99	'00	'01
WGC MatchPlay	-	-	-	-	-	-	-	17	3	-
Mercedes Ch	-	-	-	-	-	-	6	1	3	7
Tucson Open	-	-	-	6	MC	24	1	-	-	-
Sony Open	-	-	-	14	-	-	-	-	-	-
Phoenix Open	-	-	-	-	35	14	27	18	30	MC
AT&T P Beach	-	-	37	2	-	2	WD	15	61	MC
Buick Invitatn'l	-	-	-	63	MC	18	MC	-	-	-
Bob Hope Cl'	-	-	-	2	33	52	4	1	5	51
Nissan Open	-	-	-	-	33	-	5	31	-	-
Genuity Champ	-	-	-	17	WD	4	23	-	4	63
Honda Classic	-	-	-	-	-	-	-	-	-	-
Bay Hill Invit'l	-	-	77	53	-	MC	-	-	-	-
Players Champ	-	-	-	MC	4	43	18	1	13	-
BellSouth Cl'	13	-	MC	15	3	2	14	1	73	-
US Masters	-	-	-	-	18	MC	2	6	3	2
Worldcom Cl'	-	-	-	MC	-	MC	-	-	-	-
Houston Open	-	-	-	27	3	15	1	64	-	26
GG Chrysler Cl'	-	-	-	14	-	-	-	-	-	-
Compaq Classic	-	-	-	3	-	-	-	MC	-	18
Byron Nelson C'	-	-	-	3	MC	-	-	-	20	3
MasterCard Cln'l	-	-	12	12	41	14	-	-	-	46
Kemper Ins Open	-	-	-	-	-	-	-	-	-	-
Memorial T'ment	-	30	2	2	17	3	3	25	-	
St. Jude Classic	-	19	-	-	-	-	-	-	-	-
U.S. Open	MC	-	-	28	67	48	7	7	8	16
Buick Classic	-	-	-	8	MC	27	-	10	2	26
Canon GH Open	-	38	-	MC	-	-	7	11	-	22
Western Open	19	30	8	68	MC	21	-	-	-	-
Gr. Milwaukee	-	-	-	-	-	-	-	-	-	-
British Open	-	-	-	20	14	33	11	62	11	1
B.C. Open	MC	-	-	-	15	MC	-	-	-	-
John Deere Cl'	-	-	-	-	-	-	-	-	-	-
The International	-	-	5	MC	MC	MC	2	WD	24	
Buick Open	-	-	MC	-	MC	-	-	-	-	-
USPGA Champ	-	-	-	MC	41	13	MC	10	-	10
WGCNEC Inv'	-	-	-	-	-	-	-	27	-	27
Reno-Tahoe Op'	-	-	-	-	-	-	-	-	-	-
Air Canada Chp'	-	-	-	-	-	-	-	-	-	-
Bell Canadian O'	-	-	-	2	-	-	-	-	-	-
WGC AmEx	-	-	-	-	-	-	-	-	-	-
Tampa Bay Cl'	-	-	-	-	-	-	-	-	-	-
Marconi Penn C'	-	-	-	-	-	-	-	-	-	-
Texas Open	-	-	-	50	-	MC	-	-	-	-
Michelob Chmp'	MC	MC	-	-	1	1	8	19	41	
Invensys Classic	-	-	-	58	-	-	-	-	-	-
NCR Golf Cl'	-	-	-	-	1	43	-	-	-	-
Buick Challenge	-	-	MC	MC	9	6	-	1	2	
SFB Classic	-	-	-	-	-	-	-	-	-	-
Tour Champ'ship	-	-	9	15	1	8	15	6	7	

Joel Edwards
22/11/61 – Dallas, TX

On his 316th US Tour start Edwards broke his US Tour duck by winning the 2001 Air Canada Championship. He promptly dedicated it to all the players who ply their trade on the lesser tours in America. Edwards has played on the Buy.Com Tour and other feeder tours in his time and understands more than most the life of a journeyman pro. Not surprisingly, 2001 was his best year since turning pro in 1984. Edwards won on the Buy.com Tour in 1999 (Mississippi Golf Coast Open) and his game relies on accuracy rather than power.

ScAv - 70.65 (48th) – DD - 276.0 (129th) DA - 73.7 (21st) GIR - 69.1 (35th) – PpGIR - 1.756 (55th) SS - 54.3 (68th)

	'92	'93	'94	'95	'96	'97	'98	'99	'00	'01
WGC MatchPlay	-	-	-	-	-	-	-	-	-	-
Mercedes Ch	-	-	-	-	-	-	-	-	-	-
Tucson Open	MC	68	MC	MC	27	-	-	-	MC	-
Sony Open	-	-	MC	62	16	67	-	-	19	MC
Phoenix Open	-	16	MC	26	-	MC	-	-	30	49
AT&T P Beach	MC	MC	MC	MC	-	38	-	-	51	MC
Buick Invitatn'l	MC	15	-	58	MC	65	-	-	-	MC
Bob Hope Cl'	-	55	-	54	-	MC	-	-	MC	-
Nissan Open	-	MC	MC	-	34	-	-	-	-	MC
Genuity Champ	-	-	MC	MC	-	MC	-	-	36	50
Honda Classic	MC	20	68	75	59	55	-	-	50	5
Bay Hill Invit'l	-	-	-	-	-	-	-	57	-	-
Players Champ	-	11	62	MC	19	MC	-	-	-	DQ
BellSouth Cl'	41	52	44	MC	39	72	-	-	MC	MC
US Masters	-	-	-	-	-	-	-	-	-	-
Worldcom Cl'	-	33	60	MC	48	-	-	-	MC	28
Houston Open	MC	MC	MC	70	44	52	-	-	3	13
GG Chrysler Cl'	-	26	8	71	16	-	-	-	28	54
Compaq Classic	-	32	27	MC	4	11	-	-	17	18
Byron Nelson C'	MC	MC	MC	MC	MC	MC	MC	-	MC	MC
MasterCard Cln'l	-	MC	-	-	MC	-	-	-	13	MC
Kemper Ins Open	MC	-	6	42	63	MC	-	-	-	-
Memorial T'ment	-	MC	-	-	39	-	-	-	68	-
St. Jude Classic	-	23	42	MC	44	53	-	-	15	22
U.S. Open	-	62	-	-	-	-	-	-	-	-
Buick Classic	MC	WD	MC	-	-	MC	-	-	-	MC
Canon GH Open	-	-	MC	MC	6	MC	-	-	58	45
Western Open	-	64	67	50	MC	MC	-	-	MC	MC
Gr. Milwaukee	9	MC	-	MC	-	MC	-	-	-	61
British Open	-	-	-	-	-	-	-	-	-	-
B.C. Open	2	MC	22	28	56	MC	-	-	-	27
John Deere Cl'	53	MC	49	12	19	43	-	-	MC	-
The International	-	MC	-	MC	-	MC	-	-	-	-
Buick Open	19	40	26	7	88	MC	-	-	25	49
USPGA Champ	-	MC	-	-	77	-	-	-	-	-
WGCNEC Inv'	-	-	-	-	-	-	-	-	-	-
Reno-Tahoe Op'	-	-	-	-	-	-	-	-	62	19
Air Canada Chp'	-	-	-	-	-	12	-	-	13	1
Bell Canadian O'	MC	-	61	MC	42	-	-	-	-	52
WGC AmEx	-	-	-	-	-	-	-	-	-	-
Tampa Bay Cl'	-	-	-	-	-	-	-	-	MC	-
Marconi Penn C'	-	-	-	-	-	-	-	-	-	-
Texas Open	MC	-	MC	33	-	MC	-	-	19	17
Michelob Chmp'	MC	-	MC	-	MC	MC	-	-	-	-
Invensys Classic	-	60	MC	MC	34	-	-	-	MC	45
NCR Golf Cl'	-	MC	MC	MC	36	MC	-	-	34	MC
Buick Challenge	39	MC	MC	MC	-	25	-	-	5	7
SFB Classic	-	-	-	28	72	61	MC	-	MC	28
Tour Champ'ship	-	-	-	-	-	-	-	-	-	-

Ernie Els

17/10/69 – Johannesburg, South Africa

Last season was the first time since joining the US Tour in 1994 that the Big Easy failed to win a tournament Stateside. The South African pro did come close, though, finishing as runner-up once and third on five occasions. There are those who still question Ernie's bottle, but the winner of two Majors, eight US Tour titles and another 24 worldwide just needs a little bit of luck to win again. His length off the tee is a big advantage, although his putting was poor in 2001. Enlisted the help of sports psychologist Jos Vanstiphout in the latter half of last season.

ScAv - 70.30 (27th) – DD - 285.8 (30th) DA - 64.8 (153rd) GIR - 66.1 (97th) – PpGIR - 1.790 (144th) SS - 60.6 (10th)

	'92	'93	'94	'95	'96	'97	'98	'99	'00	'01
WGC MatchPlay	-	-	-	-	-	-	-	33	17	4
Mercedes Ch	-	-	-	-	14	10	-	-	2	3
Tucson Open	-	-	-	-	-	-	-	-	-	-
Sony Open	-	-	-	-	-	-	-	-	5	3
Phoenix Open	-	-	-	-	-	-	-	-	-	MC
AT&T P Beach	-	-	-	-	-	-	-	-	-	-
Buick Invitatn'l	-	-	-	-	-	-	-	-	-	-
Bob Hope Cl'	-	-	-	-	-	-	-	-	-	-
Nissan Open	-	-	-	-	MC	-	1	66	-	-
Genuity Champ	-	-	-	17	MC	MC	-	3	15	25
Honda Classic	-	MC	-	-	-	23	MC	46	-	-
Bay Hill Invit'l	-	MC	MC	42	42	MC	1	44	14	62
Players Champ	-	MC	45	68	8	10	11	17	20	MC
BellSouth Cl'	-	-	-	-	29	-	-	-	-	44
US Masters	-	-	8	MC	12	17	16	27	2	6
Worldcom Cl'	-	-	-	7	-	68	10	-	3	-
Houston Open	-	-	-	-	-	-	-	-	-	-
GG Chrysler Cl'	-	-	-	-	-	9	-	-	-	-
Compaq Classic	-	-	27	-	47	-	-	-	50	3
Byron Nelson C'	-	-	-	1	18	-	63	-	-	MC
MasterCard Cln'l	-	-	-	MC	67	-	-	-	-	-
Kemper Ins Open	-	-	-	-	-	MC	-	-	34	-
Memorial T'ment	-	-	45	13	6	38	7	7	2	63
St. Jude Classic	-	-	-	26	-	-	-	-	-	-
U.S. Open	-	7	1	MC	5	1	49	MC	2	66
Buick Classic	-	-	2	4	1	1	WD	22	5	-
Canon GH Open	-	-	-	-	-	-	-	-	-	-
Western Open	-	-	-	MC	-	-	-	-	-	-
Gr. Milwaukee	-	-	-	-	-	-	-	-	-	-
British Open	5	6	24	11	2	10	29	24	2	3
B.C. Open	-	-	-	-	-	-	-	-	-	-
John Deere Cl'	-	-	-	-	-	-	-	-	-	-
The International	31	65	4	2	19	7	42	5	1	3
Buick Open	-	-	-	3	38	2	-	6	-	-
USPGA Champ	MC	MC	25	3	61	53	21	MC	34	13
WGCNEC Inv'	-	-	-	-	-	-	-	5	12	8
Reno-Tahoe Op'	-	-	-	-	-	-	-	-	-	-
Air Canada Chp'	-	-	-	-	-	-	-	-	-	-
Bell Canadian O'	-	-	-	20	-	MC	-	-	-	-
WGC AmEx	-	-	-	-	-	-	-	40	WD	-
Tampa Bay Cl'	-	-	-	-	-	-	-	-	-	-
Marconi Penn C'	-	-	-	-	-	-	-	-	-	-
Texas Open	-	-	-	-	-	-	-	-	-	-
Michelob Chmp'	-	-	-	-	-	-	-	-	-	-
Invensys Classic	-	-	-	-	-	-	-	-	-	-
NCR Golf Cl'	-	-	-	-	-	-	-	2	-	-
Buick Challenge	-	-	-	-	-	-	-	-	-	MC
SFB Classic	-	-	-	-	-	-	-	-	-	-
Tour Champ'ship	-	-	17	16	6	26	-	26	3	2

Bob Estes

2/2/66 – Graham, TX

A best ever season for Estes who finished the 2001 term as one of the hottest golfers on the US Tour. The Texan pro didn't finish worse than eighth in his last six events in 2001 and enjoyed two victories in a season which saw him earn nearly $3million. Prior to 2001, his sole US Tour win in 322 starts came in the 1994 Texas Open. But wins in the St Jude Classic and the Invensys Classic trebled his victory haul. Neither long nor straight off the tee, Estes relies upon good putting to keep him competitive. His bunker play improved in 2001.

ScAv - 69.73 (7th) – DD - 278.3 (112th) DA - 67.0 (123rd) GIR - 68.5 (45th) – PpGIR - 1.726 (6th) SS - 57.0 (27th)

	'92	'93	'94	'95	'96	'97	'98	'99	'00	'01
WGC MatchPlay	-	-	-	-	-	-	-	33	9	33
Mercedes Ch	-	-	12	-	-	-	-	-	-	-
Tucson Open	12	34	MC	32	3	-	25	-	-	-
Sony Open	MC	MC	-	-	-	-	-	-	-	-
Phoenix Open	MC	64	2	29	MC	-	51	26	-	MC
AT&T P Beach	-	-	-	-	-	MC	MC	-	-	-
Buick Invitatn'l	53	29	6	16	MC	MC	27	11	-	41
Bob Hope Cl'	MC	12	9	49	-	-	19	4	MC	56
Nissan Open	39	66	40	14	MC	33	6	7	MC	MC
Genuity Champ	-	-	-	-	MC	-	-	-	-	8
Honda Classic	-	48	-	-	-	-	7	15	-	MC
Bay Hill Invit'l	-	-	13	53	-	-	2	5	-	17
Players Champ	70	20	35	34	MC	-	42	62	MC	MC
BellSouth Cl'	-	-	4	22	MC	14	19	-	-	-
US Masters	-	-	MC	29	27	-	-	4	19	-
Worldcom Cl'	69	12	7	MC	38	-	14	32	MC	42
Houston Open	58	MC	MC	-	MC	-	-	73	-	-
GG Chrysler Cl'	48	78	-	-	37	3	-	13	-	-
Compaq Classic	MC	18	-	-	-	8	-	-	-	-
Byron Nelson C'	29	20	50	55	MC	MC	12	MC	6	MC
MasterCard Cln'l	MC	22	MC	MC	41	MC	7	6	26	-
Kemper Ins Open	MC	5	-	-	-	-	-	-	60	22
Memorial T'ment	-	50	19	73	-	-	44	48	76	-
St. Jude Classic	57	39	24	14	MC	22	4	-	45	1
U.S. Open	44	52	-	MC	-	-	-	30	MC	30
Buick Classic	26	-	16	-	-	6	-	10	-	63
Canon GH Open	5	MC	-	8	37	-	58	-	-	-
Western Open	16	-	17	6	70	57	65	68	63	15
Gr. Milwaukee	57	MC	3	10	12	12	MC	-	-	-
British Open	-	-	24	8	MC	-	24	49	20	25
B.C. Open	MC	-	-	-	-	-	-	-	-	-
John Deere Cl'	MC	14	18	-	MC	23	-	-	-	-
The International	45	29	62	-	36	-	MC	-	MC	MC
Buick Open	-	-	-	-	-	11	-	5	-	-
USPGA Champ	76	6	47	6	MC	-	34	6	MC	37
WGCNEC Inv'	-	-	-	-	-	-	-	-	-	-
Reno-Tahoe Op'	-	-	-	-	-	-	-	-	58	-
Air Canada Chp'	-	-	-	-	MC	3	5	10	-	8
Bell Canadian O'	-	40	10	-	MC	-	-	15	-	2
WGC AmEx	-	-	-	-	-	-	-	11	-	-
Tampa Bay Cl'	-	-	-	-	-	-	-	-	-	-
Marconi Penn C'	-	-	-	-	-	-	-	-	-	-
Texas Open	MC	4	1	22	MC	MC	11	29	MC	4
Michelob Chmp'	-	-	-	-	-	46	63	-	-	-
Invensys Classic	3	3	MC	-	MC	-	32	37	MC	1
NCR Golf Cl'	-	-	-	-	MC	-	MC	-	MC	-
Buick Challenge	-	2	11	-	MC	37	MC	25	23	3
SFB Classic	-	-	-	-	-	-	28	-	-	-
Tour Champ'ship	5	-	15	-	-	-	28	25	-	7

Brad Faxon

1/8/61 – Oceanport, NJ

Bagged his eighth US Tour win in 2001 by capturing the Sony Open in Hawaii in January. Faxon has been one of the most consistent players in America over the last decade and was perhaps unlucky not to receive a wild card pick for the USA Ryder Cup team (he played in both 1995 and 1997). He has now won in each of the last three seasons. Faxon is widely regarded by his fellow pros as the best putter of his generation and many players ask his advice about reading greens and putting strokes. Ranked a lowly 182nd in the total driving stats.

ScAv - 70.53 (42nd) – DD - 274.6 (147th) DA - 64.7 (154th) GIR - 65.5 (117th) – PpGIR - 1.739 (21st) SS - 64.9 (3rd)

	'92	'93	'94	'95	'96	'97	'98	'99	'00	'01
WGC MatchPlay	-	-	-	-	-	-	-	33	-	5
Mercedes Ch	2	5	-	-	-	-	22	-	8	23
Tucson Open	-	-	-	-	-	-	-	-	17	-
Sony Open	-	-	-	-	2	MC	-	-	MC	1
Phoenix Open	24	-	39	MC	-	-	-	MC	-	-
AT&T P Beach	MC	-	52	6	-	15	56	21	20	13
Buick Invitatn'l	15	-	40	32	24	65	MC	30	MC	58
Bob Hope Cl'	-	-	-	-	21	-	-	-	-	4
Nissan Open	75	-	4	52	-	27	-	-	MC	-
Genuity Champ	MC	MC	-	MC	-	MC	MC	-	65	-
Honda Classic	66	75	MC	-	54	-	-	MC	-	18
Bay Hill Invit'l	8	17	42	2	-	MC	36	74	MC	47
Players Champ	67	DQ	6	49	-	4	35	46	77	26
BellSouth Cl'	-	-	MC	-	-	-	63	-	69	-
US Masters	31	9	15	17	25	MC	26	24	-	10
Worldcom Cl'	6	58	30	56	42	2	14	MC	50	66
Houston Open	-	33	-	-	-	-	-	-	76	-
GG Chrysler Cl'	10	MC	15	7	-	2	23	13	-	-
Compaq Classic	-	-	-	-	1	64	MC	MC	MC	
Byron Nelson C'	-	-	-	-	26	-	18	-	11	
MasterCard Cln'1	75	53	5	5	20	2	MC	-	-	MC
Kemper Ins Open	18	60	44	31	2	-	MC	-	16	-
Memorial T'ment	MC	4	9	47	6	57	51	-	33	30
St. Jude Classic	-	-	-	-	-	-	-	-	-	-
U.S. Open	MC	68	33	56	82	65	49	-	MC	MC
Buick Classic	34	13	3	29	6	11	12	-	68	6
Canon GH Open	MC	16	15	66	8	53	56	-	32	MC
Western Open	-	-	-	55	-	-	-	-	29	20
Gr. Milwaukee	-	MC	-	WD	-	-	-	-	-	-
British Open	-	MC	7	15	32	20	11	-	-	47
B.C. Open	38	54	-	20	62	-	-	1	1	-
John Deere Cl'	-	-	-	-	-	-	-	-	-	-
The International	1	7	43	MC	2	17	6	64	MC	6
Buick Open	2	63	28	46	-	-	MC	-	6	MC
USPGA Champ	15	14	30	5	17	MC	13	61	27	59
WGCNEC Inv'	-	-	-	-	-	-	-	-	-	-
Reno-Tahoe Op'	-	-	-	-	-	-	67	-	-	
Air Canada Chp'	-	-	-	51	-	-	-	-	-	
Bell Canadian O'	-	16	75	-	-	22	25	MC	14	
WGC AmEx	-	-	-	-	-	-	-	-	-	
Tampa Bay Cl'	-	-	-	-	-	-	6	-	-	
Marconi Penn C'	-	-	-	-	-	-	-	-	-	
Texas Open	-	22	-	MC	-	-	-	-	-	-
Michelob Chmp'	-	-	-	-	-	MC	MC	MC	-	
Invensys Classic	-	23	-	64	-	-	MC	27	-	
NCR Golf Cl'	MC	MC	56	-	71	-	76	28	24	-
Buick Challenge	-	-	-	-	6	-	-	-	-	59
SFB Classic	-	-	-	-	-	-	-	17	4	-
Tour Champ'ship	7	-	26	-	2	6	-	-	-	26

Steve Flesch

23/5/67 – Cincinnati,OH

Another winless year on the US Tour for this left-hander who managed 13 top-ten finishes in 2000. Flesch wasn't as consistent in 2001 but remains one of the more likely non-winners on tour to break through to the big time. His all round game is soild, with perhaps only his lack of accuracy off the tee a worry. He has won on the Buy.com Tour (the 1997 Buy.com Tour Championship) and the Asian Tour (the 1996 Malaysian Open) so his ability to succeed isn't in question. His best finish on the US Tour in 2001 was fifth in the NCR Classic.

ScAv - 70.69 (54th) – DD - 283.4 (54th) DA - 68.2 (105th) GIR - 67.9 (56th) – PpGIR - 1.755 (50th) SS - 53.2 (85th)

	'92	'93	'94	'95	'96	'97	'98	'99	'00	'01
WGC MatchPlay	-	-	-	-	-	-	-	-	-	33
Mercedes Ch	-	-	-	-	-	-	-	-	-	-
Tucson Open	-	-	-	-	-	-	MC	13	7	9
Sony Open	-	-	-	-	-	-	69	-	-	-
Phoenix Open	-	-	-	-	-	-	67	MC	7	23
AT&T P Beach	-	-	-	-	-	-	56	25	35	23
Buick Invitatn'l	-	-	-	-	-	-	35	MC	10	MC
Bob Hope Cl'	-	-	-	-	-	-	35	MC	28	MC
Nissan Open	-	-	-	-	-	-	-	23	5	-
Genuity Champ	-	-	-	-	-	-	MC	-	-	58
Honda Classic	-	-	-	-	-	-	15	-	19	7
Bay Hill Invit'l	-	-	-	-	-	-	-	-	18	MC
Players Champ	-	-	-	-	-	-	-	MC	38	40
BellSouth Cl'	-	-	-	-	-	-	3	36	10	19
US Masters	-	-	-	-	-	-	-	-	-	MC
Worldcom Cl'	-	-	-	-	-	-	-	49	MC	7
Houston Open	-	-	-	-	-	-	12	MC	-	-
GG Chrysler Cl'	-	-	-	-	-	-	23	MC	-	-
Compaq Classic	-	-	-	-	-	-	2	2	6	MC
Byron Nelson C'	-	-	-	-	-	-	25	MC	33	43
MasterCard Cln'1	-	-	-	-	-	-	10	47	31	46
Kemper Ins Open	-	-	-	-	-	-	11	-	-	61
Memorial T'ment	-	-	-	-	-	-	MC	54	5	11
St. Jude Classic	-	-	-	-	-	-	MC	-	20	-
U.S. Open	-	-	-	-	-	-	-	MC	-	MC
Buick Classic	-	-	-	-	-	-	-	10	42	56
Canon GH Open	-	-	-	-	-	-	25	MC	5	MC
Western Open	-	-	-	-	-	-	22	MC	9	7
Gr. Milwaukee	-	-	-	-	-	-	MC	31	-	-
British Open	-	-	-	-	-	-	-	-	20	MC
B.C. Open	-	-	-	-	-	-	-	WD	-	-
John Deere Cl'	-	-	-	-	-	-	41	-	-	-
The International	-	-	-	-	-	-	6	10	MC	18
Buick Open	-	-	-	-	-	-	-	54	25	35
USPGA Champ	-	-	-	-	-	-	13	34	MC	13
WGCNEC Inv'	-	-	-	-	-	-	-	-	-	-
Reno-Tahoe Op'	-	-	-	-	-	-	-	50	7	10
Air Canada Chp'	-	-	-	-	-	-	40	-	-	-
Bell Canadian O'	-	-	-	-	-	-	MC	-	6	-
WGC AmEx	-	-	-	-	-	-	-	-	11	-
Tampa Bay Cl'	-	-	-	-	-	-	-	-	-	-
Marconi Penn C'	-	-	-	-	-	-	-	-	61	22
Texas Open	-	-	-	-	-	-	45	54	-	-
Michelob Chmp'	-	-	-	-	-	-	-	35	12	47
Invensys Classic	-	-	-	-	-	-	-	32	9	13
NCR Golf Cl'	-	-	-	-	-	-	51	69	2	5
Buick Challenge	-	-	-	-	-	-	6	44	27	38
SFB Classic	-	-	-	-	-	-	-	51	-	-
Tour Champ'ship	-	-	-	-	-	-	-	-	15	-

Harrison Frazar
29/7/71 – Dallas, TX

Went under the knife in August 2001 to clear up a nagging hip problem and missed much of the last half of the season. He still managed to retain his card, though, courtesy of four top-ten finishes prior to having surgery. In four seasons on the full tour Frazar has yet to win but he has won on the Buy.com Tour (South Carolina Classic in 1997).

He is long off the tee and always ranks in the top 30 of the driving distance stats. Turned pro in 1996 and spent one year on the Buy.com Tour before graduating to the full tour in 1998.

ScAv - 70.95 (70th) – DD - 286.8 (24th) DA - 66.6 (130th) GIR - 66.5 (87th) – PpGIR - 1.772 (96th) SS - 42.0 (177th)

	'92	'93	'94	'95	'96	'97	'98	'99	'00	'01
WGC MatchPlay	-	-	-	-	-	-	-	-	-	-
Mercedes Ch	-	-	-	-	-	-	-	-	-	-
Tucson Open	-	-	-	-	-	-	MC	45	-	9
Sony Open	-	-	-	-	-	-	MC	MC	-	MC
Phoenix Open	-	-	-	-	-	-	-	6	MC	19
AT&T P Beach	-	-	-	-	-	-	25	MC	61	MC
Buick Invitatn'l	-	-	-	-	-	-	MC	-	-	10
Bob Hope Cl'	-	-	-	-	-	-	-	MC	MC	22
Nissan Open	-	-	-	-	-	-	43	MC	MC	-
Genuity Champ	-	-	-	-	-	-	46	70	15	58
Honda Classic	-	-	-	-	-	-	30	15	28	47
Bay Hill Invit'l	-	-	-	-	-	-	-	MC	-	14
Players Champ	-	-	-	-	-	-	-	MC	33	MC
BellSouth Cl'	-	-	-	-	-	-	MC	-	3	17
US Masters	-	-	-	-	-	-	-	-	-	-
Worldcom Cl'	-	-	-	-	-	-	-	MC	MC	-
Houston Open	-	-	-	-	-	-	MC	-	29	MC
GG Chrysler Cl'	-	-	-	-	-	-	16	MC	-	-
Compaq Classic	-	-	-	-	-	-	42	2	3	4
Byron Nelson C'	-	-	-	-	-	MC	2	51	67	51
MasterCard Cln'l	-	-	-	-	-	-	4	65	MC	54
Kemper Ins Open	-	-	-	-	-	-	-	52	-	-
Memorial T'ment	-	-	-	-	-	-	38	52	20	68
St. Jude Classic	-	-	-	-	-	-	MC	-	-	-
U.S. Open	-	-	-	-	-	-	-	-	-	66
Buick Classic	-	-	-	-	-	-	MC	46	-	26
Canon GH Open	-	-	-	-	-	-	56	26	MC	-
Western Open	-	-	-	-	-	-	9	49	29	MC
Gr. Milwaukee	-	-	-	-	-	-	-	70	MC	5
British Open	-	-	-	-	-	-	-	-	-	-
B.C. Open	-	-	-	-	-	-	-	-	-	-
John Deere Cl'	-	-	-	-	-	-	-	21	MC	73
The International	-	-	-	-	-	-	MC	43	MC	24
Buick Open	-	-	-	-	-	-	65	-	-	-
USPGA Champ	-	-	-	-	-	-	MC	MC	MC	MC
WGCNEC Inv'	-	-	-	-	-	-	-	-	-	-
Reno-Tahoe Op'	-	-	-	-	-	-	-	63	51	-
Air Canada Chp'	-	-	-	-	-	-	28	-	-	-
Bell Canadian O'	-	-	-	-	-	-	-	-	MC	-
WGC AmEx	-	-	-	-	-	-	-	-	-	-
Tampa Bay Cl'	-	-	-	-	-	-	-	-	-	-
Marconi Penn C'	-	-	-	-	-	-	-	-	-	-
Texas Open	-	-	-	-	-	-	73	54	19	-
Michelob Chmp'	-	-	-	-	-	-	54	-	-	-
Invensys Classic	-	-	-	-	-	-	-	15	-	-
NCR Golf Cl'	-	-	-	-	-	-	MC	-	-	-
Buick Challenge	-	-	-	-	-	-	58	20	-	62
SFB Classic	-	-	-	-	-	-	-	MC	-	MC
Tour Champ'ship	-	-	-	-	-	-	-	-	-	-

Edward Fryatt
8/4/71 – Rochdale, England

An encouraging second season on the US Tour for this Rochdale born pro whose career started off in the Far East. He was second on the Order of Merit in Asia in 1998 (and posted four wins out there in total) before moving to America and playing on the Buy.com Tour.

He won the 1999 Hershey Open on the Buy.com Tour before graduating to the full tour. Based in Las Vegas, Fryatt was one of the top bunker players on tour in 2001. His best US Tour place was third in the 2000 MCI (now WorldCom) Classic.

ScAv - 71.03 (81st) – DD - 279.2 (101st) DA - 66.8 (127th) GIR - 65.6 (107th) – PpGIR - 1.758 (60th) SS - 61.8 (8th)

	'92	'93	'94	'95	'96	'97	'98	'99	'00	'01
WGC MatchPlay	-	-	-	-	-	-	-	-	-	-
Mercedes Ch	-	-	-	-	-	-	-	-	-	-
Tucson Open	-	-	-	-	-	-	-	-	50	MC
Sony Open	-	-	-	-	-	-	-	-	MC	MC
Phoenix Open	-	-	-	-	-	-	-	-	7	13
AT&T P Beach	-	-	-	-	-	-	-	-	MC	27
Buick Invitatn'l	-	-	-	-	-	-	-	-	-	58
Bob Hope Cl'	-	-	-	-	-	-	-	-	36	-
Nissan Open	-	-	-	-	-	-	-	-	52	20
Genuity Champ	-	-	-	-	-	-	-	-	9	63
Honda Classic	-	-	-	-	-	-	-	-	MC	-
Bay Hill Invit'l	-	-	-	-	-	-	-	-	46	-
Players Champ	-	-	-	-	-	-	-	-	-	MC
BellSouth Cl'	-	-	-	-	-	-	-	-	MC	68
US Masters	-	-	-	-	-	-	-	-	-	-
Worldcom Cl'	-	-	-	-	-	-	-	-	3	MC
Houston Open	-	-	-	-	-	-	-	-	-	MC
GG Chrysler Cl'	-	-	-	-	-	-	-	-	-	29
Compaq Classic	-	-	-	-	-	-	-	-	MC	MC
Byron Nelson C'	-	-	-	-	-	-	-	-	72	77
MasterCard Cln'l	-	-	-	-	-	-	-	-	MC	MC
Kemper Ins Open	-	-	-	-	-	-	-	-	69	MC
Memorial T'ment	-	-	-	-	-	-	38	-	41	-
St. Jude Classic	-	-	-	-	-	-	-	-	-	MC
U.S. Open	-	-	24	MC	-	-	-	-	MC	-
Buick Classic	-	-	-	-	-	-	-	-	33	47
Canon GH Open	-	-	-	-	-	-	-	-	5	22
Western Open	-	-	-	-	-	-	-	-	41	MC
Gr. Milwaukee	-	-	-	-	-	-	-	-	-	-
British Open	-	-	-	-	-	-	-	-	-	-
B.C. Open	-	-	-	-	-	-	-	-	MC	12
John Deere Cl'	-	-	-	-	-	-	-	-	-	15
The International	-	-	-	-	-	-	-	9	-	9
Buick Open	-	-	-	-	-	-	-	-	MC	-
USPGA Champ	-	-	-	-	-	-	-	-	MC	-
WGCNEC Inv'	-	-	-	-	-	-	-	-	-	-
Reno-Tahoe Op'	-	-	-	-	-	-	-	-	MC	12
Air Canada Chp'	-	-	-	-	-	-	-	-	MC	8
Bell Canadian O'	-	-	-	-	-	-	-	-	-	MC
WGC AmEx	-	-	-	-	-	-	-	-	-	-
Tampa Bay Cl'	-	-	-	-	-	-	-	-	-	-
Marconi Penn C'	-	-	-	-	-	-	-	-	MC	52
Texas Open	-	-	-	-	-	-	-	-	-	MC
Michelob Chmp'	-	-	-	-	-	-	-	-	-	-
Invensys Classic	-	MC	-	-	11	-	28	56	MC	-
NCR Golf Cl'	-	-	-	-	-	-	-	-	66	MC
Buick Challenge	-	-	-	-	-	-	-	-	MC	MC
SFB Classic	-	-	-	-	-	-	-	-	55	-
Tour Champ'ship	-	-	-	-	-	-	-	-	-	-

Sponsored by Stan James

Fred Funk

14/6/56 – Takoma Park, MD

No wins in 2001 for this old-style, straight-hitting pro but another $1million+ earned after he churned out yet more top-ten finishes – four last term and 61 in a career spanning over 400 US Tour events. His career earnings now top the $8million mark. Funk has won five times on the main tour but his last victory was back in 1998 (Deposit Guaranty Golf Classic – now Southern Farm Bureau). Known for his straight driving game and nearly always finds the fairways with his tee shots – although they land some 20 yards behind everyone elses.

ScAv - 70.40 (32nd) – DD - 272.1 (165th) DA - 77.2 (3rd) GIR - 68.2 (50th) – PpGIR - 1.775 (102nd) SS - 54.1 (75th)

	'92	'93	'94	'95	'96	'97	'98	'99	'00	'01
WGC MatchPlay	-	-	-	-	-	-	-	33	33	33
Mercedes Ch	-	21	-	-	16	11	-	5	-	-
Tucson Open	59	MC	29	73	3	MC	MC	-	-	20
Sony Open	57	13	27	74	-	MC	-	12	58	5
Phoenix Open	MC	57	8	MC	41	62	34	22	65	9
AT&T P Beach	41	21	MC	21	-	33	WD	-	-	-
Buick Invitatn'l	-	69	51	26	-	25	-	-	-	27
Bob Hope Cl'	MC	60	14	28	MC	MC	43	4	7	30
Nissan Open	-	MC	-	-	MC	4	15	MC	52	MC
Genuity Champ	76	-	58	33	34	-	23	34	60	50
Honda Classic	29	MC	18	MC	-	65	MC	-	MC	-
Bay Hill Invit'l	-	MC	MC	16	MC	70	MC	44	-	15
Players Champ	60	39	78	61	13	14	69	38	13	33
BellSouth Cl'	32	13	21	66	MC	51	MC	-	-	-
US Masters	-	MC	38	-	36	17	MC	MC	37	-
Worldcom Cl'	MC	57	12	44	75	42	24	18	25	38
Houston Open	1	33	10	12	MC	13	70	27	17	46
GG Chrysler Cl'	-	MC	-	-	14	6	31	MC	54	
Compaq Classic	MC	-	39	-	-	-	-	-	-	-
Byron Nelson C'	68	MC	-	-	-	-	MC	-	68	
MasterCard Cln'	134	27	66	33	55	WD	29	2	13	20
Kemper Ins Open	60	38	65	MC	MC	MC	3	34	MC	17
Memorial T'ment	23	MC	50	13	14	54	38	35	58	11
St. Jude Classic	-	6	MC	-	-	-	36	-	-	
U.S. Open	33	7	44	MC	MC	43	-	MC	MC	44
Buick Classic	3	10	27	4	6	54	WD	18	57	MC
Canon GH Open	58	-	-	-	56	29	4	20	58	-
Western Open	WD	75	-	MC	43	-	-	-	20	-
Gr. Milwaukee	-	28	MC	-	9	26	7	-	MC	-
British Open	73	-	-	-	-	-	WD	MC	-	
B.C. Open	20	17	MC	28	1	MC	16	2	-	MC
John Deere Cl'	-	-	-	-	41	-	5	MC	50	29
The International	25	MC	32	55	-	-	-	-	-	-
Buick Open	10	6	8	11	7	49	15	19	-	21
USPGA Champ	MC	44	55	39	26	61	23	73	9	70
WGCNEC Inv'	-	-	-	-	-	-	-	-	-	-
Reno-Tahoe Op'	-	-	-	-	-	-	-	4	21	WD
Air Canada Chp'	-	-	-	-	-	-	-	2	MC	3
Bell Canadian O'	MC	-	-	-	MC	-	-	-	-	23
WGC AmEx	-	-	-	-	-	-	-	7	-	-
Tampa Bay Cl'	-	-	-	-	-	-	-	-	40	-
Marconi Penn C'	-	-	-	-	-	-	-	WD	18	
Texas Open	66	MC	-	MC	-	-	20	29	-	MC
Michelob Chrmp'	15	8	-	8	3	4	44	32	62	47
Invensys Classic	51	MC	39	-	12	MC	-	-	65	46
NCR Golf Cl'	MC	44	33	37	-	MC	7	MC	4	MC
Buick Challenge	69	19	MC	1	2	17	2	37	41	23
SFB Classic	22	-	11	MC	-	1	-	6	3	
Tour Champ'ship	-	-	27	14	-	24	5	-	-	-

Jim Furyk

12/5/70 – West Chester, PA

Possesses one of the most ungainly swings in the business but one which is very effective. Furyk has finished in the top ten of the four Major championships on 10 occasions and has won six times on the US Tour – and for each of the last four seasons (including the Sony Open in 2001). He will play in the Ryder Cup for America for the third successive time in 2002. Furyk isn't long off the tee but is accurate and is a fine iron player with a deft touch on the greens. His career earnings were pushed to over $10million in 2001.

ScAv - 69.92 (14th) – DD - 272.5 (164th) DA - 75.7 (7th) GIR - 70.5 (17th) – PpGIR - 1.738 (19th) SS - 55.4 (54th)

	'92	'93	'94	'95	'96	'97	'98	'99	'00	'01
WGC MatchPlay	-	-	-	-	-	-	-	33	9	-
Mercedes Ch	-	-	22	8	-	9	4	1		
Tucson Open	-	MC	7	5	MC	35	9	-	-	-
Sony Open	-	-	MC	18	1	2	21	19	39	14
Phoenix Open	-	-	39	12	MC	26	41	6	37	-
AT&T P Beach	-	-	29	21	-	4	3	MC	18	-
Buick Invitatn'l	-	-	MC	-	-	-	-	-	-	MC
Bob Hope Cl'	-	-	-	16	11	20	MC	-	-	22
Nissan Open	-	-	48	9	MC	MC	-	62	37	-
Genuity Champ	-	34	58	58	45	9	-	1	17	
Honda Classic	-	MC	-	-	-	12	-	4	7	
Bay Hill Invit'l	-	-	MC	MC	36	47	8	23	-	-
Players Champ	-	-	MC	13	53	35	17	61	21	
BellSouth Cl'	-	MC	MC	-	-	-	-	-	-	-
US Masters	-	-	-	29	28	4	14	14	6	
Worldcom Cl'	-	-	56	32	MC	79	-	-	-	
Houston Open	-	MC	46	-	-	-	-	-	-	-
GG Chrysler Cl'	-	44	51	7	14	11	2	42	9	
Compaq Classic	-	11	63	27	-	-	-	-	-	
Byron Nelson C'	-	MC	-	23	5	15	-	20	37	
MasterCard Cln'l	-	-	MC	38	8	2	55	8	22	
Kemper Ins Open	-	MC	MC	-	-	-	14	-	-	
Memorial T'ment	-	-	53	49	2	4	43	25	24	
St. Jude Classic	-	24	-	-	-	-	-	-	-	
U.S. Open	-	28	-	5	5	14	17	60	62	
Buick Classic	MC	40	MC	3	2	22	51	19		
Canon GH Open	-	MC	-	-	-	-	-	-	-	
Western Open	-	MC	WD	66	6	7	34	3	-	
Gr. Milwaukee	-	41	58	-	-	-	-	-	-	
British Open	-	-	44	4	4	10	41	MC		
B.C. Open	-	MC	17	-	-	25	-	-	-	
John Deere Cl'	-	MC	-	-	-	-	-	-	-	
The International	-	MC	42	17	7	59	-	-	-	
Buick Open	-	36	11	38	15	-	9	16	2	
USPGA Champ	-	-	13	17	6	MC	8	72	7	
WGCNEC Inv'	-	-	-	-	-	-	-	10	4	2
Reno-Tahoe Op'	-	-	-	-	-	-	-	-	-	-
Air Canada Chp'	-	-	-	-	-	-	-	-	-	-
Bell Canadian O'	-	39	MC	-	MC	22	37	-	-	
WGC AmEx	-	-	-	-	-	-	-	11	-	-
Tampa Bay Cl'	-	-	-	-	-	-	-	-	-	-
Marconi Penn C'	-	-	-	-	-	-	-	MC	11	
Texas Open	-	15	-	-	-	-	-	-	-	
Michelob Chrmp'	-	10	MC	-	-	39	35	19	MC	
Invensys Classic	-	5	1	22	19	1	1	17	MC	
NCR Golf Cl'	-	70	49	59	-	-	-	-	-	
Buick Challenge	-	56	14	-	MC	-	-	MC		
SFB Classic	-	MC	-	-	-	-	-	-	-	
Tour Champ'ship	-	-	15	2	3	15	-	7		

Sergio Garcia
9/1/80 – Castellon, Spain

El Nino came of age in 2001 with two wins on the US Tour and two runners-up positions. He also won on the European Tour in 2001 – his third victory in Europe. Coached by his father Victor, the young Spaniard will line up again in the Ryder Cup in 2002.

Burst on to the scene in 1999 by winning twice on the European Tour, making the Ryder Cup team and finishing second in the USPGA Championship. His game has it all, long and accurate off the tee, a superb iron player and an excellent touch on the greens.

ScAv - 69.13 (3rd) – DD - 287.8 (22nd) DA - 73.1 (24th) GIR - 68.0 (54th) – PpGIR - 1.740 (24th) SS - 56.8 (31st)

	'92	'93	'94	'95	'96	'97	'98	'99	'00	'01
WGC MatchPlay	-	-	-	-	-	-	-	-	9	-
Mercedes Ch	-	-	-	-	-	-	-	-	-	-
Tucson Open	-	-	-	-	-	-	-	-	-	-
Sony Open	-	-	-	-	-	-	-	-	-	-
Phoenix Open	-	-	-	-	-	-	-	-	MC	13
AT&T P Beach	-	-	-	-	-	-	-	-	35	59
Buick Invitatn'l	-	-	-	-	-	-	-	-	-	-
Bob Hope Cl'	-	-	-	-	-	-	-	-	-	-
Nissan Open	-	-	-	-	-	-	-	-	-	25
Genuity Champ	-	-	-	-	-	-	-	-	-	-
Honda Classic	-	-	-	-	-	-	-	-	-	-
Bay Hill Invit'l	-	-	-	-	-	-	-	-	42	4
Players Champ	-	-	-	-	-	-	-	-	MC	50
BellSouth Cl'	-	-	-	-	-	-	-	-	-	-
US Masters	-	-	-	-	-	-	-	38	40	MC
Worldcom Cl'	-	-	-	-	-	-	-	-	-	MC
Houston Open	-	-	-	-	-	-	-	-	-	-
GG Chrysler Cl'	-	-	-	-	-	-	-	-	-	-
Compaq Classic	-	-	-	-	-	-	-	-	-	-
Byron Nelson C'	-	-	-	-	-	-	-	3	15	8
MasterCard Cln'l	-	-	-	-	-	-	-	-	-	1
Kemper Ins Open	-	-	-	-	-	-	-	-	-	-
Memorial T'ment	-	-	-	-	-	-	-	11	-	2
St. Jude Classic	-	-	-	-	-	-	-	-	-	-
U.S. Open	-	-	-	-	-	-	-	-	46	12
Buick Classic	-	-	-	-	-	-	-	-	3	1
Canon GH Open	-	-	-	-	-	-	-	-	-	-
Western Open	-	-	-	-	-	-	-	-	-	-
Gr. Milwaukee	-	-	-	-	-	-	-	-	-	-
British Open	-	-	-	MC	-	29	MC	36	9	-
B.C. Open	-	-	-	-	-	-	-	-	-	-
John Deere Cl'	-	-	-	-	-	-	-	-	-	-
The International	-	-	-	-	-	-	-	13	14	11
Buick Open	-	-	-	-	-	-	MC	-	-	-
USPGA Champ	-	-	-	-	-	-	-	2	34	MC
WGCNEC Inv'	-	-	-	-	-	-	-	7	-	-
Reno-Tahoe Op'	-	-	-	-	-	-	-	17	-	-
Air Canada Chp'	-	-	-	-	-	-	-	4	-	-
Bell Canadian Op'	-	-	-	-	-	-	-	3	5	-
WGC AmEx	-	-	-	-	-	-	-	7	5	-
Tampa Bay Cl'	-	-	-	-	-	-	-	-	-	-
Marconi Penn C'	-	-	-	-	-	-	-	-	-	-
Texas Open	-	-	-	-	-	-	-	-	-	-
Michelob Chmp'	-	-	-	-	-	-	-	-	-	-
Invensys Classic	-	-	-	-	-	-	-	-	-	-
NCR Golf Cl'	-	-	-	-	-	-	-	-	-	-
Buick Challenge	-	-	-	-	-	-	-	-	-	MC
SFB Classic	-	-	-	-	-	-	-	-	-	-
Tour Champ'ship	-	-	-	-	-	-	-	-	-	2

Brian Gay
14/12/71 – Ft. Worth, TX

Texan born but Florida based golfer who enjoyed his best year in 2001 since turning pro in 1994. This former Walker Cup player has yet to win on the main tour but his third full season yielded five top-ten finishes, including runners-up position in the Master-Card Colonial. Had spent his early pro years on minor tours before gaining his US Tour playing rights through the 1999 Q-School.

Not one of the new breed of big hitters but accurate off the tee and an excellent putter. Made the most birdies on the US Tour in 2001 – 443.

ScAv - 70.43 (38th) – DD - 267.1 (186th) DA - 75.8 (8th) GIR - 66.9 (78th) – PpGIR - 1.722 (3rd) SS - 54.2 (73rd)

	'92	'93	'94	'95	'96	'97	'98	'99	'00	'01
WGC MatchPlay	-	-	-	-	-	-	-	-	-	-
Mercedes Ch	-	-	-	-	-	-	-	-	-	-
Tucson Open	-	-	-	-	-	-	-	MC	13	MC
Sony Open	-	-	-	-	-	-	-	MC	MC	10
Phoenix Open	-	-	-	-	-	-	-	-	-	36
AT&T P Beach	-	-	-	-	-	-	-	MC	MC	MC
Buick Invitatn'l	-	-	-	-	-	-	-	MC	68	MC
Bob Hope Cl'	-	-	-	-	-	-	-	-	-	MC
Nissan Open	-	-	-	-	-	-	-	-	-	-
Genuity Champ	-	-	-	-	-	-	-	MC	45	34
Honda Classic	-	-	-	-	-	-	-	38	4	27
Bay Hill Invit'l	-	-	-	-	-	-	-	-	-	56
Players Champ	-	-	-	-	-	-	-	-	-	40
BellSouth Cl'	-	-	-	-	-	-	-	-	30	WD
US Masters	-	-	-	-	-	-	-	-	-	-
Worldcom Cl'	-	-	-	-	-	-	-	-	MC	42
Houston Open	-	-	-	-	-	-	-	MC	45	13
GG Chrysler Cl'	-	-	-	-	-	-	-	MC	MC	-
Compaq Classic	-	-	-	-	-	-	-	46	MC	5
Byron Nelson C'	-	-	-	-	-	-	-	-	30	43
MasterCard Cln'l	-	-	-	-	-	-	-	-	41	2
Kemper Ins Open	-	-	-	-	-	-	-	52	20	-
Memorial T'ment	-	-	-	-	-	-	-	-	-	60
St. Jude Classic	-	-	-	-	-	-	-	42	20	MC
U.S. Open	-	-	-	-	MC	-	-	-	MC	-
Buick Classic	-	-	-	-	-	-	-	MC	MC	37
Canon GH Open	-	-	-	-	-	-	-	MC	-	36
Western Open	-	-	-	-	-	-	-	74	MC	15
Gr. Milwaukee	-	-	-	-	-	-	-	MC	14	-
British Open	-	-	-	-	-	-	-	-	-	MC
B.C. Open	-	-	-	-	-	-	-	MC	18	-
John Deere Cl'	-	-	-	-	-	-	-	MC	MC	-
The International	-	-	-	-	-	-	-	-	MC	MC
Buick Open	-	-	-	-	-	-	-	MC	47	6
USPGA Champ	-	-	-	-	-	-	-	-	-	22
WGCNEC Inv'	-	-	-	-	-	-	-	-	-	-
Reno-Tahoe Op'	-	-	-	-	-	-	-	24	42	10
Air Canada Chp'	-	-	-	-	-	-	-	MC	-	-
Bell Canadian O'	-	-	-	-	-	-	-	MC	MC	18
WGC AmEx	-	-	-	-	-	-	-	-	-	-
Tampa Bay Cl'	-	-	-	-	-	-	-	-	33	-
Marconi Penn C'	-	-	-	-	-	-	-	-	MC	22
Texas Open	-	-	-	-	-	-	-	38	MC	24
Michelob Chmp'	-	-	-	-	-	-	-	MC	-	-
Invensys Classic	-	-	-	-	-	-	-	44	MC	13
NCR Golf Cl'	-	-	-	-	-	-	-	-	MC	MC
Buick Challenge	-	-	-	-	-	-	-	MC	14	MC
SFB Classic	-	-	-	-	-	-	-	WD	20	48
Tour Champ'ship	-	-	-	-	-	-	-	-	-	-

Geiberger

? – Santa Barbara, CA

? of Al Geiberger, the first player to shoot 59 ? Tour event, has yet to achieve anything like ? father did but grinds on, and three top-five ? in 2001 ensured a sixth successive sea- ? the main tour. His sole success came in 1999 ? won the Canon Greater Hartford Open.

?ent two years on the Buy.com tour before ?ing to the main tour in 1997. The one weak- ? an otherwise solid all round game is his ? He was ranked 99 in 2000 and is outside ? 100 in 2001.

71.03 (81st) – DD - 280.5 (82nd) DA - 70.8 GIR - 66.9 (78th) – PpGIR - 1.776 (104th) ?.0 (153rd)

	'92	'93	'94	'95	'96	'97	'98	'99	'00	'01
?chPlay	-	-	-	-	-	-	-	-	33	33
?Ch	-	-	-	-	-	-	-	-	8	-
?en	-	-	-	-	-	MC	69	5	-	MC
?	-	-	-	-	-	19	21	MC	-	-
?pen	-	-	-	-	-	-	2	MC	41	70
?each	-	-	-	-	-	65	-	-	-	-
?atn'l	-	-	-	-	-	25	6	-	10	5
?Cl'	-	-	-	-	-	MC	64	MC	12	18
?en	-	-	-	-	-	20	67	13	MC	51
?amp	-	-	-	-	-	DQ	-	-	-	-
?ssic	-	-	-	-	-	20	7	15	-	-
?it'l	-	-	-	-	-	-	MC	44	73	MC
?amp	-	-	-	-	-	-	MC	46	MC	70
?Cl'	-	-	-	-	-	28	-	10	37	WD
?s	-	-	-	-	-	-	-	-	MC	-
? Cl'	-	-	-	-	-	-	39	56	-	-
?pen	-	-	-	-	-	20	MC	MC	-	MC
?er Cl'	-	-	-	-	-	19	MC	MC	28	-
?lassic	-	-	-	-	-	31	-	-	-	56
?son C'	-	-	-	-	-	27	MC	46	MC	28
?d Cln'l	-	-	-	-	-	33	41	39	24	26
?s Open	-	-	-	-	-	MC	36	18	-	-
?T'ment	-	-	-	-	-	MC	48	54	51	-
?lassic	-	-	-	-	-	MC	-	-	-	-
?	-	-	-	-	-	-	MC	-	MC	-
?ssic	-	-	-	-	-	63	-	22	-	37
? Open	-	-	-	-	-	MC	65	1	18	82
?pen	-	-	-	-	-	28	MC	3	41	57
?ukee	-	-	-	-	-	52	-	-	-	5
?en	-	-	-	-	-	-	-	-	-	-
?e Cl'	-	-	-	-	-	-	-	-	-	-
?ational	-	-	-	-	-	22	-	MC	61	32
?n	-	-	-	-	-	11	29	19	-	MC
?amp	-	-	-	-	-	-	71	MC	MC	-
?Inv'	-	-	-	-	-	-	-	-	-	-
?oe Op'	-	-	-	-	-	-	-	-	-	24
?a Chp'	-	-	-	-	-	12	11	65	8	5
?dian O'	-	-	-	-	-	MC	-	DQ	-	-
?Ex	-	-	-	-	-	-	-	55	-	-
?y Cl'	-	-	-	-	-	-	-	-	-	-
?enn C'	-	-	-	-	-	-	-	-	-	-
?en	-	-	-	-	-	2	MC	3	MC	11
?Chmp'	-	-	-	-	-	MC	-	-	-	-
?lassic	-	-	-	-	-	14	22	69	40	MC
?Cl'	-	-	-	-	-	-	3	28	41	MC
?llenge	-	-	-	-	-	MC	30	MC	5	17
?ic	-	-	-	-	-	-	-	-	-	-
?np'ship	-	-	-	-	-	-	-	3	-	-

Matt Gogel

9/2/71 – Denver, CO

Will probably always be remembered as the player who let slip a seven-shot lead with seven holes to play in the 2000 AT&T Pebble Beach Pro-Am. Tiger Woods took advantage of Gogel's aberrations on the Monterey peninsula but that second place remains his best finish on the US Tour.

Next year will be just his third full season on the US Tour and three top-ten finishes in his last four events in 2001 bode well for the future. Nothing really stands out about his game but it was good enough to give him six Buy.com Tour wins.

ScAv - 71.08 (86th) – DD - 280.3 (86th) DA - 68.6 (97th) GIR - 65.6 (107th) – PpGIR - 1.766 (77th) SS - 44.5 (167th)

	'92	'93	'94	'95	'96	'97	'98	'99	'00	'01
WGC MatchPlay	-	-	-	-	-	-	-	-	-	-
Mercedes Ch	-	-	-	-	-	-	-	-	-	-
Tucson Open	-	-	-	-	-	-	-	-	-	71
Sony Open	-	-	-	-	-	-	-	-	MC	-
Phoenix Open	-	-	-	-	-	-	-	-	MC	36
AT&T P Beach	-	-	-	-	-	-	-	-	2	27
Buick Invitatn'l	-	-	-	-	-	-	-	-	MC	-
Bob Hope Cl'	-	-	-	-	-	-	-	-	7	MC
Nissan Open	-	-	-	-	-	-	-	-	MC	MC
Genuity Champ	-	-	-	-	-	-	-	-	-	40
Honda Classic	-	-	-	-	-	-	-	-	28	MC
Bay Hill Invit'l	-	-	-	-	-	-	-	-	68	-
Players Champ	-	-	-	-	-	-	-	-	MC	MC
BellSouth Cl'	-	-	-	-	-	-	-	-	-	MC
US Masters	-	-	-	-	-	-	-	-	-	-
Worldcom Cl'	-	-	-	-	-	-	-	-	MC	MC
Houston Open	-	-	-	-	-	-	-	-	11	60
GG Chrysler Cl'	-	-	-	-	-	-	-	-	46	MC
Compaq Classic	-	-	-	-	-	-	-	-	-	MC
Byron Nelson C'	-	-	-	-	-	-	-	-	MC	-
MasterCard Cln'l	-	-	-	-	-	-	-	-	MC	MC
Kemper Ins Open	-	-	-	-	-	-	-	-	-	22
Memorial T'ment	-	-	-	-	-	-	-	-	MC	-
St. Jude Classic	-	-	-	-	-	-	-	-	-	-
U.S. Open	MC	-	-	51	-	MC	-	-	MC	12
Buick Classic	-	-	-	-	-	-	-	-	MC	37
Canon GH Open	-	-	-	-	-	-	-	-	MC	-
Western Open	-	-	-	-	-	-	-	-	41	10
Gr. Milwaukee	-	-	-	-	-	-	-	-	MC	-
British Open	-	-	-	-	-	-	-	-	-	47
B.C. Open	-	-	-	-	-	-	-	-	-	-
John Deere Cl'	-	-	-	-	-	-	-	-	-	5
The International	-	-	-	-	-	-	-	-	MC	MC
Buick Open	-	-	-	-	-	-	-	-	67	MC
USPGA Champ	-	-	-	-	-	-	-	-	-	-
WGCNEC Inv'	-	-	-	-	-	-	-	-	-	-
Reno-Tahoe Op'	-	-	-	-	-	-	-	-	MC	-
Air Canada Chp'	-	-	-	-	-	-	-	-	MC	-
Bell Canadian O'	-	-	-	-	-	-	-	-	MC	8
WGC AmEx	-	-	-	-	-	-	-	-	-	-
Tampa Bay Cl'	-	-	-	-	-	-	-	-	63	-
Marconi Penn C'	-	-	-	-	-	-	-	-	MC	6
Texas Open	-	-	-	-	-	-	-	-	-	-
Michelob Chmp'	-	-	-	-	-	-	-	-	74	-
Invensys Classic	-	-	-	-	-	-	-	-	36	11
NCR Golf Cl'	-	-	-	-	-	-	-	-	24	-
Buick Challenge	-	-	-	-	-	-	-	-	-	MC
SFB Classic	-	-	-	-	-	-	-	-	-	-
Tour Champ'ship	-	-	-	-	-	-	-	-	-	-

Retief Goosen
3/2/69 – Pietersburg, South Africa

The European Tour Order of Merit winner of 2001 (courtesy of three wins) had failed to post a top-ten finish in 27 events on North American soil before winning the US Open at Southern Hills. His shock win in Tulsa propelled the 'Goose' into golf's elite. He is a multiple winner of the European Tour and now has to decide whether to base himself in the USA or stay in Europe. He uses sports psychologist Jos Vanstiphout. Spent his amateur days battling with great friend Ernie Els and is now out of his shadow. Length off the tee is key to his game.
ScAv - 69.94 (N/A) – DD - 284.3 (N/A) DA - 60.7 (N/A) GIR - 65.0 (N/A) – PpGIR - 1.779 (N/A) SS - 41.7 (N/A)

	'92	'93	'94	'95	'96	'97	'98	'99	'00	'01
WGC MatchPlay	-	-	-	-	-	-	-	-	17	17
Mercedes Ch	-	-	-	-	-	-	-	-	-	-
Tucson Open	-	-	-	-	-	-	-	-	-	-
Sony Open	-	-	-	-	-	-	-	-	-	-
Phoenix Open	-	-	-	-	-	-	-	-	-	-
AT&T P Beach	-	-	-	-	-	-	-	-	-	-
Buick Invitatn'l	-	-	-	-	-	-	-	-	-	-
Bob Hope Cl'	-	-	-	-	-	-	-	-	-	-
Nissan Open	-	-	-	-	-	-	-	-	-	-
Genuity Champ	-	-	-	-	-	-	-	-	33	-
Honda Classic	-	-	-	-	-	-	-	-	-	-
Bay Hill Invit'l	-	-	-	-	-	-	MC	-	MC	34
Players Champ	-	-	-	-	-	-	MC	-	MC	MC
BellSouth Cl'	-	-	-	-	-	-	-	-	MC	WD
US Masters	-	-	-	-	-	-	MC	-	40	MC
Worldcom Cl'	-	-	-	-	-	-	-	-	39	-
Houston Open	-	-	-	-	-	-	-	-	-	-
GG Chrysler Cl'	-	-	-	-	-	-	-	-	-	-
Compaq Classic	-	-	-	-	-	-	-	-	-	-
Byron Nelson C'	-	-	-	-	-	-	-	-	-	-
MasterCard Cln'l	-	-	-	-	-	-	-	-	-	-
Kemper Ins Open	-	-	-	-	-	-	-	-	-	-
Memorial T'ment	-	-	-	-	-	-	-	-	-	-
St. Jude Classic	-	-	-	-	-	-	-	-	-	-
U.S. Open	-	-	-	-	-	-	MC	MC	12	1
Buick Classic	-	-	-	-	-	-	-	-	-	-
Canon GH Open	-	-	-	-	-	-	-	-	-	-
Western Open	-	-	-	-	-	-	-	-	-	-
Gr. Milwaukee	-	-	-	-	-	-	-	-	-	-
British Open	-	-	-	75	10	MC	10	41	13	
B.C. Open	-	-	-	-	-	-	-	-	-	-
John Deere Cl'	-	-	-	-	-	-	-	-	-	-
The International	-	-	55	-	MC	-	-	-	-	
Buick Open	-	-	-	-	MC	-	-	-	MC	
USPGA Champ	-	-	-	61	MC	MC	MC	37		
WGCNEC Inv'	-	-	-	-	-	-	-	24	10	
Reno-Tahoe Op'	-	-	-	-	-	-	-	-	-	
Air Canada Chp'	-	-	-	MC	-	-	13	-		
Bell Canadian	-	-	77	-	-	-	-	-	-	
WGC AmEx	-	-	-	-	-	-	25	35	-	
Tampa Bay Cl'	-	-	-	-	-	-	-	-	-	-
Marconi Penn C'	-	-	-	-	-	-	-	-	-	-
Texas Open	-	-	-	-	-	-	-	-	-	-
Michelob Chmp'	-	-	-	-	-	-	-	-	-	-
Invensys Classic	-	-	-	-	-	-	-	-	-	-
NCR Golf Cl'	-	-	-	-	-	-	-	-	-	-
Buick Challenge	-	-	-	-	-	-	-	-	-	-
SFB Classic	-	-	-	-	-	-	-	-	-	-
Tour Champ'ship	-	-	-	-	-	-	-	-	-	-

David Gossett
28/4/79 – Phoenix, AZ

Turned pro in July 2000 and became the first player since Tiger Woods to win on a sponsor's exemption when capturing the John Derre Classic in 2001. Started the season on the Buy.com Tour after failing to win his playing privileges at Q-School despite shooting a 59 – the first time that score had been achieved at Q-School. Played Walker Cup golf for the Americans in 1999 (was the youngest player on the team at 20) and has a big future ahead of him. A big hitter who can also find the fairway more often than not, his bunker play isn't the best.
ScAv - 70.68 (N/A) – DD - 282.0 (N/A) DA - 70.5 (N/A) GIR - 69.3 (N/A) – PpGIR - 1.765 (N/A) SS - 50.9 (N/A)

	'92	'93	'94	'95	'96	'97	'98	'99	'00	'01
WGC MatchPlay	-	-	-	-	-	-	-	-	-	-
Mercedes Ch	-	-	-	-	-	-	-	-	-	-
Tucson Open	-	-	-	-	-	-	-	-	-	-
Sony Open	-	-	-	-	-	-	-	-	-	-
Phoenix Open	-	-	-	-	-	-	-	-	-	-
AT&T P Beach	-	-	-	-	-	-	-	-	-	MC
Buick Invitatn'l	-	-	-	-	-	-	-	-	-	-
Bob Hope Cl'	-	-	-	-	-	-	-	-	-	46
Nissan Open	-	-	-	-	-	-	-	-	-	MC
Genuity Champ	-	-	-	-	-	-	-	-	-	-
Honda Classic	-	-	-	-	-	-	-	-	-	-
Bay Hill Invit'l	-	-	-	-	-	-	-	-	-	-
Players Champ	-	-	-	-	-	-	-	-	-	-
BellSouth Cl'	-	-	-	-	-	-	-	-	-	-
US Masters	-	-	-	-	-	-	-	-	54	-
Worldcom Cl'	-	-	-	-	-	-	-	-	-	-
Houston Open	-	-	-	-	-	-	-	-	-	-
GG Chrysler Cl'	-	-	-	-	-	-	-	-	-	-
Compaq Classic	-	-	-	-	-	-	-	-	-	-
Byron Nelson C'	-	-	-	-	-	-	-	-	-	-
MasterCard Cln'l	-	-	-	-	-	-	-	-	-	-
Kemper Ins Open	-	-	-	-	-	-	-	-	-	-
Memorial T'ment	-	-	-	-	-	-	-	-	-	-
St. Jude Classic	-	-	-	-	-	-	71	MC	-	28
U.S. Open	-	-	-	-	-	-	-	-	MC	-
Buick Classic	-	-	-	-	-	-	-	-	-	-
Canon GH Open	-	-	-	-	-	-	MC	-	-	-
Western Open	-	-	-	-	-	-	-	-	-	-
Gr. Milwaukee	-	-	-	-	-	-	-	-	-	-
British Open	-	-	-	-	-	-	-	MC	-	-
B.C. Open	-	-	-	-	-	-	-	-	-	-
John Deere Cl'	-	-	-	-	-	-	-	-	-	1
The International	-	-	-	-	-	-	-	-	MC	MC
Buick Open	-	-	-	-	-	-	-	-	-	-
USPGA Champ	-	-	-	-	-	-	-	-	-	MC
WGCNEC Inv'	-	-	-	-	-	-	-	-	-	-
Reno-Tahoe Op'	-	-	-	-	-	-	-	-	MC	-
Air Canada Chp'	-	-	-	-	-	-	-	-	MC	5
Bell Canadian O'	-	-	-	-	-	-	-	-	MC	43
WGC AmEx	-	-	-	-	-	-	-	-	-	-
Tampa Bay Cl'	-	-	-	-	-	-	-	-	-	-
Marconi Penn C'	-	-	-	-	-	-	-	-	-	-
Texas Open	-	-	-	-	-	-	-	MC	MC	24
Michelob Chmp'	-	-	-	-	-	-	-	MC	MC	MC
Invensys Classic	-	-	-	-	-	-	-	-	-	MC
NCR Golf Cl'	-	-	-	-	-	-	-	-	-	MC
Buick Challenge	-	-	-	-	-	-	-	-	MC	23
SFB Classic	-	-	-	-	-	-	-	23	-	23
Tour Champ'ship	-	-	-	-	-	-	-	-	-	-

Paul Gow
11/10/70 – Sydney, Australia

Former ANZ Tour pro who made the jump from the Buy.com Tour to the full tour in 2001. He missed 13 cuts in his first full season but two top-five finishes, including runners-up position in the BC Open, helped him to retain his card for next season. Gow played in Australia for four years before moving to the United States, winning once, and his 2000 season on the Buy.com Tour also yielded one victory (in the Hershey Open). His statistics don't highlight any real strength in his game bar that of bunker play, where he ranks in the top ten.

ScAv - 71.60 (134th) – DD - 277.6 (117th) DA - 67.0 (123rd) GIR - 64.9 (140th) – PpGIR - 1.785 (125th) SS - 60.6 (10th)

	'92	'93	'94	'95	'96	'97	'98	'99	'00	'01
WGC MatchPlay	-	-	-	-	-	-	-	-	-	-
Mercedes Ch	-	-	-	-	-	-	-	-	-	-
Tucson Open	-	-	-	-	-	-	-	-	-	MC
Sony Open	-	-	-	-	-	-	-	-	-	MC
Phoenix Open	-	-	-	-	-	-	-	-	-	-
AT&T P Beach	-	-	-	-	-	-	-	-	-	MC
Buick Invitatn'l	-	-	-	-	-	-	-	-	-	MC
Bob Hope Cl'	-	-	-	-	-	-	-	-	-	-
Nissan Open	-	-	-	-	-	-	-	-	-	25
Genuity Champ	-	-	-	-	-	-	-	-	-	40
Honda Classic	-	-	-	-	-	-	-	-	-	61
Bay Hill Invit'l	-	-	-	-	-	-	-	-	-	-
Players Champ	-	-	-	-	-	-	-	-	-	-
BellSouth Cl'	-	-	-	-	-	-	-	-	-	MC
US Masters	-	-	-	-	-	-	-	-	-	-
Worldcom Cl'	-	-	-	-	-	-	-	-	-	-
Houston Open	-	-	-	-	-	-	-	-	-	16
GG Chrysler Cl'	-	-	-	-	-	-	-	-	-	MC
Compaq Classic	-	-	-	-	-	-	-	-	-	34
Byron Nelson C'	-	-	-	-	-	-	-	-	-	-
MasterCard Cln'l	-	-	-	-	-	-	-	-	-	-
Kemper Ins Open	-	-	-	-	-	-	-	-	-	MC
Memorial T'ment	-	-	-	-	-	-	-	-	-	-
St. Jude Classic	-	-	-	-	-	-	-	-	-	MC
U.S. Open	-	-	-	-	-	-	-	-	MC	-
Buick Classic	-	-	-	-	-	-	-	-	-	26
Canon GH Open	-	-	-	-	-	-	-	32	29	
Western Open	-	-	-	-	-	-	-	-	-	MC
Gr. Milwaukee	-	-	-	-	-	-	-	-	-	MC
British Open	-	-	-	-	-	-	-	-	-	-
B.C. Open	-	-	-	-	-	-	-	-	-	2
John Deere Cl'	-	-	-	-	-	-	-	-	-	10
The International	-	-	-	-	-	-	-	-	-	37
Buick Open	-	-	-	-	-	-	-	-	-	57
USPGA Champ	-	-	-	-	-	-	-	-	-	-
WGCNEC Inv'	-	-	-	-	-	-	-	-	-	-
Reno-Tahoe Op'	-	-	-	-	-	-	-	-	-	MC
Air Canada Chp'	-	-	-	-	-	-	-	-	-	MC
Bell Canadian O'	-	-	-	-	-	-	-	-	-	5
WGC AmEx	-	-	-	-	-	-	-	-	-	-
Tampa Bay Cl'	-	-	-	-	-	-	-	-	-	-
Marconi Penn C'	-	-	-	-	-	-	-	-	-	-
Texas Open	-	-	-	-	-	-	-	-	-	-
Michelob Chmp'	-	-	-	-	-	-	-	-	-	MC
Invensys Classic	-	-	-	-	-	-	-	-	-	MC
NCR Golf Cl'	-	-	-	-	-	-	-	-	-	MC
Buick Challenge	-	-	-	-	-	-	-	-	-	WD
SFB Classic	-	-	-	-	-	-	-	-	-	-
Tour Champ'ship	-	-	-	-	-	-	-	-	-	-

Jay Haas
2/12/53 – St Louis, MO

Veteran golfer who has played on the US Tour since 1977 and can boast nine victories, the last of his wins, though was in 1993 (the Texas Open). Made the Ryder Cup team in 1985 and 1995 and his most notable achievement in 2001 was to claim fourth place in the BC Open – his best finish for nearly two years. His first win came in 1978 San Diego Invitational (now Buick Invitational). He can't compete with the younger players in terms of length off the tee but still finds more fairways and greens that most golfers and retains a fine putting touch.

ScAv - 70.40 (32nd) – DD - 273.7 (154th) DA - 71.0 (45th) GIR - 68.9 (39th) – PpGIR - 1.751 (40th) SS - 55.5 (51st)

	'92	'93	'94	'95	'96	'97	'98	'99	'00	'01
WGC MatchPlay	-	-	-	-	-	-	-	-	-	-
Mercedes Ch	25	4	-	-	-	-	-	-	-	-
Tucson Open	-	-	-	MC	-	-	-	-	-	-
Sony Open	33	30	MC	-	-	-	-	-	-	-
Phoenix Open	-	-	-	MC	-	-	-	-	-	-
AT&T P Beach	56	36	29	-	-	20	6	66	MC	MC
Buick Invitatn'l	21	4	51	MC	12	34	76	MC	MC	MC
Bob Hope Cl'	15	4	58	MC	17	41	52	43	MC	30
Nissan Open	3	45	MC	7	44	27	10	MC	12	63
Genuity Champ	-	-	-	17	6	13	36	3	21	-
Honda Classic	-	-	-	-	-	-	-	-	-	-
Bay Hill Invit'l	43	10	13	5	53	47	42	77	MC	71
Players Champ	MC	20	55	MC	8	43	MC	MC	MC	-
BellSouth Cl'	-	-	-	-	-	9	50	MC	-	-
US Masters	-	38	5	3	36	-	12	44	37	-
Worldcom Cl'	12	39	30	MC	32	20	24	72	MC	62
Houston Open	22	20	16	-	-	MC	MC	MC	60	MC
GG Chrysler Cl'	20	20	13	MC	MC	-	-	-	-	-
Compaq Classic	18	-	-	-	38	MC	-	-	43	-
Byron Nelson C'	5	63	50	MC	23	MC	MC	-	-	-
MasterCard Cln'l	40	-	-	-	-	-	-	70	41	-
Kemper Ins Open	-	33	-	31	-	11	42	-	-	17
Memorial T'ment	60	4	19	5	30	21	23	35	17	20
St. Jude Classic	1	23	15	11	MC	53	7	42	15	12
U.S. Open	23	77	MC	4	90	5	MC	17	-	-
Buick Classic	MC	63	3	MC	MC	-	-	35	MC	26
Canon GH Open	15	38	MC	-	-	MC	36	MC	MC	36
Western Open	-	-	2	MC	-	MC	-	-	-	-
Gr. Milwaukee	9	41	11	10	22	12	MC	10	70	10
British Open	-	-	-	79	22	24	-	-	-	-
B.C. Open	2	MC	-	5	MC	-	-	-	-	4
John Deere Cl'	35	48	MC	-	-	-	-	-	-	-
The International	-	-	12	3	69	5	26	8	48	45
Buick Open	16	19	-	33	13	-	MC	-	-	49
USPGA Champ	62	20	14	8	31	61	40	3	64	-
WGCNEC Inv'	-	-	-	-	-	-	-	-	-	-
Reno-Tahoe Op'	-	-	-	-	-	-	-	17	MC	MC
Air Canada Chp'	-	-	-	-	-	-	-	-	-	-
Bell Canadian O'	-	-	-	-	-	-	-	-	-	23
WGC AmEx	-	-	-	-	-	-	-	-	-	-
Tampa Bay Cl'	-	-	-	-	-	-	-	73	-	-
Marconi Penn C'	-	-	-	-	-	-	-	-	WD	11
Texas Open	MC	1	33	8	2	MC	2	5	MC	17
Michelob Chmp'	-	-	7	34	17	MC	-	-	-	MC
Invensys Classic	11	MC	65	-	-	-	-	-	-	-
NCR Golf Cl'	-	24	73	-	5	-	51	MC	62	-
Buick Challenge	-	-	-	55	5	MC	MC	MC	-	-
SFB Classic	-	-	-	-	-	-	-	-	-	MC
Tour Champ'ship	7	10	6	20	-	-	-	-	-	-

Dudley Hart
4/8/68 – Rochester, NY

A fine second half of the season ensured that this New York born Florida based pro would line up next term for an 11th successive year on the US Tour. The 'Mini Volcano', as he was dubbed in the early part of his career due to his short fuse on the course, can boast two victories on the US Tour (the Honda Classic in 2000 and the 1996 Canadian Open). He has been plagued by back problems in his career and, in fact, has withdrawn from at least one tournament in each of the last five years. A long driver, he hits plenty of greens in regulation.

ScAv - 70.38 (30th) – DD - 284.5 (40th) DA - 64.4 (165th) GIR - 69.0 (38th) – PpGIR - 1.756 (55th) SS - 56.4 (34th)

	'92	'93	'94	'95	'96	'97	'98	'99	'00	'01
WGC MatchPlay	-	-	-	-	-	-	-	33	33	9
Mercedes Ch	-	-	-	-	-	27	-	-	-	19
Tucson Open	4	3	MC	41	-	31	-	-	-	-
Sony Open	41	MC	50	65	-	51	-	-	-	47
Phoenix Open	-	45	MC	-	-	WD	8	10	41	-
AT&T P Beach	MC	MC	7	MC	-	MC	56	39	20	-
Buick Invitatn'l	66	MC	-	MC	-	MC	-	-	-	-
Bob Hope Cl'	WD	-	-	MC	-	-	-	-	-	DQ
Nissan Open	-	-	WD	46	-	-	-	-	-	MC
Genuity Champ	59	MC	MC	17	-	MC	15	-	MC	MC
Honda Classic	MC	13	MC	40	-	MC	30	9	1	47
Bay Hill Invit'l	58	MC	MC	MC	-	MC	MC	23	29	-
Players Champ	MC	WD	MC	-	-	MC	25	38	WD	MC
BellSouth Cl'	-	-	-	60	-	60	-	-	-	MC
US Masters	-	-	MC	-	-	MC	-	-	28	43
Worldcom Cl'	MC	MC	69	-	-	62	36	25	12	
Houston Open	MC	MC	WD	55	-	MC	4	-	MC	-
GG Chrysler Cl'	48	3	8	MC	-	29	11	4	3	24
Compaq Classic	18	45	-	63	-	69	-	10	-	11
Byron Nelson C'	8	43	-	MC	-	19	MC	35	-	11
MasterCard Cln'l	-	33	-	-	6	50	DQ	-	WD	
Kemper Ins Open	36	MC	MC	51	-	13	-	20	-	
Memorial T'ment	-	16	-	-	-	38	MC	35	-	
St. Jude Classic	-	-	MC	MC	21	2	43	-	MC	
U.S. Open	33	-	-	-	-	WD	17	MC	62	
Buick Classic	45	38	58	MC	-	54	-	54	-	
Canon GH Open	23	26	47	15	56	-	-	-	3	
Western Open	MC	13	MC	71	-	62	3	34	MC	7
Gr. Milwaukee	3	MC	MC	-	MC	-	-	-	-	
British Open	-	-	-	-	-	MC	81	37	WD	37
B.C. Open	-	54	MC	-	-	-	-	-	-	
John Deere Cl'	43	-	MC	WD	27	-	-	-	-	
The International	MC	26	42	-	4	35	48	-	MC	
Buick Open	13	19	MC	MC	MC	MC	12	25	6	4
USPGA Champ	MC	6	55	-	-	MC	44	MC	WD	16
WGCNEC Inv'	-	-	-	-	-	-	-	-	-	
Reno-Tahoe Op'	-	-	-	-	-	-	17	-	-	
Air Canada Chp'	-	-	-	14	-	-	-	-	-	
Bell Canadian O'	23	8	WD	34	1	MC	43	3	-	8
WGC AmEx	-	-	-	-	-	-	3	48	-	
Tampa Bay Cl'	-	-	-	-	-	-	-	40	-	
Marconi Penn C'	-	-	-	-	-	-	-	46	MC	
Texas Open	MC	MC	40	22	-	-	-	WD	30	-
Michelob Chmp'	52	MC	MC	56	74	-	MC	32	MC	MC
Invensys Classic	14	MC	26	MC	12	MC	53	3	27	-
NCR Golf Cl'	-	-	24	MC	8	-	MC	7	-	
Buick Challenge	MC	-	MC	80	MC	25	-	-	-	
SFB Classic	-	-	28	21	-	-	-	-	-	
Tour Champ'ship	-	-	-	-	-	-	-	-	-	

J.P. Hayes
2/8/65 – Appleton, WI

Two mid-summer third places were enough for this Buy.Com Tour pro to secure his card for 2002. He missed the back of end of last season but had already made enough cash to ensure he didn't have to go back to Q-School for the fifth time.

He has won just once on the main tour (1998 Buick Classic) and he also has one Buy.com Tour victory (1996 Miami Open). His putting stats for 2001 have slipped alarmingly from his 2000 figures. He did gain a modicum of accuracy off the tee last year, though.

ScAv - 71.36 (114th) – DD - 277.3 (120th) DA - 69.8 (71st) GIR - 65.6 (107th) – PpGIR - 1.778 (108th) SS - 50.7 (116th)

	'92	'93	'94	'95	'96	'97	'98	'99	'00	'01
WGC MatchPlay	-	-	-	-	-	-	-	-	-	-
Mercedes Ch	-	-	-	-	-	-	-	12	-	-
Tucson Open	MC	-	-	MC	-	-	-	-	-	MC
Sony Open	MC	-	-	MC	61	MC	-	-	-	-
Phoenix Open	-	-	-	-	-	-	10	MC	70	
AT&T P Beach	MC	-	MC	-	MC	3	MC	MC	-	
Buick Invitatn'l	53	-	16	-	18	MC	MC	10	MC	
Bob Hope Cl'	-	67	-	-	-	28	46	MC		
Nissan Open	MC	-	71	-	67	MC	35	10	51	
Genuity Champ	-	-	-	-	-	-	-	-	-	
Honda Classic	MC	-	MC	-	-	-	2	47		
Bay Hill Invit'l	-	-	-	-	-	-	33	70	MC	
Players Champ	-	-	-	-	-	-	MC	42	MC	
BellSouth Cl'	MC	-	22	-	67	MC	30	-	MC	
US Masters	-	-	-	-	-	-	MC	-	-	
Worldcom Cl'	-	-	-	-	-	MC	-	-	-	
Houston Open	64	-	32	-	8	47	5	45	72	
GG Chrysler Cl'	-	51	-	29	42	-	MC	-		
Compaq Classic	MC	-	MC	MC	48	51	-	-	MC	
Byron Nelson C'	-	78	-	38	-	MC	MC	MC		
MasterCard Cln'l	-	-	-	-	-	MC	55	58		
Kemper Ins Open	MC	-	-	-	MC	-	-	-	-	
Memorial T'ment	-	-	-	-	-	-	14	10	49	
St. Jude Classic	MC	-	MC	-	MC	68	-	-	49	
U.S. Open	MC	-	-	-	-	-	MC	-	-	
Buick Classic	MC	-	18	-	69	1	28	19	3	
Canon GH Open	-	-	MC	-	53	MC	-	-	MC	
Western Open	MC	-	-	MC	31	MC	23	MC	-	
Gr. Milwaukee	54	-	MC	MC	18	76	3	3		
British Open	-	-	-	-	-	MC	-	-	42	
B.C. Open	23	-	MC	-	MC	-	-	-	-	
John Deere Cl'	MC	-	12	-	23	-	41	-	-	
The International	MC	-	MC	-	-	MC	-	48	MC	-
Buick Open	76	-	53	-	74	49	63	MC	62	
USPGA Champ	-	-	-	-	MC	54	19	-	-	
WGCNEC Inv'	-	-	-	-	-	-	-	-	-	
Reno-Tahoe Op'	-	-	-	-	-	-	32	21	7	
Air Canada Chp'	-	-	-	-	51	-	-	-	29	
Bell Canadian O'	MC	-	13	-	MC	-	MC	-	-	
WGC AmEx	-	-	-	-	-	-	-	-	-	
Tampa Bay Cl'	-	-	-	-	-	-	-	MC	-	
Marconi Penn C'	-	-	-	-	-	-	-	MC		
Texas Open	42	-	MC	-	72	64	-	-	-	
Michelob Chmp'	6	-	45	-	25	MC	17	41	-	
Invensys Classic	MC	-	MC	-	23	MC	44	67	-	
NCR Golf Cl'	20	-	MC	-	MC	-	-	76	-	
Buick Challenge	MC	-	MC	-	52	20	MC	48	-	
SFB Classic	32	10	-	57	-	19	-	51	-	
Tour Champ'ship	-	-	-	-	-	-	-	-	-	

J.J. Henry

2/4/75 – Fairfield,CT

Superb rookie season for this young former Buy.Com Tour player. Henry posted three top-six finishes in his last four starts in 2001, including second in the Texas Open. Also finished runner-up in the Kemper Open.

He spent the 2000 term on the Buy.com Tour, winning the Knoxville Open before graduating to the main tour in 2001. Turned pro in 1998 after finishing runner-up in the NCAA Championship. Has the game to go far – massive off the tee, accurate with his irons and his driver, his putting isn't the best, though.

ScAv - 70.98 (75th) – DD - 286.6 (26th) DA - 70.7 (58th) GIR - 70.7 (13th) – PpGIR - 1.810 (186th) SS - 37.7 (190th)

	'92	'93	'94	'95	'96	'97	'98	'99	'00	'01
WGC MatchPlay	-	-	-	-	-	-	-	-	-	-
Mercedes Ch	-	-	-	-	-	-	-	-	-	-
Tucson Open	-	-	-	-	-	-	-	-	-	MC
Sony Open	-	-	-	-	-	-	-	-	-	66
Phoenix Open	-	-	-	-	-	-	-	-	-	-
AT&T P Beach	-	-	-	-	-	-	-	-	-	MC
Buick Invitatn'l	-	-	-	-	-	-	-	-	-	27
Bob Hope Cl'	-	-	-	-	-	-	-	-	-	-
Nissan Open	-	-	-	-	-	-	-	-	-	MC
Genuity Champ	-	-	-	-	-	-	-	-	-	MC
Honda Classic	-	-	-	-	-	-	-	-	-	MC
Bay Hill Invit'l	-	-	-	-	-	-	-	-	-	MC
Players Champ	-	-	-	-	-	-	-	-	-	-
BellSouth Cl'	-	-	-	-	-	-	-	-	-	53
US Masters	-	-	-	-	-	-	-	-	-	-
Worldcom Cl'	-	-	-	-	-	-	-	-	-	-
Houston Open	-	-	-	-	-	-	-	-	-	46
GG Chrysler Cl'	-	-	-	-	-	-	-	-	-	MC
Compaq Classic	-	-	-	-	-	-	-	-	-	MC
Byron Nelson C'	-	-	-	-	-	-	-	-	-	-
MasterCard Cln'l	-	-	-	-	-	-	-	-	-	-
Kemper Ins Open	-	-	-	-	-	-	-	-	-	2
Memorial T'ment	-	-	-	-	-	-	-	-	-	-
St. Jude Classic	-	-	-	-	-	-	-	-	-	MC
U.S. Open	-	-	-	-	-	-	-	-	-	-
Buick Classic	-	-	-	-	-	-	MC	-	-	MC
Canon GH Open	-	-	-	-	-	56	MC	-	-	MC
Western Open	-	-	-	-	-	-	-	-	-	52
Gr. Milwaukee	-	-	-	-	-	-	-	-	-	61
British Open	-	-	-	-	-	-	-	-	-	-
B.C. Open	-	-	-	-	-	-	64	-	-	46
John Deere Cl'	-	-	-	-	-	-	-	-	-	-
The International	-	-	-	-	-	-	-	-	-	MC
Buick Open	-	-	-	-	-	-	-	-	-	-
USPGA Champ	-	-	-	-	-	-	-	-	-	-
WGCNEC Inv'	-	-	-	-	-	-	-	-	-	-
Reno-Tahoe Op'	-	-	-	-	-	-	-	-	-	MC
Air Canada Chp'	-	-	-	-	-	-	-	-	-	8
Bell Canadian O'	-	-	-	-	-	-	-	-	-	14
WGC AmEx	-	-	-	-	-	-	-	-	-	-
Tampa Bay Cl'	-	-	-	-	-	-	-	-	-	-
Marconi Penn C'	-	-	-	-	-	-	-	-	-	-
Texas Open	-	-	-	-	-	-	-	59	-	2
Michelob Chmp'	-	-	-	-	-	-	-	-	-	6
Invensys Classic	-	-	-	-	-	-	-	-	-	64
NCR Golf Cl'	-	-	-	-	-	-	-	-	-	-
Buick Challenge	-	-	-	-	-	-	-	-	-	67
SFB Classic	-	-	-	-	-	-	-	-	-	6
Tour Champ'ship	-	-	-	-	-	-	-	-	-	-

Tim Herron

16/2/70 – Minneapolis, MN

Lumpy's haul of just three top-ten finishes in 2001 was his worst since joining the US Tour full time in 1996. His best position came last season in the Greater Milwaukee Open, where he managed third place but he slipped to 57th on the Money List – his lowest finish. Has won three times on the US Tour (his last success coming at the 1999 Bay Hill Invitational) after turning pro in 1993, following a fine amateur career (in which he once defeated Tiger Woods – one of only two players to do so). Long, but erratic off the tee, his putting was poor in 2001.

Sc Av – 70.73 (58th) DD – 288.9 (17th) DA – 65.7 (141st) GIR 70.3 (19th) PpGIR – 1,795 (160th) SS – 50.7 (116th)

	'92	'93	'94	'95	'96	'97	'98	'99	'00	'01
WGC MatchPlay	-	-	-	-	-	-	-	-	17	17
Mercedes Ch	-	-	-	-	-	17	20	-	23	-
Tucson Open	-	-	-	-	MC	61	4	20	-	32
Sony Open	-	-	-	-	74	19	35	19	39	-
Phoenix Open	-	-	-	-	-	50	MC	MC	41	23
AT&T P Beach	-	-	-	-	-	38	19	10	61	13
Buick Invitatn'l	-	-	-	-	24	16	MC	MC	-	MC
Bob Hope Cl'	-	-	-	-	61	-	-	-	-	-
Nissan Open	-	-	-	-	60	-	-	15	MC	-
Genuity Champ	-	-	-	-	-	MC	9	-	-	MC
Honda Classic	-	-	-	-	1	14	47	60	28	67
Bay Hill Invit'l	-	-	-	-	MC	6	MC	1	10	40
Players Champ	-	-	-	-	19	MC	MC	MC	MC	21
BellSouth Cl'	-	-	-	-	-	-	30	-	-	MC
US Masters	-	-	-	-	MC	-	MC	44	MC	-
Worldcom Cl'	-	-	-	-	56	54	56	27	39	MC
Houston Open	-	-	-	-	72	-	-	-	-	-
GG Chrysler Cl'	-	-	-	-	MC	MC	16	37	46	-
Compaq Classic	-	-	-	-	38	MC	-	-	-	MC
Byron Nelson C'	-	-	-	-	MC	MC	9	MC	MC	11
MasterCard Cln'l	-	-	-	-	MC	63	-	2	13	69
Kemper Ins Open	-	-	-	-	-	7	MC	-	7	6
Memorial T'ment	-	-	-	-	56	8	7	35	45	MC
St. Jude Classic	-	-	-	-	13	-	12	2	75	-
U.S. Open	-	-	-	MC	MC	-	53	6	MC	40
Buick Classic	-	-	-	-	9	54	-	-	-	-
Canon GH Open	-	-	-	-	-	40	36	8	18	14
Western Open	-	-	-	-	43	MC	31	MC	-	52
Gr. Milwaukee	-	-	-	-	71	-	-	-	-	3
British Open	-	-	-	-	MC	-	-	30	MC	-
B.C. Open	-	-	-	-	37	-	-	-	-	-
John Deere Cl'	-	-	-	-	-	-	-	-	7	74
The International	-	-	-	-	59	MC	74	51	-	14
Buick Open	-	-	-	-	-	MC	-	54	47	-
USPGA Champ	-	-	-	-	31	13	75	MC	MC	MC
WGCNEC Inv'	-	-	-	-	-	-	-	-	-	-
Reno-Tahoe Op'	-	-	-	-	-	-	-	-	12	7
Air Canada Chp'	-	-	-	-	-	6	-	-	38	29
Bell Canadian O'	-	-	-	-	52	MC	25	MC	-	-
WGC AmEx	-	-	-	-	-	-	-	16	-	-
Tampa Bay Cl'	-	-	-	-	-	-	-	-	9	-
Marconi Penn C'	-	-	-	-	-	-	-	-	-	28
Texas Open	-	-	-	-	6	1	MC	29	30	62
Michelob Chmp'	-	-	-	-	-	MC	MC	-	-	MC
Invensys Classic	-	-	-	-	MC	69	MC	MC	22	MC
NCR Golf Cl'	-	-	-	-	66	49	-	-	-	-
Buick Challenge	-	-	-	-	55	44	14	52	-	-
SFB Classic	-	-	-	-	-	-	-	-	-	-
Tour Champ'ship	-	-	-	-	-	-	-	9	-	-

Scott Hoch

24/11/55 – Raleigh, NC

This 20-year tour veteran enjoyed his best season in 2001 since turning pro. At 46-years-old, he taught the young guns a trick or two by winning two events last term. He has won 10 titles on the US Tour and his short but straight hitting game is still good enough to compete with the best around – as it has been for over a decade.

His infamous grumpyness was still in evidence in the Greater Greensboro Classic, when he complained about the height of the rough – even though he went on to win the event.

ScAv - 69.85 (9th) – DD - 275.8 (133rd) DA - 73.9 (19th) GIR - 67.0 (75th) – PpGIR - 1.739 (21st) SS - 56.1 (40th)

	'92	'93	'94	'95	'96	'97	'98	'99	'00	'01
WGC MatchPlay	-	-	-	-	-	-	-	17	5	-
Mercedes Ch	-	-	-	11	2	24	19	-	-	-
Tucson Open	-	MC	MC	32	40	-	9	-	-	-
Sony Open	-	-	-	76	-	-	-	-	-	-
Phoenix Open	-	MC	8	-	26	22	-	22	77	-
AT&T P Beach	-	-	-	-	-	-	-	-	-	-
Buick Invitatn'l	-	-	-	-	-	-	-	11	-	-
Bob Hope Cl'	-	19	1	54	3	9	MC	37	MC	MC
Nissan Open	-	-	20	23	-	3	6	7	25	MC
Genuity Champ	-	9	27	MC	-	35	7	34	30	MC
Honda Classic	-	MC	30	-	44	-	-	-	-	-
Bay Hill Invit'l	-	39	57	MC	MC	68	29	5	14	8
Players Champ	-	MC	MC	WD	19	2	5	6	13	7
BellSouth Cl'	25	-	-	7	-	-	-	-	-	-
US Masters	-	-	MC	7	5	38	16	44	MC	30
Worldcom Cl'	-	20	60	20	3	9	31	12	15	28
Houston Open	-	26	-	2	31	4	12	10	7	16
GG Chrysler Cl'	-	MC	-	-	-	-	-	MC	-	1
Compaq Classic	-	6	-	-	21	11	12	12	9	11
Byron Nelson C'	-	-	21	-	-	-	-	-	-	-
MasterCard Cln'l	63	MC	30	52	16	33	18	26	MC	-
Kemper Ins Open	69	3	10	21	2	-	2	18	34	6
Memorial T'ment	71	25	14	38	49	4	MC	-	13	10
St. Jude Classic	MC	23	42	-	MC	-	11	-	20	10
U.S. Open	MC	5	13	56	7	10	MC	MC	16	16
Buick Classic	-	MC	-	-	-	-	-	4	-	2
Canon GH Open	42	-	22	-	-	-	7	-	MC	-
Western Open	29	59	3	10	MC	13	7	MC	9	1
Gr. Milwaukee	-	24	25	1	22	1	47	84	22	10
British Open	-	-	-	68	-	MC	-	-	-	MC
B.C. Open	-	-	-	-	-	-	-	-	-	-
John Deere Cl'	35	20	-	5	-	52	-	-	-	-
The International	-	-	-	-	40	-	-	-	-	-
Buick Open	27	MC	MC	33	-	42	-	25	-	-
USPGA Champ	MC	6	MC	MC	61	6	29	21	74	7
WGCNEC Inv'	-	-	-	-	-	-	23	-	21
Reno-Tahoe Op'	-	-	-	-	-	-	-	12	-
Air Canada Chp'	-	-	-	-	-	27	27	-
Bell Canadian O'	65	MC	-	-	-	-	-	-	-
WGC AmEx	-	-	-	-	-	7	17	-
Tampa Bay Cl'	-	-	-	-	-	-	MC	-
Marconi Penn C'	-	-	-	-	-	-	2	MC
Texas Open	-	WD	11	WD	MC	-	-	64	-	-
Michelob Chmp'	11	17	14	3	1	5	22	24	9	MC
Invensys Classic	51	19	8	-	MC	-	-	-	-	-
NCR Golf Cl'	14	10	MC	21	13	33	MC	11	57	MC
Buick Challenge	-	-	MC	-	8	68	-	63	-	5	-
SFB Classic	-	-	3	-	3	-	-	-	36	-
Tour Champ'ship	-	-	20	27	18	20	21	-	-	29

John Huston

1/6/61 – Mt. Vernon, IL

His worst season on tour since an injury plagued 1997 campaign for the Florida based pro who can boast six US Tour wins since turning pro in 1983. He was unable to defend his title in the Tampa Bay Classic as the 2001 event was cancelled. Last season yielded just one top-ten finish for Huston as he struggled with most aspects of his game. He retained plenty of accuracy with his iron play but his waywardness off the tee and poor putting touch let him down. Last year was also the first season in four he hadn't won a tournament.

ScAv - 71.25 (109th) – DD - 279.7 (93rd) DA - 68.1 (108th) GIR - 70.4 (18th) – PpGIR - 1.780 (117th) SS - 55.8 (43rd)

	'92	'93	'94	'95	'96	'97	'98	'99	'00	'01
WGC MatchPlay	-	-	-	-	-	-	-	3	33	33
Mercedes Ch	-	9	-	9	-	-	-	18	-	5
Tucson Open	23	WD	9	21	MC	25	-	-	-	-
Sony Open	MC	51	3	7	63	MC	1	12	3	14
Phoenix Open	4	64	MC	MC	59	72	8	-	37	-
AT&T P Beach	-	-	-	-	-	-	-	-	-	-
Buick Invitatn'l	12	20	-	8	MC	-	MC	-	-	-
Bob Hope Cl'	22	19	9	28	2	30	10	3	7	MC
Nissan Open	-	-	MC	-	-	-	-	-	-	-
Genuity Champ	18	57	1	27	MC	MC	2	MC	36	50
Honda Classic	MC	-	35	MC	MC	26	30	54	-	18
Bay Hill Invit'l	3	60	29	MC	-	MC	MC	-	46	-
Players Champ	40	MC	35	MC	MC	68	MC	20	MC	MC
BellSouth Cl'	-	22	-	-	-	-	5	3	5	54
US Masters	25	59	10	17	17	21	23	36	14	20
Worldcom Cl'	62	-	-	72	-	-	10	5	9	MC
Houston Open	MC	2	-	-	14	-	12	-	-	-
GG Chrysler Cl'	70	27	22	MC	5	MC	-	-	-	-
Compaq Classic	-	-	-	-	10	MC	-	MC	-	-
Byron Nelson C'	MC	-	-	-	-	MC	-	-	4	-
MasterCard Cln'l	55	6	22	WD	46	9	18	7	20	-
Kemper Ins Open	-	-	MC	43	-	-	-	-	-	-
Memorial T'ment	65	48	26	MC	5	MC	31	WD	58	-
St. Jude Classic	21	65	32	11	9	MC	-	50	65	-
U.S. Open	-	MC	MC	MC	82	-	32	17	4	MC
Buick Classic	-	-	27	-	-	-	-	-	-	MC
Canon GH Open	36	11	-	-	-	13	-	-	9	80
Western Open	MC	13	74	6	26	MC	46	MC	-	-
Gr. Milwaukee	-	MC	-	34	-	MC	-	-	-	-
British Open	-	48	MC	31	-	-	11	68	MC	MC
B.C. Open	-	-	-	-	-	-	-	-	-	-
John Deere Cl'	53	5	6	67	72	-	-	-	-	61
The International	67	-	WD	MC	72	39	-	-	-	38
Buick Open	4	15	-	-	49	MC	MC	-	-	-
USPGA Champ	18	44	MC	DQ	MC	-	13	MC	71	72
WGCNEC Inv'	-	-	-	-	-	-	33	-	-
Reno-Tahoe Op'	-	-	-	-	-	-	-	-	-
Air Canada Chp'	-	-	-	-	MC	-	-	-
Bell Canadian O'	WD	22	-	74	-	65	-	-	-
WGC AmEx	-	-	-	-	-	34	-	-
Tampa Bay Cl'	-	-	-	-	-	-	1	-
Marconi Penn C'	-	-	-	-	-	-	-	22
Texas Open	MC	22	-	-	6	WD	37	-	-	-
Michelob Chmp'	MC	-	-	-	MC	6	-	48	-	-
Invensys Classic	19	6	MC	MC	MC	WD	-	-	-	-
NCR Golf Cl'	1	35	11	WD	76	WD	1	5	MC	16
Buick Challenge	23	26	-	8	MC	MC	-	-	MC	-
SFB Classic	-	-	-	-	46	-	-	-	-	17
Tour Champ'ship	13	2	10	-	-	-	11	5	25	-

Lee Janzen
28/8/64 – Austin, MN

Two-time US Open winner who was disqualified in the 2001 renewal because of a rules infringement regarding wiping dew from the fairway. He didn't manage to add to his eight US Tour wins. Janzen's last victory was the US Open in 1998 – his only success in the last six years in fact. In 1995 he won three times and finished third on the Money List. Never the longest of drivers, his accuracy off the tee in 2001 wasn't as good as in previous years. His putting was still first class though. Janzen represented the USA in the 1993 and 1997 Ryder Cup.

ScAv - 70.94 (68th) – DD - 275.3 (138th) DA - 68.4 (103rd) GIR - 67.6 (62nd) – PpGIR - 1.747 (30th) SS - 55.5 (51st)

	'92	'93	'94	'95	'96	'97	'98	'99	'00	'01
WGC MatchPlay	-	-	-	-	-	-	-	17	33	-
Mercedes Ch	-	28	20	9	7	-	-	13	-	-
Tucson Open	1	27	59	25	3	5	MC	-	-	MC
Sony Open	12	MC	-	-	-	-	-	MC	MC	-
Phoenix Open	33	1	30	63	41	14	14	10	18	MC
AT&T P Beach	MC	6	MC	MC	-	-	-	-	35	-
Buick Invitatn'l	-	37	-	-	-	2	22	-	-	MC
Bob Hope Cl'	24	-	-	-	-	20	52	-	-	40
Nissan Open	MC	14	MC	46	-	MC	-	-	12	-
Genuity Champ	MC	10	34	MC	50	-	-	-	-	21
Honda Classic	-	-	MC	27	MC	14	15	-	-	39
Bay Hill Invit'l	MC	23	MC	65	60	68	MC	MC	46	8
Players Champ	MC	34	35	1	46	37	13	MC	9	18
BellSouth Cl'	-	-	-	-	-	2	14	MC	MC	-
US Masters	54	39	30	12	12	26	33	14	MC	31
Worldcom Cl'	41	20	-	MC	15	30	18	8	34	21
Houston Open	38	-	-	59	21	-	4	-	-	2
GG Chrysler Cl'	MC	6	22	41	23	-	-	-	-	-
Compaq Classic	37	-	-	-	-	-	-	-	30	-
Byron Nelson C'	MC	-	-	-	-	-	3	62	MC	-
MasterCard Cln'l	125	11	30	MC	-	22	MC	21	MC	MC
Kemper Ins Open	-	7	4	1	58	14	21	41	16	22
Memorial T'ment	12	50	60	19	MC	4	31	31	-	11
St. Jude Classic	MC	-	-	45	-	-	26	-	-	MC
U.S. Open	MC	1	MC	13	10	52	1	46	37	MC
Buick Classic	3	3	1	18	73	17	-	10	-	MC
Canon GH Open	11	-	MC	-	18	MC	-	MC	-	-
Western Open	-	MC	-	MC	8	39	3	MC	15	MC
Gr. Milwaukee	23	MC	-	34	-	-	-	-	-	-
British Open	39	48	35	24	MC	MC	24	70	MC	-
B.C. Open	13	-	13	-	26	-	-	-	-	-
John Deere Cl'	-	-	-	-	-	-	-	-	-	-
The International	2	31	15	1	MC	44	63	-	-	34
Buick Open	MC	-	MC	-	-	-	-	19	MC	-
USPGA Champ	21	22	66	23	8	4	MC	MC	19	MC
WGCNEC Inv'	-	-	-	-	-	-	-	30	-	-
Reno-Tahoe Op'	-	-	-	-	-	-	-	-	17	44
Air Canada Chp'	-	-	-	-	2	12	-	-	-	MC
Bell Canadian O'	50	60	70	MC	MC	-	-	3	48	-
WGC AmEx	-	-	-	-	-	-	-	-	-	-
Tampa Bay Cl'	-	-	-	-	-	-	-	-	6	-
Marconi Penn C'	-	-	-	-	-	-	-	-	MC	52
Texas Open	7	-	21	-	9	31	MC	-	-	-
Michelob Chmp'	-	-	-	-	-	11	54	13	58	32
Invensys Classic	-	39	-	19	6	27	56	15	29	-
NCR Golf Cl'	6	24	24	21	-	7	-	37	48	21
Buick Challenge	MC	-	-	55	-	-	-	-	-	17
SFB Classic	-	-	-	-	-	-	-	-	43	37
Tour Champ'ship	2	22	-	20	-	26	24	-	-	-

Per-Ulrik Johansson
6/12/66 – Uppsala, Sweden

Swedish former European Tour player who just about scrambled into the top 100 of the Money List in his rookie season.

Won five times on the European Tour before trying his luck in America, gaining his US Tour card by finishing 31st at the 2000 Q-School.

Struggled in the first part of the season, missing six cuts in his first seven events. But his solid all round game saw him finish the year strongly.

His putting in 2001 was dreadful but if it improves in 2002 a first US Tour title should come his way.

ScAv - 71.16 (94th) – DD - 281.4 (74th) DA - 70.1 (65th) GIR - 68.1 (52nd) – PpGIR - 1.823 (193rd) SS - 44.2 (169th)

	'92	'93	'94	'95	'96	'97	'98	'99	'00	'01
WGC MatchPlay	-	-	-	-	-	-	-	-	-	17
Mercedes Ch	-	-	-	-	-	-	-	-	-	-
Tucson Open	-	MC	-	-	-	-	54	-	-	MC
Sony Open	-	-	-	-	-	-	-	-	-	MC
Phoenix Open	52	-	-	-	-	-	-	-	-	-
AT&T P Beach	-	-	-	-	-	-	-	-	-	MC
Buick Invitatn'l	-	-	-	-	-	-	-	-	-	MC
Bob Hope Cl'	-	-	-	-	-	-	-	-	-	-
Nissan Open	-	-	-	-	-	-	-	-	-	MC
Genuity Champ	-	-	-	-	-	-	-	-	-	MC
Honda Classic	-	-	-	-	-	-	-	-	-	57
Bay Hill Invit'l	-	-	-	-	-	-	-	-	-	-
Players Champ	-	-	-	-	-	54	-	-	-	-
BellSouth Cl'	-	-	-	-	-	-	-	-	-	68
US Masters	-	-	-	-	12	12	24	-	-	-
Worldcom Cl'	-	-	-	-	-	62	43	-	-	MC
Houston Open	-	-	-	-	-	-	-	-	-	MC
GG Chrysler Cl'	-	-	-	-	-	-	-	31	-	MC
Compaq Classic	-	-	-	-	MC	MC	-	-	-	-
Byron Nelson C'	-	-	-	-	-	-	-	-	-	MC
MasterCard Cln'l	-	-	-	-	-	-	-	-	-	11
Kemper Ins Open	-	-	-	-	-	-	-	-	-	6
Memorial T'ment	-	-	-	-	MC	-	-	59	-	-
St. Jude Classic	-	-	-	-	-	-	-	-	-	30
U.S. Open	-	-	-	MC	-	25	MC	-	-	-
Buick Classic	-	-	-	-	-	-	-	-	-	19
Canon GH Open	-	-	-	-	-	-	-	-	-	MC
Western Open	-	-	-	-	-	-	-	-	-	MC
Gr. Milwaukee	-	-	-	-	-	-	-	-	-	-
British Open	68	-	60	15	MC	66	MC	MC	64	-
B.C. Open	-	-	-	-	-	-	-	-	-	-
John Deere Cl'	-	-	-	-	-	-	-	-	-	-
The International	-	-	-	-	19	-	-	-	-	-
Buick Open	-	-	-	-	-	-	-	-	-	MC
USPGA Champ	-	-	-	58	8	67	23	MC	-	-
WGCNEC Inv'	-	-	-	-	-	-	-	-	-	-
Reno-Tahoe Op'	-	-	-	-	-	-	-	-	-	MC
Air Canada Chp'	-	-	-	-	-	-	-	-	-	62
Bell Canadian O'	-	-	-	-	-	-	-	-	-	23
WGC AmEx	-	-	-	-	-	-	-	-	-	-
Tampa Bay Cl'	-	-	-	-	-	-	-	-	-	-
Marconi Penn C'	-	-	-	-	-	-	-	-	-	33
Texas Open	-	-	-	-	-	-	-	-	-	51
Michelob Chmp'	-	-	-	-	-	-	-	-	-	55
Invensys Classic	-	-	-	-	-	-	-	-	-	MC
NCR Golf Cl'	-	-	-	-	-	-	-	-	-	MC
Buick Challenge	-	-	-	-	-	-	-	-	-	7
SFB Classic	-	-	-	-	-	-	-	-	-	-
Tour Champ'ship	-	-	-	-	-	-	-	-	-	-

Jonathan Kaye
2/8/70 – Denver, CO

A first US Tour win still eludes this Colorado born pro, who once defeated Phil Mickelson in a prestigious amateur event in a play-off back in 1992. Kaye has competed in 150 full Tour events and has finished as runner-up twice. Had rotator cuff surgery in 1996 and missed most of the next 18 months. Last season was a disappointment after such an impressive 2000 – when 11 top-ten finishes helped to bring him his first $1million+ year. Kaye ranked in the top 20 of total driving last season and poor bunker play was the only blot on his stats copybook.

ScAv - 71.05 (84th) – DD - 283.4 (54th) DA - 70.0 (67th) GIR - 67.1 (73rd) – PpGIR - 1.766 (77th) SS - 47.5 (141st)

	'92	'93	'94	'95	'96	'97	'98	'99	'00	'01
WGC MatchPlay	-	-	-	-	-	-	-	-	-	33
Mercedes Ch	-	-	-	-	-	-	-	-	-	-
Tucson Open	-	-	-	-	MC	-	48	MC	17	32
Sony Open	-	-	-	27	-	-	-	38	MC	-
Phoenix Open	-	-	-	-	MC	-	41	33	MC	23
AT&T P Beach	-	-	-	MC	-	-	-	WD	35	23
Buick Invitatn'l	-	-	-	MC	-	-	MC	18	28	MC
Bob Hope Cl'	-	-	-	-	48	-	-	43	51	75
Nissan Open	-	-	-	MC	-	-	36	MC	43	-
Genuity Champ	-	-	-	-	-	-	-	52	-	MC
Honda Classic	-	-	-	MC	-	-	-	15	6	57
Bay Hill Invit'l	-	-	-	-	-	-	-	-	14	MC
Players Champ	-	-	-	-	-	-	-	-	MC	18
BellSouth Cl'	-	-	-	MC	-	-	-	23	73	-
US Masters	-	-	-	-	-	-	-	-	-	43
Worldcom Cl'	-	-	-	-	-	-	-	-	11	-
Houston Open	-	-	-	MC	-	-	MC	5	11	MC
GG Chrysler Cl'	-	-	-	-	-	-	67	63	5	36
Compaq Classic	-	-	-	-	MC	-	-	-	MC	53
Byron Nelson C'	-	-	-	MC	-	-	MC	MC	-	MC
MasterCard Cln'l	-	-	-	-	-	-	-	62	WD	34
Kemper Ins Open	-	-	-	-	-	-	42	28	28	MC
Memorial T'ment	-	-	-	-	-	-	-	-	25	30
St. Jude Classic	-	-	-	MC	-	-	56	18	65	MC
U.S. Open	-	-	-	-	-	-	-	-	MC	-
Buick Classic	-	-	-	MC	-	-	54	DQ	-	37
Canon GH Open	-	-	-	MC	-	-	47	26	18	29
Western Open	-	-	-	-	-	-	-	MC	-	31
Gr. Milwaukee	-	-	-	MC	-	-	MC	MC	-	18
British Open	-	-	-	-	-	-	-	-	-	-
B.C. Open	-	-	-	20	-	23	51	4	18	3
John Deere Cl'	-	-	-	2	-	-	MC	41	-	-
The International	-	-	-	MC	-	-	MC	29	61	59
Buick Open	-	-	-	9	-	-	29	54	MC	35
USPGA Champ	-	-	-	-	-	-	-	-	51	63
WGCNEC Inv'	-	-	-	-	-	-	-	-	-	-
Reno-Tahoe Op'	-	-	-	-	-	-	-	9	MC	36
Air Canada Chp'	-	-	-	-	-	-	MC	57	52	-
Bell Canadian O'	-	-	-	MC	-	-	-	37	-	-
WGC AmEx	-	-	-	-	-	-	-	-	-	-
Tampa Bay Cl'	-	-	-	-	-	-	-	-	-	-
Marconi Penn C'	-	-	-	-	-	-	-	-	-	-
Texas Open	-	-	-	MC	-	-	-	29	30	30
Michelob Chmp'	-	-	-	27	-	MC	39	MC	41	15
Invensys Classic	-	-	-	30	-	-	DQ	2	3	53
NCR Golf Cl'	-	-	-	-	-	-	-	17	MC	-
Buick Challenge	-	-	-	-	MC	-	-	-	MC	46
SFB Classic	-	-	-	11	-	-	18	6	36	-
Tour Champ'ship	-	-	-	-	-	-	-	-	-	-

Jerry Kelly
23/11/66 – Madison, WI

A former Buy.com Tour graduate who has still to win in six years on the US Tour. Kelly certainly had chances to break his duck in 2001. He had a lead going into the final round of the Players Championship but blew it and was second in the Reno Tahoe Open. He did win twice on the Buy.com Tour in 1995 (the Alabama Classic and the Buffalo Open) before graduating to the full tour and was Buy.com Tour player of the year in the same year. Has a solid all round game and was in good form with the flat stick in 2001.

ScAv - 70.51 (40th) – DD - 281.3 (77th) DA - 69.0 (84th) GIR - 69.4 (31st) – PpGIR - 1.735 (13th) SS - 49.1 (128th)

	'92	'93	'94	'95	'96	'97	'98	'99	'00	'01
WGC MatchPlay	-	-	-	-	-	-	-	-	-	-
Mercedes Ch	-	-	-	-	-	-	-	-	-	-
Tucson Open	-	-	-	-	64	10	18	45	MC	15
Sony Open	-	-	-	-	MC	-	-	55	9	29
Phoenix Open	-	-	-	-	-	48	MC	MC	MC	-
AT&T P Beach	-	-	MC	-	-	50	WD	53	4	8
Buick Invitatn'l	-	-	-	-	MC	MC	35	52	66	75
Bob Hope Cl'	-	-	-	-	49	52	35	40	46	26
Nissan Open	-	-	-	-	MC	MC	20	9	MC	8
Genuity Champ	-	-	-	-	4	20	MC	57	-	25
Honda Classic	-	-	-	-	MC	MC	22	-	MC	-
Bay Hill Invit'l	-	-	-	-	MC	MC	MC	MC	MC	-
Players Champ	-	-	-	-	MC	MC	31	MC	42	4
BellSouth Cl'	-	-	-	-	10	MC	14	MC	30	11
US Masters	-	-	-	-	-	-	-	-	-	-
Worldcom Cl'	-	-	-	-	MC	MC	39	18	15	MC
Houston Open	-	-	-	-	56	6	6	17	27	MC
GG Chrysler Cl'	-	-	-	-	MC	19	11	37	34	4
Compaq Classic	-	-	-	-	-	20	MC	12	-	18
Byron Nelson C'	-	-	-	-	MC	-	-	-	-	-
MasterCard Cln'l	-	-	-	-	71	MC	33	MC	50	MC
Kemper Ins Open	-	-	-	-	-	19	25	MC	MC	-
Memorial T'ment	-	-	-	-	56	MC	MC	-	25	MC
St. Jude Classic	-	-	-	-	-	MC	71	25	80	MC
U.S. Open	-	-	-	-	-	-	-	57	37	-
Buick Classic	-	-	-	-	73	69	WD	MC	-	56
Canon GH Open	-	-	-	-	MC	MC	MC	MC	-	7
Western Open	-	-	-	-	MC	35	MC	MC	41	5
Gr. Milwaukee	MC	MC	-	34	2	8	57	3	47	47
British Open	-	-	-	-	-	44	-	-	-	MC
B.C. Open	-	-	-	-	50	MC	MC	50	5	-
John Deere Cl'	-	-	-	-	-	-	-	30	12	-
The International	-	-	-	-	49	MC	-	61	-	45
Buick Open	-	-	-	-	MC	-	-	-	-	-
USPGA Champ	-	-	-	-	-	MC	WD	26	MC	44
WGCNEC Inv'	-	-	-	-	-	-	-	-	-	-
Reno-Tahoe Op'	-	-	-	-	-	-	-	-	17	2
Air Canada Chp'	-	-	-	-	MC	-	-	-	13	MC
Bell Canadian O'	-	-	-	-	MC	MC	MC	-	-	-
WGC AmEx	-	-	-	-	-	-	-	-	-	-
Tampa Bay Cl'	-	-	-	-	-	-	-	-	19	-
Marconi Penn C'	-	-	-	-	-	-	-	-	MC	58
Texas Open	-	-	-	-	-	-	-	-	14	MC
Michelob Chmp'	-	-	-	-	37	MC	MC	MC	-	55
Invensys Classic	-	-	-	-	MC	MC	70	15	MC	-
NCR Golf Cl'	-	-	-	-	8	33	MC	81	MC	MC
Buick Challenge	-	-	-	-	14	44	MC	25	18	MC
SFB Classic	-	-	-	-	-	-	7	42	13	37
Tour Champ'ship	-	-	-	-	-	-	-	-	-	-

Skip Kendall

9/9/64 – Milwaukee, WI

Last term's earnings pushed his career cash haul to over $4million but he has yet to post his first US Tour win in seven full years on the main tour. Kendall has won on the Buy.com Tour (twice – both in 1994 – the Inland Empire Open and the Carolina Classic), one year after losing his full tour playing privileges after a poor rookie season in 1993.

He posted just one top-ten finish in 2001 and in monetary terms last season was his worst in three years. He has been once of the best putters on tour over the past two years.

ScAv - 70.71 (56th) – DD - 273.1 (160th) DA - 73.5 (22nd) GIR - 67.0 (75th) – PpGIR - 1.730 (9th) SS - 56.4 (34th)

	'92	'93	'94	'95	'96	'97	'98	'99	'00	'01
WGC MatchPlay	-	-	-	-	-	-	-	-	-	33
Mercedes Ch	-	-	-	-	-	-	-	-	-	-
Tucson Open	-	MC	-	MC	-	MC	-	-	MC	-
Sony Open	-	77	32	42	-	MC	16	MC	MC	WD
Phoenix Open	-	69	-	51	-	-	14	44	MC	49
AT&T P Beach	-	44	-	MC	-	50	MC	15	31	MC
Buick Invitatn'l	-	MC	MC	-	-	9	2	30	28	58
Bob Hope Cl'	-	51	-	40	-	45	8	6	51	46
Nissan Open	-	MC	-	46	-	51	13	69	-	-
Genuity Champ	-	MC	-	43	-	56	MC	57	MC	25
Honda Classic	-	38	-	MC	-	65	MC	-	19	11
Bay Hill Invit'l	-	-	-	-	-	54	36	MC	3	23
Players Champ	-	-	-	-	-	68	10	MC	-	11
BellSouth Cl'	-	27	-	MC	-	MC	MC	16	-	11
US Masters	-	-	-	-	-	-	-	56	-	-
Worldcom Cl'	-	-	-	-	-	45	12	70	42	
Houston Open	-	MC	-	46	-	MC	11	64	29	MC
GG Chrysler Cl'	-	74	-	65	-	49	11	17	26	MC
Compaq Classic	-	69	-	60	-	MC	-	20	-	-
Byron Nelson C'	-	MC	-	MC	-	MC	-	-	41	MC
MasterCard Cln'l	-	-	-	-	-	18	30	13	46	
Kemper Ins Open	-	33	-	38	-	MC	-	MC	-	31
Memorial T'ment	-	-	-	-	-	MC	48	68	24	
St. Jude Classic	-	43	-	MC	-	22	43	-	-	
U.S. Open	MC	-	-	-	82	-	-	-	-	MC
Buick Classic	-	44	-	DQ	-	27	-	MC	33	19
Canon GH Open	-	MC	-	59	-	MC	-	2	32	MC
Western Open	-	72	-	MC	-	MC	17	55	55	52
Gr. Milwaukee	-	MC	-	71	MC	12	23	6	9	15
British Open	-	-	-	-	-	MC	-	-	-	-
B.C. Open	-	MC	-	7	-	58	9	12	-	-
John Deere Cl'	-	MC	MC	-	18	54	-	MC	-	-
The International	-	8	-	71	-	3	MC	24	MC	MC
Buick Open	-	27	-	40	-	49	36	19	11	14
USPGA Champ	-	-	-	-	-	-	10	21	27	63
WGCNEC Inv'	-	-	-	-	-	-	-	-	-	-
Reno-Tahoe Op'	-	-	-	-	-	-	-	-	-	MC
Air Canada Chp'	-	-	-	-	-	19	-	65	MC	-
Bell Canadian O'	-	68	-	MC	-	MC	-	-	-	-
WGC AmEx	-	-	-	-	-	-	-	-	-	-
Tampa Bay Cl'	-	-	-	-	-	-	-	27	-	-
Marconi Penn C'	-	-	-	-	-	-	-	-	41	MC
Texas Open	-	MC	-	MC	-	-	-	-	-	-
Michelob Chmp'	-	MC	52	MC	-	36	48	MC	-	19
Invensys Classic	-	-	MC	-	39	-	63	36	44	27	20
NCR Golf Cl'	-	17	-	37	-	33	43	MC	18	6
Buick Challenge	-	19	-	MC	-	37	5	66	55	23
SFB Classic	-	44	MC	28	-	13	-	WD	2	57
Tour Champ'ship	-	-	-	-	-	-	-	-	-	-

Neal Lancaster

13/9/62 – Smithfield, NC

His sole US Tour win came in 1994 when he defeated five others in the first six-man play-off in the tour's history. He birdied the first extra hole to land the Byron Nelson Classic.

Over the past two years he has relied upon one good finish to retain his playing privileges. Is usually extremely busy in the year, packing in over 30 tournaments each season.

Got on the tour the hard way by playing mini tours after turning pro in 1985. Putting was his Achilles Heel in 2001.

ScAv - 71.14 (90th) – DD - 275.9 (132nd) DA - 69.0 (84th) GIR - 68.0 (54th) – PpGIR - 1.792 (149th) SS - 55.7 (48th)

	'92	'93	'94	'95	'96	'97	'98	'99	'00	'01
WGC MatchPlay	-	-	-	-	-	-	-	-	-	-
Mercedes Ch	-	-	23	-	-	-	-	-	-	-
Tucson Open	71	34	69	32	MC	MC	MC	-	-	41
Sony Open	41	45	MC	-	31	-	-	MC	26	MC
Phoenix Open	67	MC	28	66	MC	MC	MC	MC	41	MC
AT&T P Beach	33	MC	MC	-	20	56	8	15	MC	
Buick Invitatn'l	MC	51	MC	-	71	45	35	35	21	MC
Bob Hope Cl'	15	24	MC	33	44	MC	29	MC	23	51
Nissan Open	32	58	61	MC	16	MC	36	56	MC	8
Genuity Champ	32	38	58	58	MC	28	23	15	WD	50
Honda Classic	-	MC	50	80	38	65	WD	-	MC	39
Bay Hill Invit'l	MC	-	-	69	-	-	-	44	4	-
Players Champ	40	MC	35	MC	53	MC	MC	MC	-	MC
BellSouth Cl'	19	38	44	33	7	42	-	36	MC	WD
US Masters	-	-	-	MC	MC	-	-	-	-	-
Worldcom Cl'	51	47	71	33	22	MC	24	MC	MC	55
Houston Open	MC	66	55	-	MC	15	MC	MC	53	WD
GG Chrysler Cl'	MC	MC	MC	61	MC	MC	4	12	34	36
Compaq Classic	6	6	MC	-	WD	66	30	28	WD	26
Byron Nelson C'	MC	73	1	MC	-	12	MC	MC	41	MC
MasterCard Cln'l	134	-	32	MC	-	46	-	73	DQ	67
Kemper Ins Open	MC	38	65	16	63	MC	MC	WD	76	WD
Memorial T'ment	48	-	MC	MC	-	16	-	68	-	
St. Jude Classic	MC	31	45	-	65	46	12	WD	MC	MC
U.S. Open	-	-	-	4	82	-	-	-	-	-
Buick Classic	50	MC	MC	-	43	51	-	41	-	MC
Canon GH Open	MC	-	MC	37	MC	20	MC	MC	80	
Western Open	29	MC	-	MC	55	MC	48	42	61	MC
Gr. Milwaukee	69	MC	MC	67	71	52	-	73	MC	36
British Open	-	-	-	-	-	-	-	-	-	-
B.C. Open	-	48	32	15	WD	69	MC	MC	63	DQ
John Deere Cl'	MC	55	23	-	-	WD	-	MC	8	15
The International	MC	22	MC	55	59	13	41	MC	31	MC
Buick Open	MC	9	-	DQ	-	MC	-	MC	57	43
USPGA Champ	84	-	44	-	52	-	MC	-	-	WGC-
NEC Inv'	-	-	-	-	-	-	-	-	-	-
Reno-Tahoe Op'	-	-	-	-	-	-	-	MC	-	19
Air Canada Chp'	-	-	-	-	MC	51	-	MC	-	37
Bell Canadian O'	MC	MC	-	61	-	WD	43	MC	-	55
WGC AmEx	-	-	-	-	-	-	-	-	-	-
Tampa Bay Cl'	-	-	-	-	-	-	-	-	56	-
Marconi Penn C'	-	-	-	-	-	-	-	-	78	MC
Texas Open	14	-	40	WD	-	MC	-	49	-	MC
Michelob Chmp'	70	79	-	MC	37	46	44	MC	MC	7
Invensys Classic	60	MC	45	MC	MC	58	-	MC	-	MC
NCR Golf Cl'	67	MC	-	-	18	33	MC	MC	MC	MC
Buick Challenge	57	11	52	34	14	MC	8	MC	MC	3
SFB Classic	-	-	5	57	39	36	-	13		
Tour Champ'ship	-	-	-	-	-	-	-	-	-	-

Bernhard Langer

27/8/57 – Anhausen, Germany

The veteran German was back to form in 2001 after a few years in the doldrums. He won twice on the European Tour and although he didn't add to his US Tour haul of three wins (including two Masters wins – 1985 and 1993), he did post seven top-ten finishes, including third in the prestigious Players Championship and tenth in the Tour Championship. Langer finished 22nd on the Money List – his best ever position. He will make his 10th Ryder Cup appearance in 2002 for the European team. Short off the tee, his putting was superb throughout the season.

ScAv - 69.89 (12th) – DD - 269.5 (179th) DA - 68.8 (91st) GIR - 68.4 (46th) – PpGIR - 1.729 (8th) SS - 52.4 (91st)

	'92	'93	'94	'95	'96	'97	'98	'99	'00	'01
WGC MatchPlay	-	-	-	-	-	-	-	9	33	33
Mercedes Ch	-	-	-	-	-	-	-	-	-	-
Tucson Open	-	-	-	-	-	-	-	-	-	9
Sony Open	-	-	-	-	-	-	-	-	-	-
Phoenix Open	-	-	-	-	-	-	-	-	-	-
AT&T P Beach	-	-	-	-	-	-	-	-	-	MC
Buick Invitatn'l	-	-	-	-	-	-	-	-	-	25
Bob Hope Cl'	-	-	-	-	-	-	-	-	-	-
Nissan Open	-	-	-	-	-	-	-	-	-	-
Genuity Champ	-	-	40	MC	-	21	62	36	40	
Honda Classic	-	-	4	13	MC	26	22	MC	28	27
Bay Hill Invit'l	70	6	21	31	13	22	4	72	18	34
Players Champ	29	2	27	2	-	31	MC	38	42	3
BellSouth Cl'	-	-	-	-	-	-	-	-	-	-
US Masters	31	1	25	31	36	7	39	11	28	6
Worldcom Cl'	-	16	-	-	-	-	-	-	-	3
Houston Open	-	-	-	-	-	-	-	-	-	-
GG Chrysler Cl'	-	-	-	-	-	-	-	-	-	-
Compaq Classic	-	-	-	-	-	-	-	-	-	-
Byron Nelson C'	-	-	-	-	-	-	-	-	-	-
MasterCard Cln'l	-	-	-	-	-	-	-	-	-	-
Kemper Ins Open	-	-	-	-	-	-	-	-	-	-
Memorial T'ment	-	-	-	-	-	-	-	-	-	-
St. Jude Classic	-	-	-	-	-	-	-	-	-	2
U.S. Open	23	MC	23	36	DQ	MC	MC	-	MC	40
Buick Classic	-	-	-	-	-	-	MC	-	-	-
Canon GH Open	-	-	-	-	-	-	-	-	-	-
Western Open	-	-	-	-	-	-	-	-	-	-
Gr. Milwaukee	-	-	-	-	-	-	-	-	-	-
British Open	59	3	60	24	WD	38	MC	18	11	3
B.C. Open	-	-	-	-	-	-	-	-	-	-
John Deere Cl'	-	-	-	-	-	-	-	-	-	-
The International	-	-	-	-	-	-	-	-	-	-
Buick Open	-	-	-	-	-	-	-	-	-	-
USPGA Champ	40	MC	25	-	76	23	-	61	46	MC
WGCNEC Inv'	-	-	-	-	-	-	-	-	-	11
Reno-Tahoe Op'	-	-	-	-	-	-	-	-	-	-
Air Canada Chp'	-	-	-	-	-	-	-	-	-	-
Bell Canadian O'	-	-	-	-	-	-	-	-	-	-
WGC AmEx	-	-	-	-	-	-	48	35	-	-
Tampa Bay Cl'	-	-	-	-	-	-	-	-	-	-
Marconi Penn C'	-	-	-	-	-	-	-	-	-	-
Texas Open	-	-	-	-	-	-	-	-	-	-
Michelob Chmp'	-	-	-	-	-	-	-	-	-	-
Invensys Classic	-	-	-	-	-	-	-	-	-	-
NCR Golf Cl'	-	-	-	-	-	-	-	-	-	36
Buick Challenge	-	-	-	-	-	-	-	-	-	-
SFB Classic	-	-	-	-	-	-	-	-	-	-
Tour Champ'ship	-	-	-	-	-	-	-	-	-	10

Tom Lehman

7/5/69 – Austin, MN

Hasn't finished outside the top 33 in the Money List in the last ten years on the US Tour. Lehman was named the Player of the Year in 1996 after his Open win, which helped him to top the Money List. He didn't add to his five US Tour wins in 2001 but was runner-up twice – pushing his career earnings to over $12million.

His early career in America wasn't so lucrative and he went to play in Asia and South Africa in the '80s before returning to the tour in 1992. An accurate iron player who can also hit his drives a long way.

ScAv - 70.05 (16th) – DD - 286.7 (25th) DA - 68.6 (97th) GIR - 74.5 (1st) – PpGIR - 1.782 (123rd) SS - 55.4 (54th)

	'92	'93	'94	'95	'96	'97	'98	'99	'00	'01
WGC MatchPlay	-	-	-	-	-	-	-	33	17	9
Mercedes Ch	-	-	5	12	2	-	-	-	-	26
Tucson Open	-	-	-	-	-	6	-	-	-	-
Sony Open	5	30	14	2	4	6	69	-	6	2
Phoenix Open	16	9	6	22	MC	7	14	-	1	7
AT&T P Beach	4	28	6	MC	-	20	9	-	7	MC
Buick Invitatn'l	6	15	13	-	3	-	-	-	-	13
Bob Hope Cl'	8	60	-	-	-	-	-	-	-	-
Nissan Open	39	WD	15	-	6	-	36	-	MC	-
Genuity Champ	13	-	-	-	-	-	-	-	-	-
Honda Classic	29	-	31	-	30	-	80	-	-	27
Bay Hill Invit'l	58	MC	6	37	9	MC	22	2	22	43
Players Champ	13	11	MC	14	8	6	2	MC	8	12
BellSouth Cl'	MC	-	-	-	-	-	-	-	-	-
US Masters	-	3	2	40	18	12	MC	31	6	18
Worldcom Cl'	26	8	18	24	13	4	14	36	2	28
Houston Open	-	-	-	-	-	-	-	-	-	-
GG Chrysler Cl'	27	27	-	11	-	-	5	16	-	
Compaq Classic	-	-	-	10	-	MC	-	-	-	-
Byron Nelson C'	-	67	MC	-	-	-	MC	MC	-	MC
MasterCard Cln'l	MC	11	5	1	MC	MC	-	26	-	50
Kemper Ins Open	MC	-	-	33	66	-	13	-	-	
Memorial T'ment	42	MC	1	29	30	26	11	19	41	-
St. Jude Classic	MC	-	-	-	-	-	2	-	3	
U.S. Open	6	19	33	3	2	3	5	28	23	24
Buick Classic	-	5	-	14	2	-	3	35	MC	DQ
Canon GH Open	WD	-	-	-	-	-	62	-	-	
Western Open	9	MC	52	-	18	52	-	-	55	31
Gr. Milwaukee	3	-	-	-	-	-	2	-	-	
British Open	-	59	24	-	1	24	MC	MC	4	MC
B.C. Open	-	-	-	-	-	-	MC	-	-	
John Deere Cl'	2	39	6	-	-	-	-	-	-	
The International	26	-	13	14	5	25	MC	-	WD	-
Buick Open	-	MC	8	9	-	-	2	-	MC	
USPGA Champ	MC	39	MC	14	10	29	34	WD	MC	
WGCNEC Inv'	-	-	-	-	-	-	15	31	-	
Reno-Tahoe Op'	-	-	-	-	-	-	-	-	-	-
Air Canada Chp'	-	-	-	-	-	-	-	-	-	-
Bell Canadian O'	20	3	-	7	-	-	-	-	-	
WGC AmEx	-	-	-	-	-	25	-	-		
Tampa Bay Cl'	-	-	-	-	-	-	-	-	-	-
Marconi Penn C'	-	-	-	-	-	-	28	-	-	
Texas Open	-	5	-	-	MC	-	-	-	-	
Michelob Chmp'	5	-	-	-	25	-	-	-		
Invensys Classic	40	17	59	-	53	-	2			
NCR Golf Cl'	20	50	-	-	10	15	57	-	13	
Buick Challenge	23	6	-	-	-	-	-	-	-	
SFB Classic	-	-	-	-	-	-	-	-	-	-
Tour Champ'ship	13	-	28	12	1	15	15	15	18	15

Sponsored by Stan James

Justin Leonard
15/6/72 – Dallas, TX

Even though he has won a Major championship (the Open in 1997), he will always be known for his dance across the 17th green in the Ryder Cup at Brookline in 1999, after holing a monster putt that effectively won his singles match against Jose Maria Olazabal. His second successive Texas Open win in 2001 was his sixth US Tour victory. Former US Amateur champion and two-time Ryder Cup player. Made significant changes to his swing in 2001. He is still short off the tee but the rest of his game is solid and he showed fine form with the flat stick last term.

ScAv - 70.68 (52nd) – DD - 275.7 (135th) DA - 70.5 (59th) GIR - 66.9 (78th) – PpGIR - 1.742 (25th) SS - 51.6 (102nd)

	'92	'93	'94	'95	'96	'97	'98	'99	'00	'01
WGC MatchPlay	-	-	-	-	-	-	-	17	17	9
Mercedes Ch	-	-	-	-	-	22	25	5	-	8
Tucson Open	-	-	-	MC	27	27	2	-	-	-
Sony Open	-	-	-	MC	-	-	-	-	-	-
Phoenix Open	-	-	-	MC	2	MC	27	2	23	MC
AT&T P Beach	-	-	-	43	-	65	45	4	15	MC
Buick Invitatn'l	-	-	-	-	MC	MC	-	-	-	-
Bob Hope Cl'	-	-	-	14	61	-	-	-	36	40
Nissan Open	-	-	-	52	MC	51	MC	15	MC	68
Genuity Champ	-	-	-	4	38	MC	MC	15	-	58
Honda Classic	-	-	-	31	-	-	-	-	-	-
Bay Hill Invit'l	-	MC	-	MC	MC	38	42	16	-	MC
Players Champ	-	-	-	34	65	37	1	23	22	MC
BellSouth Cl'	-	-	-	61	-	-	-	63	-	-
US Masters	-	MC	-	27	7	8	18	28	27	-
Worldcom Cl'	-	-	-	44	42	30	56	MC	-	MC
Houston Open	-	52	-	32	MC	15	-	17	MC	4
GG Chrysler Cl'	-	-	-	14	-	-	-	16	-	-
Compaq Classic	-	-	-	39	MC	43	-	-	-	-
Byron Nelson C'	-	56	-	26	23	27	35	12	MC	6
MasterCard Cln'l	-	71	-	5	10	13	8	39	61	5
Kemper Ins Open	-	-	-	4	13	1	25	22	2	54
Memorial T'ment	-	-	-	MC	21	46	16	7	2	30
St. Jude Classic	-	-	MC	53	4	5	MC	-	-	-
U.S. Open	-	68	-	-	50	36	40	15	16	MC
Buick Classic	-	-	-	-	-	-	-	22	-	56
Canon GH Open	-	-	MC	MC	-	-	31	3	MC	-
Western Open	-	25	26	2	8	3	9	20	-	20
Gr. Milwaukee	-	-	MC	17	-	-	-	-	-	-
British Open	-	MC	-	58	MC	1	57	2	42	MC
B.C. Open	-	-	MC	-	-	-	-	-	-	-
John Deere Cl'	-	-	MC	-	-	-	-	-	-	-
The International	-	-	MC	62	5	39	-	57	20	-
Buick Open	-	-	-	17	1	49	MC	25	MC	10
USPGA Champ	-	-	-	8	5	2	MC	MC	41	10
WGCNEC Inv'	-	-	-	-	-	-	-	20	2	-
Reno-Tahoe Op'	-	-	-	-	-	-	-	-	-	5
Air Canada Chp'	-	-	-	-	-	-	-	-	-	-
Bell Canadian O'	-	-	MC	29	64	6	-	3	26	55
WGC AmEx	-	-	-	-	-	-	-	11	25	-
Tampa Bay Cl'	-	-	-	-	-	-	-	-	14	-
Marconi Penn C'	-	-	-	-	-	-	-	-	-	-
Texas Open	-	-	15	2	11	-	2	-	1	1
Michelob Chmp'	-	-	3	-	-	MC	25	-	-	MC
Invensys Classic	-	-	-	23	50	-	6	19	22	58
NCR Golf Cl'	-	-	-	-	-	-	-	-	-	-
Buick Challenge	-	-	19	18	MC	-	24	13	MC	62
SFB Classic	-	-	MC	-	-	-	-	-	-	-
Tour Champ'ship	-	-	-	7	6	8	5	12	16	22

J.L. Lewis
18/7/60 – Emporia, KS

Gained his third $1/2million haul on the spin in 2001 but still has just one US Tour win to his name – the 1999 John Deere Classic. Gave up the game in the '80s to work as a club pro but came back to the full tour in 1989 and had spells on the Buy.com Tour before establishing himself on the main tour in 1998. Played full time on the Buy.com Tour in 1997 finishing seventh in the Money List.

Recorded his best finish in 2001 at the Texas Open. One of the longer hitters on tour but the rest of his figures left a lot to be desired last season.

ScAv - 71.15 (93rd) – DD - 283.3 (57th) DA - 65.7 (141st) GIR - 65.0 (137th) – PpGIR - 1.786 (129th) SS - 55.2 (59th)

	'92	'93	'94	'95	'96	'97	'98	'99	'00	'01
WGC MatchPlay	-	-	-	-	-	-	-	-	-	-
Mercedes Ch	-	-	-	-	-	-	-	27	-	-
Tucson Open	-	-	-	-	-	-	69	MC	-	MC
Sony Open	-	-	-	62	-	-	MC	MC	58	37
Phoenix Open	-	-	-	-	-	-	-	52	MC	-
AT&T P Beach	-	-	MC	-	-	-	WD	MC	MC	-
Buick Invitatn'l	-	-	-	69	-	-	6	MC	38	20
Bob Hope Cl'	-	-	-	40	-	-	MC	MC	3	11
Nissan Open	-	-	-	MC	-	-	MC	MC	-	33
Genuity Champ	-	-	-	-	-	-	MC	-	15	25
Honda Classic	-	-	MC	-	-	-	MC	MC	61	-
Bay Hill Invit'l	-	-	-	-	-	-	-	-	29	56
Players Champ	-	-	-	-	-	-	MC	MC	MC	73
BellSouth Cl'	-	-	-	33	-	-	50	55	MC	69
US Masters	-	-	-	-	-	-	-	-	-	-
Worldcom Cl'	-	-	MC	-	-	-	-	MC	WD	-
Houston Open	MC	41	47	MC	MC	-	MC	MC	-	MC
GG Chrysler Cl'	-	-	-	MC	-	-	MC	9	-	MC
Compaq Classic	-	-	-	44	-	-	MC	MC	-	26
Byron Nelson C'	-	-	-	41	-	-	MC	73	41	28
MasterCard Cln'l	-	-	-	-	-	-	-	-	33	40
Kemper Ins Open	-	-	-	56	-	-	36	MC	-	-
Memorial T'ment	-	-	-	-	-	-	-	-	33	-
St. Jude Classic	-	-	MC	-	-	-	MC	MC	-	30
U.S. Open	-	-	-	40	-	-	-	-	MC	30
Buick Classic	-	-	-	60	-	-	MC	46	-	19
Canon GH Open	-	-	MC	-	-	-	36	-	44	50
Western Open	-	-	-	-	-	-	53	27	29	57
Gr. Milwaukee	-	-	34	-	-	-	34	46	MC	-
British Open	-	-	-	-	-	-	-	-	-	-
B.C. Open	-	-	MC	-	-	-	MC	-	-	-
John Deere Cl'	-	-	MC	-	52	-	MC	1	50	61
The International	-	-	MC	-	-	-	MC	45	MC	MC
Buick Open	-	-	17	-	-	-	23	63	-	MC
USPGA Champ	-	MC	MC	-	-	-	21	-	-	-
WGCNEC Inv'	-	-	-	-	-	-	-	-	-	-
Reno-Tahoe Op'	-	-	-	-	-	-	-	24	65	55
Air Canada Chp'	-	-	-	-	-	-	MC	-	11	MC
Bell Canadian O'	-	-	MC	-	-	-	65	-	10	71
WGC AmEx	-	-	-	-	-	-	-	-	-	-
Tampa Bay Cl'	-	-	-	-	-	-	-	-	MC	-
Marconi Penn C'	-	-	-	-	-	-	-	-	-	46
Texas Open	MC	77	DQ	MC	18	-	20	12	19	8
Michelob Chmp'	-	-	-	MC	-	-	13	35	-	-
Invensys Classic	-	-	MC	-	-	-	61	43	27	MC
NCR Golf Cl'	-	-	-	MC	-	-	14	41	69	
Buick Challenge	-	-	-	34	-	-	4	MC	55	72
SFB Classic	-	-	MC	-	-	-	56	23	55	MC
Tour Champ'ship	-	-	-	-	-	-	-	-	-	-

Frank Lickliter II

28/7/69 – Middletown, OH

Last season proved to be a breakthrough year for this former Buy.com Tour graduate. He won his first US Tour event – the Kemper Open – despite a shaky finish, and his haul of nearly $2million was more than he had won in his last two seasons on tour put together. He just missed out on a Ryder Cup place. Since stepping up from the Buy.com Tour in 1997 Lickliter has been placed in the top 50 of the Money List four times. He won on the Buy.com Tour in 1995 (Boise Open) and turned pro in 1991. Has a solid all-round game and shone on the greens in 2001.

ScAv - 70.28 (26th) – DD - 284.7 (38th) DA - 70.5 (59th) GIR - 68.4 (46th) – PpGIR - 1.737 (16th) SS - 49.0 (129th)

	'92	'93	'94	'95	'96	'97	'98	'99	'00	'01
WGC MatchPlay	-	-	-	-	-	-	-	-	-	-
Mercedes Ch										
Tucson Open	-	-	-	MC	MC					
Sony Open	-	-	-	39	41	7	MC	67	63	
Phoenix Open	-	-	-	-	8	MC	10	18		
AT&T P Beach	-	-	-	38	MC	2	MC	59		
Buick Invitat'l	-	-	MC	45	76	11	48	2		
Bob Hope Cl'	-	-	-	-	67	61	28	7		
Nissan Open	-	-	MC	42	20	9	MC	MC		
Genuity Champ	-	-	-	75						
Honda Classic	-	-	65	MC						
Bay Hill Invit'l	-	-	-	55	19	52	23			
Players Champ	-	-	-	MC	23	48	7			
BellSouth Cl'	-	-	7	MC	36	MC	69	40		
US Masters	-	-	-	-	MC	-				
Worldcom Cl'	-	-	-	6	49	25	MC			
Houston Open	-	-	MC	MC	-	10	38	26		
GG Chrysler Cl'	-	-	35	MC	MC	-	MC			
Compaq Classic	-	-	42	MC	51	28	30	8		
Byron Nelson C'	-	-	MC	MC	63	60	-	28		
MasterCard Cln'l	-	-	-	MC	MC	-				
Kemper Ins Open	-	-	79	MC	-	-	56	1		
Memorial T'ment	-	-	-	61	14	39	MC			
St. Jude Classic	-	-	44	68	-	10	-	-		
U.S. Open	-	MC	-	67	MC	18	-	MC	52	
Buick Classic	-	MC	67	78	-	MC				
Canon GH Open	-	61	40	70	17	66	7			
Western Open	-	MC	MC	17	17	9	10			
Gr. Milwaukee	-	12	8	MC	62	9	28			
British Open	-	-	-	-	-	37				
B.C. Open	-	MC	-	23	-	-				
John Deere Cl'	-	5	13	30	23	-				
The International	-	MC	60	MC	33	MC	-			
Buick Open	-	MC	MC	DQ	-	10				
USPGA Champ	-	-	4	MC	-	51				
WGCNEC Inv'										
Reno-Tahoe Op'	-	-	37	MC	-					
Air Canada Chp'	-	MC	MC							
Bell Canadian O'	-	20	4	MC	-	MC	WD			
WGC AmEx										
Tampa Bay Cl'	-	-	3							
Marconi Penn C'	-	-	12	MC						
Texas Open	-	MC	62	20	MC	5	MC			
Michelob Chmp'	-	17	MC	6	24	3	MC			
Invensys Classic	-	50	MC	MC	28	-				
NCR Golf Cl'	-	51	17	MC	MC	MC	MC			
Buick Challenge	-	40	MC	20	70	63	38			
SFB Classic	-	MC	19	-	36	29	-			
Tour Champ'ship	-	-	-	20						

Davis Love III

13/4/64 – Charlotte, NC

Finally got back in the winner's enclosure after an absence of two seasons by coming from behind to land the AT&T Pebble Beach Pro-Am. His victory was his 14th US Tour title – including one Major (the 1997 USPGA Championship). His last win prior his 2001 victory was the 1998 MCI (now WorldCom) Classic. His first success came in the same event in 1987. He will line up for the Americans in the 2002 Ryder Cup – his fifth appearance. Love has also represented the USA in the Dunhill Cup and the Presidents Cup. A big hitter and strong iron player.

ScAv - 69.06 (2nd) – DD - 297.6 (3rd) DA - 64.5 (163rd) GIR - 70.3 (19th) – PpGIR - 1.758 (60th) SS - 55.8 (43rd)

	'92	'93	'94	'95	'96	'97	'98	'99	'00	'01
WGC MatchPlay	-	-	-	-	-	-	-	33	4	-
Mercedes Ch	7	1	4	-	6	6	13	8	-	-
Tucson Open	-	-	-	-	-	-	-	-	-	-
Sony Open	-	7	2	-	-	-	-	-	2	10
Phoenix Open	52	-	-	-	59	-	-	2	18	33
AT&T P Beach	MC	28	24	3	-	58	22	10	20	1
Buick Invitat'l	38	-	12	1	59	3	MC	4	2	-
Bob Hope Cl'	8	12	52	-	-	-	-	-	28	-
Nissan Open	2	MC	-	35	-	WD	-	2	-	8
Genuity Champ	4	53	69	4	MC	-	7	-	-	6
Honda Classic	-	4	-	-	-	-	-	19	-	-
Bay Hill Invit'l	8	2	36	16	13	9	17	3	2	-
Players Champ	1	67	6	6	46	DQ	57	10	48	MC
BellSouth Cl'	-	20	11	22	17	-	-	7	-	11
US Masters	25	54	MC	2	7	7	33	2	7	MC
Worldcom Cl'	1	MC	MC	68	4	9	1	WD	3	7
Houston Open	38	-	-	-	-	-	-	-	-	-
GG Chrysler Cl'	1	27	MC	19	-	6	-	-	21	-
Compaq Classic	-	-	1	4	11	27	-	-	-	-
Byron Nelson C'	39	11	-	-	64	64	-	-	2	-
MasterCard Cln'l	65	42	58	5	70	-	11	2	-	-
Kemper Ins Open	-	4	-	19	-	-	-	-	-	-
Memorial T'ment	19	10	45	53	6	10	5	MC	-	-
St. Jude Classic	-	23	MC	-	67	-	MC	10	-	-
U.S. Open	60	33	28	4	2	16	MC	12	MC	7
Buick Classic	14	-	38	-	-	-	17	-	33	-
Canon GH Open	-	11	-	-	-	-	-	14	MC	MC
Western Open	MC	-	MC	60	55	7	-	-	-	2
Gr. Milwaukee										
British Open	MC	MC	38	98	MC	10	8	7	11	21
B.C. Open	-	-	MC	-	-	-	-	-	-	-
John Deere Cl'										
The International	MC	-	55	8	54	12	21	37	-	-
Buick Open	-	27	11	-	MC	-	-	MC	-	-
USPGA Champ	33	31	MC	MC	MC	1	7	49	9	37
WGCNEC Inv'								10	35	5
Reno-Tahoe Op'										
Air Canada Chp'										
Bell Canadian O'	MC	31	-	-	6	-	-	42	-	
WGC AmEx	-	-	-	-	-	-	-	16	-	
Tampa Bay Cl'	-	-	-							
Marconi Penn C'	-	-								
Texas Open	-	-	-							
Michelob Chmp'	34	38								
Invensys Classic	3	1	MC	7	2	30	5	-	40	4
NCR Golf Cl'	24	15	-	MC	-	2	-	13	2	-
Buick Challenge	14	-	60	-	2	1	14	3	18	5
SFB Classic										
Tour Champ'ship	25	27	-	16	13	2	8	2	8	15

Sponsored by Stan James

Steve Lowery

12/10/60 – Birmingham, AL

Another consistent season in 2001 and his second best ranking (27th) on the Money List since turning pro in 1983. Managed runners-up position in the Air Canada Championship but didn't add to his two full tour wins (1994 Sprint International, 2000 Southern Farm Bureau Classic). Pushed his career earnings to over $6million in 2001 (courtesy of his seasonal haul of $1.7m). Had a spell on the Buy.com Tour in the early '90s (winning once – the 1992 Tulsa Open) before joining the full tour. Has a solid all round game – his bunker play the one weakness.

ScAv - 70.65 (48th) – DD - 280.7 (80th) DA - 70.9 (52nd) GIR - 68.2 (50th) – PpGIR - 1.761 (65th) SS - 45.5 (157th)

	'92	'93	'94	'95	'96	'97	'98	'99	'00	'01
WGC MatchPlay	-	-	-	-	-	-	-	-	-	33
Mercedes Ch	-	-	-	22	-	-	-	-	-	33
Tucson Open	MC	41	MC	-	35	48	4	20	7	-
Sony Open	-	18	MC	42	MC	-	-	MC	58	22
Phoenix Open	-	11	MC	7	MC	34	WD	40	MC	3
AT&T P Beach	-	-	21	-	38	-	-	MC	-	-
Buick Invitatn'l	-	74	2	26	MC	9	MC	MC	52	54
Bob Hope Cl'	-	74	56	-	MC	41	24	MC	-	-
Nissan Open	-	14	38	14	40	MC	MC	56	MC	63
Genuity Champ	-	MC	61	10	MC	28	-	-	MC	40
Honda Classic	-	-	-	-	-	MC	MC	-	-	-
Bay Hill Invit'l	75	56	52	MC	13	MC	22	37	22	4
Players Champ	-	-	6	DQ	46	65	MC	MC	66	MC
BellSouth Cl'	MC	18	51	-	-	MC	-	-	MC	-
US Masters	-	-	-	MC	41	-	-	-	-	40
Worldcom Cl'	-	-	60	7	MC	42	34	MC	11	42
Houston Open	45	75	-	-	-	-	-	73	7	-
GG Chrysler Cl'	-	MC	15	51	MC	MC	48	23	-	-
Compaq Classic	-	20	MC	24	4	7	3	45	MC	8
Byron Nelson C'	-	33	65	11	36	MC	MC	41	33	62
MasterCard Cln'1	-	71	47	33	56	MC	69	55	-	-
Kemper Ins Open	18	55	-	42	-	-	-	-	2	31
Memorial T'ment	-	-	11	-	11	26	23	MC	5	66
St. Jude Classic	-	MC	-	-	-	12	-	-	-	-
U.S. Open	-	33	16	56	60	-	-	MC	-	24
Buick Classic	-	MC	-	14	-	MC	9	66	10	MC
Canon GH Open	-	16	20	-	37	MC	MC	MC	32	-
Western Open	-	MC	MC	6	MC	3	MC	61	20	MC
Gr. Milwaukee	-	66	-	6	9	MC	-	4	-	10
British Open	-	-	-	79	-	-	-	-	-	-
B.C. Open	-	-	51	28	-	54	39	-	-	-
John Deere Cl'	-	55	-	-	MC	-	MC	77	5	15
The International	-	52	1	MC	23	WD	WD	MC	57	MC
Buick Open	-	27	MC	-	85	-	-	-	-	-
USPGA Champ	-	MC	8	MC	58	44	-	-	51	3
WGCNEC Inv'	-	-	-	-	-	-	-	-	-	-
Reno-Tahoe Op'	-	-	-	-	-	-	MC	65	-	-
Air Canada Chp'	-	-	-	-	-	-	-	10	13	2
Bell Canadian O'	-	22	48	45	48	-	67	20	-	-
WGC AmEx	-	-	-	-	-	-	-	-	-	-
Tampa Bay Cl'	-	-	-	-	-	-	-	-	6	-
Marconi Penn C'	-	-	-	-	-	-	-	-	-	46
Texas Open	-	66	-	MC	22	14	4	-	44	-
Michelob Chmp'	-	MC	-	-	32	11	-	-	MC	-
Invensys Classic	-	68	MC	59	19	40	MC	64	17	MC
NCR Golf Cl'	-	55	MC	21	51	42	MC	11	8	59
Buick Challenge	-	MC	-	24	30	3	MC	67	-	23
SFB Classic	22	65	37	-	4	27	-	1	-	-
Tour Champ'ship	-	8	-	-	-	-	-	-	-	25

Jeff Maggert

20/2/64 – Columbia, MO

Had his best season in his career when he won over $2million in 1999, helped by winning the inaugural WGC Matcplay that was worth $1million alone. Managed only one victory prior to that – the 1993 Walt Disney (now NCR) Classic. Last season saw Maggert place 72nd on the Money List – his lowest position since joining the tour full time in 1992. Has represented the USA on three occasions in the Ryder Cup (1995, 1997 and 1999) and is a tough matchplay performer. His putting has improved in 2001 but he has lost some accuracy off the tee.

ScAv - 71.14 (90th) – DD - 279.4 (99th) DA - 71.5 (42nd) GIR - 67.5 (64th) – PpGIR - 1.767 (81st) SS - 48.4 (135th)

	'92	'93	'94	'95	'96	'97	'98	'99	'00	'01
WGC MatchPlay	-	-	-	-	-	-	-	1	33	-
Mercedes Ch	-	-	4	-	-	-	-	-	16	-
Tucson Open	MC	2	-	25	49	5	MC	-	-	9
Sony Open	3	4	8	MC	MC	-	27	2	9	37
Phoenix Open	-	11	3	MC	-	30	55	-	23	-
AT&T P Beach	12	MC	2	21	-	MC	WD	39	MC	69
Buick Invitatn'l	-	-	-	-	MC	-	-	21	-	-
Bob Hope Cl'	14	-	-	-	7	61	-	7	-	11
Nissan Open	-	6	66	-	-	17	-	-	MC	13
Genuity Champ	MC	MC	-	-	MC	MC	MC	-	-	MC
Honda Classic	29	MC	-	-	-	-	4	-	-	MC
Bay Hill Invit'l	MC	-	47	16	2	19	2	37	-	-
Players Champ	54	MC	3	18	53	MC	51	46	3	MC
BellSouth Cl'	25	-	-	MC	-	-	-	-	-	54
US Masters	-	21	50	MC	7	MC	23	MC	MC	20
Worldcom Cl'	12	-	15	-	8	MC	-	27	-	-
Houston Open	45	11	2	19	2	52	2	33	17	MC
GG Chrysler Cl'	48	MC	-	47	-	-	16	3	MC	4
Compaq Classic	4	MC	-	5	-	MC	-	-	MC	-
Byron Nelson C'	39	MC	50	32	10	-	57	-	MC	MC
MasterCard Cln'1	30	3	56	8	MC	15	18	-	-	MC
Kemper Ins Open	-	18	-	31	-	19	-	44	-	MC
Memorial T'ment	12	12	9	MC	21	67	64	-	MC	-
St. Jude Classic	MC	2	-	WD	-	-	MC	36	-	MC
U.S. Open	-	52	9	4	97	4	7	7	MC	44
Buick Classic	26	38	8	-	2	2	5	18	MC	-
Canon GH Open	-	-	-	-	-	2	-	MC	-	-
Western Open	38	MC	17	2	55	MC	-	-	6	63
Gr. Milwaukee	-	-	-	-	-	-	-	-	-	-
British Open	MC	MC	24	68	5	51	MC	30	41	MC
B.C. Open	-	-	-	-	-	-	-	-	-	-
John Deere Cl'	-	14	-	5	-	-	-	-	-	-
The International	MC	-	55	-	MC	-	-	-	63	-
Buick Open	35	MC	-	70	22	42	-	33	6	8
USPGA Champ	6	51	MC	3	73	3	44	MC	MC	MC
WGCNEC Inv'	-	-	-	-	-	-	-	7	24	-
Reno-Tahoe Op'	-	-	-	-	-	-	-	-	-	MC
Air Canada Chp'	-	-	-	-	18	51	5	-	-	MC
Bell Canadian O'	-	MC	59	-	-	-	-	-	-	-
WGC AmEx	-	-	-	-	-	-	-	48	39	-
Tampa Bay Cl'	-	-	-	-	-	-	-	-	19	-
Marconi Penn C'	-	-	-	-	-	-	-	-	8	-
Texas Open	3	32	MC	38	36	49	8	-	-	45
Michelob Chmp'	-	-	-	-	-	-	-	-	-	MC
Invensys Classic	MC	MC	MC	MC	-	-	-	-	40	38
NCR Golf Cl'	71	1	MC	-	29	10	MC	-	41	-
Buick Challenge	MC	-	-	-	-	-	8	13	2	6
SFB Classic	-	-	-	-	-	-	-	-	-	28
Tour Champ'ship	-	15	7	-	27	29	16	20	-	-

Shigeki Maruyama

12/9/69 – Chiba, Japan

Became the first Japanese player to win a US Tour event on the American mainland when capturing the Greater Milwaukee Open title in 2001. Last season was only his second on the US Tour after a very successful career on the J-Tour – including nine tour wins in his native country. A regular for the International side in the Presidents Cup (in 1998 he won all five matches) he once shot 58 in qualifying for the US Open (2000). Makes lots of birdies and eagles but not as long off the tee in 2001 as he was in the previous season.

ScAv - 70.42 (37th) – DD - 279.9 (90th) DA - 65.3 (148th) GIR - 65.6 (107th) – PpGIR - 1.750 (39th) SS - 58.8 (21st)

	'92	'93	'94	'95	'96	'97	'98	'99	'00	'01
WGC MatchPlay	-	-	-	-	-	-	-	5	9	5
Mercedes Ch	-	-	-	-	-	-	-	-	-	-
Tucson Open	-	-	-	-	-	-	-	-	-	-
Sony Open	-	-	-	-	-	-	MC	9	22	
Phoenix Open	-	-	-	-	-	-	-	61	19	
AT&T P Beach	-	-	-	-	-	63	-	-	-	-
Buick Invitatn'l	-	-	-	-	-	-	-	-	2	13
Bob Hope Cl'	-	-	-	-	-	-	-	-	-	-
Nissan Open	-	-	MC	MC	-	-	59	-	MC	57
Genuity Champ	-	-	-	-	-	-	-	-	4	63
Honda Classic	-	-	-	-	-	-	-	-	-	-
Bay Hill Invit'l	-	-	-	-	-	-	-	18	-	-
Players Champ	-	-	-	-	-	MC	MC	WD	-	
BellSouth Cl'	-	-	-	-	-	-	-	10	-	27
US Masters	-	-	-	-	-	MC	31	46	MC	
Worldcom Cl'	-	-	-	-	-	-	-	MC	-	
Houston Open	-	-	-	-	-	-	-	-	-	22
GG Chrysler Cl'	-	-	-	-	-	-	-	-	8	MC
Compaq Classic	-	-	-	-	-	-	-	-	-	23
Byron Nelson Cl'	-	-	-	-	-	-	-	-	20	43
MasterCard Cln'l	-	-	-	-	15	-	-	-	13	5
Kemper Ins Open	-	-	-	-	-	-	-	-	-	-
Memorial T'ment	-	-	-	-	WD	-	MC	10	37	
St. Jude Classic	-	-	-	-	-	-	-	-	-	-
U.S. Open	-	-	-	-	-	-	-	MC	-	-
Buick Classic	-	-	-	-	-	-	-	29	WD	
Canon GH Open	-	-	-	-	-	-	-	-	7	
Western Open	-	-	-	-	-	-	-	-	7	30
Gr. Milwaukee	-	-	-	-	-	-	-	-	-	1
British Open	-	-	14	10	29	MC	55	MC		
B.C. Open	-	-	-	-	-	-	-	-	-	-
John Deere Cl'	-	-	-	-	-	-	-	-	-	-
The International	-	-	-	-	-	-	-	-	-	-
Buick Open	-	-	-	-	-	-	-	MC	-	
USPGA Champ	-	-	-	23	65	MC	46	22		
WGCNEC Inv'	-	-	-	-	-	-	6	15	31	
Reno-Tahoe Op'	-	-	-	-	-	-	-	-	-	21
Air Canada Chp'	-	-	-	-	-	-	-	-	-	-
Bell Canadian O'	-	-	-	-	-	-	-	54	-	
WGC AmEx	-	-	-	-	-	-	-	50	-	
Tampa Bay Cl'	-	-	-	-	-	-	-	-	-	-
Marconi Penn C'	-	-	-	-	-	-	-	48	33	
Texas Open	-	-	-	-	-	-	-	-	-	MC
Michelob Chmp'	-	-	-	-	-	-	-	-	-	55
Invensys Classic	-	-	-	-	-	-	-	-	MC	25
NCR Golf Cl'	-	-	-	-	-	-	-	-	-	-
Buick Challenge	-	-	-	-	-	-	-	-	WD	23
SFB Classic	-	-	-	-	-	-	-	-	-	-
Tour Champ'ship	-									

Len Mattiace

15/10/67 – Mineola, NY

Another season in which the Florida based pro was able to keep his card comfortably. In 2001, he managed only two top-ten finishes but he missed just one cut in his last eight starts to do enough to secure his playing privileges for 2002. He has still to win on the full tour – and didn't manage to claim a victory in two seasons on the Buy.com tour either – but has finished runner-up twice (1996 Buick Challenge and 1999 Sony Open). Last season's earnings boosted his career haul to nearly $3million. His putting has improved on last year's figures.

ScAv - 70.94 (68th) – DD - 273.7 (154th) DA - 68.5 (100th) GIR - 63.5 (168th) – PpGIR - 1.770 (90th) SS - 59.5 (18th)

	'92	'93	'94	'95	'96	'97	'98	'99	'00	'01
WGC MatchPlay	-	-	-	-	-	-	-	-	-	-
Mercedes Ch	-	-	-	-	-	-	-	-	-	-
Tucson Open	-	-	-	21	13	44	-	-	40	26
Sony Open	-	-	-	16	19	49	2	MC	MC	
Phoenix Open	-	-	-	22	55	MC	65	44		
AT&T P Beach	-	MC	-	-	MC	37	MC	-		
Buick Invitatn'l	-	9	-	MC	MC	72	-	63	-	
Bob Hope Cl'	-	-	-	17	59	24	-			
Nissan Open	-	MC	-	MC	-	-	50	43	43	
Genuity Champ	-	-	MC	MC	9	MC	33	MC		
Honda Classic	-	26	-	33	30	39	MC	41	-	
Bay Hill Invit'l	-	45	-	59	30	MC	MC	57	62	
Players Champ	-	-	-	24	5	MC	9	MC		
BellSouth Cl'	-	MC	-	MC	MC	-	30	37	54	
US Masters	-	-	-	-	-	-	-	-	-	-
Worldcom Cl'	-	-	-	54	18	43	MC	12		
Houston Open	-	MC	-	14	MC	-	64	MC	6	
GG Chrysler Cl'	-	50	-	MC	MC	42	57	MC	-	
Compaq Classic	-	-	-	MC	65	19	-	-	MC	
Byron Nelson Cl'	-	76	-	MC	MC	35	MC	67	21	
MasterCard Cln'l	-	-	-	48	35	11	8	54		
Kemper Ins Open	-	60	-	MC	MC	-	MC	-	-	
Memorial T'ment	-	-	-	MC	31	65	-	24		
St. Jude Classic	-	MC	-	MC	-	-	-	25	12	
U.S. Open	-	-	-	24	-	42	-	-		
Buick Classic	-	60	-	62	MC	76	28	MC	MC	
Canon GH Open	-	MC	-	MC	MC	9	MC	32	44	
Western Open	-	-	-	MC	-	65	49	71	MC	
Gr. Milwaukee	-	81	-	MC	34	-	-	-		
British Open	-	-	-	-	-	-	30	-	-	
B.C. Open	-	73	-	26	18	MC	-	-	MC	
John Deere Cl'	-	MC	-	52	-	-	-	10	35	
The International	-	MC	-	MC	MC	MC	-	-	MC	
Buick Open	-	MC	-	-	-	49	MC	MC	-	
USPGA Champ	-	-	-	MC	MC	-	-	-	MC	
WGCNEC Inv'	-	-	-	-	-	-	-	-	-	-
Reno-Tahoe Op'	-	-	-	-	-	MC	-	-	-	
Air Canada Chp'	-	-	-	MC	24	MC	48	MC	-	
Bell Canadian O'	-	75	-	34	23	36	49	20	34	
WGC AmEx	-	-	-	-	-	-	-	-	-	-
Tampa Bay Cl'	-	-	-	-	-	-	3	-	-	
Marconi Penn C'	-	-	-	-	-	-	-	18	46	
Texas Open	-	MC	-	4	20	45	29	6	62	
Michelob Chmp'	-	66	-	43	MC	MC	MC	53	5	
Invensys Classic	-	MC	-	MC	MC	MC	-	-		
NCR Golf Cl'	-	MC	-	29	3	27	MC	MC	36	
Buick Challenge	-	16	-	2	25	MC	MC	41	MC	
SFB Classic	-	4	-	12	MC	-	9	43	73	
Tour Champ'ship	-									

Sponsored by Stan James

Bob May
6/10/68 – Lynwood, CA

Despite turning pro in 1991 after playing Walker Cup golf for the USA he has only had three seasons on the US Tour. After graduating from the Buy.com Tour to the full tour in 1994 a poor rookie year persuaded May to try his luck elsewhere. He came to Europe where his consistency earned him the name 'Top Ten Bob'. He won the 1999 British Masters and got back on the US Tour through 1999 Q-School and was second in the 2000 USPGA Championship. Last season was poor by his 2000 standards when his normally accurate game was missing.

ScAv - 70.73 (58th) – DD - 280.2 (87th) DA - 67.6 (116th) GIR - 68.9 (39th) – PpGIR - 1.776 (104th) SS - 60.3 (14th)

	'92	'93	'94	'95	'96	'97	'98	'99	'00	'01
WGC MatchPlay	-	-	-	-	-	-	-	-	-	17
Mercedes Ch	-	-	-	-	-	-	-	-	-	-
Tucson Open	-	-	63	-	-	-	-	-	MC	MC
Sony Open	-	-	MC	-	-	-	-	-	48	MC
Phoenix Open	-	-	-	-	-	-	-	-	-	36
AT&T P Beach	-	MC	-	-	-	-	-	49	-	-
Buick Invitatn'l	-	MC	-	-	-	-	-	-	33	27
Bob Hope Cl'	-	-	-	-	-	-	-	-	-	WD
Nissan Open	-	MC	MC	-	-	-	-	-	MC	-
Genuity Champ	-	MC	-	-	-	-	-	-	45	-
Honda Classic	-	MC	-	-	-	-	-	-	MC	-
Bay Hill Invit'l	-	MC	-	-	-	-	-	-	-	-
Players Champ	-	-	-	-	-	-	-	-	-	-
BellSouth Cl'	-	MC	-	-	-	-	-	-	MC	-
US Masters	-	-	-	-	-	-	-	-	-	43
Worldcom Cl'	-	-	-	-	-	-	-	-	-	21
Houston Open	-	MC	-	-	-	-	-	-	29	MC
GG Chrysler Cl'	-	MC	-	-	-	-	-	-	34	-
Compaq Classic	-	MC	-	-	-	-	-	-	50	11
Byron Nelson C'	-	MC	-	-	-	-	-	-	56	51
MasterCard Cln'l	-	-	-	-	-	-	-	-	-	52
Kemper Ins Open	-	18	-	-	-	-	-	-	-	-
Memorial T'ment	-	-	-	-	-	-	-	-	-	53
St. Jude Classic	-	MC	-	-	-	-	-	-	2	28
U.S. Open	-	-	-	-	-	-	-	-	23	30
Buick Classic	-	65	-	-	-	-	-	-	-	-
Canon GH Open	-	MC	-	-	-	-	-	-	66	-
Western Open	-	MC	-	-	-	-	-	-	-	31
Gr. Milwaukee	-	-	-	-	-	-	-	-	-	-
British Open	-	-	-	-	-	-	74	-	11	MC
B.C. Open	-	73	-	-	-	-	-	-	-	-
John Deere Cl'	-	MC	-	-	-	-	-	-	-	29
The International	-	MC	-	-	-	-	-	-	31	15
Buick Open	-	MC	-	-	-	-	-	-	-	-
USPGA Champ	-	-	-	-	-	-	-	-	2	73
WGCNEC Inv'	-	-	-	-	-	-	-	-	-	-
Reno-Tahoe Op'	-	-	-	-	-	-	-	-	3	MC
Air Canada Chp'	-	-	-	-	-	-	-	-	-	29
Bell Canadian O'	-	59	-	-	-	-	-	-	-	-
WGC AmEx	-	-	-	-	-	-	-	20	11	-
Tampa Bay Cl'	-	-	-	-	-	-	-	-	33	-
Marconi Penn C'	-	-	-	-	-	-	-	-	MC	-
Texas Open	-	46	-	-	-	-	-	-	14	17
Michelob Chmp'	-	MC	-	-	-	-	-	-	-	-
Invensys Classic	-	MC	-	-	-	-	16	13	22	20
NCR Golf Cl'	-	47	-	-	-	-	-	-	13	MC
Buick Challenge	-	MC	-	-	-	-	-	-	-	-
SFB Classic	MC	MC	-	-	-	-	-	-	-	-
Tour Champ'ship	-	-	-	-	-	-	-	-	22	-

Billy Mayfair
6/8/66 – Phoenix, AZ

Scottsdale resident who despite not winning managed his best season in 2001 in terms of prize money earned. Mayfair can boast five US Tour wins, the last of which came in the 1998 Buick Open (he also won the Nissan Open that year). Had a fine amateur career winning the 1986 US Public Links and 1987 US Amateur championship.

Turned pro in 1988 and won his first title in 1993 (Greater Milwaukee Open). A short hitter but accurate with the driver, he had one of the best final round scoring averages (69.13) last season.

ScAv - 70.38 (30th) – DD - 275.2 (141st) DA - 76.5 (5th) GIR - 69.8 (27th) – PpGIR - 1.752 (42nd) SS - 60.6 (10th)

	'92	'93	'94	'95	'96	'97	'98	'99	'00	'01
WGC MatchPlay	-	-	-	-	-	-	-	33	17	-
Mercedes Ch	-	-	13	-	19	-	-	2	-	-
Tucson Open	37	41	9	MC	56	MC	25	-	-	MC
Sony Open	12	MC	23	MC	-	31	35	-	-	-
Phoenix Open	24	MC	69	2	35	MC	41	MC	10	13
AT&T P Beach	-	-	-	-	-	-	-	-	-	-
Buick Invitatn'l	71	MC	61	48	MC	MC	35	-	MC	27
Bob Hope Cl'	-	-	-	-	-	MC	28	MC	9	-
Nissan Open	22	37	MC	35	17	27	1	23	25	33
Genuity Champ	44	24	MC	43	50	13	2	19	MC	17
Honda Classic	-	MC	-	-	-	-	-	-	-	-
Bay Hill Invit'l	MC	-	52	MC	31	MC	MC	37	10	MC
Players Champ	67	52	MC	18	MC	MC	42	MC	17	5
BellSouth Cl'	32	27	59	29	-	-	-	MC	MC	21
US Masters	42	-	MC	-	MC	-	MC	-	-	-
Worldcom Cl'	MC	54	MC	56	18	54	39	-	47	2
Houston Open	MC	MC	-	MC	MC	-	-	-	38	6
GG Chrysler Cl'	-	MC	-	MC	-	MC	67	-	21	-
Compaq Classic	40	26	MC	15	-	22	-	MC	-	-
Byron Nelson C'	29	2	14	48	MC	MC	MC	MC	81	73
MasterCard Cln'	130	22	69	8	20	54	MC	7	MC	20
Kemper Ins Open	13	7	71	42	53	47	MC	-	-	MC
Memorial T'ment	-	-	50	MC	MC	17	31	48	76	43
St. Jude Classic	39	16	MC	MC	16	MC	-	25	45	12
U.S. Open	23	-	MC	-	32	-	-	10	MC	-
Buick Classic	MC	MC	-	-	-	-	-	-	-	-
Canon GH Open	8	58	MC	51	-	21	-	-	WD	22
Western Open	-	75	-	1	26	34	65	MC	MC	15
Gr. Milwaukee	23	1	MC	34	12	MC	-	-	-	-
British Open	-	-	-	-	44	-	52	MC	-	3
B.C. Open	13	10	MC	-	-	66	-	-	-	-
John Deere Cl'	23	55	15	-	MC	75	-	-	-	-
The International	-	-	-	-	-	MC	21	5	39	MC
Buick Open	MC	MC	50	MC	MC	-	1	MC	47	14
USPGA Champ	MC	28	39	23	52	53	7	34	74	MC
WGCNEC Inv'	-	-	-	-	-	-	-	-	-	-
Reno-Tahoe Op'	-	-	-	-	-	-	-	MC	27	44
Air Canada Chp'	-	-	-	-	-	-	-	-	-	-
Bell Canadian O'	34	40	MC	34	20	MC	MC	20	MC	-
WGC AmEx	-	-	-	-	-	-	-	-	-	-
Tampa Bay Cl'	-	-	-	-	-	-	-	-	27	-
Marconi Penn C'	-	-	-	-	-	-	-	-	MC	MC
Texas Open	MC	MC	66	-	MC	-	-	-	-	-
Michelob Chmp'	52	46	-	-	MC	6	MC	MC	MC	-
Invensys Classic	MC	34	MC	2	33	2	MC	15	33	18
NCR Golf Cl'	MC	8	24	-	MC	42	-	17	MC	16
Buick Challenge	-	-	-	58	-	52	30	MC	-	MC
SFB Classic	-	-	-	-	-	-	-	51	-	-
Tour Champ'ship	-	30	-	1	-	-	13	-	26	-

Scott McCarron
10/7/65 – Sacramento, CA

A first win in four years for McCarron who managed to capture the BellSouth Classic title. It was an ultra consistent 2001 for the Californian who missed just two cuts. His Money List position was the best of his career (23rd).

Since joining the full tour in 1995, after making it through the 1994 Q-School, he has won three times, his victory last season following up successes in the 1996 Freeport-McDermott (now Compaq) Classic and the 1997 BellSouth Classic. A fine bunker player, only his driving accuracy stats didn't rank in the top 25 last season.

ScAv - 70.06 (17th); DD - 289.7 (14th) DA - 68.8 (91st) GIR - 70.0 (25th) – PpGIR - 1.737 (16th) SS - 62.1 (7th)

	'92	'93	'94	'95	'96	'97	'98	'99	'00	'01
WGC MatchPlay	-	-	-	-	-	-	-	-	-	-
Mercedes Ch	-	-	-	-	-	11	12	-	-	-
Tucson Open	-	-	-	-	MC	MC	-	39	50	32
Sony Open	-	-	-	MC	MC	-	-	-	-	-
Phoenix Open	-	-	-	-	26	7	8	22	MC	33
AT&T P Beach	-	-	-	MC	-	WD	MC	44	MC	12
Buick Invitatn'l	-	-	-	50	48	-	35	35	MC	-
Bob Hope Cl'	-	-	-	MC	21	20	-	32	51	18
Nissan Open	-	-	-	52	26	6	MC	23	66	43
Genuity Champ	-	-	-	-	-	-	-	MC	-	-
Honda Classic	-	-	-	WD	-	MC	-	-	-	11
Bay Hill Invit'l	-	-	-	-	-	30	49	37	MC	17
Players Champ	-	-	-	MC	MC	MC	35	MC	66	44
BellSouth Cl'	-	-	-	MC	MC	1	36	MC	53	1
US Masters	-	-	-	-	-	10	30	16	18	-
Worldcom Cl'	-	-	-	-	-	-	-	-	56	MC
Houston Open	-	-	-	MC	MC	15	MC	-	MC	-
GG Chrysler Cl'	-	-	-	-	-	-	-	-	21	19
Compaq Classic	-	-	-	MC	1	4	MC	12	17	MC
Byron Nelson C'	-	-	-	MC	29	54	6	MC	MC	37
MasterCard Cln'l	-	-	-	-	-	-	18	47	-	52
Kemper Ins Open	-	-	-	42	35	MC	-	60	-	-
Memorial T'ment	-	-	-	-	56	MC	MC	MC	-	MC
St. Jude Classic	-	-	-	MC	-	-	-	72	MC	3
U.S. Open	-	-	-	-	-	82	10	40	-	-
Buick Classic	-	-	-	MC	MC	-	-	MC	-	-
Canon GH Open	-	-	-	66	-	-	MC	46	-	-
Western Open	-	-	-	-	MC	-	MC	-	63	31
Gr. Milwaukee	-	-	-	MC	-	-	MC	-	47	-
British Open	-	-	-	-	-	MC	-	-	-	-
B.C. Open	-	-	-	MC	MC	-	-	-	27	-
John Deere Cl'	-	-	-	78	52	-	5	21	38	15
The International	-	-	-	-	59	11	MC	MC	MC	20
Buick Open	-	-	-	-	-	-	15	MC	32	-
USPGA Champ	-	-	-	-	47	10	MC	-	-	70
WGCNEC Inv'	-	-	-	-	-	-	-	-	-	-
Reno-Tahoe Op'	-	-	-	-	-	-	-	MC	4	24
Air Canada Chp'	-	-	-	-	-	-	MC	4	27	21
Bell Canadian O'	-	-	-	29	-	-	-	59	37	38
WGC AmEx	-	-	-	-	-	-	-	-	-	-
Tampa Bay Cl'	-	-	-	-	-	-	-	-	-	-
Marconi Penn C'	-	-	-	-	-	-	-	-	MC	-
Texas Open	-	-	-	38	28	6	-	23	61	45
Michelob Chmp'	-	-	-	34	-	MC	MC	-	41	-
Invensys Classic	-	-	-	3	22	MC	MC	-	5	4
NCR Golf Cl'	-	-	-	MC	18	-	MC	28	-	6
Buick Challenge	-	-	-	24	MC	MC	48	MC	-	-
SFB Classic	-	-	-	44	-	-	MC	-	-	-
Tour Champ'ship	-	-	-	-	12	-	-	-	-	18

Rocco Mediate
17/12/62 – Greensburg, PA

Had injury problems (back) last term, withdrawing from four events in the second half of the season, but also claimed his best finish in a Major when fourth in the US Open. Mediate didn't manage to add to his four US Tour wins (the last the 2000 Buick Open) in 2001 but claimed two runners-up positions on his way to earning $1.4million – the most in one season for the 15-year tour veteran.

His career has been plagued by injury and he missed most of 1994 with a ruptured disk. A natural right to left golfer, he is an accurate iron player.

ScAv - 70.21 (22nd); DD - 278.4 (108th) DA - 71.0 (45th) GIR - 71.0 (10th) – PpGIR - 1.753 (45th) SS - 59.5 (18th)

	'92	'93	'94	'95	'96	'97	'98	'99	'00	'01
WGC MatchPlay	-	-	-	-	-	-	-	33	33	-
Mercedes Ch	3	-	24	-	-	-	-	-	16	6
Tucson Open	MC	-	9	32	-	-	22	-	-	-
Sony Open	-	-	-	-	-	-	-	-	-	-
Phoenix Open	3	-	WD	MC	6	68	47	1	2	2
AT&T P Beach	MC	28	MC	43	-	20	25	MC	31	MC
Buick Invitatn'l	-	37	-	WD	-	54	57	-	-	-
Bob Hope Cl'	WD	MC	-	-	-	-	-	28	16	MC
Nissan Open	5	58	-	MC	34	-	-	15	18	25
Genuity Champ	78	29	-	MC	34	MC	23	-	-	-
Honda Classic	-	6	-	-	MC	39	-	-	-	-
Bay Hill Invit'l	22	2	-	WD	13	66	50	44	38	23
Players Champ	MC	6	-	55	4	MC	57	MC	MC	65
BellSouth Cl'	-	-	-	MC	-	63	-	-	-	-
US Masters	37	-	-	-	-	-	-	27	52	15
Worldcom Cl'	MC	47	-	-	8	19	14	12	MC	12
Houston Open	-	77	-	MC	-	-	-	-	-	-
GG Chrysler Cl'	9	1	-	MC	WD	9	38	17	26	-
Compaq Classic	-	-	-	-	-	-	-	-	-	-
Byron Nelson C'	-	-	-	-	33	51	MC	-	-	51
MasterCard Cln'l	59	MC	-	8	3	MC	18	62	4	8
Kemper Ins Open	-	-	61	-	MC	-	-	-	-	-
Memorial T'ment	48	30	-	-	21	32	-	MC	13	-
St. Jude Classic	-	-	-	5	-	-	20	50	-	-
U.S. Open	44	25	WD	-	-	-	-	34	32	4
Buick Classic	22	26	38	55	69	43	MC	46	WD	WD
Canon GH Open	MC	7	-	MC	25	MC	-	-	-	-
Western Open	-	-	DQ	18	52	74	-	-	-	-
Gr. Milwaukee	-	-	-	-	40	MC	-	-	-	-
British Open	45	39	-	18	-	-	-	MC	52	WD
B.C. Open	7	58	-	-	-	-	-	-	-	-
John Deere Cl'	-	-	-	-	-	-	-	-	-	-
The International	33	9	-	17	72	5	22	MC	-	-
Buick Open	-	19	-	MC	-	8	29	9	1	43
USPGA Champ	40	68	-	-	36	-	MC	49	WD	66
WGCNEC Inv'	-	-	-	-	-	-	-	-	-	-
Reno-Tahoe Op'	-	-	-	-	-	-	-	MC	27	WD
Air Canada Chp'	-	-	-	-	-	-	-	-	-	-
Bell Canadian O'	MC	-	-	-	-	MC	23	-	-	-
WGC AmEx	-	-	-	-	-	-	-	WD	-	-
Tampa Bay Cl'	-	-	-	-	-	-	-	-	-	-
Marconi Penn C'	-	-	-	-	-	-	-	-	33	2
Texas Open	MC	-	-	-	28	20	WD	49	-	-
Michelob Chmp'	-	-	-	-	-	-	-	-	-	-
Invensys Classic	60	-	-	-	MC	14	20	MC	27	MC
NCR Golf Cl'	8	35	-	-	MC	61	4	17	MC	21
Buick Challenge	26	-	-	-	MC	57	-	6	-	WD
SFB Classic	-	-	-	-	-	-	-	-	-	-
Tour Champ'ship	-	23	-	-	-	-	-	-	-	-

Sponsored by Stan James

Phil Mickelson

16/6/70 – San Diego, CA

Left-hander who remains the best player not to win a Major after three near misses in 2001. Mickelson still managed to win twice last season (Buick Invitational and Canon GH Open) – his 18th and 19th US Tour titles - and finish second on four occasions. The $4.4million he won in 2001 pushed his career earnings to nearly $18million. The only left-hander to win the US Amateur Championship (1990). He missed most of the latter half of the season due to the birth of his second child. Massive off the tee he possess one of the best short games in the world. ScAv - 69.21 (4th) – DD - 293.9 (6th) DA - 69.4 (78th) GIR - 69.9 (26th) – PpGIR - 1.717 (2nd) SS - 55.3 (56th)

	'92	'93	'94	'95	'96	'97	'98	'99	'00	'01
WGC MatchPlay	-	-	-	-	-	-	-	9	33	-
Mercedes Ch	30	-	1	19	28	11	1	22	-	28
Tucson Open	MC	8	9	1	1	13	MC	-	-	-
Sony Open	-	-	-	-	-	-	-	-	-	-
Phoenix Open	MC	45	8	35	1	7	58	61	10	MC
AT&T P Beach	-	-	-	-	MC	33	1	21	61	3
Buick Invitatn'l	MC	1	3	16	2	38	49	MC	1	1
Bob Hope Cl'	-	MC	MC	-	-	-	-	-	16	-
Nissan Open	-	19	27	MC	MC	-	52	15	-	MC
Genuity Champ	-	MC	-	-	38	20	-	-	21	-
Honda Classic	-	-	-	MC	-	-	-	-	-	27
Bay Hill Invit'l	-	-	-	MC	MC	1	MC	5	46	2
Players Champ	MC	MC	-	14	33	MC	8	32	MC	33
BellSouth Cl'	-	-	-	MC	-	-	-	7	1	3
US Masters	-	34	-	7	3	MC	12	6	7	3
Worldcom Cl'	-	28	-	13	66	20	3	36	-	-
Houston Open	-	-	-	MC	-	-	30	-	-	-
GG Chrysler Cl'	-	50	-	-	-	9	6	-	-	-
Compaq Classic	-	-	-	-	-	-	-	-	17	2
Byron Nelson C'	MC	MC	-	-	1	12	6	MC	2	28
MasterCard Cln'l	-	MC	8	33	-	22	MC	11	1	2
Kemper Ins Open	-	-	4	MC	-	14	-	-	-	3
Memorial T'ment	-	22	-	59	71	-	MC	11	-	-
St. Jude Classic	-	-	-	-	-	-	-	-	-	MC
U.S. Open	MC	-	47	4	94	43	10	2	16	7
Buick Classic	-	MC	-	-	-	-	-	-	13	-
Canon GH Open	MC	-	26	-	-	-	-	-	-	1
Western Open	38	MC	64	43	26	-	35	-	MC	42
Gr. Milwaukee	MC	-	-	-	-	-	-	-	-	-
British Open	-	-	MC	40	40	24	79	MC	11	30
B.C. Open	13	-	-	-	-	-	-	12	-	-
John Deere Cl'	-	-	-	-	-	-	-	-	-	-
The International	14	1	10	MC	16	1	2	16	2	71
Buick Open	-	48	-	-	33	-	-	-	4	10
USPGA Champ	-	6	3	MC	8	29	34	57	9	2
WGCNEC Inv'	-	-	-	-	-	-	-	2	4	8
Reno-Tahoe Op'	-	-	-	-	-	-	-	-	-	-
Air Canada Chp'	-	-	-	-	-	-	-	-	-	-
Bell Canadian O'	-	DQ	31	-	-	-	-	-	-	-
WGC AmEx	-	-	-	-	-	-	-	40	-	-
Tampa Bay Cl'	-	-	-	-	-	-	-	-	-	-
Marconi Penn C'	-	-	-	-	-	-	-	-	-	-
Texas Open	47	-	-	-	-	-	-	-	-	-
Michelob Chmp'	-	MC	-	-	-	-	-	-	-	-
Invensys Classic	MC	19	3	30	8	14	MC	37	2	-
NCR Golf Cl'	46	-	-	-	-	MC	-	-	-	-
Buick Challenge	8	-	-	-	-	-	-	-	-	-
SFB Classic	-	-	-	-	-	-	-	-	-	-
Tour Champ'ship	-	28	17	24	12	22	17	21	1	-

Geoff Ogilvy

11/6/77 – Adelaide, Australia

Australian former European Tour player who practically secured his playing privileges for 2002 with two top-three finishes in the first five starts of his rookie season. He made just one cut after June but had earned enough cash in the first half of the season to place in the top 125 of the Money List. Started on the ANZ Tour and was rookie of the year in 1999 before moving to Europe. Finished as runner-up in the 2000 and 2001 Johnnie Walker Classic. Made it on tour by coming through the 2000 Q-School. Big hitter with a decent putting touch. ScAv - 71.80 (154th) – DD - 284.8 (37th) DA - 67.3 (120th) GIR - 64.1 (155th) – PpGIR - 1.764 (70th) SS - 47.6 (140th)

	'92	'93	'94	'95	'96	'97	'98	'99	'00	'01
WGC MatchPlay	-	-	-	-	-	-	-	-	-	-
Mercedes Ch	-	-	-	-	-	-	-	-	-	-
Tucson Open	-	-	-	-	-	-	-	-	-	3
Sony Open	-	-	-	-	-	-	-	-	-	MC
Phoenix Open	-	-	-	-	-	-	-	-	-	-
AT&T P Beach	-	-	-	-	-	-	-	-	-	MC
Buick Invitatn'l	-	-	-	-	-	-	-	-	-	-
Bob Hope Cl'	-	-	-	-	-	-	-	-	-	-
Nissan Open	-	-	-	-	-	-	-	-	-	-
Genuity Champ	-	-	-	-	-	-	-	-	-	21
Honda Classic	-	-	-	-	-	-	-	-	-	2
Bay Hill Invit'l	-	-	-	-	-	-	-	-	-	51
Players Champ	-	-	-	-	-	-	-	-	-	-
BellSouth Cl'	-	-	-	-	-	-	-	-	-	-
US Masters	-	-	-	-	-	-	-	-	-	-
Worldcom Cl'	-	-	-	-	-	-	-	-	-	MC
Houston Open	-	-	-	-	-	-	-	-	-	-
GG Chrysler Cl'	-	-	-	-	-	-	-	-	-	MC
Compaq Classic	-	-	-	-	-	-	-	-	-	MC
Byron Nelson C'	-	-	-	-	-	-	-	-	-	DQ
MasterCard Cln'l	-	-	-	-	-	-	-	-	-	34
Kemper Ins Open	-	-	-	-	-	-	-	-	-	-
Memorial T'ment	-	-	-	-	-	-	-	-	-	MC
St. Jude Classic	-	-	-	-	-	-	-	-	-	-
U.S. Open	-	-	-	-	-	-	-	-	-	-
Buick Classic	-	-	-	-	-	-	-	-	-	MC
Canon GH Open	-	-	-	-	-	-	-	-	-	22
Western Open	-	-	-	-	-	-	-	-	-	MC
Gr. Milwaukee	-	-	-	-	-	-	-	-	-	-
British Open	-	-	-	-	-	-	-	MC	-	MC
B.C. Open	-	-	-	-	-	-	-	-	-	-
John Deere Cl'	-	-	-	-	-	-	-	-	-	-
The International	-	-	-	-	-	-	-	-	-	-
Buick Open	-	-	-	-	-	-	-	-	-	-
USPGA Champ	-	-	-	-	-	-	-	-	-	-
WGCNEC Inv'	-	-	-	-	-	-	-	-	-	-
Reno-Tahoe Op'	-	-	-	-	-	-	-	-	-	MC
Air Canada Chp'	-	-	-	-	-	-	-	-	-	MC
Bell Canadian O'	-	-	-	-	-	-	-	-	-	74
WGC AmEx	-	-	-	-	-	-	-	-	-	-
Tampa Bay Cl'	-	-	-	-	-	-	-	-	-	-
Marconi Penn C'	-	-	-	-	-	-	-	-	-	-
Texas Open	-	-	-	-	-	-	-	-	-	MC
Michelob Chmp'	-	-	-	-	-	-	-	-	-	-
Invensys Classic	-	-	-	-	-	-	-	-	-	MC
NCR Golf Cl'	-	-	-	-	-	-	-	-	-	MC
Buick Challenge	-	-	-	-	-	-	-	-	-	MC
SFB Classic	-	-	-	-	-	-	-	-	-	-
Tour Champ'ship	-	-	-	-	-	-	-	-	-	-

Jesper Parnevik
7/3/65 – Stockholm, Sweden

Swedish Ryder Cup star who came back from hip surgery to win the Honda Classic in 2001 – his fifth US Tour win. Parnevik will line up for the Europeans at the Belfry next season (his third successive appearance). His win on the US Tour means he has claimed at least one victory each year since 1998. Joined the US Tour after five successful years on the European Tour (can boast five Euro Tour wins).

A superb wind player, he has posted three top-four finishes in the Open Championship. Father Bo is one of Sweden's most famous comics.

ScAv - 70.12 (19th) – DD - 284.2 (46th) DA - 67.6 (116th) GIR - 66.9 (78th) – PpGIR - 1.769 (87th) SS - 54.3 (68th)

	'92	'93	'94	'95	'96	'97	'98	'99	'00	'01
WGC MatchPlay	-	-	-	-	-	-	-	33	9	-
Mercedes Ch	-	-	-	-	-	-	-	26	6	23
Tucson Open	-	-	MC	73	21	-	-	-	-	-
Sony Open	-	-	5	18	31	MC	-	29	3	MC
Phoenix Open	-	-	-	MC	35	2	1	14	37	MC
AT&T P Beach	-	-	19	MC	-	5	19	-	-	72
Buick Invitatn'l	-	-	-	41	10	2	MC	-	-	-
Bob Hope Cl'	-	-	-	-	13	3	69	70	1	-
Nissan Open	-	-	20	-	-	-	-	-	2	13
Genuity Champ	-	-	27	27	8	28	30	15	WD	17
Honda Classic	-	-	70	MC	59	5	MC	-	-	1
Bay Hill Invit'l	-	-	33	5	MC	-	-	-	-	-
Players Champ	-	-	49	53	MC	25	23	-	MC	MC
BellSouth Cl'	-	-	-	MC	-	-	-	20	-	21
US Masters	-	-	-	-	21	31	MC	40	20	-
Worldcom Cl'	-	-	9	44	-	2	18	DQ	9	28
Houston Open	-	-	-	-	-	-	-	-	-	-
GG Chrysler Cl'	-	-	MC	6	-	41	-	1	8	-
Compaq Classic	-	-	51	15	6	2	12	-	-	-
Byron Nelson C'	-	-	28	32	MC	-	-	-	1	62
MasterCard Cln'l	-	-	MC	-	-	-	-	-	-	11
Kemper Ins Open	-	-	-	21	-	MC	61	-	-	-
Memorial T'ment	-	-	38	66	18	21	11	43	-	30
St. Jude Classic	-	-	-	-	-	-	-	-	-	8
U.S. Open	-	-	-	-	48	14	17	MC	30	-
Buick Classic	-	-	MC	-	-	-	10	-	5	-
Canon GH Open	-	-	-	45	-	-	-	-	-	-
Western Open	-	-	-	-	55	-	-	-	-	-
Gr. Milwaukee	-	-	-	-	3	-	-	-	-	-
British Open	-	21	2	24	44	2	4	10	36	9
B.C. Open	-	-	59	-	-	-	-	-	-	-
John Deere Cl'	-	-	-	-	-	-	-	-	-	-
The International	-	-	33	25	-	13	22	-	-	-
Buick Open	-	-	-	-	-	-	-	-	-	-
USPGA Champ	-	-	MC	20	5	45	MC	10	51	13
WGCNEC Inv'	-	-	-	-	-	-	-	27	-	-
Reno-Tahoe Op'	-	-	-	-	-	-	-	-	-	-
Air Canada Chp'	-	-	-	-	-	-	-	-	22	19
Bell Canadian O'	-	-	45	-	7	-	-	9	26	43
WGC AmEx	-	-	-	-	-	-	-	WD	-	-
Tampa Bay Cl'	-	-	-	-	-	-	-	-	-	-
Marconi Penn C'	-	-	-	-	-	-	-	-	-	-
Texas Open	-	-	-	-	-	-	-	-	-	11
Michelob Chmp'	-	-	-	-	-	-	-	MC	-	-
Invensys Classic	-	-	-	-	-	-	-	-	-	58
NCR Golf Cl'	-	-	-	59	-	4	37	-	-	6
Buick Challenge	-	-	-	-	-	-	-	-	-	31
SFB Classic	-	-	-	-	-	-	-	-	-	-
Tour Champ'ship	-	-	-	-	-	6	3	-	22	-

Carl Paulson
29/12/70 – Quantico, VA

Topped the Money List of the Buy.com Tour in 1999 courtesy of two wins (Utah Classic and Boise Open) but had yet to translate that form on to the main tour in his last two seasons at the highest level. Also had two years at the highest level in 1995 and 1996 but didn't finish inside the top 125th on the Money List. Just crept in to the top 100 last year after two top-ten finishes. Not related to Dennis Paulson.

He is a long hitter but also has some accuracy off the tee – he ranked in the top ten of total driving in 2001 (for the second successive year).

ScAv - 71.58 (130th) – DD - 281.7 (69th) DA - 73.5 (22nd) GIR - 66.1 (97th) – PpGIR - 1.801 (174th) SS - 45.5 (157th)

	'92	'93	'94	'95	'96	'97	'98	'99	'00	'01
WGC MatchPlay	-	-	-	-	-	-	-	-	-	-
Mercedes Ch	-	-	-	-	-	-	-	-	-	-
Tucson Open	-	-	-	MC	-	-	-	-	MC	48
Sony Open	-	-	-	-	-	-	-	-	MC	MC
Phoenix Open	-	-	-	MC	-	-	-	-	MC	-
AT&T P Beach	-	MC	-	-	-	-	-	-	-	-
Buick Invitatn'l	-	-	MC	MC	-	-	-	-	52	WD
Bob Hope Cl'	-	-	-	MC	-	-	-	-	MC	-
Nissan Open	-	-	MC	MC	-	-	-	-	66	-
Genuity Champ	-	-	-	MC	-	-	-	-	MC	-
Honda Classic	-	-	MC	44	-	-	-	-	28	MC
Bay Hill Invit'l	-	-	-	-	-	-	-	-	-	40
Players Champ	-	-	-	-	-	-	-	-	-	68
BellSouth Cl'	-	-	MC	-	-	-	-	-	63	MC
US Masters	-	-	-	-	-	-	-	-	-	-
Worldcom Cl'	-	-	MC	-	-	-	-	-	57	3
Houston Open	-	-	MC	48	-	-	-	-	17	35
GG Chrysler Cl'	-	-	-	-	-	-	-	-	42	MC
Compaq Classic	-	-	MC	MC	-	-	-	-	30	MC
Byron Nelson C'	-	-	-	36	-	-	-	-	MC	-
MasterCard Cln'l	-	-	-	-	-	-	-	-	24	MC
Kemper Ins Open	-	-	MC	-	-	-	-	-	MC	48
Memorial T'ment	-	-	-	-	-	-	-	-	-	53
St. Jude Classic	-	-	64	MC	-	-	-	-	75	-
U.S. Open	-	-	MC	-	-	-	-	-	-	MC
Buick Classic	-	-	MC	62	-	-	-	-	-	-
Canon GH Open	-	-	66	MC	-	-	-	-	MC	50
Western Open	-	-	-	-	-	-	-	-	9	15
Gr. Milwaukee	-	-	MC	34	-	-	-	-	MC	-
British Open	-	-	-	-	-	-	-	-	-	MC
B.C. Open	-	-	59	15	-	-	-	-	37	-
John Deere Cl'	-	-	20	MC	-	-	-	-	MC	MC
The International	-	-	-	-	-	-	-	-	MC	-
Buick Open	-	-	MC	MC	-	-	-	-	6	MC
USPGA Champ	-	-	-	-	-	-	-	-	-	MC
WGCNEC Inv'	-	-	-	-	-	-	-	-	-	-
Reno-Tahoe Op'	-	-	-	-	-	-	-	-	36	55
Air Canada Chp'	-	-	-	28	-	-	-	-	44	MC
Bell Canadian O'	-	-	MC	12	-	-	-	-	MC	MC
WGC AmEx	-	-	-	-	-	-	-	-	-	-
Tampa Bay Cl'	-	-	-	-	-	-	-	-	2	-
Marconi Penn C'	-	-	-	-	-	-	-	-	24	61
Texas Open	-	-	79	66	-	-	-	-	-	11
Michelob Chmp'	-	-	71	23	-	MC	MC	-	-	36
Invensys Classic	-	-	MC	MC	-	-	-	-	-	38
NCR Golf Cl'	-	-	7	36	-	-	-	-	34	36
Buick Challenge	-	-	40	20	-	-	-	-	4	MC
SFB Classic	-	-	35	33	-	-	-	-	MC	6
Tour Champ'ship	-	-	-	-	-	-	-	-	-	-

Dennis Paulson

27/9/62 – San Gabriel, CA

Slipping back down the rankings after a superb previous two years. In 1999, Paulson got back on the main tour after a couple of seasons on the Buy.Com Tour and notched seven top-ten finishes on his way to earning over $1.3million, and then in 2000 he won for the first time – the Buick Classic. But his big hitting game hasn't been on song in 2001, when he posted just two top-ten finishes and eventually placed 64th on the Money List. Nicknamed 'The Chief', Paulson has won on the Buy.com Tour (1998 Huntsville Open) and the Asian Tour (1990 Phillipines Open). ScAv - 71.01 (78th) – DD - 281.6 (72nd) DA - 61.4 (185tll) GIR - 64.9 (140th)   PpGIR - 1.779 (115th) SS - 59.1 (20th)

	'92	'93	'94	'95	'96	'97	'98	'99	'00	'01
WGC MatchPlay	-	-	-	-	-	-	-	-	33	33
Mercedes Ch	-	-	-	-	-	-	-	-	-	12
Tucson Open	-	-	MC	MC	-	-	-	45	-	-
Sony Open	-	-	MC	65	-	-	-	70	-	MC
Phoenix Open	-	-	-	MC	-	-	-	26	28	WD
AT&T P Beach	-	-	12	MC	-	-	-	32	MC	-
Buick Invitatn'l	-	-	31	26	-	-	-	7	21	20
Bob Hope Cl'	-	-	74	25	-	-	-	43	36	MC
Nissan Open	-	-	-	25	-	-	59	MC	18	2
Genuity Champ	-	-	-	-	-	-	-	-	-	-
Honda Classic	-	-	MC	-	-	-	-	-	-	-
Bay Hill Invit'l	-	-	-	-	-	-	-	56	29	8
Players Champ	-	-	-	-	-	-	-	MC	MC	31
BellSouth Cl'	-	-	MC	MC	-	-	-	16	MC	3
US Masters	-	-	-	-	-	-	-	-	14	MC
Worldcom Cl'	-	-	-	MC	-	-	32	-	12
Houston Open	-	-	MC	MC	-	-	-	-	-	-
GG Chrysler Cl'	-	-	MC	MC	-	-	-	37	62	-
Compaq Classic	-	-	4	MC	-	-	-	4	MC	-
Byron Nelson C'	-	-	50	55	-	-	-	MC	-	MC
MasterCard Cln'l	-	-	-	-	-	-	-	55	MC	MC
Kemper Ins Open	-	-	24	MC	-	-	-	8	-	MC
Memorial T'ment	-	-	-	-	-	-	-	6	64	40
St. Jude Classic	-	-	MC	45	-	-	-	-	-	-
U.S. Open	-	-	-	-	-	-	-	WD	MC	-
Buick Classic	-	-	MC	77	-	-	-	2	1	52
Canon GH Open	-	-	MC	MC	-	-	-	-	-	-
Western Open	-	-	74	MC	-	-	-	55	41	-
Gr. Milwaukee	-	-	18	MC	-	-	-	-	-	-
British Open	-	-	-	-	-	-	-	58	11	MC
B.C. Open	-	-	MC	68	-	-	-	-	-	-
John Deere Cl'	-	-	-	5	-	-	-	-	-	-
The International	-	-	MC	MC	-	-	-	39	-	-
Buick Open	-	-	11	MC	-	-	-	-	MC	-
USPGA Champ	-	-	-	-	-	-	-	MC	58	MC
WGCNEC Inv'	-	-	-	-	-	-	-	-	-	-
Reno-Tahoe Op'	-	-	-	-	-	-	-	7	MC	-
Air Canada Chp'	-	-	-	-	-	-	-	-	-	16
Bell Canadian O'	-	-	53	45	-	-	-	2	MC	MC
WGC AmEx	-	-	-	-	-	-	-	20	45	-
Tampa Bay Cl'	-	-	-	-	-	-	-	-	MC	-
Marconi Penn C'	-	-	-	-	-	-	-	-	MC	-
Texas Open	-	-	MC	MC	-	-	-	-	-	71
Michelob Chmp'	-	-	46	-	-	-	-	35	-	32
Invensys Classic	-	-	MC	15	-	-	-	28	49	MC
NCR Golf Cl'	-	-	MC	WD	-	-	-	-	-	-
Buick Challenge	-	-	-	-	-	-	-	55	-	-
SFB Classic	-	-	MC	-	-	-	-	-	-	-
Tour Champ'ship	-	-	-	-	-	-	-	29	-	-

David Peoples

9/1/60 – Augusta, ME

Looked set for a big future in the game when he won the Buick Challenge in 1991 and the Michelob in 1992 but hasn't won since. Re-established himself on the full tour in 2000 after three years in the wilderness. Third place in the NCR Classic earned him enough cash to keep his card. Turned pro in 1981 and has visited the Q-School on seven occasions. Finished 25th on the Money List in 1992. Still an accurate driver of the ball and hits plenty of greens in regulation, his putting was poor in 2001 and his bunker play left plenty to be desired. ScAv - 71.08 (86th) – DD - 279.8 (91st) DA - 70.9 (52nd) GIR - 69.4 (31st) – PpGIR - 1.781 (122nd) SS - 46.6 (148th)

	'92	'93	'94	'95	'96	'97	'98	'99	'00	'01
WGC MatchPlay	-	-	-	-	-	-	-	-	-	-
Mercedes Ch	23	15	-	-	-	-	-	-	-	-
Tucson Open	59	MC	MC	-	68	-	-	-	69	32
Sony Open	-	-	66	-	MC	-	MC	-	58	37
Phoenix Open	MC	66	-	-	-	-	-	-	30	49
AT&T P Beach	-	-	-	-	-	-	-	-	-	-
Buick Invitatn'l	12	9	51	-	WD	-	-	-	MC	MC
Bob Hope Cl'	6	-	21	-	-	-	-	-	46	-
Nissan Open	17	37	48	-	MC	-	-	-	-	-
Genuity Champ	18	MC	61	-	-	-	-	-	21	MC
Honda Classic	-	-	MC	-	27	-	-	-	57	MC
Bay Hill Invit'l	51	39	-	67	-	-	-	-	-	-
Players Champ	MC	MC	-	-	-	-	-	-	-	MC
BellSouth Cl'	5	MC	4	33	MC	-	-	-	15	69
US Masters	54	52	-	-	-	-	-	-	-	-
Worldcom Cl'	29	MC	MC	-	-	-	-	-	MC	MC
Houston Open	11	66	MC	MC	MC	-	-	-	65	MC
GG Chrysler Cl'	41	-	44	55	MC	-	-	-	34	19
Compaq Classic	-	-	MC	5	MC	-	-	-	17	11
Byron Nelson C'	-	33	WD	-	MC	-	-	-	41	8
MasterCard Cln'lMC	WD	-	-	-	-	-	-	-	-
Kemper Ins Open	-	MC	57	-	MC	-	-	-	7	MC
Memorial T'ment	-	69	-	-	-	-	-	-	-	46
St. Jude Classic	-	MC	52	-	25	-	-	-	11	MC
U.S. Open	-	MC	-	-	-	-	-	-	-	66
Buick Classic	MC	-	MC	MC	MC	MC	-	-	MC	-
Canon GH Open	MC	-	WD	24	74	-	-	-	32	55
Western Open	-	-	-	-	-	-	-	-	MC	MC
Gr. Milwaukee	39	49	29	MC	MC	-	MC	39	MC	15
British Open	-	-	-	-	-	-	-	-	-	-
B.C. Open	MC	22	41	-	MC	MC	18	-	-	-
John Deere Cl'	43	MC	18	38	WD	MC	81	12	MC	WD
The International	-	MC	46	-	-	-	-	-	-	53
Buick Open	-	53	MC	62	-	-	-	-	57	49
USPGA Champ	69	-	-	-	-	-	-	-	-	-
WGCNEC Inv'	-	-	-	-	-	-	-	-	-	-
Reno-Tahoe Op'	-	-	-	-	-	-	-	76	21	MC
Air Canada Chp'	-	-	-	-	46	39	MC	-	38	21
Bell Canadian O'	-	WD	MC	-	-	-	-	-	-	-
WGC AmEx	-	-	-	-	-	-	-	-	-	-
Tampa Bay Cl'	-	-	-	-	-	-	-	-	27	-
Marconi Penn C'	-	-	-	-	-	-	-	-	-	58
Texas Open	-	-	55	-	MC	67	DQ	-	-	WD
Michelob Chmp'	1	60	MC	45	MC	MC	48	MC	41	-
Invensys ClassicMC	47	65	-	-	-	-	-	49	53
NCR Golf Cl'	29	60	76	-	-	-	-	-	66	3
Buick Challenge	MC	MC	MC	MC	MC	59	20	13	-	31
SFB Classic	-	-	26	28	66	57	MC	42	MC	13
Tour Champ'ship	27	-	-	-	-	-	-	-	-	-

Tom Pernice, Jr.
15/9/59 – Kansas City, MO

Stumbled over the line to hold off some of the best players in the world to win the International at Castle Pines in August of last year. That victory was the second US Tour success of his 18-year pro career – the other being the 1999 Buick Open. He was a regular if relatively unsuccessful member of the main tour in the mid-'80s before losing his card and playing on the Buy.com Tour in the early part of the last decade. Solid, if unspectacular, performances in the late '90s have meant no recent returns to Q-School. Lacks accuracy off the tee but is a big hitter.

ScAv - 71.14 (90th) – DD - 282.2 (66th) DA - 63.9 (172nd) GIR - 64.1 (155th) – PpGIR - 1.758 (60th) SS - 54.3 (68th)

	'92	'93	'94	'95	'96	'97	'98	'99	'00	'01
WGC MatchPlay	-	-	-	-	-	-	-	-	-	-
Mercedes Ch	-	-	-	-	-	-	-	8	-	-
Tucson Open	-	-	-	-	MC	-	MC	-	-	61
Sony Open	-	-	-	-	-	MC	MC	MC	-	MC
Phoenix Open	MC	-	-	-	-	-	-	MC	23	MC
AT&T P Beach	-	-	-	-	-	MC	2	MC	MC	36
Buick Invitatn'l	-	-	-	-	-	34	27	MC	MC	36
Bob Hope Cl'	-	-	-	-	-	MC	-	13	28	7
Nissan Open	-	-	-	-	-	MC	24	62	52	68
Genuity Champ	-	-	-	-	-	MC	-	-	-	-
Honda Classic	-	-	-	-	-	MC	MC	-	MC	MC
Bay Hill Invit'l	-	-	-	-	-	-	-	MC	22	71
Players Champ	-	-	-	-	-	-	-	MC	MC	-
BellSouth Cl'	-	-	-	-	-	19	36	MC	5	34
US Masters	-	-	-	-	-	-	-	-	-	-
Worldcom Cl'	-	-	-	-	-	-	-	MC	61	MC
Houston Open	-	-	-	-	-	45	MC	45	29	26
GG Chrysler Cl'	-	-	-	-	-	MC	MC	MC	-	-
Compaq Classic	-	-	-	-	-	MC	51	-	54	80
Byron Nelson C'	-	-	-	-	-	MC	70	MC	MC	MC
MasterCard Cln'l	-	-	-	-	-	-	-	33	55	MC
Kemper Ins Open	-	-	-	-	-	56	42	MC	-	45
Memorial T'ment	-	-	-	-	-	-	-	43	64	-
St. Jude Classic	-	-	-	-	-	MC	MC	-	-	MC
U.S. Open	-	-	94	-	-	-	-	-	-	-
Buick Classic	-	-	-	-	-	MC	MC	79	MC	50
Canon GH Open	-	-	-	-	-	21	MC	20	MC	6
Western Open	-	-	-	-	-	42	71	MC	MC	MC
Gr. Milwaukee	-	-	-	MC	-	4	18	39	35	MC
British Open	-	66	-	-	-	-	-	-	-	-
B.C. Open	-	-	-	-	-	-	-	-	-	-
John Deere Cl'	-	-	-	-	-	82	13	16	MC	MC
The International	-	-	-	-	-	33	17	59	MC	1
Buick Open	-	-	-	-	-	15	MC	1	21	4
USPGA Champ	-	-	-	-	-	-	-	MC	27	51
WGCNEC Inv'	-	-	-	-	-	-	-	-	-	-
Reno-Tahoe Op'	-	-	-	-	-	-	-	-	-	-
Air Canada Chp'	-	-	-	-	-	MC	11	13	MC	37
Bell Canadian O'	-	-	-	-	-	MC	47	-	MC	MC
WGC AmEx	-	-	-	-	-	-	-	-	-	-
Tampa Bay Cl'	-	-	-	-	-	-	-	-	-	-
Marconi Penn C'	-	-	-	-	-	-	-	-	MC	MC
Texas Open	-	-	58	-	-	-	-	-	-	-
Michelob Chmp'	-	-	-	-	-	-	MC	69	MC	-
Invensys Classic	-	-	-	-	-	MC	15	MC	MC	21
NCR Golf Cl'	-	-	-	-	-	MC	19	MC	MC	21
Buick Challenge	-	-	-	-	-	MC	MC	31	41	MC
SFB Classic	-	-	-	-	-	MC	-	MC	72	67
Tour Champ'ship	-	-	-	-	-	-	-	-	-	-

Chris Perry
27/9/61 – Edenton, NC

A veteran of 469 US Tour events but just one victory - the 1998 BC Open. Last season wasn't as lucrative as previous years – especially 1999, when Perry managed to earn over $2.1million without a victory (a record). In fact, he didn't manage to make a cut in 2001 after withdrawing from the British Open in July. Turned pro in 1984 and bar 1993 and 1994 (when he played on the Buy.com Tour – winning once, the Utah Classic) he has been a stalwart of the main tour, always claiming enough cash to earn his playing rights for the following season.

ScAv - 71.21 (102nd) – DD - 278.4 (108th) DA - 69.6 (74th) GIR - 68.4 (46th) – PpGIR - 1.782 (123rd) SS - 39.4 (186th)

	'92	'93	'94	'95	'96	'97	'98	'99	'00	'01
WGC MatchPlay	-	-	-	-	-	-	-	-	33	17
Mercedes Ch	-	-	-	-	-	-	-	20	-	-
Tucson Open	MC	-	MC	-	-	24	MC	-	-	41
Sony Open	-	-	MC	66	-	-	-	2	-	51
Phoenix Open	WD	-	-	MC	-	MC	34	MC	23	13
AT&T P Beach	MC	58	-	55	-	65	MC	-	28	-
Buick Invitatn'l	MC	-	32	66	34	72	4	MC	-	41
Bob Hope Cl'	-	MC	-	33	-	MC	16	43	36	18
Nissan Open	-	-	-	-	-	MC	-	35	-	8
Genuity Champ	37	-	58	-	13	53	44	15	25	-
Honda Classic	MC	-	66	MC	MC	30	-	-	-	-
Bay Hill Invit'l	MC	-	53	-	14	MC	23	38	8	-
Players Champ	MC	-	-	31	MC	32	33	-	-	-
BellSouth Cl'	-	WD	-	MC	-	MC	MC	-	10	MC
US Masters	-	-	-	-	-	-	-	50	14	37
Worldcom Cl'	MC	-	-	-	-	27	MC	4	15	71
Houston Open	-	-	74	-	30	-	-	-	-	-
GG Chrysler Cl'	MC	-	29	MC	MC	38	25	5	MC	-
Compaq Classic	72	-	MC	MC	31	27	12	MC	-	-
Byron Nelson C'	MC	-	-	5	57	9	MC	-	-	-
MasterCard Cln'l	-	-	-	-	-	-	-	33	-	WD
Kemper Ins Open	MC	-	-	18	MC	25	-	-	-	WD
Memorial T'ment	-	-	WD	-	57	16	24	17	MC	-
St. Jude Classic	-	-	-	-	MC	35	-	-	-	-
U.S. Open	-	MC	56	-	43	25	42	32	19	-
Buick Classic	MC	-	12	24	17	10	3	5	19	-
Canon GH Open	-	-	-	MC	-	-	-	-	-	-
Western Open	MC	-	52	MC	52	22	7	41	63	-
Gr. Milwaukee	39	MC	-	MC	34	34	3	6	9	61
British Open	-	-	-	-	-	WD	-	-	MC	WD
B.C. Open	38	21	-	50	2	1	39	-	-	-
John Deere Cl'	20	39	-	12	3	-	54	5	-	-
The International	53	-	55	-	MC	19	4	48	-	-
Buick Open	MC	-	WD	65	20	23	15	2	MC	-
USPGA Champ	-	-	-	-	49	74	10	34	MC	-
WGCNEC Inv'	-	-	-	-	-	-	-	-	-	-
Reno-Tahoe Op'	-	-	-	-	-	-	-	2	33	MC
Air Canada Chp'	-	-	-	-	-	10	-	-	-	-
Bell Canadian O'	-	-	-	WD	30	11	-	-	-	-
WGC AmEx	-	-	-	-	-	-	-	7	16	-
Tampa Bay Cl'	-	-	-	-	-	-	-	-	-	MC
Marconi Penn C'	-	-	-	-	-	-	-	-	2	-
Texas Open	17	MC	-	28	60	-	-	-	-	-
Michelob Chmp'	MC	-	MC	51	11	39	-	-	-	-
Invensys Classic	56	-	30	-	27	32	4	MC	MC	-
NCR Golf Cl'	58	-	63	-	17	MC	37	13	MC	-
Buick Challenge	49	-	70	-	21	8	13	18	-	-
SFB Classic	17	22	11	MC	26	-	-	-	-	-
Tour Champ'ship	-	-	-	-	-	-	-	-	4	8

Kenny Perry

10/8/60 – Elizabethtown, KY

No relation to Chris, and a player that had a much better season than his namesake in 2001. His win in the Buick Open was his first for six years and the fourth of his career (the last being the 1995 Bob Hope Classic).

The victory helped Perry top the $1million for seasonal earnings for the first time ($1.7million in fact, pushing his career haul to $7.6million). Ended the year on a high by finishing fifth in the Tour Championship. Massive off the tee, his iron play was top class in 2001 and his putting was way above average.

ScAv - 70.22 (24th) – DD - 292.3 (10th) DA - 68.5 (100th) GIR - 71.4 (8th) – PpGIR - 1.748 (35th) SS - 52.1 (94th)

	'92	'93	'94	'95	'96	'97	'98	'99	'00	'01
WGC MatchPlay	-	-	-	-	-	-	-	-	-	33
Mercedes Ch	13	-	-	16	15	-	-	-	-	-
Tucson Open	-	55	MC	72	-	-	31	13	13	61
Sony Open	69	MC	-	-	55	-	16	-	-	-
Phoenix Open	24	MC	54	41	10	4	27	6	23	60
AT&T P Beach	20	MC	37	3	-	50	MC	MC	20	13
Buick Invitatn'l	-	-	-	-	-	WD	-	-	-	-
Bob Hope Cl'	8	-	-	1	7	MC	MC	53	65	MC
Nissan Open	-	MC	MC	2	52	42	-	35	31	-
Genuity Champ	71	16	45	MC	MC	28	46	-	51	63
Honda Classic	29	62	39	-	-	14	MC	MC	28	27
Bay Hill Invit'l	MC	-	-	53	-	59	-	52	-	43
Players Champ	WD	65	62	55	4	MC	MC	WD	27	18
BellSouth Cl'	6	-	54	-	23	19	36	36	3	WD
US Masters	MC	-	-	12	MC	MC	-	-	-	-
Worldcom Cl'	6	20	60	24	22	MC	10	MC	MC	-
Houston Open	-	MC	-	-	-	-	36	-	-	MC
GG Chrysler Cl'	20	61	MC	36	35	MC	MC	31	8	24
Compaq Classic	-	MC	4	-	WD	-	-	-	-	43
Byron Nelson C'	MC	-	14	5	-	60	57	MC	-	8
MasterCard Cln'	159	33	18	33	MC	-	6	33	41	26
Kemper Ins Open	-	MC	7	9	-	33	14	22	-	-
Memorial T'ment	MC	19	24	11	18	67	44	11	39	7
St. Jude Classic	-	50	-	-	3	12	MC	MC	-	-
U.S. Open	-	25	-	MC	50	MC	-	-	-	-
Buick Classic	-	MC	MC	-	-	-	-	-	-	-
Canon GH Open	MC	5	15	MC	MC	21	9	MC	-	7
Western Open	-	-	MC	-	-	WD	-	MC	15	20
Gr. Milwaukee	46	55	-	-	-	-	-	-	3	5
British Open	-	-	-	-	-	-	-	-	-	-
B.C. Open	-	-	-	-	-	-	-	-	-	-
John Deere Cl'	23	8	2	-	-	10	3	21	-	-
The International	MC	MC	WD	-	8	18	56	WD	-	11
Buick Open	-	48	28	11	MC	-	-	-	16	1
USPGA Champ	-	55	49	2	23	10	34	30	44	
WGCNEC Inv'	-	-	-	-	-	-	-	-	-	-
Reno-Tahoe Op'	-	-	-	-	-	-	-	17	-	-
Air Canada Chp'	-	-	-	-	5	-	-	-	-	-
Bell Canadian O'	18	10	-	-	-	-	-	-	-	-
WGC AmEx	-	-	-	-	-	-	-	-	-	-
Tampa Bay Cl'	-	-	-	-	-	-	-	-	27	-
Marconi Penn C'	-	-	-	-	-	-	-	-	-	-
Texas Open	-	-	-	15	-	-	MC	29	-	-
Michelob Chmp'	62	MC	14	-	-	MC	-	13	-	-
Invensys Classic	56	-	MC	MC	-	-	36	-	-	11
NCR Golf Cl'	WD	50	MC	-	MC	-	-	57	MC	MC
Buick Challenge	49	16	31	-	MC	67	MC	WD	-	23
SFB Classic	-	-	26	-	-	-	-	-	-	-
Tour Champ'ship	-	-	26	20	4	-	-	-	-	5

Nick Price

28/1/57 – Durban, South Africa

Veteran Zimbabwean who has had 30 worldwide victories including 16 US Tour titles and three Majors (1994 British Open and USPGA Championship in 1992 and 1994). Winless on the US Tour for the third straight year, though, in 2001, but he still managed to claim over $1million in prize money – for the eighth time in his career (his earnings in 18 years on the main tour now top $14million). His last success in America was in the 1998 Fedex St Jude Classic. One of the best ball strikers and iron players on tour, although he lack distance off the tee.

ScAv - 69.66 (6th) – DD - 274.5 (149th) DA - 71.8 (41st) GIR - 67.5 (64th) – PpGIR - 1.755 (50th) SS - 64.8 (4th)

	'92	'93	'94	'95	'96	'97	'98	'99	'00	'01
WGC MatchPlay	-	-	-	-	-	-	-	17	33	-
Mercedes Ch	17	-	-	-	-	-	4	-	-	-
Tucson Open	33	-	-	-	-	-	-	-	-	-
Sony Open	-	-	-	-	-	-	-	-	-	-
Phoenix Open	7	-	-	-	3	22	-	-	-	13
AT&T P Beach	-	-	-	-	-	-	-	-	-	-
Buick Invitatn'l	46	-	-	-	-	-	-	-	-	-
Bob Hope Cl'	50	-	-	-	-	-	-	-	-	-
Nissan Open	MC	-	-	-	-	-	-	5	43	20
Genuity Champ	-	16	72	-	20	2	36	10	3	7
Honda Classic	11	26	1	13	3	-	-	MC	-	-
Bay Hill Invit'l	11	10	2	14	36	11	MC	-	-	-
Players Champ	8	1	MC	37	46	24	8	3	3	10
BellSouth Cl'	-	2	MC	-	3	5	30	-	MC	-
US Masters	6	MC	35	MC	18	24	MC	6	11	MC
Worldcom Cl'	3	54	-	7	5	1	6	60	39	49
Houston Open	7	-	MC	MC	-	-	-	-	-	-
GG Chrysler Cl'	MC	-	-	-	-	-	-	-	-	-
Compaq Classic	-	-	-	-	-	-	-	51	17	23
Byron Nelson C'	55	11	20	-	4	19	MC	12	15	3
MasterCard Cln'	155	45	1	12	56	-	35	-	-	MC
Kemper Ins Open	-	-	-	9	-	3	-	-	-	-
Memorial T'ment	-	-	-	10	-	-	-	-	-	-
St. Jude Classic	13	1	4	MC	-	5	1	42	25	8
U.S. Open	4	11	MC	13	-	19	4	23	27	MC
Buick Classic	-	-	-	-	WD	-	-	-	-	-
Canon GH Open	2	1	33	-	-	-	-	-	-	-
Western Open	9	1	1	13	70	-	22	20	2	50
Gr. Milwaukee	6	31	-	-	-	-	-	-	-	-
British Open	51	6	1	40	44	MC	29	37	MC	21
B.C. Open	-	-	-	-	-	-	-	-	-	-
John Deere Cl'	-	-	-	-	-	-	-	-	-	-
The International	-	-	-	-	-	10	72	48	MC	MC
Buick Open	19	-	-	17	MC	-	-	-	-	-
USPGA Champ	1	31	1	39	8	13	4	5	MC	29
WGCNEC Inv'	-	-	-	-	-	-	-	3	20	29
Reno-Tahoe Op'	-	-	-	-	-	-	-	-	-	-
Air Canada Chp'	-	-	-	-	-	-	-	-	-	-
Bell Canadian O'	3	10	1	3	WD	-	-	-	-	23
WGC AmEx	-	-	-	-	-	-	-	4	5	-
Tampa Bay Cl'	-	-	-	-	-	-	-	-	-	-
Marconi Penn C'	-	-	-	-	-	-	-	-	-	5
Texas Open	1	-	MC	-	-	-	-	-	-	-
Michelob Chmp'	-	-	-	-	-	-	-	-	-	26
Invensys Classic	-	-	-	-	-	-	-	-	-	-
NCR Golf Cl'	-	-	-	-	-	-	-	-	-	13
Buick Challenge	-	-	-	-	-	-	-	-	2	9
SFB Classic	-	-	-	-	-	-	-	-	-	-
Tour Champ'ship	13	18	20	30	-	26	30	21	3	-

Brett Quigley
18/8/69 – Ft Devens, MA

Enjoyed his best season on the US Tour despite playing in just 21 events – missed the whole of March through injury. Managed five top-ten finishes in 2001 and comfortably retained his playing privileges for 2002. His best effort came at the Greater Greensboro Classic when he claimed second place – his best finish on the main tour since turning pro in 1991. His uncle, Dana, is a member of the Seniors Tour. Is long off the tee and his length usually sets up plenty of eagle opportunities. Former Buy.com Tour player who won the Philadelphia Classic in 1996.
ScAv - 70.31 (28th) – DD - 298.5 (2nd) DA - 62.5 (180th) GIR - 66.6 (85th) – PpGIR - 1.754 (46th) SS - 49.5 (126th)

	'92	'93	'94	'95	'96	'97	'98	'99	'00	'01
WGC MatchPlay	-	-	-	-	-	-	-	-	-	-
Mercedes Ch	-	-	-	-	-	-	-	-	-	-
Tucson Open	-	-	-	-	-	MC	MC	MC	-	WD
Sony Open	-	-	-	-	-	MC	4	-	39	-
Phoenix Open	-	-	-	-	-	MC	-	-	-	-
AT&T P Beach	-	-	-	-	-	38	MC	10	MC	MC
Buick Invitatn'l	-	-	-	-	-	29	-	MC	-	-
Bob Hope Cl'	-	-	-	-	-	MC	-	-	-	-
Nissan Open	-	-	-	-	-	45	24	70	-	-
Genuity Champ	-	-	-	-	-	40	-	MC	-	-
Honda Classic	-	-	-	-	-	37	-	-	-	-
Bay Hill Invit'l	-	-	-	-	-	-	42	-	-	-
Players Champ	-	-	-	-	-	-	-	-	-	-
BellSouth Cl'	-	-	-	-	-	MC	MC	-	-	-
US Masters	-	-	-	-	-	-	-	-	-	-
Worldcom Cl'	-	-	-	-	-	MC	-	-	-	-
Houston Open	-	-	-	-	-	32	59	MC	-	-
GG Chrysler Cl'	-	-	-	-	-	MC	55	MC	MC	2
Compaq Classic	-	-	-	-	-	MC	MC	47	-	MC
Byron Nelson C'	-	-	-	-	-	56	MC	-	-	-
MasterCard Cln'l	-	-	-	-	-	-	MC	-	-	5
Kemper Ins Open	-	-	-	-	-	65	54	MC	34	37
Memorial T'ment	-	-	-	-	-	-	23	-	-	MC
St. Jude Classic	-	-	-	-	-	70	56	10	MC	-
U.S. Open	-	-	-	-	-	-	-	MC	MC	-
Buick Classic	-	-	-	-	-	51	68	54	16	69
Canon GH Open	-	-	-	-	-	MC	MC	MC	76	-
Western Open	-	-	-	-	-	42	-	-	-	-
Gr. Milwaukee	-	-	-	-	-	20	MC	46	MC	18
British Open	-	-	-	-	-	-	-	-	-	-
B.C. Open	-	-	-	-	-	41	9	67	5	8
John Deere Cl'	-	-	-	-	-	MC	17	59	12	46
The International	-	-	-	-	-	MC	MC	30	-	6
Buick Open	-	-	-	-	-	20	MC	-	28	49
USPGA Champ	-	-	-	-	-	-	-	-	-	MC
WGCNEC Inv'	-	-	-	-	-	-	-	-	-	-
Reno-Tahoe Op'	-	-	-	-	-	-	-	DQ	MC	50
Air Canada Chp'	-	-	-	-	-	12	MC	MC	MC	8
Bell Canadian O'	-	-	-	-	-	30	MC	20	MC	MC
WGC AmEx	-	-	-	-	-	-	-	-	-	-
Tampa Bay Cl'	-	-	-	-	-	-	-	MC	-	-
Marconi Penn C'	-	-	-	-	-	-	-	65	-	-
Texas Open	-	-	-	-	-	38	73	46	19	MC
Michelob Chmp'	-	-	-	-	-	36	44	MC	MC	19
Invensys Classic	-	-	-	-	-	23	-	-	-	-
NCR Golf Cl'	-	-	-	-	-	49	27	-	-	-
Buick Challenge	-	-	-	-	-	MC	39	-	MC	-
SFB Classic	-	-	-	-	-	34	MC	62	50	5
Tour Champ'ship	-	-	-	-	-	-	-	-	-	-

Chris Riley
8/12/73 – San Diego, CA

Registered his best finish on the US Tour when runner-up in the International. His performance at Castle Pines gave him the confidence to go on to a further three top-ten finishes – and no missed cuts – in the latter half of the season. He improved upon his Money List position for the third consecutive season in 2001 (since graduating from the Buy.com Tour in 1998) and doubled his pro-career earnings with last term's cash haul of $1.2million. Played on the USA Walker Cup team alongside Tiger Woods in 1995. An accurate golfer, with a decent putting touch.
ScAv - 70.67 (51st) – DD - 276.3 (126th) DA - 71.2 (44th) GIR - 65.1 (132nd) – PpGIR - 1.751 (40th) SS - 52.4 (91st)

	'92	'93	'94	'95	'96	'97	'98	'99	'00	'01
WGC MatchPlay	-	-	-	-	-	-	-	-	-	-
Mercedes Ch	-	-	-	-	-	-	-	-	-	-
Tucson Open	-	-	-	-	-	-	-	-	31	20
Sony Open	-	-	-	-	-	-	-	7	26	MC
Phoenix Open	-	-	-	-	-	-	-	52	MC	MC
AT&T P Beach	-	-	-	-	-	-	-	25	MC	MC
Buick Invitatn'l	-	-	-	MC	-	-	-	7	MC	20
Bob Hope Cl'	-	-	-	-	-	-	-	-	-	-
Nissan Open	-	-	-	-	-	-	-	MC	-	43
Genuity Champ	-	-	-	-	-	-	-	19	MC	77
Honda Classic	-	-	-	-	-	-	-	9	28	-
Bay Hill Invit'l	-	-	-	-	-	-	-	MC	-	-
Players Champ	-	-	-	-	-	-	-	-	48	58
BellSouth Cl'	-	-	-	-	-	-	-	-	-	MC
US Masters	-	-	-	-	-	-	-	-	-	-
Worldcom Cl'	-	-	-	-	-	-	-	49	50	51
Houston Open	-	-	-	-	-	-	-	-	-	16
GG Chrysler Cl'	-	-	-	-	-	-	-	25	MC	MC
Compaq Classic	-	-	-	-	-	-	-	MC	54	-
Byron Nelson C'	-	-	-	-	-	-	-	51	56	25
MasterCard Cln'l	-	-	-	-	-	-	-	MC	-	MC
Kemper Ins Open	-	-	-	-	-	-	-	-	34	12
Memorial T'ment	-	-	-	-	-	-	-	MC	-	MC
St. Jude Classic	-	-	-	-	-	-	-	MC	65	-
U.S. Open	-	-	-	-	-	-	-	MC	-	-
Buick Classic	-	-	-	-	-	-	-	MC	71	69
Canon GH Open	-	-	-	-	-	-	-	46	18	73
Western Open	-	-	-	-	-	-	-	-	-	-
Gr. Milwaukee	-	-	-	-	-	-	-	-	MC	MC
British Open	-	-	-	-	-	-	-	-	-	-
B.C. Open	-	-	-	-	-	-	-	MC	15	27
John Deere Cl'	-	-	-	-	-	-	-	MC	4	MC
The International	-	-	-	-	-	-	-	MC	14	2
Buick Open	-	-	-	-	-	-	-	MC	-	-
USPGA Champ	-	-	-	-	-	-	-	-	-	51
WGCNEC Inv'	-	-	-	-	-	-	-	-	-	-
Reno-Tahoe Op'	-	-	-	-	-	-	-	MC	62	14
Air Canada Chp'	-	-	-	-	-	-	-	42	4	8
Bell Canadian O'	-	-	-	-	-	-	-	-	MC	-
WGC AmEx	-	-	-	-	-	-	-	-	-	-
Tampa Bay Cl'	-	-	-	-	-	-	-	-	56	-
Marconi Penn C'	-	-	-	-	-	-	-	-	54	-
Texas Open	-	-	-	-	-	-	-	49	-	41
Michelob Chmp'	-	-	-	-	-	-	-	45	9	12
Invensys Classic	-	-	-	-	MC	-	-	44	MC	7
NCR Golf Cl'	-	-	-	-	-	-	-	28	-	-
Buick Challenge	-	-	-	-	-	-	-	-	-	10
SFB Classic	-	-	-	-	-	-	-	6	-	-
Tour Champ'ship	-	-	-	-	-	-	-	-	-	37

Loren Roberts

24/6/55 – San Louis Obispo, CA

The 'Boss of the Moss' fell to his lowest position on the Money List for 14 years after a season that saw him post just two top-ten finishes – and they were nine months apart. His nickname comes from his undeniable skill with the putter and he still ranked in the top 40 of that category in 2001.

He is short off the tee, however, and his iron play was poor last season. The last of his seven US Tour wins came in 2000 (Greater Milwaukee Open).

Turned pro in 1977 and made the Ryder Cup team in 1995.

ScAv - 70.95 (70th) – DD - 261.6 (193rd) DA - 71.0 (45th) GIR - 65.6 (107th) – PpGIR - 1.749 (37th) SS - 55.3 (56th)

	'92	'93	'94	'95	'96	'97	'98	'99	'00	'01
WGC MatchPlay	-	-	-	-	-	-	-	9	33	-
Mercedes Ch	-	-	24	12	24	13	-	29	19	
Tucson Open	MC	31	2	58	24	-	71	-	-	
Sony Open	-	26	-	-	-	40	7	MC	5	
Phoenix Open	33	-	MC	29	-	MC	-	-	-	
AT&T P Beach	23	52	-	31	-	MC	-	-	-	
Buick Invitatn'l	MC	63	MC	26	35	-	7	21	MC	
Bob Hope Cl'	44	MC	52	-	-	19	21	-	40	
Nissan Open	-	-	-	-	-	15	44	18	-	
Genuity Champ	18	MC	7	43	20	MC	-	-	-	
Honda Classic	-	-	-	-	-	-	-	-	-	
Bay Hill Invit'l	22	MC	1	1	MC	6	WD	MC	4	47
Players Champ	21	MC	14	34	33	3	MC	MC	MC	MC
BellSouth Cl'	-	MC	-	-	-	-	-	-	-	
US Masters	-	5	24	23	MC	-	MC	3	37	
Worldcom Cl'	MC	74	3	13	1	30	-	49	MC	62
Houston Open	11	7	26	-	-	MC	-	5	3	WD
GG Chrysler Cl'	27	67	-	14	-	-	-	-	-	
Compaq Classic	66	-	-	-	-	-	-	-	-	
Byron Nelson C'	39	26	14	9	29	19	MC	1	25	28
MasterCard Cln'l	MC	4	30	46	MC	10	MC	51	46	-
Kemper Ins Open	-	-	-	-	7	21	-	44	48	
Memorial T'ment	-	34	26	-	67	-	-	-	-	
St. Jude Classic	46	23	35	-	44	61	56	55	7	MC
U.S. Open	-	11	2	WD	40	13	18	-	8	52
Buick Classic	39	16	MC	-	24	-	-	5	-	47
Canon GH Open	MC	-	-	-	-	-	-	-	-	
Western Open	56	19	-	MC	7	22	42	-	52	
Gr. Milwaukee	17	MC	2	27	1	2	35	46	1	36
British Open	-	-	24	MC	18	MC	29	-	7	13
B.C. Classic	-	-	MC	-	-	-	-	-	-	
John Deere Cl'	2	31	-	9	-	-	-	-	-	
The International	-	-	-	-	-	-	-	-	-	
Buick Open	-	MC	-	MC	-	-	9	16	21	
USPGA Champ	28	9	58	MC	49	65	MC	58	MC	
WGCNEC Inv'	-	-	-	-	-	-	-	14	29	
Reno-Tahoe Op'	-	-	-	-	-	-	-	-	-	
Air Canada Chp'	-	-	-	-	-	MC	-	-	-	
Bell Canadian O'	18	MC	-	12	-	MC	-	-	-	
WGC AmEx	-	-	-	-	-	-	40	-	-	
Tampa Bay Cl'	-	-	-	-	-	-	-	-	-	
Marconi Penn C'	-	-	-	-	-	-	-	8	MC	
Texas Open	25	MC	-	3	-	14	4	62	9	MC
Michelob Chmp'	33	6	-	-	9	13	35	19	-	
Invensys Classic	24	-	-	-	-	-	-	-	-	
NCR Golf Cl'	8	3	74	-	51	-	57	28	-	MC
Buick Challenge	3	19	-	2	68	MC	48	13	-	17
SFB Classic	-	-	-	-	-	-	-	-	6	
Tour Champ'ship	-	-	8	11	WD	8	-	21	27	-

Rory Sabbatini

2/4/76 – Durban, South Africa

Big-hitting, South African-born pro who is based in Tucson, Arizona. Won the Air Canada Championship in 2000 – in only his second season as a pro – and nearly added to his victory haul in 2001 when finishing second in the Mercedes Championship and the Invensys Classic.

Made it through Q-School in 1998 to gain membership to the full tour and, at the start of the 1999 season, was the youngest player on tour. Lacks accuracy off the tee but can hit it out there and ranked first in the 'bounce-back' category in 2001.

ScAv - 71.80 (154th) – DD - 288.5 (20th) DA - 62.3 (181st) GIR - 66.2 (95th) – PpGIR - 1.785 (125th) SS - 50.9 (113th)

	'92	'93	'94	'95	'96	'97	'98	'99	'00	'01
WGC MatchPlay	-	-	-	-	-	-	-	-	-	-
Mercedes Ch	-	-	-	-	-	-	-	-	-	2
Tucson Open	-	-	-	-	-	-	-	MC	60	-
Sony Open	-	-	-	-	-	-	-	MC	MC	43
Phoenix Open	-	-	-	-	-	-	-	-	58	MC
AT&T P Beach	-	-	-	-	-	-	-	MC	11	-
Buick Invitatn'l	-	-	-	-	-	-	-	52	MC	MC
Bob Hope Cl'	-	-	-	-	-	-	-	-	2	74
Nissan Open	-	-	-	-	-	-	-	-	12	66
Genuity Champ	-	-	-	-	-	-	-	70	-	-
Honda Classic	-	-	-	-	-	-	-	78	16	-
Bay Hill Invit'l	-	-	-	-	-	-	-	-	DQ	-
Players Champ	-	-	-	-	-	-	-	-	MC	MC
BellSouth Cl'	-	-	-	-	-	-	-	3	MC	-
US Masters	-	-	-	-	-	-	-	-	-	MC
Worldcom Cl'	-	-	-	-	-	-	-	-	-	MC
Houston Open	-	-	-	-	-	-	-	40	72	-
GG Chrysler Cl'	-	-	-	-	-	-	-	MC	-	-
Compaq Classic	-	-	-	-	-	-	-	MC	54	-
Byron Nelson C'	-	-	-	-	-	-	-	MC	WD	65
MasterCard Cln'l	-	-	-	-	-	-	-	-	70	WD
Kemper Ins Open	-	-	-	-	-	-	-	MC	-	-
Memorial T'ment	-	-	-	-	-	-	-	-	MC	60
St. Jude Classic	-	-	-	-	-	-	-	MC	33	-
U.S. Open	-	-	-	-	-	-	-	-	MC	-
Buick Classic	-	-	-	-	-	-	-	MC	-	MC
Canon GH Open	-	-	-	-	-	-	-	MC	-	-
Western Open	-	-	-	-	-	-	-	MC	-	5
Gr. Milwaukee	-	-	-	-	-	-	-	22	-	-
British Open	-	-	-	-	-	-	-	-	-	54
B.C. Classic	-	-	-	-	-	-	-	3	-	-
John Deere Cl'	-	-	-	-	-	-	-	21	-	-
The International	-	-	-	-	-	-	-	16	MC	26
Buick Open	-	-	-	-	-	-	-	MC	-	-
USPGA Champ	-	-	-	-	-	-	-	-	77	MC
WGCNEC Inv'	-	-	-	-	-	-	-	-	-	-
Reno-Tahoe Op'	-	-	-	-	-	-	-	63	-	-
Air Canada Chp'	-	-	-	-	-	-	-	MC	1	29
Bell Canadian O'	-	-	-	-	-	-	-	58	6	-
WGC AmEx	-	-	-	-	-	-	-	-	-	-
Tampa Bay Cl'	-	-	-	-	-	-	-	-	-	-
Marconi Penn C'	-	-	-	-	-	-	-	-	-	MC
Texas Open	-	-	-	-	-	-	-	-	-	MC
Michelob Chmp'	-	-	-	-	-	-	-	77	MC	-
Invensys Classic	-	-	-	-	-	-	-	MC	73	2
NCR Golf Cl'	-	-	-	-	-	-	-	-	62	50
Buick Challenge	-	-	-	-	-	-	-	65	23	65
SFB Classic	-	-	-	-	-	-	-	-	-	-
Tour Champ'ship	-	-	-	-	-	-	-	-	-	-

Scott Simpson
17/9/55 – San Diego, CA

After an injury plagued 2000 – in which he didn't play a US Tour event due to a broken ankle sustained in a skiing accident – this seven-time US Tour winner retained his tour card for 2002 mainly due to his second place in the Greater Greensboro Classic. His last victory came in 1998 (the Buick Invitational) and the one before that back in 1993 (the Byron Nelson Classic). But this veteran pro, who played in the Walker Cup in 1977 and Ryder Cup ten years later, is still one of the best putters around. Watch out for the Hawaiian-based pro in the Sony Open.

ScAv - 71.24 (105th) – DD - 272.7 (163rd) DA - 68.6 (97th) GIR - 64.5 (151st) – PpGIR - 1.738 (19th) SS - 44.6 (166th)

	'92	'93	'94	'95	'96	'97	'98	'99	'00	'01
WGC MatchPlay	-	-	-	-	-	-	-	-	-	
Mercedes Ch	-	-	4	-	-	-	-	25	-	
Tucson Open	-	-	-	2	-	-	-	20	-	
Sony Open	28	45	20	65	4	13	MC	64	-	MC
Phoenix Open	16	22	71	-	6	58	51	49	-	-
AT&T P Beach	48	36	MC	MC	-	65	WD	MC	-	MC
Buick Invitatn'l	53	37	15	MC	3	16	1	7	-	MC
Bob Hope Cl'	MC	3	44	16	56	34	MC	-	-	MC
Nissan Open	8	45	-	4	2	33	29	74	-	51
Genuity Champ	-	-	-	-	-	-	-	-	-	MC
Honda Classic	-	-	-	-	-	-	-	-	-	76
Bay Hill Invit'l	MC	17	21	11	31	45	MC	-	-	-
Players Champ	17	MC	MC	11	MC	MC	MC	-	-	-
BellSouth Cl'	-	22	-	-	39	45	-	-	-	27
US Masters	13	11	27	-	29	-	MC	-	-	-
Worldcom Cl'	16	-	-	-	-	-	-	-	-	-
Houston Open	-	-	-	19	-	-	-	MC	-	35
GG Chrysler Cl'	MC	-	MC	29	-	37	-	-	-	2
Compaq Classic	-	-	-	8	15	MC	-	-	-	43
Byron Nelson C'	55	1	MC	55	MC	-	-	MC	-	37
MasterCard Cln'l	MC	-	2	33	-	54	MC	-	-	-
Kemper Ins Open	-	-	-	14	30	MC	25	-	-	MC
Memorial T'ment	MC	57	14	21	75	-	-	54	-	-
St. Jude Classic	-	-	39	-	53	-	74	-	30	
U.S. Open	64	46	55	28	40	MC	58	-	-	-
Buick Classic	WD	55	-	-	MC	-	54	MC	-	-
Canon GH Open	-	-	40	-	-	68	-	-	-	17
Western Open	38	DQ	45	2	MC	62	42	MC	-	36
Gr. Milwaukee	-	-	-	-	-	-	-	-	-	36
British Open	-	9	MC	MC	32	-	-	-	-	-
B.C. Open	-	-	-	-	-	-	-	-	-	-
John Deere Cl'	-	-	-	-	-	-	-	-	-	-
The International	-	5	46	MC	MC	62	-	-	-	-
Buick Open	-	-	-	-	-	-	-	-	-	-
USPGA Champ	-	6	MC	54	MC	-	MC	-	-	-
WGCNEC Inv'	-	-	-	-	-	-	-	-	-	-
Reno-Tahoe Op'	-	-	-	-	-	-	-	-	-	-
Air Canada Chp'	-	-	-	-	MC	-	MC	-	-	-
Bell Canadian O'	-	-	-	-	-	-	-	-	-	67
WGC AmEx	-	-	-	-	-	-	-	-	-	-
Tampa Bay Cl'	-	-	-	-	-	-	-	-	-	-
Marconi Penn C'	-	-	-	-	-	-	-	-	-	-
Texas Open	17	-	55	-	MC	69	-	MC	-	24
Michelob Chmp'	68	39	-	2	-	MC	MC	MC	-	-
Invensys Classic	MC	-	-	-	-	-	19	MC	-	53
NCR Golf Cl'	38	35	74	WD	MC	MC	MC	-	-	-
Buick Challenge	49	26	MC	MC	55	MC	-	MC	-	MC
SFB Classic	-	-	-	-	-	-	MC	MC	-	WD
Tour Champ'ship	-	2	-	4	-	-	-	-	-	-

Joey Sindelar
30/3/58 – Ft. Knox, KY

Left it late to secure his playing rights for 2002 but second place in the Bell Canadian Open was enough to haul this six-time US Tour winner into the top 125 of the Money List. Sindelaar's last US Tour win was back in 1990 – the Hardee's Golf Classic (now John Deere Classic). Turned pro in 1981 and has made just shy of $6million in prize money over the past 20 years. His best season on the US Tour came in 1988 when two victories helped him to third on the Money List. Hits the ball a long way – over 290 yards on average.

ScAv - 71.18 (98th) – DD - 291.5 (11th) DA - 64.5 (163rd) GIR - 67.0 (75th) – PpGIR - 1.791 (148th) SS - 45.5 (157th)

	'92	'93	'94	'95	'96	'97	'98	'99	'00	'01
WGC MatchPlay	-	-	-	-	-	-	-	-	-	
Mercedes Ch	-	-	-	-	-	-	-	-	-	
Tucson Open	-	60	-	-	56	MC	9	-	-	MC
Sony Open	-	2	-	-	-	-	-	-	-	-
Phoenix Open	MC	MC	-	MC	-	-	-	-	-	-
AT&T P Beach	66	3	-	-	MC	WD	25	MC		47
Buick Invitatn'l	MC	7	-	32	10	MC	MC	MC	-	-
Bob Hope Cl'	MC	-	-	-	MC	MC	53	-	-	30
Nissan Open	68	-	-	-	-	-	-	-	-	-
Genuity Champ	32	MC	-	WD	MC	50	23	19	MC	-
Honda Classic	MC	15	-	27	27	MC	47	MC	MC	18
Bay Hill Invit'l	18	9	52	MC	67	54	36	23	MC	MC
Players Champ	46	16	35	-	MC	31	61	10	MC	-
BellSouth Cl'	13	-	30	18	29	67	-	-	5	6
US Masters	-	27	-	-	-	-	-	-	-	-
Worldcom Cl'	29	MC	50	-	32	14	6	MC	MC	MC
Houston Open	-	-	-	27	63	MC	59	10	MC	MC
GG Chrysler Cl'	MC	78	44	MC	16	49	MC	MC	MC	19
Compaq Classic	14	-	27	MC	MC	MC	-	-	43	-
Byron Nelson C'	-	-	-	-	-	-	-	-	-	-
MasterCard Cln'l	49	MC	42	66	-	63	41	MC	MC	40
Kemper Ins Open	MC	72	MC	MC	MC	14	42	28	MC	65
Memorial T'ment	3	25	MC	-	-	44	MC	MC	-	WD
St. Jude Classic	-	-	-	MC	-	-	-	-	-	WD
U.S. Open	6	MC	-	-	-	-	43	MC	-	-
Buick Classic	58	MC	MC	MC	31	63	17	71	5	WD
Canon GH Open	MC	51	MC	45	45	53	9	MC	53	MC
Western Open	19	MC	54	-	26	78	35	68	71	37
Gr. Milwaukee	9	-	3	6	MC	52	-	8	18	MC
British Open	-	-	-	-	-	-	-	-	-	-
B.C. Open	9	MC	7	6	31	MC	WD	MC	27	WD
John Deere Cl'	6	-	MC	59	MC	MC	-	31	WD	68
The International	11	-	43	22	36	MC	35	WD	38	53
Buick Open	62	-	MC	MC	MC	MC	6	9	MC	MC
USPGA Champ	56	WD	-	-	14	10	40	WD	-	-
WGCNEC Inv'	-	-	-	-	-	-	-	-	-	-
Reno-Tahoe Op'	-	-	-	-	-	-	-	-	-	MC
Air Canada Chp'	-	-	-	-	-	-	-	-	-	16
Bell Canadian O'	4	-	MC	14	7	44	13	58	35	2
WGC AmEx	-	-	-	-	-	-	-	-	-	-
Tampa Bay Cl'	-	-	-	-	-	-	-	66	-	-
Marconi Penn C'	-	-	-	-	-	-	-	-	78	MC
Texas Open	MC	-	-	MC	22	MC	-	-	-	-
Michelob Chmp'	MC	66	22	18	MC	46	17	-	12	MC
Invensys Classic	19	-	MC	MC	MC	30	22	-	MC	-
NCR Golf Cl'	11	-	24	-	13	-	19	-	MC	-
Buick Challenge	-	-	-	-	-	59	-	41	-	-
SFB Classic	-	-	-	49	-	28	-	43	-	-
Tour Champ'ship	-	-	-	-	-	-	-	-	-	-

Vijay Singh

22/2/63 – Lautoka, Fiji

Twenty two top-25 finishes in 26 events entered in 2001 for this Fijian two-time Major winner (1998 USPGA Championship and 2000 US Masters) but no win for the first time since 1996. He did win twice on the European Tour, though. Singh has had nine US Tour victories – the last being the 2000 US Masters – and 19 other worldwide titles. Turned pro in 1982 and learned his trade in Asia and Europe before coming to the USA full time in 1993. One of the best ball strikers in the game, massive off the tee and a brilliant putter.

ScAv - 69.21 (4th) – DD - 287.5 (23rd) DA - 66.7 (128th) GIR - 69.5 (30th) – PpGIR - 1.723 (4th) SS - 58.3 (24th)

	'92	'93	'94	'95	'96	'97	'98	'99	'00	'01
WGC MatchPlay	-	-	-	-	-	-	-	17	33	17
Mercedes Ch	-	-	17	-	24	-	13	4	8	3
Tucson Open	-	-	2	MC	-	-	-	-	-	-
Sony Open	-	-	32	47	8	-	-	38	19	22
Phoenix Open	-	-	18	1	21	-	22	WD	41	36
AT&T P Beach	-	-	24	MC	-	15	WD	10	2	2
Buick Invitatn'l	-	-	61	-	-	-	-	-	-	-
Bob Hope Cl'	-	-	-	-	-	-	-	-	-	-
Nissan Open	-	-	38	-	-	-	-	50	18	-
Genuity Champ	-	-	75	12	2	13	4	MC	36	3
Honda Classic	-	-	27	31	9	30	2	1	50	-
Bay Hill Invit'l	-	2	2	20	13	35	22	11	29	4
Players Champ	-	28	55	43	8	31	54	20	33	2
BellSouth Cl'	-	-	-	-	-	-	-	-	-	-
US Masters	-	-	27	MC	39	17	MC	24	1	18
Worldcom Cl'	-	47	15	MC	5	68	24	18	3	3
Houston Open	-	-	5	8	21	43	-	5	-	6
GG Chrysler Cl'	-	9	64	7	56	49	-	9	-	-
Compaq Classic	5	-	-	-	-	-	-	-	24	-
Byron Nelson C'	-	-	WD	-	-	-	-	-	41	11
MasterCard Cln'l	-	-	-	-	29	-	MC	11	41	11
Kemper Ins Open	-	-	-	4	80	33	42	18	-	-
Memorial T'ment	7	16	MC	11	43	1	68	2	33	5
St. Jude Classic	13	-	-	-	-	-	-	-	-	-
U.S. Open	-	MC	-	10	7	77	25	3	8	7
Buick Classic	-	1	WD	1	20	12	24	5	24	6
Canon GH Open	-	-	-	15	-	-	12	-	-	-
Western Open	-	-	-	66	8	57	2	4	MC	10
Gr. Milwaukee	-	-	-	-	-	42	-	-	-	-
British Open	51	59	20	6	11	38	19	MC	11	13
B.C. Open	-	-	-	-	-	-	-	-	-	-
John Deere Cl'	-	-	-	-	-	-	-	-	-	-
The International	-	17	MC	-	69	-	1	19	9	3
Buick Open	19	MC	-	-	-	1	8	72	11	-
USPGA Champ	48	4	MC	MC	5	13	1	49	MC	51
WGCNEC Inv'	-	-	-	-	-	-	-	15	-	13
Reno-Tahoe Op'	-	-	-	-	-	-	-	-	-	-
Air Canada Chp'	-	-	-	-	-	-	-	-	-	-
Bell Canadian O'	-	-	-	-	15	52	22	-	-	MC
WGC AmEx	-	-	-	-	-	-	-	16	3	-
Tampa Bay Cl'	-	-	-	-	-	-	-	-	-	-
Marconi Penn C'	-	-	-	-	-	-	-	-	-	MC
Texas Open	-	-	-	-	-	-	-	-	-	-
Michelob Chmp'	-	-	-	-	-	-	-	-	-	-
Invensys Classic	13	-	-	40	-	-	32	-	-	-
NCR Golf Cl'	-	-	-	-	-	-	12	5	18	6
Buick Challenge	-	-	-	-	55	37	58	-	-	10
SFB Classic	-	-	-	-	-	-	-	-	-	-
Tour Champ'ship	-	16	-	6	9	10	2	9	3	17

Jeff Sluman

11/9/57 - Rochester NY

Winner of the USPGA Championship in 1988 who had to wait another nine years for his second success on the US Tour (1997 Tucson Open). Has added two more wins since then and is firmly established on the full tour. Last season he managed to end his play-off hoodoo when he finally won in extra time at the BC Open – breaking a run of six successive play-off defeats. One of the best putters on the US Tour and a deadly accurate iron player. Turned pro in 1980 and has ranked in the top 60 of the Money List every season since 1994.

Sc Av – 70.13 (20th) DD – 281.6 (72nd) DA – 64.6 (159th) GIR – 70.2 (22nd) PpGIR – 1.725 (5th) SS – 60.2 (15th)

	'92	'93	'94	'95	'96	'97	'98	'99	'00	'01
WGC MatchPlay	-	-	-	-	-	-	-	33	17	17
Mercedes Ch	-	-	-	-	-	-	19	13	14	-
Tucson Open	47	34	-	MC	MC	1	59	-	-	MC
Sony Open	-	51	50	-	8	MC	MC	1	14	10
Phoenix Open	16	57	MC	MC	56	MC	-	-	-	-
AT&T P Beach	2	MC	MC	57	-	62	25	53	42	-
Buick Invitatn'l	15	-	-	-	-	-	16	18	21	36
Bob Hope Cl'	15	60	31	MC	MC	-	59	8	23	11
Nissan Open	32	45	15	14	MC	MC	-	23	MC	2
Genuity Champ	32	45	16	12	8	71	36	-	21	3
Honda Classic	-	-	-	-	MC	-	MC	MC	-	-
Bay Hill Invit'l	3	MC	MC	26	DQ	38	MC	44	MC	8
Players Champ	40	46	MC	49	41	MC	MC	46	17	33
BellSouth Cl'	-	-	59	-	-	51	57	-	-	-
US Masters	4	17	25	41	MC	7	MC	31	18	-
Worldcom Cl'	12	12	MC	MC	13	30	34	2	39	66
Houston Open	52	41	MC	-	-	-	-	-	-	MC
GG Chrysler Cl'	10	9	56	2	58	45	-	23	WD	-
Compaq Classic	-	-	-	-	-	-	-	-	74	11
Byron Nelson C'	8	-	-	26	4	MC	12	30	MC	-
MasterCard Cln'l	110	MC	63	23	2	13	3	2	13	15
Kemper Ins Open	60	22	37	38	30	33	-	22	MC	-
Memorial T'ment	35	-	MC	19	MC	-	70	-	25	15
St. Jude Classic	-	70	MC	-	-	-	2	MC	-	42
U.S. Open	2	11	9	13	50	28	10	MC	MC	-
Buick Classic	MC	60	MC	-	24	21	WD	-	-	-
Canon GH Open	5	20	40	MC	-	21	-	-	25	36
Western Open	7	30	6	MC	13	3	35	27	29	MC
Gr. Milwaukee	MC	MC	-	34	26	1	22	-	-	10
British Open	MC	MC	-	-	59	-	-	45	60	-
B.C. Open	13	41	2	7	9	WD	-	MC	-	1
John Deere Cl'	23	-	-	-	9	18	35	52	23	4
The International	-	-	MC	-	-	-	-	-	-	-
Buick Open	27	58	-	3	13	36	15	33	28	21
USPGA Champ	12	61	25	8	41	MC	27	54	41	MC
WGCNEC Inv'	-	-	-	-	-	-	-	-	-	-
Reno-Tahoe Op'	-	-	-	-	-	-	-	-	21	44
Air Canada Chp'	-	-	-	-	-	-	-	-	-	-
Bell Canadian O'	MC	MC	MC	MC	-	-	43	15	42	30
WGC AmEx	-	-	-	-	-	-	-	34	-	-
Tampa Bay Cl'	-	-	-	-	-	-	-	-	48	-
Marconi Penn C'	-	-	-	-	-	-	-	-	18	28
Texas Open	MC	57	MC	MC	-	-	-	-	-	-
Michelob Chmp'	52	-	-	8	-	11	10	MC	MC	-
Invensys Classic	-	MC	MC	54	22	MC	-	49	17	MC
NCR Golf Cl'	-	-	-	-	18	42	54	7	7	MC
Buick Challenge	-	7	4	20	MC	48	-	-	-	14
SFB Classic	-	-	-	-	-	-	-	-	-	-
Tour Champ'ship	13	-	-	-	9	-	11	5	-	20

Chris Smith
15/4/69 – Indianapolis, IN

Former Buy.com Tour pro who is still to win on the full tour. Last season saw him register his highest finish on the US Tour when he managed to claim third place in the BellSouth Classic.

Has had a stop start career after first coming to prominence when he managed to gain 'Battlefield Promotion' to the full tour after winning three times on the Buy.com Tour. His big hitting game is ideal for many US Tour venues and his time will surely come sooner rather than later. Also ranks highly in the Greens in Regulation stats.

Sc Av – 70.70 (55th) DD – 293.2 (9th) DA – 68.4 (103rd) GIR – 70.6 (15th) PpGIR – 1.773 (98th) SS – 36.3 (191st)

	'92	'93	'94	'95	'96	'97	'98	'99	'00	'01
WGC MatchPlay	-	-	-	-	-	-	-	-	-	-
Mercedes Ch	-	-	-	-	-	-	-	-	-	-
Tucson Open	-	-	-	-	72	-	MC	MC	-	MC
Sony Open	-	-	-	-	MC	-	-	MC	-	59
Phoenix Open	-	-	-	-	66	-	34	-	-	-
AT&T P Beach	-	-	-	-	-	-	9	MC	-	47
Buick Invitatn'l	-	-	-	-	MC	-	MC	MC	-	10
Bob Hope Cl'	-	-	-	-	MC	-	52	-	-	38
Nissan Open	-	-	-	-	68	-	MC	-	-	MC
Genuity Champ	-	-	-	-	-	-	71	44	-	8
Honda Classic	-	-	-	-	MC	-	MC	78	-	11
Bay Hill Invit'l	-	-	-	-	MC	-	-	-	-	-
Players Champ	-	-	-	-	-	-	-	-	-	-
BellSouth Cl'	-	-	-	-	MC	-	MC	30	-	3
US Masters	-	-	-	-	-	-	-	-	-	-
Worldcom Cl'	-	-	-	-	-	-	MC	-	-	28
Houston Open	-	-	-	-	MC	-	MC	33	-	26
GG Chrysler Cl'	-	-	67	-	MC	-	MC	-	-	-
Compaq Classic	-	-	-	-	33	-	MC	20	-	5
Byron Nelson C'	-	-	-	-	29	-	MC	30	-	62
MasterCard Cln'l	-	-	-	-	-	-	-	-	-	MC
Kemper Ins Open	-	-	-	-	63	-	MC	MC	-	-
Memorial T'ment	-	-	-	-	-	-	-	-	-	56
St. Jude Classic	-	-	-	-	MC	-	37	MC	-	-
U.S. Open	-	-	-	-	-	60	-	62	-	MC
Buick Classic	-	-	-	-	81	-	68	46	-	16
Canon GH Open	-	-	-	-	MC	-	47	MC	-	45
Western Open	-	MC	-	-	70	-	53	MC	-	20
Gr. Milwaukee	-	-	-	-	MC	12	MC	55	-	36
British Open	-	-	-	-	-	-	-	-	-	-
B.C. Open	-	8	MC	-	MC	-	MC	-	-	-
John Deere Cl'	-	-	-	-	MC	-	66	MC	-	MC
The International	-	-	-	-	-	-	MC	MC	-	67
Buick Open	-	-	-	-	-	-	-	-	-	-
USPGA Champ	-	-	-	-	-	-	-	-	-	29
WGCNEC Inv'	-	-	-	-	-	-	-	-	-	-
Reno-Tahoe Op'	-	-	-	-	-	-	MC	-	-	MC
Air Canada Chp'	-	-	-	-	67	31	40	MC	-	-
Bell Canadian O'	-	-	-	-	MC	-	36	MC	-	-
WGC AmEx	-	-	-	-	-	-	-	-	-	-
Tampa Bay Cl'	-	-	-	-	-	-	-	-	-	-
Marconi Penn C'	-	-	-	-	-	-	-	-	-	41
Texas Open	-	-	-	-	76	38	64	MC	-	-
Michelob Chmp'	-	-	-	-	72	19	60	MC	-	MC
Invensys Classic	-	-	-	-	-	-	MC	56	-	MC
NCR Golf Cl'	-	-	-	-	-	-	60	69	-	MC
Buick Challenge	-	MC	-	-	68	-	-	MC	-	MC
SFB Classic	-	-	-	-	MC	-	7	MC	-	6
Tour Champ'ship	-	-	-	-	-	-	-	-	-	-

Jerry Smith
24/4/64 – Council Bluffs, IA

Turned pro in 1987 but only made it on to the US Tour for the first time in 2000. Spent some time in Asia and won the Guam Open in 1998 on the Omega (now Davidoff) Tour before making it to the full tour through Q-School in 1999.

Claimed third position in the NCR Classic – his best finish on the US Tour – in 2001, which helped him earn his playing rights for 2002.

His putting was the best attribute of his game last season as he is neither long nor particularly accurate off the tee.

ScAv - 71.25 (109th) – DD - 276.5 (125th) DA - 68.2 (105th) GIR - 63.9 (159th) – PpGIR - 1.755 (50th) SS - 46.9 (144th)

	'92	'93	'94	'95	'96	'97	'98	'99	'00	'01
WGC MatchPlay	-	-	-	-	-	-	-	-	-	-
Mercedes Ch	-	-	-	-	-	-	-	-	-	-
Tucson Open	-	-	-	-	-	-	-	-	13	MC
Sony Open	-	-	-	-	-	-	-	-	14	29
Phoenix Open	-	-	-	-	-	-	-	-	69	MC
AT&T P Beach	-	-	-	-	-	-	-	-	42	27
Buick Invitatn'l	-	-	-	-	-	-	-	-	MC	-
Bob Hope Cl'	-	-	-	-	-	-	-	-	-	MC
Nissan Open	-	-	-	-	-	-	-	-	-	MC
Genuity Champ	-	-	-	-	-	-	-	-	33	-
Honda Classic	-	-	-	-	-	-	-	-	36	MC
Bay Hill Invit'l	-	-	-	-	-	-	-	-	MC	-
Players Champ	-	-	-	-	-	-	-	-	-	-
BellSouth Cl'	-	-	-	-	-	-	-	-	53	69
US Masters	-	-	-	-	-	-	-	-	-	-
Worldcom Cl'	-	-	-	-	-	-	-	-	39	MC
Houston Open	-	-	-	-	-	-	-	-	53	46
GG Chrysler Cl'	-	-	-	-	-	-	-	-	78	MC
Compaq Classic	-	-	-	-	-	-	-	-	MC	MC
Byron Nelson C'	-	-	-	-	-	-	-	-	9	77
MasterCard Cln'l	-	-	-	-	-	-	-	-	-	-
Kemper Ins Open	-	-	-	-	-	-	-	-	MC	-
Memorial T'ment	-	-	-	-	-	-	-	-	MC	-
St. Jude Classic	-	-	-	-	-	-	-	-	MC	53
U.S. Open	MC	-	-	-	-	-	-	-	-	-
Buick Classic	-	-	-	-	-	-	-	-	54	56
Canon GH Open	-	-	-	-	-	-	-	-	-	MC
Western Open	-	-	-	-	-	-	-	-	MC	MC
Gr. Milwaukee	-	-	-	-	-	-	-	-	-	47
British Open	-	-	-	-	-	-	-	-	-	-
B.C. Open	-	-	-	-	-	-	-	-	15	17
John Deere Cl'	-	-	70	-	-	-	-	-	MC	10
The International	-	-	-	-	-	-	-	-	63	-
Buick Open	-	-	-	-	-	-	-	-	-	66
USPGA Champ	-	-	-	-	-	-	-	-	-	-
WGCNEC Inv'	-	-	-	-	-	-	-	-	-	-
Reno-Tahoe Op'	-	-	-	-	-	-	-	-	42	MC
Air Canada Chp'	-	-	-	-	-	-	-	-	80	8
Bell Canadian O'	-	-	-	-	-	-	-	-	-	55
WGC AmEx	-	-	-	-	-	-	-	-	-	-
Tampa Bay Cl'	-	-	-	-	-	-	-	-	33	-
Marconi Penn C'	-	-	-	-	-	-	-	-	48	18
Texas Open	-	-	-	-	-	-	-	-	33	11
Michelob Chmp'	-	-	-	-	-	-	-	-	-	MC
Invensys Classic	-	-	-	-	-	-	-	-	MC	MC
NCR Golf Cl'	-	-	-	-	-	-	-	-	MC	3
Buick Challenge	-	-	-	-	-	-	-	-	MC	MC
SFB Classic	-	-	-	-	-	-	-	-	MC	-
Tour Champ'ship	-	-	-	-	-	-	-	-	-	-

Sponsored by Stan James

Mike Sposa
5/6/69 – Teaneck, NJ

Managed to break into the top 100 of the Money List for the first time in his career in 2001. Sposa didn't manage one top-ten finish last season but he did register nine top-25 positions. Turned pro in 1991 and played on minor tours and the Buy.com Tour (winning the 1998 Boise Open) before breaking on to the full Tour in 1999.

He managed to push his career earnings over $1million with his 2001 prize money. Played on the 1991 Walker Cup team. Above average putter on the tour last season but lacked length off the tee.
ScAv - 70.90 (66th) – DD - 278.2 (113th) DA - 69.6 (74th) GIR - 66.3 (92nd) – PpGIR - 1.760 (63rd) SS - 54.3 (68th)

	'92	'93	'94	'95	'96	'97	'98	'99	'00	'01
WGC MatchPlay	-	-	-	-	-	-	-	-	-	-
Mercedes Ch	-	-	-	-	-	-	-	-	-	-
Tucson Open	-	-	-	-	-	-	-	60	56	20
Sony Open	-	-	-	-	-	-	-	19	39	-
Phoenix Open	-	-	-	-	-	-	-	-	-	-
AT&T P Beach	-	-	-	-	-	-	-	32	MC	DQ
Buick Invitatn'l	-	-	-	-	-	-	-	45	MC	13
Bob Hope Cl'	-	-	-	-	-	-	-	-	-	-
Nissan Open	-	-	-	-	-	-	-	MC	-	-
Genuity Champ	-	-	-	-	-	-	-	MC	-	58
Honda Classic	-	-	-	-	-	-	-	27	MC	18
Bay Hill Invit'l	-	-	-	-	-	-	-	-	-	-
Players Champ	-	-	-	-	-	-	-	-	-	-
BellSouth Cl'	-	-	-	-	-	-	-	20	-	25
US Masters	-	-	-	-	-	-	-	-	-	-
Worldcom Cl'	-	-	-	-	-	-	-	-	-	21
Houston Open	-	-	-	-	-	-	-	WD	7	35
GG Chrysler Cl'	-	-	-	-	-	-	-	MC	MC	12
Compaq Classic	-	-	-	-	-	-	-	82	MC	-
Byron Nelson C'	-	-	-	-	-	-	-	46	-	MC
MasterCard Cln'l	-	-	-	-	-	-	-	-	-	11
Kemper Ins Open	-	-	-	-	-	-	-	10	MC	64
Memorial T'ment	-	-	-	-	-	-	-	-	-	40
St. Jude Classic	-	-	-	-	-	-	-	55	38	30
U.S. Open	-	-	-	MC	-	-	-	-	-	-
Buick Classic	-	-	-	-	-	-	-	MC	DQ	-
Canon GH Open	-	-	-	-	-	-	-	57	MC	MC
Western Open	-	-	-	-	-	MC	-	MC	MC	MC
Gr. Milwaukee	-	-	-	-	-	-	-	MC	MC	-
British Open	-	-	-	-	-	-	-	-	-	-
B.C. Open	-	-	-	-	-	-	-	18	WD	50
John Deere Cl'	-	-	-	-	-	-	-	WD	23	MC
The International	-	-	-	-	-	-	-	61	-	45
Buick Open	-	-	-	-	-	-	-	MC	MC	MC
USPGA Champ	-	-	-	-	-	-	-	-	-	-
WGCNEC Inv'	-	-	-	-	-	-	-	-	-	-
Reno-Tahoe Op'	-	-	-	-	-	-	-	MC	36	50
Air Canada Chp'	-	-	-	-	-	-	-	31	MC	MC
Bell Canadian O'	-	-	-	-	-	-	-	58	MC	18
WGC AmEx	-	-	-	-	-	-	-	-	-	-
Tampa Bay Cl'	-	-	-	-	-	-	-	-	66	-
Marconi Penn C'	-	-	-	-	-	-	-	-	41	-
Texas Open	-	-	-	-	-	-	-	MC	48	-
Michelob Chmp'	-	-	-	-	-	-	-	65	30	26
Invensys Classic	-	-	-	-	-	-	-	-	-	MC
NCR Golf Cl'	-	-	-	-	-	-	-	MC	-	30
Buick Challenge	-	-	-	-	-	-	-	MC	MC	31
SFB Classic	-	-	-	-	-	-	-	31	36	17
Tour Champ'ship	-	-	-	-	-	-	-	-	-	-

Paul Stankowski
2/12/69 – Oxnard, CA

Still to hit the dizzy heights of 1996 when he won the BellSouth Classic, the prestigious Casio World Open in Japan and the Louisiana Open on the Buy.com Tour. But Stankowski did manage to put another £750,000 or so in the bank in 2001 to boost his career earnings to nearly $5million. His best finish last season was in the Bob Hope Classic when he claimed second spot. Turned pro in 1991 and another player to have benefited from LASIK surgery. Long off the tee at over 285 yards, he can be a bit wild with the driver.
ScAv - 71.37 (115th) – DD - 285.4 (32nd) DA - 66.3 (133rd) GIR - 66.6 (85th) – PpGIR - 1.771 (93rd) SS - 52.0 (90th)

	'92	'93	'94	'95	'96	'97	'98	'99	'00	'01
WGC MatchPlay	-	-	-	-	-	-	-	-	-	-
Mercedes Ch	-	-	-	-	29	13	-	-	-	-
Tucson Open	-	MC	17	MC	3	MC	13	40	MC	-
Sony Open	-	MC	MC	MC	1	57	MC	-	-	-
Phoenix Open	-	-	MC	-	50	12	MC	10	55	-
AT&T P Beach	-	MC	MC	-	11	WD	15	35	63	-
Buick Invitatn'l	-	31	MC	MC	-	-	-	-	-	69
Bob Hope Cl'	-	6	16	-	MC	10	-	-	36	2
Nissan Open	-	-	66	MC	-	-	MC	MC	-	43
Genuity Champ	-	-	53	-	MC	-	MC	MC	-	-
Honda Classic	-	59	27	MC	5	52	15	-	-	27
Bay Hill Invit'l	-	MC	-	14	MC	-	-	-	-	71
Players Champ	-	-	MC	-	14	WD	MC	-	-	44
BellSouth Cl'	-	13	MC	1	MC	59	23	15	-	MC
US Masters	-	-	-	MC	5	39	-	-	-	-
Worldcom Cl'	-	-	68	-	14	-	MC	-	-	-
Houston Open	-	MC	4	MC	-	47	MC	11	67	-
GG Chrysler Cl'	-	MC	61	-	14	-	6	62	WD	-
Compaq Classic	-	MC	-	33	-	-	16	53	-	-
Byron Nelson C'	-	MC	MC	40	5	MC	MC	10	25	-
MasterCard Cln'l	-	-	66	MC	MC	MC	MC	-	-	-
Kemper Ins Open	-	49	38	MC	11	MC	MC	13	MC	-
Memorial T'ment	-	-	-	6	26	-	-	-	-	49
St. Jude Classic	-	8	MC	6	-	50	71	45	-	-
U.S. Open	-	MC	-	-	19	MC	-	-	-	-
Buick Classic	-	MC	MC	-	-	-	-	MC	-	-
Canon GH Open	-	MC	-	49	77	-	-	67	-	-
Western Open	-	MC	40	MC	72	-	61	-	MC	-
Gr. Milwaukee	-	MC	MC	MC	-	MC	-	-	-	-
British Open	-	-	-	MC	-	-	-	-	-	-
B.C. Open	-	MC	-	12	-	-	-	-	-	-
John Deere Cl'	-	-	-	-	-	MC	69	-	-	7
The International	-	46	MC	MC	MC	63	MC	11	45	-
Buick Open	-	MC	MC	54	-	39	-	-	-	-
USPGA Champ	-	-	MC	47	67	MC	-	41	74	-
WGCNEC Inv'	-	-	-	-	-	-	-	-	-	-
Reno-Tahoe Op'	-	-	-	-	-	-	-	MC	MC	MC
Air Canada Chp'	-	-	-	-	-	-	11	-	-	MC
Bell Canadian O'	-	77	77	34	-	MC	MC	10	-	-
WGC AmEx	-	-	-	-	-	-	-	-	-	-
Tampa Bay Cl'	-	-	-	-	-	-	-	-	-	-
Marconi Penn C'	-	-	-	-	-	-	-	-	-	11
Texas Open	-	MC	DQ	-	14	-	MC	-	-	24
Michelob Chmp'	-	MC	MC	51	-	MC	MC	-	-	-
Invensys Classic	-	5	46	MC	MC	6	MC	17	46	-
NCR Golf Cl'	-	MC	MC	-	-	52	41	-	-	-
Buick Challenge	-	67	MC	MC	-	67	-	MC	-	-
SFB Classic	-	28	-	-	18	3	-	-	-	-
Tour Champ'ship	-	-	-	-	-	17	-	-	-	-

Steve Stricker

27/2/67 – Edgerton, WI

Started last season in the best possible style by winning the WGC Matchplay Championship in Melbourne. He only gained entry to the tournament as a reserve as many of the top players dropped out. That was his first success on tour for five years – his previous two had both come in 1996 (Kemper Open and Motorola – now Advil – Western Open), when he finished fourth on the Money List.

Had a spell on the Canadian Tour in the early '90s (winning twice) before gaining his US Tour card at Q-School in 1993. Known as one of the best scramblers in the game.

ScAv - 70.76 (62nd) – DD - 281.7 (69th) DA - 54.1 (194th) GIR - 62.8 (174th) – PpGIR - 1.733 (11th) SS - 56.0 (41st)

	'92	'93	'94	'95	'96	'97	'98	'99	'00	'01
WGC MatchPlay	-	-	-	-	-	-	-	33	17	1
Mercedes Ch	-	-	-	-	-	27	-	-	-	-
Tucson Open	MC	-	2	25	64	48	22	-	-	-
Sony Open	-	-	14	36	3	51	7	-	14	-
Phoenix Open	-	-	26	12	MC	62	22	14	MC	7
AT&T P Beach	-	MC	MC	13	-	65	-	-	-	-
Buick Invitatn'l	-	-	41	32	MC	35	MC	28	MC	
Bob Hope Cl'	-	52	-	-	-	29	21	23	38	
Nissan Open	-	-	-	74	-	MC	-	-	-	
Genuity Champ	-	61	9	-	-	71	-	MC	34	
Honda Classic	-	MC	13	-	-	-	-	-	-	
Bay Hill Invit'l	-	65	4	13	MC	6	37	-	66	
Players Champ	-	23	11	MC	MC	51	6	MC	MC	
BellSouth Cl'	-	35	12	45	-	50	-	-	-	
US Masters	-	-	MC	MC	-	38	19	10		
Worldcom Cl'	-	50	24	78	42	MC	-	-	-	
Houston Open	-	-	-	-	-	-	45	MC	-	
GG Chrysler Cl'	-	37	7	3	MC	77	-	-	29	
Compaq Classic	-	-	-	-	-	-	20	4	26	
Byron Nelson C'	-	-	-	-	-	5	MC	MC	-	
MasterCard Cln'l	-	42	-	76	-	-	-	-	-	
Kemper Ins Open	-	MC	-	1	MC	8	10	56	MC	
Memorial T'ment	-	38	66	13	38	31	24	68	37	
St. Jude Classic	-	-	-	-	-	-	-	-	-	
U.S. Open	-	83	-	13	60	36	5	5	27	MC
Buick Classic	-	-	60	-	-	-	-	-	-	
Canon GH Open	-	-	3	57	30	-	-	-	-	
Western Open	-	64	43	1	28	5	55	29	10	
Gr. Milwaukee	31	MC	37	MC	3	12	2	10	63	15
British Open	-	-	-	22	62	52	MC	MC	42	
B.C. Open	MC	62	-	-	-	-	-	-		
John Deere Cl'	MC	26	-	7	-	-	-	-		
The International	-	55	26	-	18	-	-	-	MC	
Buick Open	-	-	-	-	-	6	33	-	-	
USPGA Champ	-	-	23	26	MC	2	MC	MC	66	
WGCNEC Inv'	-	-	-	-	-	-	-	-	-	
Reno-Tahoe Op'	-	-	-	-	-	-	MC	-		
Air Canada Chp'	-	-	-	-	-	-	-	-		
Bell Canadian O'	-	4	6	MC	-	-	13	MC	18	
WGC AmEx	-	-	-	-	-	-	-	-		
Tampa Bay Cl'	-	-	-	-	-	-	-	-		
Marconi Penn C'	-	-	-	-	-	-	-	-		
Texas Open	-	-	WD	-	-	-	-	-		
Michelob Chmp'	-	31	-	-	-	-	-	-		
Invensys Classic	-	-	-	-	-	-	-	-		
NCR Golf Cl'	-	4	MC	-	-	-	-	-		
Buick Challenge	-	8	-	-	MC	-	-			
SFB Classic	-	-	-	-	-	-	-	-		
Tour Champ'ship	-	-	-	3	-	5	-	24		

Kevin Sutherland

4/7/64 – Sacramento, CA

Not to be confused with David, his brother and also a member of the US Tour – although Kevin has continually got the better of his sibling in terms of Money List finishing position since 1997. Yet to win on the full tour, he managed to equal his best finishing position in 2001 by placing second in the Tucson Open in January. Last season was easily his best since turning pro in 1987. He finished 32nd on the Money List, winning over £1.5million. One of the best bunker player on tour last season, he is an accurate iron player and a good putter.

ScAv - 70.21 (22nd) – DD - 277.7 (116th) DA - 66.2 (136th) GIR - 70.2 (22nd) – PpGIR - 1.748 (35th) SS - 63.0 (6th)

	'92	'93	'94	'95	'96	'97	'98	'99	'00	'01
WGC MatchPlay	-	-	-	-	-	-	-	-	-	33
Mercedes Ch	-	-	-	-	-	-	-	-	-	-
Tucson Open	-	-	-	-	13	MC	54	45	11	2
Sony Open	-	-	-	-	76	MC	-	-	-	-
Phoenix Open	-	-	-	-	-	51	44	10	MC	
AT&T P Beach	-	-	-	MC	-	38	56	15	MC	20
Buick Invitatn'l	-	-	-	-	48	29	3	4	5	13
Bob Hope Cl'	-	-	-	-	MC	-	MC	8	23	9
Nissan Open	-	-	-	-	21	MC	15	30	25	51
Genuity Champ	-	-	-	-	MC	-	-	-	-	
Honda Classic	-	-	-	-	MC	37	7	-	-	
Bay Hill Invit'l	-	-	-	-	56	-	22	37	MC	31
Players Champ	-	-	-	-	-	-	42	MC	MC	58
BellSouth Cl'	-	-	-	-	45	9	MC	30	37	MC
US Masters	-	-	-	-	-	-	-	-	-	
Worldcom Cl'	-	-	-	-	-	-	-	MC	-	
Houston Open	-	-	-	-	69	2	MC	40	17	9
GG Chrysler Cl'	-	-	-	-	44	MC	MC	-	28	12
Compaq Classic	-	-	-	-	33	MC	MC	MC	30	MC
Byron Nelson C'	-	-	-	-	74	27	MC	MC	25	MC
MasterCard Cln'l	-	-	-	-	-	41	53	47	20	-
Kemper Ins Open	-	-	-	-	MC	-	-	-	-	
Memorial T'ment	-	-	-	-	MC	64	72	MC	11	
St. Jude Classic	-	-	-	-	50	MC	20	6	81	MC
U.S. Open	-	-	-	-	MC	-	MC	-	-	44
Buick Classic	-	-	-	-	20	72	7	18	19	11
Canon GH Open	-	-	-	-	9	13	25	17	9	17
Western Open	-	-	-	-	MC	34	42	-	41	7
Gr. Milwaukee	-	-	-	-	40	26	14	MC	-	-
British Open	-	-	-	-	-	-	-	-	-	9
B.C. Open	-	-	-	-	MC	-	-	-	-	
John Deere Cl'	-	-	-	-	69	-	-	23	-	
The International	-	-	-	-	MC	5	69	35	28	MC
Buick Open	-	-	-	-	MC	MC	-	MC	-	
USPGA Champ	-	-	-	-	-	76	44	MC	MC	-
WGCNEC Inv'	-	-	-	-	-	-	-	-	-	-
Reno-Tahoe Op'	-	-	-	-	-	-	-	17	-	MC
Air Canada Chp'	-	-	-	-	71	31	20	27	-	
Bell Canadian O'	-	-	-	-	64	23	36	29	10	-
WGC AmEx	-	-	-	-	-	-	-	-		
Tampa Bay Cl'	-	-	-	-	-	-	-	-		
Marconi Penn C'	-	-	-	-	-	-	-	-	28	4
Texas Open	-	-	-	MC	-	-	-	-		
Michelob Chmp'	-	-	-	-	65	MC	39	MC	53	32
Invensys Classic	-	-	-	-	MC	6	45	6	56	38
NCR Golf Cl'	-	-	-	-	MC	61	-	28	-	MC
Buick Challenge	-	-	-	-	68	MC	MC	-	MC	46
SFB Classic	-	-	-	-	33	-	51	-	-	
Tour Champ'ship	-	-	-	-	-	-	-	-		

Sponsored by Stan James

Hal Sutton

28/4/58 – Shreveport, LA

Dubbed the new Jack Nicklaus when he burst on to the scene in the early '80s. Sutton won his first Major title in his second year on the US Tour (the 1983 USPGA Championship) and also topped the Money List. His career wen through the doldrums, though, in early '90s. However, he has been a model of consistency over the past five years and won a 13th US Tour title (Houston Open) last season. He will play for the USA in the Ryder Cup next season – his fourth appearance. A superb iron player and tough competitor whose putting is first class.

ScAv - 70.51 (40th) – DD - 278.8 (104th) DA - 75.4 (11th) GIR - 71.1 (9th) – PpGIR - 1.792 (149th) SS - 47.8 (139th)

	'92	'93	'94	'95	'96	'97	'98	'99	'00	'01
WGC MatchPlay	-	-	-	-	-	-	-	33	5	33
Mercedes Ch	-	-	-	-	19	-	-	-	21	25
Tucson Open	47	MC	MC	15	MC	-	MC	-	-	-
Sony Open	MC	-	23	-	-	MC	-	-	-	-
Phoenix Open	MC	57	MC	MC	-	18	MC	4	4	36
AT&T P Beach	-	-	-	21	-	MC	-	-	MC	36
Buick Invitatn'l	46	9	4	2	32	MC	MC	MC	-	41
Bob Hope Cl'	28	66	21	MC	MC	34	52	-	5	40
Nissan Open	MC	45	27	-	MC	MC	13	MC	43	-
Genuity Champ	-	-	27	33	50	70	36	-	-	3
Honda Classic	-	70	9	-	-	MC	MC	7	7	18
Bay Hill Invit'l	51	74	-	MC	-	-	MC	16	29	-
Players Champ	MC	MC	19	MC	53	50	18	4	1	5
BellSouth Cl'	MC	-	13	33	45	5	24	-	-	-
US Masters	-	-	MC	MC	-	-	MC	10	36	
Worldcom Cl'	MC	MC	-	-	4	71	-	-	-	
Houston Open	-	MC	2	41	48	4	6	2	29	1
GG Chrysler Cl'	-	MC	-	12	MC	MC	8	17	1	24
Compaq Classic	MC	MC	22	MC	15	52	MC	7	54	43
Byron Nelson C'	14	73	65	WD	10	12	2	35	56	28
MasterCard Cln'l	66	MC	66	-	-	-	-	-	-	40
Kemper Ins Open	-	MC	21	53	MC	8	4	-	-	-
Memorial T'ment	75	MC	MC	66	26	38	-	-	8	53
St. Jude Classic	MC	59	2	MC	MC	MC	32	6	-	-
U.S. Open	-	-	-	36	-	19	-	7	23	24
Buick Classic	MC	44	16	-	43	-	MC	-	-	-
Canon GH Open	71	-	-	-	-	-	-	-	53	14
Western Open	MC	MC	80	MC	MC	MC	22	9	-	31
Gr. Milwaukee	MC	MC	MC	27	MC	-	-	-	-	-
British Open	-	-	-	-	-	-	-	10	MC	-
B.C. Open	-	-	-	1	37	-	-	-	-	-
John Deere Cl'	-	61	-	52	-	-	9	-	-	-
The International	-	-	15	MC	64	-	-	-	-	-
Buick Open	MC	15	17	MC	22	42	12	8	3	MC
USPGA Champ	MC	31	55	MC	MC	MC	27	26	MC	44
WGCNEC Inv'	-	-	-	-	-	-	-	15	4	11
Reno-Tahoe Op'	-	-	-	-	-	-	-	-	-	-
Air Canada Chp'	-	-	-	-	-	59	15	-	-	-
Bell Canadian O'	MC	MC	MC	4	MC	11	4	1	10	MC
WGC AmEx	-	-	-	-	-	-	-	19	-	-
Tampa Bay Cl'	-	-	-	-	-	-	-	-	-	-
Marconi Penn C'	-	-	-	-	-	-	-	-	-	-
Texas Open	MC	MC	-	59	-	-	1	-	MC	30
Michelob Chmp'	MC	MC	22	MC	MC	MC	MC	50	-	-
Invensys Classic	MC	MC	MC	MC	MC	14	MC	-	MC	-
NCR Golf Cl'	MC	MC	33	2	-	61	-	37	-	-
Buick Challenge	-	31	40	11	3	8	-	-	-	MC
SFB Classic	-	16	-	21	34	14	-	-	-	-
Tour Champ'ship	-	-	24	-	-	-	1	9	25	26

Esteban Toledo

10/9/62 – Mexicali, Mexico

A former professional boxer who hung up his gloves for clubs in 1986. He spent the early part of his pro career on the Buy.com Tour and broke through to the full tour firstly in 1994 and then in 1998, from when he's managed to retain his card with some ease. Still to win in America, he did manage to become the first Mexican to win his national title for 24 years in 2000. His best finish in 2001 was third in the Michelob Championship – one place worse than his highest finish on tour which was achieved in the 2000 BC Open. Accurate, but short, off the tee.

ScAv - 71.24 (105th) – DD - 264.8 (192nd) DA - 72.5 (30th) GIR - 65.3 (123rd) – PpGIR - 1.765 (74th) SS - 54.8 (61st)

	'92	'93	'94	'95	'96	'97	'98	'99	'00	'01
WGC MatchPlay	-	-	-	-	-	-	-	-	-	-
Mercedes Ch	-	-	-	-	-	-	-	-	-	-
Tucson Open	-	-	MC	-	-	-	-	54	MC	MC
Sony Open	-	-	44	-	-	-	27	16	14	43
Phoenix Open	-	-	-	-	-	-	MC	78	MC	
AT&T P Beach	MC	-	19	-	-	-	MC	MC	MC	27
Buick Invitatn'l	-	-	77	-	-	-	76	MC	MC	72
Bob Hope Cl'	-	-	MC	-	-	-	-	28	51	MC
Nissan Open	-	-	-	-	-	-	MC	MC	25	33
Genuity Champ	-	-	-	-	-	-	MC	34	36	12
Honda Classic	-	-	39	-	-	-	30	-	MC	27
Bay Hill Invit'l	-	-	-	-	-	-	-	-	-	MC
Players Champ	-	-	-	-	-	-	-	23	27	MC
BellSouth Cl'	-	-	35	-	-	-	3	67	MC	-
US Masters	-	-	-	-	-	-	-	-	-	-
Worldcom Cl'	-	-	-	-	-	-	-	49	57	MC
Houston Open	-	-	MC	-	-	-	36	10	17	35
GG Chrysler Cl'	-	-	MC	-	-	-	MC	MC	MC	17
Compaq Classic	-	-	MC	-	-	-	19	MC	74	MC
Byron Nelson C'	-	-	WD	-	-	-	35	24	MC	11
MasterCard Cln'l	-	-	-	-	-	-	MC	MC	MC	MC
Kemper Ins Open	-	-	49	-	-	-	25	68	28	22
Memorial T'ment	-	-	-	-	-	-	58	-	-	70
St. Jude Classic	-	-	MC	-	-	-	26	55	MC	MC
U.S. Open	-	-	-	-	-	-	-	34	-	MC
Buick Classic	-	-	22	-	-	-	MC	41	MC	-
Canon GH Open	-	-	66	-	-	-	63	MC	66	50
Western Open	-	-	MC	-	-	-	MC	34	MC	MC
Gr. Milwaukee	-	-	MC	-	-	-	MC	MC	MC	69
British Open	-	-	-	-	-	-	-	-	-	-
B.C. Open	-	-	59	-	-	-	-	-	2	23
John Deere Cl'	-	-	44	-	-	-	MC	41	-	58
The International	-	-	MC	-	-	-	32	MC	MC	MC
Buick Open	-	-	51	-	-	-	-	7	32	MC
USPGA Champ	-	-	-	-	-	-	-	-	-	-
WGCNEC Inv'	-	-	-	-	-	-	-	-	-	-
Reno-Tahoe Op'	-	-	-	-	-	-	-	32	MC	50
Air Canada Chp'	-	-	-	-	-	-	15	57	22	21
Bell Canadian O'	-	-	MC	-	-	-	MC	-	-	-
WGC AmEx	-	-	-	-	-	-	-	-	-	-
Tampa Bay Cl'	-	-	-	-	-	-	-	-	71	-
Marconi Penn C'	-	-	-	-	-	-	-	-	48	MC
Texas Open	-	-	MC	-	-	-	37	64	6	30
Michelob Chmp'	-	-	MC	-	-	-	MC	45	-	3
Invensys Classic	-	-	MC	-	-	-	69	MC	MC	-
NCR Golf Cl'	-	-	MC	-	-	-	27	MC	13	MC
Buick Challenge	-	-	MC	-	-	-	MC	MC	41	38
SFB Classic	-	-	16	MC	-	-	21	-	13	28
Tour Champ'ship	-	-	-	-	-	-	-	-	-	-

David Toms
4/1/67 – Monroe, LA

Last season saw this Shreveport pro join the ranks of the elite. In 2001, Toms won three times, including his first Major success (the USPGA Championship), earning nearly $4million and finishing third on the Money List. He narrowly missed out on claiming the Player of the Year title to Tiger Woods. He turned pro in 1991 and spent some time on the Buy.com Tour (winning twice in 1995) before establishing himself on the main tour. His first win came in 1997 when he captured the Quad City (now John Deere) Classic. A superb iron player and putter.

ScAv - 69.97 (15th) – DD - 279.5 (96th) DA - 72.1 (34th) GIR - 72.6 (4th) – PpGIR - 1.732 (10th) SS - 43.7 (174th)

	'92	'93	'94	'95	'96	'97	'98	'99	'00	'01
WGC MatchPlay	-	-	-	-	-	-	-	-	17	17
Mercedes Ch	-	-	-	-	-	-	22	-	19	8
Tucson Open	3	MC	22	-	9	35	2	7	-	-
Sony Open	33	MC	72	-	-	-	-	-	-	-
Phoenix Open	-	57	MC	-	MC	50	34	26	18	9
AT&T P Beach	41	67	MC	-	-	58	13	MC	MC	27
Buick Invitatn'l	MC	-	15	-	MC	MC	-	11	14	MC
Bob Hope Cl'	-	-	-	-	61	45	19	24	3	18
Nissan Open	MC	-	MC	-	44	MC	MC	-	-	-
Genuity Champ	66	MC	69	-	76	68	-	3	45	21
Honda Classic	69	26	50	-	17	MC	-	-	-	-
Bay Hill Invit'l	22	MC	-	-	36	-	17	19	18	56
Players Champ	MC	MC	MC	-	MC	MC	MC	20	38	12
BellSouth Cl'	MC	27	44	-	39	5	MC	10	15	17
US Masters	-	-	-	-	-	-	6	MC	49	31
Worldcom Cl'	-	MC	MC	-	MC	-	-	-	-	-
Houston Open	-	MC	32	-	MC	MC	-	-	27	9
GG Chrysler Cl'	MC	84	MC	-	48	MC	23	MC	-	-
Compaq Classic	MC	15	-	-	MC	31	42	MC	37	1
Byron Nelson C'	MC	MC	WD	-	MC	48	MC	WD	20	11
MasterCard Cln'l	-	-	-	-	-	-	72	MC	4	8
Kemper Ins Open	25	22	MC	-	6	MC	-	4	MC	-
Memorial T'ment	26	-	-	-	-	-	51	MC	-	-
St. Jude Classic	MC	55	MC	-	25	16	74	55	15	53
U.S. Open	-	-	-	-	MC	WD	-	MC	16	66
Buick Classic	-	MC	MC	-	MC	-	-	-	-	-
Canon GH Open	26	MC	55	-	MC	-	20	MC	-	-
Western Open	72	MC	MC	-	MC	17	48	20	9	42
Gr. Milwaukee	MC	MC	18	-	34	40	23	MC	-	-
British Open	-	-	-	-	-	-	-	-	4	MC
B.C. Open	-	10	WD	-	-	-	-	-	-	-
John Deere Cl'	MC	MC	59	-	19	1	4	12	MC	-
The International	MC	MC	55	-	MC	-	11	1	MC	MC
Buick Open	MC	9	36	-	22	-	-	-	-	35
USPGA Champ	-	-	-	-	MC	MC	MC	41	1	
WGCNEC Inv'	-	-	-	-	-	-	-	-	-	13
Reno-Tahoe Op'	-	-	-	-	-	-	2	7	-	-
Air Canada Chp'	-	-	-	18	-	21	-	-		
Bell Canadian O'	MC	MC	MC	-	-	-	-	-	-	
WGC AmEx	-	-	-	-	-	-	-	11	25	-
Tampa Bay Cl'	-	-	-	-	-	-	-	40	-	-
Marconi Penn C'	-	-	-	-	-	-	-	-	-	
Texas Open	65	MC	MC	-	20	-	12	19	MC	
Michelob Chmp'	MC	MC	MC	-	15	MC	MC	59	1	1
Invensys Classic	24	64	59	-	MC	-	MC	-	-	-
NCR Golf Cl'	46	MC	MC	-	MC	-	-	57	18	6
Buick Challenge	MC	8	19	-	68	21	MC	1	MC	WD
SFB Classic	-	37	-	12	40	56	-	-	-	
Tour Champ'ship	-	-	-	-	-	-	-	12	11	2

Kirk Triplett
29/3/62 – Moses Lake, WA

Finally managed to win on the US Tour in 2000 after 264 previous tries. His victory in the 2000 Nissan Open helped him to his highest finish on the Money List (11th) but unfortunately for Triplett, he couldn't maintain the momentum in 2001. Second place in the Michelob Championship was his best effort last season. Turned pro in 1987 and played in Australia, Asia and Canada (winning the Alberta Open in 1988) before returning to the US Tour by way of the Q-School in 1989. A short but accurate driver, he ranks highly in the sand save stats.

ScAv - 70.32 (29th) – DD - 269.9 (178th) DA - 75.3 (12th) GIR - 70.3 (19th) – PpGIR - 1.757 (57th) SS - 58.5 (23rd)

	'92	'93	'94	'95	'96	'97	'98	'99	'00	'01
WGC MatchPlay	-	-	-	-	-	-	-	-	-	33
Mercedes Ch	-	-	-	-	-	-	-	-	-	16
Tucson Open	MC	55	9	76	-	13	77	3	7	-
Sony Open	-	-	-	-	-	-	-	-	-	-
Phoenix Open	MC	3	MC	35	48	MC	MC	69	4	-
AT&T P Beach	MC	28	2	21	-	MC	13	44	MC	13
Buick Invitatn'l	MC	51	6	2	15	45	72	MC	5	75
Bob Hope Cl'	38	MC	MC	16	-	17	10	18	10	56
Nissan Open	MC	MC	8	25	26	74	15	30	1	MC
Genuity Champ	-	-	-	-	-	-	-	-	-	-
Honda Classic	-	-	-	-	-	-	-	-	-	-
Bay Hill Invit'l	-	39	21	MC	13	45	45	13	22	64
Players Champ	39	MC	45	67	19	10	35	38	42	31
BellSouth Cl'	MC	7	-	68	-	-	-	46	MC	-
US Masters	-	-	-	MC	-	-	-	-	MC	6
Worldcom Cl'	41	MC	MC	44	-	-	-	-	-	-
Houston Open	2	41	MC	12	48	MC	MC	-	-	-
GG Chrysler Cl'	MC	74	67	14	16	3	MC	6	-	-
Compaq Classic	-	51	10	54	4	MC	12	6	34	
Byron Nelson C'	62	-	-	10	30	15	24	MC	28	
MasterCard Cln'l	59	22	18	33	69	15	18	21	13	15
Kemper Ins Open	-	MC	10	-	-	40	MC	-	10	MC
Memorial T'ment	MC	-	24	MC	MC	32	16	MC	-	-
St. Jude Classic	-	31	42	14	9	MC	7	15	15	MC
U.S. Open	66	52	23	-	40	-	MC	MC	56	7
Buick Classic	-	-	-	-	-	-	-	-	-	-
Canon GH Open	46	26	7	2	49	MC	31	11	3	7
Western Open	MC	MC	MC	MC	-	34	-	-	MC	
Gr. Milwaukee	MC	-	-	-	-	-	-	-	-	
British Open	-	MC	-	-	-	-	-	60	-	
B.C. Open	-	22	3	MC	-	-	-	-	-	
John Deere Cl'	-	10	-	-	-	-	3	2	15	
The International	21	MC	MC	11	MC	18	15	10	35	15
Buick Open	-	48	-	-	-	-	-	-	-	
USPGA Champ	MC	-	15	13	MC	13	MC	49	59	10
WGCNEC Inv'	-	-	-	-	-	-	-	33	DQ	
Reno-Tahoe Op'	-	-	-	-	-	-	MC	-	-	
Air Canada Chp'	-	-	-	MC	-	-	-	-		
Bell Canadian O'	60	-	-	-	-	-	-	-	-	
WGC AmEx	-	-	-	-	-	-	-	14	-	
Tampa Bay Cl'	-	-	-	-	-	-	-	-	-	
Marconi Penn C'	-	-	-	-	-	-	-	MC	-	
Texas Open	MC	-	MC	50	-	-	-	-	MC	-
Michelob Chmp'	-	25	-	11	23	6	63	MC	-	2
Invensys Classic	30	19	8	10	MC	66	8	37	40	25
NCR Golf Cl'	MC	50	-	-	54	60	MC	MC	-	
Buick Challenge	-	19	19	4	40	MC	30	MC	-	MC
SFB Classic	-	-	4	2	13	7	7	-	23	
Tour Champ'ship	MC	-	20	-	-	-	-	8	-	

Sponsored by Stan James

Bob Tway

4/5/69 – Oklahoma City, OK

After a poor 2000, this seven-time US Tour winner bounced back with three top-four finishes in his first five events in 2001. Tway didn't manage to add to his career victories, though, the last of which came in the 1995 MCI (now WorldCom) Classic. Turned pro in 1981 and has been a stalwart of the tour since 1985 – only twice dropping out of the top 125 of the Money List. His best season on tour was 1995 when he posted eight top-ten finishes on his way to 20th in the Money List. Accurate with his irons, his bunker play was sub standard last term.
ScAv - 70.40 (32nd) – DD - 279.4 (99th) DA - 70.3 (63rd) GIR - 71.9 (6th) – PpGIR - 1.767 (81st) SS - 49.7 (122nd)

	'92	'93	'94	'95	'96	'97	'98	'99	'00	'01
WGC MatchPlay	-	-	-	-	-	-	-	17	17	-
Mercedes Ch	-	-	-	-	4	-	-	-	-	-
Tucson Open	MC	WD	MC	6	2	17	6	-	-	3
Sony Open	63	-	14	-	-	-	-	-	-	-
Phoenix Open	MC	-	MC	41	21	34	MC	MC	61	MC
AT&T P Beach	-	-	-	-	-	-	-	-	-	-
Buick Invitatn'l	38	80	MC	MC	MC	11	16	MC	14	20
Bob Hope Cl'	-	-	MC	16	-	71	10	24	61	4
Nissan Open	-	31	MC	19	10	20	MC	35	25	2
Genuity Champ	44	66	39	67	42	9	9	15	15	58
Honda Classic	MC	15	39	13	-	-	-	-	-	-
Bay Hill Invit'l	MC	-	-	-	-	-	-	-	-	-
Players Champ	70	MC	MC	68	MC	MC	18	MC	MC	40
BellSouth Cl'	MC	MC	MC	MC	MC	19	5	MC	49	40
US Masters	-	-	-	-	12	MC	MC	52	MC	-
Worldcom Cl'	37	MC	MC	1	15	30	8	34	42	-
Houston Open	-	-	-	-	-	-	-	-	-	-
GG Chrysler Cl'	55	MC	MC	MC	-	-	-	-	-	-
Compaq Classic	-	MC	-	-	22	51	35	24	23	-
Byron Nelson C'	-	MC	42	9	MC	5	19	MC	49	MC
MasterCard Cln'l	MC	MC	29	12	6	35	MC	MC	46	-
Kemper Ins Open	-	-	-	-	-	-	-	-	-	-
Memorial T'ment	MC	38	29	43	10	16	35	63	37	-
St. Jude Classic	-	19	58	5	-	-	62	MC	-	-
U.S. Open	-	MC	MC	10	67	5	3	62	-	52
Buick Classic	39	34	54	14	MC	38	7	10	MC	MC
Canon GH Open	-	-	-	-	-	-	-	-	12	-
Western Open	29	MC	6	18	39	42	-	MC	20	-
Gr. Milwaukee	-	62	MC	-	-	-	-	-	-	-
British Open	MC	-	MC	MC	MC	MC	MC	MC	-	-
B.C. Open	-	-	-	-	-	-	-	-	-	-
John Deere Cl'	MC	4	MC	27	61	-	-	16	MC	MC
The International	-	MC	39	42	3	MC	6	16	-	38
Buick Open	62	70	MC	-	7	20	15	2	MC	10
USPGA Champ	56	MC	MC	MC	MC	13	13	57	MC	29
WGCNEC Inv'	-	-	-	-	-	-	-	-	-	-
Reno-Tahoe Op'	-	-	-	-	-	-	-	7	MC	12
Air Canada Chp'	-	-	-	-	-	-	-	-	-	-
Bell Canadian O'	34	68	13	9	20	36	25	13	MC	23
WGC AmEx	-	-	-	-	-	-	-	37	-	-
Tampa Bay Cl'	-	-	-	-	-	-	-	-	10	-
Marconi Penn C'	-	-	-	-	-	-	-	-	MC	41
Texas Open	-	MC	21	-	28	MC	53	29	-	-
Michelob Chmp'	33	-	-	-	-	-	-	-	36	47
Invensys Classic	MC	6	16	25	MC	50	4	61	40	38
NCR Golf Cl'	-	40	4	42	17	43	3	MC	21	-
Buick Challenge	-	MC	41	-	-	21	20	MC	MC	31
SFB Classic	-	-	-	-	-	-	-	20	61	-
Tour Champ'ship	-	-	15	-	-	8	-	-	-	-

Scott Verplank

9/6/64 – Dallas, TX

A surprising choice by Curtis Strange as a Wild Card for the USA Ryder Cup team. However, he justified his selection by winning the Bell Canadian Open the week after Strange announced he was in the Belfry line up. His success in Canada was his fourth US Tour win. He last win prior to that came in the 2000 Reno Tahoe Open and his first when he was an amateur in the 1985 Western Open. He is a diabetic and also struggled with an elbow problem in the early part of his career – missing most of the 1992 season. Accurate off the tee and with his irons.
ScAv - 69.88 (11th) – DD - 271.3 (170th) DA - 75.2 (13th) GIR - 70.7 (13th) – PpGIR - 1.747 (30th) SS - 66.2 (2nd)

	'92	'93	'94	'95	'96	'97	'98	'99	'00	'01
WGC MatchPlay	-	-	-	-	-	-	-	17	-	17
Mercedes Ch	-	-	-	-	-	-	-	-	-	30
Tucson Open	-	-	MC	56	48	44	-	17	-	-
Sony Open	-	-	-	-	-	-	-	-	-	-
Phoenix Open	-	-	-	21	-	14	33	75	4	-
AT&T P Beach	-	-	-	-	-	-	MC	-	-	-
Buick Invitatn'l	-	45	32	56	MC	MC	-	38	-	-
Bob Hope Cl'	-	-	-	MC	35	11	MC	4	-	-
Nissan Open	-	27	35	44	MC	10	MC	37	33	-
Genuity Champ	-	MC	17	20	50	MC	52	6	12	-
Honda Classic	MC	-	35	8	38	-	-	-	-	-
Bay Hill Invit'l	MC	-	-	-	-	45	-	-	-	-
Players Champ	-	MC	WD	-	11	32	20	44	-	-
BellSouth Cl'	MC	21	4	-	51	5	55	77	-	-
US Masters	-	-	-	-	-	-	MC	-	MC	-
Worldcom Cl'	-	-	24	22	30	MC	MC	11	3	-
Houston Open	MC	-	-	-	-	-	-	-	-	-
GG Chrysler Cl'	-	MC	36	-	14	2	48	8	36	-
Compaq Classic	-	44	24	15	MC	74	-	30	43	-
Byron Nelson C'	MC	-	MC	5	74	MC	MC	MC	25	2
MasterCard Cln'l	-	12	38	-	35	21	20	WD	-	-
Kemper Ins Open	-	24	-	MC	-	-	-	-	-	-
Memorial T'ment	-	29	MC	-	38	48	20	24	-	-
St. Jude Classic	MC	-	39	-	46	12	18	-	-	-
U.S. Open	-	18	21	-	49	17	46	22	-	-
Buick Classic	-	44	-	MC	-	-	-	-	-	-
Canon GH Open	MC	-	-	-	-	-	-	-	17	-
Western Open	MC	-	17	MC	-	38	9	55	MC	15
Gr. Milwaukee	-	-	-	-	-	-	-	-	-	-
British Open	-	-	-	-	-	15	MC	30	-	-
B.C. Open	58	-	32	-	23	-	-	-	-	-
John Deere Cl'	-	15	10	-	10	9	8	12	-	-
The International	-	-	39	-	MC	59	-	-	-	-
Buick Open	MC	-	WD	11	-	MC	2	MC	11	14
USPGA Champ	-	-	MC	-	-	54	34	MC	7	-
WGCNEC Inv'	-	-	-	-	-	-	-	-	17	-
Reno-Tahoe Op'	-	-	-	-	-	-	50	1	-	-
Air Canada Chp'	-	-	-	-	-	-	48	-	-	-
Bell Canadian O'	-	13	38	-	9	MC	6	1	-	-
WGC AmEx	-	-	-	-	-	-	48	-	-	-
Tampa Bay Cl'	-	-	-	-	-	-	-	-	-	-
Marconi Penn C'	-	-	-	-	-	-	8	61	-	-
Texas Open	-	-	MC	MC	-	-	-	-	-	-
Michelob Chmp'	-	4	27	-	25	32	36	-	-	-
Invensys Classic	MC	-	46	-	3	61	15	7	-	-
NCR Golf Cl'	-	37	-	17	4	46	-	-	-	-
Buick Challenge	-	-	-	MC	-	-	-	-	-	-
SFB Classic	-	20	-	19	-	-	-	-	-	-
Tour Champ'ship	-	-	-	5	-	14	5	-	-	-

Grant Waite
11/8/64 – Palmerston North, New Zealand

New Zealand-born pro who has been based in the States for over a decade, Waite has only managed to win once on the US Tour. That was in the 1993 Kemper Open (and didn't defend his title due to the birth of his first child). Spent the early part of his career on the ANZ Tour (won the 1992 New Zealand Open) and also had a spell on the Canadian Tour (winning the Trafalgar Capitol Classic in 1992).

Posted just one top-ten finish in 2001 – third in the Bay Hill Invitational. Another long hitter who is a touch loose with the driver.

ScAv - 71.41 (119th) – DD - 284.9 (36th) DA - 68.1 (108th) GIR - 66.4 (89th) – PpGIR - 1.787 (135th) SS - 55.7 (48th)

	'92	'93	'94	'95	'96	'97	'98	'99	'00	'01
WGC MatchPlay	-	-	-	-	-	-	-	-	-	-
Mercedes Ch	-	-	20	-	-	-	-	-	-	-
Tucson Open	-	MC	71	MC	13	61	31	20	MC	45
Sony Open	-	MC	-	10	MC	MC	-	-	MC	-
Phoenix Open	-	-	18	29	14	MC	MC	MC	-	MC
AT&T P Beach	-	7	MC	MC	-	65	WD	53	14	13
Buick Invitatn'l	-	20	-	-	-	-	-	-	WD	MC
Bob Hope Cl'	-	33	-	70	44	8	MC	61	-	-
Nissan Open	-	45	MC	MC	-	MC	30	-	-	-
Genuity Champ	-	-	MC	43	69	65	62	-	-	25
Honda Classic	-	MC	-	72	-	-	15	60	73	3
Bay Hill Invit'l	-	MC	29	-	56	61	13	23	MC	3
Players Champ	-	-	51	-	8	MC	63	MC	-	MC
BellSouth Cl'	MC	38	-	MC	12	10	-	-	-	69
US Masters	-	-	MC	-	-	-	-	-	-	MC
Worldcom Cl'	-	-	73	MC	-	MC	MC	32	-	-
Houston Open	-	MC	-	59	18	23	17	MC	-	-
GG Chrysler Cl'	-	39	71	MC	-	MC	MC	MC	56	MC
Compaq Classic	-	45	-	27	MC	63	-	-	MC	66
Byron Nelson C'	-	MC	65	MC	WD	-	MC	MC	-	37
MasterCard Cln'l	-	-	MC	-	DQ	41	64	-	-	-
Kemper Ins Open	-	1	-	MC	2	MC	MC	52	16	MC
Memorial T'ment	-	30	MC	-	-	-	-	-	-	30
St. Jude Classic	-	MC	45	26	-	-	-	24	MC	-
U.S. Open	-	72	-	-	DQ	36	MC	-	-	-
Buick Classic	-	MC	-	29	79	DQ	-	66	33	MC
Canon GH Open	-	-	MC	2	MC	73	16	26	66	MC
Western Open	-	50	MC	13	26	74	-	MC	-	MC
Gr. Milwaukee	-	-	MC	-	-	MC	-	55	14	WD
British Open	-	-	-	-	-	-	-	-	-	-
B.C. Open	-	MC	-	-	20	8	40	39	10	-
John Deere Cl'	-	69	-	-	-	43	MC	MC	30	MC
The International	MC	MC	52	MC	MC	36	MC	MC	WD	MC
Buick Open	-	70	64	40	MC	42	MC	MC	MC	-
USPGA Champ	-	MC	-	MC	MC	-	MC	-	-	59
WGCNEC Inv'	-	-	-	-	-	-	-	-	-	-
Reno-Tahoe Op'	-	-	-	-	-	-	37	27	-	-
Air Canada Chp'	-	-	-	-	MC	39	MC	57	2	8
Bell Canadian O'	-	MC	53	24	34	42	67	-	2	DQ
WGC AmEx	-	-	-	-	-	-	-	-	-	-
Tampa Bay Cl'	-	-	-	-	-	-	-	-	40	-
Marconi Penn C'	-	-	-	-	-	-	-	-	33	-
Texas Open	-	MC	MC	-	-	-	-	-	-	-
Michelob Chmp'	-	WD	-	-	MC	2	69	59	25	MC
Invensys Classic	-	19	MC	54	MC	23	71	MC	-	29
NCR Golf Cl'	-	-	-	15	MC	26	MC	MC	24	MC
Buick Challenge	-	MC	40	MC	9	39	20	14	54	-
SFB Classic	-	4	62	-	-	11	MC	6	57	-
Tour Champ'ship	-	-	-	-	-	-	-	-	-	-

Mike Weir
12/5/70 – Sarnia, Ontario, Canada

Canadian golfer who finished 2001 on a high by winning the prestigious Tour Championship. Always seems to play well at the end of the season – in 2000 he won the term-ending WGC Amex title in Spain. He became only the sixth left-hander to win on the full tour when capturing the Air Canada Championship title in 1999. Had a successful time on the Canadian Tour before gaining his playing privileges on the US Tour by way of the Q-School in 1997. He relies on accuracy over length to succeed. Career earnings now stand at over $7 million.

ScAv - 70.06 (17th) – DD - 284.4 (45th) DA - 64.9 (152nd) GIR - 67.7 (58th) – PpGIR - 1.761 (65th) SS - 58.7 (22nd)

	'92	'93	'94	'95	'96	'97	'98	'99	'00	'01
WGC MatchPlay	-	-	-	-	-	-	-	-	17	-
Mercedes Ch	-	-	-	-	-	-	-	-	4	12
Tucson Open	-	-	-	-	-	-	-	13	-	-
Sony Open	-	-	-	-	-	21	MC	-	-	-
Phoenix Open	-	-	-	-	-	-	-	22	10	23
AT&T P Beach	-	-	-	-	-	MC	MC	7	8	-
Buick Invitatn'l	-	-	-	-	-	-	-	-	-	5
Bob Hope Cl'	-	-	-	-	-	-	-	32	MC	-
Nissan Open	-	-	-	-	-	MC	MC	MC	MC	MC
Genuity Champ	-	-	-	-	-	46	44	-	2	-
Honda Classic	-	-	-	MC	-	MC	-	19	-	-
Bay Hill Invit'l	-	-	-	-	-	-	56	7	-	-
Players Champ	-	-	-	-	-	-	-	-	MC	44
BellSouth Cl'	-	-	-	-	-	MC	5	-	2	-
US Masters	-	-	-	-	-	-	-	28	27	-
Worldcom Cl'	-	-	-	-	-	-	10	-	-	-
Houston Open	-	-	-	-	-	MC	-	WD	-	-
GG Chrysler Cl'	-	-	-	-	-	MC	25	-	-	-
Compaq Classic	-	-	-	-	-	19	MC	-	61	-
Byron Nelson C'	-	-	-	-	-	MC	MC	MC	11	-
MasterCard Cln'l	-	-	-	-	-	72	8	58	-	-
Kemper Ins Open	-	-	-	-	-	42	MC	-	-	-
Memorial T'ment	-	-	-	-	-	-	24	4	30	-
St. Jude Classic	-	-	-	-	-	37	-	-	-	-
U.S. Open	-	-	-	-	-	-	MC	16	19	-
Buick Classic	-	-	-	-	-	WD	-	19	-	-
Canon GH Open	-	-	-	-	-	MC	-	-	-	-
Western Open	-	-	-	-	-	MC	2	51	3	-
Gr. Milwaukee	-	-	-	MC	-	-	-	-	-	-
British Open	-	-	-	-	-	-	37	52	MC	-
B.C. Open	-	-	31	7	10	-	-	-	-	-
John Deere Cl'	-	-	-	35	-	-	-	-	-	-
The International	-	-	-	-	MC	21	MC	19	-	-
Buick Open	MC	70	-	54	-	MC	MC	-	-	-
USPGA Champ	-	-	-	-	-	-	10	30	16	-
WGCNEC Inv'	-	-	-	-	-	-	24	25	-	-
Reno-Tahoe Op'	-	-	-	-	-	-	-	-	-	-
Air Canada Chp'	-	-	-	5	MC	5	1	38	MC	-
Bell Canadian O'	MC	MC	MC	MC	MC	MC	MC	MC	70	34
WGC AmEx	-	-	-	-	-	-	30	1	-	-
Tampa Bay Cl'	-	-	-	-	-	-	-	-	-	-
Marconi Penn C'	-	-	-	-	-	-	-	-	-	-
Texas Open	-	-	-	-	-	37	-	-	-	-
Michelob Chmp'	-	-	-	-	-	69	3	2	12	-
Invensys Classic	-	-	-	-	-	MC	19	12	-	-
NCR Golf Cl'	-	-	-	-	-	64	57	39	36	-
Buick Challenge	-	-	-	-	-	MC	-	-	-	-
SFB Classic	-	-	-	-	-	35	-	-	-	-
Tour Champ'ship	-	-	-	-	-	-	-	26	21	1

Garrett Willis

21/11/73 – Charlotte, NC

Q-School graduate who won on his first outing of the season in 2001 – the Tucson Open. However, in the next 32 events, he missed the cut in 20 of them. Willis played on the Buy.com Tour in 1999 and 2000 after some success on the Hooters Tour in the previous years (he actually won his first pro tournament in 1996). Possesses a solid all-round game but ranked poorly in the greens-in-regulation stats. He first taste of full tour golf came when he qualified to play in the 1998 and 1999 US Open, but he missed the cut on both occasions.

ScAv - 72.01 (164th) – DD - 279.6 (94th) DA - 69.0 (84th) GIR - 65.2 (126th) – PpGIR - 1.771 (93rd) SS - 35.7 (192nd)

	'92	'93	'94	'95	'96	'97	'98	'99	'00	'01
WGC MatchPlay	-	-	-	-	-	-	-	-	-	-
Mercedes Ch	-	-	-	-	-	-	-	-	-	-
Tucson Open	-	-	-	-	-	-	-	-	-	1
Sony Open	-	-	-	-	-	-	-	-	-	54
Phoenix Open	-	-	-	-	-	-	-	-	-	WD
AT&T P Beach	-	-	-	-	-	-	-	-	-	23
Buick Invitatn'l	-	-	-	-	-	-	-	-	-	-
Bob Hope Cl'	-	-	-	-	-	-	-	-	-	46
Nissan Open	-	-	-	-	-	-	-	-	-	MC
Genuity Champ	-	-	-	-	-	-	-	-	-	MC
Honda Classic	-	-	-	-	-	-	-	-	-	18
Bay Hill Invit'l	-	-	-	-	-	-	-	-	-	MC
Players Champ	-	-	-	-	-	-	-	-	-	MC
BellSouth Cl'	-	-	-	-	-	-	-	-	-	MC
US Masters	-	-	-	-	-	-	-	-	-	-
Worldcom Cl'	-	-	-	-	-	-	-	-	-	55
Houston Open	-	-	-	-	-	-	-	-	-	54
GG Chrysler Cl'	-	-	-	-	-	-	-	-	-	79
Compaq Classic	-	-	-	-	-	-	-	-	-	MC
Byron Nelson C'	-	-	-	-	-	-	-	-	-	43
MasterCard Cln'l	-	-	-	-	-	-	-	-	-	-
Kemper Ins Open	-	-	-	-	-	-	-	-	-	-
Memorial T'ment	-	-	-	-	-	-	-	-	-	43
St. Jude Classic	-	-	-	-	-	-	-	-	-	MC
U.S. Open	-	-	-	-	-	-	MC	MC	-	-
Buick Classic	-	-	-	-	-	-	-	-	-	MC
Canon GH Open	-	-	-	-	-	-	-	-	-	MC
Western Open	-	-	-	-	-	-	-	-	-	MC
Gr. Milwaukee	-	-	-	-	-	-	-	-	-	MC
British Open	-	-	-	-	-	-	-	-	-	-
B.C. Open	-	-	-	-	-	-	-	-	-	DQ
John Deere Cl'	-	-	-	-	-	-	-	-	-	-
The International	-	-	-	-	-	-	-	-	-	MC
Buick Open	-	-	-	-	-	-	-	-	-	MC
USPGA Champ	-	-	-	-	-	-	-	-	-	MC
WGCNEC Inv'	-	-	-	-	-	-	-	-	-	-
Reno-Tahoe Op'	-	-	-	-	-	-	-	-	-	MC
Air Canada Chp'	-	-	-	-	-	-	-	-	-	-
Bell Canadian O'	-	-	MC	-	-	-	-	-	-	-
WGC AmEx	-	-	-	-	-	-	-	-	-	-
Tampa Bay Cl'	-	-	-	-	-	-	-	-	-	-
Marconi Penn C'	-	-	-	-	-	-	-	-	-	MC
Texas Open	-	-	-	-	-	-	-	-	-	MC
Michelob Chmp'	-	-	-	-	-	-	-	-	-	MC
Invensys Classic	-	-	-	-	-	-	-	-	-	-
NCR Golf Cl'	-	-	-	-	-	-	-	-	-	70
Buick Challenge	-	-	-	-	-	-	-	-	-	MC
SFB Classic	-	-	-	-	-	-	-	-	-	37
Tour Champ'ship	-	-	-	-	-	-	-	-	-	-

Tiger Woods

30/12/75 – Cypress, CA

A history-making season for the world's No.1. By winning the Masters, he became the first player to hold all four Major titles at the same time – whether it's a Grand Slam or not is up to you to decide. Based the whole part of his early season on getting his game in shape for Augusta. All talk of a slump was dismissed when he won at Bay Hill and then Sawgrass. Topped the Money List for the fourth consecutive year and took his career earnings to over $26million. Has now won 29 US Tour titles, including six Majors and has the perfect all-round game.

ScAv - 68.81 (1st) – DD - 297.6 (3rd) DA - 65.5 (145th) GIR - 71.9 (6th) – PpGIR - 1.775 (102nd) SS - 53.5 (80th)

	'92	'93	'94	'95	'96	'97	'98	'99	'00	'01
WGC MatchPlay	-	-	-	-	-	-	-	5	2	-
Mercedes Ch	-	-	-	-	-	1	2	5	1	8
Tucson Open	-	-	-	-	-	-	-	-	-	-
Sony Open	-	-	-	-	-	-	-	-	-	-
Phoenix Open	-	-	-	-	-	18	-	3	-	5
AT&T P Beach	-	-	-	-	-	2	WD	53	1	13
Buick Invitn'l	-	-	-	-	-	-	3	1	2	4
Bob Hope Cl'	-	-	-	-	-	-	-	-	-	-
Nissan Open	MC	MC	-	-	-	20	2	2	18	13
Genuity Champ	-	-	-	-	-	-	-	9	-	-
Honda Classic	-	MC	-	-	-	-	-	-	-	-
Bay Hill Invit'l	-	-	MC	-	-	9	13	56	1	1
Players Champ	-	-	-	-	-	31	35	10	2	1
BellSouth Cl'	-	-	-	-	-	-	1	-	-	-
US Masters	-	-	-	41	MC	1	8	18	5	1
Worldcom Cl'	-	-	-	-	-	-	18	-	-	-
Houston Open	-	-	-	-	-	-	-	-	-	-
GG Chrysler Cl'	-	-	-	-	-	-	-	-	-	-
Compaq Classic	-	-	-	-	-	-	-	-	-	-
Byron Nelson C'	-	MC	-	-	-	1	12	7	4	3
MasterCard Cln'l	-	-	-	-	-	4	-	-	-	-
Kemper Ins Open	-	-	-	-	-	-	-	-	-	-
Memorial T'ment	-	-	-	-	-	67	51	1	1	1
St. Jude Classic	-	-	-	-	-	-	-	-	-	1
U.S. Open	-	-	-	WD	82	19	18	3	1	12
Buick Classic	-	MC	-	-	43	-	-	-	-	16
Canon GH Open	-	-	-	-	-	-	-	-	-	-
Western Open	-	MC	57	-	-	1	9	1	23	20
Gr. Milwaukee	-	-	-	-	60	-	-	-	-	-
British Open	-	-	-	68	22	24	3	7	1	25
B.C. Open	-	-	-	-	3	-	-	-	-	-
John Deere Cl'	-	-	-	-	5	-	-	-	-	-
The International	-	-	-	-	-	-	4	37	-	-
Buick Open	-	-	-	-	-	18	4	-	11	-
USPGA Champ	-	-	-	-	-	29	10	1	1	29
WGCNEC Inv'	-	-	-	-	-	-	-	1	1	1
Reno-Tahoe Op'	-	-	-	-	-	-	-	-	-	-
Air Canada Ch'	-	-	-	-	-	-	-	-	-	-
Bell Canadian	-	-	-	-	11	-	MC	-	1	23
WGC AmEx	-	-	-	-	-	-	-	1	5	-
Tampa Bay Cl'	-	-	-	-	-	-	-	-	-	-
Marconi Penn C'	-	-	-	-	-	-	-	-	-	-
Texas Open	-	-	-	-	3	-	-	-	-	-
Michelob Chmp'	-	-	-	-	-	-	-	-	-	-
Invensys Classic	-	-	-	-	1	36	-	-	-	-
NCR Golf Cl'	-	-	-	-	1	26	12	1	3	16
Buick Challenge	-	-	-	-	-	-	-	-	-	-
SFB Classic	-	-	-	-	-	-	-	-	-	-
Tour Champ'ship	-	-	-	-	21	12	20	1	2	13

EUROPEAN/US TOUR STATS

DRIVING DISTANCE

European Tour

Rank	Player	Avg. dist	Rank	Player	Avg. dist
1	Angel CABRERA	303.5	52	Joakim HAEGGMAN	284.5
2	Ricardo GONZALEZ	303.3		Peter HANSON	284.5
3	Emanuele CANONICA	298.8	54	Eduardo ROMERO	284.3
4	Jean HUGO	297.6		Marco BERNARDINI	284.3
5	Adam SCOTT	297.4	56	Wayne RILEY	284.1
6	Mark PILKINGTON	295.7	57	David GILFORD	284.0
7	Robert KARLSSON	295.3	58	Kenneth FERRIE	283.9
	Elliot BOULT	295.3	59	Anders FORSBRAND	283.6
9	Carl SUNESON	294.5	60	Massimo SCARPA	283.4
10	Scott GARDINER	293.4		Gary MURPHY	283.4
11	Gary EMERSON	293.1		Jarrod MOSELEY	283.4
	Sandy LYLE	293.1	63	Rolf MUNTZ	283.3
13	Greg OWEN	292.4		Paul McGINLEY	283.3
	Steve WEBSTER	292.4	65	Soren HANSEN	283.2
15	Darren CLARKE	291.8		Brian DAVIS	283.2
16	Sergio GARCIA	291.4		David CARTER	283.2
17	Roger CHAPMAN	291.3	68	Maarten LAFEBER	283.1
18	Paul CASEY	291.1		Greg TURNER	283.1
19	Retief GOOSEN	291.0	70	Mathias GRONBERG	282.9
20	Jose Manuel LARA	290.7	71	Alastair FORSYTH	282.8
	Francis VALERA	290.7	72	Wei-Tze YEH	282.7
22	Marcello SANTI	290.6	73	Christophe POTTIER	282.6
23	Nicolas COLSAERTS	290.5	74	Thomas BJORN	282.3
24	David LYNN	289.8		Henrik STENSON	282.3
25	Brett RUMFORD	289.7	76	Robin BYRD	282.2
26	Olivier EDMOND	289.6	77	Fredrik JACOBSON	282.1
27	Gregory HAVRET	289.5		Johan RYSTROM	282.1
28	Santiago LUNA	289.2		Trevor IMMELMAN	282.1
29	Niclas FASTH	289.1		David HOWELL	282.1
30	Michele REALE	288.9	81	Carl PETTERSSON	281.9
31	Des TERBLANCHE	288.7	82	Thomas LEVET	281.6
32	Stephen DODD	288.5	83	Craig HAINLINE	281.5
33	Tobias DIER	288.0	84	Simon DYSON	281.4
34	Stephen GALLACHER	287.8	85	Paul LAWRIE	281.2
	Benoit TEILLERIA	287.8		Peter FOWLER	281.2
36	Darren FICHARDT	287.4	87	Paul STREETER	281.1
37	Justin ROSE	286.6	88	Simon D. HURLEY	281.0
	Lucas PARSONS	286.6		Massimo FLORIOLI	281.0
39	John SENDEN	286.5		Hennie OTTO	281.0
40	Peter LONARD	286.0	91	Michael CAMPBELL	280.9
41	Ian POULTER	285.7	92	Stephen SCAHILL	280.7
42	Henrik BJORNSTAD	285.6	93	Russell CLAYDON	280.6
	Raphael JACQUELIN	285.6	94	Alex CEJKA	280.5
44	Padraig HARRINGTON	285.5	95	Anders HANSEN	280.4
45	Paolo QUIRICI	285.3	96	Simon HURD	280.3
46	Warren BENNETT	285.1	97	Thomas GOGELE	279.9
47	Michael JONZON	285.0	98	Eamonn DARCY	279.8
48	Desvonde BOTES	284.9	99	Paul BROADHURST	279.7
49	Lee WESTWOOD	284.8		Sam TORRANCE	279.7
50	Anthony WALL	284.6		Tony JOHNSTONE	279.7
	Marc FARRY	284.6			

Sponsored by Stan James

DRIVING DISTANCE

US Tour

Rank	Player	Avg. dist	Rank	Player	Avg. dist
1	John DALY	306.7		Andrew McLARDY	283.7
2	Brett QUIGLEY	298.5	52	Craig PERKS	283.6
3	Davis LOVE III	297.6	53	Brad ELDER	283.5
	Tiger WOODS	297.6	54	Steve FLESCH	283.4
5	David DUVAL	296.7		Jonathan KAYE	283.4
6	Charles HOWELL III	293.9		Jim McGOVERN	283.4
	Phil MICKELSON	293.9	57	J.L. LEWIS	283.3
8	Steve ALLAN	293.3		Kaname YOKOO	283.3
9	Chris SMITH	293.2	59	K.J. CHOI	283.1
10	Kenny PERRY	292.3	60	Jeremy ANDERSON	283.0
11	Joey SINDELAR	291.5	61	Andrew MAGEE	282.9
12	Jason GORE	290.5	62	Tommy ARMOUR III	282.7
13	Brandt JOBE	290.4	63	Ian LEGGATT	282.6
14	Scott McCARRON	289.7	64	Craig BARLOW	282.5
15	Kelly GRUNEWALD	289.1	65	Stephen AMES	282.3
16	Chris TIDLAND	289.0	66	Tom PERNICE, Jr.	282.2
17	Tim HERRON	288.9	67	Briny BAIRD	281.8
18	Brian WILSON	288.8		Brian WATTS	281.8
19	Stuart APPLEBY	288.6	69	Stewart CINK	281.7
20	Rory SABBATINI	288.5		Carl PAULSON	281.7
21	Fred COUPLES	288.2		Steve STRICKER	281.7
22	Sergio GARCIA	287.8	72	Dennis PAULSON	281.6
23	Vijay SINGH	287.5		Jeff SLUMAN	281.6
24	Harrison FRAZAR	286.8	74	Hunter HAAS	281.4
25	Tom LEHMAN	286.7		Gabriel HJERTSTEDT	281.4
26	J.J. HENRY	286.6		Per-Ulrik JOHANSSON	281.4
27	Brent SCHWARZROCK	286.4	77	Jerry KELLY	281.3
28	Mark CALCAVECCHIA	286.2	78	Robin FREEMAN	281.1
	Danny ELLIS	286.2	79	Cliff KRESGE	281.0
30	Ernie ELS	285.8	80	Doug DUNAKEY	280.7
31	David BERGANIO, Jr.	285.5		Steve LOWERY	280.7
32	Cameron BECKMAN	285.4	82	Steve ELKINGTON	280.5
	Paul STANKOWSKI	285.4		Brent GEIBERGER	280.5
34	Marco DAWSON	285.2	84	Michael CLARK II	280.4
35	Mathew GOGGIN	285.1		Joe DURANT	280.4
36	Grant WAITE	284.9	86	Matt GOGEL	280.3
37	Geoff OGILVY	284.8	87	Bob MAY	280.2
38	Robert ALLENBY	284.7	88	Billy ANDRADE	280.1
	Frank LICKLITER II	284.7		Shaun MICHEEL	280.1
40	Carlos FRANCO	284.5	90	Shigeki MARUYAMA	279.9
	Donnie HAMMOND	284.5	91	Mark HENSBY	279.8
	Dudley HART	284.5		David PEOPLES	279.8
	Kevin JOHNSON	284.5	93	John HUSTON	279.7
	Duffy WALDORF	284.5	94	John RIEGGER	279.6
45	Mike WEIR	284.4		Garrett WILLIS	279.6
46	Jesper PARNEVIK	284.2	96	Paul AZINGER	279.5
	Tommy TOLLES	284.2		Russ COCHRAN	279.5
48	Rich BEEM	284.1		David TOMS	279.5
49	Ben BATES	283.7		Jeff MAGGERT	279.4
	Ronnie BLACK	283.7			

DRIVING ACCURACY

European Tour

Rank	Player	% fairways hit	Rank	Player	% fairways hit
1	Peter O'MALLEY	83.7	51	Phillip PRICE	67.0
2	Richard GREEN	81.9	52	Ignacio GARRIDO	66.9
3	John BICKERTON	77.1		Carlos RODILES	66.9
4	Gary ORR	76.0	54	Michael CAMPBELL	66.8
5	Mark PILKINGTON	75.1	55	Diego BORREGO	66.7
6	Michele REALE	75.0		Soren KJELDSEN	66.7
7	Anders HANSEN	73.7		Peter BAKER	66.7
8	Matthew BLACKEY	73.4	58	Garry HOUSTON	66.6
9	Paul EALES	72.7	59	Anthony WALL	66.5
10	Sergio GARCIA	72.6		Nicolas VANHOOTEGEM	66.5
11	Ian GARBUTT	72.1	61	Roger CHAPMAN	66.4
12	Nick FALDO	71.4	62	Graham RANKIN	66.3
	David CARTER	71.4	63	Bernhard LANGER	66.0
14	Simon D. HURLEY	71.0	64	Santiago LUNA	65.9
15	Miguel Angel JIMENEZ	70.9	65	Mark MOULAND	65.7
	Nick O'HERN	70.9	66	Gregory HAVRET	65.6
17	Pierre FULKE	70.3		Massimo FLORIOLI	65.6
18	Darren CLARKE	70.1	68	Barry LANE	65.5
	Eamonn DARCY	70.1		Gary EVANS	65.5
	Dean ROBERTSON	70.1	70	Stephen LEANEY	65.4
	Henrik NYSTROM	70.1	71	Raphael JACQUELIN	65.0
22	Greg OWEN	69.9		Tomas Jesus MUNOZ	65.0
23	Jeremy ROBINSON	69.8	73	Johan RYSTROM	64.9
24	Colin MONTGOMERIE	69.7	74	Tony JOHNSTONE	64.8
25	John SENDEN	69.5	75	Christopher HANELL	64.7
26	Adam SCOTT	69.4	76	Eduardo ROMERO	64.6
27	Des SMYTH	69.3	77	Per NYMAN	64.4
	Brett RUMFORD	69.3	78	Roger WESSELS	64.3
	Shaun P. WEBSTER	69.3		Steve WEBSTER	64.3
30	David PARK	68.8		Raymond RUSSELL	64.3
31	Greg TURNER	68.6	81	Kenneth FERRIE	64.2
	Alastair FORSYTH	68.6		Justin ROSE	64.2
33	Gustavo ROJAS	68.5	83	Malcolm MACKENZIE	64.0
34	Peter LONARD	68.3		Paolo QUIRICI	64.0
	Jonathan LOMAS	68.3	85	Warren BENNETT	63.9
	Erol SIMSEK	68.3		Jamie SPENCE	63.9
37	David GILFORD	68.2	87	Graeme STORM	63.8
38	Paul McGINLEY	68.1	88	Richard S. JOHNSON	63.7
	Andrew OLDCORN	68.1		Olivier EDMOND	63.7
40	Steen TINNING	67.7		Markus BRIER	63.7
	Daren LEE	67.7	91	Maarten LAFEBER	63.6
42	Jorge BERENDT	67.6	92	Gary MURPHY	63.5
	Mark JAMES	67.6		Marc FARRY	63.5
44	Rolf MUNTZ	67.5	94	Stephen GALLACHER	63.4
	Benoit TEILLERIA	67.5	95	Stephen SCAHILL	63.3
46	Sven STRUVER	67.4	96	Paul CASEY	63.2
	Mark McNULTY	67.4		Jarmo SANDELIN	63.2
48	Jean-Francois REMESY	67.3		Soren HANSEN	63.2
49	Andrew MARSHALL	67.2	99	Francis VALERA	63.1
50	Mark ROE	67.1	100	Peter HANSON	63.0

Sponsored by Stan James

DRIVING ACCURACY
US Tour

Rank	Player	% fairways hit	Rank	Player	% fairways hit
1	Joe DURANT	81.1	52	David BERGANIO, Jr.	70.9
2	Glen HNATIUK	77.8		Steve LOWERY	70.9
3	Fred FUNK	77.2		David PEOPLES	70.9
4	John COOK	76.6		Dicky PRIDE	70.9
5	Billy MAYFAIR	76.5	56	Brent GEIBERGER	70.8
6	Olin BROWNE	75.8		Charles HOWELL III	70.8
7	Jim FURYK	75.7	58	J.J. HENRY	70.7
8	Tom BYRUM	75.6	59	Briny BAIRD	70.5
	Jose COCERES	75.6		Kent JONES	70.5
	Brian GAY	75.6		Justin LEONARD	70.5
11	Hal SUTTON	75.4		Frank LICKLITER II	70.5
12	Kirk TRIPLETT	75.3	63	Bob TWAY	70.3
13	Scott VERPLANK	75.2	64	Stephen AMES	70.2
14	Jeff HART	74.5	65	Brandel CHAMBLEE	70.1
15	Mark BROOKS	74.3		Per-Ulrik JOHANSSON	70.1
16	Blaine McCALLISTER	74.2	67	Robert ALLENBY	70.0
17	Craig PARRY	74.1		Bob BURNS	70.0
18	Pete JORDAN	74.0		Mark HENSBY	70.0
19	Scott HOCH	73.9		Jonathan KAYE	70.0
20	Brent SCHWARZROCK	73.8	71	Jeff BREHAUT	69.8
21	Joel EDWARDS	73.7		J.P. HAYES	69.8
22	Skip KENDALL	73.5	73	Ben BATES	69.7
	Carl PAULSON	73.5	74	Rich BEEM	69.6
24	Jim CARTER	73.1		Chris PERRY	69.6
	Sergio GARCIA	73.1		Mike SPOSA	69.6
26	Corey PAVIN	73.0	77	Steve ELKINGTON	69.5
27	Robert DAMRON	72.9	78	Phil MICKELSON	69.4
	Jean VAN DE VELDE	72.9	79	Bill GLASSON	69.3
29	Glen DAY	72.6		Kaname YOKOO	69.3
30	Esteban TOLEDO	72.5	81	Tommy ARMOUR III	69.2
31	Fulton ALLEM	72.4	82	Greg CHALMERS	69.1
32	Paul GOYDOS	72.3		Jay WILLIAMSON	69.1
33	Bradley HUGHES	72.2	84	Tripp ISENHOUR	69.0
34	Richie COUGHLAN	72.1		Jerry KELLY	69.0
	Frank NOBILO	72.1		Neal LANCASTER	69.0
	John RIEGGER	72.1		Garrett WILLIS	69.0
	David TOMS	72.1	88	Brandt JOBE	68.9
38	Jay Don BLAKE	72.0		Ian LEGGATT	68.9
	Lee PORTER	72.0		Andrew McLARDY	68.9
40	Larry MIZE	71.9	91	Brian HENNINGER	68.8
41	Nick PRICE	71.8		Bernhard LANGER	68.8
42	Jeff MAGGERT	71.5		Scott McCARRON	68.8
43	Donnie HAMMOND	71.3	94	Woody AUSTIN	68.7
44	Chris RILEY	71.2		Paul AZINGER	68.7
45	Russ COCHRAN	71.0		Duffy WALDORF	68.7
	Scott DUNLAP	71.0	97	Matt GOGEL	68.6
	Dan FORSMAN	71.0		Tom LEHMAN	68.6
	Robert GAMEZ	71.0		Scott SIMPSON	68.6
	Jay HAAS	71.0	100	Len MATTIACE	68.5
	Rocco MEDIATE	71.0		Spike McROY	68.5
	Loren ROBERTS	71.0		Kenny PERRY	68.5

STROKE AVERAGE
European Tour

Rank	Player	Avg. per round	Rank	Player	Avg. per round
1	Padraig HARRINGTON	69.23	41	Alex CEJKA	70.94
2	Retief GOOSEN	69.32		Jean VAN DE VELDE	70.94
3	Sergio GARCIA	69.53	43	Fredrik JACOBSON	70.97
4	Colin MONTGOMERIE	69.75	44	David HOWELL	70.98
5	Paul McGINLEY	69.82	45	Peter LONARD	70.99
	Bernhard LANGER	69.82	46	Nick O'HERN	71.02
7	Ernie ELS	69.90	47	Andrew OLDCORN	71.03
8	Angel CABRERA	69.95	48	John SENDEN	71.04
9	Ricardo GONZALEZ	70.00		Henrik BJORNSTAD	71.04
	Jesper PARNEVIK	70.00	50	Scott GARDINER	71.05
11	Darren CLARKE	70.02	51	Andrew COLTART	71.07
12	Adam SCOTT	70.12		Greg TURNER	71.07
13	Thomas BJORN	70.19	53	Brian DAVIS	71.09
14	Niclas FASTH	70.27	54	Anders FORSBRAND	71.11
15	Peter O'MALLEY	70.35		Soren HANSEN	71.11
	Anthony WALL	70.35	56	Nick DOUGHERTY	71.13
17	Warren BENNETT	70.37		Jeev Milkha SINGH	71.13
18	Robert KARLSSON	70.39	58	Mark McNULTY	71.16
19	Phillip PRICE	70.42		Markus BRIER	71.16
20	Ian WOOSNAM	70.45	60	Christopher HANELL	71.17
21	Anders HANSEN	70.47		Gary ORR	71.17
22	Richard GREEN	70.50	62	Carl PETTERSSON	71.18
23	Steve WEBSTER	70.52		Diego BORREGO	71.18
24	Paul LAWRIE	70.54		Stephen LEANEY	71.18
25	Eduardo ROMERO	70.60	65	Jonathan LOMAS	71.19
26	Dean ROBERTSON	70.62	66	Jeremy ROBINSON	71.21
	Jose Maria OLAZABAL	70.62		Soren KJELDSEN	71.21
28	Raphael JACQUELIN	70.66	68	Joakim HAEGGMAN	71.23
29	Paul CASEY	70.67		Olle KARLSSON	71.23
	Miguel Angel JIMENEZ	70.67	70	Brett RUMFORD	71.25
31	Greg OWEN	70.69	71	Mikko ILONEN	71.27
32	Thomas LEVET	70.71	72	Jorge BERENDT	71.28
33	Mathias GRONBERG	70.79	73	Raymond RUSSELL	71.30
34	Ignacio GARRIDO	70.82	74	Desvonde BOTES	71.31
35	Justin ROSE	70.83		Gary EVANS	71.31
36	Michael CAMPBELL	70.84		Jarrod MOSELEY	71.31
37	David LYNN	70.88		Roger WESSELS	71.31
38	John BICKERTON	70.89		Fredrik ANDERSSON	71.31
39	Ian GARBUTT	70.91	79	Costantino ROCCA	71.33
40	Emanuele CANONICA	70.93		Sven STRUVER	71.33

Driving Accuracy is the percentage of times a player hits the fairway with his tee shot.

Driving Distance is the average number of yards per measured drive. Driving distance is measured on two holes per round.

Stroke Average is the average number of strokes taken per round.

Sand Saves is the percentage of times a player was able to get "up and down" once in a greenside sand bunker.

STROKE AVERAGE

US Tour

Rank	Player	Avg. per round	Rank	Player	Avg. per round
1	Tiger WOODS	68.81		Hal SUTTON	70.51
2	Davis LOVE III	69.06	42	Robert ALLENBY	70.53
3	Sergio GARCIA	69.13		Brad FAXON	70.53
4	Phil MICKELSON	69.21		Corey PAVIN	70.53
	Vijay SINGH	69.21	45	Olin BROWNE	70.60
6	Nick PRICE	69.66	46	K.J. CHOI	70.62
7	David DUVAL	69.73		Brian WATTS	70.62
	Bob ESTES	69.73	48	Cameron BECKMAN	70.65
9	Scott HOCH	69.85		Joel EDWARDS	70.65
10	Chris DiMARCO	69.87		Steve LOWERY	70.65
11	Scott VERPLANK	69.88	51	Chris RILEY	70.67
12	Bernhard LANGER	69.89	52	Stuart APPLEBY	70.68
13	Charles HOWELL III	69.91		Justin LEONARD	70.68
14	Jim FURYK	69.92	54	Steve FLESCH	70.69
15	David TOMS	69.97	55	Chris SMITH	70.70
16	Tom LEHMAN	70.05	56	Skip KENDALL	70.71
17	Scott McCARRON	70.06	57	John COOK	70.72
	Mike WEIR	70.06	58	Tim HERRON	70.73
19	Jesper PARNEVIK	70.12		Bob MAY	70.73
20	Jeff SLUMAN	70.13	60	Greg CHALMERS	70.74
21	Paul AZINGER	70.14		John DALY	70.74
22	Rocco MEDIATE	70.21	62	Briny BAIRD	70.76
	Kevin SUTHERLAND	70.21		Steve STRICKER	70.76
24	Kenny PERRY	70.22	64	Jose Maria OLAZABAL	70.77
25	Stewart CINK	70.27	65	Billy ANDRADE	70.81
26	Frank LICKLITER II	70.28	66	Mike SPOSA	70.90
27	Ernie ELS	70.30	67	David BERGANIO, Jr.	70.93
28	Brett QUIGLEY	70.31	68	Lee JANZEN	70.94
29	Kirk TRIPLETT	70.32		Len MATTIACE	70.94
30	Dudley HART	70.38	70	Harrison FRAZAR	70.95
	Billy MAYFAIR	70.38		Loren ROBERTS	70.95
32	Mark CALCAVECCHIA	70.40	72	Scott DUNLAP	70.96
	Fred FUNK	70.40	73	Fred COUPLES	70.97
	Jay HAAS	70.40		Frank NOBILO	70.97
	Bob TWAY	70.40	75	J.J. HENRY	70.98
36	Jose COCERES	70.41	76	Jim McGOVERN	70.99
37	Shigeki MARUYAMA	70.42	77	Craig PARRY	71.00
38	Brian GAY	70.43	78	Dennis PAULSON	71.01
39	Joe DURANT	70.45	79	Steve ELKINGTON	71.02
40	Jerry KELLY	70.51		Dan FORSMAN	71.02

Greens in Regulation is the percentage of times a player was able to hit the green in regulation (greens hit in regulation/holes played).

Putts per GIR measures putting performance on greens hit in regulation. For each green hit in regulation the total number of putts are divided by the number of greens hit in regulation. By using greens hit in regulation we are able to eliminate the effects of chipping close and one putting in the computation.

GREENS IN REGULATION

European Tour

Rank	Player	% greens hit	Rank	Player	% greens hit
1	Greg OWEN	77.1	52	Michael CAMPBELL	69.9
	Sergio GARCIA	77.1	53	Johan RYSTROM	69.6
	Padraig HARRINGTON	77.1	54	Jorge BERENDT	69.5
4	Peter O'MALLEY	76.5	55	Anders HANSEN	69.4
	Retief GOOSEN	76.5	56	Massimo SCARPA	69.3
6	Paul McGINLEY	75.6		Roger WESSELS	69.3
7	Steve WEBSTER	75.5	58	Jose Maria OLAZABAL	69.2
8	Richard GREEN	75.4	59	Soren HANSEN	69.1
9	Colin MONTGOMERIE	75.1	60	Nick O'HERN	69.0
10	Adam SCOTT	74.6		Paul CASEY	69.0
	Bernhard LANGER	74.6		Paul LAWRIE	69.0
12	Thomas LEVET	74.3	63	Massimo FLORIOLI	68.8
13	John BICKERTON	73.4		Peter HANSON	68.8
14	Gary ORR	73.2	65	Mark McNULTY	68.7
15	Eduardo ROMERO	73.0	66	Tobias DIER	68.6
16	Raphael JACQUELIN	72.7		Justin HOBDAY	68.6
17	Ian GARBUTT	72.6	68	Stephen SCAHILL	68.5
18	Ian WOOSNAM	72.3		Jean-Francois REMESY	68.5
19	Michele REALE	72.1		Rolf MUNTZ	68.5
20	David CARTER	71.9	71	Ricardo GONZALEZ	68.4
21	Gary EVANS	71.8	72	Gregory HAVRET	68.2
22	Des SMYTH	71.5	73	Paul EALES	68.1
	Andrew COLTART	71.5	74	Barry LANE	68.0
24	Niclas FASTH	71.4		Nicolas VANHOOTEGEM	68.0
25	Jeremy ROBINSON	71.3		Trevor IMMELMAN	68.0
	Warren BENNETT	71.3		Matthew BLACKEY	68.0
27	Jonathan LOMAS	71.1	78	Daren LEE	67.8
	Brett RUMFORD	71.1		Sven STRUVER	67.8
	Anders FORSBRAND	71.1		David LYNN	67.8
30	Darren CLARKE	71.0		Craig HAINLINE	67.8
31	Jose Manuel LARA	70.8		Simon DYSON	67.8
	Maarten LAFEBER	70.8	83	Olivier EDMOND	67.7
	Emanuele CANONICA	70.8		Van PHILLIPS	67.7
34	Mark PILKINGTON	70.7	85	Steen TINNING	67.5
	Justin ROSE	70.7		Jean VAN DE VELDE	67.5
36	Peter BAKER	70.6	87	John SENDEN	67.3
	Ignacio GARRIDO	70.6		Hennie OTTO	67.3
	Simon D. HURLEY	70.6		Dean ROBERTSON	67.3
39	Peter LONARD	70.5	90	Robert KARLSSON	67.2
	Tomas Jesus MUNOZ	70.5		Phillip PRICE	67.2
41	Roger CHAPMAN	70.3		Shaun P WEBSTER	67.2
42	Anthony WALL	70.2	93	Santiago LUNA	67.1
	Henrik STENSON	70.2	94	Per NYMAN	67.0
	David GILFORD	70.2		Robin BYRD	67.0
	Angel CABRERA	70.2		Eamonn DARCY	67.0
	Diego BORREGO	70.2		Stephen DODD	67.0
47	Alex CEJKA	70.1	98	Carl SUNESON	66.9
	Jose RIVERO	70.1		Thomas BJORN	66.9
	Miguel Angel JIMENEZ	70.1		Raymond RUSSELL	66.9
50	Greg TURNER	70.0		Desvonde BOTES	66.9
	Stephen GALLACHER	70.0			

GREENS IN REGULATION

US Tour

Rank	Player	% greens hit	Rank	Player	% greens hit
1	Tom LEHMAN	74.5	52	Per-Ulrik JOHANSSON	68.1
2	Charles HOWELL III	73.5		Duffy WALDORF	68.1
3	John COOK	72.9	54	Sergio GARCIA	68.0
4	David TOMS	72.6		Neal LANCASTER	68.0
5	Joe DURANT	72.1	56	Steve FLESCH	67.9
6	Bob TWAY	71.9		Jeff HART	67.9
	Tiger WOODS	71.9	58	Jose COCERES	67.7
8	Kenny PERRY	71.4		Russ COCHRAN	67.7
9	Hal SUTTON	71.1		Frank NOBILO	67.7
10	Donnie HAMMOND	71.0		Mike WEIR	67.7
	Glen HNATIUK	71.0	62	Mark CALCAVECCHIA	67.6
	Rocco MEDIATE	71.0		Lee JANZEN	67.6
13	J.J. HENRY	70.7	64	Bob BURNS	67.5
	Scott VERPLANK	70.7		Bill GLASSON	67.5
15	Chris DiMARCO	70.6		Jeff MAGGERT	67.5
	Chris SMITH	70.6		Craig PARRY	67.5
17	Jim FURYK	70.5		Nick PRICE	67.5
18	John HUSTON	70.4	69	Brent SCHWARZROCK	67.4
19	Tim HERRON	70.3	70	John DALY	67.3
	Davis LOVE III	70.3	71	Craig BARLOW	67.2
	Kirk TRIPLETT	70.3		Marco DAWSON	67.2
22	Fred COUPLES	70.2	73	David BERGANIO, Jr.	67.1
	Jeff SLUMAN	70.2		Jonathan KAYE	67.1
	Kevin SUTHERLAND	70.2	75	Scott HOCH	67.0
25	Scott McCARRON	70.0		Skip KENDALL	67.0
26	Phil MICKELSON	69.9		Joey SINDELAR	67.0
27	Briny BAIRD	69.8	78	Brian GAY	66.9
	Stewart CINK	69.8		Brent GEIBERGER	66.9
	Billy MAYFAIR	69.8		Ian LEGGATT	66.9
30	Vijay SINGH	69.5		Justin LEONARD	66.9
31	Jerry KELLY	69.4		Jesper PARNEVIK	66.9
	David PEOPLES	69.4	83	Dan FORSMAN	66.8
33	Robert ALLENBY	69.3		Jose Maria OLAZABAL	66.8
34	Paul AZINGER	69.2	85	Brett QUIGLEY	66.6
35	Stephen AMES	69.1		Paul STANKOWSKI	66.6
	David DUVAL	69.1	87	Harrison FRAZAR	66.5
	Joel EDWARDS	69.1		Spike McROY	66.5
38	Dudley HART	69.0	89	Robin FREEMAN	66.4
39	Jay HAAS	68.9		Mark O'MEARA	66.4
	Brandt JOBE	68.9		Grant WAITE	66.4
	Bob MAY	68.9	92	Jeff BREHAUT	66.3
42	Cameron BECKMAN	68.8		Greg KRAFT	66.3
43	Bradley HUGHES	68.6		Mike SPOSA	66.3
	John RIEGGER	68.6	95	Michael MUEHR	66.2
45	Bob ESTES	68.5		Rory SABBATINI	66.2
46	Bernhard LANGER	68.4	97	Michael CLARK II	66.1
	Frank LICKLITER II	68.4		Ernie ELS	66.1
	Chris PERRY	68.4		Carl PAULSON	66.1
49	Olin BROWNE	68.3	100	Tom BYRUM	65.9
50	Fred FUNK	68.2		K.J. CHOI	65.9
	Steve LOWERY	68.2		Steve JONES	65.9

PUTTS PER GIR

European Tour

Rank	Player	Avg. per hole	Rank	Player	Avg. per hole
1	Padraig HARRINGTON	1.723	26	Jean VAN DE VELDE	1.759
2	Michael CAMPBELL	1.731	27	Paul LAWRIE	1.760
	Thomas BJORN	1.731		Ricardo GONZALEZ	1.760
4	Colin MONTGOMERIE	1.738		Gary EMERSON	1.760
	Retief GOOSEN	1.738		Lee WESTWOOD	1.760
6	Pierre FULKE	1.739	31	Greg TURNER	1.761
7	Darren CLARKE	1.742		Angel CABRERA	1.761
8	Jose Maria OLAZABAL	1.744	33	Simon HURD	1.762
9	Niclas FASTH	1.745	34	Henrik BJORNSTAD	1.763
10	Phillip PRICE	1.746	35	Peter FOWLER	1.764
	Brian DAVIS	1.746	36	Jarmo SANDELIN	1.766
12	Seve BALLESTEROS	1.747		Soren KJELDSEN	1.766
13	Joakim HAEGGMAN	1.748		Paul McGINLEY	1.766
	Mikael LUNDBERG	1.748		Andrew OLDCORN	1.766
	Russell CLAYDON	1.748		Malcolm MACKENZIE	1.766
16	Anthony WALL	1.749	41	Stephen LEANEY	1.767
17	Dennis EDLUND	1.750		Olle KARLSSON	1.767
18	Nick FALDO	1.751	43	Jarrod MOSELEY	1.768
	Fredrik JACOBSON	1.751		Bradley DREDGE	1.768
20	Robert KARLSSON	1.754	45	Soren HANSEN	1.769
21	Des TERBLANCHE	1.756		Michael JONZON	1.769
	Jeev Milkha SINGH	1.756		Ian POULTER	1.769
23	Anders HANSEN	1.757	48	Simon D. HURLEY	1.770
	Elliot BOULT	1.757			
25	Mathias GRONBERG	1.758			

US Tour

Rank	Player	Avg. per hole	Rank	Player	Avg. per hole
1	David FROST	1.708	26	Brian WATTS	1.745
2	Phil MICKELSON	1.717	27	Cameron BECKMAN	1.746
3	Brian GAY	1.722		Joe OGILVIE	1.746
4	Vijay SINGH	1.723		Corey PAVIN	1.746
5	Jeff SLUMAN	1.725	30	Mark CALCAVECCHIA	1.747
6	Bob ESTES	1.726		Tripp ISENHOUR	1.747
	Craig KANADA	1.726		Lee JANZEN	1.747
8	Bernhard LANGER	1.729		Jose Maria OLAZABAL	1.747
9	Skip KENDALL	1.730		Scott VERPLANK	1.747
10	David TOMS	1.732	35	Kenny PERRY	1.748
11	Steve STRICKER	1.733		Kevin SUTHERLAND	1.748
12	Chris DiMARCO	1.734	37	Jay Don BLAKE	1.749
13	Glen DAY	1.735		Loren ROBERTS	1.749
	Jerry KELLY	1.735	39	Shigeki MARUYAMA	1.750
15	Stuart APPLEBY	1.736	40	Jay HAAS	1.751
16	Russ COCHRAN	1.737		Chris RILEY	1.751
	Frank LICKLITER II	1.737	42	John DALY	1.752
	Scott McCARRON	1.737		Billy MAYFAIR	1.752
19	Jim FURYK	1.738		Michael MUEHR	1.752
	Scott SIMPSON	1.738	45	Rocco MEDIATE	1.753
21	Brad FAXON	1.739	46	Greg CHALMERS	1.754
	Scott HOCH	1.739		Blaine McCALLISTER	1.754
	David MORLAND IV	1.739		Brett QUIGLEY	1.754
24	Sergio GARCIA	1.740		Willie WOOD	1.754
25	Justin LEONARD	1.742			

SAND SAVES

European Tour

Rank	Player	% saves made	Rank	Player	% saves made
1	Jean VAN DE VELDE	85.2	26	Per NYMAN	63.2
2	Tony JOHNSTONE	81.6	27	Francis VALERA	63.0
3	Bernhard LANGER	78.9	28	Jose RIVERO	62.9
4	Miguel Angel JIMENEZ	78.7	29	Mark ROE	62.3
5	Brett RUMFORD	78.3	30	Trevor IMMELMAN	62.0
6	Simon HURD	76.9	31	Andrew COLTART	61.9
7	John SENDEN	76.0		Simon D. HURLEY	61.9
8	Seve BALLESTEROS	72.5	33	Richard GREEN	61.6
9	Jose Maria OLAZABAL	72.2	34	Ian WOOSNAM	61.2
10	Padraig HARRINGTON	71.1	35	Greg OWEN	60.8
11	Fredrik JACOBSON	69.0	36	Des SMYTH	60.6
12	Michele REALE	68.4	37	Nicolas COLSAERTS	60.5
13	Christophe POTTIER	67.9		Sam TORRANCE	60.5
14	Scott GARDINER	67.4	39	Peter MITCHELL	60.3
15	Dean ROBERTSON	66.9		Robin BYRD	60.3
16	Jamie SPENCE	66.3	41	Stephen GALLACHER	60.0
17	Gustavo ROJAS	66.1	42	Mark JAMES	59.6
18	Miguel Angel MARTIN	65.5	43	Niclas FASTH	59.3
19	Jarmo SANDELIN	64.7	44	Craig HAINLINE	59.2
20	Mathias GRONBERG	64.6	45	Gary MURPHY	59.0
21	Mark PILKINGTON	64.5	46	Raymond RUSSELL	58.9
22	Bradley DREDGE	64.3	47	Phillip PRICE	58.8
	Tomas Jesus MUNOZ	64.3		Benoit TEILLERIA	58.8
24	Ignacio GARRIDO	64.0			
	Christopher HANELL	64.0			

US Tour

Rank	Player	% saves made	Rank	Player	% saves made
1	Franklin LANGHAM	68.9	25	Craig KANADA	58.0
2	Scott VERPLANK	66.2	26	Dan FORSMAN	57.5
3	Brad FAXON	64.9	27	Steve ELKINGTON	57.0
4	Nick PRICE	64.8		Bob ESTES	57.0
5	Jose COCERES	63.7		Brian WATTS	57.0
6	Kevin SUTHERLAND	63.0		Jay WILLIAMSON	57.0
7	Scott McCARRON	62.1	31	Greg CHALMERS	56.8
8	Edward FRYATT	61.8		Sergio GARCIA	56.8
9	Ronnie BLACK	61.3	33	Paul AZINGER	56.7
10	Ernie ELS	60.6	34	Dudley HART	56.4
	Paul GOW	60.6		Skip KENDALL	56.4
	Billy MAYFAIR	60.6	36	Craig BARLOW	56.3
13	Bob BURNS	60.4		Willie WOOD	56.3
14	Bob MAY	60.3	38	Robert DAMRON	56.2
15	Jeff SLUMAN	60.2		Jeff HART	56.2
16	Brandel CHAMBLEE	60.1	40	Scott HOCH	56.1
17	Chris DIMARCO	59.6	41	Steve STRICKER	56.0
18	Len MATTIACE	59.5	42	Mark O'MEARA	55.9
	Rocco MEDIATE	59.5	43	Doug BARRON	55.8
20	Dennis PAULSON	59.1		John HUSTON	55.8
21	Shigeki MARUYAMA	58.8		Davis LOVE III	55.8
22	Mike WEIR	58.7		Craig PERKS	55.8
23	Kirk TRIPLETT	58.5		Lee PORTER	55.8
24	Vijay SINGH	58.3	48	Neal LANCASTER	55.7

Sponsored by Stan James

CHALLENGE TOUR RESULTS

Date	Tournament	Venue	Winner
1-4 Mar	Tusker Kenya Open	Muthaiga GC, Kenya	Ashley ROESTOFF
8-11 Mar	Stanbic Zambia Open	Lusaka GC, Zambia	Mark FOSTER
29 Mar-1 Apr	Segura Viudas Challenge	Club de Golf Villamartin Alicante, Spain	Euan LITTLE
26-29 Apr	Open Golf Montecchia	Montecchia GC Padova, Italy	Andrew SHERBORNE
3-6 May	Credit Suisse Private Banking Open	Patriziale GC Ascona, Switzerland	Greig HUTCHEON
17-20 May	Austrian Open	Murhof GC Graz, Austria	Chris GANE
24-27 May	Saint Omer Open	Aa Saint Omer GC, France	S DELAGRANGE
31 May-3 Jun	NCC Open	Saderasens GC, Sweden	Benn BARHAM
7-10 Jun	Nykredit Danish Open	Aalborg GC Aalborg, Denmark	S DELAGRANGE
14-17 Jun	Galeria Kaufhof Pokal Challenge	Rittergut Birkhof GC, Germany	Wolfgang HUGET
21-24 Jun	DEXIA-BIL Luxembourg Open	Kikuoka CC Canach, Luxemborg	Grant HAMERTON
28 Jun-1 Jul	Open des Volcans	Golf des Volcans, France	Scott DRUMMOND
5-8 Jul	Challenge Total Fina Elf	Joyenval GC Chambourcy, France	Kenneth FERRIE
12-15 Jul	Volvo Finnish Open	Espoon Golfseura, Finland	Peter HEDBLOM
19-22 Jul	Gunther Hamburg Classics	Treudelberg GC, Germany	Peter HANSON
26-29 Jul	Charles Church Tour Championship	Bowood G&CC Wiltshire, England	Mark FOSTER
2-5 Aug	BMW Russian Open	Moscow G&CC, Russia	Jamie DONALDSON
9-12 Aug	Talma Finnish Challenge	Golf Talma, Finland	Klas ERIKSSON
16-19 Aug	North West of Ireland Open	Slieve Russell Hotel G&CC, Ireland	Tobias DIER
23-26 Aug	Rolex Trophy	Geneve GC, Switzerland	Stuart LITTLE
23-26 Aug	Skandia PGA Open	Bokskogens GC, Sweden	Christophe POTTIER
30 Aug-2 Sep	Formby Hall Challenge	Formby Hall GC, England	Sam LITTLE
5-8 Sep	Muermans Real Estate Challenge	Herkenbosch G&CC, Holland	D NOUAILHAC
13-16 Sep	Telia Grand Prix	Bro BÂlsta Stockholm, Sweden	Jamie DONALDSON
27-30 Sep	PGA of Austria Masters	Golfclub Eichenheim Kitzb͵hel, Austria	Iain PYMAN
3-6 Oct	San Paolo Vita & Asset Management Open	Margara GC, Italy	Mads VIBE-HASTRUP
11-14 Oct	Hardelot Challenge de France	Hardelot GC, France	Marten OLANDER
18-21 Oct	Terme Euganee International Open	Padova GC Valsanzibio, Italy	Chris GANE
1-4 Nov	Challenge Tour Grand Final	Golf du Medoc, France	Richard BLAND

CHALLENGE TOUR MONEY LIST

Rank	Player	Events	Money (euros)	Rank	Player	Events	Money (euros)
1	Mark FOSTER	23	97,736.71	20	Andre BOSSERT	24	51,080.59
2	J DONALDSON	18	92,740.20	21	Michael ARCHER	21	50,401.93
3	Philip GOLDING	21	79,731.35	22	Benn BARHAM	22	49,664.27
4	A MARSHALL	19	75,840.90	23	Iain PYMAN	23	47,749.82
5	Gary CLARK	24	72,949.77	24	M ELIASSON	24	47,025.45
6	S DELAGRANGE	12	71,236.94	25	Alberto BINAGHI	21	46,104.04
7	Klas ERIKSSON	22	66,933.36	26	A ROESTOFF	22	44,466.12
8	R Jan DERKSEN	20	61,595.11	27	D NOUAILHAC	22	43,639.79
9	Chris GANE	25	60,778.07	28	Mattias NILSSON	21	39,392.73
10	Richard BLAND	21	60,693.27	29	D DE VOOGHT	25	38,192.88
11	M VIBE-HASTRUP	16	60,677.01	30	Euan LITTLE	25	36,965.02
12	Peter HANSON	6	60,432.40	31	J Maria ARRUTI	19	36,047.64
13	G HAMERTON	24	59,580.64	32	S WAKEFIELD	25	33,882.37
14	Stuart LITTLE	25	58,649.94	33	Sam WALKER	22	33,031.27
15	Ma OLANDER	20	58,306.44	34	Kenneth FERRIE	15	32,915.77
16	Peter HEDBLOM	16	57,680.47	35	Joakim RASK	19	32,231.06
17	G HUTCHEON	18	56,387.55	36	M PERSSON	19	31,735.98
18	S DRUMMOND	21	54,058.29	37	Kariem BARAKA	21	31,636.34
19	A SHERBORNE	25	53,173.13	38	Ian HUTCHINGS	16	31,443.68

BUY.COM TOUR RESULTS

Date	Tournament	Venue	Winner
Mar 8-11	Florida Classic	Gainesville Country Club, Gainesville, FL	Chris COUCH
Mar 15-18	Monterrey Open	Club Campestre, Monterrey, Mexico	Deane PAPPAS
Mar 29-Apr 1	Louisiana Open	LeTriomphe Country Club, Broussard, LA	Paul CLAXTON
Apr 19-22	Arkansas Classic	Hot Springs Village, AR	Brett QUIGLEY
Apr 26-29	Charity Pro-Am at The Cliffs	The Cliffs, Greenville, SC (TGC)	Jonathan BYRD
May 3-6	Carolina Classic	TPC at Wakefield Plantation, Raleigh, NC	John MAGINNES
May 10-13	Virginia Beach Open	TPC of Virginia Beach, Virginia Beach, VA	Trevor DODDS
May 17-20	Richmond Open	Richmond, VA	Chad CAMPBELL
May 31-Jun 3	Steamtown Classic	Glenmaura National, Scranton, PA	Jason HILL
Jun 7-10	Canadian PGA Championship	DiamondBack GC, Toronto, Ontario	Richard ZOKOL
Jun 14-17	Greater Cleveland Open	Quail Hollow Resort, Concord, OH	Heath SLOCUM
Jun 21-24	Dayton Open	The Golf Club at Yankee Trace, Centerville	Todd BARRANGER
Jun 28-Jul 1	Knoxville Open	Fox Den Country Club, Knoxville, TN	Heath SLOCUM
Jul 5-8	Hershey Open	Country Club of Hershey (East Course), Hershey, PA	John ROLLINS
Jul 12-15	Wichita Open	Crestview Country Club, Wichita, KS	Jason DUFNER
Jul 19-22	Siouxland Open	Dakota Dunes Country Club, Dakota Dunes	Pat BATES
Jul 26-29	Ozarks Open	Highland Springs Country Club, Springfield	Steve HASKINS
Aug 2-5	Omaha Classic	Omaha, NE	Heath SLOCUM
Aug 9-12	Fort Smith Classic	Hardscrabble Country Club, Fort Smith	Jay DELSING
Aug 16-19	Permian Basin Open	The Club at Mission Dorado, Odessa, TX	Chad CAMPBELL
Aug 30-Sep 2	Utah Classic	Willow Creek Country Club, Salt Lake City	David SUTHERLAND
Sep 6-9	Tri-Cities Open	Meadow Springs Country Club, Richland	Guy BOROS
Sep 13-16	Oregon Classic	Shadow Hills Country Club, Eugene, OR	Cancelled
Sep 20-23	Boise Open	Hillcrest Country Club, Boise, ID	Michael LONG
Sep 27-30	Inland Empire Open	Empire Lakes GC, Rancho Cucamonga, CA	D.A. POINTS
Oct 4-7	Monterey Peninsula Classic	Bayonet & Black Horse Courses, Seaside	Chad CAMPBELL
Oct 11-14	Gila River Classic	Whirlwind Golf Club, Chandler, AZ	Ben CRANE
Oct 18-21	Shreveport Open	Southern Trace Country Club, Shreveport	Pat BATES
Oct 25-28	BUY.COM Tour Championship	Capitol Hill, Prattville, AL	Pat BATES

BUY.COM MONEY LIST

Rank	Player	Events	Money ($)	Rank	Player	Events	Money ($)
1	Chad CAMPBELL	23	394,552	20	Ryuji IMADA	25	151,711
2	Pat BATES	24	352,261	21	Jason DUFNER	13	151,394
3	Heath SLOCUM	18	339,670	22	Tom CARTER	25	149,576
4	Rod PAMPLING	26	306,573	23	Ben CRANE	26	147,474
5	Deane PAPPAS	24	271,169	24	Kelly GIBSON	24	145,551
6	John ROLLINS	25	242,841	25	Chris COUCH	26	145,536
7	Tim PETROVIC	23	239,010	26	Sonny SKINNER	24	143,951
8	Jonathan BYRD	20	222,244	27	Keoke COTNER	26	143,317
9	Jeff GOVE	25	198,812	28	Brian KAMM	22	138,714
10	Brenden PAPPAS	26	188,152	29	Jim BENEPE	17	128,987
11	Bo VAN PELT	24	175,947	30	D.A. POINTS	20	126,366
12	Matt PETERSON	21	169,947	31	Jay DELSING	18	125,374
13	Richard ZOKOL	21	167,192	32	Pat PEREZ	26	124,818
14	Jason HILL	26	166,899	33	Todd FISCHER	12	118,622
15	Michael LONG	25	161,665	34	Jeff FREEMAN	24	118,038
16	Todd BARRANGER		27159,392	35	Eric MEEKS	24	117,816
17	Paul CLAXTON	26	158,920	36	C RAULERSON	25	116,966
18	T VAN DER WALT	23	155,291	37	David GOSSETT		12116,288
19	Steve HASKINS	25	153,739	38	Jason CARON	26	116,147

EUROPEAN SENIORS TOUR RESULTS

Date	Tournament	Venue	Winner
29-31 Mar	Barbados Open	Royal Westmoreland GC, Barbados	Priscillo DINIZ
3-5 May	Beko Classic	Gloria Golf Resort, Turkey	Noel RATCLIFFE
11-13 May	AIB Irish Seniors Open	Powerscourt Golf Club, Dublin, Ireland	Seiji EBIHARA
31 May-3 Jun	PGA Seniors Championship	De Vere Carden Park, England	Ian STANLEY
8-10 Jun	Wales Seniors Open	Royal St. David's Harlech, Wales	Denis DURNIAN
15-17 Jun	Microlease Jersey Seniors Masters	La Moye GC, Jersey	Seiji EBIHARA
22-24 Jun	Palmerston Trophy	Faldo Course, Palmerston Resort, Berlin, Germany	Denis O'SULLIVAN
28-30 Jun	Lawrence Batley Seniors	Huddersfield GC, England	Nick JOB
13-15 Jul	Scandinavian International	Kungsangen GC Stockholm, Sweden	Denis O'SULLIVAN
26-29 Jul	Senior British Open	Royal County Down GC, Northern Ireland	Ian STANLEY
3-5 Aug	De Vere Hotels Seniors Classic	De Vere Slaley Hall, England	Noel RATCLIFFE
10-12 Aug	Bad Ragaz PGA Seniors Open	Bad Ragaz GC, Switzerland	David HUISH
17-19 Aug	Energis Senior Masters	Wentworth, England	David OAKLEY
24-26 Aug	Legends in Golf	Crayestein Golf, Dordrecht, Holland	David GOOD
31 Aug-2 Sep	Scottish Seniors Open	The Roxburghe, Scotland	David OAKLEY
7-9 Sep	STC Bovis Lend Lease European Invitational	Woburn GC, England	Rob SHEARER
14-16 Sep	Monte Carlo Invitational	Monte Carlo Golf Club, Monaco	Cancelled
21-23 Sep	TEMES Seniors Open	Glyfada GC, Greece	Russell WEIR
5-7 Oct	Senior Tournament of Champions	Mere G&CC, England	Delroy CAMBRIDGE
17-19 Oct	Tunisian Seniors Open	Port el Kantaoui GC, Tunisia	Simon OWEN
24-27 Oct	Match Play Championship	Le Meridien Penina, Portugal	Jim RHODES
2-4 Nov	STC Seniors Tour Championship	PGA Golf de Catalunya, Spain	Jerry BRUNER

EUROPEAN SENIORS TOUR MONEY LIST

Rank	Player	Events	Money (euros)	Rank	Player	Events	Money (euros)
1	Ian STANLEY	19	287,025.14	25	Craig DEFOY	19	97,787.52
2	Denis DURNIAN	21	276,623.40	26	Terry GALE	12	94,912.15
3	Noel RATCLIFFE	19	218,685.44	27	John GRACE	14	93,615.54
4	David GOOD	21	214,500.19	28	Mike MILLER	19	89,715.49
5	Jerry BRUNER	21	214,457.29	29	Tommy HORTON	18	85,342.68
6	Simon OWEN	17	199,341.67	30	David HUISH	18	84,052.83
7	David OAKLEY	20	188,061.40	31	Eddie POLLAND	20	83,266.49
8	Seiji EBIHARA	13	187,077.15	32	Bill HARDWICK	21	82,922.68
9	D CAMBRIDGE	20	177,871.80	33	J VAN WAGENEN	21	78,943.22
10	John MORGAN	20	171,750.33	34	Bobby VERWEY	16	75,749.83
11	B GALLACHER	18	166,623.74	35	John MCTEAR	19	75,002.57
12	D O'SULLIVAN	21	165,919.98	36	Alan TAPIE	16	70,491.63
13	M BEMBRIDGE	21	143,651.84	37	Russell WEIR	10	69,548.49
14	Jay HORTON	20	134,576.93	38	Paul LEONARD	16	64,440.07
15	Priscillo DINIZ	18	126,670.77	39	Alberto CROCE	16	56,530.46
16	Bob SHEARER	16	121,619.54	40	Neil COLES	10	55,371.41
17	Barry VIVIAN	15	117,312.61	41	John IRWIN	15	51,835.07
18	K MACDONALD	19	114,243.28	42	H WOODROME	16	50,536.27
19	Nick JOB	19	111,083.86	43	P TOWNSEND	20	47,274.57
20	M GREGSON	18	107,364.10	44	Ray CARRASCO	12	42,281.87
21	Peter DAWSON	21	107,174.87	45	Brian HUGGETT	8	40,278.45
22	Bob LENDZION	16	105,483.34	46	Steve WILD	13	38,185.52
23	Jim RHODES	21	104,274.06	47	Tommy PRICE	17	36,748.52
24	David CREAMER	21	101,523.02	48	S LOCATELLI	15	35,520.20

US SENIORS TOUR RESULTS

Date	Tournament	Venue	Winner
Jan 18-21	MasterCard Championship	Hualalai Golf Club, Kaupulehu-Kona	Larry NELSON
Feb 1-4	Royal Caribbean Classic	Crandon Park Golf Club, Key Biscayne	Larry NELSON
Feb 8-11	ACE Group Classic	Pelican Marsh Country Club, Naples	Gil MORGAN
Feb 15-18	Verizon Classic	TPC of Tampa Bay, Lutz, FL	Bob GILDER
Feb 22-25	Mexico Senior Classic	La Vista C.C, A.C. Puebla, MX	Mike McCULLOUGH
Mar 1-4	Toshiba Senior Classic	Newport Beach C.C, Newport, CA	Jose Maria CANIZARES
Mar 8-11	SBC Senior Classic	Valencia Country Club, Valencia, CA	Jim COLBERT
Mar 15-18	Siebel Classic in Silicon Valley	Coyote Creek G.C, San Jose, CA	Hale IRWIN
Mar 22-25	Emerald Coast Classic	The Moors Golf Club, Milton, FL	Mike McCULLOUGH
Apr 12-15	The Countrywide Tradition	Desert Mountain, Scottsdale, AZ	Doug TEWELL
Apr 19-22	Las Vegas Senior Classic	TPC at Summerlin, Las Vegas, NV	Bruce FLEISHER
Apr 26-29	Bruno's Memorial Classic	Greystone G&C.C, Birmingham, AL	Hale IRWIN
May 3-6	The Home Depot Invitational	TPC at Piper Glen, Charlotte, NC	Bruce FLEISHER
May 10-13	Enterprise MatchPlay	Boone Valley G.C, Augusta, MO	Leonard THOMPSON
May 17-20	TD Waterhouse Championship	Tiffany Greens, Kansas City, MO	Ed DOUGHERTY
May 24-27	Senior PGA Championship	Ridgewood C.C, Paramus, NJ	Tom WATSON
May 31-Jun 3	BellSouth Senior Classic	Opryland Springhouse G.C, Nashville	Sammy RACHELS
Jun 7-10	NFL Golf Classic	Upper Montclair Country Club, Clifton	John SCHROEDER
Jun 14-17	The Instinet Classic TPC	Jasna Polana, Princeton, NJ	Gil MORGAN
Jun 21-24	FleetBoston Classic	Nashawtuc Country Club, Concord	Larry NELSON
Jun 28-Jul 1	U.S. Senior Open	Salem County Club, Peabody, MA	Bruce FLEISHER
Jul 5-8	Farmers Charity Classic	Egypt Valley Country Club, Ada, MI	Larry NELSON
Jul 12-15	Ford Senior Players Championship	TPC of Michigan, Dearborn, MI	Allen DOYLE
Jul 19-22	SBC Senior Open	Kemper Lakes Golf Club, Long Grove	Dana QUIGLEY
Jul 26-29	State Farm Senior Classic	Hayfields Country Club, Hunt Valley	Allen DOYLE
Aug 2-5	Lightpath Long Island Classic	Meadow Brook Club, Jericho, NY	Bobby WADKINS
Aug 9-12	3M Championship	TPC of the Twin Cities, Minneapolis	Bruce LIETZKE
Aug 16-19	Novell Utah Showdown	Park Meadows Country Club, Park City	Steve VERIATO
Aug 23-26	AT&T Canada Senior Open	Mississaugua G&C.C, Ontario	Walter HALL
Aug 30-Sep 2	Kroger Senior Classic	Kings Island, Mason, OH	Jim THORPE
Sep 6-9	Allianz Championship	Glen Oak Country Club, West Des Moines, Iowa	Jim THORPE
Sep 13-16	Vantage Championship	Tanglewood Park, Clemmons, NC	Cancelled
Sep 20-23	SAS Championship	Prestonwood Country Club, Cary, NC	Bruce LIETZKE
Sep 27-30	Gold Rush Classic	Serrano Country Club, El Dorado Hills	Tom KITE
Oct 4-7	Turtle Bay Championship	Palmer Course at Turtle Bay, Kahuku	Hale IRWIN
Oct 11-14	The Transamerica	Silverado Resort, Napa, CA	Sammy RACHELS
Oct 18-21	SBC Championship	The Dominion C.C, San Antonio, TX	Larry NELSON
Oct 25-28	SENIOR TOUR Championship	Gaillardia G&C.C, Oklahoma City	Bob GILDER

US SENIORS TOUR MONEY LIST

Rank	Player	Events	Money ($)	Rank	Player	Events	Money ($)
1	Allen DOYLE	34	2,553,582	11	Walter HALL	35	1,339,059
2	Bruce FLEISHER	31	2,411,543	12	M McCULLOUGH	35	1,335,040
3	Hale IRWIN	26	2,147,422	13	Ed DOUGHERTY	36	1,330,818
4	Larry NELSON	28	2,109,936	14	J M CANIZARES	30	1,191,094
5	Gil MORGAN	24	1,885,871	15	Tom JENKINS	36	1,156,576
6	Jim THORPE	35	1,827,223	16	Bruce LIETZKE	10	1,119,573
7	Doug TEWELL	28	1,721,339	17	Tom WATSON	13	986,547
8	Bob GILDER	30	1,684,986	18	Sammy RACHELS	27	932,031
9	Dana QUIGLEY	37	1,537,931	19	Jim COLBERT	29	930,096
10	Tom KITE	23	1,398,802	20	B SUMMERHAYS	34	904,617

WORLD RANKINGS

Rank	Player	Country	Pts.Avg.	Rank	Player	Country	Pts.Avg.
1	Tiger WOODS	USA	18.06	51	Stuart APPLEBY	Aus	2.32
2	Phil MICKELSON	USA	10.01	52	Miguel A. JIMENEZ	Spn	2.29
3	David DUVAL	USA	8.55	53	Billy MAYFAIR	USA	2.28
4	Ernie ELS	SA	6.79	54	Dudley HART	USA	2.28
5	Davis LOVE III	USA	6.52	55	Phillip PRICE	Wal	2.27
6	Sergio GARCIA	Spn	6.30	56	Toru TANIGUCHI	Jpn	2.26
7	David TOMS	USA	6.26	57	Steve STRICKER	USA	2.26
8	Vijay SINGH	Fij	6.09	58	Paul LAWRIE	Sco	2.25
9	Darren CLARKE	Nlr	5.43	59	Adam SCOTT	Aus	2.25
10	Padraig HARRINGTON	Ire	5.36	60	Bob MAY	USA	2.22
11	Mike WEIR	Can	5.30	61	Jeff SLUMAN	USA	2.21
12	Retief GOOSEN	SA	5.17	62	Jose Maria OLAZABAL	Spn	2.09
13	Colin MONTGOMERIE	Sco	4.90	63	Shigeki MARUYAMA	Jpn	2.06
14	Bernhard LANGER	Ger	4.84	64	Loren ROBERTS	USA	2.06
15	Jim FURYK	USA	4.67	65	Kevin SUTHERLAND	USA	2.05
16	Scott VERPLANK	USA	4.67	66	Hidemichi TANAKA	Jpn	2.02
17	Jose COCERES	Arg	4.43	67	Ian WOOSNAM	Wal	2.00
18	Bob ESTES	USA	4.43	68	John HUSTON	USA	1.96
19	Scott HOCH	USA	4.32	69	Rory SABBATINI	SA	1.93
20	Chris DiMARCO	USA	4.24	70	Dean WILSON	USA	1.91
21	Toshi IZAWA	Jpn	4.20	71	Robert KARLSSON	Swe	1.85
22	Thomas BJORN	Den	4.16	72	Taichi TESHIMA	Jpn	1.85
23	Paul AZINGER	USA	4.09	73	Andy OLDCORN	Sco	1.84
24	Tom LEHMAN	USA	4.03	74	Eduardo ROMERO	Arg	1.80
25	Mark CALCAVECCHIA	USA	4.00	75	Peter O'MALLEY	Aus	1.80
26	Robert ALLENBY	Aus	3.92	76	Mathias GRONBERG	Swe	1.79
27	Lee WESTWOOD	Eng	3.71	77	Dennis PAULSON	USA	1.72
28	Stewart CINK	USA	3.68	78	Jerry KELLY	USA	1.71
29	Rocco MEDIATE	USA	3.67	79	Notah BEGAY III	USA	1.69
30	Michael CAMPBELL	NZl	3.57	80	Gary ORR	Sco	1.68
31	Hal SUTTON	USA	3.57	81	Andrew COLTART	Sco	1.66
32	Jesper PARNEVIK	Swe	3.57	82	Ian POULTER	Eng	1.66
33	Nick PRICE	Zim	3.56	83	Brian GAY	USA	1.66
34	Angel CABRERA	Arg	3.42	84	Chris PERRY	USA	1.64
35	Paul McGINLEY	Eng	3.36	85	Ricardo GONZALEZ	Arg	1.62
36	Kenny PERRY	USA	3.34	86	Masashi Jumbo OZAKI	Jpn	1.61
37	Shingo KATAYAMA	Jpn	3.21	87	Lin KENG-CHI	Twn	1.61
38	Joe DURANT	USA	3.10	88	Duffy WALDORF	USA	1.61
39	Justin LEONARD	USA	3.05	89	Henrik STENSON	Swe	1.61
40	Niclas FASTH	Swe	2.98	90	Fred FUNK	USA	1.60
41	Kirk TRIPLETT	USA	2.95	91	Paul CASEY	Eng	1.60
42	Steve LOWERY	USA	2.90	92	Tom PERNICE, Jr.	USA	1.59
43	Frank LICKLITER II	USA	2.60	93	Nick FALDO	Eng	1.59
44	Brad FAXON	USA	2.57	94	Robert DAMRON	USA	1.59
45	Charles HOWELL III	USA	2.52	95	Mark BROOKS	USA	1.59
46	Scott McCARRON	USA	2.42	96	Chris RILEY	USA	1.57
47	Steve FLESCH	USA	2.40	97	Fred COUPLES	USA	1.56
48	Billy ANDRADE	USA	2.39	98	Warren BENNETT	Eng	1.55
49	John DALY	USA	2.38	99	Jeff MAGGERT	USA	1.52
50	Pierre FULKE	Swe	2.32	100	Bob TWAY	USA	1.52

Sponsored by Stan James